100 YEARS OF ARC MEMORIES

Celebrating the Centenary of Arcadia

(South African Jewish Orphanage)

1906-2006

David Solly Sandler

This edition first published March 2006

Cover designed by Sarah Natasha Myra Sandler

Every effort has been made to incorporate correct information, dates statistics and photos. The publisher regrets any errors and omissions, and invites readers to contribute their up-to-date or additional relevant information to David Solly Sander, E-mail: sedsand@ca.com.au

ISBN 0-646-45880-9

100 YEARS OF ARC MEMORIES - FOREWORD

The purpose of this book, like the *Arc Memory Booklets* it brings together, is to record the memories of the children of Arcadia (Arcs) and the history of Arcadia (the Arc). The Arc children of many different ages now live in many countries around the world and have followed many different walks of life. The common thread that binds the Arc children is that they spent some, or even all of their childhood in Arcadia.

The book also marks and celebrates the Arc's centenary. Finally, 100 years after its official beginning, old Arcs of at least five of the ten generations who passed through its gates have expressed a little of what the Arc meant to them. I feel privileged to be the recorder of their memories.

ARCADIA

Arcadia, known as *the Arc* to all its children, started off as the South African Jewish Orphanage (SAJO). 'Arcadia' was the name of the 26-acre estate bought from Sir Lionel Phillips in 1923 by the South African Jewish community. The name remained when the palatial villa and extensive grounds were transformed into a home to house Jewish children in need of care. Thus Arcadia, 22 Oxford Road, Parktown, Johannesburg was to become the address and home of generations of children. Arcadia SAJO has cared for over three thousand Jewish children over the past 100 years. In 1975 its name was changed to Arcadia Jewish Children's Home. In 2002 the children then in residence, were relocated to Sandringham and the property was sold in 2004.

The story actually begins more than 100 years ago. In 1902, the Jewish Ladies' Communal League founded the original Orphanage, which it continued to run in Johannesburg until 1921. In that year the South African Jewish Orphanage (SAJO) was established as a separate and independent Institution and took over all the Orphanage work, property and assets from the League. Two years later, 'Arcadia' was bought and that was where the story of the first 'Old Arcs' really began.

And if you're wondering why the Arc's centenary is being celebrated in 2006 - well, we will all have heard of how birth dates often went unrecorded. To save the Arc from this fate, its committee declared in 1931 that May 1906 would be the birth date as that was the date on which the first home owned and erected by the SAJO was established.

DEDICATION

Arcadia owes its existence to the tremendous generosity and caring of the South African Jewish community to look after their 'own'; to the captains of industry, to the donors large and small, to those giving gifts in kind or free services, to the Medical Board, Dental Board and Para-Medical Board, who gave their services free, to the Members and Subscribers and Honorary Collectors, and to the many Committee and sub-Committee Members from all over South Africa, who over the years gave so generously of their time and assistance. Every one of these people played an essential part in helping to support the running of the Arc, and mere words cannot properly express the thanks that is due to these legions of honourable people.

This book is dedicated to all the supporters of Arcadia mentioned above, to all the carers and to fellow Arc brothers and sisters especially those who bravely opened their inner hearts and shared their more sensitive and private stories.

One Old Arc Celia Kramer (Aizakowitz), a granny blessed with ten grandchildren wrote:

> "Despite the fact that I personally was not particularly happy at Arcadia, after going through the whole history of the founding of the Arc what stands out so clearly, is the tremendous caring and generosity of the Jewish community to look after their "own". Unfortunately I am sure all those good people are long since gone, as I would personally have liked to thank them."

Lastly this book is dedicated to Doc (Dr Adolf Lichtigfeld) who is the Greatest Man I have known and to his wife, Ma (Renia). Not only was Doc our Rabbi, a philosopher and a learned man who lectured at, and wrote papers for universities around the world but also for 20 years he was our friend, guardian and a warm fatherly figure who always sought to bring out the best in each of us through his kindness, wisdom and serenity.

THE CHILDREN

Although the book may seem to portray only good happy days, this of course was not the case, especially in the earlier years when life was very harsh and many ordinary people struggled to put food on the table. Judging by the standards of the day, I believe that the children in Arcadia were very well looked after.

The Old Arcs who have written in and shared their memories are in the minority. Some, unfortunately, are no longer with us or their whereabouts are unknown. But, in truth, the majority chose their silence because they cannot or do not want to remember. This book barely touches on the trauma that a young child experiences when losing a parent, or is separated from them and put into an institution. One can only imagine what goes on in the mind of a young child and how it will affect them in their future years. Also the pain a parent feels when they must place their child in an institution can only be imagined.

Many children were ashamed of being known as, and labelled as orphans at school, and even after leaving school this 'embarrassment' was something each child dealt with in their own way.

Many of the children were indeed orphans, especially in the earlier days before the advent of modern medicine. It was probably more the case that most children had one surviving parent. But there were also children who were in the Arc because their parents were unable to look after them.

The Arc Memories of the children in this book cover mainly the middle 50 years of the life of Arcadia. I do not have the recollections of the earlier Arcs who would by now have passed away and I have had very little contact with the fewer younger Arcs of the more recent years. They appear to be caught up in their own lives and have not stopped to look back and review their lives.

THE STORY OF THE BOOK

I spent most of my childhood in Arcadia from age four until 17 when I finished school. At the age of 28 I left Johannesburg and I have lived the past 25 years in Perth, Western Australia.

In January 2000, after visiting many Old Arcs in South Africa, Israel and the UK, I 'published' my first photo album containing the photos I had collected on my trip. Soon afterwards, through correspondence, and thanks to the Internet, I started more seriously collecting Arc photos and Arc Memories, initially from my contemporaries but then later from older Old Arcs. I have been at it ever since.

Over the years I have compiled ten booklets and albums that I photocopied and sent to fellow Arcs. At the time of going to print, I am in touch with over 100 Old Arcs by weekly email, sending them all the correspondence I receive. I compile a monthly correspondence booklet from these weekly emails and add photos (which I have given up trying to email out) and I post these out to Old Arcs not on the internet.

This book will contain much of what is in the booklets and other previously published Arc correspondence. For those who are interested in the historical facts, I have included the formal history of Arcadia taken from past publications such as Annual Bulletins, *The Arcadian* Magazine, newspaper articles and special publications to celebrate milestone dates. I have chosen to place this historical data at the end of the book as an Appendix, rather than turn this informal anecdotal publication into a historically accurate one.

Some of the 'children' who have shared their Arc Memories are now octogenarians and they are spread all over the world. Some have passed away. Some have written books themselves and are, in my opinion, very skilled writers`.

This book, *100 Years of Arc Memories*, is being published for the May 2006 centenary. For me personally, it completes a journey of over six years and a labour of love - though some call it a '*meshugas*'. Over these years, I have been privileged to meet up with, and get to know many many fellow Arc brothers and sisters spanning many generations across the world. I am indebted to them all, for without their memories there would be no book.

In 2002, shortly before two very close Arc 'brothers', David Kotzen and Dr Solly Farber, passed away, Solly and I had agreed to write a book on the Arc, together. Without Solly's input it will be a lesser book and will lack insights and input from his special story-telling ability and his rich experiences, including being Chairman of Arcadia for many years. Solly, however, has written the book with me, as his articles in many past Arcadia publications are included in this book.

Even today I feel inspired and encouraged by these older benevolent Arc brothers who encouraged me and helped me and contributed to the booklets and I sometimes feel that it is not by chance that I share with them my names David and Solly.

While I believe that all of the stories told in this booklet are essentially true, I must add that one older Old Arc, whose name I shall not mention, but who likes to draw illustrations, has qualified his stories and has written to a fellow Old Arc as follows:

> "I have been sending some more memories of Arcadia to David Sandler... Some are, I admit, exaggerations, some are downright fiction, but some are gospel truth..... Truth, that is, that my 80-year-plus old addled brain can recall."

I hope you enjoy the read and tripping back in time. Best wishes and good health to you all, and may there soon be peace in Israel.

Shalom

David Solly Sandler

100 YEARS OF ARC MEMORIES

Table of Contents

Note: Dates are approximate

'IN THE BEGINNING'
THE FIRST 50 YEARS - 1899-1952

The South African Jewish Orphanage owes its establishment to the Jewish Ladies' Communal League, which in 1899, began its activities among the small Jewish community which had ventured to Johannesburg.

"After going through the whole history of the founding of Arcadia what stands out so clearly, is the tremendous caring and generosity of the Jewish community to look after their own."
Celia Kramer (Aizakowitz) a granny blessed with ten grandchildren.

The Main Entry Hallway at Arcadia

"No one stands more erect than he who stoops to help a child."

Chapter 1 - INTRODUCTION TO ARCADIA

At the end of the 19th century and at the beginning of the 20th, pogroms and persecution in Eastern Europe and the discovery of diamonds and gold in South Africa encouraged many Jews to seek their fortune and a better life in Southern Africa.

While some fortune seekers and merchants prospered many did not and many fell on hard times. Death following childbirth, diseases or accidents was much more common in those days, before the advent of modern medicines, and this gave rise to the need of the community to take care of their orphaned children.

INTRODUCTION TO THE SOUTH AFRICAN JEWISH ORPHANAGE AND "ARCADIA" (THE 'ARC')
Extracted from 1906-1931 *Arcadia Jubilee Souvenir*

The South African Jewish Orphanage owes its establishment to the Jewish Ladies' Communal League, which in 1899, began its activities among the small Jewish community which had ventured to Johannesburg. In the course of its work in looking after the welfare of the Jewish school children, the Committee encountered cases of orphans in need. To provide for these waifs a house was rented in Pretoria Street, corner of Twist Street, and was opened on 18th August 1903, by the late Mr L J Reyersbach. Here, then, was the beginning of the community's efforts to provide for its fatherless.

There were but eight children accommodated at that time. However, the number of Jewish children in need of home and shelter gradually grew, and soon a larger house was rented in Esselen Street. It is indeed a credit to the efforts of the League that there was an ever-increasing demand for accommodation. In 1906 the generosity of Mrs Max Langerman made possible an expansion which had become vitally necessary, if the League were to be able to cope with the large number of cases which had come to its notice. On the ground donated by Mrs Langerman, who was then the President, the first Jewish Orphanage was established in Benbow Street, Kensington, with accommodation for 32 children. The League continued its efforts year by year, until its never-failing good work and

The first South African Jewish Orphanage in Kensington

The Official Opening of Arcadia by Jan Smuts – 18 July 1923
Mr Schlesinger is presenting the key to General Smuts.
On the right are Rabbi Dr. J L Landau and Mr. I Heymann. On the left is Mr. M I Isaacson.

service culminated in 1921 with the establishment of the SA Jewish Orphanage as a separate entity

It soon became apparent that further expansion was essential. With the growth of the South African Jewish community applications for admission had increased considerably, but owing to limited accommodation numerous deserving cases had to be refused. This fact, coupled with the advent of the Russian pogrom orphans brought out by the SA Jewish Relief, Reconstruction and Orphans Fund, made it imperative to acquire much larger premises. The Jewish community responded whole-heartedly in support of the movement and in 1923 "Arcadia", 22 Oxford Road, Parktown, was purchased at a cost of £30,000. The SA Jewish Relief, Reconstruction and Orphans Fund agreed to contribute £12,500 towards the purchase price, in consideration of the Orphanage taking charge of the pogrom children. A home had been acquired which will ever be a monument to Jewish liberality, and on the 18th July, 1923, "Arcadia" was opened by the then Prime Minister, General the Rt Hon. JC Smuts.

In 1923 the Orphanage accommodated 142 children, including the 61 pogrom orphans. Since then admissions have continued unabated, until today there are 290 children in our care.

The Orphanage authorities are happy to think that notwithstanding the increasing number of applications, since the opening of "Arcadia" no child has been refused on the ground of lack of accommodation. Over six hundred children have been given all the amenities of a Jewish home and education. They have been placed in careers and maintained until they have become self-supporting. This happy state of affairs has only been made possible by the support of the Jewish community of Johannesburg: It can only be maintained by the continued support of our people. The discharge of parental responsibility is costly and lengthy.

It would not be possible to leave the story of our Orphanage without some reference to the 'munificent' generosity of the Jewish Community. Depending so much, as it does, upon the liberality of the members of the community, the Orphanage owes a deep debt of gratitude to the community.

*****

The number of children in care increased over the years and peaked at 400 in 1939 with the greatest number of children in care during the war years 1939-1945.

In order to accommodate these children structural improvements and enlargements were necessary. In 1930 a hospital with 48 beds was opened. In 1931 "*The Joe Lewis Wing*" was opened to accommodate 100 children followed by the "Boys Wing" in 1936 and the Swimming Bath with its unique above the ground design in 1940.

The number of children actually in residence in Arcadia decreased gradually from an average of 107 in the 1950s, to 74 in the 1960s, 36 in the 1970s, 30 in the 1980s and steadied out around the 25 mark thereafter.

The number of "children in need and never in Arcadia" climbed, as the philosophy of childcare changed and it was deemed to be more beneficial to support the children in their family environment. The number of these children increased from 62 in 1950, to 127 in 1963 but generally ranged between the 80-120 children from 1960 to 1993 when the number shot up from 147 to 264 in 2001.

In 1969 a pilot scheme of The Cottage System, to house children in a family atmosphere, was introduced. A house was acquired in Rosebank and later the "cottage" was moved to

3

Greenside. The cottage housed between three and seven children.

In 1996 because of the low number of children in residence and the high cost of maintenance of the Arcadia estate *"Villa Arcadia"* was put up for sale. At the same time forward planning commenced to relocate the children residents of Arcadia into the community. In 2001 two adjoining houses in Raedene were acquired for a new Arcadia and plans were afoot to make alterations to improve the suitability of the houses.

In March 2002 the Johannesburg Jewish Helping Hand – the Chevrah Kadisha - took over the running of Arcadia and in May 2002 the children were relocated to Sandringham where there are currently 20 children living in residence – of which 18 are statutory placements.

In 2004 Villa Arcadia was sold to a large insurance company. They have demolished some of the structures and have rebuilt a large office complex and have maintained and restored the main building.

INTRODUCING ARCADIA
Written by Solly Farber 1999

To get to Arcadia you would leave Johannesburg town on the number 5 bus from the terminus in Pritchard Street just off Rissik Street. You could also take the 5A, but it ran very infrequently. At the terminus there was a large furniture store and further along the street the Juta Book Store where you could drop in and browse if the next bus was only due to leave in a while.

The electric bus would run silently as a ghost up Rissik Street into de Villiers Street, past the entrance to Park Station and then up the long hill to Hillbrow. It would pass the Hillbrow police station; go through upper Parktown along Victoria Avenue and then take a sharp turn into Oxford Road. From there it was a short run down the hill to the bus stop just opposite the ornate gates of Arcadia. Nearly there, but you would still have to cross Oxford Road, and with the busy traffic, that could be quite an undertaking. Once we had an 'extra-Afrikaans' coach who got knocked down by a cyclist right there at the gate, but that is a story for another time.

If you made it safely across you would enter Arcadia, the one time home of Sir Lionel and Lady Florence Phillips. You would walk up the driveway, flanked on your left by the playing fields and the Boys' Wing and on the right by the *koppie* rising almost straight up to St Andrews Road where the great battleship Johannesburg Hospital now stands. In the glory days of Parktown, Sir Percy Fitzpatrick lived on that hill. He wrote *'Jock of the Bushveld'* sitting at a stone table in his garden, looking down on his neighbour at Arcadia and gazing northwards to the Magaliesberg mountains. The driveway was which formerly lined by gum trees is now lined by jacaranda trees and at certain times of the year you could walk up all the way on a carpet of jacaranda blossoms which went pop-pop as you walked along. That same driveway appears on the old maps of Johannesburg as Sydney Street. It must have taken all the influence of Sir Lionel to have a street, albeit a short one incorporated into his private estate.

We Arcadians thought ourselves very important people. Our neighbors weren't your common old garden 'Joburgers.' We lived among the real elite. To the east we had Sir Ernest Oppenheimer; to the west over Oxford Road, Lord Albu and up the hill a certain Mr Potter about whom we knew very little. Our *'medinah'* was Oxford Road and its tributary, the Valley Road.

At the top end of the driveway was a large parking area, wide enough for a carriage to turn around. For us it had other uses. There on a Saturday evening we did our weekly stint of marching as Cadets of the St. John Ambulance Brigade. We also played our own Arcadian version of soccer there. At each end of the parking area was a magnificent pair of pillars, which no doubt at one time were adorned with massive gates. Now they were innocent of such gates and they served very nicely, thank you very much, as goal posts for our noisy and incessant football games.

Further along the driveway you would pass the Wolf Hillman Hospital - Arcadia's sickbay - and at the top end, the garage, the laundry, the cow stables, the bus driver, Charlie Miller's house, and Mr. Chait's shoe repair shop. On the *koppie* above these buildings was the Native compound.

The beautiful main building, the Villa Arcadia was designed by Sir Herbert Baker in 1909 just before he did the Union Buildings. The two buildings have a lot in common. I am not an expert on architecture, but having grown up in Arcadia I can feel a Herbert Baker House without really knowing why. I once visited a family member in Grahamstown. I felt utterly at home in his lounge, like being in Arcadia Villa, and I pronounced sagely that his home was a Herbert Baker house. He was amazed and delighted at my conclusion, but gently informed me that it was not strictly 'Baker', but it was in fact designed by one of Baker's pupils.

The Villa Arcadia was an architectural marvel. This is not to say that as grubby little savages we were intrigued or in awe of our surroundings. We small boys loved to roam the *koppie* exploring and looking for relics of the Phillips era and especially of the Jameson Raid in which Sir Lionel was infamously involved, and for which he was sentenced to death. The sentence was never carried and was later commuted to a huge fine, but he did spend six months in *'Cheder'*, and he nearly died there.

The Villa was built on baronial lines with countless bedrooms and sitting rooms upstairs, a formal layout downstairs and a grand staircase joining the two floors. There were big rooms and little rooms, magnificent rooms and holes in the wall, especially up the back staircase. There were tiny courtyards within the building and there were far flung outbuildings. To this day I have not been into every room in that vast mansion. Some childcare authorities decried the place as being 'a mausoleum and unfit as a residence for children', but for us growing up there it was a magic wonderland

The most magnificent rooms were the main dining room where we all ate on Friday nights and Jewish Holidays, and the synagogue. This Shul was truly God's House. It was a large pavilion-like structure with a high vaulted ceiling and huge arched windows in the east and west walls. In the north wall was the Holy Ark which contained the Torahs and which was fronted by ornate curtains shot through with gold weaving. Over the Ark, burnt the Eternal Light, which gave a deep red colour. At night when the main lights were extinguished you could see the comforting glow of that red light and know that God was there. The Shul could accommodate over 200 worshippers. It had been Sir Lionel's Music Room and had wonderful acoustics. We prayed there twice every day and we observed each and every holiday and holy day according to ritual of our ancient faith. The Shul played a very important part in our daily lives.

The Villa was truly fit for a king it was a source of pride to us that the Prince of Wales, the future King Of England stayed over as a guest of the Phillips family during his famous visit to South Africa in the early part of the century.

The Phillips family sold the property to the Jewish Orphanage in 1925. One can imagine the doubts and fears they had about changing this baronial home into a home for underprivileged children, but they went ahead and in 1926, Arcadia opened its doors to children. The grand opening was performed by no less a personage than General J C Smuts. We used to love going into the wood panelled Committee Room and leaf through the massive Visitors Book, which always lay, on the long table there. The book contained many famous signatures, but the first and most eminent was that of General Smuts with *Ouma* Smuts' signature right below his.

The gardens at Arcadia were magnificent. There were rockeries and water features. Here and there were quiet arboreal retreats to which one could slink away to read a Boggles or Tarzan book without interruption, or in times of distress shed a secret tear away from the derision of the other boys. There were also walking paths paved with stone along which one could go for a quiet amble or just go shooting the bull with earnest young friends.

Only the senior girls lived in the main building. The boys lived in dormitories in the Boys' Wing, and the junior girls and the babies were housed in yet another wing. Our Wolf Hillman hospital could have comfortably done service for a small town. We had a Sister who lived in and cared for us when we got sick.

We also had a full sized sports field, and two sandy tennis courts. Our swimming pool was wonderful in that it was built above the ground on concrete pillars. The space under the pool was a perfect meeting place for 'secret societies' or revolutionary gangs planning some mischief. We had a herd of cows that roamed around the grounds and gave our home a rural feel. It was like being on a farm or in a small village.

Arcadia was built on a flat plane, which seemed to have been cut into the side of a hill. We thus had hill above us and hill below. We referred to them as 'up the hill' and 'down the hill'. We were able to roam at will up and down the hill and all over the grounds of the estate. Down the hill we built *hoks* for our pigeons or Foofiei Slides between the huge trees there. There was plenty of opportunity for mischief and adventure and we did not stint ourselves.

Our world was in Arcadia. We were a huge family there, with all the joys and sorrows that families have. The glory of our surroundings worked its slow magic on us. Herbert Baker and the Phillips' were constantly with us, whispering to us from every corner of the estate, challenging us to find out more about them. To this day I have a sense of ownership about Baker and Phillips. They are 'my boys' and I devour anything and everything written by, or about them.

Arcadia still stands there at the foot end of Oxford Hill, slightly the worse for wear but still housing the Arcadia children and still generating lives and dreams for those who live there now.

*****

ARC HISTORY AND BACKGROUND
Written by Michael Perry Kotzen

The monogrammed 'LP' on the ornate eaves of Arcadia mansion house are Sir Lionel's initials LP "Lionel Phillips". Sir Lionel and his friend Barney Barnato were English born Jewish boys who had been fruit and vegetable barrow boys in London's East-end before they went to South Africa in the 1870's to 'hitch their wagons' to the Empire builder stars of Cecil John Rhodes and Liander Star Jameson. Both Barnato and Lionel Phillips became millionaires through their associations with the De Beers Diamond mines in Kimberley and with the great Rand Gold mining industry.

By the turn of the century both Jewish barrow boys had been knighted by Queen Victoria and King Edward the seventh for their 'sterling' efforts in financing and supporting Rhodes and Jameson and British interested in South Africa and in the war against the Boers.

Sir Lionel Phillips married a high born English Lady and had the famous architect Sir Herbert Baker build for Lady Phillips, a magnificent, ostentatious mansion house, which she named Arcadia, in the elite and select northern suburb of Johannesburg called Parktown. Closely neighboured to Arcadia were the palatial homes of Sir Otto Beit and Sir Ernest Oppenheimer, and other Gold mining magnates.

Johannesburg's wealthy Jewish community in the early 1920's recognised and dealt with the problems of the destitute Jewish children from the overcrowded, predominantly Jewish poor class slum suburbs of Mayfair, Fordsburg, Doorfontein, Judith Paarl and Bertrams where many Jews lived in cheap run-down houses and tenements, many with large families of children.

The wealthy acquired and established premises for an orphanage. At first in Kensington, then later, in 1923, Sir Lionel Phillip's Arcadia estate at 22 Oxford Road Parktown became the South African Jewish Orphanage

We had arrived at Arcadia in 1933 before "social science", "human rights" and such terms as "child abuse" and "child care" attained common daily usage in the English language. For centuries prior children were generally regarded as impositions, a 'drain on a man's finances', a 'stifling of personal liberties' or as Charles Dickens wrote; "More trouble than the bed in which they were conceived!" Particularly in the poor and the working classes, harsh orphanages and children's workshops existed. The wealthy classes placed their children in boarding schools or in the care of Victorian governesses.

In 1923 Lady Phillips' music room was converted into a dormitory for the boys. My brother Mannie and I arrived in Arcadia ten years later, in 1933. The boys' dormitory had outgrown the confines of the music room so extra beds were placed along the verandas surrounding the fishpond quadrangle. The fishpond was filled in and tarmacked over. Mannie and I were given beds. Mine was inside the hall and Mannie's was outside under the veranda canopy. At that time the Shul and the library were contained in one room inside the main front hallway.

Then in 1936 the new boy's wing and Hebrew classes were built on the West side of the main house. That allowed for the transformation of the old music room-dormitory into a spacious new Shul to accommodate all 350 children of Arcadia. The small Shul was retained as the library.

When I entered Arcadia at the age of nine in 1933 the population consisted of about 200 children, approximately 30 babies, 60 or 70 junior boys and girls and roughly about 90 seniors. The girls were all dormitoried in the main house.

Arcadia was staffed with a Jewish superintendent, albeit a Victorian martinet who then employed numbers of Afrikaans men and women to "keep the kids in line!". Martinet Louis Shaer was superintendent and Mrs Rachel Shaer was the matron.

The hospital, another new wing added to the main house, was in the charge of Sister Goldwater.

The babies were cared for by two kindly twin sisters named Kaufman and were house in the new 'Joe Lewis Wing'. The rest of the children were watched over by Afrikaans wardresses.

The 'Joe Lewis Wing' – Babies' Department

The 'Woolf Hillman' Hospital

Boys' Department

Villa Arcadia from the North

Chapter 2 – THE UKRAINE ORPHANS

This article was written in September 2004 by Lionel Slier who refers to the Ukraine Orphans as 'The Ochberg Orphan'.

Lionel is currently is the editor of 'Community Buzz' a column in the South African 'Jewish Report' about the Jews in the country communities, now mostly without any Jews and he write, "I have been involved all my life with Arcadia because my late mother came there in 1921 as one of Isaac Ochberg's Pogrom orphans and I grew up with stories of Daddy Ochberg. My mother always retained contact with 'the orphanage girls and boys' as she referred to them."

A great vote of thanks goes to Lionel who has kindly allowed his article, which is indeed a vital part of the history of Arcadia, to be included as part of the book.

BACKGROUND

Lionel's article gives us a detailed history of World War One (1914-1918) and ends as follows;

In South Africa the Jews looked on in horror at what was happening in eastern Europe. Many had come from those areas where the fighting was fiercest. Some had only come very recently and had left behind parents, wives, brothers, sisters, families and friends. Many in South Africa were in a state of shock and trauma. A few received messages from Europe detailing the death and destruction that had taken place. The war had been followed by widespread pogroms and then, in 1920, by the 'flu epidemic which killed as many people again as had died in the war. There were thousands of orphaned children, hungry, sick and dying. The South African Jews asked themselves whether there was not something that could be done. Could they not help the survivors? Or at least rescue the children?

THE ISAAC OCHBERG ORPHANS.

The saying goes "Cometh the hour, cometh the man" and that man was Isaac Ochberg, the President of the Orangia Jewish Orphanage in Cape Town. Ochberg had come to South Africa in 1895 from the Ukraine so he knew the area well and, of course, spoke the language. He was now a wealthy businessman with interests in marine salvaging, property, Foschini fashion shops, the CTC Bazaars and cinemas.

A Group of children maintained in Odessa by the Cape Jewish Orphanage.

In 1921 Ochberg contacted the Federation of Ukrainian Jews in London to get advice from them. They promised to assist him. Ochberg then went to see Gen Smuts who had become Prime Minister in 1919, to ask permission to bring Jewish orphans to South Africa. Smuts discussed it with his deputy, Patrick Duncan and the Minister of the Interior, Sir Thomas Watt.

They came back to Ochberg and said that he could bring 200 children to this country, subject to certain conditions. These conditions were: The children had to be proper orphans. Those with even one parent still living could not be taken. Siblings were not to be separated. If for some reason one did not qualify then the others had to be left behind. No children with physical disabilities were to come, nor any sick or retarded children. Finally 16 was the age limit for any child. The Jewish community had to bear the cost of bringing the children out to South Africa and they were also to be responsible for their upkeep here. The government was not to be involved in any expense whatsoever.

A Pogrom Orphans Fund was started and meetings were held around the country while people canvassed for money. A sum of £10,000 was raised and with pledges the amount reached £15,000. Many non-Jews also contributed.

There was great enthusiasm amongst the Jews here, but there were also some dissenting voices. In the March 24, 1921 edition of the Cape Town based "*SA Jewish Chronicle*" the editor wrote: "*The only hope for the Jews in Russia was emigration to Palestine. There are fears that because of the post-war economic depression in South Africa, bringing Jewish orphans to this country would jeopardise the Jewish position here*".

A correspondent in the same paper wrote: "*It would be ridiculous to bring these children out to this country as, apart from the question of them losing their Judaism here, there is no doubt that we have enough children in South Africa. Then there is the other aspect to be considered, the question of how the Christian population among whom we live, will view the matter. Will they be quiet while we are flooding South Africa with thousands of boys and girls from Eastern Europe? I think not*".

Ochberg set off for London where he organised the papers needed to go to Poland and the Ukraine. Strangely enough the papers were arranged with the help of Dr Fridtjol Nansen, the famous Norwegian North Pole explorer. Nansen was involved, at this time, in Russian famine relief and was 'persona grata'.

Poland was in a shambles after the war but Ochberg went to orphanages and Shuls looking for children. He had the heartbreaking task of choosing which children to take and which to leave behind. He wrote: "*Thousands of Jewish orphans are in need of immediate and urgent assistance and although my health has suffered by being here, I feel that no sacrifice can be too great for any Jew, if some of these unfortunate children of our race can be helped*". He found children that were hungry, weak, dirty and traumatised. They were in a wretched state, dressed in rags and verminous.

Polly (Stanger) Joffe recalled that time: "*There were seven of us in the family with only my mother left to care for us all. There was a scarcity of everything and to make matters worse for us,*

she died a little while later. Although I was only five years old I can remember that my eldest sister and I were living with a German woman. She looked after us as best as she could, but then my sister died of some sickness. I was taken to an orphanage in Stanislavov. The years in the orphanage were horrible. Often there was nothing to eat. Then fighting broke out in the town and we were chased into the countryside and a forest to escape. I remember sleeping in a filthy stable. We saw the Russians tearing the town apart looking for Poles. I was here for three years and I was about eight when Mr Ochberg came to the orphanage to choose children to go with him. I went to Cape Town and I have never regretted it*".

Eventually Ochberg chose 200 children and they were taken to Brest-Litovsk, previously a Russian fortress town on the Polish/Russian border which came under Polish rule after the peace treaty signed there in 1918. From there the children were taken by train to Warsaw and then Gdansk where a boat took them, in terribly cramped conditions to England. They went to the East End of London where they stayed at the Temporary Shelter for the Jewish Poor while they waited for a boat to South Africa.

Here I must declare my own interest. My mother was one of the Ochberg children. She was born in Brest-Litovsk in 1910, the third of five children to Leibel and Yetta Altuska. During the fighting in the city she was shot in the leg and all her life she had the scar of the bullet in her calf. My mother always said that the Germans treated the Jews much better than the Russians had. She had a younger sister, Leah, and a brother, Chaim, who was aged five. There was a problem with the two older sisters, however. The eldest, Tasha, was already 20 years old and did not qualify to be taken as an orphan. The second eldest, Faigel, was ill when Ochberg came and I believe that she was in hospital, but I cannot be certain of that now. The parents had simply disappeared. Ochberg overcame the problem of the oldest sister by making her a nurse to look after the youngest children; he literally created five nurses, whom he took along. However Ochberg broke one of the conditions of the agreement with the South African government by taking the four Altuska siblings and leaving Faigel behind. Faigel married a Polish Jewish man. Milzstein, in 1925 and they went to Argentine where they lived in Tucuman - the town, incidentally, where Eichmann was kidnapped by Israeli operatives in 1960. In 1973 my mother and Leah travelled to Argentine and met their sister after 53 years.

Ochberg and the children left Southampton on the Union-Castle liner, the 'Edinburgh Castle'. However 13 boys refused to go. They did not want to go to a jungle and a country full of lions, they said.

Jenny Bailen remembers the voyage clearly. "*We stayed in steerage class: they made bunks for us there. They cleared out everything, they had bunks top and bottom. We little ones had to climb on the ladder to get to the top. I was at the top, and there Mr Ochberg took over and looked after the children and he was with us all the time. Actually he, himself, was First Class, with his wife but he was with us most of the time. And then on the boat we always found our cushy little surprise; little biscuits, little chocolates. He was the one all the time. He loved it. We called him 'Daddy......Daddy Ochberg' He was fantastic*".

After a three-week voyage, the ship arrived in Cape Town on the 21st September to a tumultuous, even hysterical welcome from Cape Town's Jews who had flocked to the docks to meet the children.

The *'Cape Times'* recorded the arrival. "*As the children disembarked and proceeded to take their places in the motor-cars, they were besieged with people pressing all sorts of nice things upon them in the way of sweets, fruit and cakes. Everyone was struck with their happy and healthy condition and in fact, except for a case or two of measles among them on the trip, they had a clean bill of health all along, so that the half a dozen Ukrainian nurses who came over to look after them had a fairly easy time of it*".

Fanny (Schrirer) Lockitch recalls her arrival. "*Never until my dying day shall I forget our first sight of the lights of Cape Town and then the tremendous reception when we came ashore with half the city apparently waiting on the quay for us. It really made us feel at home because we came with very mixed feelings. There were so many stories told, you know – we would be sold, we would be thrown into the sea, but Daddy Ochberg made all the difference*".

The children were taken to the Orangia Jewish Orphanage but it was so crowded and 87 were sent to Johannesburg as arranged previously. In Johannesburg the children were split into two groups; some went to the Kensington Sanatorium, where there were local orphans already, and the others went to the Jewish Old Age Home in Louisa Street, Doornfontein. It was hoped that some, at least, of the children would be adopted. Solly Jossel, aged five, saw a woman whom he thought was his mother and clung to her. She and her husband adopted him.

Meanwhile in Johannesburg the Board of Deputies started looking for a suitable building for an orphanage for the new children as well as for those South African orphans. It happened that Arcadia, the home of Sir Lionel and Florence Phillips was on the market.

Lionel Phillips was born in England in 1855 and came to South Africa, aged 20, and ended up on the diamond fields in Kimberley. He gained the confidence and friendship of millionaires Alfred Beit and Cecil Rhodes. In 1884 he was put in charge of the firm, Wernher Beit, as both Julius Wernher and Alfred Beit had moved to England. In 1885 he married Dorothea Florence Alexandra Ortlepp, born in Colesburg in 1863 in a church wedding.

The following year gold was discovered on the Witwatersrand and they moved to the new mining town of Johannesburg where they lived in a house in Noord Street where the railway line to Park Station was later built (and where the bus and taxi terminus now stands).

Phillips ran the firm of Hermann Eckstein & Co representing London-based Wernher Beit as the Central Mining Finance and Investment Company which controlled Rand Mines and was popularly known as the Corner House. He later became the President of the Chamber of Mines and extremely wealthy in his own right.

Arrival of Ukraine Orphans in Johannesburg

The Phillips' moved to a house in Parktown called Hohenheim (where the Johannesburg hospital now stands) causing the suburb of Parktown to become very popular and many *Randlords* also moved into the area. In 1890 they bought a property, also in Parktown, called *Arcadia* and engaged the British architect, Herbert Baker, to rebuild it for them. The new house was called '*Villa Arcadia*'.

In 1895 Phillips was involved in the Reform Committee which plotted to overthrow Kruger's government with an attack led by Leander Starr Jameson. It became known in popular history as the Jameson Raid. The raid was a failure and Phillips was amongst those arrested and taken to jail in Pretoria where he was put on trial and sentenced to death by Judge Gregorowski. The sentence was later commuted and Phillips was fined £25,000 instead.

In 1913 Phillips was shot and wounded outside the Rand Club in Harrison Street during a labour dispute and taken to the General Hospital. After this Florence Phillips was determined to leave in Johannesburg. The Phillips' spent the First World War in England and returned when the war ended. They put '*Villa*

Arcadia' up for sale. This is where the Jewish Board of Deputies stepped in and purchased the property for £25,000.

Florence was horrified when she learnt the reason for the purchase. "*To think that my beautiful house is going to be turned into an orphanage*," she said.

In fact she was not totally wrong. The house was clearly unsuitable. Florence's private sleeping apartments with its enclosed balcony became the girls' dormitory. Between the main building and Lionel Phillips' music room there was a quadrangle. This was enclosed with blinds and this is where the boys slept. The music room was altered and became the orphanage Shul.

The South African children in the orphanage mixed freely and easily with the children whom they called "The Russians". The older girls were sent to Hebrew High School at the corner of Claim and Smit Street near Joubert Park while the older boys went to Jewish Government Primary School in Beit Street, Doornfontein.

When the children turned 16 they were sent out to work, although still living at Arcadia. The boys were put into trades, as glaziers, plumbers, carpenters etc while the girls became salesgirls at the CTC Bazaars. Those who showed academic ability were apprenticed to pharmacists or given further education.

Eventually they all passed into the larger Jewish community, married, set up homes and started families. Many kept in touch with each other and 'The orphanage boys and girls' never lost this bond that they had with each other.

In 1999 I met Leslie Wolchuk whom I believed was the last living "Russian" in Johannesburg. Wolchuk represented South Africa in 1935 as a boxer in the Maccabi Games. In 1950 he went over as the boxing coach to the Third Maccabiah. To my surprise in the August 2004 issue of "*The Jewish Report*" there was a story of Solly Jossel. He was celebrating his 90th birthday and also his 60th wedding anniversary. My mother, who went to live in Durban in 1971, passed away in 2002.

Now a story about myself. In 1948 I was invited to Muizenberg to spend the summer holidays with my mother's cousin from Brest-Litovsk, Isaac Bornstein. He had married Yetta, one of the Ochberg girls. They had two daughters younger than me. I was too busy parading around the Snake Pit and swanning it with all the other 'sharp young Jo'burg boys' to pay too much attention to the girls, Rita and Tania, who, in fact, were second cousins of mine. However they seemed to be very nice girls. I went again in 1949. Fast forward now to November 2003 and I was going to Israel on the "*Israel Now*" Tour. Imagine my surprise, when the younger girl, Tania, was on the tour as well. We had not seen each other for 54 years, as I had not been back to Muizenberg since. It was wonderful to meet her. We keep in touch

In 1921 the Ochberg orphans ranged in age from 5 to 16 years. Eighteen years later they would have been between 23 to 34 when the Second World War broke out. Those unlucky enough still to be living in Eastern Europe would probably have ended up in a trench, shot by the death squads or else, horror of horrors, gassed in a concentration camp.

In the annals of the Jewish community of South Africa there can hardly be a more momentous and wonderful achievement than the rescuing of 187 orphans from Russia and Poland and giving them a life in this country.

Here is part of a poem, written in Yiddish on the Edinburgh Castle and given to Ochberg.

"Merciful Father in Heaven
Who in His mercy towards children, left orphans
Forced to leave their homes.
Has sent Daddy Ochberg to make us citizens of South Africa.
G-d blessed us that we found ourselves amongst good people".

And what of Ochberg?.

His one daughter, Ruth, had a heart problem and died at the age of 17 in 1935. Ochberg donated money to the Hebrew University and a faculty was established in Rechovot called *The Ruth Ochberg Chair of Agriculture.*

In 1937 Ochberg took desperately ill with stomach cancer while in England. He spent weeks in hospital and continually begged the doctors to allow him to return to South Africa. Eventually, but very reluctantly, they agreed. Two days out from Cape Town he died. Usually when a person dies on a ship the burial takes place at sea, but Ochberg's wife begged the Captain to allow them to bury her husband in Cape Town. Being so close, the Captain agreed. Ochberg was 56 years old.

In his will Ochberg left money to the Hebrew University in Jerusalem where there is now an Isaac Ochberg Wing.

On his tombstone in Cape Town is written; "*He was a good South African and a great Jew*".

The quotations are taken from an article by Jonathan Boiskin in "Jewish Affairs" (Winter 1994)

Some of the Orphans and nurses on their way to South Africa

Chapter 3 – ALEX MANDERSON (1921–1990)

Alex Manderson was born in Volksrust as Alexander Mendelson on 28 June 1921 and was in the care of Arcadia from age five to age 16 from 1926 to 1937. Initially he entered Arcadia with his older brother Isadore (Sonny), their sister Lillian followed them about a year later.

Alex was on active service and in the Army from 1940 to 1945. He served in Kenya, Abyssinia, Egypt and Libya and was a prisoner of war in Libya, Italy and Germany.

In 1946 he arrived in Australia to make a new life for himself. Today children and grandchildren of the three siblings live in Australia.

Here are his memories of his life in Volksrust as a child and then in Arcadia as extracted from his book 'AFRICA and EUROPE 1921-1946 a Memoir' which was edited by his daughter Lenore and has been reproduced here with her kind permission.

Alex May 1945

PREFACE FROM LENORE MANDERSON, MELBOURNE, FEBRUARY 2006

Alex wrote these memoirs in 1990, drafting them in long hand and passing them to Mardi, his wife, our mother, who then keyed them into a computer. The last pages of this manuscript – concerning his arrival in Australia – were written on 7 December 1990. On the 8th, he took Mardi out to dinner, celebrating her birthday as much as the completion of the work. On Monday 10th, the two of them drove from Canberra to Longbeach on the south coast of New South Wales, stopping in Braidwood for morning tea en route. Alex had a small new project in preparation of our gathering there over Christmas: the pailings of the balcony needed to be repaired to ensure their safety. He was below the balcony when he last spoke to Mardi, in response to her suggestion that she join him to clear away the tools. "Everything is finished now; I'm really satisfied." By the time she had reached him he was gone, dead from a massive heart attack at the age of 69.

The memoirs were nearly complete when I saw him the end of November. I was in Canberra for work, having flown down from Brisbane for a few days. Usually he drove me to and from the airport, but this time I had a hire car. I was about to drive to the airport at the end of the visit when Mardi ran out, camera in hand, to photograph us. It was the last photograph taken before his death; the only one of just the two of us taken since I was a small child. Richard, Roland and Desmond have similar precious poignant memories.

None of us knew he had a health problem; he may not have known. We will never know whether uneasiness about his health propelled him to write the memoirs. We will never know whether he might have then turned to write of his early life in Australia: winning a three mile race, swimming breast stroke

against others' free style, along the Yarra River in Melbourne, 10 weeks after his arrival in 1946; meeting Mardi while he was working as a road labourer and she a bush nurse; working with Ian Potter and Company or studying commerce at The University of Melbourne; moving to farm first in south Gippsland then in the Riverina. Nor, in late 1964, of our move to Canberra when he joined the public service, or his final rise to be head of the Division of Water Resources in the Department of National Development.

We do know a few things now, not mentioned in the memoirs but worth a footnote. Alex returned from the savagery of Europe to South Africa at a critical point in its history. He discovered his home country gripped by escalating racism: black and coloured men and women thrown out of work as white soldiers returned. The Nationalist Party was on the rise, under the banner of the Swastika, anticipating the defeat of Smuts and the institutionalisation of apartheid in 1948. The environment was strongly anti-Semitic, an echo of Germany. Alex, scarred by the war and the fear it engendered, left South Africa to a country as far as possible from that continent and Europe, changing his name from Mendelsohn to Manderson in the process.

The six day war in 1967 was cathartic, a turning point from which Alex felt able to reconnect with Judaism, Jewish history, family and Israel. He and Mardi went to South Africa, Israel and Italy late 1972 – early 1973, a visit that gave him an opportunity to show her the environments that had so profoundly shaped his life, and hers and ours.

He was an extraordinary, talented and funny man. His memoirs offer just a glimpse.

VOLKSRUST 1921-1926

I was born Volksrust, 28 June 1921. That is what I have always believed, and still do. Nevertheless, my birth certificate, which I first saw when I was in my sixties, states that I was born at Wakkerstroon. In the absence of a birth certificate, I have sworn innumerable statutory declarations to the effect that I was born at Volksrust. So much for statutory declarations. The answer to the conundrum may be that the regional Registrar of Births, Deaths and Marriages was located at Wakkerstroon, which is only about 20 kilometres away. Together with nearby Platrand (flat ridge), the other two towns figured prominently in my mother's recollections of our early family life.

Volksrust was a typical *platteland* (outback) town, dominated by Afrikaners whose farming activities provided the economic backbone of the town, its centrepiece and social hub being the local Dutch Reformed Church. As in most similar towns in those days, the church faced a large open square, provided specifically for the faithful from the neighbouring countryside for use during their attendance at *Nagmaal* (Communion). They would, at the time of my birth, arrive in their ox-drawn wagons and camp out for a few days on the square, all sleeping and eating around their individual wagons, still essentially the same means of transportation used by their forebears, the *Voortrekkers* (pioneers), when they left the British-controlled Cape Province to settle in the Orange Free State and the Transvaal. Nagmaal was a social as well as a religious occasion, even more still a political event. The link between Afrikaner politics and the Dutch Reformed Church has always been strong. In fact, one could say without exaggeration that the Church preached liberation theology long before it became fashionable in Latin America. The Dutch Reformed Church was the guardian of Afrikaner culture, hope and ambition for many decades after their devastating defeat in the Boer War.

Our house was at 90 Hoogstraat (High Street), which ran along one side of the church square. I can still clearly recall the sight of numerous ox-wagons camped on the square and Mom telling me that the 'Dutch' people had come for Nagmaal. It was only a good while later that they became universally called Afrikaners.

Volksrust has no particular claim to fame. It was a Customs post when the Transvaal was an independent Boer republic and neighbouring Natal was a British colony. Obviously, it was a potential flashpoint when hostilities broke out, but nothing much eventuated, although at nearby Majuba Hill in Natal the British suffered a major defeat during the first Boer War in the early 1880s which the Boers won.

As far as I can recall, we were the only Jewish family in Volksrust. There were others at Platrand – my father's relatives – and quite a few at Standerton some 80 kilometres westward, which also had a small synagogue. At that time there were small Jewish communities scattered throughout South Africa, but later on, with the growth of Afrikaner nationalism and its unfortunate fellow traveller, anti-Semitism, most disappeared, preferring aggregation in the main cities. Society was rigidly stratified by racial origins and religious affiliations – blacks, coloureds (mixed bloods), Indians, Afrikaners and English, the last including the Jews. There was very little social intercourse and little intermarriage.

The Afrikaners were in general still brooding on the loss of their independence and their current economic impotence. After all, at the time my parents settled in Volksrust, probably around 1914, the Boer War and its immediate aftermath was not long over, memories of the British Army's scorched earth policy were still vivid, bitter memories of the death of thousands of women and children in concentration camps (the first to be known by that name) were still strong, as was also the banishment of Afrikaners to remote prisons such as St Helena in the mid-

Cover of 'Africa and Europe 1921-1946 A Memoir'

Atlantic. Many Boers had left the Transvaal to settle in South America and other far away places.

My father, Abraham George Mendelsohn (I knew nothing of Abraham in his name until I first saw my birth certificate only comparatively recently) was born in Riga, now capital of Latvia, but then an integral part of Tsarist Russia. The Latvian Jewish community was mainly of German origin and settled there along with the Germans when the Baltic was the mercantile preserve of the Hanseatic League (mainly Hamburg, Lubeck, Cologne, Breslau and Cracow) during the period spanning the 12th to 17th centuries. My father arrived in South Africa during 1908 and was probably brought out by his uncle and aunt, AJ and Rose Kuny (Rose was his blood relative). We only knew AJ and Rose when they were old and lived at Hillbrow in Johannesburg. Rose was then almost blind and AJ was an Inspector of Hebrew

Schools which were attended by Jewish children for religious and cultural instruction after normal school hours and at weekends.

The Kunys still lived at Platrand during my infancy and I recall their daughters, Dora and Freda, visiting us at Volksrust. AJ must have arrived in the Transvaal during the 1890s and set up medical practice at Platrand. He had no recognised medical qualifications, but apparently he knew something about medicine; the availability of medical services being at such a premium in the Transvaal Republic, his qualifications to practice were never queried. All their children were born in the Transvaal. They spoke Dutch at home – Afrikaans had not yet developed to a distinctly recognisable and acceptable language – and probably some Yiddish. They referred to their parents when the latter had become grandparents as *Oupa* and *Ouma,* Dutch for grandparents, and in fact this is what is inscribed on their tombstones. The two sons, Alex and Ben, became doctors, Ben lived to a good age at Springs, near Johannesburg, but Alex, after serving in the trenches in France during World War I as a medical officer, died in the 1919 flue epidemic on his return to South Africa. The daughters, whom we, as adults, got to know better, died in Johannesburg, nearer 90 than 80.

My mother came to South Africa at the invitation of her uncle, Abram de Wilde, and his wife Flora (nee Phillips). De Wilde was originally de Wylder, the family emigrating from Holland to England last century. My grandmother, Caroline de Wilde, was born in Holland in either Rotterdam or Amsterdam, (my mother was not certain) and still spoke Dutch, particularly when annoyed. Mom was one of 13 children. I once knew all their names but can now only recall Esther, the oldest girl, Solly, the oldest boy, Adelaide, Alex, Becky, the youngest, and of course, Miriam, my mother. The patriarch was Isaac Rosenburg, nicknamed 'Black Ike'. He was a tailor. He came from Warsaw. My mother once mentioned that he was also a ritual slaughterer (*schochet).* Perhaps he augmented his paltry income with whatever seasonal work was available.

As far as I know, Mom came to South Africa in 1912 and met my father at a place called Balfour. They married in 1914. Mom was 25 and Dad 34. Sonny was born in 1916, Lillian in 1918, and I in 1921.

I don't recall much of life in Volksrust. I do remember the almost weekly ritual of Mom dragging the three of us – wind, rain, or shine – up what seemed at the time to be a steep hill to visit the Derricks. Lillian my sister most resented this imposition of pleasure, and invariably got a hefty slap for her protestations and sulked all the way there and back. The Derricks lived in a corrugated iron house – roof and sides – which was like a furnace in summer. I recall Mrs Derrick's use of grass at seeding for floral decorations. We met up with one of the Derrick boys during the War.

Our house at 90 Hoogstraat was tiny, and the yard at the back almost completely taken up with a shed in which my father kept oxhides while they were being cured. The ample application of coarse salt in between the hides could be smelled throughout the house and beyond. It was not offensive, but very pervasive. The horse-drawn trolley was parked alongside the shed but no longer in use, as my father had acquired a T-Model Ford, one of the first in the district. We three children would jump up on the

seat of the trolley – I, the smallest, in the middle – and pretend to be urging or restraining the two horses which once pulled the load of hides and wool.

I cannot recall our family being very happy. I do not recall any outward sign of affection from my father. I do recall, though, receiving a good strapping from him for nagging my mother to distraction, seeking a commitment from her that, as soon as circumstances permitted, I would get a suit with a waistcoat, just like the one Sonny had.

Our circumstances were becoming increasingly straightened. At one stage, according to Mom, we were very well off indeed and they were making ambitious plans for the education of all three children. My father's fortunes depended on his success in predicting future wool prices as he often bought wool on the sheep's backs, offering a price that would yield him a profit when shorn. In later years, his market predictions, not too surprising in an era of communications primitive alongside those that now prevail, were very much astray. At the time when he entered hospital for a prolonged stay for the treatment of alcohol-aggravated illnesses, we were practically penniless and Mom had to make plans for the future of the three children and herself which might exclude the participation of her husband.

One day in 1926, Mom took me to Johannesburg by train. I later learned that the purpose of our visit was for an interview with the Committee of the South African Jewish Orphanage with a view to the admission of Sonny and me. I was astounded at the state of the art transport system – trams! I wondered how they could run along the streets without traction by oxen, horses, or a steam engine. I marvelled even more at my mother's ability to alight and descend at the right places. We stayed a few days with the de Wildes and then returned to Volksrust for the final break. We arrived back in Johannesburg, this time with Sonny and Lillian, late in December 1926 when Sonny and I were to enter the orphanage 'Arcadia'.

Mom did not prepare me for entry into the orphanage. I was told that we were going to Johannesburg to visit the de Wildes, whom we called Grandpa and Grandma. Perhaps Sonny, then aged ten, knew the truth.

Looking back on those first five years of life, they did not have a strong influence on me. I do not think that I had close white friends of comparable age, given the rigid demarcation of society in an Afrikaner dominated town. I do recall black playmates, probably the offspring of visiting black servants. I spoke reasonably good Zulu – so my mother told me – and in fact this was a constant source of amusement to the black servants at the orphanage. I can still see the look of amazement and howl of delight when I went into the scullery and asked a black man in Zulu for a drink of cold water – *Mina funa makaza manzi.* His eyes popped out.

ARCADIA 1926-1937

"Lillian did not come with Sonny, Mom and me to Arcadia on 23 December 1926. My lasting recollection of that fateful day is sitting with Mom on a bench in an alcove, one of many along the numerous terraces of the beautiful home that was Arcadia in its heyday. A trellis of grapes ran alongside this particular terrace. They were of the Isabella variety and in late December they were already starting to turn black. The vines were heavily laden. One of the white staff – we called them nurses, although they had neither health responsibilities nor qualifications – engaged my attention to draw me away from Mom, as I must have sensed something drastic was imminent. It was late afternoon. I suddenly looked around and saw Mom running away as quickly as she could. The nurse restrained me from following. I cried almost continuously for the next eight hours or more. Naomi Shaer, the daughter of the superintendent at Arcadia, sat at my bedside in the dormitory trying to comfort me and get me off to sleep. Exhaustion was finally her ally. Naomi and her elder sister Ruth lived at Arcadia but were not on the staff.

The next day, Christmas Eve, was my first day as a Jewish orphanage boy. The previous day all the children had been to the full dress rehearsal of the Christmas pantomime. This was an annual event attended by children from all charitable institutions in Johannesburg, and each received a small carton of lollies with the compliments of the Mayor and Mayoress of Johannesburg. So, on 24 December 1926, they were all singing the pantomime song of the year, which they had learnt from the Principal Boy [often a young lady] or the Ugly Dame [who was often a man] in a singalong, so characteristic of pantomime in those days. The song went:

> All I want is a proper cup of coffee
> Made in a proper coffee pot.
> Tin coffee pots and iron coffee pots
> They're no use to me.
>
> If I can't have a proper cup of coffee
> In a proper coffee pot
> I'll have a cup of tea.

The first few days at Arcadia, I spent wandering around, getting to know my new environment. Most of all I remember exploring the magnificent landscaping, featuring rock quarried on the site.

Arcadia was originally the home of a gold-mining magnate and his wife, Sir Lionel and Lady Phillips. They were in residence from 1910 to 1923. The South African Jewish Orphanage Committee bought the house and its extensive grounds in 1923, moving to the more desirable and sought-after address in Johannesburg from its former base in one of the least desirable suburbs, Doornfontein. The orphanage was already in existence pre-World War I, as evidenced by a Roll of Honour commemorative wooden tablet which was moved to Arcadia in 1923.

Sir Lionel Phillips was one of the most prominent figures in the gold mining industry that was established following the discovery of gold at Langlaagte in 1886. They were the leaders of the Uitlanders [foreigners] who flocked to the Witwatersrand. They were a constant thorn in the side of the Boer administration, agitating for civic rights but unwilling to abandon their nationality, mainly British.

The British Colonial rulers, from their bases in Natal and the Cape Province, cast envious eyes at the Transvaal and to a lesser extent the adjacent Orange Free State. Officially, their concern was to forestall a German invasion from its base in South-West Africa [now Namibia], but their concern was in reality more gold-driven than strategy-driven.

The infamous Jamison Raid that took place in 1895 implicated a number of prominent Uitlanders, including Sir Lionel Phillips. It was an attempted coup d'etat instigated by Starr Jamison [later knighted], a member of the Cape Legislative Assembly, involving the dispatch of a relatively small troop of armed raiders into the Transvaal. They were to seize vital installations and leave the rest to a general uprising on the Witwatersrand – the 100 km ridge of gold-bearing reef either side of Johannesburg. Unfortunately for the raiders, the Boers intercepted a telephone conversation involving one of the plotters, and they were ready to welcome Jamison's men when they crossed the western border of the Transvaal.

Sir Lionel Phillips, along with others, was put on trial for his life. He was found guilty, but was offered the option of buying out the sentence for a king's ransom. He could well afford it, and he did. Four years later, on the pretext of protecting the civil rights of the Uitlanders, most of whom were British subjects, Britain formally declared war on the Boer Republics. This they won in 1902, after heavy losses, concentration camps and brutal treatment of civilians. That was the background of the man whose mansion I inherited, to some extent, for eleven years, and called home.

'Arcadia' at 22 Oxford Road, Parktown, was one of the choicest bits of real estate in Johannesburg. Opposite was the mansion built by Sir George Albu; behind, that built by Sir Otto Beit; and to the east, 'Brenthurst', built by Sir Ernest Oppenheimer whose son, Harry Oppenheimer, a well-known anti-apartheid activist and the current chairman of de Beers, the international diamond marketing monopoly. Phillips came from England, but the other three were German Jews who converted to Christianity for social advancement after they had made their fortunes.

In its heyday, 'Arcadia' must have been a magnificent estate. It was designed by Sir Herbert Baker who also designed the Union Buildings in Pretoria, administrative seat of the national government, and a number of buildings serving the same purpose in New Delhi. These structures won worldwide acclaim at the time. Arcadia was of Mediterranean architectural design. It was painted white, it had long colonnaded verandahs and open terraces, fluted chimneys and U-shaped terracotta interlocking roof tiles. There was an extensive driveway that took off from Oxford Road. It was lined with eucalypts, ending in a high archway that protected the mansion from view. As one passed under the archway, the magnificent main building appeared alongside a gravelled area large enough for carriages with four in hand and later, luxury limousines to make a full circle with ample room to spare.

When Sonny and I were admitted in 1926, the buildings had not yet been modified much from the condition in which Lady Phillips had left them in 1923. Some of the balconies had been glassed in to provide accommodation for the growing number of children, and a fairly large room had been built on to the main structure to provide a dining room and play area for the Babies [two to about six years of age].

In addition, the changed purpose of Arcadia was already evident as one came through the main entrance. There on the walls of what was the reception area were affixed numerous boards of highly polished wood, enumerating in golden paint the names of the Arcadia's benefactors under the heading 'Beds Kindly Donated By'. In those days a 'bed' represented a donation of at least £50. Even during the Depression, names were still being added, although at a slower rate, to join those of Sir Ernest and Lady Oppenheimer, Sir George and Lady Albu, Sir Alfred and Lady Beit, and many of the wealthy but untitled South African Jewish families.

One entered through two large wooden doors swung on cast iron hinges, protruding about a third the width of the door. The reception area – a long passage – was tiled in black and white, at one end a sandstone staircase leading up to what were bedrooms in the original plan. The central block contained a huge formal dining room with a large sandstone block wall and exposed oak beams holding up the ceiling. Alongside was an informal dining and sitting room, much of the walls lined with lead-lighted built-in cupboards. On the other side of the formal dining room were the kitchen, servery, scullery, cellars and storage rooms, some with thick steel doors. Further along were living quarters for white staff, I suppose – housemaids, kitchen staff, etc. – during the Phillips' occupancy.

On the other side of the sitting room was a quadrangle, the centre of which was sealed with bitumen when we arrived, but was originally a fishpond and lawn, and on the far side of the quadrangle was a large ballroom with high arched ceiling.

On the northern flank of the main building was a long colonnaded verandah with what seemed to be endless arches, facing the Magaliesberg Mountains, from where one could clearly see the controlled winter bushfires to stimulate, spring and summer grass growth, as well as the uncontrolled summer fires which sometimes spread with alarming speed.

Adjoining the main building were stables, a small dairy, and the Bantu servants' quarters, which were primitive but in line with then prevailing standards. Space seems so unconfined when one is very young, but I would think that Arcadia covered at least 15 acres in its original state – 15 acres of prime residential location.

Arcadia was developed by the Phillips' in four main tiers. The highest tier was level with the top of Oxford Road and was largely untouched, except for a small area excised to provide the small 'top' orchard. There was also a stone swimming pool that was never in use while I was at Arcadia. The main buildings were on the second tier. Gardens and open space occupied the third tier, and more undisturbed rocky ridge descended to the fourth tier, largely occupied by a very comprehensive 'bottom' orchard. The northern boundary of Arcadia coincided with the end of the steep slope of Oxford Road.

There were two cottages on the property, well away from the main buildings, probably originally built for senior white staff such as property manager or staff supervisor. One was close to the Oppenheimer's 'Brenthurst' and the other adjoined the bottom orchard. In our time, they were used for isolation purposes when an infectious disease such as mumps or chickenpox broke out; but when, through a generous benefactor, the Wolf Hillman Hospital was built, the cottages were used for other purposes, including rental for revenue raising purposes.

The various tiers were separated by skilfully constructed and aesthetically pleasing stone walls. They were everywhere and led to pleasant surprises such as a small alcove with seating for three or four, or a flight of steps leading to a concealed garden feature. The gardens must have been magnificent at one time but they were gradually allowed to deteriorate, priorities being elsewhere.

I started life at Arcadia in the Babies but moved to the Boys when I was about six. We were then housed in the former ballroom that was icy cold in winter. Even colder was the accommodation of the older boys on the open verandahs of the quadrangle alongside the former ballroom. A few years later, another benefactor provided funds to build a wing for the Babies and Junior Boys, which had become necessary with the growth of numbers. At one stage there were about 200 children in residence. I then moved over to the new building and returned to the Senior Boys when I was ten and a half, and was about to start High School.

All children were allotted a number that was written on clothing in marking ink for identification purposes after laundering. Clean clothes were then stored on shelves according to numbers and issued on Friday afternoons or before festive days. At various time my number was 35 [Boys], 14 [Junior Boys], and 53 [Senior Boys].

I did not have too much contact with Sonny whom I now had to call Isadore, with great difficulty for a start. He probably found me to be a nuisance, particularly for the first six months when I was not allowed to see any visitors, including Mom, in case the settling-in process was disturbed. I knew that Sonny was permitted to see Mom and I kept on nagging him to pass on messages to her, such as 'Please come and take me out of here and put Lillian in, in my place'. After he had promised to pass on my messages, I'd follow him around pleading 'But don't forget', to which he'd reply, 'No, I won't forget', to which I would add 'But you mustn't forget,' and the sequence was repeated until I felt the full impact of his boot. I was teased 'Don't forget' for many years.

Lillian stayed with Mom at York Lodge under very difficult conditions, at one stage sharing a room with her in the black servants' quarters. However, much as Mom would have liked to keep Lillian out of Arcadia, she eventually succumbed to the inevitable, about a year or so after Sonny and I entered Arcadia. I had more to do with Lillian than with Sonny when upset; she was like a bantam hen – small but ferocious when guarding her family – and she sorted out kids twice her size who were giving me a rough time. I saw a lot of her when I was in the Junior Boys and she used to help with the Babies who shared the same separate building. In fact, she became a lifelong friend of the two German sisters, Henny and Zelma Kaufman, who devoted much of their lives to the little children.

Religion played a dominant role in our lives. Or, perhaps I should say, the customs associated with religion. Of itself religion, in its ethics and philosophy, ceased to mean very much, as enforced adherence daily to its practice whittled away any enthusiasm or inquisitive interest which might otherwise have developed. However, the customs and privileges associated with each feast day – or fast day- broke the monotony of institutionalised life.

After the synagogue service on Passover eve – all festivals started on the preceding evening – we sat down at long tables, each participant having his or her own Hagaddah, literally the story which is devoted mainly to the circumstances surrounding the Exodus of the Children of Israel from Egypt under Moses. The tables were laden with matzo – unleavened bread – bottles of home-made wine of nearly zero alcoholic content, parsley in remembrance of the bitter Egyptian captivity, and other symbolic food items I have since forgotten. Bread, lollies, or any food made in everyday utensils is forbidden for the eight days of Passover, and by the eighth day the craving for fresh bread is almost uncontrollable. The superintendent of the orphanage, Louis Shaer, would start the evening's proceedings leading off with the recital of the Hagaddah and its opening statement, pointing to the matzo. 'This is the bread of our affliction.' We went through a description, almost blow by blow, of the ten plagues visited on the Egyptians, reluctant until the end to 'Let my people go.' Then, finally, came dinner. As with all festivals at Arcadia, our culinary treat was boiled poultry thanks to the generosity of benefactors living in country areas. I recall many an occasion being rostered to catch chooks a day or two before a festival and to present them to the schochet for ritual slaughter by cutting the main artery at the throat. Then we'd have an unenforceable bet to see which headless chook flapped around for the longest period of time.

After the Seder meal we would be allowed to have an additional ration of wine, the first having been sipped away at prescribed passages in the Hagaddah, and then the singing really began, some pretending they were under the influence of alcohol. I only realised many years later why Sonny, at Mom's request, kept an eye on how much I drank, in case I got a taste for it! One Passover, I was selected to read the scene-setting question and answer statement customarily delivered by the youngest family member, in Hebrew and English. It starts: 'Wherefore is this night different from any other night? Any other night we may eat leavened or unleavened bread, but this night only unleavened bread', and so on, enumerating the customs that differentiate Seder night from less important nights. The payoff for the chosen young person was a congratulatory joke from Louis Shaer and a sip of wine from his table, which was not of the current year's home-made vintage.

The Jewish New Year, Rosh Hashonah, occurs in September/October. We received some new items of clothing – children lucky enough to be in well-off homes generally received complete new outfits – boiled poultry and special dishes consistent with the Russian/Polish Ashkenazi traditions in force at Arcadia. The synagogue service was more solemn than usual. It is then that God is reputed to open the Book of Life and start to inscribe therein the fate of every human for the coming year. In fact, the traditional Rosh Hashonah greeting is 'May you be inscribed for a good year.' Furthermore, a cantor from the general community conducted the service, which was also attended by many wealthy families living in the affluent suburb of Parktown and nearby locations. In the middle of the three-hour service, eight of the visitors are in turn invited to

ascent the Bimah – an enlarged pulpit – and watch the cantor read an apportion of the Torah, handwritten on a parchment scroll. At the end of each incantation, the cantor invoked God's blessings on the person concerned, and in reply the visitor pledged donations, all in guineas, to his favourite charities, Arcadia always having priority. We all knew enough Hebrew to gauge the generosity or otherwise of the person concerned.

Just over a week later came Yom Kippur, the Day of Atonement, the holiest day in the religious calendar involving 24 hours of total fasting. On this day, the Book of Life is closed and everybody's fate sealed for another year. The cantor reads with chilling certainty 'Who will live and who will die.' Many elderly people or those with chronic sicknesses cry openly and one cannot but help being moved by the occasion. God's forgiveness is asked for broken vows promises, commitments, etc, available only if every step is taken to seek the forgiveness of those aggrieved by broken promises, etc. This particular prayer 'Kol Nidre' has been set to orchestral music and Block's composition has been recorded by all the world's best orchestras. The cantor proclaims the end of the fast with a long blast on the shofar – the ram's horn – and at Arcadia, everybody rushed to partake of the boiled poultry-dominated meal, prepared by the non-Jewish staff, of course.

Succoth, the Feast of Tabernacles, takes place eight days later. It symbolizes the transitory nature of life during the long march through the Sinai Peninsula and beyond before entering the Promised Land. The Succa at Arcadia was built of newly felled pine saplings, still smelling of their newly released resin. Their leaves were still on the poles when the outdoor Bantu staff erected the succa, subsequently blessed by the Chief Rabbi. It was large enough to accommodate the tables necessary to seat us in rotation for a meal. The festival, coinciding as it does with the Holy Land autumn, is also a harvest festival, and many fruits were suspended from the succa ceiling. These were rather limited in the South African spring. The last day of this festival is Simchat Torah, the Rejoicing of the Law. On this day, the last portion of Deuteronomy is read, thus completing a cycle of reading a portion of the Torah every Saturday from Genesis to Deuteronomy. Traditionally, the Rabbi, cantors, and the congregation rejoice physically, dancing with the Torah scrolls. The gradual Anglicisation of the Russian-Polish tradition in South Africa seemed to have inhibited this outward manifestation of joy. That's how it was at Arcadia, but we had another school holiday and boiled poultry.

At the personal level, everybody at Arcadia, boys, girls and babies, had to recite aloud prayers before and after meals. I remember clearly the first time I heard the Babies singsonging their way through these prayers. I became familiar with the rhythm of each – particularly the acceleration towards the end – long before I parroted the words and even longer before I knew the correct Hebrew pronunciation and what they meant. They were very pragmatic prayers. What could be more basic than the prayer before meals: 'Blessed art Thou, O Lord our God, who bringeth forth bread from the earth?' There were special very much longer prayers for Sabbath and the holy days.

The older boys were always in a hurry to get through the after-lunch prayers on Saturday in order to race off to see First Division soccer. Nevertheless, one particular segment of those prayers and its haunting tune still lingers on. It is Psalm 126, which describes the feelings of the exiles returning from Babylon [now Iraq] to Israel [or was it then Judea?] under the prophet Ezra. It is a paeon of hope, joy and thanksgiving, and contrasts so pointedly with Psalm 137 [which should logically have preceded it in numerical order of the Book of Psalms] when the exiles first reflected on their sad fate, a century or so earlier:

> By the waters of Babylon
> There we sat down, yea we wept
> When we remembered Zion.

All boys, except those in the Babies, had to attend prayers every night and every morning before meals, and Barmitzvahed boys [over 13] were required to don the tefilim [phylacteries] every morning except on Saturday and festival days. These consist of a small cardboard box, about 40 mm square, containing a small piece of rolled up parchment on which a relevant extract from the Bible has been hand-written. Attached to the box is a long leather strap, the box is placed on the upper left arm and the strap wrapped around the lower arm and hand in a particular manner all having a religious significance that I have long forgotten. A box and two leather straps are also placed on the head. I skipped this procedure that had become a bore, as often as I could get away with it. Girls did not have to attend week-day prayers, but those on Saturday and holy days were mandatory for everybody. Only the sick were exempted.

On turning thirteen, boys were confirmed in the Barmitzvah ceremony, the spiritual gateway to manhood. Each Barmitzvah candidate is taught to chant a small part of that portion of the Torah due to be read on the Saturday nearest to his birthday, preferably if it can be calculated according to the lunar calendar, and also to chant part of the excerpt taken from the rest of the Old Testament which is also due to be read on that Saturday. On my Barmitzvah, I read [in Hebrew, of course] Numbers 28, verses 26 to 31, and Habakkuk 3, verses 1 to 9. The numbers portion was all about sacrifices on a specific occasion – two young bullocks, one ram, seven lambs, etc. It had no uplifting effect whatsoever, nor indeed relevance to the occasion. Still, it was a tradition. The Habukkuk segment was a dire warning of disaster awaiting the sinning Israelites but with redemption available for those who repented. While the Barmitzvah ceremony was and still is a great family occasion in Jewish life, the Barmitzvah boy generally receiving lots and lots of presents, it did not mean much to me except added responsibilities. My sole present to mark the occasion was a pair of monographed cuff links from Mom and Sonny, who was then working, and a Hebrew/English Bible from the Superintendent. One of my sons now has the cuff links.

The older boys took turns to conduct religious services, except the very important ones. Chanting and responses were mechanical, the objective being to get through the service as quickly as possible, but the Superintendent would intervene if the speed got out of control. But occasionally I did pray fervently [in English], at examination times. I made all sorts of rash promises in exchange for outstanding results. I always rationalized the abandonment of my promises.

Religion was also a source of much welcome income for me when I became a senior boy. I was asked to teach some of the

prospective Barmitzvah candidates to chant their portions of the Torah. For each successful candidate, I received five shillings, an enormous sum of money in those days in the orphanage. The Torah, written on parchment by hand, includes notations above each word indicating how it should be chanted. I was never taught how to interpret these notations, so I made up my own system, but once a Hebrew scholar attended a Barmitzvah ceremony involving one of my pupils. He was aghast with the liberties I had taken with the holy script. But nobody else raised objections, and five shillings was a lot of money in those days and I would have willingly endured far more criticism before I would have been prepared to forgo such an easy source of income.

The greatest burden imposed on Jewish children in those days before the advent of Jewish day schools was attendance after secular school at Hebrew school for religious and cultural instruction. It was an hour spent at the end of a long day when powers of concentration are frayed and tired bodies want to relax. We were taught Biblical interpretation, progressing through the Old Testament by rote and rule. I well remember the sing-song repetition line by line in Hebrew and then in English. I recall particularly passages from Genesis to do with the creation, and most of all Genesis 2, verse 21:

> And they were not ashamed
> Before each other.

We also learned about post-Biblical Jewish history, the tragedies of the Crusades, the pogroms in Eastern Europe, the Enlightenment, the phoney allegations which surfaced throughout the Middle Ages of ritual murders, and dearest to my heart, the Golden Age of the Sephardi Jews in Spain under the Moors from about 700 to 1000 AD. The Spanish Inquisition and finally the expulsion of Jews from Spain and Portugal by King Ferdinand and Queen Isabella in 1492 sent shivers down my spine. I regarded it as one of the most fateful events in post-Biblical history coming, as it did, after centuries of complete integration and harmony between people of different faiths. The Sephardim held the most important public and private positions available in Moorish Spain. They were Grand Viziers, Commanders-in-Chief of Armies, they designed and built the most outstanding buildings of the time, including the Alhambra, they were philosophers, poets, surgeons, etc. Despite all this, their bona fides were ultimately rejected and their achievements and commitment counted for nothing in their hour of need. We even shared the horrors of English Jews massacred at York in the 11th century.

I often think back as to what influence religion played in my life. There were not many positive aspects. Judaism is a celebration of history as much as a philosophy and a moral code, but what remains mainly in my mind from my formative years is the historical highs and lows, and in my own lifetime and that of my parents, the pogroms in Russia and later the emergence of Nazism in Germany and its tragic evolution. It is no wonder that the antagonistic and brutal side of the Jewish interface with Christianity, or more accurately I should say with nominally Christian nations, left the more enduring impression on me.

While the daily enforcement of religious observances turned me against the practices of institutionalised religion, it did not turn me into an agnostic or an atheist. I believe that spiritual faith is so personal that there is an infinite variety of perceptions of this faith, and, like Tevye in Fiddler on the Roof, I believe that there is always an open line right to the very top.

I did not make any lasting friendships at Arcadia. I got closest to those surrogate siblings with whom I vied for scholastic achievement. The monthly mark sheets issued at Parktown High listed every pupil's achievements in every subject, and Mom's main interest was as to how I had performed vis-a-vis the other two Arcadians in the class. The standing of the other 27 pupils was of scant interest. If one from Arcadia had excelled in science, she wanted to know why I could not do as well and reverse the situation next time around. As a result, she got to know my competitors, and to some extent, their parents too.

Visiting day was every first and third Sunday of the month from 2 p.m. to 5 p.m. If there were a fifth Sunday, it meant a break of three weeks between visits. At about 1.45 p.m. on visiting Sundays, eager children would congregate at vantage points with a good view of Oxford Road, and, in particular, the bus stop. Most children could recognise their parent from the moment they stepped off the bus, probably from their walk, dress, and the number of carrier bags filled with cake, fruit, sandwiches, etc. Mom's carrier bags were near bulging; mainly they contained leftovers from the de Wilde-Cowan boarding house where she lived and worked while at rest from her daytime job.

Every family group had its reserved spot for visiting day. We had a secluded stone seat at the head of a short flight of stone steps, but not that secluded that Mom could not observe which Mothers were sporting new boy friends or Dads introducing new women friends to the children, or who was pregnant again and even who was drunk! One family in particular occupied her constant attention. They were the 'Black' Kotzens, as distinct from the 'White' Kotzens who had fair hair. Mrs 'Black' Kotzen always seemed to have three small children permanently attached to her; one just learning to walk, one in her arms, and one bulging out from behind her ample skirt. As the youngest of the three became a little less dependent on its mother's support, it joined the five or six or more already in Arcadia. There were eventually twelve or thirteen children. While Arcadia was called an orphanage, it was rather a refuge for the children of parents who could not support their broods. There were very few real orphans at Arcadia. Mr 'Black' Kotzen's claim to fame was his Army service in the trenches in France in World War I, and many of the soldier songs of that era I learned from him through his older sons.

I never asked Mom for money as I know how hard things were for her, but when Sonny started work I used to get sixpence each Saturday to spend at the soccer, or to see the latest movie at the 'Hippodrome'. I remember well standing in an agreed spot every Saturday afternoon, watching and waiting for Sonny. Far in the distance I'd see a small figure on a bicycle pedalling for all his worth to deliver my weekly allowance. He never failed me.

At visiting time, Mom would not only keep her eyes open but also her ears, and if she heard somebody talking loudly in a foreign language, she would mutter disapprovingly 'Bloody Peruvian'. They certainly were not from South America, but generally from Russia or Poland. This nickname for foreign

Jews was unique to South Africa and there is a very interesting story behind it. It appears that a member of the Cape Legislative Assembly, Mr. Lima, a former migrant from Central Europe, incurred the wrath of a colleague from the Anglo-Saxon establishment, who dismissed as irrelevant Mr Lima's comment on a matter under discussion. As Lima is or was the capital of Peru, he assumed a link between Peru and his adversary and referred dismissively to the ramblings of the 'Peruvian' Jew. Thereafter, all foreign Jews were referred to, by Anglo and other English-speaking Jewry in particular, as Peruvians. The louder one spoke a foreign tongue in public, particularly Yiddish, the more disgust seemed to go into the denunciation as 'a Peruvian'.

I started school in January 1927 at Hebrew High School. It was probably once a private school attached to the main Johannesburg synagogue opposite, but when I started there it was a government secular school with probably an hour a day for Hebrew lessons. The highlight of the day was the arrival at lunchtime of the 'Old Lady', wheeling her pram converted to a mobile mini-tuckshop. The orphanage kids generally flocked around to see who had money to spend and to window shop. The 'Old Lady' [she was originally from England] was old and frail and, with no social security safety net in those days, she was constantly on the verge of starvation. Even we realized that, living as we were at Arcadia on public charity, we were far better off than she was. I once saw the miserable sordid circumstances under which she lived, and poverty took on a new meaning.

After two years at Hebrew High, together with most of the orphanage children, I became part of the inaugural intake of a new school that had just been completed, only about a kilometre at the most from Arcadia's north-west boundary. It was called Forest Town School. Hebrew High eventually closed down, but later became an Afrikaans-medium school. I often wonder what, if anything, they then did with the foundation stone in Hebrew and English, consecrating the building for non-Christian purposes. Forest Town School had barely been completed when we moved in. One could smell freshly applied paint. The grounds were totally undeveloped, except for the construction of night-soil toilets. I remember the first day there, sitting under a eucalypt – probably a Victorian Bluegum – and squashing the leaves to enjoy the pungent smell. We had sat near an ants' nest and in no time we were being attacked in fury. We boys, dressed in short pants and no underpants, called them ball-biters for obvious reasons. The girls too then called them ball-biters, with a daring very rare in those days.

The school was strictly secular. My teacher in the first two years, a Miss Morrison, basked in the reflected glory of her two brothers who were outstanding sportsmen – soccer and cricket. Miss Kotze, a frustrated embittered Afrikaner spinster, was a disaster in my third year, 1931. I think she deeply resented her posting to a school composed almost entirely of Jewish children. After a few months, she informed a few of the brighter kids, including me, that we could do what we pleased for the rest of the school year as we would have no difficulty passing the exam at the end of the year. As we shared the classroom with the grade above, we asked whether we could then join that grade. Her response was to please ourselves, but we would then have to repeat that grade the following year because of our younger age. It meant utter boredom for that year in the classroom, but for Miss Kotze it meant fewer children to bother about. It did not occur to her to suggest challenges to develop whatever talent we had. As a result, I spent much of terms two and three running messages for the principal, mainly to the Education Department headquarters in Central Johannesburg.

The principal was a lovely Scottish lady, called Miss Brotherhood. No name could have been more apt. She usually gave me sixpence for my excursion to town. Out of this I paid twopence each way on the bus, and the remaining twopence was for my own enjoyment, generally cheap lollies. One day she gave me a long list of things I had to do in town, and pinned to the note, was a five pound note – an enormous sum of money for a young boy to be entrusted with in those days. Somehow I lost the note and, consequently, the money. Miss Brotherhood was very upset. She probably had to make it up from her own salary, which would not have been very much more than the lost fiver. I was upset too because I felt I had betrayed her unquestioned and absolute trust. She called us all together and explained what had happened and asked us all to pray for the recovery of the lost money. Her simple Presbyterian prayer would have been acceptable to the adherents of any faith, and it was not in vain. A few days later, she received a letter enclosing the lost shopping list with the five pound note still attached. And that during the depths of the great Depression. What pleased her almost as much was that, judging from the accompanying note, the honest finder was a fellow Scot.

Thankfully, Miss Kotze was relieved of her posting and another Afrikaner, a lady in every and the best sense of the word, took over responsibility for the joint Standards 3 and 4 classroom. Miss Kruywagen soon noticed a number of us disinterested in what was going on. We informed her of our understanding of our situation as expounded by Miss Kotze. She rejected the situation out of hand and told us that, if we worked hard during the final term and passed the Standard 4 exam, we would proceed to Standard 5, thereby skipping a year in Primary School. Not only did we do that, but we filled the top positions.

Standard 5 was an awkward year as Forest Town only went up to standard 4, and the equivalent of Standard 6 was the first year at High School. So we had to be found a school to cater only for that year. It was Spes Bona Intermediate School, the name signifying that it went up to Standard 8, mainly for children unable, unsuitable, or unwilling to go to High School.

The worst part of attending my new school was the physical process of getting there as we had to walk. The orphanage bus was reserved for the girls, the walking sick, and the convalescent. It was uphill all the way. Oxford Road just outside Arcadia had a slope now reminiscent of Clyde Mountain, there was a further drag up to the Children's Hospital and an even steeper climb past the Infectious Diseases Hospital, reaching 'The Fort' at the top of the hill practically breathless. Spes Bona was a hundred yards or so further on. Opposite Spes Bona was the walled rear of the South African Institute of Medical Research.

Spes Bona is the Latin for Good Hope and refers to the first permanent settlement by the Dutch of the south-western tip of the continent. The Portuguese under Bartholomew Diaz were the first to circumnavigate the continent, and named the south-west tip the Cape of Storms, using it only for re-victualling purposes. The Dutch landed there in 1652 and took up permanent occupation under Jan Van Riebeeck, who renamed the area the Cape of Good Hope, making his headquarters on the side now occupied by Cape Town. Spes Bona drew its pupils mainly from the lower socio-economic stratum, mainly Afrikaners from the semi-slum suburb of Braamfontein and neighbouring areas. I saw Braamfontein again in 1972 when Mardi and I visited our relatives in Johannesburg. It is now high value inner city commercial real estate – a far cry from the depressing sight it was in 1932. Although it was an English-medium school, Afrikaans was the main language of the playground, and it was there that I first came in contact with Afrikaners of my own age. To a small degree, this was my introduction to their hang-ups, prejudices, chips-on-the-shoulder, and sometimes to their humour and kindness.

Apart from the orphanage kids, there were six or so other Jewish children, and probably for our own well-being, we were placed in the same class under the sole Jewish teacher at the school, who received a very rough time from the senior pupils in Standards 7 and 8. The headmaster, Mr Harris, was a delightful, reserved, kind and courteous Welshman, with a lift in his step as well as in his voice. His eyebrows would have made those of Bob Menzies look like pencil lines. He was a staunch Methodist and every morning at assembly we would sing a hymn from the Methodist hymn book. There I learned to sing and love many of those hymns such as 'Abide With Me,' 'O God Our Help in Ages Past', and my favourite 'O God of Bethel,' with regard to which I must admit that the second line was very relevant to one living on public charity during the Depression:

> O God of Bethel by Whose hand
> The people still are fed.

I am sure that it was in deference to the handful of Jewish children that he only selected hymns with minimal obvious Christian references. Never once was the assembly asked to sing 'Onward Christian solders'. How he would love to lead the choir celestial in that rousing call to arms! I never felt guilty of betrayal in joining in the singing, though hesitantly at first. To the contrary, I had at last found something in common with the world at large. In later years, I realized why Roman Catholicism has never and can never take hold in Wales. The rigid Catholic liturgy provides little scope for the choral ability and enthusiasm of the Welsh.

One Afrikaner used to call me 'ten-in-five' as I was a year younger than normal for Standard Five, but possibly three years or so in size and maturity. I also rejoiced in the nickname of 'Jack' for most of my stay at Spes Bona. This followed the special attention once received from the gym master at our weekly physical training exercises when, noticing me for the first time alongside a gawky lanky boy as inept as I was in following his instructions, he bellowed to the delight of his entire audience, 'Hey, you two there! Jack and the Beanstalk! Get those knees up! Up! Up! Up!'

I once witnessed with horror a vicious fight between two Afrikaners, one of whom had called the other a bastard. This word had a double meaning in South Africa. Firstly, it reflected on the non-marital status of one's mother at the time of birth,

19

which to the strictly observant Calvinists of the Dutch Reformed Church was insult enough, but it also referred to a community in the Cape Province called the Bastards, the progeny of miscegenation with native inhabitants during the early years of Dutch settlement. Its use in this context, or rather its interpretation in this context, implied doubt as to the purity of one's genetic heritage. Even in jest, it was an unbearable insult, even in those pre-apartheid days.

'The Fort' and its associated public activities pre-occupied everybody. 'The Fort' was the main prison in Johannesburg. Every Monday morning, we would watch what seemed to be an endless procession of blacks shuffling along towards The Fort for contravening the pass laws over the weekend. Only recently have these iniquitous laws been repealed. They required blacks to carry an identification card and, if away from their residential address after specified hours, to carry a signed authorization from their employers. Blacks coming in from the countryside in search of employment were prime targets. Then there was the infamous Daisy de Melker. She was up on a charge for murdering three husbands for their insurance policies. It was alleged that she poisoned them with arsenic. We often stood outside the Fort waiting to catch a glimpse of her as she stepped up into the back of the Black Maria for conveyance to the Law Courts. She was eventually found guilty and hanged. Once she turned to us, rudely staring at this notorious woman, and calmly said 'Now that you have seen me, I hope you all feel better.'

The South African Institute of Medical Research was also an area of considerable interest, mainly to the more daring and adventurous. Some said that if you lifted yourself to the top of the seven-foot high brick wall, you could see parts of human bodies, decaying animals, and all sorts of ghoulish things. I was not that daring or adventurous, and besides, I had a weak stomach.

I entered Parktown Boys High School in January 1933. Sonny had matriculated there in 1932 and Lillian, two or three years ahead of me, was still at Parktown Girls High School, a couple of miles away. I had never before been particularly conscious of the school clothes all boys at the orphanage wore. While the girls wore the gym dresses and white blouses generally worn at all schools, the boys wore khaki shorts and trousers and black boots. The Arcadia uniform, because that is what it was, did not stand out in a school that did not have a specific uniform all were required to wear. At Spes Bona, for instance, the combination of clothing was endless – one girl even came to school once in an evening dress! But at Parktown High, our khaki clothes and boots stood out starkly against the black blazer, white shirt, black shorts, and socks topped with the black and red school colours, which everybody else wore almost without exception. Many of the Parktown High pupils came from affluent homes, but even those from modest homes avoided the Principal's wrath reserved for those not wearing full Parktown High regalia. Our identity was bared for everyone to see; anyone dressed in khaki was a kid from the orphanage. It was the first time that I encountered discrimination which seemed to continue every day.

Many of the teachers at Parktown were sensitive to our isolation and did their best to make us feel just like any other schoolboy.

But it was not easy. Firstly, we had to leave school immediately after classes to attend Hebrew classes back at Arcadia. This made it virtually impossible to take part in organised extra-curricular activities such as sport and cultural activities, including debating. There was also the financial problem of being able to buy sporting equipment even for those who might have been chosen on ability alone. One could be excused from Hebrew classes for special purposes, but one could not plan on exemption as an ongoing special privilege.

I do not think that the orphanage authorities had us dressed as outsiders at Parktown High for any sinister purpose. Perhaps it was cheaper to have everybody at Arcadia dressed alike, and so not create an elite group just because they were brighter than their fellows. Perhaps they did not even think about the psychological implications of discrimination by dress.

The only sport I took part in was boxing, which formed part of our weekly session in the gymnasium. For all first four of my five years at High School I boxed in the same division – under 70 pounds, in weight ranging from 65 to 69 pounds. Even in my matriculation year I was the second smallest in the whole school and still only slightly above the weight limit I had boxed in previously.

The annual boxing tournament results were recorded *in The Parktonian*, the school magazine, the division in which I boxed, being the lightest division, was recorded at the start of the tournament report. Mostly I was recorded as the loser in the final – there were always only two of us in the division, But in one of the four years I took part, I won the division. To my horror and disappointment, the result was not reported in *The Parktonian*. Robbed of my crowded hour of glorious life!

The school activities were organized along the lines of the English Public Schools, even to the point of sometimes identifying brothers as, for instance, Smith Major and Smith Minor. A third brother would be identified as Smith Tertius, etc. All were organized into 'Houses'. As Sonny was in Trojans, I automatically became a Trojan. The other Houses were Romans, Spartans, Thebans, and Tuscans. At inter-house sporting competitions, everybody was expected to wear a rosette in the house colours, and Mom always obliged with a large brown rosette.

I once turned up to play cricket for Trojans' Junior 'C' Team, which generally fielded less than the full complement of players for lack of interest. I faced only one ball, which hit me on the thumbnail. It turned black and then septic, which caused no end of pain and inconvenience. I remember the concern and kindness of my Afrikaans teacher at the time, at my failed cricket career and its painful aftermath.

I once took part in an inter-class friendly rugby game – or so I thought. I was waiting very patiently for the ball to come my way, scorning the hooliganism in the scrums. Eventually it did come my way. I was hopelessly offside but I still grabbed the ball to register a try, even though I knew it would be disallowed. I had taken only a few strides towards the opposition's goal posts when its full-black, 'Boer' Watermeyer, who played for the schools First XV, bent down, grabbed my ankle, and effortlessly upended me. I fell on my nose, which bled profusely. So ended another failed foray into the world of sport.

Miriam Alex and friend - June 1940

BIOGRAPHICAL and EDITORIAL NOTES
Written by Leonore Manderson from AFRICA and EUROPE 1921-1946 A Memoir of Alex Manderson

Alex Manderson was born Alexander Mendelson on 28 June 1921. This Memoir is his account of his first 25 years: as a small child in Volksrust and an older child in a Jewish orphanage in Johannesburg; as a young man who for two years worked and studied while he lived with his mother, brother and sister; as a member of the South African Irish Regiment in Kenya, Egypt and Libya; as a prisoner-of-war in southern Italy and in numerous locations in Germany; and finally, again, as a student in South Africa, leading to his migration to Australia.

Alex's migration to Australia followed his earlier efforts to find freedom – from the injustices of apartheid South Africa, the rigidity of its social structure, and the added layers of conservatism and constraint, complicated post-war by guilt and fear of being Jewish. In this memoir, the interpersonal and societal tensions of family, nation and army are gently told. Alex provides a wry account both of his childhood and South Africa's war effort – largely a comedy of errors, in which he casts himself as an accidental clown. His description of his regiment's trek in tanks across the Libyan desert, often heading in the same direction as those of the enemy, worthy of Dad's Army, and explains to his family his delight in television slapstick accounts of the war. Other sections of the memoir are more poignant and wonderfully honest: the pervasive theme of hunger; the repetitious failures at various ordinary everyday

achievements (sport for example); his innocent and rare encounters with young women; his boredom, rather than fear, as a prisoner-of-war; his awe of the scenery as he crosses Italy to a camp in Germany; his self-doubts, speculations and regrets; his desperation for adventure, for personal and intellectual freedom.

The memoir does not present us with easy good and evil characters neatly aligned to Allies and axis forces. South African racism and anti-Semitism are sketched in relief by the unexpected humanity of various Italian and German guards. Alex's jailor, circumstantial friend and tutor, Nappi Giovanni, is one of the most memorable characters in his account. His mother – a constant figure throughout, admonishing him, singing music hall songs, struggling, fooling in the kitchen, begging him not to leave – is no less memorable.

Alex arrived in Australia on 12 November 1946. He married Marjorie Hannah Hogarth [Mardi] in Melbourne on 4 May 1950. They lived on a farm, Blyvoor [blue hills in Afrikaans], at Yannathan Upper, South Gippsland, Victoria, from 1950-1960, then Langlaagte [low flat country] at Logie Brae, near Jerilderie, the Riverina, New South Wales, from 1960-1964. With Lenore [b. 1951], Richard [b. 1954], Roland [b. 1955] and Desmond [b. 1960], they moved to Canberra in October 1964. Here he joined the public service, working variously with the Bureau of Agricultural Economics, the Department of External Territories, and the Department of Natural Resources. He remained in Canberra for the rest of his life.

Alex wrote this memoir in 1990 and it was Mardi who converted his semi-legible longhand to a typed manuscript. The shared task was completed three days before his untimely and unexpected death, on 10 December 1990. In editing the manuscript for Mardi, Richard, Roland and Desmond, I have made minor corrections only, such as rare spelling or grammatical errors. Alex wrote as he spoke. This is his voice at multiple levels. We make it public for those who mourn him, and especially for his four grandchildren – Jake, Tobi, Kerith and Alice Bach Ngoc.

OLD ARCS REMEMBER ALEX MANDERSON

Mannie Osrin

I remember Alec very well, but the last time I ever saw him must have been when he just left school. He must have been one of the most brilliant of people ever to have been in the Arc, and reached a high level of Public service / Government officialdom.

All this I learned from his late brother Isadore, who was a patient of mine for many years, before he went to live in Perth, to be with his son, who is a very prominent G P in Perth, Ralph Mendelsohn.

*****

Bertha Kronenberg (Klevansky)

I remember the Mendelsohns very well, and in fact recall their mother when she used to visit.

The Mendelsohns were considered clever, and Alec I think was at school, at Parktown with my brother Hymie while Isadore would have been at school with my brother Vicky.

I seem to remember Lillian being friendly with my sister Rae. I being, what seemed at the time, much younger, didn't know any of them personally.

*****

Alex Orange Grove March 1940

Freda Cheilyk

I met up with Alec Mendelsohn's daughter Lenore some years ago.

Lenore had taken her young child to the Jewish Kindy and asked Clare Goldstein who is the Director of the Kindy whether she knew if Arcadia still exists. I was on a visit in Brisbane at the time and Clare said if she wanted information she should get in touch with me. We met for coffee and we had a most interesting discussion. Lenore told me that her father had written a book and she was to edit same and publish the book. I told her I did not actually know Alec but knew the name also that of Isadore Mendelsohn.

I also told her that Molly Levine often spoke of Alec and told me that Alec said that when he grows up he would go to Australia and become a rich sheep farmer. Lenore said her father hated

sheep. I also said that Alec's name was on the Roll of Honour when he served in the army in the second World War. I sent one of the Arcadia Bulletins to Lenore so she could see the picture of Arcadia and her father's name on the Roll of Honour.

Lenore proceeded to tell me that they never knew that her father was Jewish until the end of the six day war when Alec became very emotional and called his family together to inform them that he was Jewish.

Lenore Manderson is at the Queensland University and holds a high position there. I will try to get in touch with Lenore again as I feel sure she would be delighted to see what has been written about Alec.

LILLIAN AND ISADORE MENDELSOHN
Written by Graeme Finberg

Lillian, my Mom, was born in 1918 in Volksrust and was in the care of Arcadia from 1927 to 1935.

She married Hymie Finberg who was born in Golders Green London in Cape Town 5th March 1944 and has two Children: Janice and Graeme. Janice is a travel agent lives in Johannesburg had two daughters Arlene and Helena both of whom live overseas. Graeme an accountant has four sons Craig Anton Matthew and Saul and lives in Perth Western Australia

Isadore (Sonny) Mendelsohn was born 5th December 1916 in Volksrust and was in the care of Arcadia from 1926 to 1932

He married Doreen Leiman in Johannesburg. They had three Children Geoffrey Ralph and Karen. Geoffrey is Prof of Pathology and has two sons Kevin and Clifford lives in Cleveland Ohio. Ralph is a highly respected medical practitioner has a son and daughter and lives in Perth Western Australia and Karen has a daughter Jodi and lives in Irvine Califormia USA

Sonny (Isadore) Mendelsohn never came to settle in Perth. He went to visit his eldest son in Cleveland and took ill and passed away there in August 2000 just before he was due to come and live with my family. He was very close to us. He lost his wife in 1991 and became a very integral part of our family unit. We nursed him through a multiple heart bypass operation in 1994 and subsequent heart episodes thereafter, I can recall being called out a few times in the middle of the night when he was ill.

I would call in and take him to my home most evenings and after dinner would take him back to his apartment. I never wanted him to be alone and he loved the trips to the Kruger National Park and Warmbaths with my family. He was a surrogate Grandfather to my four sons. If we were invited out for Shabbat or on a Sunday for lunch Sonny came with as he was a member of our family.

To ensure that my family are never forgotten I have dedicated various items of Judaica in our Shul in their name. I have placed Plaques on the Memorial Board and dedicated Chumashim and Siddurim to honour them.

Chapter 4 – BERTHA KRONENBERG (KLEVANSKY) (1924)

Bertha was born in 1924 and lived in Arcadia from 1926 to 1940. Bertha was the youngest of five siblings, Isaac born 1915, Sydney 1916, Rachel 1919 and Hymie 1921.

Their parents both came from Lithuania in the late 1900s. Their father was from Shadova and their mother from Tels.

Her eldest brother Isaac (Ike) (now deceased) left the home when he was fourteen to go to work and is deceased. Interestingly he married Lily Aginsky, also an Old Arc. They have family of six who are professionals in the sphere of education, law, medicine, physics and computer science, one in Europe and one in Australia.

Her brother Sidney (Vicky) spent many, many years in Arcadia looking after the children in numerous capacities and is well known by Arcs of many generations.

Rachel went to work in Europe for the American Joint Distribution Committee and later the American Jewish Committee. She is married, is now 86 and still lives in Paris.

Hymie is a Dermatologist, lives in Port Elizabeth and at 83 still practices there.

Bertha matriculated while at Arcadia and at one time Wolf Hillman agreed to sponsor her to go to University. He changed his mind –' you're only a girl and will get married. She worked as a shorthand typist; later joined the Air Force (Sergeant Meteorological Section). She then worked in the "Welfare Department" of the S.A. Jewish Board of Deputies. In 1946 Bertha married Gerhard Kronenberg. She emigrated to Canada in 1987. They have three sons and four grandchildren.

Bertha studied for her BA Hon (English) when her boys were growing up, and was working part-time.

Michael Perry Kotzen writes that Bertha is an excellent, poetic and prolific writer and that her reminiscing of Arcadia and Arcadians and her love and devotion for her brother Vicky are moving, nostalgic and colourful.

AN ADDRESS BY BERTHA TO THE MIZRACHI COMMITTEE TORONTO 1987

Firstly I want to outline briefly the history of the orphanage as it was then known. The South African Jewish Orphanage was officially founded at the beginning of the century to accommodate orphans from Russia. It had a modest beginning but in time as the numbers grew it began to expand. In the mid-twenties the Jewish Ladies Communal League bought the home of Lord and Lady Lionel Phillips, mining magnates of the time. The property extended over 25 acres and was indeed a type of paradise for the orphans who were placed there. I came to the Home at the age of two and left at the age of sixteen when I went work and when I supported myself. The orphanage was my home, it moulded my being, gave me warmth when I needed it; provided the basis of my culture and had a tremendous impact.

1929 Bertha & Isaac Klevansky

Mid Thirties – Vicky as Cub Master And Bertha

1934 Nita Friedland, Rachel And Bertha Klevansky

Mid Thirties Bertha Ruby Stoller & Vicky

I think at this stage I should tell you that I am the youngest of five children, all of whom grew up at Arcadia. The eldest was ten years older than I am. Arcadia is the name given by the Phillips to their home situated then in the most affluent section of the city. As a child I remember gardens laid out exquisitely, with mazes of neatly clipped lavender hedges surrounding beds of roses. At its centre was an idyllic spot, a fishpond surrounded by benches, the background a riot of flowering mauve and white wisteria in spring, and in summer a shady escape from the heat. With time all of this was to change as new buildings were added for extra accommodation. The main building had a sweep of marble stairs, ornate balustrades, and the huge ceilings were borne on mighty fluted columns with Corinthian and Doric plinths. There was a magnificent panelled library that served as our Shul. I remember many a Sabbath morning sitting at the services with one eye on the Chazan (usually an older of the Home) and listening to the drowsy buzzing of the bees outside. My home was a far cry from the austere drab room where my father stayed in downtown Johannesburg.

Most of the children were the offspring of immigrants from Lithuania – folk who were simple, spoke mainly Yiddish and had fallen on hard times either financially or because of poor health, or where one of the parents was deceased.

The highlights of the year – twice annually we were allowed to go out to family. On each such day we rose early, polished our shoes once again, and waited expectantly for parents to fetch us. These days were marvellous in the true sense of the word. I come from a large family, but sadly none of my aunts, uncles or cousins visited me in the home. They made up for it on the days out when we were spoilt and plied with food. Later when I discussed this with family the explanation came out – there was just not sufficient money for the fare to the home. Another highlight of our year was Pesach and Rosh Hashonah when we had special food; in winter, around Pesach a new winter dress and on Rosh Hashonah a summer dress – both of which were made by a seamstress on the premises – and all the same material and the same pattern.

We also had picnics from time to time when we were bundled into large open trucks and yelled our lungs out singing songs. Perhaps the most magical times I spent at Arcadia were when we went to the Sea Side. Now Johannesburg is situated 6000 feet above sea level on a plateau. The air is rarified. What a difference at sea level. This camp took place every four years – a whole train was booked and we kids were almost mad with excitement. We wore khaki shirts and shorts, slept in tents on the soft sea sand, and had campfires every night. It was a time of magic, of wonder unrestricted fun and enjoyment. I attended three such camps that lasted six weeks each.

But back to basics, let me tell you how Arcadia was run. We children were housed according to our age and sex. Up to the age of six one was a baby, seven to 12 was the Junior Department and the Seniors were children over this age. In the early years I remember sleeping in rooms with about eight beds. I remember attending a kindergarten run at the home by two ladies from Frankfurt.

From them I heard my first German, some of which I later learnt were derogatory "*schweine hund*" is one that comes to mind, and at the same times little tunes that we little ones sang with

gusto. My early years up to the age of about eight were extremely happy, there was enough stimulation, plenty of open gardens and fields to enjoy. We were, I think, extremely fortunate.

The Home stood on a hill overlooking a broad valley and we children lived in the main building, upstairs, overlooking African veldt where we could see the mauve-blue of a distant mountain ridge. I developed a love of the outdoors. In more ways although our lives were regimented, when I look back I know that although we lacked a great deal materially and socially, we had a lot more than children who were brought up by their parents in the very difficult years of the Great Depression.

I have written several anecdotes about Arcadia which reveal that my experience was not a strict black and white picture, neither was it straight up and down. It varied. These anecdotes show a child who was at times terribly unhappy, who in my preteens felt a terrible void, a lack of genuine motherly love. The system had a housemother for about 40 children, who slept next to their dormitories and supervised them. I feel in retrospect that some were unsuited for this task. Their method of discipline was harsh; at times a smack with a brush dipped in salt water, at others group punishment was tried. This usually involved us sitting with fingers on lips, forbidden to move or speak for what seemed like hours. I detest any form of group punishment.

This brings me to schooling. Nearby within walking distance we attended a Government School, which was also attended by a couple of kids in the neighbourhood. We kids all wore the same clothing, and the children from, whom we called "private" homes, dressed with white socks and brown shoes. We wore black socks and black shoes. Our hair was cut en masse by the same barber and whether the hair was curly, wavy, thick or thin, it was cut in the same style; straight fringe, straight all around. We all looked the same.

There was uniformity about our lives, clothing for the week and special clothing for the Jewish holidays – all made of the same material and of the same design. Each child's clothing bore an allotted number. No.1 was my number as a baby; and later no.8. In a sense we were depersonalised. There was no feeling of having anything really, nothing that was essentially one's own, and I feel that this was to manifest itself in the in-between years, namely nine to 11. Some of my friends cherished their physical possessions to the extreme.

This in-between time was important in another sense, for it was the time of innocence with an occasional occurrence of sexual awareness. Any discussion of sex was taboo: there was never any contact with boys who were housed in separate quarters.

Please don't let me leave you with the impression that my childhood was unhappy. We had dancing lessons, some had piano lessons, we had a brownie and guide pack, were instructed in First Aid, and a showing on Saturday night of Films. I think there were children in Johannesburg who did not enjoy these benefits. This did not make up for the lack of social intercourse, and the estrangement from family.

We didn't know how to buy food and had no idea of the cost of things. Although limited in variety these were always there for us, however humdrum. This was wrong. What was good in those days is that we had to be able to help ourselves, certain duties were allotted; we either had to prepare tables for meals, serve the food, or sweep and dust areas.

Arcadia is still a strictly orthodox institution hence I grew up in a total Judaic environment and knew no other. The boys attended Shul morning and nigh, the girls on Friday night, Saturday morning and night, and of course on all Jewish holidays. I think to this day, I know Minchah, Maariv and Neilah by heart. From the age of six we attended Chedar in premises set aside for Hebrew lessons, every day of the week except weekends.

Nothing was easy when you were one of 40 girls. There really was no privacy to study or do homework. Winter times we sat on the hot water pipes in the washroom – the floor concrete, the silence broken by the soft scuttle of cockroaches. We had battles to overcome – coming face to face with the wealthy girls at school. School projects were a challenge, any pictorial material hard to come by, no books to consult, no magazines to read. I was fortunate in that I loved math and science but my lack of contact with adults stifled my knowledge of language. I made up for it in other directions.

I never lost my thirst for knowledge and with three teens, at the age of forty-four I started studying, 26 years after I finished school. Majoring in English and Psychology and English, I obtained honours in English studied French, German, Zulu and Philosophy.

I was a conscientious student but in my final year started to worry about where I could stay when I left Arcadia. I had lost my father in the same year.

My life in an institution would be lacking if I did not mention the aftermath of this experience. I finished my schooling in Matric, and although boys were sent to University it was felt, at that stage, unnecessary for girls, however brilliant or gifted. Members of my family were all living in different places and Arcadia arranged a rental of a room in a Jewish home. Nothing, but nothing was as traumatic as this transition in my life. I was virtually thrust into an alien and strangely silent world where I was desperately lonely and unhappy. I must confess that I cried bitterly when I, aged 16, left the home that I had known and loved.

Retracing my steps, we girls received our higher schooling in one of the best schools at that time. Here I was happy and thwarted. I felt deeply conscious of the fact that my classmates spoke about their homes, their parents and evaded questions from them. At times the children from the home were invited to concerts and other musicals. We would arrive in a large bus with the Institutions name on the side, deeply conscious of people staring at us, all dressed in the same colour and style dress with long black stockings.

When I left Arcadia I experienced a deep sense of shame for having been brought up on charity. I learnt quickly to survive; paid my rent for board and lodging (five pounds) at the time, clothed myself and paid my fare on the balance of three pounds. I found a job quickly after an intensive three month secretarial course but never stopped trying to improve myself. Somehow I managed to pay 50 pence a month for shorthand lessons in the

evenings, and saved money on transport by walking to and from work (maybe five miles each way). They were difficult yet happy years and I experienced the frustrations of adolescence but coped. I was 21 years of age when I met the person whom I later married, and the first thing I had to make clear was the fact that I had been brought up in the Jewish Orphanage.

There are some of my peers who are still ashamed of their background, but for me and countless others we are proud of this fact, proud to have made it in a world where everybody was jostling to be somebody. We have an Association of Old Arcadians scattered across the globe.

This brings me to the last stage of my talk. I met Charlotte Sasto the first time when I joined the Arcadia Committee in 1973, her name was synonymous with Jewish charitable work. Her loss to the Arcadia Committee is your gain: Her loss to other Jewish organisations is immeasurable.

With me on the Arcadia Committee were many of the young boys I had grown up with, boys who studied at night after work as I did and made good. Many are specialists in their fields, medicine, architecture, law, and business while others are leaders of their congregations.

The following is a collection of Bertha's Arc Memories

WHO IS THIS BABY?

The child, aged two or so, is the latest arrival in the Arcadia records, year 1926. She has an olive skin and brown eyes; a pleasant child, the youngest of five Klevanskys. That's who I am, and now over 76 years later, this is a picture of my early days.

In the main building, upstairs in a large corner bedroom, facing north with two ornate balconies, there is a fireplace with an elegant fireguard – and dimly, ever so dimly figures around me come and go. Is it my ear being rinsed with a kidney basin placed under it? Days go by – vaguely, nudging my memory I recall the name of Dr Rose Baranoff – I hear myself talking in baby language, sounds that have no meaning except for me – I'm a slow talker, I believe, but when I do start to form words and sentences they erupt urgently and cogently.

There is a rustling sound, of freshly starched linen and Henny Kaufmann is there, uniform white, cap on head and a thick stiff belt adding order and authority. Under the trees on the large lawn in front of the main building we played "Ring-a-Roses, pocket full of Posies"................and there I was to learn the German words that echo down the years

> "Hanchen Klein geht allein
> in die weiter weld hinein…."
> Little Hans ventured forth
> all alone in the wide world

We small ones clapped hands in rhythm to the song.

Did you ever glance in the built-in shelves in the panelled dining room? Did you see displays of our work? Dressed in cotton dresses, each small figure with apron and floppy hat we little ones spent many hours threading coloured strips of paper through slotted sheets of paper.

These early years may be coloured with my fancy, but Arcadia is the only home I remember, where my consciousness of my world seemed to start, and from where some 15 years later I unwillingly left her embrace.

BEYOND THE WALL

Once a year the children were allowed 'out', that being the manner of saying that the children were allowed to visit parents or relatives for a whole day.

The six-foot wall around the Children's Home had been there for as long as Rita could remember, and although daily she walked to and from school, it was not the same thing. School days saw the children, in pairs, walking in double file, perhaps some 40 of them, an anonymous collection of navy blue pants, white skirts, black shoes and socks.

On the day out coloured dresses made their appearance, hands clutched adult hands of a mother, father, aunt or uncle. Black shoes were replaced by brown, and black socks by white.

This special day started weeks before with preparations and childish boasts and exaggerated accounts of what the day held. The more extended the family, the greater the possibilities.

The children experienced the thrill of getting up earlier than on school days, so early it seemed foolish, for there was a long wait before their folks would arrive.

The departure was a mosaic of passengers alighting from the bus to fetch their offspring, and for each child the adult was special. The particular thing about this going out was the return.

Now for Rita the excitement was intense, and the journey almost overpowering. Big lumbering buses transported people to the city centre terminus. From there narrow upright double-decker trams clanged and noised their way down Main Street, rushing madly down the Fordsburg Dip.

Although the temptation was strong to sit on the top balcony of the tram, the greater fascination existed in watching the driver. Rita watched him clanging the bell, foot tapping confidently on the large metal button, nothing stopping the tram in its flight.

The driver was magic as he wound the large wheel, and then with disdain let it whirr back. Shoplet and shoplet would fly past, a kaleidoscope of shirts lined up methodically, and other goods crammed for all to see, people walking unconcerned with the passing traffic, and the whole world crammed into the child's vision.

On alighting from the tram her hand tightened its grip for experience had taught her that now the real danger started. The dog business started and somehow, although terrified, she endured this stoically, for the thought of the excitement and love that awaited her was her shield against the canine onslaught.

As the old man and his children walked along the street, dogs barked, came up to them, sniffed, dawdled and loped alongside. It did not bother the little girl that her aunt and uncle spoke both English and laughed and talked in Yiddish with her father.

The impersonal atmosphere of the Home was replaced by one of love and laughter, and boy and girl cousins and the enchantment of small beds in cosy rooms. It was a day of child play, of bountiful portions of food and huge blobs of jam in black tea.

Experiences on day-outs differed over the years. The old man and his children did not go to family in Mayfair or Rosettenville as usual, but to a fair at Boksburg Lake, where there were small stalls with this and that, and marvellous things of amusement. There was also a pen with goats in it.

Rita was attracted to this strange animal with small horns, and totally fascinated as it ate some paper which had been blown into the enclosure. Running through a maze of adult legs she searched all over for bits and pieces which the animal greedily annihilated. Time was of no consequence to her. Darkness was descending, the crowd thinning, and the child was oblivious of all. She watched the goat, totally absorbed.

Who would look for a child outside a cage when murky waters abound. When the father and siblings could not find her, all efforts were directed at the lake, and some even swore, when questioned that yes, they had seen a little girl throwing stones in the water. The goat nudged the child through the railings, urging it to forage something at least. The child slept unaware of the turmoil around her.

Johannesburg downtown in the 20s on a Sunday late afternoon was usually deserted except for an idler or two. On the day-out there was usually a collection of parents and children at the terminus waiting for the last bus home. The children sit close to the man and the eight year old holds his hand tightly, swinging legs back and forward, backward and forward.

She thinks of the place where her father lives, not far form the bus stop in Loveday Street. One room in a narrow arcade, one room with one black spindly iron cot, stone floor, stark and lonely, a coffee-stained mug on a side table, an enamel jug and basin nearby.

As happens every year, at this time, the child experiences a hollow feeling in the pit of her stomach, an emptiness, for she has to go back.

Passers-by, regular commuters on this bus, saw the motley crowds that alighted from the bus as darkness fell, pushing and shoving with great fuss as children were bundled off.

Some had big packets and others nothing. The parents were simple people, mainly immigrants from Eastern Europe who had not made good in this land of their dreams. Here their strangeness inhibited their laughter, here sickness seemed more severe and more catastrophic.

So it was that many of the children had lost a parent, a mother or father, and life was difficult.

But momentarily, on an occasion, food was the magical remedy for everything. Food softened the agony of parting, food made a child smile and the parent happy A child who ate what he liked and plenty of it, had love. This was almost a legacy from the ghettos of Eastern Europe.

Rita wondered about parents, about the joy and contentment that her friends who had food showed... it lasted while the food was there. She wondered about the old man, waistcoat spotted with food, who would seat her on his lap and sing in a measured sing-song way 'pum, pum, pum' rocking her up and down. He loved her, that she knew for certain, so it made no difference to her when she returned empty-handed.

Rita is a persona I adopted and this is one of her experiences. I have a collection of them and at one time thought I would publish them in a slim volume. I wanted to give them a universal appeal so didn't actually mention Arcadia at all.

MY BOBBA'S GIFT

There were two things that I, in my pre-teen years, lacked. Both were fundamental to my happiness, so I remember them well.

The first was, it seemed, never solved. I felt very much out of place when I had a cold. Sniff, sniff, a cold trickle, and then slyly, but ever so quickly, I wiped my nose on my sleeve. How long did a cold last, and did it happen each year? It seemed so for me, and was a given as the seasons changed. But kids are tough and I'm sure there were many sleeves that bore traces of a running nose.

I wasn't unique though with the second problem - the matter of being hungry, for this seemed to be a constant with us kids in Arcadia. Fridays were special though. I had a Bobba with brains. Looking back it was the tactics that were employed that place this benevolence in some time slot. One of my beloved cousins who lived in Mayfair and attended Parktown High School was the messenger, the recipient my brother Hymie who attended the same school. Now my Bobba lived with my Uncle Tevia and Aunt Ida Goss in Mayfair, and I guess she must have patiently prepared the week's Bagel, delivered to me on Fridays.

Friday was the day I followed my brother's instructions. "Pup" he would say (Pup was my nick name) "Bobba has sent a Bagel for you with Bill Goss, it's in my locker" and that's where I found it. "Where was the locker" you may well ask.

Well in those days the boys slept on the verandah around the quadrangle, easily accessible, and particularly for a nine-year old with a mission and an appetite. Those bagels, so it seemed, were extra big, extra fresh, overflowing with jam, they were wonderful.

For me Bagels, Bobba and Love go together.

OF FLOWERS, PETS AND BIRDS

Before Arcadia was split and in the beginning, as I remember it, it was vast, upper and lower orchards, grape vines, the hills, the trees, and the cows feeding down where the tennis courts were later built.

I write of a time buried in mists it seems of the 20s and the 30s of the last century. I think of peace, of tranquillity, of green lawns, neatly manicured hedges.

Arcadia had many, yet to be explored treasures, secretive places, and I discovered some, and in so doing I found simple things.

Let me take you with me, follow me carefully and we'll enter through an archway to the lavatories. There were two or three, another space where we polished our shoes, and nearby, just outside was a grape vine, twisted, gnarled, the width of an arm. This provided a good step to get a look on top. I cannot recall the particular structure but hearing mewing I saw nestled on top a mother cat with her kittens, a most endearing sight. The discovery was a personal secret, I thought at the time.

My first glimpse of the birth of a living creature was when returning from Rannoch Road School, climbing the staircase leading to the quadrangle I saw a cat in the act of giving birth to kittens. I watched fascinated as they literally tumbled out, to be cleaned and licked with great concentration.

Night-time upstairs was a scary time for not many a night passed without the cries and noise of wild cats above the bougainvillea growing alongside the high southern wall bordering the parking grounds. Sleeping on the verandah I felt exposed and many a night pulled my blanket over my head. I don't think I imagined it but I would see two eyes glistening there and later a cat slinking down the broad passages. As fearful too were the wildcats that seemed to dash out of the undergrowth, hissing and scaring the living daylights out of me when at times I ventured "down the hill". They were a monstrous sight.

Night-time held other secrets – at one time I heard an owl that seemed to be perched very close by. Night-time held other terrors. My first experience of an encounter with a bat was when we slept in the end room, overlooking the quadrangle to the west and the large lawns to the south. It was the night that Matron Shaer died, the blackness was mysterious, and this winged thing flew in. Screaming we girls scrambled into bed covered our heads shouting that it would get into our hair. It settled, unbeknown to us, in somebody's shoe, to be discovered the next morning.

Down the hill, if you looked carefully, under small low bushes nestled usually near a big rock shiny leaves hid "*steenvrugte*". These were small round shiny fruits with a large brown pip reminding me of the loquats that used to grow liberally in the lower garden abutting the northern colonnade. *Steenvrugte* were a delicacy, white flesh, smooth and sticky, sweet while the other wild fruit we garnered from our searches revealed low spindly trees with some dried larger fruit. I cannot recall the name but the bland taste.

I think we kids grew up tough, we were scroungers, and nobody that I knew of suffered through eating these wild fruits. I enjoyed the taste of nasturtium leaves on my bread, and knew that wild sorrel that we called sour leaves had a good taste.

And while writing about the *koppies* what else did I see. Huge spiders that claimed the territory with their nets; I smelt dry faeces, and hated any thorn bushes with a passion.

I loved the *koppies* above the drive, and enjoyed the solitude in my mid-teens where I could sit on a jutting rock and survey in peace the activity below, read a book and watch the comings and goings on the drive.

I know that the boys had "hoks" where they kept poultry, but this was territory I dared not venture into. They never seemed neat structures to me with their sheets of zinc and wire netting.

I loved dogs with a passion. The Shaers had a dog, Brownie, a small lion-coloured tawny terrier. He never seemed hungry and I considered him privileged.

On the other hand we had a dog Tommy, an Airedale type of dog, always pleasant, fed with scraps from our plates, never bathed, never brushed, and a wonderful friend who slept with Ekie or myself. I have wonderful recollections about our faithful dog who joined us when much smaller as we teased the calf out of the stable, encouraging it to chase us. I was fearful of cows and to this day keep my distance. Arcadia had many treasures. Much has been written about the orchards, the upper and the lower, the illicit pinching of half-ripe fruit, the punishment that followed – these are stories of adventure and daring.

FUN MOMENTS IN THE ARC IN THE 1930s

I think there were about 40 girls in the Junior Department - housed in "The Joe Lewis Wing", and our fun and games were mainly home-grown. It was the time of the Depression Years. So what did we do for fun. I'll tell you - and I hope those of my friends who read this will get the same pleasure as I do recalling them.

The tarmac driveway through Arcadia ended in a cul-de-sac where the stables were. Housed here were also the laundry, Charlie Miller's house, Mr. Chait's Shoe Repair Shop and where we had our Chedar Lessons.

But it's the stables I want to concentrate on. After supper some of us kids followed by the canine pet of the moment, a dog that may have been short of food but not love, used to go there. Our aim was to get the latest calf to chase us. It was wonderful - the shouting, the giggling, the mayhem, the absolute terror as it chased us, the dog barking and we fled down along a steep path by the Wolf Hillman Hospital scattering in all directions, egged on by the dog's excited barking. The calf of course couldn't follow us as it kicked up its heels. We usually ran for cover to the outdoor lavatories.

On a more restrained note I can see us in the long grasses at the bottom of the steps in the dusk tying knots together and playing hide-and-seek, with someone ever so often going flying as they were tripped by the knotted grasses. This was more civilised of course.

Life was somewhat boring so any diversion was welcome. I think my favourite game was when we took some potatoes from our supper and then smeared the floor of the small room connecting the dormitories. Normally this was a highly polished red concrete floor but for our purposes it became a potato rink. Can you imagine skating on potatoes, well we did it. I don't remember any casualties, and I don't recall either why we ever stopped.

GOING UP AND GOING DOWN

"Steps and Stairs" the teacher wrote on the blackboard.

There were plenty of steps in her life, some concrete, some even marble lined, and they all led to different places – for the child's world was one that encompassed hills and orchards, gardens with terraces, places secret, great halls, and places where little people had to tiptoe and be quiet.

But outside in the grounds of the Home, the world was free, with winding paths and steps that had to be negotiated at intervals, not one or two or three in an orderly progression of different levels, but one here, and one there, created as mysteriously convenient platforms. And paved stones that jig-sawed, their resting places shifted by countless feet on their way to school in double-file, one year, two years for each pair, and for many others all the years of primary school. This was the way through the vast grounds that led outside of the big walls to the red-brick Government School whose student population was 95 per cent orphanage children.

Steps that weren't steps to anywhere but just an aid on the descending path through the grounds of the home, and steps that brought you back. And then there were steps that seemed to be hewn from the side of embankments, winding steps, fashioned from the heavy rocks that typified these *koppies*, that towered above the six-year old, and promised mystery and perhaps fun at the bottom or the top. Steps that, at times, led to an encounter with a wild cat that would hiss and challenge and also the place where the wild berries grew nestling their fruit in crevices.

And steps were places when, on your way to the communal dining room, you could giggle with your best friend and stick out your tongue too at your latest enemy knowing that the passage-way protected you for the time being, for there was not much space on either side to move freely, not for much pushing and shoving others out of the way.

I once saw a photo of a family, father and four children, not a happy photo mind you for the father looked sad and the children mildly obedient. I knew that family for I was the youngest, awkward at age nine, and my father already with thinning grey hair, a soft-spoken man, most at ease when he conversed in Yiddish – which I just could not understand. I loved the "pum-pum-pum" he sang when he had me on his knee, or the clap hands we played, old man and child sharing a strangely intimate bond.

The last time I visited the children's home the steps were still there, and somehow they looked so narrow. Does another family sit there now? I doubt it for times have changed over six decades, the hundreds of children are scattered who knows where, and the handful of boys and girls who call this place home can be counted on two hands, for those little ones who need a home are bundled off to foster homes and anything that hints at institutionalisation is frowned upon.

I lived there for the whole of my childhood – 15 years, and with the lack of entertainment at hand – and a degree of imaginative curiosity – explored my home.

It was at the top of the steps that one looked at the servants' bells. Evidence of the great servant-full mansion this once was. Twelve at least, I think, and 12 buttons to summon service – in the wood panelled library, the beautiful blue room with cathedral windows, bedrooms, great halls where, I fancy, banquets were served.

The steps in the servants' quarters were grey concrete, high and narrow, not like the white marble steps that wound down to the imposing entrance hall. Here the railing of wrought-iron scrolls had felt smooth pampered skin.

A reminder of more genteel times was a swimming pool, reminiscent of the ancient Roman baths, with large concrete pillars, now dank and damp, waters algae-bedecked, green and slimy, but once upon a time who knew what secrets lingered there? Access to the top hill was by way of a flight of steps jealously guarded by a bees nest, a narrow passageway that dared me to enter, to dart up, heart beating, and to flit unseen, so I thought through the trees to the swimming pool. Shaded from the sunlight, the steps to the pool were well constructed, now bestrewn with leaves and the flotsam and jetsam of tangled bushes and the droppings of pigeons and doves that had made this their haven. It fascinated me and in later years there was an elevated swimming pool like some huge concrete bath, admission by a flight of steps, steep and practical. Here there were no overhanging trees, but iron spikes on the gate, and the smell of disinfectant and chlorine, waters sparkling beneath blue skies.

Privacy was impossible and highly sought when I tried to study for my final school-leaving exam – the challenging Matriculation. Rising at four-thirty in the morning I would wander down the hill among the trees trying to memorise this and that – many a time distracted by the silence and the peaceful, the precious atmosphere I had sought. But it was at night when the steps in the servants' quarters became a haven for me. I ignored the cockroaches for here was a place where I could concentrate without interruptions.

Over time steps changed their appearance and regular, factory manufactured steel steps made their appearance, being like ugly excesses on a once classical building.

With some three hundred children plus to accommodate sleeping space was limited and so use was made of a long balcony where twenty iron beds stood on a concrete floor, and which unheated in the high veldt winter was adequate for hardy teenagers. To gain direct access to these quarters a steel staircase was built – rudely puncturing the building shell, strictly functional – a passageway into the darkness, unprotected day or night as it elevated itself above the once exotic gardens. A similar structure was built on the other side of the building, inadequate for sitting on, ugly to look at but functional leading down to an equally functional quadrangle.

The marble has long since vanished, the steps from here to there in the large grounds have disappeared as vast traffic passageways slicing overhead ignore what once was.

CAMP TIME IN PORT ELIZABETH

When Moses was, When Moses was,
A little child, a little child
He floated down, he floated down
The River Nile. the River Nile

And Pharoah's daughter,
and Pharoah's daughter..........

These words come back to me, the tune recalling camp, the year 1934, the place Port Elizabeth. It was not the first "Orphanage" camp I had enjoyed for there was an earlier time, a huge tent housing us little ones and somehow I see a picture of low-slung hammocks in which we small ones slept. This was 1930.

Four years between camps now seems like a wisp of time, fleeting and yet forever remaining. The train journey, the jolting at night in the silence of the African night, the chugging of the train, the click-clicking over the rails and the intimacy of the compartment with its six bunk beds to be identified. There is charm and wonderment in childhood when imagination runs havoc as it did for me in Port Elizabeth. I saw magic flashes of light, tantalizingly beautiful. Years later in Barberton I was to see a bedroom lit up by a single flitting flame of light. In New York, many years later, I enjoyed the same spectacle but casting childish thoughts aside I learnt how magic was made.

We juniors were housed in bell tents. These were secured by ropes anchored into wooden pegs driven into the beach sands of Pollock Beach area. I know one had to be careful not to trip over guide ropes, to know your way to the open bucket toilet at night. Sing-alongs took place in the huge communal tent, and we soon learnt the words of the songs. We had a wonderful Master of Ceremonies, the name Lyons springs to mind, his voice echoes over the decades.

And when I die, and when I die
Don't bury me at all, Don't bury me at all
Just pickle my bones, Just pickle my bones
Alcohol, In Alcohol

The song went on, the laughter increased

I still have a photo of Happy Valley, my personal Shangri La which I have revisited over the years, and although changed by weather and other factors harbours the dreams of my childhood.

1938 Port Elizabeth Camp

HARSH TIMES

You asked for my memories of Arcadia growing up there in the twenties and thirties to 1941.

I do recall a degree of anti-Semitism in various spheres. There were times when we kids went for a long, long hike that little kids would throw stones at us calling us names. I was conscious of this and associated the language of Afrikaans which I hated, never quite understood, and which had an effect on my final Matric results and hence my failure to earn a bursary for higher studies. However I became totally *tweetalig* in later years and enjoyed wonderful TV dramatic presentations and excellent programs in later years.

Memories are subjective. The Hararys came to Arcadia in the 30s; there was an element of harshness portrayed by the Shaers. Somehow I think I was somewhat favoured by Rachel Shaer and her two daughters Noami and Ruth. I have a picture of us kids, aged I think ten, eleven and somewhat younger having to sit still, perched for what seemed like hours, without talking. That was punishment. I can recall our being kept upstairs at one time on the small balcony facing the quadrangle where the boys slept while "Lulu Le Roux" occupied herself with some handcraft or another.

For me they were overall very happy days. I knew no other. The stigma of being raised on charity that I experienced as an adolescent was erased when I guess I became more mature, and gave way to a sense of achievement of a personal triumph over adversity.

ARCADIA'S HOSPITAL

I can't remember when the magnificent grounds of Arcadia were piecemeal changed for there was a time when the magnificent main building with its adjoining buildings occupied the 25 acre property, which included various cottages and the stables. On these grounds which covered *koppies* a Hospital was built, a "Boy's Wing" and then a building that housed the Juniors.

1933 was an auspicious year at Arcadia. The hospital was opened. Situated towards the eastern side of the property it was a low-slung building. From the patio on the northern side a panorama of Johannesburg stretched extending in the distance to the Magaliesberg, to the South it was walled in by a high embankment. Its formal approach was from this side, from the concrete drive Stepping inside the entrance on the eastern side we children used, I recall, what was a long passage. There was always an aura of quiet.

When admitted, the ensuing one-on-one contact and care was relished for here one received special attention. The anonymity of being one of many vanished. This was the time of the Great Depression and the number of Arcadians ran into the hundreds. Here there was a hushed quiet. I don't remember being too sick to care and relished the times when I was in a small ward by myself, after all recurring swollen neck glands could be a portent of mumps. In a sense I enjoyed my hospital stays, the food seemed to be better. Many was the time that a throbbing witlow was attended to, scars of my misadventures carry memories of raucous games and rusted tin, of caring hands and

big bandages. Somehow boils were part of my sufferings and I think I endured with others the intense heat of some grey-like ointment. I swear it came on liniment straight from the oven onto my painful neck. I have never again seen the spout-like container through which we used to inhale steam laced with Friars Balsam and would have found it handy treating my youngsters.

I pay tribute to so many, long since gone, to those women who attended to us, to Wolf Hillman for financing this institution, to Nursing Sister Goldwater who later became the Matron of Arcadia. I recall the many people in the medical profession who gave of their services, the dentists, the doctors. In the early years there were dental clinics on Sundays and operations performed to remove tonsils and adenoids

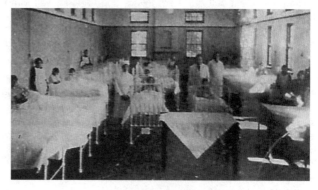

The Arc Hospital

Who would have guessed in those days that numbers would thankfully dwindle, the different healing purpose, and be converted to comfortable quarters providing emotional support in a home-like environment.

THE BLACK BUS

It was the black bus with its rows of seats, sliding windows and heavy capitalized identification S.A.J.O. on both sides that heralded the comings and goings of us children. We were the resident Jewish Orphans of Johannesburg.

Now there was a double identification – poor orphans – cast-offs of society. Ask any casual (gentile) acquaintance if they know of poor Jews, and it's almost as if you had asked whether it is a myth that boys are basically more intelligent than girls. Of course everybody knew this was baloney, so why parade this stupid bus around with those kids.

But then society was generally made up of situations that didn't fit the norm. The bus driver was a man of "mixed Blood" indicating that in some former generation there had been cohabitation between white and black – result, Charlie, amiable, capable, wife Dolly – a wasted symbol of fertility. With her wispy frizzy hair, bare gums, she appeared either with swollen tummy or baby on hip. With no knowledge of family life there was a certain fascination with the goings-on in the Miller's house.

Opposite the Millers, on the other side of the courtyard, Hebrew lessons occupied our afternoons; climbing up the narrow steps there this house seemed cosy, its smallness being in direct contrast to the huge vaulting ceilings of our living space in the main building.

I should mention that the Millers occupied that end of the semi-circular formation of small buildings slap-bang adjoining the cow stalls. At one time this enclave must have provided accommodation for staff plus stalls for cows, and horses. In fact cows still grazed the upper hills of the property.

We relished the fun we had up in those quarters, from watching the African workmen "white-wash" the walls, sloshing great blobs of paint, to our after dinner escapade of the day. We planned and looked forward to the thrill of the day when we would venture into the cowsheds accompanied by our pet dog, enticing the latest calf out. Feet flying, dog barking, calf almost twisting its body in frenzy it would chase us, screams of terror mixing, flying feet as we escaped down a steep embankment. Safe in an outside washroom we gathered, dog noisily pleading for another round, children giggling.

The 25 acre estate where we grew up once housed the gentry of Johannesburg. The home of a mining magnate it was originally built outside the city limits, the backdrop forest of indigenous trees on rocky *koppies* it was a gathering place of society in the early gold mining town Johannesburg and records show a scene of magnificent balls with lavish entertainment. Guests were enthralled by the African veldt stretching gloriously beyond vast valleys to the azure-tipped Magaliesberg mountains in the north.

My childhood memories are coloured with vast grounds, elegantly curved walkways cooled in the summer heat by vines of grapes crossing beams overhead. Here I fancifully imagined lovers sought secluded bliss for at intervals niches in the wall provided seating.

For those who chose to ample washrooms were provided discreetly accessible through an arched aperture in the wall.

The whole layout of Arcadia then suggested languorous hot summers, cool evenings where a child, one among hundreds could find a space for fancy speculation. The real world often intruded with a strict curriculum of activities.

Afternoon Chedar lessons were held every day, after formal school, Monday to Friday. It was a time of boredom interspersed with episodes of great fun and mischief. On reflection it must have been vanity or a fashion of the times that led our teacher to have a great shining yellow blob on his front teeth. That gold led one astray and instead of concentrating on the lesson at hand speculation on the wondrous tooth made for daydreaming and laziness. I don't know who thought of the idea of locking the teacher in the cupboard, but it happened one day, not with any ill effects however. The culprit was never found – I don't think the teacher tried too hard.

Hebrew classes were held in the small house opposite Charlie and Dolly. A tall Eucalyptus tree gave shade. Nearby was the home laundry with its massive cylinders, steam and heat, mounds and mounds of clothing, sheets, towels. It seemed to me a place with a life of its own with machines hissing steam and sheets forever peeling out of gigantic rollers.

Ever tried to mix sand, stones and water to make a workable concrete. First came a pile of cement, nearby a pile of stones and then there was the water trickling slowly from a nearby hose. Instead of any drums to mix concrete there was fascination in watching the process, piling sand, stone to contain the water. Then followed an energetic mixing of cement, shovels scraping to control the water seeping out. It had an element of excitement about it for water is wilful and man is clumsy.

I ramble and should get back to the bus. When does the age of innocence stop and the age of experience start?

I think our bus carried tens of kids, down the long drive, up Oxford Road and wonders of wonders to Park Station. We were on our way to a seaside camp, a wonderful treat every four years. What a time of mystery, will it be the lower, middle or top bunk, and what about the clickety-click of the rail track, running up and down the passages, looking out of the window for what seemed days and days. I never took note of the bus then "have a good time" Charlie shouted, and off we went, laughing kids in khaki shirts and pants.

At the time we knew that prisoners were transported in "The Black Maria" a black bus, and we, well we were transported in our black bus.

We were fortunate to enjoy entertainment and I recall circuses and pantomimes high on the list. With time, as innocence gave way to awareness, we experienced trepidation instead of enjoyment. We were submitted to the stares of curious bystanders as we trooped, clothed in identical bottle green serge dresses from our bus. I shuddered at the thought of any of my classmates seeing me. The final blow to my dignity came when the Black Bus took me, a lone passenger, with my possessions in our large case, and dumped me at my new home; I was to rent a room with a family. Close to 17, and on my own for the first time in my life, I rang the doorbell and someone with curlers in her hair, said "yes". "I'm from the Jewish Orphanage". "Oh yes come in the room's ready for you." I watched the bus pull away and heard laughter from my childhood fading.

The Black Maria (Arc Bus)

LEAVING THE ARC

I found too a tremendous sadness on leaving as if I was being pushed out of the nest, my haven of safety, and experienced great loneliness and uncertainty in the early years, and coupled with that were other factors. I, a serious-minded and studious person had my dreams shattered of furthering my education because of my sex which resulted in years of turmoil and rebellion.

A VISIT BACK TO THE ARC

We came flying down Oxford Road, through the massive gates, past the name "Arcadia", my home for fifteen years, and into the driveway, the wind blowing my hair, my brother urging me to sit still on the handlebar. I loved my brother. I loved living, I loved the world.

But it wasn't always so, and as for the beginning I have no sense of time, or of myself being registered in my memory but assume that the two-year old child was taken with her siblings

from their home in the narrow streets of Mayfair. Not the London Mayfair of moneyed folks but a working class area west of down-town Johannesburg, accessible from the city centre by a rickety tram. Down Main Street it clattered, running through a street lined with narrow shops whose windows were crowded with merchandise.

In later years I recall visiting aunts and cousins, of hearing tales of miners' strikes, of bullets flying, of mayhem, for Johannesburg was in its early years in the 1920s, a mixture of immigrants, tough pioneers, and poor whites shadowing the indigent people. Evident too were people of colour, and Indian folk who had settled earlier in the country to work the great sugar fields of Natal. The magnet, money, trade, the discovery of gold.

"Arcadia" was situated on 25 acres, overlooking the great valley where one could stand on the rocky *koppie* and gaze at the distant Witwatersrand. "Arcadia" the once magnificent home of mining magnate Sir Lionel Philips and his wife and now the home of children called orphans, not true orphans in most instances but children of impoverished parents.

The Home known then as the S.A.J.O. or the South African Jewish Orphanage was a haven for these children, a well-run institution with its imposing manor, manicured gardens, winding lanes and imposing trees.

A great ample courtyard greeted the visitor allowing entrance through massive doors to an imposing hallway. Ceilings were high, and a curved marble staircase led to the upper floor, panelled walls were evident everywhere. Facing north an imposing colonnade graced the balcony, an architectural example of the mining magnate's magnificent living style where no expense had been spared. Children's sounds were everywhere and as the depression overtook the country in the 30s so the admittance numbers rose to some three hundred plus.

It was a life of fun and fury, of loneliness and liveliness, a life indeed of contrasts, which saw dormitories with rows of black iron cots, children standardised, both in dress and haircut, of untold stories and untold merriment. It was my life where fantasy and harsh fact mixed.

AN OCTET OF CHANGE
Written by Bertha on the occasion of her eightieth birthday.

Days of joys and sorrows cannot be encapsulated in any particular decade for over the years of the sun rising and setting one single soul is lost in the glory of it all. I see no starting point as I enter the eighth decade as faces flit past, and incidents tumble over one another. I cannot recall a time of innocence for my childhood was rich with impressions, and the reality of changing circumstances.

Adulthood did not denote maturity; body changes did not evolve into completeness for there was much complexity involved. My innate competitive spirit was jostled, my adolescence saw much emotional conflict, borne stoically as I look back, for each individual in the institution was regarded more like a unit of the whole.

This collective security disappeared as I was jostled into the reality of having to make my own way. Clerical work was the order of the day for me, coloured with nights jitterbugging, weekends hiking, as I moved from one boarding facility to another. Earnings were carefully husbanded, my upbringing veiled for I experienced a sense of shame in my background.

Thriftiness and hard work propelled me along. Morning rides to city and suburb for work were a joy, downhill through suburban Hillbrow with its small cottages and low-rise buildings, the return home a tough push uphill on my newly acquired bicycle.

My sister, older by a few years, endured my bouts of liveliness and unruliness for I rebelled against years of conformity. Soper Road, Berea, became a base for the Klevansky sisters. Here we rented a room, escaping its four walls with a Hiking Club early Sunday mornings. A sturdy lot we were. Park Station was our meeting place; Little Falls, Kings Kloof, Strubenvale Valley, Sterkfontein Caves come to mind.

This was the era of World War II, of soldiers in uniform on the streets, khaki as well as the blue of the Royal Air Force. There was a panorama of humanity, love affairs intense and brief, stirring patriotic rallies at the City Hall; the tragedy of Tobruk.

I escaped the humdrum of work, enlisted and served in the Meteorological Unit of the Air Force. Those were days of challenge, as I flew in the Hudson and Hind bi-planes to make note of cloud formations and their altitude high in a blue sky, foam-white cumulus clouds soaring majestically upwards.

It was at Castle Gorge with a Hiking Club where I met Gerd Kronenberg, my husband. This was a magical place, not easily accessible, with hidden narrow paths between high rock formations, where baboons chatted and screamed, where waters tumbled serenely over rocky beds.

Our marriage is a continuation of our venture in the mountains where we met over 60 years ago. There were the bitter -sweet memories of his childhood in Germany, the tragedy that enfolded his family.

After the War many years work in the "Welfare Department" of the Board of Deputies honed my sensitivity, as the cruel realities of life's ups and downs were revealed. The days of joys and sorrow saw the dramatic unfolding of society's progress, mores and values changed, the War had changed the calm social stability.

To chronicle the ensuing decades is to deal with raising family, establishing a home against a climate of political instability. Stable as our lives were, circumscribed by work and school, we were always mindful of the whirlpool of changing mores and values.

The years have seen changes in fashions, the mini, the midi, platform shoes, dresses replaced by slacks, henna giving way to highlights, the pageboy replaced by the razor cut. Lisle stockings were a thing of the past, nylons became commonplace, plastic was the magical material.

My generation referred to as "The Greatest Generation" had eliminated the evils of fascism with a "Big Bang" as technology released this potent force. We faced a future bright with hope accompanied by a lingering doubt as to the potential of the "genie" that had been released.

However life continued peacefully, we saw the great changes of the 60s, the jive and jitterbug were replaced with rock and roll, "hippies" was a new word in our vocabulary and it seemed as if our orderly social world was coming apart. Mores and values were changing. Our old fashioned ideas on behaviour, politeness, were replaced with a certain brusqueness. We were relegated to the status of "the then generation", and the era of the young adults of the baby boomer era had begun. It was a time of adjustment.

It has been 17 years since our arrival in Canada where we joined our eldest son and settled near Lake Ontario in Scarborough. This is a peaceful area, almost pastoral where neighbours over the years have helped to colour the tapestry of our lives, helping us so many years ago to adjust to a changed climate.

Hot sunny blue skies of the *Highveldt* winter were replaced with a whiteness that blanketed streets, driving became a double challenge, and so we weathered the early years. We revelled in the changing seasons, and still do, the weather forecast, the high and low pressures; still marvel at the size of this country, still glory in the fall colours and the utter stillness of winter nights. Separation from family was like a gnawing emptiness and over time has been eased with the at-your-finger-tips availability of e-mail, reasonable phone rates, and the occasional visit when excitement reaches fever pitch and the glory of it is captured on film.

Eight decades of change and the days continue, our obvious physical change balanced with the richness of mental, and emotional growth. Fortunate to be beneficiaries of a generous medical system, fortunate too to have many facilities open for us, we two feel blessed in our second home.

MY HUSBAND GERD KRONENBERG

Bertha has written about a fascinating piece of Jewish history concerning her husband Gerd. This is a tribute to a man with guts and a reflection of a horrible time in our history. His father was an officer in the Great War, and he and Gerd's mother were murdered at Auschwitz. Many people will not visit Germany but they went to the small village where his family had lived for centuries, speaking to people who hid his parents - a harrowing tale of suffering, of bravery in face of unspeakable horror.

My husband Gerd Kronenberg was the son of a World War 1 ex-officer, a member of the RJF - Reichsbund Judische Frontsoldaten, and as such was accorded the honour of representing Germany in the 10,000 metre race. While he was on one year's compulsory military service in the German Army he was called to Berlin where he met the champion florette fencer Helena Meyer. Both of them were told that they could be officially accepted to represent Germany in the 1936 Olympics if they renounced their Jewish Faith. Helena Meyer complied and Gerd refused.

On his return to the barracks he was told by his Sergeant Major that he would be granted a weekend pass (unheard of in those days) and advised not to return on Monday as the Gestapo would be waiting for him. He then fled to Amsterdam, stayed there for a couple of months and then went to London. From there he sailed for South Africa arriving on 4 January 1937.

When we were holidaying in Margate in 1951 we met some folk there who hearing the name Kronenberg asked whether we were related to the well-known Jewish gymnasts, the Kronenberg brothers. I learnt then something of his past excellence in sports.

Bertha and Gerd Kronenberg – Married 1946

Chapter 5 - MICHAEL PERRY KOTZEN (1923)

Michael was born on October 10th 1923 in the Eastern Transvaal town of Bethal while his older brother Mannie was born in October of 1921 in Springs. Asher, their father, had arrived in South Africa in 1917 after fleeing war and persecution in Russia. He came from Riga in Latvia.

Michael's mother, Sadye-Jane was a young girl from Manchester England. She had come to South Africa to visit her older sisters who lived in Pretoria and Johannesburg. There she met and married Asher Kotzen and went with him to his farm in Bethal District.

After his idyllic babyhood on the farm, in his 10th year, 1933, his 48 year old father, Asher, gravely ill through kidney failure and dropsy, passed away. Sadye-Jane was a destitute widow at age 34 with two small sons. She took them to Johannesburg and placed them in the care of the South African Jewish Orphanage.

Mannie and Michael were in Arcadia for the ensuing eight years. Mannie went into the army in 1941 and Michael followed him three years later in 1944.

In 1963 at age 39 Michael married Roz Simson of Cape Town. They named their first born Asher. He was born in 1964. Adrian, their second son, was born in 1966. Their daughter Jessica was born in 1968. Michael made Aliya to Israel in 1978 at the age of 54, together with his wife and three small children." In 2005 Michael and Roz migrated to Sydney Australia following their three children who had left Israel and settled in Sydney.

While I believe that all of the stories told in this booklet are essentially true. Michael, who is a prolific writer and likes to draw sketches, has qualified his stories by writing to a fellow Old Arc "I have been sending some more memories of Arcadia to David Sandler. Some are, I admit, exaggerations, some are downright fiction, but some are gospel truth.....Truth, that is, that my old addled brain can recall."

Here is a selection of Michael's countless recollections and Arc Memories, together with his illustrations.

FAMILY HISTORY

Asher Zalman Kotzen (my father) came to South Africa from Latvia in 1919 after he had suffered the indignities and traumas of Tzarist and revolutionary pogroms. Asher was born in Riga in 1885. Asher succeeded in bringing four of his brothers and his brother-in-law from Russia to South Africa. One brother, Phillip, mistakenly boarded a ship in Holland that was sailing to America. Phillip could not read English and he mistook the word 'America' for 'Africa'. Phillip remained in New York till his death in 1970.

My grandfather, Shlomo Behrer Kotzen was a horse trader and a farmer. His farm was on the Riga to Moscow road. In the 19th

Michael, Sadye and Mannie. Babies wing in background. Stompie Shaer is with Hymie Cohen on left and Maurice Hurwitz on right.

century stage coaches and carriages would stop at the Kotzen farm to change their tired horses for fresh, and the passengers could get a meal and a bed for the night. The Tzar's Kossacks and police frequently used the wayside restroom facilities.

The Kotzen children were six boys and two girls. Asher was the third child. In 1902, when Asher was 17 years old, the Tzar's police scoured the countryside and villages for young Jewish boys, to press-gang them into army service. Asher and his brother Shmuel avoided capture by hiding inside the large bake oven in the farm yard. The boys would crawl to the very back inside the oven and conceal themselves there behind a brick wall which shielded them from the burning logs. But the hiding place was discovered and Asher was arrested, flogged by the police and sentenced to hard labour in an army camp deep inside Siberia.

He spent 14 years in the army camp, virtually a slave labourer, together with some six or seven other Jewish boys from Latvian shtetles. He would never see his parents again or get back home to Shlomo's farm near Riga... The Bolshevik revolution in 1917 and the murder of the Royal family caused the Kossacks to abandon their camps and to take flight with the thousands of refugees. Asher and his friends made their way through Russia and Poland working on farms for a day and a meal and attaching themselves to Polish, French and British cavalry units, tramping through war-torn Poland.

Hundreds of men and horses were being moved across Europe in trains and ships… Asher worked on a ship with a cargo of horses from Danzig to Rotterdam in Holland. In Rotterdam he worked with horses, loading horses onto ships… In November 1918 the war ended. Asher was employed on a ship that was to carry many horses. War survivors, to South Africa… He sailed with the horses. The ship made a number of ports for refuelling and refoddering – Portugal, Spain, through Gibraltar, Italy, Greece, Alexandria, Egypt, each port meant a couple of days of loading and unloading for the deckhands and also a chance for Asher to mail a letter to his parents in Riga… Through the Suez and the Red Sea, down the East Coast of Africa, Mozambique, Madagascar, Durban. East London and finally Cape Town. Asher 'jumped' ship and went with the horses to a horse ranch at Paarl. From there he found a job as a stable hand and sulky jockey at Milnerton racecourse. It was 1919, Asher was 34 years old.

With the money Asher had won at Milnerton he travelled up to Johannesburg. His cousins, the Nestad and Goldstein and Gore families were on the East Rand. Asher joined his friends the brothers Hirshovitz, farming in the Springs and Bethal districts. He was introduced to Sadye Jane Becker, who came from London with her parents to visit her older sisters in Johannesburg. Asher and Sadye were married in Johannesburg in 1920.

BEFORE THE ARC

Early childhood was a careless and happy time for Mannie and me. Our parents had a farm twelve miles north of the village. Our playmates were Dutch farmers' barefoot children and Bantu picaninies. Our Jewish parents, Asher and Sadye Kotzen, would make the 12 miles journey to and from Bethal in a two wheeled Cape-Dutch cart drawn by a pair of Asher's magnificent, beautifully groomed horses. Asher bred horses. He had acquired the skills of horse breeding from his father, Shlomo-Behr Kotzen, in Latvia. Mother Sadye was the daughter of an English-Polish immigrant family. Sadye had come to South Africa in 1920 together with her parents, sisters and brother. Her father, Yechiel-Maishe Becker, was a rabbi. He had secured the position of Hebrew master and Shamus (Sexton) for the Great Synagogue in Fordsburg, Johannesburg. Sadye and Asher were married in Johannesburg in 1920. Their first child, Menachem (Mannie) was born in October 1921. And I, Menasheh (Michael) arrived in Bethal in October of 1923.

We cherish sweet memories of our stone farmhouse and the servants and the horses and all the farm animals. Especially our memories of the wonderful journeys in the Cape cart.

Mannie and I sat behind our parents in the cart with our bare feet dangling over the back board. Asher named his magnificent carriage horses "Sweetheart" and "Darling". Ostensibly to tease Sadye who always laughingly pretended she did not know if Asher was talking to her or to one of his horses.

Horse and Cart

and relatives, English and Afrikaans from the white children and teachers in Bethal, and Zulu and Sasutu from the black kids I played with on the farm. My dear brother Mannie and I came to Arcadia from our early childhoods in the Eastern Transvaal. Our parent spoke in English and Yiddish. Our playmates were Afrikaans and Bantu kids. In Arcadia we were ridiculed by the other children and by Stompie Shaer for our usage of our own Kotzen-patois. Our private 'Esperanto'. We used broken English and Afrikaans words interspersed with Jewish and Sasutu Zulu expressions.

The ridicule of the children in Arcadia contributed greatly to my determination to learn to speak (what Stompie called 'proper' English). Mannie and I took to reading English literature and I happily discovered the geniuses of Shakespeare and Dickens and Oscar Wilde and Mark Twain and RL Stevenson a host of wonderful writers. My increasing desires for reading eventually urged me into a theatrical career.

Mannie went to Israel in 1961. I followed 18 years later in 1978. Our brotherly reunion in Israel was a blessing to behold. Much enjoyed by family and friends. In Israel our childhood lingo had acquired and adopted some common Hebrew terms and some slang four letter words. We would chatter away with our sons contributing further popular expressions, and everybody giggling, in our 'language' that only the Kotzens could fully understand.

MY FIRST DAY IN THE ARC

How do I remember my first day in Arcadia?

In 1933 my 11 year old brother Mannie and nine year old me, were brought by car from our grandmother's little bungalow in Fordsburg to 22 Oxford Road, Parktown. I remember we wore snow-white silk shirts and white knickerbocker trousers with white stockings and shiny red shoes. It was a mid-week morning. The driveway and the gardens and orchards were devoid of people… an occasional black gardener perhaps, but no children. We were told that the children were in neighbourhood schools and that they return in the afternoon.

The car pulled up in front of the imposing front portals. The sound of the gravel crunching under tyres and underfoot engraved pleasantly forever in my mind's ear. We were escorted into the building… our driver and escort, a kindly Christian gentleman named Derek, rang the heavy front door bell… we heard a scraping and a shuffling within and the door was opened slowly by (to us) a very strange looking young woman… She was Essie (We learned her name later). Essie was about 15 years old. She did not go to school with the other children as she was unfortunately "disabled". Essie was a spastic sufferer. She suffered from excessive muscular convulsions. Her movements were sudden and severely erratic. Poor Essie spoke in a slurred difficult manner and she nervously shook her shoulders and shuffled her feet. Essie was one of a few 'disabled' children who did not attend school, but stayed in Arcadia. Essie and the others used to help in the kitchen and the cleaning staff, maintaining the floors and corridors of Arcadia.

It was merely incidental that morning of my arrival that Essie answered the front door. But I do admit that her convulsive appearance behind the slowly creaking opening door was kind of spooky for a nine year old country-bumpkin little boy dressed like little lord Fauntleroy.

That was my very first impressionable memory of Arcadia. Further first impressions followed in that first week - each one uniquely mine.. Mannie's first impressions differ from mine.

I did not return to Bethal before my 30th birthday in 1953. To my surprise, as I rediscovered the scenes of my origins, the old homestead and outbuildings of the farm seemed so much more smaller and 'shrunken' in my adult perspective than they were in my childhood memories. People and places and artefacts in my child's eye-view were considerably larger and more imposing.

ARC HISTORY AND BACKGROUND

Arcadia, at 22 Oxford Road Parktown, became the South African Jewish Orphanage in 1923. The year in which I was born on a farm in the Eastern Transvaal. When I entered Arcadia at the age of nine in 1933 the population consisted of about 200 children.. approximately 30 babies, 60 or 70 junior boys and girls. And roughly about 90 seniors. The girls were all dormitoried in the main house.

The babies had a new wing specially built on the lower lawn. Junior boys shared the babies building. And the senior boys, boys over the age of 12, slept in the hall that had been Lady Phillip's ballroom and in the open quadrangle verandah and fishpond garden adjoining the ballroom. Martinet Louis Shaer was superintendent and Mrs Rachel Shaer was the matron. The hospital, another new wing added to the main house, was in the charge of sister Goldwater. The babies were cared for by two kindly twin sisters named Kaufman. The rest of the children were watched over by Afrikaans wardresses.

The wardresses called themselves "nurses" or "Verpleegsters". I always suspected that they were farmer's daughters and widows who had come to Johannesburg from the platteland to find jobs. (Working for the blerry Jews!) They were unskilled, untrained, unprofessional, cruel, sadistic women. A far cry from the kind and gentle child care kindergartens of today… Normally there were eight nurses… two for each department…The four watching over and controlling and

persecuting the boys department were unfortunately four Germanic sadistic female 'dragons'. Battle-axes!

One was Juffrou Josie Le Roux. She had a good healthy masculine figure, stony faced, tight-lipped, flaxen haired, bespectacled. Neatly and smartly uniformed in white. She viciously slapped and beat boys who were not her current favourites. "Julle stout kinders" were locked in solitary confinement and denied meals. We all "loved" our Josie Le Roux!

Then there was Verpleegster Bruin - (Nurse Brown) a fat woman. A nasty tub of sweat and lard! On a par with sadistic Josie.

Every second Sunday in the month was visitors' day at Arcadia. Visitors were permitted on a Sunday afternoon every fortnight. On visiting Sunday many of the children would line the drive-way waiting for their visitors. Scores of people alighted from the JMT buses at the bus stop in Oxford Road. They would walk up the drive through the 'gauntlet' of eager children, carrying packets of food. The visitors would be greeted by excited orphanage siblings and cousins, then all would proceed down to the lawns and rockeries there to have their picnics. Many children used to save sweets and fruit with which to bribe their nurses. Nurse Le Roux had a 'pantry' in her bedroom in which she stored sweetmeats (lekkergoed) purloined from 'arse-creeper' kids!

One day Clippie Hesselburg and I were work detailed to clean Le Roux's room and to make her bed… Clippie stole one of the lush red apples from her cupboard.. Later when she missed the apple she summarily blamed me. (Daardie Yookie dief Michael!). I was not going to snitch on Clippie. She slapped me and dragged me screaming and protesting to Stompie. Dragged me by the ear, without hearing my side of the story Stompie called to his assistant Swanepoel to "hold the little bugger down" while he thrashed me nine vicious cuts across my backside. "I'll give you thieving you dirty crook! Take that! And that ! And that!"

The boys developed their skills of bunking out. Escaping the confines of Arcadia into a fine art. There was not a boy in Arcadia who had not bunked out. Gone over the hill or down the bottom hill, or sneaked past the Zulu watchmen at the gates. One boy would distract the Zulu with talk and sweets while a half dozen boys slipped out and away. Bunking out presented Stompie Shaer with, what he termed 'an insolvable problem!' Till he boastfully conceived the idea to employ a white Afrikaans policeman, a "bad boys restrainer", "to teach these kids their proper place!"

Enter drill sergeant, ex-Salvation Army, Swanepoel. Experienced child disciplinarian. I cannot recall Swani's first name. It may have been Heinrich or Adolf or Herman! He straight away proved his metal worth. Imposing strict rules of silence and deportment and behaviour on the boys. On visiting Sundays Swani would don his sergeant's uniform and with a riding crop smartly tucked under an armpit he would parade up and down the driveway. Glaring at visitors and daring any boy to try, "just try Yookie!" to bunk out!.. How we loved him. Our dear ole Swani!

Sergeant Swanepoel had his quarters in two rooms under the ballroom. In later years when the ballroom was converted into the Shul, the quarters underneath, which were originally cloakrooms for Lady Phillips' Ball guests, were converted into an apartment for Mr and Mrs Harary. Swanepoel had a gramophone ('His Master's Voice' made in U.S.A.) and a collection of records. Most of his records were German marching music and songs. He also had a few of Al Jolsen and Eddy Cantor. ("Yerra man. But those Yookies can moss sing hey!") His favourite song "Swani, how I love you, my dear ole Swani!

"Why don't you little *Yookies* also sing like Al Jolsen? Hey?" We would cower in Swani's presence. Always afraid that he would suddenly lash out at us with whatever came to hand, his riding crop or a rolled newspaper or a plate or a stick of celery or a belt or just his banana fingers back hand!

I wander what eventually became of Swani. Probably long dead and buried by now.. Perhaps his ghost still parades up and down the ancient driveway at Arcadia.

Last night I dreamed that I went back to Arcadia. The rusty gate hung skew on a broken hinge. The driveway was overgrown with weeds. The buildings were cracked and peeling and broken windows. A broken shutter banged against the
dusty wind. Rats scurried across the kitchen floor. Stoves and bits of furniture broken by looters and thieves!!!!!!!!

For my Arcadian memories it is not really fair to condemn all Afrikaners who peopled my childhood as anti-Semitic sadists. In truth there were many who were kind and considerate and respectfully disposed towards the Jews. There were teachers at Rannoch Road School and Parktown High whom I admired and

respected, whom I did not fear, who never ever displayed any anti-Semitic sentiments. And in my adulthood I was happily involved in the theatres with some of the finest most noble Afrikaans men and women, some of whom are still my correspondents to this day. My good friend Patrick Maynhard, a most talented and most well known Afrikaans actor, who can play an orthodox Jewish Rabbi or a Jewish soldier saying the Kaddish over a slain friend with absolute and complete sincerity and conviction.. I am proud and happy to be his friend. And the many many Afrikaners of my South African acquaintance and my good memories.

I fondly remember the good times. But I sadly cannot forget the bad times of my nine year Arcadia odyssey. The good times included the wonderful comradeship, the special holiday treats, the Friday night fried fish and mashed potatoes, the gardens and orchards and the spacious aesthetic building accommodation.

The bad times were the perpetual pangs of hunger, the painfully cold winters, the awkward and uncomfortable clothing, the boots that were either too big or too tight, the sadistic supervisors and cruel nurses, the corporal punishment, the whippings… all these bad things had been diminished and eradicated or improved in Arcadia in the 50's and 60's.

In the 1940's the old guard was replaced, renewed by kindly and benevolent, compassionate Jewish fatherly and motherly social workers. Fascism had been defeated. The holocaust was over! A new order for peace and love was abroad in the world. Peace, goodwill, human rights, democracy, Israel, civilisation, social sciences, all having a therapeutic influence and effect on the institution Arcadia in the good persons of Mordechai Harary and Doc Lichtigfield and Fickey Klevansky and their fellow Arcadians.

1950s and 1960s Arcadians are fortunate to be post- holocaust children.

ARC MATES

My list of lost Arc-mates is quite long…one by one we are shuffling off this mortal coil!….

For starters I will tell you something about my very best and dearest Arc-mate David Rushovich. David passed away in 1999 in Johannesburg. Little Russy and I were pals in the Rannoch Road School and in the Hebrew Chedar classes. Mr Mann, Mr Rotstein and Miss Factor were our Hebrew teachers. In 1933-34-35 the Hebrew school was held in the ramshackle, tumble down, decaying three storey Dickensian building which stood precariously opposite the dairy and cowsheds and the laundry and the bus garage and bus driver Charlie Miller's cottage where he lived with his wife Dolly and their children.

David Russy and I first "cottoned on" to one another in the junior boys. Russy's older brother Issy was in the Seniors together with my brother Mannie. Russy had a junior girl sister, Judith and a baby brother Boris. The only department sans a Russy was the Senior Girls. Their older sister, Justice, a very beautiful film star like teenager used to come and visit them with their mother on visiting Sundays once a month. My older brother Mannie and Issy Rush, together with Alec and Louis Nerwich the "Pip" brothers, and Sam and Issy Lipschitz the 'Lip' brothers, formed the "Big brother's feeding scheme". The big brothers used to sneak down to the Juniors after lights out with scraps of bread and meat and biscuits which they had purloined from the Senior's dining room and from the committee room tea trays, to feed their kid brothers. Dave's kid sister Judy was also in our Hebrew class. We used to save sweets and titbits to give to our "beloveds". Quite often a sweet that I gave to Judy would gradually make the daisy-chain round and eventually come back to me via Molly…Often a little the worse for wear and tear!

In '34-'35-'36 the boys and girls in Arcadia were in a perpetual state of hunger. Food was for us the beginning and end all of survival. We polished off every scrap of every meal in those austere days when the quality and the quantity and the menu of the children's feeding programme left much to be desired. We would barter and trade our meagre rations. The food bartering was a cursed part of our nourishment.

At one stage I bartered half of all my mince meat to Sambo Manashevitz in return for half of all his bread pudding… That was a bad deal as the mince meat was a little better in taste and quality than the bread pudding…But a deal was a deal… we spat and shook on it… Sambo and I struck to our deal for 6 months, till Mr Harary put a stop to bartering. The main trouble was that we had bread pudding about 4 times a week. And meat loaf only once or twice a week.. at every supper time each table's appointed waiter of the month brought in the steaming dishes. The head boy of each table dished up the 'skoff'…according to his own rules of favoritism…I got to be a head boy by 1936… and I behaved in exactly the same way towards my table mates…

After each child had his rations on a plate before him, some boy would call out "trading time!" and almost everyone, head boys and everyone would be up and running every which way with plates of food from table to table. I would get up and charge over to Sambo's with half my mince. Sambo would be collecting or paying food elsewhere in the dining room. He was a prolific wheeler-dealer. But never once did he fail to leave half a dollop of soggy bread pudding in my plate or at my place. Some boys 'organised' a food 'Mafia'… and grew fat and food-prosperous. Some others were unlucky speculators and gamblers and became starving beggars - begging from table to table with empty plates. It was a Dickensian scene from Oliver Twist. The supervisors and Afrikaans 'watchdogs' did nothing to stop it. They used to laugh at the antics of "the hungry little *Yookies!*"…

Eventually by 1937-38 a new Hebrew teacher Mordechai Harary, joined the supervising staff. We called him "*Speedcop*" because he was often running around blowing a whistle. Mr Harary made drastic changes for the betterment of Arcadia. He fired the cruel Afrikaans 'watchdogs'.. replaced them with kind hearted Jewish men and women. He outlawed the food bartering practices. The rations were increased and greatly improved in quantity and quality. He replaced the Zulu cooks with matronly, motherly Jewish women.

Harary completely eradicated bullying and 'enslaving' smaller boys by bigger boys. One or two 17 year old drop outs and lay abouts were expelled from Arcadia. Harary and his wife took a parental personal involvement with the children. A new era of enlightenment and human dignity and human rights had dawned in Arcadia.

In 1941 Dave Russy and I followed our older brothers out of Arcadia and into the army and the wide world. Before leaving Arcadia the kid brothers of the Pips, the Lips, the Russys and the Kotzens had formed our own gang. We used to wander the hallways and garden paths of Arcadia singing our gang song "Little Lip and little Pip and Little Russy's gang. We'll never get out of this gang. Bang! Bang! Bang!"….

About six years ago Dave and Claire Rush visited us here in Israel. One fine day we were in Zikron Yaacov at a beach sea-food restaurant…I had ordered fried sole and chips. And Dave had ordered boiled Bream and mashed potatoes. Our wives were enjoying vegetarian salads. Suddenly Dave said "Tell you what, I'll give you half my boiled bream for half your fried sole!" We all burst out laughing. The other diners in the restaurant and the waiters wanted to know what was so funny about the sea-food!

PIP

Many Arcs had nicknames. In my generation there was Panzy and Pip, Ghandi and Shiney-nose, Kiviet and Kloggo, Du-du and Dovy and Dobby, Loutoo and Lou-Lou and Lipka, Skinny and Popeye and Humpty Dumpty, Dopey and Doc and Stinky, Clippie and Starkey, Fickey and Khunya and Puppy and many others.

I don't think I have told you the story of how the Nerwich family, Louis, Alec, Ray and Fanny, came to be nicknamed the "PIP" family. Louis was called BIG PIP, Alec, Little Pip and the sisters were Ray Pip and Fanny Pip.

From time to time a "craze" invades the children's lives. In the 1930's we saw the yo-yo craze and the Diabolo craze and even the craze for collecting bottle caps or matchboxes. In the late 30's a marbles craze hit the playgrounds. At school the Arc boys could not keep up with the "private" boys who had limitless supplies of expensive (to us) marbles. The orchards of Arcadia were rich in apricot trees. The boys used to raid the orchards, mainly for apricots, the pips were then saved in lieu of marbles. The rules of pip-pip were basically the same as for marbles, except of course that pips did not roll and had to be flipped. At school we still vied for marbles against the privates, but back at home in Arcadia the name of the game was 'pip-pip'. Some of the boys became master pip gamblers. Pip millionaires. Louis and Alec were exceptional pip winners. They together amassed pillowcases full to overflowing with apricot pips.

The Nerwich brothers were renowned Kings of pip-pip. It was with great respect and reverence that we referred to Louis as BIG PIP. King of Arcadia's pipulation. And Alec was with equal reverence recognised as the Prince of pippery, Little Pip. Their sisters were the princesses Ray Pip and Fanny Pip. A right Royal pipular family.

In the 1940's Louis and Alec and their older brother Barney were soldiers in the South African army 'up North' and the other old Arc men in uniform would salute them. It was customary in the army to salute pips (Officers) The PIPS were life long friends of my brother Mannie and myself. Alec used to visit Mannie regularly on Moshave Moledet in Israel. They would sit by a barbecue fire roasting pecan and chestnuts and talk about "the days of yore".

Arcadia. Alec and Becky PIP Nerwich have a very special place in the Kotzen hearts and memories.

OUR PRIVATE ESPERANTO

My dear brother Mannie and I came to Arcadia from our early childhoods in the Eastern Transvaal. Our parent spoke in English and Yiddish. Our playmates were Afrikaans and Bantu kids. In Arcadia we were ridiculed by the other children and by Stompie Shaer for our usage of our own Kotzen-patois. Our private 'Esperanto'. We used broken English and Afrikaans words interspersed with Jewish and Sasutu Zulu expressions. The ridicule of the children in Arcadia contributed greatly to my determination to learn to speak, what Stompie called 'proper' English. Mannie and I took to reading English literature and I happily discovered the geniuses of Shakespeare and Dickens and Oscar Wilde and Mark Twain and RL Stevenson a host of wonderful writers. My increasing desires for reading eventually urged me into a theatrical career. Mannie went to Israel in 1961. I followed 18 years later in 1978. Our brotherly reunion in Israel was a blessing to behold. Much enjoyed by family and friends. *Ou boet* Menachem and his *klein-boet* Menasheh entertained family and friends with our *geselskap*-indaba, mish-mash *fariables*, our *koeksusters* and *Oy veys,* our 'plaasjaap se moer!'. In Israel our childhood lingo had acquired and adopted some common Hebrew terms and some slang four letter words. We would chatter away with our sons contributing further popular expressions, and everybody giggling, in our 'language' that only the Kotzens could fully understand.

"LES ENFENTS PERDU"
Written in 1955

What was once the Manor-house and country estate of Sir Lionel Phillips had become a home for children and where, in Johannesburg's early days, the elite had once wined and dined and danced in crinolines, the little parentless people now sat in orderly rows at their meals and their scripture lessons. And neatly made their rows of beds. And obediently polished their rows of boots. And quietly filed to and from their classes, or patiently stood in line for an apple at four o'clock. Life for them was orderly and duty bound and somewhat bewildering.

But the children were nevertheless happy and healthy in their Manor-house, with its vast halls and spacious grounds. And the present day elite were more than proud of the facilities and amenities, which they and the late Sir Lionel, had so generously bestowed upon these homeless ones.

The Home had been in existence for some years before the committee of well to do city fathers and mothers, secured the services of professor Worthington, a most distinguished English gentleman. The professor was in his late 70s when he came to Arcadia, that was the name given the estate by Sir Lionel, and was happily, and comfortably ensconced in a small cottage, formerly the gate-keeper's lodge, situated below the orchard off the Oxford road.

The aged professor had been the headmaster of a public school in England for many years. And had come to live in South Africa upon his retirement, as his asthmatic constitution craved a dry climate. Besides which, he found himself very much alone in his old age. His dear wife having passed away, when he was not quite 60: And their only child, a son, was lost in action somewhere in France.

The old man came to love the children. And the little boys would swarm through his cottage and about his garden in quest of tools and watering cans and all sorts of things. And he taught them all about seeds and showed them how to plant them. And he let them into the many secrets and mysteries of gardening and the mechanics of everything that surrounded and encompassed their young lives. And, more officially, he gave them lessons in English literature, and corrected their speech defects.

Young Michael, perhaps the most precocious of the urchins, who doted on the professor and literally worshipped the very ground on which the old man walked, was always well to the fore at story telling time. And when the professor took his wheezy walks through the orchard and about the grounds, he was invariably accompanied by Michael and one or more of the other boys, not forgetting the professor's ever present Major, a catarrh ridden old bulldog, who was devoted to his mater, ignored the children completely and growled ferociously at everyone else.

Professor Worthington opened the windows to the world for the tousled headed Michael. Mark Twain, R M Ballantyne, Richard Hughes, Anthony Hope, Hans Andersen and a host of wonderful story tellers, were brought to glorious life by the professor's brilliant talents. His magnificent dramatic ability and complete command of the English language. With his enraptured little audience, he world re-enact the works of Alexander Dumas, with swashbuckling sword in hand and the daring skill of a Douglas Fairbanks.

They sailed the treacherous seas with Jack London, and battled the vicious Touregh rebels with P C Wren. They sped into the future with H G Wells and to the floor of the Atlantic with Jules Verne. They outwitted Edgar Wallace and vividly transplanted Stevenson's Island into the orchard off the Oxford Road.

They were Black Beard and his pirates, then they switched to Robin Hood and his merry men, then Ivanhoe and the knights of old England, and Ghengis Khan and the Mongol lords, and Shakespeare's crew of patches. Michael delighted in always being Puck, who could girdle the earth in 40 minutes. Or Peter Pan leading the lost boys, or Tom Brown solemnly taking his beating from the bully Flashman. Sometimes he saw himself as a mixture of many heroes. A sort of fearless wonder boy. With the intelligence of Kipling's Kim, Toomi's command over the elephants and the energy of Stalky resplendent in shining uniform and mounted on a magnificent steed, he would charge with the Light Brigade.

On one of their numerous Arcadian walks together, the professor accidentally, and quite unconsciously, walked over a pathway that had only that morning been cemented. Michael drew the old teacher's attention to the fact that he had left a trail of footprints behind him in the unset cement. After showing a little surprise at his folly, the professor chuckled out loud as he lit his pipe, saying 'Never mind Michael, We shall call them, footprints in the sands of time ...'

A short fortnight after the cement incident the professor was confined to his bed and Michael and his friends were told that he was not to be disturbed and that they were to keep away from the cottage.

Suddenly the walks were no more. The story telling had ceased. The play acting came to an end and Michael and the urchins prayed for their friend to return but he never did return. After breakfast, one Sunday morning, the children were told to observe a few moments of silence, because Professor Worthington was dead.

For many days Michael and the faithful Major, sat near the footprints in the sands of time. He cried a bit, when the other boys were not there to see him. He pined for the old English gentleman, and Michael secretly wished that he was not what he was, or where he was, but that he were someplace else. He wished he was on the other side of the world.

You write that you can see how my story "*Les Enfents Perdu*" ties in with my life on the stage. Admittedly I penned it while sitting in my dressing room, between entrance cues at the Reps Theatre, but my inspiration was my boyhood in Arcadia. The books and films and authors I mentioned stemmed from the stories and teachings and books of dear old Professor Worthington. Professor Worthington was a retired old English schoolmaster whom Mr Stompie Louis Shaer had employed to give the children extra curriculum homework lessons.
Prof Worthington was a very dear and kindly 'grandfather' of the old aristocratic type.. someone like the wonderful character that Ralph Richardson played in "Greystoke", the English film version of the Tarzan story. Prof Worthington had a dry, straight-faced sense of humour. He was a marvellous 'mine' of Oscar Wilde and Bernard Shaw and Winston Churchill quotations. He could recite whole passages from Shakespeare and paragraphs from Dafoe's Robinson Crusoe and Swift's 'Gulliver's Travels'. We ten year old urchins loved and respected him. Suddenly one fine day the professor suffered a

heart attack and he was no more. Robert Bushkin, Tommy Green, Freddy Fuchs, Sambo Mannie, David Rushowich, Paisie Meyers, Morris Hurwitz, Hymie Cohen, Ghandi Sacks, Jonah Perkel, Clippie Hesselburg, Abe Starkowitz and Michael Perry Kotzen were among those who mourned the professor and revered in his memory for years to come.

GOD BLESS MISS KRUYWAGEN OF RANNOCH ROAD PRIMARY SCHOOL

1934 was my year in standard one in Rannoch Road Primary School in Parkview near Arcadia. This was the nearest Government primary school to Arcadia. Nearly all the pupils at Rannoch Road were from Arcadia. The insignificant number of "private kids" were but a mere handful. Junior boys and girls between the ages of seven and 12 plus a few seniors of 12 and 13 assembled in the Arcadia quadrangle after breakfast at 7.00 am. Then we walked in long 'crocodile' lines, the boys in khaki shirts and khaki shorts and black socks and black boots.

The girls in pale green or faded blue cotton dresses, white socks and "sensible school-shoes". One or two of our Afrikaans nurses and our indomitable Mr Swanepoel accompanied us down through the northwest point of Arcadia estate.

There the padlocked and chained gates were opened, the children's street patrol, a specially selected band of boys and girls carrying stop signs on long broom handles, would hold up the busy Oxford Road traffic, enabling the hundreds of children to cross the road and proceed down Rannoch Road. The school was situated on the right side of Rannoch Road. A large single storeyed bracket shaped building of five or six classrooms on either side of an assembly quadrangle.

A spacious playground stretched from the classrooms to the north side fence. The two long toilet blocks occupied the North end of the playground. In 1934 Rannoch Road School had not yet been fitted with "sophisticated" flush toilets. This was still the old fashioned night-soil bucket variety that was 'cleared' by a mule drawn sanitary cart twice a week. Mr Jacobs was the headmaster. We referred to him as 'Jakey'. Miss Kruywagen was vice principal and Afrikaans mistress. Jakey himself taught arithmetic and history and his pet interest Nature Study. There were three or more other teachers or student teachers. We were taught English, Geography, basic science and other primary school subjects. The school covered standards one, two, three, four and five. After standard five the pupils would graduate to form one in Parktown High School or to standard six in other Johannesburg schools.

In 1934 Jakey planted a number of bluegum eucalyptus saplings around the playground perimeter. There were about 15 of these saplings lining the school grounds. "For the boy or the girl who shows special interest or aptitude in nature study!" said Jakey as he gave me the honour and special privilege of caring for one of the saplings. He put each shrub and tree and flowerbed into the special care and maintenance of a different child. I was very happy to be given a tree for my own 'responsibility' for my five years at Rannoch Road School…. To water it and to rake it and care for it every school day. The ten o'clock tea break was always a time of watering cans and rakes and child-gardening. If Jakey found a plant that was neglected he would "fire" the gardener and replace him or her with someone more efficient.

After I had left Rannoch Road in 1938 my tree was looked after by a succession of new generations of pupils…. 30 years later I had the occasion to revisit the Rannoch Road School. By then it was a rehabilitation centre for Cerebral Palsy victims. But the grounds and gardens were beautiful. A lush green lawn surrounded by 15 huge, tall, magnificent bluegum trees.

My tree, the third one on the 'upper' side, was as tall and as handsome as all the rest. The trees had been very well cared for. I noticed a heart and arrow and some lettering carved in the trunk of 'my' tree. "HE LOVES BS"… I have often wondered who HE and BS are. Recently I learned from Alec Saul that the bluegums of Rannoch Road are no more. They have been felled and removed to make room for building development. The trunk with "HE loves BS" is probably part of a kitchen table or propping up a mine shaft now!

KITE BUILDING

In 1934-35 there was a kite building-flying craze fascinating children all over. Competitions were held to determine the biggest and the best of kites. Miss Kruywagen encouraged the school to enter the competitions. She taught us how to build the kites and what accessories to acquire. She copied plans and instructions from encyclopaedia and from Oriental manuals. I and five of my friends formed a kite-cartel.

Mark Kobrin, Tommy Green, Clippie Hesselburg, Sambo Manasevich, Basil Samson and myself. Miss Kruywagen got us the special paper and string and strips of wood and helped us decode the blue-prints and the Chinese instructions. We finally assembled our 'enterprise' in the senior boys quadrangle, eagerly aided and abetted and heckled by an enthusiastic crowd of Arcadians. Some of the girls helped us with the pasting and threading and snipping …….Eki Levine, Judy Rushowitz, Molly Michelow, Freda Kotzen. The kite was a large

cupboard size box kite. Jokes and jibes from the spectators called us "the Kite-brothers of Kittyhawk!"…as it did a bit resemble the Wright brother's first flying machine.

The construction was finished and we carried it triumphantly in procession – like a Christian pageant in Rome, singing and chanting, out to the driveway. There amid cheers and jeers and funny catcalls from all Arcadia lining the driveway we launched our giant masterpiece. Tommy and Mark running holding the large box aloft. Clippie and I tripping over one another with the string winder. Sambo and Basil bringing up the long flapping multicoloured rags tail.

We all ran and stumbled down the drive. Miraculously, thanks to our careful obedience to dear Miss Kruywagen's instructions and suggestions, the huge box kite took off. We had a lift off! It rose magnificently skywards. We deftly played out the string. First one ball then a second ball.. The beautiful monster soured high above Arcadia. Over tree tops and rooftops and high above the chimney pots to cheers and cries of delight from hundreds of happy children… The six of us jockeyed for control of the string winder, keeping the string clear of trees and overhead wires.

Upstairs windows were flung open. People put their heads out to see what all the cheering was about. Stompie and Matron Shaer came out of the front door followed by Mr Swanepoel, Arcadia's head of security. They gazed skywards and pointed at the flying box kite. We manoeuvred the kite over the driveway and started winding it down. Suddenly a sudden unexpected gust of wind sent it spinning and spiralling drunkenly. Twisting and turning its long raggy tail every which way. We battled the wind and wrestled each other to get control of the drunk whirling monster. Six boys pulling and tugging and shuffling and arguing but we were no match for the big box kite, and it plunged end up, like the great Titanic going down, into the thick orchard above the driveway. Tangling itself in the branches of a heavy pear tree. Of course we six kite-brothers dashed into the orchard to save our enterprise.

And Swanepoel and Stompie Shaer and Speedcop Harary were after us with whistles and whips as the orchard was strictly out of bounds to boys, with or without kites.

How we retrieved our kite and repaired it… and gathered windfallen pears… and suffered under the lash… is another story. Another Arc-memory

THE BLUE-GUM TREE HOUSE

In 1936 or 37 my brother Mannie, Tommy Green and I built a tree-house in one of the high blue-gum trees growing on the west side of the new under construction Boy's department building. That was before the raised swimming pool on stilts was built.

It was a large and high blue-gum tree. A thick strong trunk rose branchless for about 20ft. Then the high canopy of leafy branches extended upwards for quite another 30ft.

We nailed pieces of wood slats onto the trunk to make a ladder to reach the lowest branches. When we were twenty feet up we

Arc Kite and Tree House – M Perry 1999

could climb through the branches to a height of fifty feet from the ground. At the dizzy swaying height of forty feet we built a plank platform in the arms of a couple of strong branches.

We had purloined or 'borrowed' the planks from the rubble of the under construction scaffolding on the new Boys wing. Also lengths of rope with which we hauled planks, one at a time, to our blue-gum eyrie on high. With purloined nails and wire and makeshift iron pipe hammers we constructed a firm, solid and secure platform over 40ft above the ground.

Then we attached four 6ft long corner poles on which we tacked hessian walls. The roof was left open to the leafy green leaves spreading canopy over our tree shack.

Tommy "invented" a secret ladder system meant to deter other children from invading our tree hideout. Tommy's patent consisted of only three rungs. Each wooden rung had strong cuphooks screwed on to it. Strong eye-hooks were left in the tree trunk like clampons on a cliff face. The first of us to arrive would dig out the three rungs from a garden hiding place. Then hook them on the clampons as he ascended. Reaching down for the lowest rung and reaching up to hook it over his head. Leaving the bottom of the trunk un-runged as he worked his way upwards.

We hid a homemade rope ladder in the crook of the branches under the platform. The first person up the tree would lower the rope ladder for the other two boys.

Our tree house served us well for five years. We retreated up to our tree house almost daily from 1937 to 1941. It was our private sitting room, study room. Our homework haven for

Tommy and me during our years in forms one, two and three in Parktown High School.

Till one afternoon in 1941 we came home from school to find that a dozen of the trees, including our tree with the tree house, had been cut down. Felled. Cut up for firewood and removed from Arcadia by the builder's lorries to make room for the proposed new swimming pool.

Mannie and I left Arcadia before the pool was ready for occupation. Tommy Green stayed on in Arcadia for two more years spending much of his free time at the poolside where he did his reading and his homework.

Some 40 years later, in 1980 in Israel, on a happy visit to Mannie on Moshav Moledet, I climbed up a tall tree, with the assistance of Mannie and his son Joel, to admire the tree house that Mannie and Joel had built for Mannie's grandchildren.

Tommy was a Johannesburg lawyer. Eventually he immigrated to Australia with his wife and children. Sadly Tommy died of a heart attack in 1983. He was 60 years of age. On my yearly visits to my family in Sydney I always intend to visit Tommy's grave. Perhaps he lies buried in the shade of a blue-gum tree.

I SPY WITH MY LITTLE EYE

At age 12 I was one of a number of children hospitalised in Arcadia's hospital to have our tonsils removed. It was 1936. About a dozen boys and an equal number of girls. In the boy's ward we recuperated and regained our voices and we were fed ice cream and mild soups. As we lay there in white hospital beds we took to playing at a guessing word game. "I spy with my little eye something beginning with…………" Of course we had to spy objects inside the ward. Like 'D' for door, 'B' for bed, 'L' for locker, 'W' for window and so on… Close beside each bed stood a steel hospital locker. The locker had a shoe cupboard, two or three shelves and a glass top. The beds and lockers were the only furniture in the ward. Our I spy game progressed happily for most of the day.

Then came Mickey Gordon's turn to spy. Mickey reflected for a moment and then he piped up with "I spy wiff my little eye something beginning wiff Eff Gee!… Hyphenated or double words were allowed.. We started to guess. "Flower Garden" said Robert Bushkin. "No" said Mickey. "Four green grapes!" said Clippie Hesselberg. "Wrong" said Mickey. "Funny Groove" Sambo offered. "Fat Groin" said tubby Harry Edelman. "Wrong. Wrong". The guessing continued round the ward… "Fat Geese" said Tommy Green. Louis Hurwitz came out with "Fancy Gloves" and I rudely inserted "Filthy Guessing Games" which solicited "Farty Gasses" from Marky Kobrin. And "Fat Gravy" from Pasey Meyers. And "Flat Girls" from the buxom nurse Brown who walked in to the ward. We guessed and guessed on into the night and half the next day in our throaty hoarse tonsillectomy voices, exhausting every possible Eff Gee possibility. But to everyone Mickey croaked "No' and "Wrong". One by one we waited for Mickey to tell us what he spied beginning with Eff Gee. Mickey took his time. He pointed to the thick glass locker top beside him and proclaimed "FICK GLASS!".. We had overlooked the fact that Mickey Gordon had difficulty in pronouncing <u>TH</u>. He used to say, "Mickey Gordon fats my name. So fere. I bet you a fousend pound!" (Eff Gee could have stood for "Fat Guts" Stompie.

THE RINGWORM EPIDEMIC IN ARCADIA IN 1935.

Ringworm or Tinea is a contagious skin disease caused by a species of fungus. In the 1930's it was most common among children of school age. Dogs and cats and other animals are subject to ringworm, which can easily be communicated from pets to human beings.

In 1935 in Arcadia many of the boys had pet farms in the rocks and crannies of the Arcadia hills. Some bred chickens or ducks and enjoyed egg and poultry cook-outs from time to time. One enterprising "farmer", Hymie Ekovitz, sold a boiled egg for a tickey, a fried egg cost fourpence. Other boys had kitten farms and puppy nurseries.

One of my best boyhood friends and food-bartering associate was Sambo Mannie. At eleven years of age Sambo successfully maintained a small cat-breeding farm. Sambo and his partners built an enclosure in a rock cave on the lower hillside in which they 'imprisoned' stray cats that they caught and found. They fed their cat stock on milk stolen from the Arc dairy and food scraps salvaged from the garbage.

One hot summer's day in 1935, Sambo met me as I was emerging from the old Hebrew school. Sambo and I were two eleven-year-old 'business associates' in the Arc food and goodies market! We respected each other's business interests and endeavours. Our brief conversation in passing went something like this; Sambo: "Hello there Mr Mike, how's the bread pudding business?" Me: "Hello mister Sambo. Fine thanks. Doing well. And how's the 'lion taming' business?" Sambo: "The kitten farm is thriving. I have a new batch of beautiful ginger pedigrees. Can I interest you in a couple or three?" Me: "Not today thank you mister Sambo. Maybe next week, after visiting Sunday". (meaning that I would probably have some gift from a visitor to trade for a kitten) Sambo: "Do us a favour mister Mike" Me: "Sure thing mister Sambo. Whatever, if I can". Sambo: "Lend me your cap. I left mine down the hill. Old Mannieballs (Hebrew teacher Mr Mann) will kick me out if I don't have a cap". Me: Sure thing. Only with pleasure." I said removing my cap and plonking it on Sambo's head…"Thanks mister Mike" said Sambo as he ascended the steep stairs into the old Hebrew school. "I'll give it back to you tonight at Shul time." I was happy to oblige my good associate Sambo.

That evening Sambo duly appeared outside the Shul and gave me my cap back. Donning our caps we entered the Shul. But I did not realise that that afternoon Sambo had used my cap in which to transport a half dozen newborn kittens.. The kittens had infected my cap with ringworm and I had inadvertently transferred the tinea infection to my scalp. By next morning I was suffering a dreadful case of very itchy scalp… Sambo too was scratching his head and so were six other boys. All of whom were pet farmers, associates of mister Sambo… Nurse Molly Cohen herded the eight of us into Sister Goldwater's hospital. The eminent skin specialist Dr Henry Gluckman who later became Smut's Minister of Health, did voluntary medical treatment at Arcadia. Gluckman declared us an epidemic.. Our

heads were shorn bald. Salves and ointments were plastered all over our bodies and we were quarantined in a ward, kept away from the other children and from school. Food trays were passed to us through the window by African servants wearing cover-alls and rubber gloves and facemasks.

The quarantine lasted two or three weeks. Then one morning we were head bandaged and dressed and loaded onto the Arc bus and taken to Dr Gluckman's clinic in Jeppe Street. Nurse Josie Le Roux accompanied us. We alighted from the bus in busy up-town Johannesburg. Crowds stopped to gape in amazement at the sight of eight small skinny boys in baggy trousers and bandaged heads and clumsy boots with a uniformed nurse in charge. We were shepherded into Lister building. Someone asked if we had been in an accident. A kindly lady touched my shoulder and said "Oh you poor thing." She then gave me a sixpence, which I meekly accepted. After our medical check up inside Gluckman's clinic we were herded back down to the pavement to board Charley Miller's bus. Curious by-passers stared at us through the bus windows. More people started passing coins to the "eight wounded soldiers". "What happened to your heads Sonny boys?" asked an elderly gentleman. "'Twas an accident!" said Sambo pocketing the shilling the man gave him. The Gluckman treatment cured the ringworms and dispelled the epidemic. In another fortnight we were all discharged with clean bills of health. My hair grew again and I resolved to never lend or borrow articles of clothing. Especially caps… especially to mister Sambo the "lion tamer!"

A HAPPY JOURNEY FROM JOHANNESBURG TO PORT ELIZABETH.

I well remember 1935 and 1936 when I was 11 and 12 years of age. In December of 1935 the children of the Jewish Orphanage in Johannesburg were taken on a three weeks holiday to Port Elizabeth. There was eager anticipation and much preparation and great excitement in Arcadia from October onwards. The boys and girls were given special lectures and instructions by teachers, scoutmasters and by Matron and 'Stompie' Shaer on how to conduct themselves in the seaside beach camp and on the train, what to do and particularly what not to do. Not to go into the sea or anywhere outside the camp without proper adult authority and supervision. Not to make fires or pick berries or steal fruit or eat anything other than what we were fed on in the camp's dining tent. And special instructions on how to behave on the train and in public places. We were grouped six or eight children per group. Each group appointing a leader and a second in command.

The much looked forward to day of departure finally dawned. Almost the entire compliment of Arcadian children and staff would be transported to Port Elizabeth. The very small babies were to remain at home in Arcadia together with their nurses and sister Kaufman.

Each child going to Port Elizabeth had been given a cardboard school-case in which to carry personal belongings, a towel, soap, toothbrush, a tin plate and tin mug, pyjamas etc. Some lucky boys and girls had Kodak box cameras and packets of sweets and small gifts from relatives.

My 14 year old brother, Mannie, whom I adored and doted upon, and I stuck close together in the 'herd' of about 300 children as we boarded the buses that took us to Park Station. Groups of relatives and benefactors cluttered the station platform where our train stood waiting for us. We were allocated compartments with six or eight boys to a compartment. There were six bunks in each compartment and each boy was given a bunk for himself. Though there were some small brothers who were permitted to double up with their big brothers. Mannie and I took separate bunks. Mannie on an upper berth while I was beneath him on a middle berth. I remember being carefully warned by older boys to see that the compartment windows were shut when the berths were folded down. As the person occupying the middle bunk could very easily slide out of the open window, blanket, bedding and all.

Excitedly we settled in stowing our cardboard cases under the lower bunks. The time was early morning. The middle and upper berths were folded flat against the wall during the day.

There was a colour picture of Hex River valley on the underside of the middle bunk. Our compartment companions were senior boys Hymie Ekovitz and Maurice Wolfsohn. Hymie was group captain. Maurice was first lieutenant. Willy Gresak and Colin Noren, Mannie and myself were Hymie's "soldiers". The train whistle blew two long toots. That set off a cheering and a singing from three hundred children's throats. With a great clanking jerk the train started to move. The people on the platform waving and shouting "Bye, Bye!". The chuff puffing

engine picked up speed, the carriage wheels clickety clacked, the shrill voices of the girls sang out "*Hava nagillah hava nagillah vay nissmachah*" to be topped by the boys singing "The bear went over the mountain to see what he could see!" to the tune of "Should auld acquaintance be forgot!" Onwards we sped. Clickey clacking through Braamfontein railway yards, on through Mayfair and Langlaagte and Randfontein. Telegraph poles moving past our windows. Telegraph wires forming patterns overhead like the lines on a musical stave, with birds and enamel bottles on the pole crosstrees like musical notes.

We sat with our noses pressed to the windows happily watching the passing landscape. Vast fields of green mealies and potatoes, dusty sand roads, ox wagons and lorries loaded with farm produce and picaninies reminded Mannie and me of the good life we had enjoyed three years previously on our father's farm in Bethal.

The engineer blew his whistle. A long wailing toot. The children responded with more songs and cheers. The train slowed or stopped for short minutes only at sidings or at stations to allow up-train traffic to pass, much to the excitement and pleasure of the noisy chattering boys.

This was our boy's dream come true. A great train ride. As the day wore on we unfolded the table over the washbasin and our Arcadian Zulus came down the corridors trundling bread and jam and boiled eggs and milk and apples for our marvellous compartment picnic lunch. Hymie and Morris were kind and

By M Perry Kotzen

helpful and considerate. Mannie, who was 14, was a Senior Boy. I, at 12 was a pre-Barmitzvah "inbetweener". After lunch we played "I spy with my little eye, something beginning with…! "whichever letter. There was so much to see both inside and outside the train. So many things beginning with the letter espied that the guessing went on endlessly with much humour and funny jokes and boyish pranks.

By evening we were travelling across a vast desert region. We saw sheep and cattle and an occasional Bushman and a bearded man riding a donkey. The red setting sun was on our right hand so we knew that we were travelling southwards towards the Cape. Our Zulus brought us more food. Stewed fruit and cheese sandwiches and tea. Nurse Molly Cohen and some senior girls came down the corridors bringing us cakes of soap and toiletries, even toilet paper. As night fell we folded down the bunk beds and folded up the table. We washed our tin plates and tin cups in the wash basin. Working the basin was a four hands affair. The push button tap had to be held down by one boy while another boy washed. For the second one released pressure on the tap the plughole opened and all the water drained out. We brushed our teeth each in turn. Ekovitz, our leader, called out our names for our turn at the basin.

He was a good leader, was Hymie Ekovitz. He always called himself last and the smallest boy, me, the first. Hymie was to be our tent leader in Port Elizabeth. We six and another two for tent mates. Mannie and I were very happy with this, as we were both very fond of Hymie Ekovitz. He was a kind hearted older boy; he was 15 or 16 in 1935. He was not a bully like some of his contemporaries were. There were a number of sadistic bullies among the Arc boys in 1935 who ill-treated and exploited the younger boys. But there were also some exceptionally kind hearted, considerate, big-brotherly boys. Notably Hymie Ekovitz and Sydney Fickey Klevansky and Maurice Wolfson and Basil Levit. The small fry or "*kleinspan*" as we were known in Afrikaans, admired and respected the "*grootspan*" boys and girls who were not bullies. But we lived in fear and trembling of those who had bully reputations. In our berths on the train clicking through the *veldt* at night, we sang together or we played "I spy" and we were happily lulled to sleep by the rhythmic swaying and clacketing of the train.

In the early morning we saw the sun rise on the Karoo's vast and beautiful landscape. We took turns to the toilet in the corridor and for the wash basin. The Zulus appeared with warm milk and porridge and bread rolls and cheese. And nurse Molly came by with a couple of senior girls who handed each of us a handful of toffees. By the afternoon we were in the mountains of the Northern Cape.

As the train rounded curves through the mountain passes we could wave to people in other carriages. There was great excitement during a tunnel or running through a deep cutting. Everything was exciting and unusual and happy and memorable, a small boy's dream come true. A wonderful memory for the orphanage kids of 1935. I for one would remember that train trip to Port Elizabeth for the rest of my days.

On our second day in the train my brother Mannie suddenly complained of earache. Molly Cohen put some drops in his ear but the pain persisted. Early the next morning we were in Port Elizabeth. Many Port Elizabeth people had come to the station

in private cars to help 'ferry' the children to Humewood Beach. A kindly old English gentleman and his wife took Mannie and me and two other children in their Model T ford. A beautiful 'vintage' car that he had kept in perfect pristine condition and proudly driven since 1928. They drove us through the city and pointed out landmarks such as the famous Camponile Tower.

We sped along the coastal highway, honking and overtaking slower cars, to Humewood Beach. There we found Hymie Ekovitz and Colly Noran and Morry Wolfson and our tent-mates and we moved into the bell-tent that Hymie had reserved for us. There were eight camp bed stretchers inside the bell-tent. As we all excitedly settled in, brother Mannie, in agony, went with nurse Molly to the "Hospital tent" in the camp. A doctor there examined Mannie and immediately rushed him off to the Port Elizabeth Children's Hospital where Mannie underwent an emergency operation in his ear to remove an inflamed mastoid. Mannie was hospitalised for the three weeks in Port Elizabeth.

While devastated and completely at a loss, I, unhappily moped about the camp, hardly taking part in any of the activities and the fun. The boys and Molly Cohen tried their best to cheer me up but I was inconsolable. Mannie was brought back to Humewood the day before our final day. We were all busy packing up. 229 sun-tanned children and one pale untanned Mannie were ferried back to the train station, entrained and clickety clacked back to Johannesburg and Arcadia. For me and Mannie, the train journeys were the most memorable and the best adventure of our boyhood lives.

'A PASHA TWICE SUNG'

One of my most poignant memories perhaps of Arcadia is my recollection of my Barmitzvah day on the first Saturday in October of 1936.

Two senior boys, Morris 'Bull' Wolfsohn and my brother Mannie Kotzen, were elected by the Hebrew teacher Rothstein to rehearse me in the Pasha. Mannie and Bull started training me two months ahead of the date in October. From mid August I was rehearsed daily for over an hour each afternoon and by October I knew the Pasha by heart and I could sing it loud and clear. Anticipation of my Barmitzvah was further enhanced by the knowledge that my dear Mother would come to the Arcadia Shull on Barmitzvah Saturday to hear me sing the Pasha.

At that time my mother was boarding in a room in Mayfair - the western suburb of Johannesburg. She was employed in a dry cleaner depot in the main Mayfair Road. Mother's 26 year old nephew, Ben Kessel, was a newly qualified pharmacist, who worked in the General Hospital Clinic in Hillbrow. Benny was a handsome young man about town. He was well dressed, drove a snappy Model T Ford, and had a flat in Hillbrow. Benny played tennis in the private courts of the Houghton and Parktown nobility. He squired the rich and beautiful girls from Houghton and Saxonwold through the night life of Johannesburg. Mother asked her nephew Benny to kindly escort her to Arcadia on little Michael's Barmitzvah day. She made this request of him a few weeks in advance of October 10th. Benny readily agreed. He often professed a love and admiration for his beautiful Aunty Sadye, and he promised faithfully that he would call for her on Saturday, October 10th 'around eight or nine' am.

The Barmitzvah day dawned bright and sunny. Happily expectant looking forward to greeting my mother when she arrived at the Shull, I was very early ready, scrubbed, polished and dressed in a new white shirt with a blue tie and new blue shorts, blue socks and my boots highly polished. The Shull hall started filling up at 8.30 am. Girls to the right hand side. Boys to the left. Mr Rothstein entered followed by Mr Shaer and Matron Shaer making their grand entrance. As Rothstein called out 'Stand', we all rose from our seats as a sign of respect for Mr and Mrs Stompie. Matron seated herself amid the senior girls while Stompie and Rothstein took their places in the 'Presidential box' in front of the Bimahh. Senior boys Basil Levett and Hymie Wolchuck, the Arc chazzans, took their places up on the Bimah. Basil and Chuck were the forerunners of Starkey and Osrin and Perkel and Samson. At a signal from Mr Rothstein the male congregation donned tallaysim in unison. 'Sit' ordered Rothstein and the congregation sat down, many of the boys noisily slamming their seats down in the process.

The Saturday morning service began. But as yet there was no sign of my mother. I glanced over to my brother Mannie. He signalled me in body language 'Don't worry. She'll get here in time.' It was early yet. Meanwhile, clear across Johannesburg in Mayfair, mother was dressed and ready waiting for Benny to fetch her. 9.00 am and then 10.00 am came and went with no Benny tooting his Model T for mother.

At Arcadia the service proceeded. At 10.00 am the Oren Kodesh-Ark was opened with song and prayer and the Torahs were carried through the Shul to the Bimah. In my seat between my friends Tommy and Peysy, I was feeling increasingly apprehensive. Where was my mother? What could have happened to delay her??

A Barmy Day in 1936 – by M Perry 2001

Some of the senior boys were called up to make brochas on the Torah as Hymie Wolchuch chanted the haftorah … I kept looking to the doors and windows to the quadrangle, but still mother did not enter the Shul.

The call came from Basil Levitt. '*Ya Amode ha Barmitzvah Menasheh Ben Asher*'. That was my cue to go up on to the Bimah. Some of the boys whispered 'Go on Michael. That's you!' 'What about my mother?' I whispered back as I rose and sidled down the passage. 'Get a move on boy' commanded Mr Stompie Shaer. 'Don't you want your Barmitzvah?' 'He wants his mother sir' piped up my friend Robert Bushkin. 'What utter nonsense!' Stompie shouted. 'You become a man today. From today you must do without your mother!'

I mounted the Bimah. Basil Levitt led me through the blessings and Chuck pointed the silver hand indicator at the opening word of the Pasha.

I gave a tremulous glance at the Shul doors hoping that mother would still be on time. All eyes focused on me. I timidly launched my high falsetto voice into the song, starting softly but increasing in tempo and volume with each painful stanza. And with each phrase I would look beseechingly for a sight of my mother. I finished the Pasha. I remained up on the Bimahh until the haftorah was completed. And still no sight of mother. The Torah was rolled up and dressed in ornate cover and ornaments, while I sat holding it. Then as the congregation sang '*Etz chyim hee lama chazeekim bo …*' it is a tree of life to them that grasp it' I carried the Torah through the Shull back to the oren kodesh.

Across the city in Mayfair, mother finally realized that Benny had stood her up. She hurried from her room to the main road and caught a tram to town. In town she had to wait a half hour for a bus that would take her to the Oxford Road in Parktown. All the while she was tearfully ashamed of having missed Michael's Barmitzvah. By the time she got off the bus in Oxford Road it was after 12. Then she ran and stumbled up the long drive. Adon Olam was over and the service had ended. Everyone filed out of the Shul and dispersed to their departments. Only Mannie and Michael stood forlornly in the deserted quadrangle. I was still expecting mother to pitch up. 'Don't cry little brother' said Mannie gently. 'I'm sure mother tried to get here in time, but she had difficulties.' Just then we heard a sobbing moan coming through the big door to the gravelled courtyard. It was mother sobbing 'Michael, I'm here, I'm coming!' She stumbled through the doorway, distraught, dishevelled out of breath, sobbing. We ran to embrace her. She hugged us both. 'Your Barmitzvah?' she asked 'What about your Barmitzvah?' 'I did it already' I said. 'Where were you? You said you'd be early!' 'I came on the bus and I had to run all the way' she panted. 'Oh Michael, I am so sorry!'

It was then that my wonderful brother Mannie took charge of the situation. 'It's all alright. It's alright' he assured us. 'It's no big tragedy. It's no big deal. It's only a song sung in the Shul. So now we will go back inside the Shul and Michael will sing his Pasha over again, a special encore for his special mother. 'Come on' said Mannie taking mother's arm and guiding her into the Shul. Mother had stopped sobbing. Mannie sat her down in Matron's seat on the girl's side and I ascended the steps of the Bimah. Then brother Mannie, standing at the lectern in front of the *oren kodesh-ark*, called out loud and clear, '*Ya amode, ha barmitzvah Menasheh Peretz ben Asher Zalman.*' I took a breath and sang out the Pasha. I noticed that boys and Mr Rothstein had gathered at the French windows.

As I sang, rolling each word melodiously, the boys came through into the Shul, Basil and Ronnie Levitt, Hymie and Leslie Wolchuck, my friends Robert Bushkin and Pasey Meyers and Tom and Jonah and Pasey's kid brother Barney, and Basil Samson and Starkey and Fickey Klevansky. I sang out with full baritone strength and utter confidence giving every word my very best rendition. Rothstein and Bull Wolfsohn came up on to the Bimah. Pride and joy registered on their beaming faces. Mother sat enthralled. I hit the high notes and ended the Pasha with a long held tenor crescendo climax. The boys burst into applause. One by one they approached mother. Each boy, Mr Rothstein as well, shook mother's hand and wished her 'Mazel Tov Mrs Kotzen.'

Mother's tears were tears of happiness and gratitude and I had a very happy and proud Barmitzvah.

A GOLD SOVEREIGN FROM I.W.

I was one of 15 boys to celebrate Barmitzvah in 1936 in Arcadia. My personal Barmitzvah ritual was performed on an October Saturday morning in the new Shul, which had formerly been the Senior Boy's dormitory on one of the great halls of the old Sir Lionel Phillips' mansion house. The new Boy's wing was built and opened in 1936 and the synagogue was transferred from the library in the main entrance hall to the spacious ballroom on the West side of the quadrangle. Although my Barmitzvah ceremony was in October I would however be celebrating in a joint party at Chanukah time together with the other 14, 1936 Barmitzvah boys.

The long, looked forward to, Chanukah of 1936 finally dawned in December. All of the more than 300 children of Arcadia were assembled on the lower lawn where long trestle tables were covered with white cloths and set with plates and cups, large enamel tea pots and bottles of orange juice. Each child was given a slice of fruit cake, a handful of sweets and nuts and a cup of liquid .juice or lemonade or tea with milk and sugar.

The 15 1936 Barmy-boys stood in line together dressed in white shirts and blue shorts, black socks and black laced up boots. The elegant party of invited benevolent guests attended by Superintendent Mr Louis Shaer and his good wife Matron Shaer and committee members Woolf Hillman and Eddy Kohn with their bejewelled wives and chubby children, were seated at an elaborately arranged table laden with dishes of cream cakes and fruit bowls and fancy Spode china crockery. The assembled ladies and gentleman of Johannesburg high society sipped their tea delicately, many a manicured pinky raised prudishly, and munched at neat little cucumber sandwiches or nibbled at creamed crumpets while enjoying the prospect of three hundred happy Jewish children singing and dancing or self consciously prancing on the lawn.

Mr Eddy Kohn introduced one or two special guests who rose in turn to make short complimentary speeches of praise and admiration and encouragement for past and present benefactors of Arcadia. Matronly and motherly Matron Shaer introduced a pretty senior girl, Sylvia Ostrovick, who shyly sang

a solo Hebrew song accompanied by Sister Goldwater on the piano. The piano had been carried and wheeled out on to the lawn by the six burley Zulus who were employed in the kitchen. Then the children stood together to be conducted in chorus-concert by Matron to sing the well loved song of Chanukah. "*Mor ows tzur ye shoe owsee!*" The cat's in the cupboard and you can't catch me!" sang little Hymie Cohen.

Eddy Kohn then boldly announced that the "lucky" 1936 15 barmy-boys were to be presented with special Barmitzvah gifts from the committee members and their families. "A handsome embroidered tallit bag, a magnificent silk tallit, a new set of leather tefillin, a magnificent leather bound chumash-siddur prayerbook and a proper orthodox yamulkah"

"But!" he added… "Before we call out the names of the 15 "lucky" boys, it gives me great pleasure to introduce our special, SPECIAL guest of honour the right honourable Mr I W Shlashinger.. Who has something to add for these lucky boys".

Acknowledging rounds of polite appreciative applause, IW rose from his chair. Short, chubby, ruddy faced, brown double breasted suit, brown snap brim Fedora hat at a jaunty angle, sparkling diamond cufflinks, manicured, polished, dapper, non-practicing Jew, philanthropist, míllionaire I W Schlashinger. Mr "moneybags" of the South African Anglo-Jewish society.

IW spoke briefly of his patronage and association with what he referred to as "Dish Joovish Offenhouze" in a high pitched falsetto voice. He went on to point out that as 1936 was also the Barmitzvah year of his own son, Johnny Schlashinger; "My Johnny is unfortunately not able to attend dish morning's heppy paarty.. As he is down in der Sous Coast on his holiday!.. Nebberderless… Johnny is mit us in our thoughts and in our hearts!" IW went on to say that "on Johnny's behalf each vun of the 15 Jooyish Offenhouwze Barmitzvah boys would be receiving today, a gift of a golden sovereign!" "So vot do you tink bout dat, hey!"

This magnanimous announcement was greeted with much joyful approving applause. Woolf Hillman thanked and embraced IW, Eddy Kohn and the Shaers rose to clasp IW's hands while the scout master "Aunty" Greenblatt, called for three hearty cheers for IW Shlashinger and his son John. "Hip … Hooray!….hip, hip…….hooray!……hip, hip, hip…….HOORAY!"

The Barmy-boy's names were called out one by one in order of our birth dates. "Bushkin, Hurwitz, Karp, Green, Cohen, Sachs, Meyers, Swerzick, Manashevitz, Kemp, Hesselberg, Kotzen, Nochumsohn, Adler, Perkel.." We each in turn approached the main table.. Charles Dickens called it "Mounting the scaffold one by one!".. To receive a handshake and a gift tallit-tefillin bag from Mr Rotstein. We moved along the table to Mrs Wolf Hillman, a stout smiling powdered lady under a flowery hat, who handed to each a handsome leather-bound Chumash-siddur prayerbook. Each Barmy boy looked around with anticipation. Looking for I.W. or Eddy Kohn with the 'golden handshake'.. But the Shlashingers and the Kohns had left the garden party during the first round of applause. "Don't worry boys!" assured Stompie Shaer. "You'll get what's coming to you later …. much later!" With our hands full of prayerbook and tallit bag we all assumed that our promised gold sovereigns were in the committee's safe keeping for us. "You'll get that when you turn twenty-one." Not one of us dared or ventured to inquire for his sovereign that day! It was a day to remember. A happy Chanukah in Arcadia in 1936.

As for our promised golden sovereigns, our measly 20 shillings apiece? In spite of some feeble and tentative approaches by various Barmy-boys through the ensuing years, to Eddy Kohn and the committee, or to Stompie and even Johnny Shlesh himself, nothing ever came of it.. Not to any of us, except being told off by the 'powers that were' for being the 'grasping little beggars' that we were. There was not ever one brass farthing. Not a penny oil rag! "Let's face facts boys!" said Speedcop Harary. "What is it you are looking for? Twenty lousy mingy shillings worth of scrap!" "Forget about it!"

ROSH HASHANA 1937

In 1937, in preparation for the high festivals of Rosh Hashana, Mr Rotstein, a Hebrew teacher, selected a dozen boys to be trained as a choir…'The unlucky 12' we thought, because choir boys would be put to suffer about two months of intensive practice and rehearsals and then have to spend the two long hot days of Rosh Hashana and the longer hotter day of Yom Kippur, standing on the crowded Bimah behind the monotonous chazan. Octogenarian Mr Aginsky was the chazan for 1937. He came to Arcadia through the courtesy of the Bella La Chagiya Shul in Doornfontein.

The long Senior boys dining room was converted into a temporary Shul to accommodate the many honoured guests as well as the more than 300 orphan children in the High Festivals. A wooden rostrum Bimah was erected at one end of the dining hall. Dozens of folding chairs were brought, hired from a catering company in Fordsburg, to fill the hall in neat rows.. On the first day of Rosh Hashana sage old Mr Aginsky, dressed in white robes, a silk tallit and boxlike white silk cantor's hat, was assisted up on to the rostrum. The girls and boys of Arcadia filed into the hall. The boys in clean white shirts, blue shorts, black socks and black boots. The girls in neat blue and white 'school-outfits' and blue ribbons in their hair.
Blue double breast suited Mr Rotstein led the 12 choirboys up on to the rostrum behind Mr Aginsky. The elegant and notable guests and visitors took their seats in the hall centre reserved for guests. Mr Shaer and Mr Rotstein and Matron Shaer and Miss Factor all called for "Silence please" and old Mr Aginsky began the service.

Mr Rotstein, deftly and with poise, conducted the choir in long humms and long aahs backing Aginsky's "Veyimaroo Amein's and his ever creaking, monotonous chazonis. The crowded hall grew stiflingly hot inside. The long French windows North facing had been thrown open by the usherettes.

The French door window immediately behind the Bimah was opened by Mr Rotstein. But Mr Aginsky, pausing in mid-chazonis, turned to Mr Rotstein and said "Pleeze! Da vinhinow! Vats a matter you!".. The service dragged on slowly. The opening and shutting of the errant window was an often repeated distraction for the children, especially the choir boys. Everyone grew hot and bothered and very bored. Mr Aginsky

wheezed away ending each prayer stanza with a croaking "El raachoom ha cha-a noon, erech a paayim verav chesed ve-emet!" and the humming choir would come in with "Adanay elohaynoo ud she hanaynoo" and Aginsky would belt out his "ve ne emaar aa main" with dreadful monotonous repetition.. Till finally, the window was open again, and Aginsky whirled round angrily to face Rotstein and instead of "venemaar amain" he sang out loud and clear "KLOYS DA VEWINDOW!".

The children exploded into laughter and that Rosh Hashana 1937 service went down in Arc history as "the great Aginsky fiasco!"

'Aginsky Fiasco' – by M Perry 2002

"IN 'CROCODILE' TO THE WANDERERS"

I was a senior boy during the days of 1936-37-38-39-40 and 41. The senior boys numbered about 100 in those years before the Klevansky-Harary-Lichtenfeld reformation. After passing standard five in Rannoch Road School the boys graduated, some to Parktown Boys High School, others to Jewish Government School in Doornfontein and some to Cyrildene School.

At the end of 1938 I went into form one at Parktown Boys. We used to walk from and to school from Arcadia each day. In the mornings walking down the Arcadia drive and up the Oxford Road, each boy carrying his satchel of books and his lunch. The lunch consisted of two or four thin slices of brown bread smeared with either peanut butter or mashed vegetables or sometimes minced meat.

Most days we returned to Arcadia from school at about 3 or 3.30 pm. We had to take off our school uniforms, black blazer with a rampant red lion on the breast pocket, grey socks, grey shorts, white shirt and red and black tie, and our Arcadia black boots. Then in patched khaki shirt and shorts we went down to the terrace under the Shul's west windows where we had "our four o'clock" which was a wedge of bread and jam and a tin mug of scalding hot tea. The boys liked very sweet tea so they used to put four or five teaspoons of sugar in the cup. The contents of the mug was so thick that the teaspoon would stand up unsupported.

We then went to Hebrew classes. From 1937 the Hebrew classes were in the "new" wing, on the north side of the boy's department. The girls and the boys were mixed in the Hebrew classes. That was about the only time that we could 'fraternise' with the girls. All the boys of my class had "sweethearts" with the girls of the class. I fancied Judy Rushowitz, but Judy herself fancied Mickey Gordon. Mickey in turn thought that Ekie Levine was "something special" but Ekie had eyes for David Rushowitz. While David found Molly Michelow attractive… and Molly on the other hand thought that Michael Kotzen was worth attention… it was a daisy chain.

After an hour of Hebrew we did our homework in the dormitory or in the library.. or we forgot about homework and we played soccer with a tennis ball on the lower lawn west of the Babies department, or some of us attended to our hobbies. Kitten farming, puppy farming, egg hatching and frying, or a kite factory or a tree house. The swimming pool was established only in 1940 on the west side of the new wing.

Some boys 'bunked' out after school and went to visit relatives in the suburbs. After Shul service on Saturday mornings boys used to bunk out, scrambling up the hill to the Queens Road and on to Yeoville and Berea and Doornfontein. But our very efficient and very strict chief watch-dog, Afrikaans Salvation Army Sergeant Major Swanepoel and his sadistic team of Zulu watchmen that patrolled the driveway and the Oxford Road boundary wall and the hillsides above the orchards were most adept at arresting bunkers-out.. and dragging the unfortunates they caught to the office where Stompie Shaer administered his dreadful "six of the best"…"Bend over you dirty little scoundrel!"

However, on Saturday afternoons 30 or so boys would be elected and escorted by Sergeant Major Swanepoel in a "walking crocodile", a long line two abreast, to the Wanderers football stadium near Park Station to see a first division soccer match. The list of names selected for the Saturday crocodile was compiled by the nurses in charge during the week. The, mostly Afrikaans, nurses, would gather the names of 30 "lucky" boys who, they maintained, "deserved" to go to the football on Saturday. This resulted in unfair favouritism on the part of the nurses. Those boys who ran after the nurses, helping them to clean and tidy the dormitories, or to *shlepp* bundles of laundry to and from the Arc laundry way up on the top of the driveway, boys to whom we referred to as "arse creepers", usually made the lucky list each week.

The 'arse creepers' consisted of only about 10 boys. The other twenty were chosen more or less at random or as payment for favours. If a nurse of the calibre of our anti-Semite Josie Le Roux, liked the look of a boy or liked the way a boy smiled at her and bade her "*goeie more juffrou!*" then she would put his name on the crocodile list. There were boys who got on the list every week. While others were never ever listed. But in any case most of the senior boys got out of Arcadia on Saturday afternoons.. If not on the crocodile walk then over the hills and over the wall. Smarter boys would engage a watchdog with chat, creating a diversion enabling his pals to sneak off… or get a Zulu to chase them while friends walked out of the gate.

One Saturday afternoon my brother Mannie and I both succeeded in getting on to Swanepoel's crocodile list. We dutifully walked along on the tail end of the 30 boy crocodile,

hoping for an opportunity to sneak off down a lane, as some of the more daring boys would do. But Sergeant Major Swany was far too alert. He seemed to have eyes in the back of his head… That Saturday afternoon he had already caught Sambo Manesevich trying to bunk off and he had whipped Sambo viciously across his bare legs with his dreadful willow cane. We were compelled to stay with the crocodile all the way to town, to the Wanderers.

There Swany allowed us to go to the urinals, two or three boys at a time while the rest waited in croc-line at the turnstiles. We were then herded into the stadium bleachers and made to sit, all 30 boys, in two rows close together "*Waar ek julle kan dop hou*" (Where I can keep an eye on you!) A soccer match kicked off. After some two or three minutes play Swany instructed an older boy, might have been Fickey Klevansky, to "Keep an eye on these buggers!" "I'll be back in ten minutes" And Swany went out of the stadium, not as we may have imagined, to visit the toilets, but he left the grounds completely. A boy spy watched from the top tier of the stadium and saw Swani hurrying away from the Wanderers in the direction of Braamfontein. Now we all knew that Swanepoel had a lady friend who lived in Braamfontein. We also knew from experience that he would not return to the stadium till about 5.00 pm. Last whistle time.

"Gone!…He's gone! To Braamfontein!"… the word went out among the boys. Whereupon 25 of the 30 boys were up and running out of there. Out of the Wanderers. Some going to Doornfontein. Others to Yeoville and Berea. All intending to be back at the stadium before Swany returned at 5.00 pm.

Louis and Max Rosengarten and Mannie and I raced down Rissik Street to Market Street where we jumped on a tram going to Mayfair. The conductor took tuppence from each of us. Tuppence was a schoolboy fare from Market Street to the Mayfair tram terminus. We sat upstairs on the open balcony and enjoyed the rattling ride through Fordsburg and all the way to the Mayfair tram terminus. The driver whistled as he clanged the bell and the conductor gave the strap two sharp ringing tugs at every stop.

In Mayfair the brothers Rosengarten went to visit their mother in 8th Avenue… Mannie and I visited our cousins, the Binder family in Battery Street. The cousins gave us lemonade and biscuits and showed us all their toys and books. Rhoda Binder played the piano for us. At 4.15 pm we said our goodbyes and we ran back to the tram stop. The tram was slow in arriving and then it was delayed in Fordsburg. We got back to Market Street at 4.55 pm. Five minutes to whistle time. We sprinted fast down Rissik Street and through the subway to the Wanderers. It was 5.05 pm and all the boys were assembled on the pavement outside the stadium. Swanepoel was there lividly glaring daggers at us. The Rosengarten brothers had made it back before 5.00 pm.

"*Waar was julle!*" barked the sergeant major.

"We went to the Gents *meneer!*" we whimpered.

"Gents se *moer*" he shouted… "*Vloek* stronde! *Blerry* liars!" he yelled as he flogged my bare legs with that terrible willow cane, making me yelp with pain and dance about the pavement..

much to the amusement and pleasure of the many Johannesburg citizenry streaming out of the stadium. *"Slaan hom dood!"* *"Gee hom goeie pak!"*.. came the encouraging comments from some well dressed gentlemen. The Sergeant Major then ordered the crocodile to *"Stap voor. Yookies!"* (Forward March little Jewboys!) as he led us up the hospital hill to Clarendon Circle and Queens Road and down the Oxford Road to Arcadia.

'OUR SURROGATE ZAIDA'

In 1933 and 1934 I was a ten year old in Arcadia. The aged eleven and upwards 'senior boys' were dormitoried in the Lady Phillips Ballroom. The large east wing of the main mansion which would, in 1937, become the Shul. The boys filled the hall and the quadrangle in rows and rows of iron cots. The verandahed quadrangle with its central fishpond, was the most noticeable feature of the east wing. A three stage iron fire escape stairway linked the quadrangle with the upper floor of the mansion where all the girls were dormitoried. Many an Arcadian rendition of the balcony scene in Romeo and Juliet was enacted inadvertently on that fire escape. With boyish David or Louis or Hymie or Woolfy or Harry playing 'Romeo' down beside the fishpond, while Esther or Rita or Ekie or Judy or Gertie or Sylvia or Molly played 'Juliet' up on the top fire escape platform.

Their dialogue, although pure Arcadian-South African lingua, was not far removed from Shakespeare's poetry, with warm whispered phrases such as: 'Psst. Come down here for a little while why don't you?' from Romeo and an anxious reply from upstairs, 'No. Don't be crazy. Do you want sister Goldwater and Matron to catch me??' ,,, 'But don't you love me?' … 'Well, I like you!' … 'How much?' … 'I like you a lot!' … 'So, come on down and give us a little kiss!' 'Don't be mad. *Cavey* – here comes matron!' …

Ten years later, when I was a 20 year old drama student, I was somewhat convinced that the Bard of Avon had been inspired by conditions in some mediaeval or Stratford on Avon institution similar to our Arcadia.

In Arcadia the boys were provided with boots which had been donated to the orphanage by various footwear manufacturers, mostly second graded, factory quality-control rejects, because of faulty workmanship or machine errors. We had to accept what footwear was given to us. A right size, a good fit, or a comfortable feel were considerations of no importance. If your boots pinched or gave you blisters or hindered your walking, you were ordered to 'Swap 'em with another boy!' My boots were too tight so I swapped them with a bigger boy who had bigger feet. Consequently the boots were then too loose for me, while my swapper had to endure too tight boots. So we swapped back and forth never finding comfortable satisfaction.

The boys kicked tennis balls and stones and anything around daily. Boots quickly became scuffed and worn down. A very dear old Jewish cobbler who had a shoe repair shop in Jeppestown, a central Johannesburg suburb, used to voluntarily spend one day each week at Arcadia mending the children's shoes. Kindly old Mr Chait would come on the bus to Arcadia carrying his bag of tools and spare parts with him. Zaida Chait

set up his workshop in a ground floor room of the old two storey Dickensian building at the top of the Arc driveway. Mr Mann's and Miss Factor's Hebrew classes occupied that old building. In between learning our *aleph-beth-gimel-daled* we would go downstairs to visit Zaida Chait.

He was an adorable Jewish grandfather. We all loved him and we squabbled among ourselves to help him carry his tools and to repair the boots. He rewarded us with toffees and fruit and Jewish idioms. He usually repaired a pair of boots while the wearer waited bare feet. Zaida Chait called some of us 'Tatingkeh' – Little father or 'Mameleh' – 'little mother. He was our surrogate Zaida. The zaida that the orphaned boys and girls would have liked for their own.

Many years later I met a business associate named Chait in Johburg. After doing business with Mr Chait for a number of yeas I happened one day to mention Arcadia in passing conversation. To which Mr Chait told me that his late father was the old cobbler who devoted a day each week to the children of Arcadia. It was then I saw the strong facial resemblance. Mr Chait looked a lot like his wonderful father, our surrogate Zaida at Arcadia.

With genuine tears in my eyes, I thanked Mr Chait for lending us his Tatta for our Zaida those years in Arcadia. My business relationship with Mr Chait took on a new meaning from that day. I'm sure that many of my generation of old Arcs remember our dear kind, loveable Zaida Chait, the boot repair man.

Zaida Chait, the cobbler was already an old man, or he seemed so in my ten year old eyes, when he repaired shoes in that room opposite the laundry, back in 1933-34-35-36. I now learn that that dear old grandfather was still there repairing broken shoes and broken hearts as late as 1964. He must have been very old by then. And his son would have been a grown man by 1964. When I spoke with Mr Chait, the son, in 1969-1970 he spoke sadly about his late father. So old Zaida Chait had by then gone to his repose.

A COMPULSIVE EATER

Quite often these days my wife and my children rebuke and scold me for over eating. My family are all small eaters. My wife is a strict vegetarian. More often they leave half the meal on their plates. The family garbage disposal is enormous. But I am of the habit of consuming every last morsel of food on my plate. Even to wiping the plate clean with a piece of bread., and then to asking for a second helping.

My friends tend to tease me for having a "healthy appetite". Any slight loss of appetite on my part is seen as a signal to my wife that I am 'coming down' with something ailing. A cold or a fever or an upset stomach or perhaps a toothache. Or my good wife demands to know from me "What is wrong with the dinner?" putting me on the defensive against accusations of 'bad cooking'.

I know full well that I am a compulsive eater. It probably stems from the nine childhood years I endured a "starvation diet" in old Arcadia. Happily I am neither overweight, nor do I suffer indigestion usually. So why do I like to eat?? Like Sigmund

Freud I search my childhood and adolescence for possible cause.

The first nine years of my life were spent on my late father's farm and in the village of Bethal, Eastern Transvaal. My dear mother was the daughter of a London East End Yiddish family. Mother and Grandmother happily and generously fed us on wonderful ample helpings of delicious Jewish dishes. Fried fish, various herrings, cheeses and chopped liver, cakes and strudels and jams, *kreplach, taiglach, imbilach, farfel,* tsimmus and chicken soup, roasted polkas and *kneidlach* and beetroot borscht, and all the mouth watering traditional Jewish food recipes from the East End of London and from Poland and Russia.

In 1933 when I was nine years of age, my food paradise suddenly ended with the untimely death of my father. Within a month of father's death brother Mannie and I were placed in the care of the South African Jewish Orphanage in Johannesburg. 1933 Arcadia was an austere, harsh and drab institution housing some 300 perpetually hungry, ragged, scruffy, aggressive children who were watched over by a Victorian martinet superintendent and his staff of Afrikaans anti-Semitic female wardresses who referred to themselves as "nurses". In 1933 the children were fed half-cooked, half-boiled, half fresh vegetables, the cast-off from the Newtown market.. coarse brown bread – no butter.. a gruel porridge laxative and perhaps a once a week dollop of mince meat or minced fish. And an occasional stale bun with a mug of scalding milkless tea at 4.00 pm.

Needless to relate I sorely missed my mother's Jewish dishes and the bountiful table on the farm.

In October of 1934, at my 11th birthday, brother Mannie and I were summoned to Mr Shaer's office one Sunday morning. We were told that a Mrs Sarovich of Jeppestown had donated some money to the orphanage. And that she and her husband would be visiting Arcadia that afternoon. Mrs Sarovich had specifically asked to see the "little Kotzen boys". "Apparently she is a relative of your late father" said Stompie Shaer. We were happy and excited to be getting a visitor. Visitors usually brought sweets and biscuits and sometimes toys.

We washed and cleaned up. Our wardress Miss Josie Le Roux gave us clean shirts. Clean but patched and frayed. Le Roux inspected us. Ears? Nails? Necks? "Go polish your boots!" Off we went. Two skinny small boys. We had been in the orphanage then just over a year. Our heads were close cropped bald. Our shining blonde curls had been clipped away two months earlier as a precaution against the ringworm epidemic which prevailed that year. Mannie wore a cloth cap. I look back now many years later at a faded snapshot that Rae Sarovich took of us that day in 1934. Patched and faded khaki shorts and shirts, outsize black cast-offs boots.

We waited outside the front doors for our visitors. We were joined by three other children. Max and Norman Rosenfeld and their beautiful doll-like baby sister six year old Shulamith. The Rosenfeld children were expecting a visit from their father. They had arrived in Arcadia that year. Their father had brought them to Johannesburg from Beira in Mozambique, East Africa, where they had lost their mother.

Presently a battered and dusty Chevrolet sedan (1930 vintage) pulled into the gravelled front area. Three adults stepped from the car, Mr Roselfeld, and Mr and Mrs Sarovich. Mr and Mrs Sarovich, she was our father's cousin Rae Gore who had visited us on the farm in Bethal two years previously. Rae was now married to Mossy Sarovich. They lived in Jeppestown.

Mossy and Rosenfeld carried a wicker hamper from the car. We all walked through the quadrangle and along the long verandah and down the stone steps towards the Baby's department. We found a shady corner of the lower lawn and Aunty Rae spread a large blanket on the ground for us to sit on.

Some orphanage children crept through the shrubbery to peep at us. Two adult men and one adult woman, well dressed, and four scruffy orphanage boys and one small pretty doll like girl Shulamith, picnicking on a rug in the Arcadian garden.

Aunty Rae unpacked and unwrapped the hamper. Enamel plates and tin mugs and metal spoons. 1934 was still a time before plastic or paper crockery and cutlery had been introduced.

Rae produced sandwiches made from delicious fresh white bread, filled with cream cheese, or gefilte fish or potato latkes or chopped liver. She unwrapped chicken polkas and wings roasted and *shmaltsy*. Apple strudel, cheesecake, salt beef, a jar of pickled herring, fried fish, boiled eggs, *babkah*, an assortment of jams and biscuits. She poured honey sweetened milk from a large bottle that had a clip-on ceramic stopper. We five happy kids and uncle Mossy and Daddy Rosenfeld responded admirably to Aunty Rae's magnificent picnic. I ate to bursting. (But I remained skeletal!). What food we had not eaten was distributed to friends and the inevitable army of hungry scroungers attracted by the aroma that curled across the gardens of old Arcadia.

I look back at that snapshot now. Little doll Shulamith and I are the sole survivors. *(Shulamith passed away in 2004.)* Aunty Rae and Uncle Motty and Daddy Rosenfeld and Max and Norman and brother Mannie are all angels now picnicking together somewhere on cloud nine. I wonder if they have potato latkes and chopped liver, and fresh white bread and gefilte fish.

I last saw dear Max Rosenfeld in the 1950's. He ran a bicycle shop near Roodepoort. Norman worked in a bank in Tel Aviv till his death in the 1980's. Brother Mannie died at age 72 in 1994 on his farm Moledet in Israel. Our dear Aunty Rae Sarovich visited us here in Israel in 1979 after Mossy had passed away. She passed away in Johannesburg in the 1980's. Baby-doll Shulamith Lowenstein-Rosenfeld was a beautiful and a glamorous grandmother in Johannesburg. Shulamith sadly passed away in 2004 in Johannesburg.

HONOUR GUARD AT FUNERALS

In my days in Arcadia, once or twice a month, usually on a Sunday, a contingent of senior boys were selected by Stompie and his minions and taken to Brixton or Braamfontein cemetery to 'honour guard' at a funeral. Those were the days before West Park became the Jewish cemetery. The funerals to which the boys paid homage and honour guard were of some benefactor or benefactor's parent who had bequeathed money to the

Jewish orphanage. The names of 12 or 15 or 20 boys would be called during Saturday night's supper or at Sunday morning's breakfast or in the Shul at tefillin laying time. The chosen boys would then dress themselves in shabass-best, white shirt, blue pants, black socks, black shoes highly polished, and black yamulkeh. Some of the boys who did not want to go on 'funeral parade' simply deputised a 'fag' or a kid brother in his place.

Most of the big boys had fags. A fag is a smaller boy who helps with their 'labours', like waiting on them at table, or polishing boots, or stealing fruit, or raiding grub, or making beds and taking care of clothes and even doing homework. I was happy to fag for my brother Mannie and for his friends Mark Wulfsohn and Alec Pip. And I willingly took Mannie's place on a funeral parade or at any 'unpleasant obligation' he did not care to take part of. I enjoyed the outing - the bus ride to and from Brixton in Charley Miller's bus.

Consequently I became a regular funeral-parader. When I was a child, even before coming to Arcadia, I heard about and saw first hand some people die of terminal illnesses. Friends and relatives of my parents. I do not remember if cancer was ever mentioned. In those days people died of heart failure or a stroke or influenza or 'dropsy' or malaria or pox. All the 'old fashioned' diagnoses. I only heard about cancer in my adult years.

In Arcadia there was a boy, Issy Miller, who died at age 14 from 'Sirvitus Dance'. Do any old Arcs remember Issy Miller? And there was our wonderful 'Goodbye Mr Chips' old English schoolmaster Professor Worthington. Professor Worthington's death was blamed on asthma and 'pulmonary consumption'. Doctors today tell me that I have a malignant cancerous tumour, but they cannot tell me where it comes from or, indeed, at the beginning, if it's even really there! Cancer does not seem to discriminate as to age or sex or season or geographical location. As with all modern afflictions, both good and bad, it comes alike to the wicked and to the just. And to those who sacrifice and those who do not!

MY ACTING CAREER

I really started acting and entertaining and telling stories at about 11 years of age in Arcadia. I still am, and I was, a prolific reader. My book-worm tendencies were fostered and encouraged by Professor Worthington… An elderly retired English schoolmaster, Professor Worthington, was engaged by Stompie Shaer and the orphanage committee to give extra curriculum lessons to the children. The Professor, was housed in the small stone cottage (which later became Stompie's house) at the lower Oxford Road - a gatehouse of the Arcadia estate, opposite Rannoch Road. He was a widower. He lived alone, but for a Zulu servant and an aged bulldog called 'Major'.

Some 15 boys and three of four girls became Professor Worthington's special "merry gang of rogues".. We would trail after him, six or seven of us at a time, with his faithful bulldog, on his walks "of discovery" through the gardens and rockeries and orchards and "secret pathways" of the great Arcadia estate. I enjoyed many afternoons for more than two years "under the tutelage and the wing" of dear old Professor Worthington. He would lend us books and introduced me to England's boyhood heroes.. Robin Hood, Beau Geste, Gulliver, Robinson Crusoe, David Copperfield, Oliver Twist, Tom Sawyer, Huckleberry Finn. And many many more. (My story "Les Enfants Perdus" is in memoy of Professor Worthington, which I wrote for the SA Jewish Times in 1966.)

In the boy's dormitory at night I would sit up late relating the stories and yarns I had heard and read from the Professor. More and more I would try to tell the story with facial expressions and animated action. I would jump up and sword fight like Captain Blood or talk to an elephant like Toomiy and put the words into action. I acquired a regular appreciative audience… some boys also joined me in the play-acting. I became a "star raconteur" among the Arc boys… Sadly the old professor died in 1936 around the time of my Barmitzvah.. I remember that he was too ill on my Barmitzvah Saturday to come to the Shul to see me perform my 'pasha'.

The "gang of rogues" mourned him and missed him. We said "Goodbye to our own Mr Chips!".. However, I continued recounting and acting out the stories that I had read or seen in the 'bioscope'…

At Parktown Boys High School I was a member of the school's drama department.. In forms two-three-four and five I was cast as Mark Anthony in Julius Caesar and other Shakespearean characters… As a Parktown old boy I returned to play Shylock in their production of Merchant of Venice…

I joined the Johannesburg Reps and the Jewish guild drama groups… I auditioned or, when cast, played for Taubie Kushlick, Brian Brooke, Adam Leslie, Cecil Williams and other South African producers. I studied elocution voice with Miss Muriel Alexander and I won applause and considerable kudos in eisteddfods ….

In 1948 January I went to London to audition and attend at the Royal Academy of Dramatic Art. The 'better' parts I played while at RADA were "Puck" in A Midsummer's night dream and PEER GYNT, and Uriah Heep in David Copperfield. Numerous small parts "walk-ons" and "bits".. I remained in England for six years in professional theatre and in films and I stage-managed an opera "Albert Herring" for Benjamin Britton. For the British Arts Council I toured England and Wales, Holland and Germany. I returned to South Africa in 1953 to work for the National Theatre Organisation. I played leading rolls for Leonard

Schach in "Volpone", "Antigone" and "Twelfth Night".. I acted in "The Tempest" in Cape Town's Maynardville open-air theatre. In Johannesburg I performed for the Reps and most other theatres and worked at Killarney and Kinekor Fox film studios acting and scenario writing… At age 54 in 1978, my wife Roz and our three children Asher, Adrian and Jessica and Roz' mom Paula and myself sold up and packed up in South Africa and we went on Aliya to Israel…. Now at the age of 82 I am retired-pensioned but still available for auditions. "Have grease paint, Will travel.". "Once a raconteur, always a raconteur!" said Professor Worthington as he and his faithful major left their footprints in my sands of time!

AFTER OUR DISCHARGES IN 1946

After our discharges in 1946, I, ambitious, and desirous of a career in the theatre and encouraged by my amateur successes in high school and with the Johannesburg Repertory Players, I sailed to England in February 1948 to audition for the Royal Academy of Dramatic Art in London. Six years later in 1954 aged 30 I returned to South Africa. For the next 25 years I made a precarious living as a professional actor, scenario writer and travelling salesman. Professionally I used my two 'Christian' names Michael Perry. In England I was advised to drop 'Kotzen' as the name so I was told, conjures up and invites anti-Semitism! Jewish friends and fellow thespians were discarding their Jewish names for English sounding equivalents. Harry Skikne became Laurence Harvey, Daniel Danilovitz became Kirk Douglas, Myrvyn Dunsky was Mervyn Douglas, Daniel Kamenski became Danny Kaye, Doris Kappelhoff became Doris Day, Berny Schwartz turned into Tony Curtis. Old Arcadian Michael Aronstam became Michael Preston and Menasha Peretz Kotzen became Michael Perry!

My late brother Mannie lies buried on his Moshav in Jezreel valley. Moshav Moledet where he had farmed for 33 years.

Another old Arc, Louis 'Sauce' Sullivan's grave is a close neighbour to Mannie's grave. Solomon Meyers attended Mannie's funeral in 1994. Now alas Solly himself has gone to that Arcadia in the sky. Many of my close Arc friends are now the dear departed. David and Boris Rushovich, Sambo Mannie,

Phil Kemp, Aaron Karp, Syd Nochumsohn, Norman Rosenfeld, Robert Bushkin, 'Ghandi' Hymie Sacks, Basil and Nita Samson, Bobby Friedlander, Hymie 'Digs' Cohen etc etc. However there are yet old Old Arcs who still know that I am alive and well and living… Jonah Perkel, Syd Adler, Willy Isaacs, Effie Segal and Bertha Kronenberg.

Since I came to live in Israel in 1978 I have stayed in correspondence contact with Mordechai Harary and Doc Lichtenfield and Ficky Klevansky as well as with Bertha Kronenberg in Canada and Dave Kotzen in Florida and Alec Saul in Johannesburg. My late-correspondents were Dave Rushowich of Van Der Bijl Park, Basil Samson, Strathaven Johannesburg, Hymie Digs Cohen, Australia. Occasional correspondents were Dr Sol Farber of Johannesburg. Solly Bayer in East London, South Africa, Willy Isaacs in Texas, Ekie Litvan-Levine and her sister Edie in Johannesburg.

I have been in letter writing touch with Bertha Kronenberg in Canada for a number of years. We exchange letters two or three times a month. Her letters are beautiful, poetic and nostalgic as compared to my mundane complaining, depressive attempts.

In Israel I have met with the late Solly Meyers, the late Norman Rosenfeld, Toby Spector, Hymie Sacks, Sheila Aizakowitz-Dror, Freda Cheilyk, the late Hymie Ghandi Sacks and some few others.

Michael and Roz in May 1963 on honeymoon

Michael with his sons Asher and Adrian in Jan 68
(Daughter Jessica was born in June 1968)

Chapter 6 - MENACHEM (MANNIE) KOTZEN (1921-1994)

Mannie, Michael's brother was in the care of Arcadia from 1933 to 1941.

IN BLESSED MEMORY OF MY DEAR BROTHER MANNIE KOTZEN
Written by Michael Perry Kotzen - August, 2004.

Mannie passed away in 1994 in his home on Moshav Moledet. He was 72. He lived on Moshav Moledet for 33 years from 1961. His wife Zillah and their children are still on Moledet. Mannie lies buried in the beautiful Moledet Garden cemetery. The cemetery and orchards and livestock facilities in which Mannie had a significant role in establishing and nurturing and maintaining.

Moledet pauses today to salute the memory of their popular-pioneer - Moshavnick Menachem Kotzen. The children of Moledet loved their Dod Menachem. Mannie's favourite project was his Children's Zoo in which he collected tame animals, rabbits, budgerigars, canaries, geese, ducks, chickens, goats kids, lambs, calves, fowls and baby donkeys and calves and horses and camels for the children to ride and to feed, tortoises and honeybees, a large pond with ducks and geese and herons. Menachem's zoo is still in existence today but sadly it is a mere shadow of its former Menachem glory. Moledet has found Menachem hard to replace. There have been a few short lived candidates for the Zoo's management in the past ten years since Mannie's demise, including Matan Gadri, Mannie's 21 year old National Hero grandson who was killed by Palestinian terrorists two years ago. Matan lies buried close by his grandfather in Moledet cemetery.

Mannie's children have presented me with a package of memorabilia. The package contains a few personal items such as a hat and a cardigan. Also some photographs and papers and letters, and a fob-watch-compass on a gold chain that had once belonged to my late father and to his father before him in Russia.

Among the papers I found a poem that I had scribbled when I was aged 14 in Arcadia. I never knew that dear Mannie had kept my draft in his scrapbook all those years. I remember that Mannie always scoffed at my juvenile attempts at poetry and [what he called] sentimentality.

A frequent quip of Mannie's was 'All that cloying sugary sweet sentiment is not my cup of tea brother moon!' Brother Moon was his pet name for me. On present reflection, I now detect the influence of Oscar Wilde's *'Ballad of Reading Goal'* in this poem. I was reading 'Ballad' in form one at Parktown High School.

Asher Zalman, Sadye, Michael and Mannie – 1933

Here is the poem:

The boys stood on Arcadia's drive
Waiting for their mother
A thin and hungry bald headed boy
And his bedraggled brother
Their mother was a counter hand
In a town department store
And when she stepped down off the bus
Her boys on the driveway she saw
At first she did not know her sons
For they had changed since when
She'd seen them three long months before
And not seen them since then
The sight of their pathetic looks
Reduced the mother to tears
And other people on the drive
Accosted her with jeers
The boys embraced their mother
And tried to shield her from the jeering
They sat her on a stonewall bench
Away from the vicious leering
She had brought a chocolate and some cake
Which she unwrapped for her boys
They kissed her on her tearful cheeks
And ignored the jeers and noise

I seem to recall having written a second page - but brother Mannie unfortunately salvaged only the first page!

'How did the second page go?' asked my nieces - 'It was probably sugary sentimental cloying stuff!' I told them 'That Mannie deliberately discarded!'

MANNIE MY BROTHER AND BETHAL – EARLY MEMORIES
Written by Michael Perry Kotzen

My dear late brother Mannie, were he with us today, would have delighted in contributing childhood memories to the 'Arc Memories' magazine. Mannie loved to sit of an evening with children and grandchildren, telling beautiful nostalgic stories of events that he and his kid brother Mike had experienced when we were small boys on a farm in the Bethal district and later in Arcadia and Johannesburg.

Many of these memories, though perhaps vague and dim or non existent in my memory bank, are nevertheless vividly recollected for me in my recalling, not the actual events, but the telling and retelling of it years later by my dear departed brother Mannie.

Arcs who knew Mannie in Arcadia will attest that he was indeed a yarn-spinner par excellence. His fascinating yarns might have been slightly embellished and exaggerated with repeated spinnings in the passage of time, but basically they were true stories. Brother Mannie was the very paragon of honesty and truthfulness and viability in Arcadia.

I am looking back 75 years at the things I have witnessed, the tremendous changes I have seen, the times I have lived through, the yarns I heard from Mannie, the water under the bridge, the yesteryears, the sisters and brothers Arcadian, the memories.

The place of my beginning was the Bethal district in the Eastern Transvaal. I was born on 10 October, 1923, Paul Kruger's birthday. I was the third baby, but the very first boy born in the newly built Bethal maternity home…"That's my brother Mike" said Mannie, "Always following the girls!"

Early childhood was a careless and happy time for Mannie and me. Our parents had a farm 12 miles north of the village. Our playmates were Dutch farmers' barefoot children and Bantu picaninis. Our Jewish parents, Asher and Sadye Kotzen, would make the 12 miles journey to and from Bethal in a two wheeled Cape-Dutch cart drawn by a pair of Asher's magnificent, beautifully groomed horses. Asher bred horses. He had acquired the skills of horse breeding from his father, Shlomo-Behr Kotzen, in Latvia. Mother Sadye was the daughter of an England-Poland immigrant family. Sadye had come to South Africa in 1920 together with her parents, sisters and brother. Her father, Yechiel-Maishe Becker, was a rabbi. He had secured the position of Hebrew master and Shamus (Sexton) for the Great Synagogue in Fordsburg, Johannesburg. Sadye and Asher were married in Johannesburg in 1920. Their first child, Menachem (Mannie) was born in October 1921. And I, Menasheh (Michael) arrived in Bethal in October of 1923.

We cherished sweet memories of our stone farmhouse and the servants and the horses and all the farm animals. Especially our memories of the wonderful journeys in the Cape cart. Mannie and I sat behind our parents in the cart with our bare feet dangling over the back board. Asher named his magnificent carriage horses "Sweetheart" and "Darling". Ostensibly to tease Sadye who always laughingly pretended she did not know if Asher was talking to her or to one of his horses.

Daddy Asher would find a shaded spot. Usually near a river, where we would break our journey, give the horses a rest and have our picnic. Asher would unhitch the horses and let them roll happily on the grass. Or they would splash about in the water. Then Asher himself would stretch out in the shade of a tree and take a nap. Meanwhile, Sadye and her little boys would unpack the picnic hamper on a spread-out rug. We would pick wild flowers and splash naked in the stream. We were two very happy, healthy little boys in our rural paradise.

I remember one sunny day in 1928, Sadye called to us excitedly, "Boys, boys, look, look" as she pointed skywards. We saw a tiny aeroplane flying high up in the sky. Way up in a cloudless blue sky, droning away into the wide blue yonder. That was my very first sight of an aeroplane. I had seen pictures and drawings of aircraft, but never before seen an actual real aeroplane. It was 1928. Aircraft were still a rarity over the vast expanses of the *highveldt*.

When we got into Bethal town later, the town was buzzing with excitement. People everywhere excitedly talking about the miraculous flying machine that had earlier swooped down over the rooftops, hedgehopping the tree tops, causing black servants to run screaming to hide under tables and beds, dogs had barked madly and chickens had run apanic and children had fled their schoolhouse. Bank and stores and houses had emptied. People were running up and down the streets waving towels and sheets and hats. Quiet rural Bethal was in a state of high anxiety. People had hitherto heard about these flying "devils" of the wars in far away Europe, but the *backveldt* and the *platteland* had never yet seen one close-up. The *Dominee* of the Dutch Reform Church rang the bells and called the Christians to kneel in prayer to ask God to deliver us from this evil. "Come to church to pray with us Asher!" called out a friend of Daddy's. "Sure thing Piet!" said Asher. "Just as soon as I have fed and rubbed down my horses!"

On our way home to the farm we scanned the heavens for another glimpse of an aeroplane. Night was falling. Asher lit the two side lamps on the cart. We trotted along the gravel trail quietly. Sadye humming one of her English songs. Asher puffing his pipe and murmuring sweet nothings to Sweetheart and Darling. The sparse traffic we encountered on the trail in those days consisted of an occasional ox-wagon or mule drawn carts. We seldom encountered a car in 1928, though there were numbers of model T-Fords, box shaped Chryslers and Dickie-seat Chevrolets in the streets of Bethal. Under the canopy of a blue black night sky sprinkled with a million sparkling stars we reached our farm homestead.

Thirty odd years later I returned to Bethal with my wife Roz in our convertible Peugeot roadster. I tried to retrace our old Cape cart route from Bethal to the farm. The old gravel trail out of Bethal was a macadamised highway lined with telegraph poles. Smooth concrete bridges spanned the river and our former picnic spots. And high overhead huge four engined Dakota airliners crossed the sky flying between Johannesburg and Durban or Cape Town. No one, then in 1960, took any notice of the aeroplanes. Not even the stoic rural Bantu. The shops and banks and buildings in Bethal were modern seven storey high erections, air conditioned and soundproof.

Back in 1928, inside our stone farm house, Sadye and Asher used to light paraffin lamps which were suspended from hooks in the ceiling. Sadye would heat up a large cauldron of water on the wood-stove. A stack of firewood was kept under cover in the back yard…. splitting logs and chopping wood was one of Asher's daily morning chores. Mom and Dad would pour the hot water from the cauldron into a tin bath tub on the kitchen floor. Asher would add cold water from the bucket to bring the temperature down to 'little boy' level.

We would bath, scrubbing and soaping ourselves in the middle of the kitchen floor. Asher and Sadye joining in the fun and games and happy splashing, while cleaning our ears and scrubbing our necks and washing our blonde curls. The old house did not have a bathroom as such. The house was only three rooms. The large middle room was the kitchen-main living room-bathroom-dining room-office-rumpus room - the bedrooms were one on each side of the main room.

The toilet was a crude old fashioned wooden 'privy' situated a hundred yards from the kitchen doorway, across the back vegetable garden and surrounded by a heavy cactus jungle. The privy was a wooden box with a round hole cut in the top. A wood and tin roof framed over it. It had a hinged wooden door and a wooden step for small boys to climb up. The box with the round hole perched over a 10ft deep pit.

Asher shovelled spadesful of quick lime down the privy hole every other week. Sadye kept a pile of old newspapers in there for use as toilet paper. Come to think of it I don't think I ever saw a roll of toilet tissue anywhere before about 1936 in Johannesburg.

The stone house had been exceptionally well built by the Dutch farmer, and Boer war general, Christoffel Lochner around about 1902. Lochner junior sold the farm, called "Yster Vark Fontein" (Pig Iron Fountain) to Asher in 1920. Asher then changed the name, officially through a lawyer's office, to "Ysterfontein" (Iron Fountain) removing the offending word "Vark" (Pig). "We were Jewish!" explained Asher. "Jewish people object to pigs!"

One wall in the master bedroom had been wood-panelled in white knotted deal slats. Asher considered this very odd and most peculiar. "Why only the one wall panelled??" He decided to remove the panelling and revealed the white washed stone face beneath. To his surprise, on removing the slats, he saw scruffy marks and boot prints on the stone wall clearly indicating where a ladder had given access to a trapdoor in the ceiling. Asher and his Bantu assistant, Big Tom, stripped open the ceiling to expose the trapdoor. Inside the ceiling they discovered a wooden coffin. Keeping a reserve coffin in storage was a known Dutch farming habit…. But the coffin in our ceiling was packed full of rifles and ammunition. It was an arms cache from the Boer wars…

At that time there had been another Boer War relic discovered on a farm close to *Ysterfontein*. A coffin full of guns and bullets was "exhumed" from the family-plot cemetery on a neighbouring farm. Asher immediately contacted the Bethal police constabulary on our party-line handle-crank telephone. Our "number" was two short turns and one long… and the dozen or more phones of the neighbourhood were able to listen in on our conversations! The police duly removed the arms from the farm. We were fortunate there had not been a fire or excessive heat in the house in all the 20 years since 1902, or we would have had a terrifying fireworks display.

In 1960 when I returned by the Hipkin family, Hipkin, an English gentleman, had acquired Ysterfontein some years after Asher had passed away in 1933. "I knew your Dad well." Old man Hipkin greeted me, "I bought some horses from him when you were still a baby!" Mr and Mrs Hipkin and their handsome family showed us around the homestead. They had a bright new modern house with a spacious three sided verandah and a beautiful English rose garden. House and garden stood some distance from the old stone house which had fallen into ruin back in the 40's. It had been repaired and rebuilt into a barn-garage-stable for the Hipkin cars and ponies. They had added a tennis court and a swimming pool to the homestead complex. They had running hot and cold water on tap, electric light from a diesel engined generator, flush inside toilets, glass cubicles showers, tiled and scented bathrooms, a cold storage pantry, refrigerators, sophisticated furniture and appliances. Mrs Hipkin showed us through the well tended vegetable garden. the cacti still grew at path's end, but there was no sign of the privy …"There used to be an old privy here!" I meekly remarked. "Yes", said Mrs Hipkin, "It was struck by lightening one stormy night many years ago! So we ploughed it under!"

Mannie and Michael on Moshav Moledet - 1988

That was in 1960. I have not visited the farm of my roots again.

My dear mother Sadye eventually came to Israel to live on Mannie's farm Moshave Moledet. Sadye passed away in 1984 at the age of 84. Brother Mannie followed Sadye ten short years later in 1994. Mannie was 72. They rest now eternally side by side in Moledet's beautiful garden cemetery.

My young and very dear father Asher lies buried in a corner of the Bethal Jewish cemetery these past 70 odd years.

My 30 something sons Asher and Adrian and my lovely daughter Jessica are all successful, prospering Sydneysiders in Australia today.

Here is a picture of my late brother Mannie and his family in 1970
Mannie , Joy, Ashle,y Joel and Zillah on Moshav Moledet
Joy married Eli Gadri in 1980. Their son Matan was killed by terrorists in 2001.

MATAN GADRI

Michael Perry Kotzen writes about Matan Gadri the grandson of his late dear brother Mannie.- 8 June 2003

Matan Gadri was killed on Saturday night in Hebron. Twenty one year old Matan was the grandson of my late dear brother Mannie. Before Mannie passed away ten years ago on Moledet, he said to me "Michael, I am not going to be around any longer. Please 'keep an eye' on my grandsons for me! "Now I am devastated by the dreadful news that Matan, handsome, happy, clever, adorable, only a boy, Matan is no more... killed and snuffed out. The funeral was at Moledet. The entire Kotzen family and extensions are shocked and grief stricken. Matan's sister Dafna flew back from Brazil where she was backpacking, to be in time for the funeral.

Last Saturday night, brought very sad and dreadful shock to the Kotzen family in Israel. My dear late brother Mannie's grandson, Matan Gadri, lost his beautiful young life to the bloody Arab intifada that is plaguing Israel. Matan was a Staff Sergeant on an army patrol in Hebron. Satanic suicidal terrorists fired down on the soldiers from a roof top. Killing our dear boy Matan and consequently getting themselves killed by the Israelis. The Kotzen-Gadri families are grief stricken. Matan was given a

tremendous military funeral on Wednesday June 11, with full honours and attended by about two thousand people. There were troops in battle dress, officers in full dress, VIPs, celebrities, chaplains, rabbis. There were many making speeches, laying wreaths, words of regret and sorrow and condemnation, praise and admiration, weeping and wailing. Sobbing calls to heaven above. Rifle shots in salute that startled the doves out of the trees. Matan was 'laid to rest' as flocks of birds swept the sky above the cemetery and the hundreds of vehicles and scores of half masted flags clogging every inch of Moledet estate.

The cars and the people took hours to disperse from the funeral. It was nightfall and I sat there on my brother Mannie's flower covered grave, a few paces from grandson Matan's fresh new grave. I communed with Mannie telling him of my grief and my regret. As he did in life he merely lay there and listened and said not a word. Though the trees and the throngs of spectators murmured. 'Michael! Michael! The 80 year olds are supposed to go before the young innocents!'

Mattan Gadri, an Israeli Soldier

Chapter 7 – HYMIE (DIGS) COHEN (1923-1999)

Hymie was born on the 28th of August 1923 and was in the care of Arcadia from 1925 to 1940.

A TRIBUTE TO MY LATE DEAR FRIEND HYMIE 'DIGS' COHEN
Written by Michael Perry Kotzen

I would like to start off with a tribute to my late very dear Arc-friend Hymie Cohen (Digs). My good pal Hymie "Digs" died in Australia a few years ago. Digs and Louise and their children left South Africa in the mid 1980's. They went to live in Broadbeach Waters on the Queensland Gold Coast.

I was especially fond of Hymie. We called him "Digs". He played soccer for Arcadia old boys. How did Digs Cohen get to be called "Digs"? In the mid 50's the Arcadian old boys formed a soccer team. We called the team "Arcadia" which confused us with the first league Pretoria Afrikaans team of Arcadia. But we played only in second league matches. One weekend we went to Pretoria to play in the suburb of Arcadia against a local 2nd league Afrikaans team.

In the pre-match changing rooms the Arc boys were approached by some Afrikaans lads who asked; "Are youze guys Arcadia?" "Yeah that's right" we chorused. "But" they insisted, "Youze is not from here. We are from here see! We are Arcadia." Our Hymie Cohen, naked except for his under briefs, bravely stepped forward. "Actually you see" said Hymie, "We just call ourselves Arcadia. That's all!" "So where are youze from then?" they demanded. "We are from the Chevra Kadisha Old Boys!" said Hymie.. "The gghev-what"? they asked. "The gghevra Kadisha! The grave diggers of Westpark cemetery!" Hymie elucidated. "Grave Diggers!" said the puzzled Afrikaner "*Waar die donner is dit?*" "Grave diggers" repeated Hymie.. "Are you the captain!" asked another. Hymie replied "That's right. I am the head grave digger!" of Arcadia, Pretoria. And from that day on Hymie's nickname would be "DIGS".

In our bachelor singles days Dave and Boris Rush and 'Digs' and Tommy Green and 'Toots' Maurice Bernard and myself were frequent habitués at the Wigwam Rustenburg. Digs was a star comedian and dancer. The husband hunting girls (he called them kugels) were crazy for him.

One year I was contracted to act in Shakespeare's "The Tempest" at Maynardville open air theatre in Cape Town. Digs came with me. We stayed at the Imperial Hotel in Muizenberg. I was acting at Maynardville every day and night for five weeks while Hymie took over the snake-pit beach. It was over Pesach time and he organised and ran a magnificent Pesach seder in the hotel. His effort was praised and admired and tape recorded. The first night was mainly the hotel residents and guests. But on the second night a huge crowd came. They blocked the streets outside the hotel. More than half of the crowd could not be accommodated. Many people merely listened to the seder over the loud speakers, but those inside were served kneidlach and matzo balls and gefillte fish and roast chicken, and wine and matzo.

In Arcadia and in our after Arcadia bachelor heydays, Digs was a master raconteur and a star-quality clown and magnificent practical jokester. I, always an avid film fan, had made a study of famous comedians and noteworthy clowns, easily and proudly and happily compared my friend Digs to such comic luminaries as Milton Berle, Bob Hope, Danny Kaye, Jerry Lewis and Lou Costello. And I proudly proclaimed Digs much better than all those stars put together.

Digs had an intelligent sense of fun. He was not a fool or an idiot or a 'monkey', but always an intellect who knew right from wrong and distinguished smart from stupid. His talent, I was sure, equalled and surpassed the talents of the world's great laugh makers. I was with Digs one Saturday afternoon at Turffontein racecourse. A crowd of multinational fans followed Digs as we proceeded from the car park through the paddocks to the grandstands. The fans were all eager to talk to him, some wanted his autograph but most wanted a racing tip from him as Digs had a reputation for picking sure winners… Digs and I had devised a comedy cabaret act, a sort of Abbot and Costello or Martin and Lewis duet. I played the straight man and Digs was the funny guy. We performed our act quite regularly in some night club floorshows and on our "singles" weekends at the Wigwam in Rustenburg.

After Digs' sad and untimely death, my wife and I were visiting relatives in Queensland. We called on dear Louise. She told us that on that fateful day she and Hymie had taken their usual afternoon stroll. They stopped at the Broadbeach public library to read the overseas newspapers in the reading room. Digs, who, never ever complained of not feeling well, excused himself and went from the reading room into the Gent's room. Louise waited for a while for him to return. He failed to do so, so Louise asked an attendant to please call Mr Cohen from the men's room. The attendant then discovered that poor old Digs had collapsed in the men's room.

A doctor and an ambulance were called but sadly Digs had passed away. Louise went into shock and hysteria. When Louise told me the sad story I could not help thinking to myself how Digs the comedian would have recounted the story himself. Digs' scenario might have gone something like this: *He made his way from the reading room to the men's room, passing the librarian's desk he asked her "Do you perhaps have a copy of 'Gone with the Wind?" "No" she replied, "But we have 'Exodus' and 'The Way of all Flesh!'…"Or how's about 'The Greps of Wrath!" "Hows about "Joke of the Bushveld!' suggested Digs… "Take 'From Here to Eternity'" said the librarian!!!*

The ghost of our dear departed Arc-brother Hymie Digs Cohen continues to get a smile and a hearty laugh from his old Arc-brothers and sisters everywhere. As Sid Caesar and Milton Berle used to say "Always leave them laughing. Always make your exit on a laugh!"

Chapter 8 - THE RUSHOVICH FAMILY
DAVID (1923-1998), BORIS (1928-1971), JUDY (1925) AND ISSY (1922)

David was born in 1927 and Boris in 1930 and they together with their older brother Issy born in 1922 and sister Judy, born in 1924, were placed in the care of Arcadia in the 1933.

JUDY (RUSHOVICH) ROSENBERG RECALLS

I was only in the Arc from 1933 – 1936 – eight to 12 years old and was Junior Girls No 42!

I have three three brothers: Issy, David and Boris.

I have on my bedroom wall a photo of the Johannesburg Old Arcadian Association Football Team, who were the winners of the Yeoville Sunday Soccer League 1940-1947. Boris is goalie, David is also in the team and Issy is Chairman. Sydney Nochumson was Hon. Secretary.

Michael Kotzen was a very good friend of my late brother David and I met Michael again in 2003 in Tel Aviv at David's grandson's Brit.

Hymie Grevler and I live on the same street. He was very happy to hear that someone remembered him, but said he was not in the right frame of mind to write. However, he sends his love to you all. Hymie came to Israel for the War of Independence 1948 and joined the Israeli Air Force as an aircraft mechanic – and a jolly good one at that I was told a long time ago by Tev Zimmerman who worked with Chaim (as we know him) and hailed from Winburg, Orange Free State.

We were all Machalnicks (overseas volunteers) including my husband Sam Rosenberg and I. We lived in army barracks in an Air Force camp. Sam as an aircraft maintenance engineer and I as a civilian working in the production control office.

I'm sorry that Michael left Israel, but nevertheless I wish him and his family all the very best!

Sheila Aizokowitz' and I were very good friends in the Arc, and I've often thought of her.

The Old Arc Association Soccer Team - Winners of the Yeoville Soccer League 1940-1947
Back Row l to r: Joss Lipschitz, Mannie Osrin, Goalie Boris Rushovich, Isaac Grevler, Morris Getz
Second Row l to r: , Barney Meyers, David Rushovich, Donald Goldman, Beans Levine, and Aaron Karp
Front Row l to r: Sidney Nochumsohn, (Hon. Secretary) Willie Isaacs, Sambo Mannie, his brother Meyer and Chairman Issy Rushovich
Insets – top: Solly Meyers above and Phillip Kemp, below, and on the bottom we have Morrie Bernard and below him, Mr. Harary (Superintendent.SAJO)

Here's a list of the Old Arcs (which I know of) that came to help the Nascent State of Israel.

Syd Chalmers, Phillip Kemp, Sidney Lipman, Max Rosengarten, Solly Meyers and Tamar, Harry (Tzvi) Vass, Boris Rushovich – 1956 – Sinai War, Hymie Grevler, Eli Zagoria and me, Judy (Rushovich) Rosenberg and my husband Sam (not an Old Arc).

ST JOHN'S PARADE
Written by Freda Cheilyk

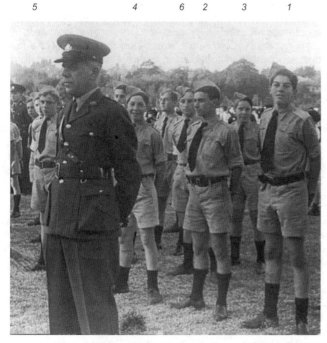

St John's Parade
1. Moris Sidlin, 2. Dave Rushovitz, 3. Gerald Colman, 4. Ronnie Sacks, 5. Mendel Strime, 6. Percy Nochumson

Morris Sidlin was an only child and joined to fight as a pilot for the Israeli War of Independence. He must have been 21 years of age and died in 1950. I remember it was 1950 as I was pregnant and wanted apples. My brother sent some with Morris Sidlin. There were, I think, seven or eight young men who joined the Air Force. One of the pilots got polio and they were all in isolation, so I of course never got my apples. The others, with the exception of one volunteer pilot remained alive and was sent back to Cape Town. Morris Sidlin stands tall and first on right.

'2' is Dave Rushovitz and he has passed away. Between Morris and Dave, slightly behind is Gerald Colman (passed away in Sydney). Slightly behind Dave Rush is Percy Nochumson who is now in the Hospital of Sandringham Gardens. Just behind the St John's Captain, smiling is Ronnie Sacks (died many years ago). His sisters are Sheila and Hazel Sacks. On the other side of the Captain, looks as though he is without a cap, is Mendel Strime. He lives in Johannesburg.

Hank Epstein after seeing the above photo wrote:

I believe I am in the photo, showing a picture of a St John's parade circa 1943-45. I distinctly remember it being taken. Ronnie (Zoopy) Sacks, Percy Nochumson and I were friends. I believe that it is I, standing to the left of Mendel Strime. Only half of my face is showing. It may be that the boy between Percy Nochumsohn and Ronnie Sacks is Abe Lazarus, but I'm not sure.

Zoopy and I had a pigeon hock "down the hill", where we raised a dozen or so common birds. Percy had a larger hock, higher up on the hill. He bred fantails and homing pigeons. Then there was Jacob Kemp, who had the biggest hock. He also raised common pigeons. Each day we would let them out and enjoy seeing them fly and tumble. They sat on our shoulders and ate from our hands. It was Jacob who got Zoopy and me interested in keeping pigeons. He helped us acquire the wire and build our *hoks*.

Then one night, a large wild cat made a hole in our hock and killed all our birds. We were, of course, heartbroken, and gave up keeping pigeons. Percy and Jacob continued keeping theirs--I don't recall for how long.

JUDY RUSHOVICH
Written by Michael Kotzen

Judy and I were in cheder class together in 1936. Judy was the very attractive sister of my buddy David. I had made a special appeal to Geveret Factor, our Hebrew teacher, to seat me next to Judy. Miss Factor did so happily and I was a very happy cheder pupil that term. David sat beside the lovely Ekie Levine, and they whispered sweet nothings to each other all afternoon in class. I wonder if Judy remembers? Probably not since Judy had eyes for handsome Mickey Gordon while Mickey in turn was bent on out ogling David for the affections of the beautiful Ekie.

All of these cheder shenanigans however did not leave me completely out in the cold as I was sympathetically consoled and encouraged by Molly Michelow, Judy's best friend.

Ah, memories sweet memories.! Do you remember Judy? Ah yes, I remember it well!!

DAVID AND BORIS RUSHOVICH ARC FRIENDS
Written by Michael Perry Kotzen

In memory of my very dear Arc-friends David and Boris Rushovich - David who passed away at age 70 in 1996, and his kid brother Boris who passed away at age 43 in 1971.

It is now eight years since late David, my lifelong friend and penpal passed out of this life. I fondly remember him and I miss him sorely.

David and his brothers Freedom, Issy and Boris and sisters Justice and Judy were very close friends to my brother Mannie and me in Arcadia and in the years after we left Arcadia. I have nurtured a 'crush' on Judy Rushovich since I was 12 years old. After Arcadia, David and I shared rooms in Yeoville and

Hillbrow, and holidays and weekends at resorts, we shared our circles of friends and parties and motor trips and hotel accommodation. At times brother Boris was with us. Boris had grown into a tall and extremely good looking teenager and twenties. Whenever Boris was with us we were ogled at and smiled at by every female in sight. Handsome debonair gallant Boris exuded a magnetism that women found irresistible.

I was lucky to share my happy bachelorhood with the Russy brothers. We laughed at each other's corny jokes and we jointly cooked up practical jokes to play on our circle of friends. I attended their weddings. David married Claire Kline in the Cyrildene Shul in 1960. Boris' first marriage was to Jackie van der Berg in Bulawayo in about 1964. They divorced after a year or two and Boris then married Yvonne, in Johannesburg in the Greek Orthodox Cathedral in Joubert Park. I married Roz in Cape Town in 1963.

The Kotzens continued our close friendship with the Rushovichs. We played tennis with David and Claire, and they came to see me performing in the theatres. They visited us in Israel and we tried to attend each other's simchas and mitzvott. David kept up a witty and humorous and nostalgic penpal correspondence with me for 50 years. We enjoyed reminiscing and laughing at ourselves and at our Arc memories often to the puzzlement and amusement of our wives and our children.

One time we were all having lunch together in a Zikron Yaacov restaurant. David and I were remembering our 1930s in Arcadia. A waiter took our orders, David ordered fish and chips with salad on the side. I then ordered a steak and chips. Our wives, both vegetarians, ordered salad lunches. David and I were happily reminiscing about the boys' dining room in the 1930s Arcadia, when juniors and kid brothers ate together with senior and big brothers in the boys' dining room. There was, in those days in Arcadia a 'stock exchange food bartering' system among the children. We recalled how Robert Bushkin owed all his bread to Ghandi Sacks. And Ghandi had 'pledged' half of all his apples to Sambo. And how Sambo manoeuvred every meal into a heaped and overflowing plate. And how some small boys were left hungry and empty plated every dinnertime.

Then our waiter returned with our orders. The platters of lunch were put before us. David looked down at his fish and chips and then said to me: 'I'll give you half my fish for half your steak!' Keeping my face deadpan straight I replied: 'Half your fish plus three long chips - you've got a deal!' Deadpan David glared back; 'The smallest half, and one half chips!' I considered the offer then I said; 'Deal! - Shake! No taking back!' We shook hands and exchanged half the fish for half the steak and we both burst into laughter. Our wives and the other diners in the crowded restaurant could not figure out what it was we were laughing about. 'What was so funny about the food?' The restaurant manager came to inquire, what was wrong with the service? How could we explain that we were reliving our grub bargaining days of Arcadia long ago?

TRAVELLING AROUND EUROPE IN MY YOUTH
Written by Dave Spector

I haven't been to Paris these past couple of years, but of course I lived there at different times for a total of about ten years. I arrived in Paris for the first time on 1 January 1950, coming from London, where David Rushovich (Russy) and I were living from March 1949. Russy joined me in Paris about May 1950 and remained for two or three months. Russy and I went to the Island of Jersey to pick tomatoes, but because of the terrible drought that summer, the tomatoes were very late in ripening and there was no work for us. We were almost penniless, although we both had a little money in a Post Office in London.

We bought the local Jersey newspaper in search of employment and saw an advertisement for a Hotel Porter. We tossed up a penny to decide who would apply for the job and I won the toss and in my letter of application I mentioned that I had been the Publicity Manager in a large company which was quoted on the Johannesburg Stock Exchange. The response was immediate and I was called in for an interview. No questions were asked and I was taken for a tour of the hotel which terminated in the kitchen where I was presented to the cook and told that I would be the dishwasher. I complained, but the manager told me that it was the only job available and I would have lunch and supper in the kitchen. As Russy and I were almost starving, I had no alternative, but to accept the job. At least I could save half my lunch and supper for him. It was a terrible job as water was rationed and in fact turned off at about 12.30 pm, so I had to work first in a full sink of steaming water which progressively was transformed to stinking water as it lost its heat. Fortunately the residents of the hotel were unaware of the drama in the kitchen. I was paid weekly and weakly.

A few days later Russy managed to find a job as a building labourer on the extension to the Jersey hospital, but it was not without anguish, because he had to convince them that he wasn't a Polish or Russian spy, bearing the name of Rushovich. He found the job very exhausting carrying bricks and wooden boards, while the tough Irish labourers were carrying twice his load. After a week he decided or perhaps was asked to leave. However he very soon managed to find another job as a building labourer on the extension of houses in another area of the island where he met a girl, whose 'co-operation' made his labour bearable. As a lover Russy was far more experienced than me.

I returned to London in March 1951 with my newly wed wife for a few days to collect the rest of my luggage and withdraw the £20 I had invested in the Post Office. Josette and I remained in London for only a few days before catching the train for Southampton to embark upon a Dutch ship bound for Cape Town.

I saw Boris several years later when I was the Secretary of The Council of Natal Jewry which is the Natal section of The SA Jewish Board of Deputies and he called at my office. I think he was selling jewellery at that time. My next meeting with him was in Cape Town in the 1970s when he was married to a Greek lady and they had two lovely young sons. We visited them quite a few times at their Muizenberg residence. His father-in-law was a wealthy man. Unfortunately Boris died from a heart attack in the ambulance taking him to hospital. I was on a month's business trip around SA when this happened. Josette attended his funeral. Boris was definitely talented and it was a great pity that his life was cut short so suddenly. We kept in touch with his wife until our departure for France.

Chapter 9 – ROSE GATTER (MAFCHER) (1915)

Rose was born in 1915 and she and her younger brother Abe were in the care of Arcadia from 1928 to 1932. Rose arrived at age 13 and left when she was 17 while Abe arrived when ten years old and left when 14.

ROSE GATTER (nee MAFCHER)
Letter dated 6 October 2005

Dear Old Arcadians,

Let me begin by saying THANK YOU most sincerely for the unexpected and much appreciated Yom Tov gift, delivered personally to me at Sandringham Gardens, and beautifully presented per Selwyn Segal's Gift Shop. This was particularly dear to my heart, as my eldest son now lives there.

November 2005 will be my 90th birthday, and my memories of Arcadia and all my friends from those bygone days are still very vivid. Of course, many have already passed on, and over all these years, I have lost contact with their relatives and families.

Unfortunately my eyesight is now impaired, but my daughter Pearl had been reading all the newsletters to me, which I enjoyed and brought back many fond memories.

My brother (Abe Mafcher) passed away almost two years ago (in December). He had his Barmitzvah at Arcadia. I have his two (Rosh Hashanah & Yom Kippur) Prayer Books, that he kept all these years with the following inscription: "Presented to A Mafcher on the occasion of his Barmitzvah by the Committee of the SAJO …Chanukah 5691 December 9th 1931."

I married Solly Gatter, a Jeweller, in 1938, had three children, two sons and a daughter. Solly passed on 15 years ago, and Jules, our younger son, passed on 13 years ago.

Children at Humewood Beach – circa 1935

Chapter 10 – DAVID AGINSKY (1918)

David was born in 1918 and was in the care of Arcadia from 1928-1935 together with his younger sister Lily and his brother Harry.

David writes as follows:

"I was very surprised to receive your letter, but nevertheless I am grateful that you did, as I have lost contact with all ex Arcs. I have just returned from a tour of Israel with my wife Beatty where we visited her brother Rabbi David Fir, his wife Leah and his children and grandchildren.

We were astonished at the growth and progress of Israel. They have the most modern cities, sky scrapers, four lane traffic and are ahead of many countries in the world. We were lucky to be there for Yom Yashua, Yom Yerushalayim, Yom Ha'atzmaut and partake of the festivities and visit all the important sites – the Western Wall, the Great Synagogue, the Tomb of Hertzel etc.

Here I give you a little of my personal history. Firstly I was born in Fordsburg on 1 September 1918 and had my Bris in the Fordsburg Shul on the 2nd day of Rosh Hashana. My wife Beatty was born on 13 September 1926. We have three very talented children. Our eldest son Allan is a Pharmacist and general chemist and he lives with his wife Debra, two daughters Danielle and Shira and son Saul in Toronto, Canada. Our other son Phillip and his wife Karen and his two daughters, Laura and Kerry are in Atlanta America. He passed first in the Board Exam for Accountants and Auditors in South Africa and has many degrees. He owns a huge electrical business in America. Our daughter Adele, husband Solly and grandchildren Hayley and Taryn live in Jo'burg. Our daughter has been working at Wits for 25 years.

As far as Arcadia is concerned, I and my sister Lily and my late bachelor brother Harry entered Arcadia in 1928. I was told to leave in 1935 without any means of support by the late Stompie, Louis Shaer, but I managed to survive by doing all sorts of odd jobs and I think this is what made me successful in my later years. We have lived most of our lives in Johannesburg and were foundation members. I was a warden of the Pine Street Synagogue. I also worked for the Yeshivah College helping to raise funds and my son was the first outstanding College student, my daughter Adele was one of the first girls to enrol at the Yeshiva.

We moved to Durban 25 years ago, where I was appointed Chairman of Ward 1 Ratepayers for two years. I also helped to establish the Vryheid Memorial Synagogue in the Durban Club and am the retired Chairman and President after serving 22 years.

We returned to Johannesburg two years ago as I was suffering from ill health. I had three operations on my eyes for cataracts and I also had a pacemaker operation. I thank Hashem for my recovery.

I will close off by recollecting certain inmates that I know:

Harry and Basil Levitt, Mark Woolfson, Levy and Bimmie Woolf, Solly Nankin, Leslie and Anita Friedlander, Leslie Bushkin and her brothers. Harry, Barney and Paisie Meyers, the Kotzen brothers, Isaac and Reuben Maisnik, Alfie and Phillip James, Lipman Cohen, Leslie and Fred Walchuk, Mende Goldstein, the Goodman brothers, Abe Mafcher, Chalmers, Smith, Hymie Eckovitz, Donald Goldman, Issy and Alec Mendelson, Toots Bernard Galvin, Mannie Snaid and his brother, Mick Gordon, Simmy Kark, Sam and Max Paikin, Leslie and brother Nawran.

My brother in law was the late Isaac Klevansky, brothers Vicky, Hymie, sisters Bertha and Ray.

Selwyn Chalmers writes

I had a visit from David Aginsky yesterday. He was at the Arc from 1928 to 1935. He told me he remembered my father well and they were good friends. It is the first time I have met an Old Arc, apart from Vicky Klevansky who remembered my father.

Chapter 11 - SAM GORDON (1919-2003)

Sam Gordon was in the care of Arcadia from 1931 to 1937.

SAM GORDON
As remembered by Effie Segal.

The Gordons were in Arcadia in the 1930s. Sam was the oldest brother of Hilda and Mickey of 'Fick Glass' fame. There was another brother [maybe a twin of Mickey] who was never in Arcadia. Sam was the boxer who fought wrestler Eli Zagoria. He was an older senior boy when I became a senior in 1937 and there was little contact with him as he went to another school [maybe Spes Bona]. I seem to remember him with a cricket ball in his left hand as if he were a spin bowler.

Sam married Marcia Rosenkowitz, older sister of Colin and Edith [Cohen] and stayed in Yeoville. I met him a few years ago and a few years after his wife had died. He told me a hilarious story of his new girlfriend and her sons trying to inveigle him into transferring his house to their ownership. He also mentioned that his two brothers were in business in Cape Town.

From Old Arcadian Association Newsletter Aug/Sept 2003
Editor Mannie Osrin

In September 2003 we lost Morrie (Itchy) Shain and Sam Gordon. Both were in their eighties, and our condolences and good wishes go out to their families and we wish them too long life.

Chapter 12 - MARK WULFSOHN (1920-2003)

Mark was born in 1920 and was in the care of Arcadia from 1931 to 1937.

REMEMBERING MARK WULFSOHN
Written by Alec Saul

Rather than write about the fact that Mark Wulfsohn died, I prefer to write how he lived.

He used to act as a hard nut and, in his approach came over rather aggressively, that is to people who did not know him. My dealings with him always came out on the positive side, I would phone him to help Old Arcs with spare parts for their cars and tyres and batteries. He would give me an address to which the person in need would go and he would then pick up the invoice and pay for the goods himself. The number of times he gave money to individuals was numerous, without a word of complaint.

I remember an incident where an Old Arc developed a system to grow food-producing plants in water. It did not turn out as expected. Nevertheless he spent time trying to develop the system at no charge to that person. His concern for his family was remarkable, and he would rather go without himself than have them short of anything.

He was an outstanding boxer (an Air Force champ) and was football coach for the Old Arc Sunday league team, which dominated the league for some years. In his presence nobody could castigate the Jews and get away with it, despite the fact that he was not religious.

Old Arcs have lost a very sincere brother.

His family has lost a wonderful husband, father and grandfather. I wish them all long life."

Old Arcadian Association Newsletter May/June 2003
Editor Mannie Osrin

Mark Wulfsohn passed away at the age of 80 and was buried on the 13th April 2003.

A sprinkling of Old Arcs attended the funeral.

Another sad loss and to his wife Dorette and children Lawrence, Bruce and Pippa, we extend our condolences and wish them long life.

Chapter 13 – MORRIE SHAIN (1922-2003)

Morrie Shain was in the care of Arcadia from 1926 to 1937

MORRIS SHAIN
As remembered by Effie Segal.

Morris [Itchie] Shain was in the Junior Boys when I came to Arcadia in February 1931. He left at the end of 1940. He had two older sisters, Bessie and Eva and a younger sister, Hilda. An older brother, Harvey was not in Arcadia. Sister Eva may still be alive as the sole survivor.

Itchie always seemed to be doing things. He ran a '*hok*' with chickens for quite a few years. I remember his ginger hen had a brood of chickens, which gradually dwindled to two. These two he named after Ginger Ladier whom he called 'Owlie' and me, Effie.

When I became a Senior Boy, Itchie took me to the Wanderers on a Saturday afternoon to see the soccer match. In summer we were supposed to watch the cricket, but if we had a sixpence [5 cents] we went to the cafe bioscope where we could also have a cold drink or ice cream and watch the films for as long as we liked. On the way Itchie would stop at Wings in Eloff Street where his sister Eva worked to get some money.

He was artistic and matriculated in the Art School. His older brother, Harry ran a crockery factory and I think Itchie joined him. However, Itchie did have a pottery factory named Zeniths where he produced work popular with the tourist trade using his artistic talents to make his pieces distinctly African in style. He was also a great appreciator of South African artists and he had a fine collection. He was married and had at least one daughter. Unfortunately I never knew much about his family.

1933 Juniors

Chapter 14 – ELI ZAGORIA (1922)

Eli was born in 1922 in Riga, Latvia and in 1936, at age 14 his mother put him in the Arc where he remained for two years. Being from Latvia, his English was non-existent. At that time children normally left the Arc at age 14 but Eli says his mother was able to arrange that he stay until he was 16. He attended Jewish Government School as well as Spes Bona School.

Eli Zagoria is an artist who lives in Perth with his wife of 56 years Estelle Kaplan. He still does portraits and paints and has a small studio at the back of his house and estimates he has drawn over 15,000 portraits over his life.

He remembers that Stompie Shaer encouraged him with his art and gave him a room upstairs in which to do his art and sculpture. This room he shared with Issie Nicholaaff who was very good at maths and was his friend in the Arc. Stompie tried to arrange lessons for him with Rene Shapshack, a very famous Johannesburg artist, but this was too expensive.

In the Arc he remembers Louis Nicholaaf was a very good musician and he also showed me photos he had of Boy Robinson and Freddy Fuchs and several of Issie Nicholaaff.

He remembers getting into a fight with Issie's older brother who had mocked him about his very poor English. The beds in the dormitory were moved back and there "was standing room only". While Eli came out expecting to wrestle, his opponent was expecting to box. Eli says once he got hold of his opponent he gave a good account of himself. He also fought another Arc who mocked him for the same reason.

After he left the Arc he served in the South African Army in the Medical Corp and was captured in Tobruk and was a prisoner of war returning to SA in 1946. His name was recorded as 'Sagoria' on the plaque of Arcs on active service that used to hang in the dining room.

He was given a full three year scholarship in the Art College in Johannesburg and then volunteered to go to Israel and join the Israeli Army in the 1949 War of Independence. In the Israeli Army he once again was in the medical corp helping the wounded and sick with a Dr. Rosenberg (now Kidron).

Since Eli had second World War experience in managing a medical post in the desert in North Africa and Dr Kidron had just become a doctor, they complemented each other in the maintenance of the infirmary of Gedud 79 in the western Galilee. Eli later joined another small unit during a lull, which was formed at the Misrad Habitachon by some hair-brained officers to prepare for a big victorious celebration commemorating Israeli Defence Force victory.

At age 28 in 1949 Eli returned to SA to get married to Estelle Kaplan and they together helped establish Moshav Habonim (Shi tu fi) with mostly members of Benoni Habonim. Also on the Moshav was David Teperson (Migdal).

Eli in his Workshop.
Portrait of his Mother on the wall.

He spent seven years in Israel and over 23 in Zimbabwe before returning to Johannesburg for 13 years. During the time back in JHB he did portrait sketches at Eastgate shopping centre. He came to Perth in 1992. He has two sons Michael and Ilan born in Israel and a daughter Karen born in Zimbabwe. Ilan is a musician and also teaching English at a university in Perth.

ELI STILL WORKS

At my age, I find that I have to devote my time to certain priorities. The first being in helping Estelle, my wife, maintain our home here in Perth. Secondly, I am totally occupied with my art, with painting and framing which I do myself. Believe me it takes considerable effort. The logistics involved in exhibiting are quite involved. Paintings have often to be packed well for exhibitions all over Western Australia. They also have to be delivered to many venues. Altogether I exhibit at 22 exhibitions annually. Unsold works have to be collected - the whole process is time consuming and tiring.

Estelle and I are also avid bridge players at club level, three times a week. We do not play with each other as that could lead to a quick divorce. So for the last ten years or more we have had other partners. We are extremely fortunate to have our son and daughter living here in Perth, and we see them frequently. Luckily I am in good health and since my paintings are selling, I have to keep painting.

As for telling other Arcadians about one's life since leaving Arcadia, where does one begin or stop. Before coming to Australia, I was encouraged to tell my life story. So I wrote it all down. For 13 years in Johannesburg, I sat at Eastgate Shopping Centre doing portraits. There was much time in between models to do it. The result is a book, which my children and grandchildren may find of interest one day. There are enough Arcadians no doubt with just as interesting stories. On the other hand I only spent two years there. They were certainly crucial for me to start a new life in South Africa. I was grateful for the time and to have lived there.

Here is just a line I wrote 20 years ago in my memoirs:

The best possible thing, for me, anyway, was the Orphanage where I had a home, better than I ever had in my life, friends, good food, care and even encouragement for my art.
The men in charge mentioned above, I feel did their very best for us.

ZAGORIA SPELT WITH AN "S"

When I first met Eli Zagoria I showed him the photo of Arcs "On Active Service", the one that used to hang in the dining room, and records the name of all Arcs on active service in World War II. We could not find his name and we thought it was simply omitted. Freda Cheilyk pointed out that Eli's name is indeed on the list of Arcadians on active duty the only thing is that they spelt it with an "S" and not a "Z".

Weekend Markets – by Eli Zagoria

Forrest Place – Perth by Eli Zagoria

REMEMBERING ELI

Ephraim Segal (Effie)

Eli slept across the main senior bedroom from my bed. The wrestler versus boxer fight was in the same bedroom at the foot of his bed. The other guy was Sam Gordon who was a bit lighter than Eli and was easily pinned to the floor and that was that.

Eli one night suddenly started reciting a poem in his previous home language. I never heard it again but it stuck in my mind for some strange reason. I obviously remember it wrongly but I'll write it down how it sounded to me:

> "Sturra burra unstic
> Sturra burra bunsic
> Krepcol krepcol
> Krepcol spull
> Spull plus noolsa
> Pirri Virri noolsa
> Ipa tomba
> Oplets spull"

I thought he gave us the sounds of a drummer.

Eli used to exhibit in *Artists Under the Sun* in the Pieter Roos Park in Parktown and at the Zoo Lake, which were held once or twice a year.

Both Jonah and Eli came from Israel. Jonah was born in Israel. They conversed with each other in Hebrew, and with the rest of in Hebrew-accented English. In Arcadia I once asked Eli in which language did he think in, to which he cleverly replied "I think in pictures". No wonder that he is a good artist-illustrator.

Jonah Perkel

I enjoyed looking at Zagoria paintings. Zagoria was the person I befriended on coming to Arcadia on 10 October 1936 - as I could only speak Hebrew, French and Arabic and he could speak Hebrew - so he became my mentor. Anyway I was also surprised that he married a girl who was my friend staying a corner away from my house. I and a friend visited their house meeting her parents and sister. The father worked in a men's clothing shop in Rissik Street.

Michael Perry Kotzen

The artists of my Arc generation – I remember that Eli Zagoria was an exceptionally talented artist. The boys envied Eli's ability to draw. Other Arc boys artistic, were Izaak Maiznick and Benny Gruzin. Maiznick did an impressive oil painting of the Prince of Wales in full regalia, which he copied from a small photograph. Stompie Shaer and the committee were so impressed with the painting that they had it handsomely framed and displayed in the committee room. Benny Gruzen, on leaving Arcadia, became a successful commercial artist in Johannesburg.

Both Jonah and Eli came from Israel. Jonah was born in Israel. They conversed with each other in Hebrew, and with the rest of in Hebrew-accented English. In Arcadia I once asked Eli in which language did he think in, to which he cleverly replied "I think in pictures". No wonder that he is a good artist-illustrator.

Eli's father and Alex Manderson's father were both from Riga Latvia. Eli himself was born in Riga. My late father Asher Zalman Kotzen was born in Riga in 1885. My grandfather, Slomo Behr Kotzen had a farm and a highway inn about 20 miles from Riga on the road to Visaginas and Moscow. My father was the third of eight siblings. He went to South Africa from Rotterdam in Holland in 1918.

FATHER AND DAUGHTER ART EXHIBITION IN PERTH

Eli Zagoria and his daughter Karen Frankel who both live in Perth held a "Father and Daughter Art Exhibition" on the 9th and 10th of April 2005 at the local Dianella Hotel. Eli has for many years been an artist, but his daughter Karen Frankel gave up

her computer business and decided to follow her dad and be an artist too.

Eli at around 83 looks very fit and trim. He has a strong handshake and also does the framing of all their artwork. It was a family affair with wife Estelle at the door and son Ilan playing the guitar. Grandchildren Sarah and Jeremy were helping out too.

For someone totally unqualified to comment on art I thought the artwork looked very good. I liked the bright colours and the tissue paper art medium used by Karen.

Eli, Estelle and Karen at Father & Daughter Exhibition 2005

Eli Zagoria

Father Daughter

Karen Frankel

Dianella Hotel
Cnr Alexander Drv. & Waverley St.,
Dianella

ART EXHIBITION

10 - 5 **9th & 10th April**
email: artist@karenfrankel.id.au
tel: 9375 8103 or 9275 3085

Chapter 15 – MINNIE HURWITZ (LEVINE) (1922)

My young sister Edie, my baby brother Sidney (known as Beans Levine) and I were brought to Arcadia at the beginning of 1935. We came from a background of poverty and deprivation, living with our parents in a small house in Doornfontein, Johannesburg.

The morning after the day of our arrival I was absolutely delighted to find at my bedside, a full school uniform and brand new shoes, all of which I had never had before in my primary school years.

FOND MEMORIES OF ARCADIA

During the June and December school holidays, those girls who had parents or relatives living in the peripheral towns of Johannesburg (such as Boksburg, Germiston and Krugersdorp etc.) were allowed to spend the full holidays with their families, whereas, those of us whose families lived in Johannesburg had to remain in the Arc. Consequently those of us left behind, were encouraged to develop hobbies, one of which was bead - collecting.

Donations to the Arc of clothing, shoes etc were stored in what was known as the Curiosity Shop. Sister Goldwater, who succeeded Matron Sher, was sitting with us one afternoon excused herself and reappeared holding an exquisitely beautiful evening dress - a French 1922 model of black velvet with glittering silver bugle beads and diamonte. She wanted to cut it into squares to provide each girl with a piece. The girls proceeded to cut off the beads and diamonte from their pieces but I did not. I treasured my piece. The year was 1936 and after 69 years I still have mine intact. I sometimes wonder if any of my contemporaries still have theirs.

On many a Saturday afternoon, two of my friends (Sylvia Rabinowitz and Lily Barlin) and I would "bunk" out and walk to the zoo with one objective in mind. The zoo authorities would, at several places on the lawn, place a cage to trap the little "mossies" which would be fed alive to the snakes. We would release these birds and hurry away. On one occasion a couple and their children were having a picnic nearby. They beckoned us to come over and asked where we had come from. Obviously the fact that we were wearing bottle green dresses, black stockings and black shoes, raised their curiosity. We told them that we lived in Arcadia and they took a photograph of us. They promised they would send each of us a copy by post, which in fact they did. I had mine for many years but, sadly, I have misplaced it.

I too was given the opportunity of seeing the musical Forty Young Australians. I recall the visit to the Arc of Larry Adler, a master at playing the Harmonica. Also a visit by "Afrique" a brilliant magician who thrilled his audience.

On the occasion of the Barmitzvah of John Schlesinger, his father who was very prominent in the early days of the film industry, presented each child at Arcadia with a half guinea and an accompanying gift. The gift I was given was a Conway Stewart fountain pen.

Another happy event at Arcadia was a party given to us on the occasion of the engagement of Inez Kaumheimer to a Dr Gordon. She was the daughter of a prominent member of the Arcadian Committee. Some weeks prior to the party the children were requested to endeavour to contribute their pennies and tickeys towards the cost of a silver tray that would be appropriately engraved on their behalf. In the mid 1950's I met Inez Gordon - she was a highly prominent member of the Women's Zionist movement in South Africa and I was involved in working for the love of Israel. Over the next few years we enjoyed a close relationship. Sadly Dr Gordon passed away, and Inez married a Dr Bernstein and they planned to go on Aliyah to Israel. She mentioned to me that of the few household items she was taking to Israel, was a silver tray given to her by the children of Arcadia. Although I had never before mentioned that I was an ex Arcadian, I was certainly very proud to claim that I was a "contributor" of the tray. She became very emotional and just hugged me.

Morris Hurwitz, my late husband, was a gifted pianist although he was self taught. He was the accompanist at the various Arc concerts for those girls (my late sister Edie being one of them) who had lovely singing voices. On several occasions Matron Shaer would request Morris to come to the cottage where she and Mr Sher (the superintendent of Arcadia) lived. Morris would play the piano and sing Hebrew and Yiddish lullabyes. Her favourite was My Yiddish Mamma.

Mr Harary also appreciated Morris's talent. He was responsible for the lyrics in Hebrew and Morris composed the music and sang. In fact, before Morris passed away, we (the family) had a video recording made playing classical music and singing those lovely Hebrew and Yiddish songs. We also had some tapes made for family members and close friends.

One of my memories that remain indelibly on my mind is this: At the end of each year we had a lovely concert at which talented children performed. It was a time when those boys and girls who had completed their education were ready to leave Arcadia. Wolf Hillman, after whom the hospital is named, would deliver a speech ending his remarks with the following words of wisdom: "We don't want you should have a superiority complex and we don't want you should have an inferiority complex". Did he perhaps feel we could develop our own personal complexes?

I wish to record my deepest appreciation and gratitude for everything that was done for me in my young years, and I salute those generous donors who contributed and those who continue to contribute magnanimously to the security of the existence of our beloved Arcadia.

THE OLD ARCADIAN ASSOCIATION

May I mention that the Old Arcadian Association was formed in 1948. Morris Hurwitz was appointed Chairman and Philip Kemp and Hymie Cohen were two of the committee member. I cannot recall the names of the others. In 1949 the committee organised an Arc dance which was held at the Ginsberg Hall in Doornfontein. It was an overwhelming social success, attended by many Old Arcs.

I would very much like to mention that Doreen Kapeluschnik is one of our top workers for the Old Arc's monthly book sale held in aid of raising funds for our cause. She worked at the Arc from February 1972 and left in May 1988. Initially she was the house-mother for a few years and was promoted to matron, working together with Vicky Klevansky. She was then co-opted to serve on the general committee of Arcadia that she did for a number of years, and then appointed as Chairlady of the after-care committee.

In 1999, I was retired after 45 years' service with the South African Zionist Federation and the Israel United Appeal, most of the time serving as Personal Assistant to the Director General. I then immediately joined the Occupational Therapy Section of Sandringham Gardens where I am presently involved in fabric painting, knitting of dolls, making items of importance required by the patients in the frail care section of the hospital and also for the hospital itself. I am the Secretary/Welfare of the Old Arcs Committee. I take Old Arcs shopping for groceries every three months, I arrange gift parcels to be sent to the old Arcs resident (or those in hospital) every Pesach and Rosh Hashanah, all the money for which is provided by the Committee.

Minnie is an active member of the Old Arc committee, conducts regular book sales to augment the funds, and also visits and spends time with the Old Arcs who are being cared for at Sandringham Gardens.

Book Sale at Pic n Pay Norwood
Abe Starkowtiz, Miinnie Hurwitz, Bernice Katz, Alec and Gootie Saul

Chapter 16 – LOUIS HURWITZ (1923)

Louis was placed in the Arcadia in December 1931 with his older brother Morris (Born 1922) and younger sister Judy (Born 1926). Louis left Arcadia in December 1940. Morris left about a year earlier, and Judy about six months later.

Morris married an Arc Girl, Minnie Levine (Born 1922) and she would have lived in Arcadia at the same time as the three Hurwitz siblings.

"I was in the Arc from December 1931 to December 1940, and, like most of the inmates was not an orphan, but one of four children whom my mother had battled to support after being abandoned by my father. In desperation, my mother placed in the care of the Jewish Orphanage three of the children, my older brother Morris, our youngest sibling Judy and myself. She kept with her my brother Selwyn, the oldest, and brought him up as best she could until he was old enough to leave school and go and work"

ARC MEMORIES

I could, but won't write page after page describing my life during those formative years. I think everyone of us who spent time in Arcadia could write volumes about their experiences, and indeed many have, in the memoirs that you have so diligently and devotedly collected.

But when I read through these collections, especially relating to my era, from Louis "Stompie" Shaer and his wife Leah to Abba and Ima Harari, there appears to be a common theme that runs through them. They differ only in minor details depending on what years were spent in Arcadia, whether through the almost Dickensian approach of the committee for which the Shaers were well suited, through to the more enlightened and humane approach of the Hararys. I speak only of course, of my sojourn in Arcadia, which ended in 1940.

In later years the changes that occurred were dramatic, and the home really lived up to its name Arcadia, a name that was frowned upon by the well meaning members of the committee and the supporters around the country. They much preferred the name South African Jewish Orphanage believing that any deviation would affect donations in cash, food and clothing on which the very survival of the home depended.

In the decades that have passed, I have often thought back to my days in the Arc, told my children and grandchildren endless stories of growing up in that unusual environment. And how, for better or for worse, that made me what I am.

One year my wife and I took our kids to celebrate the first night of Seder at the Arc, and to put it mildly I was stunned at the changes that had taken place, and was at a loss to explain to my daughters how different it was from what I had related to

Young Louis Hurwitz

them in the past. They could well have asked of me *"ma nish tana ?"*

On another occasion I took my daughters for a service at the Shul, which had, I indicated to them, previously been the dormitory where I had slept in my early years as a senior. And I showed them the beautiful palm trees flourishing along the driveway, and the memories that they evoked. I had helped Mordechai Harary plant the seedlings which he had nurtured from seeds obtained from a Jewish settlement in Palestine, the first time, or so he told me, that this had been done in South Africa.

But I digress. What I wanted to say was that, for some reason that I cannot explain, whenever my thoughts wandered back to those distant days, they somehow never included Rannoch Road School, where I spent four of the most formative years of my childhood. That is, until I read some of the memoirs from old

Arcs, and suddenly what was hidden away in the recesses of my mind became vivid images of the past. I found myself reliving incidents and events most of which have been related by my contemporaries of that period, with probably more wit and wisdom than I can muster. What intrigues me is how my memories differ, in minor ways, from those related by some of your correspondents. Perhaps this is because we may have seen it in a different perspective, understandably after 70 or so years. Or could it be that over the passage of time our memories of particular incidents have become a little fuzzy around the edges, and the core, the very essence of what happened on such and such an occasion has become the cornerstone of myth and urban legend as generation followed generation.

For example, that farting incident at Rannoch Road School, which took place, depending on which version you read, Effie's or Heinz's, in Miss Coetzee's classroom or that of Miss Kruywagen, both versions differing from what I remember. Not that I would vouch that my memory is correct. Not at all. I was in Miss K's class when this memorably smelly incident occurred, or maybe it was a similar one, this farting thing being anything but an isolated incident, and taking into account our diet rich in starches and fats, was, understandably, a pastime indulged in by most of us at one time or another.

But, as I remember it, Miss K, displeased by the sulphurous fumes reaching her desk, took up a position near the door, and ordered us to exit the class room one by one, while she sniffed at each hapless student as they hastily made their way out. After about a dozen or so had made it to safety, she stopped one of the boys in his tracks and proclaimed that he was the culprit, sent him outside and told the others to return to their seats and continue with their work. The alleged culprit was of course reported to Shaer, and as punishment for his malodorous deed had to forgo eating cabbage for one month.

This was quite a stiff sentence, because in those days our dinner menu for five days of the week consisted of meat, potatoes and cabbage, so this meant not only a loss of about a third of the meal, but also the competitive edge for a nightly dormitory pastime. Effie mentions that as a further deterrent against future gas attacks in school, Friday school sandwiches with polony would be replaced by jam, same as the other days of the week. Here, I must confess, either my memory or Effie's is at fault or distorted by time. Polony?? In the orphanage? Surely not! Unless of course we were better off in those days than I imagined.

I started out to write a short letter to introduce myself, and now it spans a couple of pages, so I will close now, perhaps to hit the keyboard again in the not too distant future, G-d willing that I do not run out of time.

POLONY – written by Michael Perry Kotzen

I would love to read more from Louis Hurwitz… About Rannoch road school and his talented brother Morris…Louis there actually were occasions that we DID get polony… a couple of thin slice between two slabs of course brown bread… I vaguely remember that the source of Arcadia's polony supply was a polony factory in Doornfontien, "Crystals Kosher Polony"…

They used to sometimes send parcels of shop leftover or date-expired or second grade meat products to the orphanage. I remember once helping Charlie Miller carry parcels from the bus into the kitchen… these were gift-food parcels that Charlie collected from various shops and factories…

One day Effie Segal and Mark Kobrin and I, while helping Charlie, stole one of the parcels. I tossed it into a hedge shrub. We later retrieved it and sneaked it down the hill to our hide out. It was a polony wrapped in brown paper. We devoured it secretly in our hideout. But Hymie Ekovitz and Sambo Manashevits saw us and threatened to split on us unless of course we gave them a chunk of polony… so we had to carve that sausage five ways!

You may think it strange that I remember such an incident. But I really recall the telling and retelling of the story. For years after Arcadia, Sambo and I were close companions, and would retell our polony story and other Arc adventures… What I actually remember now in the 80s is the repeated telling and retelling not so much the actual deed… The same applies to all our childhood memories… We remember the retelling more than the actuality… Each retelling adds a little more embellishment and exaggeration and dramatic license… The more that your audience approve and applaud and enjoy the more embellishments the story acquires. Were I now to tell it now to Sambo, he died 30 years ago, I am sure he would not recognize the story. I'd love to know what Arc readers think about my theory of memories?

Polony

FORTY YOUNG AUSTRALIANS

Louis sent us this letter addressed to Michael Perry Kotzen:

"Dear Michael, I sometimes wonder if there is not a strong spiritual link, ESP perhaps, between old Arc contemporaries such as ourselves. I ask this because on more than one occasion I have been thinking of some incident or person from those memorable days and sure enough before long I hear or read a glancing reference to what has been occupying my thoughts for maybe days on end.

For some reason, I know not why, I found myself thinking about the show Forty Young Australians for days on end, wondering whether any of the cast were still alive, what they may have experienced in the tumultuous years that followed. And lo and behold when I downloaded Dave Sandler news-letter 26th June, there was your query whether any old Arcs remembered their visit. Well, now you have the answer to your question, or is it?

I cannot remember them performing at the Arc, but Bertha does, and she remembers falling in love with all of the 40 boys!! I saw the show at the old His Majesty's, that theatre with the two crowns that lit up at night. I can remember the opening scene, the backdrop was a liner and down the gangway came the forty boys and "girls". The show was in the form of a revue, sketches, dancing, singing and so on, and that requires both sexes, and about a third of the troupe played the part of girls throughout the tour.

In the opening scene the one boy sported a black eye, and when asked about it he replied that it was a birthmark. "A birth mark?" "Yes. I got into the wrong berth!!" A risqué joke for those days, and one that requires the cast to be both sexes, as you would know from your theatre experience. The "girls'" make up and costumes were superb, and like Bertha, I too fell in love with those sexy creatures, the raging hormones of a sixteen year old blotting out the fact that those gorgeous "girls" were not for real.

Now your question begs another. I have not the slightest doubt that I saw the show at His Majesty's, my memory of that occasion is still clear. What I am not sure about is this. You will remember that we used to get free admission to movies during the school holidays, and now and again to stage shows. I seem to think that this show was one of those occasions, and that there were other Arc guys as well, but I cannot be sure. If it was in 1938 then I was still in Arcadia, and I certainly would not have had the money for a ticket.

Michael Perry Kotzen remembers

Louis Hurwitz in Canada confirms my memories of the Forty Young Australians. Louis is right. The Australians performed in His Majesty's theatre. Arcadia was given a limited number of complementary tickets. Something like 20 tickets for each of three or four matinee performances. There were 350 children in Arcadia. The 60 or 80 lucky kid recipients were carefully chosen by Stompie and matron Shaer with recommendations from nurses Le Roux and Swanepoel. As I was never a favourite neither of the nurses nor of Stompie's I did not make the selected few. But the young Australians gave a special Sunday performance at Arcadia for the benefit of the 270 kids who did not get complimentary tickets. Louis was obviously one of the lucky 80 who did

Louis Hurwitz remembers 40 young Australians

MPerry 2005.

CATASTROHPY

Recently I met with Ekie Litvin (Levine) and her husband Maish who were visiting their son and family in Toronto. Ekie was a contemporary of mine, and we spent a few hours reminiscing about our days in Arcadia, and how we used to smuggle out food to feed the feral cats that lived in the shrubbery near "The Old Curiosity Shop" on the east side of the main building.

We used to hide the kittens, not always successfully, in the hope that they would not be found by sadistic Swanepoel who delighted in disposing of them in the fish pond, then summoning us to unknowingly witness the results of his handiwork. Not a good memory, but happily a rare one, and when I get down to putting on paper the memories, myths and legends of Arcadia, as I hope to do, there will be nothing as distasteful as the above incident.

REMEMBERING FELLOW ARCS

David Aginsky is one of the many names that I am familiar with, but cannot remember personally as he is five years older than me, and so were many of the people from Arcadia that he mentions. Of particular interest to me was mention of Reuben Maisnek and Abe Maftur, both of whom I had heard of while in the Arc, but they had long left before I entered the exalted ranks of the senior boys.

But talk about fate! In 1950 when I was courting the young lady who would later that year become my wife, I was introduced to her sister and husband Reuben Maisnek, and thus began a close association of nearly 40 years until Reuben's death.

Reuben often talked about his best friend Abe Maftur, and I might well have met him during those years, but I am not sure. But I did know that Abe had a sister, Rosie, who was also in the

Arc, and here fate takes a hand as well.

As I mentioned to you in my earlier letter Minnie visits at Sandringham Gardens regularly, and a couple of weeks ago she mentioned that Rosie (married name Gatter) had been admitted to Sandringham. She has made a point of seeing Rosie every time she visits, usually three times a week. She tells me that Rosie is very frail, barely able to walk even with the aid of a walker, and is 91 years old!! We think she is the oldest surviving Old Arcadian.

Chapter 17 - ABE STARKOWITZ (STARKEY) (1923)

Starkey (as he is known to all Fellow Arcs) was born in 1923 and was in the care of Arcadia from 1930 to 1938.

Starkey is well know by Arcadians of many generations as for over 50 years he was the cantor (with a magnificent voice) at Arcadia over the high holidays.

Over many many years (in fact all my life) I have always seen Starkey's familiar face on the Bimah leading the Rosh Hashonah and Yom Kippur services. We have heard his wonderful and familiar singing.

Below is a photo of Starkey at age 16 holding the Torah and on the right a recent one of him on the Bimah.

Starkey on the Bimah

Starkey at age 16 holding the Torah

THE IMPORTANCE OF KNOWING
Extract From Old Arc Newsletter – Editor Alec Saul
By Abe Starkowitz

In 1940 as a young man I decided to join the army to help get rid of the scourge of Nazism embodied in Hitler's regime and his armed forces. In the campaign I was taken prisoner in North Africa, whilst fighting in the desert, I was incarcerated in a POW camp in the town of Marciano in Italy. I considered it my duty to escape which took me three months to do and made my way into the hills to hide.

The local farmers were friendly to me and arranged caches of food to protect themselves and at the same time enable me to feed myself and in the ongoing process they taught me the language in which I became fluent.

One Friday night I was passing the house of a family I knew well. I heard talking and listened. To my amazement I heard the Friday night service being conducted in Hebrew. Finding the door unlocked I walked in intending to join in the service. The next thing I knew I was bound to a chair and was told by them that they were going to kill me to protect the people in the house.

Imagine how scared I was and thought my end was close. What to do now. Then it struck me. In Arcadia I was taught to conduct the service and anything you learn always comes in useful and is never lost. I asked them to please give me a chance. I told them I was Jewish and to prove it would continue the service from where they left off without a book, which I promptly did. Then I was accepted like a brother.

That Sunday a most amazing thing happened. I went to visit the local priest in his church. He was one of my protectors and sitting in the front row was the family who I had continued the Friday night service for. This was not a new theme and has been used by Jews to protect themselves from anti-Semitism over the ages. Apart from the town, I have named no names to protect the people involved.

Starkey – R2 million in the bag

OUR CHARITY MILLIONNAIRE

STARKEY, THE LION [HEARTED] HAS RAISED R2-Million

Abe Starkowitz, known as 'Starkey', what else, in his private time has raised R2-million over 40 years for charity./ - Now that's one hell of an introduction to a story.

So who is Starkey? He is the warm, kind-looking guy that joined Pretoria Wholesale Druggists in July last year. He has been in the pharmaceutical business all his life – and loves it.

Money kick
Adapted from material supplied by Scribe Woolf Getz

So what[s with the money raising kick?

He loves that too. He's a Lion. Lions are like Rotarians, only more so. That puts him into community service.

As a member of Lions International, and past chairman of the Cyrildene/Observatory Lions Club, he led the campaign to raise enough money three years ago to build a nursery school for underprivileged children in Doornfontein.

So how did he do it? By organising two motor shows similar to those held at Earls Court, London, which together raised R55 000.

And as chairman of a stage production company for the last eight years he has raised about R90 000 for charity.

Starkey saw active service with the South African Second Division in North Africa and Europe between 1940-43.

He was captured by the Germans in Nights Bridge. He didn't like that and escaped. To join the partisan forces in Yugoslavia.

When he wasn't fighting and before he went behind the wire, he represented his battalion at soccer, hockey and baseball and later played for the Transvaal *Moths* hockey XI.

He is also a great one for stamps. He specialises in collecting the stamps of South Africa, South West Africa, and homelands and Canada.

He was the first person to open a stamp club at a school for the deaf and one for the under-privileged, naturally.

Music Lover

Starkey also loves music and is gifted with a lovely voice which he uses to great effect when conducting synagogue services at the Jewish Orphanage. For the past 50 years, no less.

And for 41 years Johannesburg-born and bred Starkey has been married to Lillian. They have two children, Cheryl and Lionel.

Enough is too much, the man's human.

Chapter 18 – MAX (GINGER) LADIER (1923)

Max Ladier was an only child and was born on the 18th of September 1923 in Jerusalem Palestine. His mother Miriam Ladier (nee Margowsky) was born in Russia and immigrated to Israel at the age of two.

When Max was two years old he and his mother immigrated to South Africa. Max was placed in the care of Arcadia in August 1931 and left in March 1940.

I was in Arcadia from April 1932 until January 1940 and I was known as "Ginger". I was educated at Parktown Boys' High school and matriculated at John Orr Technical College.

I married Gittel (Gertie) Spark in 1956 and she passed away in 2002.

After several jobs I decided to open my own business and in 1958 I opened my own hardware business "*Woody Woodman*"

Max Ladier

in Rosettenville. I was well known in the area and specialised in hardware and traded for some 25 years. I thought I would retire but after working for such a long time, found it extremely difficult to retire. I then took on a job working for the Nussbaum family first with locks and keys and then stationery until I decided to make aliyah at the end of December 2003.

I also served for almost 30 years on the Arcadia Committee as Chairman of Estate Committee.

In December 2003 I immigrated to Israel to be with my daughter Carole who lives with her family. She has two children. My son Geoffrey immigrated to London with his family and also has two children. I have once again reinstated my friendship with Alec Saul in Israel.

Max lives in a retirement place called Ahuzah Beit in Raanana and Alec Saul says he sees him regularly. They go for coffee twice a week in Ahuza Street and Alec reports, "There is a magnificent little waitress whom we both fancied and we were competing with each other to catch her eye. What we would have done if one of us got it right I do not know."

Max Ladier in Israel

Chapter 19 – HANK (HEINZ) EPSTEIN (1929)

Hank was born in Europe on 24th April 1929. His mother passed away in Paris, France, in 1934 and he came to South Africa with his father in 1935. He was placed in the Jewish Orphanage in Cape Town until 1936 and he remembers that Bernard Aronstam and Bessie Firer were also in the Cape Town Jewish Orphanage at about the same time.

At the age of seven he was put into the care of Arcadia. He left the Arc in 1948 after completing his Matric at Parktown Boys' High.

RANNOCH ROAD PRIMARY SCHOOL

I always thought of Mr. Jacobs, (Jakey), the headmaster of the Rannoch Road Primary School, as a very strict man. As he walked up and down the isle between benches, we would slide in our benches away from him to avoid a slap on the head. Once he asked me a question for which I had no answer. After slapping me a couple of times on the back of my head, I had the answer he wanted. "You see" he said, "all one has to do is give a slap to the head, and out comes the answer!" His favourite verse was the one about the village master and his school. It ran something like ---------- *the village master taught his little school. A man severe he was, and stern to rule* --The "severity" and "sternness" was what he enjoyed.

Then there was Miss Kruywagen, (Kravy). I think we all liked her. I venture to say that I learned more from her than any teacher I ever had. She taught English, Afrikaans, arithmetic, and spent many hours reading to us. I remember reciting after her--"*met my hande speel ek. Met my tande byt ek. Met my oë sien ek.*"

I also see her suddenly exiting the classroom holding her nose, with the rest of the class following. Somebody made a smell. Kravy kept a chart on the wall with all the pupils' names. Whenever exceptionally good performance was achieved, the pupil received a star. On the tenth, one got a gold star. I would compete with David Rodin for the most stars for which, at the end of the term, the winner received a prize, usually a book. David got most of his stars for his handwriting. I got most of mine for arithmetic. For that I was assigned to "grading" the arithmetic of the rest of the class. But I sure envied David's handwriting. I would have traded my skill in numbers for his beautiful writing.

Mrs Yates taught 1st and 2nd grades, and Lucy Pincus Std 3 and 4. I still remember many of the children's songs Mrs Yates taught. I believe that Ms Pincus is a cousin of Abe Stoller.

CHAZANIM

Between 1944 and 1947 Samuel Adler and I were Chazanim at our Shul in the orphanage. We would alternate officiating Friday nights and Saturdays for the Shabbath services.

Young Hank Epstein

Particularly taxing were the services on the high holy days of Rosh Hashanah and Yom Kippur. Usually Mr Harary himself chanted the Kol Nidre, but on one occasion he let me do it. As you probably know, the Kol Nidre is sung three times, very slowly, and with great feeling I was a little nervous at first, especially since we had a large congregation, and on the first time around my voice broke on the high notes, which made me even more nervous. But Mr Harary calmed me down and the next two times went off perfectly. Samuel left Arcadia a year or two before me.

SOME ARC MEMORIES

Thinking of the Arc brings back memories, both good and bad. I remember Mr. Potter --he never associated with any of us. One thing I remember about him--his dog. Every afternoon he would carry his master's newspaper all the way up our driveway, to his house. Very cute!

I remember more distinctly the heavy-set one of the Oakey brothers. He farted a lot. Every afternoon he would arrive by bicycle with his box of sweets. Peppermint crisps and beehives, which I could not afford, were a tickey (about two and a half cents!) each. When "cop" Harary saw the profits Oakey made, he kicked him out and installed his own "Tuck Shop". Mrs Harary (Ima), ran it, and the quality definitely suffered. She usually hired one of the boys to sell the goods, paying him a very meager salary. Sidney Adler was one of the salesmen, and was dismissed for eating some of the goods. The worst sweets were "*Talk of the Town*", and *Butterfingers*". They seldom sold. We longed for Oakey.

Boy, this sure brings back memories!!

And don't forget to write about the nurses of Arcadia.

There was sister Gabelsky, who was the sister at the hospital when I came to Arcadia, circa 1936); sister Kime; (I may have her name wrongly spelt), who was really rough on Jacob Kemp, and would beat him for any excuse; sister Edith Pels, and Lucy Joynson, who left at about the time I did, in 1948.

50 YEARS LATER

I did not correspond with anyone for 50 years, from 1948, when I left Arcadia, until1998.

It was on the spur of the moment that I decided to come to South Africa in 1998. I had no idea who, among the many people, I knew, were still around. I booked a hotel in Sandton, after the South African embassy, here in Los Angeles, warned me against staying in downtown Johannesburg. I immediately began searching the phone directory for any name that might be familiar, but had no luck, mainly because the phone book did not list first names. So then I rented a car, bought a map of the local area, and searched for Arcadia, or the South African Jewish Orphanage.

Driving on the wrong (er, left) side of the road was an experience I shall never forget. More than once did I end up facing oncoming traffic, with horns blowing and people yelling. I can't even remember how I overcame the chaos I caused, but I swore I would never rent a car here again. Anyway, I found Arcadia, but was flabbergasted to discover a freeway passing through much of the grounds. Gone was the hill, the orchard, the path to Louis Shaer's (Harary's) house and the house itself! It was a great disappointment to see how dilapidated so much of Arcadia had become. But enough of this theme.

While looking at a photo hanging on the wall of the "committee room", of a group of people, whose names were written below, I came across my dear friend Hakkie Kabe. Not having seen him for 50 years, I was unable to recognise him, so I matched the names with the position of the faces, and yes, I saw a resemblance! The name of Vicky Klevansky also came up.

I met some lady in the hall and asked her if she knew any of the guys in the photo, and of course, she identified Vicky. When I met him, neither of us recognised one another at first. That soon changed. Vicky rightly noted that my hair was much more blond than now, but I was amazed at his recollection of so many events of the past.

Through Vicky I was able to find Sadie Lurie (I knew her as Sadie Segal), and through her, the location of Hakkie's company. We did not tell him that I was coming, and the event

was an overwhelming, emotional moment, that I will never forget. For the rest of my visit, I stayed with him at his house. Through Hakkie I then met Solly Farber, Mannie Osrin and Barney Meyers. I also attended an evening service at the Shul in Arcadia, where I met many of my old friends Basil Samson, Alec Gavson, Isaac Goldman, Starkey, but I was indeed sad to learn of the passing of so many of those I once knew.

Hakkie's death hit me very hard, as did the recent passing of Leonard Lipschitz and his brother, and Hymie Lemmer.

Just recently I came to Johannesburg (I can't get used to Gauteng) again, and was delighted to see and spend some time with Solly, Mannie and Barney, and their wonderful wives. I knew Mannie's wife Sarah, (nee Epstein), when she was about 16, and she is as lovely as ever. I again rented a car, but this time I was super careful about driving in the right direction. I also attended an Arcadia committee meeting headed by Tim Cohen, whom I met for the first time in 50 years. We recognised each other immediately. Vicky also attended the meeting, and I promised to write and give him a little history of myself. I hope that this letter to you, David, will fulfil this promise, as I'm sure he will get to see it.

SINCE LEAVING THE ARC

I left South Africa in January 1950, together with my father and stepmother. We arrived in New York in the midst of a terrible winter, after enduring the worst hurricane of the century while on board the Queen Elizabeth. On top of that, New York had a blackout due to a coal strike. I was so miserable, that for two cents I would have returned to sunny SA! Well, after a 3-day train journey to Los Angeles, California, I felt much better, especially after seeing my aunt and uncle who met us at the station. We had not seen them since leaving Germany in 1933.

Both jobs and apartments were scarce in those days. The war had ended only five years earlier, and millions of repatriated servicemen were looking for work. I was only 20 years old, without skills, and only a high school education, but through my uncle, who had a top management position as a food chemist at S E Rykoff & Co, I got a job washing bottles and mixing foodstuff ingredients into vats, for 60 cents an hour. I stayed with my parents in a dingy apartment, and slept in the living room in a bed that was hidden in the wall, and had to be pulled down and sat on, so that it would not snap back into the wall.

Then came the biggest change in my life. In June 1950, the North Koreans invaded the South, and America entered the war. I won't dwell on the details concerning the aspects of the conflict, but suffice to say that, as an emigrant having taken out first papers toward citizenship, I was eligible for the draft. I had a number of choices. I could wait to be drafted into the army, (at the time it was for two years), or I could enlist into the Navy or the Army Air Force, (subsequently called the Air Force), for a period of four years. Getting shot up in Korea did not exactly appeal to me, so I decided to go Navy.

All around me were these recruiting posters showing jets zooming off carriers into the wild blue yonder, and the pilots just having a ball! I thought, "that's for me". Boy was I naïve! At the recruiting office the first two questions they asked me were whether I was US citizen, and a college graduate. Being neither, my ambition as a carrier fighter pilot vanished. Only officers could be pilots, and one had to be a citizen and university graduate to become an officer. I was not about to enlist as a sailor, since my stomach and a ship aren't in sync. Well there was still the Air Force. Again, I naively assumed that Air Force personnel flew. Not until after I enlisted did I learn that for every pilot there were perhaps 100 persons who supported him.

I was sent to Lackland AFB in Texas for eight weeks basic training, during which time they put us through detailed testing to see where we best fitted. I excelled in mathematics and physics, which gave me a choice of careers. I chose electronics. That brought me to Scott AFB, Illinois, for 26 weeks training in the maintenance and repair of airborne radio and radar communications equipment. At about this time, some French students arrived in the USA for training in navigation equipment, and since I was the only one around having a working knowledge in French, and, showing some skill in the ability to teach, I was sent to an instructor training school. For about one year, I taught both American and French classes in the theory and maintenance of airborne navigation receivers and transmitters. Then came my turn to go overseas.

As a staff sergeant, I was sent to an Air Force base in Kyushu, Japan. The war was not going well, with the North Koreans knocking at the door in Pusan. We worked around the clock repairing damaged airborne equipment carried in C-46 and C47 cargo planes, and radar gear in fighter aircraft. But I must say that my entire career as an Air Force enlisted man, was satisfying, fulfilling, and very happy. I made a lot of friends, in particular a man and his wife, who also was in the Air Force, and who are now retired and living in Hawaii.

The war ended in 1953, and a year later, I was discharged from the Air Force and returned home to California. But I already made up my mind to pursue a technical career. I applied for entrance to the university of California, (UCLA), as an undergraduate in engineering, and received a BS in electrical/electronic engineering in 1958. Later I went on to receive a Masters degree from the University of California at Fullerton. All during this time, I stayed in the Air Force reserves.

This I did for two reasons. First, I received a small payment which supplemented the money I got through the "GI Bill of Rights". This was a program giving a supplement to all honourably-discharged armed forces personnel for educational purposes. (American spelling differs from English). Second I wanted to pursue a more ambitious Air Force career as a commissioned officer, since I was getting nowhere as a non-com. in the reserves. Virtually all avenues to a commission were closed for me. ROTC was out because I was no longer a student. I was too old (30) for Officer Training School (OTS), and too old and without influence for the Air Force Academy. The only possibility was through something called the "Outstanding Airman's Commissioning Program".

This was tough to get into, and even tougher to get through. There were less than 50 yearly vacancies, and you had to compete with selected "outstanding" airmen from bases all over the USA. Well luck was on my side and on 19 April 1959, at a

ceremony at the Space Division in Los Angeles, I was made a first lieutenant. (I skipped 2nd lieutenant because I was over 27).

Incidentally, I applied for, and received, my US citizenship in 1954.

Hank Epstein - 4-star USA General

After graduation from UCLA, I went to work at Autonetics, a division of North American Aviation, subsequently called North American Rockwell after the merger between Rockwell and NAA, and subsequently renamed Rockwell International. You must have heard of us, since we were responsible for the B-1 bomber, the Space Shuttle, and guidance for the Minuteman missile I married shortly after graduation, but my wife passed away not long ago, after 28 years of marriage. We had no children.

After 31 years with Rockwell, I retired in 1989. While I enjoy retirement, I miss working because my work was always interesting and fulfilling. I was a senior research engineer, primarily involved in the design and development of electronic equipment for testing of guidance components for the control of missiles, submarines and aircraft. I specialised in automatic control systems. While I am no longer involved with such heady work, I keep active in the fields of science and engineering. I regularly meet with friends and ex-colleagues over luncheons and the subjects are mostly engineering and politics. We are always in harmony when it comes to science and mathematics, but politics? ---well we don't fight, but we can be heard all over the dining room.

Everyone has a computer, and much of the discussion revolves around the latest upgrades and downloads. I use the computer mainly for keeping tabs on my financials. I also trade on-line. I also use it for keeping records, data and appointments, and writing letters such as this. It is easier for me to write with the computer than by hand, because some 30 years ago, I lost much of the use of my right hand when I damaged both the radial and ulna nerves at the elbow. I banged my elbow at work, on a console I was building, and this damaged the nerves, which in turn caused muscle atrophy. It is a big handicap, but I'm used to it. My bowling and tennis days are over, but I keep fit walking. Up until 1995, I ran between five and eight miles a day at a school track near my home. Now, with a minor back problem, I only walk. I try do go five miles/day at 15min./mile. Gee, I almost forgot! You probably don't remember what a mile is!! (just kidding). Just in case- - five miles is eight kilometres.

From 1958 until I retired in 1989, I pursued a parallel career in the Air Force reserves. To cut a long story short, I worked my way up through the ranks and retired as a colonel. As an engineer, my work with the Air Force also involved military electronics. As a colonel, the assignments were in an advisory and supervisory position, but I did not miss the hands-on engineering because I was still doing that at my civilian job.

I have a house in Anaheim, California, in which I have lived since 1978. I also have a house in Hawaii, on the big island. My two best friends, Earl and his wife Helen Cooper whom I met while stationed in Japan back in 1952, live on the big island, in a place called "Hawaiian Paradise Park", about 15 miles from Hilo .I visited them in 1992 and became so enthralled with the island that I bought an acre of land, (0.4 hectare), across the road from them. A year later, I built a house on one half of the land. I stay there three times a year for two weeks at a time. The house is fully equipped, and I keep a car in the carport. All I need when going there is my airline ticket. It takes five hours to fly the 4,000 km from Los Angeles to Honolulu.

I have never corresponded with any of the "old boys" from Arcadia, not even those living in the United States, the reason being that I don't know where they are. I believe that my friend Jacob Kemp is somewhere in California, but no one in South Africa knew of his whereabouts. I also understand that Bernard Aronstam, whose career in the U.S. parallels mine, (he was in the navy), is living somewhere back east. I get all of my inputs from Solly, Mannie and Barney. The quarterly publication of the Old Arcs is not too informative for me. I am not acquainted with most of the people written about. Still, I look forward to receiving it because familiar names do pop up.

CATCHING UP WITH ARCS IN THE USA

A couple of months ago I got a real surprise. An e-mail arrived from none other than Bernard Aronstam. It caught me completely by surprise because I have long wondered where Bernie was. Of course I immediately answered his letter and we became acquainted again, after about 55 years! We now correspond by phone and e-mail quite often.

Earl Cooper and Hank in Japan 1953
This is how most people will remember Hank. He was 24 years old.

Earl Cooper and Hank in Hawaii

Bernard also sent me a complimentary copy of his book which I took with me to Germany, where I had the opportunity to read it from cover to cover. It was fascinating. What struck me most was how parallel our lives ran. We both enlisted in the Air Force, I, at the start of the Korean War, he a short time after. We took basic training at Lackland AFB, then we went into electronics, he at Keesler AFB for training as a radar technician , and I to Scott AFB for 26 weeks of training as a navigational equipment technician. I stayed on to become an instructor in that field, then was sent to Japan for a two year hitch. At about the time I graduated from the University of California at Los Angeles (UCLA) in engineering, Bernie was at the University of California, Berkeley studying law. What is really galling is that in all these years, we were so near to each other, yet never even knew where the other was, except that I knew Bernard was somewhere in America. Some time this year I will go to New Orleans to visit him.

Another surprise came a few days after Bernie called me. I received a call from someone in Florida, who spoke in Afrikaans. Not having spoken this language for some 55 years, I was amazed how much came back to me. The man said he knew me and my father in South Africa and asked if I wanted some biltong. The conversation was a little nutty, and I asked if he could speak English. *"Nee"* he said. Then he rambled on and finally burst out laughing and told me he was Jacob. Yes, it was Jacob Kemp, the first and my best friend I had on coming to Arcadia in 1936. We didn't speak too long, but he tried to sign me up for a telephone subscription. I wasn't biting, but he managed to sign Bernie up, at a higher cost than he was paying. Jacob seems to be heavily involved in scientology. Although I did not ask for it, he said he would send me some literature on the subject.

I am in contact with Jacob Kemp (by phone). Again, I have not seen (nor spoken to) Jacob, until recently, since about 1945. Jacob may be coming to California. It will be a great reunion.

MEETING AFTER 55 YEARS
Heinz and Bernard – from the French Quarter of New Orleans

Here we are in New Orleans---"we" being Bernard and Heinz (Hank). Thanks to you, David, because without your input, we would never have found each other. Who could believe that we would meet after an absence of 55 years?

We had a hard time finding each other when Hank arrived in New Orleans from California because we had no idea what the other looked like. I only remember Bernard from a picture of him as a 13 -year-old, and Bernard had the same picture of me as a 16-year-old. So what do we look like after 55 years. Well after a little searching and waiting we finally found each other. Miracles never cease.

Hank is only able to stay here for five days, so we did not accomplish much in sightseeing because we had so much to talk about. So much of what we had forgotten suddenly came back to us. Even minor seemingly insignificant events were suddenly expanded into all directions. That kept us talking into the wee hours of the morning. In the process, we were flabbergasted to discover how our lives paralleled from the time we left Arcadia. We both came to America in the 50's, joined the Air Force during the Korean war, went through the same boot camp at Lackland AFB, then on to electronic school for 26 weeks, Bernard at Keesler AFB, and Hank at Scott AFB. After a four-year stint, we got out and attended university, Bernard at the University of California at Berkeley, and Hank at the University of California at Los Angeles, (UCLA). Bernard studied law, and Heinz engineering. Remarkably, our paths never crossed, even though at some point of time we were at the same location at the same time. But we digress, back to our visit to New Orleans.

We didn't just talk about old times, we also took in some of the sights that are renowned the world over, such as Larry Flint's Hustler's club, (of course we only viewed it from the outside), and the sights and sounds of Bourbon street---whose sounds are still ringing in our ears. The Champs Elysées it is not. We saw the Mississippi River, Jackson Square and had coffee and beinets at the cafe du Monde. On this, Hank's last day, we will take in the Mississippi River Bridge, and visit the West Bank of

New Orleans, then dine in style for the last supper. By the way, you may be interested to know that the state of Louisiana has a large number of Arcadians in its population----not from the Arc, but from Arcadia in Canada. We call them "Cajuns" who have the reputation of being typical Louisianans. I, Hank, am so impressed that I have become a confirmed Cajun. We recently had another pleasant experience. We contacted both Willie Isaacs in Houston, and Jacob Kemp in Florida. This was the first time that Hank had contact with Willie since about 1946, but he talks with Jacob regularly. We don't know when our paths will cross again, but rest assured, we will keep in touch.

ENGAGEMENT, MARRIAGE AND A DAUGHTER ELIZABETH MAI LAN

I visited Vietnam with a Vietnamese girlfriend of mine, not just to accompany her, but to visit her four sisters, one to whom I am engaged to be married. Her name is Oanh. We have been corresponding with each other over the phone, by mail and e-mail for some time, and it became time that we met. It was a wonderful experience. She lives in a town called "Go Cong", some 70 km from Saigon. (Ho Chi Minh City). Our engagement party was a great success with about 60 relatives and friends attending. Even though I cannot speak Vietnamese, (except for many words and phrases), I felt quite at home. The people were all exceptionally friendly. Of course I had my friend Patty to interpret for me

Hank married Oanh on the 23rd of October 2003 and they now have a daughter Elizabeth Mai Lan - DS

Hank and Oanh on their engagement

Chapter 20 – JONAH PERKEL (1924)

Jonah was born in Israel on the 14th July 1924, and his mother died some days later. His birth certificate states that he was born in the Jewish Community of Jaffa, as Britain refused to recognise Tel Aviv as a Jewish city or the Jewish community as an entity. Jonah came out to South Africa in 1936, and due to their circumstances his father had him admitted to Arcadia. Being Hebrew speaking, it took him a while to adjust to school and conditions at the Arc. Jonah was in the Arc from October 1936 until 1941.

JONAH'S HISTORY

I left Palestine in 1936 and it took us about six weeks to get to South Africa as the only means of transport was by ship. There was an Italian liner that used to ply between Haifa and Genoa on a ship known as Julius Caesar and a ship from Genoa to Cape Town called the Dulia. Apparently there were two ships plying on that route, one leaving Haifa and at the same time one leaving Genoa to Haifa and the same with the Cape Town Genoa route.

If you recall, 1936 was the height of anti-Semitism in Europe and the world and I believe we were the last boat that was allowed to enter South Africa due to the foreign minister DF Malan closing the gates to all immigration especially from Europe.

My brother Nathan, who is still alive and lives in Haifa, came out to South Africa unaccompanied by ship. My other two brothers are deceased. Due to the depression at the time and my late father not having the ability to earn enough, he placed me in the orphanage where I could not talk English or any other language other than Hebrew or Jewish so I was sent to a Jewish Government School.

When I arrived at the Arc, Stompie felt I should go to Professor Worthington for English lessons as I had no knowledge of English, having come from [those days] Palestine, so I was fully aware of this elderly professor who resembled my late brother-in-law in looks and speech.

The late principal Mr Harris, because of my lack of English and the subjects that was needed, put me in Std 3 which was a class with an average age of about 10, when I was 12 and a half. However with a bit of diligence I caught up by skipping Std 6 and only stayed in Std 3 for about six months. Mr Harris in his wisdom did not want me to go to high school because of my age, so Stompie took it upon himself to override the Principal. However by the time this was sorted out it was too late to enrol in high school so I went to Observatory Junior Boys' High which started in Std 6 which class I skipped and went to Std 7 thus matriculating at the normal age of about 18.

Jonah Perkel

Harary was reluctant to let me leave the Arc, as he was keen that I continue reading the Torah every Saturday and Yomtovim. I continued to do this even after I left, and that was my way of giving back to the Arc.

As with everybody, it becomes a problem as to what to do after Matric. I started engineering at the university and at that time there were very limited outlets for engineers and working on the mines. I saw that many overseas qualified engineers from English and German universities were doing the same work as I was, cleaning centrifugal pumps and joining electrical wires in breakdowns and I decided that the engineering profession was not for me. By sheer chance I met my late brother's bookkeeper, a Mr Serebro, who invited me to join his firm as an articled clerk. I met him on a Saturday morning at the Post Office and Monday I began serving my Articles.

I wrote all the exams which by comparison to today were extremely easy in all subjects. I passed my Final A in two and a half years but had to write my Final B, if my memory confirms, approximately three times. However it is the end result that counts.

I am now also a registered Public Accountant in Israel. I proceeded to take the Israeli accountancy exams as I felt that if there were an upheaval in the world situation, Israel would be the only country where I would not have to prove myself for acceptance. So one plans life as best one can and in hindsight one can easily detect the right and the wrong path taken and the only consolation one can have is that the children have all got professions and are all married with their own families and if that is a test of success then I suppose I have been successful.

Senior Boys 1940.- Abe Lazarus, Issy and Benny Gavson in front. Horace, Woolfie Getz, Donald Goldman, Issy Pleban and Jonah Perkel at back.

I am now deeply involved with the grandchildren who call on me more than on their own parents as they note that grandparents cannot say "no" to their requests. It is quite an interesting experience to note that when they phone to ask you to take them out for a cup of tea or coffee you end up paying for a dress or some other expensive article which they see in a shop so the cup of coffee or tea that they are requesting you to have with them mounts up with a cost of R200 if not more.

However one takes this into account in giving them more confidence as they are reciprocated in their little ways that grandchildren do, always happy to be in the company of their grandparents as well as wanting to swot or come to the house. We are fortunate in having the facilities for them by way of a tennis court, swimming pool and a huge garden so at this stage it is still a question of the facilities or the relationship between the grandparents and themselves.

My wife Maisie finished her BA at Unisa about five years ago so she has now a lot in common with some of the grandchildren who are also pursuing their professions through Unisa. We have celebrated our 54th anniversary so I suppose like everyone else we have managed to overcome the downs and enjoy the ups which all marriages go through. We have five sons, all now married, and 14 grandchildren.

Unfortunately Vicky will be the only one who could really get the full benefit of the Arc history, as he appears to have been a Mr Chips in the Arc. I believe that he came to the Arc as a little boy and was involved until 2002. He reached the position of Vice-Principal at Parktown High School as well.

It is rather sad that an Arc child is spending his live in jail with life sentences for drug dealing etc. Since reading about Krebs, I made contact with a local Rabbi who has in-depth contacts in Thailand through the Lebavich community, and who promised to take him into his normal caring embrace. The Rabbi hopes to use his influence to alleviate the difficult conditions Krebs is experiencing. There is always hope that the congregation in Thailand will visit him with parcels for his needs, and comfort. So once again your efforts in making contacts may prove to make a big difference.

My son who is a journalist in Canada, with the Canadian press, has been assigned to report on a place called Walkerton, where there has been a tremendous outcry on the polluted waters with the government of Canada who simply turned a blind eye. He was approached by a leading publisher in Canada, to write a book on his experiences. I understand that at present the book is complete and receiving reviews by the publishers so hopefully from the feedback he has had which apparently is very favourable, one of these days we will have the publication. Colin has been with the Canadian press for some 20 years and has now been seconded to the Canadian Federal Parliament so presumably he seems to have the ability having qualified with a Master's Degree at the University of London in Toronto which was given to him by way of a scholarship having qualified as a doctoral degree which is the equivalent of an MA in Holland.

Jonah, Mark Kobrin and Tommy Green

I was fortunate enough to visit Louis Hurwitz a few years ago at his home in Canada and we enjoyed a couple of hours on two occasions with each other's company and historical past times.

Also on my last visit to Toronto, my wife Maisie and I were entertained by Bertha and her husband, and it was pleasant to see them well settled there. Joe Siegenberg has made his home in Vancouver where I met him when I visited the Rocky Mountains.

I read recently a psychology article that in later life friends and acquaintances of youth, become closer friends than even family and this could be the reason why your Arc correspondence is taking such a hold on the Old Arcs. This is a rather interesting aside as everybody who gets your letters and correspondence has nothing but praise in how you manage to handle it, especially holding out by yourself such an expensive enterprise.

A YOM KIPPUR STORY

Some time in 1953 when I was a resident in Windhoek the cantor in a place called Keetmanshoop, which is almost the capital of the Kalahari Desert, apparently had a heart attack between Rosh Hashana and Yom Kippur. To replace a chazzan in such a short period would have been impossible so I was asked to go down to take the service for the Day of Atonement.

An older Jonah Perkel

Nobody told me that the heat of the desert becomes unbearable in the train. I decided to sleep on the upper bunk of my compartment to get some of the air to cool off. As soon as the sun sets the desert air becomes almost like an ice chest so I woke up about 3 o'clock in the morning, freezing, coughing and sneezing and I was thinking to myself how can I take the service with a cold and a cough.

Hoever, when I got off the train in Keetmanshoop, the committee that looks after the Jewish affairs welcomed me and allowed me to go into one of the houses of the committee to rest in the afternoon, shower etc. The wind that blew the desert sand penetrated into one's clothes with desert sand all over the place adding to the difficulties of the afternoon.

However, at about 5 o'clock that afternoon the skies began to get cloudy cooling off the whole area as though an umbrella suddenly appeared. The howling wind stopped at about

5 o'clock in the afternoon and both the weather and the general climate became cool and comfortable. My cold and cough suddenly disappeared as though God's hand had something to do with the whole situation.

The climate changed to a very breezy evening that almost every person in the area and further afield who could come to the Shul decided to arrive with the machzorim from about 6.30 pm as the sun sets at about nine o'clock.

I was quite surprised that nobody left the Synagogue either for the kol nidrei night or the whole day of Yom Kippur except before neila. I remember that day as it was the Russian Sputnik that came over Windhoek and before we went back to the Synagogue we were watching it. The dog Laika was on board at the time.

If one is very religious one can say that God put the white cloud over the whole of Keetmanshoop and stopped the wind whining as though it was just switched off, giving everybody the opportunity to come to the Synagogue. My voice came back, my sneezing and coughing ceased almost instantly and I took the service from approximately 7 o'clock Yom Kippur night to about 9.30 the next morning without even feeling the strain.

A very religious person would obviously call it God's hand that all these occurrences such as the stopping of the wind, the light cloud in the sky covering the whole sky and people telling me they had never had a cloudy sky like this for some 50 years and it all happened on Yom Kippur night. It remained like that for almost 30 hours.

So fate has its unusual passages.

Chapter 21 – SIDNEY (1924-1971) AND HARRY (1925-1945) NOCHUMSOHN

There were five Nochumsohn siblings; Sidney born 1924, Harry born 1925, Percy born 1927, Jeanne born 1929 and Judith born 1933. They were all put into the care of the Arcadia in 1937 and left when they had finished their schooling when they were about 17 years old.

Sidney Nochumsohn left the Arc in 1941 at the age of 17 and initially studied and became an accountant. At age 47 he qualified as an advocate. He served on the Arc Committee and was Chairman of Arcadia. Sidney Nochumsohn has three sons all lawyers. His one son lives in Israel and the other two sons live and practice in Johannesburg. Sidney passed away very suddenly at the age of 72 in 1996.

Harry Nochumsohn left the Arc in 1943 at the age of 17 and was killed in action in January 1945 at the age of 19 years. Of all the many Old Arcs who served "up North" he was the lone casualty.

HARRY NOCHUMSOHN'S GRAVE
Written by Michael Perry Kotzen

Harry Nochumsohn

Photo of Harry Nochumsohn's Resting Place

The picture of Harry's resting place in the South African military cemetery in Como, Italy was taken a short time after Harry's death. It was taken by my brother Mannie to send to General Smuts after Smuts had ordered that the Cross be replaced by a Magen David. Mannie and Berny Adler had petitioned Smuts. and Hofmeyer to change the wooden marker when they discovered that poor Harry had been Christianised in death.

The sad story was reported in South African newspapers with considerable praise and credit to both Mannie and Berny.

Today the Como Military cemetery is a vast field of the graves of South African and British Empire soldiers who fell in North Africa and in Italy. Harry's grave is a lone Jewish marker in a sea of crosses.

However there were many other Jewish men who died for king and country. Destined eternally in Christian anonymity.

May our Arc Brother Harry Nochumsohn rest in peace.

LEST WE FORGET

This poem was written by Barney Meyers to honour the memory of Harry Nochumsohn an Arcadian who was killed in action in January 1945 at the age of 19 years. The last two lines refer to the time when Harry Nochumsohn was a prefect at Arcadia.

> *Faithfully, truly, unflinchingly strong.*
> *Didst thou endeavour to uphold the cause*
> *Of righteousness, against the fangs of wrong.*
> *As thou didst plunge into troublesome doors.*
>
> *In sight of victory and glorious peace.*
> *A blow on the undaunted soul befell.*
> *A cursed blow which made thy blood to cease.*
> *And stopp'd that which thou wouldst've done well.*
>
> *O! that thy rest be tranquil as in days*
> *When first we knew thy joyous sounding words.*
> *And may we all recall thy faithful ways*
> *In which the willing deeds did lead the herds.*

The poem was first published in *The Arcadian* in January 1951.

ARMY DAYS

Extract from Arcadia – 90 years of Memories
Editor Solly Farber

In the 1939-1945 War and in the various wars of Israel's struggle for survival, Old Arcs played their part.

During the war years visiting servicemen and women stayed in Arcadia and they were billeted in the hospital for the duration of the High Holy days.

Vicky, who is probably the best know Arcadian of all times, was Regimental Sergeant Major in the Air Force at Roberts Heights, later called Voortrekkerhoogte.

ROLL OF HONOUR OF ALL ARCADIANS WHO SERVED IN WORLD WAR II.

Here is the Roll of Honour of all Arcadians who served in World War II. For many years the plaque and the photo of Harry Nochumsohn hung in the main dinning room at Arcadia.

Old Arcs on Army leave attend High Holy Day
Festival Services at Arcadia

SOUTH AFRICAN
JEWISH ORPHANAGE

ON ACTIVE SERVICE

Barlin H	Goodt J	Landsman H	Rosengarten M	Cowen Ruth
Bernard N	Green D	Landsman W	Rubenstein M	Cohen L
Barlin B	Goldsmith S	Landsman M	Roden M	
Bushkin A	Grevler H	Lockitz W	Robinson A	Klevansky Bertha
Bernard M	Grevler I	Lurie M	Robinson D	Kotzen Ethel
Bushkin J	Greenberg J	Levitt M		Kotzen Fieda
		Levitt B	Smith T	
Cohen S	Harris H	Levitt H	Smith B	Levine Minnie
Cohen H	Harris Henry	Levitt R	Shain H	Levine Edith
Cohen J	Hellman B	Lipman S	Sagoria E	
Cornick I		Levi A	Steiner C	Michelow Mollie
	James A		Sullivan L	
Edelman H	Jacobson M	Mendelsohn A	Starkowitz A	Newman Sophie
Echowitz H	Jacobson H	Maisnik R	Slater M	
Engelman J		Mafcher A	Sacks M	Ostrowick Sylvia
	Kotzen M	Mussman I	Slavin C	
Friedlander L	Kotzen R	Meyers P		Potash Pearl
Friedlander B	Kotzen L	Meyers S	Wulfsohn M	Pearlman Hannah
	Kotzen M	Mogrobi J	Wulfsohn Mark	
Goodman H	Katz S		Wilson L	Rubinowitz Eve
Goodman J	Kobrin M	Nerwich A	Wolchuk L	Rubinowitz Sylvia
Goldman J	Kobrin H	Nerwich B	Woolf J	
Gellman M	Kemp P	Nerwich L	Woolf S	
Goldstein M	Klevansky H	Nauren L	Woolf L	
	Klevansky S	Nauren C		
		Nochumsohn H		
		Nickolaaff L		
		Nicholaaff I		

South African Jewish Orphanage — On Active Service (Roll of Honour plaque)

Chapter 22 – EPHRAIM SEGAL (EFFIE) (1925)

Effie came to Arcadia in February 1931 as a six year old, spent a year in the babies, five years in the juniors, and five years in the seniors and left in February 1942.

His father came to South Africa in about 1908 and was naturalised in 1913. He went back to Lithuania in the early 1920s, got married there and brought his wife back to South Africa.

This picture was taken by my father when I was about 17. He was a street photographer at the zoo gate after he had lost his shop in Bedfordview, which was set on fire by a burglar upsetting a candle. The shop was not insured. I don't think he was still there when the Farber family spent the day out at the zoo (but might have been).

BEFORE COMING TO THE ARC

My mother died when I was 3½ years old and my father, who was running a shop at the diamond diggings near Lichtenburg, put me in the care of a neighbour, Mrs Hope, in Doornfontein. There my mother and I had stayed as there were no houses at the shifting sites of the diamond diggings. After about a year and a half I found myself on the diggings helping out in my dad's shop and was then put in the care of an Afrikaans farmer in the district. Here I helped cut the wheat with a sickle and tie the sheaves.

Hereafter we went by ox-wagon on a two day journey to the nearest town, stopping overnight at a friendly farmer's place with a prickly pear plantation. I was given a prickly pear which I promptly put in my mouth, thistles and all. Luckily butter was a known remedy to remove the thistles. We encamped in the town square and went to the *Nagmaal* church service. I could not understand a word the preacher said but was impressed by his strong voice.

After this I stayed with a cousin in Ventersdorp. My memories there were of a clear water stream (maybe the Schoonspruit for bottled water) and seeing a film in the town hall with Al Jolson – perhaps the first talkie film ever.

I was then taken by lorry to Johannesburg, where I was loaded on to a rickshaw with a suitcase and taken to another cousin in Doornfontein. How the rickshaw runner found the place is a mystery. He must have asked people where to go.

My next memory is of being in the bus going down bluegum lined Oxford Road and then in the baby department upstairs of the main building on the side nearest the boys department, later the Shul. The place echoed and re-echoed to the sounds of the children which was absolutely strange to a child who had been alone before with almost no contact with other children. In tears I went to a balcony overlooking the lawn and was immediately impressed by the lush vegetation and trees of Arcadia and the suburbs and open country beyond. Before that I had known

Young Effie Segal

only the dryness of Doornfontein and the flat veldt of the Western Transvaal. This was like a paradise.

I came in February 1931 aged six, next came "Ginger" Max Ladier in March, Ivan Kurland in April, Isaac Grevler with younger brothers Hymie and Jackie.

EARLY ARC MEMORIES

Initially all the children stayed in the one building as bought from Lady Philips.

The girls and babies were upstairs in the main building and the boys in the old ballroom – now the Shul – and the quadrangle round the fishpond in front of the Shul. The open parts of the quadrangle were blocked off by blinds or boards for protection from the weather. The Shul was in the library. How we could all get in is a mystery.

However within a few months of my arrival the Joe Lewis wing was ready, so the junior boys and we babies moved into the new building. The tennis courts were also built in that year as I saw from the hospital when I had mumps.

Whenever there was an epidemic of children's diseases I always caught them. The worst was the measles, which filled the hospital with juniors. In our ward, to fill in time, we played I spy with my little eye something beginning with....... After we had exhausted all the objects in the ward we started more difficult ones requiring two letters. Mickey Gordon had us all baffled with his words beginning with F.G. Eventually we gave up. His answer was "Fick Glass".

The two Kaufman sisters looked after the babies in those days. The matron, Mrs Shaer, took a lot of interest in the babies. We also had an elocution teacher, Miss Kay, and a senior girl, Leah Meltzer helped organise games for us.

The grounds were still landscaped and planted with many varieties of trees and shrubs with scenic walks both up and down the hills where the babies were taken for walks. The two orchards were never given a chance to supply fruit for the home as the kids raided them before the fruit had a chance to ripen, except once because we were away in a holiday camp in Port Elizabeth in the school holiday of Dec/Jan of 1934/5.

When we returned home we used to pick a bunch of grapes from the pergola above the walk-way of the lower orchard on our way back from Forest Town School in the afternoon. I was promoted to the junior boys but was considered too small to go to a camp in Standerton where all the boys spent the school holidays. However I was taken to a filmed pantomime "Puss in Boots" at the Carlton Bioscope and also taken to the Zoo Lake swimming bath in the care of two senior girls who ducked me in the water and probably put me off swimming for a long time.

In the Junior Boys it was important to know who was the strongest. The strongest juniors were Solomon Wigeson and Colly Noran and the strongest seniors were Levi Woolf, Basil Levett, Vicky Klevansky and Solly Nankin.

The juniors' nurse was Jossie le Roux assisted by senior boy Hymie Wolchuck (Chuck). We felt they were tyrants. Chuck looked after us for less than two years but it felt like centuries. Jossie le Roux had an infallible method of punishing the boy who would not own up to peeing on the floor in the lavatory. She lined us up in the passage and we had to hold out our hands. She then hit every hand with a stick from one end of the line to the other. As she hit so the kids started crying till the crying chorus was in full spate in the whole line. I never cried from pain; only if my feelings were upset.

Lights out at night was always 8.00 pm but some of the boys used to fall asleep before then. One of them was Philly Kemp. One night Chuck played a trick on him. He shouted "up, up" to wake him (Philly) as he did every morning at 6.00 am. Philly got up and started making his bed while we all watched in astonishment. We didn't see it as a joke as Chuck intended.

The oppression the Junior Boys felt under Jossie and Chuck I feel was more a verbal than a physical thing. But the Senior Boys had a real problem in the shape of a reform school type martinet, a man of strength and a loud voice, a Mr Swanepoel. I assume he used physical punishment because the boys eventually revolted. They gathered up the hill and refused to come down until he was removed from his post. In this they succeeded.

Usually we juniors were quite content. We played from morning to night. At school we played soccer with a tennis ball on at least two grounds, before school, small break and big break. When we came home, after tea – more soccer before Hebrew lessons (cheder) and after cheder.

Then we had our baths, played marbles or pips (apricot season) in the passage till suppertime. We also played wicket with tennis balls (take out go in) hide and seek, kicking the milk tin, cowboys and crooks. (As cowboys we took the names of famous film stars. Mannie Rodin always wanted to be Buck Jones, so that became his nickname for the rest of his short life). We explored up and down the hills, picked the wild fruit in season, *steenvrugte, mispels* and wild peaches. At school we also played horsey.

If we had money we used to buy sweets from "Okey" who used to come with about four varieties of wonderful penny sweets to Arcadia every weekday afternoon. How he could make a living from us kids is a mystery. We had very little money, most of the time not at all. A couple of juniors used to sometimes bunk out to the zoo to buy sweets. Invariably they were caught because Goldie Cohn, a committeeman, lived in Forest Town in Cowie Road, just off Rannoch Road, always seemed to be on the watch and reported them. How he could identify them is a mystery. My guess is he phoned the home and a reception awaited them on the way back. This was in 1933/4.

RANNOCH ROAD SCHOOL

Most of the primary school kids of Arcadia in the early 1930's went to Forest Town School, Rannoch Road down the road from Arcadia.

A few incidents come to mind; In grade 1 at Forest Town School our teacher, Mrs Brotherhood, asked us to spell feather. Isaac Grevler knew how and was immediately promoted to Grade 2. On another occasion the teacher asked who had done something, about which I knew nothing, but for some strange reason I also owned up to. I got two cuts with a stick, which taught me never to own up to anything again.

The class ahead of me, Std 3, had a sharp-nosed teacher, Miss Coetzee, who seemed to smell every silent fart let off in the class. Her expression of disgust never varied. I always felt that the polony sandwiches, which we enjoyed every Friday, were stopped because of her complaints. I think this teacher had left the school. Perhaps she had got a compassionate transfer as a gas victim of the class war.

In Std 5 we had a teacher, Mr Jacobs (Jakey), who had a certain sense of humour but not of the kind to appreciate the puerile efforts of my special friend Ivan Kurland, who tried to be a bit of a humorist. There used to be an expression: between me and the lamppost I don't know. When we were asked where does the lion live, Ivan said in a lamppost, short cutting the expression. Jakey, all serious, took Ivan to the window, pointed to a lamppost and asked if he could see a lion there. On another occasion when the phone rang in the office, Ivan said he'll take it, as we were not used to the phone it was quite a new experience for us to speak on the phone. Jakey followed him and instead of taking the call immediately rushed back to tell the class, "the idiot is speaking through the earpiece".

Because of these incidents and possibly others, Jakey was probably prejudiced against allowing Ivan to go to high school; so Ivan had to go to Jewish Government in Std 6 before rejoining us in Form 2 in Parktown Boys High. Here he also got into trouble because of his misplaced sense of humour. We were obliged to stand up if the headmaster, Mr Druce (Dux) walked into the classroom (as a sign of respect). One day Pinky Yates our maths master walked in to our Latin class taken by Bull Smith and Ivan stood up as if for the headmaster. Pinky who had no sense of humour was annoyed and asked Bull Smith if he could talk to Ivan. He then ranted and raved for quite a few minutes until Ivan was in tears. Strange to say, in later years Pinky did become headmaster. He was a good maths teacher but I doubt his headmastership.

Ivan Kurland, son of Latvian Jewish parents, is married to Doris, daughter of Lithuanian Jewish parents, who have fourth daughters, the second oldest Vickie (Victoria) is teaching Spanish dancing (Flamenco etc) to Spaniards in the south of Spain near Cady – Andalusia the home of Flamenco. Vickie is married to a Spanish dancer. So is tradition maintained! Ivan and Doris are living in retirement with this daughter.

REMEMBERING FELLOW ARCS AND EVENTS

Vicky, as cubmaster, used to end each meeting with a yarn, including some of the cubs as characters in the adventure. As we scouts and adults passed by, we also stopped to listen and when he said he would continue next week the cubs were not the only ones to show dismay with "Ah Vicky!"

Vicky was the spark that kept things alight at the 1938/9 camp in Port Elizabeth. Every morning we had to fold up our beds and smooth the sand floors of our tents. Louis Bayer who was in our tent also initiated clearing away leaves and raking paths in the little forest on the edge of our camp. His one big main path was called Louis Bayer Avenue. On one of the windy days – a P.E. special – a cricket match was arranged against a local team. The wind was so strong it blew the matting wicket away, so we played on the concrete base. I remember one ball hit to mid-off was blown back and caught in the slips. When I batted I was bowled first ball because the wind pressure on my bat slowed my shot resulting in my being too late to hit the ball. I like good excuses for making a duck.

If you managed to get some photographs of the 1934 camp in Port Elizabeth you might have seen one snap of the junior boys playing cricket in their pyjama jackets and khaki shorts. We all

had such painful sunburn that we could only tolerate the softness of the pyjama material.

Louis, Solly Bayer's older brother was a complete individualist. In the Arc bus he used to read a boy's magazine, The Hotspur, giggling quite oblivious of the others in the bus. I don't think he ever joined in to play soccer or cricket etc, but he was a great swimmer. He swam 400 lengths in the Arc pool at a good pace doing the crawl all the way. When we went for a picnic to Germiston lake he immediately donned his swimming costume and swam across the lake and back. When he left Arcadia we never heard from him again. I think he even cut himself off from his brother. He might have become a ship's engineer.

Michael Kotzen was an entertainer even as a small boy. About four of us used to sit round his bed after lights out and listen to the story of a film he had seen. In the early hours of the morning we had a different form of entertainment as we listened to the lions roaring in the zoo.

We played marbles, if available, nuts over Pesach and with apricot pips in season. One year Erwin Badler (Bradler?) a fairly new boy might have lost the few pips he had but was very keen to get back into the game so he begged for just one pip. "Give me jou pip, just von pip" he pleaded but in vain. What he did get was a nickname – Von Pip. He didn't stay long in Arcadia but I believe he became a judo expert. So mockers beware!

Other boys came to Arcadia with their nicknames – Boykie Cohen, Pickles Robinson, Herring (Harry), Latkes (Sidney) and Peachy (Percy) – the three Nochumsohn brothers, Klugg, Kiewiet and Handsman.

The best sportsman in the juniors was Sambo Manaschewitz, a crackshot in marbles, fast bowler (yorkers and full tosses), smashing batsman and a good dribbler in soccer. When we played in the Yeoville Sunday soccer league he was the captain of the team ("Old Arcs"). We usually won all matches and the league but one year we were beaten by a team in which one of the stars was Aaron Kapp, also an old Arcadian.

Here are two snippets from later life in the Senior Boys:

"You think this is teaspoon tea?" Harry Nochy to the chap who didn't fill his cup to the brim.

There was a popular dance in which one sang at the same time called "The Lambeth Walk". It went as follows:

Any evening any day, when you go down Lambeth's way you'll find them all doing the Lambeth Walk.

The Senior Boys' version was: You'll find them all Karp, Rodin, Saul."

Alec Saul the sole survivor can confirm.

Issy Nicholaef mentioned by Eli was Issy Lipschitz (Little Lippy) – his brother Sam was Big Lippy. Issy was adopted by an uncle who was a musician and so the name change. He, Issy, learned to play the harmonica from music and once played at a concert given in Arcadia by he old boys.

A friend of Little Lippy was Little Pip (Alex Nervitz) (Big Pip – Sam Nervitz; Sister Fanny Pip). Fanny who was deaf used to sing a song at every concert. She must have learned it when very young before she became deaf; similarly with her talking.

A story, not confirmed by me, that Little Lippy, a bigger senior boy, was playing chess with Max Rosenfeld, a small senior boy. When it seemed that Max was winning, Little Lippy gave a look at Little Pip who then walked past upsetting the chess board 'accidentally' with profuse apologies. Little Lippy said not to worry as he remembered where the pieces were placed but then failed in his attempts to put them back.

I knew Alec Mendelsohn as a brilliant classical scholar who to the dismay of 'Daisy Wallis' the classics master at Parktown Boys High, took up accountancy or similar. Strange to say, Daisy himself became secretary of the Black Cat Peanut Butter subsidiary of Tiger Oats, because he felt badly treated re promotion by the school authorities. Alec was an enthusiastic soccer player and controlled play as an energetic and attacking centre half. He must have been one of the hungry Arcs as his non-complimentary nickname 'Alec Guts' implies. I remember him as being friendly enough to teach me to sing my Barmitzvah portion of the Torah.

(Maybe you are mixing Alec with his brother Isadore (Sonny)?)

Although we were not "demeaned" by wearing different clothing at school, we nevertheless kept separate to a certain extent during the school breaks by sitting in the *'jiffeuage'* [orphanage] corner on the steps of the far side of the gymnasium. In our class in Form 2 our Latin Master Bull Smith used us as a good example to one or two slack ones in the class, eg that we made our beds, polished our shoes etc. In the class there were five of us, Max Ladier (Ginger), Morris Bernard (Toots), Bernard Barlin (Bunny), Ivan Kurland and Ephraim Segal (Effie). With the exception of Ivan, who was in Jewish Government School in Standard 6 and Ginger who left school after Form 3, we were all in the same class from Grade 1 to matric. The last time I heard we were in the following countries; Canada – Bunny, Spain – Ivan, Australia – Toots, and South Africa – Ginger and Effie.

I wonder how many old Arcs still make their beds when they get up in the morning. Sometimes when I battle to make the bed as tidy and straight as I would like, I think of Bunny who in the junior boys, got a prize for making the neatest bed. We were also invited to one of our close mates' Barmitzvah party at his home in Saxonwold. All I remember was someone playing badminton on the lawn. I have no memory of refreshments or anything else.

Myer Rabinowitz married Tillie Aires, also an old Arc. We have been friends ever since. For about 30 years I was invited every Pesach Seder and Rosh Hashanah to their home in Victory Park. For the last two years they have lived in Baltimore, USA near their two younger daughters' families.

BARNEY SMITH

Thank you once again for the regular supply of Arc news and email letters. You asked in one of them re Barney Smith. I think it was Freda Cheilyk who told you that the Smith brothers shuttled between Meyerton College and Arcadia. I was not

aware of this as I thought that they were in Arcadia all the time since they arrived, but as they were a bit younger than me, I did not keep track of them most of the time. Hearing about Barney working as a stoker on a ship to work his passage surprised me as he always struck me as living on his wits and definitely not the hard labour route.

He once ran a modelling agency where he probably offered to train would-be models. Obviously young girls thought of modelling as a glamour job, and one of these was the daughter of Sir Francis De Ginguard who came to South Africa to manage the Raleigh Cycle Factory in Springs. When Sir Francis heard of his daughter's antics he gave Barney a real military dressing down, reminiscent of a cross sergeant major, for daring to demean his upper class family. Incidentally Sir Francis was General Montgomery's Chief of Staff during the war.

ISSY LIPSCHITZ, HARRY KOBRIN, WOLF LANDSMAN AND MORRIS RING

You asked about pupils at Jewish Government School, known to Les Meyerowitz 1933 to 1935, namely Morris Ring, Wolf Landsman, Harry Kobrin and Issy Lipschitz. They were all younger Senior Boys when I was still in the juniors; so the contact and knowledge of them was limited.

Issy Lipschitz, who was adopted by his uncle and changed his name to Nicholaef was the friend of Eli Zagoria. I wrote about him before. Morris Ring had a younger brother David who was my contemporary in the babies. Their mother remarried and took the boys out of Arcadia. They changed their names to Slater. Morris later went into business as a caterer. His slogan on his vehicles was 'Cater with Slater'. David used to work in the 'rag' trade; material wholesalers and clothing factories. I saw him a few times in the area but I never asked him precisely where he worked.

Wolf Landsman nickname Kloggo, was the older of twin brothers in Arcadia, the younger brother's nickname, Kiewiet. As one can guess these were the sons of a farmer - who grew potatoes in the Zeerust district - hence the Afrikaans nicknames. Wolf was quite a friend of mine later on. After Shul on Saturday mornings he always picked me to be his opening partner for the cricket at which he was a good batsman and bowler. Also, as was custom that two boys shared a bath, sometimes on an afternoon we sang all the songs we knew as our bathroom entertainment. He was a clever boy, his classmates used to copy his maths homework; also he was not beyond a few sly tricks. When bowling in cricket he sometimes burst out laughing - my assumption was that he threw instead of bowling. In penny penny he 'spun' the coins in such a way that the coins wobbled as if they were turning but always kept the same side up that he had called. I think he became a tradesman after leaving Arcadia. He was too clever to join his brothers when they started a furniture factory - Landsman Brothers, which eventually folded.

Harry Kobrin was the older brother of Mark. He must have had a quick temper because one day he punched Cop Harary who punched back and a fight resulted. Stompy Shaer came on the scene - saw what was going on smiled and walked away. That was all I knew of the matter.

The last I heard of Harry Kobrin was that he lived in Cape Town. His brother Mark was a year ahead of me in school, a contemporary of Solly Meyers, Morris Hurwitz and Sarah [Soika] Pearlman. In his matric year, Mark got a winding gramophone and some terrific records - a tribute to the good taste of the donor, maybe Harvey - which I for one appreciated to the full. Mark was a quiet and pleasant character. He had the best freestyle swimming style and probably the fastest swimmer in the Arc. He settled in business in Welkom as did another Old Arc, Freddy Fuchs. Bertha Klevansky was probably another contemporary of Mark.

Hymie Landsman [Kiewiet] and his friend Lionel Lipman didn't feature much on the soccer field, but in dormitory soccer they were tops. [A sport in which I had the dubious distinction of breaking a window by kicking too high for a goal - a pair of socks the ball.]

EFFIE THE HARMONICADIAN

In 1938 we were all assembled in the committee room to hear two Jewish entertainers 'Afrique' and Larry Adler, but first, lo and behold, the first harmonica band in Arcadia played to us, who never knew they even existed. Larry Adler, as always, asked bandsman to play a solo. Bobby Friedlander said he wanted to play 'Tippy, Tippy Tin' but did not know it all and

Adler said 'Then just play Tippy'. I remember the four members of the band were Abie Levy, Bobby Friedlander, Alex Kaplan and Mannie Rodin and possibly one other? Abie and Bobby proved later on to be good musicians.

Effie taught the harmonica at the Arc for many years.

The "Harmonicadians'- Selwyn Dembo, Donald Goldman, Effie Segal, Solly Farber, Charles Segal and David Kotzen.

Gershon Rochlin Donald Goldman and Effie Segal.

EFFIE THE LIMERICK KING

Michael Perry Kotzen writes "Effie was the uncrowned limerick king during the great limerick epidemic of the 1950s." and Dave Spector writes "By the way, Effie Segal is a talented writer of 'limericks' which would be appreciated by your readers. I suggest that you invite him to furnish you with his talent."

Effie has sent us these two modern day limericks;

> *The Wizard of Wanneroo*
> *King of the Koala and Kangaroo*
> *is collecting the Arc story*
> *Sometimes of love and glory*
> *and sometimes of pure ballyhoo*
>
> *The Old Arcs, cobber from Wanneroo*
> *Has now become a jackaroo* [1]
> *Fast on his pony, not to be late*
> *To the outback for a dinner date*
> *With his latest jillaroo* [2]

(1)   Cowboy
(2)   Lady Cowboy, Cowperson, personaroo?

After leaving the Arc I then went to Wits University to study engineering in which I was a hopeless failure and definitely not suited to the profession. Subsequently I worked in various wholesale and retail firms and gradually got interested in the stock exchange as a means to independence on retirement from work.

In 1973 I semi-retired by working half day while building confidence on the stock exchange as I had relatively little to live on, no pension or medical aid. In 1976 I took the plunge to retire full time, treating the stock exchange as a regular mornings work, in one of the cafes of Hillbrow. The afternoons were for shopping, visiting, tennis or sleeping. At last I found what I was most suited for – a full time loafer. At one stage I depended for living expenses on bank overdraft.

In 1987/88 the interest rate rose to 25%, compounded monthly this was about 32% per annum. So in 1990 I took a job in a men's outfitter at age 65 – a good age to start working – and in 1994 retired again as the stock exchange was again coming to life and I had learned a good lesson. Being single, my troubles were not inflicted on any family members.

I still stay in a flat in the Joubert Park area where I have been for over 40 years. Hymie Lurie, another ex-Arc, has probably been here even longer than I. We are probably the only Old Arcs in the area and probably the only Jews. In my building I am the only white. In most buildings in the area as well as

Hillbrow, Town, parts of Berea, only blacks stay; so I don't have to travel to see how a third world people are gradually and often rapidly, transforming to first world attitudes and status.

Effie now retired

Chapter 23 – MABEL BRITTANY (GOLDSMITH) (1927)

Mabel was born on the 14th January 1927 in Germiston, a gold mining town just outside Johannesburg.

Ten days after giving birth to Mabel her mother, Anne Sino, aged 27, died of septicaemia. The poison had also gone through Mabel leaving her very ill and fighting for survival.

Initially, Mabel and her brother Stan, who was three years her senior, were looked after by their maternal grandmother and then by their Aunt Jenny and Uncle Harrold Hoffman who also had four children of their own. Mabel was very ill and it was touch and go between life and death and she was nursed back to health with the care of her family.

After the children had lived a relatively peaceful two years in Brakpan in the care of their relatives, they had a very unhappy year going backward and forward between these kindly relatives and their Dad who had remarried.

There was a tug of war over the children between the relatives who wanted to adopt the children and their father who was not able to properly look after the children.

After this very unhappy period it was decided that the children would be better off in the care of the orphanage and an application was made to the South African Jewish Orphanage.

Mabel and Stan had a very traumatic time prior to coming to Arcadia. The following is Mabel's recollection of her life in Arcadia where she lived from 1930 to 1941.

IN THE BABIES

The mansion Arcadia had once belonged to Sir Lionel and Lady Phillips. When purchased in 1922, it was altered to accommodate about 121 orphan children. The entrance was very impressive. Big gates led into a long gravel driveway with tall, impressive gum trees gracing its sides, intermingled with jacarandas which covered the road with a violet carpet, every spring, which was a very inspiring sight. At the top of the driveway was the entrance to this stately mansion. The institution was commonly known as "Arcadia", but nicknamed 'The Arc' by the children.

The year was 1930 when my brother Stan and I were taken to the orphanage. I was now three and a half and my brother Stan seven years old. The depression was felt by many families. Life had become very difficult, and people were starving. The orphanage now referred to as "Arcadia", had close to 270 children. Very few were orphans, but there were many children from one parent families who needed help. In some instances there were as many as six to eight children from the one family, who would be part orphans with only the one parent alive, or when one parent would be very ill, and the other unable to take on the responsibility of running the home. Most were families of

Mabel at age 8

two, three, or four children. This was an era when it was regarded a disgrace for parents to divorce, therefore very few children were from divorced families.

When we arrived, my brother was taken to the Junior Boys, whose aged ranged from six years to 12 years. I was to be put into the Babies' Section which housed boys and girls up to the age of six years. As I was being taken from my aunt Jenny and given to the nurse in charge I started screaming and holding onto her.

"Don't leave me", I cried. "I'm afraid." Clinging harder, holding tighter, screaming louder, with fears returning of being locked up again. The nurse kept trying to pull me loose. My Aunt gently loosened my grip on her. Wiping the tears from her eyes, she quickly made her escape, completely heartbroken, as she could not handle the situation.

Here I was once again thrown into a situation I did not understand. The only feeling I had was the fear of the unknown, returning and engulfing me again.

No Mother to love, hold me and say, "My darling baby, don't cry I'm here with you."

Mother would kiss all my tears away and with the loving warmth of her arms would enfold me with her security, but alas, this was not to be. The turmoil was overwhelming me. Eventually, exhausted from sobbing, I fell asleep.

The Babies' dormitory normally consisted of 30 babies. In my age group I was the smallest and youngest. There were also about 50 junior girls, ages between six and 12 years, and about 60 Senior Girls aged from 12 to 18 years. The Boys' Section, other than the babies, was split in a similar way as the girls. Several of the older senior girls used to assist the nurse with the babies. They would bath, dress and feed the very small ones, help to teach the bigger babies how to do everything for themselves, and in the evenings, put us to bed. Most of the babies of my age were partly independent, but I certainly needed help as already the trauma of the past three years had taken its toll. Eventually I would be taught to become independent.

The first few nights I was terrified, there were no lights and no familiar faces. I was afraid of the dark. The other babies had in their own ways, learnt to accept their position with all the attached insecurities. I still had to learn acceptance. Every time I fell asleep I would have nightmares, and wake up in a state of panic.

"Help me, help me!"

All my screams would be unheeded, whether I screamed aloud or in my dreams.

No mother came to hold me in her arms, rock me, soothe my fears and gently whisper to me. "Don't cry my baby, we will chase those nasty bad dreams away, no harm will come to you. Do you think I would let anything hurt you?" She would then rock me off to sleep, kiss my brow and put me back into my cot.

Instead, I would once again cry within myself, then I would go back into a restless sleep, only to find myself in the same position the next night. Eventually learning that you did not cry aloud because you would wake the other babies. I would have to learn how to cope with situations. Survival became the name of the game.

Arcadia was only about a half an hour's walk away, from the zoo. Many a night I would hear the roar of the lions, which would wake me up in a panic. I did not understand these strange noises which were causing me further nightmares. When it was explained to me about the strange sounds coming from the zoo, I slowly overcame my fear of noises.

My nightmares remained part of my life and, together with walking in my sleep, were to be part of my insecurity for many years. Eventually I would, many years later, learn to overcome some of my insecurities.

I started to grow up in a world where there was no love nor understanding, though many restrictions. I did have a home, sufficient food and clothing, whereas during the depression years, many children did have loving parents, though very little

else. My first year in the orphanage taught me to become fairly independent. I could now feed, dress and help myself.

Whenever I was hurt, bleeding and trembling with fear, there would be no mother to pick me up, to carefully wipe my tears and wash the blood away, then gently allay my fears with. "You are such a brave little girl," holding me so close that I would not feel afraid.

This was never to be. I would pick myself up and there would be no sympathy other than the tormenting of another child who would laughingly shout. "Cry, baby cry." Instead panic started building so that by the time I arrived at the hospital section, I would be in a state of anxiety and apprehension. Even though the nurse would feel sympathy for the babies that had hurt themselves, she was always too busy to do more. By the time you had been treated and left the hospital, you would feel very sorry for yourself.

I was to be at a disadvantage because of my size, and remained all my years in the orphanage, the smallest of the babies and the Junior girls. I would often be excluded from outings or games, with the following comments. "Oh, you're too small to come with us," or "You will never be able to keep up the pace."

This only added further, to my frustration and insecurities, for now I had found the girls who were to be my playmates, in particular Martha and Jill who were around my age, but both were very tall girls.

I do not recall many incidents in my three years as a 'baby' in the orphanage, but I vaguely remember that this was the beginning of the regimental training of my life. Whenever we had to go anywhere or do anything as a group, we would first have to line up from the smallest to the tallest. Being the smallest I had to be first to lead, holding hands with the girl next to me, and the rest would follow. Whenever any visitors from the committee came to see the Baby Section, I would always be the first approached. It became automatic for me to keep my head down hoping no one would notice me, but to no avail. I would be asked to recite a nursery rhyme.

"Mary had a little lamb," I would mumble under my breath. This was never heard. Then I would be patted condescendingly by the lady, who wanted to know if such a small child was clever. Besides being afraid and insecure, I had now become self-conscious of my size.

"Mummy," I would cry within. "What do I do?" Instead, once again I would only withdraw further into myself.

Boys will be boys and when one of the younger junior boys and his friends got hold of some matches, they would go down to the bottom of the orphanage hill, and light a fire. You would then hear shouts and screaming. "There's a fire, there's a fire!"

There would be lots of excitement. Bigger boys could be seen running and scrambling to get hold of tree branches, then start trying to beat the fire out. This happened several times a year, so they became quite efficient in handling the fires. There would be no need to call the fire brigade. When the culprits were caught and punishment meted out, the person responsible never lit a fire again. This did not stop the fires, as there was always someone else to experiment with matches.

The fires added further fears and nightmares to my already overloaded insecurities, as the Baby Department was on top of the hill, which seemed to me to be always in danger of fires, whether they were small or large.

What would happen if everything was burnt? Where could I go? My small brain would ponder. I'll get burnt, how do I handle this?" I cried within, very confused.

Regrettably, there was nobody to explain to me that I was safe. No Mother to reassuringly tell me that no harm would come to me. Years later when the bushes and trees were cut down, and there were no more fires, my nightmares about a fire stopped. I was always to remain sensitive about fires.

Our meals, bathing and bedtime were always at the same time. You could tell the time by what we were doing. I had been given a bed to sleep in, as my cot was needed for other younger babies who had arrived at the home. Some of my playmates were reaching six years old and were to be transferred to the Junior Girls. Once you went up to the Junior section you did not associated with the babies as you were a big girl, but this did not matter because there were always other playmates.

Once again I found myself being left out on account of my size. I can recall being very upset, that Mary who was my age, and Jill, who was at least six months younger than me, had become junior girls several months before I did. If I had had the courage to approach the nurse and ask. "Why has Jill become a junior girl before me? I am older than her," I would probably have received a very curt reply. "She is bigger than you and that makes her more capable." This meant that, because she was very much taller, she could cope better and could accomplish anything, whereas small girls could not. This taught me at a very early age, that size mattered. I would always be at a disadvantage, and would subconsciously learn to have the strength within, and become both a fighter and a survivor.

IN THE JUNIOR GIRLS

I turned six and six months later I became a Junior Girl.

The Junior Girl's section was in the upstairs wing of the main building. The panorama you saw was amazing, as you could see the unspoiled hills in the distance, as well as the undeveloped part of the area, which at this stage, still belonged to nature. In fact on a clear day you could see the outline of the zoo.

This was a wonderful day for me as I would no longer be regarded as a baby, and would be with Jill and Martha again. The Senior Girls section was in the same building, but as you were separated, you hardly saw any of the older girls, unless you had a sister that you visited.

We all had to be inoculated against small pox. This was done when you became a Junior Girl. Unfortunately when I had my inoculation it started to itch, scratching the inoculation I developed an infection that had to be treated at the hospital. It took several months to clear and heal. It was understandable that very little was explained, as trial and error were your teachers.

As a Junior Girl you now had added responsibilities. You started to make your own bed, which had been done for you as a baby. You learnt to bath yourself, but this was watched over by either the nurse or a Senior Girl. There would be three girls in one bath, so you were not allowed to play or stay too long, as there were still many more girls to go through the same ritual.

Your program stated at 6.00 a.m. winter or summer. The nurse would come into your dormitory, which consisted of about 30 girls. "Get out of bed, you'd better hurry up!" she would shout out at the door of your dormitory.

One minute later another shout. "You lazy good for nothings, can't you hear me? Hurry up, it's getting late."

Should you not have heard or been quick enough, she would pull down your blankets, and then you would be yanked by the ear out of the bed. If you yelled "Ow!" you only got a further yanking on the ear.

Where was my mother, to come in quietly, shake me lightly, to wake me with "It's time to get up for school. Go and wash quickly, then go and have breakfast." Then gently hurrying me with "You don't want to be late." This thought was an illusion that was never to be.

Freezing cold in winter you learnt very quickly to jump up and make your bed properly, which meant to have neat corners, not just pull the sheet and blanket up. If checked by the nurse and found incorrect, the bed would be stripped right down, to be redone. This could happen once or twice teaching you very quickly to make a bed almost perfectly. You got dressed in your school uniform, rushed into the bathroom, washed your face, cleaned your teeth hurriedly, all the time being reminded with "Hurry up, don't dawdle."

Time was running out so you hurriedly lined up in the corridor. You were taught that punctuality was very important early in life, if you did not want to be punished, you were very quick with whatever had to be done.

In winter you lingered longer in the mornings hoping not to be caught. Somehow, if you were lucky, there would always be someone slower than you, who would always be in trouble.

You would be marched in single file into breakfast. Should you be heard talking to the girl next to you, a hard slap at the back of your head from the nurse with the following "Don't you know you're supposed to be quiet in line? Should I hear any more talking you'll be in big trouble" Since you were afraid of the consequences you would continue to march in silence.

Breakfast consisted of a plate of cooked porridge, bread and butter, and a cup of tea. This was given day in and day out. Many a morning you just found you could not face the same breakfast. Hungry you were, but you could never starve.

Straight after breakfast you were each given two sandwiches for school. Then everyone who was in the Junior School, would line up in the quadrangle for your overall inspection, before you were sent marching off to school. This consisted of having everything checked, for cleanliness and neatness. "Let me see your nails" the nurse would call out.

Then "Ow!". Someone had been wrapped on the knuckles for having long dirty finger nails whereas they should be short and clean.

"Your hair is too long, see that you have it cut," would be the remark made to one of the girls, as you had to have short tidy hair.

Clean and neat navy blue serge gyms for the girls and navy blue pants for the boys, white shirts black shoes and socks, shoes polished like a mirror so that you could see your face in them, heaven help you at inspection if you were found wanting.

A further comment by the nurse who was on duty that day would be. "Why haven't you cleaned your shoes, I suppose you'll tell me that there is no more polish."

"You did not put your gym under your mattress over the weekend" would be another remark. Then punishment, which was always a threat hanging over your head. You developed very early in life the art of being clean, tidy and punctual. Arcadia's very strict daily routine also instilled a great sense of discipline into the youngsters.

Once a month your hair was cut to ear length with a straight fringe. The only noticeable difference was the very straight or very curly hair, which gave some distinctive character to the girl. Hair was also checked for lice, often referred to as nits. Should you possibly be found to have even one nit, through outside contact, or from new arrivals to the orphanage, your hair was shaved, or cut very short. A special oil rubbed in, then hours of having your hair combed with a special fine comb, that scratched and hurt your tender skull. To avoid an epidemic, precautions were always taken.

Girls could be catty and jealous, especially when there were so many together and you were pretty. If you were one of the unfortunate one to have had lice, on top of the humiliation of having your hair shaved, you became very aware of your bareness and ugliness. You were teased with the following remarks. "Doesn't she look ugly? Just like a convict in prison." Or. "She is such a pretty girl, and look at her now. Serves her right. If she would spend less time looking in the mirror she would not have lice."

However, you did have your special friends, who would make you feel better by sympathising with you. "Don't take notice of the others. Our hair will grow very quickly, and you will be just as pretty as you have always been." This, however, did not console her, and she would feel miserable until her hair had grown, and then this episode would be forgotten.

Every Friday morning you would fold your sheets and blankets and air your bed. When you came back from school, you would clean and brush down your gym, then put it neatly under your mattress. This was the natural way of getting out all the creases, without having to iron your gym. You then remade your bed, tucking on top the clean sheet you had been given, and replacing the blanket and a white counterpane covering. Every

bed was identical, making the room always looking neat. With very little effort, on a Monday morning you would have a neat clean gym to wear, which surprisingly had no creases. Just imagine the problem if everyone had to iron their gyms.

Once again no mother to build up your confidence by gently saying. "My goodness, look how capable you are doing everything for yourself."

Carrying your suitcase you started to walk down the hill to school in double file, which seemed to you like hundred of steps. Midway you would pass 'The Cottage,' which was the home of the superintendent of the orphanage, Mr Shaer, who lived there with his wife, and two daughters, Naomi and Rachel. There would be singing, talking and often the boys telling one another jokes. The girls kept together. Occasionally one of the boys, who liked a particular girl, could be seen walking with her. Many a time your ears would be burning with the gossip that you would have overheard. "Do you think he really likes her? He is always making a play for my friend Lily." Someone who was envious would remark. "She could have fancied someone better," would be the reply.

We walked to school whether the weather was below freezing, hot, cold or raining. You became hardened to the elements. In the winter, should you did not have gloves, by the time you arrived at school your fingers and suitcase had to be pried away from each other, vigorously rubbing your fingers and trying to blow warm air from your mouth to warm them up. Some children were luckier than others, as their parent had bought gloves for them. Eventually you would arrive at school still chattering, as there was always so much to tell.

A government school was situated two blocks from the orphanage, which was about a 15 minutes walk. There were many who discussed this phenomenon some decade later in as much as the children were unintentionally protected against the outside world. In a school which catered for 150 children, ten came from private homes and the balance from the orphanage. With a few exceptions, you had no contact with other children. This tended to make you very aware of the difference between yourselves and the private children. It would tell on you in later life.

If only my mother was around to explain to me, why I should not feel any different to any one by telling me. "You never need ever to be ashamed of who, and what you are. You are just as good as anyone else." Regrettably this was not to be.

Sandwiches were jam, cheese or egg every day and occasionally a treat of salami, week in and week out. By the time you had your lunch break the sandwiches would be stale and hard. At times you could not stomach them, so you dumped them in a dustbin on the side of the pavement, which was on the way to school, where an African boy hungrier than you, would take them home, very thankful for something to eat, as he would really be starving. Three times a week at school, you were given a small piece of cheddar cheese and a half a glass of milk, which was subsidised by the government.

You arrived at school and when the bell rang you lined up in the quadrangle for morning prayers, which was always one of the Psalms that had to be learnt by heart. "Let's begin with Psalm

23," called the principal, who always seemed very stern and threatening. In chorus you would hear. "The Lord is my shepherd." By the time I had left primary school, I was to remember at least half a dozen psalms that had been recited at school.

In the classroom there were six rows of desks, one behind the other. Two children shared a desk with its ink-pot holes and a lid that thumped noisily when closed. The teacher's table, which was a large polished one, stood on a raised platform, that nobody touched. You showed a lot of respect for your teachers, or was it fear?

From school, which finished at 2.00 p.m. you did not always go back the way you came. Often you took a short cut scrambling up a steep hill which landed you on top of the lawn so that you would be one of the first girls in the line. A nurse would be on duty. You would help yourself to a cup of tea and piece of fruit, to which you took off the trays. The last few in line would get the measly pieces. Many a time a bigger girl would push in front of the smaller ones while standing in line. When this happened to me I would be annoyed and would try to defend my position. "I got there before you," I would shout. "You think I care?" would be the reply. If she was both older and bigger, I would, in this instance let her get the better of me, knowing that I would not be able to defend myself as I realised I was not match for her. Discretion is the better part of valour. You learnt when, and where not to defend yourself.

Religion became part of your life. You went every Friday night, Saturday morning and evening to the synagogue, which was one of the larger rooms in the main building. Several years later one of the committee members donated a sum of money for the purpose of building a new synagogue, which would be part of the quadrangle. Even the babies would be marched in for half an hour, every Saturday morning. All the different religious holidays were observed.

In the afternoon, after school you would go to Hebrew, to be taught history of the Old Testament, where a special teacher taught you all about your religion. Boys and girls would be together. One year our class had a fairly old teacher. Whether you listened, talked to your friend, played the fool or were teased by the boys sitting at the back of you, made little difference. This teacher could never control the class, and was often laughed at by the boys, who would throw paper pellets at him while he was writing on the board. "Who threw that paper." He would shout. "What paper?" the boys would reply very innocently.

The teacher knew he could never outwit them. Being very clever he simply pretended to ignore the boys. You also had exams once a year, to test what you had learnt, and to enable you to go into a higher class. I personally enjoyed the history and the psalms. After Hebrew you were left to do your homework or play, but nobody bothered or cared. However, your report told its tale.

The one purpose for the Hebrew classes was to prepare the boys for turning 13 years, which meant that the boys had a Barmitzvah and had to learn a portion of Hebrew law. This would be celebrated once a year with a party. Everyone looked forward to this event, as this was the only time a party would be given to all the children. Presents would then be presented to all the boys who had had a Barmitzvah that year. Parties were very rare, and only for exceptional circumstances.

Your evening meal, was at 6.00 p.m. when a bell was rung. If you were late, you could miss your meal. The dining room seated eight children at a table. The girls separate from the boys. Meals were served by the boys or girls who had that particular duty. A different meal each night of the week would be served.

Monday night consisted of soup, cottage pie with a vegetable and sago pudding called frogs eggs. For many years after I had left the orphanage I could never eat sago in any form. There were never any surprises because you knew what you were going to have the same meal every day, week after week. If you did not like any particular meal, you passed it on to one of the girls at your table; as there were always willing takers. Friday night's meal was the only meal already put on the table, which was always fried fish and mashed potatoes. This, to me and to many of the children, was the best meal of the week.

Certain games were made up and only played by the Junior Girls. When you came back from prayers on a Friday night, the girls often played a game called "I opps you." You would be walking down the corridor to the dining room, with one of your friends, who would be at your table. As soon as you entered the room, if she said "I opps you," first, you would have to give her your piece of fried fish. If you said it first, she had to give you hers.

Another game was not walking on the lines that separated the squares in the corridor leading to the dining room. If you did, you forfeited your fish to the friend with whom you played the game. These games were played only by the Junior Girls in the Arc, and were not known to children outside the orphanage. There would be times when you would run into the dining room quickly and change your small piece of fish for a larger one at your table before any of the others saw you. If caught there would be very strong condemnation like "You thief you stole my piece of fish. If I catch you again I will tear you apart." Knowing your reputation could be ruined if caught a second time, you decided not to try again, and accepted pot luck.

By 8.00 pm it was lights out and no talking. Believe me you were afraid of the consequence if caught talking, so you went off to sleep without any sound. Many a night I spoke and screamed in my sleep from a nightmare, one of the girls would wake me saying. "For crying out aloud will you shut up? You're waking us all up."

The next night the shoe would be on the other foot. I would be woken by someone else screaming from a nightmare. Not being bothered to get out of bed, and ignoring the noise, I would try to get back to sleep. I could not help anyway and being the smallest, I did not want to get involved in a fight.

You became very responsible for all that you did. On becoming a junior girl you were given a number that was clearly marked on all your clothing and had to be put neatly into a locker with your number written on top, so that each one kept to their own sizes and shapes. My number was 38. If anything was broken you were taught when you became a Junior Girl at the tender age of six to mend and darn. The older girls would be responsible darning the boys' socks. In the afternoons you would spend what you thought was hours darning and, if not correctly done, the area would be cut away making the hole much larger. You would not be allowed to go to bed until you were finished. It did not take you very long to learn to do all your mending and darning correctly.

I was the smallest and thinnest Junior Girl and often found myself in a position where girls taller, though not necessary older, would start bullying me. One day Pearl, who was always teasing me, started with, "Look how small you are, you're still a baby."

She would taunt me, then start hitting me and pulling my hair. By now I had had all I could take. Boom! Bang! I was into her, hands legs and the rest of little me. I started to hit, scratch and kick her back shouting. "You think because you are bigger than me you can bully me," while every part of me hit back.

I was now becoming very aware that there was nothing wrong with fighting for one's survival, which also taught me self preservation. Pearl landed up in hospital with blood poisoning from my dirty nails, but never again started with me.

Just under seven years, I was the size of a very small and thin four and half year old. As usual this was to my disadvantage. In 1933 the Empire exhibition took place at the show grounds at Milner Park, which was only a few miles from the orphanage, approximately half an hour's quick walk. I was the only junior girl kept back from walking to the exhibition with the following remark from the nurse. You are too small to go with the bigger girls, you would never be able to keep up."

Very unhappy with tears falling down my cheek, I started crying and pleading with her. "Please let me go, I promise I'll keep up." The nurse completely ignored me, which left me with a definite impression that if you were small, you would not be able to cope, and I certainly felt this throughout my young life.

No mother to tell me with gentle understanding, "Size does not matter; it's what's inside that counts."

Instead I was left with the babies for the day, very unhappy with myself, resenting the fact that I was small. When the girls came back and related all the wonderful stories of what they had seen and done, I was made fully aware that small meant missing out.

I had been a junior girl for almost a year when excitement was great. Preparations were being made for everyone for the December holidays which was just a month away. The babies were to remain behind in the orphanage. We were all going to a camp at Port Elizabeth, a coastal town about 800 miles away. It just happened to be where my Aunt Sarah and family lived. A camping spot had been prepared not far from the beach, and further arrangements were made for a special train for all the children.

This was the first time many of us had ever been in a train. Keeping an eye on 270, high spirited children, was the headache of those who were in control, consisting of nurses, a few committee members who had volunteered to help, and several older senior boys and girls. The coaches were split between the girls and the boys. There being one senior girl or boy in charge of each junior compartment.

One special task was to see that no-one got off at the different stations, unless permission had been granted. A few boys did get off the train at one of the stations without permission, and almost missed the train. Their punishment was, that whenever we stopped at a station, they were not allowed to leave the compartment. By the time we arrived after two and a half days and two nights travelling, the seniors and nurses who were in charge of controlling the children, were all mental wrecks, thankful that not too many emergencies had occurred. I'm sure they must have vowed to themselves. "Never again!"

For most of the children this was the first time they had ever seen the sea. The first time they went into the sea was a wonderful experience with all the excitement and "Oohs! Ahs!" which expressed how they felt.

A few of the younger boys would creep up on the girls and shout to one another. "Let us pull them under the water." The girls would be too quick for them shouting to one another. "Watch out! The boys want to duck us under the water." There would be lots of splashing, shouting, jumping around, between the girls and boys. The mornings would be for swimming in the sea. Early afternoons for resting, then later on, lots of fun and games.

Stan and I had an added privilege as my Aunt Sarah and family lived in Port Elizabeth. Arrangements were made several times for them to take us out. After having been made a fuss of and given lots of sweets, we were sorry to return to the camp.

Theresa, one of the older junior girls, was bitten by a scorpion, which created a lot of fear in us, as she landed in hospital, fortunately she soon recovered, her mishap was forgotten in a couple of days with the wonders of all our new experiences. This holiday was to be remembered by all the children and organisers of the camp.

There were to be changes in the orphanage and it was decided to split the junior girls from the seniors, as there were now close to 300 children. A new wing at the bottom of the playground was to be built onto the Babies' wing, combining the babies' and Junior Girls' section. The Joe Lewis wing was donated by his wife, and was to be known as the Babies and Junior Girls wing when it was completed. There was lots of excitement as we were going to be independent from the seniors.

Responsibilities were very significant in our lives. Every one of us had duties to perform. The general running of the home was done by the children and the following were only some of the duties that had to be attended to. Keeping the dormitories neat and clean, setting the tables, serving up the food, helping in the baby department, assisting in the kitchen, making sandwiches, and many more. The boys had other responsibilities, such as looking after the gardens, sweeping after meals and attending to their own section.

Once a month a list of your duties was called out by the nurse through your number that had been allocated when you first became a Junior. We would assemble in the main room, where the nurse would start calling out the numbers and the duty assigned to you for that month. You then waited in anticipation to know whether you had, what we called, a good or a horrible duty. You were not allowed to change your duty with anyone whether you liked it or not.

You often heard the following comments. "Oh no, not that one!" Or, "You're lucky, sandwiches."

This particular duty was regarded as the pinnacle of the duties. You were envied by the girls who were unhappy with their lot. You would be involved in the kitchen making sandwiches for all the school-going children. Four girls would be assigned to this duty.

The main reason why it was so prized, was that should the opportunity arise you could steal, or as we termed it, pinch either an egg or anything else that your eye noticed, other than bread, which always seemed to be in abundant supply. Most of the times it was an egg, which you never ever had, and was to you a luxury.

We had developed the art of stealing an egg. When the sandwiches were almost finished and ready to put into a special cool room for the night, while the cook was busy and had his back turned, you would quickly slip an egg from the basin where they were kept and put it into your big baggy bloomers. These were the size of a miniature parachute. You would then hobble out of the kitchen very slowly, making sure that the egg did not break, as this would have been a catastrophe.

The moment you were out of the kitchen and no-one was around, you would very gently slip the egg out of your baggy bloomers, keeping it safe. It was your special treasure, which you revealed only to your best friend with whom you promised to share, whenever you had an opportunity to fry or boil it.

Adjoining the Junior Girls' building was a boiler room, looked after by an African named Jim. The top of the boiler was always hot, so you would put an old tin top on the stove and then you could make a fried egg in one minute. The boiler was coal-fed so that there would be enough hot water in the morning and evening for the Junior and Babies Section.

The room was used by many of the girls who had managed to steal an egg. Many a time the egg would turn out to be a big mess. At this stage, too many eggs were disappearing from the kitchen. Jim a very reliable African, who used to assist in the kitchen, had been instructed by the superintendent, to try to find out who was stealing the eggs.

Having been assigned the kitchen duty the day before, and having stolen an egg, I gently placed it in a safe place. Early the next morning, together with Martha we started frying or should I say making a big mess of the egg. Mary had run back to the dormitory to fetch something.

I felt a hand put on my shoulder with the following threatening words. "Caught you in the act". Terrified, I was marched upstairs to the office of the superintendent of the orphanage. He was short and stout, hence the nickname Stompie. I came into the room, trembling with fear. Looking very threatening he yelled in his loud voice. "Where did you get the egg?"

In this state of fear I managed to stumble out with the following lie. "My friend Joyce's brother Alec has fowls, he gave me the egg."

At this particular period, the orphanage was still fairly rural. There would be cows that grazed on the lawns up on the hill which supplied some of the milk for the babies. Fowls near the bottom of the hill that gave the eggs. The Senior Boys' duties would be to look after the fowls, which taught them a certain sense of responsibility.

I doubt that Stompie believed me. I was so terrified at having been caught for the first time, he decided not to punish me, which would have been several hidings to my hand with a thin narrow piece of bamboo rod, that most of the younger girls were afraid of, as it really hurt. He assumed that I would be an example to the other girls who were lucky enough not to have been caught. The news travelled fast, so everyone knew about my mishap. For a short time only, it solved the case of the missing eggs. No eggs went missing, but after a while the eggs started to disappear, taken by other girls who took their chances, who knew how to be a lot more cautious. I on the other hand, never stole eggs again.

Life in the orphanage settled down to a routine pattern, giving me a certain sense of security. We did not have swimming pools, tennis courts, movies, TV and radio.

Several years later these would be donated for the benefit of the children. We did make our own amusement, and games that we enjoyed, like *Kennetjie*, *Bok-Bok* also known as Horsey, games not known today and were often played together by both boys and girls.

Cricket and other ball games like soccer were played by the boys. The younger girls found other interests, such as playing school, where one of the girls would be the teacher who presided over a class of three or four girls or "housie housie", where we would make believe we had been invited for tea, and enjoyed our little mime. If you were lucky enough to have a doll, you would protectively play with it.

Every Saturday you went to the Synagogue which had several years earlier, been specially built. All the services were conducted by the children, after which you were each given about three to four sweets. We received no pocket money from Arcadia, though a child could possibly be given 10 pence by their parent on visiting day.

The Senior Boys were allowed on a Saturday afternoon to walk to the centre of town. They would buy sweets to sell to the youngsters, who if they had any money would be only too pleased to pay whatever was asked. The bigger boys would always be winners.

On School holiday, my Aunty Jenny and Uncle brought Stan and I to Brakpan for a week's holiday. I was now very self conscious, doing what ever anyone told me, and always being obedient wherever I went.

On another school holiday we were taken by my grandfather to Germiston for a week. The story that preceded him was he had once had a bet with a friend in Germiston that he could bend a heavy railway line with his two hands. He won his bet, as he was a big strapping man known in his young days as Goldsmith the Blacksmith. In actual fact he was a blacksmith by trade, but as horses were replaced by the motorcar, he became a second hand dealer by buying and selling steel and junk.

We had a wonderful time and used to play hide and seek, as his steel junk yard also had old broken down cars and trucks. We would go to the cinema which was around the corner of his house, this being the highlight of our stay. When it was time to go back to the orphanage we were disappointed that the time had been so short. The only thing I did not like about my grandfather was the sloppy wet kisses which he would give me, and I would always try to wriggle out of his clasp.

On another holiday I went to Ladysmith on my own, to be with Uncle Solly and Aunt Minnie, my mother's younger sister, who had a general dealer shop that sold just about everything. Their daughter Ruth, was a year younger, though very much taller. At this particular time, it was considered, that the reason why I was so small, was because I did not like, nor drink milk. The only way I would drink a glass, would be when Aunt Minnie, in desperation would bribe me with the following proposal.

"Ruth knows where all the sweets are, after you have finished your milk, you can go with her and take a handful." This always worked wonders. After all, which child did not like sweets!

The time spent with them was wonderful. We went to the cinema, played lots of games, went exploring on the open grounds nearby, and just had a lot of fun together. I felt very sorry when I had to return to the orphanage.

I was very close to my brother Stan, as he was all I had. He was a very quiet and shy boy and certainly no fighter. It would always be upsetting for me to see the older boys fight with him. One time, when he was at school being teased I found this to be very upsetting and when I came into class I was crying. The teacher asked "What is wrong!" I replied, "The bigger boys are fighting with my brother."
"Go and sit down, don't be such a baby," she said.

Where was my mother to run to and cry on her lap, soothing me with. "Don't cry I know how you love your brother, and don't want to see him hurt?" Instead I had to realise it was a hard and hurtful world, but again survival was the name of the game of life.

In the younger classes we had a teacher named Miss Kruvwagen. She was the typical teacher of the era. A spinster, thin, tall, strict and threatening. To my small mind she either had a very sharp sense of smell or an obsession with smells. In the middle of a class she would jump up.

"Who made that bad smell?" She would ask very sternly. No one would answer. She would then file us out of the room one by one and announce that the classroom was being aired. This seemed to happen almost once a week, regardless of which class she had. Becoming the butt of the children behind her back, she was eventually referred to as the bad smelling teacher.

I was about eight years old and looked like a very small five-year-old, together with a boy by the name of Larry who was eleven years and looked like a nine-year-old. We were considered very small for our age, and for some reason or other, neither of us seemed to grow. At that time only small people were considered different. There were several girls and boys who were very tall, but that was acceptable.

Tests were being conducted at the medical research regarding retarded growth. The orphanage was approached and asked if they had any particularly small children. Larry and I were singled out. In those days no consent was necessary, so we became the guinea pigs. Every Monday, we were taken to the section where tests were being carried out at the Medical Research Institution. Each given an injection of some experimental monkey gland hormone and sent home. As I was too small to reach the dining table, I always sat on a cushion at meal times so when I came back after the injection with a very sore bottom, I was only too pleased to have something soft to sit on.

These injections were given to us for about six months. I dreaded going as I hated injections and the after effects of a very sore bottom, besides the fact that I was made more fully aware that I was different by being so short. Neither of us grew, and the injections were discontinued, to our relief. We both remained very small. With today's knowledge of genetics, being small would be acceptable.

Still very thin and small for my age, when playing with friends on the lawn playground, I would notice a few of older junior boys and girls pointing towards me, one of them holding a blanket. I would then hear them shouting to one another. "Let us catch Mabel and toss her in the air."

I knew that I had to run for my life, but there were too many chasing me, and anyway where could I hide. As they caught me, I would start crying. "Please don't toss me in the air."

Knowing what they were going to do, being overpowered and too small to do anything, I would continue crying and pleading: "Please, don't throw me in the air, I'm afraid."

Four of them would hold the ends of the blanket, another would pick me up, which was not very difficult as I weighed very little. Once caught I would then be thrown into the middle of the blanket and tossed high into the air. A crowd had gathered and were enjoying all the fun.

Screaming and crying, I would shout. "Help me, please put me down!" Nobody took notice of my agony.

Getting tired of me, they would find another small girl or boy to terrorise. I would be left alone in a state of exhaustion feeling very frightened, until one of my friends would come and pacify me. One day they missed the catch and a small boy was hurt, fortunately not seriously. They were forbidden, even to throw anyone up in a blanket again, to my utter relief.

By 1935, the old orchards had disappeared, to make way for alterations and expansion for accommodating 370 children.

Vegetable gardens were laid out. There were now no orchards left to steal fruit from. This did not deter the children from having their sights set on the surrounding neighbour properties.

During the spring season when the fruit would start to ripen, most of the owners of the big neighbouring mansions, which had large orchards of various fruit trees, dreaded this time of the year, as they knew without fail that unless they were lucky they would enjoy very little fruit from their trees. There would be large dogs guarding their houses behind various types of high fences, but no matter how many precautions they took to prevent the fruit from being stolen, they knew they would be outwitted.

After school, or on a weekend, a few boys and girls would get together, and slip out of the orphanage grounds, even though this was forbidden. A scheme would be worked out amongst themselves. The boys were required to climb the trees while the girls would fill their big baggy bloomers with this half-ripened green fruit, later to share the spoils. It was amazing to see how much fruit our bloomers could carry. It was also arranged between us who would keep "cavy" which meant, watching out for the dogs or the owner.

The boys would pick the fruit off the trees and throw it down. If you were agile, you caught the fruit, if not you kept on bending down and stuffing the fruit into your big baggy bloomers until they could hold no more. Someone would shout. "*Cavey*" the call to alert you to get down from the trees and to start running for your lives.

You would hear the dogs barking, followed by the owner of the house shouting. "Will you children get out of my fruit trees? I'm going to phone up and report you!"

Even before the sentence was finished, whoever was in the tree would climb down. Then finding the hole in the fence that had originally been made, start pushing and shoving the person in front of you through the hole, running so fast for your life, that neither the dogs nor the owners could catch you. Still running down the pavement with fruit dropping out of the now bulging baggy bloomers, you did not dare look back until you got to what you thought, was the safety of the orphanage.

By now the owner had phoned through to Mr Shaer, who had instructed a couple of the African staff to try and catch the culprits. Fortunately for us, they would only manage to catch a couple of the children, the rest getting away. On one occasion I was one of those who had been caught, then taken to the office Mr Shaer was waiting with his stick.

"Stealing fruit, how many times have I warned you children that this is not allowed? You are a disgrace to the orphanage. Have you no shame? Put out your hand!" he would shout.

The girls got a few hard cuts on the hand; the boys had to bend down, and were given three of the best on their bottoms. Then roaring like a raging lion, he would continue. "If I ever catch you again you will get double punishment. Go straight to the hospital. I have already phoned the nurse".

With his anger still echoing in our heads, we would run all the way to the hospital, where a nurse was waiting for our arrival, having been completely instructed what to do. "So you've been caught today." She would smugly say, enjoying giving you two tablespoons of castor oil. Then, adding insult to injury, "I hope this teaches you a lesson not to steal fruit again."

By now, I was sore from the hiding, sick from the castor oil and only wanted to find a corner to feel very sorry for myself, vowing never to steal fruit again. A friend who had been through the same sympathised with me, making me feel it was not the end of the world. Memory was very short, and the next year I would be involved with the crowd again, but a lot wiser, this time, making sure I did not get caught.

Those who were not caught would find a comfortable spot on the lawn to share the spoils of green peaches, apricots and plums, which were the most common fruits grown. They would discuss the misfortune of those caught, while relishing the green fruit.

By the time evening arrived, those who had a weak constitution, would be suffering with stomach aches. Doubled up with pain, they would arrive at the hospital. Never admitting it was the green fruit, the nurse knew that these were the children who had avoided being caught. Like a spider in its web trying to lure a fly. She would be waiting: "What's wrong with you?" would taunt. "I've got a stomach ache?" would be your inaudible reply. "Why have you got a stomach ache?" she would goad you on. Seeing that no answer was forthcoming, she would continue. "Open your mouth". Then two tablespoons of castor oil went down your throat.

"This should teach you not to steal fruit." She would smugly add. It tasted terrible, but at least it took your stomach ache away. In the end, whichever way it was, very few escaped the consequences of stealing fruit. This did not deter us, and the same episode was repeated the following year.

All the girls learnt dancing. Lessons were given by an honorary qualified teacher. The days we had dancing all the girls would go into a special hall where there was a piano. The teacher would bring her own pianist, instructing her which music to play, generally light classical. She would demonstrate how to do various dance movements to the music. Most of the girls did dancing, as no homework was involved. If you did not want to participate, it did not matter, as it was not compulsory. Your classes were divided into the juniors and seniors, each lesson lasting an hour. Among the older girls there were a few excellent dancers, who seemed to be naturals, and would be commended by the teacher. We all wore special dancing tunics. Every year you did a test to determine how you had progressed.

I was a fairly good dancer, being small and light on my feet, but no-one other than the teacher, took any notice. Once a year, a concert would be given by the dancers for all the children, parents and committee. This was one way to raise money for the home. It was always a success, and enjoyed by all. I'm sure had my mother been there, she would have been very proud of me.

A couple of years later, we began to have elocution, also given by an honorary qualified teacher. Not many girls attended, especially if they felt it was too much to cope with, as homework would often consist of learning either poetry or prose for exams. I enjoyed the elocution and liked to do my share of acting.

Concerts were given by the children, for the children. The older girls and boys were both the directors and the actors, and many talented younger ones were also allowed to take part. I recall my first concert where I participated with Jill. We were ten years old when we did the following act together.

> Little man you're crying, I know why you're blue.
> Someone stole your kiddy cart away.
> Better go to sleep now.
> Little man you've had a busy day.
> You've been playing soldier, the battle has been won.
> The enemy are out of sight. Come along you soldier.
> Put away your guns, the war is over for tonight.
> Time you stopped your scheming,
> Time your day was through.
> Can't you hear the bugles softly say.
> Time you should be dreaming.
> Little man you've had a busy day.

Jill did the singing, as she had a lovely voice, and together we did the acting, which we both enjoyed. During the act some smart little boy, trying to upset and confuse us, would shout, "She sounds like an old fog horn!" Pretending we did not hear, we would ignore all remarks. Then another smart Alec would call out loudly. "She's not a boy but a silly girl. Throw them off!" A chorus of girls would shout even louder. "Shut up, you boys. We can't hear with all your stupid remarks."

Then all would be quiet, until some other act was on, and a repeat of funny little remarks would be made again. Talents went unheeded; your potential, never realised.

The highlights in our entertainment would be when we were taken occasionally to see a pantomime or to the cinema during the school holidays. We would be taken by a special bus into the centre of the town where the theatre and cinemas were. Filing down the aisle two by two, we would sit down and gaze at the wonders around us, particularly at the Colosseum, which after the lights went out had tiny twinkling stars in the ceiling that looked like the night sky with all its stars.

Many a film we identified with, and you would hear sobs and nose blowing from the girls. In the back you would hear the silly remark from one of the clever junior boys, who at any opportunity would try to annoy us. "Hey boys! Let's lend then a few of our hankies, they don't seem to have enough at the rate they're crying." As usual you ignored them.

Films were specially selected for us. We were rarely subjected to any violence. The films were mainly musicals, children and *Lassie*. The favourite of the younger girls was Shirley Temple, the younger boys preferred *Lassie*, and everyone, especially the older girls and boys, enjoyed the musicals.

By the time we got back we were in our own wonderful world of dreams, the girls would be walking on air, discussing what had been seen, felt and heard. This set certain standards for the young girls, who had not been exposed to very much violence as the orphanage was very insulated, and in my case growing up with a gentle nature, yet a fighter for survival.

Visiting days were only two Sundays a month from 3.00 pm to 5.00 p.m. We waited expectantly at the bottom of the drive as parents or other relatives arrived. They then would be eagerly snapped up by their children. Sweets, biscuits and fruit were usually brought, which were devoured by the child. Many a time there would be much too much to eat all at once. The remainder would be taken to the child's dormitory, and was either shared with their friends, or stored in their locker. More often than not, whatever was stored in the locker, would somehow disappear. You never discovered who the culprit was. When it was time to say good-bye, there would be many a tear and heartbreak for both parent and child.

The main visitor for Stan and I, was our grandfather who lived in Germiston, and tried to see us at least once a month. Occasionally Aunt Jenny, Uncle Harry and one or two of their children would visit. Stan and I would wait at the bottom of the driveway. Many a visiting day, especially if my grandfather was ill, no one would arrive. We would join the rest of the children in the same position, with disappointment all over our faces.

Within myself I would cry to my mother. "How do I cope with disappointment." Eventually I learnt to try and accept the different circumstances that arose.

Twice a year, relatives were allowed to take their children out for the Sunday. The evening before you did not sleep. Through the night, you could hear the girls talking softly to one another discussing what they thought they might do. Early next morning, you dressed hurriedly in what was your best dress, and being so excited, some of the girls would miss breakfast. A bus had been donated. It was named "*The Black Mariah*" by the children, as it was a black bus. It would take the children to the Union Grounds, which was an army training depot just off the centre of the city, near the main gardens known as Joubert Park. Here they would be fetched by relatives. Those that did not go by bus, would wait at the bottom of the Arc driveway for their relatives.

Stan and I would be fetched by my grandfather, who was the only person to take us out. He would pick us up in his old rattling lorry. What a wonderful experience this was driving to Germistion, and passing all the old gold mine dumps on the way.

He had now expanded his second hand dealers business with many more steel and allied goods. As usual when we were with him, we would play in his old junk yard, specially in the many derelict old cars. In the afternoon we would either go to the cinema around the corner, or go visiting with him to a lady friend who lived nearby. By 6.00 pm, the time we had to be back, we would be completely exhausted. The girls would tell one another how amazing the day had been, where they had gone and all that they had done.

When my grandfather was unable to take us out, we would feel so lost and disappointed. Realising that we were not the only ones, and that there were others in the same position, we made the best of the day. This taught us that there was a lot that we had to accept.

Grandfather Morris Goldsmith, with Stan and Mabel

rest huts. This was a very popular picnicking place for families to spend a Sunday. There would be singing, laughing, shouting and a lot of noise in the open lorries and cars that helped transport all the children to the lake. Games, competitions and other entertainment was arranged. My grandfather would arrive to visit Stan and me at the lake as he lived nearby. By the time we got home we had all had a good time.

Another outing which was organised by a club called the Sunshine Club, formed by various members of the public together with the committee, arranged to take the children with their own transport for the day, to a hotel on the Vaal River in Vereeniging, which was approximately a two hour drive from the orphanage. During the drive we would be given sweets, and made to feel good by committee members and other volunteers, who were kind enough to give up their time, so that we could have an enjoyable day.

The Junior Girls were sometimes taken on a Sunday by a few of the older senior girls to the zoo, which was about half an hour's walk away. A band would play light classical music in the afternoon. The popular hobby was collecting discarded chocolate wrapping paper thrown on the ground, or from the dustbin, where visitors to the zoo had rolled the silver paper into little balls and thrown them away.

Many a fight would be started, when two friends saw the same silver paper. Jane would pick it up and Freda would say, "I saw it first" "Too bad, I picked it up first" would be the answer. The next moment each one would be pulling on the other girl's hair, shouting and fighting over this little piece of silver paper, which you treasured as though it was a piece of jewellery. Then one of the older girls would separate you. "Stop it immediately. This is a public place and people are staring at your. Now behave yourselves."

It would either be split in half, or for the rest of that day you would both be bad friends. However you never remained bad friends for long. When you came back, the silver paper would be opened up painstakingly with the scratching of your nail, all the different patterns smoothed out then put into a book. Duplicated papers would be swapped among the girls. This to us was a very fascinating hobby.

Occasionally during the school holidays the junior girls would be taken to the zoo by the nurse in charge. There was a children's playground where we could play. As the orphanage had no playing equipment at that time, the playground was a special treat.

On one particular day it had been raining and everything was wet. The nurse had to go somewhere for several minutes, and warned the girls not to go on the slide as it was wet and dirty. When she returned, she took one look at us and was very annoyed. "You girls who disobeyed me will be punished!" She marched us back and those of us who had disobeyed her were told "No supper, and straight to bed." This did not worry us, as we had enjoyed the afternoon on the wet and sloppy slide, having gained more than missing the usual supper.

Every Sunday morning we were given a dose of Epsom Salts. You would all stand in a line, and a nurse would give each child one tablespoon of concentrated Epsom Salts. If you were

Opposite the entrance to the orphanage, near the top of the hill, were two cottages. In the first one lived the shoemaker, Mr Chait, whose job was to repair all the children's broken shoes and suitcases. The other cottage was occupied by Charley Miller, his wife Dolly and their eldest daughter Alice, who was my age. Eventually there were five other children added to the family. Charley was the driver of the black bus, nicknamed the "*Black Mariah*". He was coloured, but to all the children, he was just our friend and part of our lives. We grew up with no prejudice regarding other people – on the contrary, we felt we were the under dogs.

Everyone had to belong to either Brownies and Girl Guides for the girls, and Cubs and Scouts for the boys. Meetings took place every Sunday morning. The most enjoyable part of our activities was the Jamboree. Brownies from all parts of the country would meet once a year during the school holidays in different parts of the country. Whenever it was held in Vereeniging a town on the Vaal River, about two hour's drive from Johannesburg, you camped out on the banks of the river for the weekend. Meeting and making new friends, you felt that life was wonderful.

One special outing was going for a picnic to Germiston Lake which was a big beautiful lake surrounded by trees, lawns and clever and knew how to hold the salts in your mouth, you would seek out a nearby plant, very skilfully spit it onto the plant, and walk away just as innocently. Apparently the plants needed the booster as they flourished, whereas most of us landed up with stomach aches or running tummies. I on the other hand suffered with very bad stomach problems.

There was the hospital section for the ill children, and it was not unusual to find many children together in this section with either one of the four common illnesses. Measles, mumps, chicken pox and whooping cough. At this stage inoculation for these diseases was not given. However, at this stage one could often see children walking around, with big bandages under their chin for the mumps, or the final spots clearing from the measles and chicken pox. I had had the four children's main illnesses, as well as having had my tonsils taken out.

Doctors could do small operations like taking out tonsils as the hospital had recently been updated. As you could not swallow anything else, ice cream and jelly was given. For that reason alone you did not mind having tonsils out, as this was one of the few occasions you were given these special treats. If you had any serious illness or a severe contagious disease, you still had to go to the main children's hospital, situated near the centre of the city, several miles away from the orphanage.

Several honorary dentists looked after our teeth. Either a nurse or a Senior would take a few of us by bus, into the centre of the town where the dentists rooms were. Very few children looked forward to this visit. Being afraid of the dentist I would find myself in a very bad state when I knew I had to go to the dentist. He somehow or other always seemed to hurt me. A couple of years later, one very generous committee member paid for a complete dental surgery which was to be built adjoining hospital section. This solved a lot of administration problems; arranging when the dentist could accommodate you, as well as relying on either a nurse or an older senior boy or girl, to get you safely to the dental rooms, either with the "Black Mariah" or the bus that stopped just outside the orphanage.

It was not unusual for us to practice our own therapies, especially when we had colds. One of the most common medications was to pick a couple of eucalyptus leaves off the one and only tree that was in the school playground. We would then wrap it in our wet handkerchief and inhale, hoping it would clear our nose. Many of us could swear that this is what cured our cold. Others again said it was only because a cold could not last too long.

When one of the junior girls was diagnosed with diphtheria, we all had to have a swab taken. As a precaution, 20 of the girls who had been in contact, were isolated in a ward for a week. All we had to do to keep occupied was to play games, and read. The nurse in charge was driven crazy by the mischief we created, and the bickering and fighting between the girls. The girls were not ill, but were not allowed to mix with anyone else. Keeping us happy was a relentless and impossible task, as we were confined to a very small area. By the time the week was over, the poor nurse was ready to have a nervous breakdown.

The sister in charge would often take us for walks past the top part of the orphanage. "Hello Dolly" we would shout as we passed her house on our way to the koppies, which was a little hill. At the top was an open field covered with chestnut trees, that seemed to be waiting for our arrival. They had dropped their fruit, or we would shake the trees and then pick them up, as usual, put them into our baggy bloomers. However, as they seemed to belong to no one, we never had to run, or feel we were stealing. We always enjoyed this outing.

About six different friends, who were now a lot older, would gather close together, often discussing different issues that we now found occurring in our lives. We would get into a huddle, and in whispers discuss certain changes that would take place at about 12 years old. Myrtle who was only 11 years old, had gone up to the senior girls because she was in this position. We expressed different opinions on what we thought. This was a very sacred discussion, and all our sexual education, had been handed down from a sister or overheard from a senior girl. By the time we had finished debating what would happen, nobody understood anything anyway.

You had contact with the boys at school, after school and weekends. Occasionally an older junior boy was becoming aware of one of the junior girls. Many a romance between the senior girls and boys took place, and you would see a young couple walking down the drive in the evening or weekend. Years later, several of the couples would marry. Many a marriage did not last, and ended up in a divorce, and others remained for life.

At the end of the year we would all gather in the main hall. Stompie would arrive with our reports. Was this the day of reckoning! There would be complete silence. Then in front of everyone, he would read each report out loudly. The very clever and studious boys and girls had nothing to fear. For many of the other children, however, this would be a terrifying ordeal. Those with a bad result or had failed would be made to feel very vulnerable with the following sarcastic remarks. "What do you think you were doing at school, playing funny games. Do you always want to be stupid. I'll see you in my office at the end of the session." You knew there would be punishment.

One year, Stompie had read out my report, on which the teacher had written "Talkative", he called me up in front of everyone. I was only eight years old at the time. "Talkative!" he bellowed. "What have you to say?" I was so afraid that I just stood there, looking down on the floor and wanting to burst into tears, but how could I cry in front of 350 boys and girls? By now I had learnt a certain amount of controlling my feelings.

"Go back and don't let me see this remark again on your report!" he barked. The humiliation of the situation certainly had an effect on me. The following year's report, had no comments. Those who did well would be commended.

Only the very clever boys went to High school to matriculate, the rest went to Junior High school, which only went to standard eight. None of the girls, that I knew of, ever went to far as matric. Many years later a few girls who were regarded as brilliant, were given the opportunity of matriculating. The average boy or girl went to work at the age of 15 years, with no qualifications in anything.

I grew up very slowly and remained most of my life very naïve. Could this be because of my size, which I felt was keeping me back? Was it a veil that I had developed at a very young age as protection? What ever it was, I somehow knew instinctually, that I had to survive my own individual way.

The gardens were very well kept, and gardeners looked after the grounds. Near the hospital section, there were outside toilets for the girls, where there was an open stand, which was divided into small portions and the junior girls who were interested in growing vegetables or flowers, were given a small piece of ground. This created a lot of problems. Often someone would steal your vegetable, and no-one would know who. Should per chance the person who stole, be caught, there would be a lot of trauma, and eventually no-one was allowed to grow anything, and the whole idea was scrapped.

Nasturtiums were a popular flower grown, as we used to eat the leaves on bread and butter, or just on their own. This was regarded as a delicacy.

When it was a friend's birthday, you would have kept a special trinket for this occasion

Instead tears would come into your eyes. You knew the sacrifice your friend had made to give you her most treasured possession, with a little note wishing you many happy returns of the day. In turn she would feel the same about your present. Both of you knowing it came from the heart. You built special friendships, some lasted a life time, others stopped when you left the orphanage.

Friends changed like the weather. There would be times when you would be upset with a friend. Finding another would not be difficult as there were always other girls around.

Whenever one of my friends had upset me, there would be no mother to run to, to cry on her shoulders. My only cry would be within, where no one could see or feel my hurt. Later you forgot you had been upset. By now I had accepted my lot like most of the other children in the same position.

THE SENIOR GIRLS

Having turned 12 years, I now had become a Senior girl. Here the Matron in charge was Sister Goldwater who had been with the Seniors a long time. She was both respected and loved by many of the girls. We had more independence. You were taught sewing on an electric sewing machine, and you made your own clothes. You also dressed slightly differently, and felt more like an individual. You could listen to records, which were played with a gramophone that had been donated. Life was starting to become a lot easier.

The middle of the year that I turned twelve I became ill, with pains in my legs. The doctors could not seem to diagnose the problem. I was put into the hospital section, and for a month was told to stay in bed. During the day I was taken out of the ward and put into the enclosed verandah on the side of the hospital

Days were long and I was never a reader. I used to look out at the garden and notice the flowers growing outside the window.

It was autumn and I became aware of nature in its natural splendour. The leaves were gently changing into golden brown. The many beautiful flowers dropping their faded petals onto the ground, which slowly shrivelled up. Birds chirping their songs, and the gentle whisper of the breeze through the trees.

I started to feel the inspiration to write poetry. Most of them were about nature, fairies, and occasionally about my longings. My first was about my garden. A few are recorded below.

By my little Garden.

By my little garden there is a tree.
What do you think I always see.
I see some birds that sit so long.
And don't even give us a little song.
I see bees buzzing here and there
They all are so busy they have not time to spare
There are flowers right round the tree.
Though some time you can't even see.

London Town.

As I went through London town. In a shop I saw a gown.
It was so bright and gay, though I had no money to pay.
I went on further, but what did I see, a little toy not meant for me.
I came to a shop with cake so nice, and only wished I'd had a slice.
At last I saw my brother in town, and asked him if he'd buy the gown.
He bought it for me, and now I'm happy as you can see.

The Fairies

At our fields at night come the fairies so bright.
In a silvery dress but what shall we guess
The king and the queen are also to be seen
They do look so bright when the moon gives light.
A bird does sing while in a ring.
The fairies go round but not one sound.
But when a sunbeam is to be seen.
They run up the moon ever so soon.

Now I was starting to express my feeling in what I felt was poetry. But regretfully no one was ever to see or know about my writing. It was never shown to anyone. No mother to read and say with encouragement. "*My goodness, such an imagination and feelings. This is what poetry is about,*"

Instead, over the years, different traumas and joys of life, coming from within, were expressed in poetry

Days were passing by as I watched the blending of the autumn shades of the golden leaves dropping and gently swaying to the ground. The frosty bitter cold winds began blowing in the winter, awaiting the gentle anticipation of the opening of the early spring flowers yet to come. By now I had not got any better. The doctor's verdict was "Rheumatic Fever." It was decided that I would need to be admitted to the children's hospital, situated on the outskirts of the central area. Arcadia at this stage could not cope with any serious illnesses.

A week after the decision was made, I arrived at the children's hospital, and went into a ward for girls only, nothing contagious, though the illnesses were more serious than the normal run of the mill ones. Next to me was a girl by the name of Fran, who also had Rheumatic Fever. Even though she was the same age as me, she was more than double my size. We were not allowed out of bed at all, as rest and medication were the only cure.

I had very strong dislikes of certain vegetables that were associated with Arcadia. One of them was cabbage, and whenever we would get cabbage, Fay who also detested cabbage and I would wrap it in some paper, and throw it out the window which was situated in between our beds. For some reason, no-one ever noticed what we were doing. It probably became compost, and I imagined that it grew better and bigger cabbages.

Once a month, the boys who were in the ward next door, would have their beds pushed into the girl's section to watch movies. There would always be someone who would be teased, especially if they had mentioned that a certain girl or boy was nice.

Sundays were visiting days, my grandfather who was ill, or my Aunt and uncle would occasionally visit me. Many a week there would be no-one to visit me. I would look around and feel very lonely. There was nobody to make me feel better!

I was ashamed to tell anyone that I was in an orphanage, therefore I did not make friends easily. Fran noticed I very rarely had visitors. On day she asked me. "Why don't you have visitors." "I don't have any parents." I told her.

At this stage I never ever mentioned my father as he had never visited my brother and I since we were admitted to the orphanage, and I had forgotten I had one, and for my part he could have been dead. Neither my grandfather or my aunts and uncles ever spoke to him.

"No mother". She exclaimed! As her mother was always visiting. Very timidly I continued. "I live in an orphanage, where I have been brought up from the age of three years. I have been unaccustomed to having family around, besides when occasionally grandfather, and my aunt and uncle visit".

Days became weeks, and all of a sudden it was Christmas time. I was still in hospital. A very happy Santa Claus, dressed in his special clothes, came visiting the wards, giving us all presents. It was the first time I had had seen a live Father Christmas. He came around into the wards and gave me the complete set of Snow White and the Seven Dwarfs figurines, which I loved. At this stage the film was on at the cinema. Later in life, whenever I saw the film, I associated the Christmas in the hospital with the film. I had now been ill for six months, and the doctors felt that I was a lot better. They decided that I could go back to the orphanage, as I had been cured.

I had missed six months of schooling. It was the December school holidays, and the middle of summer. The orphanage children were going for their second camp to Port Elizabeth. As I was not strong enough to go, it was decided that for the duration that the children were at camp, I would go to the Hope Home, which was a convalescent home, situated on the top of the hill. You could see the orphanage just below the hill on the opposite side of the street.

The majority of the children in the home were physically handicapped. Some through accidents, others had been born with some crippling defect and had to be taught to walk. The building was very dark and dreary, it gave one the impression that this was the place where ghosts seemed to live. This left me with a very depressed feeling.

When I came out of the Hope Home and retuned to the orphanage, the children had just returned from camp. Listening to all the stories about camp, from my friends, who were now a lot older than the first camp of six years ago, I realised I had missed out again. To compensate for my disappointment my grandfather gave me a gold ring for my twelfth birthday. To this very day, I still have the ring.

My grandfather had been corresponding with his sister whom he had visited in England so that she could come and live with him to look after Stan and me, enabling us to leave the orphanage. This was not to be, because at this stage the Second World War between England and Germany was declared. Normal holiday travel by ships had stopped on account of the dangers of torpedoes sinking them and his plan was never to materialise.

The year was 1939. War had been declared, and South Africa, which was a commonwealth country under the government of General Smuts, was completely aligned with the British. Our position was not threatened, and the defence force took on a whole new meaning, with lots of men and women joining the forces on a voluntary basis. There was also a strong alliance of the Afrikaner who supported Hitler, and were anti everything. Often scuffles would take place outside the city hall where the two different opinions would clash, ending in riots and the police would be involved in keeping the peace.

There were stories circulating, about children who were to be brought out of Germany, and were to come to the orphanage. A dormitory was being prepared, but this fell through as these children were unable to escape from Hitler's Germany, and at the end of the war, we were told, that they had all been killed. There had also been threats to place a bomb in the grounds of the Arc, and this created a lot of fears among the younger children. Fortunately this did not eventuate.

As I had been away from school for so long, I had to redo standard. All my regular friends had passed into a higher standard and went to a different school. At 13 I was the eldest in the class. The principal, whose name was Mr Jacobs, was also the teacher of the standard fives, which was the highest class of the primary school. He would always open school with morning prayers for assembly, which were psalms that we had to learn off by heart. In my case a love for them was instilled, from the very beginning of my school days. The most noted one being. "The Lord is my Shepherd" Psalm no 23 and no 91.

I do not recall much about the early days of the war as we were isolated, but every now and then we would hear snippets of what was happening. One morning having just settled into the class Mr Jacobs came in and mentioned very down hearted that Holland and Denmark had fallen to the Germans. Even though most of us did not understand, we were all upset. This remained one of my most vivid impressions of the early days of the war.

At this stage the war had made very little impression. Only the elder boys and girls would listen to the radio, and would understand what was happening with the war, as well as life outside the orphanage. The rest of us were too young to fully comprehend. By the end of the war about 90 boys and 14 girls who had been in the orphanage had joined the Army, Navy and Auxiliary Service.

Regrettably one was killed. There is a plaque today in the hall with all the names of those who were in the Army. At the bottom of the plaque is his picture, and written underneath 'In memory of Harry Nochumsohn who was killed in action.' He was remembered by many of the boys and girls.

One day during the school break, I was called by one of the children and told that there was someone at the school fence who wanted to see me. Arriving at the fence, I was greeted by a man and a woman whom I did not know. He told me he was my father and was married to Rose, the woman standing next to him.

This was the first time I had any connection with my dad for over 10 years. Very soon the bell went. By the time I had gone into class, I had forgotten them. After school a few friends asked me who the people at the fence were. When I told them it was my father and stepmother, they were surprised, as I had never mentioned him. It was the first time in 10 years I had seen him, I felt very awkward and did not know what to say.

Stan who was now 16 years old, was called into Mr Shaer's office and told that our father had remarried, he would be leaving the orphanage to live with them.

Several months later Mr Shaer called me into his office, and told me I was to leave the orphanage and live with my father and his new wife, as he had not paid anything towards our upkeep. As my grandfather was ill and not able to pay either, the committee felt that I would have a home, and I would be better off living with them.

I had very mixed feelings and was once more was very afraid, as I would be leaving all my friends and security behind. Starting a new challenging episode in my life, during the next few years, would be very traumatic.

*L to R Mary Millman, Mabel Goldsmith, Lilly Cohen.
Taken in the quadrangle by the fish pond.*

The girls' hostel in Harrow Road - Mabel Brittany in centre front with Marcia Rosenkowitz on her right. Alma Lipman standing

A week later, my father came to fetch me from the orphanage. I managed to fit all my belongings into one small suitcase. While waiting for the bus, which was just outside the orphanage driveway, I once again experienced this feeling of insecurity. Looking back at the gates and driveway I started to feel very apprehensive about what was happening to me.

Mabel was married first to Ruby Klitofsky who passed away.

Mabel is now living in Melbourne Australia with her husband of 48 years Morris Brittany. Between them they have three children and 13 grandchildren

Chapter 24 - TOBY UNTERSLAK (ROBERTS) (1925)

My stay in Arcadia began in December 1934.

My father passed away in November of 1934 at the young age of 47, leaving a young wife with three small children to fend for.

I was the eldest of the three and was nine years old at the time, my sister Miriam was six and my youngest sister Yetta was three. My mother was suddenly forced into a situation of having to support a family after having never worked in her life. She found a job in a factory but was forced to put us into Arcadia. We had an uncle on the Jewish Welfare committee at the time who helped to get us into Arcadia and a very wonderful lady, Annie Isaacs of the Jewish Welfare was of great support to my mother.

Arcadia became the life line for us. We were educated both in English and Hebrew. We were given the opportunity of learning dancing, singing, sewing and above all were given a strong foundation in Judaism, always going to Shul on Shabbos and Yomtov and keeping the foundations of our heritage.

I made many wonderful friends in Arcadia. Bertha Klevansky (Kronenberg), Soeka Perlman, Rosa Cohen were just a few of the very special ones.

I left Arcadia in 1941 to live with my mother who was living in Doornfontein with her sister.

My sister Miriam passed away in October 1981 and Yetta in September 1996.

I married David Unterslak in 1946. We had two wonderful children.

My daughter Denise Swimmer had four children and now has four grandchildren. My eldest great grandchild is already 15 and I was privileged to celebrate his Barmitzvah with him.

My son Rodney is a very influential doctor and he has five children and four grandchildren. I am the very proud grand mother of nine and great grandmother of eight.

All my children are Lubavitch Jews and are warm, caring and very loving. I live in a cottage which my son and daughter-in-law built, connected to their house when my husband was stricken with Parkinsons disease with which he suffered for five years. I needed the moral support and help from my children and so we moved there. I have my own life. We do not encroach on each other, but I know that they are always there and I get to see them all every day.

My husband passed away in August of 2002. He lived at home with me right up until his death.

Hashem has been very good to me and has blessed me and for this I am very grateful.

I am also grateful to all those who shaped my life whilst in Arcadia - Mr and Mrs Harary, Stompy Shaer and Sister Goldwater.

Chapter 25 - HENRY HARRIS (1925-2002)

Henry, born in 1925 and his younger brother Ralph, born in 1930 were placed in the care of Arcadia in 1930 and 1935 respectively.

They both left Arcadia in 1941.

REMEMBERING HENRY HARRIS
Written by Mannie Osrin

On Wednesday 13th November 2002 I went to the funeral of a truly wonderful Old Arc, namely that of Henry Harris. I'm not too sure just how well Henry would have been known to those Arcs, who, say, are 55 years old or younger. He was a most generous soul and would never refuse a request for assistance from anyone, over and above a large monthly donation to Arcadia, which had been going on for many years prior to his death.

My recollections of him in the Arc have been dimmed by the passage of time. It is after all more than 50 years ago.

I do remember him as one helluva nice guy, always willing to help the younger blokes. I remember him as an all-round sportsman, with boxing as a distinction. He went to Parktown High and almost immediately upon leaving school, joined the Army, where he once again did a lot of boxing.

Henry was later in life to become 'famous' as one of the co-founders of the highly successful Northern Medical Aid Society.

Perhaps the most enduring memory of Henry is the generosity he displayed towards helping others, in both a financial and spiritual giving of himself to those less fortunate. He was especially kind to Arcadia and it should be mentioned that he was made an Hon Life member of the Arcadia Committee quite a number of years ago.

Henry had an older brother, Harvey, who passed away some time ago, and a younger brother, Ralph, whom I saw at the funeral for the first time in about 20 years.

He leaves his wife Cybil, and a son and daughter, and grandchildren. We wish them all 'long life'.

He will be sadly missed by all who knew him.

Written by Willie Isaacs

My condolences to Henry's Family. It is a very long time ago that we were good friends but my memory of that time is still very strong.

Written by Edith Cohen (Rozenkowitz)

I was very sad to hear that Henry had passed away. I did know him. I also know Sybil. We worked together art Aetna Insurance Co. and remember how excited she was when she got engaged and for me to learn it was Henry. That seems like an awful long time ago. I didn't know their children and wish them all long life and deepest condolences.

RALPH HARRIS
Letter from Ralph Harris - January 2006

My brother Henry Harris passed on about three years ago which left me as the sole survivor of the Harris family.

My wife Nita, known to all as Feigie Harris has been my eyes as I have a lot of trouble with my eyes.

My stay in Arcadia was from year 1934–1941. I can only say that I had many friends at the Arc. Some have passed on but my memories are very dear to me.

In 1947 I moved to Israel. I have lots of memories about my stay in Israel as I was very successful in the Army.

Best wishes to all ex Arc boys in Israel

Chapter 26 – ALEC SAUL (1925)

Alec was born on the 29th of August in 1925 and was in the care of Arcadia from 1933 to early 1942.

Before Alec came to the Arc he went to Bethlehem Junior School, Orange Free State and Junior School City and Suburban Johannesburg. While in the Arc he attended Jewish Government School, Rannoch Road Forest Town School, Observatory Junior High and John Orr Technical College up to standard 8.

Alec went back to school in later years and gained his Matric at Damelin College at age 42.

Alec's Mom, Fanny Rachel Bentel, was born in Rumania in Chernowitz and was a refugee from the 1914-1918 war. She came to South Africa in 1920 and passed away at age 87.

Alec's father, Mark Saul (original name was Shuvall or Shoval) was born in Kovno in Russia in 1879. He came to South Africa at about age 19 and passed away at 82.

ALEC'S ARC MEMORIES

THE KEYS

I had a friend Sydney Silver and between us we had the run of the Arc. We had keys for every lock in Arcadia including the pantry, the big refrigerator and the sweet room. We used to go into the sweets room and help ourselves, taking one or two sweets at a time so they would not be missed. He and I were shrewdies.

A bunch of senior boys decided to break into the sweets room to raid it, They invited us to join them. Sydney looked at me as if to say do we need this, so we turned them down. That night they broke in and stole all the sweets. The guard caught them and called cop Harary. The first ones he looked for were Sydney and I but of course we were not there. We knew he knew we had a set of keys but could not prove anything.

One Friday afternoon he sent for Sydney and I who were the Arc handymen and fixer uppers. I have a big problem he explained as the housekeeper has lost her keys and they could not get in anywhere.

"Sir, would you like us to take off the locks?" we said in all innocence and starry eyed. "No," he said, "I want to borrow your keys". "Sir", we said, "we don't know what you are talking about". "Come, come" he said, "I will give them back when the housekeeper finds her keys."

The story moves on about 50 years later when we went to Manuel Lipschitz' house for his 80th birthday. We had over the years become very good friends and we were having a great time. I said to him, "I don't want to upset you but I have a big

Alec at age 3 and his Mom

grouse and I am very annoyed with you." "Why?" he said "I want the keys back." I leave the rest to your imagination !

BEDLAM

There is a dearth of amusing stories between 1935 and 1940. So most of the stories would not be known. This particular story has a very unusual twist at the end. Let me relate the story of Bobby Poop (Friedlander) and his special police force.

In the senior boys' dormitory, the boys would get together for a blanket tossing experience. What we would do is, we would lay four mattresses on the floor and take a blanket, lay it on the mattresses. We would get one of the guys to lie on the blanket, and then we would toss him up in the air, with about twenty of us holding the edges of the blanket, to see if we could put the blokes head through the ceiling.

Now Bobby's job was to keep watch on all the entrances where cop could come in and catch us. Bobby's police force, was the equivalent of the Israeli Mossad and just as efficient. He would post his guards and at the first sign of Cop coming up from his flat downstairs, he would pass on the warning through his chain of command. The boys were that organised when somebody shouted. "Watch it, cop's coming!" the mattresses would be put back on the beds, the blanket spirited away and most of the guys back in bed.

Suffice to say, they were so quick, that sometimes the poor Arc that was suspended in the air had no protection when he fell. Please understand that I exaggerate slightly. In any event, if cop walked in and caught the guy who was being tossed on the blanket, on pain of death, he would not split on anybody. His answer was, "Sir, I fell out of bed."

Now where is the twist? This Bobby Friedlander (Poop) additionally to being a top lawyer became Minister of Finance in the Swaziland Government and that is a fact. There are many instances of old Arcs holding high office in Government, business, and all the professions.

THE LAMBETH WALK

The following stories should provide memories, and a few laughs, to the old old Arcs this will bring to light incidents that happened in our time. Did you know that Alec Saul was immortalised in the song Lambeth Way, the song had a repeating line which went this way:"

*When you go down Lambeth way, any evening any day,
you will find them all, doing the Lambeth walk.*

This was around 1938. I went to visit my mother in Klerksdorp on holiday and on returning home to Arcadia, I found the song still widely sung, however, the end words had been changed from you will find them all and then concluded with the three names Karp, Rodin, Saul. The names were Maurice Karp, Mannie Rodin and Alec Saul.

The two first people Maurice Karp and Mannie Rodin were both killed in car accidents, and the superstition was that it would also happen to Alec Saul. So far at the age of 80 I have beaten the devil.

WINING

Sydney Silver and I were great mates. We were the handymen for Arcadia and had a huge bunch of keys that fitted every lock in Arcadia so we were free to come and go as we liked. Sydney Silver started work as a cinematograph operator and used to come home at night around 11 o'clock.

One day, he said to me, "Alec we are going to raid the wine cellar." It was Pesach time and they were laying in and making stocks of wine so I heartily agreed because we did everything together. That night he came home and woke me up. "Ok Alec lets go". I said to him "Sydney I am tired and want to sleep." He said to me "Ok if you don't want to come I will take someone else." With that I went back to sleep. About 20 minutes later, I hear him and his accomplice tearing up the stairs and he says to his accomplice, "Quick, lie on the bed and start groaning." Then I hear another set of feet running into the dormitory. These belonged to the Zulu night watchman who said to him, "*Hau*, what have you been doing?"

Meanwhile, the Arc is lying on the bed groaning his head off, and the bottles of wine are going clink clunk. Sydney says to

Alec at age 15

the guard, "He is sick and I took him to the hospital" and the guy is moaning and groaning. The Guard then asked what the bottles were for and Sydney replied, "This is the medicine that the hospital gave me for him," and still the groaning went on. I had to stuff my foot in my mouth and hide underneath the blankets in order to control my laughter. The guard swallowed the story and left.

I got up and was most disgusted when he refused to share his booty with me. Sydney and his accomplice proceeded to stink heartily of wine for the next month and I regret to say that I cannot remember the name of his accomplice and for accuracy I am unable to present names which will not be factual.

TOOLS

Our committee member, Mr Wolf Hillman used to send the foreman from his company, Hillman Brothers, to teach us carpentry once a week. We created a workshop up in the old cheder rooms, next to the stable. The company provided us with a large cupboard that we filled with tools to be used for our lessons.

The foreman found that the boys had been helping themselves to the tools and not returning them. This was one thing which Sydney and I never did. If we borrowed tools, we made damn sure that they were always returned. The foreman however, in his wisdom decided to put two locks on the cupboard so that no-one could help themselves to the tools. He was the only one who had the keys to these locks and only opened the cupboard when he came to teach us.

It must however be understood, that Sydney and I had very few tools and we were the Arcadia handymen, so we hit on a plan. We simply obtained a very thin nail, and placed it on the pin that held the hinges in place and knocked out the pin. We then opened the door backwards. We used what we had to and replaced them thinking no one would be the wiser. However, our foreman was one smart guy, he had arranged the tools in a certain order and knew that somebody was using them, what he did not know was how the crime was being committed, and one day he pulled us aside and said what do you guys know about this. We came clean and explained to him, our position as handymen and the fact that we really had no tools to work with

He then made the decision to give us the keys to the locks simply because of the fact that we had always returned the tools to the cupboard and were honest about why we had needed them. So sometimes CRIME DOES PAY.

AFTER LEAVING THE ARC

Alec was first employed as a Cinematograph Operator for African Consolidated Theatres and was later promoted to sound department and trained as sound engineer. He left to open his own business in Kempton Park, "Radio sales and service". He moved to JHB due to lack of business in Kempton Park and opened premises in Kerk Street for three years. He then moved to King George Street for ten years and finally to Commissioner Street where he traded for 35 years under the name "Motor Radio".

During this period, he opened a motor accessories warehouse under the name "Automobile Radio Dealers Association" with

50 owner owned outlets and share holders, He was Chairman for 35 years and sold "Motor Radio" 1993. He then joined a book wholesale company for eight years.

Alec was a member of Arcadia Committee for 11 years and news editor for Old Arcadian Association Newsletter for seven years. He immigrated to Israel in November 2003 at age 78.

He achieved his amateur radio licence (HAM) and Sensei 2nd Dan Judo when 36.

Alec says he made the best decision of his life when he married Gootie Saul (nee Golach) and they have two daughters, Ava Katz and Marcelle Saul Sheimann, and five grandchildren.

Alec with wife Gootie – 1955/56

Chapter 27 - MARY FLAX (ARONOVSKY) (1926-2005)

Mary's parents were Maximillian and Rochel (nee Stein) Aronovsky and they came to South Africa from Kovno.

Max arrived first in around 1927 and Rochel and Mary came later in 1930.

Mary was placed in the care of Arcadia when she was four years old and lived there until she was 16 (early 1930 to the end of 1942).

Mary's parents moved to Durban and opened up a cafe for sailors at the harbour. In Durban they had another daughter (10 years difference between her and my Mary) Esphere (Essie) (nee Aronovsky) Ratzer. Essie was brought up in Durban in foster care -luckily with one family of German origin. Mary and Essie hardly knew each other in their youth but in later years did and become close.

Essie married Gerard Ratzer and they have three children; Sherrie unmarried and living in the USA, Robyn unmarried still living in SA and a son Mark Ratzer who has remarried and lives in Pretoria. His first wife lives with his two boys in Australia.

Mary married Michael (Mot) Flax and they have three children Helene, Sharmaine and Richard.

Helene, a Doctor, married Rabbi Dovid Shapero. They live in Detroit and have three children; Shira, Yaacov Boruch and lastly Mordechai Menecham.

Sharmaine married Chaim Tuvia Palmer and live in Baltimore with five children; two girls Namae Shifra Ester and Elisheva and three boys Tsvi Gedelaih, Elchanan and lastly Mordechai Eliyahu.

Lastly Richard Flax married Maya Kor, an Israeli, and they have two kids Leah and Nissanel. They live in Golder Green in London.

The three children and 10 grandchildren of Mary and Mot are all frum - a wonderful merit for them.

Sharmaine Palmer, daughter of Mary Flax (nee Aronovsky), who lives in the USA wrote this on behalf of her Mom in 2003.

Mary with her mother Rochel (nee Stein)

I was visiting my Mom Mary Flax (nee Aronovsky) in SA. She lives in the Rantjieslaagte Retirement Village in Johannesburg RSA and has lived there since my father Michael (Mot) Flax a"h passed away about five and a half years ago.

She had recently received a mailing from Arcadia, a largish brown envelope. She has failing eyesight and between that and her not being that well told me to take it. I managed to read it on the flight home.

My Mom, Mary Flax (nee Aronovsky) has a sister who is ten years her junior. Her name is Espehere (Essie). She was not put in the Arc but rather a foster care program - she lived with a German family and went to a convent in the Durban area. My Mom and her did not really have a chance to be close, but in later years they did both live in Johannesburg and have now a much closer relationship. My Mom and Dad had three kids, scattered all over: I in Maryland, my sister in Detroit, Michigan, and our brother in England.

I often tell my kids the stories from "The Arc". They get a lot out of hearing them. Such a different time and place.

MY MOM'S ARC DAYS

I wanted to write stories and events that my Mom told us when we were kids. My Mom was placed in the orphanage when she was four years old and lived there until she was 16 (early 1930 to the end of 1942). My Mom realised at an early age that this was not an ideal situation to be in, but as it was her only option she decided she just may as well make the best of it. She did, and to this day reflects back on the Arc days as good old days.

My mom remembers the practices they had for Shul services. This was done during the week, and on Shabbos they all dressed up in their best and went to Shul. My Mom remembers being called the "chocolate boxes' as in those days boxes of chocolates came wrapped with a stiff ribbon and people would save them and send them to the Arc and they would wear them as hair bows. After Shul they all got one candy; all the left-over candies were then thrown into the air and everyone scrambled for them. My Mom remembers the song that someone made up for Yom Kippur:

> For a while we must fast
> And we fast till the last
> Till the shofar blows and Shul is through
> We say we're feeling faint
> But it's a lie we really ain't
> Cos we fressed the night before you see
> We keep our toffees near us
> and when the shofar blows
> We hope that the Lord will hear us
> As into our mouths it goes
> For a while we must fast and we fast until the last
> And we hope to fast again next year

When asked by someone what Pesach meant to them they all shouted "chicken!" Chicken was only for holidays. Most times, she says, when she came back from school they went into the kitchen to get some of the food that had been left over for them. She remembers it being a brownish mush being kept warm on the stove.

My Mom does remember being hungry a lot of the time and like a lot of others raided the pantry when they were able. She told us of hiding potatoes and eggs in their bloomers and going down to the bottom of the garden to make a fire to cook them. Often they did not know what they were eating---a bit of burnt potatoes or ashes!

Bioscope was sometime worthwhile sneaking out for. They would sneak out to the tearoom bioscope and afterwards they paid their admission and were given a saucer to show they had paid. My Mom does not remember where the money came from, but does remember that they would often get a bus with a conductor with one eye. They tried to get on without paying at times, but she said it was amazing what he saw with his one eye. She remembers that when they snuck back into the Arc everyone of course knew immediately if the movie they had seen was happy or a tearjerker.

After school they used to get bus fare for the return trip and sometimes they would spend it on "fish crumbs" (the dregs that were left over from the fish and chips stores---it was mainly oil) then they would have to make the tiring walk up the hill.

The girls were allowed to sleep on the balcony during the summer, as it was cooler. She waited her turn and when it came she says that they made so much noise hardly anyone could sleep. They were not allowed to sleep there again.

Some of the stories are not that happy. On visiting day they would sit near the Arc building and watch for parents who would come to visit. My Mom remembers one day they watched as someone got off the bus. He was obviously drunk and soon the girls were imitating the way he was walking. Later my Mom said one of the girls was upset and said that that was her father.

Mary Aronovsky at age 9

My Mom remembers the names of Arc girls' parents who, when they came to visit, took a different kid out with them for the day. Another incident that I remember being told was that once the girls passed by the office and they heard the phone ringing. They were not familiar with phones and picked it up and all had a grand time yelling in the mouthpiece and earpiece. Also my

Mom remembers the Arc girls going to the office when someone had mistakenly left out The Book (the book of everyone's histories or information about the kids). She said that one girl looked up her name, read the page, and then tore it out of the book.

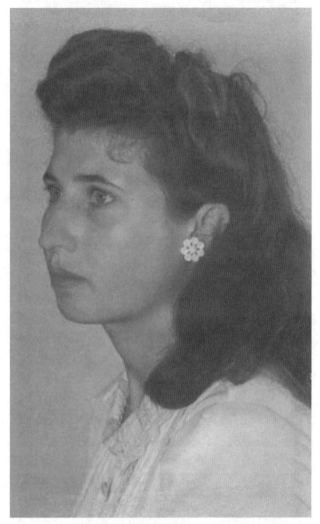

Mary at age 25

Many people sent their old clothes to the orphanage to "help" clothe the kids and they had to go down to the "schmatter" room to pick something out and then to unpick it and remake it. My Mom at first refused to do this but was really forced to. To this day my Mom will sew a button and maybe a hem but nothing else.

My Mom has not mentioned anything much about the infirmary. She was one of the kids affected with the ringworm infestation and had to have her head shaved, which she found embarrassing. Once a month they all had to line up to get either one tablespoon of caster or mineral oil.

My mother speaks of her Arc experience with fondness--- it was her home during her formative years. To this day she has maintained contact with the "old Arcs", some of whom are her life-long friends. The traditional Jewish values that were instilled in her during her formative years enabled her to establish her own home imbued with the same. All her children and her grandchildren are *frum*---may it be a source of merit for her.

Mary sadly passed away on Monday 24th January 2005 after spending eight months in the Hospital Section at Sandringham Gardens. Her two daughters from the USA and her son from London sat Shiva for her in Johannesburg.

Michael (Mot) and Mary and their first Grandchild

Chapter 28 – ESTELLE (EKIE) LITVIN (LEVINE) (1926)

Ekie was born in 1926 and together with her sister Molly were in the care of Arcadia from 1930 to 1941.

In 1930 after the death of their parents the two younger sisters Molly and Ekie were placed in the care of Arcadia. As Arcadia could only take the two younger children the eldest, Fanny went to live with an Aunt and Lilly went to live with a cousin.

In 1941 when Molly and Ekie left Arcadia they went to live with their married sister Fanny Fix.

In about 1947 Lilly got married to Mully Levine and they left to live in Palestine.

Lilly and Molly passed away recently.

THESE ARE MY PAINTING MEMORIES OF ARCADIA

Absolute desolation

Boys playing marbles

*My first memory – Going up the drive in a horse and trap at night
Me, my Father, an Uncle and Molly, my sister*

*Children running from the bees.
The boys disturbed the bee hive when the babies came by on their Saturday walk
The wall, archway and steps leading up the hill opposite the main building.*

Two Junior Girls taking washing to the laundry

Trees in the top orchard

Artist in a bottle
(Inspired by the situation of Shani Krebs)

A new life with old
A bird feeding her chick in a palm tree at Sandringham Gardens

The Wrigleys in their yellow car. They were an English couple that lived in the top cottage past the laundry and had a cheeky fox terrier. They used the sand road from the cottage to get to the top of the drive by the laundry and then drove past the hospital and main building and on to Oxford Road.

MY FAMILY HISTORY

My mother and father came to South Africa from Upina, Lithuania separately and met and married here. I do not know if it was an arranged marriage as used to be in those days but I know that the wedding took place at the house of my mother's sister in Turfontein, Johannesburg. I am the youngest of four daughters of that union. My mother had to have a gall bladder operation at the General Hospital in Johannesburg. She was 34 years old at the time, and she died as a result of the operation.

I understand that my father and mother had a shop on the diggings at the time, and my eldest sister who was 15 years older than me brought me from the diggings to my mother's sister in Turfontein. I have absolutely no recollection of my mother at all or living on the diggings. Arcadia must have just been purchased from Lady and Sir Lionel Phillips and there must have been many applications for children to be accommodated there. It was the time of the great depression in South Africa. My father must have applied for the four of us to be accepted, but only Molly and myself were taken in. The date of our admission to Arcadia was March 1930.

ARC MEMORIES

My first actual memory was going up the drive in a horse and trap with my father, an uncle, Molly and myself. I do not remember going through the front door and my next memory was myself being in a cot crying my heart out. Molly was by the cot with a lot of other people. The next day I remember running down a verandah and children running behind me shouting – 'the new girl, the new girl'. The Babies Department then was the north west corner room upstairs of the main building and we must have used the bathroom and toilets in that section of the building. What I gathered later on, as I was growing up, was that the Joe Lewis wing was being completed and they then started building the Woolf Hillman Hospital. After that the Babies' dining room was built. Until the Babies' dining room was built the Babies ate their meals on the North East verandah that came off the main building.

I remember when us Babies were moved into the Joe Lewis wing. There was a big celebration From then on I remember the Kaufman sisters being our nurses. Henny was the eldest one and Zelma the youngest. Henny was the stricter of the two and many an ear was boxed and a bottom was whacked by her. Zelma was always a gentle soul.

They came from Germany and they had a brother who had a hunch back. He was a wonderful violinist and used to play for us kids very often. They were young women at the time. Henny played the piano and ran a nursery school with us kids in one of the rooms in the building. She made a band with us kids. Some of the boys played drums and tambourines. The girls rang little bells and played the triangles and we all used to sing and have lots of fun. I'm sure there are some of those folks still around who will remember the favourite song - *"Have you heard our band, have you heard our band? With its tingle*

ling a ling and its rubba dubba dub with its tingle ling a ling and its rubba dubba now you've heard our jolly band."

The next building that was completed was the Woolf Hillman Hospital. It was a fully equipped modern hospital with a modern (then) properly equipped theatre for operations etc. The building, when I last saw it, was changed into beautiful flatlets for the kids still in Arcadia. There were two medium sized wards and one very long and large ward, a bedroom for the matron, sister in charge, room for a nurse, a kitchen and a fully equipped dispensary. Matron, Sister Ethel Goldwater was employed and was in charge of the hospital. She was a very dedicated and wonderful person and we all loved her very much. The doctors of the Jewish Community used to give their time voluntarily, and there was a roster kept, and those doctors were always on call if needed. It included specialists and dentists, optometrists etc. The children got very good medical care. Soon after the hospital opened for a couple of Sunday mornings, a number of children had their tonsils removed. Those days we were all very quiet, and must have been in a bit of shock. However, the dispensary was always very well attended from cuts, scratches, broken limbs, whatever ailment befell the kids they were attended to immediately with professional skill.

Louis Shaer and his wife Rachel, were in charge of the children of Arcadia, as Superintendent and Matron from when Arcadia was opened as the Johannesburg Jewish Orphanage. I think they were both school teachers in England somewhere. Rachel Shaer was a tall, attractive slim woman very strict and her dark hair was cut with a fringe, short sides and I personally did not like her. She wore black rimmed glasses and always a long black dress. We were all terrified of these two people - always. Stompie was a short balding man with a very rounded tummy. I often wondered how he could tie his shoelaces. Slip slops were unheard of those days.

They had two daughters, Ruth and Heather Naomi. They were grown up and were teachers. Neither was married and they each had a room in the quarters where, I'm sure, the personal attendants of Mrs Phillips resided. It was a portion of the mansion that was above the kitchen. The very last room of this section was what we called the sewing room. This was where a Mrs Amery was employed and she made dresses for the girls, mended all the linen and sewed everything that needed stitching or making. She was there for many, many years and was a very kind and helpful woman. Matron Shaer was not a well person. She wore glasses and was going blind. She and Stompie occupied the Phillips' quarters upstairs.

There was a bathroom in a round room, with windows opposite the door. It had a sunken bath with gold taps, in the middle of the room. It was the first sunken bath in the country. There were also the most beautiful delft tiles edging the white tiles which covered the walls of the bathroom. There are some funny stories to be told with regards to this bathroom.

Matron Shaer eventually became very ill and could not carry on her duties anymore, so she had to resign as matron and the

Shaers then moved into the bottom cottage in the grounds of Arcadia. It must have been the home built for the gardener in charge of the bottom section of the grounds and the bottom orchard and vineyard, and the big room which held the water pumps (in the Phillips' days). Naomi and Ruth moved with their parents. Stompie remained the Superintendent and Sister Goldwater then was made the Matron of Arcadia. A woman by the name of Mrs Hammerschlag who also came from Germany and was a qualified nursing sister, was engaged in Sister Goldwater's place in the hospital.

By then there were almost 400 children in Arcadia and accommodation was very tight. They then planned and built that monstrous building which became the Boys Department and it included large chedar classrooms. This building was constructed where there was, what we called, *the little lawn* and leading from this lawn were steps down to an English styled rose garden surrounded by lavender bushes, oleander trees (pink and white), a lovely fish pond in the middle of the garden with marble pillars around a pathway and wisteria growing up the pillars which made a roof covering of gorgeous purple blue when in bloom in the summertime.

In this new building there were quarters for Mr and Mrs Harary who were then employed in Arcadia. Mr Harary I think was in charge of the boys Senior and Junior and he was also a chedar teacher. Until these chedar classrooms were built, Hebrew classes were held in the beautiful cottage that was part of buildings where the laundry was, the shelter for the bus (the first one called "The Black Maria") then years later came the green bus.

There was a cow shed and the cows were milked every day. There was also accommodation for Charlie Miller, his wife Dolly and their children Calia and Norman. He was the bus driver and very important in our lives.

In that area, a bit up the hill, was a compound for the African staff, consisting of Zulu men, who worked in the gardens, cleaned and polished floors, windows, lights etc. They were amazing people, and very kind to us kids.

There was a swimming pool built on stilts, the first of its kind in SA – boys swan separately to the girls, on weekends. Harary also planted palm trees along the driveway. He wanted to pull out the jacaranda trees, thank goodness he was not allowed to as the drive was so beautiful in the summer. He always spoke of "when I get the reigns of Arcadia "I'll do this and that!" He eventually destroyed the magnificent orchard (top) that was halfway up the driveway, nestled at the first of the top hill. It was the most beautiful sight to see when it was in full bloom with its pink and white blossoms. Of course the fruit itself never ever really reached maturity when we kids were around, and caused lots of cramps etc. There were fruit trees of every kind – rows upon rows. I have seen a painting of that orchard. The bottom orchard was just as wonderful and a joy to all of us.

There was a coloured cook in the beginning called Annie Wenzel, succeeded by an African. George. Kleinboy was a gardener or looked after the cows and there was an old sheepdog called "Mekulu".

Ethel Goldwater, when Rachel Shaer got ill, became the Matron of Arcadia and was a tremendous influence on us girls. She was a lady from the tips of her fingers to her toes. And she taught us a lot of finesse. She was a very compassionate person and very understanding, and always looked to help and guide us. She played the piano beautifully and we used to love to listen to the classical music she played.

When I left, some of the girls that left at the same time, used to get together, and visit her. Quite a while after I left she got very sick with cancer and passed away in the Jo'burg General Hospital.

In about 1940-41 the Woolf Hillman Hospital Theatre was equipped as a fully functioned dental clinic manned by two of us Senior Girls as nurses, and dentists used to come every Sunday morning to check the kids' teeth. There were lists made, and a number of kids were checked each week. Mrs Hammerschlag was then made the housekeeper.

The Arc children were eventually used as the trials for diphtheria and polio injections when that serum was first put together – they had to have a lot of kids all different ages. It was a three in one series of injections spread over a few months. They were damn sore and our arms were very painful. Those Sundays were very unpleasant for the group having the injections that day. The results of those tests were miraculous and kids today are beneficiaries. I'm sure those of that era still around can remember this episode.

When we started school, we all went to Rannoch Road Primary School. It was a Government School, down the road from the bottom gate of Arcadia, across Oxford Road and within walking distance.

I remember the grade teacher Miss Yates so well still. She took grade one and two.

Std 1 and Std 2 were in the second classroom and a Miss Kruywagen was the teacher – a holy horror of a woman. I think I had a mental block with Afrikaans.

Std 3 and 4 was a Miss Rosen – a wonderful kind and caring woman. She got ill and was then replaced by a Mr Jacobson, who was a marvellous English teacher, but a holy horror. He gave us kids bad complexes.

When I finished primary school, Toby Roberts and I were sent to Commercial High School. They were trying out new schools at the time. Some boys were sent to Trade School.

As a junior girl of about eight or nine, we were taken to what used to be the showground near Wits University. Some member of the British Royal family was visiting SA at the time and all school children had been learning to sing songs to welcome his highness, as well as "*Land of Hope and Glory*". We were taken very early in the morning and had to hang around for hours. It was hot and we got tired, so some of us lay on our backs in the grass and slept a little.

The Friday after this event, we were having our hair washed before out baths for Shabbat. About six of us were around the bath tubs and a nurse named Lulu le Roux was in charge, all of a sudden one other girl and I were yanked out of the washing procedure and yanked into one of the bedrooms. We had to get up on two chairs, around which was placed newspapers, towels were put around our shoulders and Lulu le Roux proceeded to shave off our hair with barber's clippers. We were both shaved to the scalp – our hair collecting – falling onto the newspaper. We had lice. The shock and the shame cannot be described. We were given berets to cover our heads with, and the biggest fun for the other kids was to pull these berets and run off, especially the boys. You can imagine the scraps both verbal and physical that took place, and the anger we both felt. Today it amazes me that lice has become a very common thing that happens to kids in the summer season, and is taken by parents so casually and that all they do is use special shampoos.

The Joe Lewis wing was built under one roof, but had two complete sections with their own entrances and exits, ablution blocks and the Junior Boys were moved into the second section. They had till then occupied what is now the Shul. The senior boys slept around the quadrangle in front of the Shul. The boys, both senior and junior had ablution facilities underneath the new Shul. There was a staircase going down to the bottom section. The Shul's "Bimah" is on top of the staircase. (The Shul was Lionel Phillips' music room).

The Shul was in the new library to the left of the passage from the front door next to what was closed off as Stompie Shaer's office. The committee room was always used as such, and Shaer, Matron and their daughters always had their meals in that room. The big room (hall) was used for the girls. At various times these rooms were changed in occupation depending on numbers of girls to boys.

These rooms had doors leading into them from the hallway and were inter-leading from each other and from the big room, doors on either side of it lead out onto a verandah that ran from one side of the north side of the building to the other.

There was a scullery that was next to the small dining room, and opposite the kitchen. This is where there were bread cutting devices, where bread and jam sandwiches were made daily for kids to take to school and where bread was cut for each meal for all the children every day. Two boys (Senior) and two girls (Senior) had the duty which was rotated each month. As a Senior Girl, I had had two fist fights with the nurse in charge of our department, and from then on I was given the bread duty every second month, and an unpleasant duty the alternative month.

As a very young child, for some reason, I became besotted with the main building, its beauty and the materials put into the place. The grounds and the gardens were a paradise for me and should have been for any child. They were still kept in excellent shape for many years. I used to often pretend I was Lady Phillips entertaining guests as meal times. Maybe that helped me through growing up.

I wonder if there is anyone around who remembers a child actress Sybil Jason, who was a hit at the time of Shirley Temple, and her visit to Arcadia. Also "Yehuda Menuhin" who came to play the violin for us. There were many artists, both local and international who came to entertain us.

We girls learnt dancing with a top teacher Polly Solomon and then Ray Duchan took over. Elocution lessons were taught by Hetty Feitelberg, Hebrew lessons were conducted by Miss Factor, Mr Mann and Mr Harary.

The Nothern Verandah by Ekie Litvin

124

The Senior Girls had sewing lessons. We had to make our own dresses and one item for a Junior or Baby. Our times were pretty busy, but we still had time to skip, play all sorts of kids' games, *bok bok, kennetjie*, marbles, table tennis, and ordinary tennis and swim. Baseball was also a favourite game.

I then had a problem with one of the nurses in charge of the Senior Girls department (Cookie Nelson), and after a couple of years of her I left Arcadia to go and live with my eldest sister, after nagging her to take me out of Arcadia – I lived with her until I got married in1950.

In our time matric opportunities weren't given so easily to the females, and university was unheard of. Bertha Kronenberg, who was a brilliant student was not given the opportunity of university, which she deserved without question. We were lucky if we could go to College for a few months, and then we had to go to work.

It has given me such pleasure to realise that the younger generations all had wonderful schooling and great opportunities in the foundation of their lives.

THE KAUFMAN SISTERS

For many years the Kaufman sisters were in charge of the Babies, and during this time they became involved with the father of one of the children in Arcadia and his friend. Henny married Mr Metzger and Zelly married the friend, a Mr Leiman. When I left Arcadia they were still there. I think at various stages of their stay in Arcadia, they were transferred to look after the Junior Boys. Eventually, when they were retired the Arc set them up in a flat in Bellevue and paid them both pensions each month. Henny passed away, and Selma stayed on in the flat. At this stage I had been married for a number of years, my children were at Primary School and we had been in our house for a long time. I always made the Yomtovim – Rosh Hashana and Pesach, I wanted my children and the children of various relatives to know their Yiddishkite.

Just before one such Yomtov - I think it was Rosh Hashana, I got a phone call from Sarah Brenner (Benatar) and she told me she always had Zelly for Yomtov but could not have here that time and asked me if I would have her over, which I did. The flat was not far from my house. So started a very long association with Zelly and my family. Some time later Zelly got ill and had to have a big operation to her stomach. When she was discharged from hospital, the people of the Committee of Arcadia decided it would be best for her to go to Sandringham Gardens as a resident. So for may years it became routine, every Sunday morning, to pick her up, and take her out for coffee. We used to visit my eldest sister, various friends who were always very kind and made her very welcome.

Eventually Balfour Park Shopping Centre came into existence, and thank goodness for that. We ended up being the Wimpy's best clients on Sunday mornings. Zelly loved to have anchovy toast and coffee each time. The waiters got to know us so well that they kept a certain table for us and automatically brought the goodies. Zelly used to tell everyone I was her daughter.

On her 90th birthday I phoned some of Old Arcs to donate a few bob towards a cardigan that I bought for Zelly at a Pringle Outlet that I had entré to. She was so delighted with it. She had her full faculties, and walked upright and we used to have wonderful conversations. She was always so grateful to be in Sandringham Gardens and also always had a smile and cheerful disposition. She was hardly ever ill – a cold occasionally.

At the beginning of April 1993 I went to see her one day during the week. She had a bad cold. Friday 10th April 1993, I went to see her – she was in the hospital section. My husband and I were going to Durban that evening to celebrate the 70th birthday of one of our best friends. It was the first time that Zelly didn't know who I was. I was very distraught and thought to myself "Do I go back again to see her when I come back from Durban." We came back Saturday late afternoon and my son gave me a message to phone Sandringham Gardens immediately. The woman who spoke to me when I phoned told me that Zelly had passed away that day and they could do nothing about moving her or arrange her burial until I came and signed the permission for them to do so. I did so and they arranged the funeral and I got as many ex Arcs that I could contact to attend. It was such a sad event. She was 90 years old when she died. She had not a family member in this world.

The home eventually gave me Zelly's belongings, amounting to two little suitcases, with some pictures, a few letters, a communist member's card and also her handbag. I kept these items for a long time, and then decided to throw them out. How sorry I am now, because the bits and pieces and pictures could have been very useful for the book. I didn't mention that both Henny and Zelly were divorcees after a short while of marriage, but both kept their marital names till their departures.

MY ART

I have made a number of lovely paintings of memory pictures of childhood in Arcadia. I have done a graphic drawing of Stompie Shaer that I copied from a snapshot I found in an album. Also I have done a drawing of the verandah that runs along the north side of the main building.

I also have pictures of Arcadia which are so very special, which were taken by an associate of mine. I am going to try to paint these pictures and so make a story out of my paintings.

I have often wondered where some of the folk are, and it was good to read about the Aizakowitz sisters Sheila and Celia and also about Eli Zagoria. I remember him and was always amazed at the fact that he was an artist then.

Chapter 29.--BARNEY MEYERS (1926)

Barney's parents arrived in South Africa at the turn of the century and came from Zeimel and Razalia in Lithuania.

Three older brothers, Harry, Philip (Pacey) and Solly were placed in Arcadia in 1929 following the death of their father.

Barney was born on 9th August 1926 and came to Arcadia in April 1933 as a six year old following the death of his mother. He spent almost 12 years in Arcadia and left in December 1944.

From all accounts Barney was an excellent sportsman both in Arcadia and after he left the Arc.

For more than 40 years Barney served on the Arcadian Committee and was in charge of the Education sub-committee. He is an honorary life member of Arcadia and a trustee. He also served as secretary of the Old Arc Association for five years in the 1950s

Barney is very well known in the Jewish community in Johannesburg as he was the Principal of the King David Primary in Victory Park for 24 years. He would also be known for the handwritten calligraphy invitations he does as a hobby in his spare time.

Recently a room in the newly restored 'Villa Arcadia' was named after Barney, honouring Barney as a man that has served the community well. Barney we all salute you!!

MY HISTORY, WHICH I'M PROUD OF AND HUMBLE TO RECORD

My late parents came from Lithuania and settled in Benoni. I was the youngest of six children, a sister and five brothers. The eldest Esther and eldest brother, Israel, were not in Arcadia. Three brothers, Harry, Philip (Pacey) and Solly were placed in Arcadia in 1929. I was kept at home with my late mother until she passed away and then I was taken to Arcadia in 1933. My mother was a widow and had lost her husband some four years previously. I spent 11 years and eight months in Arcadia.

Initially I was housed in the Baby Department in the Joe Lewis Wing. The Kaufman sisters looked after us and I remember Bertha Disler, a senior girl who took a great interest in me.

My number was 14 in the Baby Department and 18 in the Junior Boys and there Molly Cohen and Jossie Le Roux were the assistants. My number was again 14 in the Senior Boys and I've always regarded 14 and 18 as lucky numbers.

We had no nursery school but I was a pupil at Forrest Town Primary School. We walked down Rannoch Road every morning and back every afternoon. In Standard 5 we wrote an entry examination for Parktown Boys' High where I spent my five high school years from 1941 to 1945.

Barney Meyers and David Rushowitz

At Parktown Boys' High I enjoyed sport and was a Prefect in Matric.

During my time in Arcadia I was cared for by Housemothers, and Superintendent and Matron, Louis and Rachel Shaer. My sister and brothers showed great love for me and I'm greatly indebted to them. I would like to express my gratitude to the many family and friends who assisted me and influenced me in my life.

At six and eight years I had rheumatic fever, and over the years my health has been quite normal and sound. I did my schooling at Forrest Town Government School and Parktown Boys high. I was made prefect in matric and played Rugby in the first team achieving colours and an honours cap. I participated in cricket, boxing, athletics and cadets.

I received a BA degree at Wits (majoring in Latin and Greek) and doing a teaching course at the Teachers College, received the TTD. I played soccer for the 1st Wits team and received a half-blue. I played soccer for Old Arcadians as well. I had board and lodging with my uncle and aunt in Mitchell Street Berea, my brother Harry had a house in Webb Street, Yeoville. He was determined to house all the family there. He looked after me like his own son. I'm forever grateful to my family for the great concern and care they had for me.

I'm grateful to The Committee, Staff and all connected to Arcadia for looking after me for 11 years and eight months that I lived there. I made lifelong friends, was taught to stand on my own two feet and was cared for and had a very happy upbringing.

I was also assisted by Arcadia during the years that I was at University and Teachers College. I did qualify for a loan and bursary for my tuition, but I am most grateful to my family for board and lodging with an aunt and uncle in Mitchell Street, Berea.

After I qualified as a teacher I taught at Benoni West Primary School for just one year I was seconded to the Germiston High School in 1951 where I taught for five years. In 1956 I was made Vice Principal at the King David Primary in Linksfield where I was for ten years under two wonderful headmasters, Abe Lipschitz and Dr Beron.

In 1966 I was appointed headmaster of the King David Primary in Victory Park where I spent 24 years until I retired in 1990.

I was secretary of the Old Arcadian Association for five years in the 50's and I've been a member of Arcadia Committee for about 40 years – I'm an honorary life member and recently appointed as a trustee as well.

I married Bess Caplan in Bloemfontein in 1960 and we have two daughters - Tammy and Ingrid, a doctor and speech therapist respectively. Tammy married Greg Morris and has two children; Simone and Adam. Ingrid married Musa Shilrit in Israel has two children; Gabi and Mika.

Bess has worked as a conveyancing secretary for lawyers all her working life. She likes reading and solving bridge problems. I do some calligraphy, read the daily newspaper and try to work out the cryptic crossword puzzle in the "Star". Bess and I watch TV for news and sport but Bess watches some "soapies" as well.

I played hockey for many years starting with a couple of years in Benoni. I also played hockey for Balfour Park 1st team for many years. I also captained the team. We had a Balfour Park Jewish Guild reunion dinner and it was a pleasant, nostalgic affair.

I also played hockey for Maccabi in South Africa and at one time captained the Maccabi Mens' hockey team.

I've been a member of the Northern Suburbs Hebrew Congregation (Waverley Shul) for at least 45 years.

I'm particularly grateful to all the many people who have assisted me in my life- brothers, sisters, friends, associates, relatives and parents and pupils of the schools I worked at.

PLAYING SPORTS

At Parktown Boys High, Barney played cricket for the third team and played first team rugby for which he received colours and honours. Mannie Osrin reported that Frikkie Marais, Science master and 1st team Rugby coach (and later Head Master of Parktown) used to say "give me 15 Barney Meyers and I'll beat any school team in the country!"

Barney was a Prefect in his Matric year. He participated in boxing where he won his own weight division from Form 2 until Matric and his name and many other Arcs are mentioned in the copies of the Boxing Section of the 1943 and 1944 Parktonian. The Arcs, highlighted in bold type, were excellent boxers taking five out of ten of the senior weight divisions in 1944.

Barney Meyers graduation 1948 at Jhb City Hall

King David Primary School

Victory Park

My daughter, Dana-Lee, attended King David Primary School in Victory Park, Johannesburg. We fondly remember Barney Meyers as a very friendly, caring and wonderful Headmaster who knew all the pupils and their parents by name. I'm sure many South Africans living around the world share this view.
I heard that he was doing calligraphy and he did my daughter's batmizvah invitations meticulously by hand with style and character. She is almost 21 and I still have a copy of the invitation. Best wishes to you and your family, Mr Meyers!
Marcelle Plaut – Perth, Western Australia 23 August 2001

PARKTOWN BOYS' HIGH ANNUAL BOXING COMPETITION – 1943 and 1944

Rubinowitz and Joe Siegenberg

PARKTOWN BOYS' HIGH ANNUAL BOXING COMPETITION - 1943

Extracted from *The Parktonian* - November 1943

The Boxing Competition proved to be just as successful as in previous years. The juniors were mainly responsible for the large number of entries which were received. The great number of spectators, who attended the preliminary bouts, were well entertained by the brilliant display of boxers.

The finals were held in the school gymnasium on Wednesday, 29th September. **Gavson** and Kruger, both Thebans, were the first boxers in the ring. The bout was very evenly contested, and in the end Kruger narrowly gained the decision. Much entertainment was provided by **Willie Aizakowitz (Tusc.)** and **(Gavson Theb.)** who put up a vigorous, yet skilful performance. The Tuscans won by a small margin.

Wannenburg and R. Stuart, in spite of the fact that they were both Thebans, fought with unrelenting tenacity, but Wannenburg proved to be the better fighter. Klein (Rom.) defeated Lazarus (Theb.) in an exciting bout.

Other interesting fights were those between **Rubinowitz** and Viljoen, Karp and Croucamp; while Spilkin, Purchase, Joffe and Siegenberg, proved to be good fighters.

Great excitement prevailed when Adler (Rom.) and **Meyers (Theb.)** entered the ring for the final bout. At the moment Romans and Thebans were leading with 80 points each. A hectic battle ensued in which the boxers excelled themselves. The crowd stood breathless while the decision was considered. A great roar emanated from the Theban supporters when **Meyers was declared the winner.**

Thanks are due to the masters who so kindly acted as judges.

The results were as follows;- Thebans 85 points, Romans 83 points, Spartans 66 points, Trojans 55 points and Tuscans 46 points

School Champions

Under 75 lbs	Kruger (Theb.)
Under 82 lbs	Wannenburg (Theb.)
Under 89 lbs	Spilkin (Spart.)
Under 96 lbs	Purchase (Rom.)
Under 103 lbs	Klein (Rom.)
Under 110 lbs	**Meyers (Theb.)**
Under 117 lbs	**Aizikowitz (Tusc.)**
Under 124 lbs	Karp (Troj.)
Under 131 lbs	Spector (Spart.)
Under 138 lbs	**Rubinowitz (Tusc.)**
Under 145 lbs	**Siegenberg (Theb.)**
Under 153 lbs	Joffe (Troj.) - J.A.B.

PARKTOWN BOYS' HIGH ANNUAL BOXING COMPETITION - 1944

Extracted from *The Parktonian* - November 1944

The Finals took place on the 20th September; as usual, the gymnasium was packed. The first bout between Stuart (Theb.) and Gavson (Theb.) both experienced boxers, supplied first-class entertainment, and were both well-applauded. Stuart, R gained the decision.

The next pair in the ring were **Siegenberg Jnr. (Theb.)** and Kruger (Theb.). Again two experienced boys were putting up a brilliant exhibition of clean and skilful boxing. **Siegenberg** won by a close margin.

Wannenber (Theb.) beat Alter (Tusc.) after having an extra round. Other interesting bouts were between Klein (Rom.) and Spilkin (Spa.), (the latter demonstrating to the audiences the effective use of the 'straight left'; **Meyers** (Theb.) and Kannemeyer (Spa.), Dando (Tro.) and Grobler (Rom.); and **Rubinowitz** (Tusc.) and Viljoen (Spa.). In the 121lbs. senior class, **Aizikowitz** (Tusc.) and **Rushovich** (Tusc.) fought four hard and exciting rounds, the latter gaining the decision narrowly.

In the heavy weights **Siegenberg** (Sen.) (Theb.) gained the decision over Steytler (Theb.) and Smith (Spa.) over Michelow (Spa.).

It could be plainly seen that the Theban House had the majority of finalists. Their victory, which brings them the Ralston Cup, was naturally a foregone conclusion. The successful finalists are congratulated, and the masters who officiated thanked.

The results were as follows:- Thebans 86 points, Tuscans 59 points, Romans 41 points, Spartans 38 points and Trojans 15 points.

School Champions   Juniors:

Under 72 lbs	Delport (Troj.)
Under 79 lbs	**Siegenberg** (Theb.)
Under 86 lbs	Stuart (Theb.)
Under 93 lbs	Wannenberg (Theb.)
Under 100 lbs	Hellman (Theb.)
Under 107 lbs	Marais(Tusc.)
Under 114 lbs	Barnes (Thes.)
Under 121 lbs	Grobler (Rom.)
Under 128 lbs	McMurchie (Spar.)
Under 135 lbs	Cohen (Tusc.)
Under 142 lbs	Revelas (Tusc.)

Seniors:

Under 93 lbs	Brophy (Rom)
Under 100 lbs	Spilkin (Spa.)
Under 107 lbs	Purchase (Rom.)
Under 114 lbs	**Meyers** (Theb.)
Under 121 lbs	**Rushovich** (Tusc.)
Under 128 lbs	**Gavson** (Thes.)
Under 135 lbs	**Rubinowitz** (Tusc.)
Under 142 lbs	Kulwinsky (Tusc.)
Under 149 lbs	**Siegenberg** (Theb.)
Open Smith (Spa.)	

Note. The names of all Arcadians above are in bold.

Prize Giving Day at the Arc

ANNUAL PRIZEGIVING PROGRAM

This is a program of the 1931 Chanukah Barmitzvah celebration and Annual Distribution of Prizes (at Arcadia).

.. PROGRAMME ..

1. *Evening Service*
   Obercantor S. Inspektor and Joint Choirs of the Yeoville and Park Synagogues (Choirmaster and Conductor Mr. S. Kantor, Organist Miss Kantor).

2. *Kindling the Lights ("Hanairos Hallolu").*
   Cantor N. Lopato and Joint Choirs.

3. *Mizmor Shir, Psalm xxx.*
   Cantor N. Lopato and Joint Choirs.

4. *Mo-oz Tsur*
   Joint Choirs and Children.

5. *Address of Welcome by President.*
   B. Kaumheimer, Esq.

6. *Presentation to Barmitzvah Boys.*
   Mrs. W. Sachs.

7. *Address*
   Chief Rabbi Dr. J. L. Landau.

8. *Speeches by the Barmitzvah Boys.*
   (a) Nathan Bernard, in Hebrew.
   (b) Harry Aginsky, in Yiddish.
   (c) Sidney Woolf, in English.
   (d) Harry Myers in Afrikaans.

9. *Distribution of Prizes.*
   Mrs. A. Atkins.

10. *Address by the Vice-President.*
    Bert Mendelsohn, Esq.

11. *Hebrew Singing and Recitations.*
    By the Children.

12. *New Membership Campaign Awards by the President.*
    B. Kaumheimer, Esq.

13. *Refreshments.*

In the program you'll see that my late brother Harry had to make a speech in Afrikaans (Myers spelt without (er)). I was not present as I only arrived at Arcadia after my three brothers had come to Arcadia in 1929 – I arrived in April 1933. I thought this program item might be of some interest to you. Many years later I think I had to make a speech in Hebrew. The Hebrew teacher at the time was Miss Factor (Mrs Lax). She coached me.

Alec and Benny Gavson, Barney Meyers, Mike Rabinowitz and Zummy Isenberg with Tilly (Aires) Rabinowitz

Gathering of Old Arcadian and Old Parktonian Boys in 2001 Benny Gavson, Solly Farber, Jeff Esakoff, Barney Meyers, Mannie OsrinAlec Gavson, Max Goldman and Fickey Klevansky.

130

Chapter 30 - PHILIP (1920-2002) AND SOLLY (1923-2000) MEYERS

Barney's older brothers Philip (Paisie) and Solly were in Arcadia from 1929. Philip left in 1937 and Solly in 1941.

PHILIP MEYERS
Written by Barney Meyers - 20 February 2002

Philip, who was a widower, (having lost his wife about 18 months previously) passed away in Zimbabwe Bulawayo, on 31 January 2002.

He was my senior by six years and the fifth of seven children. Now I am the only one left of my family of seven children. He came to Arcadia in 1929, four years before me. He was educated at Parktown Boys' High School. Philip worked hard throughout his life.

In the Second World War, he joined the army and was Lance Corporal in the mounted signals brigade. With many other soldiers who fought in North Africa during the war, he was captured at Tobruk in October 1942. When Italy withdrew from the war, Philip escaped the POW camp and spent many days in the Italian hills until he was able to be repatriated to South Africa

Philip married Stella Kirsten in 1952. They had a daughter Marilyn, son-in-law Jeff Sasinsky and two grandchildren Ariel

and Michal. They moved to Zimbabwe (Rhodesia) and lived there for more than 40 years. Philip was very versatile, being fond of music, reading, stamp collecting, doing woodwork and being au fait with world politics.

As a brother, he helped me in my life, like an interested father. From his army and prisoner of war camp, he persistently requested me to continue my studies. I am grateful for all his care and consideration for me in all my years.

I wish his daughter, Marilyn, son-in-law Jeff, grandchildren, Ariel and Michal comfort in their mourning, sincere condolences and "long life".

LETTERS FROM LANCE CORPORAL PHILIP MEYERS
Extracted from *The Parktonian* Magazine of Parktown Boys' High - November 1942

Before I go on to tell of my experiences since leaving the Union, I wish first to thank "the Old School" for a copy of *The Parktonian*, and also for a Christmas parcel I have just received. I'd like to say that we do appreciate all you are doing for us.

After mooning around in Union camps for over a year we were at last informed that we were going "North". A last glorious week of embarkation leave and then we were aboard ship and

Old Arcadian Committee 1951-1952   Front: Barney Meyers, Sid Nochumson, Izak Weiner.
Back l to r: Alec Gavson, Len Lipschitz, Gerty Kemp, Phil Meyers

away. We had all conjured up visions of a few small cargo ships, into which we were to be crammed like so many cattle. Imagine our surprise when we were marched into what is one of France's largest luxury liners, or rather "was", because today she sails under the red ensign and the cross of Loraine. During the whole voyage a strict blackout was imposed, and all air-raid and other necessary precautions were taken. We had many practice air alarms, and boat drills took place almost every day.

On crossing the equator we held a "Crossing the Line" ceremony. All of us were ducked in barrels filled with flour and sea water, and the climax came when we ducked King Neptune himself, who happened to be one of our sergeant-majors. Certificates were issued to us, which stated that, after having suffered the prescribed punishment for crossing King Neptune's Line, "we were now proper persons to mingle with his mermaids."

At first we were camped in the interior of the Egyptian desert, from where originated the stories concerning all the flies, fleas, bugs and dust. I'll not bore you with any more tales on those subjects.

It was in this camp that we enjoyed our first experience of an air raid. I say "enjoyed" because it was not our camp that was bombed, but a "place" near by. The flares, bursting shells and flaming onions and the searchlights made a really beautiful sight. At first we were a little scared and ran for our slit-trenches at the first sound of the alarm, but later we only turned over and slept all the more soundly.

Re "slit-trenches": They are long, narrow holes about three feet deep in which we lay during air raids. They are ample protection against shrapnel and stray bullets. Against a direct hit the action taken – so the joke goes – is to reach up and unscrew the detonator before it reaches the ground!

At one place our forces had surrounded a pocket of the enemy, who were strongly entrenched in underground defences. I was at a wireless post between our artillery and the Jerries. Our artillery meant to keep the enemy underground, and every time one of them popped his head up, bang! went our artillery. A sudden blinding flash followed by a deafening crash, and the whole desert air reverberated to the whining song of the shells singing their way overhead to 'Iti' and Jerry.

The night was cold, and the little light given by the stars shining down through cottonwool clouds was not enough to prevent Jerry from taking advantage of the dark to fire some rounds at us. A few shells landed near us but did no harm. About twenty yards from my van lay an unexploded shell which was liable to pop off and explode at any moment. Fortunately it didn't, but I felt pretty awkward all the time that I was in that spot.

After this came Bardia. No doubt you already know all about it, so that I need not bore you with anything more about the actual battle. At the end of the battle I had not washed or shaved for days, and my clothes had not come off for a week, so that when at last we returned to base the first thing was a wash.

SOLLY MEYERS

Solly Meyers in 1947

Address given at the burial of Solly Meyers written by a close friend in Israel.

Extracted from Old Arc Newsletter – Editor Alec Saul

For over 50 years we were neighbours and friends – more like family. We shared our celebrations and comforted each other in times of sorrow and tragedies. Our families were always together or the chagim. Every Shabbat after Shul the 'boys' automatically came and sat on your lawn and this past year on your new verandah. Tamar served refreshments and discussions took place sometimes very heated ones, about things on the Meshek, the state of the country, politics and even Parshat Hashabuah to mention a few. Jokes were told which caused laughter and joy. This relaxing and pleasant gathering became a weekly habit which everyone enjoyed. In your memory Solly, Tamar and your friends have decided to continue this special Shabbat gathering even though you will be missing. How we all miss you Solly. How heartbroken we all are.

In spite of your biggest tragedy – the untimely loss of your beloved daughter Yael – and occasional heart problems you managed to put up a good front. You realised that life goes on and that is what we in our sorrow have to do now.

May your soul rest in peace! - Leah

Chapter 31 - THE KOPPEL FAMILY
FREDA (1927), MONTY (1928) AND HYMIE (1930)

Freda was born in 1927, Monty in 1928 and Hymie in 1930 in Czechoslovakia. They went to South Africa in 1936 and following the death of their mother were placed in the care of Arcadia in 1940. Freda left the Arc in 1943 followed by Monty in late 1944 and Hymie in early 1945.

Freda is a mine of information; she seems to know everyone and their connections and has a seemingly endless supply of Arc photos and other Arcadiana.

THE HISTORY OF THE KOPPEL FAMILY

We were born in a small village called Teresva, in Czechoslovakia. There were seven children, but the youngest died at about 14 months from blood poisoning, caused by a rusty needle. It was a hard and primitive life. There was no electricity and the evenings were spent by the light of a lantern. Water was collected from an outdoor pump, as there was no running water indoors. We lived next door to the Rabbi of the village who had 10 children. There were about 300 Jewish families in the village all of whom were Hassidim. Except for a fortunate few people who somehow survived the Holocaust, the rest including all our uncles, aunts, cousins and grandparents were murdered by the Nazis.

We were ultra Chassidic and my brothers all had payot and wore tiztzit. The boys davened three times a day from a very early age and attended Cheder before school each morning from about the age of three. During the winter months it was still dark and they would go by the light of a lantern. They then returned home to have breakfast, before rushing off to school. After lunch they would again attend Cheder and daven Mincha and Ma'ariv. On Friday nights and Shabbat we all attended Shul.

Monty, Morris (16 yrs old), Leibi (with hat, 14 yr old) Mother, Anthony (12 yrs old)
Freda (9 yrs old) and in front Hymie (wearing tzitzis -5 yrs old)

Passport Photo
Anthony, Leibi (with hat) in front of Leibi is Hymie (in sailor hat) Mother, Monty and Freda

Our mother worked hard. She cooked, baked bread and washed and ironed for the whole family. I remember too the garden with vegetables which our mother planted. In addition she also worked in the family store, which was attached to our house.

Our eldest brother Morris helped out in the shop often, while he was still a schoolboy. It seemed that our father was never around as he was always travelling somewhere.

Our father had visited South Africa in 1928 when he acquired a residence permit, thus entitling him to bring his family later. In 1934 he returned to Johannesburg in South Africa, where we were to join him in November 1936.

Our mother was reluctant to leave the only life she knew, as well as her mother and siblings. We children were keen to go and excited by the prospect of a new adventure. Our mother relied on our eldest brother, who was just 16 years old, to help with the younger ones. It was very difficult for her.

We began our long journey on a Sunday afternoon. It seemed that the whole town was at the station to see us off. We arrived in Vienna where we saw electric lights for the first time. In Genoa we embarked on a three week trip to Cape Town on the "Julius Caesar" (this boat was subsequently sunk during the second world war). It was a beautiful ship, but we could not enjoy its amenities. We were all sea sick, we couldn't communicate and we would not eat the food as it was not Kosher. We ate bread, hard-boiled eggs, sardines and fresh fruit, which we recognised. We did not eat the many tropical fruits that were available as they were unknown to us.

In Cape Town, the Czech consul took us to the railway station. As it was Shabbat, we sat there till 10.00 pm till we embarked on the Johannesburg bound train arriving there at 6.00 pm on Monday.

Our first house seemed wonderful. It was in Doornfontein, next door to the Shul with its impressive lions at the entrance. Also, the sight of pink lights with "BREGY PHARMACY" twinkling on and off all night was magic.

Our top priority was to start school and learn English and we immediately attended the Jewish Government School. Our eldest brother Morris started to work in a shop and didn't go back to school.

Our father sold cigarettes and not having a motorcar had to carry a heavy suitcase laden with cigarettes on and off the tramcars to the various suburbs wherever his customers were.

Then we moved to Judith Paarl and attended Bertrams School, which was small and only went to Standard 3. There were many other immigrant children at the school so communication was always a problem.

Our mother became ill and suffered and at times had to be hospitalised. We were in South Africa just over three years when she passed away, one week before Purim 1940.

Our father was unable to take care of us young children as he worked long hours, getting home as late as 8.00 pm or 9.00 pm. I was 13 years old, Monty 11 and Hymie nine years old when we all went to live in Arcadia before Pesach of 1940. The children at Arcadia were told to expect a group of ultra religious children. They were curious to see us.

We then attended Forest Town School together with all the children from Arcadia. Our headmaster was Max Jacobs. He was a hard taskmaster but the other female teachers were very nice. Because of our lack of English we found schoolwork hard. In fact when Monty left to go to Observatory High School the headmaster, Max Jacobs, wrote in his report that if he was not any good in the first three months he should be sent straight back. The three orphanage boys who had gone into in Standard 6 at Observatory High School, Monty, Percy Nochumson and Manfred Herman always came 1st, 2nd and 3rd and nearly always in that order. When Monty met Max Jacobs later by chance in Clarendon Circle he asked Monty how he was doing and when Monty said he was doing very well as he was top of his class Max Jacobs kept a straight face and said "self-praise is no recommendation". Monty says he remembers those words to this day.

As I was a Senior Girl, I was always able to see my brothers and spend time with them without a problem. We were very close. Shortly after we arrived in Arcadia, Hymie got mumps and was placed in quarantine in the hospital. Monty and I were only allowed to see him through the hospital window.

Our father visited us regularly every Sunday and we looked forward to this. During the school holidays we would often go 'AWOL' and visit my brother who had a shop where we stuffed ourselves full with chocolates and ice creams, before returning to the Arc. We were happy not to be caught out! I think back of the times I bunked out on Shabbat and shudder to think that I

used to take little June Bartlett with me into town to visit her mother. June could not have been more than nine years old. The girls had to wear aprons and we would hide these behind the big rock in the front until we returned. I would have been expelled had I ever been caught, taking this little girl with me. I can hardly imagine how we walked the long distance there and back. Monty, together with one his three good friends, either Mike Romer, Freddy Joffe or Nathan Friedman, used to bunk out of the orphanage on a Saturday afternoon and go over to Morris' shop in Vrededorp walking all the way from Oxford Road. The fruits of the outing made the long walk worth while as they drank and ate to their hearts' content and brought back various treats with them. Nathan Friedman, who was Monty's best friend unfortunately lost his life as a pilot in the War of Independence. Monty also lost another good friend in that war, Morris Sidlin, who was his close friend after they left the orphanage as they lived close to each other in Berea Road, Bertrams.

During school holidays we had regular, twice a week outings to the Cinema in the City. Charlie drove us to town in the green SAJO bus. We were most privileged to enjoy this special generous treat.

After school one Friday afternoon, instead of going directly home, I went into the City. By the time I took the bus to get back home, it began raining and hailing heavily. The bus driver kindly stopped outside the gate of Arcadia, but I had to cross the road. As I attempted to jump over the gushing water in the gutter, I fell in and was immediately swept along by the strong current. I had a harrowing time, with the hailstones beating against my body. I desperately tried to get out but I couldn't. As I neared the Valley Road Corner where the water was gushing into the storm water drain, I thought that I would drown. Suddenly there was a black man in front of me holding onto the pole waiting to pull me out of the water before I entered the drain. I then ran into the house where the people took care of me.

Monty kept pigeons as pets in a cage down the hill. However one day he arrived to find his pigeons all dead, as a cat had got into the *hok* and killed them. He was devastated and this had a terrible effect on him. From then on Monty never wanted to keep a pet. Monty loved his Kodak box camera, which he got as a Barmitzvah present. He took many wonderful photos. Hymie was a good student, although his eyesight was always a problem. Monty was always very protective of his younger brother.

I left Arcadia at the end of 1943 and did a Secretarial Course. I married in 1947 and our daughter Rina was born in 1948. We then immigrated to Israel in 1949 and lived on Timorim. Gideon was born there in 1950. My husband passed away suddenly in 1955 and the children and I returned to Johannesburg to be with our family.

Monty was 16 years old when he left Arcadia in 1944 and began work as an apprentice jeweller in Johannesburg despite having received five distinctions and despite Arcadia trying to persuade him to continue his studies. Monty felt he wanted to get out into the world. After one year, he decided this was not for him as he was bored and it was not stimulating his mind and he went to night classes to complete his matric. One of the subjects he chose to study for his matric was a legal subject and he passed his matric in six months. He decided that if law was so easy he would become a lawyer. He then studied law and later joined a firm of Attorneys to take his Articles. He was first articled to a man called Bernard Guttenberg who later merged his practice with another firm so Monty joined another lawyer, Mr AH Cohen (whose daughter Louise Tager was for many years the Dean of the Law Faculty at Wits University). He quickly became very successful and well known as a lawyer and was offered a partnership in the firm straight after qualifying and the firm was renamed as AH Cohen and Montague Koppel. Subsequently two old Arcs, Freddy Joffe and David Green did their Articles under Monty in this firm.

Monty left Johannesburg many years ago with his wife to live in London where their three married children and seven grandchildren now all live. Monty has always been outgoing and popular among his friends and has been very successful in law and business in a variety of undertakings, in particular in television and high-tech ventures. Monty has always regarded his success as being attributable to the foundation that was laid for him during his five years at the Arc.

Hymie was the only sibling remaining in Arcadia, so it was decided that he should live with our eldest brother who had married. Hymie continued at Parktown Boys' High School and was a top student. He matriculated in 1948 with a few distinctions. Arcadia agreed to send Hymie to University and Mrs Bella Lubner was instrumental in sending Hymie on holiday to Durban to reward him for his hard work. Whilst studying, he gave extra lessons both private and at Mr Harary's Ulpan. However, Arcadia would not allow Hymie to give lessons in his final year and thus subsidised him. After completing a BSc Degree, he worked at Adcock, Ingram Laboratories where he remained for 25 years until he left to go on Aliyah. Hymie's wife died a few years ago and due to his poor eyesight he now cannot take care of himself. He now lives at Golden Acres in Johannesburg. He has a daughter Tamara living in Melbourne with her husband and four children.

Parktown Boys' High 1944. Front Row Left to right: ?? ?? Mannie Osrin, Alec Gavson, Hymie Koppel, Josh Lipschitz, Harold Siegenberg, ??
Back Row: Barney Meyers, Willie Isaacs, Dave Rushovich, Mike Rabinowitz, Benny Gavson, Woolfie Getz, Joe Siegenberg, ?? and Dave Specter.

I have been most fortunate that both Monty and Hymie have been very caring brothers and uncles. We maintain a very close relationship even though we all live in different countries. I now live in Australia at the Gold Coast, having been here since 1994. My son and his family live in Brisbane, Australia and my daughter and her family live in London. I have four grandchildren and two great-grandchildren as well as our extended family of Old Arcs all over the world.

OLD ARC GATHERING

A few of us got together with Gloria Burman (Rubinowitz) while I was visiting Johannesburg. There was Jenny Nochumson, Shulamith Lowenstein (Rosenfeld) Hazel Danker (Fish) Mary Flax (Aronovsky) Sam Bartlett and his wife and myself. Gloria's daughter prepared a lovely afternoon tea for us. Also Mannie Osrin and his lovely wife Sara (Epstein) were also at the afternoon tea.

Left to right: Zelva Bartlett, Freda (Koppel) Cheilyk, Dr Mannie Osrin, and wife Sarah (Epstein) in the dark glasses, Sam Bartlett behind, Shulamith, Mary Flax (Aronosvsky) and Gloria Burman (Rubinovitz)
Front: Hazel Danker (Fish) and Jenny Nochumsohn.

CHAPTER 32 - WILLIE ISAACS (AIZAKOWITZ) (1926)

Willie and his older sister Sheila were born in Lithuania and came to South Africa, with their late mother in 1931. Their father arrived about two years before them. Celia, their younger sister was born in July 1932.

Sheila and Willie arrived in Arcadia during the last few months of 1932 sometime after the death of their mother on Yom Kippur. Celia could not be accepted as she was only six months old.

Willie left the Arc in December 1944 after he matriculated.

BEFORE COMING TO THE ARC

I was born on the 2nd September 1926 in Posvel, a very small village in central Lithuania, about two years after Sheila, my older sister. I have in my possession the original birth certificate in Lithuanian and Yiddish with a copy of an accompanying English translation signed by TH Preston, the British Consul at that time. How did this document come into my possession? At the age of 21 I became eligible for South African citizenship, and had to make a formal application, which included the production of my birth certificate. This seemed to be an insurmountable problem at that time, as both my parents were deceased and the signatures of my uncles and aunts confirming the date were not acceptable.

My lawyer consulted some colleagues, one of whom suggested that he write to the department of Coloured and Asiatic Affairs in Cape Town, South Africa which was in control of all immigrants from Europe and Asia at that time. They might well have retained the document on our entry into South Africa in 1931. Lo and behold one of the miracles of all time occurred as this certificate was received in less than two weeks time.

Back to life in Pasvalys. Sheila and I shared a very small part of the living quarters, situated at the back of our tiny family general dealer store. The store was situated on a corner facing a small vegetable market, which was infrequently used by the surrounding farmers. Living conditions were very difficult for all Jewish families at that time, and like everybody else my parents were exploring opportunities to emigrate to South Africa.

Father's brother, Louis, who had left home some years before, had become very successful in Johannesburg, South Africa and offered our family financial assistance to get out of Lithuania. Father left Lithuania in the late 1920's and sent for us in 1931. I have only one vague recollection of the trip and that is of being bathed in a wash basin at what must have been one of our many train stops.

Winnie, my wife, in one of her genealogy searches, established that we most likely came across Europe, by train from Pasvalys to either a European or English port. The rest of the trip was

Young Willie Isaacs and sister Sheila

obviously from the port of embarkation to Cape Town, South Africa. I should have discussed these details with my aunts and uncles who had also emigrated to Johannesburg in later years, but unfortunately never did so. It never entered my mind at that time. I was far too busy with all sorts of activities.

Our Uncle Louis, who had so generously helped us to get to Johannesburg, also provided us with accommodation when we arrived. He made a small unused house available to us located on his business premises. My recollections of events in Johannesburg relating to our new surroundings are very sketchy. Uncle Louis, father's brother, had built an enormous house for himself and his family in one of the most affluent suburbs. I only appreciated how big it was and how much it must have cost when I visited it again some years later.

One experience that will always be with me occurred the first time we were invited to dinner at my uncle's house. Even at such an early age I commented to my parents about being offered milk in my tea after dinner. My remark to my parents was simply that I thought all Jewish people kept kosher like we did.

I was always mindful of my debt to my Uncle Louis and made the opportunity later on to thank him for saving my life and the lives of my family. My memory of the first year in Johannesburg is of a blurring, continuous activity. We met aunts and uncles from my mother's side who made us feel very much at home, notwithstanding their lack of wealth. They were also from Lithuania and their outpouring of love for us was demonstrated by the hugs, kisses and their wonderful meals. The time passed by very quickly indeed and we were delighted when our younger sister, Celia was born on July 15 1932.

The happy and carefree days came to an end very abruptly. I can still recall standing at the foot of my mother's bed and asking my family, who were present, when she was going to get up and be well again. Unfortunately, that was not to be. She was taken to hospital, never to come home, and passed away on Yom Kippur day, 1932. When our mother died our father could not possibly take care of us, and our other relatives, besides the Kessler family, were too poor at the time to add three children to their homes.

My next experience and remembrance was of Sheila and I travelling in my uncle Hirsha's car on a steep winding downhill road, shaded by trees feeding into the driveway of what was to become our home for the next twelve years. Arcadia, as the South African Jewish Orphanage was known, was settled on approximately twenty five acres, at 22 Oxford Road, Parktown, in one of the most affluent suburbs of Johannesburg.

Celia was not so lucky. According to then existing rules of the South African Jewish Orphanage, no child under the age of eighteen months could be admitted. She was sent from one gentile home to another until she reached the correct age.

THE ARC

The main building could best be described as overwhelming. It was a two-storey structure, with the ground floor being a mixture of rooms of different sizes. The larger were suitable for dining rooms separating the girls and boys and the smaller ones for a library and committee meeting room. A substantial kitchen and pantry adjoined the boys' dining room. On a lower level, directly in front of the main building, was a large, reasonably flat open space that became the area in which most sports could be accommodated. The boys played, soccer, cricket and a form of baseball on it very regularly, while the girls watched. A double tennis court, constructed behind the junior wing, was available to anybody that had the time and inclination to learn how to play the game. Racquets and balls were supplied by the administration, but very few took advantage of the opportunity.

One of the rules that was strictly enforced was that there could be no fraternising between the sexes in the living quarters. The romances were all evident on the playing fields, before and after meals in around the dining rooms but, to my knowledge, this rule was always strictly obeyed.

The main entrance to the building led into a large hallway and we always felt very hesitant opening the door as we expected to find the superintendent, Mr. Shaer waiting for us. He was a strict disciplinarian but very fair in all his actions and decisions. The inner walls of the main entrance were covered with endless lists of names, which were meaningless to me as a child, Years later found I out that they were the names of major donors to Arcadia.

As I never visited the upper level of the building I assume that after the necessary alterations were originally carried out, the premises were suitable for housing the girls of different ages that slept there.

The primary School for children ages six through 12 was within walking distance of Arcadia. Parktown Boys High School was about a mile and a half away and also considered to be within walking distance but seemed much further in inclement weather.

The girls High School was a good bus ride from Arcadia and so was the Middle School, where the rest of the older children were educated before leaving Arcadia to take up jobs in the open market. The "Arcadia bus" was used to transport those children who needed the service.

The upper level of the main building was big enough to house all the school going girls, and there was sufficient space downstairs to separate the boys and girls at mealtimes. The inter-leading doors between the dining rooms were opened on very rare occasions.

Information gleaned from literature of those times reveals that, in the very early stages, contact between the parent and child was very limited; Visiting was allowed on the first and third Sunday afternoon of each month, (3-5pm). The emotional state of the child was rarely considered. Children were being cared for in very large groups with no appreciation of each child's individual needs.

I do believe that our father visited as frequently as he was allowed and that at the outset it was only twice a month. Seaside camps were organised for all the children during the summer school holidays in 1930, 1934 and 1938. The approximate one thousand mile train rides from Johannesburg to the seaside camping resort in Port Elizabeth and back were the highlights of the vacation. I attended two camps and still have very fond but vague memories of those vacations. The daily activities on the beaches were very strictly controlled.

Adoption of any of the children was very rare indeed. Freddy Joffe, at about ten years of age was the only boy adopted during my eleven years in Arcadia. I do remember losing Freddy as one of my friends and feeling very despondent and possibly even envious of the fact that he would become a member of a family, with parents to look after him instead of a superintendent and his assistants. I thought a lot about it for a while and ultimately realised that it would not be likely that any family would adopt three children. I concluded that, in the circumstances, my sisters and I were better off together in Arcadia.

A few years later, when in high school, adoption was discussed in class and the full realisation brought out that the Jewish population was not well off enough to take on the additional costs of extra members to their families, we came to the conclusion that, at Arcadia, we had many advantages that the struggling Jewish families could not afford for their children.

Over the years I learned to box, earning my first medal at the age of 11, but so did my opponent, Barney Meyers, and he was only ten. I still have the medal, which I treasure dearly. Our instructor, Roy Ingram, was a former professional boxer who taught us boxing, always stressing that we should be able to defend ourselves and in addition reminding us that we had a longstanding tradition of winning nearly all the titles at the annual Parktown Boys High School boxing tournament.

In 1933, when Sheila, my older sister and I first arrived in Arcadia, the paved road from the entrance gate to the parking lot in front of the imposing mansion was 150 yards long. An unimpressive and bedraggled looking fruit orchard was on the right hand side and unkempt grass lawn on the left. Sheila was taken to the girls' quarters in the main building and I to the boys section, which was in one of the new buildings constructed away from the main building. We only saw each other for very short periods over the weekend.

Celia, our younger sister, because of Arcadia rules, was too young to be accepted and was cared for in gentile homes for the very young until she was 18 months old, and then transferred to Arcadia. The babies and nursery section was in the same building as the junior boys' section and from the outset I made time to visit Celia very regularly. However shortly after arriving in Arcadia I was hospitalised for a number of months.

The records reflected the illness as being Rheumatic Fever and I was bedridden for about six weeks. While writing these memoirs it has suddenly occurred to me that I must have had the surgical removal of an abscess behind my left ear at that time, which information I had repeatedly disclosed to many doctors and hospitals, but could never give them a date of the surgery. The scar behind my left ear has been examined by many doctors, over the past 72 years, who have all expressed surprise at the success of the surgery, and told me how lucky I was to have come through so successfully. I now doubt the veracity of the report about having been treated for rheumatic fever at that time.

After I was released from the hospital I was accompanied by a nurse for a number of weeks, particularly at or near any sporting activities. She was instructed to make sure that I did not participate in any sports at all. However as time went by the nurse became very lax in her attention and I started taking part in some events, at a slow pace, speeding up as I felt my strength returning. I believe today that the participation in some sporting activity, albeit at a slow pace, at that time, helped my recovery and introduced me to sports.

My introduction into Arcadia's activities was slow and tedious. I could not speak English and my Yiddish was understood by very few of the other children. I kept very much to myself, making few friends until I started school in July 1933. This was a little later than the other children, but I did not have any trouble keeping up with them in any of the subjects. The school was only a few blocks from Arcadia and we all walked together, in good or bad weather. At the end of five years at the junior school my grades in all subjects, were good enough to enter high school.

Arcadia's educational policy was a very simple one. If a child showed the ability to succeed in the preparatory school, then High School was automatically offered. Unfortunately, at that time, 1940, only fourteen of the boys and a much lesser number of the girls of my age were sent to high school. The rest were educated at what was known as a commercial school, with the emphasis on being able to start working directly after school.

Because Arcadia was governed by orthodox Jewish religious laws, and about 90 percent of South African Jews were orthodox, learning Hebrew and attending Synagogue services regularly were strictly observed. All children attended the regular Sabbath services, that is Friday evening and twice on Saturdays. Boys of Barmitzvah age and over attended every morning and evening.

During the week daily Hebrew lessons were provided for all the boys after regular school and we were all automatically enrolled. Somehow I was not treated like everyone else. I completed the first year of Hebrew school satisfactorily, or so I believed, and when the second year began I went with the other boys to the next class. The names were read out and I told the teacher that my name was missing. She unhesitatingly told me that I had failed the first class and had to repeat it. I did not argue and went back to the first grade classroom, where I was told that I was not on that list of pupils either. I sat outside the classroom, waited for the class to end and then went to play soccer with the boys after their classes were over. I continued waiting outside the classrooms each day for about a week and all the time felt that I was not wanted there. I never returned to Hebrew lessons for the remaining ten years. That is how long it took the administration to find out that I was missing from the roll.

For the first four years, while waiting for the Hebrew classes to end, I spent time with Celia, my younger sister, and then went to play with the boys on the sports fields. When I was called into Mr. Shaer's office and confronted with the fact that I had not attended the weekday afternoon Hebrew lessons for some time and he wanted an explanation as to how it could have happened. I told him the truth and also how I had occupied my time all those years. I was not punished in any manner and told to attend the final class with the others, the same age as myself. I learned to read Hebrew the practical way. We all recited our prayers in Hebrew, before and after every meal as fast as we could. It took me some time to distinguish the words. I also attended the Sabbath services regularly, and after a while I could read the prayers very easily. I also had no problems with the Hebrew requirements for my Barmitzvah. In fact, after my Barmitzvah, the Principal of Arcadia asked me if I would like to join the other boys who were leading the Sabbath services regularly. I politely declined, using my inability to sing well as the excuse.

I have often thought about my Barmitzvah and how different it was to all the others, during my years in Arcadia. One of the Seniors taught me to read the prayers and chant my Torah portion. As both my parents had passed away before my Barmitzvah, I advised my uncles and aunts of the date and time and eagerly anticipated their arrival on that day. They arrived very shortly after I had completed reading and chanting my part of the service! Mr Shaer, the superintendent, did not hesitate! He pointed to me, called me to the "Bimah" as if I had not been there a little earlier that day and softly said " do it all again". There was not a murmur from my friends. They all understood the situation and accepted that my family was there for that purpose and I did it all over again.

PREPARING THE WINE FOR PASSOVER

I have fond memories of the annual Jewish Passover festival that gave all of the kids tremendous enjoyment and also provided us with more food that we could eat at one sitting. That was one of the times that all the inter-leading doors were opened to make one big room, accommodating everybody for the occasion, girls separately from the boys. The Passover "Seder" was led by one of the senior boys. Home made wine was available to the seniors only and drank at the traditional times as laid down in the "Haggadah", our Passover prayer book.

Willy's CHAG-PESSACH SAMEACH.

M.Petty. 2005.

In my last year in Arcadia, I was invited by the Principal, to help make the wine for Passover. The work began six weeks before

Passover festivities. The special grapes grown in the Cape vineyards, about 1 000 miles south of Johannesburg, had been purchased a few days before at the city fruit market and brought to Arcadia for this purpose. The instructions were very simple. Pluck the grapes off from the stems, throw them into a large steel basin and then take off shoes and socks and bare footedly grind the grapes into a pulp. The pulp was placed in wooden barrels and left to ferment for six weeks.

We were invited back at the end of the fermentation period to help pour the wine from the barrels into bottles that were to be used at Passover. As the supervision of the procedure was non-existent, my fellow prefects and I were left to complete the job. I was in charge of filling the bottles from the barrels and handing them over to my fellow prefects to be corked and stacked. We felt that we had an obligation to taste the product every now and then and I believe that I did more tasting than the others, because at the end of the procedure when everything was completed I tried to stand up from my half sitting position and keeled over. My first inebriated experience.

SUNDAY, SEPTEMBER 3, 1939

Travelling in the Arcadia bus to and from a Boy Scout Rally and seeing the Newspaper Posters on the tree trunks starkly giving us the news, "War Declared". I clearly recall that General Jan Smuts led the Boy Scout Rally and addressed the very large crowd in attendance. At that time I was very confused about the war and how it would affect us in South Africa.

Shortly thereafter the anti-Semitic Afrikaners made it obvious that they supported the Germans in the war and threatened all Jews in the country. It was a hollow threat but the Arcadia administration took it seriously and the older boys were given the responsibility of guarding the outer perimeters of our home. Our "guards" paraded around Arcadia for a few nights which were incident free and then the administration called off these activities.

JOUBERT PARK

One incident that stands out in my memory and I sincerely hope can be confirmed by another Old Arc and that it is not a figment of my imagination. Saturday afternoons, in my high school days, were spent walking to the "Wanderers Soccer Fields" and watching the games of the day. Entrance was free and we generally went together in a crowd. In order to get to the Wanderer's playing field we had to walk through Joubert Park, a public area beautified by gardens, trees and water fountains. We were generally a crowd of about ten to 15 boys ranging in age from ages 15 to 18.

Late one Saturday afternoon, we were accosted by a group of roughnecks who were intent on beating us up. Their average size and age was very much to their advantage and their numbers much greater than ours. In the discussion that followed we agreed to bring a few more of our friends the following Saturday afternoon and we could all enjoy the "rumble".

On the following Saturday, late afternoon, about 15 Arcadians and a number of the roughnecks met and before we started fighting, one of the Arcadians suggested that each group nominate one person to represent each side and the outcome of their fight would settle the dispute between the two parties.

Somehow this was accepted and our representative Bobby Friedlander was to fight one of them. They chose a much larger person who towered over Bobby. Well, the fight was over in about 30 seconds. Bobby was a very good boxer and could handle himself like a street fighter, when necessary. Needless to say, we had no further problems from them.

VALLEY ROAD EXCURSIONS.

Valley Road will always remain in my mind as one of the most beautiful roads in Johannesburg. The eastern end bordered on Oxford Road, which ran in front of Arcadia. The tall, evergreen shady trees grew along the length of Valley Road, which seemed endless as the homes and surroundings were unusually large. Most of the homes had huge orchards as frontages. As many Johannesburg residents were looking for, and found relatively quiet streets on which to walk during the weekend, Valley road was a gem. We heard a lot about Valley Road from our seniors in Arcadia but also were warned about the dogs patrolling the orchards, particularly during the night and early morning.

Three of us decided that we would attempt to steal some of the peaches, plums and apples early one morning. We surveyed the layout one Sunday afternoon when there was some pedestrian traffic on the street and sidewalks. We selected a house with fruit trees near the sidewalk and a reasonably low wall to clamber over in a hurry, if necessary. Our first early morning trip down Valley Road led us to believe that there were no dogs or watchmen present and that we could be successful at this location.

At five o'clock the next morning we clambered over the wall, got to the trees relatively quickly and started picking the fruit as quietly as possible. After about five minutes we sensed, heard and then saw movement of a large dog and its handler coming toward us from the house. We jumped down from the trees, with our bags of fruit and ran to the wall. The dog and handler were still some yards away when we clambered over the wall and ran from the house. We were fast enough to get to the corner of the street, running away from Arcadia and when we looked back found that we not being pursued. That was not the end of the story.

A report was made to the superintendent of Arcadia and we had to confess our misdeeds. Fortunately there had not been a raid on their fruit trees for about two years so a written apology sufficed. However, we kept our spoils and distributed some to our closest friends.

One other "fruit" story is also worth telling. The pupils who attended Parktown Boys High School had to walk up a very steep incline, on Oxford Road, directly after leaving the gates of Arcadia. At the top of the incline was a very beautiful corner house, with about six fruit trees in the front garden, one of which was an apple tree growing a single apple. Every Arcadian passed that corner and saw the apple growing bigger and pinker daily.

The subject of the pink and then red apple was one that came up daily at the lunch breaks. We looked at each other and very frequently asked who was going to be daring enough to jump over the fence, grab the apple and get away with it. The redder the apple got the more tempting the dare. The house was on a very busy corner and anybody bold enough to jump over the fence would obviously be seen and reported to the police, or so we thought. One morning the apple was no longer there and there were many discussions among us as to the identity of the thief or if it possibly was plucked by the owner of the house who was totally oblivious of the discussions among us Arcadians.

1937 AGE ELEVEN

Age eleven, was a very memorable year and there were many milestones that made it so. In July, my father was killed in an accident while peddling his wares around Johannesburg. Sheila and I were called to the Superintendent's office and in a very brief comment told about the accident. We were quite stunned as he then gave us the details about the funeral which was to take place the following day.

I can still vividly recall my Aunt Dinka hysterically crying, in Yiddish, "What will happen to the children?" That cry was indelibly etched in my mind and stayed with me through all the other times that I attended funerals, and they were plenty. It was deemed necessary for all boys passed Barmitzvah age to attend the funerals of the Arcadia's benefactors, and like most of the other boys, I simply accepted that as a required chore. I have attended many funerals all over the world, since then, and truthfully have never felt any remorse whatsoever.

After not having had any visitors, other than my father, during the first five years in Arcadia, we suddenly found ourselves getting a lot of attention. Harry Kessler, the oldest son in the Kessler family, visited us for the first time, on the Sunday after the funeral, which was also the day he was to be married. He made it very clear that he would have liked us to attend the wedding, but in the circumstances thought that it would be better if we met a few weeks later.

He was a man of his word. He visited us regularly and I do believe that he was responsible for my attendance at the Young Israel Boys Camp, in Port Elizabeth in December 1937. As it was essentially a camp for boys, who had Matriculated and were of University age. I was, at age eleven, very much out of place. However, I was treated like a mascot and encouraged to join in all the daily activities except for the evening parties. I clearly remember being escorted to my tent daily, after the evening meal, tucked into bed and left on my own until the next morning. The evening entertainment was, evidentially not for me.

I enjoyed the two weeks very much indeed. The food was plentiful and very different from the daily menu at Arcadia. I was under close supervision on the beach but generally, enjoyed the freedom attached to the daily activities.

School vacations during the following years were spent at the homes of distant relatives who lived about 20 to 30 miles from Johannesburg. Some had children my age, which made my stay much more enjoyable. They taught me how to ride a bicycle, introduced me to their Jewish friends and got me invited to some very interesting parties.

One of the most enjoyable daily events that I experienced with them was going out delivering milk, very early, every morning. The deliveries were to homes as well as businesses and generally were to the customers that had not yet started their daily activities.

There was however a very unpleasant turn of events that made me realise how protected we were at Arcadia. Krugersdorp, a small town, is about 25 miles west of Johannesburg and the white population, at that time, consisted mainly of Afrikaners. My family were well known to their neighbours and accepted by everybody. I, however, was a stranger, also a Jew, and fair game for molestation. As soon as I stepped out of the house, onto the sidewalk and alone, I was called all sorts of names. Cuss words followed by "Jew".

I went back into the house and asked my family if I was in any danger as the tone of the words did not indicate any friendliness whatsoever in fact they were very belligerent and angry. The answer came back that I was protected while in their company but also that I should not leave their house alone.

Initially I was very careful and ensured that I always left the house with them. That was for the first week and I felt safe thereafter, stupidly thinking that they would recognise me and not molest me when I was on my own. On a beautiful sunny day I decided to go to the public swimming pool, just a few blocks distant and as nobody else was home took only my towel and swimsuit and left for the pool. I had walked about two blocks when I was accosted by about five young men, speaking Afrikaans very loudly and threateningly. As I could not understand what they wanted from me I tried to continue walking. It did not take very long for all of them to attack me with their fists and then with their feet. I tried to fend off their blows, but to no avail.

After about five minutes they laughingly cursed and left me. I got back to the house, changed my clothing and showered. I felt a pain in my ribs and found breathing quite difficult. There was very little point in letting my cousins know about the incident as they had to live in their neighbourhood and I would go back to Arcadia soon afterwards. I had suffered a cracked rib in the incident, but knew that it would heal in time. As this was the only incident in about four visits to my family, I decided that I would stay in Arcadia for the future school vacations.

MY MATRIC YEAR - 1945

The highlight of my matric year was the March 1943 concert that I helped produce. One of the set works that we had to study for the year end Matric exam was Shakespeare's 'Macbeth'. I volunteered to produce a section of the play and also to take the part of Macbeth, thinking that learning, acting and understanding my part would also help me in my final exam.

I was always very serious minded in everything that I attempted and in order to ensure the success of our production I coached all the other participants in the play. Unwittingly, I learnt everybody else's parts as well as my own, while coaching them. We all made a very serious attempt at studying our parts in the play and this was evident from the obvious enjoyment that we all displayed during the performance.

A visit to the local library helped me in my studies as well as letting me know that royalty fees were due and payable by any organisation producing the play. I wrote to the organisation mentioned in the book, requesting permission to produce the play, at the same time mentioning that we did not have the funds to pay them. A reply came back very promptly requesting payment in full. The total amount was 15 pounds sterling. I immediately went to Mr. Shaer, our Superintendent, explained the situation to him advising that we did not have the funds, but that we would very much like to continue the production. We heard nothing further from the organisation and Mr. Shaer advised that he had explained everything to them and that they had waived the fees.

The concert was a tremendous success.

I got the best award of all that resulted from my constant rehearsals of Shakespeare's Macbeth Play. The midyear Matric English literature test was written about three months after our Concert and our English teacher made Macbeth his main area of questioning. It was very easy for me to get the highest mark as I knew it all from my coaching. I felt it was an apt reward for all my work.

My last year in school was without doubt, my most enjoyable one. I was not pressured at all to get a first class passing grade as I knew that I was going to study for my accounting degree on a part-time basis. Furthermore I had agreed to work for my cousin Cecil Kessler in his Accounting practice and his brother Harry had arranged board and lodging for me with friends of his, in a house in Berea, which was within walking distance of downtown as well as Witwatersrand University.

My casual attitude to the final exams was reflected in my acceptance to play in a game of cricket the day before the exams began. Our school was invited to play against a representative team of the armed forces and our cricket coach had accepted on behalf of the school feeling very confident that he could get 11 players to participate. We had a wonderful afternoon. The result of the game was unimportant but the opportunity to play against members of the armed forces was an opportunity not to be missed. My attitude bein,g that if I had not done enough studying by that time then it was too late to catch up anyway.

1945 closed in very happy circumstances for me. Joe Siegenberg, a fellow Arcadian and I had become very close friends as well as fellow members of the Parktown Boys' High School's first team in both Rugby and Cricket. At the end of most games Joe and I would visit his mother's flat to enjoy the wonderful food, which was always plentiful and her obvious happiness at having her son visit her. I was always made most welcome and when she heard that I was going to work directly after finishing High School she offered me the opportunity to join her two sons, Joe and Harold, who would be going on a two weeks vacation on a farm in the Orange Free State.

We had a very enjoyable time and I was very grateful to Joe's mother for her generosity. I visited her from time to time thereafter and she was always very thoughtful and encouraging about my studies and sporting achievements.

FOOD FROM THE FAMILY

My Aunt Dinka, Uncle Manna and son, Itz Kalmanowitz boarded with Sam Edelman and his mother in Doornfontein for some time. It was a wonderful coincidence that Sam attended Parktown Boys High School at the same time as I was there. Sam found me one morning before school began and handed me a paper bag full of the most wonderful delights. My Auntie Dinka found out that Sam was attending the same high school as I was and from that day ensured that I would not go hungry. I had my sandwich from Arcadia and a plentiful supply of the most wonderful food from my Aunt. That was totally unbeatable. Unfortunately, Sam was in his last year and I had just started, so my wonderful lunches continued for only one year.

BOXING AND OTHER SPORTS

1943 and 1944 seems like a lifetime away and yet when you bring up those days in Parktown Boy's High School, it truly seems like yesterday. In the true tradition of Arcadia, I, like all the others, felt that we had to take part in the annual boxing tournament and make sure that we swelled the ranks of the winners of titles. In my five years in High School, I participated, and if one reached the finals, it was quite an achievement.

In 1943 Willie won the under 117 lbs weight division and in 1944 he was beaten by Rushowitz, another Arc.

Donald was the boxing coach in Arcadia, but I cannot tell you which year. My memories of high school sports participation revolve around cricket, all five years and rugby, the last two, when I played fullback for the first team. What does come back to me is that particular day in assembly when Frickie Marais, the first team coach announced to the full school, that anybody who plays soccer on Sundays and gets injured, would not be eligible for the first team selection. It did not take very long for all the other Arcadians and I to know that that message was addressed to me. Frickie was a leading first class soccer referee and I was always delighted, later on in my Balfour Park soccer career, when I found that he was to referee the game of that particular day. He was strict but always fair.

The cartilages that were removed from my left knee in 1956, in Windhoek, SWA, help remind me of those better days. The

more than occasional tingle helps to let me know about the days of long ago. It is not with any regret whatsoever. I learnt about soccer on the lower lawn at Arcadia and developed the skills that carried me through my playing years at Balfour Park and the Sunday, Yeoville League, with Sambo as our Captain and me as Vice Captain. I still boast about our seven unbeaten years.

Mark Wulfsohn brings back some wonderful memories of our Yeoville Sunday soccer league. We won the league for seven consecutive years and were unbeaten during that period. I took out the photograph to remind me of those days and of my fellow team mates and thought back to the great times we had. We needed Mark for protection many times particularly when we played away in the Southern Suburbs. I recall our arrangements that at the end of some games we grabbed our suitcases containing our change of clothing and ran to the tram or bus to get away from the area.

Willie Isaacs

AFTER LEAVING THE ARC

Winnie and I are married over 50 years. We lived in Windhoek, SWA for seven years, where I tried my hand at coaching soccer and where I had surgery on my left knee to remove the cartilages. As a result of my inability to be connected with soccer, I took up golf and finished playing off a four handicap. Not too shabby for four years of golf activity.

After Windhoek came London England, for four years and Toronto Canada, for one year. Returning to Johannesburg I could not afford the time or the money to play golf so I switched to lawn bowls and played in four National Championships representing Allenby Country Club. Thinking about the South African and South West African sports activities makes me realise how easy it was to have the time and money for sports in the Old Country.

My wife, Winnie, and I have two married daughters and their families living within five miles of us. Most unusual for American and former South African families. We see enough of each other to have a continued very healthy relationship. One unique feature is that we have met for Shabbat meals continuously for the past 21 years and that it started in South Africa when our eldest daughter Sharon got married in 1975. Linda our second daughter is a qualified Radiation Therapist and X-Ray Technician from Johannesburg General.

Winnie, a librarian retired about eight years ago. I am now a retired Chartered Accountant, having stopped work at the end of last year. I practised from home for the past 16 years and prior to that worked as a controller for a South African owned chain of Jewellery stores. Before that I had my two introductory years with a firm of CPA's in America.

I have two sisters, both living in Israel. Sheila Dror, and her daughter and family, live in Haifa, Eric passed away a number of years ago. Celia Kramer and her husband live in Hertzlia. Their children and grandchildren are scattered in Israel. Winnie and I have visited Israel a number of times since 1961. We have quite a large family there on her side as well. We have travelled extensively and have also lived in different countries during our lives.

REMINISCING

In 2004, Winnie and I visited Israel, particularly to be present at Monty's, Celia's husband, 80th birthday celebration. Our nieces and nephews prepared a wonderful spread and invited all members of the family that lived in Israel, as well as just a few friends. It was a wonderful evening, with unsurpassed weather.

The tables were set outside and, as generally happens, all the South African members of the family congregated at one table. The main topics of discussion were the old days in South Africa. I used this opportunity to remind Itz about the magnificent lunches that I received from his late mother every day for that year. I did share my lunches with some of my fellow Arcadians, but not very much.

In addition to the School days of the past some other very interesting questions were asked by my cousins. They recalled my visits to their homes in Judith Paarl and Doornfontein but

wanted to know how I got there as they were about eight to ten miles from Arcadia. I reminded them that my visits to their homes were always made on beautiful sunny days as I had no money for bus or tram fares. As I was always in very good physical condition, an eight mile walk was not very difficult for me. The reward for the long walk was always the same. The warm welcome, wonderful food and the occasional tram and bus fare back to Arcadia was always well worth the effort on my part.

My cousins and I discussed life in Arcadia as compared to theirs at home with their parents and while there were some similarities we found that there were major advantages and disadvantages on both sides. It was very clear to me then that having parents, their own home and individual rooms, was the main advantage. As none of my cousins took part in any form of sport I realised that they could not afford that activity and that studying was far more important to their parents.

Family Photo
The left side of the photo shows Paul and Linda Metter, and
their children, Kevin and Jennifer.
On the right you have Arnold and Sharon Kagan and their three children, Melanie,
Ryan and Julie. I am in the middle with Winnie on my left.

CHAPTER 33 - CELIA KRAMER (AIZAKOWITZ) (1932)

Celia, the youngest of the Aizakowitz siblings, was born in July 1932. When she was three months old Celia was placed into the care of Cotlands after the death of her mother. At around age two Celia was then placed in the care of Arcadia where she lived until she was 13.

FAMILY HISTORY

My father was helped to get to SA from Lithuania, by an older brother, Louis, who had already started up the ladder of success in Johannesburg. My mother, sister Sheila and brother Willie were left behind in Lithuania for a few years until my father managed to save enough money to bring them to South Africa. I was born nine months after they joined my father, in 1932 and my mother died three months later. I was put into "Cotlands" baby home and my brother and sister were placed in Arcadia. My father was killed five years later by a runaway horse and I was in Arcadia by then, aged five years at the time of the accident. All my formative years were spent in Arcadia.

ARC MEMORIES

The late Mr Shaer was the Superintendent at the Arc when I arrived and he was followed by "Cop" Harary, who we were all terrified of. He walked around with a whistle, and when he blew it you had to stop dead. I have warm memories of both the Kaufmann sisters, Zelma and Henny, who took care of us when I was in the Babies Department.

"Sister" Goldwater was promoted to being in charge of the girls. Previously she was the matron in charge of the hospital. We also had a "nurse", Miss Durston, who was a farm girl, put in charge of the Junior Girls. I remember how she knocked hell out of us. We were terrified of her.

We used to go to primary school in Forest Town, just outside the orphanage gates. No one from the "neighbours" would allow their kids to go to school with us. We used to see the kids, who lived in the area, being driven to school, further away, by the chauffeur driven cars. There was one kid by the name of Sylvia, whose parents did not mind her being "contaminated" by the orphanage kids. We had great fun stealing fruit in the very early hours of the morning from Lord and Lady Albu's estate, across the road from the Arc.

Mr Mann was the Hebrew teacher and he hated the smell of onion, so we used to eat onions deliberately before 'Heder' in order to be kicked out.

THE JUNIOR DEPARTMENT

One of my grandchildren, Rut, a beautiful vivacious 17 year old Sabra said to me one day, "Savta" which means grandmother

Sheila, Willie and Celia

in Hebrew, "I feel so sorry for you when you were a child" and when I asked her why, she replied "because you had no TV and no computer!!!". Well, I started telling her about the games we played at the Arc, and the imagination we used to amuse ourselves, of course, she was absolutely fascinated, some of them I will relate to you. This happened when I was still in the "Junior Department".

Every day, someone came down with measles, every time we thought we would be let out of quarantine, someone else got sick, all except me. It was six long weeks of being "locked up" and we were all dying of boredom. Out of desperation we thought up a new game. To hold a funeral. One of the boys took a fish out of the fishpond, someone else provided a shoebox for a coffin, the boys took a prayer book, yarmulkes and Talitot out of the Shul, and we dug a grave and buried the fish. The boys said "Kaddish". It was so sad burying the fish we were all "heartbroken", the service was so real, we shed bitter tears. Anyway this took all afternoon.

After a couple of days, again we ran out of games, so we decided to do something happier than a funeral. We wanted to have a wedding. It never came off because no "boy" wanted to marry one of the "girls" so even though we tried all kinds of persuasion it was no go.

Anyone who owned a tennis ball was King or Queen. We invented unbelievable games, using this tennis ball. Of course, the owner of the ball had absolute say about all the rules, and who was permitted to participate and who was not. We also got hold of old tins and piled them one on top of the other, to see who could jump the highest, until one of the kids got badly cut and we were forced to throw away our "toys" – the tin cans.

Besides the various games we played I became a voracious reader and read anything and everything I could lay my hands on. Although it is a "life-time" ago, there are other incidents I remember very clearly.

More than half a century has gone by since I was in Arcadia, which is a long, long time, but nevertheless one never forgets one's basics. On reading different life stories, I realise that I really missed out by having to leave Arcadia, at the age of 13 years – 1945. I have to admit I never felt any warmth or love or interest in me whatsoever from anyone in charge at the time. The late "Sister" Goldwater, whom I have mentioned before, was promoted from matron of the hospital to matron of all the girls. I always remember her as being very overworked and harassed. "Doc" Lichtigfeld and his wife seem to have been a definite improvement on all their predecessors.

I remember being in the junior girls, when I was about six years old. There was a rumour that a white polar bear had escaped from the zoo. I cannot remember which Afrikaans nurse was in charge of us at the time, but they told us that the bear would definitely come after us if we misbehaved. We were so frightened that everyone was fighting to keep the broom under his bed for protection. In the early hours of the morning we could actually hear the lions roaring in the zoo.

I also remember during the war years refugees were going to come to the orphanage. Very suddenly a lot of mattresses were brought in and a lot of new dresses, the refugees never reached the Arc but the dresses remained. They were pretty, floral material and we always referred to them as "refugee dresses". Every girl from school age received two dresses, same style, and same material. The dresses were made very big, so we had a few years to grow into them. The material was green, very strong and very durable, no matter how often they were washed, nothing ever happened to them, consequently we called them "bomb proof dresses".

The time of the year we most dreaded was just before the "Chaggim", Jewish Holydays because after the usual Saturday morning service in Shul, we all had to stay and have a full rehearsal of the service for whichever Jewish Holyday was coming up. The Shul, the section where the girls sat, was next to the French windows, so after breakfast we would race down to the Shul and book our place next to the French windows, gradually, the pews filled and the service began. Those of us in the back row slipped out, went for a swim and came back towards the end of the service. I was never caught out.

I also remember we used to line up after Shul to get our "five sweets". Whoever had misbehaved, was not given sweets. I was punished a few weeks running, so I took the law into my own hands. I was about 11 years old at the time. I organised a

few other "offenders" and we came close to the sweets, we were told to go away, so I hit the sweet box hard, from underneath, so it "rained" sweets and we were all scrambling to pick them up. I never got any sweets for a good few weeks after that episode.

We also had Saturday night "bioscope" which we looked forward to all week and then discussed it all week. Again, offenders had to be in bed, in pyjamas, before the others went to the film. We went to bed, and lights were put out. When everyone had gone, we rolled up our pyjama legs, sleeves of pyjamas too, slipped our dresses over our heads and sneaked up to the big dining room where the film was being shown. We sat in the last row, hid under the seats when the reel was changed and ran as fast as we could before the last ten minutes of the film ended, quickly got undressed, and back into bed, in time for inspection to see if we were fast asleep. Afterwards we had to beg someone to tell us the end of the film.

I also remember that we all looked forward to Friday night supper, because we were served dessert. We particularly liked stewed guavas. There was this youngster, Billy Robinson; he was crazy about guavas, so he told us that he had seen some worms swimming in the guavas. Of course he put us off completely, but then he said he did not mind eating worms, so we all gave him our dessert.

One of the more enjoyable events was that occasionally one of the committee members had a family celebration. We were all brought into the dining room on a Sunday morning, and given a piece of cake and a cold drink, that was a rare treat. The best was when it was my brother Willie's Barmitzvah and he sat on a platform with a lovely, rich cake, we were all eyeing it, and he called me over to give me some cake.

We were very sensitive to committee members bringing family or friends to visit the Arc, and see us kids. We felt we were in a zoo, so whenever we were told to be on our best behaviour because of these impending visits, we used to disappear by climbing high into the trees or climbing hills. It was the same when we were due to have our once a month haircut. Barbers would come to cut our hair short above our ears, with no shape or style, we dreaded it, so again we did the disappearing trick, however we were somehow outsmarted and landed up with these dreadful haircuts. We were threatened that if we did not comply, then one of the Afrikaans "nurses" would put a saucer on our heads and cut around it.

I looked very forward to our Sunday morning dancing class. We had teachers from the finest studios teaching us tap dancing, ballet, acrobatic dancing and Russian dancing. I loved it so much, that the teachers took a special interest in me. I was entered into the eisteddfod, competing at the age of nine years old in the age group of nine – 16 years. I won first prize and it was quite a sensation. I was asked to dance in a special prestigious competition of winners of all sections but the Arc flatly refused, because they said, "children must be children". Soon after that the war broke out, so that was that.

As much as we looked forward to Sunday's dancing lessons, Sunday was also something to dread, because that was the

145

time the dentist came. We all had our teeth checked once in three months. We also had the best dentists volunteering to check our teeth and if necessary we had treatment too.

One of the most mischievous things we did was to frighten the wits out of Tilly Airs and Eva, I cannot remember her surname. They were swotting for matric and sitting in the office, at night, alone. Three of us took a feather duster with black feathers, crept under the window, made a noise and then rattled the black feathers and ran for our lives. There was a witch-hunt the next day to find out who the culprits were and we got a severe telling off.

I remember wishing I could eat some more food. I was never really hungry. I just would have liked a bigger portion of food. We sometimes managed to sneak into the kitchen and got hold of some bread and raw onion. We had a midnight feast on that and we thought it the most delicious food under the sun.

I remember little things like not ever having any money to spend. There was a tuck shop and I would watch some of the kids buying those long toffees, and die for one. At the Rannoch Road Primary School, an African would come on a bicycle, selling cartons of delicious ice cold milk and it was like wishing for the moon, to be able to afford one. I knew there was no way I ever would have money to buy anything.

Also I remember Mr Jacobs from Rannoch Road School, who was a very stern disciplinarian, and never had second thoughts about giving the girls as well as boys, cuts on the backside. Yet I respected him.

Lucy Pincus was also a teacher I had at Rannoch Road School. I remember her as a nice young woman, who always came to school with her hair in rollers, bound by a scarf, because she could not get up in time to comb out her hair properly.

I remember having been promoted to the senior girls, and that week, Sister Goldwater, the matron would not allow me to go with the senior girls to bioscope. The orphanage had been given a certain number of free tickets, so she made me stay alone whilst all the other girls went off in the bus to enjoy themselves.

I also remember the shoemaker, Mr Chait, he was forever asking those of us who might have been given a doll or toy as a present, to give it to him for his children. There was a kid by the name of Freddie Joffee, who was very naughty and was caught swinging on a cow's tail, and Molly Berer who ran away and was brought back by the police. Then there was Sarah Geber who was very undisciplined and her father sent her to the same convent where I landed up a few years later. The nuns loved her and filled a big void, as she later became Catholic.

TWO PAINFUL EPISODES

My last year, in Arcadia was marked by two very painful episodes. I was 13 years old at the time. The first was at the beginning of the new school year. I was in Standard 5, a "senior" in my last year in primary school, Forest Town. A new boy had arrived, a refugee from Europe. He and I were chosen to be prefects. I will not mention names but if he should read this story, he will readily identify himself. Being a prefect meant that the two of us were privileged to go into the teachers staff room to prepare tea for them, or fetch anything that they might need.

A few days went by and suddenly, in the middle of our lessons, the headmistress, a Miss Kruywagen, called the entire school out to assemble in the school playground. In a loud voice she announced that a pupil who had been trusted, and allowed into the teachers' staff room, had breached their trust, and stolen money from their bags. I innocently wondered who on earth she was talking about. She pointed a finger at me, and called me a thief and a liar. I was absolutely thunderstruck. I had no idea what she was talking about. She even accused me of looking guilty, and would not allow me to defend myself. I was absolutely mortified.

The rest of the year was a complete misery, and of course I did very badly at my studies. When I left Forest Town, Miss Kruywagen said she would write thief in large letters on my transfer to another school. I was like a beaten dog with my tail between my legs. My biggest shame was that my brother, whom I revered, would find out that I was labelled a thief.

When I had left the orphanage and was at boarding school, at a Roman Catholic Convent in Bloemfontein, one of the Arc girls, with whom I was corresponding, wrote to me. She told me that my "partner" prefect, who had gone to Parktown Boys High School, had been caught stealing red handed, with his hand in a coat pocket, in the cloakroom and expelled. This did not help me one bit. The label stayed.

Celia as a Junior   Celia as a Senior

The second episode occurred towards the end of the school year. It was a Sunday morning, and a lot of children had family visiting. I had no-one. Shifra Bortz asked me to help share out all the "nash" her father had brought, between her various siblings. In the middle of doing this, the Afrikaans caretaker, called Miss Durstan came up to me and very insultingly accused me of once again being a "*shnorrer*". I was stung and answered her back, she grabbed hold of me and said for once and for all, she was going to teach me a lesson. She had a feather duster in her hand and beat me with the cane end. I was struggling to get away from her, but she thrashed me so hard that the insides of my thighs were bleeding.

It so happened that that particular Sunday morning was the monthly committee meeting and senior boys and girls were posted around the grounds to make sure that there would be no noise or disturbances. "Sister" Goldwater was the matron and to be fair to her, probably did not know how Miss Durstan was beating us into shape. She was delighted that the junior girls were so "well behaved" with Miss Durstan. I by this time was completely hysterical from the beating I was getting and managed to wriggle away. I ran screaming at the top of my voice to the committee room.

Tobie Roberts tried her best to prevent me getting there, but I was in such a rage, no one could stop me. I burst into the committee room and pandemonium broke out. Sister Goldwater was furious with me for spoiling her reputation and tried to get me out as fast as possible but Mrs Lubner insisted on hearing what it was all about.

I was eventually sent out of the room by which time I was dead scared to go back to the Junior Girls because Miss Durstan said she would "get me". What I did not know was that she was trembling in her boots. For a week I was too scared to go into the dining room to eat, but most of the kids saved bits of food for me. Soon after I left, the kids wrote and told me that Miss Durstan was duly fired. So in actual fact I did them a big favour, because she terrified us.

Despite the fact that I personally was not particularly happy at Arcadia, after going through the whole history of the founding of the Arc etc what stands out so clearly, is the tremendous caring and generosity of the Jewish community to look after their "own". Unfortunately I am sure all those good people are long since gone, as I would personally have liked to have thanked them.

GOING OUT

We had three sets of aunts and uncles on my mother's side, two living in Doornfontein and one in Judith Paarl. Whenever there was a day out, Willie and I would automatically head for one of those families. We felt at home with them and I always remember the delicious food we ate there. The fourth family who lived in Houghton, and were our legal guardians were the once in a blue moon visitors.

The aunt and uncle who lived in Judith Paarl once invited me for a school holiday. I was about six years old. She was a very strict lady and both her two sons and husband knew better than to argue back. She made the most delicious chicken soup with 'perogen'. However, the soup had a parsley root swimming in it. I told her I did not want the vegetable in the soup, but would have the soup and perogen. She answered that in her house, everyone ate everything placed on the table. I refused, was very cheeky, so she gave me a good slap. I jumped up from the table, it was a Saturday and the maid's day off, so I ran to her room and hid under her bed.

The entire family searched for me all afternoon and were very worried when I could not be found, and were considering going to the police. By evening I was so hungry, I crept into the kitchen and was stupid enough to switch on the light. My aunt grabbed me by the collar, and out of frustration and relief gave me a good few more slaps.

Anyway, as you can imagine, I was dispatched back to the orphanage as she felt she could not handle me. I think my aunt felt very sorry about the whole episode and on many occasions tried to invite me over, but for years I would not go into her house. She was Willie's favourite aunt, but I always went to one of the others. Only when I got married and lived near her for a while, I got to know her much better.

When I was nine years old, a distant relative, living in Brakpan, invited the three of us for a school holiday. Fanny and Shollen had married relatively late and had no children as yet. They had chickens and ducks and a vegetable garden and were a very warm, Yiddisha couple. Willie and Sheila were already teenagers and as they were not used to handling children, invited me on my own, every school holiday, five years running. I was very lucky as Fanny sewed new dresses for me, baked and cooked all the things I liked and was very good to me. This all stopped when I was sent to a Roman Catholic Convent in Bloomfontein when I was 13 years old.

Shollen and Fanny had a son and after I was at the convent and many years later, a second son. Both are in Israel. However, the parents are no longer alive. I discovered that even during the years I was growing up at the Convent, they continued inviting children from Arcadia for school holidays. Shollen died in South Africa and Fanny moved to Israel to be near her sons, and lived a few years in Israel too, before she passed away. As you can see, there are good people in this world.

AFTER LEAVING THE ARC

Willie and Sheila left the Arc when they finished school and I was on my own till the age of 13 years old.

For reasons best known to themselves, Uncle Louis, who was appointed my legal guardian when my father died, pulled me out of the Arc at the age of 13 years just when I was ready for high school - overnight I was living in Houghton. They sent me to a Roman Catholic Convent in Bloemfontein for three years of my high school. I was like a fish on dry land. My biggest saviour was Willie, who felt very responsible towards me and was my mentor all through my childhood. He gave me my values and strength to face all adversity that came my way.

After three years in high school, I was brought back to Johannesburg. Willie and I were very fortunate that Sheila had married and she and her husband very kindly made a home for us. Willie graduated as an accountant and married, I worked in an office and was very fortunate to have met my husband, who was very understanding of the complexes one usually has from being in the orphanage and the fact that he had a large, warm and very close family.

I lived with Sheila and Eric until 1954 when Monty and I married, and we lived in Johannesburg for the first eight years of our married life, and had three little girls at that time.

MAKING ALIYA

Monty was always a keen Zionist, so we decided the time had come to pack up and leave for Israel. Sheryl, our eldest daughter was ready for school and we wanted her to start school in Israel.

We had a very adventurous journey to Israel. Sheryl was 5½ years old, Mickey was three years old and Carmel four months old. Everyone we knew around us told us we were quite mad to make 'Aliya' and that we would be back within a month. In those days El Al flew in conjunction with Sabena. We flew from the then Jan Smuts Airport to Leopoldville in the Belgian Congo. It was so hot and humid that when we were asked to leave the plane for refuelling. I had to get permission to fetch a towelling nappy from the plane to hold the baby who was slippery from sweat.

From Leopoldville we flew to Athens, then to Israel. This all took 24 hours. The airline had promised me a hammock for the baby, and when we were in the air told me they did not have one. Fortunately I had a blanket with me, so the baby slept on the floor of the plane all the way. When we had stopped to refuel in Athens at 4.00 am my sister, Sheila (who had decided at the last minute to also go on Aliya with husband and two children) took Mickey by the hand and walked towards the plane. Monty had Sheryl and I held the baby. There were so many kids on the plane it was chaos.

As we were given instructions to land, I suddenly saw Mickey's seat in front of mine was empty. I rushed to Sheila to ask where Mickey was and she said Mickey had run away to look for me. Whilst the plane was still grounded, I got into a panic and started running up and down the plane calling out Mickey's name. The air hostess was furious and told me to sit down, we were coming in to land. Eventually I found her stuck in the toilet.

We finally landed in the early hours and a good friend who had made Aliya a year earlier came to the airport with her mother, who was visiting. In those days you could stand above and shout down to the passengers as they disembarked. It was time to give Carmel her last bottle of the journey and Hellen agreed to find somewhere to warm it up and feed her until we were through customs. The air hostess took Carmy and only after a few hours we came through customs. Hellen was feeding and holding a huge baby in her arms and both she and her mother exclaimed that she looked more like a boy, nothing like Monty or I and was very big for four months. We took a look and realised it was not our child. Before we could open our mouths,

a woman who must have copied us, and sent her baby through the customs yelled in Yiddish "Voo is mein kind?" She grabbed the baby (who had finished all of Carmy's food) from Hellen and threw our little mite at us. She was very very hungry and yelling.

We had a nightmare journey to the Ulpan outside Natanya until we could lay our hands on some food for her. Today, she is a mother of three beautiful sons and says in a joke that perhaps she does not belong to us.

The next day we sent Sheryl off to school and we were not told that she was too young to start school in Israel. The teacher told her to go home. She got up and on her own started walking in the wrong direction and was found by a strange man who judged by her clothes and the fact that the Ulpan was close by, that she was a new immigrant. He kindly brought her back to the Ulpan. So as you can see, we had a very adventurous and you could even say, hair raising first week in Israel.

We have been here since 1962, been through many experiences, made wonderful staunch friends, our kids have grown up and married, and between the three girls we have ten wonderful grandchildren. A bonus, after the girls were already all at school, we had a son. Although he is the only *Sabra* I can easily say all of my children are free *Sabras*.

My brother Willie lives in Houston, Texas and my sister Sheila also lives in Israel. Shortly after arriving in Israel, Sheila and Eric changed their last name to Dror.

Sheila's husband, Eric, was a highly skilled motor mechanic, specializing in Volkswagens. On arrival in Israel got a job with the Volkswagen Franchisee and a few years later was able to open up a VW workshop for himself and a partner. Eric passed away in 1989.

Sheila had a job with the port of Haifa for a number years after which she retired. Their two children, Sandra and Michael, both of whom married in Israel have one son each.

Celia and Husband Monty - 2002

Chapter 34 - DAVE SPECTOR (1927)

David was born on the 3rd of November 1927 and at age five, together with his elder brother, came to Arcadia in 1933 soon after their Mom died. David left the Arc at the end of 1944 aged 17.

BEFORE THE ARC

We were living in Bloemfontein in 1933 when my mother died in July. I was five years of age and my brother eight years. My father had a Bottle Store, which brought sufficient income for us to survive, but was adversely affected by the 1929 and 1933 World Economic Depressions. During six days of the week we scarcely saw our father, who left for work early in the morning and returned after dusk. I was in fact, in the hands of an African Nanny during the whole day and my brother for half the day. We had the pleasure of being with our father on Sundays and Public Holidays. Apparently our Nanny was inefficient and didn't survey us sufficiently and we were seen playing in a fairly busy street which was dangerous. When this was brought to the attention of members of the Jewish community in Bloemfontein, it was suggested that we should be sent to Arcadia in Johannesburg.

ARC MEMORIES

We arrived at the Arc at about the end of September with my brother placed in the Junior Department and me in the Baby Department. My father had agreed to pay the Arc an amount that he could ill afford and Stompie Shaer always referred to us as the millionaires.

In December I suddenly felt ill and I vomited in the Babies' dining room at supper. I was immediately taken to the hospital a few yards away. Sister Goldwater immediately summoned a doctor, who diagnosed scarlet fever, which became so serious that my father was called from Bloemfontein and a cousin of ours came up from Cape Town. I have no recollection of having seen them so I must have been unconscious at the time. However, the Good Lord decided that I should survive. After my recovery and the long period of quarantine, it was probably in March when I was discharged from hospital, placed in the Junior Department and sent to school.

When the teacher and Headmaster of Rannoch Road School saw me they decided that as I was too small and feeble and that I had missed about 1½ months of school, I should be sent back to the Arc and start school in January of the next year – 1934. I was taken back, but that good soul Sister Goldwater, sent me back to Rannoch School, with a note declaring that I was six years of age and must start school regardless of the circumstances.

I was placed at a desk shared with the late Norman Rosenfeld

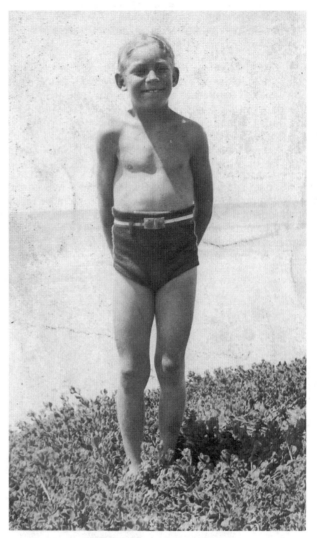

Dave Spector as a Young Boy

and I simply copied everything that he was doing during the first week or two, before slowly, but surely I began to understand.

By the end of the school year I had progressed sufficiently to be put up on trial to Grade 2, where I managed to hold my own, though I wasn't among the brightest in the class, but good enough to be promoted to Standard 1.

There ill-fate struck me once again, when it was discovered that I had a ring worm on the back of my head, and sent to the Arc Hospital in quarantine and kept away from school for several weeks. So once again, I was behind with my school lessons, especially with the reading and writing exercises, not to mention the arithmetic, but I managed to be promoted once again on trial, to Standard 2. There a change came upon me and I decided to work hard at school, which resulted in my coming first in the class in Standards 2, 3, 4 and 5 from where I went on to Parktown Boys High School. There I was always among the forefront of the class, gaining the distinction of being awarded the literature prize in Standard 7 (Form 2). This was the last time during the war when prizes, which were in the form of books, were available from England.

My Arc contemporaries at Parktown High were all pretty good scholars and we were practically all involved in the various sports events – athletics, boxing, rugby and cricket. Joe Siegenberg, Willie Isaacs, Meyer Rubinowitz played for our First Rugby Team during their matric year, 1944. Joe Siegenberg and Willie Isaacs were also in the 1st Cricket Team. In that same year Meyer Rubinowitz and I were awarded colours for athletics.

In 1945, our last year at school, Barney Meyers was in our 1st rugby team and I eventually managed to be promoted also. It was obvious to me that Mannie Osrin would be selected for the 1st rugby team the following year, but I couldn't guess that he would also be the Head Prefect of Parktown High School, presumably the only Arc scholar to have achieved this distinction.

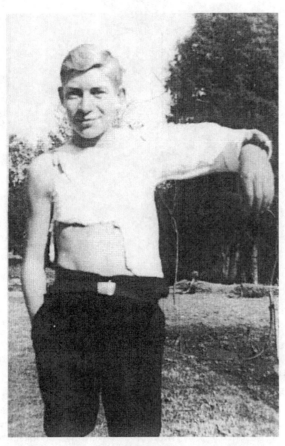

Dave Spector

The photograph goes back to 1942. During the 1942 July holidays we were playing soccer on the lawn in front of the main building. I don't know why it was called a lawn, because there were as much stones and rocks as there was grass. On that day, the 16th July, which happened to be the 9th anniversary of my mother's death, I came to grief when running at full speed after the ball which I tried to kick, but missed, lost my balance and came crashing down, not on lawn or grass, but on a rock on which my left shoulder landed. The pain was unbearable, I could hardly move, but nobody paid attention and the game continued. I couldn't move my arm at all.

When I eventually managed to get up on to my feet, I simply walked off the so-called soccer field and up to the hospital, where the good sister Goldwater realised that I couldn't move my left arm and the seriousness of my wound. She phoned for an ambulance and I was taken to the General Hospital. I had crushed the neck of the humeris of my left shoulder, which kept me in hospital for more than a month.

Ten days of traction failed to pull my humeris into shape, so an operation was inevitable and the enclosed photo shows the aftermath of my operation. The first thing I did when I left the hospital was to kick a football on the Arc 'lawn'. The next act was to go into the swimming pool. I had been advised by the doctors at the hospital not to play rugby, soccer, cricket and particularly not to box. I observed this advice for about 1½ years, but that was too long to deprive myself of our youthful pleasures and I bounced back into the forbidden sports.

At the end of 1944 the Arc Committee decided that boys who had passed to the matric year should leave the Arc and rejoin their families in Johannesburg. Wilfred Getz and I had no family in Johannesburg so we shared a room in a boarding house in Hillbrow, arranged by the Arc. My father was still paying the Arc who in turn paid the boarding house. Unbeknown to me Cop Harary had a good impression of my abilities and had suggested that after finishing school I should be sent to the USA to study plastics, a newly developed material. Unfortunately the Arc Committee didn't share his enthusiasm regarding me.

At the Arc I was involved in the usual adventures, such as stealing a loaf of bread between 11.00 pm and midnight. On one occasion the late David Rushovich and I stole a watermelon from the kitchen on a Saturday morning after Shul. When the dear Mrs Hammerslag saw us with it we explained that we were practising for a school rugby match in the afternoon and we would return it later, but of course we didn't. She was not surprised and made no fuss about it.

Russy and I had also noticed an apple tree 'pregnant' with fruit in the garden of a wealthy owner of a house near the other side of Oxford Road, so we decided to lighten its burden. The property was surrounded by a stone wall about 10 feet high, so I climbed on Russy's shoulders, jumped over the wall and climbed up the tree. Within a few minutes not only the tree, but also my shirt was pregnant with apples, when suddenly I heard a dog barking and I espied a viscous bull dog under the tree. He looked as though he was even hungrier than us. An apple a day may keep the doctor away, but a shirt full of apples didn't keep the bull-dog away. Almost immediately the bull dog was joined by an African in uniform with his *knopkierie*, who ordered me to descend from the tree, which I refused to do while the bull dog was still there licking his lips as though he hadn't had any breakfast and lunch.

It took me a few minutes, which seemed like hours to convince the African guard to lead the unfriendly bull dog back to his barracks before I climbed down from the tree and ended my pregnancy by delivering all the luscious apples to the African guard.

Another old memory was an occasion when the Arc children were asked to distribute 'daylight saving' instructions to residents in Johannesburg.

Alec Saul, Sydney Silver and I were in a group sent to the Houghton area, which was occupied by wealthy families living in expensive houses and flats. Very soon a gentleman living in a house or flat threw down a 2/6 shilling piece to thank us. This gave an idea to Silver and Saul and I, although frightened, did not disagree that we should charge 2/6 pence for our future deliveries, which brought us a tidy sum of money that we shared. Unfortunately for us, the fact that we had charged money for distribution of 'daylight saving' instructions was reported to Stompie Shaer's office and he called for the culprits at dinner time to 'own up'. I stood in fear and so did the other two, but we didn't budge. To this day I am still ashamed of that incident. I hope that Alec Saul, who has done so much good work for the Old Arcs Association, will pardon my describing this incident.

I was a friend and an admirer of the late Harry Nochumsohn, who was killed in action in Italy on 13th January 1945. At that time we thought it was on the 1st of January. I was also very friendly with the late Percy Nochumsohhn. At the Arc I was very friendly with Alec Saul and I have memories of him lifting me off my feet clinging to his hair.

AFTER LEAVING THE ARC

After I matriculated my father had fallen on hard times and couldn't afford to send me to University. This didn't upset me greatly, because my real ambition was to become a newspaper reporter. Unfortunately there were no openings in Johannesburg, so I found a job in the office of a shipping company, where I remained for a few months, before accepting a job with my family in Cape Town.

I had lost touch with the Arc, having lived in Cape Town, Durban, England and France. Basil Sepel recognised me in Paris in 1962. Later both of us returned to South Africa and we met once again in Cape Town. Our destinies once more took us back to France and we met again when my lifelong friend Donald Goldman, on a visit to his son in London crossed over to Paris to visit us and brought Basil Sepel, who, unknown to us, was residing in Paris once more.

I remember Eli Zagoria and Alec Mendelsohn of whose brilliant brain I was aware. Vicky was our Cub Master and we worshipped him and could never hear enough of his brilliant yarns. He is indeed an exceptional person, who has devoted his life to the service of others, seeking no gain. What a wonderful person he is!

I have a regular correspondence with Effie Segal that we have maintained for years and I have suggested that he contribute his limericks of which he is a wizard, to the "Arc Memories" produced by David Sandler. Donald Goldman and I have never broken our link. He sent me the current issue of "Arc Memories", which my wife and I found most interesting.

Also I have always kept in touch with my contemporaries particularly Barney Meyers and Tilly and Myer Rubinowitz, who now live in Baltimore USA. I have had some correspondence with Dr Joe Siegenberg who lives in Canada and Willy Isaacs who lives in Houston, USA. I keep in touch with Barney Meyers exchanging letters once or twice a year.

I have now entered into regular correspondence with Michael Perry Kotzen, another exceptional person, blessed with the three A's - author, actor, artist. I remember Michael Perry Kotzen from the Arc days and on the one occasion thereafter when we met on the Durban beach in 1952 or 1953. So, in fact, the first gap was not 65 years, but 49 or 50 years.

On that occasion Michael was in Durban with his actor colleagues, touring with the performances of *Valpone*, which my wife and I were pleased to be amongst the audience. We were living in Durban, where I was the secretary of the Council of Natal Jewry, the Provincial Representative of the S.A. Jewish Board of Deputies.

As you know Russy and I left SA for London in May 1949. I crossed over to France on 1st January 1950 and Michael Perry Kotzen met Russy in London shortly thereafter. He obviously recounted our adventures in London and the English country-sides. I remained in touch with Russy until his tragic end. We still keep in contact with Claire by correspondence, although this year I have been negligent because of my wife's grave illness and at present I am recovering from a double hernia operation.

Hank Epstein is now living in California. He and I used to walk to Parktown High School together. Of course we lost touch when I left the Arc at the end of 1944 and I was in a Hillbrow Boarding House for my matric year, ie 1945. I later heard that he became a pilot in the American Air Force during the USA-Korean war. It is amazing how many ex Arcs scattered all over the globe.

Alec Saul, who settled in Israel still edits the Arc newsletter. I was very friendly with him at the Arc where he wasn't at all academically and religiously inclined and he was physically very strong. I imagine that his wife uncovered his hidden philosophical powers and steered him into religious and academic trends.

The Wanderers Dream

As dusk approached I saw the sea
And on her white sands I bent my knee
To rest my weary limbs and bones
From yet another full days roams
The place was deserted but for me
The sinking sun and pale blue sea
The gush of the wind and roll of the ocean
Was all that remained to beckon a motion
Then on my visions edge
I saw a painted hedge
Of sun and clouds and coloured water
T'was beautiful and satisfied all I sought for
And as I watched the decline of day
I felt in my heart inclined to pray
To thank my God for this inspiring sight
In that moment I forgot my plight
A haze of beauty dazzled my eye
And comfort and friendship seemed ever so nigh
I was no longer that unaided enchanted wanderer
So I laid me down preparatory to slumber
While I lay stretched out on the heat radiating sands
My body in comfort, beneath my head my hands
With my gaze in the sky I saw the moon appear
Full and round, a disc so mighty and sincere
Then one by one followed the stars
Was that Venus, Neptune or Mars?
I saw the veil of darkness over me spread
T'was the only blanket over my earthly bed
As over her infant bends the mother
So over me night bent her cover
I was so overjoyed that I began to weep
But ere I could wipe my eyes I fell asleep
Yes! I was asleep to the world, but awake in heaven
And about me stood angels. There were seven
They sang with one voice a song so dear
As ever in my life I could hope to hear
I stood aback, ablushed, amazed in sheer wonderment
Was this my useless life's reward or covenant?
Then each in turn my astounded gaze did seek
Until the song was ended and the first, smiling this did speak
"Fear not my child, for we have come to teach
And what you hear now this you shall preach
Love thy neighbour as they love thyself indeed
But show that love not in emotion, but in deed"

Then spoke the second in a voice serenely sweet
"The food from the earth thy and thine brethren shall eat
But remember the earth must thou never maltreat"
"Aye! Said the third. Live, love, labour and learn
For thus only canst thou a just reward earn
And departing this life to heaven return"
"There's enough in our world for all to have and none to want
This in thy mind must ever remain forefront"
These words, those of the fourth with such feeling were spoken
That they flowed into my heart and stayed as a token
"Ahe me! Said the fifth, "enough men have fought

Happiness can neither be won nor bought
Show the Lord your gratitude with less words and more thought"
Said the sixth, "Jealousy is but a grave groundless greed
Against infection of this malicious snare, take heed
For "tis not born within us or even inflated
But through weakness of character is it created"
"Now" said the seventh, "Get ye up" and as she spoke
There appeared on the horizon a burning ball of smoke
Slowly, silently the growing fire approached
As though in others land it had encroached
"Arise, go forth, take heart and do as thou art bidden
So that thou mightest clear thy brethren the sin beridden
By planting God's laws, his wish his seed
Amongst thou evil wicket forgetful creed
Only then will the ear by God be hallowed"
And the words were scarce spoken when the angels were swallowed
In that fiery ball, the chariot of Elijah I deemed
Then I awoke and discovered that I had dreamed
And putting my hand to my brow, I felt it was moist
Had I in sleep wept or had I rejoiced?
Was my face so wet with sweat or were they tears?
It was the first time I awoke thus in all my years.

PART II

With that same feeling of sacredness I arose
And defying the sun I stood erect as though to pose
On those lonely sands, before the Almighty the most high
For with hope and much anxiousness I gazed into the sky
But though my secret wish was not fulfilled
My heart, my soul, my mind were yet enthrilled

Note Bene: I never completed this, my first and favourite poem
Dave Spector - November 1946

Master of the Mountain, Victim of the Mound

What a mighty world this seems!
What a small part we humans are!
How distorted our dreams
What a hopeless failure so far!
Yet, we have made mountains disappear
Seas we've calmed, storms we've curbed
Slight things aroused, great things severed
In all, the whole earth we've greatly disturbed
We command the seas, we control the lands
We subdue the birds, the beasts and the elves
With but a point of a finger, a touch of the hands
We are master of all things except ourselves
Until such time when man understands man
When one not only knows his neighbour but loves him well
And, when good is done, it is done for the clan
Then and then only can man in happiness dwell
David Spector - France 1947

152

Thinking of Shani Krebs, who is a gifted artist and courageous person, I was reminded of a poem which I wrote way back in 1947, so I enclose 'Thoughts in a Prison cell'. I was inspired to write it after reading Lord Byron's magnificent poem 'The Prisoner of Chillon' which covers 392 lines. Lord Byron died at the early age of 36 years in 1824, but he will be ever remembered in the annals of English literature. In January 1950 I was in Switzerland for three days and I saw the prison, but I could not visit it.

Thoughts in a Prison Cell

Oh dark and dreary is this prison cell!
Oh dank and dirty is this captive smell!
This lonely lazy life I lead
Where day nor night know no speed,
Where night and day are one,
Because I never see the sun.
Merely existing in perpetual darkness,
The helpless victim of another's smartness.
I see the same sight, I hear the same sounds.
Beyond these four walls is out of bounds.
One kindness they have given me, that I know
Above my bed, some eight feet high a small window
Rations the light and air, but brings me joy
'Tis all I have, 'tis my only toy
I can't play with it, I can just watch it
But every night I thank my God I've got it
Oh that someone should throw a gleam of light
To ease the burden of my onerous plight!
Do I really subsist on hopes and doubts and dreams"
T'would be ill-true to think that, but so it seems.
Being alone it behoves one in himself to find comfort
And ofen, very often hope is passionately sought
In deep, profound, melancholy, triumphant thought
In schemes and dreams and castles in the air
In soft, soothing, strengthening prayer
For who will encourage me if 'tis not my own deed?
Who will spare a thought if 'tis not his own need.

David Spector – 1947

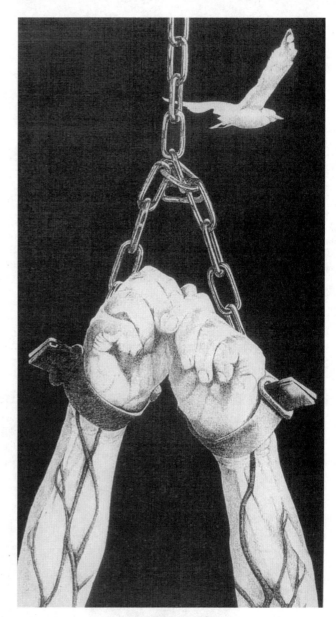

Painted by Shani Krebbs

My Ideal Self

Would that I could return a smile for a snarl
Exchange fairplay for play which is foul
Reciprocate with kind thoughts for unkind words
Look on all alike, the individual and the herds!
Oh that I could treat a loss like a gain, in good spirits
Face a threat and deem that a handshake it merits,
Give praise when praise is due, even to deadly foes
Make merry in company though buried in private woes.
If failure would do nothing else but spur me on
To greater heights, then greater happiness would be won

Dave Spector - 1948

I can only refer back to my poems of yesteryear, so I enclose a poem I wrote in 1948 expressing hopes to which I have never achieved. I enclose another of my poems of yesteryear. Sadly age is taking its toll both physically and mentally and I now have to rely on my youthful efforts.

MY FAMILY

My wife, Josette and I have two adorable sons, Denis who is a geologist with a Masters Degree from London University and Gerald who has a doctorate in Chemistry from the University of Paris. We have two lovely granddaughters from Gerald who unfortunately returned to RSA. Denis lives in Maryland, USA.

On the 3rd and 10th November 2005 my wife Josette and I reached our 78th birthday anniversaries and on the 17th November we celebrated the 55th anniversary of our marriage. Alas our sons can't be with us for the occasion, because Denis lives in Silver Spring, USA and Gerald lives in RSA.

Denis, the elder is a Geologist. He graduated and did his Honours Degree at the University of Cape Town and he had to practice as a geologist for a minimum of four years before being accepted by the University of London where he went on to graduate for his Masters Degree. Gerald obtained his degree in Chemistry at UCT and we then sent him to Paris where he continued his studies until he obtained his Doctorate in Chemistry. He is now working in RSA. He has two lovely daughters, who are excellent scholars and are distinguishing themselves in dancing and musical instruments. Denis doesn't have any children and perhaps that is better in this crazy mixed-up world as we survey it today. I can understand Monty Python when he said "*Stop the world from rotating, I want to get off*".

Dave Josette Gerald and Denis

154

CHAPTER 35   WOOLF (WOOLFIE) GETZ – (1927)

Our family has a Russian background. My late father, Barnett Harris, came from a small town in Latvia called Schubitz and arrived in S.A. in 1919. He was 53 when he passed away.

My late mother, Alta Eva, came from a small town in Lithuania called Ponedel. She came to SA in 1914 and was 86 when she passed away.

I was born on 8 March 1927 in Pretoria in Paul Kruger's former House. My father passed away on 16 March 1936. I was placed into the care of Arcadia on 24 of January 1937 together with my brother Morris, who was born on 16 December 1925.

Natie who was the oldest in the family was never in the Arc and he passed away in 1958. My sister Nancy was born October 1922. She also was never placed in Arcadia.

As my late father left my Mom in a very bad position, she had no alternative but to send Morris and me to Arcadia. This was a very wise decision as she could not look after three small children and still have to work. Thank G-d Morris and I were placed in this phenomenal institution. I thank Hashem every day of my life for Arcadia.

BEFORE COMING TO THE ARC

I always remembered how hard my parents worked for their children, and how much love they gave us. I always felt that one day when I grew up, I would be able to return the love that they gave me and that life would be much easier for them. Unfortunately, this was not to be. After my Dad passed away my brother Morris and I were sent to Arcadia. I was very upset about this. I knew I would miss my mother and my sister as well as all my friends. At first I could not wait for the school holidays to come because I knew I was going home to my family and friends in Pretoria. In those days, if you came from a town outside of Johannesburg, you were allowed to go home for the school holidays.

A LITTLE FUN IN ARCADIA

When I was still a kid, I was a real little "Zoolik". I used to get up to all sorts of pranks and nonsense. Bless Arcadia. They made something of me.

The late Manny Rodin and I were dormitory soccer champs. We beat everybody that we came up against. The soccer ball was a pair of black socks rolled up into a ball. If a game was in progress and somebody shouted that cop Harary was coming, we would all jump into bed and make as if were fast asleep

I remember the late Louis Rosengarten as a senior boy looking after us junior boys in the dormitory. He used to hit us on the head with his boot when we were in bed and we bluffed that we were sleeping.

Woolf (left) and Morris Getz – 1938

Then there was Joseph Stoller and myself. Joseph was a master at getting into the sweet room, the fruit room, opening the bread cupboards, as well as getting into the wine cellar. We used to get into the bread cupboards often, and a number of hungry kids used to have lots of bread. The fruit room and the sweet rooms were never a problem. As for the cellar we often took wine and matzo for some of the kids.

One night at about nine o'clock when we were making a L 'Chaim and eating matzos cop Harary came upstairs very quietly and caught us.

As senior boys we were allowed to go out every Saturday afternoon. We were not allowed to catch buses on Shabbat and the condition was that we had to go to the old Wanderers to watch soccer. However most of us used to walk to the top of Oxford Road and get the bus there. Most of us used to go to the cafe bioscopes and watch movies: all this included a cool drink. Price was sixpence (5 cents).

I remember scaling out of Arcadia one Saturday morning to play in an inter-schools soccer "six-a-side soccer" competition which we won, but all morning I was worried that Cop Harary

Camp at Port Elizabeth - 1938

would notice that I wasn't in Shul. However, I got away with it and I got my medal.

Camp in 1938/39 was always a breeze and we kids had an absolute ball. I well remember how our marquee was blown down by the strong Port Elizabeth winds. For a few days we ate lots of sea sand mixed in with our meals. The last day of camp was very sad, and I can still see Stompie Shaer standing there and saying "well children, all good times must come to end".

ARC MEMORIES

I went to Forest Town primary school, (1937 to 1940), Observatory Junior High School (1941 to 1943), and finally Parktown Boys' High School (1944 to 1945) where I matriculated. I applied to university to become a dentist, but unfortunately Arcadia would not help me.

The next thing that happened was that Mr Harary called me into the office and told me that I should become a rabbi and that he had made an arrangement for me to see, I think, Rabbi Kossowski. Much as I told Mr. Harary that I did not want to become a rabbi, he insisted that I go and see Rabbi Kossowsky.

When I arrived at the Rabbi's place which was on the ground floor, I rode straight into his classroom on my bicycle. He asked me what I wanted and I told him that Mr Harary told me to tell him that I want to become a rabbi. "And do you want to become

a rabbi?" asked Rabbi Kossowsky. I replied, "Definitely NO". Rabbi Kossowsky told me to get out of the classroom and I couldn't get out quick enough.

There was a funny twist to this story. Years later, my wife and I went to our son's graduation ceremony at Wits University and whilst waiting for the proceedings to begin, we found a machine which gave you your IQ and what your calling in life should be. My IQ was alright, but, my calling in life said that I should be a teacher or a Rabbi.

Willie Isaacs and I formed a great pair of soccer full-backs for Arcadia and it was always difficult for our opponents to pass us. Whilst in Arcadia I played lots of soccer, cricket, rugby, boxing, any sport that was going.

Some Saturday nights I remember we had dances or movies and occasionally we would put on a concert. I can still remember dancing a "Kazatska" with Abe Lazarus. Everybody loved it.

During our school years, the late David Rushovitch and I were in the same class from standard two through to matric.

In 1952, I qualified as a pharmacist and in 1954 I married a young lady by the name of Suzanne Kursman. We have been married for 51 years. During this time we had two sons; Hilton and Neil. Our son Hilton has two lovely sons, but Neil has never been married. On November 28, Hilton will turn 50. Neil will turn 47 on February 11th. 2006.

Cubs

One person who always was my good friend was Vicky. This is a person who only knew goodness and kindness. How we kids loved and adored him, and how we used to wait for him at the bottom of the driveway on Sundays because we knew he would tell us a yarn at the end of cubs. It was always Vicky who encouraged me when I had made my mark in the community. I well remember his many visits to the pharmacy and how he always gave me wonderful words of advice. G-d bless this saint.

The book "My Struggle" by Bernard G Aronstam brought back many memories. As for Vicky, I can speak of him only in the highest regard. What happened in the Harris era I don't know, but what a "great" person I found Vicky to be.

One thing that stands out in my mind is my Hebrew days. In my first year I was top of the late Mr. Mann's class and the following year I came last in the late Mr. Harary's class. What a turn around.

The guys whom I associated with in my time were Dave Spector, Barney Myer, Myer Rabinowitz, Joe Siegenberg, Manny Osrin, Benny Gavson, the late Donald Goldman, and lots more.

I was Bunny Barlin's "*Skievee*". I made his bed for him many times and I would stay up at night and run his bath for him. Jackie Mekler. used to get up early in the morning while the other children were still asleep and he would go for long runs. He was a great marathon runner and great Springbok.

My one and only girlfriend I had in Arcadia was Joyce Levy. What a lovely person she was. She got married and became Mrs. Meyerowitz. It was very distressing and upsetting to read that she had passed away.

I remember Bessie Firer was junior to me when we were in Arcadia. I seem to recall that her sister Miriam was in my class at school. Miriam was a good looking girl and also pretty bright.

There is just too much to say about this wonderful and outstanding place called ARCADIA. This institution made something out of me and something that I can never forget. G-d bless Arcadia and all those wonderful people who I was privileged to be there with.

Woolfie is now 78, his wife Sue 74 and they have been married for 51 years.

They have two children. His brother Natie had three children, his sister Gerty has four children while Morris has no children. The children are now in different parts of the world.

"Woolfie Getz, was in Arcadia at the same time as I was and he was the same year in Parktown High as Barney Meyers and Dave Spector. I had to fight him in the boxing tournament at school, and he gave me a bloody nose. When he batted at cricket, it was impossible to get him out, unless you happened to make him laugh! He ran a Pharmacy in Hillbrow for many years. He is married to Suzanne and now lives in Canada ."Mannie Osrin.

I found this photograph of the late Donald Goldman and myself when we played soccer for Balfour Park Under 21. This was an outstanding photo of the two of us. There is a lot of sentimental feeling attached to this photo

Chapter 36 ~ DONALD GOLDMAN (1927-2004)

Donald spent all his childhood and most of his youth at Arcadia – his father died when he was just one year old and he knew no other home. He actually learnt to box at the Arc under Alfie James in the mid 1930's. Alfie and Donald both grew up in the Arc, and when Alfie left to pursue his boxing career, Donald took over training the youngsters at the Arc.

In this capacity, boxing teacher, Donald was known to many Arcs over many generations and his connection with the Arc was maintained throughout his life.

In later years he became synonymous with raising funds for Arcadia through his organisation of box-and-dine evenings which he did for many years.

A LETTER FROM DONALD

Dear Dave

Please, please forgive me for taking such a long time to reply to your letter and "booklet", but you know I'm the worst letter writer in the business.

I'm still travelling on the road selling furniture. I have been repping for 45 years now. David you realise I am writing this letter to you from a hotel in Lichtenburg. Last night I slept in Mafekeng and P.G. tomorrow in Klerksdorp and then home on Thursday. I do quite a bit of country travelling as you see. I still do country about six nights out. My wife is so used to it by now. Do you know a Hilton Dembo? He stays in Perth. I used to work with his late father "Lou".

I thank you for the letter from Basil Sepel. I last saw Basil in Paris years ago with Dave Spector who you know stays there,

Donald age 23 at the Maccabi Boxing Trials in 1950. He won the first fight but lost in the final.

who writes to me twice a year, we have always kept in touch. Talking about Basil he was quite a good boxer, he could use himself well.

I'm sure you know they are still trying to sell the "Arc". I think "Donny Gordon" from "Liberty Life" bought two houses in Raedene near Orange Grove and the kids will move in there some time or later.

It's a great pity about Shani Krebs. I still cycle with the Bloch brothers, Selwyn and Mervyn, I mentioned to Mervyn on Sunday about you. His two sons are fantastic cyclists, Shaun is in London and I saw Garon at a wedding last Thursday.

This photo with me teaching boxing is with Abe "Duck" Kupferberger and I'm sure you will recognise his opponent, I can't remember his name!!! (Sidney Elcon)

Donald Teaching Abe Kupferberg and Sidney Elcon boxing

Derek my son, lived in London for 19 years and is now back in Cape Town with his wife. They are not interested in children. They are in the "computer game". Janell, my daughter, is married to a Hollander and T.G. stays two kilometres from us and has one of each, Katja 15 and Tyrone 13.

Goldman Family (From l to r)
Janell, Donald, Katja, Chookie, Tyron and Derek

Then there's the picture of the late "Larry Adler" (who passed away last month) with the "Arc Harmonica Band". From left to right is Pawpaw DuBois, Ellie Osrin, David Kotzen, Larry Adler, me (Donald Goldman) and Solly Farber who wishes he had that head of hair today.

Solly, Effie Segal and I used to have "jam sessions" on our harmonicas now and then, but not for a while now. I play now and then just for myself, I love it!!! I have all Larry Adler's records and a signed photo of him and us.

The Arc still call me the "sweet man" as every "Simchas Torah" I get the sweets to distribute after the service which "Starkey" still runs.

These two articles, where you can read a little bit about Donald, were published in the Jewish Report and Boxing World Magazine.

THE BACKROOM BOYS OF BOXING
By Leonard Neill

The death of Gerry Atherton recently left a void in Gauteng boxing that will be hard to fill because he was among three backroom boys who have been vital to the sport.

Most people outside of those with whom this trio have come into contact have hardly heard of them by name, though may have seen them. But along with Gerry Atherton, there was Donald Goldman and Simon Khumalo who have been an indispensable part of Gauteng boxing.

Leonard Neil and Donald Goldman at Sun City

Gerry and Donald have been gloving stewards for as long as the regulars at boxing can remember. Simon has been a man about the commission offices – especially when South African and Transvaal were linked – for the past decade. But all three have more than that to their records in fistic activity behind the scenes.

Anybody who has been a part of Gauteng boxing – and a good few others worldwide – has had the attention of Donald Goldman at some stage or other. He seated thousands of media members at the bulging Superbowl ringside throughout the Sun City fight days, working as a press liaison assistant, with similar tasks elsewhere. And promoters worldwide know him.

He has walked into the offices of Mickey Duff in London and Bob Arum in Las Vegas and emerged with tickets for their next shows. No argument, they were compensating him for the services he had given them in bygone days.

But Donald, a healthy 72-year-old today who cycles kilometres equal to his age every weekend to keep fit, goes back a long way in the fight game.

"I actually learnt to box at the Arcadia Orphanage in Johannesburg under Alfie James way back in the mid 1930's," he tells you. "Alfie and I both grew up there, and when he left to pursue his boxing career, I took over training the youngsters at the orphanage."

He staged amateur tournaments there as well down the years, and counts among the outside opposition who fought on his bills none other than Sol Kerzner, then a student at Wits University. Kerzner was once South African Universities' welterweight champion.

Donald has never forgotten his orphanage upbringing. "My dad died when I was a year old, and so I knew no other home," he says.

Today he runs regular events to support the institution, including an annual box and dine, the latest having been attended by 600 paying guests.

With Donald around, one set of orphans in Johannesburg will never go without.

But in the professional sphere of boxing he has worked with all the top promoters, sat at ringside in Las Vegas alongside Kirk Douglas and Bo Derek watching Hagler fight Duran, and has a wall in his home filled with photographs of himself and the top dogs of the fight game and the cinema world.

Yet the moment in his life that stands out most prominently has nothing to do with boxing. It happened on the soccer field, when the then 34-year-old Donald played for South Africa in the Maccabi Games.

"We beat Brazil 4-0 and I scored all four, "he proudly proclaims. "There was a riot on the field, with Brazil walking off and the game abandoned, but the score and the result stood. That match stands out as the highlight of my sporting career."

DONALD GOLDMAN SA BOXING'S "MISTER NICE GUY"
Story and photograph by Brian Gaitz

Ask anyone in South African boxing circles who Donald Goldman is and you will find that this charismatic, enthusiastic and youthful 73-year-old is practically part of the furniture.

Goldman is in fact a furniture sales representative and a man with an absorbing love of boxing.

"When it comes to sport, my two passions have been boxing and soccer," says Goldman, who made a name for himself when he represented the South African Maccabi soccer team at the Maccabi Games in Israel.

Goldman reminisces with fondness about moments in his amateur soccer career.

Goldman spent most of his youth at the Arcadia Orphanage – "I feel I have a lot to repay Arcadia for and I would do anything for them.

"It was wonderful growing up there and I owe them so much. At one stage I had 300 brothers and sisters there.

"The Arc has done wonders for me and raising money for the orphanage is the least I can do to show my gratitude," said Goldman, who raised over R150 000 for the orphanage where the young Goldman's interest and love for boxing was first nurtured.

"I began my amateur boxing career at the Arcadia under Alfie James in the 1930's and when he left to pursue his boxing career, I took over the training of the youngsters at the orphanage," he recalled.

Goldman is well known by most boxing promoters worldwide, including the likes of Bob Arum and Mickey Duff overseas as well as local promoters Rodney Berman and Mike Segal.

One could say that the likeable Goldman has "forced" his way into the lives of these people.

"I used to gate crash so many boxing tournaments when I was young that eventually the promoters got tired of it and gave me a job. I guess they reckoned that as they were never going to get rid of me, they might as well give me something useful to do," said Goldman, whose perseverance at boxing tournaments rewarded him with the job of gloving steward and seating people.

His current standing in boxing circles is one of acting as a "behind-the-scenes" boxing impresario. While the boxers fight it out in the ring, Goldman makes sure that everything outside of the ring runs smoothly.

"That was the best fight I have ever been witness to," he said.

Goldman has managed to get himself photographed with some of the world's most renowned celebrities, but the photograph that he treasures above all else is the one with him and boxing icon Sugar Ray Leonard, which was taken in Las Vegas.

"Sugar Ray has always been, and always will be, my boxing hero. In my opinion he was the greatest boxer ever, so to get a photograph with him was a great thrill," said Goldman.

He attributes his youthful disposition to his "absolute love and zest for life", as well as the support of his wife Chookie – whom he has been married to for 44 years – and his two children and grandchildren.

One of his clients in the furniture business once told Goldman that when he walked into the room, the furniture started dancing.

That description would aptly describe a man who always exudes a positive and exuberant attitude towards life and this shows in his youthful features, making it hard to believe that he is in fact 73 years old.

Donald Goldman with Pastor Ray McCauley at the Nashua "Night of Legends"

TRIBUTES TO DONALD – NOVEMBER/DECEMBER 2004

I'm sure you all join me in wishing Chookie and Family "Long Life" and that you share the feelings expressed below by our Fellow Arcs and Friends from all corners of the world:

"Donald Goldman, like Doc and very few others, is one hell of a decent guy.

Donald giving boxing lessons

The kind attention he gave us as a boxing teacher was the only reason why I continued boxing so many years. My respect for Donald was so deep that at the age of seven for my first ever boxing tournament against the inevitable Alf James club - I actually destroyed my "professionally garbed "frightening opponent, after only a minute or two of the first round. And while they were rushing him to hospital or elsewhere, Donald gave me the most humiliating mouth wagging accompanied by an unusual knock or two. He was right but it unconsciously cost me my devastating knock-out punch.

I gave up the sport some eight years later because it's frustrating to be in a ring with the right arm kind of tied to your body just unable to use it effectively. Fortunately I recuperated it again after leaving the Arc and country - cutting the umbilical cord kind of thing - as it was the case with several other blockages that many of us develop in similar growing up circumstances."

Donald's passing away is very sad. Donald I will always love and remember you with warmth. Chookie just continue going because that's what your husband would want.
Basil Sepal - Paris France
******

"Donald I remember you very well and remember you teaching me to box when I was about eight years old - that was 40 years ago, under the Shul. I still remember the smell of the leather and the punching ball and the bag too, and I remember you scolded me for hitting Max too hard and then you got me to spar with Raymond Lang who was about 12 years old. When

we were a bit older we used to go into that room quite often and had a secret key.

Also I remember once when I was with Leon Goodman (we had just started working) bumping into you in town at lunchtime (say 1973) and you had quite a big briefcase and we teased you that it was only full of sandwiches. When we challenged you to show us what was inside you did but there were no sandwiches, which we were trying to bum off you."

"A truly great man" who with his bubbling personality was friends to and known by many Arcs over many generations:
David Sandler – Perth Australia
******

"I always open emails from you with great anticipation, expecting news about Arcadia, mostly good. However life is not always kind and as time goes by we get a blow, meant in boxing terminology, that hurts. Donald was a great friend to everybody and although we had not made contact for many years, I always felt pretty good when reading about his successes. I have just pulled out my copy of the photo titled "Johannesburg Old Arcadian Association", Winners Yeoville Soccer League. 1940-1947. Donald is in the centre of the middle row, and that is how I have always thought about him. Right in the centre of everything. Looking at the photo of those wonderful years I cannot believe that all of that started more than sixty years ago and that I was fortunate enough to have participated in them. My best wishes to Donald's family and as we always say in South Africa, "long life to all of them"
Willie Isaacs - Houston USA
*****

I first heard from Freda Cheilyk about Donald's death, and was very saddened at this news and the fact that he had suffered so badly. Louis Hurwitz and I both remarked on his jovial and friendly nature; he brought laughter with him whenever he went. To his wife Chookie and his family I extend my deepest condolences and wish them Long Life.
Bertha Kronenberg (Klevansky) - Toronto Canada.
*****

Lennox Lewis and Donald

I was very saddened to hear about the death of Donald Goldman. I did hear from my brother Colin that he had been very ill. Of course I knew him and remember his beautiful smile always. My sincerest condolences to his family. I am sure he will be sorely missed by all.

Sorry also to hear about the passing of Percy Nochumson. I was friendly with his sister Judy.
Edith Cohen (Rosenkovitz) - UK

*****

Donald was an Old Arc very much involved with Arcadia. He often organised chocolates and other goodies for the kids at Arcadia.

He was a boxer in his youth and always had a very strong connection to boxing. He organised Arcadia's Box and Dine evenings which we had a few times. He could virtually sell all the tickets himself as he was so well known and well connected. He was also involved with a campaign called "Stay alert- stay alive" sponsored by Pick n Pay amongst others.

Donald always had a smile and was always positive and upbeat. He will be sorely missed. RIP Donald. I'm sure that by now all Old Arcs in Johannesburg who knew Donald will have heard the news.
Selwyn Chalmers – JHB RSA

*****

Very sad news on Donald.....a man in a million!!!!
Max Goldman – JHB RSA

*****

"What a sad event the passing of Donald Goldman has been. Such a wonderful person. Such an Icon of all that we who were brought up in Arcadia have come to be proud of. Part of our personal heritage, and therefore part of our personal pain and loss. To Chookie and family we say 'long life' and extend our heartfelt condolences. He will never be forgotten and will always be loved.

Willie Isaacs referred to the photograph of that "all conquering" Old Arcadian Soccer side that swept all aside in the tough Sunday league of the mid forties. I remember the picture very well as I was in it, and was very proud to be in it, as I was not the greatest footballer ever and to have been chosen to be there was a tremendous personal achievement. But the reason I mention it now is the background to what actually happened when the photographer tried to take the shot. As he was about to press the button, Donald said something so funny that we were thrown into convulsions for about ten minutes, and the poor bloke had to start all over again. Eventually, when we had all regained sufficient composure, and the button was again about to be pressed, Donald came out with another wisecrack that sent us all off holding our stomachs. Well, it took about half an hour to take the picture, and whenever I see the end result I always remember what went on at that photo shoot.

Most Old Arcs are known only to the age groups they belong to. I think it's fair to say that Donald Goldman was known and loved across the entire spectrum of Arcadia's history and memory. He will be sorely missed."
Mannie Osrin - Melbourne Australia

*****

"I remember Donald very well, as he also taught me to box, specifically with Alan Levy who was even shorter than I am, but was a good little boxer. He always gave me a headache. I could never really take too much of a knock on the head. Donald loved kids and he was always there for us, a gentle giant. I am sorry to hear of his passing on and wish all his family long life and lots of loving memories".
Louis Schreeuwer - Sydney Australia

*****

It was with great shock that I read of his passing. It has been many many years since I last had contact with him, probably 30 odd years ago, but I still remember him coming to the Arc and giving the 'boys' boxing lessons. He was always smiling and friendly, and all the 'girls' adored him. Please pass on to his family, our deepest condolences as this sad time."
Lesley Becker and family (nee Mark) – Kibbutz Revivim Israel

*****

"I was very distressed to hear about Donald's demise. Truly indeed a great guy and a thorough gentleman. We often played soccer together at the Arc and I also played goalie for the Old Arcs team. Boxing wise I still vividly remember him at many ringside bouts. I also fondly remember the days when I first met Don at the Arc. He used to joke about and gave me the nickname of BALA. To this very day I am still bemused by the name and what it meant. Incidentally Don also worked for a long period at the furniture store by the name of Victoria Lewis who happened to be my late wife. Don was quite intrigued and excited when I relayed this bit of news to him. We salute you DON alias Clint Eastwood. You will be sorely and sadly missed. A giant of a man and a true legend in our time (R I P)
Barney Segal - JHB RSA

*****

My state of mind was shattered by the death of my dear life-long friend, Donald Goldman. I was glad to read the most deserved praises to such an exceptional man.
Dave Spector - France.

Durbachs and David Catching Up With Donald - Dec 2001

CHAPTER 37 - SAM BARTLETT (1928)

Sam was born in 1928 and on the 3rd of April 1936 at age seven he was placed in care of the Arcadia together with his sister June and brother David. Sam left the Arc in 1942.

MY FIRST DAY IN THE ARC

The very first day I came to the Arc - I ran away. I found my way to where my mother lived in Gold Street, Johannesburg. My mother immediately went out and bought me some slabs of chocolate, which I assume she hoped to pacify me with but completely forgot that the Pesach started that evening. So it was when I was later sent back to the Arc with a friend of the family and walked into the Seder carrying chocolates in my hand. The look of horror on the face of the Superintendent remains with me to this day.

The chocolates of course were immediately confiscated. Day one in the Arc was not a good start for me.

WHO DONE IT

At the swimming pool one day five senior boys (including Phillip Kemp and Morris Bernard) grabbed me and were going to throw me into the pool as part of my initiation. As I was struggling and fighting they did not throw me cleanly into the pool and I hit myself on the side of the pool and injured myself and landed up in hospital.

When I was in hospital Mr Shaer came and asked me who threw me into the pool, but as I could not tell him as it was forbidden to "squeal". Mr. Shaer then told the sister to carefully watch who came to visit me and, sure enough, he caught the five senior boys who came to visit me.

BROTHERLY LOVE

I was once in hospital with Joe Siegenberg with chickenpox. One Friday night the visiting doctor, Mr Shaer and Mr Harary were around Joe's bed while doing their rounds. In the middle of their examination they heard a voice calling "Joe! JOE!! J-O-E!!!" and all of a sudden a hand appeared through the window with a kitke and fish sandwich. It turned out to be Joe's brother Harold.

DOUBLE CUTS

Ralph Goldberg and I bunked out to bioscope one night and we made our beds look like someone was still in the beds by putting things under the blankets. We got back at about 11 o'clock at night and just as we were climbing over the wall a voice rang out. "What are you doing at this time of night?" It was Mr Con from the committee. Thinking very quickly I replied that we were training for athletics for sports at school. "Don't talk rubbish to me "Mr Con said "You will be dealt with later!!"

Sam and granddaughter Shana

The next morning Mr Con reported it to the superintendent and we got cuts. To make the matter worse Mr Jacobson, the school principal at Forest Town School also invited us to his office and also gave us cuts.

A VERY BIG BUNK

I wanted to bunk out one day and I told the Hebrew teacher Mr Mann that I had to go and see the doctor, as I was not feeling well. He said that it was all right to go.

The next day I repeated the request and he once again gave me permission to go. The following day I repeated the request adding that I had to see a specialist and he once again gave me permission to go. The next day I told him that I had to go for treatment every day and once again he gave me permission to go.

One year later Mr Mann bumped into Sister Goldwater and said that he was very sorry for Bartlett and asked what was wrong with him. Sister Goldwater asked "What are you talking about?" Mr Mann told her how Sam was going to a specialist daily for treatment and had missed Hebrew lessons for about a year. After the initial shock of being told this story, I was reported to Mr Shaer who gave me six cuts, however judging by the look on his face I think he was quite amused to discover that I had bunked Hebrew for a whole year without anyone realising it.

UPSTAGED

It was Barmitzvah time. Gifts of pens and books were being given out by members of the committee to the Barmitzvah Boys. The stage, which was prepared by the staff and where all the committee sat on suddenly, collapsed.

All one could see were committee members thrown backwards with their feet in the air. To us Arcs it was the most hilarious thing we had ever seen and we screamed with laughter. Of course to Mr. Shaer the superintendent this was a disaster and the more he shouted "Order ! ORDER!! Stop laughing!!" the more we laughed. I'm sure that someone had to answer as to why the stage collapsed.

A collapsed hilarious Committee

M Petry 2005

HAVING YOUR CHIPS

One day one of the senior boys talked three junior boys, including myself, to steal potatoes from the cellar in order to make chips. The senior boy was to 'keep *cavey*' while us three junior boys went into the cellar to get the potatoes. While we were busy a nurse came along and caught the senior boy unawares and he immediately told her the whole story to save his own skin.

GOLDEN FISH

I remember once walking passed Marshall's Pet Shop opposite the law courts in town, looking in the window. One of the items that caught my eye was the goldfish.

It suddenly struck me that the Arc had an endless supply in its two fishponds. I walked into the pet shop and enquired whether they bought gold fish. They told me they pay two shillings a pair.

I now had a buyer and an endless supply of goldfish.

I devised a plan. I got hold of some fly netting and made it into an oblong basket. I put this into the pond by the Shul and threw

in some breadcrumbs. The next morning lots of fish had congregated in the net. I simply lifted the net and put the fish into a tin and took them to Marshall Street Pet Shop, where I did a roaring trade.

One day I passed the superintendent's home carrying my tin. I knew he never went up to his office before 4 o'clock, but unfortunately for me, for some mysterious reason, which I have never understood to this day, I suddenly saw him walking up the pathway towards me.

He stopped and looked at me and said "Bartlett, what are you doing here?" I said to him" I am making a garden" which quite a lot of us did at the time planting beans or some other kinds of vegetables. He asked what I had in my tin, which was now hidden, behind my back. "Nothing but water " I said. But he demanded to see it. Panicking, I flung the tin of water with the fish onto the side of the pathway. The look of horror on his face when he saw the gold fish wriggling on the ground terrified me. He made me put all the fish back in the fishpond and told me to wait for him at his office. I returned the fish to the pond and walked to his office and waited terrified knowing what was in store for me. I waited and waited but he never came so I realised that he would not come before 4 o'clock.

I decided then to go down to the Shul knowing there were a number of comics in the shelves at the backbenches. It was while I was looking at a comic that I suddenly heard a voice saying. "You're a very lucky boy; the fact that you are praying for what you have done is what has saved you from getting six cuts." He walked out of the Shul and at that time I did pray, giving thanks that I had got off the hook.

A BAD CUT

At Forrestown Primary School we had a teacher Kruywagen and one day I arrived at school with a bandaged finger. I had taken iodine and a bandage from the Arc hospital. I had put the iodine on my finger on my right hand and then wrapped the bandage around.

After we were seated at class, I put my hand up and I told the teacher that while I was walking I'd fallen and cut my hand and the doctor had said that I could not write with it. The teacher gently took my hand and started to unwind the bandage. I told her that the doctor had said that I must not unbandage the finger but she told me she would do it up exactly as she found it. Despite my protests she continued to unwind the bandage. I just wanted the ground to swallow me up because of my fear and embarrassment.

After it was all unbandaged she got the whole class to come up and look at the "terrible cut" that never existed. Needless to say I was sent to the headmaster and received a caning for my trouble.

THERE AND BACK

One day a few Arcs encouraged me to see what was going on in an upstairs room opposite where Dolly and Charlie stayed next to the cow stable. I climbed up along the drainpipe. I climbed up to the gutter towards the open window to see what they were doing and as I was climbing along I came to a rusted part of about three feet. As I grabbed the gutter it gave away in my hand. I nearly died of fright as it gave way and to make matters worse I was on the second storey. I held on with my other hand and grabbed further where the gutter seemed to have not rusted and then climbed along until I came to the window where these blokes were. I was only too pleased to get there where the window was opened because I was scared I was going to fall.

As I put my hand to go in a voice said to me "Go back the same way you came!!" I now had to go all the way back and pass that broken gutter. I swore I'd never climb another gutter again.

HELP YOURSELF

A couple of Arcs were caught stealing fruit off the fruit trees in one of the houses near the Arc. The owner who caught the boys told them it was not nice to take things without asking and told them in future that all they had to do in future was ask. One week later, two Arcs knocked on the door and asked the if they could pick fruit.

"Of course", said the lady, very pleased she had been asked and told them to take as much as they wanted and went back into her house. What she did not realise was that the Arcs assumed that permission was given to the whole of Arcadia, with the result that half the Arcs were all over the trees picking fruit.

When the woman discovered her trees had been stripped of fruit she reported the matter to the Superintendent, who apologised but explained that children can have their own interpretation of what is meant by "taking as much as you like." Of course we were never invited to partake in the picking of her fruit again.

RUNNING AWAY TO DURBAN

Another Arc and I decided to run away to Durban

Our first stop was to visit my aunt who lived in Johannesburg. When we told her we were running away to Durban she was very excited and told us that my Dad had run away too. She went to the post office and took out some money, and gave it to us. This enabled us to buy train tickets to Durban. We took the train from Park Station and were on our way to Durban. It took us ages because we had caught the milk train, which stopped at all stations to deliver and pick up the post.

We were very quickly out of money and were starving. We lived amongst the sandbags, which were part of the trenches dug for the war, and ate the crumbs thrown out by the fish and chip shop.

One day we were picked up by the military police who asked for our passes and then insisted we were AWOL as we had on khaki pants and boots the same as army issue. After a very long time and much questioning they let us go…

We decided we were going to join the navy and a collection was made for us by a group of men, mainly sailors, who we had befriended from the Venereal Disease Hospital. We did not really know what the hospital was for, but had accepted the money and went for our first big meal with the money.

We kept some money and bought some bananas, as our plan was to catch a small monkey. We went down to the beach and walked along to where the monkeys were and started to feed them. When we got to our last banana a little monkey came right up to us and I caught it.

The little monkey let off a scream, which was immediately echoed by thousands of other monkeys. We immediately released the baby monkey and ran into the water until we were neck deep. The screaming was terrible and the monkeys followed us along the edge of the water as we slowly made our way down the beach where other people were and the monkeys slowly dispersed. I have never taken my children to see the monkeys at the zoo because of this experience.

One day we picked up an old newspaper which reported that two boys had run away from the Jewish Orphanage. It also mentioned that it was believed that they were heading for Durban.

Later on we were picked up by the police and were taken to a holding house for children who had run away from home, where we had to dig six-foot holes and bury banana leaves. We also met a girl, a stowaway on a ship, who had run away from Turkey, as she did not want to marry the man her father, had chosen for her. We got into a fight when we were called "Bloody Jews."

After a while we were taken in handcuffs back to Johannesburg by train and were then held in the prison with other prisoners until we were taken up in front of the magistrate. He was very angry with the police for putting children in handcuffs and for holding us in a cell with other prisoners. Eventually we were released into our parent's care - my mother then took me out of the Arc. I was only 15 years old.

THE BARTLETTS – MY OTHER FAMILY
Written by David Sandler

The first connection I had with the Bartlett's was through my brother Brian and that was when he introduced me to someone in the playground when I was about 11 years old and still at Roseneath Primary School. This was Jackie Herman and Jackie told me that when he was big he would be very rich and that he had an older brother Sam who used to be in the Arc. I think Brian first met Jackie because on Friday afternoons us Arc kids used to go out with Jewish families. I think Brian went with Jackie who stayed with Granny, Sam's mom in Hillbrow in a little house in the middle of Hillbrow between all these flats. So Brian went visiting there on the Friday afternoons and that's how the connection started.

The next thing I remember was one Sunday afternoon walking out of the main entrance out into the parking area and there under the bougainvillea on the one side was this parked station wagon. Zelva was in the front with Sam and lots of kids at the back and Brian, my brother, was there too. Zelva called me over and she said, "Hello, how are you?" and I think she invited me to come and sit in the car or something like that. I did not really like her. I was very suspicious because I'd overheard my Granny saying that the English were two faced and they never spoke the truth in front of you. I saw Zelva as English and not Jewish and well, they were two faced the English and they were never up front and honest with you. So that's how I first saw Zelva and I would have been about 11 or 12 at the time. For the record Zelva is really Scottish and Jewish.

At that time Zelva and Sam started coming to the Arc regularly. Every Sunday afternoon they would come and sit on the grass by the pool. There was a little embankment and they used to sit there. Zelva always used to bring little cakes and little things to eat and also tea in a flask. Slowly, slowly over time, over many many weeks I warmed up towards her. Initially I was very shy, suspicious and untrusting but slowly, slowly over time she won my confidence and so did Sam. Jenny, my older sister explained that you could be English and Jewish and that Zelva was Jewish and Scottish.

Sam was, and still is a great storyteller. He would always treat us all as equals, not as kids, he would talk to us as adults and he could talk very well. He was very interesting to listen to and

here was an adult who treated us as adults and spoke to us as adults. He gave you his attention and this was a rare thing because usually we were treated like kids but here he was treating us like an adult.

I remember around that time also Sam and Zelva and their kids coming to a Seder night at the Arc and Zelva was very friendly towards us little kids. I remember her giving us wine which was a big no no. She gave us wine from the main table where they had a lot. She half sneaked it to us when Ma was not looking and we all thought it was a lot of fun. We would have had just like a single little glass of wine. The wineglasses were empty fish paste containers. I remember getting a little drunk from the wine.

Not only the boys but the girls really liked Zelva as she gave us a lot of attention. We all really started to like her and Sam and she seemed to be very very friendly and nice and we did not really have that so that was very special for us.

I remember Sam and Zelva taking us for a picnic on a Sunday. We had a nice picnic and talked and had a lot of fun and maybe even sang songs. I remember there was this hypnotist which they took us to see. My brother Brian was there and he got hypnotised and also Zelva's son David. Zelva asked the hypnotist to unhypnotise Brian and David during interval. After interval the main show started and it was great fun to see what the hypnotist made the hypnotised people do.

The Embankment by the pool
Vicky talking to Sam Bartlett. Minnie and Gary in background and seated are David, Shelley Bartlett, Peter, Les, Jenny Bartlett, Jenny Sandler, Zelva Bartlett and Errol with Graham in foreground. Mike Saiet and Danny Lasker are playing Tippie in the background and you can see the tennis ball in the air

Jenny and Shelley were there always too and they were little kids at the time but they were friendly and Shelley was very chatty. We always fun during the family outings and they treated us like one of their kids.

When Jenny, my older sister, finished school she went to stay with the Bartlett's. She was called "Big Jenny" to distinguish her from Jenny Bartlett. Zelva would talk of "Your David" that's me and "My David" for David Bartlett or even added our surnames when it got a bit confusing.

Zelva and Sam made their home open to Big Jenny, my sister, and she went to live with them. I don't know how long she lived with them. It was for around a year and it would have been very difficult for them as Zelva had her own three little kids too. Jenny, my sister, was quite a headstrong girl and she wanted to go out and conquer the world and it would have been quite a difficult time for them all as Jenny was in those difficult growing up years.

I remember Jenny used to wear her miniskirt right up to almost her belly button. I remember my Dad once saying she should wear knickers the same colour as her dress because whenever she bent down you could see her knickers. Once during Yomtov Jenny went to Shul with a very short miniskirt.

I found out years later that the Arc committee called Zelva and Sam in. How could Zelva let Jenny go out like this, they asked. I think Zelva explained that you can't crush the girl you have to let her have a little bit of freedom and I think Zelva did speak to Jenny and initially Jenny's reaction was really negative but then later on she lengthened her skirt. It is very difficult looking after children.

I remember when I was about 14 or 15 and I was still in the Arc I used to go to Sam and Zelva almost every second Sunday or three out of four Sundays. I used to go there and they always treated me like one of their kids. They gave me lunch and tea and if they were going out somewhere they would take me with them. It became a regular thing, every Sunday morning; they would come to the Arc and pick up the kids who weren't going out. We really all enjoyed going there.

I remember they had a house in Orange Grove and that's where Jenny stayed with them and then later on Jenny really needed her own place to stay so she went to stay in a hotel in Hillbrow. I felt really so much at home with Sam and Zelva that even on some Sundays when they didn't come (because maybe they were busy or Sam was sick or something) I caught a bus to their house. They were always very nice to me and made me welcome. Even although they had not come to the Arc to pick us up, I felt close enough to them to go there anyway and they made me welcome and we had a nice day together.

After Jenny left Paul Cohen went to live with them and he used to come to school (Parktown Boys High) by bike.

When I left the Arc and I was in the army I used to write to Zelva. When I had leave I'd visit Sam and Zelva. I remember going there with Leon Goodman, who was also in the army, and after walking for ages we found their new house in Bramley Park. They made us welcome and fed us.

After the army, once again their home was always open to me. They were always very friendly, always asked me to stay and have a meal, to stay for dinner etc. They asked me to go with them to Granny where we would watch the movies. If they were going out to their friends I would go along too. Zelva always used to introduce me as her adopted (or stepson) and it was a little embarrassing for me but then later on I grew to accept it. When Shelley or Jenny had to introduce me, I think they wanted to say that also. I think they felt that very much also. Shelley would say, he is like my brother.

Later on when I was at university I used to visit them very regularly and I would never phone and say look I am coming. I think I would just turn up. I was just expected and if I was not there on a Friday night Zelva would ask, "Where were you??!!"

On Friday nights we would see a movie and Sam's mom, Granny, would be there too and then afterwards I would give her a lift home. Here once again, if I visited them and they were going out I would always go along. I would be introduced as, I think Zelva said, the adopted son. I think that is the word she used and not stepson. I was always just part of the family and they treated me as part of the family and I was close to Jenny and Shelley. I wasn't so close to David as he was like a teenager growing up and he had his own friends.

The Bartlett family treated me as part of their family and always made me welcome. I remember spending some time with Zelva in the kitchen watching her cook and helping her cook and I liked that very much. She would always give me little chores to do and she would talk to me and explain things to me. It was always very special for me and made me really feel part of their family. Afterwards she would say, come lets have some tea and we would sit and talk.

I remember spending lots and lots of time with Sam and he would explain to me what he was doing and tell me stories from the Arc or just current happenings. He was really a master storyteller, he could really tell a story very well and command and capture an audience. Sam, at that time, had a film library and I used to do the books of the film library and I would often go there to see them. What was very interesting was to watch Jenny, who was still very very young, serve the customers. She could handle them so well and she was maybe only about 12 at the time. She could explain the movies and talk to them and deal with them like the best of adults.

On Sundays we would go to their house and they would have a friend who is a pianist over and we would sing songs. The pianist would play and Sam would play the drums and we would all be singing these songs and it was really a lot of fun. We had a great time. I also met up with Hymie (Digs) Cohen and his family at Sam and Zelva and also Tex and Raymond who were also old Arcs. Hymie always had a long string of jokes to tell.

At that time I had a flat in Bellevue and we had a few parties there. I remember when Jackie came out the army we decided to have a party and Jenny and Shelley were there too. Also at my 21st, Shelley was there. I treated them like I was their older brother and was a little bit protective of Jenny and we would do things together. I remember once we went to Kyalami with Paul Cohen and we spent the day together. I suppose they treated me like an older brother and me I treated them like younger sisters and we were always very kind to each other, I don't remember every having arguments or fights with them, so it was a very special relationship.

Later on when I went overseas for 27 months I used to write to Zelva regularly and she used to write back regularly. She followed what I was doing keenly and kept in touch all the time. I got married overseas and then came back to South Africa and there Barbara (my wife) and I used to visit Zelva and Sam who once again made their home very open to us and treated us always like family.

Later on we went to live in Australia and I always kept in regular contact with Zelva. When my daughters were born she was the first one I wrote to and I'd always send her photos of the girls growing up. All the time over the last 20 years we have kept in contact and I am sure if Zelva looked in the bottom of her drawer she would find many photos of the kids and lots and lots of letters.

Their daughter Shelley came to Australia and one time she came and spent a holiday in December with us with her son, Kevin. Shelley and I have always kept in contact here in Australia.

Sam, Stephen, Shelley holding Shana and Zelva

Whenever I go across to South Africa I always make sure I put a day or two aside and I catch up with Sam and Zelva and when they go to Sydney to visit Shelley or return to SA they stop here in Perth for a day or two and we catch up

Another time when Jenny went over to Sydney for a holiday with her husband Johnny, and kids Jessie and Jared, I took Esther and Sarah across to Sydney also and so we were all together and we all stayed together in the same hotel.

So Zelva was always a very special person to me, I think she sees me as a son but even maybe with rose coloured glasses because I could not do anything wrong in her eyes. She is the closest I have ever had to a Mom because she just accepted me. I don't think she had a harsh word for me and has always been hospitable, always warm and always friendly. Sam too is also always very friendly and we would always sit and talk and talk and talk. Mainly he would talk and I would listen as Sam can tell a good story.

Johnny, Esther, Jarrad with Friend, Sarah and Jenny at back

So they are my other family and I regard them as my family and also Shelley and also Jenny. By coincidence we are related like all good Jews. Florrie the Granny, Sam's Mom, is first cousin to Monty Tepperson who married my Aunty Fay who is my Mother's sister.

There you go we are all related.

Chapter 38 - JUNE DU BOIS (BARTLETT) (1931)

June, born 1931, her older brother Sam and a younger brother David, born 1932, were placed in the care of the Arc in 1936. David had a twin brother who had passed away at about 15 months old and he passed away when he was almost seven years old.

June remembers they arrived in the Arc at about Pesach time and that they were all very ill and went directly to the hospital. Sam left the Arc in 1942 June left in 1940.

JUNE REMEMBERS

June remembers going to Girl Guides as a "brownie" when Fanny Nerwich was in charge of them. Also on Thursdays the girls went to dancing lessons, which June loved as she said they each received two sweets for attending dancing. She also remembers hiding chewing gum under the desks and this was chewed again the next day. On Sundays all the girls were made to line up and given Epsom Salts which of course they all hated. They eventually learned to keep it in their mouths and spit it out in the toilet.

She remembers the Jewish Holidays as being fantastic, especially Pesach and Succot. She remembers the Succah being decorated with wine and fruit, however the boys came and stole the wine and the fruit so plastic decorations were used. There was a Mrs Hammerschlag who ran a "curiosity shop" and the boys opened the locks and pinched the stock.

When June was very young she was chosen to present the Mayor of Johannesburg with some flowers, so her mother had to go into "town" to buy her a dress and new shoes for the occasion.

June's friends at the Arc were Jenny and Judy Nochumsohn, Shulamith Rosenfeld, Blanche Barker, Phyllis Adler and although older than June, Freda (Koppel) Cheilyk. She remembers Freda sneaking her out of the Arc and taking her to the zoo. Freda said that when she arrived at the Arc June was the only one to make her feel welcome. There was also a girl called Sarah Gebe who was known as "Fowl" Gebe because she killed the chickens.

There was a nurse in charge of the junior girls - a Miss van der Merwe - who was a terrible anti-semite. All the junior girls were absolutely petrified of her. June says that the orchard at the Arc was fantastic but the fruit never had a chance to ripen as the children stole it all while it was still green. She remembers Vicky Klevansky standing at the staffroom window and giving her a sandwich.

She says that there were good days, bad days and sad days at the Arc, but she remains always grateful to the Arc for taking her in, giving her a roof over head and giving her a start in life.

June married Sydney (Pawpaw) Du Bois and has three sons and several grandchildren. They were later divorced and June now lives in Sandringham Gardens.

1986 80th Anniversary Reunion of Arcadia (Photo from Freda Cheilyk) Front Row: Sarah Brenner, Selma Kaufman, Abe Starkowitz (Starkey), Mary Aronovsky, Judy Nochumsohn, Bertha Kronenberg (Klevansky) June Bartlett Back Row: Freda Koppel, Eli Benatar, Mot Flax, Hillary and Max Rabinowitz, Willy Jasven (Shreeuwer)

Chapter 39 - SHULAMITH LOWENSTEIN (ROSENFELD) (1928-2004)

Shulamith was born in 1928 and was in the care of Arcadia from 1931 to 1946.

Shulamith passed away on the 14th of August 2004.

I write to inform you of a farewell luncheon to Mannie Osrin who has left to join his son in Melbourne. Of course, I should have mentioned that Sarah, Mannie's wife, has gone with him.

Shulamith [Rosenfeld] Lowenstein was the chief organiser of the luncheon for Mannie and Sarah. The luncheon was on 1 August at Denzil's Restaurant in Edenvale. There were 30 or more Arcadians present. Unfortunately on 14 August 2004, Shulamith passed away after having an aneurysm.

The following Old Arcadians and spouses were present. I apologise if I leave out somebody's name who may have been present.

Sam Bartlett and his wife, Mervyn and Bernice Katz, Joe Klug and his wife, Gerry Levy and his wife, Shulamith Lowenstein, Sadie [Segal] Lurie, Barney Meyers and wife, Louis Nerwich and his wife, Mannie Osrin and Sarah, Eli Osrin and his wife, Jonah Perkel and his wife, Issy Rush, Claire Rushovich, Effie Segal

Mick Swercik, Donald Goldman and his wife, and Lipka [Lorraine - Perlman]

Shulamith made a fitting appropriate and pleasant speech to Mannie and Sarah. Mannie replied well.

Some of the above attended Shulamith's funeral. Ekie [Levin] Litvin, Bennie and Betty Garson and Alec, Simon, Ross and Rose Oskowitz also attended the funeral.

I have to write how wonderful Shulamith was in organising the function for the farewell to Mannie and Sarah Osrin. She was always so friendly, so warm and so efficient. It was so sad that her passing away was so soon after the get together of the Old Arcadians. Heartfelt condolences and deepest sympathy go to Toby and his family.
Barney and Bess Myers RSA 24 August 2004

Bertha Kronenberg (Kevansky), Anne Disler, Max Goldman, Mabel Britany (Goldsmith) , Shulamith Lowenstein (Rosenfeld), Mary Flax (Aranovsky) and Ekie (Levine) Litvin at the 1979 Arc Fete.

Chapter 40 - MANNIE OSRIN (1929)

Mannie (born 1929) came to the Arc in 1936, at the age of seven, and left there when he finished Matric in 1946. He arrived at the Arc together with his sister Rita, who is six years his senior. His younger brother Elli, came to the Arc at the age of two, about a year or so after Rita and Mannie.

While there were actually quite a number of Arcs who were prefects at Parktown Boys' High, Mannie distinguished himself by being the only Headboy.

It was in Arcadia that Mannie met his wife to be, Sarah Epstein, as she was then. After leaving the Arc Mannie went on to become a doctor and was a well-known GP in Johannesburg. Mannie, together with Solly Farber and Abe Starkowitz were the three Arc Tenors and conducted the High Holiday services at the Arc for many decades.

Mannie and Sarah have one son, a clinical psychologist, living in Melbourne, and he has twin sons of 11 years old and a daughter aged seven. Mannie and Sarah migrated to Australia in 2004 to be with their son and grandchildren

In the Synagogue - Mannie with Torah and Colin Rozenkowitz

ARCADIA

I have never been able to find out who it was who gave the name Arcadia to the Orphanage, or why indeed that particular name. After all it's not a biblical name or a Hebrew name, for that matter. Surfing the web for answers, the nearest I could get was that Arcadia was originally a district in ancient Greece, and was proverbial for the contentment and simple happiness of its people. The name came to be used figuratively for any scene of rural simplicity and peace. For those of us who spent our childhood in Arcadia, the feeling must be that the name was well chosen.

MY FIRST DAY IN THE ARC

So here I am at the age of seven, in a car with my sister Rita, driving up this strange driveway, which we'd later know as "the drive", at 22 Oxford Road, Parktown, the address of the South African Jewish Orphanage. My younger brother Eli was barely one year old and was being looked after elsewhere, by other family members.

The cousins who had brought us this far, handed us over to the 'nurses' who had been waiting for us. It is about eight in the evening and the main building is quiet. We get given tea and sandwiches in the nurses' dining room. Rita, aged 13 says, by way of cracking the ice, "So it seems like you're all part of one big family." The nurses laugh. I feel nervous. Rita gets taken one way, and I another. I am very confused and frightened. I'm not quite sure as to what's going on. All I really know is that my father has died in Port Elizabeth, and that my Mother is too ill to take care of us, and that we'd be better off in this home, where there are lots of other children.

Another nurse takes me to a bed, helps me get into some strange pyjamas and after putting me between the sheets, says "Good night. I'll show you how to make your bed in the morning". I pull the blankets over my head, and cry myself to sleep. I also proceed to wet the bed for the first time in my life. The year was 1936, and I can't remember what month it was.

The following day I discovered that I was Junior Boy No 41, an "identification" that I kept until the day that I 'graduated' to the Senior Boys. I also discovered a whole host of other Junior Boys. I had never been in the company of so many children, and it sort of frightened and encouraged me at the same time.

I learned, too, that I was not going to see my sister Rita every day. She was with what they called the Senior girls. It was very upsetting, and I can remember the first few times that I did see her, I usually ended up in tears.

The next few years are quite hazy in my memory. Suffice it to say that the years did pass without any major mishaps or catastrophes. Apart from the fact that I was not part of a household with parents, brothers and sisters, I think I had quite a good life. One could almost say a normal upbringing, under the circumstances.

SCHOOL

I went to a good school, Forest Town, and I have memories of some very good teachers, among them Miss Kruywagen, very strict but fair, who was for ever saying (shouting) "one thing at a time, and that done well is a very good thing, as many will tell."

Also there was Lucy Pincus, quite a looker, as I recall, who was always very nice to me, and another chap, whose name escapes me, but who used to be in the British Army in India at one time of his life. As these were the War years he would try and teach us what Army life was like. He used to march us up and down the street, in formation, and we all felt very important.

And, of course, there was Jakey (Mr Jacobs) headmaster and English teacher. He was a wonderful man, dedicated to his art and to the children. I will never forget how proud I felt when he awarded me the English prize in Standard 5. And I will never forget that he was instrumental in me going to High School.

Quite a number of years later, I think I had just finished University at the time, I bumped into Jakey in Hillbrow, and hesitatingly exclaimed "Hello Mr. Jacobs. How nice to see you again. I don't suppose you'd remember me after all this time. I'm...." and he finished my sentence for me, by saying "Osrin, of course I remember you." I will never forget how awful I felt at not having kept in touch with this man, who had helped shape my life. Most of the others in Standard 5 elected to go to Observatory Junior High School, as they would then be finished with School at the end of Standard.8. Some of them, however, did switch to Parktown for the form 4 and matric years.

The night before I was due to start my first day at Parktown High School, I was sitting on my bed, just before lights out, with a knot in my stomach, nervous and worried, when in walked one of the Seniors, by name Ivan Kurland, and asked " Where's Osrin? " I held up my hand as he hadn't seen me at first, and he came and sat on my bed and proceeded to give me the kind of encouraging talk a parent or older brother might give to someone about to embark on a strange future.

I will never forget that he said to me, "Mannie, if you ever need any help with anything, don't be afraid to ask. And if I'm not here, ask one of the other Seniors." I never ever forgot that little chat, and how kind he was, and how much I appreciated it.

The five years that I spent at Parktown High were probably the most enjoyable and rewarding consecutive five years that I ever spent in my entire life. I took part in all sporting activities, not always making the A team.

My best sporting achievement, I suppose was starting the Rugby season in form IV in the 4th side and working my way up through 3rds, 2nds and then playing a few matches for firsts at the end of the season. My only real claim to fame, however, was, when playing against Jeppe High, I tackled Des Sinclair

(who was later to become a Springbok centre) so hard, that he had to leave the field.

In that match against Jeppe, I played alongside Barney Meyers, of whom Frikkie Marais, Science master and 1st team Rugby coach used to say "give me fifteen Barney Meyers" and I'll beat any school team in the country!" The following year when Barney had left, I took over the number eight position in the scrum, but was dropped after we suffered a huge defeat against King Edwards, our "arch-enemies". I've often thought that had it been some other School, I would probably have retained my place.

I was very lucky to have some truly wonderful Arcs with me at Parktown. I felt very privileged to be in their company, and to count them as my friends and brothers. I also felt humble in the face of their achievements, both academically and on the sporting field. There were quite a few 1st class matrics and other scholastic honours that came the way of Arcadia. One felt rather proud to be known as "one of the boys from the orphanage".

There are, of course, far too many Arcadians who went to Parktown, for me to even think of mentioning all their names, each and everyone of them have brought honour and distinction to the school, and by extension, to Arcadia. However, just to name a few whose scholastic, and or sporting prowess spanned a period of quite a number of years, without any prejudice, of course to those not named, I salute the following: Hymie and Sydney (Vicky) Klevansky, Alec Mendelsohn, Harry and Bunny Barlin, Effie Segal, Jonah Perkel, Sydney and Harry Nuchomsohn, Meyer Rabinowitz, Joey Siegenberg, Willie Isaacs, Barney Meyers, Dave (Herbie) Spector, Izzy and David Rushovich, Benny and Alec Gavson, Zummy Isenberg, Gerry Levy and, of course, Solly (Shalom) Farber.

At Parktown Boys' High
BACK: Willie Isaacs, Aaron Karp, Sid Nochumson, Solly Meyers, Mike Rabinowitz, Joe Siegenberg
FRONT: Dave Spector; Barney Meyers, Josh Lipschutz, Mannis Osrin, Benny Gavson.

Of all the sports in which the Arcs participated, at Parktown, it was probably in the boxing ring that they excelled. This of course was in no small measure due to the boxing program that was an ongoing weekly exercise at Arcadia. Certainly for as long as I can remember, with boxing instructors drawn from the ranks of ex champs, amongst whom of course, was our own Alf

James, a truly amazing pugilistic talent, who brought great honour to Arcadia. Sometimes, because the tournaments were run according to one's weight, it happened that an Arc would come face to face with one of his Arc friends, and I will never forget having one hell of a scrap with Woolfie Getz! I can't even remember who won. But I do remember having a very painful nose for a long time afterwards.

I make mention quite a lot of Parktown High, as a most memorable event took place in late November of 1945. Picture the scene. The school hall is packed in the early morning prior to classes commencing. The Headmaster, Mr. Logie, announces, "The head prefect for next year will be Osrin of the Trojan House." All around me friends are slapping me on the back, on my head, my ears are ringing and the blood, I swear, has left my brain. Now I had to negotiate the steps from the

Mannie Osrin, Natie Romer, Alec Gavson and Manual Lipschitz

upstairs area that Trojans occupied, to the ground floor to re-enter the hall, walk to the raised platform and shake Mr Logie by the hand.

Me, Mannie Osrin, a boy from the Orphanage, appointed Head Boy of one of the most prestigious schools in Johannesburg. Let me hasten to add, in case I be accused of blowing my own trumpet, that the reason I mention so much about Parktown, and the accolade that came my way, is because I've always firmly believed that when Logie made me head boy, he was bestowing the honour, not only on me but on Arcadia and the long list of truly wonderful students from Arcadia that had graced the halls and playing fields of Parktown Boys High.

Before I leave the above subject, allow me to tell you an amusing, related story. Many years after leaving school, in 1996 to be exact, Hymie Sachs (who now lives in Sydney with wife Pam and their family) came to see me as a patient, in my consulting rooms. He seated himself across the desk from me and said, "Mannie, before we start, could I just ask you to clear up an argument I had last night with some friends. They said that you had been Head Boy at Parktown, and I said that you hadn't. So tell me, who was right?"

To which I replied, "Well, actually, Hymie, you were wrong and they were right", at which point Hymie jumps to his feet, extends his hand to shake mine, and exclaims "Hell, shot, Mannie, well done, congrats. Bloody good going, fantastic!" This little scene, of course, took place 50 years after I'd left school!

AFTER LEAVING THE ARC

I matriculated just after the war had ended, and ex servicemen who wanted to study Medicine had only to apply in order to get into Medical School. That left a great number of us who had to do a year in the Arts faculty, with the promise that if we passed all five subjects at the end of the year, we would automatically get into 1st year Medicine. I didn't know if the Arc would allow me to do this, but Harary came out on my side, and persuaded the committee to let me do it. And the rest is history as they say.

And so it was that I ended up at Witwatersrand University, studying Medicine. One of my dreams was being fulfilled, thanks to Arcadia. The Varsity years that followed were interesting, exciting, difficult and a bit scary. Perhaps, because I had been confined to Arcadia most of my life, and the Arc itself, of course, being a close knit community, I found that I had certain minor problems socialising with non-Arc people, and found myself often drifting back to the comfort of the Arc environs, which, of course, was most fortuitous, as I really got to know and fall in love with the one who was to become my wife and soul mate, Sarah Epstein.

On 3 December 2004 we celebrated our 50th Anniversary. Suffice it to say, of our relationship, that if I was ever to have been judged a "success" then it gives credence to the old adage of "behind every successful man is a good woman". We are very proud of our only son, Steven, who is a Clinical Psychologist, living and working here in Melbourne, Australia. We have three grandchildren, twin boys of 11 years old, and a granddaughter of seven. They are the best kids in the Universe, and Sarah is Granny, and I am Grandpa.

RITA AND ELLI

My Sister, Rita, resides now with her husband Solly, in St Louis, USA. Her two sons and their families are also there, and certainly keep her busy. She is a highly successful Wife, Mother, Grandmother, and Great Grandmother. One of her daughters lives in Israel with her family and the other daughter and family live in Johannesburg.

My brother, Elli, is also still in Johannesburg with his wife, Sara. His daughter and family live not too far away from him, but his one son and family live in Cape Town, and the other son and family reside in Perth, Australia. So he too gets plenty opportunity to play Grandparent. For those who are not aware of the fact, I make mention that Elli was Chairman of Arcadia for quite a number of years, a position he filled with great energy and enthusiasm, earning the respect of all who had anything to do with the institution.

CHAZAN

I have always been enthralled by the story of Brigadoon, the film of which I must have seen about six times. It concerns a mythical village in the Highlands of Scotland, which comes to life every 100 years, but each awakening is as though it was simply the next day. This is the feeling I used to get every year on Rosh Hashana and Yom Kippur. The same service, the same songs, the same solemnity and, of course, basically the same congregation who would attend year after year, and every year it would feel as though the previous year had only happened yesterday. I was very proud, when Leonard (Joss) Lipschitz relinquished his position as Chazan, to have been asked to take his place and to become part of the three chazonim, namely Abe (Starkey) Starkowitz, Solly (Shalom) Farber and me. I have a most treasured photograph of the three of us taken on the Bimah, together with the Shamas, Basil Samson. It gives me a warm feeling to think that somehow or other we added to the lives of Arcadians.

The three Chazans; Solly Farber, Abe Starkowitz and Mannie

MEMORIES

I think we all, at some stage or other, experienced the thrill of "bunking out". My first and most daring was at about the age of 12. Mookie Romer and I bunked out to see Alexander's Ragtime Band at a cinema in Doornfontein, one Saturday afternoon. We re-entered the Arc near Charlie Miller's house, and were in time for supper. We were never found out. I can still feel the excitement.

There are so many fleeting images of things that happened in connection with Arcadia, and most of them I'm sure, I share with most Arcs, not only of my time, but with those who went before me and those who came after me. Some, however, may be a bit different, and I'll just jot down a few.

I'm sitting in the stands at the old Wanderers grounds together with hundreds of Wits University students at the inter- varsity athletic meeting. There is one runner far ahead of the rest of the field, running the 10,000 metres, and every time he passes our stand, the cheer rings out, "WITS, WITS, RabinoWITS" That, of course was Meyer Rabinowitz, and my chest nearly exploded with pride. Meyer won numerous long distance races, and from the time that he was winning the mile at Parktown to his University triumphs, and in between becoming Southern

Transvaal cross country champion, he left behind an impeccable record of guts and endurance. I've often wondered just how much Jackie Mekler, whose feats in themselves are legendary, may have been influenced by Meyer's achievements.

I myself was never much of a runner, but I do remember once coming second to Sam Bartlett, when we held our own long distance race, starting at the tennis courts, up past the Stables, down the drive, across the field where the swimming pool was, on to the big field, around the back of the babies department, and finishing again at the tennis courts.

And now, dear reader, allow me to play the "what if...?" game with you. What if there had not been a place like Arcadia? What would our lives have been like? Who would have looked after all of us? Would I even have gone to Parktown High, would I have gone to Medical School, and would I even ever have been in General Practice? It seems very unreal to even think of not having met my wife, Sarah, or the very many Arc brothers and sisters we all have, had there not been an Arcadia.

Would Vicky still have been Vicky, and to whom would he have spun his yarns? Would Starkey still have been the great Chazan he was, and in which Shul would he have davaned? Would I ever have heard Jonah Perkel reading and singing from the Torah? Would I ever have witnessed the wizardry of 'Beans' Levine on the soccer field, or the all round sporting achievements of Donald Goldman or Gerry Levy? And would I ever have had the great privilege of knowing and being a friend of Solly Farber, the quintessential Arcadian?

Countless images and corresponding questions, impossible to answer.

The physical Arcadia, as we knew it, the buildings, the grounds, the driveway, the 'up the hill' and 'down the hill' the Girls' department, the Boys' department, the Babies section and the Hospital, have all, according to recent reports, changed quite a lot. It had to come eventually, and one could almost think of it as having passed on. By the same token, however, it is true to add that nothing is ever gone, as long as it lives in our memories. And David Sandler has become the man to do it with his endeavours in creating this book of Arc memories. I would like to endorse a sentiment that I expressed a while ago, regarding David, that he has certainly emerged as the Arc Mensch of the decade. His clarion call to all Old Arcs to contribute to the bank of Arc memorabilia, for him to collate, is truly a labour of love, and in itself will become an everlasting memory. May the force be with you, David.

Sarah and I left South Africa in August, 2004, to be with our son and the grandchildren in Melbourne, Australia. A few weeks before we left, Barney Meyers and Shulamith Loewenstein (Rosenfeld) arranged a farewell luncheon for us. There was quite a number of Old Arcs present and it would be difficult for me to mention them all, but it was truly a wonderful gesture on the part of Barney and Shulamith and all those who attended. One name I will mention is that of Donald Goldman, who in spite of being so ill, showed great fortitude and determination in turning up to wish us bon voyage. We will never forget it.

My last words to Shulamith were "see you in Australia". She was due to come out to be with her daughter in Melbourne at the end of the year. Alas, it was never to be. The lovely, cultured and refined lady Shulamith was struck down with a cerebral haemorrhage and died a week later.

So here we are in Australia, home now strangely enough to a growing number of ex Arcadians, some old and some not so old. As you all know, David Sandler is in Perth, and Michael Perry Kotzen is in Sydney. There are others scattered all over Australia. David (Tommy) Green lies buried here as does Hymie (Digs) Cohen. Doubtless there are others. Maybe somebody, sometime will get round to writing the book "Arcadians in Australia!"

Mention soccer to any Old Arc and I'm sure there would be a flood of stories for your book. I've got two little tales for all to chuckle at.

The first concerns my very first game. I had only been in the Arc a few days and had never even heard of soccer, let alone played a game. Stompie Shaer himself had taken me down to the "big lawn" where the boys were already playing. I was all of six years old and quite terrified of what I knew was coming. He barked out an instruction to someone to let this new boy play. I was told to stand near the goalie and kick the ball the other way if it ever came to me. Unfortunately when it did come to me it hit my leg and rebounded into my own goal. The goalie gave me a *klap* (hit) on the head and told me to go and stand somewhere else!! That was my inauspicious introduction to the "beautiful" game.

My second tale is one of "phantom" soccer played in front of the main building. This area had just recently been tarred and Cop Harary had given strict orders that no soccer was to be played there. We decided to play a trick on him and proceeded to play a game without a ball, if you can imagine that. Someone would dribble the imaginary ball and someone else would pretend to tackle him. The "ball" was then "passed" to another, and another before being slammed into a goal. During this exercise Cop came out, looked at what was happening in direct violation of his orders and was about to throw a fit, when he realised what was going on, and to his credit, saw the funny side of it all and had a good laugh.

Mannie wrote the above article for this book and I include other prior articles of his below.

PYOTTS BISCUITS

It really is great reading all the e-mails going back and forth. Even though most of you are not known to me, I never realised until now, just how many decades span the lives of all the kids who lived and played in the Arc. Even though large age gaps exist, it actually feels as though I'm meeting long lost brothers and sisters and cousins.

It feels quite eerie to know how many children walked the same paths as I did, sat in the same Shul, and ate meals at the same table as I. Some of the stories we've read could quite easily have had been me, and some of my friends, as the main

characters. When Solly told of his family outings to the Zoo, well, it could have been me and my family. As though it happened yesterday.

We've all got lots of stories to tell, some relating them much better than others. I thought I'd kick off with a scary one.

A few of us 'senior boys' decided to 'relieve' the Arc storeroom of a large box of Pyotts biscuits. And by 'big' I really mean of a much larger size than the usual box of biscuits. It must have measured at least 55cms x 30 x 25. Imagine how many biscuits were inside!!

Getting the loot down to the Boys Department was a feat in itself but I won't bore you with details. The real problem was where to keep this 'treasure' so that we could feed off it when hungry (which was most of the time) and also avoid detection. Well we came up with this ingenious plan. We decided, believe it or not, to hide it on the roof of the building!

Now for those of you familiar with the Boys' Department you'll know that the only way up to the roof was through the windows which over-looked the quadrangle in the centre of the building. You'd climb on top of the lockers which lined the corridors of the upstairs area, balance precariously on the open window itself, lift yourself slowly until you'd reached up and managed to get an arm on to the roof, and with a mighty heave, pull yourself up. You'd then locate the booty, help yourself to a few biscuits of your choice, rest a while, and then prepare yourself for the even more daunting task of getting down again!! The whole process would have to be reversed.

Now the box of biscuits lasted a long long time as our enthusiasm for repeating the crazy journey slowly but surely got replaced by a realisation of the risks we were taking every time we went out of that window. I cannot remember with absolute certainty who my co-conspirators were, but I seem to recollect that Joss Lipschitz and Basil Samson were two of the 'gang'. Also I think Alec Gavson was there. In the many years that passed since the above escapades took place, I have on occasion been up to the Boys' department, and gazed with awe and wonderment at the actual place, the very window, where the above all took place.

How on earth could we have allowed ourselves to do such a thing, when one tiny slip would have resulted in a tragic fall. I can only conclude that we must have been very very hungry, indeed!!

WINNERS YEOVILLE SUNDAY LEAGUE, 1940 - 1947

At last our lift arrived from South Africa, and this has made us feel a bit better, having all our old familiar things around us. Amongst the goods to arrive was a certain photograph of the "real" Old Arcadian Football side,

The other thing of interest, which is impossible to tell just from looking at the picture, is how we had all been collapsing about in laughter a few minutes before the taking, from the jokes and wisecracks that kept coming from Donald Goldman. I'll never know how we managed to get so serious!

Mannie Osrin in soccer gear - 1947

MISSING THE ARC SHUL

Situated now as I am, at seemingly the other end of the world, (in Melbourne Australia) I must admit to having bouts of loneliness and certainly there was a lot of "longing" when it came to going to a "strange" Shul in a "strange" country. The high Holy days of Rosh Hashona and Yom Kippur have always meant a lot to me in my personal life style (apart from the Religious, that is) and to be 'separated ' from my roots, so to speak, left me feeling, at times, very homesick indeed.

Where was Vicky Klevansky's Erev Rosh Hashona sermon? No Jonah Perkel Torah 'leining'. And Abe Starkowitz. Starkey, Oh, Starkey, where were you? And all the Arc tunes? And all the friends living and parted. How I used to love davening with our home-made "choir" behind me, the shamas Basil Samson, baritone Manuel Lipschitz, and Beans Levine and Alec Gavson bringing up the rear.

And as if these memories weren't painful enough, along comes a new Poet, by the name of Hymie Pearlman, with the most beautiful, most powerful and most moving poem in memory of our dearly beloved Solly Farber. What a lovely effort Hymie. It meant so much to me to read your dedication to someone who meant such a lot to all of us. Like you, I will never forget him.

LIFE IN MELBOURNE

On the 22 August 2004 it was exactly one year since we arrived to take up residence in Australia. It is truly amazing how quickly the year has gone by. I would be lying if I said it's all been a "piece of cake". We have certainly had our ups and downs. Fortunately the 'positives' seem to be gaining the upper hand. We still meet people who tell us that it took them a long long time to 'settle', some as long as a couple of years!! But we have survived, and hopefully we'll continue doing so. Not all the battles have been won, and there is still some work to do.

For instance, although it was never my intention to find some work as a Doctor, I soon realised that I wasn't very good 'retirement material', so to speak. So I applied for registration in the State of Victoria, and was successful. But then, because of a host of bureaucratic rules and regulations and *meshugas*, I was not able to get a Provider number, the Holy Grail of General Practice in Australia, unless I went to work out in the countryside. And of course this wasn't the reason that I came to live here. But, fortunately, I have been able to secure a job as a Medical examiner in the Insurance field, which is a part-time job, and suits me down to the ground. And I have actually earned some Australian dollars. I have only been with this company for three weeks now, so I haven't earned all that much, but enough to allow me not to have to multiply everything by five, as one does when working with South African Rands.

One of the requirements of my job is that I travel to clients' houses to do the Medical. Because of this I have been to places that people who have lived here for a long time, didn't even know existed. This Melbourne is truly a huge place. I always used to think that Johannesburg was big. But this is really something else. Fortunately I'm getting a petrol allowance, as with the price of fuel these days, I wouldn't be able to do the job without it.

Just a parting word about the weather. I never ever thought I'd write about such a subject! I remember that in Johannesburg winter used to last about three weeks, ie three weeks in which we were really cold enough to wear extra clothes, or to switch on some heating in our homes. Here in Melbourne I've experienced for the first time in my life what it's like to go from month to month in cold, grey conditions with no sun. All is compounded by confounding rain, which comes at you parallel to the ground, so you should really have two umbrellas, one over your head, in the usual way, and one in front of you.

Chapter 41 - ELLI OSRIN (1936)

Elli was born in 1936. He spent almost all his childhood in Arcadia. He arrived in the Arc in 1938 age two and left in 1953 aged 17.

In high school at Parktown Boys' High Elli captained the school athletic team and was also a 1st team rugby player and both Elli's sons were prominent Rugby players at King David in Linksfield.

Elli was Chairman of Arcadia for quite a number of years, a position he filled with great energy and enthusiasm, earning the respect of all who had anything to do with the institution.

AN ARCADIAN GROWS UP

Arcs have got characteristics about them that single them out as Arcs. In this article Eli, who spent the first 17 years of his life in Arcadia, attempts to get at the reasons for the build-up of Arcadian characters

As children we did not receive the individual devotion and attention of a mother but had to share 'mother' with 50 other babies. Big brothers and sisters took most of our troubles to heart. The kindergarten days went swiftly by and we soon joined the procession of children on their way to the big school where we learnt ABC which Sister Goldwater had tried so hard to teach us. Promotion from babies to juniors was indeed a great event that can be compared to a child sleeping in his own room for the first time. Whatever dreams we cherished about being juniors were soon realised but also now the hardships began as the youngest had to stand up to quite a lot.

The savage laws of the jungle played an important part in this period of life. Fifty boys ranging from the ages of seven to about 20 lived together. Every lad had to fend for himself. This moulded us into the tough little fellows who could look after themselves in the hardest of circumstances. Initiation ceremonies were the order of the day and the new fledglings took the pillow-gauntlet, blanket throwing and constant fagging for seniors as every day happenings. Arcadia's very strict daily routine also instilled a great sense of discipline into the youngsters. Weakness was not tolerated and even less so unfitness. A run of seven or eight miles was nothing even to the youngest junior boys. Boys often took canings for other boys' crimes. To 'squeal' was unheard of.

The next phase of life was really the beginning. Slowly we matured and forgot about 'cops and robbers' and started to take an interest in school sport and school work. As a senior boy you were looked up to by the juniors. During this period of life the fierce Arcadian feeling begins to grow. The sense of loyalty of Arcadians would put the revolutionists of 1848 to shame. It has to be seen and felt to be believed. Arcadia is a small town and the seniors interest themselves in various activities such as pigeon breeding, stealing fruit, doing electrical

Elli Osrin

repairs, carpentry, projector operating and also conducting of Shul services.

Thus as the years pass a character is moulded. The large number of Arcadians who attain prefectships and captaincies at the schools which they attend bears witness to the fine type of person produced by Arcadia. Maybe Arcs are hard, but once you become friendly with the Arcs you'll never be able to break away from the group. My years in Arcadia were so many years of moral training and from them I have a good training for life and indeed an eternal treasure of memories.
(Written around 1950)

Elli and his wife Sara have three children and seven grandchildren.

The oldest son, Alan, lives in Perth, with his wife Robyn. They have three children, two boys and an older daughter. Elli's other son, Brett, lives in Cape Town, where he is in business, and has two children.

His youngest daughter Kim, a primary school teacher, lives in Johannesburg with her two children.

Arcadia Barmitzvahs 1948
Dave Gordon, Elli Osrin, Cyrl Touyz, Sam Berer, Colin Rosenkowitz and Cyril Fanaroff

ELLI REMINISCES

Despite the fact that the years' have passed so quickly the bonds of family and friendship of all Old Arcadians remains as strong as ever, both locally and internationally. To be introduced to anybody as an "Old Arc" still carries a tremendous belonging.

My Barmitzvah was in 1948, the same year in which the State of Israel was born. Because I was a Barmitzvah boy I was chosen to raise the flag of Israel on the day of statehood in front of the main building that is the Herbert Baker building at Arcadia. Years later while visiting Israel, my wife Sara, and I attended a South African exhibition at the Museum of the Diaspora in Tel Aviv. The original photograph of the "Raising of the Flag" stood on the wall of the Museum. Imagine our surprise and joy to discover, we and Arcadia, had somehow made our mark on the history of Israel.

After leaving Arcadia I became involved with the Old Arcadian Association and was co-opted onto the Main Committee in 1960 where I served as Honorary Secretary, Honorary Treasurer, Vice-Chairman and eventually Chairman in 1980. I presently hold the position of Life President of Arcadia.

My involvement has always been a privilege, especially to be surrounded by so many dedicated workers who give up so much of their time. On reflection Arcadia was indeed a haven of peace and tranquility and a tribute to the Jewish community who served it with a giving heart!

My sister Rita and her husband Solly Bortz live in St Louis with their sons and grandchildren. Rita and Solly have recently celebrated 60 years of marriage.

The picture is historic. This was our celebration on the day that the State of Israel was founded. I see many faces I recognise. The winsome little guy on the extreme left is Woolfie Kotzen (David's late brother after whom he named his son). Next to him is Sam Berer; next to him is Ralph Brooks; behind him is David Gordon (Bobby's brother):

The chap behind the hand holding the flag is Benny Touyz, who went to Israel where he was known as Ben Zion Touyz and he became the Quartermaster General of the Israeli army.

Just to the right of the flag at the back is Bernie Aronstam. The fair-haired guy in the middle of the picture near the bottom of the flag) is Colin Rosenkowitz (father of the famous sextuplets). Just behind Colin is Gerry Levy; on Gerry's right and slightly forward is Basil Sepel; behind and above Basil is Eli Osrin. At the top behind Eli is Harry Cohen who was Chairman of the Arc at the time

The fair-haired with the fringe in the middle of the picture is Zelda Gordon and next to her is Bella Bortz. The two little girls in front are Bortz Girls. Bessi and Eva (Written by Solly Farber)

Chapter 42 - BARNEY SEGAL (1929)

Barney was in Arcadia between 1943 and 1945.

Arcadia is a very special place for me as I spent two years there (from 13 to 15 years) that were significant and memorable for me, having come from a disturbed and unsettled family unit. I enjoyed the environment there as it built up my character and I also enjoyed the sporting scenes, having played a lot of soccer, my favourite sport.

I attended Bertrams Junior School up to Std 3, and then I went to Jewish Government School doing Standards 4 and 5 there.

One of the teachers there was Miss Shaer, and 'Stompie' Shaer, her father, was superintendent then before 'Cop' Harary. After Jewish Government I went to Observatory Junior High where I completed my Junior Certificate. Obervatory was my first opportunity to meet the guys from 'Arcadia'.

Having not had a very happy and stable home life, I then made application to be admitted to the orphanage. I was very pleased to gain admission at the Arc, even though I wasn't an orphan at the time. I spent more than two years there, leaving there at age 16. I was very happy being part of this great institution.

Arcadia taught me plenty and for that I am truly grateful, especially in my formative years. The boys at the Arc always used to get up to naughty escapades, like raiding the food cellars at night but unluckily when we were caught by the guard, we had to appear before 'Cop' Harary and get severely reprimanded.

Sport was a great leveller and also a big event at the Arc and we always looked forward to our game of soccer on the weekends. I enjoyed playing soccer alongside players the calibre of Sydney (Beans) Levine, Max Robinowitz, the late Manual Lipschitz and without question, the late and great Donald Goldman, a truly lovable and sincere human being if ever there was one.

I do recall a certain guy by the name of Ralph Goldberg who used to sleep walk at night and scare the daylights out of us in the dormitories. I also often recall how I used to sneak out on a

Barney Segal – September 2001

Sunday afternoon, to visit my younger sister up the road who was sick at the time in the Hope Convalescent Home. At the time I was very keen on religious studies and for a long period of time I used to conduct the morning Shul services.

Such were the good ole' days there.

When I left the Arc I became a printer. I have been married with two children. I was part of a family of five children. I lost a sister age four years, and many years later another sister aged 55 years who was living in Australia, passed away.

I still maintain my links with the Arc being on the Old Arcs committee. I still keep active, doing the Publicity and Advertising work as regards the home. I enjoy writing different articles to the newspapers. And so we keep the campfires burning as long as we can. G-d willing.

In Conclusion I pay homage to the great Arc institution.

Arc soccer players in the SAPDC Social Soccer Side 1967

| *Reuben Lipschitz* | *Barney Segal* | *Hymie Sacks* | *Jeff Esekow* |

Chapter 43 - IZAK (ISAAC) WEINER (1929)

Izak was born in 1929 and was in the care of Arcadia from 1939 to 1946.

ARC MEMORIES

In 1936 my mother and I (seven years old) went to visit my dad who was terminally ill at the Otto Beit Convalescent Nursing Home, which was situated on top of the hill, near the new General Hospital in Parktown. One of the sisters suggested that while we were waiting to see my dad that we take a walk down the hill to go and visit the "poor orphans" in the orphanage, which we did, not realising that I would soon be admitted to the orphanage.

During our era at Arcadia, amongst the most accomplished "all round" sportsmen were chaps such as Willie Isaacs, Donald Goldman, Louis Kreser, Gerry Levy and Max Rabinowitz. Springbok status was achieved by Sarah Sundelowitz (Soika Perlman), Jackie Mekler, Max Rabinowitz - names that come to mind. Others who were big of heart on the sportsfield were Willie Isaacs, Barney Myers, Alec Gavson and Sidney (Beans) Levine.

Percy Nochumson taught me my Barmitzvah portion. At school Percy was usually in the top three academically. He was a prefect and cadet company commander and a fairly good sportsman. In later years things took a turn and Percy struggled. Percy Nochumson passed away. He was a resident of the Sandringham Gardens. Percy would have been 77 years old his next birthday. I am sure he is now at peace with himself.

Robert Furman was one of the fastest chaps when it came to playing bobbies and thieves. Robert stayed in Pretoria after leaving the Arc, and was successful in the motor industry. About 10 years ago he emigrated, I think to the USA.

My last year in Arcadia was 1945. Each year we would vote for the most "popular boy", who would then receive a certain amount of money at annual prize giving. Bernard Aronstam took a liking to me and unknown to me became my "campaign manager" and mustered support. The result was that a probable 7/1 chance (that was me) received the award. This certainly proved that a good campaign manager is essential for elections. Well done Bernard!!

I read and reread extracts from "My Struggle" by Bernard Aronstam. As an Old Arc I am sure we can all relate to Bernard's experience. The Harris' at Arcadia were after my time but the negative reports of them are well known. This contrasts with Doctor and Mrs Lichtigfeld's term at Arcadia. I recall an incident when the boys were playing soccer with Doc in goals. Vicky came to call the boys to evening Shul, "now", to which Doc replied "After the next goal Vicky".

When I first arrived at Arcadia the late Manfred Herman befriended me. What a wonderful person he was, as was the late Miriam Wiener (Roberts). I am sure there are many other wonderful Old Arcs but the two I mentioned made an indelible impression on me.

When I was in Arcadia we had a Hebrew teacher who replaced Mr Mann namely Mr Shalit. My contemporaries and I learned much of Modern Hebrew from him. Mr Shalit was a wonderful person, a great human being. and probably amongst the best teachers that I had in all my schooling. He also had a son-'Maishe' who is practicing medicine in Houston. Maishe and his wife recently joined the same Shul as Willie Isaacs they meet at services infrequently, mainly because neither of them attend regularly.

When I left Arcadia, I went to stay at "The Bermans", a residential private boarding house in Berea, opposite the Berea Shul, facing Barnato Park Girls School. Some other Arc boys who stayed there included Donald Goldman, Gerald Colman, David Green and Max Rabinowitz. Woolfie Getz stayed in the next street, behind the Bermans with a family called Gower.

I was recently asked to commiserate with Gerry Levy who unfortunately contracted Shingles about a year ago. His right arm was badly affected, and could not drive his car for a considerable time. I spoke to Gerry recently and he says he has about 60% use of his arm. Another case where his condition was not correctly identified.

I quote from Shakespeare's-Julius Caesar- Mark Anthony is allowed to speak with certain restrictions after Caesar has been murdered. "I come to bury Caesar, not to praise him. The evil that men do lives after them, the good is oft interred in their bones - so let it be with Caesar". I pose a question excluding Doc of course; can this be said of some of the past superintendents and others in charge at Arcadia over the years?

Hakkie Kabe was in the care of Arcadia from 1943 to 1946 together with his younger brother Abe.

OBITUARY
Solly Farber – Extract from the 1999 Bulletin.

We record with great sadness the recent death of Hakkie Kabe, a true friend and leader of Arcadia. Hackie was an Arcadian in every sense of the word. He spent a number of years as a youth in Arcadia. After leaving Arcadia he went out into the world and slowly but surely made his way to the highest levels in commerce. He became a captain of industry and was most prominent in the sewing machine market.

In spite of his great success, Hakkie never forgot his roots in Arcadia. He returned to Arcadia by joining the committee in 1982. His ability was soon recognised and he rose through the ranks and became Chairman in 1993 and subsequently an Honorary Life President of Arcadia.

Hakkie was a man of great compassion and unbounded charity. He always stood up for the 'underdog' and he helped many of our youngsters by providing employment or other assistance.

He contributed to Arcadia by freely giving to us his precious time and by contributing goods or funds whenever he perceived that these were needed, and his perception was very finely tuned.

We thank his wife Beryl and his children and grandchildren for sharing him with us for so many years. We share in their grief at his passing and we rejoice in the splendid life of this dear and wonderful man.

Farewell dear Hackie, we will remember you always.

HAKKIE KABE
By Alec Saul

Let me begin by saying that the death of Hakkie Kabe was a tragedy is not true. We all have to die eventually. What is true is he will be almost impossible to replace. I personally was in contact with him frequently. In his business dealings, a deal was a deal and he was one of the toughest businessmen I have come across. I do not know of a case where he did not keep his word.

An Old Arc Committee member related an incident to me. As a young man Hakkie had to borrow R50 from the Old Arcs. When it came to paying back, his condition was that he would return it providing he could give it back to another Old Arc who was in need at the time. His charitable attitude was apparent even

then. His efforts on behalf of Arcadia were legendary. The number of Old Arcs he helped was numerous. The various Jewish institutions he helped with money and his own personal time were considerable. The number of times he interceded for me on behalf of poorly placed people are many. My own daughter who worked for Selwyn Segal Hostel needed three sewing machines for the Hostel. She asked where she could get them. I told her to phone Hakkie and he did not know she was my daughter when she mentioned Selwyn Segal. They were there the next day.

In my opinion Hakkie packed two life-times in his own life. Rudyard Kipling in one of his poems relates if you have left the world a better place than when you entered it, then you have achieved mightily. To his family I say his achievements as a father and a provider were immense. I sympathise with you in your loss, as all Old Arcs do, and wish you long life.

HAKKIE'S SIBLINGS.
From Freda Cheilyk (Koppel)

The eldest of the clan is a brother named Louis who was a Signwriter and a Sister Goldie who was already married when the two boys came to Arcadia. Goldie got married when she was about 17 and left to live in America many years ago

Abe is Hakkie's younger brother and was killed in a motor accident a few years before Hakkie passed away. These two brothers were both in the Arc

ABE KABE
By Mannie Osrin

Here's a little old Arc story. A true story, good for a little laugh. It must have been in the mid sixties. I had been in general practice for a few years and was staying in a block of flats with my family in Berea. One evening at about 7:30 the phone rang. It was Abe Kabe asking me to do a house visit on a friend of his, who had suddenly taken ill. I took down the address, got into my car and very shortly arrived at Abe's flat. He greeted me warmly as we hadn't seen each other for a while and introduced me to another friend.

I then asked which room the patient was in, whereupon Abe said "Oh no, he doesn't live here. He stays a few blocks away!!" "I then said "So, Abe, why have you asked me to come here?" Abe replied, "So that you could give us a lift to our friend!!" How's that for chutzpa?

Unfortunately the loveable rogue is no longer with us. I remember him with fondness, and whenever I think of the old days and the Kabes in particular, I always think of the above story.

Chapter 45 - BESSIE (NEWMAN) FIRHER (1930-2002)

Bessie was born in 1930 and was in the care of Arcadia from 1937 to 1948.

Lawrence Newman, Bessie's son, has written a tribute to his Mom that is printed below.

Lawrence also writes about the book he wrote about Bessie; a very sad story about going to Israel to find her after he lost contact with her and plans to combine that story with two others.

TRIBUTE TO MY MOM
Written by Laurence Newman (Bessie's son)

My Mom was a staunchly loyal, kind hearted, generous and fun parent. She was an immensely talented person with a wicked sense of humour and a great sense of compassion and feeling for the people around her. She was a lady with deep humility and an innate 'olde worlde' graciousness, no longer seen in the 21st century world of today.

As a small child, growing up in the sixties, I see her bent over the piano in the dining room of our house in Greenside. She played passionately, her deft fingers flying across the keys as she moved in time to the ticking metronome.

The intensity of the feelings and emotions she conveyed as she played the great masters, Chopin and Beethoven, remain locked in my mind forever. The immense technical mastery of iconic music, such as that of the revered Rachmaninov (immortalised in the movie "Shine"), was her absolute speciality.

The fire that ignited those hugely talented fingers was discovered at Arcadia when she was a small girl. It carried her through the Conservatoire of Music, to a short lived career as a concert pianist, performer and music teacher.

It in turn had a huge effect on my childhood. It motivated me. As a small boy I wanted to emulate my mother. I begged her to teach me to play the piano. She agreed with the stipulation that I was to be taught by another teacher. She felt that a multiple role would be confusing. So I took lessons elsewhere and matriculated with music in the mid seventies.

Having a musical mother was a veritable nightmare for a young student practicing daily at home on the piano. Every single missed note, slurred pedal or muddled arpeggio received loud sanction from the kitchen, scullery or garden or wherever Bessie happened to be!

When she was satisfied that I had made progress and had potential, she arranged an audition for me with a famous concert pianist who had studied under Noel Coward. She offered me the chance to become a concert performer myself. To my mother's great delight after the audition that doyen of the concert halls agreed to coach me.

Bessie Firher

Mom's glee was cut short by my acute shyness. The prospect of facing bright lights and the public eye put me off. I declined.

Nevertheless, today I have a BA Degree majoring in Music from Wits. I also worked for many years for the world renowned Royal Opera and Royal Ballet Company at Covent Garden in London amongst the musical greats of our time.

Ironically it was only by means of that same music in later years that Bessie was able to communicate any emotion or feeling whatsoever. The tragic illness that beset her in her prime deprived her of her senses, her reality, her family and ultimately her life.

That a vociferous, dynamic and very beautiful woman ended up as a shell, a wisp of a human being, without any will to live or interest in anything at all was a waste. Sadly not for her would the story end as with Russel Crowe in *A Beautiful Mind*. She lost the battle to schizophrenia in an unevenly matched set.

She left behind though, the marvellous, reverberating sound of magical harmonies that continue to this day to echo in my fond memory of her.

Once in later life she fixed me with her characteristic quizzical gaze and asked me why I had chosen to study music. I remember answering her something like this: "Goodness me Mom, that's what I knew best!"

I should have added "Without your music I would never have felt the rapture of feeling and creating magic through it!" I would never have gone to the places I had, known the people I met or lived the life I did. I would never have appreciated the extraordinary mother that I had had or been able to communicate with her when nobody else could.

Senior Girls; Front Row; Bessie Fihrer, Sifra Bortz, ? , Joyce Friedman, ? ? ?Judy Nochumson, Gertie Kaminer,? and Hilda Ellis.
Second Row; ? ? Jeannette Clous, Sophie Kukulis, ? and Audrey Sepel. Yetta Roberts and Lilly Lipschitz at back.

LAWRENCE WRITES ABOUT HIS BOOK ON BESSIE.

The script was written last year (two years after my Mom had passed away). It was written as three stand alone stories, each one written at a different time.

The first section was about the years she was missing in Israel. When I finished it a friend of mine who read it said she felt I should write about how my Mom had been found and what happened afterwards. So I wrote another story. When I completed it another friend of mine, a psychologist, suggested I write a third section to give an insight into the trauma that resulted in the illness and subsequent disappearance of Bessie.

Writing the three stories was a source of comfort to me and enabled me to put the whole sequence of events into some kind of perspective and to try to make sense of it if that's at all possible. It disrupted my life enormously and caused me immense distress. However, it did help me to put her finally to rest. I had hoped to gear it towards helping other people who may have found themselves in similar situations.

I also went to see Mrs Harary in Israel before she passed on. She was deeply concerned about my late Mom and wanted to know everything that was happening.

Of course, I do not know what I would have done without wonderful Freda who has, since I was a child, taken an interest in me and helped me out in many ways over the years. She is a beacon of wisdom, kind heartedness and has been an absolute and genuine gem. So it was natural that I gave her the story when she was here a few months ago.

Chapter 46 - EDITH COHEN (ROSENKOWITZ) (1933)

Edith's parents came from Vilna where her eldest brother Meyer and sister Marcia were born.

Edith was born in Windhoek, Namibia in 1932 and when she was still young, her family moved to Mossel Bay where Colin, her younger brother was born. Their father was a tailor and mother a dressmaker.

After their mother passed away, at age 43, they moved to Jo'burg staying with family. There Edith contracted Scarlet Fever and spent six weeks in isolation in the Fever Hospital.

Edith was placed in the care of Arcadia in December 1942, two weeks after her older brother Colin and sister Marcia had arrived, and she spent seven years in the Arc until March 1950

Audrey Sepel, Jeanette Claus and Edith

ARC MEMORIES

On the first day of arrival at Arcadia I went straight into the glassed-in isolation room in the big ward. - I had already spent four weeks in the Fever Hospital as I had Scarlet Fever and then had to spend another two weeks in isolation again. The sister in charge was Sister Edith Peltz (how could I forget her name). She was so frightening and so strict I wasn't able to talk. I was given a colouring book and crayons and coloured one page a day so that I would have something to do for another day. It was so lonely.

I had no visitors except peering faces through the window looking when I noticed my brother Colin and then felt better. Colin and my sister Marcia had arrived two weeks before me. I still remember how I used to wash the porridge down the drain. Everything I possessed had to be taken away from me to be burnt, which left me with nothing, but I got through it all.

I must have lost track how many times I must have sat with my foot in a basin of hot water as I always suffered with witloes on my toes. I still remember Bertha, who was always very kind to me, calling me Granny as I had to wear a slipper as I couldn't wear a shoe over the thick dressing!

I was in the Juniors for some time and remember Miss Durstan with horror and the fish oil or some such we had to slug down.

In the Senior Girls we were under the watchful eyes of Sister Goldwater whom I remember with fondness. I used to make her bed in the mornings together with – if I can remember rightly – Hazel Fish and Judy Nochumsohn, and she used to give us a few "shillings".

Also I recall the time when Alf James had a boxing match and it was being broadcast on the radio. We could hear the commentary from her room as the door of her lounge lead onto the balcony where we slept, and she didn't mind us listening. She did tell us off once when a couple of us girls bunked out

one afternoon to see "Random Harvest" and we arrived back late for some St Johns Ambulance Brigade ceremony

How I looked forward to our trips to the bioscopes twice a week during the holidays to see the latest movies in Charlie's bus also the pantomimes and circus. I remember Natie Roamer being blindfolded in the circus ring and trying to catch a pig. What good times we had at camp in Lakeside – Muizenberg.

Looking at the photos of the building - how beautiful it was and can see where I slept outside on the verandah watching the mice running along the top of the blinds.

Abe Kabe always teased Colin and me by clicking his heels and making the sign of Heil Hitler, calling me Sister Canary and Colin, Brother Budgie. I got so used to it that I didn't take any notice at the end of the day but of course still remember it as I always thought he was a "bit odd". I do remember his brother Hakkie and sorry they are no longer with us.

I remember most of the Birer family and was more friendly with Molly and Mary Aronofsky was a friend of my late sister Marcia.

I remember I was always so shy.

There are good and bad memories but what I shall never forget is the wonderful care I was given throughout the seven years I was in the Arc for which I am forever grateful.

Celia was the ringleader of a group of about five of us. We called ourselves red/blue or something rose and also can't remember the others. I still remember what a beautiful Russian dancer Celia was and can still visualise her doing the "*gezatzkah*". I was such a lousy dancer and always felt like a baby elephant with no grace. She has so many memories of things gone by. I am sure I must've been together with her for some of the mischievous things we got up to, but I think I must be reminded of them. Perhaps "old age has crept up with me.

I remember the excellent treatment I was given by my dentist – Dr Gorvy. He used to give us a tube of sweets after each visit. I also had orthodontic treatment to straighten my teeth. I am also very grateful for being taught First Aid, Hebrew, sewing, dancing, elocution and going to Girl Guides amongst so much else. This has given me such a good grounding. I was also put through College. I know my father could never afford what Arcadia had given me.

I remember Mr. Shaer for a short while, Mr and Mrs Harary and then barely remember Mr and Mrs Harris.

LONDON AND ANTIQUES

I left Arcadia early 1949. After a couple of years I moved to Salisbury where I met my husband Gerry who was from London. While I was there my father, who was 65 years old, passed away. I returned to Jo'burg, got married and went to London on honeymoon to meet the in-laws and never returned home so, we are still on our "honeymoon"!

Before we got married, Mrs Bella Lubner, one of the committee members took me to a wholesaler to choose some linen and bedding towards my trousseau. It was a wonderful start and very much appreciated and I think of her whenever I use the tablecloths (Yes, still in good use).

I remember Shirley Bortz being in London many years back when I did speak to her and didn't think she was still here. Don't know the whereabouts of Sandra Berlin. I know Nettie Kofsky lives in London but don't know where. She is a short and small lady and has a sister Becky in Johannesburg. Did see her once but she has since moved and don't know her married name.

Since Gerry retired we do antique fairs dealing mainly in Victorian and late 19th century glass, also deco glass. We go out almost every Sunday and sometimes we do a two day fair and stay overnight. We travel quite a distance away so it is always up at the crack of dawn. Summer time it is OK but not so clever in the winter, as some days we get up at 3.30am. At least we do avoid the heavy traffic at that hour, but coming home is not very pleasant when you have a tiring day. So it is going in the dark and coming home in the dark. When we go out buying, we have to use a torch, so you have to be so careful what you buy and it is always a chance. We traders are all mad but what can you do when it is in our blood.

At least we keep ourselves busy, although not making our fortune. We also have a unit in a shop here in Southgate where six of us share space. We take it in turns to be in the shop for a day so you see we keep out of mischief

We have had so many early mornings getting to our fairs when we have to get up at 3.30am to get to Nottinghamshire by 6am. It is still very dark and we walk around with torches to see what we can buy. I look like a Michelin tyre with so much gear on to keep me warm. There are about 4000 stalls. There are five indoor pavilions and the rest of the dealers are out of doors. We are all such a crazy lot and I think I am getting too old for this game. I don't seem to get the time for housework so the house is always like a tip.

We have two daughters, Cheryl and Tracy. We have been in London for almost 47 years. It must be about 56 years since leaving Arcadia. I have been in London for 46 years and don't know where the years have gone. It is terrifying. It is a life time.

COLIN AND THE ROSENKOWITZ SEXTUPLETS

Colin is my brother and is the father of the famous sextuplets born in Cape Town.

ColinRosenkowitz

Extract From Old Arc Newsletter – Editor Alec Saul

Colin Rosenkowitz of sextuplets fame, writes on his experience with Dave Kotzen mentioning how he taught him to carry three plates as a waiter in London, got him to come to Canada and take up a job as a plumber on the mines. They were in business together delivering cars in 32 states in the USA.

When he said goodbye in New York he little realised that Dave would meet his wife in that city. Clin writes how he was paid to referee soccer matches and was paid to write by the local newspaper of his experience of reffing and how Dave was classed in every instance as man of the match. In the cup final there was a punch-up with the players. The spectators ran onto the soccer field, but Colin controlled the game at all times and was commended by the newspaper for his grip on the game. The sports writer was lyrical in his praise of Dave and his soccer ability. Colin attributes his and Dave's abilities to their upbringing in the Arc.

COLIN ROSENKOWITZ
Extract From Old Arc Newsletter – Editor Alec Saul

Colin Rosenkowitz of sextuplets fame writes on his experience with Dave Kotzen, mentioning how he taught him to carry three plates as a waiter in London, got him to come to Canada and take up a job as a plumber on the mines. They were in business together delivering cars in 32 states in the USA.

When he said goodbye in New York he little realised that Dave would meet his wife in that city. Colin writes how he was paid to referee soccer matches and was paid to write by the local newspaper of his experience of reffing and how Dave was classed in every instance as man of the match. In the cup final there was a punch-up with the players. The spectators ran onto the soccer field but Colin controlled the game at all times and was commended by the newspaper for his grip on the game. The sports writer was lyrical in his praise of Dave and his soccer ability. Colin attributes his and Dave's abilities to their upbringing in the Arc.

ROSENKOWITZ SEXTUPLETS
From the SA Jewish Times January 1974

South African family makes history

CAPE TOWN – With the birth in Cape Town of sextuplets, three boys and three girls, a South African Jewish couple has made history and has hit the headlines of the world's press.

The six are progressing very nicely. The three boys are fairly strong and the proud parents, Mr and Mrs Rosenkowitz, Susan and Colin, should, according to an attendant paediatrician, be able to celebrate a triple *bris* within the next three weeks.

FIRST EVER?

The birth of the sextuplets is the first in the history of South Africa and is believed to be the first ever recorded in Jewish history. Mr and Mrs Rosenkowitz are both members of the Cape Town Jewish Reform congregation. Mrs Rosenkowitz converted to Judaism.

They have two older children, Samantha, aged seven and Anthony, aged five. Samantha attends the Weizmann Primary School in Sea Point.

Mr Rosenkowitz was born in Mossel Bay. His mother died when he was six years old and he spent the next ten years at Arcadia, the SA Jewish Children's Home, in Johannesburg. He met his wife in London, where they were married in 1966.

Mrs Rosenkowitz has been active in the Young Sisterhood of Cape Town's Temple Israel and was secretary of the Sisterhood at the beginning of last year.

ALMOST ALL-JEWISH

The birth of the sextuplets was well nigh a Jewish affair. At the birth there was a Jewish gynaecologist in attendance, two Jewish anaesthetists and a Jewish paediatrician.

To crown it all, Cape Town has a Jewish Mayor in the person of Cr David Bloomberg, and he was quick off the mark, expressing the delight of the citizens of the mother city.

"Cape Town," he said, "is proud and excited".

On the question of the *Bris Milah* of the boys, Rabbi David Sherman, senior Rabbi of the Cape Town Jewish Reform Congregation, told a newspaper reporter that there would be no problem regarding the circumcision of the boys.

"These children were premature and underweight. No Jewish child is circumcised until he has reached a weight of six lb."

THE ROSENKOWITZ SEXTUPLETS
Update in 2005 from Edith

Colin, my brother, is still in Cape Town. Only one of the sextuplets, Grant is in Cape Town, three of the girls, Emma, Liz and Nikki are in London as is Jason. David is working in Ireland. Anthony the eldest son who is married is also here in London. Samantha who is married is in Cape Town.

MARCIA MY SISTER

I have two daughters Cheryl and Tracy and but no grand children.

Marcia is my sister who passed away in 1999. She was married to an old Arc, Sam Gordon. He passed away in Jo'burg aged 83 in 2004. They had two children, Ralph who has three children and Lorraine who has one child.

Marcia my Sister at the Arc swimming pool

Chapter 47 – BERNARD G ARONSTAM (1933)

Bernard Aronstam was born in 1933 and together with his older brother Mike (DOB 1931), were placed in the care of the Cape Town Jewish Orphanage. In February 1942 they were placed in the care of Arcadia. Mike left Arcadia in 1946 but Bernard stayed until 1949.

Bernard after leaving the Arc found his way to Europe and then to the USA where he qualified as a printer, spent two years in the US Navy where he was a boxing Champion. He later went on to qualify as a lawyer on the GI Bill of rights. Subsequently he capped his achievements by gaining a doctorate in law.

In 1999 he published an autobiography "My Struggle" where he devotes two chapters to Arcadia and these have been copied below with his kind permission.

In August 03 Bernard met up with Hank Epstein in New Orleans after 55 years and they discovered that they had both been in the US Armed Forces. They have both been in touch with Jacob Kemp, another Old Arc living in the US.

In 2005 Hurricane Katrina destroyed his house in New Orleans. Bernard and his wife were rescued from their house and were in a shelter in Port Gulf. They then flew to and lived temporarily in Cape Town, South Africa with Bernard's brother, Michael. They plan to return to New Orleans briefly to settle his affairs, and then plan to go to California and live with Hank Epstein for a short time. Then are unsure what he will do thereafter.

LETTER FROM BERNARD G ARONSTAM   Attorney-at-Law March 2003

Let me assure you had I had your book as a reference when I wrote mine, the Chapter on the orphanage would have been a lot different and maybe a lot better. I think I am the only Old Arc that writes disparagingly of my days in the Arc and as best as I can remember, we were not a lot of happy campers as your book appears to intimate.

Before you jump to any conclusions let me give you my take of the entire set-up. You can divide the Arc history into BH and AH. Before Harris and after Harris. When I was at the Arc we had Shaer, Harary and Harris. All of whom ran a snake-pit. They didn't know about love and care and kindness and believed in the iron boot. Vicky was Harris' master-at-arms and was nothing more than an image of his master.

Then came Doc and Vicky changed his spots. He rolled with the punches and Doc proved himself up to the task and the Orphanage became what it should have been all along. A place for displaced children where love and kindness ruled the roost.

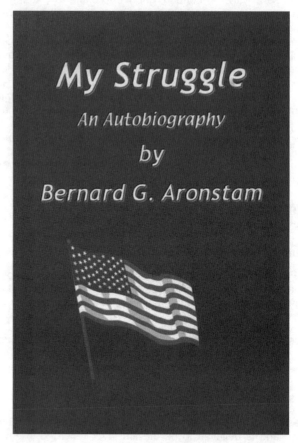

Front Cover of Bernard Aronstam's Book

Let me emphasise that at the present time I bear no malice toward anyone. I made my own life and I answer to no one but myself. Thanks to David Sandler I have been able to contact Jacob Kemp and he seems to me, just the same old Jake. I am still interested in contacting Hank Epstein so if you have his address please forward it on to me.

In conclusion let me thank you once again for your kind consideration in putting me on your mailing list. I would like to make a special request of you. Please disclose my address to any Old Arc who might find himself in this neck of the woods as my home is open to any and all old Arcs who might need my help.

MY STRUGGLE an Autobiography
By BERNARD G. ARONSTAM

FOREWORD

I would be less than candid if I were to say that a great deal of planning or research preceded the writing of this book because it didn't. On the contrary, I would say this book was written on the spur of the moment with very little preparation going into it. As a consequence, I was obliged instead to dig down into the deep recesses of my memory to recall the events of yesteryear.

And so, while I have strived to the utmost for accuracy, this book comes with no guarantee on that score. While I have spared no effort to be candid, open and truthful, it is possible that the ravages of time have wreaked havoc with my memory and that in some instances, events recounted in this book bear little resemblance to reality.

If that has indeed occurred let me assure you that it has not been intentional. In any event it should be of no consequence. This book was not intended as a treatise, text or manual. It is nothing more than what it purports to be, and that is a personal recounting of the events of my life, splattered with a healthy dose of my perception of history and philosophy. This book is designed to entertain and amuse and that is all that it is intended to do. It is as simple as that.

It will become evident to the reader, early in the book, that I have written disparagingly of certain people that have in some way or another touched my life. In this regard, let me state categorically that I bear malice or ill-will toward no-one. It has not been my intention, throughout this book, to harm or hurt anyone.

It has been my experience, throughout my life, that good can sometimes emerge from adversity. Indeed we learn from our experiences whether good or bad. Perhaps in some instances an unpleasant experience can do more to shape and build one's character than all the good fortune that might cross one's path.

In the last analysis I consider myself fortunate indeed. In fact I consider the ill-wind that has befallen me to be every bit as important in moulding my character and shaping my outlook as all the good things that have blown my way.

And so I want to avail myself of this opportunity to thank the many people, too numerous to mention here, who in some way or another, small or great, have touched my life, lighting it a little hour or two, and then going on their way, but leaving me a better person for it.

There were my teachers in primary and high school who moulded my character and in their way prepared me for my great struggle as an adult. There were my college and law school professors who took great pains to inspire me and prepare me for the vicissitudes of the real world.

There were my superiors in the Air Force, officers and NCO's alike, who brightened my life and taught me that without discipline, life can indeed be hollow. To all of them, and to the numerous others who have faded from my memory but left me a better person that I was, I express my deepest and heartfelt appreciation.

And last, but certainly not least, I would be remiss in my duty if I did not express my deepest and most profound appreciation to my dear wife, Olive for the help she provided me in writing this book. She advised me and counselled me on it. She encouraged me when I was ready to throw in the towel. She has been my friend and most ardent supporter for more than 35 years and I count myself fortunate indeed because of it.

My favourite poem is Abou Ben Adhem by Leigh Hunt. Like Abou I prefer to think of myself "as one who loves his fellow men." I really do. True, I have not always been as understanding and as considerate as I should have been, but pride cometh before the fall.

Today I understand, more than ever before, that we are all part of the human race and that all people everywhere are our brothers and our sisters. And so in conclusion I would make a plea for tolerance. For surely without it we are all doomed.

Bernard G Aronstam

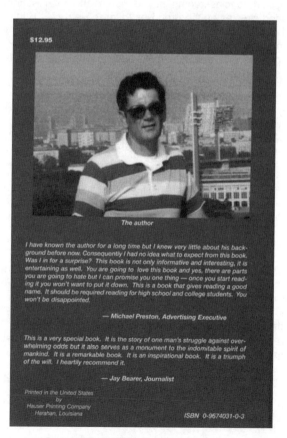

The author

I have known the author for a long time but I knew very little about his background before now. Consequently I had no idea what to expect from this book. Was I in for a surprise? This book is not only informative and interesting, it is entertaining as well. You are going to love this book and yes, there are parts you are going to hate but I can promise you one thing — once you start reading it you won't want to put it down. This is a book that gives reading a good name. It should be required reading for high school and college students. You won't be disappointed.

— Michael Preston, Advertising Executive

This is a very special book. It is the story of one man's struggle against overwhelming odds but it also serves as a monument to the indomitable spirit of mankind. It is a remarkable book. It is an inspirational book. It is a triumph of the will. I heartily recommend it.

— Jay Bearer, Journalist

Printed in the United States
by
Hauser Printing Company
Harahan, Louisiana

ISBN 0-9674031-0-3

Back Cover of Bernard Aronstam's Book

MY STRUGGLE an autobiography
by BERNARD G. ARONSTAM

CHAPTER III - THE JEWISH ORPHANAGE

I spent ten years in the Jewish Orphanage in Johannesburg and I hated every minute of it. It was terrible. I understand no institution could substitute for a loving home but that was not the real problem. The real problem with living in the orphanage was the people who ran it. We had a superintendent who more or less set the policy and laid down the rules. While I was there we must have gone through four or five of them, but unfortunately no-one was more enlightened than any other.

The ironic thing about the orphanage is that it could have been a nice place. It could have been a happy place. It should have been. At one time they had as many as 300 children of all ages there. You would have thought that someone in high places would have realised that a little kindness, love and understanding would be an imperative in our upbringing. But we never got any of that.

Instead we were dished out a harsh regimen of discipline coupled with a healthy dose of religion. It was religion for breakfast, religion for lunch and religion for dinner. Actually, the orphanage had its own synagogue and we were required to attend services in the morning and evening.

We also had classrooms at the home and after school we attended classes on the premises to learn Hebrew. To this very day I can read and write Hebrew and although not fluent, I can still mumbo-jumbo my way through a conversation in Hebrew. The powers that be must have believed that idleness is the devil's workshop.

Our Hebrew teacher was Mr Mann. He always carried a long cane with him in class and would strike out at you without warning if he felt you had misbehaved. One time he caught me unawares and dished out three or four stinging "cuts" with his cane before I was able to elude him but I had my revenge a few days later.

The restrooms were nearby. One was reserved solely for the staff. Mr Mann was in the stall when I came in and I could see his feet sticking out on the floor. I took a paper sack filled it with water and threw it over the top. There was a loud splash I was outta there. Classes were cancelled for the rest of the afternoon.

Even on weekends we were kept busy. Saturday afternoon it was bible study. Saturday night it was St John's classes for an hour before the movies. (St John's was South Africa's answer to the Red Cross and we were taught first aid and stuff like that.) Sunday morning it was boy scouts and boxing lessons while the girls were taught to sew and had ballet dancing classes. It was go, go, go.

The orphanage was located on one of the choicest pieces of land in Johannesburg. It occupied 27 acres which had once been the estate of Sir Lionel Phillips. In fact the gutters of the complex still bore his initials, "LP" embossed on them.

The orphanage had its own orchards, laundry, shoemaker shop, auditorium, and it even had its own bus. On weekends we saw some of the latest movies in the auditorium and in the summer holidays, we were taken to the movie houses downtown to give us an outing away from the facility. In fact the orphanage had its own stables and cows which provided the daily supply of milk for 300 children.

The orphanage had a large compound of African employees who performed all the menial work at the facility and I imagine they did so for a mere pittance. But that was the way it was back in those days.

We had or own swimming pool and tennis courts and we had a soccer field and a cricket pitch. So what am I really complaining about. It sounds like a country club. As I said it could have and should have been our Garden of Paradise instead of the Black Hole that it was.

The orphanage hired an assistant to the superintendent. He had the tongue-tying name of Vicky Klevansky. I suppose his first name was a nickname but I never did know his real name. As far as I know Vicky is still alive and well but he must be quite old by now.

Vicky was in charge of the senior boys and he loved the power that went with it. In those days the authorities still believed in corporal punishment and I suppose that would have been okay if we would have been spanked or caned or had some other civilised punishment meted out to us.

But oh no, Vicky's idea of corporal punishment was to punch you out. Have you ever seen these pictures of physical hazing in the military where the drill instructor punches the recruit in the stomach and kayos him? Well that could have been Vicky. Vicky loved to punch us out. How he loved it. He should have been a drill instructor. He missed his calling.

I remember one time some of us arrived late for synagogue service. The service was scheduled for 7.00 in the morning and of course it was always a chore to get up and get ready in time. So anyhow, some of us arrived late after the service had already started. Well, no-one will disagree I am sure, that we were amiss in being late and should have been punished but Vicky had his own way of punishing us. He lines us all up outside the building and made us pray with our heads bowed looking into the prayer book.

The main idea was that we were not to lift our heads from the bowed position and of course some of us did from time to time. That was a big mistake, POW! As soon as we lifted our heads Vicky would punch us in the mouth. It was no fun and not something I can look back to with any joy or happiness. If we were living in today's world it would be an outright case of child abuse. But then who knew about that? For that matter who cared?

Vicky, you might say, was the master-at-arms. The captain of the ship at that time was Arnold Harris. Harris and his wife had been brought out from England specifically to run the orphanage. Arnold was a slight wisp of a man weighing, probably no more than 125 pounds dripping wet.

His wife, a huge buxom matron weighed close to 250 pounds. They were an unlikely couple. He a milquetoast and she a brazen shrew. I don't think they were really evil people but they were incompetent and their fault lay, I suppose, in letting Vicky run the establishment. We hated the Harris' almost as much as we hated Vicky.

On Friday nights all the boys and girls used to dine together in the auditorium. After the meal was over we would sing Hebrew songs and generally engage in good fellowship with readings from the Talmud and the sidur (Hebrew prayer book). It was quite pleasant. One song we sang in English went like this: "I met a girl in Palestine, the land I thought was really mine, till we met those British swine, give me a gun and sparks will fly."

As I said the Harris' were from England. So every time we came to the part "till we met those British swine" everyone shouted it out with added gusto. The Harris' could have died. They flushed. They seethed and I suppose they plotted revenge. I don't know. That was the way it went in those days.

While we were in the orphanage we attended the public schools. This provided a welcome relief from the rigors of the orphanage and as unhappy as I was in the orphanage I still have fond memories of my time in high school. I attended Parktown Boys' High School, one of the elite schools in Johannesburg although there were others too, to be sure. The girls had their own high school.

South Africa basically follows the English system of schooling. Primary school encompasses the first seven years of schooling and then it is on to either junior high or high school depending on the ultimate goal of the student. If the student plans to pursue a trade or does not plan to go to university, then it would be logical to attend junior high, which generally taught vocational subjects. Students who planned to go to university would, as a general rule, attend a high school that went from Form I to Form V and covered a curriculum necessary to qualify for admission to university.

We wore our school tie that was red with black stripes and our school blazer which was black with a red badge portraying a lion on the breast pocket. Under the lion was the word "Arise" which was the school motto. Boys who had excelled in sports were awarded their "colours' to great fanfare and had the distinction of wearing a jacket with a red stripe embroidered around the edge of the sleeve.

Our teachers in high school were wonderful. They took a great deal of interest in our welfare and were anxious to see that we got a good education. There was, to be sure, discipline in the schools but it was not sadistic. Mostly a sharp rebuke was sufficient to correct any disciplinary problem that a teacher might encounter, and on rare occasions, very rare indeed, the teacher might feel compelled to send the student to the principal's office for chastisement. If and when this did occur, the student would feel such humiliation and embarrassment that you could bet he would make certain it wouldn't happen again.

I remember our teachers hated for you to chew gum in class. They hated ballpoint pens and they hated most of all, comic books that they called "American trash". But we loved them, especially the "classic comics" because it would help us to avoid having to read our set books which were required reading.

If I have any criticism at all of the South African educational system, at least at that time, then it must be that the curriculum was just too rigorous for the young minds that were expected to grasp all the material offered to us.

For instance, in Form I, which I suppose would be about the eighth grade equivalent in the United States, we were required to study arithmetic, geometry and algebra, we had to take English and Afrikaans, we had to study biology and chemistry, we had history and geography. In the next year we had to take an additional language, either Latin or French keeping in mind that we were still expected to learn Hebrew back in the orphanage.

Our English and Afrikaans was doubly compounded because we had set books which had to be read in both languages. In fact one of the greatest novels I have ever read was The Cloister and the Hearth, a setbook assignment in my second year in high school. We were also expected to memorise poems in both languages and to this very day, I still remember Gray's Elegy in a Country churchyard which I learned in Form II and which just might be the greatest poem ever written.

So, as I said, the curriculum was difficult, very difficult. It was arduous. We finished our last class in school at 3.00 pm and often had to spent the rest of the afternoon sometimes until 11.00 at night doing our homework. So it wasn't easy. But it was wonderful.

I have only the fondest memories of my public school education. We had such wonderful teachers. Mr Marais taught us science. Mr De Klerk taught us Afrikaans. Mr Bredenham taught us mathematics. And Mr Potter, who was from England, taught us English.

I will never forget to this very day, and I can recall it as if it were yesterday, about a story Mr Potter told us of when he was growing up in the old country. He told us that when he was 16 he took a national exam to determine if he could gain entrance to university.

On a cold and miserable day, he was lying sick and infirm in bed in the attic when the results came out. He said he could hear his father's heavy footsteps clomping up the stairs. His father came into the room waving the letter. He announced, "99 out of a 100, the highest in the land, but there is room for improvement."

When I heard this story I was horrified. In fact I even felt some pity for Mr Potter. I thought for sure it wasn't true and that he had just made it up, well you know, to make a point. I waited until after class and went to talk to him.

If I was an American kid I would have said, "Mr Potter please say it ain't so. It never happened." But I didn't say that. I just said that what he had told us had bothered me because I felt his father should have praised him to high heaven.

Mr Potter stared at me in disbelief. I don't know what he was thinking but he assured me that it had occurred precisely the way he had related it to us. He said "that is what happened, my boy, I assure you". I know I walked out of the classroom that day with my head down and a sad countenance. Now I wonder what he thought but I never know because the matter was never brought up again.

As can readily be seen, obtaining a high school diploma in South Africa was no easy accomplishment. It was a highly-prized possession. In fact to matriculate all candidates had to take a provincial exam (equivalent to a State exam in the United States). It was like taking the Bar Exam at the high school level.

The school year in South Africa runs from January to December. After the exam was over the examiners repaired to Pretoria, the administrative capital of the Republic, to grade the papers. In those days you weren't notified by mail whether you passed or failed. The results appeared in the local newspaper, The Star, on New Year's Eve.

You can imagine the excitement. Most students attended parties or dances on New Year's Eve. At midnight they all rushed down to the newspaper offices and waited at the dock for the first edition to roll off the presses.

It was exciting. Hundreds of students all gathered around clawing and scraping to get hold of a paper to check the results. The schools were listed in alphabetical order If you passed your name was in the paper. If you failed you weren't listed as a failure but your name just did not appear.

There was whooping and hollering and screaming and shouting as students found their names. Others who weren't so fortunate looked disconsolate and forlorn. You could always tell who passed and who failed without a word being said.

Despite our heavy schedule of studies at school we also had a lot of sports programs. We had a beautiful gym, we played rugby and cricket and we were noted for our outstanding track team. There was intense rivalry between the different high schools. There were English and Afrikaans speaking schools and the rivalry was especially intense between us and Helpmekaar Hoër Skool vir Seuns (Helpmekaar High School for boys) which was Afrikaans-speaking and was located just across the way from us.

For some reason the Afrikaans speaking schools excelled in rugby and we excelled in cricket and track and we were never able to beat them at rugby while I was at school. I played rugby and cricket and I was quite a good cricket player in my young days.

At that time General smuts was Prime Minister and the United Party, which was pro-British held sway. South Africa was pro-British and we strongly supported the British way of life. As I said our school system paralleled the English school system and we learned more about English history at school than we did about South African history. In fact the history of the Boer War was completely obliterated from our history books.

At that time there was a custom throughout the country to play the British national anthem at the end of every movie showing. At the end of the movie everyone stood up and a stirring rendition of God Save the King was played while a picture of King George VI was displayed on screen with the Union Jack waving proudly in the background. I stood up with the rest of the audience and sang along with the rest of the audience. At least I did at first.

It became fairly obvious early on that the Afrikaners in the audience, who had no love for the British, failed to wait around for the National Anthem to be played. They skedaddled out of there without so much as an 'excuse me'. After a while I started thinking I could get a head start to get my bus back to the orphanage and avoid the crowds by pretending to be Afrikaans. So as soon as the movie ended I skedaddled out of there along with the Afrikaners.

In 1947 South Africans became agog with excitement when it was announced that the Royal Family was to tour the country. All kinds of arrangements were made for their entertainment and many towns bedecked the streets with neon lights to honour the Royal Family's presence.

Pictures of the royals were displayed in store windows and big welcome signs were posted everywhere. Receptions were planned nationwide and city officials were falling all over themselves in an effort to outdo their rivals. Something this big had never happened in South Africa for quite some time and most government officials were agog with excitement about it.

Excitement heightened as the Royal Navy's Battleship HMS Vanguard departed the United Kingdom with the Royal Family on board destined for Cape Town. I can distinctly remember the day they arrived. I was at school. It was about mid-morning. There was no television back then but each class had acquired a radio for the occasion and we all sat excitedly listening as the announcer related the events.

The King was walking down the gangway followed by the queen and the two princesses, Elizabeth and Margaret. First his right foot then his left. Then the announcer could barely restrain himself with excitement. "The King's right foot has touched South African soil" he virtually screamed into the microphone. I remember how thrilled we were also.

The royal Family was shown a wonderful time in South Africa. They made public appearances all over the country and everywhere they went they received many gifts. Princess Elizabeth celebrated her 21st birthday in the Union and she was showered with gifts including priceless diamond necklaces and bracelets. It was insanity. In the meantime the blacks in the townships lived in squalor and poverty and there were many poor whites too.

Of course when the Royals visited Johannesburg they were entertained lavishly. We were also afforded the opportunity to see the Royal Family when it was announced that they were to pay a visit to the Rand Show, a trade fair held at Milner Park near where I went to school. As it so happened, the road to Milner Park ran directly behind Parktown High School and the royals were to pass by on their way to the fair.

So, at 8.30 in the morning we were all marched out to the back fence of the school so that we could view the Royals as they passed by. After a two-hour wait their motorcade finally arrived. The King and Queen were in the lead car followed by the two princesses. They must have been travelling about thirty miles an hour and all I can remember from that morning was now they were here and then they were gone. I guess we must have seen them for about fifteen seconds.

I can recall seeing the backs of their heads as they disappeared into the distance. I must confess that as young as I was, and as enthusiastic as everyone else was about seeing these great figures, I began to wonder what all the fuss had been about. I remember the most enthusiastic viewers were our teachers. They seemed to revel in the pomp and circumstance more than the students did.

Meanwhile, back at the orphanage we had boxing lessons on Sunday morning and I began to take a little interest in boxing. We had intra-mural boxing at school and I always managed to win my division.

I remember one time I was matched against a youngster by the name of Ron Spring. Spring was tall and gawky but I had never actually seen him fight. He was always a winner too and since I had won all my fights it was inevitable that there was quite some interest at the school when we met in the final. My friends warned me that I was in for a heap of trouble.

It was a scream. I climbed into the ring with a pair of walking shorts tied with an old school tie. I didn't have boxing shoes but used an old pair of sneakers (which we called *tackies*) and gray socks. Spring stepped into the ring looking like Sugar Ray Leonard.

He wore a beautiful pair of white silk trunks with a black stripe as well as a white silken robe. He wore boxing shoes with tassels on his laces and white socks with a blue stripe. In short he looked the consummate professional. I started to feel some misgivings. I thought maybe he was something special. I was beginning to think maybe I was in the wrong place and that my friends were right.

But I learned a good lesson. I gave him a good drubbing and learned in the bargain that things are not always what they seem. After the fight was over I have to give it to him. He came and congratulated me and asked me if he could buy me a coke or whatever South Africa's version of a coke was at that time. Talk about the age of innocence.

I also learned another lesson by being in the orphanage. I became, in my own way, streetwise. I mean I did things that I am not too proud of today although, in retrospect, they appear to be more humorous than mean-spirited.

I loved boxing and I loved movies. However, it was not always easy for us to attend these activities because we had very little money back on those days. But we did devise a way to attend some of the big boxing matches that were held at the Rand Stadium in Johannesburg.

I saw many, many boxing matches, from ringside seats and yet I never paid a dime to get in to see them. Back in those days we never had the money to spend to watch prize-fighting. We would "scale" in to the fights.

This meant climbing the fence, negotiating some strands of barbed-wire at the top and dropping down about ten feet on the other side. Sometimes we got cut or sprained our legs but mostly the injuries healed fast. We were young and we didn't care about small things.

Sometimes "scalers" would bring wire-cutters and actually cut big holes in the fence for us to crawl through. One time I crawled through a drain outlet. It had been raining a day or two before and by the time I got into the stadium I was soaking wet. But my favourite way of getting in didn't involve acrobatics at all. Youngsters were hired to sell programs and hot-dogs.

They had ingress and egress to the stadium. They wore white coats to signify their status. They were on the inside and we were on the outside. They would hand their coats and programs to us through the fence. We would then don these coats and walk through the turnstiles as the gatemen acknowledged our status. We would then return the jacket and programs to the original program seller and give him a shilling for his trouble. So it worked out nicely for all of us. That was the way it was back in those days.

We also discovered during those days that brazenness has its virtues. Without tickets we would head straight for the ringside seats. No-one ever asked us to substantiate authorisation to be where we were. I guess those in authority who were assigned the task of verifying our tickets, automatically assumed we were there because we had a right to be.

Sometimes we ran into problems by sitting in people's seats who came to claim them but mostly we would find a place and not be subjected to harassment by the authorities. Friends of ours who had paid to get in sat in the bleachers. We had "scaled" in and had the best seats in the house.

We also attended movies on a regular basis. At that time, as did most countries around the world, South Africa had magnificent movie palaces. There was The Twentieth Century, The Metro, The Colosseum, His Majesty's, The Empire and so on. They were all magnificent in their own right. My favourite was The Colosseum which had, what looked to me like stars in the sky. They were just small lights placed on the ceiling but they appeared to be stars and they even blinked.

Going to the movies on a Friday or Saturday night was truly a special occasion. Everyone dressed up in their finest array. Short programs, cartoons and newsreels were shown. I remember American Movietone was my favourite newsreel and there was also the British Movie Tone News "Presenting the world to the World". South Africa also had its own newsreel called the African Mirror but it was so inferior to the American and British newsreels that most people scoffed at it.

At intermission everyone assembled in the lobby for refreshments. It was like going to the opera today. It was a special event. Liquor was not sold but vendors hawked candy, chocolates and ice cream outside on the sidewalk and you could obtain a 'pass-out' to leave the theatre. A buzzer rang five minutes before the show was to begin and everyone scurried back to their seats.

But unique to South Africa as far as I know, we also had what was commonly referred to as "cafe bioscopes". These were movie houses showing mostly "B movies" on a continuous basis. A cafe bioscope, as its name suggests, was a combination of a cafe and a movie house. They actually served meals while you watched the movie. Each row of seats had a ledge affixed to it on which the crockery could be set.

The system was ingenious. There was no box-office where you could purchase a ticket. You simply came into the theatre and took a seat. Waitresses would scour the aisles looking for anyone without a saucer in front of them on the ledge. Where the patrons had no saucers the waitress concluded they hadn't paid and she would take their orders. A glass of soda, came with a saucer and was part of the base price.

You could however, order a full course meal, for which of course, you paid extra. There was sausages and mash, sausages and sauerkraut, fish and chips and hamburgers and chips. Custard pudding was standard dessert with every meal. The choices were varied but the food was simple and relatively cheap.

One disadvantage of ordering a meal was the actual process of getting the food to you. If you were sitting in the middle of the theatre your plate had to be passed down from the aisle to you. That means it would be "handled" by several patrons prior to reaching you. Their eyes would be transfixed on the screen but their hands would be groping at your plate while they passed it down the line. God only knows how many fingers went into your potatoes or custard pudding by the time your order reached you.

The theatre was often patronised by bus drivers and conductors who worked split shifts and who utilised the cafe bioscopes to while away their dead hours. Also the homeless, the hobos and people down on their luck found a home away from home in the cafe bioscopes. These were not the great palaces of the era but they were cheap and they did afford the dregs of society a place to park their weary bones for a while.

And so I suppose it was not surprising that we, at the orphanage found a place where we could go to the movies, and we could go for free. How did we do it? The answer was simple. We simply took a saucer from the orphanage, tucked it under our shirt and after we had sat down we pulled out the saucer and placed it on the ledge in front of us. I am amazed to this day that of the numerous times we utilised this procedure to get in to these movie houses we were never apprehended.

I am sure now that the saucers we used were not of the same brand or design used by these theatres. I am also sure that the waitresses must have seen us come in and knew we hadn't ordered or paid for our seat. But of all the many times I attended the cafe bioscopes without paying, not one time was I ever called on the carpet about it. God knows how many saucers the cafe bioscopes must have accumulated from the orphanage boys. I suppose they also must have been wondering at the orphanage why there was always a shortage of saucers.

It was during this same period that my potential acting career came to a screeching halt. I had always held out the hope of one day pursuing my father's unrealised dream of becoming a professional actor. I had recited poems before live audiences and in truth had felt quite comfortable on stage. It had never bothered me. But I had a strange quirk which was to prove my undoing.

I had this inexplicable propensity to giggle or laugh in a dire situation. While others were fretting or stewing in a perilous situation, I would start laughing. Ask me why. I can't explain it. For example, on one occasion I had a small part to play. I was to play the role of a waiter. My brother had the lead in the play and at some time in the opening scene he was to call for "waiter". At that point I was to come on stage and take his order which was for two drinks.

In due course I heard the call "waiter" and for some reason I got the giggles and was unable to come on stage. Fortunately one of the stage hands had the presence of mind to grab the tray from me and go out on stage to fill my part. Something should have told me then to give up but oh no, I was to try again.

The next disaster occurred in a play given at the orphanage at the end of our summer holidays. I had the starring role along with Benny Touyz in a play called "*The Married Couple*". I can't recall everything about this play but I recall the opening scene. Benny and I are on stage when the curtain goes up.

Benny is dressed like a little old lady. He is wearing a wig and a dress and hose and high heel shoes. His opening line addressed to me is "darling, we have been married for thirty years and we have never had a quarrel." I am supposed to retort that it has been wonderful except for this or that which triggers a big argument.

Well, as soon as Benny started out with "Darling" I just lost control and burst out laughing. Down went the curtain and out came Vicky on stage. And he wasn't smiling either. He announced the play would start over and it did but with the same result. This time Vicky was steaming. He announced, and he was flushed with the one corner of his lip quivering, "We are going to give Bernard once more chance."

I am sure that the only thing that would have given Vicky satisfaction at that point was to punch me out. But he didn't. I was given another chance but needless to say it happened again and a substitute was found for me. If I felt sorry for anybody it was Benny. He was almost in tears. He announced that he would never act with me again and so my acting career drew to a close before it really had begun.

I was doing fine in school but my bad reputation at the orphanage was at a point where I was branded a trouble-maker. Things reached their zenith when Vicky refused to let a close friend of mine, Morris Farber, have breakfast because he arrived five minutes late. I was irate. I was seething. Morris was very ill. He had a heart condition which we all knew about.

I felt Vicky was arbitrary and unfair. I don't know how it came about but I announced that if Morris didn't eat none of us would. Morris was not allowed to eat breakfast and we all walked out of the dining room at my instigation.

It was a calamitous action and branded me as a firebrand. I remember all the food for sixty or so boys being taken back to the kitchen. Vicky and the superintendent, Mr Harris, were standing there seething. I know they would have just loved to throttle me. But that action sealed my fate.

I was definitely persona non grata. Thereafter things went down and down for me at the orphanage. It seemed like I was always in trouble. It was bound to happen. I resolved to run away.

Chapter Iv - The Runaway

To this day I don't know how it happened but happened it did. I ran away from the orphanage. But even worse than that I took two other boys with me, which I suppose compounded the felony. I must have just turned fifteen. It seemed like things were going from bad to worse. I was only in the 11th grade. I was making the grade at school but not excelling. It seemed like I was always in a heap of trouble at the orphanage.

Where I should have been a leader and setting a good example it seemed like I was always in the soup moving from one disaster to another. And the more trouble I found myself in, the more rebellious I would become. We were always up to derring do. Always up to mischief. I don't think we were really bad kids. Certainly we were angels by today's standards.

It seemed like I was always late for dinner. I was always late for services at the synagogue. For some reason or another, no matter how chastised I was, I never corrected the problem. Maybe it was psychological.

Before and after dinner we said a short prayer. To say prayers Jews must cover their heads. We all wore caps for this ritual as our heads were required to be covered. The procedure was for all of us to stand and the senior boy would say, "Caps, bend your heads and close your eyes, begin". We would don our caps. Bend our heads and then in unison we would all say the prayer together in Hebrew.

It was quaint. I can see that now. But count on me. When it came my turn to lead the procedure I would say, "caps, bend your eyes and close your heads, begin".

No matter how many times I went through this same procedure everyone would burst out laughing and of course Vicky and Harris would have a fit. I remember one time, Harris became extremely irate. He screamed at the top of his lungs, "blackguard" which was a saying we were not all totally familiar with since it was one he had brought with him from England.

I knew it wasn't a compliment though. Let us just say I had not endeared myself either to the Harris' or Vicky. I am sure they would have liked to see the end of me and I can assure you it wouldn't have broken my heart to see the end of them either.

And so I resolved to make a break from the orphanage. My decision was to have tragic consequences for one of my dearest friends who fled with me. Morris Farber. I am sure now, as best as I can recall that I was the ringleader.

But anyhow somehow, I persuaded two friends of mine, the previously mentioned Morris Farber and David Gordon to accompany me on this venture. It was a foolhardy escapade. We had no money to speak of. We resolved to run away to Durban.

Durban is a popular vacation resort on the Indian Ocean approximately 300 miles east of Johannesburg. It is indeed a beautiful place and it is not at all surprising that thousands of people from Johannesburg flock there for their annual vacation. So our goal was to run away from the orphanage and go to Durban. What we were going to do there when we got there we didn't really know. We had just a few dollars with us, perhaps enough for a night or two at a hotel, and that was it.

So off we went. It was the summer holidays and we started out hitchhiking with barely enough clothes or money to keep us going. It didn't take us long to get a ride. In those days hitchhiking in South Africa, as it was back then in the United States, was not arduous. We were young and I suppose people could recognise that we were just high school kids heading out. It didn't take us long before we got our first ride and were on the road to Durban.

Then, by a strange quirk of fate, luck intervened. Unbeknownst to us, as soon as the authorities at the orphanage realised we had flown the coop, they notified the police and an all points bulletin to keep a lookout for us was posted. But we had gotten a ride with a Boer farmer on his way to Ladysmith.

He asked if we wanted a ride and he explained that Ladysmith was out of the way but we could get to Durban from there in a roundabout way. We accepted the ride. Law enforcement officials were on the lookout for us but their search was chiefly restricted to the main roads. By being on one of the back roads we were not spotted.

It was kind of interesting because on the way to Ladysmith our benefactor began relating the history of the Boer War to us. He explained that being English, we would appreciate the significance of the great battle that had been fought at Ladysmith between the Boers and the English in the Boer War and that the English had been victorious.

We quickly corrected him. We told him we were Jewish and had no love for the British who had treated our own people with less than respect in Palestine. This was after the close of World War II and the British had interned fleeing displaced Jewish refugees on the Island of Cyprus.

We were not unmindful of the fact also that the British had been less than supportive of the Jewish cause in obtaining Palestine as a Jewish homeland. Of course the Harris' only reinforced our hatred for the British so we were not hesitant to vent our spleen on the British.

We could tell this immediately triggered a reaction from our driver. He warmed to us immediately. He became far more friendly. He asked us a lot about our personal lives. He inquired of us where we were going and must have detected that something was amiss because he put us off at a hotel owned by a friend of his in Ladysmith.

Strange as it may seem, the innkeeper fed us dinner without exacting a fee. He put us up in a private lounge where we spent the night and for which service there was no charge. So go and figure this out. We counted ourselves lucky because we had no plans for that night and as I recall, the weather there was frightfully cold that evening. So we were blessed by an unknown divine intervention, one might say.

The following morning, after a breakfast on the house once more, we were off to Durban. We didn't even have to hitchhike a ride. Someone at the hotel was going to Durban and they offered to take us there. So it was all cut and dried. No sweat. No problem.

Durban is a fabulous city. In a way it is like Miami. It is very hot in the summer but has a mild moderate temperature in the winter. Thus it is a favourite winter vacation resort. We arrived there at close to noon and immediately checked into a rooming house. Talk about naiveté. We gave our real names.

Off we went to swim without a care in the world. When I think about it now I am simply befuddled. It made no sense. Other than an act of rebellion it was just plain ludicrous. I mean what would we have done? What could we have done?

Unbeknownst to us everyone and their brother was on the lookout for us. There were reports that we had been spotted on the way to the Kruger National Park which was in another direction. We should have suspected something when our landlord served us dinner on the house. But we didn't. We just weren't thinking. We were naive and we were, maybe stupid but we weren't criminals as we were later made out to be.

Somehow, while relaxing in the lounge that evening, I picked up the evening paper only to read a big headline screaming at me, "Missing Boys Sighted." Of course it was us. It gave a detailed description of us and stated that we had been seen on the road to the Kruger National Park. It urged everyone to keep on the lookout for us.

We knew at this point the jig was up but we didn't panic. In fact we were amused that we had been identified heading for the Kruger Park. We went to bed that night without a care in the world.

What we were thinking of I have not the slightest idea. All I know is it didn't seem to make much difference. The way I looked at it then was whatever will happen so be it. As best as I could tell, Morris and David felt the same way I did. At least neither of them seemed to be overly concerned by the consequences.

Things came to a drastic head at about 5.00 o'clock the following morning. We were all sound asleep only to be awakened by Mr Harris. Apparently he had, along with a chauffeur, driven all night long to arrive at our hotel at that early hour. We were rousted out of bed, made to dress and hauled back to Johannesburg in the van that they had come in. But when we got back to Jo'burg we weren't taken back to the orphanage. Oh no. We were taken down to Marshall Square. Marshall Square is the police complex in the City Centre where there are lockup facilities along with magistrate and trial courts. We were promptly incarcerated.

I will never forget that experience. We were locked up in a cell with bars on the windows. Other miscreants who had occupied that cell prior to us had carved various messages on the wooden table or written graffiti on the walls and we whiled away

the hours reading what others, similarly situated, I suppose, had to say.

A lot of the scribblings were in Afrikaans. The word "fuck" and "fok" were freely used. There were hearts carved in the table. "Mom" and "Ma" were used repeatedly in the inscriptions. I will never forget one of these inscriptions. It said "General Smuts is an ass". I wondered why and who said that. We would have laughed if we hadn't felt like crying.

We were in there for at least five hours. During that time we weren't given permission to go to the bathroom or have a drink of water. It was scary for us because we had never been exposed to that type of treatment.

Unfortunately too, for Morris Farber, he was very ill and the experience must have been deleterious to his health. Just how deleterious we were not to discover until a few months later when he died at the age of 15. It was a tragic unnecessary consequence of a foolhardy venture.

In retrospect I feel an awesome responsibility for his death. Perhaps his illness would have resulted in his death regardless of our trip to Durban and its aftermath. No one knows the answer to that and no one ever will. Suffice it to say that our experience was totally unnecessary.

We were taken before a magistrate and interrogated. We were intimidated and led to believe that we were going to be sent to a reformatory. I didn't know much about reformatories back then but I knew they weren't nice places. I was intimidated. I was frightened. I wasn't the tough guy they were portraying me to be. I wanted to get out of there and breathe the fresh air of freedom. I think at that time my hatred was directed more at the orphanage than the magistrate hanging the sword of Damocles over my head.

The long and the short of it. It was just a big bluff. They had no intention of sending us to a reformatory. They just wanted to scare the hell out of us and they sure as heck succeeded in doing that. Instead they expelled us from the orphanage. We were left to manage on our own.

Within six months Morris Farber was dead. Living a life without care and kindness he succumbed to his illness at the tender age of fifteen. Was it my fault? It was a great tragedy. It is one that I will never overcome.

The orphanage and I must take a great deal of the responsibility that lies in the death of Morris Farber. Morris' death lies heavy on my heart to this very day. I will never recover from it. I will never cease blaming myself for it. I feel responsible. I feel guilty. It is a guilt trip I will never get over. With my expulsion from the orphanage things would never be the same for me again. My mother and my sister, Stella shared an efficiency apartment. I was expected to go and live with them. Indeed there was no other place for me to go.

It was just a matter of time and I would be off again. This time I would start on an even greater journey which would lead me to the United States of America. But this was just the start. There was a long long way yet to go.

COMMENTS ON BERNARD ARONSTAM'S BOOK

Heinz (Hank) Epstein USA

A couple of months ago I got a real surprise. An e-mail arrived from none other than Bernard Aronstam. It caught me completely by surprise because I have long wondered where Bernie was. Of course I immediately answered his letter and we became acquainted again, after about 55 years! We now correspond by phone and e-mail quite often. Bernard also sent me a complementary copy of his book which I took with me to Germany, where I had the opportunity to read it from cover to cover.

It was fascinating. What struck me most was how parallel our lives ran. We both enlisted in the Air Force, I, at the start of the Korean war, he a short time after. We took basic training at Lackland AFB, then we went into electronics, he at Keesler AFB for training as a radar technician, and I to Scott AFB for 26 weeks of training as a navigational equipment technician. I stayed on to become an instructor in that field, then was sent to Japan for a two year hitch. At about the time I graduated from the University of California at Los Angeles (UCLA) in engineering, Bernie was at the University of California, Berkeley studying law. What is really galling is that in all these years, we were so near to each other, yet never even knew where the other was, except that I knew Bernard was somewhere in America.

Some time this year I will go to New Orleans to visit him. Another surprise came a few days after Bernie called me. I received a call from someone in Florida, who spoke in Afrikaans. Not having spoken this language for some 55 years, I was amazed how much came back to me. The man said he knew me and my father in South Africa and asked if I wanted some biltong. The conversation was a little nutty, and I asked if he could speak English. "Nie" he said. Then he rambled on and finally burst out laughing and told me he was Jacob. Yes, it was Jacob Kemp, the first and my best friend I had on coming to Arcadia in 1936. We didn't speak too long, but he tried to sign me up for a telephone subscription. I wasn't biting, but he managed to sign Bernie up, at a higher cost than he was paying. Jacob seems to be heavily involved in scientology. Although I did not ask for it, he said he would send me some literature on the subject.

Izak Weiner RSA

It is with great humility that I read and reread extracts from "My Struggle" by Bernard Aronstam. As an Old Arc I am sure we can all relate to Bernard's experience. The Harris's at Arcadia were after my time but the negative reports of them are well known.

This contrast with Doctor and Mrs Lichtigfeld's term at Arcadia. I recall an incident when the boys were playing soccer with Doc in goals. Vicky came to call the boys to evening Shul, "now", to which Doc replied "After the next goal Vicky".

My last year in Arcadia was 1945. Each year we would vote for the most "popular boy", who would then receive a certain amount of money at annual prize giving. Bernard Aronstam took a liking to me and unknown to me became my "campaign manager" and mustered support. The result was that a probable 7/1 chance (that was me) received the award. This certainly proved that a good campaign manager is essential for elections. Well done Bernard!!

Estelle And Eli Zagoria Perth Australia

From the little I have so far read in Aronstam's, *My Struggle*, it appears he certainly is a chap of character. Institutions and bureaucrats hate people like him. Anyone who questions the status quo is their enemy. Personally I can only admire his intelligence and the courage to follow his inclinations. It is people like him who first cry 'The king is totally nude'. His path is full of obstacles and always will be. Most of us are after an orderly, safe, peaceful existence. We are careful not to shake the boat. Provided his conduct does not hurt innocent individuals, I say good luck to him.

Basil Sepel France

Bernard Aronstam - Welcome back to the Arc Circuit. Yeah how about exchanging books, yours for one of mine. Do you remember The Belfast, OK Jo'burg and London 1961???

The cyclic nature of life is a pointer to the fact that succeeding generations experience basically similar happenings in more or less identical environments. And so Arcs of one decade were the Arcs of the next etc. So Bernard Aronstam's sad experiences with the Harris' and Vicky were rather what most went through more or less depending on age and character. If you stood up to them they'd try to knock you down to preserve their own unfortunate skins and vice versa. But all this 'fighting' definitely made it easier for those of the future resulting in Doc and Ma replacing Archie and Maggie and with Vicky moving in Doc's direction, something new to him because he too went through a rough time growing up, including becoming a military instructor during the war.

Personally I had no serious grudges against either simply because I was too young and at that Volcanic epoch. I nevertheless did experience a couple of humdingers: I was the first Arc ever to be caned by Archie for bunking out (poem in my book) and Archie cheated me by pretending the extra long haphtorah I was learning was for my Barmitzvah while in fact it was for a Yom kippur morning service. And so I had to learn another Torah reading in only several days because my real Barmitzvah was about only a week later.

On top of all that then had to learn a three page English typed documentary speech by heart in some twenty four hours for the annual prize giving ceremony attended by the then Chief Rabbi of South Africa (Rabinowitz a cousin of Harris, the former bringing him out from England). Archie was a smart crook but if I didn't have a photographic memory he would have fallen on his arse.

The result was that I understood neither the Hebrew nor my English speech and as for religion!!! However Doc put me right - just his presence and decency alone turned me in the right direction. By the way, Cop Harary was a cause of my foreign language problem by smacking me across the ear, nearly taking my head off, because at the age of five and something I came late to my first ever Hebrew lesson - preferred climbing a roof as I still do today.

Vicky gave me no trouble either. Except when he was my Latin teacher where at every lesson without a doubt he threw a question my way - 'Flower' what is the absolute ablative of ..? The result quite a good mark in Latin - but I spent some 50% of all my matric swotting time learning the veni vidi vici. Once while visiting the Arc after passing my first year at university Vicky asked me "Basil what's the use of Agriculture - it's a strange course you're studying?" After a few seconds of reflection I replied, "Vicky people can't live without food but they certainly can without Latin."

Today Vicky is a very old man thanks to AFL - Arc Food Latin and I'm teaching in Frogland where Latin definitely helps. However something should also be said about the Arc bullying Arc thing. As far as I'm concerned it's as worse as the Controllers bulling kids. Human beings can be terribly cruel with one another that's why we're in the condition we're in today and as it will be tomorrow unless we try do something about it even if there is nothing we can really do. But; lets try after all that's why we're here 'est pas?

Alec Saul In Israel

AS regards BERNARD ARONSTAM'S guilt re Morris's death, I hardly think he was in any way responsible for that. The influence that he bore on Morris to run away from the Arc can hardly relate to the fact that Morris had suffered from rheumatic fever. Any number of reasons could be advanced as to the cause of his death but for Bernard to take this on himself does not allow for the logic of the matter and is certainly no reason for his guilt trip. So for me he should cast that aside forthwith, even Arcadia's fault in this matter can be questioned. When I think of the number of kids who passed through its portals it is remarkable I can only recall three deaths in all the years.

In an age were child fatalities were high and specifically in other orphanages they were much worse. This coupled to the fact that the number of children who passed through Arcadia must have been at least 5000.

Mannie Osrin

Thanks for printing that extract from Bernard Aronstam's book, and Bernard, wow, not bad at all! I must get a copy to read at my leisure. In a strange way, although I never ever entertained any thoughts of running away while in the Arc, I felt that I could identify with your escapade. I'm sure a lot of other Old Arc's feel the same way.

David Sandler, Perth, Australia

I know of quite a few ex Arcs who really did not enjoy their time in the Arc but a common thread amongst them is they don't talk or write about it. (I include my sister and my Aunt). I tried to write about it in the last booklet under "Harsh times in the Arc".

Its very interesting how you saw Vicky....I saw him as a very strict but less severe man....and in later more recent days a very gentle old man. But there are a few who saw him as you do...as much too strict a disciplinarian.

I have now read your complete book and found parts of it very interesting...the parts about the Arc, the boxing and the story of the French Officer Dreyfus.

Hopefully by now you would have received the package of Arc Memory Booklets and Photo Albums. If memory serves me correctly I sent them about a month ago.

In the one dated Feb 2002 you will see the articles written by Solly Farber and the one he writes about Morris (Moozy) ....I do not detect any blame or fault attributable to you in Solly's article and as a 15 or 16 year old yourself at the time while you may have been naughty for running away and for doing other things as I see it you should not hold yourself guilty in any way for Moozy's unfortunate death.

Reply From Bernard Aronstam

Initially I would like to apologise for not writing sooner but we took two trips out of town and I wanted to digest the material you sent me before responding. Now I want to tell you how much I appreciate you running excerpts of my book. Of course I am interested what others think about it and I appreciate your kindness and consideration in attempting to alleviate my guilt feelings over the untimely death of Moozy. I still think about him and our trip and I still wish I had been more mature and more able to deal with the situation. Who was that who said *the moving finger writes and having writ moves on, nor all your piety nor wit shall lure it back to cancel half a line, nor all your tears wash out one word of it?* Yes I know its water under the bridge but I will never forget Moozy.

I was, to be quite candid, a little surprised that Solly never mentioned Moozy's trip to Durban and its aftermath. I only wish now, when it is too late, that I would have talked to Solly a little more about Moozy when I visited him back in 1992.

By the way I am very interested in establishing contact with Shani Krebs. No I didn't know he was incarcerated in Thailand but I will sure write to him. I would like to get to know him and of course to help him in any way I can.

Bernard Aronstam

Hank Epstein sent me a picture taken, who knows when, which included me and my brother Mike which of course I was thrilled to receive. I guess I am just a sucker for nostalgia. I was very pleased to hear that you had received my book and of course interested in your perception of it.

You may (or may not) believe this but I harbour no animosity toward Vicky or anyone else for that matter. Vicky had two careers you might say. The post Harris and ante-Harris periods. Unfortunately I knew Vicky as a very strict authoritarian under the Harris'.

When Doc took over Vicky rolled with the punches and proved, as I like to say, that a leopard can change its spots. But hey, that is all water under the bridge. I value my time in the orphanage. I look back at my time at the Arc as a great adventure and although I wish I could say it was a happy time, as I understand it was when Doc was in charge, there is no use crying over spilt milk.

By the way you have my authorisation to copy any and all parts of my book as you might see fit.

You might be interested to know that there was quite some interest shown in my book locally although I have never really pushed it. Maybe I will get the inclination to push it a little more. If there are any old Arcs who knew me and would like a copy of my book (and I have plenty copies available) let them contact me and I will be happy to oblige, free of charge of course.

Otherwise there is not much else to write about. The main thing is that we keep in touch. By the way I don't have the book where Solly wrote about Moozy but I sure would like to see what he had to say. Of course, when it is too late, I would like to talk to Solly again and especially talk to him about Moozy. Moozy and Wolfie Kotzen were my two best friends in the Arc. Wolfie was killed in a car accident the day before I arrived back in South Africa in 1961. I think it was in April of 1961.

Battling Bernie at San Jose State-1961.

BERNARD A BOXER IN THE US AIR FORCE
News cuttings provided by Solly Faber

Bernard Aronstam was in the US Air Force. As can be seen from the copies of the news cuttings below, he was an excellent boxer.

ARONSTAM CAPTURES FIRST AF FIGHT
Extract From US Newspaper

Local Boxer Displays Power punching in TKO

Bernie Aronstam, the Pacific Coast Conference light-welter weight boxing champion from Edwards AFB, won his first bout in the Air Force World-Wide Boxing Championship at Mitchel AFB in Long Island, NY on Monday.

Aronstam, the lightning-fast boxer from Johannesburg, South Africa, stopped his opponent, Peter Hoefl, on a TKO after 43 seconds had elapsed in the second round of their scheduled three rounder. A head-puncher, Aronstam consistently worked on his opponent's face, scoring time and again with direct blows.

The winners of the four light-welter elimination bouts were to square off against each other during the week, with the two finalists meeting in the ring today for the AF Title.

In qualifying for the AF tourney, Aronstam won over Wilfred Tucker of Travis AFB, Calif, the Northern District Champion, on a TKO in the second round, not on a three round decision, as was stated in last week's WINGS.

Aronstam's experience in the ring ranges from the 1954 Canadian territory championships in Toronto and Ontario, to the AF World-Wide fracas of last year.

He annexed the Canadian titles in April and May of 1954, eliminating all opponents and advancing up to and through the finals. In other Canadian fighting, the stout Aronstam fought in the International Meet, at the Maple Leaf Gardens in Toronto, losing in the finals to "Stan Fitzgerald, the 1954 A.A.U. champion from the US.

After enlisting in the AF, he participated on the Lackland AFB boxing team, while undergoing basic training. He was then transferred to Keesler AFB, Miss., where, in February of 1956 he travelled to Shaw AFB, S.C. and won the light-welter championship of the South Eastern Conference.

Also in that tourney, he was awarded the Outstanding Fighter Award for his display of superior skill and aggressiveness. That title won him a berth in the AF World-Wide meet, at Bolling AFB. He advanced to the semi-finals before he lost to Willie Morton, now a promising professional light-welter, on a three round decision.

Aronstam was assigned to the AFFTC in June of 1956, when he resumed training for another shot at the world-wide affair.

The 23 year old fighter, who was born and raised in South Africa, moved to Canada in 1952, where he made his home until he enlisted in the U.S.A.F.

Local Fighter at AF Tourney

Bernie Aronstam of the Edwards AFB boxing team is at Mitchell AFB, NY to participate in the AF-World Wide boxing tournament, representing the Pacific Coast Conference in the light-welter division.

Bernard Aronstam the Boxer

Aronstam shot at fistic glory came after an unanimous decision over Wilfred Tucker, the Northern District champ from Travis, in PCC finals held recently at Fairfield.

The win over Tucker came after two sound victories in the Southern District finals at March. The first one saw Aronstam, who hails from Johannesburg, stop Long Beach's Larry Hughlett in the second round. In the second fight, Aronstam won a unanimous decision over Manuel Amaga of Vincent AFB.

The AF tourney starts March 4, runs for four days, and will feature top AF boxers from all districts. Results will be published in the Desert Wings when available.

UPDATE ON BERNARD'S WHEREABOUTS

From Mike Aronstam

This is to let all Old Arcs who knew my brother know that we have located him and his wife in a shelter in Gulf Port. He was rescued from his home on Sunday. How we found him was an absolute miracle.

His wife's son went to America and put a notice on the internet. Someone in California saw an article about refugees in a Gulf Port newspaper and recognised his wife. They contacted his stepson. His home has apparently been destroyed and we hope to soon have him back in South Africa.

From Hank Epstein

Hurricane Katrina wiped out Bernard Aronstam. His house is a total loss. He and is wife are temporarily living in Cape Town, SA with his brother, Michael.

He will return to New Orleans briefly to settle his affairs, then, come to California and live with me for a short time. He is unsure what he will do then. Jacob Kemp lives in Florida. He, Bernard and I correspond regularly.

Chapter 48 - MIKE ARONSTAM (1931)

Mike was born in 1931 and was in the care of Arcadia from 1942 to 1946.

ARC MEMORIES

I was in the Arc with my brother Bernard during the forties - first under Shaer, and later Harary, having first been in Orangia, the Cape Town Orphanage. I don't have too many specific memories of the years I spent there. In fact I have never seen a photograph of myself at Arcadia. So if anyone has one of me in a group I would be grateful to get a copy.

One memory I have is of a whole bunch of us going on strike because we were getting chicken dinners too often. (WOW!)

I was in the Arc at the same time as Mannie Osrin, the Koppels, Mannie Lipschitz, Beans Levine, the younger Nochumsons

When I was 11 or 12 years old I decided to produce a "Circus". I enrolled five or six of my friends and we rehearsed for a few weeks and finally one Saturday morning we "Opened" to about ten or 15 kids. We used one of the Hebrew school rooms placed the chairs all around and performed at one end of the room. We charged three sweets as an entrance fee. The performance lasted about 45 minutes and when it was all over our audience left and we started packing up the equipment we used for our tightrope walks, acrobat acts etc.

One kid however remained seated in his chair. I am not sure who it was. It might have been Natie Romer. Before I could ask him why he had not left he shouted at me saying: "If you don't start the Circus I want my sweets back." I think, even at that age, I saw the funny side and burst out laughing. I don't remember if I gave him his sweets back.

When I was older I was the leader of one of the two gangs in Arcadia. The leader of the other was Mannie Lipschitz. We arranged (I don't know why} to fight it out one against one. I had to fight Mannie whom I beat and my brother Bernard was pitted against Hugo Bamberger. Hugo was much bigger than Bernard and he really beat him up. I demanded a rematch with Mannie to get my revenge but it was refused and I think we stopped the whole thing then and there.

I remember the custom of couples strolling down the drive every evening after supper as part of life in Arcadia. I remember Mannie Osrin and Sarah, Myer Rubinowitz, Joey Siegenberg, and others.

After I left Arcadia I went to Canada. Ten or so years later I returned and a couple of years after that I joined the Arc Committee. I think we were the only committee of its kind that totally consisted of Old Arc inhabitants. During my time on the committee a number of children were expelled and I called a special meeting to express my disapproval.

I remembered Morris Farber being expelled and dying shortly afterwards because he had no knowledgeable person to take

care of him. Solly was on the executive committee at the time and I reminded him of that fact. We agreed that no one would be expelled without the consent of the full committee.

A couple of months ago I went with my wife to the "new" Arcadia and walked around the main building. I admit that tears came to my eyes. I don't know if I will be able to go back again so that was my last farewell.

SINCE LEAVING THE ARC

I know Michael Perry Kotzen, not from the Arc, but from having acted with him in a number of plays in Johannesburg under the name of Mike Preston, before he went to Israel, Michael brings back a lot of memories. He was a very fine actor. "One More River" and "Abraham Lincoln" were two of the plays we were both in.

I came with my wife Dorothea to Cape Town about seven years ago after my wife was mugged and shot at and her friend killed in front of her. Today I am semi retired but still produce some TV commercials and industrial videos. I don't think there are any other old Arcs living in Cape Town, except Colin Rosen.

Needless to say we enjoy living in this city despite the tremendous tourist invasion which is happening right now.

Because I have a bit of spare time on my hands I have formed an NGO, Non-Profit Organisation called SPAIDS, Society for the Prevention of Aids. I have produced, at my own expense, a television commercial and radio spots and have commissioned an ad agency to design newspaper ads and billboards, posters and leaflets.

The concept of the campaign is simple: instead of teaching children how to have sex using condoms, which I am against because I believe it is counter-productive, (and not working anyway) I will be telling them to "stop sleeping around".

The ads are very hard hitting and I will be producing a short video showing people suffering from Aids-related illnesses to be screened in schools. I will soon be looking for young volunteers and part time paid workers to help organise the campaign across the country.

We have three children who have three children each so what started as a small family has grown rapidly.

My daughter also lives with her family in Johannesburg. My son Marlon lives in Johannesburg and is a sports bookmaker. Another son Seth lives with his wife and three children near Jerusalem in Ramot Beit Shemesh.

So we don't see them too often but try to get to Johannesburg every now and then. Because of our health we have difficulty in the rarefied air on the highveldt. Anyway we love Cape Town so don't mind being stuck down here.

Chapter 49 - ZUMMY ISENBERG (1933)

Zummy was born in 1933 and was placed in the care of Arcadia in 1939 together with his older sister Jessie. He remained in the Arc until age 15 and left in 1948.

After completing high school he became a dentist and joined the Dental committee of Arcadia, as well as Sandringham Gardens providing free services to the Arc children.

MY FAMILY

My Dad died a month after my sixth birthday in February 1939. We lived in Brakpan. My sister, Jessie was 11 years old. My brother Abe was in matric in Benoni High School. My Mom took my Dad's death with great emotion and sadness. I remember her crying and screaming for what seemed like many days and nights. I also remember being taken to see my Dad what was possibly a few days before he died. Of course I never understood much. He died of pneumonia at the age of 39. Penicillin was discovered six months later. He would possibly have survived. My Mom had to re-arrange her life, as well as ours. In those days there were no insurance policies. She had to survive. She had to get a job. She had to find new accommodation. World War II started a few months later that same year. My brother Abe had to leave school and look for a job as well. My Mom and Abe shared a room in a house in Mayfair (Jo`burg) with a Jewish family. My Mom got a job as a seamstress I think, and Abe sold shoes at ABC shoe stores in town. But first my Mom took Jessie and I to Arcadia soon after my Dad died.

MY FIRST DAY IN THE ARC

I remember vividly, though I was only six, standing at the top of the driveway by the main building with Stompie Shaer holding my hand, while my Mom walked away from Jessie and I, down the driveway, her back to us, to the exit gate at Oxford Road.

I can't remember if I was crying. I probably was howling. I must have been angry and confused. I did not know why my Mom had left me. I could not understand. It took me another 30 years to realise and understand the emotions my Mom was going through while she was walking away from Jessie and I. It was only when I became a father, a parent, that I looked back to my Mom deserting me, walking away from me, leaving me. I never, ever, thought of how she felt at the same time, when she had to turn her back and walk away, leaving her two children to be looked after by others in an orphanage. To any woman, to any mother, imagine the trauma, the heartache, for whatever reason, of giving your young children away to be cared for by others. And yet we were very lucky, very fortunate indeed. History unfortunately has shown the ghettos and persecutions of Jews in Germany before the war followed by the murders after it started. There must have been thousands and thousands of children in orphanages all over Europe. There were probably very few if any survivors. As I said, we were very

Zummy, Abe and Jessica

lucky. We were clothed. We were fed three meals a day. We were schooled. We had a Jewish education and taught Jewish values. We all had hundreds of brothers and sisters. Arcadia was a truly wonderful home.

But while I was at the Arc, I probably did not realise how lucky I was to be there at that particular time in history. Life was hard, certainly by today's standards. In winter we were cold. Very often we were hungry. We were all poor. Nobody had any money. It was many years later and many years older that I was thankful for the years I spent at the Arc. I was lucky that a place like Arcadia existed. There was no other Jewish institution of its kind anywhere in the world. It is of the greatest credit to the South African Jewry, with their foresight and generosity, that they started and subsequently maintained Arcadia for 100 years.

When I first arrived I seemed to remember that there was a discussion with my Mom and Stompie Shaer whether I should go to the Babies Department or Junior Boys. At this time the cut off age was six, and I had just turned six. I was probably small for my age, but was anyway sent to the Junior Boys (six – 13 years.) which meant I was the youngest and smallest. How I wished they would have sent me to the Babies' Department. I must have lived a very sheltered and protected life before I came to the Arc, because now I was thrown into the deep end.

I had to fend for myself from day one, but I soon learned we all had to fend for ourselves. I had to make my bed every morning. It had to be neat. We had no help. If not done properly it had to be done again. But we all learned very quickly. You learned that at night when you went to bed, you got between the sheets very gently and when you fell asleep it was very restfully, so that the next morning you slid out of bed, which was then so much easier to make.

I remember every night (once or twice), for the few kids who used to sometimes wet their beds, I was not one of them, an enormous Zulu "watchboy" would come and wake them up. He had an enormous *knop kierie* and would bang it at the bottom of the metal bed and shout "*Vooga, Vooga*! Go Piss!" And they would all walk off in their sleep to the toilets. Of course the Zulu would wake up the whole dormitory with his shouting. If this happened to me tonight I would wet my bed immediately.

BOXING

One of my first memories, which I will never forget, when I arrived was that every Sunday morning we all had to learn boxing. I remember the teachers were at first, Roy Ingram, and later Alf James who was an Old Arc. They were both South African champions. Anyway at the age of six and coming from a protective environment, I never knew what boxing was. I soon learned. For the next many months I disappeared every Sunday morning and hid in the toilets. I was not prepared to have my head knocked off once a week. However my absence was eventually discovered. Two older fellows (I think I remember who, but not too sure) held me by my feet, upside down, with my head in the toilet. If I did not promise to come to boxing lessons, I would be flushed down the toilet. So I promised. I was absolutely terrified.

One soon realised that your opponent was the same size and weight. You were never really hurt, and he was as scared of you as you were of him. But as the years passed by we all gradually learned to box quite well. So much so, that Arc boys did extremely well at the Annual School Boxing Championship at Parktown Boys High. Many pupils, who thought about entering the competition would first come to the Orphanage Corner behind the gym to find out our weight before they entered. In my five years I won three finals and lost two. In my last final in matric the fight was stopped in the 1st round, otherwise I would have been murdered!!

The Arcs that I recall who excelled the most were Joe Siegenberg and Barney Meyers, Alec Gavson, and of course Bernard Aronstam who, a few years after school in 1960 in the USA, was I think in the finals to choose the team to represent the USA for the Olympic Games. I think Bernard won some special award at the championships. He was such a classic orthodox boxer. It was the same tournament that Cassius Clay (later Mohammed Ali) won the heavyweight division and go on to win a Gold Medal for the USA By co-incidence I was there (in Rome) and saw the fight.

SPORT

Sport, especially soccer and cricket, was very important in our lives. It was almost everything. Every minute, other than sleeping, eating, school, etc. was spent playing sport. If we never had a ball, we used an old open tin, or a pair of folded socks and played in the dormitory, even under the bed. If we never had a bat, we used a plank or a stick and played *kennetjie*. There was always something to play.

One of my big sporting achievements was at the age of 14. I bunked out on a Saturday afternoon to go to the Balfour Park under 16 trials. Towards the end of the game a much bigger fellow, (I think over 16), bumped me while I was in the air using my head. I fell on my arm. Both bones fractured. I know his name and in later years I hoped he would come to me as a dental patient, no such luck!!

Anyway, someone kindly took me to the General Hospital. After X-rays I was told it would have to be set that evening under general anaesthetic and would have to stay overnight. Remember I had bunked out of the Arc that day and they had to know what was going on and give permission etc. So when I got back the next morning I thought Cop Harary would break my other arm

I must have played quite well in the trials because a few days later I got a postcard from Balfour Park saying I was chosen for the under 16A side, and must report next Saturday at some place or other. But after that traumatic week I decided to quit soccer for a while and stick to school rugby in my own age group. It was more of a gentleman's game and not so rough.

Throughout school I played rugby and cricket in the A side of my age group. In matric I got my colours for cricket (wicket keeper). My mentor a few years earlier was Alec Gavshon.

But this was an average achievement by Arc standards. All the Arcs did well at high school level. I remember that Barney Meyers (rugby), Mike Rabinowitz (athletics), and Jacky Mekler (athletics) were all a great credit to Arcadia.

But of course the best all-round sportsman from the Arc was Gerry Levy, whose school blazer never had enough room for all the scrolls he was awarded.

Zummy and Jessie

SCHOOL

Although we were all involved with sports we realised there was an academic side to our lives. But there was nobody to encourage us, to advise us. There were sometimes extra lessons if we needed them. What we never had and what we needed most of all was a parent to encourage and congratulate us when we were good and pull us up when we were bad. Nobody really swotted. We were never reading books. It was sports, sports, sports. I remember in high school we had to choose our matric subjects in the last three years. Some Arc, many years before my time, chose Latin and Ancient Greek. So these two subjects were handed down from year to year. What an absolute waste of a school career. I had two more languages (compulsory) in English and Afrikaans, Maths, Science and Hebrew as an extra subject. I studied five languages and today I only use one.

ARC MEMORIES

Arcadia was a way of life with a daily and weekly and monthly routine. I used to wait for Sunday afternoons. My mother would visit Jessie and I every Sunday without fail. I don't think she missed a Sunday in nine years. Visiting hours was at 2.00 pm. and she was on the first bus. She naturally arrived with her packets of sweets, biscuits, cakes, etc. While she was there I ate as much as possible because I knew the minute she left the vultures would arrive. While she was there she and the other parents would sit on the lawns adjacent to the driveway and watch us play soccer. There were many Sunday afternoons that we played against mostly Jewish kids of all ages outside of Arcadia. I remember how Colin Stein, whose mother was for many years a great committee lady, would come to Arcadia week after week with a soccer team of friends to play against us. Some of these kids were very good but we never ever lost. The scores were rugby scores to nil. Colin was the goalkeeper. He must have broken all records for goals let through him. But I can tell you that Colin was loved by us all. We looked forward to Sundays and the arrival of his soccer teams. I don't think he realised it in those years, but it was a great mitzvah that he performed for the kids at the Arc.

I remember one day playing cricket in front of the main building. Joss Lipschitz was bowling downhill to me. He was very fast. He was older and bigger than me. He had no pity. I was shit scared. His first ball was a full toss. I closed my eyes; I connected, and hit him for a six into the downhill area on the way to Oxford Road. He was as annoyed as hell.

I remember Sunday suppers. For years that I can recall it was always mealies and curried fish. I love mealies but to this day I hate curried fish, especially on Sundays. I remember one Friday afternoon having to help the kitchen peel guavas, either for a fruit salad or compote. I pealed one, ate one, pealed one, ate one, for hours. In Shul that evening I was as sick as a dog. To this day I hate guavas in any form. I remember how we had duties to make sandwiches, hundreds of them, for school the next day. Jam, peanut butter, Marmite. Nothing exciting, the most un-appetizing sandwiches. But the next day at school, and you were hungry, they were great.

I remember how some evenings we used to steal bread from the bread cupboard - especially the rye loaves. It was so easy maybe because of its shape. We unlatched the cupboard with a finger at the bottom, pulled the doors forward, and pulled out a loaf. It may have been because we were a little hungry, or bravado, or a dare, or just naughty but to this day I love rye bread.

I remember school holidays, going to the bioscopes in town, in our own Arc bus. We were packed into the bus much like our taxis today. It was one of the few times, other than school, that we ever left the security of Arcadia, to go into the outside world. I think many of us felt uncomfortable as we got out of the bus, filed into the bioscope, and all the time being stared at by everyone in the vicinity.

I remember the winters. We had no track suits. It was usually bitterly cold while waiting for breakfast, the Arc bus, or whatever. We only had khaki shorts and shirt and a very thin jersey. We used to play a game to keep warm. About 20 kids lined up behind each other, with say their right shoulders against any wall. You would then try push the fellow in front of you (who was doing the same thing to the fellow in front of him) out of the line. In which case you went to the back of the queue, and started all over again. If you were bigger and stronger you would eventually get to the front. Otherwise you were usually towards the end but either way everyone kept warm.

I remember when I was about nine and had to have my tonsils out. I went with Donald Goldman (who was a few years older than me) who needed to have his adenoids removed, to the old General Hospital, and not the Children's Hospital. Being older, Donald looked after me. For a whole week they kept us there and we lived on jelly and ice cream. It was great. Coming from Arcadia it was like a five star hotel.

I remember an incident with Boris Rushowitz. He was older and much bigger than me. For some reason I must have seriously annoyed him. It certainly wasn't physically. I must have said something and he was cross. We were on the Senior Boys balcony. He picked me up and held me over the side, and threatened to drop me unless I apologised. I screamed in panic "I'm sorry, I'm sorry." He pulled me back up but I honestly thought he was going to drop me.

One of the strange things I remember was when I was seven, but only put two and two together approximately 25 years later. I remember there was talk amongst all the kids of a boat coming from Europe full of Jewish kids who had escaped from the Germans. The rumour was that they were coming to Arcadia and we would all have to double up. That means two in a bed. Nothing ever happened. However many years later, a movie was made about a boat, The St Louis, in 1940, carrying Jewish refugees from Germany to Cuba. At the last minute Cuba changed its mind. The boat then travelled back close to the east of America. They wouldn't take them. The Canadians also didn't want them. Nobody wanted them. It was perhaps at this time that there were these rumours at Arcadia.

I remember while still at primary school we were all concerned at the way the war was going. Perhaps because we were not really affected it was exciting to us, but I remember we were asked to learn how to knit so that we could make scarves for the soldiers fighting up north. I actually remember making many scarves.

Zummy knitting scarf with Jessie standing behind.

It is seven years later. I can never forget my Barmitzvah. It was the 1st or 2nd Saturday of January, 1946. My only visitor in my family was my Mom. Abe and Jessie were at Habonim camp. There were no uncles, aunts or cousins. But at the time I never cared. It never bothered me. Vicky taught me my Maftir and Haftorah, and the rest we all knew off by heart. Vicky must have done a great job, because soon after my barmy Harary said I have to be one of the Arc Chazzans. I was so small I could hardly hold the Torah, and could barely be seen when holding it. I told my Mom I didn't want to be a Chazzan and if Harary made me, I would run away from the Arc. Anyway I became a Chazzan and never ran away. Actually, I think I was quite a good one. You had to do the service quickly because immediately after was a brocha and then of course was soccer or cricket. All in all, I think I quite enjoyed being a Chazzan. I remember after my barmy going to Shul every morning before breakfast, and putting on tefillin. I remember how at every meal, we first stood behind our chair in the dining room, with our hands covering our heads, and saying the 1st verse of the Shema before sitting down to eat.

After my barmy I went upstairs to the Senior boys. Again I was the youngest and smallest, only this time it was very different. At this stage nobody was really a bully and we mostly coped. But just to cover my tracks in case of emergencies, I was a "fag" for one or two older fellows. Just in case there is a mis-

interpretation, when you were a fag all you did was make his bed every morning, and maybe clean a pair of shoes. Not even that. I was a fag for Mannie Osrin who at this stage had become Head Prefect at Parktown Boys High School. An extremely great honour and achievement for a Jewish student and even more so for someone from Arcadia. Mannie deserved this honour. He was very successful and very popular. And I was his fag!! Unfortunately it also meant carrying his suitcase to school every morning, all uphill for about 20 minutes. It wasn't easy, but I was well protected going to my new high school.

Mannie Osrin, Zummy and Emmanuel Lipschitz

I remember the Pesach Seders very well. We all loved Pesach. It was much harder and more meaningful than today. I remember all the songs and tunes. We read and sang till the very end. I remember one year saying the ma nishtana through a microphone into three halls (two dining halls and the committee room). Senior boys, Junior boys, Senior girls, Junior girls, Old Arcadians, families and Committee members. There must have been 500 people there. I have never missed a Pesach seder, and have always sung the Arc tunes. But in the last few years I have had to take a back seat. My kids now do the Seders, and the older grandkids who are all at King David School, want Zaida Zum to do it their way, not my way.

I remember the Annual Barmitzvah days together with prize giving. We all got something. There were five of us my year. There was Bernard Aronstam, Nicky Friedlander, Matta Levy, Jacky Mekler and myself. I remember having to learn my speech in Hebrew.

I remember an incident, with no name mentioned. He was playing with his pellet gun and I saw there was one pellet left and told him so. He said "no there isn't" and he pointed the gun an inch in front of my left eye. Instinctively I turned my face away to the right as he pulled the trigger. The pellet hit me on my temple at the side of my left eye. I was so lucky. A little bump and no bleeding. But the idiot was nearly murdered by my buddies who saw it happen. To his credit he was running around shouting, "I'm mad, I'm mad, I could have killed him".

I remember one year we had our own boxing tournament. There were three of us in my weight. Eric Herr (who was my best friend), Matta Levy, and myself. I was by far the weakest and the worst. I first fought Matta who was giving me a hiding, so I had no choice but to keep turning my back to him. So he was disqualified for continually hitting me on the back. Then about one hour later I had to fight Eric who refused to fight me because I was still in a bad state from the hiding I got from Matta. So I was declared the winner!!

LEAVING THE ARC

In later years when I was at university, I corresponded a lot with Eric who was at the University of Cape Town studying law. He was a very good soccer player and played for UCT (1st side). He later settled in Durban as a lawyer. Matta has been a loyal patient for 35yrs.

Something every Arcadian looked forwards to, but also feared, was the day you left the Arc, to go into the real world. It was, for many, especially for some of the girls, a frightening experience. Some left the Arc at about 16 years, before doing matric. They wanted to get a job and earn money. Some had nowhere to go. They would rent a room with a friend, or a family, if they were lucky enough they could go to family. Some would finish matric and then get a job. Some would go to the Technikon, or university. It all depended on individual circumstances. But leaving Arcadia was almost as frightening an experience as arriving at Arcadia.

I left Arcadia when I was 15. I had just over two years to finish matric. My Mom had remarried and lived in a rented semi in Mayfair. My stepfather's name was Abe Goldman. He was good to my Mom and Jessie and I, and I shared a bedroom with my younger stepbrother, Leslie, for the next seven to eight years. My two older stepbrothers Ivan and Cecil were studying Medicine and Dentistry and living in Benoni. We all got on well and it was nice having an extended family. So I was lucky. I left the Arc and had a home to go to, and could continue my schooling at Parktown Boys. Instead of walking for 20 minutes, I would go by tram to town and another tram to Wits. In these last few years at school I spent every lunch break at the Orphanage Corner behind the gym. I never left my Arc friends, or forgot my roots, even though it meant my mother's magnificent Jewish sandwiches would disappear in seconds.

When I lived in Mayfair, because of my brother Abe, I became involved with new friends in the community, in Jewish groups and societies, like Bnei Zion, Habonim, Hachsharah with a determination to eventually go on aliyah. I wanted to learn a trade and go to Israel but my Mother, being a Jewish Mother, had different ideas and ambitions. She had heard about bursaries for university and I must apply to Arcadia, which I had to do. I never even had any idea of what I wanted to study.

Varsity was never ever part of my hopes or ambitions or aspirations. I was a poor kid from a poor family. The committee of Arcadia wanted me to get letters of recommendation from various people. The headmaster of Parktown School, Mr. Yates, gave me a great letter. My CV at this particular stage was not too bad. I played 1st. team cricket and rugby for the school. I was a prefect, involved in boxing and athletics, a lousy swimmer, and not really a great academic scholar either but I got my bursary.

DENTISTRY

I decided to apply for Dentistry, being influenced by my stepbrother Cecil who at this stage was a final year Dental student. It would be very difficult to get into Dentistry as at that stage every Jewish boy wanted to become a Dentist. It was certainly the best profession in those days. How times change!! As luck would have it, this year for the 1st time, the Dental faculty, because there were so many applications, decided to accept every application, regardless of matric results. The only proviso was you had to get a matric university pass. There were about 120 students in 1st year and the best 40 would go into 2nd year, even if we all passed. While I was in 1st year, I realised I had to graft. I was a student with a bursary from Arcadia and I would not let them down. I swotted very hard, weekends as well and every night till midnight and later. I took no drugs to keep me up and I could not afford a cigarette. My only recreation was playing for Wits. under 21 soccer on Saturday afternoons. I was determined to work harder than my colleagues.

When the mid-year exam results were displayed I was absolutely devastated. I failed two of four subjects, and didn't do well in the other two either. Something was wrong. Was I out of my depth? Were my nine years in Arcadia the reason?. I just knew I had to work harder.

At this time I was very friendly with a classmate from Muizenberg, Alec Rifkin. It was a few weeks before our finals, and Alec and I would often meet lunch-hours to discuss what we had just been swotting. I never knew a single thing. Alec was extremely bright and a certainty to be in the top 40. He showed me and taught me how to swot. I thought that if I stayed up till midnight and stared at my books, often daydreaming as well, then I was swotting. Without going into details I passed. I think I was probably number 39 or 40. But I have no doubt that I would not have made it without Alec's help. I wish to add that Alec also played rugby (centre) for Wits under 21 and later the 1st side as well. There may also be many kids who were at Arcadia in those days who knew Alec, as he was very involved for many years with Bikkur Cholim camps. Anyway I made it into 2nd year.

While I was a Dental student, I always had to report to Dr. Morrie Schneider. He was the chairman of a very big and dedicated panel of Dentists who would come to the Arc, usually on Sunday mornings. At the beginning of each year we would get a list of books required for every subject. These text books were extremely expensive. For each subject there was often a choice of two or three different books, and most students would get 1one. When I showed the lists to Dr. Schneider he would tell me to get them all. Each year I would have the best selection in the class. In the later clinical years when we had to get instruments etc. he would let me get whatever I needed. He was very good to me and very helpful. There was I, the poorest student in the class, with the best selection of books and instruments. I think it was his way of levelling the playing fields.

When I started varsity we moved from Mayfair to Yeoville. My big regret during my fivers as a student was the fact that I became distant to my good buddies I grew up with at the Arc. I never had the time to be an Old Arc, and visit Arcadia on Sunday afternoons. I also missed many of the friends I had made in Mayfair. The friends I now had were mostly my colleagues in my class. It was swot, swot, and swot. But I'm proud to say that as the years went by, and I got nearer the end, my swotting became less and less. I had also learned that if you don`t understand something you can't swot it. My crowning glory in the finals was to get the top 1st pathology. Second place was a tie between four other students. I swotted better than they did.

In my five years as a student I went every year in the December holidays to the Young Israel Camp, in Lakeside near Muizenberg. I had five wonderful holidays there, of which I think the last two or three I was on the camp executive, in charge of entertainment, as well as in charge of the camp train, from Jo`burg to Cape Town, with over 100 campers. It was during my days at camp that I realised I had the confidence to mix with many kids as a group, perhaps because of my years at Arcadia. But I always felt a little less confident on a one to one basis, but this changed when I eventually qualified and started work as a Dentist at last. I was very proud for my Mom, and that I never let Arcadia down.

LONDON

Immediately after I qualified, I first went to camp, and then by boat to England. I went to London for what I thought would be a year or so, and planned to come home via a few weeks in Europe. I somehow stayed for 13 years.

Dentists earned a lot of money in those days. The patient paid the first pound and the Government paid the rest. My first job in London was for a Jewish dentist, and I signed a six month contract. Within a few months of signing there was trouble in Israel, and it seemed that there was going to be a war. I told my boss I wanted to go to Israel, to do what I can. He said to me that if I broke my contract, he would see to it that I would be struck off the roll, and never be allowed to practice again. To my regret I should have told him to xxxx off. Instead I panicked and saw out my contract, at the end of which he asked me to stay and be a partner. I told him what he could do with his partnership, but I was still ashamed at my actions. I realised I needed my father to help and advise me.

Every week I earned a lot of money and spent it as fast as I earned it. Having never had it, when I did eventually get it, I spent it. As long as I was a bachelor it was always like that. I had nobody, but nobody, to keep me in check, to advise me about saving for a rainy day. I was still in my early twenties and on top of the world. But I never forgot, every now and then, sometimes often, sometimes not often enough, to send money to Arcadia.

Towards the end of my first year in London I was now on my 2nd job as an assistant, and the Overseas Visitors Club in Earls Court had started. It was to become famous and very popular for young tourists especially from the Commonwealth. The average age was early twenties. Nobody needed work permits. There were jobs for everyone. Life was great in London. Every night at the OVC you met new friends from all over the world, especially from South Africa which at that time was still part of the Commonwealth.

I was in fact building up the practice for my new boss from friends at the OVC It was at this time that the owners of the OVC advised me to open a surgery in Earls Court. I had no money, having spent it all, but I knew it was the right thing to do. My return to South Africa would have to wait. I opened my practice early 1957 with a friend, Harry Friedman - a class mate - as a partner. I lacked the confidence, to my regret, to go for it on my own. But I started the first surgery. Within a few months I was fully booked for over a week working every day from 9 am to 9 pm and Saturday till 3 pm. By the end of the year I was finished. We opened the 2nd surgery next door and Harry joined me. He was married, and already a father, was more responsible than I was, so I was quite happy for him to take over the main administration of the surgery. I was still a bachelor, sharing a flat with an Israeli navigator on El Al, and enjoying life. Within a few years we had seven surgeries (two within the OVC itself), and another partner.

During this time I spent a lot of time with Emanuel Lipschitz. He was on a working holiday like many others. I remember once a week we decided to go out together without dates. We would alternate in choosing a restaurant in London, the only proviso being that neither of us had been there before. We found some magnificent places. I also saw many Old Arcs as patients over the years. There were some who even lived there. Chalkie Adler and Mookie Romer. At one stage I had the boss of the South London mafia as a patient. Mookie once saw him in a betting shop, showing his teeth and telling his buddies to go to his little Jewish dentist in Earls Court. The funniest thing about Mookie was how someone from the Arc could acquire such a beautiful English accent.

After eight years in London as a bachelor, I met the most gorgeous girl from Jo`burg. Denise Bloom. She was friendly with Emanuel and Ethne Lipschitz, and related to friends of mine in London. So it was inevitable that we would meet. For me it was love at first sight. Why else would I have taken her out every night for the next six weeks. I wined and dined her. We danced at clubs and discos, often till the early hours of the morning. We had a wonderful courtship, so that when I proposed to her after six weeks, I knew she could not say no. We were married a few weeks later in Jo`burg, and came back to London to settle down.

For the first time in my life I realised I had responsibilities. Something I never learned at Arcadia or even the few years after when I lived with my Mom. Denise and I had two lovely kids in London, Ian and Tammy. We would manage to come to Jo`burg once a year to see the family, which was one of the conditions for settling in London. It was good to see Old Arcs again.

BACK TO SOUTH AFRICA

After a few years, I was becoming unhappy with my work, my partners, and the fact that because of the British weather, Ian and Tammy were forever indoors. Denise loved London and was happy to stay. But I gave her the choice. We go to Israel or South Africa. She chose her family. We had to sell our house at a difficult time. We sold it fully furnished at the same price that we bought it - five years previously!! My problems with my partners were worse. They were not prepared to negotiate or arbitrate. Their attitude was, if you want to go to South Africa, then go. Twelve years ago I started the first surgery, and seven surgeries later I left without a penny or a goodbye. Anyway, after 13 memorable years in London I came home with my family, to our families and roots. I think this was the only decision I made in our married life without discussion.

Soon after we returned, Denise renewed a life-long friendship of hers, since primary school-age eight - with Barbara Ginsburg from Arcadia. They went to high school together. They shared the same wedding dress. They corresponded while we were in London and Barbara, who married George Geer, was in Rhodesia. I'm sure there are many Old Arcs who remember Barbara and her two brothers David and Howard. Regrettably they both passed away in the prime of their lives. David at 38, and Howard at 21. For the last 25 years. Denise, Barbara, George and I go almost every Sunday to the Zoo Lake for a long walk and then for breakfast. Guess what Barbara and I are always talking about?

Within a few months I started my surgery in the Hyde Park Shopping Centre. I was busy from day one. It was now about 21 years since I had left Arcadia, and was out of touch with many Old Arcs, and what was going on inside Arcadia. However, I immediately joined the Dental committee of Arcadia, as well as Sandringham Gardens. Soon after joining, Dr. Morrie Schneider passed away, and I was asked to be the Chairman of the Dental Panel. To me it was a great honour, because the Chairmen of the Medical and Dental Committees, as well as the Chief Rabbi of South Africa, were all honorary members of the main committee. The amount of work which my Dental colleagues and myself put in, was a fraction compare to the work done by the Dentists when I was at the Arc, mainly because there were now so few kids in the Arc. But I was also pleased that many Old Arcs came to me as patients, their kids as well.

I soon settled in to the normal Jewish South African way of life. We had our third child – Shani - who would later become a Dentist. Life was good. We bought a house with a pool and tennis court in Birdhaven. Denise had her tennis school. I had mine. I very often played with Sammy Birer against Beans Levine and Emmanuel. It was great fun. Our three kids were all at King David School in Victory Park whose headmaster at that time was Barney Meyers. I was a member of Kyalami golf course. We had a holiday flat in Muizenberg, which we went to annually with the kids. The surgery was doing well. I had just completed my fourth Comrades Marathon, and mentally and physically I felt like superman. It was 12 years since we had come back from London. It was three weeks after my fourth Comrades that I decided to run 21 km with my good friend and Doctor, Ian Schapkaitz, who was on the Medical list of Arcadia.

At the end of the run, I was having a coke and fainted. Anyway after a night in hospital, ECG`s, effort ECG`s, second opinions, etc, I was told that I should have a by-pass. I didn't even know what a by-pass was. I just knew it was major cardiac surgery. My world came crashing down. How could it happen to me, I was so fit and strong. I thought I was Superman!!

The night before the operation, after Denise had left me, and I was all alone. I prayed to G-d, I begged, I bargained, I even argued. Please don't let happen to my kids what happened to me. I wanted them to have a father a little longer. I wanted to be a father a little longer. I think (I hope) for the most part I have stuck to my bargain. I recovered quite well, and within a few weeks was back at work. There was one very big lesson I learned from this episode in my life. Never take anything for granted!! Something else happened a few weeks after my operation. A very good friend of mine - Alex Zingol - asked me to go and see a Rabbi Tucazinsky who was his Rabbi visiting from Israel. I met him, had coffee with him, had a lovely evening. When I left he looked me in the eye and said. "Don't ever pray for money, only good health." From that day for the rest of my life I was to learn exactly what he meant.

I will not go into the full and boring medical details of the next 24 years following my double by-pass. After many operations I was able to come back and continue work. I continued my daily running which regrettably - with age - has turned to daily walking. I think I had a mental block after these ops, I would ignore it. They never happened. At the Arc I had a broken finger, a broken arm, and my tonsils out. I cannot remember ever having any of the usual childhood illnesses. I must have had the occasional cold. Also some form of asthma. Did my years at the Arc help me recover in any way? I don't know, but I know G-d was with me all the way. When you look around and see blind people, severely disabled people, strokes, paralysis, and many other irreversible diseases, then I realise that there are conditions worse than cancer.

In my twilight years, I was tired of the responsibilities of running my own surgery, but wanted to continue working, but at a more relaxed pace. At the same time as I was advertising the sale, Shani, my daughter, told me that her other boss, (Dr Trevor Wasserman), who had the dental surgery in a private clinic in Melrose Arch, a new up-market shopping complex in the northern suburbs, was looking for an assistant who could bring his own patients. It was ideal for me. I would not have to pay rent, or a nurse or secretary, or running expenses, or anything. I just had to bring a nucleus of my own patients. Not even to bring my own equipment. I wrote to my patients I treated in the last five years, to inform them I was relocating in two months. I never gave up my phone number, which was an invaluable asset, for the next 12 months, and left my new phone number on a message. But this meant I had no goodwill to sell. I was not giving up my patients or my phone number. All I had was very good second hand Siemens equipment. This proved very difficult to sell.

I somehow felt there may have been the hand of G-d in what followed. A dental rep told me there was a dentist looking for equipment for a dental surgery in a home for black kids with Aids. All he was able to do was extractions on a chair. No fillings were possible. I did not hesitate. I donated my entire surgery to a home of mostly black orphans. I closed my surgery with nothing but good memories. Had I not been in Arcadia, and later educated by Arcadia, would I have done such a thing? Who knows?.

My children, Ian, Tammy, and Shani, are all married with three kids each. They are still living in South Africa, all living near each other. They are all members of the same Shul and their kids have been or are at the same nursery school or King David School. Their ages range from 1 to 12 years.

When I see what I have just written, and when I think of my prayers over 24 years ago, the night before my by-pass, I know G-d was listening very well. I have received a great deal of nachas from my children and grandchildren. Denise and I have been truly blessed.

While on the subject of Denise, I have kept her for last. Behind every great man is a woman. In my case, behind a very ordinary man is a great woman. When we met it was a wonderful courtship. She came from a wonderful family, with very close family ties. I came with no family background. So it was a meeting of two very different people which you don't see in a courtship. Settling down to married life in London at first was great. It was an extension of our courtship. But after Ian and Tammy were born, and the joy we had with them, came added responsibilities. We were now a family. Something I was never familiar with. But I soon learned about big decisions and little decisions. I basically took a back seat, and opted out, leaving Denise to decide about most things. Her family background made family decisions easier than if left entirely with me. But she would always discuss things with me. Anyway, the few times I did interfere I was usually proved wrong. It's been like this throughout our marriage. She ran the home, the kids, schooling, paid the bills, and I looked after the surgery. You all know who did the better job!! She has done a wonderful job. Besides being a wife to me, and mother to my children, with all my ops and chemo, she has also been my nurse. I often say this to Denise. I will say it once more. Nisi (I call her Nisi). Nisi, I love you and appreciate you.

I want to end with a line from my wedding speech:

IF I HAD MY LIFE TO LIVE OVER AGAIN I WANT TO GO BACK TO ARCADIA.

Entire family. November 2006

John was born in 1934 and was in the care of Arcadia from 1943 to 1945.

OBITUARIES
Article and photo sent by Solly Farber

World-renowned South African photo-journalist John Brett Cohen has died in Johannesburg at the age of 66. Cohen, who survived some of the most vicious wars of the past century, both as a front-line soldier and as a photographer, was run over by a truck while walking along a tranquil country lane near Hertford Estates in Lanseria, north of Johannesburg, where he had lived for 30 years.

His best work, comprising photographs taken during a lifetime of travel, appeared in Images of *My World*, published in 1973, Israel Front Line, published in 1974, and Images of *My World (Two)*, published in 1998. Images of *My World*, one and two, are in the permanent collection of the Museum of Modern Art in New York.

Most of his pictures are in black and white and are so good that those familiar with them wonder why he was not more widely recognised. The answer lies partly in the fact that they were ahead of their time, and partly in his maverick personality and almost constitutional inability to play the system.

Only more recently, with photography of the non-special effects and overtly aesthetic kind increasingly recognised as art and sought after by collectors, has his work shown signs of coming into its own.

Cohen, who was never as famous or commercially successful as his fellow photographer and one-time collaborator David Goldblatt (a fact that irked him no end), was described recently by Goldblatt as one of South Africa's "most original yet least appreciated photographers". At its best, said Goldblatt, Cohen's work was "sardonic, lyrical and raw". In a piece in Leadership magazine last year, Goldblatt wrote: "Except by a number of discriminating buyers and devotees, his photographs have tended to be overlooked or forgotten by editors, art directors, collectors and arbiters of 'relevance'."

Cohen published and supervised the final quality of every picture and line of copy in his books (each one a limited edition of 600 signed copies) himself, "not because I don't believe in publishers but that no one would know what I was talking about", he said.

His life was a constant battle for money, and he was forced to do things like corporate profiles, interviews and surveys to get by. When he died, he had just accepted a commission from the mining executive Brett Kebble to do a book about mining in Africa.

Cohen could never come to terms with the marketplace. His best pictures were not about things so much as about

Sensitive artist was a poet with a camera

themselves. They were poems. And the marketplace in the 1950s, 1960s, 1970s and 1980s was not attuned to the kind of work he was doing. Magazine editors and publishers wanted more accessible stuff that he, a poet with a camera, was unable, or not prepared, to deliver.

He described his existence as a constant battle against "indifference, commercial platitudes and the incessant paraphernalia of daily life, where not paying the rent can destroy [one] overnight".

Cohen was born in the rough, poor-white Johannesburg suburb of Mayfair on May 10, 1934. When he was four, his mother, Rosie, was committed to a mental institution. He was told she had died, and he spent some years at an orphanage before living again with his father and then his grandmother, whom he adored. Only at 21 did he discover his mother was still alive. He visited her regularly until she died in 1979.

Another side of Cohen, the exquisitely sensitive artist, was Cohen, the warrior. He could never get over the way the Jews had, as he saw it, submitted to their near-extermination by the Nazis.

He decided that never again would they be victims if he could help it. When the Sinai War erupted in the wake of the Suez crisis in 1956, he left his (first) job on the Jewish Herald in Johannesburg, rushed to Israel, became a paratrooper in a crack commando unit and was in the thick of the fighting. In recognition of his talents as a fighter, he was shown the signal honour of being awarded the standard of his unit's battle colours by his commander, Mordecai Gur, Israel's future chief of staff. He later wrote an autobiography, which he called Memoirs of a Standard Bearer.

His photo-journalism started from this time and kept him on the move for the next 30 years - living with a family of Bedouin nomads in the Negev, touring Angola before the civil war, and taking pictures in Mozambique and of fishermen in Walvis Bay, "great chunks of men who knew the toll of time", as well as in doomed but vibrant District Six.

He photographed the Six Day War in 1967 and was in Paris when the Yom Kippur War erupted in 1973. Armed with a letter from Anglo American (he did assignments around the world for the corporation's magazine Optima) to the Angolan government, he talked his way onto an El Al flight with doctors and reservists and went straight to the frontlines.

What is remarkable about his war pictures, and indeed all his photography, is the way they capture the human condition without ever resorting to the sensationalism that would have made them so much more commercially viable. His accompanying words read like free verse rather than prose. Poetry and philosophy were as much a part of him as photography, and he published a book of poetry.

Cohen married in 1963 and divorced in 1968 after his wife, Ann, and her parents tried to have him committed to an asylum. He is survived by two children.

FOLLOWING THE ARCS TO TEL AVIV
Written by John Cohen – Extract from the 1959 Arcadian

Conditions in Israel in 1956 were 'understated' by saying they were 'tough'. Amongst those boys who were in the Young State were also those who had spent a greater part of their youth in the South African Jewish Orphanage, better known to all as the 'Old Arcs'. By sheer coincidence this descendent of Noah found himself in the promised land, but make no mistake, the only

John Brett Cohen – Photographer

guys who believe in promises would take this expression seriously.

I met some of my fellow Arc friends Benny Touyz, Linky, Bernard Klingman, Louis Lopatkin, Hymie Krut. All had come to devote themselves to serving Israel for a year or so. They all had a spell of time on strategic border kibbutzim. It is amazing how one adopts the everyday 'come what may, what will be, will be attitude' in Israel. I spent three weeks with Linky Klingman in Tzorah, a miserable place in the cold, muddy Jerusalem winter, surrounded by the forestation of trees - planted by the Keren Kyemet, the sponsors of that little blue box with the big Magen David sign.

One of my first duties was clearing the weeds from these trees; (these mountains were the biblical birthplace of Samson) and lugged around those old fashioned slings that modern day shepherd hurled at me while wandering around one peaceful Shabbat (needless to say he missed). Benny Touyz was also billeted at this Kibbutz as well as on Kfar Blum in Northern Israel, close to the Syrian gun-emplacements that wreaked such havoc on kibbutzim in that area last November.

He and Linky spent nearly two years there before going to Europe, Linky was studying interior design when I left him in London Benny is married and is likely to return to Israel. Louis Lopatkin had everyone on their toes and the episodes he got into defy description; even the dead-end kids could have taken lessons. Football and Tel Aviv appealed to him most.

Hymie Krut, who is studying in Cape Town, spent a lot of his time on Hassollelim, writing for a paper we produced of the humorous and serious side of daily living. The kibbutz lies in the heart of Western Galilee. Nazareth is the nearest town and the centre for most of the Israeli Arab population. I was accorded the special privilege of helping in the work of removing boulders that resembled Moore-creations. The whole idea of this work of removing masses of stone is to clear the fields for planting crops. The broken stones are loaded onto trailers and are used in the construction of roads.

Purim was in the air during my stay and having had the good fortune to be left off from lugging stones and helping to inoculate chickens, I painted the background of the scenery for our Purim play and party. Israelis, Canadians, Americans, South Africans, North Africans and my friends from Bombay, all dressed in the variety of festival garb. They danced and sang until the morning.

This country of which so much has been written and talked about is, to say the least, a border country; for no part of Israel is far from the border, and there is the constant preparedness for all emergencies.

The people have no time to waste their lives in aimless existence; to them one must always have an aim, to work, strive and study. Since the common denominator of their existence is based on survival, militarily, technically and spiritually, they have an almost unexplainable will-power, as we were taught 'Ein Davar Omed Neged Haratzon', nothing can withstand human will.

JOHN COHEN AND LINKY KLINGMAN - PHOTOGRAPHER AND ARTIST *Written by Basil Sepel*

I met John in Durban Jewish function in July 60. He was photographer reporter and womaniser despite having a pale white face and dark ringed eyes. I ,beach sleeper was preparing for a South African Universities soccer match against Natal in Pietermaritzburg where I was finishing agricultural science course.

Then from 30 February to May 61 (the day I left South Africa .and the golden day it became a republic) I worked and

lived in the Johannesburg city centre where I befriended Linky. Linky, who was the Arc art teacher for a couple of months, was artistically creating new children's games. Of course being used by his selfish boss while only peanuts paid - this indeed made him a great deal sad.

John and Linky both did their Israeli military service almost simultaneously and together returned to Europe then South Africa. Through Linky I met John a couple of times in his photographic studio where they discussed Pasternak and other subjects while I hungrily gobbled it all.

BOOK'S WRITTEN BY OLD ARCS
Written by David Solly Sandler

In 2003 I was aware only of the two poetry books written by Michael Basil Sepel:

> This Magnificent Universe in 1998 and
> High Fly in the Sky Lets Try in 2001

Over 2004 I learned of four more books written by Old Arcs:

o Africa and Europe 1921-1946- A Memoir - An autobiography of Alex Manderson (Mendelsohn) who after World War II made a new life for himself in Australia.
o My Struggle - An autobiography by Bernard G. Aronstam, a proud U.S citizen.
o Know the Seasons of your Womanhood, a medical book written by Solly Farber (Shalom Abe Farber) and
o Know your Risks – the STDs a medical book written by Solly Farber which he co-authored with Ron Ballard.

In addition Basil Sepel informed me about John Brett Cohen, a photographer, who has published many books of his photography:

o Images of My World was published in 1973,
o Israel Front Line, published in 1974, and
o Images of My World (Two), published in 1998

Images of My World, both one and two, are in the permanent collection of the Museum of Modern Art in New York.

The chapters from the autobiographies of Alex Manderson and Bernard Aronstam relevant to the Arc have been reproduced in this book with the kind permission of the authors.

Selections of Basil Sepel's poetry and also some reviews of his books have also been included as well as the covers of Solly Farber's books together with several of his short stories.

Chapter 51 - ALF JAMES (1912-1993)

Alf was a senior boy in Arcadia in the 1920-30's. His two sisters, Kathy and Esme were also in Arcadia.

Alf saw active service in the Army in WWII and was the South African Bantam Weight boxing champion.

He was always good, kind and considerate to the old Arc boys and girls.

WAR'S USELESS SLAUGHTER
Written by Alf James (1942)

I'll remember the day we started this job.
My mother's farewell, a smile and a sob.
We left the old country, sailed the sea
To the glamorous East where the enemies be.

I'll remember the first battle and our part,
We struck in the West at the enemy's heart,
Many fell there on that fateful ground,
As the enemy guns in their frenzy pound.

I'll remember too, that last hundred yards,
We were boys no more, as we made that charge.
Blood curdling screams we uttered all,
As bayonet we thrust through gullet and gall.

I'll remember always that sickening spell,
When all eyes looked round at that bloody hell,
It could not be that this was right,
That God meant man to kill and fight.

I'll remember now, and always will,
This Gazala battle, we're in it still,
A slit trench is the place we lay,
From dawn until the end of day.

For overhead it will come soon,
There it is! Far distant boom,
You start to shiver and to pray!
As that scream grows shriller on its way.

It's nearer now and you know real fear.
As you cringe and grovel to the earth so dear,
But no, it's past and you live again!
Till the next one comes with all its pain.

I'll remember now, and always shall,
The vow I take to all to tell,
Of the useless slaughter and bloody strife,
By man turned beast in war's hideous strife.
Alf James [1942]

Alf James

ALF JAMES
From 1949 Arcadian
By Jimmy Arnison

After James' crushing defeat at the hands of George Angelo in which the ex-welter king suffered a KO, it came as no surprise when shortly afterwards he announced his retirement from active boxing. It will be remembered that two weeks prior to this defeat he lost his crown to Don Carr on the closest of margins, but was handicapped by having to reduce to make the weight limit.

Although James is far from being an idol, he can always be relied upon to give his best, and was rated as South Africa's cleverest boxer. It will be remembered that James' fight with Stevens, in which he earned a draw, brought the boom back to boxing; and since then James has held the Lightweight and Welterweight titles, beating Willie Miller and Angelo respectively.

During James' brilliant career he has beaten such men as Catteral, Bradley, Voster De Roode, and earned draws with Heinhold and Stevens. While he has suffered 11 defeats, his brilliant exhibition against Boon won him the admiration of all boxing fans. James has now earned a considerable sum in purses and with the money well invested, he has taken a wise step in announcing his retirement.

OBITUARY

Alf James died in London at age 81 and was a South African boxing legend. Alfie was born in Pretoria and raised in Arcadia. He was one of the cleverest and shrewdest tacticians in his chosen sport. His first coach was Jim Tuner who gained his experience in the bare-knuckle days. Alfie won his first title as a senior lightweight at 17 in Natal. He worked his way to London after arriving in Edinburgh with less than two pounds in his pocket.

In London he had a job as an usher in the Trocadero in Elephant and Castle. He then joined the La Bohemia Club in Mile End Road. He won his first fight at the Black Friars against Alf Hayman on 30 January 1938. In 1939 he joined the Rand Light Infantry and saw service in Egypt. After suffering from malaria he returned to South Africa and transferred to the Royal Air Force. At the end of World War II Alfie fought the well known Laurie Stevens for the SA Welterweight title conceding weight. He came out with a well-fought draw. He became SA Light Weight champion in scoring a 12 points lead against Willie Miller. Near the end of his career he defeated the slick and scientific George Angelo. Sadly to say he was stopped by Angelo in their next fight in the second round in Salisbury which effectively stopped his career. His record was 67 fights with a loss of 15.

Over the years Arcadia produced many great boxers. Alf James was, arguably, the best of this wonderful lot. He was the SA champion in his weight division and a strong contender for the Empire title.

Vicky Klevansky and Alf James at Braamfontein Station, leaving for December 1934 Camp

Chapter 52 - MEYER (MIKE) RUBINOWITZ (1928)

Meyer (Mike) was in the care of Arcadia from 1935 to 1944

A NEW HEADMASTER FOR KING DAVID VICTORY PARK
From SA Jewish Times, 1969

Mr Mike Rubinowitz, Principal of Herzlia Primary School and Deputy Headmaster of the Herzlia High School, Cape Town, has been appointed to the post of Headmaster of King David School, Victory Park, Johannesburg.

Meyer Rubinowitz the runner

Meyer Rubinowiz – The Headmaster

Mr Rubinowitz, an Arcadian old boy, matriculated at Parktown Boys' High School and graduated at Witwatersrand University and the Johannesburg Teachers' Training College.

During the years 1955 to 1961 he was Principal of the Sydenham/Highlands North Talmud Torah. For the past eight years Mr Rubinowitz has been Deputy Headmaster and Principal of the Primary School of Herzlia, Cape Town. In 1964 and 1965 he was appointed examiner in Hebrew for the Cape Senior Certificate.

At the third Maccabiah, Tel Aviv, in 1950, Mr Rubinowitz won the 5 000 and 10 000 metres track titles and repeated this success in 1953.

Mr Rubinowitz is married and has three daughters.

He will take up his new post at King David High School at the beginning of the fourth term of this year.

MEYER RUBINOWITZ
As remembered by Mannie Osrin

I'm sitting in the stands at the old Wanderers grounds together with hundreds of Wits University students at the inter-varsity athletic meeting. There is one runner far ahead of the rest of the field, running the 10 000 metres, and every time he passes our stand, the cheer rings out, "WITS, WITS, RubinoWITZ" That, of course was Meyer Rubinowitz, and my chest nearly exploded with pride. Meyer won numerous long distance races, and from the time that he was winning the mile at Parktown to his University triumphs, and in between becoming Southern Transvaal cross country champion, he left behind an impeccable record of guts and endurance. I've often wondered just how much Jackie Mekler, whose feats in themselves are legendary, may have been influenced by Meyer's achievements.

ARCADIAN SPORTING ACHIEVEMENTS
Arcadia Supplement to the SA Jewish Times Friday July 25 1986 – Editor Solly Farber.

Arcadian kids have always been crazy about sports. It is really not surprising then to recall how many fine sportsmen and women have come out of this Children's Home. We've had stars at every level of endeavour.

Among our Springboks we mention Jackie Mekler the greatest long distance runner in the whole world in his prime; Leon Nahon who represented South Africa in swimming and water polo; and more recently we have one of our girls wearing the Green and gold in bowls

In the annals of Arcadia one Alfie James looms very large. He learnt how to box right here. He went on to become the national champion in his weight division and was a serious contender for the Empire title.

Les Wolchuck was one of "our" boys who did well in the ring. He became a Maccabi boxer and later also went to Israel as manager of the SA Maccabi boxing contingent.

Bernie Aronstam fought his way to fame in the USA and became a regional Golden Gloves Champion.

When you talk Arcadian sport then you are really talking soccer. Stars we have had aplenty. Many years ago Levi Wolf made his way over to the UK and ultimately played professional football for one of the top teams.

Rarely did a Springbok Maccabi Soccer team leave these shores which did not contain at least a pair of Old Arcs. Basil Lipschitz attended two Maccabiahs. "Beans" Levine and Donald Goldman are two others who achieved SA Maccabi status. Mannie Lipschitz was selected but didn't get to go as FIFA ruled our team out of the Games.

Louis Kreser achieved local fame as a pro for the then famous Rangers team.

Our Old Arcadians soccer team was famous in Johannesburg in the 60's and 70's. They won both the League and the Cup in the Sunday Yeoville League for seven years running! What an outstanding achievement.

In cricket we had Gerry Levy visiting Israel with an SA Maccabi XI. What a sportsman he was that Gerry. Under different circumstances he could have been an international at any one of a number of different games, soccer, cricket, athletics, boxing and hockey. He excelled in them all.

Mike Rubinowitz is an Old Arc who dazzled on the athletic track. He attended at least two Maccabiahs and each time took the gold medals in the 5 000 and 10 000 metre events.

Max Rabinowitz was our table tennis ace, and I believe at one time held the national men's singles title.

We even had our stars in ice hockey. Len Lipschitz and Max Paikin made their names in this, the swiftest and most dangerous of games.

At school level our kids have really excelled. We've had boys in First XV teams down all the years up to the present time. They would be too numerous to mention. For inexplicable reasons our boys do not seem to continue rugby after school. Mind you, the late Woolfie Kotzen played Transvaal under 19 and also first XV at Leeds University in the UK.

It seems then that the Arcadian kids will always have this love for sport and we will continue to send out potential champions into the big wide world.

PS   Eddy Stern who was in the Arc for a short time as a baby represented South Africa and Great Britain in Shooting. He had Springbok colours from 1983 to 1996 and then later Protea colours from 1997 when the SA emblem changed.

Chapter 53 - MAX ROBINOWITZ (1931)

Meyer Shuman Robinowitz who is known as Max Rabinowitz was born in Cape Town on the 13th of July 1931 and was placed in the care of Arcadia in 1933 after his father died and he remained in Arcadia until 1948.

Max's older sister, Mary Robinowitz was also in the Arc. She passed away 15 September 1993.

First of all, my name is Meyer Schuman Robinowitz. I'm known as Max Rabinowitz. Why I was called Max in the Arc, I haven't the faintest idea. Maybe they didn't want me mixed up with Meyer Rubinowitz who was also in the Arc. They never told me why.

I remember my Mom who was an opera star in Europe and gave quite a few concerts for charity in South Africa. She used to entertain the Arc kids with gypsy songs and Russian songs. She used to play the piano in the hall. She didn't speak English well. Most of it sounded like Yiddish with a Polish accent. She came from Vilna in Lithuania. She sang a Russian song, *Orchichornia* and danced with it.

THE BABIES

I was handed over into the care of one of the Kaufman sisters, at the big oak tree on the field below the main building. That to me was traumatic.

In the Babies, I remember pictures like humpty dumpty and Queen of hearts on the wall. We were washed or bathed standing up in a bath. I think Morris Samson fell in that longish bath and hit his eye or eyebrow on the side of it. We were always washed with red soap.

I remember going to camp in Port Elizabeth, I think in 1933 or 1937 and being held in the sea right up to my chin.

I remember collecting tennis balls from below the tennis court. Some were old and some pretty new. To hide them I climbed a little bit up a tree with a hollow. One night there was a storm and it rained a lot. The next morning some kids were screaming outside, "Come see, It rained tennis balls!" I never used the tree for a hiding place again.

Arcadia was near the zoo. When I heard the Lions roar and the elephants trumpet, I got scared because I thought they could get out.

THE JUNIOR DEPARTMENT

I went to primary school in Rannoch Road. I remember convicts working at the school with a white guard with a gun watching them. Does anybody remember that? There was a time when Natie Roamer and I went to the compound by the cowsheds.

A Young Max Robinowitz

They gave us something to drink and that was *skokiaan*. We landed in hospital and what we swallowed they ended up taking out of us with an enema. It was not pleasant at all.

I still remember Vicky telling us yarns. One was about pirates on the open seas. One piece I learned went something like this:

> *"Were four cut-throat pirates, come back from the ocean!"*
> *"Were four shady characters who've taken French leave."*
> *"But who is the shadiest? I haven't a notion…We argue the point as we plunder and thieve."*

I remember Bernard Aromstam and his brother Michael well. That scary show called "A day of the Triffids. "Something to do with trees and branches doing creepy things to people and property. That night it was raining. And I saw some trees moving outside. I was falling asleep when Bernard jumped in my bed. Well we both let off a hell of a scream at the same time, AAAHHHH! It really was a scary show.

People used to donate old toys and bikes. I received a bicycle. When I got to the top of the drive, I couldn't believe my eyes. The front wheel came off and went rolling between the jacaranda trees and I nearly did a somersault.

I used to run sometimes with Jackie Mekler down valley road.

Yes I remember *Kennetjie*, Loquats, the *'Steenvrugte'*. I got into trouble one day as they caught me cooking down the hill. The wind came up and the bushes and trees caught alight. I was then a senior. Six of us were told to be at Harary's office. The next morning, being the smallest and thinnest of the group, I just heard some 'klaps' being dished out by Cop Harary. When I went in he said, and what did you get. I said I got the potatoes for the chips. His words were, why did you do it why? (Following the grammatic principle of Hebrew). And he gave me a 'klap' across my face with his thick hands. I decided to stay down. We did this because we were hungry.

When we had spending money, we would jump the wall, go to Hillbrow and buy polony and pickled cucumbers. I would go and steal a loaf of bread from the shelves that were near the pantry. My hands were thin and I could just get my hand in underneath and squeeze out a loaf, and put it in the big oven which was still cooling from supper. It was one risky effort. To this day, I still think of that delicious hot rye bread with polony and pickled cucumbers.

Yes I remember the day we sat on the wall calling out the make of cars coming down Oxford road like Ford, Pontiac, Chevrolet, Hudson. It was approximately around 1939 because suddenly there was a Scottish band and many soldiers marching. I was so impressed. I had never seen anything like it before. We jumped over the wall and marched behind them. Eventually we landed up at zoo lake grounds, at the big eagle. Jan Smuts gave a speech to the soldiers. They were smart in their uniforms going up north.

At my Barmitzvah, we all had to make a speech on the lawn. They were done in Yiddish. I didn't know the difference because Cop wrote it for me. I still remember it off by heart. There were seven of us that year including Manual Lipschitz, Barnie Kotzen and Jackie Mekler. They gave us a watch, a Chumash, a Tallis, and a big book on the folklore of the Jews as well as a fountain pen. To us it was valuable. I swapped my watch for a pair of soccer boots, as they were more useful to me at the time. I went to Observatory Junior High.

The walls of the Arc made me feel closed in. Does anybody remember a guy called Robert Furman? Forgive me if it's the wrong guy as I do not remember names well. Well to me he was a real champion when it came to passing wind. Knowing him, this guy was a one man band. He could play tunes real well.

There was an incident at Rannoch Road School. We were playing soccer when suddenly lightning struck. Some kids were hospitalised, but they all recovered.

I also remember the crush that I had on a few girls. Like Sarah Epstein, Celia Aizakowitz, Yetta Roberts, and a girl called Daniella whose surname I don't remember.

Yes I remember the good times and the bad times and the tough times people had when they left. But they all made it. There's just too much to write about.

My sister Mary was also in the orphanage. I didn't see much of her as they kept the girls and boys apart. She worked at Ackermans in Rissik Street and I used to visit her there. She passed away a few years ago from lung cancer.

MY FATHER
Written by Carol Hasday

My father left the Arc at the age of 16. A few years later he met my mother, they married and they had three children, my brother Joel who now lives in Sydney Australia, Julie my sister who lives in Maalot in Israel and I, Carol live in Metulla Israel which is situated in the North of the country on the borders with Lebanon and Syria. When we were very small my parents divorced and a few years later my father remarried to Hilary Levine who has four children: Gary, David, Rina and Elana.

Before I was born my father reached the number one position in South Africa in table tennis and again a few years ago. He then began playing squash and excelled in that sport as well. However, his sports always had to come second to making a living and spent most of his life as a diamond cutter. When he was in the Arc he excelled at soccer and was doing very well when he fell and fractured his back, the doctors told him he wouldn't walk again, but he did - I am so proud of him and all he achieved with his sports.

He now lives quite near my sister in Maalot. My stepmother passed away a few years ago and he is once again alone. He spends his days at the beach in Nahariya and playing chess in a chess club and even plays tennis with young men (around the ages of 20-25) and then says to me, "Well didn't win the game this time - maybe next time"

MAX'S SPORTING ACHIEVEMENTS

Max is indeed one of the most talented Arc sportsman and he has a most impressive list of sports achievements.

Cricket

Observatory Junior High
1946 Winners Open Cricket Team

Dancing

Wells Sisson Dancing School (All Novice Class)
Passed	Bronze
Passed	Silver
Passed	Gold

Football

1946	Observatory Open Soccer Team
1948	Balfour Park Soccer Club
	Joint Winners Southern Transvaal under 18 league
1949	Played for Marists Brothers under 19 B side
	Reached finals at Rand Stadium in Curtain Raiser to Germiston Callies. Full house of 40,000
	Wolfhampton or Newcastle against S.A. (Losing 1-0).
1950	Transvaal Sunday League Div. 2 (Winners)
	Played for Old Arcs.
1951	Transvaal League Div. 1
	(Winners of League + Cup Final)
1950-51	Saturday League 1st Div.

Played for Marists Brothers 1st team after playing 4 matches. Then I hurt my back and had three operations for a slipped disk.

Teams I played against were Arcadia (Pretoria), Rangers Ramblers – Delfos Germinston.
I took Hymie Kloners Place when he got hurt.
Bennie Mechanic – Charley Hurley – Wally Warren – Botha Motgomery all played in that side.

Table Tennis

1959   Won SA Open Singles title
        South African Champion Graded No. 1 in Country
        In Final (Beat Mike Fry 3-1)
1957   South African Maccabi Team to Israel (5th Maccabia)
        Lost to Ficklestein in singles 26-24 in 3rd set)
        (No 1 seed in Maccabi Games)
1960   In Jewish Guild Magazine in June
        Transvaal Closed Championships
        Won Mens' Doubles + Mixed Doubles With Mike Fry and Hester Botha
        Runner up to Mike in Singles
1959   Won Transvaal Mens' Open Singles Title
1959   Won Maccabi Open Title
1959   Lost Transvaal Closed (to Rex Edwards) very narrowly in Final
1959   Played in Transvaal Table Tennis Team - Won 1959 Foster Trophy in Durban + Sofer Trophies. Won all games (lost only one to Ken Stretton of Eastern TVL)
1959   Jewish Guild Closed Tournament
        Won Mens' Singles + won doubles with Ruby Eilim
        Jewish Guild Open – lost mixed doubles final to Stretton+ Foldy
1968   SA.Table Tennis Championships Robertsham JHB.
        Reached finals with Olof Burwitz against Oscar + Calie
1960   SA Open at Wanderers Club
        Reached I think semi finals or finals lost against Sol Phitides
1959   No record – not sure – Won Wanderers Open
        Did win against Mike Fry – Eastern Province Open
1964   Played for Hillbrow Club. A Team in Transvaal League - Won 3rd Div. Men
1965   Won Mens' 1st League with Wanderers Club Joint
1959-60 Played Exhibition Game against World Champion Barna when he toured SA

Squash

Dec 1979 Jerusalem Post Israel
Age 48   Israel 3rd National Squash Tournament
         Won Israeli Open
         Graded 1 in Country
1978   Lost in Finals by one
1977   10th Maccabia Games
         Played for Squash Team (Veterans over 40) to Maccabia Games in Israel
         Our team won gold for SA in singles and team event
1980   Returned to SA

1986   Protea SA Veterans Inter Provincial Squash Tournament JHB
        Our team won (four players – two of whom were ex South African champions Cecil Kaplan and Leo Melville)
        Reached 2nd League – played for Summit Club in Hillbrow
        Played in Summit Club final against Bruno Campbell
        Lost in 5 set 10/9

No record   Won 3rd League (Business League) with Bruno Campbell + Mike Roberts

I played squash for about 30 years

Alec Saul and Max Robinowitz in Israel - 2005

OUR DAD
Written by Carol Israel Metulla and Julie Israel Maalot

We have contacted Wingate Sport Institute in Israel and they are interested in seeing Dad's sporting achievements and will most probably put it in their archives - of course if we have something to say they will put it all into the Hall of Fame - however that is quite difficult as they are only interested in Olympic winners. You must remember that S.A. did not compete in Olympic games during those times.

He hasn't had an easy life - what with our mother leaving three tiny children - she just upped and left and he was left to pick up the pieces - he had to work, he had to play sport to keep himself sane and we all suffered because of that. He then remarried and onto his three children another four became his children and he had to support all of us by working really really hard every day of his life – I do believe that if he had the chance and time he would have been a world sports achiever and champion!

When we were young we watched our dad dance and his grace is just amazing – he taught us to dance and we've never ever danced with someone like that – all the ballroom dancing – no words can be added.

Believe it or not - even in his seventies he sometimes gets paid by youngsters in their twenties to play tennis. Yes he was also a tennis player - and a wonderful swimmer too. Amazing yes - he is our dad.

Chapter 54 – JACK MEKLER (1932)

Jack Mekler was in the care of Arcadia from 1941 to 1948 together with his sister Hannah.

END OF A GLORIOUS ROAD
Arcadia Supplement to the SA Jewish Times - Friday ,July 25 1986 – Originally from the Sunday Express –1969

The end of a long, long running road – a road that stretched for nearly 60 000 miles, or nearly twice around the world – has come to Jackie Mekler, the most dedicated athlete in South African history who has decided to retire at the age of 37.

Mekler's brave effort to win the gruelling "Comrades" Marathon of 54 miles for the sixth time, which would have raised him above the other three immortals of the race – Wally Hayward, Arthur Newton and Hardy Ballington – failed.

But it was a glorious try when he finished third, and he can now relax in his retirement secure in the knowledge that he leaves the long distance scene as one of the greatest runners the world has known.

Yet it is now known that the little, freckle-faced athlete, then a 13 year old at the Jewish Children's Home in Johannesburg, decided to run because of his fragile build and the fact that he was a weaker than average youngster.

Nature did not bestow on him dazzling running gifts as she had, for instance on Jan Barnard, Mekler's contemporary. Barnard leapt to the forefront of athletes in swift, spectacular fashion. For Mekler success came slowly, agonizingly. But history has shown that champions who reach the top the hard way stay there longer. Other champions have flashed like stars across the firmament with startling rapidity – only to plunge to obscurity as quickly.

Mekler has been at the top for decades – but he had to compete in well over 100 events before tasting the sweetness of his first victory. That was in 1953. And from that point he swept ahead irresistibly to gain fame not only in South Africa but in many overseas countries.

At one time he held three world records – 30 miles (2hr 58 min) 40 miles (4 hr 18 min) and 50 miles (5hr 25min). He still holds the record for the classic London to Brighton road race at 5 hr 25 min 26 sec – a time which the greatest British runners have tried to lower year after year since 1960.

And he still retains the gruelling "up" record in the "Comrades" marathon of 5 hr 56 min 32 sec established also in 1960. It was only in 1963 that the English runner Bernard Gommersall beat his "down" record of 5 hr 51 min 20 sec.

He wore the Springbok vest in England, Finland, Canada and Greece and has run more than 70 standard marathons.

Jackie Mekler

Although one thinks of Mekler and the "Comrades" in terms of glittering success, few people know that at his first attempt he finished seventh and in his second he came fifth. He won his first "Comrades" at his third attempt and he also finished third (twice) and once second – and he has also dropped out.

His list of successes is an imposing one. He won the Southern Transvaal marathon title seven times, the South African championship twice, the Durban Athletic Club's marathon three times, the Jackie Gibson Memorial marathon three times, the King William's Town to East London 38-miler once and the Pieter Korkie Memorial race from Pretoria to Germiston six times.

We bid farewell to one of the most distinguished long distance runners the world has known. And also to a modest, model sportsman. I do not think Mekler has ever uttered one word of recrimination or resorted to excuses in the races in which he has not finished first. His first instinct was to congratulate the winner and praise him.

WELL DONE JACKIE!
By Solly Farber

By just looking at the headlines from newspapers which are reproduced below one can gather that Arcadia's Springbok, Jack Mekler, has not been idle this year.

Since he went to England last year with Wally Hayward and Fred Morrison, Jackie has added an impressive list of titles and records to his name.

Shortly after his return to South Africa, Jackie showed that he had gained a great deal of experience on the trip and won both the Natal and Southern Transvaal Marathon titles. In the latter race he won in record time, breaking the 14-year-old record set up by the late Jackie Gibson, and in the former he broke Johannes Coleman's records.

The best was yet to come. At the South African Athletic Championships Jackie beat Wally Hayward, Jan Barnard and others to win the title and bring him a chance to get into the Empire Games team.

Arcadia demanded a share in Jackie's triumph, and on the following Friday night Jackie dined at Arcadia and delivered a never-to-be-forgotten speech about his athletic career, making special reference to his trip to England.

As was expected, Jackie did gain a place in the Springbok Empire Games team, and away he went to Canada with the rest of the Springboks.

Sportsmen and sports writers were doubtful of Jackie and Jan's chances of achieving anything at the Games, but the Arcs,

knowing the indomitable character of both Jackie and Jan, were almost dead certain that both of them would gain places in the Marathon. Needless to say, the faith of the Arcs was repaid, and in they came – Jackie second, Jan third.

Less than a week after the Springboks' return Jackie visited the Arc again and held the Arcs spellbound while delivering a speech about the Games and Canada.

In a few months Jackie had risen from being practically an unknown to become one of the best long-distance runners in the British Commonwealth. But Jackie has an insatiable appetite for running, and three weeks after his return, when the other Springboks were all still settling down to normal life, Jackie was on the Delville track, where he set up world records for both the 40 miles and 50 miles. I doubt whether anybody, including Jackie, was expecting this. Everything was against him, the notorious Rand altitude, the great heat in which he ran, and the monotony or running around a track 200 times; but, to his credit, Jackie has what he himself described as the greatest asset of a marathon runner in his invitation article in last year's issue: "a courageous heart and indomitable will to keep you going long after muscle and bone have cried for rest."

In this run, which took place on Sunday 5th, Jackie ran the 50 miles in 5hr 24min, 57.4sec, and at the 40-mile mark his time also bettered the existing world record.

I can only conclude this article by saying, "Well done, Jackie, and may you continue to have the success which you deserve."

PS   Jackie gained more glory when he broke his own Southern Transvaal marathon record at the Scottish Gathering.

Chapter 55 - GERRY LEVY (1935)

Written by Mrs. Mona Levy - December 2005.

My husband, Gerry Levy and his brother David Levy were children who grew up in Arcadia. Gerry was born on the 25th October, 1935, and was put into the Arc at the age of four and David was seven.

Their father, Hymie Levy, was from Rhodesia and their mother, Sally, was from Pretoria. Their parents got divorced and their father remained in Rhodesia. Sally and the boys returned to Johannesburg. She then put them in Arcadia as she was unable to support them.

Gerry's years spent at the Arc were very happy years. Perhaps the fact that he excelled at sport was a great advantage. He went to Saxonwold Primary School and then on to Parktown Boys' High School where he started in 1949.

He played 1st 15 Rugby: 1953-1954; 1st Team Cricket 1952-1954 and received colours for Cricket and Rugby and also received Honours for Rugby. He received athletic colours and won his weight in boxing five out of six times. His boxing coach was a very loved Old Arc, Donald Goldman.

Gerry Levy

Gerry Levy

Gerry was voted the most popular boy at Parktown Boys' High, and the cherry on the top was, that he was the only orphanage boy to be chosen for the Transvaal Nuffield Cricket Eleven.

When he left the orphanage he went on a Goodwill Maccabi Tour for Cricket in 1955 and was chosen to play Maccabi Soccer in 1961. He feels that the Arc was very instrumental in helping him reach his goals in sport, and he made wonderful friends while living there.

While he was at the Arc, it was run by Dr .Adolf Lichtigfeld (known as Doc), as well as Morderchai Harary. The housemaster of the boys was Vicky Klevansky, who was also one of his teachers at Parktown Boys' High.

His memories of his days at the Arc are only good memories. His friends included the late Dr Solly Farber, the Kreser Brothers, Alec Gavson, Dave Kotzen, Dr Mannie Osrin, Eli Osrin, his mentor Donald Goldman and many others, too numerous to mention.

Some of his fondest memories of the Arc are when they were visited by the featherweight boxing champion of the world, Robert Cohen, who he actually sparred with, as well as Reg Parks the body builder. These visits were, of course, great highlights to him as he is a sport fanatic.

He does not feel that being brought up in the Arc was anything but a privilege, and is very proud to be an Old Arcadian.

I come from Ermelo and am the daughter of the late Rev Bloch. We were married on the 10th February 1963, and he feels that his greatest achievement in life are our three wonderful children.

They are all married and we have six lovely grandchildren. Gerry loves to tell the grandchildren of his days growing up in the Arc. We have had a wonderful life together and have been very blessed. Gerry recently celebrated his 70th birthday and we had a lovely party with all our friends and family.

SPORTS IN ARCADIA
By Gerry V Levy - Extract from 1954 Arcadian

This is the second article in the series, 'Sports in Arcadia', and I hope that this series will be continued as long as there is an Arcadian.

Cricket - Every Saturday morning after Shul the Arcs hold practice matches among themselves, and during the week the verandah is the favourite cricket pitch. The Arc team played two matches and were victorious in both. In school cricket only a few Arcs take part: Gerry Levy has been playing for Parktown 1st XI for three years and has gained colours. Reuben and Louis play for Parktown 3rd, David for Athlone 2nd and Charlie and Norman for Athlone Under 14a.

Rugby - This is perhaps the most popular sport amongst the Arcs. Once again, through the kindness of the Athlone rugby master (Mr A Malan) the Arcs' team played against an Athlone 3rd XV, and won easily by 34 points to nil.

In school rugby the Arcs have a record of achievement that warrants much honour. Four boys, Gerry Levy at Parktown and Selwyn Dembo, Woolf Kotzen and Cyril Touyz at Athlone all play for their respective 1st XV. Gerry gained a re-award of colours and honours, while Woolfie, Selwyn and Cyril gained colours at Athlone. Louis Kreser, Reuben Lipschitz and David Kotzen represented their school 2nd XV. David was captain of his team. Arnold Levitan, Benny Kreser and Allan Dubois play for their school Under 15b team. Arnold is captain of his team.

Last year the Arcs scored 111 points for their schools. This year they surpassed their record and between them scored 134 points. Not Bad!.

Soccer - Here again the Arc juniors are prominent in their school teams. Owing to a lack of under 18 teams the Arcs senior team was this year an under 17 team. This team played a number of matches and was unbeaten and here is a critique on the players;

Arnold Levitan [goal]: Although this position is a new one to Arnold he acquitted himself very well during the season, but he must learn to come out of the goal when necessary.

Marek Stein [right back]: A most improved player, but one who is inclined to use rough tactics.

Solly Farber [left back]: Solly is a good player and he tries very hard. Does not stop playing until the final whistle.

Selwyn Dembo [right half]: A very good player who tries his utmost. Selwyn is very keen and is all over the field.

Dave Kotzen [centre-half - captain]: The best player in the side. Very good with his head and plays an attacking game. Is, however, inclined to be a bit selfish.

Basil Sepel [left half]: When he feels like playing, Basil is an excellent player. Must play harder.

Charlie Segal [right wing]: Charles does not know much about playing on the wing and only plays in bursts. Should develop into a fine player next year.

Alan Dubois [inside right]: 'Squeeky' is a very fast and clever player, but must not persist in trying to shoot from difficult angles.

Louis Kreser [centre-forward]: An excellent player who has a terrific shot in both feet. 'A soccer player in the making'.

Benny Kreser [inside left]: Has improved immensely, but is a bit slow. He compensates this slowness by always being in position to take the ball.

Norman Sacks [left wing]: Has not shown the form we know he is capable of. He does not centre the ball but tries to shoot from the wing. A bad habit.

The following also represented the team in one or two matches: I Levitan, Y Bortz and E Dembo.

Swimming: As a competitive sport, swimming is only favoured by a few in Arcadia. Nevertheless the Arc Sixth Annual Gala was a great success. The few who do take interest were noticeable at their school house galas, and Solly Farber represented Parktown on numerous occasions and David Kotzen represented Athlone.

Life Saving: Congratulations are due to Solly for gaining three awards from the RLSS and Isadore and Arnold for gaining their Intermediate Certificates.

Netball: Arc girls represent their schools and have made quite a name for themselves. Congratulations to Bella for gaining her braid and to Anne, who already has her braid. Well done, girls!

Boxing: The Arcs have been showing great keenness in this sport. A tournament was held at the Youth Centre last year between the Arcs and the YMCA. At last year's Parktown Boxing Championship Louis Kreser and Basil Sepel won their respective weights. Gerry was narrowly outpointed by the South African junior welterweight champ.

As you can see from the above report, the Arcs have quite a name in sport, and I sincerely hope that Arcs will continue in this way in the years to come.

Chapter 56 – EDDY STERN (1937)

I arrived at the Arc in December 1940 and left in August 1941. So, being very young I don't unfortunately remember individuals, which I very much regret. My date of birth was 22 May 1937.

I don't have any siblings. After my birth my mother was expecting another, so she told my wife once (never revealed to me) but with all the terrible goings on back in Germany, the pregnancy was terminated. Once in Mocambique and then Northern Rhodesia, as penniless refugees the idea of a larger family was out of the question.

The 10 November 1938 marked the turning point in the lives of our family in Essen, Germany. My father, a doctor of law who had been barred from his professional calling by one of various discriminating decrees by the Nazis, together with my young uncle, were rounded up at six in the morning and arrested. After incarceration at the local cells, they were sent to Dachau concentration camp.

The preceding five years had seen the rapid erosion of constitutional law and the aggregation of total brutal power in the hands of Hitler and his chosen coterie of delusional misfits.

My grandfather, Kurt Stern, who owned a large industrial undertaking, had to watch his world crumble under the imposed boycott of Jewish businesses. The plant and workshops were located in Essen, the Ruhrgebiet, the home of Krupp, the mainstay of Industrial Germany and the developing war machine.

Kurt, who had many non-Jewish friends and was popular with his workers, had always believed things would come right and that they would have a future in Germany. He now had to concede that this was not so.

My father Werner's younger brother, an engineer, fearing the worst, had emigrated to South Africa in 1936. My mother desperately sought to get my father and her brother out of Dachau. After several fruitless efforts with the authorities, she travelled to Bonn. There, a sympathetic British consular official gave her visas to enable us to emigrate to Northern Rhodesia. At this time, prior to the "Final Solution", if Jews were able to persuade foreign governments to accept penniless refugees, the Nazis would let them go.

My Grandfather by this time was physically handicapped and arrangements were made for him to be cared for in a home. Not long after he, together with many others were murdered in a death camp. We had previously left for Beira, Mocambique, but on arrival there found that the visas were invalid. Their issue was simply a charitable act by the consular official in Bonn to enable us to get out of Germany.

We had to spend some time in Mocambique before being allowed into Northern Rhodesia a British protectorate. Having German nationality we were classed as enemy aliens and my father had to report to the police once a week. The authorities rescinded this requirement once they realised the futility of it. During this time, I contracted malaria badly. People were dying of Black Water Fever. This affected my health and after a year in Northern Rhodesia the doctor advised that I should be removed to a more moderate environment to recover.

That is how a little German speaking $3^{1}/_{2}$ year old suddenly found himself in an English-speaking environment far away from home. Oddly, the only memory I have of Arcadia (and I do remember experiences prior to that time), is of a friendship with an African staff member and communicating with him in the grounds higher up behind the main buildings. My stay at the Arc was relatively short, I was there for just under a year by which time my health was fine and I could return to Northern Rhodesia. I was only there for almost a year and left with a good command of English.

It was in Broken Hill (since renamed Kabwe meaning "Stones", the mining connection) in Northern Rhodesia, in the late 1940s and early 1950s, as a teenager that I met Bunny Barlin (from Arcadia), through my parents' friendship with him, even though he was of a younger generation to them.

As a still very young man Bunny Barlin had a very senior job with the Anglo American owned mine in the town. He was a young Wits metallurgy graduate He distinguished himself as a bright plant superintendent and was well thought of in the Anglo American Group. He was an able sportsman and became the national diving champion, and coached his wife, Una to ladies champ. Besides being a superb sportsman, Bunny was an exceptionally bright and talented person also interested in classic music.

I do believe the Arc was a useful interlude in my life. Apart from the crash course in English, it fitted me for institutional life and getting on and communicating with others. I have since been in just about every institution known to Man apart from prison and I have thoroughly enjoyed the experiences.

As a matter of interest I have had a number of bouts of malaria since but with each subsequent one the level of intensity has diminished to the extent that I believe I have luckily achieved a state of immunity now. During my last fishing and camping trip up to Lake Tanganyika practically all in the party contracted malaria whereas in my case it was just a case of being a little off my food for two days.

At the age of 68 I take part in Masters Athletics, sprints and javelin with pleasing successes and I have Springbok and Protea colours for shooting and continue to participate in Internationals. For the record I first achieved Springbok colours in 1983 and currently have Protea colours, I have also captained our team a number of times. From 1986 to 1990, through having dual citizenship, I was fortunate to represent Great Britain in international shooting as South Africa were banned at that time. My wife Erica, son Marc and I live on a small farm outside Johannesburg while my daughter Yael lives in Fairlight, Sydney

The team photo was taken at the culmination of the World Muzzle Loading Long Range Championship held in Cape Town in 2001. I had successfully made the bid at the 2000 World Short Range in Australia, where I placed 7th, for us to hold the match in Cape Town. I am at the extreme right of the 4 man long range (800 and 900 metres) team wearing our silver medals on our lapels. We beat all the major nations except France who pipped us for gold.

with David Gold and their infant son Jamie. We left Zambia for South Africa to obtain treatment for my oldest son David in 1970 but he succumbed to leukaemia. Subsequent to 1994 the new political order was anxious, in keeping with trends elsewhere in Africa, to change names and minimise the contribution and role of Europeans (whites) in SA. After serious negotiations the politicos agreed that as a temporary measure they would allow the Springbok name and logo to be used only by the national rugby team. All other national teams were to be known as the Proteas. Thus 1996 was my last appearance as a Springbok at the World Champs and in 1998 at the subsequent Worlds in the UK I captained the Protea team.

1983 to 1996 I was a Springbok, 1997 to present I am a Protea, and in 1986 to 1990 I also represented Great Britain.

The 1921 Annual Bulletin mentions Isaacson as one of three members of an advisory board that drafted a new constitution for the South African Jewish Orphanage so that it became an institution on its own and was no longer just a part of the Jewish Ladies Communal League where it had been for 17 years.

It also mentions that the Orphanage (64 children) are in the charge of the Matron, Mrs Myers, (Mavis's mother) who is assisted by a staff of three.

The 1921 and 1922 bulletins mention Mr M I Isaacson as a member of the committee and in the 1924 Bulletin he was Chairman. In that year he married Mavis Myer who was the daughter of the then matron of the South African Jewish Orphanage then housed in Kensington.

Mr Isaacson was also the Treasurer of the Relief Fund that negotiated to bring to South Africa 200 Orphans from Poland and the Ukraine. Mavis took charge of 88 of the Orphans and they were temporarily housed at the Old Aged Home.

At the same time while plans were afoot to build a new Orphanage in Kensington the palatial residence "Arcadia" became available and it was acquired as the new home of the South African Jewish Orphanage and Mavis was then appointed Matron.

In 1926 they retired to Warmbaths and the 1927 bulletin mentions Mr & Mrs M I Isaacson as subscribers with the address as Warmbaths Hotel, Warmbaths.

RAND PIONEER WHO ESTABLISHED "ARCADIA"
By Richard Feldman

Morris Isaac Isaacson

Some there are who have served the community for the lifetime but have not left their mark or in any way influenced the development of the organisations or institutions which they have served. Others there are, though few, who may have devoted only a limited period of their lives to the welfare and improvement of the community, yet have been creative and much achievement to their credit. Morris Isaac Issacson, MII to his friends, belongs to the latter category.

His is the story of those who at the turn of the century sought to find a new home in South Africa. It is a little different from the average story, because "M.I.I." came with a social consciousness which he did not suppress in his pursuit to establish himself economically. Rather did he develop it in the new home he found.

A distinguished looking gentleman with the white trimmed moustache, who can be taken for a retired English colonel, Morris Isaac Isaacson was born in Varsan, Lithuania. His father was an innkeeper and when the old Russian

Government introduced a monopoly in the sale of alcohol products, one more avenue was closed to the Jew, and it was decided to send young Morris to South Africa.

Johannesburg "Played Out"

The family wrote to a relative in Johannesburg, and it is significant that the reply said – and that was in the year 1896 – that Johannesburg was "played out"; but within a few years it was considered that Matabeleland (Rhodesia) would be a place with a future.

Nevertheless, he left that year for South Africa. On his way from Memel to Bremen he travelled in a train for the first time. The usual hardships and exploitation by "Agents" were experienced. An attempt was made to delay the departure of the group of immigrants of which our Isaacson was a member, and "M.I.I" had his first experience in organising a protest. They were a young and somewhat spirited crowd of immigrants, and it is interesting to note that an offer was made by an "Agent" to sign then on as miners, it being contended that a "Kaffir War" was imminent in the Transvaal, and they might not be otherwise admitted. Besides, if they agreed to work as miners, their travel fare would be less. They proved a troublesome lot, and were sent off to London, where the authorities of the Jewish Shelter did not detain them for long, either, and so to South Africa.

Mavis Myer

"MII" had two relatives in Johannesburg. At the station he was casually met by a "landsman" who took him by carriage to one of the relatives. This relative gave him a lunch and two golden sovereigns, and indicated that as he had recently married he could not put him up. His second relative, a poorer man, received him more hospitably, providing him with place to sleep, though he had to provide food for himself.

After a period spent in hawking, young Isaacson took a job as a shop assistant in Brakpan. He tried about a dozen different occupations, ranging from working in a mineral factory to selling insurance before establishing himself in business.

Joins Labour Party

In 1910 he joined the S.A. Labour Party, and for many years took a leading part. He knew little of the theory of Socialism, but his friends said he was "a born Socialist" as he acted and preached as one. He took a prominent part in the famous 1913 strike.

In 1914 he was elected a member of the National Executive, and was a candidate in the elections for the Town Council, which owing to the Rebellion, was cancelled.

At the outbreak of World War I, "M.I.I." was amongst the small group that formed the War on War League, later to emerge as the International Socialist League. At one of its stormy mass meetings, held at the Gaiety Theatre, Mr Isaacson presided.

He had, however, not severed his connection with the Labour Party, and while a member of the Party's Administration committee, took a prominent part in the Rand strike of 1922. In 1924, together with Messrs G Weinstock, M Kentridge and B Jenkins, he established the Labour weekly, "Forward," which was to become the mouthpiece of Labour, which had then entered into a pact with the Nationalists.

Jewish War Relief Fund

Simultaneously with his activities in the Labour Party, we find "M.I.I." at the beginning of World War I, together with the respected representative of the orthodox Jews, Reb. Chaim Yankel Kark, as chief protagonists for the formation of a Jewish War Relief fund, which was at first strongly opposed by Mr Harry Graumann, at that time the leading spokesman of Johannesburg Jewry.

At the end of the First World War, Mr Isaacson was amongst the most prominent and active leaders of Johannesburg Jewry. He was President of the Jewish Guild, Treasurer of the Jewish War Memorial fund, Treasurer of the Jewish Relief and Reconstruction Fund, and chairman of the S.A. Jewish Orphanage.

Orphanage "Revolution"

His connection with the Orphanage needs to be written up at greater length, as it is the story of a bloodless "revolution" to establish democratic rule in one of the community's institutions. Briefly the facts are these. The Orphanage was not an independent body, and had no separate constitution, but was an activity of the Jewish Ladies' Communal League. Males could not have a say in the way the Orphanage was run. The League leadership was unsympathetic to the recent immigrants from Eastern Europe. Orphanage contributions had no legal rights, membership fees were regarded as donations. Attendance at an annual meeting was a courtesy, not a right.

Mr Isaacson, in collaboration with Mr David Getz (now of Cape Town), the late Mr W Jacobson, and other supporters, attended an annual meeting - by courtesy of the Committee – and demanded the independence and democratisation of the Orphanage. Seeing that the rebels had strong support, the Chairman adjourned the meeting for ten minutes, and on its resumption announced that the League was prepared to "abdicate", and an Interim Committee to draft a constitution was adopted. The old leadership refused to participate in the new Committee. "M.I.I." found himself with an Orphanage on his hands. Here he met Mavis Myers, the daughter of the Matron, and he married her in 1924.

The Relief fund was negotiating to bring to South Africa 200 orphans from Poland and Ukraine, and Mr Isaacson played a prominent part as Treasurer of the Fund in the bringing together of the local and the overseas orphans.

Mavis Myers took charge of the 88 overseas orphans, who were temporarily housed at the Jewish Aged Home, and soon became "Mummy Myers" to them, as indeed "M.I.I." became "Pappa Isaacson". Their devotion to the young strangers was without bounds.

How "Arcadia" was acquired

Plans were ready for the building of a new Orphanage at Kensington at the cost of 35,000 pounds but the late Bernard Alexander, leader of South African Jewry at the time, and Chairman of the Relief fund, sent for Mr Isaacson and the late Peter Kaplan, and told them that Sir Lionel Phillips' palatial residence, "Arcadia", was for sale and it was bought for 30 000 pounds.

There was considerable opposition to this purchase on the ground that poor orphans should not be housed in a palace amidst beautiful surroundings. This opposition persisted until the official opening by General Smuts, who pointed out that the beauty of the surroundings was some compensation for these children who had no parents and no home of their own.

Mavis Myers was appointed matron and until her marriage she and Mr Isaacson devoted their spare time, their energy and love, to making "Arcadia" a home for its young residents.

In passing, it may be mentioned that Mr Isaacson wanted the Orphanage to be known as "Arcadia", and not the "Orphanage". He had witnessed some of the overseas children, when brought to the Cape Orphanage, reading the word "BET YESOIMIM" (House of Orphans) and crying: "So we have come from one Orphanage to another". This impressed him so much that his main endeavour was to free "Arcadia" from any institutional atmosphere.

Memorial to his wife

In 1926 the Isaacsons left for Warmbaths, and their active association with communal institutions stopped for some years, but many there are who have cause to remember them with affection and gratitude for the paternal care and assistance they rendered.

During the last war, Mrs Isaacson gave voluntary but full-time service to the Johannesburg Hospital, and at her death in 1949, sincere tributes were paid to her by the Hospital authorities for her devoted services.

As a memorial to his wife, Mr Isaacson, under the auspices of the City Council, built a Nursery School at Moroka Township – truly a fitting reminder of a partnership of service to different sections of the community.

Illuminated Address Given To Morris Isaacs And Mavis Myers On The Occasion Of Their Wedding In Thanks For Their Service Given To The Ukraine Orphans.

United South African Jewish Relief Reconstruction and Orphans Fund
To M I Isaacson Esq

Dear Mr Isaacson
On the occasion of your marriage we wish to place on record our deep appreciation of your great services to the cause of our people in Eastern Europe in your capacity as Hon Treasurer and Vice President of the Fund, particularly in the cause of our destitute orphans.

After the pogrom period in the Ukraine when the news of the terrible plight of hundreds of thousands of pogrom orphans reached us and South African Jewry deeply felt the great national tragedy, you placed yourself at the head of the Save the Orphans Campaign and since then you have worked wholeheartedly on behalf of these destitute orphans of ours. When the eighty eight orphans brought out by our Fund arrived in Johannesburg you entirely devoted yourself to caring for their well being and happiness. Indeed you have been like a father to them.

It is not for us to thank you for your great and noble work, but we feel sure that on this your wedding day as well as all your life time you will feel happy and compensated in the knowledge of having to such an extent been instrumental in saving so many young lives, ensuring them of a happier future than that which faced them.

We also feel happy in the thought that your life's partner has also been associated with us in the caring of our orphans. Indeed Miss Mavis Meyers has as Matron been a true friend to them giving them a mother's care and love.

We wish you both a very happy life – a life full of joy and sunshine.
With kindest regards – On behalf of the Central Executive Committee.

The document is signed by the President, whose name is not clear (it may be Hollander), the Vice President, Natie Kirschner, the treasurer, I. M. Gordon, the Secretary, Ray Cowen, and Richard Feldman, the chairman of the Propaganda committee.

JEFFREY ISAACSON (THEIR SON) WRITES

Now some personal facts: Mavis Myers (born in Manchester) was my mother, and she was 24 when she married my father, Morris Isaac Isaacson, (born in Kovno), who was 46 or so (he wasn't sure). She must have been very capable to be matron at so young an age. She tragically died of cancer in 1949, and my father who must have been 76, died in 1954.

They adopted me in 1933, one week before my first birthday, but they never mentioned it to me. When I was over 50 I discovered I was the illegitimate son of my mother's younger brother, and a blond Russian lady called Lena Max. When I visited South Africa in 1985, my wife begged me to look for her, but I never had the guts.

In any case I never had a complaint, having what I would consider a privileged upbringing, although we were nearly stranded in Europe in 1939, sailing from Southampton on 1st September 1939. I already had a gas mask, and didn't get another one, until the Scuds were fired in 1991. I know I should be embarrassed, but I was educated at Michaelhouse, and studied Geology at Wits.

With my mother's urging, my father left most of his money to black education. The Isaacson trust educated hundreds of black pupils, apart from building one of the first nursery schools in Soweto, and the Morris Isaacson high school, which was the focus of the 1976 uprising and was partially destroyed.

It was the site of the film Seraphina, which you may have seen. I opened the school in 1961. In 1997 I visited the rebuilt school, and was given an emotional reception, which I wished my parents could have been alive to experience. After all, it was their show, not mine.

My father, who had been a wholesaler in Market Street and a Labour politician, gave it all up and bought the Warmbaths Hotel in 1927. They sold it in 1947. Apart from boarding school, I then lived on a farm in Warmbaths, where we grew flowers, and raised livestock. Not what I would call a conventional upbringing.

One story my father told me of was concerning a plot to assassinate General Jan Smuts at the opening of Arcadia. I'm sure it is not generally known, and if the plot had been carried out, it would have caused a pogrom

My father, who was an active member of the Labour Party, was involved in the 1922 general strike, and when Smuts, good democrat that he was, had some of the strikers shot, he went and hid on a health farm in Natal for some time.

When Smuts was invited to open the orphanage, the remaining ex-strikers thought it was a good place to assassinate him, but when my father heard about it, he had enough influence to talk them out of it.

In the photo of General Smuts opening the orphanage my father is on the left hand side behind General Jan Smuts.

Family Photo

229

Chapter 58 – LOUIS AND RACHEL SHAER
At Arcadia – 1924–1943

Louis (Stompie) and Rachel Shaer who were from England were appointed Superintendent and Matron of Arcadia in October 1924, about a year after the move to Villa Arcadia.

Louis Shaer was referred to as "Stompie" Shaer by the children as he was very short.

This arrangement continued until Rachel Shaer passed away in 1937 and Sister Goldwater was promoted to Matron. In 1938 Mordechai Harary was appointed as Assistant to Stompie Shaer and in 1943 Stompie Shaer retired.

Louis and Rachel had two daughters, Naomi and Ruth, both School Teachers. One of them became Principal of an Indian school.

Louis Shaer

THE LATE LOUIS 'STOMPIE' SHAER
By Woolfie Getz

From what I can remember about this man, (may he rest in peace), he was a hard man not really suited to run an institution of this calibre. He knew how to use the cane. That was always to his advantage. He never liked the boys to be friendly with the girls. I remember he used to refer to Morry (Toots) Bernard as "Sissy Bernard". If a kid was late for anything he would always say to him "If it was chocolates, you would be there first."

It is hard to try and think of a man in those days as compared to the present day. In today's times "Stompie" Shaer just would not shape. I just found "Stompie" a very hard man who was out of touch in the running of Arcadia. Of course, he and the late Sister Goldwater could never find it easy to control such a big organization. In actual fact I don't really remember much of him as I was too young.

Louis Shaer

IN MEMORY OF MRS RACHEL SHAER
Extracted from Annual Bulletin 31 March 1938

It is with deep regret that we record that on August 23 1937, Mrs Rachel Shaer, wife of our Superintendent, who had been Matron for ten years from October 1924, passed away after a lingering illness. She was indeed a 'true mother in Israel' to the hundreds of children that had passed through her hands during the period of her Matronship, and her memory will ever be treasured by them and by us. On Sunday, April 10 a Memorial Plaque, erected to her memory in the entrance hall of Arcadia by the Committee and children of the Orphanage, was unveiled by Mr Wolf Hillman.

entrance hall on the lines in an odd way, slapped my face and said, "You'll break your shoes! They cost money!"

Rachel Shaer I believe, wrote for some weekly Jewish publication - my memory of her is coloured with two incidents. Friday nights, for some reason, she used to call me to read to her and her two daughters Naomi and Ruth in their private lounge upstairs.

The second incident is one I recall vividly - she used to come out of her upstairs quarters, stand on top of the stairs leading to the main entrance hall, clap her hands and shout "Somebody, Somebody" until one of the girls came running to her.

She was always addressed as Matron Shaer. This era in my life represented conformity and discipline. My memories of the Shaers are pleasant and I see him still with his big paunch, grey thinning hair blowing in the wind when he ruled the roost at the Port Elizabeth Camps.

Stompie Shaer - Sketched by Ekie Litvin

LOUIS AND RACHEL SHAER
By Bertha Kronenberg (Klevansky)

I remember Louis and Rachel Shaer as being very English in their ways.

Louis Shaer was strict and harsh, and on occasions would shout at children, sometimes commenting on their parents in front of all the kids. He once caught me walking along the

Sketched by Michael Perry Kotzen

Chapter 59 – HENNY AND SELMA KAUFMAN
At Arcadia – 1927–1957

Henny and Selma, sisters from Germany, looked after the children at Arcadia for 30 years. Most of their time was spent looking after the Babies and they are fondly remembered by all their children.

LOOKING BACK
Extracted from the 1951 Arcadian
Miss Kaufmann reminisces to representative of The Arcadian

We were sitting in the staff room one evening. It was after lights out, nobody was there except Miss Kaufmann and one other member of staff and I. We talked casually of the Home, the children. Miss Kaufmann was in very reminiscent mood and talked of her long career at Arcadia.

"In my early days here about 23 years ago, I had 50 babies in my care. There was no Joe Lewis Wing in those days. The babies were upstairs. I looked after the babies for about 14 years. We had a percussion band at one time. I taught them to play. It was very nice. There were five boys later on in my senior boys who all matriculated the same year. They were Effie Segal, Maurice Bernard, Bunny Barlin, Philip Kemp and Ivan Kurland.

"The boys slept in the quadrangle by the fish pond and also in the place which is now the Shul. The Shul then was in the library and the babies sat on the benches in the hall. All the children wore uniforms and they had to change when they came home from school. Lights out for the whole house was 8 o'clock, not like today, 9 o'clock and even later. Matron Shaer corrected me many times – in my English, I mean."

"I remember when the whole house went on a seaside holiday to Port Elizabeth. I think we went three times. We took everything with us and locked the house. In those days the swimming suits were made of all kinds of pieces of linen. We didn't buy any.

"My babies have grown up; some are married. I went to their weddings. There is Alma Kemp, Harry Barlin, Bertha Klevansky. Yes, I had all the Kotzens. I'm a grandmother. You know Esther Kotzen, Alma Kemp, Bertha Klevansky have babies of their own. I remember how Flora Kotzen was lost at the seaside. No-one could find her, so we had to inform the police. Then there was Freda Kotzen. She was called 'The Water Baby' and she's married too and living in Cape Town."

A COUPLE OF UNFORGETTABLES
Extracted from 1957 Arcadian
Written by Reuben Lipschitz

You must have something if you can withstand the Arcs, as they ripen from naughty little boyhood into naughty big boyhood. You must have something extra and quite a bit more, if you can

Mr Hepker making a presentation to the Kaufman sisters

perform this feat of physical and mental endurance, this trial of patience and understanding for a full 30 years.

Henny and Zellie Kauffy did just that. For 30 years they moulded and shaped the characters of the Arcs, and helped to give them an equal start in life. Henny gave me such a start, that it took her a whole week before she could catch up with me and slam me with her feather duster. These two ladies were made to order for the pen of Charles Dickens.

Just after the Ark settled on Mt Ararat (22 Oxford Road), these dear ladies settled down and started looking after the babies, at the Arc. It was Henny's proud boast, that the boys, who were in the babies with her, were only about half as naughty as those who were not.

After a period Henny graduated to the senior boys and Zellie became 'Zellie of all trades', ranging from sister in the hospital to boilermaker in the laundry. At about six each morning Henny woke up the Senior Boys. I doubt if any of the boys ever mistook her for a lark, but nevertheless she got us out of bed. A feat on its own. At meals Henny saw to it that her Senior Boys were well fed. If ever the Senior Girls' roast potatoes looked slightly bigger or slightly better done, the culprits in the kitchen knew all about it.

Besides mending the clothes and supervising the general comings and goings of the boys, Henny organised a musical band. I hardly need draw your attention to the fact that Elvis, Bill Haley and other famous artists only became famous after the Henny's Arc band chucked up.

That 'something extra and quite a bit more' I mentioned in the first paragraph were extra large helpings of physical fitness, energy, experience, understanding of children (especially Arcs) and golden hearts overflowing with kindness. I know Henny and Zellie look back on their 30 years of good hard work well done with very few regrets, for generally their Arc charges have been a credit to them.

The day after Henny and Zellie left the Arc to live in their comfy flat in Yeoville, every Arc knew that they were going to be very hard to replace, and so time has proved them right. Thank you very much for everything, Henny and Zellie. I feel sure that the Kaufys are visited frequently by many of the old Arcs.

THE KAUFMAN SISTERS
By Bertha Kronenberg (Klevansky)

I must have known the Kaufman sisters for many, many years for I remember singing German ditties on the big lawn with us little ones standing and clapping hands as we stood in a circle. For me they seemed to rustle as they moved in their starched white uniforms, and had the smell of peppermint about them. They seemed to be a fixture.

HENNY AND SELMA KAUFMAN
By Freda Cheilyk (Koppel)

Henny and Selma came from Germany in the late 1920's and were already working in the baby's department for a long time when I arrived in Arcadia in 1940.

Henny Metzger (nee Kaufman)

Henny was a strong character and it seems she gave the orders. Selma was quiet, unassuming and sweet-natured. Henny too was likeable and treated the Babies well. They had a brother Benno who was a hunchback, and played the violin. He often came to the Arc to visit his sisters.

At the time there were no less than 35 children all under the age of six and as young as two years old. There was just one maid to help. These babies were to be bathed daily dressed in the mornings teeth brushed, and hair combed. Many of them still needed to be fed. Imagine all these children and they were always clean and tidy. These sisters worked very hard and slept in a room next to the baby dormitory.

On a Saturday morning the Babies in their Shabbat clothing would be brought to Shul for one hour of the Service. After Shul the Babies would be taken for a long walk and I invariably joined them. One occasion sticks in my memory: I was holding Solly Farber's hand as he was walking with a calliper. Solly' sister Flora about eight or nine years old came along and slapped my hand away and said to me "He is my brother not yours."

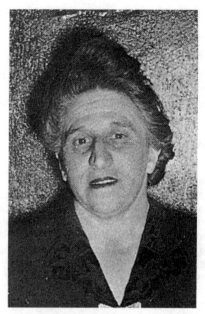
Selma Lehman (nee Kaufman)

I often went to the Baby Department of an evening to help put them to bed. I cannot claim that I was either smitten with children or that I was looking to be helpful. I was just very lonely. I had not made any special friend and everyone else seemed to have their friends. I remember also seeing Sister Goldwater being in the Babies' dining room to check on them regularly.

Selma was a Mrs Lehman and her sister Henny a Mrs Metzger. Henny and Selma would get off one Sunday a month and spend the day visiting their respective husbands.

Mr Metzger had a son Gunther in Arcadia who in 1940 would have been a Bar-Mitzvah boy. Gunther who later called himself George was a very nice person and in later years became a printer and lived in Brakpan until he and their family emigrated to Texas U.S.A.

After Henny and Selma retired they shared a flat in Yeoville. In later years after Henny passed away Selma went to Sandringham Gardens where she lived until her passing at the age of 95. Ekie Litvin (Levine) was in the babies with the Kaufman's and also in later years Ekie used to visit Selma on a Sunday morning and often took her out when she was at Sandringham Gardens. Selma was always very particular in her dress and fussed about how she looked.

Many of the boys and girls of Arcadia remember both Henny and Selma with nostalgia as both sisters were taking the place of a mother.

Chapter 60 - SISTER E GOLDWATER
At Arcadia 1932-1947

Sister Ethel Goldwater came from Ireland and she was initially employed in 1932 as Sister in the Wolf Hillman hospital.. It is an educated guess that her original name was Goldwasser and was Anglicised to Goldwater.

On the death of Rachel Shaer in 1937 she was promoted to Matron, a role she continued after Louis Shaer left and almost all of the time while Mordechai Harary was superintendent.

SISTER E GOLDWATER
Extracted from the 1961 *Arcadian*

It was a great shock and sad loss to all Arcadians, present and past, to hear of the passing away of Sister Goldwater - a great lady - matron over a period of 15 years who left Arcadia in 1946. She started her work at Arcadia as a Nursing Sister and then took on the onerous and responsible position of Matron, which position she filled with great distinction and capability and endeared her to all who came into contact with her. A lady of great integrity and understanding. She will be greatly missed by all who knew her.

SISTER GOLDWATER
By Freda Cheilyk (Koppel)

Ethel Goldwater was a trained hospital Sister and her only brother was a Doctor. She was tall and a very refined and dignified lady. We used to refer to her as Polly behind her back because of her long nose. When we girls would gather in the cloakroom which opened onto her balcony we would think nothing of discussing her, when suddenly Sister would appear.

I remember Sister doing the rounds of the Hospital as well as the baby department. Sister was pleasant but always aloof. She did not want to be called Matron out of respect to Mrs Rachel Shaer so she was always known to us as Sister Goldwater and she lived in the suite of rooms as one walked up the white marble staircase

On Friday nights we would have the privilege of gathering in Sister Goldwater's lounge and just have an informal chat. I recollect when Sister was away on holiday and Mrs Harary replaced her in her duties. The Friday nights spent with Judith Harary had a warmth that we never felt with Sister Goldwater. Sister Goldwater remained a spinster

MATRON - SISTER GOLDWATER.
MPerry. 2005

SISTER GOLDWATER
By Bertha Kronenberg (Klevansky)

Sister Goldwater first came to Arcadia as a nursing sister at the hospital. There she was with her white uniform and flowing white veil, efficient and helpful. I never got to know her well. I think she found me somewhat tiresome with some of my wild ways, jumping down a flight of five steps, whistling all the time. She too, I think, believed one should behave properly - she was always known as "Sister Goldwater" even when she assumed the role of Matron.

SISTER GOLDWATER
By Mabel Brittany)

Having turned 12 years, I now had become a Senior Girl. Here the Matron in charge was Sister Goldwater who had been with the Seniors a long time. She was both respected and loved by many of the girls.

Chapter 61 – MORDECHAI AND JUDITH HARARY
At Arcadia 1938-1948

In 1938 Mordechai Harary was appointed as Assistant Superintendent to Stompie Shaer and in 1943, on Stompie Shaer's retirement, Mordechai became the Superintendent. During this period Sister Goldwater remained the Matron of Arcadia.

Mordechai was referred to as "Cop" Harary by the children as he walked around with a whistle, and when he blew it you had to stop dead.

The Hararys resigned in 1948 and they where followed by Archie and Maggie Harris

A TRIBUTE TO MORDECHAI HARARY
Extracted from Arcadia Supplement to the SA Jewish Times, Friday March 7, 1986

We record with deep sadness the death of Mr M Harary a former superintendent and lifelong friend of Arcadia and Arcadians.

Mr Harary came to South Africa from Palestine (as it was then). He first served with Louis Shaer as his assistant, and when Mr Shaer retired succeeded him as the director of the Home.

The years of his tenure of office were Arcadia's golden years. The number of children under his care in Arcadia ran to hundreds and were an energetic bunch of kids.

Mordechai Harary was a disciplinarian who managed to impose his authority with warmth and love rather than with a big stick. His love for the Jewish faith and tradition was so vivid that he imbued us, his charges, with the same zeal.

He had had a background in agriculture and likewise gave us a feeling for the earth and for growing things. The beautiful palm trees growing outside our Shul were planted by him and will forever remain living reminders of a wonderful man.

As master of the home his duties included supervising the Arcadia Hebrew School. To attend a class of his when he recounted the epic tales from the Bible was a pleasure beyond telling. He could make the characters really spring to life. His explanations of the weekly Torah readings in the Shul were just as thrilling.

To generations of Arcadians he was "Cop" Harary, possibly because he carried a police whistle on his person and used it when necessary to summons anyone within hearing distance or to issue a mild rebuke to any evident wrongdoers.

After leaving Arcadia in 1949 he founded his own "ulpan". The ulpan Harary, which in time became famous in Johannesburg. After a life time of service to our Jewish youth he retired with his charming wife, Imma (as we called her) to Israel.

Mordechai Harary

In recent years the Hararys made frequent visits to Johannesburg. No sooner would they be settled in their flat in Berea than the Old Arcs would stream in to pay their respects to their beloved mentor.

On December 7 1985 a get together was held by the Arcadians to celebrate Mr Harary's 80th birthday. They came in droves, the old boys and girls, to be with him and proudly to show him their kids. It was a nostalgic afternoon for those who were there and must have made him very happy. Sadly it was that evening that he passed away. Somehow it seems so fitting that his last day was spent surrounded by Arcadians whom he knew and loved so well, and who had been so deeply influenced by his tutelage.

Cop Harary has passed on but, his kids will never forget him.

LETTER TO HARARY'S DAUGHTER ILANA
Written by Freda Cheilyk (Koppel)

The following is related by Freda Cheilyk in a letter to the Harary's daughter, Ilana, who was born at Arcadia.

"Your parents worked hard and your poor brother Zohar had a hard time. The children did not befriend him because he was the Hararys' son and they were in charge of us. Your parents then got Zohar to also eat with the boys in their dining room which must have been very hard on him. They tried their best to make things right but it did not work. However when you were born they moved into the Cottage on 22A Oxford Road so at least your life could be made easier. I left Arcadia in December 1943 and only remember you as a one year old baby, being wheeled on the driveway.

Your parents were always very pro Israel. Your Aba in his great pride at the establishment of the Jewish State, made a decision to hoist the Israeli flag on the birth of the State of Israel. He gave the honour to five boys who had celebrated their Barmitzvot that year. This caused a conflict with some of the committee who did not want any pro-Israel activity at the Arc.

The saga of the flag goes on. At one of the tea parties we had, I remember Elli Osrin's wife relating the following story. Elli's wife's name is Sarah - the same as Dr Mannie Osrin's wife. Elli and Sarah were visiting Israel and went to visit the Diaspora Museum in Tel Aviv. While Elli wandered off, Sarah recognised a picture of Elli holding the Israeli Flag on the day of Independence outside the main Arcadia building. She called Elli over who confirmed same. You can imagine how all the people in the museum stopped to listen to this.

On Sunday mornings we had Girl Guides, Brownies, Boy Scouts and Cubs. Once a week we also had St. Johns where we learned First Aid. Your husband's uncle Harry Ostroff used to take the boys for this and his fiancé Golda would accompany him. Of course you cannot remember anything if you were so young when your parents left after they resigned in 1948.

There were a few people who sided with your parents and helped them when they left Arcadia. In their first year they lived in Honey Street, Berea. Your Mom taught Hebrew at King David and your dad taught Barmitzvah boys their portions.

After Honey Street, they opened the Ulpan Harary in Observatory, which catered to boys and girls of mostly wealthy Jews from the various small country towns and farming communities whose parents wanted them to have a Jewish education.

As King David School had become established but had no hostel, Ulpan Harary filled the gap by providing a place to live, Kosher food and a couple who had proven themselves in the upbringing of school going children. The Hararys would call in a doctor when needed, buy them clothes and were aware when a child needed extra lessons and provided same. For all those parents this extra care left them free of concern.

When my brother Hymie Koppel was at University, in order to earn some money he used to give extra lessons to the children at Ulpan Harary.

Many ex-Arcadians would regularly visit them in Observatory and later were always visiting when your parents came to South Africa from Israel. Alec Saul and Hymie Koppel were amongst your mother's regular visitors in her latter years.

The Hararys returned to Israel in 1972 and Ilana and her family made Aliyah in 1974. Mordechai passed away in Johannesburg in 1985 the day after a party celebrating his 82nd birthday which many ex-Arcadians attended. Yehudit passed away in Israel in 2000, at the age of 88."

THE LATE 'COP' HARARY
Written by Woolfie Getz

'Cop' Harary was quite different from 'Stompie' Shaer. For starters, he was a much younger man who had his family with him at Arcadia. His children were with him at Arcadia and they were growing up with the kids in the Arc. I know that he had to use the cane pretty often and he had to move with the changing times. I think he took more notice of the kids growing up in the Arc. Testimony of this is born out by the fact that he remained friends with a number of the kids after they had left Arcadia. I know that he and the late Mrs Harary often visited my family when they would in later years come to Johannesburg. There were many times that he would visit me in the pharmacy, and he and Mrs Harary would come and have dinner with us. When they came to dinner with us they were made to be the parents by placing them at the top of the table. The late Mr and Mrs Harary, I think, took far more interest in the children.

Mordechai and Judith Harary

MORDECHAI AND JUDITH HARARY
Written by Bertha Klevansky (Kronenberg)

It was in the mid thirties that I first remember this young Israeli couple, very different from Louis and Rachel Shaer. Whereas my memories of the first ten years of my stay in Arcadia seemed to be very English-orientated, Girl Guides etc. the young Israeli couple brought a whiff of change in the mid-thirties.

The staidness of the Shaers was replaced by a different era as I saw it. This occurred on many levels, the social was very important.

There was always a strict division between the sexes. This was eased somewhat when we were encouraged to organise tournaments between us – table tennis comes to mind. I think lectures that both boys and girls attended bordered on sex in a very discreet manner.

I do remember approaching them about introducing extra ingredients in our food, items such as fresh fruit which we seldom enjoyed. I noticed too the palms being planted on the side of the driveway – plants that as they grew enhanced the grounds.

Mordechai and Judith Harary and the children.

Shul services also changed. Instead of the Ashkenazi pronunciation of Hebrew we learnt the Sephardic. We learnt to dance the Hora and I became very aware of the Zionist dream and the state that was still to be established.

I knew that the boys referred to Mr Harary as Cop but I considered him and Mrs Harary as good friends and many a time we were invited to their quarters. I felt as if somebody was taking a personal interest in me, and that I was being treated as an individual.

As the Godfather of my youngest son I was to continue my association with him and his family – remembering with great respect the Ulpan he established in Observatory, and his excellence in Agriculture.

He was a man of many talents and Mrs Harary, a loving and gentle person

A POEM "ARCADIA"
By Mordechai Harary
From the Commemorative Bulletin of Arcadia's 75th Jubilee

You are Home to many children, present and past.
Arcadia, you must forever last and last
Arcadia

You are both Father and Mother
Forlorn children find in your precincts sister and brother
Arcadia

You have given rise to many stalwart citizens
Of our South African Jewish population.
Arcadians represent a creditable cross section of artisans,
businessmen, doctors, nurses and lawyers.
here are even among them Tom Sawyers.
Arcadia

You are quite well represented in Israel,
In Kibbutzim, Moshavim and in the valley of Jezreel.
Arcadia

Your sons and daughters' motto is to render service
A marked percentage serve on public committees.
An Arcadian can even officiate at any Shabbat or Festive Service
Arcadia

Congratulations on reaching Seventy-Five
Your open portals have saved many a life
Arcadia

A veritable Garden of Eden, for needy Yiddishe Kinder a true Haven
And He who saveth a life, young or old, is as if he saved a whole world.

Chapter 62 – ARCHIE AND MAGGIE HARRIS
At Arcadia 1948-1952

UNANSWERED QUESTIONS
Written by David Kotzen

The story I write about is one I rarely repeat. Almost 40 years have passed and I still don't know the answer. Those of us who lived those years with the Harris family quickly learned what "hell was like". I believe the dilemma the Harris family experienced in the daily running of Arcadia, was due to their assumption that the same ground rules they utilised in England would work in South Africa. The plausibility of entertaining the notion "when in Rome do as the Romans do" was never an option. Discipline was considered the absolute necessity for all problems. Unequivocally, no deviation from this principle would be acceptable. If rules were disobeyed, punishment would follow immediately. Sometimes the punishment meant being turned away from the dining table. Expulsion from the dinner table often included being late by a few minutes.

There are many stories (some in all probability worse than mine) Arcs can tell about their different experiences with the Harris family. I will relate only two. The latter left a physiological scar that endured with me for years until adulthood.

I reckon we were about 12 years old when a few of us decided to "bunk out and go to Ellis Park to watch the cricket. The Springboks must have been doing very well for we were obviously unaware of the time. Once we concluded how late we would be, we realised punishment would follow. Archie Harris used a tactic that completely threw us off guard. "So boys what was the score when you left", in unison we all blurted out the score. "Report to my office in 15 minutes". The punishment assuredly was a caning.

I devised a plan, I would borrow about five pairs of pants, I figured this would create a bullet-proof effect. My major mistake was not pretending to be hurt when Harris lifted his cane to me. He quickly concluded what I had done, and proceeded to whack me on the legs, arms, and face area. I begged him to stop, which seemed like an eternity. It took me a long time to recover my injuries. In retrospect, I must confess I was not an easy kid. I hated the Harris family, and did everything in my power to show my resentment- including not showing up for my Barmitzvah celebration.

One day, Archie Harris called me into his office. I figured "Okay" another caning". He went on to make clear that I was not a well-behaved child and was causing many problems to him and Mrs Harris. They decided if I did not rectify my behaviour immediately, my brother, Woolfie would be sent away to a reform school. I couldn't believe they were using my brother to discipline me for my behaviour. I recall how shattered I felt, aware that my actions could be used against my brother. I lost part of myself in that office that day.

These stories are the ones that made a significant impression with me during the Harris tenure. As a result, it is extremely difficult to comprehend what motivated me to visit them in England. I arrived in England a 20-year-old man and decided to seek out the Harris family. Perhaps I was trying to say, "Well Archie and Maggie Harris, I've come to show you that, indeed, I had become a well-adjusted young man", or maybe, I felt I wanted to forgive them the anguish they had caused me as a youth.

I recall so vividly knocking on the door and Archie Harris looking at me in such dismay and disbelief. He yelled, "Mrs Harris, you will never believe who has come to see us". I remember they both had tears in their eyes. After a short visit, I walked away never looking back, much in the same way that Lot had done in the Bible. I never visited them again; I never made inquires about them; I just walked away. To this day, the question of why I went to visit them remains a mystery to me.

CHAPTER 63 - CHARLIE AND DOLLY MILLER AND FAMILY AT ARCADIA 1928-1969

Charlie Miller would be well known by all Arc children who were in the Arc between 1928 and 1958.

He passed away suddenly in 1958 after being our friendly bus driver and part of the Arc family for over 30 years.

Charlie was married to Dolly and they lived for many decades in the little cottage next to the cow stable. Dolly was in charge of the laundry and continued to live in the house for many many years after Charlie died.

They had an older daughter Doreen, a daughter called Funu and two sons Eddie and Willie (Miggie) who sometimes played soccer with us on Saturday mornings.

Above Dolly's house was a loft full of pigeons. She gave us some, which we kept in hoks when we were in the Junior Boys.

CHARLIE MILLER'S DEATH
A tribute to Charlie by Freddie Lichtigfeld (Doc's Son)
From 1959 Arcadian

I heard of Charlie's death. I can't get over it - I still see the man tell me: 'Not so fast, Freddie, not so fast - you will get there in time'.

He always gave me a feeling of being so solid and long-lasting, and what he used to tell me of his life made me understand him as a human being. His roots were very deep in the Arc, and his natural loyalty, good sense and hard work in serving the Arc, not as a servant, but as part of the family. A driver is always a thing of excitement and imagination to little children, and for the thousands of Arcs, Charlie drove hundred of thousands, perhaps millions, of miles, always safely, always friendly. He must form part of the unforgettable web of memories that an Arc has of Arcadia. His life, his habits, his stories, his accents, his horses, his idiosyncrasies, will be recounted for years and years, and I am sure to many - I will be one of them - he'll always be an unforgettable character.

CHARLEY MILLER

The Arc Bus by Michael Perry Kotzen

A TRAGEDY IN ARCADIA
From 1959 Arcadian

It was indeed a sad day for us when we heard that Charlie Miller, our bus driver had passed away.

It seems strange now for us to look at the driver's seat in the bus, and not to see Charlie's face or hear his quick and ready laughter. Charlie had been with us for a very long time, over 30 years. Charlie saw boys and girls mature from Babies to Juniors and, so on to Seniors. Boys and girls who had left and had their own children have always come back to see him.

How well we can all remember laughing and joking with him on the way to school and hear the familiar little sayings, 'Cockys' riding Moses' and 'H-e-l-e-v-a Jack' which will forever be associated with him.

In all Charlie's many years of faithful service, he was always punctual, no matter whether it was to take us to school in the early morning, or to fetch us late at night after going to a theatre or concert and thank God, which is most important of all, he never had an accident.

To his widow Dolly, his daughter Doreen and sons Eddy and Wilie, we extend our deepest sympathies on their sad bereavement. We sincerely hope that they will be consoled by the fact that Charlie was a wonderful man. He was loved by each and every child who ever lived in the Arc. He will never be forgotten.

REMEMBERING CHARLIE AND THE OLD ARC BUS
A tribute to Charlie by Audrey Shraga
Written by David Sandler

Charlie Miller was the bus driver who used to drive us to school when I started Jewish Government School in 1957. He drove the old Mac Arc bus (the Black Maria) with the bulldog in the front on the bonnet.

I remember on one occasion pointing out to Charlie a handicapped person who was driving a funny contraption on the road and then laughing. Later on Brenda Scopp told me that it was not a nice thing to laugh at the handicapped. This was at a time when Charlie was not actually driving the bus but was showing the new driver Christopher (Dice) the ropes.

On the bus we would have competitions to see if you could stand without holding on when the bus was driving along and we would often kneel on the bench and look out the windows and watch the world rushing by. I remember one day on the bus Jenny was slapping me and I was crying and Bessie suggested I hit Jenny back. I did this. I gave her a punch on the lips and she started to cry. I was very upset too. The final outcome was that she never hit me again.

240

Chapter 64 – OTHER STAFF

MRS HAMMERSCHLAG
Written by Freda Cheilyk (Koppel)

Mrs Hammerschlag was a refugee from Germany and a dignified and cultured lady. In the 1930s with so many refugees and not being able to speak English, most people were only too happy to get work.

Mrs Hammerschlag was the Housekeeper at Arcadia and I always remember her with her big bunch of keys. She occupied a room upstairs where the Senior Girls slept. She was a cheerful but strict lady and had the pleasure of 300 hungry children to feed. We were always looking for food and had no problem stealing anything we could find that was not locked away.

I remember the bread pudding being our Sunday night supper. Friday night was always fried fish, mashed potatoes and spinach. Sunday lunch was meat and I seem to remember we even got jelly. For our school lunches it seems we always got jam on the bread and on a Friday we had the good fortune to get Polony sandwiches

Mrs Hammerschlag took ill around 1941 and was unable to return to work.

GIRL GUIDES AND SCOUTS TEACHERS

SOPHIE HURWITZ
Written by Freda Cheilyk (Koppel)

This lady was our Girl Guides teacher when I arrived. A lovely person and I remember being taught all those special things like tying a knot, and to light a fire and there was lots of singing. In later years Miss Hurwitz worked in the Arcadia office.

Some time around 1970 I remember having seen Miss Hurwitz waiting for a bus so I stopped my car and offered her a lift home. This was the last time I saw her.

QUEENIE ISRAEL (NEE FRIEDLAND)
Written by Freda Cheilyk (Koppel)

This lovely lady was the Cubs teacher and when she was leaving them to get married, the little boys collected their sixpences and bought her a weekend case which she has kept all these years.

Queenie now lives in the Cape. I had the privilege of meeting up with this lovely lady, when she was on a visit to Brisbane. I immediately remembered her as the very pretty blonde lady who was at Arcadia every Sunday.

FANNY NERWICH
Written by Freda Cheilyk (Koppel)

One other special person was Fanny Nerwich. Fanny was deaf but she used to take the Brownies on a Sunday morning and loved to sing and taught the little girls songs. Fanny always worked and earned a living. Her married name was Dick and when her husband got ill and they had no phone as they would not hear it ring as he too was deaf. They both went to Sandringham Gardens and died there. There was also Mr Chait the shoemaker who was in Arcadia for donkeys years fixing all our shoes.

DANIEL CHAIT - Served Arcadia 1927-1965
Extracted from 1970 Arcadia Bulletin

We mourned too, the death of Mr Daniel Chait a former employee who at the time of his retirement, in 1965, had served Arcadia faithfully and well for 38 years.

Written by Solly Farber

"Whenever we had visitors to Arcadia they would remark about the beauty of the gardens. One man, Mr Chait, was responsible for this. He had worked for many years to bring the gardens to a state of perfection."

Sketch of Mr Chait by Michael Perry Kotzen

PERCY COWAN - Served Arcadia 1924-1956
From 1961 Arcadia Bulletin

It is with deep sadness that we refer to the passing of Mr Percy Cowen, a former Secretary of Arcadia, who retired in 1956 after 32 years of devoted service and who had been elected an

Honorary Life Member of the Institution in appreciation of his devotion and long service.

OTHER STAFF
Written by Bertha Kronenberg (Klevansky)

We had a variety of people in charge of us. There was one Molly Cohen (a former Arc girl herself) who looked after the Juniors. There was the strict Lulu Le Roux who was very, very strict and tried to restrain our boisterous behaviour en masse punishing all of us for the misbehaviour of an individual. There was a Miss Nelson who comforted me when I lost my father.

Back row: 1940 Staff – Molly Cohen and Zellie and Henny Kaufman
Front row: Miss Le Roux Junior ? Miss Nelson and Josie Le Roux

MOLLY COHEN
By Solly Farber

Molly Cohen grew up in the Arc and then later on she became a nurse in the Arc and looked after the kids. Her great thrill was to bet on the Durban July and she would put all of one pound on a horse. When it came to getting the results she would disappear because the anxiety was a bit too much for her so off she would go down to the zoo. Apparently there were two boys waiting for her on the corner to tell her the results that her horse had won.

One was oolfie Kotzen and the other one I don't know. While they were sitting there on the corner waiting a car on Oxford Road ran out of control, mounted the pavement and hurt Woolfie very badly and it was apparently blamed on her because of her *meshugas* that the kids had to wait for her there.

PROFESSOR WORTHINGTON
Written by Heinz(Hank) Epstein

I remember Prof. Worthington very well. Between 1936 until he passed away, (I was seven in 1936), I spent many an afternoon

with him .I would fill and light his pipe and he would read stories to me. I recall one book, *The Elephant's Child*, which I particularly enjoyed. There was the story about how the elephant got its trunk, *The Cat who Walked by himself* (and made an enemy of the dog), and about a dog named Dingo. Prof. Worthington would sing some of the parts of each story.

He always had bottles of seeds which he gave to anyone interested in gardening. Jacob Kemp and I often went to the professor for seeds and advice.

Although he was not Jewish, on High Holy Days he would attend Shul services, dressed in a professor's gown and cap. He sat in front of the dais I don't recall him living in a cottage down the hill, but he had a room under the grapevine near the hospital. I never understood why he was not taken into the hospital when he became ill. I recall the day he passed away because on the previous day, he called my name as I passed by his room. He asked me to get him some water. It really upset me to see how little care he was given. He would take long walks and particularly liked to go to the zoo. Jacob and I often accompanied him. He taught us much about animals.

AUNTIE GEENBLATT THE SCOUTMASTER.

"Auntie Geenblatt for many years was the Scoutmaster.

Chapter 65 - THE ARCADIAN (THE CHILDREN'S MAGAZINE)

The Arcadian was a magazine written by the children themselves. While it had a very modest beginning in 1949, over the years it grew into a sophisticated publication worthy of any association.

Initially it included articles written by the children and staff and letters from dignitaries connected with the Arc and later it included articles and letters from Old Arcs and Committee Members and others associated with the Arc.

The Arcadian is a treasure trove of Arc history and keeps alive not only the events of the day but also the children, many who would now have children and grandchildren and many who would have sadly passed away.

While the 1949 and 1951 editions appear to have been just run off on plain paper the 1955 editions and those following were professionally completed and printed editions with beautiful brightly coloured covers.

In these later editions one can see the invisible hand of Doc and his influence and encouragement at work through the editors over the years and also through his son Freddy who for many years edited the 'Post Box'.

Extracts from these publications follow.

THE ARCADIAN – THE CHILDREN'S MAGAZINE
Extracts from the February 1949 *Arcadian*

This was the very first edition of the *Arcadian* consisting of 11 pages and edited by Bernard Aronstam and Morris Farber

EDITORIALS Vol I, No 1   February 1949 – Shevat 5709

The Editors greet you with a new venture in the life of Arcadia; namely a Magazine. History records that the Scout Troup once published a magazine; but the present issue is the first of its kind. Errors will of course be found; but as time goes on these will be rectified – as far as possible. All suggestions for improvement will be welcome.

This, the first issue, includes quizzes, competitions and items of interest. Contributions in the form of articles, stories, sayings, jokes etc are invited from everyone – big and small, and if approved will be published.

There will also be columns for readers' views and questions about sport.

The editors trust you will enjoy this first number and make further issues possible by your contributions.

Birthdays

Many happy returns of the month - Bertha Aires, Leah Berer, Holda Ellis, Solly Farber, Louis Moris, Eli Osrin, Judy Nochumsohn.

'Arcadia' Broadcast

Hullo!   Hullo!   Hullo!   This is Arcadia calling

Forest Town School - has finally closed down, and our children now attend Jewish Government and Doornfontein Schools.

Sydney (Vicky) Klevansky - an old Arcadian, is back in Arcadia. We extend a hearty welcome to him.

Cricket – After much arduous work, Mr VN Hepker, who will be coming to coach the boys, has succeeded in having nets put up. Much improvement will be shown after a few months at the nets.

Back to School – After an enjoyable holiday at Camp, many of the boys and girls were sorry to be back at school. However, we settled down quickly and everything is returning to normal.

The Pigeons – Thanks are due to Sister for her much needed help in looking after the pigeons, whilst we were at Camp.

St John's – Before the holidays, the under teen girls had inspection by Mrs A A Hopkins. The report is not yet out. Parades for all have again started. The seniors don't seem to be greatly interested. We wonder why?

Dancing Class – for girls, under the direction of Miss Sackheim, has restarted on Sunday mornings. We look forward to a spectacular display shortly.

Boxing – Donald Goldman, our instructor, is struggling valiantly to keep his team together. Seniors, Juniors, you must support him!

Swimming – The Gala just before holidays is described on another page. Among the spectators were Mr and Mrs Sam Bartlett, who are now giving instruction every Sunday afternoon.

Message From President of the Jewish Orphanage

My dear Children, I am delighted at the opportunity of sending your first Arcadia Bulletin a message of goodwill.

It is significant that the issue comes with the New Year and with the successful conclusion of a well-enjoyed holiday. This year has seen great changes in the history of our Jewish People; and with the State firmly established and recognised by almost the entire world, we can all look forward with hope to one day visiting or perhaps settling in the Land of our dreams.

I want to congratulate all those who conceived the idea of issuing this Bulletin, thereby giving each and every one the opportunity of expressing their views on the various aspects of the Home as well as School, Sport and Social activities.

It is my hope and the hope of every member of my committee that you will all continue to enjoy good health and uphold the excellent reputation of Arcadia, to which you are all contributing, and your Bulletin shall be a link between you and other groups of children in South Africa and aborad.

Sincerely yours - *Harry Cohen*

Junior Swimming Gala

The presence of children, parents, friends and members of the Committee, transformed Arcadia Swimming Baths into a hive of activity on Sunday, 28th November 1948, when the Junior Swimming Gala was held. The two houses participating were Maccabi – Captain Joey Klug, and Bar Cochba – Captain Solly Farber.

The program of events was varied, and included such items as Walking the Breadth, Swimming the Length, Under water Swimming, Back Stroke, Breast Stroke, Diving, Long Jump and Relay Race. The Pyjama Race was the most humorous event and the final items were an Old Boys and Girls Race, and Water Polo.

The trophy was won by Maccabi House with a total number of 98 points, Bar Cochba having attained 62.

Thus a very enjoyable and successful afternoon ended off with the presentation of prizes and trophies by Mrs Harris to successful competitors. The Cup for the best performance – boys, was won by Joey Klug, and the one for the girls by Sarah Farber.

Our thanks are due to all participants and to those who so ably assisted. Our hope is that in the very near future a similar gala will be arranged by seniors. - *Vicky*

Arcadia Hebrew School

New term began on Sunday, January 23rd with an Assembly in the School. The examiner at the Annual Examinations at the end of last term was highly satisfied with the standard of work of the pupils, particularly with the correctness of the writing.

Best attendances last term were as follows:

Grade I	Yechiel Bortz	Grade II	Ann Gordon
Std I	Shirley Bortz	Std II	Mervyn Harris
Std IV	Bella Bortz	Std V	Colin Rosenkowitz
Std VI	Shifra Bortz		

Emulate their example and be equally awarded

Arcadian Boxing Club

The highlight of the Junior Boxing Tournament held at Arcadia was undoubtedly the exhibition bout by Alf James, then Welterweight Champion of South Africa, an old boy of the Orphanage.

Before the tournament commenced, Alf James talked on clean sportsmanship, etc.

The tournament was held in the main dining hall, and was attended by a large number of parents and old boys. Searching

around the spectators, we found such prominent boxing personalities as Harry Ralston, Bunny Barlin, Harry Isaacs and Joe Siegenberg.

The tournament provided some enjoyable fights, although the absence of the senior boys was noticeable; more will be expected of them in the future. A fight well worthy of mention was that between Woolfie Kotzen and Ruben Lipschitz. Ruben gave a game display and was eventually awarded the Cup for the best loser. However, Woolfie's hard hitting earned him the decision. Another enjoyable fight was that between Jerry Levy and Joe Klug. Jerry's orthodox stance and footwork earned him a well deserved decision, although Joe was always in the picture.

Prizes were distributed by Mrs Harris, who congratulated the winners of cups, etc. The tournament ended on a successful note and all thanks are due to Donald Goldman who was the organiser.

If Boxing at Arcadia is to live up to the reputation which we have already gained, boys must be encouraged to join. The addition of proper facilities and better attendance by members would be steps in the right direction.

'Arcadia' Under Habonim Canvas

With the hectic preparations at Arcadia for new term at school, one would have thought that holidays were entirely a matter of a dim past. But the first spark of the Camp Fire held in the grounds of Arcadia the other evening, rekindled the holiday spirit. Indeed, recaptured in a flash, the comradeship of the three weeks of camping with Habonim. For three weeks we lived and learned that individual happiness and individual fulfilment can be achieved by living a co-operative life; by taking an active share in every essential activity of the groups. A grand experience, but not unique for Young Arcadia: Daily life here is Home life; a family life of co-operative effort.

It was a Sunday morning, 19th December 1948, that they went off to camp. And hence one may permit a retrospection. On the Monday morning, there was a hollow emptiness at Arcadia. Except for the shrill echoing voices of a few infants and the cooing pigeons, Arcadia was deserted.

On that Sunday morning the 'over nines' went off to camp. After a short period of a few weeks of intense preparation, 54 boys and girls of the SA Jewish Orphanage went off to camp with the Habonim at Nahoon. Preparation meant the making of garments, measuring up for skirts and shirts, for *tackies* and macintoshes, etc, etc. The marking of thousands of articles, literally meant the organisation of teams of children equipped with bottles of marking ink and uncountable yards of tape. It is a satisfaction to know that a great deal of the preparation was accomplished by the children. Arcadia was a hive of industry, centring round Matron's room which presented a veritable warehouse scene.

At last Sunday morning, 19th December arrived and by 10.30 am every boy and girl was dressed in the appropriate uniform of the age group; Hashtilim with green scarf and beret: and the Habonim with blue scarf and blue beret. Assembled in the forecourt of the Main House, they were given a warm send-off by many members of the Committee. Cameras clicked, refreshments for the journey distributed, the 54 campers boarded the Arcadia bus to join the rest of the 500 Johannesburg Habonim at the railway station.

Three weeks of camp at Nahoon Beach came to an end too quickly. Three weeks crowded with new and refreshing experiences; new friends, new ideas of Jewish life and Jewish struggle, Jewish hope and Jewish fulfilment.

Tuesday afternoon, 11th January, platform 4 is again crowded with anxious, eager and impatient parents: The Habonim Special steaming in 'on the dot' at 1.49 pm. The sun tanned, freckled faces of our children wore a look of internal contentment, although of physical tiredness. Luggage collected, sleeping bags trailing along to an appointed spot on the platform, young Arcadia was ready for the last stage of homeward bound. They boarded the bus singing, singing through the town, and continued lustily the Hebrew songs they had learned at camp. Back again to Arcadia, where a refreshing tea awaited them and a welcome from the President and all members of staff. Enriched by the experience, they look forward with impatient anticipation to Camp 1949.

Extracts From C Camp Diary

Monday – We got up extra early to make our tent look very neat. Ozzie, one of the Madoichim, took inspection. He found a feather on the floor, so he gave it to us for cleanliness. We went to the beach in the morning. In the afternoon we finished building our Maon. Everyone in the Shevet was very proud of it.

Saturday – Had School. Then went to the beach. After lunch, rested 'till 4 o'clock. Had an Oneg Shabat. After supper had a fancy dress.

Monday, 10th January – I was very sad because Camp had ended … When the buses came I began to cry … I kissed some of the Cape Town people 'goodbye', but I just could not kiss my Madrich goodbye. I didn't want to leave her … Then we left for the station. I was crying in the bus.

Back From Camp

On the 11th of January we came back from Camp, after having had a glorious time. We all miss now the Camp fires and other camp activities we enjoyed so much.

At camp we learnt many songs and dances and many other interesting things. We also made many new friends. We are very sorry to come back from camp, and to go back to school is even worse. We thank Mr and Mrs Harris and our House-mothers who helped us go to camp, and hope we will go again in the future. - *Solly Farber*

A Memorable Friday Evening

On Friday evening, January 28th, Zvi and Batya from Habonim Camp came to pay us a visit and have supper with us. After supper we had a medurah.

First we all sang a few Hebrew songs. Then some girls danced Palestinian dances. Mr Harris also sang a song. Then we danced a 'Yadanu' in which everyone joined. We ended the sing-song with taps, followed by Hatikvah.

Then everyone said: Goodbye to Zvi and to Batya as they are going to Aretz and getting married in March.

Good luck to all of them, and as we say in Habonim, Chazak Ve-ematz. - *Solly Farber*

Camp Fire

A very enjoyable camp fire was held on the lawn of Arcadia on January 16th, the last Sunday night of the December holidays. It started at 8 o'clock and ended at 10. The opening ceremony was very impressive and the camp fire was dedicated to the State of Israel.

Songs were sung, individual items were given and games played. There was a short interval for refreshments. As the embers of the fire burnt low, we formed a large circle and danced the Horah. A very enjoyable evening ended with the singing of the national anthems and the Hatikvah. - *Woolfie Kotzen*

Just A Few Names!

As an old boy of Arcadia, I'm exceedingly pleased to see that at long last an attempt is being made by the children to produce a home magazine.

I have actually been asked to write about a few of the children – now no longer children – who have passed through Arcadia's care. One hardly knows where to begin on such a task. It's like asking a veteran of the ring to tell you of some of his fights.

Anyhow, to make things much simpler I'll just jot down a few items that have occurred of late. There's Myer Rubinowitz and Tilly Aires, now happily married, to whom go our very best wishes. Myer, by the way, is now a qualified teacher. Then, talking about teaching, we call to mind Vicky, who has also now qualified and who is helping out at Arcadia; and also Barney Meyers who is going into final year teaching. Barney got his half-blue last year for soccer, having represented the SA Universities. Congrats Barney! Then there's Joey Siegenberg who now, with a BSc degree in Anatomy goes into third year Medicine. Both Joey and Bunny Barlin, who is now a qualified engineer, have got their full blues for boxing. Congrats again! Samuel Adler is going into his final year at the Seminary and Bernard Klingman is also doing exceptionally well at the same place. Monty Koppel, studying law, has been making considerable progress and congratulations go to his brother Hymie who just recently got a 1st class pass in Matric, with three distinctions. So much for scholastic achievements.

Donald Goldman is doing good work for the Home, taking boxing every Sunday morning, and thanks go to Sam Bartlett for coaching the kids in swimming.

Our sincere good wishes and thoughts are for these of our old boys who have gone to Eretz to join Haganah or to settle in the Kibbutz. A few of the names that come to mind are, Solly Meyer, Phillip Kemp, Ralph Harris and Eli Zagoria. - *Mannie Osrin*

Extracts from the February 1951 *Arcadian*

This was the eighth edition, consisted of 23 pages and was edited by Phyllis Adler and Samuel Berer

EDITORIALS Vol I, No 8   February 1951 – Shevat 5711

Im Tirzu Ain Zu Agudah Dirchu Na Oz

The second birthday of *The Arcadian* is celebrated by this eighth issue. Two years ago this month, the Magazine made its first appearance in a 'new venture in the life of Arcadia' under the editorship of Bernard Aronstam and the late Morris Farber. Their hopes that further copies would be possible by your contributions have been partly fulfilled in that the Magazine becomes thicker in volume with every issue.

The last number appeared six months ago – a long time ago. So it is obvious that much that has happened has been omitted as 'dated'. Nevertheless, several phases of our life and doings have been included to justify our purpose to give a faithful reflection of the life of the Youth Community of Arcadia.

We would suggest your enjoyment of this number will be enhanced by testing your skill and knowledge in the competitions.

We take this early opportunity of wishing all readers a pleasant Pesach.

Birthdays - 'Yom Moledet Sa-Maiah'

Edmond Blumberg, Harry Jacob, Rose Bortz, Jeanette Sous, Leah Berer, Fay Fanaroff, Zelda Gordon, Cynthia Lipschitz, David Berman, Norman Sacks, Cyril Fanaroff, Solly Farber, Eli Osrin.

'Arcadia' Broadcast

Hullo!   Hullo!   Hullo!   This is Arcadia calling

The Family – Since we last broadcast, there have been goings and comings. Among those who have left the family circle are Bertha Aires, Joey Klug, Colin Rosenkowitz; Bertha and Joey are still at school and Colin has 'gone into the world' as an apprentice in the printing trade. Good luck! The family is larger – we are now 97.

School – With piles of new exercise books, new text books and new blazers and new time tables, term is in full swing. Everyone has started with a determination to do a year's good sound work and so make the 'excellent lists' much bigger. Congratulations to those who did very well:

Excellent	Very Good	
Benny Kreser	Gordon Cameron	Minnie Fanaroff
Fanny Blecher	Charlie Segal	Judith Berer
Jeffrey Esakov	David Berman	Shirley Bortz
Reuben Lipschitz	Norma Sacks	Yechiel Bortz
Solly Farber	Basil Sepel	Rose Bortz
Bella Bortz	Mirian Gordon	Morris Bortz
	Fay Fanaroff	Isla Sepel

Honours – David Kotzen has been made a Prefect at Doornfontein and Basil Sepel, Zelda Gordon and Fanny Blecher are Prefects at Jewish Government. Well done, Arcadians!

Boxing – At Parktown High School last term, Gerald Levy won his weight in the Inter House tournament. Jerry shows much promise. Benny Touyz and Zummy Isenberg reached the finals in their respective weights.

In response to our appeal for gloves, one reader has sent us a pair, and once again Vereeniging has come to the rescue, with four pairs. Excellent! Thank you very much. Donald, the coach, tells me that he still needs a couple of sets of 12 oz gloves. Any offers?

Cricket – There has so far been no cricket to speak of this term. Not one match has been played. This is a poor show. At the sports meeting which was held at the beginning of the season, it looked promising, with Gerald Levy, Captain Leon Klingman and Sammy Berer, Vicky, and Solly Farber, Manager. Admittedly we've had lots of rain. The Manager will be pleased to arrange matches with any outside teams

The Library – Since our last broadcast Miss Ethel Wix, the 'young lady silently working in the library' has completed her part of the job. She has gone through every book, prepared a catalogue, sorted the books, framed suggestions and rules. Now it is your job to use the books carefully, of course. To add to your comfort the promised lighting, carpets, curtains and arm chairs have been installed. Visitors to Arcadia are cordially invited to visit our library.

Hankies – A tickey a week! A suggestion from Matron is not only saving hankies and keeping tidy noses, but is adding a little income to the Junior boys and girls. Those who can produce a hanky every day for a whole week get a tickey. It has created much competition between the boys and girls and incidentally is quite good fun.

Football Medals – On the Sports Day, souvenir medals were given to the Junior Arcs Football team for having played two successful seasons, without losing a game. These medals were provided by Mr Albert Greenblatt. Old Arcadians will remember him with affection as their Scout Master Roxy.

Visitors – We were pleased to welcome a number of boys and girls from the Hope Home one Sunday morning. Several of our boys and girls acted as hosts and hostesses. Come again!

On Duty At Arcadia

An early morning ride along a magnificent drive lined with shady Jacarandas and waving palm fronds led me to an imposing building which could have easily masqueraded as a luxurious establishment at a fashionable resort. Was this really Arcadia? My first impression was indeed a good one and one which has continued right throughout my stay here. Although most of my time has been spent in the Baby Department, I have been able to experience something of the carefree, happy atmosphere which prevails among Arcadians.

During the mornings a sort of expectant hush hangs over the grounds. This is short-lived however and abruptly quietness is shattered by the first of the home-coming children. Soon the lawns are scattered with sun-tanned little figures clad in swim suits all heading in the general direction of the swimming bath. Every facility is provided for recreation both indoors and out-of-doors.

Perhaps the event which I shall remember longest was the Fancy Dress party organised for those who were not at camp. The laughter and shrieks arising from our preparations for this occasion were only surpassed by the uproar on 'the night' itself. Safety pins, cotton wool and masks flew in all directions. Excitement increased by the minute to reach a climax in the general stampede to the meeting place. The babies suddenly became shy, but with a little encouragement soon began to enjoy themselves with the rest. It was a most entertaining and enjoyable evening and one which I should like to experience again.

Finally a word to students: Be wise. Book early for your Practical at Arcadia! - *By Auntie Pam*

Third Annual Sports Day

Herzl Wins House Trophy

Amidst the delightful surroundings of garden and rockeries, which on Sunday afternoon, 5th November were bathed in summer sunshine, Arcadia held their Third Annual Sports Day on the spacious and carefully prepared Sports Ground.

The throng of visitors included parents and relatives of the children; members of the Committee, who took part in 'running the events' and many Old Arcadians, among whom were Basil Lipschitz and Myer Rubinowitz who recently took part in the Maccabi Games in Israel. The children turned out in full force, all appropriately attired, wearing their respective House Colours: Bialik with yellow ribbon and Herzl with blue ribbon. Each House was proudly captained: Herzl by Shifra Bortz and Eli Osrin and Bialik by Audrey Sepel and Leon Klingman. Judges, starters, announcers, recorders and competitors at their

respective places, and at approximately 2.00 pm the races began.

Event number one – Senior Boys Flat Race – was won by Herzl, who kept the lead right through; finally carrying off the laurels with 162 points against Bialik's 109.

Every competitor, although of course eager to win his or her prize, was more concerned with the honours of the House –

House loyalty reigned supreme; and to encourage the competitors, the groups lustily sang the House Cries, which were specially composed for the occasion by the more literary stalwarts of the House groups.

Space does not permit to give a detailed list of all winners; but the honours of scoring the highest points go to Audrey Sepel of Bialik and to Eli Osrin of Herzl, who were, later in the afternoon each presented with the 'Best Effort Cups', being the first recipients of these new trophies, kindly presented by Mr and Mrs D Stein.

The afternoon was tinged with sadness. A cup trophy given by his father, in memory of Morris Farber, was competed for in an open half-mile race and won by David Gordon, a senior boy and a friend of the deceased. To add further interest to this particular event, Myer Rubinowitz, the 10,000 metre champion of the Maccabi Games, ran with the boys.

Perhaps the most delightful racing event – though not of point value – was the Babies Race. They all took part, from the age of two to six years. Their house mother told how for days they had been putting on odd slippers and *tackies* and practising on the lawns.

After an interval for refreshments, the races were resumed: Obstacle, long jump, three legged and relay – all offering good sport and fun. And the events concluded with an Old Arcadian race round the course and lastly with a race for the African staff.

After a very delightful afternoon's sport and good fellowship, Mr Maurice Porter, President of the Jewish Orphanage, presented the trophies. He explained that the 'Harry Cohen House Trophy', not being ready, would later be handed to Herzl House, the victors of 1950.

The singing of Hatikvah concluded yet another memorable event in the life of Arcadia – the Third Annual Sports Meeting.

The Sports Day

On Sunday morning we were practising very hard because The Sports was taking place in the afternoon. It became quite crowded after a while, and then at last it came to the time when the Sports was about to begin. Vicky announced it through the mike. Well the first race was the Flat. Bella Bortz came first and so on. Well we had a lot of lovely races, specially the three-legged race, which was the most exciting of all. Refreshments at interval were served, after the obstacle race. Then before the babies ran, Mr Harris took photos of them.

At interval we had cold drinks and for the adults, tea served to them. Then we had the war cries of Bialik and Herzl; they were both very good, but I suppose we nearly broke the mike; but it was a very enjoyable day. It was great fun watching Myer Rubinowitz run, who gave them half the course start and afterwards caught them all up, and I felt very sorry when he cut his foot, but luckily Sister Benjamin was there with her First Aid. Only a few were hurt. Then Mr Harris gave out the medals to the boys who played soccer. Well, we ended with Hatikvah - *Basil Sepel*

Sing A Song Of Arcadia

I never took a lesson in my life	Wolfie Kotzen
My Yiddisher Mama	Mrs Harris
My curly headed baby	Shirley Bortz
Nightingale	Sheila Berer
She's foolish but she's fun	Freda Levine
Breathless	Eli Osrin
You couldn't be cuter	Louis Kreser
Smiling through	Karen Shrager
I don't want to set the world on fire	Sidney Klevansky
Enjoy yourself	Sammy Berer
Wish me luck	Before interviewed about reports
Could it be wrong	Kinds planning mischief
Night and Day	Phyllis Adler at her knitting
In a Persian Market	Seniors dining room
Since you went away	Judy Nochumsohn
Fascination	Bella Bortz
Nature Boy	Morris Bortz
The bells are ringing	For Shul and Hebrew
Yellow Rose of Texas	Abe Kreser
It had to be You	Zelda Gordon
Busy Line	Arcadia
Beautiful Dreamer	Shifra Bortz
I'm my own Grandma	Cynthia Sasson
Temptation	Anne Gordon
Can't you hear me calling	Flora Farber

Compiled by Joyce Friedman

Arcadia 'At Home' To Maccabi Springboks

"When I was about 13 or 14, I used to think it was all rubbish about Rachel's Grave and King David's and the Wailing Wall, but when I saw them all in Israel I felt I was living in Biblical times"; thus spoke Basil Lipschitz, the Maccabi soccer player and an old Arcadian.

The occasion was an 'At Home' at Arcadia for its three graduates who have made a name for themselves both here and in Israel in the Maccabi Games.

The 'At Home' began with the evening service which was ably conducted by 15 year old Cyril Fanaroff. Kiddush in the dining room was followed by a tasty dinner and Basil with the unselfconsciousness of a son returning to his family related his impressions of Israel.

"The children grow up there without ever being called ugly names because they are Jews, and they grow up free and without fear". He spoke of the dairy in the Negev which is larger than any in the Karoo and he said that the sight of the Israel Army display at the closing ceremony of the games was 'gripping'. He concluded: "We have come back better and wiser Jews".

Mike Rubinowitz, the scholarly long distance runner said he could not interest anyone on the team to visit the historical places with him, such as the homes of Bialik and Achad Haam, nor the Bezalel Museum, so he went alone. He was much impressed with the masterpieces of Antiquity in the Museum and with the City of Jerusalem.

Regarding the five mile race which he ran and won, he remarked "It wasn't too hard. I was a bit bothered by the heat."

The third of the old Arcadians, Les Wolchuk, is perhaps in a large measure responsible for the South African victories at the Maccabia. He trained the boys and generally kept them fit. He said: "I was there in Israel on leave from the Army in 1945, and the change that has taken place since then is unbelievable."

Reproduced by kind permission of the 'Zionist Record'

Musical Quizzing – An Appreciation

We've had three very interesting and entertaining musicals on recent Saturday evenings, thanks to Miss Rae Papert. Her enthusiasm and radiant personality combined with magical fingering of the piano was infectious. Everyone entered into the spirit of song and game. Her debut was a sing-song. A song was mentioned or hummed by a child and immediately she produced it on the piano and everyone sang. The other two occasions were musical quizzes. They were great fun and the children did show that they have 'ears' and some knowledge. The following were the winners of the third quiz: Leon Spiegler, Anita Kupernick, Hymie Sacks, and Audrey Schraga. We are looking forward to more of your original musical evenings when you return from your holidays, Miss Papaert.

The Last Night at Camp

The funniest night at camp was on the last night at our camp fire. It was very big and many people came to it. The person who entertained us was Hymie Shapero, who has now gone to England to study. He took part in most of the entertainment. We sang many songs. When we had finished singing a few plays were performed by the children. They were very enjoyable plays and I liked them. After all the plays there was a song by a girl named Edith Freed; I liked it very much, and at the end of the camp fire a boy named Leon sang 'Camp has Ended'. Then we stood and sang Hatikvah and 'Day is Done'. Then after that they announced welcomes from Israel. Then we went to the 'mitbach' and we got cocoa and buns. After that we had to go to bed very tired. - *Shirley Bortz – aged 10*

Kroonstad

Kroonstad – A town some 130 miles from Johannesburg - to 22 young Arcadians a word recalling a fortnight of happy days.

Again a group of South African Jewry has made history as far as Arcadia is concerned. Last year the prize went to Vereeniging. This year Kroonstad deserves more than worthy mention for the thought and the action which gave a happy holiday to the 22 youngsters who would otherwise have stayed home, whilst their bigger 'brothers and sisters' were enjoying themselves at Habonim Camp.

Sixteen Kroonstaders were 'father' and 'mother' to these boys and girls from the ages of five to ten years. In addition, every child returned laden with gifts which they still treasure, and which are a constant reminder of the 14 happy days. It is hard to believe that in so short a while, the 'parents' became so attached to the children, that the farewell gathering at the Communal Hall at Kroonstad was a poignant parting. No-one need feel ashamed of the deep sentiments expressed, of the tears shed or surreptitiously brushed away.

Amidst the frantic waving of hands, shouts of goodbye, strains of 'They are jolly good fellows' our bus moved off and left behind the host of dear friends, who look forward to having 'their children' again. Thank you all, 'mothers', 'fathers', 'brothers', 'sisters' and friends! We hope to reciprocate when you send us a few of your children to join us on holiday at Arcadia. - *Matron*

My Holiday At Kroonstad

We used to go to bioscope and go for walks. Once we went to a concert in the night. We used to stay up till about 11 o'clock. The food was marvellous. We made lots of friends and we were sorry to part with them. On Sunday we left Kroonstad. We were all crying when the bus came to fetch us. But the people who looked after us said we must all come again. That cheered us up and we all hope to be at Kroonstad once more. - *Roselyn Folb*

Chanukah at Arcadia

No excuse need be offered for writing of this Festival although several months after the event. This was the first Chanukah in three years that we had been able to celebrate completely, because all the children were at home.

A full week of celebrations reached its climax on the eighth night of the Festival – it was a Sunday – with a grand concert arranged and compered by Mr Arnold Daniel, who brought to Arcadia a group of artists imbued with the happy desire to entertain the children; the program consisting of songs, instrumental music, piano, accordion and harmonica and dances.

The concert was preceded by an impressive service, conducted by the children. Leon Klingman, Captain of Bialik, recited the 'Al Hanissim' and pronounced the blessings. Then four boys and four girls, equal numbers from each House, kindled the lights. The eighth night of Chanukah was unique in that it was the first occasion on which the massive brass menorah had been used.

On the Friday evening the kindling of the Lights 'Kabalat Shabbat' and the full Maariv Service was conducted by Colin Rosenkowitz.

Among other performances in the Chanukah program were items presented by the boys and girls; Dramatisation of 'The Miracle' poem: by Fay Fanaroff, Bennie Kreser, Sylvia Gordon and Chanukah Dredl sketchy by Shirley Bortz, Sarah Farber, Miriam Gordon, Basil Lipschitz, Charlie Segal.

Arcadia Hebrew School

Once again the girls did better than the boys in the December Term Examinations – the girls head the lists:

Std	First	Second	Third
1	Audrey Schraga	Ian Hirschsohn	Elaine Levine
2	Yechiel Bortz	Zelda Gordon	Sidney Lipschitz
3	Shirley Bortz	Fay Fanaroff	Sylvia Gordon
4	Bella Bortz	Cynthia Sassen	Reina Slovo
5	Flora Farber	Audrey Sepel	Morris Bortz
6	Jeanette Clous	Shifra Bortz	Benny Touyz

Attendance - The attendance during the period Aug-Dec was quite satisfactory, 28 pupils getting over 90% attendance – most girls again. Of course the boys have the battle of dual loyalties – school games and Hebrew classes.

Special mention must be made of Yechiel Bortz, Leah Berer and Bella Bortz – 100%. Audrey Schraga, Fanny Blecher, Judith Berer, Anita Levine – 99%. Ian Hirschsohn, Elaine Levine, Jeffrey Esakov, Isla Sepel – 97%. Shirley Bortz, Miriam Gordon – 96%. Zelda Gordon, Minnie Faranoff, Sylvia Gordon – 94%.

Rosh Hashanah

When the night of Rosh Hashanah came you could imagine how happy I was. We were all very excited because all of us dressed up in our best dresses and suits. And of course honey and apples to eat also, but Shul took a long time. Lots of visitors came, especially old boys and girls, and the Shofar amused me a lot. The person who blew the Shofar was Barney Myers. He turned red like a turkey.

Eli and Linky said the prayers, and to our surprise they did very well. It was a very pleasant New Year. Our Post Box was very nice. David Kotzen was the Postmaster this year, and he did it very well. There were also other boys and girls who acted as sorters and postmen for giving out the new year cards. It was great fun. - *Sarah Farber – aged 10*

Seven Bat-Mitzvahs

Shabbat Chol Hamoed Succoth was an historic occasion for Arcadia, being the first time in its history that girls became Batmitzvah. It was a 'Woman's Day', as Matron called it.

The Mayor and Mrs Mincer and Chief Rabbi Dr Rabinowitz were among the guests who attended the special functions to mark the occasion.

The seven Batmitzvahs were dressed in white frocks and hats relieved by the colours of their respective Houses – Blue and Yellow – approached the pulpit as each name was called in Hebrew: Judith Berer, Anita Kupernick, Bella Bortz, Freda Levine, Zelda Gordon, Rene Slovo and Sylvia Gordin

They recited the 'Aisbeth Chail' after which the Chief Rabbi addressed them.

On Sunday at the Annual Speech Day, each Batmitzvah was presented with a certificate and Anita delivered a speech in which she stressed the part that Jewish Women of worth have played in the past; and how today too they are standing shoulder to shoulder with the men in the rebuilding of the ancient Homeland – Israel.

A weekend of festivities beginning with the Batmitzvah Dinner on Friday evening at which the Mayor and members of committee and old girls and boys were present, continued through Saturday and culminated with the very large gathering on the grounds of Arcadia on Sunday for the Speech and Prize Day.

The significance of the occasions displayed itself in the two large cakes, sugared and lettered in the yellow and blue of Bialik and Herzl. The celebrants were privileged to cut the cakes and help themselves and distribute largesse to all the other boys and girls. Indeed an unforgettable three days.

The Ten Day Holiday

The first few days of the October holidays we enjoyed ourselves in the swimming bath. The baths had just opened. On Monday we went to bioscope to see 'The Lost Tribe'. Tuesday was a public holiday, so we were allowed out the whole day. That night we were so tired that the moment we got in our beds we were all fast asleep. All the junior girls and a few senior girls went to see Ballet dancing on Wednesday afternoon. It was very enjoyable, and most interesting. About 30 of us entered for a talent concert, which was organised by the Women Zionists. Before going to the first trials, we had a practice concert in our dining hall. Matron acted as judge, and all the staff was there. It was good fun! On Tuesday the tests took place at Coronation Hall and a number of us managed to get into the final. Friday, Saturday and Sunday we stayed home. Then on Monday we all went to the Israeli Cavalcade, where the finalists took part in a concert. - *Bella Bortz*

The Old Arcadians Club House

After a recess of a couple of months, the Club House opened again on Sunday, January 28th with a Social and Dance.

Several programs of a literary and musical nature are planned for the coming months.

The Club is open on Sunday evenings from 8 o'clock. The Hon Secretary, Max Ladier, will be pleased to give Old Arcadians information about the Club's activities. Write to him C/o Arcadia.

1950-1951 Bulletin

Mazal Tov And Congratulations

Myer and Tilly Rubinowitz, on the birth of a son.
Jonah Perkel on the birth of a son.
Molly Rich (nee Friedman) on the birth of a daughter.
Rumour has it that another Old Arcadian is being entangled into matrimony. We've met the girl. Lucky chap!
Philip Kemp, on his engagement.
The Club looks forward to the wedding celebrations of its Chairman.
Miss L Coleman on passing Final Nursing Exams with honours.

Chapter 67 - SOLLY FARBER - (1937-2002)
Past Chairman and Honorary Life President

AU REVOIR
Extract from the 1957 *Arcadian* -

Solly was born in 1937 and spent all of his childhood from age two until age 18 in Arcadia – 1939 to 1955. His older brother Morris (Moozy), and his sisters Flora and Sarah were also in the Arc.

"Solly played the mouth organ, was one of the founders of the now extinct photographic society and was chief 'Chazen'. He was also chief editor of the Arcadian for the past four years and, apart from all these hobbies, Solly still had time to go steady three times. Our mistake, it was only twice.

You will agree with us when we say that Solly was truly a wonder boy, because Solly was unfortunately born a cripple. Doctors had given up hope that he would ever be able to play sports. He really had guts and proved that their theory was wrong. Today he excels in both the sports and scholastic fields for he was a prefect at Parktown Boys and swam for the A Swimming Team. He also played for the 3rd XV Rugby Team, where he captained it on many occasions.

During his stay at Arcadia, he gained his Life Saving Instructor's Certificate. Solly's matric results were first class with distinction in Latin and Mathematics.

SOLLY FARBER
By Selwyn Milner and Jeff Esekow

Shalom Abe Farber was born in Vryburg in the Free State on 11 March 1937 and died in Johannesburg on the 24 July 2002. After matriculating from Parktown Boys' High School in Johannesburg, Solly obtained his MBBCh at Wits University in 1961.

Solly Farber

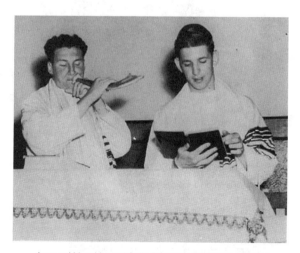

Leonard Lipschitz and Solly Farber on the Bimah – 1955

While working at the Queen Victoria Hospital as registrar, he met and married Heather McComb and in 1966 they moved to London. Upon his return to South Africa, he headed the Obstetrics and Gynaecology Department at Natalspruit Hospital. After commencing his private practice in Johannesburg, he continued as consultant and teacher at the Natalspruit and Coronation Hospitals. In 1982 he was elected Fellow of the Royal College of Obstetrics and Gynaecology.

Solly was an active and committed member of the Medical Association. In 1986 he was elected to the Gauteng Branch Council and served as Treasurer for six years and was Chairperson from 1999-2001. He was the Editor of the Gauteng Branch Newsletter. In 1993 he was elected Federal Councillor, and became known for his feisty deliberations. At national level, he served on South African Medical Association's (SAMA) Committee for Science and Education for two years, and more recently on the Committee for Human Rights, Ethics, and Legal Affairs. Solly was a good debater who would often take an opposite view merely to establish a point, thus playing devil's advocate.

The above description of his life is in itself quite unusual, but it does not convey the real essence of the brilliant and wonderful person that was Solly Farber. Few people know of the difficult circumstances that beset him in his early life which moulded his personality, character, and sense of fair play. At the age of two, he and his two sisters were placed in the care of the Arcadia Jewish Children's Home. There he made lifelong friends and mentors who influenced him in a most profound manner. He was literally thrown into the mainstream of life after his matric year when he had to leave the children's home to become independent. He struck a good balance between that and his studies.

His hobbies included reading, writing, and working with computers. He loved jazz, jogging, swimming and walking. He was passionate about education, both learning and teaching. The incredible diversity of the courses he took tells something of the breadth of his interests and achievements. He obtained the highest marks in a radio-ham course. He completed the Management Advancement Program at the Wits Business School in 1991 and obtained a postgraduate Diploma in Tertiary Education from UNISA in 1994 cum laude. Solly also completed a course in creative writing, one of his passions, and was one of the first to complete SAMA's course on Medical Ethics. The book *Know the Seasons of your Womanhood* was written by him, and he co-authored *Know your Risks – the STDs* with Ron Ballard. He was well known for his contributions to local SAMA publications and his column *Borgorygmi* was greatly appreciated as much for its medico-political content as for its tongue-in-cheek style. His sense of humour was legendary, and he could always be relied upon for witty comment.

He never forgot his roots and devoted many hours to supporting charitable organisations. After growing up in Arcadia Children's home, he returned to serve on its Committee for many decades. He was elected Chair of the Arcadia Committee for a record of four terms and became Honorary Life President of Arcadia. In addition he acted as a 'chazzan' in the Arcadia synagogue services where he enjoyed leading in singing and prayer for more than 30 years.

Despite his remarkably full life, he was a committed family man. He was devoted to his wonderful and supportive wife, Heather, and his adoring daughters, Lisa, Yael and Tanya. One could always sense the enjoyment his family brought to him.

Solly was a man of great inner strength, even when his illness and treatment were starting to affect him adversely. He tried not to impart a feeling of distress to anyone around him. He was so dedicated that he attended Branch council and Exco meetings until his health precluded this. It was this spirit of fortitude that allowed him to celebrate his daughter Tanya's wedding only a short while before his final admission to hospital.

SHALOM ABE FARBER - *By his daughter Yael*

Ever since I was a little girl, I have been coming to this beautiful Arcadia Shul with my family on the High Holy days. I would sit with my sisters and my mom somewhere near the front of these benches - for a clear view of the Bimah - where Mannie Osrin, Starkey and my dad Shalom would daven the service. My father would be deep in the raptures of prayer - but I would wait for the moment when his green eyes would lock with mine and he

Photo of Cover - Know The Seasons Of Your Womanhood

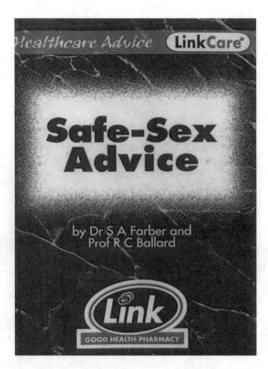

Photo of Cover - Safe Sex Advice

would somehow contrive a wink, or pull of the tongue - or lift the top corner of his mouth so that no one but I saw and felt like his chosen one. It was only much later that I realised that often all three of his daughters believed themselves to be the beneficiary of that look. And we were. He somehow managed to make us feel like the most precious gift he had.

The frame of this room is like a series of images I have of my father as he navigated his years on this earth. I remember a handsome man with olive skin and deep green eyes singing proudly up there on the Bimah opposite me. There was something about my dad's eyes that captured the consistent effort he made to live a world that was not always easy. My father believed that we were all equal in this. Life is easy for no one it is simply your choice to do with it what you will.

I recall one particular evening when I was still young enough to sit on the male side of the room close to my father on the Bimah. I couldn't have been more than five or six years old - but I remember with total clarity his eyes as he began to sing. I was so moved by the mixture of joy and soul that I saw in his eyes that I started to cry and had to feign a tummy ache. He abandoned the service to take me home, leaving the conclusion of the prayers in Starkey and Mannie's capable hands. I noticed he never offered me any medicine for the so called ailment. He simply took me past the Dolls House on the way home and we sat in silence eating our toasted cheese and tomatoes. My dad was a talker - but he always knew when to say nothing.

Each year offered a new opportunity for me to watch my father from a distance - up on the Bimah. To sit back on those benches and look up at how another year had passed over my dad. I was always aware that the walls of this room had witnessed far more of my father's life than I had.

Shalom Farber was born into the dust and tin of Vreiberg in 1937. He entered the world feet first as if already anticipating a crash landing. I would imagine he contrived the incorrect position in utero because he was already aware that no one was going to catch him and he would have to take care of his first drop all on his own. The doctor - may be a little over-enthusiastic - pulled too hard and broke the tiny left ankle he was tugging on. That was just the beginning of his luck - he always claimed. Because if it wasn't for that bugger up I would never have had the brace from ankle to thigh put on my leg until I was 12 years old. And if it wasn't for that brace - I would have been playing in the sun with the other kids, instead of in the library looking for another way to pass the long summer afternoons.

He decided that if he wasn't going to perfect soccer skills like the other boys, he would read the library. And so he began at one end of the room and didn't stop until he had read every book those walls had to offer. From ship cruise booklets donated by rich powdered ladies to the orphanage - to Dickens, Mark Twain and Shakespeare - my dad devoured every written word in sight. It is from these first dabblings in literature that my father imbued my sisters and I with a deep love and respect for books, the written word and knowledge. Until late into the nights you would have found our family around the table arguing passionately about some intricate literary or current issue that had caught our attention. Indeed

it was the numerous visits to the doctor in town to straighten his tiny damaged leg that created a deep respect in my dad for the medical profession. It was in these early dealings with medical magicians that propelled him forward from an orphanage to become one of the most respected Obstetricians and Micro surgeons. I can imagine my father as a boy, delighting in each examination he had to endure as a new adventure. My father had a unique gift of turning the most unpleasant aspects of life into a new challenge to be faced. I believe he has passed this on to his daughters and many others.

I don't believe I ever witnessed an insincere moment from my father. He had a morality that had nothing to do with institutionalised religion. He simply had a deep integrity. This is something that he had gleaned at an early age from his own father. One afternoon after a visit to the doctor - my dad told us that he was walking back along the pavement in his brace. After the five tram rides and two buses to get to town - his father Jankel Farber - realised that the man at the corner cafe had given them too much change - it was the equivalent of a couple of cents - but my grandfather piled all four children back onto the bus and made them walk the interminable journey back into town to repay the owner.

My grandfather never spoke morality to his children. He simply lived it. And they witnessed it, as did my sisters and I.

My father had a unique passion in the world that touched many people's lives. It is a common experience for my sisters and I to meet someone who feels compelled to tell us how he impacted upon them. I was opening a bank account the other day when the manager noticing my name, asked if I was the daughter of her Doctor Farber. On confirmation she proceeded to tell us how she had only continued her education because my father asked her every time she went to see him. Somehow he had made her accountable to him and she felt that she couldn't disappoint him. He believed she was destined to manage the bank. Not just be a clerk, for the rest of her life. She told me - with shining eyes - how my dad would tell her "if you managed to get this far in your education - despite growing up in a South African Township you owe it to yourself to go as far as you can". He told her he had faith in her. She did the rest. My sisters and I cannot count together the amount of people who have related similar stories to us. From his medical students to our friends - who would make special requests for a walk with my dad to chat about things - to his patients and younger colleagues - there are an infinite amount of people who have used the word 'mentor' and 'inspiration' when talking about my father.

Perhaps it was because my dad knew the power of another human being's faith in another. He told us about a Mr Harris and his wife who looked after the Arcadian Children for a certain period. They were a harsh couple whose approach was unsympathetic and rigorous. One day my father as a child wandered into the auspicious committee room - which still holds a magnificent and awesome air about it. He was standing in the room looking at the stately paintings and busts in reverence when Harris came in and accused him of being in there to steal money from the safety box in the room. He called Jankel - my dad's father in - and accused his son of being a thief. My grandfather looked him square in the eye - a courageous thing for this modest man - and simply said "My Solly a thief? Never." It was many times that my sisters and I were recipients of this inherited integrity that no one can tell you more about your own child that you already know.

Harris declared that my father would be in jail by his early adulthood. From all accounts my father was fiercely spirited, and his prediction could have become a self-fulfilling prophecy. He was a wild young thing. When you are that young and your spiritual clay is still wet, the temptation may be there to fulfil someone's worst expectations of you. But after Harris came two very special people into my dad's life. Doc Lichtigfeld and Harary. Two men who impacted profoundly on my dad's young spirit. Doc - as they called him was a man of numerous degrees, doctorates etc. He marked my father as someone he expected the best from. And my father never forgot the power of that faith. A legacy he has touched countless people with.

It was on that Bimah that my father had his Barmitzvah over 50 years ago. And it was in these benches that he sat a bewildered 12 year old trying to come to terms with the death of his brother Morris - Moosey as he was known to the Arcadia kids.

My father never discarded the difficult memories. He was not someone to idealise the past. He held onto the painful memories, not for the sake of bitterness, but for compassion. His approach to people has always been informed by his own pain - and his unique ability to transform the experience into something that would heal instead of harm the inheritor of his own experiences. The numerous experiences that could have thwarted his own potential, instead were used by him as an insight into how to overcome these both for himself and others.

Pablo Picasso once said: "It takes a very long time to become young." My father was the youngest spirit I have ever known. Old in his wisdom, old enough to know that we actively have to keep our spirits open and young. The single defining quality in my father was his endless capacity for delight in the world. My sister Tanya defined it as follows: "He never behaved as if his potential had been fulfilled. He never failed to absorb a new story or fact or experience in the belief that there was nothing new in the world for him. Everything was new." Indeed, he was the hungriest person I have ever known.

Shalom knew how to live in the moment. Tanya and I discussed this and it was very far from the hedonistic and reckless meaning this phrase has taken on in modern life. I never once in all my life saw my father intoxicated by anything artificial. But he was consistently intoxicated with life, with hope, with hunger for the world. He simply knew how to be entirely present for each moment. For each new gift the world offered him, for a balmy summer's day at the pool, or a fat novel he would devour in a matter of hours, or a walk with one of his three daughters, or a piece of music that would suddenly bring tears to his eyes and a smile to his lips. If my father was reading a book he was enjoying, we would take care to avoid wandering anywhere within his radius - or we would be trapped for hours while he read copious passages

to us and tried to share each delight the author offered. He understood the delicate currency of joy, and grief. My father knew how to integrate these two colours. He never hid pain from us. Funerals for our pets were a simple but meaningful affair in which he would talk not of loss but of thanks for the time we had with whichever fuzzy creature had just died. My father walked amongst Princes and Paupers with equal respect - understanding that we are all just people. When his dog was killed by a car, I remember the solace he found in his friendship with Jackie the young guy who used to sell the paper on the corner. Jackie put his arm around my dad and my father cried as he told him how it had happened. I watched as these two people stood, a doctor of 60 from the northern suburbs - and a newspaper boy of 17 from Alexandra Township reaching out beyond different worlds to be sad together. I don't believe my father ever thought himself above any person or experience. He understood intrinsically that there is only love and pain. And we all land in these situations at some point - without exception.

My father had a wicked sense of humour. At times he was positively 'lavatorial' to the delight of his three daughters and the constant horror of his wife. He never wore socks that I ever witnessed. He only wore a tie when there was no way around such dress codes. He loved nothing better than swimming for hours in the sea. Lying until dark on the beach reading - way after any decent hour to be on the beach in South Africa. He had an appetite for food, life, books and knowledge that I have never witnessed in anyone before. Until my father fell ill he used to function on three hours of sleep a night - maximum. At any hour if you wandered into his room he would have the lamp on filling his brain with some new story or subject matter or crossword puzzle or late night talk show. He studied constantly and held too many degrees and diplomas for us to count. He had eyes like the sea. Green and grey. Sometimes blue like the sea depending on the present climate. He had hands that were square and tanned and brought countless thousands of new born babies into this world. He suffered fools lightly - but never foolishness. My father had a keen sense of irony and loathed hypocrisy. He cared little for saying the correct or fashionable thing. He cared only that things were fair. And right. If my father thought you were not being any of these things, he would look you clean in the eye and tell you. That kind of intense honesty and integrity was the source of much love by some - fear by others. But he was respected by all.

My father has entirely unique relationships with each of his girls and his wife. To Lisa, my dad was a friend and companion as well as a father. He was her mentor in all aspects of her life. He was her guide through her education and she followed his footsteps into the medical field. This was a huge source of pride for him. She has memories of many happy hours of academic guidance, philosophical conversations and long walks on the beach. She holds in wonder his appreciation of nature's creatures no matter how great or small and of all people no matter how humble or great. She knows that his fathering couldn't be improved on and he provided perfect amounts of nurturing and limits, as well as a strong push for independence. He provided her with a model for parenting that she will strive to emulate with her children - Shalom's two beloved grandsons Gabriel and

Aaron. It was a privilege to have him as a father and she is proud to be his daughter.

Tanya his baby loved the cerebral connection they had. She called it "exercising each other's brains." When my dad got really ill or down due to his illness and there was nothing any of us could say, Tanya would move in with the pen and the crossword puzzle. They had an understanding that sometimes it is best to rely on the intricate facts the world is made up of. The same things mattered to them in the physical world. The origin of a word or its meaning. What's the capital of some obscure country, or the population of a tribe in the Amazon.

Tanya is as candid as my dad was. Fearless in making observations about people regardless of the consequences. As long as it was honest, irreverent and candid, but still somehow respectful of the recipient. In my dad's illness they did a university course on creative writing together, where they would share writings with the class. It was a great gift to both of them to share these scholarly hours together despite my dad's encroaching illness.

I like to think I was his soul daughter. I had the great privilege of going to Israel with my father. It was the first visit for both of us. I watched front doors opening and my dad being embraced by cousins and family. He had never met anyone outside his immediate family. Something opened in my father in Israel that I am blessed to have witnessed. I include long buried grief that he had never touched. I saw him acknowledge the gap where his mom couldn't be, or his father. I saw him acknowledge the ancient grief of Jewish History. These were never intellectual concepts to my father but experimental realities. We visited Yad Vashem together and my father sat down on a rock, suddenly overcome with emotion and wept. I had never seen this force of grief in him. My father's identify as a Jew defined him. He carried like a light inside him, and a weight. Of course it is this unique combination that defines the Jewish path in the world. And my dad embodied that.

He watched over my unfolding career with care and joy. Whenever I opened a new theatre production, as the actors were applauded on stage - he would somehow locate me up in the catwalks and shadows of the theatre and nod and clap for me. I keep his shining eyes as a memory of each time I began a new story in theatre.

Heatherkie - the daughter of Rebecca who worked in our home for two decades - became my father's fourth daughter. She grieves with us for a man who she regarded as her father. Even when my dad was really ill recently, he noticed Heather looking sad about something in her personal life. He hugged her and told her only ever to ask for the best for herself. At his most ill he was still concerned that we never undervalue ourselves.

My father made it very clear. Once you have left home you will take care of yourself. But when it comes to education, I will deny you nothing. He never questioned my desire to go into the dramatic arts. He paid for an education for each of us without a single emotional invoice being issued. It was his daughters' right to be educated by him. But he had his bottom line. When I called home one winter's night from a small town in Ireland to say I had £8 left to my name, he was silent for a moment and then said "I know you'll make a plan." And I did. He had his boundaries and knew when to challenge us to use our own resources.

Lisa, my older sister once quoted a book that she thought encapsulated my father's impact on us. The description of a character read as follows:

"She had the confidence of a woman who knew she was loved by her father."

Shalom blessed us with this confidence.

My father was husband in the Old World sense. Like everything else he knew that there are not short cuts. And glamour is for the pages of magazines. My mom and dad met when he was doing his housemanship at the Queen Vic in Jo'burg. Having seduced every other lass in the hospital he laser sighted on my mom - a pure little rose from the eastern cape. He used to sit barefooted, legs dangling off the trolley watching all the girls go by. My mom remembered his big green eyes and his wild reputation. She was told to go nowhere near him. Of course this is a fatal thing to say to any woman. She was drawn despite herself. They went through thick and thin together. In his last birthday card to her he wrote, "We have climbed the hill together".

Both from broken backgrounds, he promised to look after her. And he did. Together they created a complete home - where their own backgrounds had been difficult. When I went out onto the balcony today to ask my mom, as I write this - what my father was to her, the answer was simple, Everything!

A month before my father died, he walked my youngest sister down the aisle. Only now in retrospect do we all appreciate how ill he was and how much courage and determination it took to do so. After the ceremony - he said his speech, ate his dinner - excused himself and went to lie down. He deteriorated rapidly after that. But he honoured his commitment to Tanya with courage and dignity.

I don't think in the two years of his illness I once heard him ask Why me? Or complain. I don't think we ever really knew how bad he was feeling. After nine major surgical procedures, chemotherapy, radiotherapy and a final three intensive weeks of hospitalisation, he had shown us in his illness what he had always taught us in life. To give it everything you've got, face into your destiny with courage, be honest with yourself and those around you - no matter how hard the truth.

We were devastated when days before my father passed away, he could no longer talk to us. This man who had always used the beauty of words and thoughts and ideas to communicate the delicate workings of human emotion, could not reach us with language. We wanted to catch any word he spoke to carry it into our lives, to live whatever clues he gave us in the final moments. But my father was his most eloquent in his silence. He simply squeezed our hands to let us know he was there. Everything that needed saying had been said - throughout the course of our lives. He was not a fast food kind of man. He had not suddenly become a good father when he became ill. Words were irrelevant. Only his love remained. And we all carry it with us always. We are his heritage.

And like my Dad - we will take both the joy of his life and the devastation of his loss and knit them together as he taught us to.

He died as he lived. Surrounded by the people who loved him more than possible to express. Sleep well Shleima. Yours was a life thoroughly lived.

SOLLY FARBER - *by Mannie Osrin*

I think it is the most appropriate that I should be standing here in this very same spot that Solly stood, year after year delivering his *drosha* [his sermon] on the High Holy Days of Rosh Hashana and Yom Kippur.

Solly on Bimah

Every year he would look out of this window here on my right and comment on the height to which the palm tree outside had grown and mention that when he had first noticed it as a little boy it wasn't much taller than he was, then he used to say "look at it now." I think it represented some form of stability for him.

These sermons of his were always enlightening. Forever the story teller and teacher. He taught me, personally a great many things. One of the lessons I will never forget. Shortly after joining him and Starkey as the Chazonimj, I approached Solly and told him that I was not at all that happy about giving a Drosha on Rosh Hashana and especially Yom Kippur, after all I said, I wasn't a Rabbi and in fact was not all that religious in the strictly Orthodox manner and as such felt a bit uneasy standing in front of the Arc and delivering a sermon. Solly immediately referred me to a prayer in the book headed "to be said by the reader prior to the commencement of the

service." It was basically a prayer and I'm paraphrasing here, in which the Chazan tells Hashem that he doesn't consider himself worthy of such an honour and that Hashem should not judge the congregation by his [the Chazan's] shortcomings and should regard him purely as the messenger. My feelings standing here in front of you are very much along the same lines. How does one give tribute to such a legend as Solly - Shalom Abba Farber. I hope I can do justice to the task.

Solly's life, I feel, had three major facets to it. There was Solly the family man, the medical man and the man from Arcadia. He was well and truly loved by all his family. He has wonderful relationships with his wife whom he adored. He was so proud of his children, his three daughters. Over the years he would tell me of Lisa's progress at medical school. "She's going into third year", "she's in fifth year now", "Lisa just qualified" and then of course when he told me how she had specialised as an ophthalmic surgeon. How proud he was! And Yael - he would say "have you seen the play she's got on at the Market?" He would phone me and say, "have you read the critics' reviews".

Proud and joyful! And of course Tanya, his youngest, the journalist. How often didn't we discuss her writings in the Star newspaper. Again, how proud he was!

Solly, the medical man, a role he filled with great distinction. He became a well known Gynaecologist and Obstetrician and ran a highly successful practice. He became very involved with the Medical Association and was chairman of numerous committees and editor of their journal. More recently he filled the position of Chairman of the Gauteng branch of the SA Medical Association - a wonderful achievement.

Then the third facet of his life - Solly Farber - the man from Arcadia. How marvellous it was for him to have been Chairman of Arcadia on so many occasions. He touched so many lives and was loved and respected by all who came into contact with him. I always thought of him as the link, the conduit through which flowed the connection between young and old Arcadians. Those who were presently in the Arc and those who had left a few years ago, a long time ago and some many years ago. He was one of those responsible for creating a medium through e-mail for old Arcs in many different countries to keep in touch.

Those three facets of his life intermingled to such an extent that I often wondered how he managed. I would phone his home and Heather would tell me that "if he wasn't at his rooms, he must have left for a meeting at Arcadia and that afterwards he had to go to a Medical Association meeting". She used to laugh when I asked if she knew when he'd be back!

On a personal note I must say that I have lost a very dear friend, never to be replaced. He taught me so many things. He was my computer buddy. He was the only one who knew what I was talking about when I came with a computer problem. He was the first one of my acquaintances who surfed the net!

He was truly the most remarkable individual it has ever been my privilege to be associated with. He was a legend in his own life time. We have all lost heavily. His family has lost a wonderful husband, father and grandfather. The medical association has lost a most devoted servant and Arcadia has lost its most distinguished son.

We talk about a man for all seasons, Solly was truly that. However I prefer to remember him as a "man of all senses".

He had a most delightful sense of humour. Who of you ever had a conversation with Solly that didn't end with a joke! He had more common 'sense' than most of us put together. He could usually make 'sense' of any problem and in all walks of life had a great 'sense' of direction. Fortunately, even in his suffering he never took leave of his senses.

Robert Louis Stevenson said "That a man is a success who has lived all, laughed often, and loved much; who has gained the respect of intelligent men and the love of children; who has filled the niche and accomplished his task; who leaves the world better than when he found it; whether by a perfect poem or rescued soul; who never lacked appreciation of earth's beauty or failed to express it; who looked for the best in others and gave the best he had." That in essence was Shalom Abba Farber.

At the end of it all we ask ourselves the age old question of why? Well I have my own pet theory about this, and I hope I will not offend anybody by saying it, nor blaspheme in any way.

You see, with the world being in such a sorry state, Hashem has realised that he must have someone at his side to help Him, someone to run the various committees and get them into shape, to bring about a better world. Who better than Solly Farber?

STORIES WRITTEN BY SOLLY FARBER

Besides the medical books, journals and columns written by Solly he was very much involved in writing about Arcadia in the 80 year and 90 year commemorative books and in Arcadia Calls which was a Supplement to the SA Jewish Times in 1985 and 1986.

As Bertha Kronenberg wrote after reading some of Solly's stories, "It's difficult not to react with intense emotion. Student No.0112141J has a magical pen, and somewhere up there, way beyond, Dr. Farber, I greet you and say hello. Where did you hide this treasure Solly? Where did you learn your art? What a gem to be savoured many a time."

Solly completed a course in creative writing - one of his passions. Here are some of the stories written by him.

JACOB'S LADDER - *By Solly Farber*

It's a lovely Sunday afternoon sometime in March of 1944. The big War is raging 'up North' and here in Johannesburg a much smaller war is being waged between two junior boys in Arcadia, the famous Children's Home in Parktown.

The boys are dressed in khaki shirts and trousers, their feet are clad in black socks and their shoes built to last forever with thick leather soles expertly applied by Mr Chait the resident bootmaker. As they argue, they wander around the extensive grounds of "The Arc". Up the driveway, past the main building, up to the laundry right next to Charlie Miller's house, and hard by the cowshed and the adjacent large 'carriage house' where the big Arc bus rests at night.

The argument has progressed some way and the actual cause of the fray is already lost in the froth of the fight. The belligerents themselves cannot remember why they are at the point of coming to blows and are beyond caring.

"Hey you little squirt, I will knock your block off, I'll knock you 'assholes', to kingdom come."

"Is that right you cockroach? You and which *bladdy* army?" "I don't need a *bladdy* army, I will have Barney Kotzen on my side!" "So what? I will have Hugo Bamberger on my side." Now Barney and Hugo are the biggest guys in the Junior Boys Department, and to the little chaps they are only marginally less awesome than the Big Senior Boys.

The verbal battle continues. "I will get Len Lipschitz" "....Basil Lipschitz" ; "Mannie Osrin" ; " Aaron Karp, Philly Kemp" and so on, and so on, with ever bigger and fiercer senior boys being drawn onto the battle field.

Sooner or later they have exhausted all those worthies and perforce have to move on to Old Arcadians, especially those on active service "Up North". From there it is a small jump to the more prominent soldiers strutting the arenas of WWII in Europe. And so the game goes on. There is an unwritten understanding that one has first to invoke the South African military heavyweights before proceeding to the British, French, American and whatever else...... but heaven forbid, never -absolutely never - someone from the Nazis or Axis Powers. Everyone knew that THEY were going to be buggered up by the Allies.

"I'll have General Pienaar" "... Sailor Malan" "....... General de Guingaund" .... ultimately ... "General (or rather Field Marshall)....Smuts; so there!." "What can bloody Smuts do against Winston Churchill ? .....or General McArthur .....or - (spat out triumphantly) General *Bladdy* Eisenhower?

From the generals extant to those long assigned to history. "I'll have Napoleon on my side!" "Is that so?" Now the opponent can sneeringly deride Napoleon, "but he's long dead, you silly bugger!" or he can gallantly choose to entrench the principle of including heroes from the past by trumping Napoleon with : ".... Alexander the Great " or "..Atilla the Hun" or ".. Bar Kochba" or even "Hannibal with his ruddy great elephants."

From soldiers to other warriors and soon they will be bringing on the sporting heroes, and the greatest of those was indubitably Joe Louis, the Heavyweight Boxing Champion of the World. "Beat that you basted!"

On and on and up and up they go. From the boxers to Movie Characters; Spencer Tracy (and his cousin Dick Tracy!), to

Comic Book denizens; Captain Marvel, Superman or Batman. Neither of them would dare throw in Supergirl for fear of total and utter disgrace. "You want a *bladdy* girl on your side?"

This mode of interaction could and often did go on for hours on end; but finally would come the coup de grace, the final word; " Listen you and listen well, I WILL HAVE GOD ON MY SIDE". End of story, nothing more to say. The unbeatable, the insuperable…. The final word. Whomsoever threw that awesome Name onto the table was the winner.

The rules of the early phases of the game were subtle and subject to ad hoc change, but the endplay was eternal and unchanging; with God on your side you could not lose. To play the 'God Card' too soon would invite derisive laughter; "How can you mention God and Barney Kotzen in the same breath?" (no offence intended against Barney- you never know, he might be in hearing range!). "You simply can't do that, it is unfair". And yet if you waited too long. He would land up in the opposing team and that would be that.

Sometimes the discussion as to the validity of a 'checkmate' would become so heated that a whole new argument would break out and Junior Boy number one would threaten "Hey you *bladdy* lousy crook, I will get Barney Kotzen to bugger you up"

And once more they would enter into that ever ascending spiral stairway.

WILLIE TORTOISE MISSES THE BUS - *By Solly Farber*

My head and heart are full of stories such as this from my Arc Days.

The long driveway at Arcadia stretched from the gates on Oxford Road up to the main house and continued up from there to the outbuildings: the laundry, the compound, the carriage house for the big Mack Bus and right next to that the stables for the herd of cows which roamed free about the grounds and provided plenty of milk. Each day the cowherd would stagger down the driveway from the stables to the main kitchen, straining under the weight of a huge can filled to the brim with milk fresh from the udder. Whether the milk was pasteurised or not, I cannot say. None of us ever got TB so either the milk was pasteurised or perhaps our cows were just plain healthy.

On the north side of the property running from the soccer field down to a smaller gate further along Oxford Road there was a pathway of flagstones that wound its way down the hill and past a small stone cottage which was probably a guest house or perhaps the groundsman's home in the glory days. As time went by the pathway came to be known simply as 'The Cottage'.

The contrast between the main driveway and the Cottage is echoed in the stark difference in the three stairways in the main House. Ascending from the entrance hall was a grand wide marble clad staircase with a highly polished wooden balustrade and banister. We often pretended to be important visitors to the Villa. One khaki clad junior boy would stand on the lower stairs and announce with pomp and ceremony that "Lady Phillips is about to make her entrance" and Lady P – looking for all the world like just one of the junior girls - would make a grand sweep down the staircase to the genteel applause of various junior girls and the guffaws of the junior boys.

Just beyond the kitchen was a less grand staircase and further back was the narrow wooden "Back staircase" which presumably was never graced by the slippered foot of the real Lady Phillips, nor for that matter by any latter day Lady P in the garb of a Junior Girl.

The grand Driveway was the route into Arcadia for larney visitors in vehicles.

For the black staff and the children, the humble Cottage was the way in and out. Each morning we would line up in pairs and snake-file our way down the Cottage on our way to school. At the gate the whole long snake would come to a halt and Willie Tortoise who was then the 'boss-boy' would spring bravely into Oxford Road and like a latter day Moses, raise his hand to halt the tidal wave of cars rushing their owners into Town, and allow us to cross over and run helter skelter down Rannoch Road to the local Primary School.

Whenever we went out we would make our way along this same jewelled pathway to the bottom gate and to the Municipal bus stop just some yards from the gate. Not more than ten yards away from this bus stop was another bus stop, the 'Second Class Bus Stop' where the bus for the Natives stopped. If one happened to wait at the wrong bus stop and tried to embark on the wrong bus, the conductor would soon tell you to "*Voetsek*".

When we needed solitude or wanted to do some serious thinking or just stroll with a friend, we would take an amble along the Cottage. I did much of my studying for various school exams, walking book in hand, kicking a stone along the pathway and drilling the required facts into my thick stubborn head.

Once, while on such an amble, I saw Willie Tortoise rushing hell for leather down the cottage. Willie Tortoise was also sometimes referred to as Willie Skilpad. "Why has he got two surnames" I enquired from one of my cohorts and he explained that '*skilpad*' is the Afrikaans word for tortoise, and that was the very first Afrikaans word that I ever learnt.

We were in awe of him. He was tall and strong and most importantly very friendly to us kids and would always stop for a little chat when he encountered any of us.

This day he was obviously in a huge rush to catch a bus, so I was not upset that he did not stop and talk. As he hurried on I saw something fall out of his trouser pocket, but on he ran. The something that had fallen proved to be a small book with a photograph of him and some official looking writing and rubber stampings. I picked up the book and raced for all I was worth after him, through the little gate onto the Oxford Road pavement. "Hey Willie Tortoise" I shouted, "you dropped your book!" He already had one foot on the platform of the big red, number 5 bus, but he stopped in mid air and made a catlike leap off the bus.

He came over to me and I handed the precious document to him. Willie Tortoise, the mighty Willie Skilpad, fell to his knees before me, hugged my legs in a huge embrace and thanked me again and again "Thank you little Solly, thank you, you saved my life, you saved my life.

We waited together in mutual embarrassed silence for the next Second Class Bus to come along. He hopped onto the bus and I made my confused way back along the Cottage.

GIDEON'S WATCH - *By Solly Farber*

It was one of those bright summer mornings when the sun is already high in the sky by half past five. Over Arcadia there was the quiet peace of the dawn, punctuated only by the occasional call of a *Piet-my-vrou* or the cooing of the doves under the eaves of the main house. A discerning listener might also have heard the quiet sobbing of a small boy in a secret place somewhere on the estate.

At 6 o'clock precisely, the boys in the dormitories and those sleeping on the open balcony were aroused from their slumbers by Vicky, the housefather.

"Up, up, up. It's Monday and you've got school today. At half past six you must be in Shul and by quarter to seven in the dining room. Up, up, up." There was a wild rush for toilets for washbasins, boys in every direction, this one looking for his shoes, that one for his school tie and another desperate to find his schoolbag.

Amidst all the din, Vicky sensed that something was wrong It gradually dawned on him that one of his boys was missing and the missing one was Gideon. This realisation caused a thrill of anxiety. Gideon was a lovely boy, but he was 'special' and needed extra care and vigilance. "Gideon, Gideon, where are you?" Now the anxiety was very real. There was no knowing where Giddy might be and what harm he might have come to.

I was the prefect and I set out on a tour of Arcadia to try to find Gideon. Down by the soccer field I went, in the swimming pool, up the hill and down the hill, but no sign of the missing boy. It was almost time to go to Shul for the morning prayers so I headed towards the synagogue. On the way there I heard the weeping of Gideon and found him in a stony recess or alcove set in the north wall of the building, just below the Shul.

The previous owner of the Villa Arcadia, Lady Florence Phillips, probably sat in that very alcove from time to time, looking over her magnificent rockery or gazing northwards at the blue haze of the Magaliesberg. Now there sat one tearful little boy, cross-legged, with his handkerchief spread out before him. On the hankie were placed the myriad pieces of what was once a wristwatch, now forever separated.

The day before had been Giddy's birthday and the watch a birthday present from his father, which had come as no surprise because Dad had announced the gift weeks before and indeed it had been sorely anticipated. Gideon had been besotted with the idea of having his own watch. He had gone around Arcadia involving any senior boy or girl in his mission

to learn to tell the time. They had sensed his enthusiasm and responded in like manner.

"Come Giddy, have a look at my watch. What's the time now?" Or "Giddy, if the big hand is on the six and the little hand on the five, what time is that?"

With so many willing teachers he had made rapid progress. Some days before the birthday he could already tell the time accurately - well, fairly accurately.

At last the special day had arrived. The day of his birthday was Sunday, which was also visiting day at Arcadia. Gideon had set himself on the wall at the bottom of the driveway await his dad's arrival on the number five bus.

In due course the bus arrived. "Where's my watch Dad? What's the time?" "What no hullo no kiss for your Dad? Come Giddy let's first settle down, let me kiss you happy birthday and then we shall see your new watch.

As they did every Sunday afternoon, the different family groups dotted themselves on the soccer field or on the grassy embankment surrounding the field. My family took up our usual spot near the water tap at the corner of the field - so that we could wash the grapes that my Dad always brought. The grapes would be brought in a sturdy brown paper packet. I would add water to the packet and then allow the water to run out by making a small tear in the bottom of the packet. I would tear the packet open and take the whole glistening feast to my dad and my siblings.

I watched Gideon and his dad from my vantage point at the edge of the field while I fulfilled this personal ritual. His Dad got a reluctant kiss and a hug and finally the great moment arrived, the gift was unwrapped and immediately placed on the waiting wrist. Giddy was in a frenzy of joy. He ran from group to group showing off his prize. "Look I've got a new watch. It's a Roamer', "Listen to the tick", "See I can tell the time" and he went on to declare passionately: "I love my watch". Few Arcadians or their visitors managed to avoid him that afternoon.

Late in the afternoon it was time for the visitors to leave. Gideon saw his dad off at the gate and pointed meaningfully at his wrist as Dad alighted the bus. He went to sleep that night with the delicious anticipation of another whole day of telling the time (every five minutes!) and showing off his watch to his schoolmates. Oh the joy of the new watch.

Now, not even 24 hours later, here he was sitting in the alcove, his face streaming with tears and his watch in a thousand pieces.

"Gideon " I enquired, " what's going on?" "We've been looking all over for you, What happened to your watch?" "It's broken." "Yes, I can see that but who broke it?" "I did, I pulled it to pieces."

"But why, Gideon? You absolutely loved that watch?" "'Cos it wasn't working this morning when I woke up" "How did you know it wasn't working?" "Well, I looked at the watch. The small hand was on the four and the big hand was on the twelve, so it showed four o'clock, but we always wake up at six o'clock. So it wasn't working." "But Giddy, how long have you been sitting here? It is only ten past six now."

At these words, Gideon jumped up, tied the hankie with its demolished contents into a knot and hurled it down the hill. He burst into a fit of laughter, "So it was four o'clock when I woke up! The watch was working."

His enjoyment was short lived, for it suddenly dawned on him that even if the watch was okay at 4.00 am it was certainly beyond repair now at 6.00 am and he was the agent of its destruction. He burst into loud rasping tears again and rushed off down the hill to try to retrieve the precious parcel.

THE DAY OUT- *By Solly Farber*

Arcadia was our home. We rarely spent non-school days away from the home. Three or four times a year on Public Holidays we would be allowed to be taken out by a family member for a whole precious day. We would plan a long time ahead and discuss between ourselves how best to spend the day.

"Let them take you to town. You can have lunch in a café, a mixed grill only costs half a crown. Afterwards you can go to a bioscope." We didn't care what was showing at the bio; the real thrill was going out with Dad or Uncle or Auntie or a grandparent or even just a family friend.

On one such day, we went to the zoo. Father came early to fetch us and we set off walking, down the Cottage, through the bottom gate, over Oxford Road and down Rannoch Road past the School. From there we strolled through Forest Town all the way to the main gate of the zoo in Jan Smuts Avenue. We headed for this gate for a good reason. There was a street photographer who spent his days at this particular spot with his old bellows-type camera taking "family photographs, for your grandchildren to see one day."

We four siblings were shepherded together by Father in front of the camera. The photographer disappeared into the folds of the black shroud attached to his camera and, with much pomp and ceremony, took our picture. It was too amazing, but the greater marvel was that he would develop and print the pictures right there on the pavement outside the zoo. Of course it would take a couple of hours, so he advised Father to "Take your lovely children into the zoo, go to the kiosk for a meal. When you come back here later this afternoon I'll have your pictures ready for you."

So off we went. We roamed past the monkeys and the chimpanzees. We went to see the colourful parrots and the snakes and the polar bears. We roared back at the lions and shouted and whistled at the bears in their enclosure.

Best of all we went to have a ride on the elephant. To get onto the elephant's back we had to climb up a staircase onto a platform. The elephant was brought alongside and we had to step over into one of the seats forming part of a canopy-like structure over the elephant's back. This was all high up above the ground and I was rather frightened. Once all the seats on the howdah were filled, old Jumbo was taken

Morris, Flora, Sarah (in front) and Solly

lumbering around the area. It was a rather bumpy ride as he listed alternatively heavily to port and starboard as his massive shoulders rose and fell as he extended and brought down his front limbs. We were all screeching with delight. To this day I remember the pleasure of it.

Our next port of call was the kiosk, which stood hard by the eastern wall of the zoo grounds. We found a table and had great fun deciding what to eat. Just in front of the kiosk stood an old Howitzer cannon mounted on a raised platform of stones. The cannon faced along the long main avenue of the zoo towards the War Memorial, which stood at the far end of that avenue, perhaps 600 yards away.

The War Memorial was a massive structure consisting of four broad pillars holding aloft a vaulted dome. On top of the dome was an angel with huge wings, standing on a disc of concrete. The cannon at the kiosk looked like it was aimed directly at the angel.

"They say that at midnight on New Year's evening this cannon is fired at the angel and the shell makes the angel spin on that concrete disc, just like a ballet dancer" I mused. "Oh that's rubbish. If you bombed the angel, she would be shattered, she would not go spinning around like a bloody ballet dancer. What a bullshit story" said my big brother. In spite of his scepticism I preferred to hold the story as true.

None of us had ever seen this midnight miracle, so we could not confirm the myth; but on the other hand we were never awake at midnight on New Year's Eve - let alone any other night - so we were equally unable to refute it. I spent long minutes standing at the cannon, gazing along its barrel up the avenue to the angel and imagined her spinning away on her plinth on top of the War memorial.

We continued meandering around the zoo. Every now and then father would delegate one of us to go to the main gate and enquire from the photographer if our photos were ready yet. The duration of our stay at the zoo was not determined by any needs of ours, but rather by the final declaration by the photographer that our pictures were ready and available for our perusal. Then we finally exited the zoo and Dad paid for the pictures. We huddled around him on the pavement discussing the pictures at great length and in loud voices. I got crapped on for closing my eyes as the picture was taken.

Just then a tram came trundling along and stopped right there beside us. "Quickly kids, jump on" said Dad. So, even though Arcadia was a 15 minute walk from there, we had the special treat of the tram ride all the way into town and from there we took the number 5 bus back to Arcadia.

Another favourite day out activity of father's was to take us on Dingaan's Day to visit Uncle Selbst in Boksburg.

Sarah, Solly, Flora and Morris

He wasn't really a blood uncle, but he came from the same *shtetl* as my dad and we regarded him as an uncle. We went by bus to the Park Station and then by train to Boksburg. Uncle would fetch us from the station and take us to his home, which was a paradise for me. Uncle ran a general store with the family living quarters at the back of the store. It was a scene straight out of a Superman Comic, a scene from rural America in the 1940s, when Superman landed on earth and was brought up by the Kent family. The front door of the shop was fitted with a spring-loaded bell, which rang loudly if anyone opened the door. This would summon Mr Selbst from his quarters to serve the client. If he failed to come out quickly enough, the customer would call out "Shop, shop!" in a loud voice.

The shop and house were near a railway crossing guarded by booms, which came down as a train was approaching. It was a busy suburban train line and trains were frequent. A loud siren would go off to warn the motorists not to enter the crossing, the booms would come swinging down, like a belly dancer's fringed skirt. The mighty train would roar past and finally peace would reign again, but only for a short while. I was besotted with trains and would run outside to watch each and every one as it passed that way.

During one particular visit I absentmindedly put a group of small wood carved elephant figurines into my pocket. My father was aghast when we later discovered the little animals in my pocket.
"We will return them as soon as possible" he announced. But somehow we never did get to return them and I still have them up on a high bookcase in my study.

As if all this was not enough, these outings to Boksburg held an extra delight for me. Each year on Dingaan's Day they held a Fair at the Boksburg Lake and we always went to that Fair. There were the usual stalls such as the Fish Pond, Ringing the Hoop, Odds or Evens, dart-throwing and the likes. For us there were rides galore: the Merry Go Round, The Whip, the Ghost Train and, best of all, the Ferris Wheel, which stood tall and proud, towering over the whole fair. We would all climb together into a gondola and be strapped in. The gondola would travel upwards as the huge wheel went through the arc of its circle and we would wait, trembling in anticipation, for our gondola to stop at the apogee of the arc. From way up there you could see for miles around.

One year my sister was given a watch for her birthday, which, luckily for her, was on December 16th. For some mystical reason the watch stopped just as we reached that highpoint on the Ferris Wheel. Back on terra firma she insisted that Papa allow her to go up again. "Perhaps the watch will go again up there." She insisted. I was allowed to accompany her and we thoroughly enjoyed the ride. But the watch did not start again.

Another memorable outing occurred in 1947 during the visit of the Royal Family to South Africa. There was great excitement in the land. The streets of Johannesburg were decorated with brilliant lights, right from the city centre out into the suburbs, especially along Empire Road.

That Easter Monday father took us to the Rand Show which in itself was an adventure. At the end of a long tiring day we set out to return to Arcadia, where the rules of the Home required that all children had to be back by six o'clock. We hopped onto a tram and my dad was happy that we would be home well within the time laid down by the rules. Unfortunately (for me it was most fortunate) we soon realised that we were travelling in the wrong direction, we were heading out of town. Dadda decided we should stay on the tram all the way to the terminus. The trams were very infrequent on Public Holidays and we would be more comfortable in the tram than waiting in the cool evening air for another tram. "We shall", he announced "come back on the very same tram."

At the terminus the tram stopped for a full half-hour before the conductor ran up the aisle, flinging the seat backs to face the other way. The tram driver took off the driving wheel and went to the other end of the tram, to what was now the front of the tram, applied it to the driving shaft and prepared to drive the tram back along the same path we had traversed just the hour before.

By then it was getting late. The sun had set and the Royal Visit lights were twinkling all the way back through the outer suburbs right into the City. For me this was a small miracle. I had had no hope of seeing the lights and here we were, going along on the tram, seeing the lights in all their glory. And we saw the lights in the city itself. From town we got a number 5 bus back to Arcadia where we arrived well after eight o'clock. My father had some explaining to do.

For most of the children a day out was a chance to go with a parent or family member to the bioscope. To make sure that you would get a ticket to see a particular show you'd go early to town and go to the cinema of your choice, and stand in a queue. The cinemas (the Metro, the Twentieth Century, the Bijou, the Savoy and the Plaza) were large theatres and held up to 1000 people. Waiting in the queue was as much part of the outing as seeing the picture. There would be buskers strolling the pavement entertaining the queuers, and vendors selling sweets, biltong and rather warm cold drinks. A camaraderie would develop among the queuers and there would be good-natured bantering and conjecturing about the film to be seen, or scandalising about the actors in the film. Did you know that Clarke Gable had bad halitosis? His breath could strip the paint off a wall from 20 feet away.

The popular films for children then were the Three Stooges, the Lassie Films, and horror movies of the Frankenstein ilk. The movies were escapism of the highest order. We always knew that the 'baddies' would come to a sticky end and the good guys would come out on top. The pleasure of the film was carried forth after arrival back home. We would indulge in endless discussions about the movies we had seen that day.

In our dormitory we had three designated 'yarn tellers'. These were chaps who could string together a few coherent sentences and would not get stage fright if they had to tell a story to all the 20 boys in the dormitory. I was one of the yarn tellers and would have to relate any movie I had seen, scene by scene and in fair detail in the dormitory after 'lights out'.

The other guys would listen, but every now and then I would ask "Who's awake? Is anyone awake?"

Quite often you'd get no response and wonder how long you'd been talking only to yourself. But, heaven forbid, if you fell asleep while telling a yarn you would soon be roused out of your slumber by having your blankets pulled off, or by a loud shout in your ear. The horror movies were best loved, and at times you would be required to repeat a particularly scary scene again and again and again.

Fay Fanaroff, Solly and Sarah Farber

Some of my pals had no one to take them out on these 'day outs' and I would plead with my dad to take my best friend, David, along with us, which made the outings even more delicious for me.

Now all these years later:

I still have some of my family's 'zoo' photos.
I still have the elephants from Uncle Selbst's shop, high up on a bookcase in my study.
I still have the memories of the elephant rides at the zoo.
And that same David is still my best friend.

On special days I take my grandsons to the zoo. We go to the kiosk and stare along the barrel of the howitzer towards the War memorial. We walk together along the avenue up to the War Museum and gaze up at the angel on her plinth, and I wonder that the shells from the cannon at the kiosk never destroyed her.

Donald Goldman and Solly Farber with Larry Adler

Chapter 68 - MORRIS FARBER (MOOZY) (1933-1950)

Written by Solly Farber

Morris was in the care of Arcadia from 1937 to 1949 when he was expelled for running away with Bernard Aronstam and David Gordon. He died soon afterwards.

I remember it was a Friday, the last day of the school term-June 30th 1950. The previous night we had been taken to see a play. I haven't the faintest idea what the play was about, but I do remember the name: Hellfire Corner.

Some of Moozy's friends had gone to the hospital to see him the previous night, but I had seen him on Wednesday and did not go with them. David Gordon told me that they would not allow them in to see him and this was already a source of anxiety.

In the dining room, the matron came over to me and told me to see her in the Committee Room after breakfast. "You're really in deep shit this time, Boykie. What the hell have you been up to?" asked one of the fellows at my table. I had been in trouble with the matron many times, but I had no notion as to why she would want to see me that particular day.

After breakfast I went to the Committee Room where I found that the matron, had also summoned my two sisters. Without any preamble or gentle introduction she announced: "Your brother passed away at five o'clock this morning." I was stunned but was not really aware of the impact of those words on my life thereafter. My younger sister did not understand at all. "What's she saying, Solly, is something wrong with Moozy?" I was too confused to be subtle and just translated, "He's dead", at which she broke down and wept.

My life changed forever that day.

I went with my sisters from Arcadia on the municipal bus to my father's room in Hillbrow. I was shocked to find all the mirrors turned to the wall. That day I saw my father cry for the first time ever. Until then I did not know that adults also cry. Before then my father was a god, that day he became a man, he became my father, my dad.

I remember the funeral: I remember my jersey being cut with a razor as a sign of mourning. I remember every detail of that day. Solzhenitsyn opens his Doctor Zhivago with the funeral of Zhivago's mother. I have always understood this. Deep in my heart I have always seen my life as divided into two segments: the time before Moozy's death and the time after.

This was 1950 and people did not know how to comfort each other. We had no Psychologists, or social workers then. My friends were sad for me for a day or two, but quite surprised when my sadness got progressively worse as the realisation dawned on me that he wasn't ever coming back. One afternoon some weeks later I was feeling very sad and lay down on my bed in the dormitory. My best friend, David, came through.

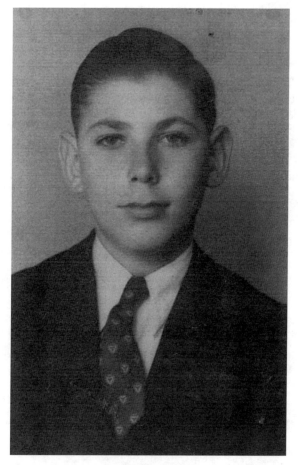

Morris (Moozy) Farber

"What's going on, Boykie, why are you here on your bed on a Saturday afternoon?" I had no desire to explain. My friends had no time for a grieving pal. They sensed a need to get me back to life, back to normality. Perhaps it was good that it was so. There was good common sense in their approach. Many year later I was to learn as a doctor that the best cure for sadness is to be active, do what you love doing, put one foot in front of the other and start your journey to healing. My friends knew that instinctively.

I learned also that happiness and sadness are not constant chronic states. It is more a matter of how often you feel happy each day in between the pervasive feeling of sadness. Inexorably and surely as the days go by there are more occasions to smile, to laugh, to be happy. Slowly I learnt to laugh and smile and am happy again.

In the home we were housed and fed and lived with our peer groups rather than in families. So, even though we were siblings, the four of us had not really spent much time with each other. I had not been with my older brother, but I knew and loved him fiercely. Boys will be boys and big boys bully little boys, but if a little boy has a big brother then he has some protection. Moozy had been my protector.

Nature looks after us in strange ways. My deep sense of loss was lightened at times by my dreams. For many months after Moozy's death I had the most comforting dreams in which my subconscious mind would devise scenarios which were improbable, but which provided perfectly plausible reasons why Moozy was thought to be dead, when in fact he was very much alive.

"They had made a mistake, it was someone else they buried on that bleak sad day in June." In my sleep I sobbed with joy, "Moozy is alive." But of course day would break and I would have to go through the bereavement all over again.

On the very night he died I came out of our synagogue at Arcadia and looked up at the star-filled sky. In my mind's eye I pictured him on one of those stars. I still have that same image in my mind all these years later. It has been an ongoing source of comfort for me.

My relationship with Moozy has been constant. He died at the age of 16 years. Now I am four times that age - an ancient man by comparison, but he remains my older brother. My image, my 'feel' of him is yet that of a brother three years older than me.

He has walked the path of life with me. I 'introduced' him to my wife and my children as they came into my life. They all say they feel as if they know him.

My family are short in stature, but Moozy was very tall, over six foot four. When he started having pain from the rheumatic fever that ultimately caused his death, the doctors said it was 'growing pains'. My father told me that he had had a half brother who was also very tall, in fact "the tallest infantryman in the whole of the Russian Army." Maybe that was so, and maybe that is where Moozy's tallness came from.

Moozy was a gentle person who avoided arguments and abhorred violence. I, on the other hand was a typical middle child: cheeky, argumentative, belligerent and inordinately fond of a good *barney*. People often found it difficult to believe that we were brothers. And yet the bigger boys often called me by his name and even now when I meet one of the chaps from those days they greet me as "Morris Farber". It used to make me mad, now it comforts me.

Many of my teachers, friends, family members and colleagues have come to their final rest in Westpark Cemetery. The only one at whose grave I cry is the first one I ever laid to rest in that 'Garden of Eden'. When I visit there, I immediately become again a devastated, bewildered 13-year-old boy who has just lost his big brother.

Moozy wanted to be a journalist. Perhaps my literary yearning grew out of a need to fulfil vicariously his dream. Another strange idea beset me as a child. My brother was in Standard 9 when he died. He had not totally committed himself to journalism and was not completely sure what he wanted to do

after completing his schooling. I got a crazy idea, a '*meshugas*' (as they would say in Yiddish) that if you are hesitant about your future, you may never get to enjoy that future. You will die young. I was determined not to suffer this fate and I laid my plans for my post school career very early in my high school days. I can write this dispassionately now, but at the time I had no deep insight into this attitude of mine.

I can recall only once that I had a serious altercation with Moozy. One Christmas Holiday my father took us, Moozy and me, to Warmbaths for a vacation. This was then an eight hour train ride with arrival in Warmbaths at 4.00 am. For me it was wonderful. I love trains, and the longer the journey, the better for me. In Arcadia we were in different sections, in Warmbaths we were in the same room, and Dad was there as well. I can't recall why my sisters were excluded from the outing.

That year at school I had learnt the Marseillaise - the French National Anthem. It is a beautiful tune and I still love it. On that holiday in Warmbaths, I took to singing, whistling or humming it all day long. Inevitably it began to irritate big brother. After ignoring some vivid threats as to what would happen if I did not desist, I got a resounding smack across the ear, which came as a real shock. He had never ever hit me before. After a while I acknowledged that it had been well deserved. We became friends again after a few sulky hours.

My chronicles go on. He was not there in the flesh to share my senior years at Arcadia and the long full years I have known since. But in my head, in my heart he is ever-present.

Come now Moozy, help me write the rest of my story

Moozy Farber

Chapter 69 - CHARLIE SEGAL (TSATSKE) (1940-1984)

Extract from the 1959 *Arcadian* – Au Revoir

Tsatske was born in 1940 and was in the Arc from age two to age 17, 1942 to 1957.

"Tsatske was a very popular boy which is proved by the fact that he won 'the most popular boy award' twice. He was regarded as one of the finest sportsmen ever to be produced by the Arc, until he gave sport up in favour of his trumpet and school work. Tsatske did exceedingly well in both these things, passing matric with a University pass and receiving colours for the orchestra and military band. Tsatske was prefect and chief Chazen at the Arc in his last year."

CHARLIE SEGAL (TSATSKE)
By Solly Farber

Here is a new story about Tsatske. It is a true story and goes back more than 50 years.. He was as lean as a beanpole and had a head of tightly curled blond hair. As a small chap he was extremely cute and was nicknamed Tsatske, which in Yiddish is a plaything, a toy a bauble. For Charlie this was a very suitable name. Our friendship was based on a mutual passion for music and specifically for the harmonica or the mouth organ as it is referred to by Philistines who don't know better. We had a harmonica band at the Home. Charlie played melody in the band and I played countermelody.

One December day when we were both very young we bunked out of Arcadia and went to the Jo'burg zoo, 15 minutes by foot from the Home. Some days before, Charlie had bought a pet white mouse in Town. The little mouse was a sensation amongst the kids.

"Can I hold him?" "Can I feed him?" "Oh he is cute, even cuter than you Tsatske"

By common consent the little mouse was named Squeaky.

We took little Squeaky with us on the outing, in Charlie's jacket pocket. As we went on our way to the zoo, Squeaky was removed from the pocket every now and then and shown familiar landmarks. "Look here's our school'
"Here's the garage where they have compressed air to pump up our soccer ball when it goes 'Pap'. The mouse took no notice.

 "Here's the entrance to the zoo where your cousins and brothers are fed to the snakes twice a day. You'd better get back into my pocket before they get you too, and you end up as snake shit tomorrow" said Charlie with a chuckle.

Once inside the zoo we made our traditional calls. We teased the monkeys, we roared at the lions and sneered at the bears. We passed by the Amazon parrots enclosure and headed for the kiosk to buy ice cream. There we met some other youngsters who immediately fell in love with Squeaky.

Charlie Segal

"Pleez sell him to us. He's so cute. We'll give you two bob for him." As he had only paid one shilling Charlie was keen to sell. I was aghast that he could even think of selling Squeaky and said so in no uncertain terms. Charlie refused the offer and I would later regret my part in his decision.

On the large lawn near the elephant rides we encountered a large group of children being given a party by a group of adults who were wearing 'bibs' showing that they were from Rotary. We mingled in the crowd and joined in the festivities. Father Christmas arrived on the back of a lorry and went about Yo Ho Ho-ing among the children.

"Queue up, queue up children" said one of the uncles'. We were caught up in the general melee. We tried to move away from the area, but one of the adults grabbed us and moved us into the queue. "Come on boys, do what you're told. Stay in line", so we stayed, but as two good little Jewish boys were none too comfortable attending a Christmas party and even more insecure about accepting Christmas gifts on false pretences. "They're probably from a home just like us. But they are definitely not Jewish kids" said Charlie. We stayed in the line, but our hearts were thumping with the fear that any second we would be revealed for what we were, little Jewish imposters. We finally got to the front of the queue and were each given a large packet which contained a variety of games and sweets. Our earlier fears were soon dispelled by the joy of ownership of the toys and the sugary sweets. As soon as we decently could,

265

we moved away from the merriment on the lawn and headed for the playground area, where we swung on the swings, went round and round on the merry-go-round and we made repeated descents on the huge slide there. During all this, little Squeaky remained secreted in Charlie's pocket.

The time was moving on, the shadows were lengthening and we headed once again towards the main gate, which took us past the animals in their dens and pens. We got to the anteater and moved up close to get a really good look at this strange creature with his elongated snout. "See Charlie", I said "his snout is long and mobile. It's made for seeking out ants and snorting them up."

As I said this, the anteater lifted up his head and faced us, almost as if he had heard what I had said and was obligingly showing his wonderful 'little trunk' full face to us. As he turned he opened his mouth and at that precise moment a loud wailing sound seemed to emanate from his mouth. This frightened the hell out of us and we took off in a wild panic and didn't stop running until we were out of the zoo and halfway back to the Arc. Then we stopped and burst out laughing .We had realised that the noise which had frightened us was not the wild cry of the anteater, but the closing-time siren which was sounded each day at quarter to five to warn visitors to the zoo to head for the exits or run the risk of being locked in for the night.

"How stupid are we Tsatske, I said. "We can hear that siren at the Arc. We hear it every day and we know what it means. We

Charlie blowing the Shofar

Gerry Levy, Colin Rosenkowitz and Charlie Segal

even use it as a 'chaila or quitting time signal to stop our afternoon soccer games or to put aside the homework for a while" and we continued our walk home laughing at ourselves as we crept stealthily through the small gate at the bottom end of the 'The Cottage'. As we wended our way along that pathway we suddenly thought of Squeaky in Charlie's pocket. Charlie took the little mouse out of his pocket only to find that poor little Squeaky would squeak no more. He was stone dead.

"Aw Gee Solly, he's dead. I must have crushed him on the slide. Oh why didn't you let me sell him to those guys we met at the kiosk? Oh hell, he would still be alive now. And he burst out crying. I felt really bad.

The mourning phase lasted for a full ten minutes. We decided to do the decent thing and give Squeaky a fitting send off on his way to mouse heaven. We first had to find eight other chaps to make a minyan- a quorum of ten males- required by Jewish law for a religious service. It did not bother us that strictly these had to be ten males who had been Barmitvahed. We decided that for a white mouse's funeral ten little guys would be more appropriate.. We found a nice spot down the hill and buried his little body deep in a hole there. We even said Kaddish for him.

Now the M1 motorway has encroached on Arcadia and the M1 passes right over the tiny sacred plot and many cars and huge trucks go thundering over Squeaky's grave every hour of every day. When I drive along there myself, I think of that eventful day at the zoo. I think of little Squeaky and how he died and most of all I think about Tsatske, my friend Charlie and the tragic end he came to much later in my life story. It is a story for another day.

CHARLIE (TSATSKE) THE TRUMPET PLAYER

David Sandler Remembers

I remember Tsatske Segal as tall with curly blonde hair, and always smiling. I remember him wearing a jacket and playing a shining silver trumpet. He played very well with crisp and very clear and loud notes. The two songs "Oh my Papa" and "Danny Boy" spring to mind. Also as I remember it, he spoke very fast and swallowed his words.

I am nearly 52 and was in the Arc from when I was three, so what I remember is about 47 years ago when I believe I was four or five years old so you have to put a small "caveat" on it.

Ronny Schreeuwer Remembers

That's about what I remember of Charlie as well. I used to sit and listen to him play on the steps behind the middle dormitory and was always fascinated by the beautiful sound that came out of that trumpet. I never knew that his nickname was Tsatske.

Solly Farber - Charlie's other favourite tune was "Cherry pink and apple-blossom white"

*David Sandler - A*fter many many enquiries I found someone who knew the tune "Cherry pink and apple-blossom white". It is very familiar and I recall Tzatske playing it and how he used to really hold onto the 4th note.

Charlie playing the Harmonica

Charlie playing Trumpet

MY THREE YEARS OUTSIDE ARCADIA
Charlie Segal - Ex-Arcadian

It seems like an eternity since I left Arcadia. I feel that the first three years of an Ex-Arcadian in the outside world is one of the most important periods in his life.

While we are at Arcadia, we are bound together like one inseparable family. Should a problem arise, we need only to turn to one or more of our companions for help. Once out in the open world, we very often are confronted with problems we must solve alone.

I therefore think that it is most important for us to set ourselves a goal in life and take full responsibility for the outcome, come what may. By instilling in us this sense of duty, not only to ourselves, but to our family, friends and business associates, we are bound to succeed in life where every opportunity for success exists.

It requires our sincere and undaunted initiative to achieve it.

Chapter 70 - DAVID KOTZEN (1938-2002)

David is the second youngest of 12 Kotzen siblings; Louis (Bill), Reuben, Esther, Flora (Florrie), Freda, Julie, Abe, Koppel, Barney, Woolf, David (Abraham) and Diana Kotzen the youngest child.

They were all in the care of Arcadia starting with the oldest Louis who was born in 1921 and who was in the care of Arcadia from 1929 to 1935 to the youngest Diana, who was born in 1942 and left Arcadia in 1959.

EXTRACTED FROM THE 1957 ARCADIAN

David Kotzen was the Valentino of the Arcs and broke the hearts of many senior girls. Unfortunately there is not enough space in this magazine to mention names. David, too, was one of the founders of the past photographic society, played the mouth organ, and gained his Life Saving Instructors certificate.

Somehow David couldn't decide what sport appealed to him most and therefore during his stay at the Arc, his sports included at one time or the other, swimming, running, rugby, tennis and cricket. Anyway David excelled at all the sports mentioned above and will always be remembered by the Arcs as a remarkable sportsman. At school David played in the 1st XV Rugby and in the 2nd XI Cricket teams.

David, as you can see, has a restless disposition. This is proved by his first going to settle in Cape Town and then trying to become a steward on a boat so that he could travel overseas. We wish David Bon Voyage!

Woolf passed away in 1961, Esther Feldman (Kotzen) passed away on 20 November 2005 and Bill on 28 November 2005. Florence Kotzen who is aged 81 has spent the last 40 years in New Zealand.

I was placed in the care of Arcadia at age three and left in 1955, at almost 18 years old.

It would be fair to say I was never exposed to family life. The Kotzen family was rather extensive made up of seven boys and five girls, I being the second youngest. Due to the considerable age differences many of my brothers and sisters were strangers to me.

My brother Woolfie was two years older than me. We grew up in the Arc together and so did my youngest sister Diana.

Michael Perry Kotzen, is no relation. He is a pen pal who wrote to me when he noticed my address posted in an old Arcadian newsletter. As a result we write to each other from time to time.

Solly Farber is my dearest friend whom I consider as family. We have been in touch for 40 plus years. I have been out of South Africa for more than 40 years, yet my roots will always be there.

A Young Dave Kotzen

It occurred to me when reading many of the Arc stories, that although our eras reflect different times, the stories are essentially the same. The only element that changes are the names of the Arcs relating their former lives experiences. Therefore, one might conclude "if you are an arc boy or girl you will always remain one"

RUNNING AROUND ARC MEMORY LANE

I reckon I must have been about 14 years old when I decided to become a world- class marathon runner. I think it would be fair to say I was seriously influenced by Jackie Mekler an Arc boy who at the time was quite famous as a Springbok marathon runner. I figured I would run about 20 miles around the circumference of the Arc. Solly Farber was my coach and mentor. He ensured that after every four times around the Arc I had plenty of fluids in my system and measured my pulse to ensure I was doing OK. (Solly's medical curiosity was evident then as, sure enough, later he went on to become a very successful gynaecologist and college professor.)

My run started at the Arc gate on Oxford Road and moved past the soccer field and the Junior Senior Boys' building. The good old soccer field, the battle-ground for Saturday's game after Shul.

Doc Lichtigfeld made his debut to the game of soccer in those days. He wore those heavy rugby type boots. His competitive spirit was intensely high, and if your foot happened to be where he thought the ball should be, a blistering "*skop*" to your shins would be the result. It soon became crystal-clear that around Doc you had better be careful. Seeing the Arc in my mind's eye, I recall as you continued down the hill you would see a house that at one time was the home of the Matron and Superintendent's family. But this was before my time. The Harris family and Lichtigfeld family lived in the main building during my time in the Arc.

Continuing along the path, my run soon took me to the heart of "down the hill territory." I could relate endless stories about down the hill but I will portray only a few. If you happened to be down the hill and the dinner bell rang you were expected to immediately report for dinner. If you missed dinner you were certain to be confronted by the matron for an explanation. The excuse passed down from generation to generation was "I was down the hill and didn't hear the bell". Looking back now, it seems inconceivable that this excuse, which never worked, was always used, especially considering how the noise of the bell echoed through the area and was probably heard in the zoo about four miles away.

The zoo was easily accessible. All you had to do was scale the wall. This was an on-going adventure for most of us, and the rewards were significant. The main shop at the zoo allowed us to purchase cigarettes. It was Louis Lapatkin who taught me how to smoke a cigarette.

I will never forget how Chalky Bortz and Mark Stein decided to bring a huge empty water tower to the down the hill area to be used as a fortress. The tower was about 10 feet high and measured about 14 feet in diameter. They managed to loosen it from its foundation and rolled this huge tower from its original location up the hill to its ultimate destination down the hill. This was an extraordinary engineering feat and, in retrospect, I am still amazed at this accomplishment.

The most vivid memory, which still remains with those of us who shared the experience, was the "Foofie slide" .We attached a hollow pipe about 12" in length through a heavy-duty wire, which extended from the top of the precipice to the bottom, and anchored it to a tree. One would hold on to the pipe and get an awesome ride to the bottom.

This was during the time when Johnny Weismuller was our famous Tarzan hero. Evidently, Abe Kreser had a special feeling in his heart for Tarzan. He decided to emulate his hero and dive after the pipe in a Tarzan- type fashion. Indeed, he missed the pipe and landed in the cacti below. It seemed weeks passed before all those cactus needles were finally removed. I believe that Abe might have been killed had it not been for those cactus plants.

This precipice was also the ideal location for a urinating contest. To this day, I'm still convinced that Reuben Lipschitz hid in the rocks above the cliff waiting for someone to pass below so he could urinate on them.

Looking back, I recall the ordeal with poor Linky Klingman. Somehow we managed to steal a chicken and decided to cook it. I don't recall who was the one elected to kill the poor bird, but after the poor bird had its head chopped off it began to run around. Linky went berserk and ran away in terror. Later, he came back and asked if rigor mortis had set in. None of us knew what "rigor mortis" meant. It was only years later I finally figured out what he was talking about.

I continued my run working alongside the tennis courts and up toward "up the hill" area. The tennis courts were used by Parktown Boys High School as practice courts. David Gordon, one of our own Arc boys, was quite a tennis player. I recall how much bigger one of his arms was than the other because of the high velocity serving power etc. I always thought him "deformed" hence I decided there was no way I was going to be a tennis player.

My run took me past the backside of the laundry and cow stables. Charlie Miller, the Arc bus driver, lived with his family in the building adjacent to the laundry. How well I remember his daughter Funu. Her name took on special meaning because of her mother yelling, "FUNU, FUNU" at the top of her lungs when she was looking for her daughter. She had a high soprano voice that would have pleased Puccini or Verde.

I continued my run behind the servants' quarters to the famous up the hill territory. This area faced the girls' lodgings, but more specifically, the senior girls' bathrooms. Obviously, we would sneak up at night to spy on the girls when they took their baths. One time, Audry Sharaga almost caught us and we figured we were done for. However, she was uncertain, and to our delight the spying was allowed to continue.

By this time I had neared my 360 degree turn, I passed the vegetable garden farm, then worked my way back to the gate to see Solly Farber, who had been attentive to my every move.

Needless to say, I never became a marathon runner. Vicky stopped my training, explaining how Polio had struck in Johannesburg and all extended exercise had to be curtailed. But, the memories of my running around the Arc, and all the wonderful observations which went along with it, will cause me to reminisce forever and keep me on the path running around "Memory Lane."

AL JOHNSON

On Sunday afternoon parents visited their respective children. Part of the visitation would include bringing candy and other treats. Obviously, I realised Ma could not favour me with such "treats" as this would show favouritism with kids in the same dilemma as myself. I decided I needed a plan.

At the time Al Johnson was a name to be recognised. We had all seen the Al Johnson story at the Saturday night "bioscope". Many of us believed we had voices to carry on his tradition. Hence it occurred to me if I paid a visit to the various parents and sang a rendition of Al Johnson songs I would gain favour and be offered candy. My goodness, it worked. Solly Farber's father was my best customer followed by the mother of Reuben Lipschitz. For years I was on a roll.

My dearest friend Solly Farber and I have often reminisced at past events at Arcadia and in particular had a good laugh with my Al Johnson interpretations. Needless to say my singing career never flourished yet the experience I had on those Sunday afternoons is something I will always cherish.

THE ARC SHUL
Written by David Kotzen in 1954

The Shul is a beautiful Shul. Four beams extend from the one wall to the other. From the middle of each beam hangs a huge globe. The Shul can seat a great number, and during the High Festivals every section is full. The boys sit on one side of the Shul and the girls on the other. In front of the Bimah there are three seats for honoured guests.

Above the Arc, and extending over the Ten Commandments, hangs the eternal light. When all other lights in the Shul are turned off the red light really creates an unbelievably beautiful scene in the Shul.

The services are led by some of the senior boys, under the supervision of Doc. The Chazanim are Solly Farber, Gerald Levy, Basil Sepel and Reuben Lipschitz.

The services are shorter than the services in other Shuls, but that is easily understood, as our synagogue is a youth synagogue. Everybody takes part, of course, with the exception of the sopranos (Senior Girls).

Before making the Friday or Saturday sermons, Doc gets the usual signs and remarks from the Senior Boys: 'Shor-r-r-rt, please Doc', 'Remember your game of soccer after Shul, you great guy.' Then comes Doc's 'Okay, you guys', and the sermon begins.

The festival services are the most enjoyable and most awe-inspiring. The beautiful Yomtov tunes are sung, with the old Arcs outdoing even the young Arcs in their singing.

Saturday night services are comically known to all as 'pairing time', for at these services Doc has to choose a boy and a girl to hold the candles while the Benedictions are being said. If Doc makes a wise choice there is a cheer of approval all round, coupled with the usual 'So-and-so likes So-and-so', and 'Well done, Doc!'

Many personalities visit Arcadia and almost invariably attend the Shul services, and if the personality wishes to, he may address the children.

In June 1953 one old boy, Max Rosenfeld, was married in the Shul. This was one of the very few marriages that have taken place in the Shul.

Another old Arc was married in our Shul. Sadie Segal was married to Gerald Lurie.

In the early days of Arcadia the Shul was a dormitory, so if an old Arc tells you that he was married in a dormitory you know that he really means the Arc Shul.
.

Habonim 1948-49
Linky Klingman, Solly Farber, David Kotzen, Louis Kreser, Unknown and Chalky Bortz

MY FRIEND SOLLY FARBER

Written by David Kotzen

David and Solly

I feel it necessary before starting this story to outline a short synopsis of Solly's history.

He came to the Arc at age two in 1939, and stayed until he matriculated in 1955 from Parktown Boys' High School. He went on to Wits Medical School to further his studies, qualifying as a Doctor in 1961. After his internship in the Johannesburg group of hospitals he started his specialist training as an Obstetrician and Gynaecologist. He continued his studies in the UK and wrote his specialty examination in January of 1967. He worked in London as a registrar and then as a Consultant in Obstetrics and Gynaecology.

In between all of this, he married Heather in 1964. Lisa his eldest daughter was born in London. The family decided to return to South Africa in 1970 and Solly became head of the Department of Obstetrics and Gynaecology at Natalspruit Hospital. In 1972 Solly went into private practice and at the same time was appointed to a part time post at Coronation Hospital and has been there ever since. His two other daughters Yael and Tanya, were born in Jo'burg. He joined the Arc committee soon after returning to SA and has been an active member ever since.

Many may know him as one of the Chazanim at the High Festival services which he has done for close to 50 years; and he is one of our own Arc "Three Tenors"; Starkey, Mannie O and Solly.

His daughters are all exceptional individuals. Lisa who has two kids, is an Ophthalmic Surgeon. Yael has reached extraordinary heights as a director and writer in the Theatre and her work has been viewed in London and New York. Tanya is a skilled writer and has a resume almost as long as her father's.

Solly is the most exceptional individual I have ever known. We grew up together in the Arc and have kept in touch ever since. There are many stories I can write about him, however, I will refer to some that are very special for me.

To begin he was the champion of all "farters" in the Arc contests. He even beat the likes of Mutta Levy, who seemed to be able to come up with one more when all of us were exhausted. As far as the Guinness book of records is concerned, I believe Solly should be there for a continuing "pee along the Arc driveway". Starting at the bottom he made it to about the half way mark-- an inconceivable feat as far as I was concerned.

One could never accuse Solly of being a bookworm, for he did very well in sport. In all the years at the Arc I was never able to beat him at the swimming gala. He influenced me into continuing my swimming by joining a life saving group, and indeed we both qualified with various awards from the Royal Life Saving Society.

I was always able to relate to him on any level; how well I remember when I discovered masturbation for the first time. I recall running up the stairs of the Senior Department yelling, "Solly, Solly Farber guess what happened to me?" As clear as day, I can still remember the smile on his face as he said "Yeah Davie Kotzen I know".

These are special moments when one reminisces about the past. I recall walking to Parktown School with him and he offering words of wisdom far beyond his age. He was someone very special to me.

Later in life when I visited South Africa I would go for jogs around the Zoo Lake with him. We would share of our family experiences and reminisce about our days at the Arc.

The last time I was in S.A. was about 10 years ago. Obviously, my day started with Solly picking me up at my brother's house and off we went for a jog around the Zoo Lake. We would then return to his home and have a peeing contest along his driveway (which he still continued to win), this was followed by a *"kaalgat"* swim in his pool". Heather would then make us breakfast.

He would leave for his office and Heather would drive me to my brother's. My last day before leaving for the States, I said goodbye to him. Soon thereafter I had the most devastating feeling of emptiness I had ever experienced in my life. It was as if someone close to me had died. I sat in the dinning room and began to cry; the tears seemed to come from the bottom of my heart. For a while I had no control of my emotions. It somehow occurred to me I would not be returning to SA This meant I would not be seeing the Farber family again. To this day I don't know whether Heather heard me crying, but it was something I will never forget.

There is a love I feel for this man that goes beyond anything I can explain. The distance that separates us has very little bearing. We share a bond that knows no time or distance. In life, we cannot choose our family, but can choose our friends. I have been blessed to have chosen Solly. Notwithstanding, there are times I wonder about the very thin line that exists between the two of us and contemplate that perhaps he is my brother after all.

Frenchie Paw Paw David and Solly

EXTRACT FROM OLD ARC NEWSLETTER *Editor Alec Saul*
Written by Solly Farber

My life at Arcadia gave me many dear friends, but when all is said and done I must say that my dearest friend was Davie Kotzen and we have remained friends and brothers over the years, and over the vast geographical space that intervenes between us. In recent years the email has been our lifeline.

David is right about two things... he could never beat me in the farting contests nor at the Arc swimming gala; but in every other sport David was superb. He was a soccer player, a rugby

player, a cricketer, an athlete and more. He had the potential to reach international level at any one of these sports.

DAVID KOTZEN
By Colin Rosenkowitz

Colin Rosenkowitz of sextuplets fame writes on his experience with Dave Kotzen mentioning how he taught him to carry three plates as a waiter in London, got him to come to Canada and take up a job as a plumber on the mines. They were in business together delivering cars in 32 states in the USA.

When he said goodbye in New York he little realised that Dave would meet his wife in that city. Colin writes how he was paid to referee soccer matches and was paid to write by the local newspaper of his experience of reffing and how Dave was classed in every instance as man of the match. In the cup final there was a punch-up with the players. The spectators ran onto the soccer field but Colin controlled the game at all times and was commended by the newspaper for his grip on the game. The sports writer was lyrical in his praise of Dave and his soccer ability. Colin attributes his and Dave's abilities to their upbringing in the Arc.

HOW DO YOU EXPLAIN THE GAME OF CRICKET TO AN AMERICAN?
Written by David Kotzen

On several occasions I have tried to explain the game of cricket to Americans, and in most cases they think I am absolutely mad. Confusion, continues when you try to tell them how the game is scored, including bowlers bowling from both sides of the wicket Then I try to explain the various positions of the game such as "silly mid on, mid off or 3rd man etc". By this juncture they are completely baffled. I point out how fiercely competitive the sport is both on the local and international level. Try telling them a high school game begins on a Wednesday afternoon and continues all day on a Saturday, including breaks and lunch. International matches last five days and can end in a draw. Clearly by this time they are totally convinced people who play this game are totally mad. Baseball on average takes about 3½ hours to complete, this has caused much discussion as to how to speed the game up

For many old Arcs that live in the States we remember cricket fondly. How well I remember the pick up games on the veranda on the second floor of the Senior Boys' Department. A wicket was either a chair or three lines drawn on the wall. The game was played with three a side. I recall one time I bowled to Gerry Levy, a phenomenal talent who played in the Nuffield team for the Transvaal and continued his career playing for 1st division in Johannesburg. I got him to pop the ball up, and I believe it was Joe Klug who missed the chance. Obviously, you did not give Gerry a second chance. We struggled for hours trying to get him out. We finally gave up and didn't even bother to bat ourselves.

Then of course there were the games/war played on the field opposite the main building. Choosing sides was a major deliberation. Who would captain? Who would decide the bowlers, or the batting order? The 3rd world war came close on those occasions.

Many years ago I visited SA with my eldest son and took him to a cricket match. I told him if he got bored we would go home. Guess what? He loved the game. Therefore, one might conclude; perhaps Cricket will take over from baseball in this country.

AFTER LEAVING THE ARC
Written by David Kotzen

I came to the Arc at age one and left at age 18 to face the world. I spent 40 years living outside South Africa. The impact the Arc made on me I will treasure for the rest of my life. I have returned to Africa over the years the last occasion six months before the ANC came into power. The South Africa. I once remembered was obviously not in existence. ver the years I have maintained a very close relationship with some of my family and especially Solly Farber, hence my soul and roots have never left SA.

The Arc found me a job working for Hendler and Hendler. I recall vividly how difficult I found this endeavour particularly having spent 17 years with 200 plus kids, and suddenly thrust into freedom, independence and sharing experiences which made a significant impact on my life. To suddenly be laid open to the outside world trying to cope was indeed a challenge. Returning home after a few days work to a small room was difficult to comprehend for an 18 year old.

Fortunately, after three months of trying to live under this environment I moved into a flat with some other Arc boys in Hillbrow. Once again I recall with clarity how Sammy Bearer took on the responsibility of keeping our house in order. He ensured everyone had the appropriate duty to perform, thereby maintaining a successful household. One year later I was called up to the reserves to do my military training. Having spent 17 years of discipline in a controlled environment, I decided I did not need this experience. Consequently I hitch-hiked to Cape Town and worked in the galley of a cruise liner arriving in Southampton a few weeks later.

Once again luck was with me. I met Tony Factor in London. We had known each other during my stay in Cape Town. We shared a room and worked together selling vacuum cleaners door to door. The alliance I had with Tony was similar to that of a brother. We shared some extraordinary times together including "bumming" around Europe. It was shortly after one of these trips Tony returned to SA and of course the rest is history. (I recall visiting him in SA; it was like seeing a long lost family member. We shared a special relationship even up to his unfortunate death).

I decided to immigrate to Canada to work in the Uranium mines in Elliot Lake some G-d forsaken place in North Ontario. I had to wait until late May for the Saint Lawrence River to thaw out sufficiently to allow a boat to be navigated. Arriving at the mines it seemed the Arc would never leave me. Colin Rosenkowitz had staked out in these mines. He had worked there for some time accumulating a fortune and after a year went back to England to open a restaurant in London.

Obviously Colin was a great help explaining the ground rules and assisting me to get settled. At the time the Canadian government welcomed anyone willing to work in the mines. I became a miner's helper which meant a "plumber". My job was to position the pipes which carried water and air from the surface. After three months and almost losing my life due to injury I felt I needed a new venture. I decided, along with a few other guys (including Arc boy, Colin Rosenkowitz), to leave the mines. I crossed the American border at Detroit explaining it was my intent to stay for the week (38 years later I am still here).

We then began to drive cars around the United States for companies or people who required the cheapest way to move their cars. Upon arriving in New York, I decided that I would remain there. The rest of the group headed back to South Africa and England. In New York I took various jobs working as a waiter, then finally decided to work for the airlines at Kennedy Airport.

My life underwent a transformation while working for the Airlines, for it was there that I met the lady who would soon become my wife. Meeting my wife has its humorous side. At the time I worked for British Airways, who had asked me to accompany a passenger who arrived from London illegally.

Due to his illegal status, he had to be escorted to the airline taking him to Canada. Only I knew at that time that I was also living in New York illegally. Nervously I took the passenger through the Custom and Immigration areas of the airport where many of my acquaintances worked. After escorting him to the American Airlines desk, I chose this lovely young women to process him. Needless to say, a romance brewed between the lovely agent and me. We married shortly thereafter, and have been married 40 years and counting. Obviously, my new wife and our marriage made me "legal."

My illegal status was made official when I married my wife soon thereafter. During our stay in New York we became the unofficial South African ambassadors. Many people would visit us from SA including old Arcs Alf James, Donald Goldman, Solly Farber, Louis Kreser, Bernie Aronstam, my brother Barney and sister Julia, hence the Arc endured in my blood.

I later took my family to South Africa, but after a year, both my wife and I realised this was not the environment in which we wanted our kids to grow up. When we returned to the States, I felt the Airlines held little future for me and pursued a career in Retail Management, where I began to work my way up the ladder. I held several different positions with various companies, my first real break coming when I was promoted to Regional Supervisor, which made me responsible for 48 stores in the New York and Washington, DC area. That position carried tremendous responsibility, stress, and strain that eventually led to my having a heart attack. Shortly thereafter I required bypass surgery. Despite this setback, the company wanted to promote me to Vice President. My wife said she did not want to "drag me out feet first" and suggested that the time had come to move to Florida, which she felt would provide a less stressful environment, and a friendlier climate

David with his pet dogs

We relocated to Florida 16 years ago. I took a few jobs in a much lesser capacity, but soon realised I was still under unnecessary stress. For health reasons, I gave up working full-time and pursued part time retail employment. Now I work about 15 hours a week selling clothes for the Gap. I love this job for it allows me the opportunity to keep my foot in the retail door and also to interact with young people. My wife, Mary, also works part time in a family store selling clothing. She is very involved with our pug dogs. She also teaches pet responsibility in the local schools, libraries and scout groups. We have two wonderful sons; the younger one lives in Cleveland. He is the youngest senior Chemical Engineer his company has ever had. He has a wonderful wife and three kids, two girls and a boy. Our eldest son lives in San Francisco. He is the Senior Human Relations Officer for Applied Material, a company that makes the machinery for silicon chips for the computer industry. When we reflect on our lives, both Mary and I are content we gave our kids a solid foundation and, as a result can enjoy our golden years together.

The Arc continues as Louis Kreser lives nearby and we see a

great deal of each other. I also share correspondence with Michael Perry Kotzen, Hymie Sacks and of course Solly Farber who has stayed in contact with me for some 40 years.

In conclusion I can with all sincerity say my childhood is a time I will appreciate and cherish forever. The Arc played a distinct part in my life and helped me to identify the significance of family and unity and for this I will be eternally grateful.

David sadly passed away in July 2002 almost the same day as his great friend Solly Farber.

DAVID KOTZEN'S ELDEST SON, LEN DE LLANO, WROTE IN 2003

I returned from a short weekend trip to Florida to check in and visit my Mom, Mary, Dave's wife. I have been travelling down to Florida every few months since last July when Dad passed away. On most of these short trips, we meet up with family and friends for casual dinners and this time was no different. Penny and Louis Kreser took Mom and I out for dinner on Saturday night and we had a wonderful time, as usual.

This now brings me to the purpose of my writing you this note... Louis gave Mom a copy of the January 2003 "Arcs and Arc Memories" booklet that you created, for her to keep. Again, I must state that we were at a very busy, noisy restaurant when Louis handed over the booklet and while we both looked at it very briefly, I certainly did not delve too deeply at that moment. Later that evening, we returned home late from the dinner and were tired and we both retired early.

However, the next day, while relaxing on the sofa, I picked up the booklet and began to read, and read, and read, and read and look at the pictures, and read. What an amazing work you have crafted!

I cannot fully describe to you the intense interest and fascination with the stories, the articles and the history of so many people's lives that I enjoyed for, what became, several hours, as I read this practically cover to cover. I only went to South Africa once as a boy in 1964-1965 and never knew most of the people mentioned in the booklet (although many of the names are familiar to me as I vividly recall them being mentioned by Dad), but I cannot tell you how incredibly interesting this was as I went from page to page to page. I told Mom she must read this and see the pictures, not just those related to Dad but also of all the other people, the other "family" that was touched by Arcadia.

I knew that I had to just send off a brief note to you to commend you on this wonderful work you have done - an amazing chronicle of life and living and survival and family and love. Thank you for doing this – I know Dad is enjoying it as well

Chapter 71 – WOOLF (WOOLFIE) KOTZEN (1936-1961)

Woolfie was in the care of Arcadia from age three and left in 1955, at almost 19 years old.

'ARC' CINEMA (BIO)
Written by Woolfie Kotzen in 1954

Entertainment plays a big part in every person's life; therefore bio is a thing looked forward to by any Arc. Every Saturday night we have a film show at Arcadia.

We are supplied with films by MGM and African Consolidated Theatres. Beside the main feature we get a serial, and periodically we get films on Israel or other educational themes. The films that are shown are chosen by the children, and therefore it is seldom that the children do not enjoy these films.

If one goes to a proper theatre you are shown to your seat and proceed to see the film in a quiet, relaxing way - but not so at Arcadia.

The Arc bioscope is a noisy and sometimes nerve-racking affair; what with juniors crawling all over the place throwing things at each other, screaming and shooting the villain of the show. Sometimes the noise becomes so unbearable that David 'Owner' Kotzen stops the film until the noise has subsided. The acoustics in the Arc 'theatre' are very bad, and add the noisy Arcs to this and you get the reason why the sound is usually on full blast.

Like at all other bioscopes, certain seats are occupied by fellows and their women loves. If you look hard enough you will see the happy couples sitting in certain corners of the 'theatre'. Some of the senior girls try to keep order in the hall, but their soprano 'Oh! Shut ups' and 'Please keep quiet' only help to make more noise.

Every week there are arguments as to how the serial is going to begin, and sometimes the triumphant cries of people who have won sweet-bets on the serial can be heard. Nearly as regular as the 'serial' arguments is the argument that goes on between Vicky and Norman Sacks. The former always 'parks' himself behind Norman and rests his feet on Norman's chair, he in turn asks Vicky most politely to remove his XXXX (censored) feet. Vicky then starts with his usual 'Bobba, Norrman'. Norman answers with 'Spy, Schloop' and other unmentionable names. Then Vicky starts naming the actors with Arc names.

The projector operators are often cursed in none too mild terms when the film snaps or slips at a critical moment. During the interval Ma hands out sweets, which often change hands because of lost bets on the serial. As the show ends some lousy, selfish people slip out and leave just a few to set the seats straight.

The Arcs drift down to their departments discussing the show, and peace reigns over Arcadia, where the Junior Boys dream about Tarzan, the Senior Boys about Marilyn Monroe, the Senior Girls about Monty Clift, and the Junior Girls dream about that amiable character - Butch Jenkins.

A TRIBUTE TO A FRIEND
Extract from *The Arcadian* 1961
Written by Solly Faber (During his final medical Exams)

With a sense of utter grief and a still unbelieving heart, I record here the tragic death of a true and dear friend and brother Woolf Kotzen, whose young life was ended in a motor accident on February 9th of 1961.

Woolfie had but a few months before returned from England where he qualified as a textile engineer at Leeds University - and was hopefully venturing out into the world where he could only have been a great success. It is not, however, as a budding scientist that I will remember him, but as a true friend with whom I shared the bittermost change from toddler to young adult.

How well I remember Woolfie, as a baby in the Joe Lewis Wing, as a sturdy junior boy, playing soccer with all the earnestness it required and equally patiently queuing up for his 'four o'clocks' on those long Saturday afternoons. How many times we walked around Arcadia together planning and wondering what the future held.

Woolfie was a person of many talents, and he applied his forceful character equally to sport and to the more mundane business of study and the other secular activities.

At the old Forest Town Government School and at Doornfontein School he acquired his primary education. From there he proceeded to Athlone Boys High School for his secondary education. At Athlone he figured very prominently in all aspects of curricular and extra curricular activity. Among other things, he was a member of the 1st XV Rugby side, the Choral Society, the dramatic society and even when time permitted represented the school at Chess! In his senior year at school, he was appointed vice head boy of the school - a well deserved honour.

In Arcadia, where he spent the greater part of his all too short life, he was no less prominent.

As I sit here trying to conjure up a composite picture of Woolfie, many things pass before my mind's eye like a kaleidoscope. I see him as a sportsman, forceful and intelligent, a useful left-winger on the soccer field, and extremely powerful batter at cricket (many time he hit the ball 'down the hill' and over the wall into Oxford Road). Woolfie also made his presence felt at Arc swimming galas and at our own and school athletic meets.

The library reverberated many a time to the tones of Woolfie discussing the Napoleonic Wars, or the geography of this or that country or the Theorem of Pythagoras or the countless other subjects which a matric student must commit to memory.

Woolfie was equally at home on the stage - how well one remembers his portrayal of the Bishop in one of our end-of-holiday concerts, and who will say that he does not remember Woolfie's powerful and sonorous rendering of 'Old Man River' in so many concerts, or in the bath.

His oft-expressed desire to become a writer was in no small way accomplished by his helping to revive 'The Arcadian' which he was wont to call 'The Mouth of Arcadians'. He wrote many inspired articles under the pen-name 'Adoone' which to him signified a wild carefree desert nomad.

Perhaps if one had to choose a single word to describe all his attributes it would be 'sturdiness' … As a very small junior boy he once had his jaw broken by a ferociously delivered cricket ball; while he was being carried off the field, he managed a painful smile and mumbled: 'at least he didn't bowl me out, he knocked me out'.

A juggernaut on the sport field he was as kind as could be when helping fellow Arcs over personal difficulties or giving sound advice where he could not help personally.

To his brothers and sisters I extend on behalf of his many many friends, our heartfelt sympathy. He came upon our horizon like a bright star and when he was burning brightest was cruelly extinguished, but the horizon in which he shone so brightly will never be the same for his having been there.

A MESSAGE FROM ABOVE.
Written by David Kotzen

My brother Woolfie was two years older than I and we grew up in the Arc together. Although two years apart, seemingly, this represented a significant maturity level. He symbolised a father/mother/sister image combined. I looked up to him with great respect and worshipped the very ground he walked on. He was truly an extraordinary individual and I owe much of my life inspirations to his efforts. He gave me emotional stability when I needed it most. He helped to explain the importance of family unity. Over the years he was always there for me.

I recall one specific incident when Abe Kabe, who used to play games in which he was always the German General fighting the Jews. G-d forbid, that you should not want to be part of his German force! On one occasion he tied the reluctant Gerry Levy to the soccer goal posts for hours. Gerry was extremely lucky he did not face serious injury as a result, since his blood circulation had nearly come to a standstill from having been tied to the posts so tightly.

One day Abe decided I should become a German spy. I assured him I would not join his forces, so he began to bully me savagely. Fortunately for me, my brother was nearby and, without thinking of the consequences dove into the melee and rescued me. I can still see him now warning Abe, who consequently had backed down, that if he ever tried that again he would be in serious trouble.

My brother was tragically killed in a car accident in 1961. I made a promise that, if I ever had a son, he would be called

Woolfie after my brother. My son Woolf was born in Brooklyn, New York in 1963. Woolfie is a name not unusual in South Africa but not widely understood or used in the United States. When he was a mere infant, some of the neighbourhood kids wanted to see the new baby and had difficulty with his name. They asked my wife if they could see the new baby "Foxy".

When my son was about 12 years old, we went on a visit to South Africa. I wanted my wife and son to see Arcadia. We were approaching the Arc Shul and I was giving them both a serious dissertation about all that transpired in the Shul. We covered Barmitzvahs, to Yom Kippur services, etc., etc. The one area I went into in great detail, was how during the sermons, to offset the boredom, some of us would carve various images into the back of the pews. On one of the pews is a heart that reads DK loves ZG (Zelda Gordon). My brother had carved "Woolfie 1952".

As we approached the Shul, it was midday. We all decided to look through one of the windows. At that precise moment the sun cast a glow through the window, and came to rest on a carving, illuminating it distinctly, and as plain as day, we could read "Woolfie 1952."

Obviously, I was perplexed for a moment, all I could say to my son was see I told you your uncle's name was Woolfie. This unbelievable, yet true story leads me to believe my brother was saying to his nephew "Hi pal; see we are linked together".

Rubbings from benches in Arc Shul done by Alec Saul and Max Goldman

Chapter 72 - LOUIS KRESER (1937)

Louis Kreser was born in 1937 and was placed in the care of Arcadia in 1947 together with his younger brother Eddie who was born in 1943. Louis lived in Arcadia until he finished school in 1955

EXTRACT FROM 1959 ARCADIAN

"Louis Kreser spent a good part of his youth at the Arc. Generally he was always a very quiet lad, but he certainly proved himself on the sports field. Louis had his eye on a few of the senior girls, but unfortunately, he was such a shy character, that someone else always stepped in before him.

Louis was a prefect at Parktown Boys and represented his school in 1st XI Cricket team for two years and 1st XV Rugby team for the same length of time. He also won five finals in Boxing.

In 1956 he received the Anthony Blatt Memorial Cup for the best Rugby player at his school. He was also awarded the Rotary Cup - a Cup awarded to the most popular boy at Parktown.

Louis Kreser in school uniform

He was a prefect at the Arc and was voted the most popular boy in his time.

Louis is now working in a stationery firm."

Louis was described by 'The Jewish Herald - 29.5.1959' - as one of the Stars in the Maccabi Soccer side".

THE STORY OF AN OUTSTANDING ARC BOY
By Dave Kotzen

Louis Kreser's life in South Africa has been well documented. He was eminently successful as a sportsman and business entrepreneur.

At Parktown Boys' High School he played in the 1st rugby and cricket teams, proving to be very successful in both endeavours.

After high school Louis continued his abilities on the sports field by playing in the Premier cricket league for Old Parks achieving some great results. He played professional soccer for the Rangers Club. He met his wife Penny during this time when she was the club's secretary.

Louis on Solly's shoulders

He entered the business world as a young stationery salesman shortly after leaving the Arc. It did not take him long to realize he could go into business for himself. His extraordinary character came into focus at this time. He demonstrated grit and determination in building his own business. His Company *Louis Kreser Stationers and Printer's* not only flourished under his steady guidance, but became one of the foremost companies in its field both in Johannesburg and South Africa.

In 1979 Louis moved his family to England, he purchased five dry cleaning establishments in London. The lifestyle, and more specifically, the weather soon wore on the family.

In 1982 Louis sold his businesses and moved to Florida in the USA. He purchased Stuart Plastics, a business that specialised in custom work in the making of signs and various items made with plastics. Although the business was well accepted in the area, Louis' ingenuity came into focus once more.

Today he has expanded the business to include the making of T-shirts and highly sophisticated signs made in vinyl. He is also known for his fine workmanship and some of the jobs he has created are quite extraordinary.

In summary when one takes into consideration Louis left the Arc a young man, unsure what the future would hold, one assuredly has to admire his guts, accomplishments and tenacity.

LOUIS KRESER REMINISCES

Taken out of school by social workers, my brother Bennie and I were taken to an undenominational home for about two months. The time seemed like two years. On Sundays we were taken to Church. We had to make the sign of the cross as we walked into the Church. It was the only time of my life that I hated being alive. Thankfully we were taken to the Arc where we adjusted much better with the Arcadian family.

I spent about 11 years at the Arc, and if I was to have it all over again, I would choose the Arc again no doubt about it. I recall the senior boys needed clothes and me, being very small and light, went onto the roof of the stock room where the clothes were kept. Elli Osrin held me by my ankles lying on his stomach as I negotiated opening up the attic window some two floors up. Thank you Elli for not letting go.

I was always very interested in my sport and I was very lucky to achieve my goals. Playing cricket once I was the wicket keeper. Standing up close to the wicket, the ball was bowled down the leg side I moved across to catch the ball. The batsman was Bennie. He swung at the ball as hard as he could, missed the ball and hit me with the bat across my nose. There was blood everywhere, and I remember Abe Kabe putting me in a wheelbarrow (his ambulance) and rushing me to the Arc hospital. I was transferred to the General Hospital to have my first broken nose fixed.

Louis playing Soccer for Rangers

My third broken nose occurred when I was playing soccer for Rangers at Durban against Durban City, I clashed heads with George Barrett. I played the game with a broken nose. After the game I was taken to the Durban Hospital, they said nothing could be done for me. I would have to have an operation in the Johannesburg hospital. Being a non-drinker and with the pain excruciating I had two beers. On the plane home I sat next to a police officer he said I was "too drunk to drive". He sat with me at the airport till after 12 am. At that point he said I had recovered enough to go home. When I got home guess what it was about 3.00 am. As I walked into the house my wife Penny's water broke with our second daughter. I had to rush her to Mary Mount Maternity Home. In the waiting room I heard the nun say "I so hate these drunks that come here".

We have been in the USA for 20 years and live in a small town named Stuart, Florida. It is about 15 minutes away from Dave Kotzen's home. We have three beautiful daughters and three grand children with a new baby expected in October 2001. The eldest daughter Kim is a professional nurse. Leigh the middle daughter is also in the nursing profession. Lani the youngest daughter currently works in the business.

THE HURRICANE OF SEPTEMBER 5th 2005

As you know September 5th, 2004 we had a massive hurricane touch down in Stuart, Florida. About eight miles from where we live and six miles from the business. Penny and I decided to hunker down and not drive up north as recommended by the powers that be. The storm was approximately 60 miles south of us in Palm Beach. It stayed just off the coast for three days, dropping rain the whole time and the wind was blowing around 80 mph. The storm moved north towards us, the winds had picked up to approx. 140 mph, causing it to be an extremely powerful category four hurricane. It finally hit land with the eye of the hurricane touching down in Stuart. The outer bands stretched about 60 miles from the eye, making it one of the most frightening experiences we had ever encountered. We opened the door to look out and there were trees falling over - huge old oak trees, small trees, all trees. The wind was so strong it lifted cars and trucks down the road. The electricity went out, we had candles and flash lights to see. All electric appliances were off, refrigerator, television and worst of all the air conditioner, the heat was stifling at 98 degrees. Needless to say it did not take long to start sweating. We were very blessed as we had no severe damage to our home or business.

The next morning the rain was still falling. We went to assess the damage. Roofs were blown away, houses were knocked to the ground, trees completely uprooted, traffic lights lying in the middle of the road, landmarks were gone. No gas to buy for our vehicles. Business signs and trees covered the roads. Massive clean up crews did a great job clearing the debris. Several days later there was still no electricity. More than 3 million people without power. Water supply was off, no bathing or showering. Normally the wildlife, ducks, birds numerous animals are all over the place, but there were none to be seen. Not sure were they go when hurricanes arrive.

We are approximately in the middle of the state and had work crews come from all over the country to help, clean up and rebuild. Not to mention our saviours who helped get the power back on.

It was two weeks later and unbelievably we were hit with yet another hurricane in approximately the same track as the previous one, doing more damage to our already devastated town. Again we decided to hunker down, not truly believing another hurricane would hit us. In our twenty plus years here we have never experienced a hurricane. Again we had no electricity, water or gasoline.

Fellow old Arcs, count yourselves lucky that you do not live in a hurricane or tsunami area. It is now over a year and our roofs, houses and landscaping is just getting the repairs needed after fighting with insurance companies, who do not like to pay up. It took the government stepping up and telling them enough is enough!!

I have been in touch with Bernie Aronstam in New Orleans but have not been able to get in touch with him since the devastating hurricane hit about a month ago.

Mary Kotzen (Dave Kotzen's widow) no longer lives near us, she relocated to Albuquerque, New Mexico, she has a new house and is very happy there

Chapter 73 – EDGAR (EDDIE) KRESER (1943-1963)

Eddie was born in 1943 and was placed in the care of Arcadia in 1947 together with his older brothers, Louis Kreser who was born in 1937 and Abe and Benny.

Eddie left Arcadia in 1960.

Extract from *The Arcadian* 1961

Eddie Kreser follows his elder brother's (Louis) lead in soccer. He was a quiet yet well-spoken boy. He kept forcefully dreaming about girls; yet the result of his many attempts to make his dreams come true are not known. He is now with Pashley."

Extract From *The Arcadian* 1964
Written by Merwyn Lampert

The news of the death of 'Eddie' as he was known to all of us in Arcadia, on the 11th September 1963 after a long illness, was heartbreaking to us all. For many years, Eddie had lived in Arcadia, and even after he left, he still maintained contact with us by regular visits.

Despite his many activities, such as working, and his intense interest in sports, in which he could partake only in a mild form, his thoughts were frequently with us.

To his family, we wish to extend our deepest sympathy in the untimely death of Eddie, who was only 19 years at the time.

LETTER FROM ABE KRESER
Written by Doc – Dr Adolf Lichtigfeld

The tragic and lamented event of Eddie Kreser's death is touched upon in Abe's (Eddie's eldest brother) letter from London in which he says:

Eddie Kreser

Thank you very much for your letter and for all you have done for my mother and all of us and for the kind words you said. I still feel very upset, but hope to get over it. It was the will of G-d and we must live by it. Arcadia has done a lot for Eddie and all of us, and I am sure wherever he is, he will keep an eye over us all. Doc, please thank the boys and girls for me for their prayers and wish them a Happy New Year.

When reading Abe's letter, we were reminded of Longfellow's immortal words: *'Believing in the midst of our afflictions, that death is a beginning, not an end, we cry to them … and send farewells.'*

In the Library - Eddie standing in the middle

Chapter 74 – SELWYN DEMBO (1937)

Selwyn born 1937 and his brother Erroll born 1944 were both in the care of Arcadia from 1951 to 1954.

Selwyn was one of the Harmonicadians together with Donald Goldman, Effie Segal, Solly Farber, Charlie Segal and David Kotzen.

In later years after leaving the Arc he served for seven years on the Arc Committee. He was a Committee Member in 1984, Honorary Secretary 1985 -1986, Vice- Chairman 1987-1988, Chairman in 1989-1990 and then became an Honorary President.

They both now live in Australia.

THE ARC DRIVEWAY
Extracted from the SA Jewish Times 25 July 1986
Written by Selwyn Dembo in 1955

Never before in *The Arcadian's* history has an article been written about a part of Arcadia's grounds. I have chosen to write about that little talked about and widely used place - the drive.

It is the driveway which greets the newcomer to Arcadia or the old inmate returning after a hard day at school or elsewhere. To anybody walking along it, the driveway must present an awe-inspiring sight. On the gate is a sign "Arcadia, 22 Oxford Road". On either side of the drive are rows of Jacarandas which cover the road with a violet carpet early every spring.

Geographically the drive is the dividing line between "up-the-hill" and "down-the-hill" which are so often referred to in Arc memoirs. It is also regarded by those bunkers who have neglected to keep bus fare as the last lap between Clarendon and home.

I do not think that any sports field has come in for more varied use. It is the regular venues for Saturday morning races and plays an important part in all Arc cross country races and training runs of our local athletes. Thus sports played on the drive include "horsey", cricket, soccer, rugby and sometimes even an occasional scrap.

The drive is always a hub of activity when there is a Barmitzvah or when the Arcs leave for their periodic visits to outside Shuls. On the later occasions the human snake wends its way along the grey road, however, the tail very often shows a great tendency to fall off but unfortunately for the laggers, Vicky is always in the rearguard and he keeps the body intact.

The drive is used as a house of learning by the boys and girls in the higher forms at school. These poor unfortunates can be seen at all hours during "swotting season" repeating facts to themselves and toiling over the hard path of knowledge. The drive has been forced to hear of the campaigns of Napoleon, Bismarck, the Voortrekkers and other historical figures and has countless times been subjected to the preparation of oxygen properties of chlorine.

The activities on the drive at night are as different from those during the day as the senior boys' verandah is from the soccer

The Arc Driveway

field. The great discussions of the century have been held there. There, Arcs and during festivals, Old Arcs, gather on the drive and talk and talk and talk. All the world's problems are settled there. Most famous of the drive orators is Basil Lippy.

A familiar scene in the evening is also that of Henny and Zelly taking their evening walks along the Highway of Arcadia.

Some readers may think that I have forgotten the primary role of the drive – Lover's Lane. "Young Love", it is said "has a mouth of gold". The whisperings of lovers are indeed the sweetest words spoken.

Many Old Arcs who are now married, first expressed their love on the Arc drive. Formerly in spring and summer the drive would be occupied by pairs and groups of Arcs walking together and talking.

For many the drive has been a sympathetic listener to all their troubles and it is to her that Arcs resort when they have some great trouble weighing on their shoulders.

If the drive could only talk we would have access to the history of Arcadia itself. Here the plans, hopes and dreams of the youthful inhabitants of Arcadia have been whispered, spoken out loud and wrung out in tears.

SOME ARC MEMORIES

We were admitted together in 1951, Erroll to the Junior Boys and I to the Senior Boys. I cannot speak for him on these matters but for me The Arc was a very positive experience. I enjoyed the institutional environment and more than anything benefited from being one of the 'boys'. The transition to Arc life was made all the more easy for me as I had already become friendly with other Arcs who were also at Athlone Boys High School.

My contemporaries were the late Woolfie Kotzen, the late Solly Farber who became a life long friend and was responsible for me joining the Arcadia committee, Reuben Lipshitz, Gerry Levy, Leon Spiegler, Chalkie Bortz, Marek Stein, Louis Kreser, Sydney (Paw-Paw) du Bois, Robert Krause, the late David Kotzen, Arnold Levitan, Ann Gordon, Rene Slovo, Cynthia Sassen, Sylvia Gordon, Faye Fannaroff, Audrey Shraga, Zelda Gordon and Judith Berer to mention a few.

I should also add that the Late Linky Klingman and also Eli Osrin, Sam Berer, Punky Fanaroff, and Abe Kreser were in the Senior Boys at the same time though we 'overlapped' for a very short period of time.

Without going into too much detail, incidents which come to mind were:

o Incarceration in the Hospital for a week of quarantine on admission and before being 'released' into the general 'population';
o Cynthia Sassen yelling in annoyance at being left on the pavement without assistance to climb the stone wall after a 'raid' on the George Albu orchards;
o Assisting the Old Arcs in putting on a concert at the Jewish Guild in Joubert Street. Basil Lipschitz's marvellous telling

of the Jewish immigrants' exposure to American Baseball has been imprinted on my mind forever;
o Bunking out together with Dave and Woolfie Kotzen to play Rugby for Athlone in Krugersdorp on a Shabbos morning and then going to watch Transvaal at Ellis Park in the forlorn hope of escaping detection by arriving home during the Saturday night movie;
o Our pigeon *hoks* (which in hindsight resembled a squatter camp) on the side of the hill – I was in partnership with Dave Kotzen;
o The 'foofie' slide from the big Oak tree near the Shul;
o The Harmonicadians with Effie Segal and in particular the Larry Adler concert where he joined us in playing a short Mozart piece;
o A performance of Les Miserables (very condensed) during which Sam Berer stabbed me in the hand with his sword while we were fooling around having sword fights during rehearsal;
o Swotting for Matric until the wee small hours in the Library together with Woolfie, Gerry, Ann and Leon though we suspected that Gerry was boning up on Wisden rather than his academic responsibilities;
o Vereeniging Branch picnics;
o Bikkur Cholim camps;
o Saturday morning soccer and cricket matches after Shul and particularly in the latter years when Doc also joined in;
o Jewish Guild concerts; and last but not least
o Those amazing Pesach Seders.

SINCE LEAVING THE ARC

I have been married for over 40 years to Sandra Gomer and we have four children.

Bradford, our eldest is married and lives in Melbourne with his family, which includes three of our nine grandchildren. David, our second eldest was married in Sydney at the Central Shul to an Australian girl in January 2000 and lives in Sydney but will be relocating to Melbourne in March of this year. He and Suzanne have a son and G-d willing will soon be blessed with a second.

Anton, our youngest and third son also lives in Melbourne with his family, which includes another three of our grandchildren. Janene, our daughter and youngest child was married in Melbourne last August to a Cape Town based Israeli and they too live in Melbourne. They have one year old twin boys.

In South Africa I was an Architect in private practice and since coming to Australia I have abandoned the profession and worked for Multiplex as a design manager/co-ordinator. I was made redundant and now own and operate a chicken shop together with my son in law in St Kilda.

Erroll my brother lives in Sydney and is also married for more years than he would care to mention. He has two children both of whom live in Sydney. His daughter, Nadine is married to a South African who she met in South Africa when visiting us for Anton's wedding. She has three boys, the two youngest being twins. Their son, Searle is as yet unmarried. They, as a matter of interest, have been in Australia for about 24 years.

Chapter 75 – MICHAEL BASIL SEPEL (BASIL) (1938)

Basil was born in Cape Town on the 10th of October 1938 and was in the Arc for 15 years from 1941 to 1956 with his two sisters; Audrey and Isla.

Extract From The 1957 *Arcadian*

Basil was tiny when he first came to the Arc and nobody imagined he would ever grow. Basil thrived on the Arc food and is now a tall, well built handsome lad.

At first he played 3rd Rugby for Parktown Boys, but he later gave it up for hockey, in which he gained a place in the 1st team. Basil was a keen boxer and won three finals.

At the end of last year he gained a University Pass which enabled him to take Agriculture at the Natal University

REMEMBERING ARC CARERS/THE BOSSES

My only experience with Harary was at the age of five when I came late for my first ever Hebrew lesson, because I preferred climbing roofs. On entering the class I was struck by a hard slap which is still wringing to this day. A few months later I accidentally burnt down the lower hill. Fortunately the slapping man was abroad for a few months. I was too young to feel or judge the man.

Sister Goldwater took over the Arc for only a short period after the Hararys left. She was like a saint in comparison with Maggie and Archie Harris who came after her.

Archie Harris was another cup of tea. Briefly you cannot run Arcadia on Oliver Twist-like reasoning. Bullying and cruelty are for the stupid. Funny enough Harris liked me, more precisely he needed me. Now this cousin of Chief Rabbi Rabinowitz taught me over a long period of time a torah reading which was supposed to be for my Barmitzvah but in fact was for a haphtorah reading for Yom Kippur.

Maggie used to beat the girls and boys alike. She would have had perfect results had she used kindness, love respect and toleration, which Doc achieved a couple of years later.

Henny Kaufman in my time was the senior boys' nurse. By then she had been in the Arc for many a year and so had become an old frustrated spinster with a volcanic cough that eventually killed her. However there were rosy moments too: Teaching us to play percussion and other metal striking musical instruments which she brought out with her from Germany.

Zelly her younger sister on the other hand was a very polite, calm and effacing gentle lady who was in charge of the laundry for many a year. I was too young to really understand any of the above bosses except Doc and Ma.

Basil Sepel with Ralph Levinsohnon on his Shoulders

FAGGING
Written by Basil Sepel

I was the fag of two guys. Benny Touyz who later became Quarter Master General of the Israeli Army. I only volunteered to do it because he was kind enough to teach me how to raise pigeons.

Then I switched to Jackie Mekler who later held many very long distance running world records. He is probably the only Arc ever to be a medal winning Springbok and world record holder. However at the age of nine I discovered responsibility after my first ever holiday with my mom and sisters. So I told Jackie I was too old to be a fag. Anyway he was nice to end it all with a slight slap to my face.

Fagging, slaving, serving just isn't my cup of tea – however Solly Sachs begged me to let him look after my pigeons as well as making my bed etc. So I allowed it for a short while because it pleased the little guy. Now Solly is the Director General of the Worlds Zionist Federation.

BASIL SEPEL
Written by Hymie Pearlman

One of my great heroes in the Arc was Basil Sepel. A man with volcanic power in his veins and the best brake-system to stop a truck when it came to self-control. One look into Basil's molten eyes when he was cross, was enough to turn anyone into a sheep and made many a man think twice. I don't think Donald wanted a "demolisher" on his hands because Basil would have annihilated anyone in the ring if he had been encouraged to box on.

Nevertheless, Basil went on to great heights with his BSc (Hons) Degree in Agriculture as well as his place in the Natal Hockey Team (approx. 1960) – a man for all seasons – Traveller, Philosopher, Lover, Poet, Raconteur and Thinker.

I remember Basil saving the day at Bikkur Cholim Camp in 1959 when he was one of the Midrachs. Some of us had bunked out of camp one night, but we got caught because of a roll call. There were other non-Arc leaders and they were very strict and wanted to send us back to Johannesburg, but Basil used his persuasive reasoning powers and we stayed on to finish the holiday.

If Basil set his mind to do something, you can bet he would achieve his goal. He must definitely have French blood in his veins because we know how passionate and unique the French are. Those traits definitely apply to him and his French ancestors.

Viva Basil "Seprich", Viva

AFTER LEAVING THE ARC
Written by David Solly Sandler

Basil says he was dumb at high school because it never interested him, but that changed after leaving the Arc. Basil was one of the top students in graduating class at university and completed a BSc Agric (Hons Equiv). He obtained University colours at 18 and was a first team South African Universities Soccer player.

Basil works for himself as an English teacher in private companies and develops subjects of conversation etc for creative professional intelligent students.

Basil wrote that his free way of life in Paris has resulted in his books - *This Magnificent Universe* - an autobiography in poetic form, as well as its sequel *High Fly In The Sky Lets Try*

MY FAMILY
Written by David Solly Sandler

Basil met a French woman while travelling overseas –"voila my French connection" and has four children – Eric nearly 42 lives in France and has three girls (twins Nina and Daniella and Celina and a son David. They are bilingual, speaking Spanish and French and David was the top Junior Mathematician in SM de Tucunum in Argentine where they were living.

Eric is an accountant but prefers running Companies than accounting. Steve 41 is a Physical Therapist - works in a hospital where he does research and lecturing. Steve came top of his class of 300 in France's elite Military Service while doing his military and he led Les Chasseurs Alpine down the Champs Elysees on a Bastille day. He has two kids Josephine and Sophie. Sophie has a very high IQ of 149.98 (maximum 150).

Lisa 26 has degrees in History and Art History and is completing her year of Museumology hoping to eventually become a curator, something extremely difficult to achieve. Ken 24 is doing computer engineering part time.

Audrey, his older sister is four years older than Basil. She was in the Arc for about nine years and is married to J Wiegand and has three kids – Wally who passed away few years ago and twins Wayne and Wanda.

EXTRACT FROM THE 1959 ARCADIAN

Isla, his sister, younger by two years was in the Arc from 1943 to 1957. Isla came to the Arc when she was a babe and what a 'babe' she turned out to be. Isla was above average at everything she tried, but she excelled in sport. At Athlone Girls High she received colours for netball and gymnastics and won the most popular girl award twice at Arcadia. "

Isla was married to Roberts and has a daughter Laureen and son Brad. All work in the family business and remain in South Africa for the time being. She was one of the best ever Arc school sports girls and captained most team sports when only still in Form 1V. Isla died in June 2000

Basil Sepel

BASIL'S POETRY BOOKS

Photo of Book Cover - This Magnificent Universe

Photo Of Book Cover - High Fly In The Sky Lets Try

SELECTIONS OF BASIL'S POETRY

This poem is an Arc story –

GROWING UP

*The Pigeon Cages Are
To Be Pulled Down
Diseases Dangerous For The Health
But Really Needing The Parts
For Protecting Young Orchard Plants
To My Surprise Found Myself On My Feet
Yelling At The Top Of My Voice
At The One And Only Adult I Loved
If You Touch My Hock
I'll Break Every Window Of The Schul
He Rushed At Me As Did
Two Large Adults From Either Side
Leapt On To The Dining Room Table
Sending Cutlery And Plates
Clattering Shattering To The Floor
Two More Leap On To Two Other Tables
And Out Of The Window Did I Speed
Down The Hill Did I Run
Picking Up A Long Metal Pole
And There In Front Of My Hock
Did I Stand A Threatening Menace
To Any Would-Be Destroyer*

Moral of the story is that years later when I visited the Arc Mine was the only *hok* still standing. Doc had the Genius not to interfere, hence the rapid happy ending.

LIFE AND DEATH ETERNITY

*Life is the eternal beginning
Of something new
Whether man flea flower earth
Sun galaxy universe or whatever
Death is the eternity of that
Which has come and gone forever
Time is the factor erasing even
Death itself from memory
All life must eventually disappear
To make place for other life
All death is permanent and eternal
For there is no beginning again of
That which has been, except
The temporary genetical transmission
Thus it is only natural to respect
Both life and death
To permit everything living an equal
And just chance in being*

March 1995

BOXING

Step into this ring and fight like a man
But I'm only a skinny five year old
This big guy knocked me one
My head exploded
But stood on my feet
Hating to do down or cry
He hit me again and again
So started throwing punches
To try and save my little self
Ten years later finally gave up the scene
But not after fighting mostly
Somebody much larger
Who hurt me real bad
But never gave up
Returning blow for blow
At the end of which down the hill
Did I go to cry alone
Until the wicked pain subsided
May 1995

ETERNITY

The galaxies go on forever
In multiple universe forms
Other earths are already there
And all that is therein
Including mighty man
Is never quite the same
Life is only genetically eternal
There is nothing else after death
So death itself is the eternity
Forever

I sent "Eternity" to Doc who answered that death was not the end of it all. And so I wrote "Life and Death Eternity". Doc then replied that at least I had thoroughly thought it through.

WHEN I RETURN

Would gladly be a moving wave
Travelling many continents brave
Tapping slapping caressing thighs
Twirling whirling curling highs
Coming grounding singing byes
Washing wetting dripping bouts
Smoothing grinding rounding mounts
Fondling grooving spurting spouts
Coasts sculptured by constant lapping
Lapping wave pleasantly playing
Playing forever joyful wave
Returning

GRANDFATHER

Around four was playing in cactus garden
When a long white-bearded stranger
Beckoned me actively to his side
Fear sent me deeper into cactus protection
Soon man people were running around
Calling me to come out or else
But to no avail
As I snuggled deeper into
My safe cactus paradise
They then changed the tune
By offering me sweets and more
But stubbornly I remained
Safe in my cactus world
Finally they all went away
And I never saw the bearded man again
Who was probably my grandfather
Stranger

UPBRINGING

I was raised to hate hell
Hell hated all that Evil
Evil that dominated so many
Many persuaded by fear and stupidity
But I was vaccinated against Evil
Fighting Evil or being fried
Burnt for being unwanted being
So fight against Evil had to
Had to do it or die
Die or fry or left to cry
Cry belittled by bully
Devil bully hate your hell
So to hell did send all Evil
May 1966

THANKFUL

Pleasantly awakening tingling and bare
Taking in the clean refreshing morning air
Joyfully breakfasting on tea and fruit fair
Watching a lizard scampering up the wall
A hawk gliding then darting in free fall
The sun warming and making one feel tall
A walk through the open relaxing countryside
Feeling the green grass tickling the underside
A rabbit nibbling the fur of another beside
Looking far through the widely empty space
Giving a heavenly feeling to the place
One can only be very thankful with Grace
This glorious day coming to an end
It is only fair that we should bend
To that unseen power in which we spend
Grateful

SOME APPRECIATIONS OF THIS MAGNIFICENT UNIVERSE

An autobiography in poetic form - M B SEPEL

- One of the greatest living writers of the English language

  Finely Heated Verse (AMERICAN - Gore Vidal)

- A Warner Brothers senior President

  *Read It Twice - Wonderful (*English - Julian Senior)

- An Adjointe au Directeur Général

  Votre livre est comme une source refraichissante gui jaillissent toutes les emotions de la vie, avec pureté, brio simplicité, un humour revivifiant, et toujours l'espoirs (Belgium - Dominique Lund)

- The strongest man in the world

  Thank you for thinking of us

- The Convener of *The Bay Poets*

  Your observations, based on incidents in your life, were to the point and based on acute philosophical perceptions

- An excellent Musician

  Ecoutez, c'est poéme! Mais oui, ils chantent! Symphonie de l'instant, symphonie de toujours (French - Etienne Weber)

- A top Educationalist

  It covers everything. It's about your life, about my life, it's about everybody's life. It really is universal (Dutch - Eric Verhulp)

Basil with his four children and granddaughter Josephine

LICHTIGFELD 'ENLIGHTENMENT' (1952-1972)
A NEW ERA

Adolf and Renia Lichtigfeld (known as Doc and Ma to all the children) ushered in a golden age of enlightenment and caring which left behind the era of harsh punishment.

They believed in gently talking and appealing to our better senses, rather than using threats, force and beating.

Copy of a portrait by Shani Krebs

"The winds of change in regard to childrearing were but a mere breeze yet,
but they anticipated them by 20 years or more." Solly Farber

Chapter 76 - ADOLF AND RENIA LICHTIGFELD (1952-1972)

Dr Adolph and Mrs Renia Lichtigfeld (affectionately known as Doc and Ma by all the children) were appointed Superintendent and Matron in August 1952 and quickly won the affection of the children with their caring and enlightened approach.

Doc besides being our friend, guardian and Rabbi was also a philosopher and a scholar of world-renown.

Ma, in her turn, handled all the more difficult matters of discipline and instilled in the girls a knowledge of Jewish domestic matters and custom.

Over their 20 years of service to Arcadia they proved themselves indeed as father and mother to the many at Arcadia who passed through their hands.

At the end of February 1972 Doc and Ma retired on pension. This decision was due to Ma's ill health and was much regretted by the Committee.

They lived for many years in a flat in Yeoville and visitors were always made welcome. Ma passed away in March 1980 and Doc in September 1985. They were indeed both very honourable people who will forever be remembered by the children they cared for.

Doc ready for soccer

'DOC' - A GREAT GUY
By Solly Farber

Now to come to Doc the brightest light in my life. Dr A Lichtigfeld came to Arcadia in 1951. The winds of change in regard to childrearing were but a mere breeze yet, but he anticipated them by 20 years or more.

His approach to us was (to borrow a phrase from modern psychology) 'I'm OK you're OK', which was then a rather revolutionary concept. I truly believe that Doc did not see any bad in any child. He was not blind to our failings but he accepted them as human. I cannot recall him ever belittling or putting down any child in his care. Prior to his arrival we had been through a rather rough patch. Arcadia had been without a Master for some time and we were rather unruly.

One day this learned man and his loving wife arrived to take charge of us. We were rather bemused that such a man of learning should be our new 'parent'. Let it here be said that Doc is indeed learned - he has a doctorate in Jurisprudence from Bonn University, doctorates in literature and philosophy from most of the universities in South Africa and to boot he is a man of the cloth.

Initially we were overawed and shy of him but within a short while he won us over, not by any fancy psychological ploys or by being permissive - no he and 'Ma' (as we soon dubbed her) brought a sense of caring for each and every Arcadian, a sense of peace. I still marvel even now at the way in which the whole atmosphere changed, Arcadia ceased to be an institution and became a 'Home'.

Of all my days in Arcadia I remember Doc and Ma's era as the happiest and most joyful. Doc got to know each child's strengths and weaknesses and he made the most of the strengths and forgave the failings. If any one showed any talent in any direction he fought tooth and nail to give that talent a chance to flower.

Education was his special forte and he was totally committed to seeing that each of us achieved the maximum we were capable of. Prior to his time it was not expected of Arcadians to matriculate but under his guidance many Arcadians did indeed do so and went on to higher education. In this he often had to fight not only with a rather doubtful committee and our parents but even with us, his erstwhile charges. He insisted on our full attention to our school work and arranged extra lessons at every turn. He believed that everyone could do better and even the brighter pupils had to attend these coaching sessions.

My personal view of life was completely turned over by this wonderful man and his equally marvellous wife. I had been somewhat of a rebel under his predecessor whom I have not mentioned in these writings before. From being an 'incorrigible brat' I became a favoured son. 'How' you may ask 'was life different'. We still lived in dormitories, we were still Arcadia children, we were still subject to the myriad restrictions that this implied. Let me now tell you.

Doc became in a way one of us and yet he was the boss. He did not order this or that to be done but rather requested or suggested a particular line of action and usually led by his own example. In the mornings he was in Shul with us to lay teffilin; He saw us off to school with a warm greeting and good luck wishes if we were writing exams or taking part in sport activity.

He knew how we were faring in the school room and helped where necessary. Should one of us be ill he and Ma came to the hospital to visit and we felt that they really cared. On Saturday mornings we played soccer after Shul.

Doc would be on the field in his togs and join in and on the field he was just another player and would protest loudly if he felt he wasn't being considered as such. On one particular Saturday he and I were playing on the same side. I passed the ball along the wing to Louis Kreser who was a superb footballer. (Louis went on to play professional soccer in later years.) 'Well done' shouted one of our team but Doc protested 'That was by no means well done, Louis is being marked by three players and I am unmarked here in front of the goals'.

Now Louis even closely marked by 10 let alone three players was a better prospect than Doc in that situation, but Doc did not see it that way and he let me know how he felt. We were wont to raid the pantry in the evenings when we felt hungry. One evening Doc actually instigated such a raid and accompanied us. The Yale lock was easily opened with a knife and we had a hearty feast with Doc receiving his fair share of the swag.

As I recall it the night watchman came to investigate the noise in the pantry but Doc sent him off with an explanation that he was already dealing with us. The next day we found a new and impenetrable lock attached to the door; so there were no more raids on the pantry; but each evening sandwiches and tea were put out for anyone who was swotting late. This was Doc's way.

He was proud of our every talent. Whenever visitors came to visit for example on a Friday evening the after dinner hour was turned into an impromptu concert and the visitors had to hear every singer and every musician make music. We had a harmonica band at the time of which I was a member and we had perforce to perform on such occasions. On one such occasion I felt that the band had not practised for some time and would not give a creditable performance. I refused to fetch the instruments and Doc became very annoyed. When I tried to explain my reasons for not wanting to play, Doc would not have it 'What matter' he said, 'You may know that you haven't practised but the visitors won't - so nu play', and we did!

At prize-giving time Doc would be loath to leave anyone out and he somehow managed to see that nearly everyone got a mention somehow even if it was only for trying or for improving. Often when we went on our interminable runs around the streets of Parktown, Doc would don his own special outfit and join us.

If the school authorities were threatening to fail one of the boys he would go to the school personally and plead the case for the boy and he often succeeded if only with a stern promise to the headmaster that so and so would work the following year; and work so and so did - Doc saw to that.

In the Shul Doc was another person altogether. As he walked to the Bimah to preach his sermon we would encourage in loud stage whispers 'Make it short Doc'. He would start off intending to make a short sermon but then his wonderful mind would take him down all sorts of side paths and one had to listen very carefully to keep up with these convolutions .In the main we were not up to this task and then the congregation would become restive. Doc would soon realise this and would return to his central theme. It often came as a shock to us that Doc who was always otherwise at our level was suddenly meandering along philosophical pathways where we were unable to stay the pace with him.

I know that some of the chaps would not or could not comprehend his sermons but I personally found that by close attention I could understand what he was driving at and even marvel at the wealth of knowledge and wisdom he was trying to share with us. And then after Shul we were all on the soccer field again and Doc was there playing inside left and being bawled out by one of us for missing a sitter of a goal.

These small incidents give an idea of how things were under Doc's benevolent wing. He has retained his interest in Arcadia and the Arcadians. At our various functions he is always there in his black beret. He can usually be spotted by the group of Arcs, old and young, clustered around sharing their latest joys and sadnesses.

THE PERSON I ADMIRE
By Charlie Segal - An extract from 1959 Arcadian

As we pass through life we meet various kinds of people. Some we tend to like and others we tend to loathe. One should never express an opinion of a person, and the only way really to know somebody is by coming into frequent contact with the person.

I have lived in an institution for nearly 16 years, and during this period I have met a good many people. Of all these people, the one I admire most is the present superintendent of our home.

In most institutions the people in charge are usually very stringent and unfriendly. They think that the only way to control children is by inflicting heavy punishment on them. In our home we are very fortunate to be superintended by a man who has had a great deal of experience with children.

They say that no matter how wonderful a person may appear he always has some bad characteristics. I waver that this is definitely not the case with our superintendent. Our superintendent happens to be a doctor of philosophy. All the children know about this and have nicknamed him 'Doc'. I have been embroiled in many difficulties during my stay at the home and each time I asked Doc for help he was only too glad to be of assistance. Doc is very friendly and lenient with the children. I think that is why there is such a homely atmosphere in our institution. Such a great love has been established for Doc by the children that there are hardly any children who take advantage of Doc's leniency. Those that do are flouted by the rest.

New children are admitted to our home every year. These children are usually children from broken homes. One has to be very patient with them, for the majority have been influenced by their parents and have very belligerent and quarrelsome attitudes. At first these children seem to be incorrigible, but owing to Doc's patience and attention to them, the bad memories of their former homes are gradually obliterated and they adopt the happy and peaceful habits of their fellow inmates.

Sometimes, during the fruit season, some of the boys filch fruit from the neighbouring orchards. After a few of them have been caught on these ventures they are handed over to Doc to administer some sort of punishment. I am sure that at any other home a boy would be severely caned or punished for committing such a crime. Doc is greatly prejudiced against punishment to children and by using his patience and kindness with these boys, he inveigles them to renounce their filching.

I only wish all homes could have superintendents like our Doc. If they did, I'm sure there would be much happier orphaned children in this world.

[This essay was originally published in 'The Athlonian']

DOC - By *Basil Sepel*

As we all respect and love DOC and all he stood for I wrote THE ARCADIAN because if anybody ever deserves that title it's DOC. I mean DOC represented DECENCY. To this day I've never ever met a person with Doc's qualities.

THE ARCADIAN

An outstanding morality
Always Ready To Give Hope
The Perfect Guide And Example
Treating Everyone Alike
Whether Ignoramus Or Intellectual
Always Ready To Encourage
A Dynamo Of Decency
A Happiness To Others
Always Available Despite The Work
Never Expecting Compliments
Nor Wanting Them At All
Of Course You Guessed Right
It's The One And Only Doc

HOW 'MA' GOT HER NAME
By David Kotzen

Sometimes I wonder if I am a celebrity of some sort, due to the fact I was the one who named Doc Lichtigfeld's wife "Ma". A name she evidently inherited throughout her stay in Arcadia. There was speculation if she in fact had any other name. To the best of my recollection I am going to try and explain why I felt she symbolized a mother I never knew.

I came to Arcadia at age one and left at 18 years old. It would be fair to say I was never exposed to family life. The Kotzen family was rather extensive made up of seven boys and five girls, I being the second youngest. Due to the considerable age differences many of my brothers and sisters were strangers to me. The concept of motherhood was something I quickly learned to do without. However, when Ma Lichtigfeld came into the picture something from deep within responded to this kind woman. Without provocation I suddenly acknowledged for the first time what a mother might be like. I called her Ma and the name stuck.

DOC AND MA
By David Sandler

When I arrived in the Arc in 1956 Doc and Ma were already there and when I left in 1969 they were still there. I always saw them as simply part of the Arc as much as the buildings were part of the Arc. I don't remember them taking days off as` the other staff were, in fact, on weekends when other staff had time off and all the kids were at home they were always there covering for the other staff. Doc and Ma were always there for us.

Doc was a Rabbi, a scholar and our guardian and friend.

When I remember Doc the Rabbi I see him standing on the Bimah in Shul blessing us all as follows:

> *"May the Lord bless you and keep you. May the Lord make his face shine upon you and give you peace and happiness. Amen."*

The sun would be streaming into the Shul behind him through the large windows and he would have just finished his sermon which very few of us could follow. I lasted maybe the first few sentences and then my mind was somewhere else.

Doc would lead the service and singing, read the torah, teach us our bar and Batmitzvahs, lay tefillin with us every morning, conduct the daily evening service for the boys and make sure we went to Chedar. At the oneg on Saturday afternoons, he would ask us questions on Judaism and then have to give us endless clues until we got the answer correct.

When I remember Doc the scholar, I see him in his study, upstairs in his flat. Around all the walls of the study were bookshelves with books going from the floor to the ceiling. Stacked on his desk were very tall piles of books. Sticking out of the books were markers and notes with scribbles. Doc was delving into and researching another subject.

Doc was a doctor of philosophy. He not only knew many languages, but also wrote articles on philosophy for European universities where he was also invited to lecture. He was a lecturer at The University of Witwatersrand. and was associated with the university long after he retired.

He was a voracious reader often borrowing the latest James Hadley Chase paperback from Muffy (Michael Goldstein) and then reading it, and giving it back the next day. I remember him learning Afrikaans and then Italian (I think) in a very short time. What took us years to study would take him weeks.

When I remember Doc as our guardian, I see him visiting us in hospital and taking a personal interest in how we were each doing at school and the occasional reprimand and caning. We always looked forward to Doc visiting us in hospital. He would bring us comics and stop and chat with us. It was almost worth bunking school for the comics.

Doc was always concerned to ensure we did well at school and we had extra lessons in English (remember Mrs Dritz) and Afrikaans (Mr Nelson) whether we needed them or not. He encouraged us at school and always tried to get the best out of us through education.

Doc did not reprimand us often and he was even kind to us when it came to caning us. He had a thick bamboo cane which was dry and split and which he kept behind his office door. It did not hurt no matter how hard he hit us.

I have many memories of Doc as our friend. He used to play soccer with us every Saturday morning after Shul. He would chat and joke with us and know us each well. He knew who smoked and which kids had a girlfriend and generally who fancied who and what was happening.

I remember, on one occasion, at Arc bioscope, Doc asked me for an apple and cool drink. I readily obliged and stole an apple from the fruit room for him and reported that I could not reach the cool drinks. He thanked me and had a big knowing smile on his face. I could not understand why he scolded me on another occasion when I offered him carrots stolen from the Arc orchard.

I also remember Doc driving me in a great rush to the general hospital in his own car when I broke my arm. I remember him crunching gears and I was quite scared, as Doc was not known as the best of drivers. I was spared the full trip as when we got to the bottom of the Arc drive the driver appeared and he was turned around and sent with Sister Conway and me to the hospital.

At one of the Hebrew School Sports Days when we won all the prizes a teacher of one of the other Hebrew schools threatened to complain that we were including runners who were older than the age group for the race. Doc took the teacher aside and whispered a few words into his ear and although the other teacher was correct, he did not take the matter further. I would have liked to be a fly on the wall to hear what Doc had to say.

Hebrew Sports Day with the Arcs (standing at back) showing off all their trophies with the younger other prize winners in the front.
L to r Marian Shrager, Harry Kupferberg, Julius Gordon, Stanley Stein, Les Sacks, Doc Keith Lang, Jenny Sandler, Estelle Langman and Brenda Stein.

When it came to some of the real tricky things we wanted Doc would wriggle out of it by saying "ask Ma" with a big knowing smile on his face.

Even after Doc had left the Arc and he was staying in Yeoville he still took a great interest in us. Doc would always welcome visitors and would always stop and chat and insist we stay and "at least drink some tea". He lead the prayers at the funeral of Thelma Durbach and after I went overseas he would always promptly answer any cards or letters I sent him…always wanting to know how I was getting on.

Ma never had the same rapport with the kids as Doc, and I think that when you are responsible for other people's kids you have to be stricter than with your own kids. She was strict with us, especially with the girls, and had a very onerous task keeping us all in line. Behind that strict facade, however, she was very sensitive and caring.

We would see Ma every Friday night when she came down to the Babies Department to light the candles. She was also there when it was our birthdays to give us a brown paper bag of sweets (Arc boilies), that we shared with the other children, and also to give us a birthday present. I remember once receiving a submarine and on another occasion a magic robot that answered questions by pointing a little rod.

On the first Sunday of each month Ma made sure we all went out and she would ask parents who did come to sometimes take also the children who had nobody visiting. I remember going out with Les and Tony Mark and their Mom, with Leon Goodman and his Mom and also many times with Mrs Feldman. I remember Max coming with me on one or two occasions too.

On Sundays that were normal visiting days for parents there were some children who never received visitors. At around four in the afternoon we would all gather in the bread room and wait for Ma to come down with her big bunch of keys. Ma would always find us a bun or a piece of cake to eat and milk, *Lecol* or even a cool drink to drink. If we were lucky we would even receive a few sweets.

Ma always told Jenny (my sister) and I not to fight, but that we should love each other and be good to each other as we only had each other. It did not make much sense then, but I find myself saying it to my two daughters now.

Ma once related a story to me, to the effect that, when she was a child she was lonely and always wanted to go to a school (or was it a home?) with lots of other kids but that this never happened. Only when she was married and grown up did it happen that her wish was granted when she came to the Arc - a home with kids.

After Sister left, Ma would look after the hospital and would come and visit us and take care of us. She always seemed to have the exact tablet to take right there in her pocket when you complained of a headache or some other minor ailment. I once heard another younger Arc say, "Yes, Ma really cared" and that when she was sick Ma used to sit next to her bed until she fell asleep.

I think of Ma and I regret being rude and cheeky to her. She had to put up with a lot of our nonsense but this did not stop her from caring for us.

OUR CHILDREN
By Ma – from the 1957 Arcadian

When one speaks about Arcadia, one cannot help seeing children with their good and bad habits - with their consideration and love for each other - with great tolerance for each other; just like in every family, only a larger one. There are children gifted and not so gifted, all trying their very best in school, sports, sewing, art, dancing and home activities. Some excel and some manage just to make the grade. One tries one's hardest to make them feel at home, and I hope they feel the same as we want them to feel.

We would like every child to achieve a high standard of education - as this is the only thing in life that nobody can take away from them. No matter where you may arrive later in life, it is not like money that comes and goes; it is with you to the end of your days. Education is something that cannot be appreciated while you are young but certainly is something which you realise the value of in later life.

Therefore my dear Children, try and follow our desire - do well in school, work hard, let encouragement stimulate you - so that you can enjoy later the fruits of your labour.

Ma with the 'Babies'

MESSAGE FROM DOC (DR A LICHTIGFELD)
"Doc" former Superintendent of Arcadia - 1981.

I gladly follow Dr Solly Farber's kind invitation to write a message for the Commemorative Bulletin of Arcadia's 75th Jubilee.

Let me first heartily congratulate the President, Executive and Committee of Arcadia who are playing such a prominent part in Arcadian affairs, including the present principal and matron.

It gives me personal great satisfaction to have been privileged, together with Ma, of blessed memory, to labour in the vineyards of Arcadia. Those who know Ma's character and saw her at work will readily acknowledge the fact that she fulfilled her duties (for her a labour of love) with great devotion. When thinking back, I dare say we did contribute to change the then-prevailing climate insofar as we tried to imbue each child, of whatever talents, with the strong feeling that there will eventually be a place in the sun for them. Of course, we were privileged, too, to have the support of an understanding and hard-working committee. Those were the days when we had about 120 and more children at the Home.

Just as we were helped in making the transition from one form of administration to another, more suitable for Arcadia at that time, so too, since our time, it appears that much progress has been made. In addition, some of the Old Arcs rising to positions of great responsibility in running the affairs of Arcadia have also enabled it to meet the challenges of today constructively. In our time, we were fortunate in having had the support of members of the committee whom it would be invidious to name in particular since they all participated fully in guiding the destiny of Arcadia. But of those who made it possible for all of us to work together harmoniously for the benefit of the children of Arcadia, I am pleased to see some are

still active in giving their support and wisdom to the people who are at the moment steering Arcadia on its destined path of service to the Community.

In retrospect, nothing that one has done in life is anywhere near perfection, but I would like to crave your indulgence and mention my satisfaction (which was always Ma's pride as well) at having opened some doors that had previously been closed to Arcadians.

I may conclude with a statement of a famous contemporary philosopher (Emmanuel Levinas) whose lines of thinking converge upon this focal point of his dialectics which he called: "On the trail of the Other". I can't think – at this momentous occasion of Arcadia's 75th – in no other way than refer to Levinas' message to our time which reads as follows:

"To go toward Him (G-d) is to go toward the Others" and in helping Others, the eternal impulse to return to G-d is being brought without our reach".

May all who help Arcadia be blessed to achieve this aim in their lifetime.

The Batmitzvah Girls of 1952. Shirley Bortz, Sarah Farber, Miriam 'Mickey' Gordon, Cynthia Lipschitz, Anne Gordon, Devorah Weinek, Sheila Berer with Ma and Doc.

FREDDIE LICHTIGFELD

Freddie is the son of Doc (Adolf Lichtigfeld) and Ma (Renia). Freddie lived in Arcadia in the early to mid 1950s while he was a medical student at the University of the Witwatersrand. He was responsible for editing the 'postbag' (all the incoming letters) in the 'Arcadian' magazine that was produced by the Arc Children of the day. I'm sure many of Arcs from that era remember Freddie. After he left the Arc and was visiting, he was always invited by Doc to play soccer with the boys on a Saturday morning so younger Arcs would know him too.

About 30 years ago, when I was auditing in SA, I did hear the Matron at a Sanatorium speaking very highly of Freddie. Also Doc mentioned Freddie in a letter he sent me many years later.

Like Doc, Freddie was completely devoted to his work far beyond the call of duty and I imagine like Doc he had a different understanding of the world and was not too concerned about some everyday things that would be of concern to you or I.

LEADING COMMUNITY PSYCHIATRIST DIES
Sent in by Ros Kupferberg

A pioneer in his field and a man who took psychiatry deep into the Southern Kwa-Zulu Natal rural areas, Dr Fred Lichtigfeld, who died recently, will be sorely missed. Dr Lichtigfeld was still a practising psychiatrist when he died in Port Shepstone at the age of 71. He was on his way home from a rural clinic when he was killed in a motor accident.

His colleagues believe that he never earned the acknowledgement he deserved for the ground-breaking work he did in his field. A humble man who never sought money and fame, he lived abstemiously, drove battered old vehicles and was known to dress shabbily. However, he always maintained a lively interest in his work, keeping abreast with any new developments in psychiatric medicine. For many years he was the only psychiatrist to attend to patients in the many rural clinics of Southern Kwa-Zulu Natal and he also consulted on the north coast. Twice a month he held consultations at Port Shepstone Hospital, as well.

Born in Dusseldorf, Germany, Dr Lichtigfeld left his country of birth as a child, in 1935, after his Jewish father was warned to leave Germany. The family settled in England then moved to South Africa after the war. Dr Lichtigfeld attended Germiston High School then studied psychiatry at the University of the Witwatersrand.

After qualifying, he spent four years in the USA, where he pioneered the use of Lithium as a treatment for bipolar disorder. He was also one of the first psychiatrists to treat patients with lysergic acid diethylamide (LSD) a substance that was later banned. However, he always believed that it could have a place in medicine.

Freddie Lichtigfeld

In the 1970's he worked at Sterkfontein Mental Hospital in Krugersdorp before moving to Kwa-Zulu Natal in the early 1980s where he set up community psychiatric services in the rural areas. He also teamed up with Dr Mark Gillman, researching the use of nitrous oxide as a psychotropic agent. They developed the hypothesis that nitrous oxide interacted directly at neurotransmitter receptor sites and could be used to treat alcohol addiction. Although they published their findings in *The Lancet,* their groundbreaking work received little notice.

In 1989 academics at John Hopkins University in the USA found that nitric acid as opposed to nitrous oxide was involved in neurotransmission. No mention was made about the work the two South Africans had already done in this area.

In 1982 he became a founding director, with Dr Gillman, of the SA Brain Research Institute.

FREDDIE LICHTIGFELD'S LETTER - Dated 17 March 2002

I am sorry to have waited so long to reply to you, but I was taken aback by what you had achieved and the memories of the long past when I lived in Arcadia while I was a medical student. Of course I was a bit older than the oldest Arc there at the time, so distanced myself somewhat from the goings on. Of course at meal times one heard all about the Arcs but I never came close to having a real friendship with one of the Arcs – it would have been very difficult and shown favouritism.

To keep the distance, I even did not attend the morning and evening services, but now so many years later I realise what wonderful opportunities I might have lost by my attitude. Certainly I did in some way relate to some of the Arcs and still feel good that I had the time and interest to do so.

One thing I had in common with all the Arcs of that time is that Doc was with me, and I found his passing some years ago a great jolt from which it is still difficult to adjust to. Donnie's children and wife still live in the States, and we rarely contact each other now.

I think your scrapbook is a labour of love and hope that you will be able to one day publish the whole idea of the Time of Arcadia in the form of a book. Solly Farber wrote an article to commemorate the passing of Doc, so he could let you have a copy of it. It has taken me two years to reply so be kind to me in at least trying to put on paper some few thoughts about that time. I will of course keep the scrapbook handy and if I can find the energy to relate something else about those times in the future, I will send it along to you.
Best regards

TRIBUTES TO FREDDIE

From Mannie Osrin

How sad it was to read of the tragic death of Freddie Lichtigfeld. He was a lovely person, and a truly devoted practitioner of the art of Medicine, keeping out of the limelight and preferring to work amongst the poor and less fortunate. Until next time, cheers and be well

From Basil Sepel from France

The death of any DECENT person is always sad and so it is for Fred Lichtigfeld. I hardly knew Freddie who was some six years older and therefore in Medical school when I was in form 1.

I did see him in Shul some of the high festivals and once in about 1954 he dissected several dead pigeons trying to find out the cause of the epidemic that within weeks killed every pigeon in the Arc - he was a natural born scientist. Doc too would have studied medicine if he hadn't been put off by the blood - so he was proud of his Fred.

Fred was passionate about his profession. Spoke with him on the phone in Dec 89 while I was visiting Doc.

He finally wrote me a short note in '95 (after Doc's death) asking what he should do with the unopened mail I had sent Doc. I replied "Do with it what Doc would have done with it".

From Hymie Pearlman

Very sad to hear about the tragic death of Freddie Lichtigfeld. I remember him very well from my Arc days, and he came across as a "gentle giant" because of his good nature and elusiveness and being very tall. MHDSRIP.

LETTER FROM LAWRENCE LIGTICHFELD (DOC'S GRANDSON) TO DAVID SANDLER - November 2005

There is no need to apologise for mistaking me for being Fred's Son Since he was my G-d Father and as much a Father (teacher) to me as Don. Fred did not have any children of his own either and was divorced.

I have three sisters Tamar Michelle Dob 1971, Gina Natalie Dob 1975 and Berdine Simone Dob 1979. I was born in 1969. My Mum, Corinne, is doing well and lives nearby, and is as stubborn and independent as Doc.

My Dad, Don, passed away in June 1997 in Pennsylvania where we had lived since 1985. I was in South Africa living in Yeoville were I had been since December 1993. I was privileged to have lived next door to Doc for those last few years and was able to learn a great deal that could never have been taught in any school.

This afternoon Bean, Corinne and I searched for more Arc memories in the Container and found more photos. One of the special memories is a Photo Album that was presented to Doc and Ma when they retired from the Arc. There is also a tree certificate that always hung at the front door of Doc and Ma's flat that is signed by many of the children.

Amazingly enough one of the photos I found today had a letter along with it, you might be surprised and interested in receiving it, you are the author- I am sure you know who it is in the photo. Gramps did not get rid of anything that was important.

I know very little about the Arc but each day I learn a lot more especially from all your hard work – thank you.

Chapter 77 – BELLA AND MORRIE LUBNER

Bella served Arcadia from 1941 to 1986 and her generosity to Arcadia and friendship with the children had no bounds. She always had a smile, a kiss and a kind word for each child.

It was very appropriate that Bella and her husband Morrie gave Tamara Salaman away when she married Hymie Pearlman in the Arc Shul.

BELLA LUBNER AS REMEMBERED BY THE CHILDREN

Remembered by Edith (Rosenkowitz) Cohen

Before we got married (in the early1950s), Mrs Bella Lubner, one of the committee members took me to a wholesaler to choose some linen and bedding towards my trousseau. It was a wonderful start and very much appreciated and I think of her whenever I use the table cloth. Yes, it is still in good use. (2005)

Remembered by Shelley Segal (Grishkan)

When we finally progressed to the Senior Department Mrs Lubner escorted each girl annually to purchase a new outfit at stores of her choice with a set limit. Well she took a shine to me and Bev Collet and we blew the budget and told us not to tell. Needless to say at the first opportunity to show how special we were, even just to Mrs Lubner, we bragged how much our outfits cost. Very swiftly Mevrou had our very special dresses returned to the store. Upon our squealing to Mrs Lubner she then had our outfits returned to us. Mevrou promptly showed us who was boss and sent Bev and I to bed at eight o clock sharp every night for about six months. We peeped through the keyhole and salivated while the rest of the senior girls stayed up and had biscuits and tea each night.

Remembered by David Sandler

After coming to the Arc and after leaving the hospital we went down to the Babies and I remember Mrs Lubner coming to see me and my sister (aged four and six) and giving us each a hug and a kiss. She told us that she was bringing some other kids to the Arc and that they would play with us. These turned out to be the Durbachs. It was only Esther, Les and Hilda at that time.

Mrs Lubner, as I remember her over the 14 years I was in the Arc, was always friendly and would always have a smile and when we were younger would kiss us saying "Hello Luvvy. How are you?" As young children, Max Goldman and I would giggle in reply.

I remember us all receiving from the Lubners, items of furniture from time to time, metal lockers in the Babies in which to put our clothes which we had previously hung over our chairs next to our beds.

As we grew up we realised that Bella was short and she used

Bella and her husband Morrie giving Tamara Salaman away

to smoke a little cigar, but it´is always her big smile and warm friendly face that I will remember.

LETTER FROM BELLA LUBNER FOR THE 1955 ARCADIAN

You have no idea how pleased I am to have been asked to write to *The Arcadian*. Just as a daily newspaper expresses the atmosphere, opinions and happenings in our world, so I am delighted to say, does your magazine express very adequately the above attributes in Arcadia.

I would like, through the medium of *The Arcadian* to express a fervent wish that Doc and Ma may continue in their unselfish and unstinting work for the Arcadians for many years to come.

Indeed, I am almost apologetic in mentioning this to you, for I know you are fully aware of this fact. But I would like to assure you boys that Doc and Ma's interest in, and work for you, does not end when you take your leave of Arcadia. On the contrary, their whole aim is to guide you to that day when you can come to them and say as a mature man or woman 'Doc and Ma, I have made it'. And even then you will know that although their active care is a thing of the past, their hearts will be with you always. I consider myself extremely fortunate to write so freely and confidently to you, knowing that 'love labours are not in vain'. With kind regards and all the best for your future in Arcadia.

BELLA'S OBITUARY

From the 1987 Arcadia Bulletin

We record with deep sadness the passing away of our beloved Bella Lubner, a mother to thousands and a legend in her time, on March 16 1987. Bella of the sparkling eye, happy sense of humour and a heart as big as a house.

Auntie Bella became interested in Arcadia a long, long time ago. After some years as a very active member of the Kensington Branch she joined Arcadia's Committee in 1945; and remained a member until last year, a total of 41 years!

The years 1951-53 and 59-60 saw her in the Chair of the House Committee, in 1963 she was honoured by being elected a Life Member and in 1965 an Hon Life Vice President. From 1972-73 she held the portfolio of Chair of the Branches and Boxes sub-committee.

The list of high offices which she held does not reflect the true essence of Bella Lubner. It made scant difference to her what title she was given. She always gave her all and was a pivotal member and a trend setter.

A tireless champion of the children, it was always Bella who pleaded for extra comforts for the children, for the ever better facilities and for leniency when a child needed to be punished.

For generations of Arcadians Bella was the one who cared. She was not content to sit in the boardroom and discuss the children. She went to the children's quarters and got to know each child individually and made each child feel as if he or she was special.

Indeed to Bella each child was unique. She knew every child's strengths, weaknesses, hopes and aspirations and most importantly their dreams. If it was humanly possible, Bella made it her personal duty to make those dreams into reality and often she did just that.

After children left Arcadia's safe walls it was to Bella they most often turned for help in coping with their new situations. Once you were one of her 'babies' you remained that forever after.

We have lost one of our leading and brightest lights. Our loss is shared by the many other organisations which she blessed with her special grace.

In all her good works Bella was warmly supported and encouraged by her equally warm hearted husband, Morrie Lubner whose philanthropy was as magnificent as Bella's.

Morrie's death some years ago deeply affected Bella, and yet she continued with her work. We mourn her passing. It is just impossible to try to imagine the world, our world Arcadia, without Bella. Farewell dear mother of Arcadia.

MORRIE LUBNER'S OBITUARY

From the 1984 Arcadia Bulletin

Morrie Lubner was so well known in the Jewish Community that it is unnecessary to list his many achievements and his wonderful support of local and national charities. Morrie was truly a champion of the underdog and his name is revered in service organisations such as ours, far and wide. He served Arcadia as Trustee from 1970 until 1983, but his interest in Arcadia goes back many years prior to that.

We mourn his passing and already miss his gentle warmth and wise counsel. To his wife our beloved Bella and to his children Ronnie, Bertie and Pam we extend our sincerest sympathy. He was truly a great man.

Bella Lubner opening the Bella Lubner Library – 1982
Shirley Edelman at the back on left hand side, Mrs Stein behind Mrs Lubner and Mrs Duchen to the right

Sidney was born in 1916 and was in the care of Arcadia from 1924 to 1935. So too were his siblings Rachel (born 1919), Hymie (Born 1921) and Bertha (Born 1924)

After leaving the Arc in 1935 he assisted as a Cub Master and maintained his association with Arcadia while working, in the Army and training as a teacher.

He served in the South African Defence Force (SADF) during 1940-1945 and rose to the rank of Warrant Officer (Sergeant Major). After the War he qualified as a teacher and was appointed House-Master in 1951, looking after the boys until 1976 when he became Director of Arcadia. He served Arcadia looking after the children until 2002, when Arcadia was relocated from Parktown to Sandringham.

At the same time he was a Latin teacher at Parktown Boys' High from 1949 to 1982, a total of 33 years, where he also served as assistant to the principal.

THOSE WERE THE DAYS
By Vicky Klevansky 2002

December 1924 – As a small boy aged seven, I trudged up the sandy drive graced by attractive, tall gum trees – a new admission to Arcadia. The buildings and beautifully laid out grounds fascinated me. There were marble statues, a summer-house, alcoves, bee hives, grape vines, lily-covered fish-pond, lavender and rose bushes, bowers, pigeon coups and two orchards with a large variety of fruit. Most of the 142 children were orphans and the home was divided into three departments – Babies, Boys and Girls.

Since the Baby Department went up to six years of age, I was allotted to the Boys Department which consisted of boys from seven to 18 years. We all had numbers, mine being 31; my worldly possessions consisted of one shelf in a cupboard in the sewing room and one shelf of a shared locker. We all dressed the same so all my clothes were kept on shelf 31 in the sewing room. A housemother looked after about 35 boys. She had one afternoon off a week and one day a month; the staff dressed like nurses in a hospital. As was the custom, I served my "apprenticeship" as a fag to an old boy and learned to fight my battles and face frustration. School reports were read aloud at a gathering of children and one soon learned to accept praise or criticism equally. Rising bell daily was at 6.00 am except on Saturday and Sunday at 6.30 am. The present Shul was a dormitory housing about 35 boys, and senior boys slept outside on the verandah; the shelter from the rain was canvas blinds, while heaters were unknown.

The library was the Synagogue and about 100 children managed to pray there every Shabbath and Holy days. There was no hospital and Nurse Balkind attended to major aches and pains. Minor ailments were seen to by the Housemothers

Vicky Klevansky – Regimental Sergeant Major

who had medicine cupboards in each department; not being a drug ridden age, the popular remedies usually were Epson salts, castor-oil, aspirin, iodine, cod-liver oil etc. We received opening medicine weekly whether needed or not. We wore boots – shoes being a luxury reserved for the lucky few – new shoes were a rarity. I wore short trousers up to the age of 15.

Barmitzvahs were homely affairs held in the "Library" Shul with very few visitors attending. In the Shul after the service we received sweets and a piece of sponge cake. However the Annual Prize Distribution and Barmitzvah celebrations were grand affairs where the participants received many Barmitzvah gifts. At all public functions at Arcadia the motto was FHB "Family Hold Back" ie. visitors received priority treatment.

During school-term the boys' queue on the drive was a daily occurrence. It was a healthy routine walking in twos to Twist Street and thence Hebrew High or Jewish Government. In the afternoons there was an hour's compulsory attendance at Arcadia Hebrew School. Extra lessons in weak subjects were virtually unknown and one soon realised that success or failure depended on oneself.

On High Festivals services were held in the dining-room, when members of the public attended. Then all meals were eaten on the verandah – sometimes amid a summer storm of thunder, lightening and rain.

The "permissive age" had not yet dawned, and like the tribal Black we enjoyed the simple pleasures of life. A pastry, extra sweets, the Annual Pantomime show, the occasional outings meant a great deal to us. Saturday night without bioscope and TV presented no problem; we were quite contented to amuse ourselves in various ways at home.

As we received no pocket money from Arcadia and very little from elsewhere (maybe 10 cents a week), some enterprising boys would buy a pocket of oranges or bag of monkey-nuts at the Indian Market and sell them at a profit to the children. Some even made homemade toffee and sold it.

The perennial problem of litter was even present in those days; one solution was that often oranges and bananas were pre-peeled before distribution and wrappings removed from sweets.

Holiday time – generally meant staying in Arcadia and organising our own holiday activities. One of the most popular holiday pastimes was cooking "on the hill". Unofficially small groups who had "borrowed" vegetables, bread and meat from the stores spent part of the holidays cooking mainly stews, mash potatoes and bread pudding. What pleasure it gave us to eat this concoction served in jam tins. We "bunked" out occasionally and if found riding on the Sabbath received six of the best. A popular place visited was the Café Bioscopes of those days, where we saw silent pictures; the admission price of 5 cents included a cold drink or an ice cream.

As there were no public swimming pools, we enjoyed swimming in the remainder of Sir Lionel Phillips' swimming bath which was perched on top of the hill. Silently we would sneak up to have our daily dip, no matter whether the water was slimy or green or contained a dead mouse or frog – filtration unheard of.

I can still remember the food served in those days. Friday night, - always fish and mash; Saturday mornings – cold fish and salads; Saturday evenings boiled mielies etc. Our health on the whole was good, occasionally large numbers of children contracted mumps, measles, chicken pox or whooping cough and were isolated in the "top" and "bottom" cottages of Arcadia.

The hospital was built in 1929 and I can remember having had my adenoids removed in its operating theatre; many children had their tonsils extracted there.

The only visiting days were the afternoons of the first and third Sunday of each month. If a month had five Sundays, the fifth was not a visiting day and was readily accepted as such. On these afternoons the main lawn was dotted with family groups partaking in refreshments, family talk and Arcadian gossip.

The luxury of high school education was reserved for the lucky few as a public High School Entrance Exam had to be written in Standard 5, many children went to work at the age of 15 years and to date apparently had made a success of their lives.

A duty roster was a sine quo non of each month. One of these duties consisted in sweeping the dining room after the evening meal when about 100 children had eaten. Today the child tends to live by the pleasure principle and is socially pressured to a great extent.

Give me back those days of 1924 to 1934 – in retrospect I enjoyed them!

CAMEOS OF THE PAST
By Sidney Klevansky 1959

To children who seldom went, out the annual picnic was a long-awaited event. It was not as today in the comfort of the motor car or bus, but in open lorries, kindly lent to Arcadia for the occasion. Cramped, and with legs dangling precariously over the sides of the lorry, we children enjoyed every moment as the lorries raced each other to their destination – be it Germiston Lake or Van Wyk's Rust.

Perched on top of the hill the remains of Sir Lionel Philips' swimming bath was indeed a landmark. Silently we would sneak up to have our daily dip, no matter whether the water was slimy and green – filtration unheard of. But who cared; as long as the pipes (primitive by modern standards) which were visible all along the sides, filled the two baths, we could splash around to our hearts' delight.

Today the drive resounds with the clatter of wooden carts – a pastime at the moment, but there was a time when the drive was made of sand with tall, sedate blue gum trees gracing its sides. Then we children watched the convicts at work, gradually paving the whole drive with concrete blocks which have now become a legacy of the past.

The face of Arcadia has also undergone many changes. The pigeon coops, beehives, summerhouse, lily-covered fish pond, lavender and rose beds bowers, all relics of Sir Lionel Philips estate, have given way to the march of time.
Even the Shul has had its vicissitudes; the library was its original home, and on the high festivals services were held in the dining room when members of the public attended. One year high festival services were held in the large ward of the hospital, then in its present abode to displace the boy's dormitory when the boys' wing was built. How often have I sat in Shul and the past has appeared before me.

I can still see the Shul again as the original dormitory with white-quilted beds, evenly spaced – the senior boys sleeping on the verandah, and the quadrangle minus its small fish pond and lawn used daily as a soccer venue for the majority of boys; the games usually terminating in the breaking of a window-pane of the committee-room and the scurrying away of the culprits.

Downstairs was the bathroom and toilet, and there was a staircase leading down to it from the present Shul. After being converted into a flat it was first used for residential purposes, then as Scout rooms and, finally, to house boxing, art and Hebrew quarters as at present.

A pause on the drive in front of the vegetable garden brings back to mind the beautiful orchard with its great variety of fruit trees which was once there. A similar orchard was near the bottom cottage. These two were affectionately known as "the Top and Bottom orchards" and were guarded day and night by garden boys against the intrusion of both girls and boys to whom such a variety of fruit, ripe or unripe, was an unending temptation.

The native-girls' quarters opposite Dolly's home has also had its different uses. Originally it was a self-contained cottage for the working girls of Arcadia, then, it became a Hebrew school and finally lapsed to its present use.

During school-term in the early morning, the boys' queue on the drive was a daily occurrence; it was a healthy routine walking in two's to Joubert Park, whence to school – Hebrew High or Jewish Government. Occasionally lifts on carts were accepted; these being at the price of our pockets of sandwiches.

Municipal buses were practically the only means of transport and, at one stage, due to complaints from visitors about buses being full when passing Arcadia, arrangements were made for two or three buses to come to the home to take people into town.

Illness and children's ailments unfortunately have always been with us and, prior to the building of the Hospital, each department was equipped with medical supplies. Minor ailments were attended to by the house mothers. The top and bottom cottages were used as isolation houses in case of contagious disease. Miss Hurwitz's office and adjacent rooms were the sickbays, and there was a trained nurse in attendance.

The first broadcast in Arcadia was indeed a memorable experience – relayed from the City Hall of Johannesburg; it was a boxing match between Kid Lewis and a South African. We all sat at the main entrance to the hall and listened intently. The atmospherics were bad, but broadcasting was in its infancy and the experience was indeed moving.

FICKEY'S STORY
Witten by Sidney Klevansky in 1976

In 1924 a little boy of seven trudged up the long drive to the main building of Arcadia to a new and unknown life, in a home. There was no Cottage system and the home was divided into three departments: Babies up to the age of six, a Boys' Department and a Girls' Department. He grew up among boys aged seven to 18, without swimming pools, tennis courts, bioscope, TV and radio.

The children enjoyed friendly games of soccer and cricket by 'picking up sides' and played kennetjie, swartmannetjie, horsie, *bok-bok;* games generally unknown to today's youth. Daily activities consisted of going to secular schools in the morning, Hebrew lessons in the afternoon and strict religious observance of Sabbaths and Holy days. Compulsory activities were Scouts and Girl Guides, dancing and sewing lessons for the girls; there

were occasional outings and visits by notable musicians and personalities.

Being small of stature, the young boy asserted himself by daily fights with other boys - a source of joy to the beholders. The years passed quickly, and at the age of 15, a small incident happened that he was to remember many years later. The then superintendent told him that one day he wanted to see this boy Superintendent of Arcadia - indeed prophetic words.

After matriculating very well, he was, for financial reasons unable to study further at University, and obtained employment at a wholesale firm at five pounds a month. In 1935 he was approached to assist as a Cub Master at Arcadia. He continued with night studies at the Technical College, and obtained his 'Associate of the Chartered Institute of Secretaries' ACIS Diploma.

War had broken out in 1939 and he joined the South African Air Force in 1940 as an Air Mechanic and rose to the rank of Warrant Officer (Sergeant Major). After serving for four years and five months, he was discharged.

During all these years he had maintained a link with Arcadia by occasional visits. In 1945, on his discharge he was approached by the chairman of Arcadia to work in Arcadia. He took up the challenge but owing to 'internal politics' he was kindly asked to leave. This proved to be a blessing in disguise because he now applied to study for a BA degree at the University of Witwatersrand and Teacher's Diploma at Johannesburg College of Education.

He qualified as a teacher, but as an old Arcadian he felt his loyalty lay with the home that had brought him up for eleven years. So although living elsewhere and teaching primary school, he regularly helped out at Arcadia when needed. Finally a new principal and matron were appointed and approached him to continue with his government school teaching but to live at Arcadia as a House-Master, and he has been part of the home ever since.

During the 40 years that he has worked in Arcadia he has seen hundreds pass through its portals. Little did he know when he reprimanded Solly Farber as a boy that the latter would one day be a chairman and president of Arcadia. He didn't realise that the slightly built boy Colin Rosenkowitz would one day be the father of the famous sextuplets.

As Cub Master he did not dream that the children listening to his yarns would include Len Lipschitz (a president of Arcadia), Barney Meyers (Principal of King David Primary Victory Park), Meyer Rabinowitz (Principal of King David Primary School Linksfield).

And so the years rolled on till 1976 when he became Director of Arcadia. Today at committee meetings he looks with pride at Solly Farber, Eli Osrin, Selwyn Dembo, Stanley Stein, Hocky Kabe, Geffrey Esekow - all dedicated members of the committee who in their youth were praised, raised and scolded by him. His association with the home is now 52 years.

MY BROTHER VICKY – A UNIQUE PERSONALITY

By Bertha Kronenberg (Klevansky)

When I think of my brother Vicky I feel I was blessed with someone who, in all respects, was an inspiration to me. Who else had a brother who brought sweets back for his kid sister on a Saturday afternoon, who else had a brother who regularly sent his sister ten shillings each month after she had left Arcadia, a lot of money in those days and who else was generous in many other ways. I treasure table-cloths which he lovingly gave me to embroider helping me during weeks of convalescence at Johannesburg General Hospital. I think back to his unstinting generosity when I needed financial help, and to cap it all, the holiday of a lifetime.

"I'll take you to see your sister when you're better" he promised me, and there we two were on a three-month tour of the UK and Europe. He fired my imagination and boosted my confidence. He has been a great friend to both my husband and I, and a wonderful uncle to my three boys.

There is eight years separating us, and the bond I formed with Vicky, one of three brothers, was and is unique. He is no ordinary person, and I became aware of his talent when he became Cub Master at Arcadia. He had a special "den" in a room in one of the rooms where Mr and Mrs Harary later lived. Because of the separation of boys from girls I really only got together with my family when my Dad visited. Outstanding at this event for me was the sight of my sister Rachel and my brother Sidney, walking on the big lawn engrossed in conversation, my sister ever the idealist, my brother practical, organised.

I think as I matured I became more aware of his innate decency and concern for others. He displayed a sense of enjoyment of life's magic. He entranced us kids at the Port Elizabeth camps with the yarns he spun. In Durban, as we motored along the Marine Parade everybody in the crowd knew him, "hey Klev" would ring out from all directions. I remember him staying at a Kosher hotel in Durban owned by Kerzner, popular with the young crowd. I heard tell that Vicky "apple-pied" beds much to our amusement. Whether he was welcome there after that I don't know. There were many among the holiday crowd at "The Wigwam" a resort near Rustenburg who came to enjoy the entertainment there, organised by the popular Master of Ceremony, one Vicky Klevansky.

Always an excellent organiser, his abilities covered the field of education, where he excelled as a Latin Teacher at Parktown Boy's High. Ever a devoted servant, reliable and enthusiastic, his pupils were taught with thoroughness, and those who needed it received extra coaching.

He coached cricket there and was a stern instructor at Cadet training at the school. His skill at instructing and leading was put to the test as a Regimental Sergeant-Major in the South African Air Force.

Loyal to Arcadia, loyal to his school, his personality reveals a person of deep religiosity and generosity of spirit.

EXTRACT OF LETTER TO VICKY – April 1999

Letter from Shani Krebbs who is serving a 40 year sentence in Thailand.

I can still clearly visualise your image and general manner to everything and the people who came in contact with you. You were a man of the highest standing, your unyielding kindness and consideration for others was part and parcel of your exceedingly friendly nature, a distinguished gentleman who I've always respected and looked upon as more like the father I never had, or perhaps should have had. Your memory will live on in many generations to come.

I was wondering if you wouldn't mind sending me a black and white photograph of yourself, it should be close-up of your face, ensuring the clearness of your physiognomy, the photo shouldn't be smaller than postcard size and no bigger than A4. It would be a great honour to draw your portrait. I would also go as far as asking if I could keep the photo, which I would always treasure.

Unfortunately I cannot specify a date for the completion of the portrait, at this present time I'm in solitary confinement for fighting. I've been here since the 2nd February and will most likely stay in solitary till the middle of July. I've discovered that solitary wasn't about being alone but rather about spending time with yourself, strangely enough one would have thought that the circumstances would trigger a tense purpose of self-expression, yet I haven't found the inspiration to draw, I'm lost in thought.

I trust that you are enjoying good health, may Hashem always be with you. I look forward to your response if one is forthcoming.

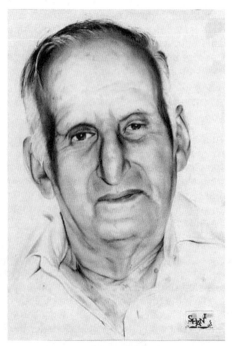

Portrait of Vicky By Shani Krebs

FICKEY - *By David Sandler*

I got to know Fickey when I went from the Babies up to the Junior Boys and he and the housemother used to look after the Junior and Senior Boys. As with Doc and Ma I saw Fickey as part of the Arc even though he was also a teacher of Parktown Boys' High. I knew Fickey in two capacities: looking after the boys in the Arc and as my Latin teacher at school.

In the Arc Fickey always woke us up in the morning at 6.00 am. He would come around twice, once to wake us and then a few minutes later to check that we were out of bed. At 6:30 he called us to line up for inspection in the long dormitory. At around 5.00 pm he came around checking that we had bathed or had had a swim. At 6.00 pm he would call us to supper by blowing his whistle. After supper he would sit with us in the homework room until 8:30 pm and check that we had done our homework.

Fickey was very strict with us and I'm sure all the boys at one time or another received a caning from him. Most times he disciplined us by giving us a stern telling off and then some time later he would make a point of talking to us normally again, as if to tell us the matter was now over and forgotten.

Fickey also had a friendly side where he would discuss some topical issue and joke and chat. He gave the senior boys a bit more latitude than the younger boys and had extra time and patience for the more troubled kids. He would give a few of us a lift to school in the morning, as many as his vintage Austin could carry.

I remember him once catching a few of us cooking *mielies* in an old paint tin under the pool. Because my sister Jenny was there, a senior girl and 'in charge', he let us carry on. The paint-flavoured *mielies* were really not so nice.

I think at that time Fickey was under a lot of pressure as he set himself very high standards not only at school, but also at the Arc. He used to drink milk (which he called his vodka) to help his ulcers which used to play up.

At school Fickey was a stern teacher who was always very affectionately remembered by his pupils. In the class there was no nonsense. However, the challenge for us was to get him off the subject by asking a very topical question right at the beginning of the lesson. Many a lesson was shortened this way and we would be spared having to translate our set work. You would know his mood at school according to how he addressed you. If he used your first name he was friendly and relaxed. If he used your surname it was School work only.

We were always mimicking our teachers as schoolboys do, and "Klev" (as he was affectionately referred to by the school kids) was no exception and he was in fact rather favoured. At the end of one year I remember Fickey inviting us to show him how we mimicked him and a few of the mimics I can remember are:

"Every time I open my mouth the same fool speaks"
"Shut up! Shut up! I don't say shut up twice."
"Er carry on …er…little…."

Telling the next person to translate the set work.

What I have related above is only seven years (1962 to 1969) a very very small part of Fickey's association with the Arc. Fickey's association started about 38 years earlier when he arrived at the arc in 1924 as a seven year-old child and continued a further 33 years up till 2002. He is the superintendent and very much respected and a loved fatherly figure. This association has therefore been for around 79 years.

It is very difficult for me to talk about the 38 years before I knew Fickey and his role with the Arc. Sam Bartlett (now around 73) once told me how he used to really look forward to going to cubs with Fickey, especially to the stories that Fickey used to tell them and the concerts they used to put on. I know Fickey was a sergeant major in the army and that he worked in an office as a bookkeeper/accountant at one stage before going to teaching.

Over the last 30 years Fickey has mellowed from being this strict House Master in charge of the boys to being a very much respected and a loved fatherly figure to all the children in the Arc. This I have only managed to glean from snippets: a letter from an old Arc full of respect and praise. An article in an Arc publication from a child leaving the Arc full of affection and love. A short visit to the Arc and hearing Fickey talk very caringly about the children and some of the problems they face.

Vicky Klevansky

Sydney Klevansky (Fickey) officiating at an Arcadian Swimming Gala circa 1956

Old Boys Visiting on High Holy Days - 1947g

CHAPTER 79   THE GOLDSMITHS (THE GEES)

The Gees are the Goldsmith Family; Stan and Goldie and their two children Maxine and Adam who were both brought up living in the cottages in the Arc. For about fifty years (early fifties to late nineties) the Gees were part of the Arc. Their house was always open and their children, especially Adam, mixed freely with the Arc children.

Stanley Goldsmith was born on the 11th of June 1923 and his sister Mabel on the 14th January 1927. Their Mother Anne died 10 days after giving birth to Mabel. They were placed in the care of Arcadia by their father Harold Goldsmith in 1930 when Stan was seven years old and Mabel was three.

Stan left Arcadia in 1940 at age 17 and then joined the Army until the end of the war. After the war he worked as an office boy for a firm of lawyers, the OK Bazaars and for Standard Canners.

During this time he studied part time and obtained his CIS qualification.

Stan married Goldie on the 26th of December 1948 and joined Arcadia as the assistant Secretary in 1953 and later became secretary. He retired in 1998 after 44 years service to Arcadia during which time he helped dozens of Arc kids.

Selwyn Chalmers (as Administrative Director of Arcadia) in the Annual Bulletin for the Year ended March 31st 1999 wrote, " I wish to take this opportunity to say a public thank you to Stan Goldsmith. A great thank you from Arcadia for almost 44 years work as Secretary. A true gentleman of integrity and dedication."

Goldie grew up in Jo'burg and her parents were Harry and Janie Kruger who were both from Seduva in Lithuania who came out to South Africa in 1911 and who got married in Oudtschoorn in June 1913.

GOLDIE'S ARC MEMORIES

For a long time I have wanted to write my memories about the Arc and the children. Where do I begin?

First we lived in the cottage at almost the end of the Arc grounds, where the cows and sheep used to meander, and the boys used to kick the ball over the fence. Anybody remember this? Later when they built the highway we moved to a newly built cottage just above the driveway and at the top of the 'orchard' which was really the vegetable gardens.

Remember the concerts at the Arc where the kids used to act, sing or dance. Well the boys used to pinch cakes, bring them to our house, and when the guests left, they fetched the cakes and had a ball. Remember all the picnics at the Vaal - they were great. One sports day the Junior Boys decided to let Georgie Marshak win the race and remember the time Muffie Goldstein - who was driving - went into the wall.

Mr and Mrs Goldsmith

I am sure that there are lots of boys who will remember the raids on the pantry. Adam would put his long arms thru the mesh, get cold drinks out. The boys would drink the drinks, put water in the bottles, and then Adam would put the bottles back. The kids would complain to Ma, "this tastes of water not cold drink". "Don't be silly it is not water, drink up" Ma would say.

Remember the Chags and the high holidays. The Babies used to sit right at the end of the Shul, on the benches, and when the Shul got too full the babies left. Then there were times when the Shul was so full that the boys sat on benches along the aisles. Remember Doc used to walk around showing everyone where the place was in the prayer books, and Ma kept an eagle eye on all.

Remember Vicky - the Legend with his sayings at a Barmitzvah taking the letters of the persons name and enlarging on these.

Abe Starkowitz, thank you "Starkey" for all those wonderful Chag services.

Remember Doc's sermons on Chags. Doc and Ma were one of the best. Doc played soccer with the boys on the playing field, after Shul. Sometimes his son Donnny would join in and also Freddie the older brother.

I remember the school days, especially Parktown Boys, when I used to fetch Adam. The Arcs used pile into our *Volksie* Station wagon. If they were staying at the school, their bags used to get a ride home. Some of the boys used to come to our house to study for their matric. Then there were days when the Arcs used to come to our house for "tea with Mrs G" and sometimes they used this as excuse to bunk out. At one time the kids planted fruit trees in our garden - now there is a three storey garage in place of the house.

I remember the kids over the years (not in any order) - Sandra Nestadt, Gary and Dianne Joffe, Gary and Desiree Creighton, The Bortz family, the Kotzens, the Lasker Boys, the Schreewers. I see Willie at Balfour Park at times. Tony and Lesley Mark, Shelly and Sharon Gruskan, the Flies Girls, Max and Charles Goldman. The Edery Family. David Jenny and Brian Sandler. Julius Gordon, Hilton, Rene Laurain and Michael Rothaus, the Stoller Family, Adela and Vera Lazinsky, Ruth and Allan Jacobs, Shaun and Mark Jacob. The late Leon Goodman, the Mayer Family, the Durbach Family, Michael and Adele Saeit. It was a very sad day when Martin Lasker and Thelma Durbach passed away. Helen and Lynette Sheer, the Goldsteins, the Miller Girls, the Segals, Beryl Sacks. The Salaman Girls, The Sedacca Family, Laurie Feinberg and Sister, the Oscher's, Langermans, Wasserman, Nedemeyers. Kupferberger Family. The Steins, Joan and Shaun Krebs. Melvyn Katz, and his ex wife Sandra. The Hough Boys, Pauline Kruger, Hymie and Myrtle Aronoff, The Schraga Girls, Paul Con-Clarke, the Bates Girls, Eddie Isaacson, Weinstein Boys, Gershon Rochlin, Mabel Goldsmith, Eckie Levin, Bernard Tanner.

In later years I met Donald Goldman, the late Solly Farber, Freda Cheilyk, Bertha Disler, Leslie Bushkin, Barney Meyers (who I see quite often at P & P.) Jonah Perkel, Max Ladier. The late Len Lipschitz, Wille Isaacs, Alec Saul and Toby Unterslack and her sisters.

It is quite a shock when one reads and sees how the 'Old Arcs' have grown up, to see them married with grown up kids - almost getting married - and one wonders 'where have all the years gone?' I am sure that there must be an Old Arc in every part of the world, most making a success of whatever they are doing.

Since coming to live at the new address we have discovered that Pauline Kruger lives close by. She never spoke or laughed when she was young. She married Johnny Lees, whose mother worked in the Arc office. Then there is Julius Gordon, who also lives nearby.

At the year end we holiday in Cape Town. Stan, Adam and I travel by train -. Adam puts his car on the train, it is necessary to have a car here. We leave Johannesburg station at 12.30 and arrive in Cape Town at 2.30 the following day. We do not mind the long trip, as we eat, sleep, and read and relax all the way, but oh all the parcels, we carry all our meals with us.

REMEMBERING THE GEES
Written by David Sandler

When I was in the Arc my association with the Gees was very limited. When I was younger they stayed "down the hill" below the soccer field. On Saturday mornings when we played soccer we would at times have to retrieve our soccer balls from their loudly barking dogs. They would come out of their house and return the ball with a smile. Only Hilton Rothaus was brave enough to jump the fence and retrieve the ball. One always saw them in Shul and greeted them, but from my point of view it was formal and a bit removed.

Later when the freeway came they moved to a new house built at the top of the drive above the veggie gardens. At around this time Adam their son was going to high school and his Arc school friends started visiting the Gees and the Gees' house became a sort of open house frequented by many of the younger boys. Over time a very close bond has been formed with some of the kids.

It was common at the time to hear that so and so was "at the Gees". From what I gathered the Gees' house for some Arc kids was a place of refuge and a home they could always go to. With some of these kids these bonds have continued over many many years and over oceans.

Many years after leaving the Arc I got to feel the warmth and hospitality of the Gees in my infrequent visits to the Arc over many years. It has been like visiting some older friendly relatives and we would sit and drink and eat and talk about the good old days and catch up to how the Arcs were now faring. They were always very interested in Mike Rothaus and I would have to take a gift for him back to Perth.

Over the years their barking dogs seemed to have changed to cats and Adam was always there visiting his parents. Maxine living in Cape Town has three sons,

Stan has been associated with the Arc for most of his life. He was in the Arc as a child and then later worked as secretary. Stan and Goldie his wife (The Gees) have become an integral part of the Arc. Not only do they know all the kids who have passed through the Arc over many many years, but they are very close to many for whom their house was an open home.

Written by Shelley Segal (Grishkan

I remember Adam and his wonderful parents the G's as we all called them and of course Maxine. It was always to your home that we kids sought refuge and respite and the G's were always a listening ear for us all. I don't know if the G's really understood just how important and valued you were to us kids and the kindness and care you showed was something special. When a housemother was mean it was also the G's phone, our lifelines to the outside world that enabled us to squeal to our parents.

Written by Allan Jacobs

I remember the vegetable garden at the bottom of Mr and Mrs Gee's house and the warmth and love of the Gees.

Written by Michael Rothaus

I remember spending a lot of time at the Gee's house together with some of the Lasker boys. The Gees were always good to us and their home was always open to us. We always used to fight for the best seat in the Gees van to get a lift home when Mrs G came to fetch Adam. I am still in regular contact with them and phone them regularly. They always send chocolates to me with a friend of theirs who visits their relatives here in Australia.

MAXINE AND ADAM
Written by David Sandler

Maxine's married name is Nerwich. Her ex-husband's father co-incidentally was in Arcadia at the same time as my dad. She lives in Cape Town and is a teacher at Herzlia Primary School for the last 22 years. She has three sons, Russell turning 30 this year, Craig turning 27 this year who is married and expecting their first child P.G. in June and Brett turning 23 this year.

Adam is the manager of the CEO's office at the Johannesburg Development Agency. He is involved in the regeneration of greater Jo'burg with projects such as the new Constitution

Adam, Goldie and Stan

Chapter 80 – RUTH DIRE

Ruth worked in the Arc from 1951 to 2001 when she retired. She spent most of her years working in the hospital with Sister Conway, but in later years was given other duties.

Over the five decades Ruth got to know all the children very well and the Old Arcs would always make sure they saw her when they visited.

RUTH 'CONWAY' AND THE HOSPITAL
Written by David Sandler

Ruth was in the Arc when I first came in mid 1956 and she was still there on my last visit in December 2001. That's 45 years but in fact Ruth has been working in the Arc 50 years, 1951 to 2001 and was very recently commended for her 50 years service to the Arc.

I can clearly remember Ruth, Sister Conway and the hospital and the hospital routine. We were woken up early in the morning and in winter that was while it was still quite dark outside.

We would all be brought a steaming basin of hot water and the smaller ones would be washed and the older ones would wash themselves. The beds would then be remade and the sheets changed if necessary. It was very comforting to be tucked up tightly with clean sheets covered by the starched bedspread. After the bed making came the breakfast and I always looked forward to the porridge (usually jungle oats) covered with cold milk and lots of sugar. I liked lots of sugar and when I was in the junior and senior boys I used to sneak extra sugar onto my porridge.

Ruth was quite strict with us as little ones. She would never hit us or even threaten to do so, yet we all had a very healthy respect for her. From my point of view Sister Conway and Ruth ran a very smart efficient hospital, always sticking to a very high standard. Ruth was always an expert splinter remover and instead of her digging it out she used to take it out by sticking the needle into the top of the splinter. Ruth also used to play tennis with us and had a very good cross-court stroke.

I remember once going to hospital with a dog bite which I think Sister Conway treated with much hidden amusement. I had been nipped by a dog on the back of my heel while climbing over a stone wall with stolen fruit. Boris Sedacca had terrified me by telling me what happens when a dog with rabies bites you. Boris said that the dog had dripping saliva which was a sure sign of rabies. I thought it was better to face Sister than to go mad.

I remember us all having chicken pox and mumps and German measles. Those kids who had not yet caught the latest sickness

Ruth Dire – 50 Years Service to Arcadia 1951 - 2001

were encouraged to play with those who had so that we all had it and that we would not get it when we were older.

Hospital was a nice place to be on the bitterly cold winter days and I used to get in by rubbing my eyes and reporting in sick with pink eyes which was some kind of allergy. I think Sister got wise to me as I always had recovered by mid morning when the sun was shining and we were busy reading comics. She would then send me to school telling me that I had a little allergy, which was not contagious. Later I would have to invent "sore throat, sore tummy and headaches" to gain admittance.

While I enjoyed the days in hospital as a kid, I was terrified of the nights alone in the hospital. I had heard stories from the older Arc boys of the hospital being haunted. I remember Henry Shippel telling "true stories" about ghosts in the hospital and to this day I still remember very vividly two of my nightmares in the hospital.

As we grew up over the years Ruth got to know us all very well and was our friend. She still remembers me as a "cry baby" and Brian as "very naughty but not a bad boy". She reminds me of this in a very matter of fact way whenever I have seen her (five times over 22 years). She always gives me a big hug and I feel like I am a little baby in the Arc again. She tells me how the Arc has changed and when she last saw Joe Balloy and Lillian who used to look after us in the junior and senior boys. She tells me that she is getting old too and that one day she will also leave the Arc.

On my last visit in December 2001 we searched around for Ruth but could not find her and had some tea and a good chat with Vicky and had a brief look around. Much later when we did find Ruth she explained that she had bunked out to Killarney with the driver "but they won't fire me because I work very hard" Even if I go to sleep for a whole afternoon they won't fire me because they won't find anybody who works like me." she said.

Ruth explained that she had her last four more days to work before she left the Arc. She added that she had started working in the Arc in 1951. Ruth said she was 70 and explained she was going to stay with her sisters and their families. She had an older sister of 76 and a younger one too and they would look after each other. She told me she planned to sit down quietly under the shade of a tree and read all the booklets I had sent her.

On looking through some old Arc photos she could name most of the children. When asked about Basil Sepel and David Kotzen, she explained she only knew them for maybe two years and then they left the Arc. "They were naughty, naughty, naughty but they were not bad boys... just very naughty!" she told me. I asked her if she remembered the Fliess girls and she rattled off Jennifer's name but could not remember Elisabeth. She explained that it was hard to remember details of some children especially if she had not seen them for many years.

Brian Ruth and Max

She remembered on one occasion Brian saying he wanted *boerewors* and not wanting the scrambled eggs being given out for breakfast.

Ruth showed us the cell phone she had recently bought and told us only to phone her only at night as she was too busy working during the day to speak on the phone.

David and Ruth

50 YEARS SERVICE - VICKY AND RUTH DIRE
Written by Solly Farber in 2001

You may recall that we have a Thanksgiving Service at the Arc every year which has become an important date on our calendar. Each year we honour a person or two or an organisation who have done a lot for the Arc. In 2001 we honoured Vicky and Ruth Dire.

Ruth who ran the hospital with Sister Conway and has been at the Arc for 50 years and will be retiring at the end of the year.

Written by Barney Meyers 2001

I attended the annual thanksgiving service at Arcadia. It was a very impressive evening. The Shul service was very pleasant with Sydenham Shul Chazan and choir singing like an opera event. Rabbi Harris, Chief Rabbi, gave an appropriate sermon. After the service, a dinner was provided. Stanley Goldsmith said a few words (Solly Farber would have done it, but could not be present) about Vicky. Vicky replied in a long discourse which was both interesting and humorous. The evening was to commemorate 95 years of Arcadia and to pay tribute to Vicky and Ruth who had been with Arcadia for 50 years.

Chapter 81 – OTHER COMMITTEE AND CARERS (1956-1975)

IN THE BABIES
Written by David Sandler

When I was in the Arc, boys and girls from the age of two went into the Babies Department till age ten and then they were separated into either junior boys or junior girls. I spent six and a half years in the Babies from July 1956 to December 1962.

The house mother before Auntie Botha

While I remember the housemother before Auntie Botha I cannot remember her name. She had dark hair and I remember every morning she used to go and sweep around the babies. I think she did that as a kind of therapy. It was soothing for her and so she would go around with a straw broom and sweep the concrete pathways that were just around the Babies. She just did it, maybe it was nice and relaxing just to get out and clear her head and enjoy the fresh air.

I remember eating a mango one night for dinner. I ate the mango and obviously I did not wash my face afterwards. The mango was all over my face and dried on my face and then the next morning my face was really very sore and very chapped and chafed. I must have been very young at the time (three or four years old) and then the next day the housemother saw that my face was covered with this dried mango paste because we hadn't washed our faces the night before. She appointed one of the older girls to take me and make sure I washed my face properly. I think it was Sonia Skopp that she asked to wash my face.

Auntie Botha

I remember Auntie Botha very well. She was a divorced English-speaking lady who had landed up marrying an Afrikaans man. In fact she did not like Afrikaners, did not speak Afrikaans and did not like it when people pronounced her name the Afrikaans way. She did not get on with the other "Afrikaans" staff and did not have her meals in the staffroom with the other staff. She came from Queenstown in the Cape and could speak Xhosa.

She had a daughter Mary who would visit and stay occasionally and I believe Auntie Botha was quite a lonely person. Over the years we got to know her quite well and she would open up to us when we were allowed to stay up late at night till half past eight. It was a treat when Auntie Botha allowed us to stay up and I remember staying up quite often and so too did Liz (Elizabeth Fliess). I think she allowed us to stay up late as she needed our company and someone to talk to.

There was also the African staff; Suzie, Gladys, Rachel and Elias. Suzie and Gladys looked after us, Rachel did the ironing

at night, and Elias cleaned the floors and washed the dishes and carried the food down from the main kitchen. Later Minnie came and Daniel, a gentle giant of a man, replaced Elias.

Suzie

Suzie was a very tiny person and would not have been very much bigger than the largest of the babies. I remember catching grasshoppers for Suzie. We then had to pull off the legs (which were not eaten) and then they were cooked under the grill and were in fact very tasty. I can clearly remember the taste. It was a little bit like a potato chip with some meat. In fact it was quite a delicacy if you forgot what you were eating.

I also remember Suzie making sour milk by putting covered milk at the bottom of the cupboard, and then leaving if for a few days to go sour. She gave me a taste once but I did not like it.

Suzie looked after Max and me as babies and encouraged us to suck our thumbs (I suppose to comfort ourselves and to make us sleep) and Max always had a very clean white thumb. Max used to suck his thumb all the time. I also used to suck my thumb too but not to the same extent. She never smacked us but she was at times a little impatient with us and sometimes spoke harshly to us so we did as she asked.

All the African staff treated us well except for Rachel who would pinch us with her long nails and leave bruises and even draw blood. I remember her being warned to stop it. I remember helping Elias clean and dry the dishes in the scullery. Gladys, who came later, told us stories about ogres, which were like giants she explained, and she would keep our attention for a very long time.

Pat Macleod

I also remember Miss Pat Macleod who arrived when I was about seven or eight. She was there to help Auntie Botha. Ma asked what we should call her, Pat or Mrs Macleod. I said Mrs Mc Clown as I had heard her wrong. She used to take us on hikes with Leone Meyer and was strict with us. We had to march two by two and hold hands and I felt tense and uncomfortable and it was not fun. Also when we played she was very strict and it was not fun. I remember her giving Liz and me a smack for some reason and then sort of saying sorry to Liz for hurting her feelings. I felt my feelings were hurt too but she did not say sorry to me. I did not like her and I think she took pleasure in hitting us and bossing us about. She was more like a harsh man and lacked the more gentle feminine side.

One of the things we did with Pat McLeod was go around and gather succulent plants, including quite a few different kinds of cacti and we planted them in the top of the stone wall that ran

310

along the back of the Babies Department and on top of the hill. It was quite interesting to observe what happened to the plants as they grew and that was our first experimentation with plants. I remember her telling us not to play with ourselves in bed and then telling us we had to sleep with our hands outside the bed covers. I could not understand why I could not play with my dinky cars in bed. The folds of the blanket made really good roads, ideal to play by myself in bed. I did not know why my hands and arms must be cold and why I could not put them under the blankets in bed.

Mrs de Winnaar (Auntie Helen)

Later I remember Mrs. De Winnaar came and we used to call her Auntie Helen. She replaced Pat Macleod. She used to get us to pull out her grey hairs and was stricter than Auntie Botha and eventually replaced Auntie Botha but that was after I had left the Babies. She would put the smaller ones in the dark little room for punishment. While this did not really worry me, the younger children were terrified by this punishment and many recall it even till today.

I remember her refusing to give Sammy Lasker (who was very young and had just come to the Arc) some food until he said "please". She once smacked me for something I did not do and then later when she realized I was not the guilty party she said that next time I was naughty she would not hit me.

If we put aside the "dark room" treatment I think she was alright.

Mr Kukuliwitz

I remember when I just started school that a Mr Kukuliwitz (then quite an old man) used to come on Friday afternoons and give us tennis lessons. I was told that in his younger days he had played at Wimbledon. I would chase tennis balls all Friday afternoon and would try in vain to hide them in my shirt and at the end of the afternoon I would get my turn to hit the balls back to him. I remember Eva Bortz playing and encouraging me to hide the balls in my shirt and laughing and giggling when I did so. This was in the earlier days.

Mrs Edelman (Auntie Shirley)

When we were a bit older but still in the Babies I remember that on Friday afternoons we used to be invited to the homes of friends in our class. Mrs. Edelman (Auntie Shirley) who was on the committee organised it and we would go to their home and have lunch and then spend the afternoon with them until about 5.00 pm. Sometimes during the holidays we would also be taken out by these friends for the day. We all also had our turn to go out for the day with Mrs Edelman (Auntie Shirley) too and I remember her inviting us all to her house for a swim and an afternoon party.

At one time we had two dogs brought to us by Mrs Edelman, (Auntie Shirley), from the committee. They had long black hair, and we called them Lucky and Sooty. We got a lot of fun out of them and then after quite a long time one of them died. They were friendly and very placid dogs. They never got excited and

were good dogs for kids. Max used to spend hours patting the dogs and I resented this as he then would not play with me.

JUNIORS AND SENIORS - 1963-1969

Mrs Stelzner

Vicky and a housemother looked after both the Junior and Senior Boys. For most of the time we had Mrs Stelzner in the Junior Boys. She passed away soon after we moved to the Senior Boys and was followed by Mrs Lucas who stayed a very short time and then later by Mrs Marques

Mrs Stelzner was quite old when I arrived at the Junior Boys. She was very strict and had to be very tough to keep all the boys in line. She would not stand for nonsense and it would be very difficult to fool her. She had a son that used to come and visit her with his wife and child and although I did not know for sure I thought that her husband had died many many years previously.

She gave us all a number to mark our clothes and for "roll call". She could very quickly see if we were all present by counting off the numbers.

I remember after school we used to have to polish our shoes and sometimes we took a short cut and you did not really polish them you just dusted them off. Stelzner would come around and she would check and she could see there was no polish on the shoes. She could see if we had not properly cleaned our shoes and we would be punished with no sweets or a slap on the face if we denied the offence.

If your pinkie pointed up while you ate or drank your tea, you could get a smack from Stelzner. She would say, "Vots met de fency finger?" Paul Cohen and I copped it sometimes. My Auntie Fay used to tell me it's a sign of royal blood.

We could get into big trouble if we asked for extra food at meal time and got it and there was no more left to give extra to a senior boy. It was quite hard to judge whether to risk asking for more. Mrs Stelzner realised this as sometimes when we had our hand up for extra we would suddenly put it down. This was when a hungry older and bigger boy than yourself gave you a certain threatening look.

Mrs Stelzner would often have scrambles. She would throw sweets down the passage or into the dormitories and we all would scramble to collect them. Basically what we collected was yours. Leslie Sacks, a senior boy, did not really like the idea that a German woman threw sweets and all us Jewish kids chased after them. I remember him discussing the matter and the instruction went out to us that we would not touch the sweets that were thrown. I am not too sure of the outcome and I think most of us younger ones at that time did not really understand Les's objections.

When we were older and it was holidays or on Friday nights we often played cards with her for money. There was Stelzner, Michael Saiet, Leon Goodman and me and very occasionally Vicky played too. We used to play poker and a few other card

Mrs Stelzner and the Boys 1961   Standing: Harry Kupferberg. Jackie Levine, Brian Langman, Neville Merwitz, Raymond Warshowsky,
Martin Katz, Leslie Sacks, Howard Ginsberg, Max Rochlin, Jules Gordon
Kneeling at Back: Henry Schippel, Abe Kupferberg, Manfred Stein, Mrs Stelzner, David Ginsberg, Keith Lang
Three boys kneeling on left front: Hilton Rothaus, Robert Langman, Hymie Aranoff
Front: Joe Lurie, Arnold Salmonsonn, Michael Goldstein, Paul Cohen, Raymond Lang and Charles Resnick.

games. I remember Leon Goodman often winning. Mrs Stelzner and I would generally come out square while Michael Saiet generally lost big. I remember him once losing one rand on one card game which was a fortune for us children at the time. We had good times playing, it was good fun and exciting entertainment for us.

I remember after school we would walk home and then we would have our lunch. It would be about 3 o' clock in the afternoon and we would sit under the shade of the peppercorn tree. The food would be on the stone table and we would sit around the stone benches and on the stairs and on the landings or the embankments or on the grass and have our lunch. Stelzner would be there and there would be talking and joking and a little bit of banter. She would pick on the boys and the boys would come back a little bit at her but it was relaxing, all sitting together and having our lunch.

In the Junior and Senior Boys I remember Joe Baloy and Lillian helping to look after us. We were all very friendly and respected them and would joke with them. Lillian would always complain

about Borris letting off and we would often tease Joe Balloy about "drinking too much skokiaan"

I remember Joe telling Keith Lang once that his wife and children were killed when their hut back home caught alight and burnt down.

One morning Mrs. Stelzner was not at our morning inspection at 6:30 as was her custom and despite knocking of her door Vicky was unable to wake her. We went off to school as per normal and later when we came home we found out that they had to break into her room, which was locked and that she had passed away. Doc at dinner mentioned her passing and said a few words and we stood a minute in silence. We were all sad for a few days and after a time Mrs Lucas arrived to look after us.

Mrs. Lucas

Mrs Lucas was a more gentle person and that was both good and bad. I remember coming home from school one day and after changing, going up to the stone table to collect my lunch, which should have been a couple of slices of corned beef, a few quarters of tomato and two slices of brown bread, enough to make up a filling sandwich. I only received a small slice of meat, a thin slice of bread and a small quarter tomato and there were still a few other plates with even less food on. I somehow imagine that Les Durbach who burned up all those extra calories to play rugby got there before me and re-dished out the meals.

Being hungry and annoyed I took the serving dish and marched up to the kitchen to speak to Ma and to get more food. Ma obliged and opened the large cool room took out a hunk of beef and cut some thick slices. She also cut some more bread and tomatoes and soon I marched back down to the Boys Department and filled up the plates. Mrs Lucas complained to Vicky that I was being disloyal. He then spoke to me but accepted what I had to say. This would never have happened with Mrs Stelzner. Mrs Lucas did not stay very long but while she was here she taught us to play 'cheat' a card game we really enjoyed.

Mrs Marques

Mrs Marques followed Mrs Lucas. She was a very gently Portuguese lady who befriended us and worked more on gentle persuasion than strict discipline for the older boys. She was stricter on the younger ones and while she knew that the older boys bunked out, she overlooked it. She also knew exactly how we used to get out at night. One of the dormitory doors looked very secure with a hasp and staple and a big lock. The only trouble was that the staple was not screwed to the door but only held in place by the lock. She would not let the younger ones go out and would appeal to the older ones to prevent the younger ones from going.

Mr Chait the Shoemaker

Mr Chait was in charge of the grounds and staff and repaired our shoes and had his shoe shop just opposite the stables. I remember on one occasion going to have my shoes repaired and watching him in amazement as he very skillfully cut the sole to size from a piece of leather and then stuck it onto the shoe and knocked in a few tacs to make the shoes like new again.

I remember him rebuking me in a very soft voice after I had walked down the driveway slashing off all the flowers with a stick like a knight slaying dragons.

William the Handyman

I remember the fence around the kraal. William, the handyman, put it up and it was interesting to watch him working, because you learnt and saw how things were done. I remember he had this hole digging tool and he would put it down and turn it around and around and dig the hole. Then he would put in the post and then join the posts with cross beams and then off those cross beams he would put up those little poles and then it would be painted nicely. It was also interesting to sit and watch because he went about his job methodically and of course he was very handy.

William was quite sour sometimes. He wasn't always the friendliest but sometimes he would joke and he used to talk about your "matonda" (your penis).

We used to build scotch carts and race down the Arc drive and we were always scrounging materials for our carts. I remember us wanting to get into William's workshop. We wanted tools, nails and prams for their wheels and axles for building our scotch carts. Michael Saiet said he could tickle the lock and he opened it with a piece of wire. We helped ourselves and then faced the music when we came back from school on the Monday.

Mrs Stelzner asked us when we came home from school if we broke into William's workshop and when one or two of us owned up she would ask who else was there. We would never squeal on each other and got a hiding not only for doing the deed but also for not dobbing on each other in. We were sometimes questioned individually and holes would be picked in our different versions of what happened. It came out that Michael Saiet had tickled the lock. We agreed not to insist that Les Durbach own up as he was mad keen on his rugby and he feared the punishment would stop him playing.

William had already taken the law into his own hands by chopping our newly made scotch carts into little pieces.

Doctor London

Also we watched when the buildings were being painted and it was very interesting to watch whoever was painting. Sometimes it was William or sometimes "Doctor London" who was always a very cheerful character. The job may have taken two or three weeks (who knows how long?) and we would watch and look on.

"Doctor London" was friendly and would talk to us and would make jokes. He also was sometimes the nightwatchman and stood guard days with his stick at the top of the driveway during the High Holy.

Dr Kussner – our Dentist

Our teeth were examined at the hospital on a Sunday morning at least every six months. Dr Kussner would come in and Rosie or Bessie Bortz would act as the dental assistant. He would gently tell us to 'open wide' and poke around at our teeth. I often needed extra attention and would have to have an appointment at his rooms at Ingram's Corner in Hillbrow. This was a treat even though the drilling and filling of the teeth was sometimes painful and you had to sometimes wait a very long time for your turn. I remember first going to see the dentist when about four years old and over the years my minders included Sister Conway, Sharon Getz and Anne Flink. Most times after seeing Dr Kussner I ended up with a few sweets that I could 'only suck'.

I remember other children were terrified of the dentist and specifically remember hearing Sharon Getz screaming while being treated even though I was sitting in the waiting room. Dr Kussner was always very gentle and soft spoken. I remember he got a new drill that 'didn't hurt so much' and sprayed water on your tooth as he drilled.

I had the pleasure of catching up to Dr Kussner in Sydney in the late 1990s.

Adon Shalit, our Chedar Teacher

I did have Adon Shalit as a Chedar teacher for about five years (1964 to 1968) and he was then a very old man. I always wondered why he encouraged us to go to Israel while he lived in SA. I found out only recently that he suffered from malaria when he made Aliyah to Israel and could therefore not stay there. While he was kind (he only hit me once when I first started lessons with him) I did not learn how to read Hebrew.

I think this is partly attributable to the fact that I had my lessons from three to four, but, as school only finished at 2:30 pm, it was okay to be a half hour late. Also the teachers then taught by repetition and did not have the art of stimulating the learning juices of us really uninterested and bored kids who were forced to go to lessons.

Leslie Teeger

When I left the Arc in 1969 there was no doubt about me going to university. This seed had long ago been planted by Doc and

he arranged for me to see Mr Teeger. Mr Teeger the one time chairman of the Arc and also a partner at Leiman Teeger Gaddin Sifris & Co, a firm of chartered accountants, gave me a job. He suggested I work for three months until the year end; during which I could decide whether I wanted to do a Bachelor of Commerce full time or do a certificate in the theory of accountancy part time.

After the three months were up I agreed to do a certificate in the theory of accountancy part time. I was partly influenced by what Mr. Teeger had said, "It was better to be a 'mensch' and earn your money than to go to university full time and live on a pittance of an allowance."

Les Teeger employed many Arcs in his accounting practice back in Johannesburg, including Lesley Marks, Leon Goodman, Max Goldman and me. In 1969 I started working for R100 per month and when it came to paying R5 for tax a month he kindly added this on to my pay so I still cleared the R100. I worked for his practice for about six years and he always had a friendly word and kind smile for us.

I also remember Leslie Teeger visiting us at the cottage in Birt Street in his capacity as a member of the committee. I completed five years of articles at Leiman Teeger Gaddin Sifris & Co.

Les Teeger's brother Dr Joe Teeger was on the Arc medical board for many many years too.

1966 Committee
Seated: 1ˢᵗ Row: (L to R): Dr M Franks (Hon President), Mr M S Zulman (Hon Treasurer), Adv L E M Goldsmid (Chairman), Mrs J M Edelman (Chairman, House Committee), Mr S J Nochumsohn (Vice Chairman), Mr L Teeger (Hon Secretary)
2ⁿᵈ Row: (L to R) :Mrs P Duchen (Hon Vice Presiddent) ,Mrs B Jaffee (Hon Vice President)< Mrs D Stein, Mrs C Sasto, Mr S Tolkin (Hon President,), Mr C Braudo (Trustee)
Standing: 3ʳᵈ Row: (L to R): Mrs V Rabinowitz, Mrs D Palm, Mrs A Marks, Mrs A Parness, Mrs G Leiman, Mrs S Lopis, Mr I J Distiller
4ᵗʰ Row: (L to R): Mr I S Levy, Mr C A Michalson, Mr B A Jacobson, Mr M L Dickson, Mr W Michel, Mr E Osrin
Back Row: (L to R): Professor P Levy, Dr C P Nelson (Hon Preside

The 1955 edition consisted of 60 pages including illustrations and was edited by Solly Farber with sub-editors Reuben Lipschitz and David Kotzen.

THE WOLF HILLMAN HOSPITAL
By David Kotzen

Arcadia hasn't always had a hospital. In the early days if boys or girls were ill they were simply separated from the other children, and attended to by one of the staff. Then on June 1st, 1930, the Wolf Hillman Hospital was opened. As the name of the hospital implies, it was built by the Father of Arcadia, Mr Wolf Hillman. The furniture in the hospital was presented by Mr John Schlesinger. Arcadians are and will always be grateful to these two men. The opening of the hospital was not only a great and memorable occasion, but a very enjoyable one.

When the operating theatre was closed down, all Arcadians were taken to one of the general hospitals when operative treatment was needed. Today the dental room replaces the operating theatre. Every Sunday one of our panel of dentists visits the Arc and examines the children's teeth. Every Arc has been in the hospital at one time or another - sometimes with *'chaferlitis'*. As I am writing this article in hospital, I can do nothing more appropriate than describe a day in hospital.

If I happened to wake up early I could forget about getting some more sleep, but if by some miracle I did get back to sleep it is only to be woken by Charlie Miller's bus - hooting of course - as it made its way to pick up the Arcs. After washing, I turned on the wireless and waited for breakfast. I was listening very enjoyably when Sister pokes her head into the ward and shouts 'Not so loud, you'll wake the babies'. As if the babies weren't awake already! After the Arcs had gone to school everything is strangely quiet, and for amusement I depended upon chatting with Sister, reading, and the radio.

Charlie's hooter signals that the children are once again home. Now I wait for my friends to come to see me at the window. A nice chat is going on when Sister, bless her soul, walks in. The Arcs scatter, but a few of the brave ones slip behind a wall to wait until Sister goes. When Sister does go the Arcs reappear, but not for long, for Sister knows their tricks and sends them away.

The evenings are spent in the same way and are therefore not worth describing. At night I usually listen to the wireless and then I go off to sleep until Dolly Miller's fowls begin their morning serenade.

Many Sisters have rendered their services and their names remain enshrined in the annals of Arcadia. Sister Johnson, Sister Pels, Sister Wheel and many others are remembered by Arcs. At present Sister E Conway is in charge, and a tough job she has, for sometimes she has to cope with 36 patients at once. In conclusion, a word of thanks to our doctors and dentists who serve Arcadia unflinchingly.

OFF TO ISRAEL!

More than six years ago little Freda Levine arrived at Arcadia, the Jewish Orphanage in Johannesburg. It is customary at Arcadia for older children to be given responsibility; and for girls it generally means helping matron and nurses in escorting little ones to the dentist, or doctor, and here it was that Freda excelled herself.

And so she grew up, helping the nurses and encouraging the children and the day came when her studies were drawing to a close and it was time to consider seriously her career. The general consensus of opinion was that Freda was a 'natural' for the nursing profession.

Dr Lichtigfeld, Superintendent of Arcadia, who has very definite views on doing everything possible to help Arcadians in their careers, preferably with the object of their settling in Israel, where he feels, they would integrate with ease and not be faced with the complexities of a life in which, due to their institutional background, they would be 'different', wanted to see Freda settle in Israel too.

And so, Freda at $16^1/_2$ years of age, became a candidate for the nursing profession in Israel. Then came the question: 'But where in Israel was she to study?' The answer was self-evident: WIZO's Mothercraft Training Centre in Tel Aviv.

A few weeks ago, in fever pitch of excitement, she arrived at Lydda Airport, where she was met by Mrs Fan Raphael, one-time member of the Council, who will 'keep an eye' on Freda during her first few months in Israel. Three months will be spent at an Ulpan - studying Hebrew in the mornings and working in the afternoons at one of the immigrant camps. And so on to the Mothercraft Centre for training, and thence to a future where she can dedicate herself to the fine profession which she has chosen, for which she has a natural bent, and for which she will be fully equipped.

We wish Freda Levine the very best of good luck!

LETTER FROM ELI ZAGORIA

We have received a letter from Eli Zagoria, an old Arc in Israel in which he disputes the statement of Rabbi Rabinowitz at the Annual General Meeting that Freda Levine is the first Old Arc to settle in Israel. He gives names and addresses of Old Arcs living in Israel. These names can be obtained from the Superintendent of Arcadia by request.

SURELY THIS IS ALSO A WORLD RECORD!
By Solly Farber

Many years back Barney Myers amazed Arcadians by heading a ball against a wall 2,521 times. This feat became almost legendary in Arcadia and was almost always brought up when Arcs got talking.

Then almost a year ago a new 'headerer' came on to the scene - Morris 'Chorky' Bortz. Week in, week out Morris practised against the wall. At first he managed a few hundred, and there was great jubilation in Arcadia when Morris first reached the thousand mark.

From that day on Morris never looked back, and not long after he reached his goal - Barney's record. 'Chorky' shattered the record by a good few hundred, and has since bettered that record so many times that the old record of 2,521 looks silly. Being an enterprising boy, Morris 'Header' Chorky determined to double the record, and sure enough not long after this decision he raised the record to above 5,000.

He has this 'sport' so completely taped that he stops once he has started' only to have lunch or something, and it is now not a case of how long he can continue, but of how much he can header before he has to stop for lunch. Every Sunday morning 'Chorky' can be seen, his head working like a machine heading the ball against the wall outside the library.

In the last three weeks he has done successively 6,009, 6,120 and last week he amazed even himself with a score of 7,734. If any of the readers can inform us of anybody who has performed such a feat we would appreciate if they would do so. Imagine heading a ball against a wall 19,503 times in three attempts! It's a pity that there is no association that could ratify this as a world record.

Readers will be pleased to hear that at the time of going to press 'Chorky' performed the amazing feat of heading the ball 13,500 (repeat 13,500) times.

CHORKY Heading for World Fame.

AU REVOIR, ARCADIANS
Written by Solly Farber, Reuben Lipschitz and David Kotzen

Arcadia is like the world - children come and children go, but Arcadia carries on just the same. At the end of the last school year six people bade farewell to the Arc and went out to take their places in the world. Those who left were Sam Berer, Cyril Fanaroff, Morris Bortz, Sidney Dubois and two girls, Sheila Berer and Rene Slovo.

Sam Berer - Sam didn't spent any time in the 'Babies' as he was already seven years old when he came to Arcadia. He has represented Arcs in soccer and cricket for quite a few years now. In his past two years he was vice-captain of soccer and proved to be an invaluable centre-half. Sammy attended the Parktown Boys' High School where he was a prefect and played 2nd XV rugby. Last year Sammy was a prefect at Arcadia.

Cyril Fanaroff - Although Cyril only came to the Arc when he was nearly Barmitzvah, he played quite a big part in Arc life. He was a prefect with Sammy last year and was a senior chazzan in the Shul. Like Sammy, he played soccer and cricket for the Arcs. Cyril obtained a university pass in the recent Matric exams and is now articled to study law.

Morris Bortz - Has been in the Arc since God knows when. He will always be remembered as the boy full of ideas. He was exceptionally good at building *ho*ks and "Buks' Cathedral" still stands down the hill as a monument to Morris' architectural abilities. Morris represented Arcs at soccer and cricket on various occasions, and in cricket proved to be a very acrobatic fielder. He is now doing clerical work.

Sidney Dubois - Sidney came to Arcadia soon after the war. Blessed with a very clear head, Sidney astounded many by his common sense. Like the others, represented Arcs at soccer and cricket and was coach of the junior boys' soccer team. He is a member of the Arc Harmonica Band. 'Paw-Paw' is now apprenticed to become a manufacturing jeweller.

Sheila Berer - Sheila spent considerable time in Arcadia. She was most popular for her beautiful soprano voice and will, we are sure, one day become world famous. Sheila is no mean performer in the swimming bath and excelled in past Arc galas.

Devorah Vainik - Devorah only spent two years in Arcadia, but during that short time she endeared herself to everyone. In 1952 she was voted 'most popular girl'. Devorah has taken up a clerical career, and we wish her the best of luck.

Reina Slovo - Last, but by no means least, we have 'Bhudda'. Reina has been in the Arc practically all her life and has been brought up in the true Arc fashion. She was outstanding at school when she bothered to work, and wasn't bad at sport. With Sheila, she is studying bookkeeping, typing etc.

These six people have spent certain periods of their lives at Arcadia and now leave, taking with them years of coaching and lessons in life and Jewish knowledge. God grant them success and let them carry on the tradition of Arcadia.

Chapter 83 - THE 1957 ARCADIAN

The 1957 edition has a silver cover consisting of 64 pages including illustrations, and was edited by Sandra Berlin and Shirley Bortz with sub-editor Norman Sacks.

SOME ARC STAFF
By Sarah Farber

Sister

We are very fortunate to have Sister with us as she is very capable and understanding.

Sister is very popular amongst the children. She often helps us in other ways besides her hospital duties by solving many of the little children's problems. The Arcs are therefore very lucky to have such a good person in our midst.

Miss Gray

A newcomer to the Arc from Holland is already very poplar amongst the Arcs. We sincerely hope she will remain with us for a long, long time.

Mrs Benhail

Was once a former Junior Boys' housemother and is now a general relief. Mrs Benhail is liked by the children.

Mrs Bridges
By Rose Bortz

Mrs Bridges is the Junior Girls' housemother and is loved by all, for she is very understanding. She gives up much of her precious time, helping us with our homework, especially English because she comes from England and has a very good vocabulary. She can imitate languages from many countries and proves to be quite a good ventriloquist. We hope that she will remain in Arcadia for many years to come.

Mrs Stelzner
By Hymie Sacks

The Junior Boys are very fortunate to have a good lady like Mrs Stelzner.

Sometimes when we are naughty she will explain in a loud and quick voice 'I'll give you *Ottie Bottel* if you don't behave yourselves'. Usually, we would behave ourselves in order to give Mrs Stelzner a bit of rest. Nevertheless, the Junior Boys still like Mrs Stelzner and often say to her 'Mrs Stelzner, you are the best housemother we have ever had'. Then Mrs Stelzner would give a friendly smile and say 'Thank you'.

Editors Sandra Berlin and Shirley Bortz

Mrs Sowerby

Special thanks for devoted services are due to Mrs Sowerby, our very popular housekeeper.

MUSICAL ACTIVITIES AT THE ARC
By Charlie Segal

Since the existence of Arcadia there have been many magnificent sportsmen and also some brilliant scholars, but, as far as I can gather, there have not been any outstanding musicians.

During my stay at the Arc, I have known quite a number of boys and girls who possessed great musical ability. Undoubtedly some of these could have become first-class musicians had they had the opportunity of training, without which, of course, no one can expect headway in the musical world, where technique must count as much as artistry. Some lucky few do learn an instrument, but why don't more?

I therefore trust that in the days to come many will be encouraged to do so, thus forming the nucleus of our own orchestra. I think I'm right in saying, that without exception, all enjoyed the concerts given by Mr S Aronowsky of the SABC and Mr E Dunn, former conductor of the Durban Philharmonic Orchestra.

If we could have lectures on Musical Appreciation from time to time, these would enable us to appreciate music in an interesting way and would greatly help the enjoyment of our leisure hours.

PS Charlie himself plays the piano, trumpet, and mouth-organ.

THE BABIES

Sarah Farber - The Arcadian – 1957

If there's anything I adore it is the small children in Arcadia. I consider myself very lucky to be able to see the little ones every day. I derive a great amount of pleasure by just going over to see them and I usually reserve Saturday mornings for a visit.

As I walk down the steps there they all are to greet me. What a welcome. I first hear little Nadia call out 'Hello Selah' this makes me feel warm and I want to stay all the time I can with them. I love each and all and I understand all their pretty little ways and odd little habits. I usually sit and listen to all their little stories. The one is always quick to tell tales on the other but I soon settle them. If I promise to do something for them then the next time I visit the first thing I hear is Sarah you promised me 'this' or you promised me 'that'. There's no escaping. The one thing I hate to do is to disappoint them. Sometimes one comes to me and says that the other is hitting her. Little arguments between them are not so easy to settle as it means listening to both sides of the story and passing judgment, however it comes right for I always make or at least try to make them see what is right, never mind the outcome.

I often stand on the balcony of our department and watch them play. I try to do this unobserved but should any one of them see me, they call me until I just can't help going down even if I am very busy.

One day I went to watch them swimming. This was really enjoyable as they like to show off in front of anyone, it's part of their make-up. They all call you simultaneously to watch them dive, so my eyes try to be everywhere at once to give them all encouragement. Well in conclusion I must say I have great pleasure in all my experiences with the dear ones.

MAZAL TOV

Mr and Mrs I Heyman celebrated their Diamond Wedding early this year. On behalf of all the Arcs we would like to congratulate them both. In addition, we want to thank Mr Heyman for all the unselfish work he has done for us and the great interest he has always taken in Arcadia.

Hearty congratulations are also due to Mr and Mrs D Stein on their Silver Wedding Jubilee; to Mr and Mrs V Gratus on their 30th Wedding Anniversary; to Mr and Mrs V Hepker on the Wedding of their Daughter (we often had the pleasure of welcoming Lyrice in Arcadia); to Mr and Mrs L Aschheim on the Wedding of their Daughter; to Mr and Mrs M Cowen on the Wedding of their Daughter; to Mr and Mrs M Lubner, Mr and Mrs B Jaffee, Mr and Mrs D Stein, and Mr and Mrs S Tolkin, and Mr and Mrs H Bradlow (Mrs R A Bradlow's son), on the birth of Grandchildren; to Mrs B N Levy on her Grandson's Barmitzvah (son of Dr and Mrs Doris Cohen, our Hon elocution teacher); to Mr and Mrs A H Stodel, on the Barmitzvah of their son; to Mr and Mrs A B Klipin on the Barmitzvah of their Grandson; and to Mr and Mrs S Tolkin on the engagement of their son.

Jackie Mekler has been chosen to represent South Africa at the Empire Games to be held in Greece. We wish him the best of luck. Congratulations Jackie!

Good luck also to Mr and Mrs J Bloom's son who has been chosen for the Maccabi Team, Athletics.

At this time our heartiest congratulations go out to Freddie, older son Doc and Ma, upon attaining the degree M.B., B.CH. We wish him good luck in Israel.

Congratulations to Jock and Audrey Wiegand (nee Sepel) on the birth of a son, and to Tony and Devorah Collet (nee Vainik) on the birth of a daughter.

Other items to be noted are the recent engagements of Fay Fanaroff to Dully Nissenbaum, the weddings of Joss Lipschitz to Dora Said, of Zelda Gordon to Bert Schoenberg, and Naomi Bernstein to Donald Goldman.

Arcadia wishes them the best of luck for the future.

We apologise to those Arcs whose names do not appear here, but would like them to know that they all have our good wishes, and we trust that in future the 'would-be-marries' would let us know in time of these coming events.

Hearty Congratulations on the election of Mr Percy Cowen, Mrs R Bessarabia (Dr R Getz), Mrs H Jaffee and Mr John Massey as Hon-Life Members.

AU REVOIR

By Sandra Berlin, Shirley Bortz and Norman Sacks.

When a newcomer comes to the Arc it is often with a tear in the eye and with little faith that all will be well, for the child knows not what it is like to live with other children. It is often suspicious of the very ones trying to help it. However, as the years go by, it soon feels quite at home and actually when the day dawns that he or she must be ready to say goodbye to Arcadia, it is with a sad heart and a great deal of reluctance that they bid farewell to those whom they lived with those past years.

Since there was no magazine last year we now have to say farewell to a large group of Arcs, each of whom deserve a short note on their respective merits.

Reuben Lipschitz - The Arc welcomed Reuben at a very early age. Then he was a quiet, short boy and nobody ever thought that he would be blessed with such flowing humour, as he has today.

This auburn haired, freckled lad played for the 2nd XV Rugby Team for three years and for the 3rd XI Cricket Team. We feel sure he would have gained a place in the 1st XV Rugby Team had he not become ill during the latter half of form IV. Reuben, despite his illness, gained a University pass at the end of December 1955. Reuben now holds a good position in a stationery firm.

Solly Farber - Solly played the mouth organ, was one of the founders of the now extinct photographic society and was chief 'chazen'. He was also chief editor of T*he Arcadian* for the past four years and … apart from all these hobbies, Solly still had time to go steady three times. Our mistake, it was only twice.

You will agree with us when we say that Solly was truly a wonder boy, because Solly was unfortunately born a cripple. Doctors had given up hope that he would ever be able to play sports. He really had guts and proved that their theory was wrong. Today he excels in both the sports and scholastic fields for he was a prefect at Parktown Boys and swam for the A Swimming Team. He also played for the 3rd XV Rugby Team, where he captained it on many occasions.

During his stay at Arcadia, he gained his Life Saving Instructors Certificate. Solly's matric results were first class with distinction in Latin and Mathematics. Solly is now in second year medicine and is doing excellently. We hope he will keep up this good work.

Congratulations Solly.

Bella Bortz - Bella came to the Arc when she was still a youngster, and although she hasn't grown very tall since then, she certainly has matured into a charming and beautiful young lady.
Bella represented her school in netball, for which she obtained her colours. At the Arc prize-giving days she won many prizes for achievement at school and at Hebrew. In her last year at the Arc (1955) she was voted the most popular girl. Bella gained a University pass.

She is now working as a Medical Technologist at the Coronation Hospital and is taking BA by correspondence with a view to doing medicine.

Allan Dubois - Usually all the new Arc boys are given nicknames. Allan a shy boy from England was nicknamed 'Squeeky' and this name has stayed with him ever since.

The following incident concerning Squeeky, which very few of the Arcs will ever forget, deserves mention: He was hypnotized by the Great Marco; while he was under the power of Hypnosis, the magician told him to jive. He did so and what a performance! We laughed until our stomachs ached and tears were rolling down our cheeks. After he was brought around and told what he had done, Squeeky was more than amazed. In those days he couldn't jive but we would like to inform you now that Squeeky is a celebrated bopper.

At school he played for the under 15B Rugby Team. Squeeky now does Commercial Art.

David Kotzen - David was the Valentino of the Arcs and broke the hearts of many senior girls. Unfortunately there is not enough space in this magazine to mention names.

David, too, was one of the founders of the past photographic society, played the mouth organ, and gained his Life Saving Instructors certificate.

Somehow David couldn't decide what sport appealed to him most and therefore during his stay at the Arc, his sports included at one time or the other, swimming, running, rugby, tennis and cricket. Anyway David excelled at all the sports mentioned above and will always be remembered by the Arcs as a remarkable sportsman.

At school David played in the 1st XV Rugby and in the 2nd XI Cricket teams.

David, as you can see, has a restless disposition. This is proved by his first going to settle in Cape Town and then trying to become a steward on a boat so that he can travel overseas.

We wish David Bon Voyage!

Louis Kreser - Louis spent a good part of his youth at the Arc. Generally he was always a very quiet lad, but he certainly proved himself on the sports field.

Louis had his eye on a few of the senior girls, but unfortunately, he was such a shy character, that someone else always stepped in before him.

Louis was a prefect at Parktown Boys and represented his school in 1st XI Cricket team for two years and 1st XV Rigby team for the same length of time. He also won five finals in Boxing.

In 1956 he received the Anthony Blatt Memorial Cup for the best Rugby player at his school. He was also awarded the Rotary Cup - a Cup awarded to the most popular boy at Parktown.

He was a prefect at the Arc and was voted the most popular boy in his time.

Louis is now working in a stationery firm.

Benny Kreser - As far back as Benny can remember, his home has been the Arc. He was a real scoundrel as it was him and his mates who were the chief instigators of the raid performed so successfully by the Male Department on the Female Department. Benny, like his brother, was attracted to the opposite sex (senior girls), but because he never took action, nothing ever materialized, and so he is still an Arc Bachelor.

At school Benny played 2nd Cricket and 3rd Rugby at Parktown Boys. He is now working at a wholesale tobacconist.

Zelda Gordon - Zelda came to the Arc at the age of eight and even then she was a pretty blue-eyed blonde and very popular. At school she played for Athlone's open netball team.

Zelda left the Arc at the beginning of 1956, and we are pleased to report that she has recently married. Mazeltov Zelda!

Fanny Blecher - Fanny began her stay at the Arc at the tender age of six years.

Her artistic abilities were known to no-one until she began school She was a good second to the previous old Arc artist, Hannah Mekler. Fanny took a dress designing course at the Technical College for a few months, but unfortunately gave this up for a secretarial course and is now working at the Zionist Federation.

We hope Fanny will continue doing art even if only as a hobby.

Basil Sepel - Basil was tiny when he first came to the Arc and nobody imagined he would ever grow. Basil thrived on the Arc food and is now a tall, well built handsome lad.

At first he played 3rd Rugby for Parktown Boys, but he later gave it up for hockey, in which he gained a place in the 1st team. Basil was a keen boxer and won three finals.

At the end of last year he gained a University Pass which enabled him to take Agriculture at the Natal University.

Arnold Levitan - Arnold was already in High School when he came to the Arc. He introduced bopping into the Arc, being an expert at it himself.

He was a prefect at Athlone Boys where he played 1st XV Rugby. He was a keen athlete and won cups at the Inter Hebrew School Sports.

He passed his Matric at the end of last year and is now working at the Modderfontein Dynamite Factory and intends doing engineering next year.

Issadore Levitan - Issy was very popular among the boys and girls at the Arc, but his leaving was felt much more deeply by the girls. While at Athlone he was a member of the under 13A Rugby team and also a prominent scorer for his team.

After passing Form I, he left Athlone in preference for Parktown, where he was Vice Captain of the under 14A Rugby team. Issy was a good athlete and scored second place in the Junior Cross Country Race. He received many cups at the Inter-Hebrew School Sports. He was also a keen swimmer and offered valuable assistance in looking after the Arc swimming bath.

Issy is now staying with his sister and brother-in-law in Durban, and we wish him all the luck for the future.

Fay Fanaroff - When Fay came to the Arc her greatest worry was how thin she was. Her stay at the Arc certainly did wonders, and we can assure her that she has nothing to worry about, because Fay is now a very attractive girl with a lovely figure.

Fay represented her school in the open tennis team. She also spent much of her Saturday and Sunday mornings on the tennis courts.

Fay was the first girl prefect at the Arc and looked after the Senior Girls, when they did not have a housemother. As co-editor of *The Arcadian* Fay rendered valuable assistance.
Fay left the Arc last year only to be engaged a few months later. We wish you Mazeltov Fay!

Anita Levine - Anita may be called an old timer of the Arc. She came at a comparatively early age. Anita was a keen dancer and performed in dances on many prize-giving days. Anita gave up much of her time to take the younger children to the dentist and was generally a willing helper.

She left school to do a secretarial course at college, but recently left college to become a Shorthand Typist.

Cynthia Lipschitz - Cynthia came to the Arc when she was very young. Although Cynthia did not excel in the sports sphere, she was a good scholar. She will be remembered for the way she willingly helped the girls with their work.

Lorraine and Glenda Cohen - These two sisters didn't remain long with us at the Arc, but during their short stay, their charming manners won everyone over, and we were all quite sorry to say farewell to them so soon. Lorraine and Glenda were keen dancers. Lorraine had a flair for tap dancing, while Glenda proved herself to be apt in both Tap and at Ballet.

They are staying with their father in Springs where Lorraine is at College doing a course of Shorthand and Typing and Glenda at the Primary School there.

We wish them both all the best of luck in their future lives.

Solly Farber, Bella Bortz and Reuben Lipschitz

The 1959 edition consisting of 78 pages including illustrations has an orange cover and was edited by Bernard Edelman, Yechiel Bortz, Jeffrey Esekow and Hymie Pearlman.

DAILY ROUTINE
By Karen Shraga and Sandra Solomon

Under the supervision of Mrs Field we have in the Girls Department what we call the 'Daily Routine'.

The silence of the morning is broken at six, when Mrs Field wakes us up with a stern voice, 'Morr-ning girls, Get up' and she then goes directly to the wireless and switches it on to her favourite program. The minute she goes out, we find LM. Before going upstairs, Mary starts nagging us to collect our things - lying around - and to shine our shoes.

At a quarter to seven we go upstairs and enjoy our tasty breakfast which consists of cereals, scrambled eggs, brown bread, butter, jam and coffee. After breakfast we collect our sandwiches and pile into the Arc bus in which we are taken directly to our respective schools.

By three o'clock most of the girls are home, except those playing sports. No sooner are we in the Department when Mary starts shouting 'Take your counter-panes and uniforms off before eating your lunch, and wash your socks'. The girls do their homework during the afternoon and in the evening.

Later in the afternoon Mrs Field comes downstairs from the smaller girls, and as all the girls have a habit of lying on their beds, she makes us get up, and at the same time, sees to it that we attend the Hebrew classes.

At six o'clock the siren is sounded, and we all go up to the dining room for supper. After supper we go back to our Departments where either the Afrikaans or Maths coaches are waiting to help us in our work.

After everyone had a bath, we get into bed, switch off the lights and start talking about one hundred and one things. As there is often a racket, the girls do not hear Mrs Field come in. She stands there without saying a word, listening. Only when one of the girls says 'good night' do we know that she's there, because she crossly calls out 'Never mind, good night and go to sleep', and with that she slams the door and walks out. By then, we are dead-beat and decide to go to sleep.

Apart from the seemingly automatic routine, there is however plenty of leisure time left for the girls to do anything they wish. (knitting, embroidering, sewing, swimming, tennis, netball, gym etc.

The Editors (l-r) Bernard Edelman, Yechiel Bortz, Jeffrey Esekow, Hymie Pearlman

MEAL TIME
Written by Jeffrey Esekow

Mrs Stelzner 'Bobby Gordon, are you talking?' Bobby: 'No Mrs Stelzner." Mrs Stelzner: 'But I saw you speaking.' He is slapped. Mrs Stelzner to Arthur: 'Are you laughing?' He is also slapped. Bobby to Arthur: 'I'll kill you afterwards.'

Silence reigns in the dining room while the children eat. Next thing Doc storms in with a visitor. Doc: 'Three cheers for Mr B ...' Wild cheering and whistling. They go out. Silence again.

Later on: Mrs Stelzner to Keith: 'Why is your dirty little paw in the air.' Keith: 'I want some more meat.' Mrs Stelzner: 'Can't you see I have only got two hands.'

Suddenly Ma comes in. Ma: 'Put your legs under the table. Why don't you eat that" Don't make such a mess on the table ...' She goes out again.

Next Doc comes in again. Doc: 'This is the list for the dentist ... Begin prayers.' Somebody: 'But Doc, we haven't finished eating.' Doc: 'You can finish afterwards. Say prayers. Prayers are said.

Mrs Stelzner rushes up to Max. Mrs Stelzner: 'Max did you say your prayers?' Max: 'Yes Mrs Stelzner. I said it silently.' Mrs Stelzner: 'Don't ever ask me for a favour again.

The meal is finished; everybody leaves the dining room.

EX-ARCADIAN SPORT SUCCESSES
Written by Hymie Pearlman

The old Arcs had a most successful soccer season last year, winning the Southern Transvaal Division Three. They have been promoted to Division Two. Loius Kreser plays for Rangers, the crack Transvaal 1st Division team, and is a possible candidate for Southern Transvaal under 23. Gerry Levy plays for Old Parktownian 1st XI league cricket.

BOXING IN ARCADIA
Written by Donald Goldman (Ex Arcadian)

Everybody knows that boxing at Arcadia is a clean, healthy and useful sport since Alf James (Ex South African Welter-weight Champion) started the ball rolling. Boxing has steadily progressed in the Arc. We haven't had any champions like Alfie, but let's hope that Donald Goldman, the boxing instructor, will produce one or two champs in the near future.

Boxing is held every Sunday morning in one of the rooms under the Shul. If one would visit a Sunday morning class he would either see the boys sparring or punching the punch bag or punch ball. Boys have been entered in tournaments. Recently, Bobby Gordon fought a well-contested, hard hitting bout, narrowly losing on points for which he won the best loser's cup. At another tournament Abram (Mike) Kupferberg fought a gruelling battle in which both boxers excelled - decision: a draw.

In this connection, I may mention that Mike 'K' is the most improved boxer amongst the Arcs.

From these two fights one can see the Arcs are learning to defend themselves both in and out of the ring.

10TH ANNUAL SWIMMING GALA
Written by Bernard Edelman

The Gala was held on 23rd March. In the morning it seemed as if it would rain, but luckily it didn't. The two teams, Herzl and Bialik, were captained by Hymie Pearlman, Rene Rothaus and Frank Berman and Lilly Solomon, respectively. The committee, with the aid of a few old boys of the home, were the judges, while Vicky announced the winners with his megaphone.

Styles and speed have improved slowly year by year, to the enjoyment of all. This is, however, taken seriously by only a few. The hat and dress race was a comical race. Another event in an entirely different vein was the Water Polo, in which the boys had their friendly brawls.

Bialik won the gala, but the loser, Herzl, took it in good sportsmanship. The prizes were handed out for the best performances and cups for the winners of certain events. Everyone was then invited for tea, cold drinks and eats.

THE BARE TRUTH
Written by Reuben Lipschitz (Ex Arcadian)

Its funny how a story changes with the passing of time. With each telling it becomes slightly more dramatic, a bit more involved, and a bit more of a '*chaff*'. I have worked out a theory for the stories which the Arcs tell. 'The truth of a tale is universally proportional to the amount of time which has passed since the incident occurred.'

Let me give you a few examples: If an old boy of ten years ago tells you he was caned until the superintendent's arm became lame and his cane splintered into a thousand pieces, he most probably received one soft cut.

If an old boy of 15 years ago tells you he received such a caning that two garden boys were called in to carry out the superintendent who had collapsed from sheer physical exhaustion and that his own hardy frame had been reduced to a state resembling minced meat or fruit salad, you can safely assume that he was reprimanded in a rather loud tone of voice.

In the interest of truth I would like to clear up a few incidents concerning myself. It is definitely true that I was very shy and weary of girls when I was in the Junior Boys. It is definitely not true that I hit and kicked a certain girl because the other fellows teased me about her. I have always considered myself a gentleman and have never lifted my feet against any woman.

Joe Klug sometimes exaggerates when he tells of the hole we dug up the hill. He stretches his six foot frame to its full and points far above his head, saying 'that's how deep it was'. I must admit that it was deeper than we were tall, but, at the time, neither of us was belly button high to a grasshopper.

Emily Chi-Chi's memory must be playing tricks with her when she recalls that she had to clean out our bath with a shovel. I can swear that the mud was never more than two inches deep.

While on the subject of bathing, contemporary Junior Boys hold the record for bathing. They claim that there were 22 boys and two tablespoons of water in the one bath. This is definitely a lie. There was only one tablespoon of water in that bath.

Solly Farber does not think much of my ability as an actor. I admit that I did not know my part as well as I could have, but at least, I did know the name of the play in which I was supposed to act. It is definitely not true that we had a stand-up fist fight in front of a large and distinguished audience on the opening night. All that happened is that we stopped the play for a few moments, while we had a verbal argument. That drama turned out to be the best comedy ever produced in the Arc.

Sadly I admit that Woolfie Kotzen scored the record against me on the Senior Boys' cricket veranda. I would like to point out that Chalky Bortz, my co-fielder, dropped about 50 catches that day. Also Woolfie only scored 362, not 364 as he sometimes claims.

I must admit that our *hoks* were bigger and better built than those of today and our pigeons were better bred. But it is definitely not true that the pigeons were so large that they were sometimes mistaken for hens, nor did they ever attack hawks. So Arcs, if your own adventures seem somewhat tame compared to those of your 'elders' do not become unduly perturbed. Time and age will teach you to exaggerate your tales when you tell them to the Arcs that will follow you.

When they sit wide-eyed and believing as you retell some adventures of your youth, you will probably add the maxim of all generations before. 'You fellows of today would never have survived in our time'

'NOT WOOD, NOT STONE, BUT MAN'
Written by Jeffrey Esekow

Suddenly there was a red flash and then shadows of darkness appeared before his eyes. When he again opened his eyes, he saw anxious, sweat-stained faces peering down at him. For a long moment he looked up at them. He tried to rise, but a pang of pain shot through his stomach and then everything began to grow dim. Feeling something warm trickling down his cheeks, he rubbed his hand across his mouth. When he held his hand before his eyes, he noticed a red smidge across his fingers and the palm of his hand. Blood! He was bleeding internally. He was going to die.

Tears began to stream down his face. He again looked at the sympathetic eyes that were fixed on him, and then, realising that he was making a fool of himself, wiped the sleeve of his shirt across his eyes. Again he tried to rise, but his left leg buckled under him. His knee seemed to be made of jelly and

would not bear his weight. He sat down and held his head clasped between the palms of his hands. He wanted desperately to burst out into tears and get over it. Why were they standing here and watching him as if he was a lost little boy? Why didn't they go away and leave him alone? For his whole body was throbbing with a dull pain.

He felt as if he had been run over by a steam roller, but he wasn't going to show them that he was hurt. He made a third attempt to rise. This time he was successful. When he tried to take a step, he nearly collapsed, but two of his friends caught him. They helped him to make a few uncertain steps, but growing angry with himself, he pushed them from him and began to stagger away. He turned around and looked at the group staring at him with admiration. As he hobbled away, one of them shouted after him 'Well done, Joe, by tackling Jerry you stopped him scoring a goal'. As he hobbled to the hospital with blood streaming from his nose, he mumbled to himself 'I'm never going to play soccer in the Arc again'

MA AND DOC'S ARRIVAL HOME
Written by Barbara Ginsberg

Ma and Doc left on the 2nd of December for a well-earned holiday overseas; they were away about three months. We all wrote to them, and from the letters and post-cards received from them, we knew that they were thoroughly enjoying themselves, and having a good rest.

Before Ma and Doc returned to the Arc, the art class, supervised by Freda Baker, painted a banner to welcome them back. On the day, when they were due back, some of us were walking up and down the drive, while a good many of the Arcs were waiting in the quadrangle. Every few seconds someone would give a false alarm by shouting 'Here they come', and everyone would start to whistle and shout until they realized that it was a 'chaff'.

When Mrs Rabinowitz's car finally came up the drive with Ma and Doc, the Arcs whistled and screamed madly, each one trying to out-scream the other. After Ma got out of the car looking as brown as a berry, she kissed everyone, and Doc thanked us for the letters they had received.

We were all glad to see them back, and I'm sure that they were glad to see us.

LETTERS RECEIVED

Mrs Gluckman - "I am on the way now to dear Old England and my family I so often think of you all in Arcadia";

Ex-Arcadian David Kotzen - "Well, I am here in Stanleigh Uranium Mines, Elliott Lake, Ontario, Canada, working as a Miner, eight hours a day, seven days a week. Colin Rosen is also here and doing well. The life here is very difficult and consists of the same monotonous pattern: eat, work, sleep, and more work. I will be here until September and will then go to Vancouver or New York:

Mr and Mrs Zulman – "As you can see, we are in Vienna – a beautiful city. We met Mrs Duchen and Mrs Sive in Nice – also phoned Freddie in London and saw Woolfie Kotzen in Leeds. We are sailing on the Randfontein from Amsterdam on 25th June for home. Hope this finds you both, the Children and the Committee, all well";

Joyce Zasler (Ex-Arcadian) (Joyce Friedman) - now happily married in Los Angeles, USA, "Thank you for your Mazeltov on the birth of our son, Nathan David. My husband received his diploma in Air-conditioning and Refrigeration and is working for a tremendous engineering company. I am still fascinated by the wonders here My regards to those who might remember me – Sandra Solomon must be a senior by now and it makes me feel quite ancient. I can remember how I practically used to hold her in my arms. My warmest regards to all Committee members and both of You."

Mr Effie Segal, Ex-Arcadian, teaching the Harmonica to Arcadians

AU REVOIR
By Bernard Edelman, Yechiel Bortz, Jeffrey Esekow and Hymie Pearlman.

During the last two years a great number of our brothers and sisters left. Although they are called Old Arcs, and we are called Arcs, they still form an intricate part of our lives. Whether they start working, or studying at University or College or whether, like ourselves, they remain in school, we wish them luck and ask them not to forget us at home because we will be forever thinking about them and hoping for their success.

Charlie 'Tzatzke' Segal - Tzatzke was a very popular boy which is proved by the fact that he won 'the most popular boy award' twice. He was regarded as one of the finest sportsmen ever to be produced by the Arc, until he gave sport up in favour of his trumpet and school work. Tzatzke did exceedingly well in both these things, passing matric with a University pass and

receiving colours for the orchestra and military band. Tzatke was prefect and chief chazen at the Arc in his last year.

Norman Sacks - Norman is first class at making laws, as anyone who ever played with him in the Babies swimming pool can confirm. This Draco of modern times is a versatile sportsman. He received his colours at Athlone for cricket and was also selected to play in the Transvaal Nuffield Cricket Trials. Although soccer is his game, he represented 3rd XV rugby. Norman's sense of humour is something not to be forgotten, with a quick quip he would change a serious situation into a light hearted one. Norman is apprenticed to be a radio mechanic.

Sandra Berlin - I think Sandra would make an excellent librarian because she is so quiet by Arc standards of course. Sandra was prefect of the Senior girls in her last year and was very reliable and consistent. Although she has been in South Africa only six years, she passed Matric including Afrikaans. As well as being a co-editor of the last Arcadian, an outstanding artist, she is the best ballet dancer ever to be produced by the Arc.

Shirley Bortz - A pretty girl who was outstanding at everything she tried. Besides being an excellent sportswoman, promising artist, and co-editor of the last Arcadian, Shirley got a first class matric, including a distinction in Latin. Shirley is studying Pharmacy at Technical College. I promise to buy all my Aspros from her when she qualifies.

Isla Sepel - Isla came to the Arc when she was a babe and what a 'babe' she turned out to be. Isla was above average at everything she tried, but she excelled in sport. At Athlone Girls High she received colours for netball and gymnastics and won the most popular girl award twice at Arcadia.

Audrey Shraga - Audrey endeared herself to all the Arcs. When she left many tears were shed. Audrey is a reliable girl, who everyone trusts. At Athlone Girls High Audrey played hockey and swam for the school where she bust a few records. Audrey is training to be a nurse where I am sure she will show the same unselfishness as she did in the Arc.

Hazel Phillips - Hazel's motto 'Arc first, self after' made her the one girl who could honestly say she worked hard. Hazel helped in the dentist room, often took the babies to the dentist in town, served the Senior girls at every meal. She quite deservedly won the Arc's most coveted award 'The Good Fellowship Cup'.

Frances Blumenfeld - Frances is a girl with a latent personality, with occasional blazes, revealing her sense of humour. She is a very bright scholar, passing well each year. Her principles, however, deterred her from even greater glory. The main theory of her principles is that the human mind and body must not be driven too hard.

Julian 'Big Bull' Allmeier - During Julian's stay at the Arc, he faithfully kept three loves: The love of the girls especially Elaine; the love of a reflection he saw in the mirror, and the love of his hair for which he cared more than any loving father could have cared for his beloved son.

Bernard Scop - This white haired, blue eyed lad (Um SHLUP ogods) showed an early interest in photography and through continuous research, Bernard soon reached the standard of a professional photographer. As well as being in charge of the Arc tropical fish, Bernard was the shamas in his earlier days.

Vernon 'Short Man' Levy -This Little Man served the Arc unselfishly, he was shamas and in charge of the boxing room. He is a clever boxer and if he concentrates on this sport we shall see a second Alf James. Vernon's interests do not only centre on the fistic world, but also on entertainment. He has a beautiful singing voice which should take him far. Vernon will be missed by everyone, especially the girls.

Merle Schneider - Came to the Arc at a comparatively old age and endeared herself to all, especially the Junior boys. Jumbo as she was fondly called (please do not let this nickname give a wrong impression of her) has a warm personality and a friendly smile. She was an above average scholar and should go far.

Minnie Fanaroff - Since the day Minnie 'Moaner Lisa' arrived at the Arc she was ranked amongst the three prettiest girls and this is no mean achievement when you look at the Arc girls.

Elaine Levine - A very popular girl known for her long spells of 'going steady'. The lucky victims were Isadore Levitan and 'Big Bull' Allmeier. Elaine always treated everyone with respect, and whenever she was seen talking to anybody she was listening to their troubles.

Molly Flink - Molly has the saddest eyes and warmest heart of all the girls. In her first year at the Arc she was voted the 'most popular girl'. Molly was one of the first and best exponents of rock and roll at the Arc.

Sarah Farber - Sarah loved and was loved by the Babies. She gave up a lot of time, both in schoolwork and in sport, just to be with the babies. Sarah is training to be a nursery school teacher. I am sorry that I was not born later so that I could have spent my nursery school days under Sarah.

Jimmy and Gordon Cameron - These two brothers had great sporting talents. They excelled in their respective teams at school, and both played soccer and cricket. Gordon won the cup for being the best swimmer, and we wish them the best of luck in their respective careers.

Frank 'The Border', Berman - Frank was somehow attracted to Arcadia. He left on several occasions, but soon returned. He was musically inclined and achieved excellent results on his harmonica. He accompanied Larry Adler on the harmonica, when the latter visited Arcadia. Frank was equally at home on all instruments he played. He was twice captain of Bialik house in swimming. He won the cup for the best boy in swimming in 1957. He was also a keen athlete doing well at the 'Arc' and at school. Frank can go far if he pursues his aims.

Solly 'Sepel' Sacks - Solly possessed the type of personality which enabled him to mix with almost everyone in the 'Arc'. He put himself out tirelessly to run the swimming bath. He was also the first-rate shamas and gave a valuable start in the upkeep of the aquarium at Arcadia. He received his nick-name 'Sepel' because he was Basil Sepel's compatriot in keeping fowls and pigeons.

Sydney Lipschitz - Sidney was a small chap when he came to the Arc and immediately became integrated into his new environment. He had a great liking for animals, as shown by his rearing of pigeons and fowls as well as helping others with their animals. Sidney also excelled in scholastic achievements and obtained the highest mark ever obtained in Hebrew in Matric by an Arc. Besides all this, he was also the most popular boy for 1958. We wish Sidney luck in the years to come.

Diana Kotzen - Diana, the youngest of the Kotzen family, like her elder brothers and sisters spent most of her childhood in Arcadia. She was well liked by everybody and gave a helping hand in rearing the babies. She also showed potential in sports and captained Herzl in swimming. Diana will be missed by all, especially her younger friends.

Leah Blecher - When Leah came to the Arc she seemed to depend entirely on her sister, but as time went on she made friends, with the result that she no longer depended on her sister. She was also very popular, as shown by her becoming a runner-up to the most popular girl in 1958.

Sonia Scop - Sonia, from the moment she stepped into Arcadia, mixed well with the boys. She showed great sporting abilities on the athletic track.

Louis Kreser [Ex Arcadian] who was Prefect at Parktown Boys' High received in 1956 the Anthony Blatt Memorial Cup for the best Rugby player at his school, and the Rotary Cup in 1957. Being the most popular boy at Parktown he is now described by 'The Jewish Herald - 29.5.1959' - as one of the Stars in the Maccabi Soccer side'.

Chapter 85 - THE 1961 ARCADIAN

The 1961 edition consisting of 115 pages including illustrations with a blue cover was edited by Eva Bortz, Marcel Getz, Merwyn Lampert, Sylvia Meyer, Hymie Sacks and Gary Salkow.

THE HARMONICADIANS
By Effie Segal [Ex Arcadian and Hon Teacher of Harmonicadians

The members of Arcadia's latest Harmonica Band at present are Geoffrey Lewis, Manfred Stein, Howard Ginsburg, Abraham Kupferberg and we hope, more will join; but bravo, Geoffrey, is the only one to have been a member of the 'Band' for nearly two years! Remember there was once a spark, then a very small flame, then perhaps.

If not much more emerges from your efforts, you have at least learned a wonderful lesson - the value of teamwork - the results that can be obtained if you all work towards a common goal. None of you may be an incipient virtuoso; together you as a whole, are better than the individual parts.

Some of the Editors – Marcel Getz, Sylvia Meyer and Eva Bortz

NEVER ON SUNDAY
Sandra Marcus and Bessie Bortz

> *Away behind the tall Arc Trees*
> *Sat Violet and 'Duck' as busy as Bees*
> *And after four (o'clock) joined two more*
> *To do as Arcs did in years before.*
> *They chattered and chirped as happy as Birds*
> *And with their eyes of love they gazed on the Arc-herds.*
> *And as the evening would draw near,*
> *They would whisper in each other's ear.*
> *Never mind, we'll meet, once more,*
> *As we have done in time before.*

AT THE ASSEMBLY CLOCK
By Jenny Sandler

> *Sandra and Geoffrey were in love,*
> *Wandering about like deluded doves.*
> *They never refused each other's call,*
> *To Arcadia's Assembly hall.*
> *She would go downstairs at five o'clock,*
> *And meet her Geoffrey at the assembly clock.*
> *She would gaze upon his eye,*
> *Till his mood softened to a sigh.*
> *She.then, would say 'Oh Geoffrey, I love you,*
> *Will our love always be so true.'*

AU REVOIR
By Eva Bortz, Marcel Getz, Merwyn Lampert, Sylvia Meyer, Hymie Sacks and Gary Salkow and Ex-Arcadians Reuben and Sidney Lipschitz.

Our first duty is to bid farewell to our four distinguished Editors, now all at Wits. University, of the last Arcadian:-

Ichiel Bortz - was a keen scholar and sportsman, in short an all-rounder; he was known for his unique sense of responsibility and co-operation in all Arcadian activities.

Bernard Edelman - known as 'Chook' - a most likeable boy whom also the girls found hard to resist. His placid nature made often the butt for many practical jokes, but nothing has ever ruffled his calm temperament for more than a few seconds. Besides being the star of many Arc-galas, 'Chook' broke long-standing backstroke records at Parktown Boys' High.

Hymie Pearlman - One of the Old School Arcs who would have measured up to any of the Old Timers in the Arc. He ruled the boys with an iron hand. He received colours and re-award in rugby; he was Prefect both at Parktown Boys' High and Arcadia. Being 'King' of the Junior Boys, it was only natural for him to join hands with 'Queen' Sandra, and -occasionally being rejected by the 'Queen' resorted to her princesses. Hymie was recently selected to play under 19 in Transvaal rugby.

Jeffrey Esekow - A fine sportsman and avid reader, a boy with strength of self-discipline and imagination, and - yet unrevealed - great talents. His love affair with Sylvia came - for some still unexplained reasons - to a violent end.

Max Markus - He was a well-liked boy. He put some of his energy into tennis and the rest he spent while dreaming of girls. Max, though not specifically interested in sports, was a temporary Prefect at Athlone Boys High. The interest he lacked in sports was manifested in his desire for coffee-parties at night. He is now a printer's apprentice and happy in his work.

Rose Bortz - was a keen scholar, a great dancer and a well-liked girl, though she never was observed to fall in love with anyone, even not with the old die-hards. The often secret advances of a Gary and a Mervin left no visible trace in her mind. She is now at College.

Barbara Ginsburg - A redhead and a hard worker at Parktown Girls' High who won the admiration of nearly all Senior Boys, only to lose it as a result of the fiery temperament, common to red-heads. The only faithful ones - to the bitter end - Max M and her secret admirer Hymie S.

Tamara Salaman - At one time most popular girl; a first rate mixer, though she did not make full use of her charming talents, faithfulness being one of her strong points. She was also known for her artistic talents. She is continuing her education at College and still not to be seen without Jeffrey Goldstein.

Gary Salkow - A scholar and co-editor of this Arcadian, whose untimely departure from Arcadia caused undue joy to his colleagues. His often too critical opinions, though disturbing, were accepted with tolerance by all. A proper Arc-boy, always ready for a game of soccer or cricket, Gary may be the only boy who has not fallen -officially - in love with anyone yet. Gary is at College and intends to take up Law.

Sandra Solomon - The 'Queen' of the Arc-girls who ruled her followers with a rod of iron, her faithful princesses being Karon and Lily. She is a very good-looking and intelligent girl. Sandra is a natural leader with a terrific sense of humour. She completed her studies at Technical College.

Renee Rothaus - is a very friendly, generous and likeable person. A star dancer during her time in Arcadia. Renee was never taken in by the shrewd approaches of the die-hards, but nevertheless appreciated their efforts.

Loraine Rothaus - A friendly yet often mischievous girl. Everybody liked her. She was a clever, but lazy scholar who preferred lying on her bed reading a book than working. Her dark black eyes are enough to capture any boy's heart.

Karen Shraga - Heir to Sandra's throne. Karen was an exceptionally fine athlete; a Form Captain at Parktown Girls'

High on man occasions. She also, like Sandra, Lily and Renee, completed her studies at Technical College. She has gone to London (October 1961).

Lily Solomon - A carbon-copy of her sister Sandra. Lily seemed to enjoy physical exercises somewhat more than Sandra did; a far above average boxer (remember a bout of fisticuffs on the drive with another young lady?) She distinguished herself in swimming both at Athlone High and at Arcadia.

Molly Valnik:- If speech is silver and silence gold then Molly should be a rich girl. Never a big talker, she let her deeds talk for her. Nursing the profession she has chosen, will benefit from her sweet and gentle nature.

Jeffrey Goldstein - In many spheres he followed Hymie's footsteps. He became a most popular boy despite the fact that he was a very conscientious Prefect. In his earlier days he was known for his enormous grub-parcels. Jeffrey's and Tamara's love affair will go down in Arc-history as one of the love-marathons. Jeffrey is now at College.

Bobby (Robert) Gordon - One of the Arcs who will definitely not get ulcers, for he is blessed with a happy disposition. He, too, was a Sportsman of no mean achievement (boxing, running, cricket and often loving). He surprised all – and still does – by his keen interest in spiritualism and psychology. Bobby is now with Reliable Cycle Works (Ex-Arcadian, Penzik).

Eddie Kreser - Eddie follows his elder brother's (Louis) lead in soccer. He was a quiet yet well-spoken boy. He kept forcefully dreaming about girls; yet the result of his many attempts to make his dreams come true are not known. He is now with Pashley.

Ethnie Seinker - A co-operative girl in all aspects of Arcadian life; her sweet voice in Shul was everyone's delight. She set a good example to the younger girls. She was often chosen a Form Captain in Parktown Girls' High and is now completing her studies at Technical College.

Gershon Rochlin - Although Gershon has never shone in any particular field, he is probably one of the best known Arcs. Gershon's specialities were a talent for remembering birthdays, number plates, cricket scores, including the matches the Boksburg soccer club is arranging. We wish 'Mr McGoo' Happy Returns for March 4th.

Arthur Stander - "The Arc goal-keeper' and no record in love affairs, due to his youth. He is a very conscientious worker in school.

There are also a number of boys and girls – too numerous to mention – who stayed just for short periods in Arcadia. We wish both them and those who have left the best of luck in their proposed career.

Chapter 86 ~ THE 1964 ARCADIAN

The 1964 edition, with a red cover consists of 64 pages including illustrations and was edited by Merwyn Lampert assisted by Bessie Bortz, Keith Lang, and Manfred and Stanley Stein

REFLECTIONS ON ARCADIA
Bertha Kronenberg (Klevansky) Ex-Arcadian

On the curve in stately Oxford Road
Where tall trees grace the tarred way
You will find wide open spaces
Occupied by children in their play.

Further on there is a notice
'Slowly please, do not hoot',
and you the motorist feel this,
so gently now, proceed on foot.

Proceed on foot, yes shed the years
Erase the dust of a decade or two,
Let a mantle of dreaming brush away cares,
You are back at Arcadia, the sky is blue.

You day-dream as you used to do
And let a wintry afternoon go by,
You are lying on the dry-brown grass
You look at the cedars brushing the sky.

You think of the space of fifteen years
And try and condense it into one,
You laugh with the memory of a thousand days
And chuckle at the merriment and fun.
The joy of roaming through rocky koppies
Where nature seemed to hold sway,
Where every rock held a magical secret
Known to you only in your play.

And then there were the Sabbath days
Drowsy with a peaceful quiet,
Arcadia was transformed into a place of calm
As if angels had descended to this Parktown height.

In this home that you knew for years
There were no boundaries to your pleasure
The verdant grasses and open spaces
Were yours to wander through at leisure.

Spring and summer, cold and rain,
Night and day over all the years
Arcadia stands, its portals ever open
To a child ... a haven without tears.

OUR DEBT TO THE ARC
By Mervyn Lampert

With or without realising it, we in Arcadia owe a great deal to 'Our Home'. One has to be in the Arc a long time to really understand what our debt to the Arc is. For many of us it has been our only home. We owe it much. They have looked after our physical and spiritual well-being, taught us manners, and cared for us in many ways. I take this opportunity of thanking Doc and Ma, Superintendent and Matron respectively, for being such wonderful 'parents' to us.

The Arc provides every basic necessity. They take great pains to provide us with a very sound education, which includes a course in Hebrew. In this connection, they have sent children, wherever possible, to a college or university for higher education. For those who are too weak in certain school subjects, they arrange extra lessons to assist the children and in addition, there is ample provision for extra mural activities and hobbies.

We also enjoy, through the Arc, many of the amenities of life. They provide us with entertainment in the form of a film on Saturday evenings. During school vacation, the Arc arranged for us to attend film shows and cultural activities, like plays, in town. One of the highlights of life in the Arc is the holiday at the coast at the end of the year. This the Arc plans for us, and the organisation is done months ahead.

When one leaves Arcadia, the Arc Committee still worry about him or her until they are sure that that particular Arc who has just left, is securely established in his or her niche. All this work is undertaken by a branch of the committee known as the 'After Care'. The only payment the Arc ever asks of us is to become worthy citizens of the Jewish Community, and of the State. When I leave at the end of this year, I shall realise even more than at present what I and other Arcs really owe to the Committee, and Doc and Ma.

DAILY ROUTINE
By Brenda Stein

Up in the morning at six o'clock,
Miss Durward wakes us with a helleva shock,
Up we get, it's not much fun.
To know that your homework is not done.
Down to the dining room we now all flock,
The whistle is blown and we know it's Doc,
Breakfast is served, O munch, munch, munch,
And the time is changed to crunch, crunch, crunch.
Off to the bus we all go.
And good morning is said to all we know.
Off to school we sadly go,
Telling our miserable tales of woe.
The school is opened by the Arcs,
And we go in as merry larks.
Lessons go by with a deep, deep sigh.
And the Arcs just wave a merry goodbye.
Back to the Arc we all return
To the daily routine, for which we yearn.

LETTER FROM SAM BARTLETT IN ISRAEL

Israel', writes Sam Bartlett, who recently emigrated with his family, 'is a strange but fascinating country. The old blending with the new. At times one is carried away with the past and searches spiritually deep into the very air to try and visualise our inheritance of this small piece of land called Israel. Then suddenly one is rudely shaken by what must be the greatest rebuilding of any decayed country in the world. Where desert and erosion through thousands of years of neglect have devastated the land, lush green pastures and orchards have sprung up. And where the land is unproductive, enormous factories are being built, and so it has been with Maayan Baruch which was one swamp and barren land and which has become one of the most beautiful parts of Israel.

It would take months to write and relate some of the stories I have heard of Maayan Baruch. The toil and tears. The fires which devastated most of the farm, leaving in its wake death and destruction, which Kibbutzim for miles around mustered whatever help and assistance they could to those who watched years of their work destroyed in a matter of hours. Yet Maayan Baruch still stands like a monument to those who fought for her and those who worked and watched her regrow. It is interesting to note that Maayan Baruch was started by South Africans and still possesses some of the original Kibbutzniks. Kibbutz life is not entirely new to me, as I lived a communal life in Arcadia. The difference, of course is, here you have to work hard.

At the moment I am picking apples in the orchard in a temperature of 100° in the shade, a job I do not particularly enjoy, but it is one of those unenviable jobs that must be done and besides if the Israelis can do it so can I. In fact I suspect that I am under the perpetual observation of every Sabra on the Kibbutz, and as such my pride cannot allow me to face, not only myself, but all those connected with the Federation who arranged our trip to Israel, and besides, it is a good and full life, where one develops a sense of security, not only for oneself, but for the whole family.

At the moment we are studying Hebrew and I am told as soon as the apple season ends and I have learned to speak Hebrew more fluently, I will be placed in the poultry section which will, of course, include study in that field by way of short courses at one of the numerous agricultural colleges. I am happy about this, as I have always been interested in poultry, having done quite a lot of reading on the subject.

Zelva has not been placed in any particular work yet, as plenty of time is given for the kids to accustom themselves to the climate and new environment. However, they will eventually be placed in houses among children of their own age, and once they have learned the language I feel there will be no difficulty. David already sleeps with his own group, while Rachelle has already made tentative attempts of sleeping one night at home and one night with the children of her group. Jennifer, the youngest, will take a little longer, but as I have said, there is no rush. But what is most important is, we see more of our children than we ever did, and the children are loving it. They have wonderful playgrounds built by the kibbutz from scrap tractor parts, etc. They have a swimming bath and a farm of 1 500 acres which consists of 150 dairy cows, 2 500 fowls, huge apple orchards, cotton fields, evergreen pastures, fisheries in which thousands of fish are bred in small lakes. Incidentally, we are now exporting this fish which I still have to acquire a taste for, to America, where it is considered a delicacy. And, of course, not forgetting the numerous workshops and modern implements. All these things spell paradise to any child. I must also point out that the education is of the highest standard and the children are well cared for by highly qualified teachers.

TRIBUTES
Dr Lichtigfeld – Superintendent (Doc)

A special tribute goes to our friend, Mr Sidney Klevansky, ex-Arcadian, who is a renown Senior Latin master at Parktown Boys' High and assists whole-heartedly in Arcadia's activities, particularly in supervision of the boys' homework. Sidney, also called Vicky, has proved a tower of strength and encouragement to all.

Apart from this, a word of tribute to salaried staff, amongst them Mr D Chait, loyal, beloved and oldest member of the staff; Mrs M Stelzner, who has again demonstrated the value of having a devoted and skilled housemother in charge, particularly where the stay is a long one, enabling her to build up stable relationships with her boys; Mrs W Westraadt, for her most capable and efficient house-keeping, ably assisted by Mrs Schonburn; Sister Conway, who devotedly attends to the sick; Mrs H De Winnaar who has endeared herself to the babies; to the new members of staff (Mrs I de Plooy, Mrs F Westley and Mrs P Roodt), who have joined us recently and are proving to be an asset to the Home, too; to Miss S Hurwitz, for her able work in Arcadia's office, and Mrs Safier, for her charming way of teaching the girls the art of sewing, and Mrs C Simpson, for her expert tuition in dancing and ballet.

Finally, a word of appreciation also to the members of the non-European staff, some of whom have served Arcadia over a period of thirty years.

Congratulations: To all those Arcadians and members of the Committee who celebrated Simchas in their families; I may mention here the privilege given to me to officiate at the wedding of Advocate and Mrs L Goldsmid's daughter and of ex-Arcadian, Mr John Cohen.

Acknowledgements: We would like to thank Miss S Hurwitz for typing this Arcadian. We are very grateful to the Editors of The Jewish Herald, The SA Jewish Times, and The Zionist Record, for the loan of photographic blocks.

We also wish to record our indebtedness to Mr E B Levenstein, Chairman of the Branches, for his very generous donation of the paper for this Arcadian and we wish to extend sincere thanks to Mr and Mrs M Shuster for their enjoyable annual parties for the children [on Batmitzvahs].

Chapter 87 – JEFF ESEKOW (1942)

Jeff was born in 1942 and was in the care of Arcadia for 11 years from 1948 to 1960 together with his younger sister Moira.

Jeff is a Chartered Accountant living in Johannesburg and served on the Committee of Arcadia from 1985 to 2002 mainly as the Treasurer.

MY FIRST DAY IN THE ARC

It was 1948 and I was six years old when I was placed in the care of the Arc. I had been gently briefed by my mother that I was going to 'stay at another place' but I was totally oblivious of what was happening and why it was happening.

My Aunt Sadie, my Uncle Hymie and my Mother drove me from Mayfair to the Arc on this Sunday afternoon. I was introduced to a few grown ups who didn't really take too much interest in me. We walked around this "biggest house" I had ever seen, and we were shown the Woolf Hillman Hospital Wing, where I was shown my cubicle. It was now getting dark and we walked back from the Hospital Wing under the overhanging grape vines, past the stationery room, past the fruit room, past the outside of the kitchen to the forecourt of the Lionel Phillips building.

I remember an emotional farewell by my Mother, my Aunt and my Uncle and I watched the car vanish down the driveway. I stood there all alone in the fading light in the forecourt, not understanding what was happening and I had no idea of how to get back to the hospital.

But I did, and I had a great 11 years in the Arc.

MY LAST DAY

It was January 1960 and Polly Pearlman, Yechiel Bortz, Bernard Edelman and myself, had just finished writing Matric. As a reward three of us were sent down as advance guard to Bikkur Cholim Camp in Lakeside by the Sea. Our leaders were Solly Farber (to this day the greatest man I ever knew) and Basil Sepel.

The advance guard episode, the camping holiday itself, the rear guard episode and the two weeks I spent with family in Cape Town after the camp, was my first real taste of not being in the Arc. Although it was a great holiday, I was looking forward to getting back to the Arc.

When, without notifying the Arc I arrived back at the front door, I was met with total astonishment, on my part and on the part of management. I was told I had already left. My bed and my locker had been given to someone else. My possessions were in storage. I could stay the night in the hospital and I must go to my mother the next day.

Jeff Esekow - 1967

The next day I left the Arc, I don't remember saying goodbye to anyone. I don't think I did say goodbye to anyone.

From then to now, I kept up my association with the Arc. Every year i attended Arc Shul on Rosh Hashana and Yom Kippur. I was on the Arc Committee from 1985 to 2002, most of that period as honorary Treasurer.

JEFF
Written by his wife Phyllis Esekow

I have been married to Jeff for 36 years - that alone surely puts me on a higher plain and I deserve a good few gold medals. In fact I met Jeff through my late Mom's sister, Sybil Stein of the late Bella Lubner's crew. Sybil is still going strong, with her little Arc tin, collecting with vigour and determination at the grand age of 94 years, whilst silently bad-mouthing the Chev!

Jeff is over 60 and Baruch Hashem, still working as hard as at the start of his auditing practice. He also is the oldest and founder member of the Wanderers' touch-rugby club. The guys play every lunch hour, notwithstanding what the weather is like. Whenever he is unable to get in his game, he actually goes through heavy withdrawal.

I think one of his best buddies was and is Hymie Sacks, living in Sydney. We went to Australia in 1995 and Hymie and Pam have come to South Africa a couple of times. Hymie, in fact has a criminal record regarding various driving offences, having taken the rap, as Jeff drove without a licence for many, many years, and I would not vouch that he is an adept person, behind the wheel!

Jeff was intrigued reading excerpts of Danny Lasker's letters, and is also overwhelmed with the dedication, time and effort David Sandler has managed to put in and to re-unite the Arc boys and girls, by way of correspondence.

Jeff resided at the Arc from age six years to 16 years and only has good, happy memories of Ma the disciplinarian, and Doc (one of the boys). I have heard numerous stories of scaling Oppenheimer's fruit; singing your own versions of the Pesach songs, and peeping through holes to catch a glimpse of the girls bathing. Audrey and Karen Shrager come to mind. I don't envisage Jeff ever becoming a "grown-up".

We still have dinner outings with Keith and Dianne Lang, and nostalgically remember when Shalom and Heather Farber, and Hackie and Beryl Kabe who used to join our outings. Keep the fires burning eternally. To reiterate I believe that I deserve a good few gold medals, living with Jeff. He is not the most gregarious or observant of the male species and I become slightly upset in view of my rating in Jeff's life. Jeff is a total workaholic, a beer drinker and a touch rugby participant. I sometimes feel he envisages me as the proficient housekeeper, with perks.

Now for the 'highlight'. We have our first grandchild. The most beautiful, intelligent, intellectual baby girl, Alli, , born to our son Jeremy and Shelley (nee Lurie) Our daughter Martine is besotted with her, as I am, and I am probably the most unmaternal woman I know. Jeff pretends to hold the 'stiff upper lip', but I watch him melting.

So great to have a "simcha" in this very mad, troubled world,

we now live in. Just had pink streaks put into my hair although I am trying to become like a proper Gran.

JEFFREY ESEKOW
By Tamara and Hymie Pearlman

Jeff is one of those unsung heroes, and was very dedicated to Arcadia. He tells me he was on the Arc Committee for 13 years, and that must have taken a lot of his personal time and effort. Jeffrey was a great supporter and 'brother' to Solly Farber, to the letter. He has done many mitzvoth.

I remember he was such an avid reader in the Arc, no wonder he always got such good marks for English. Jeff and Gary Salkow were "bookworms". Jeff was always good at Soccer and I think that he and Norman Sacks were also great farters. I remember his sister Moira. What a tough bundle of muscle she was, no nonsense with her. Quite a little beauty, but just like a wild kitten, so watch out!

Jeff could also play cricket for hours in the empty Babies Pool, with Sydney Lipschitz or upstairs, (on the balcony with the wire mesh, facing the swimming pool). Benny Kreser also loved those games as did Reuben Lipschitz and Louis Kreser. Those were great times and great days, but how restricted and isolated we were from the 'real world', and so we evolved in our little world, as best we knew how, until the great exodus at last set us free to taste the fruits of life.

I cannot deny that I was glad to be free from the Arc and it was something like burning your bridges and going forward to excitement and adventure. Nevertheless, after 40 years, when the mind goes back to Arcadia, some special ingredient, unbeknown before, is suddenly released and you are suddenly reliving your life and seeing everything clearly and especially recognising how much each person lived up to the situation we were all in.

Jeff Esekow, Solly Farber, Donald Goldman and Barney Meyers - 1999

Tamara (Tammy), Noel, Seymour Salaman was born on the 23rd of December 1943 and was placed in the care of Arcadia in the winter of 1947 when three years old. She left when 17 in the summer of 1960 after 13 years at the Arc.

Hyman (Hymie) Louis Pearlman was born on the 7th of June 1942 and was placed in the care of Arcadia in January 1952. He left the Arc when he was 17 at the end of 1959 after eight years.

Violet Jardine Salaman, sister to Tamara, was born on the 30th of September 1947 she was in the care of Arcadia from 1951 to 1964 from age four to age 17, a total of 13 years.

Hymie Pearlman and Tamara Salaman left the Arc after finishing off their schooling at the time when Doc and Ma looked after us. I remember Violet Salaman, Tamara's younger sister from Jewish Government School and she was a talented artist.

I always remember Hymie who is ten years my senior as a strapping young man wearing his colours for playing rugby at Parktown Boys High and he was "the prefect" in charge of the Junior and Senior boys under Stelzner and Vicky.

From the 1961 Arcadian

"Hymie Pearlman is one of the Old School Arcs who would have measured up to any of the Old Timers in the Arc. He ruled the boys with an iron hand. He received colours and re-award in rugby; he was Prefect both at Parktown Boys High and Arcadia. Being 'King' of the Junior Boys, it was only natural for him to join hands with 'Queen' Sandra, and occasionally being rejected by the 'Queen' resorted to her princesses. Hymie was selected to play under 19 in Transvaal rugby."

"Tamara Salaman was at one time the most popular girl. She was a first rate mixer though she did not make full use of her charming talents, faithfulness being one of her strong points. She was also known for her artistic talents. She is continuing her education at College."

Hymie Pearlman and Tamara Salaman got married in the Arc Shul and Tamara was given away by Bella and Morrie Lubner. Doc and Ma also were there and no doubt very proud of 'their' children. They have lived in Muizenberg for many many years and I visited them there a few years ago and they made Les Durbach and family and me very welcome.

Doc, Tamara, Hymie and Ma

Tamara and Hymie's wedding. Violet is standing next to Tamara with Donny Lichtigfeld behind. Bobby Gordon is third from right.

A WEDDING OF ARCADIANS IN ARCADIA
By Donnie Lichtigfeld - 1964 Arcadian

A hearty Mazeltov to Hymie Pearlman and Tamara Salaman on their wedding in November 1963. The event took place at Arcadia.

This happy function was attended by a very large number of well wishers. The dignified ceremony was conducted by Doc and Rabbi Altschuler. The bride was given away by Mr and Mrs M Lubner, thus cementing further their great attachment to Arcadians.

In their choice of each other, I doubt if Tamara and Hymie could have wished to do better, as they are both two very mature and well adjusted young people. Hymie, whom I knew before we met again in Arcadia, is a young man of very high qualities. Tamara is the quieter complement of Hymie, and I am sure we all join in wishing them lots of Mazel and fulfilment in the years to come.

VIVA ARCADIA
By Hymie Pearlman

Tamara and I got married in the Arc Shul on 3rd of November 1963. Tamara is a loving, caring, patient, strong and straight partner and friend, always ready to please and always with a positive attitude and much more. I always admired her strong character long before we got married. Also a wonderful mother to our sons Lance Seymour Pearlman born 15th March 1965 and Athol Spencer Pearlman born 23rd March 1968.

No doubt, our stay in Arcadia was part of the divine plan for all of us. We will never know why it had to be that way. We have thought about it over and over again. Perhaps there is some clarity in our search for answers. Are we richer or poorer personalities because of the experience? If Charles Dickens had been an observer of all that went on in Arcadia there would, no doubt, have been a huge volume written. And so it has been for us Arcadians to live in, and play a part in, an extraordinary time and situation, that is absolutely unique to us. We were there.

I hope that as time marches on, more and more Arcs will write about their lives, in and out of the Arc and tell us something about how they handled themselves and what life had to throw at them. One word, one line, one story. Step by step and in no time at all, we will all be running to the post box. The Arc story is a never-ending story and "100 years of Arc Memories" will go on and on for a very, very long time.

A TRIBUTE TO MY MOTHER, ELSIE PEARLMAN (1900 – 1991)

My Mom is coming to visit me today because it is Sunday. She will come on the double-decker, electric bus and probably arrive about 2.00 pm I will wait for her near the main gate or watch from the hillside. Mom usually arrives wearing her winter coat and carrying a large black, leather bag. We sit under the trees near the Soccer field on the grassy slope, or on the wall near the goal posts on the south side. Visiting time is from 2.00 pm to 5.00 pm and then we walk to the bus stop and say goodbye". (Never missed a Sunday visit over all the years).

Doc would walk around to all the visiting parents and friends, always putting in a kind word and encouragement to pupil and parent.

Every Sunday, same time, same place.
Something special about those visits;
A LINK, A BLINK, IN TIME

GOING BACK IN TIME

I recommend to all Old Arcs to dig into their psyche, and go back in time to the good times and things in the Arc, and draw strength from there. The good will always outweigh the bad. Climb into your tree house, build a hock or a scotch cart or bunk out to the zoo. Just keep triggering your memory with the fun-times and you will begin to feel the magic. How many times did you run around the soccer field trying to get fit? How many mulberries did you eat, and can you recall all the different kinds of trees that were planted and growing all over the Arc? And do you remember eating 'stunnies', and picking loquats and scratching your name on a large, white magnolia flower that grew next to the Shul steps going down to the polish room?

Here is a poem of reflection:-

My iron bed, on the veranda beckons to me
Warmer to sleep between the blankets, than the sheets.
I pull my pillow over my head,
and sleep with only a peeking-space to breathe.
How fresh the air, the stars are watching,
I love my bed, I am warm and snug,
And very soon, sound asleep and dreaming.

Six on the dot, up, up, up, up.
Its cold, but up to Shul I go.
God is there, as I say my prayers.
Then to breakfast's warm delights.
I love those glorious greasy eggs.
Now, time to get ready for school.
Better start walking, not to be late.
Get there before they close the gates.
The walk back home is slow.
We take our time as we go.
Sometimes a lift from Mrs. Bean.
And many a time a lift from Louis Bolnick.
On his Meccano-like moped we go.
A tribute to that frail-framed two-stroke machine.
That gave my walks a touch of ease.

Thank you Louis and thank your Mom Sarah,
For many the times she stopped to fare us.

Here is another poem of reflection:-

Change of clothes and into the trees.
Tarzan's the man we saw on the screen.
So many branches and so many leaves.
Places to play and not to be seen.

DOC AND MA AND BUNKING OUT

Any request to Doc (Lichtigfeld) of blessed memory, to do something out of the ordinary, like going to a party on a Saturday night, at one of your "outside" school friends' house was always met with the reply, "go and ask Ma" (of blessed memory).

As soon as he said that you knew what your chances were. NIL! Inevitably, Ma would say something like, "we'll see" or "we'll think about it" or "what means you?"

So, after a while one stopped asking, and although night excursions were out, the days held a lot of promise to do your own thing, without anyone's permission. As long as your timing was right, you could get to Hillbrow for a hamburger at the Hamburger Club and be back in time for Oneg Shabbat.

We never took the main roads, it was always up the hill, along the back roads with the same route back. There were beautiful houses along the way and I remember most of them being double storeys with beautiful gardens. I was always looking out for fruit trees!

Saturday afternoon was a good time to go to the zoo or fruit-raiding, although the latter applied throughout the week. Excursions to the Wilds via the back of the Arc were also a favourite, especially when the "Stunnies" were in season.

IN MEMORY OF SOLLY FARBER

From Poverty to Prominence
Mother seeker to Mother maker
Barefoot boy to Barefoot hero
Lover of Life, Lover of Hope
Lover of Arcadians.
Sportsman and Swimmer
Doctor and Healer and Seer.
God fearing and God praiser
In service to Mankind.
Why did you go so soon?
So strong your pillar stands
Always to remind us
Of your efforts and drive,
And achievements so proud.
Your pride is our pride.
You stand for us all.
You are our flag – Solly Farber
You are our Arcadia for evermore

A VISIT FROM DOC

I had a wonderful visit from Doc the other day while I was resting/sleeping on my bed in the afternoon. Doc suddenly appeared, he was alone, nothing was said. I got the feeling he was missing the Arc because the dream ended with him looking out over the Arc grounds towards the swings. November 2005

HYMIE'S LETTERS OF ARC MEMORIES

Shalom my Chava.

You are like a lighthouse to all the Arcs sailing the sea of life because you bring us together in spirit, and we are once again able to communicate and hold hands across the world.

Donald Goldman was such a regular figure on Sundays at Arcadia when he came to teach boxing. I am also going to miss his familiar face on the TV whenever there was some major boxing tournament being broadcast. We would say, "there's Donald" and to me, boxing will never be the same. What a great sportsman and dedicated person he was. Strength to Chookie and his family at this sad time, and we will always cherish his memory in our hearts.

I also remember Percy "Peachy" Nochumson. Peachy was a regular Sunday visitor especially when the swimming bath was open. He would swim "hundreds" of lengths in the pool and afterwards go and have a good hot soak or shower upstairs in the Senior Boys Department. Mrs Stelzner used to freak out if she found him upstairs because he was always in the nude and looking for towels to dry himself. These are my personal memories from the 50's.

They say he was also an avid newspaper reader and collected so many newspapers that he eventually ended up with a room full of newspapers on which he slept. He was also a great Court Room observer and spent a great deal of his time listening to Court Cases.

Another hobby of Peachy's was horseracing and he seemed to know the horse's lineage. A man of many colours and a very colourful person. I have no doubt that he was a great philosopher and a very humble person and did not allow his mind to be cramped and controlled in the pursuit of material wealth. He was a legend in his own lifetime and lived "as free as a bird".

By the way, it is a small world! Michael Perry Kotzen talks about Harry Skikner. My sister, Fay Levin (Nee Pearlman) used to go out with Larry Skikner alias Lawrence Harvey. He used to arrive at our house, in Derby Road, Judith Paarl, Johannesburg dressed up elaborately or in masquerade as a toff, usually with a long cigarette holder and spat shoes and tuxedo. No doubt Larry took his drama teacher very seriously and started practising straight away for his climb up the ladder.

I remember he acted in "The Manchurian Candidate". My sister was actually in Larry's class at Athlone High School (1942) and my mother convinced him not to run away from home, on his bicycle, when he wanted to join the Navy. He was always putting on an "act" so I guess he was bound to succeed at or on some stage.

The same goes for you David, because you have persevered, and one of your successes is the Arc correspondence which has given so much pleasure to us Old Arcs and brought an otherwise lost epoch about a famous lost tribe onto a tangible historic record.

My sincere wish is that more Old Arcs from that unique lost tribe will take up the inclination and tell their stories and become part of the invisible threads that connect us all.

I believe every time an Old Arc puts pen to paper and reminisces about his or her life in Arcadia another brick is added to the monument of our existence.

ARC NEWS LETTERS

I observe all the Holidays and Festivals at home, but I wish I could go to Shul. We are not short of Kitkes and Bagels because Tamara is always baking. The big plus here is the tranquillity, serenity and isolation. Something like we had in the Arc, in a way. The Old Arc news and Arc correspondence has definitely filled a void and I find myself being rejuvenated with the enthusiasm and drive of yesteryear.

What a treasure Arc Correspondence – May 2005 is. I could not put it down, it was so interesting. It is so good to hear from all the contributors from everywhere and about what they are doing and all their beautiful stories and sentiments. How else would we be able to keep in touch and share a bit of ourselves?

David, you are our conductor and let us hope your orchestra will continue to grow and get louder and louder for all Arcs all over the world to hear and come and join the party. Once again thank you for your magnificent efforts and time and energy and dedication, because you deserve the accolades and more.

THANKS TO UNSUNG HEROES

Sam Lasker said it all when he wrote in Arc Correspondence April 2005. "We all received a good education, good upbringing and nachas from an excellent Jewish Organisation".

These words really got me thinking and I believe that the unsung heroes of Arcadia were those people who made up the committees of Arcadia from its inception. I am speaking on behalf of Tamara and myself. There are not enough words to thank all those people who sat on all those committees with only the welfare of the children of Arcadia at heart. Remember, that the funds from the public had to be spent wisely.

Arcadia would not have lasted so long if it had not been for the generosity of the public and these dedicated captains of industry. They gave their time and their expertise and their dedication helped steer our home in the right direction at all times. We will never know how much work they did behind the scenes.

How will we ever be able to thank the Jewish public and all the Committee Members for what they did, except to say a prayer of gratitude and praise to heaven above and follow their example by doing good deeds?

ASTON BAY

Hymie and Tamara recently moved to Aston Bay in the Cape after living for many many years in Muizenberg..

There are no Postmen only Post Boxes next to a couple of essential shops. We love our new house because Aston is very much in the countryside. You cannot live here without a car. Perhaps a big plus about this place is that there is no pollution whatsoever. A lot of bird calls and singing throughout the day and tons of frogs croaking at night.

We have the original virgin bush-forest on our west side right outside our boundary wall. Sitting here in the lounge we just see the forest of Acacia trees, giant aloes and vine creepers interlacing the canopy. Everything is evergreen and growing in profusion. Occasionally we catch sight of some exotic bird in the branches or coming out of the bush on the ground, similar to partridges. The beach is a two-minute drive away and is very flat, so the sea pours in at high tide and fills the estuary, which again pours out at low tide. No sand crabs or seaweed or even sea gulls, but very clean and warm shores. There is always a breeze from the east or west during the day and a lot of moisture at night, and this, no doubt, is responsible for the clean environment. You can walk for miles along the beach. A lot of homes are closed up at the moment and there are a lot of new homes being built all over.

We do all our shopping in Jeffreys Bay (JB) and it takes us 10 minutes to get there. Only one robot in JB, mostly four-way stops. At about 9.00 am I am off to the beach in the car with the dogs, a walk around then back home. There are lots of B&Bs

and Guest Houses and Jeffreys Bay and Aston are geared for lots of holidaymakers. There is also a substantial local population so the economy is vibrant. Usual 'Townships' but not growing out of control as in Cape Town.

The human race seems to be at ease here and all stratas of society are represented. There is a small industrial area, but no car dealerships. We have now been here 11 months. All the animals have settled down (including our three cats). The sudden upheaval was strenuous but we are now back to a normal pace and the change was definitely worth it. No stress, no rush, no noise. Radio reception is good but no short wave during the day. TV reception is also very good.

One strange phenomena is the number of large brown garden snails that come out of the bushes onto the roads when it drizzles – an entrepreneurial opportunity! We heard that one waiter earned twenty big ones over the season – not from snails, but they might have been on the menu.

Tamara and I are settling in for another year in Aston Bay. We are right next to Jeffreys Bay and both these holiday spots are to the Afrikaners what Muizenberg or Plettenberg Bay are to the Jewish people at holiday time. We are about 90 km from PE and double that from Plett. We have been trying to rent or buy in Plett, but do not qualify because of the astronomical prices. Big, big, big bucks required.

So I have sour grapes and wrote a poem about it:-

Dreaming and Scheming.
Kicking and Screaming.
Begging and Pleading.
Paying and Praying.
Plettenberg,
Platzenberg,
Why the pain,
There is no gain!
Back to reality.

Junior Boys – 1953 1954 - Seated; Solly Sacks, Jeffrey Lewis, Morris (Butch) Levine, Arthur Stander, Jimmy Cameron, Merwyn Lampert, Yechiel Bortz, Ralph Brooks and Sydney Elcon. Back Row; Paul Strauss, Geoff Goldstein, Bobby Gordon, Michael Strauss, Bernard Scop, Isadore Leviton, Geoffrey Esakow, Hymie Sacks, Gordon Cameron (behind) unknown hidden, Hymie Pearlman, Eddie Kreser and Gerald Sacks

Bernard, Sonia born 1943, Brenda 1945 and Louise born 1947 were placed in the care of Arcadia in 1953.

Extract from 1959 Arcadian

"Sonia Scop from the moment she stepped into Arcadia mixed well with the boys. She showed great sporting abilities on the athletic track."

ARC MEMORIES

Bernard, myself, my two sisters, Brenda and Louise were sent to the Arc in 1952-59.

I remember that day so clearly. It seems like yesterday. My mother looked so smart and I still see the tears running down her cheeks as she waved goodbye to us and said that she would see us on the Sunday, the visiting day. I still don't think that we knew what was going on then, but I smiled and waved goodbye thinking to myself, well we are now going on a holiday. At seven who knew that.

Then Sister Conway came and took us to the Hospital wing where we were given the once over from head to toe (especially checking for lice) then came those awful blood tests etc. I remember Brenda and Louise crying and screaming. I wanted to murder someone for hurting my little sisters. Bernie seemed to handle it. Anyway after that we were given a sweet to calm us down. I then decided that no one was ever going to hurt us again.

We are all still very close and my Mom remarried when we had left the Arc. She is well and they live about two kilometres from us now. She is an amazing woman considering all that she has been through. My own father died when Bernie was 5, I was 3½, Brenda 2 and she was pregnant with Louise. My Mom was only 25. She is now 83 and well and healthy.

My days in the Arc as far as I was concerned were great. I loved being with so many girls and boys. We were one big family, and we all protected one another especially when we went to school. My family was sent to Jewish Government and then to Athlone High Girls. It was sort of crazy because we made friends there as well, but every time the green bus arrived to pick us up from school, the kids outside of the Arc would say, "Shame here comes the orphanage bus." And there we were getting on the bus feeling a bit "*skaam*". But who cared. We all still had each other.

During my younger years I was sent to the junior girls' dormitory which faced the tennis courts. My friends were Barbara Ginsberg, Tamara Salamon, Lily and Sandra Solomon, (They now live somewhere in Canada) Karen Shraga and Ethne Seinker.

Shame on me. Once I broke Tamara's arm by accident by swinging her in the overhead bars and going too fast and she fell off. She started to scream as we rushed her up to the hospital and then they had to take her to have her arm set. I was punished by not being able to go to the movies on a Saturday night. That was really a big thing. As far as the boys went I had many friends. I was a good sports woman and the Arc always helped us with good coaches. Tennis was the late Tom Kukuliwitz, swimming was Ralph.

Gosh I remember those days so well. We used to have the Inter Hebrew sports days at the old Wembley Stadium and the Arcs never lost in all the years they had it. Karen, Renee Rothaus, Barbara, Marion Shraga and I were the fastest runners and we always won our races especially the relays. No one could touch us. Of course the Arcs also had their own sports days. Houses were called Herzl and Bialik. Swimming galas were also great. They were at the old pool right next to the boys' dormitory.

MORE ARC MEMORIES

When I was about 10, I grew beans, firstly in cotton wool and then when they were big enough planted them against the fence by the tennis court. A little boy used to eat my beans and then one day broke my beanstalk down. Hey I was going to be like *Jack and the Beanstalk*, climb up the stalk and make lots of money by stealing the giant's golden goose. I think that the little boy was David Sandler. Well I never grew beans again and I don't think I shouted at him. I realised then that it was only a fairy tale.

Next to the baby dormitory there was a boxing ring and every Sunday morning Donald Goldman used to come and give the boys boxing lessons. I first used to watch and see what the boys did and then I begged Donald to let me also box. I was the only girl boxer in the Arc. Wow what fun I had. Sometimes I used to knock out one of the boys and eventually Donald stopped me from boxing.

We also used to play kennetjie there plus baseball. On Saturday afternoons Arnold Levitan and the late Solly Farber used to come down to the bottom of the stairs. There used to be a stone sort of bench and a big tree. I remember them sitting there and giving us the Saturday morning's Shiur and then they used to give us sweets (Today they call it Seuda Shlishit). Can you believe where I'm at? Starting all over again because I have learnt so much from my own kids and of course through the Rabbi's that I work with.

Thinking about that I remember going to Chedar after school. My first teacher was Mr Shalit and then a Mrs Gerber who lives in Melbourne with her son Les and daughter-in-law Helen. I won a book called *My Glorius Brothers* and kept the book for many years, but then when we made Aliyah in 1986, a couple of cartons went missing and the book wasn't there.

I remember Gershon Rochlin, Bobby Gordon and Isadore Levitan. Gersh I see around and to this day he still remembers birthdays, cricket scores and everyone he meets he never forgets. I believe Bobby and Isadore went to Israel and have been living there. Also Marion Shraga, she was married to Martin Goldberg and I used to see her often when we lived there.

I also remember the upstairs Senior Girls' dormitory facing the field where the juniors and babies were allowed to play. The highway wasn't there at the time and we used to climb down a place called Montgomery's Cliff. Then I thought I was a girl scout and a few of us used to dress up, in what I can't remember, and go marching around singing the *Yellow Rose of Texas*. We made a flag on a pole and then marched with that. Who said the Arc was bad? I have precious memories.

BERNARD SCOP

Extract from 1959 Arcadian.

"This white haired, blue eyed lad (Um SHLUP-ogods) showed an early interest in photography and through continuous research Bernard soon reached the standard of a professional photographer. As well as being in charge of the Arc tropical fish, Bernard was the shamas in his earlier days."

By Hymie Pearlman

"One of the most enterprising boys ever, even while in the Arc, was Bernard Scop.

While we were all concentrating on sport, Bernard was specialising in photography. Not only did he set up his own laboratory in the empty house down the hill on the Arc property (I think the Arc Secretary, Mr Stanley Goldsmith once lived there), but he even worked after school in the Chemist shop (Monte Carlo Chemist) next to the Monte Carlo Cinema in Jeppe Street at the Photographic counter, to get experience and money to pay for his equipment.

Now that is what I call enthusiasm and dedication, and that is why he was always one step ahead.

He had one of the first and biggest video distribution shops in Claremont, Cape Town and even had movies on tape a few days after they came out in London! One of his best customers was Wendy Ackerman!

In spite of him always being so busy, he invited Tamara and I to dinner, at his home with his wife Gail. Their daughter Sharon was just a baby at the time.

We also remember his wonderful mother, grandmother and sisters. Bernard once took me to his house in Houghton, with the tiled swimming pool, where they used to live.
Memories, memories."

By Sonia Margolias

I actually forgot that Bernie had a dark room at the Arc. In the old days it was between the dance studio and the hospital and he really spent many happy hours there. Bernie was a great guy and very very clever, even though at School they thought that there was something not right with his learning. He became a food technologist and computer boffin besides many other things. He also had a photographic memory.

When we were living in Israel in 1987, (we made Aliyah and then returned to South Africa in 1991), I worked for Dow Chemicals and my boss wanted to make a certain washing powder but couldn't find the formula. I asked if I could phone Bernie and he spoke to him and Bernie told him to look up in a book on technology and told him to go to page 586.

While Michael was looking this up, I asked Bernie if he was working on the computer and he said no, but he remembered exactly where it was. Michael came back and was flabbergasted as he had been looking for the formula for five years and here comes Bernie over the phone and tells us exactly what to do. Today, this is a major washing powder in Israel. It seems unbelievable, but he could do so many different things. I really miss him. We were very close and saw and spoke to each other almost daily.

Gail, Bernard's wife passed away in 1987 through negligence after an ordinary ulcer operation.

My late brother Bernie has one daughter Sharon, who lives in Port Elizabeth, and we haven't seen her for a while, but speak to her often. It so sad, she lost her mother and father within 12 years. She is now 36. I am sure lots of old Arcs will remember him. He was very quiet but very clever. Bernard passed away in October 1996 from a massive heart attack at age 54

LOUISE AND BRENDA SCOP

My sisters, Louise and Brenda (Scop) both remember David Sandler I think that Louise said that she was in the same dormitory as him. That was in the Babies. She was blonde and beautiful even at a young age. Brenda is the darker one.

Louise has been married twice. From her first husband Ronnie she has three daughters, divorced and then married Lionel they have one daughter together. Then Lionel's two daughters lived with them. So all in all six daughters and Louise treats them all the same.

Louise's youngest daughter is 22. She has nine grandchildren all together and P.G. is expecting another one soon (June).

Brenda is married to Harry Badler has three daughters and one grandchild Her youngest daughter has been married and divorced and is now engaged, and maybe some time early next year they will be getting married

MY FAMILY

I have been married to Cecil Margolias for 37 years and have two kids (not actually kids but parents themselves and seven grandchildren.)

My daughter Laureen is married to Chaim Shalpid and they have three very talented and beautiful girls who are always acting in shows. They are seven, five and three years old and they just love to be on stage

My son Vaughan is married to Ilana Lewus. They made aliyah in December 2002 and live in Ra'annana. They have three boys and a girl. Both families are very frum. We miss them like crazy.

I work for Ohr Somayach with my daughter Laureen. . Have been here for eight years fund raising and also office work and I have just finished working on a banquet which is called "*Next Year in Jerusalem.* It's really a great organisation and we do tons of unbelievable work.

Laureen and I have been very busy with our fundraising and had a most successful Horse Racing Charity day for the SMILE FUND. This fund helps children from disadvantaged homes who need facial reconstruction, due to birth defects. Cleft palate, myoebus syndrome and burns.

The Chairman of the fund is Marc Lubner. His grandparents, were the late Morrie and Bella Lubner and his parents, Bertie and Hilary. They were on the committee of the Arc and then they opened up Kibbutz Lubner. They are the most wonderful kind and generous people and great philanthropist.

REMEMBERING OTHER ARCS

I actually went to Polly and Tamara's house in Muizenberg not knowing that they had left and gone to live in Aston Bay

Donald's passing was terrible, I really felt very sad for Chooks and the family. He was an amazing man. I used to see him running around Norwood and Highlands North sometimes, I would stop and chat. I was Donald's first girl boxer and he gave such encouragement and was amazing with all the kids. We all loved him dearly and his passing was felt by so many. Never a bad mood only smile at you and make you feel so special. Another era has gone by. He will be sorely missed.

We recently drove past the Arc and it's not the same. There is this massive office block going up which I can see from the Highway. Montgomery's Cliff has now gone. (Do you remember the name and where it was) just facing the Highway. Rocky little cliff that we thought was a great big place to enjoy our climbing. How life has changed. What fun we used to have. Maybe Tamara and Barbara will remember that place because we always used to go climbing there.

Barbara Geer (Ginsburg) and George we see from time to time as well as Norman Sacks. His TV and Hi-fi shop is across the road from the office and He remembers people so well. He showed me where I was and also my late brother and my sisters on one of the *Arc Memory* booklets

Bobby Gordon was really a good friend of mine whilst in the Arc. I did see him many years ago in Israel whilst walking down Ahuza Street in Ra'annana and then never heard from him again.

I also remember Michael Rothaus and his sisters Rene and Lorraine. I haven't seen Rene for years. We used to play tennis together.

Recently, I drove on the Highway past the Arc, with one of my granddaughters and explained to her that this is were I lived as a child and she could not believe it. The old main building is looking whiter than ever and Hollard Insurance Building has taken up most of the other part of the old first swimming pool and all the soccer and sports grounds.

One of these days I will drive up to the old building and see what is going on inside the main old buildings. What memories these hold for me.

My mother is going to be 84 P.G next month and we were sitting talking about the Arc only recently. She and my stepfather come to me every Shabbos and she also can't believe that so much time has past and so much has happened over the years.

Chapter 90 – BOBBY (ROBERT) GORDON (1943)

Bobby, born 1943, was placed in the care of Arcadia in 1947 and his sister Cerisia, born in early 1947 was placed in the care of Arcadia in late 1948 as a baby.

1961 Arcadian

"Bobby (Robert) Gordon is one of the Arcs who will definitely not get ulcers, for he is blessed with a happy disposition. He, too, was a Sportsman of no mean achievement (boxing, running, cricket and often loving). He surprised all – and still does – by his keen interest in spiritualism and psychology. Bobby is now with Reliable Cycle Works (Ex-Arcadian, Penzik)."

BOBBY GORDON MARRIES JUDY
By Ronny Schreeuwer

Well we went to Bobby and Judy's wedding. Didn't know anyone there except for Hymie Aronoff. All the other people were the inmates of Beit Protea, a rest home for the South African elderly.

After not seeing Bobby for maybe 40 years I could still see a resemblance of how I remembered him as a kid. I was asked to be a pole holder at the last moment and Hymie was the best man.

Judy and Bobby both work at Beit Protea. He works mainly in the evenings at the main desk and sorts out all the problems that may arise. Judy is a free lancer and sometimes travels as a companion overseas.

Judy and Bobby

THE FIRST CAR PHONE
By David Sandler

I remember Bobbie Gordon and from the stories I heard I can tell you he was a real heart breaker in his day. I heard a story about a very unhappy father who wanted to kill him for his on-goings with their daughter. He was always a very live spark, full of fun and practical tricks. I'm sure Arcs who were his contemporaries would confirm this.

I remember him visiting the Arc once on a Sunday (which he did quite often) and he invited Jenny, my sister) and I to sit in his car and listen to some music on a tape. This was when I was say 12 so it was 35 years ago.

He had a large old bakelite phone on the console (between the two front seats) and then in the middle of the music the phone rang. He proceeded to answer the phone and talk and then put it down and carry on talking to us and we continued listening to the music. He had preset it all up.

He was years ahead of us all with the car phone.

Rafi Schreeuwer, Bobby Gordon, Hymie Aronoff and Ronny Schreeuwer

Chapter 91 - BARBARA GREER (GINSBERG) (1944)

Barbara born 1944 and her two brothers Howard born 1946 and David born 1948 were put in the care of Arcadia in 1955.

Extracted from 1961 Arcadian

Barbara Ginsberg is a redhead and a hard worker at Parktown Girls' High who won the admiration of nearly all Senior Boys, only to lose it as a result of the fiery temperament, common to red-heads. The only faithful ones - to the bitter end - Max M and her secret admirer Hymie S.

BARBARA REMEMBERS

I arrived at the Arc in 1955 with my two younger brothers, David and Howard Both my two brothers went to live in Durban. Howard was electrocuted when he was 21 and David passed away at 38. David left a wife and two children who now live overseas.

The weird part is that Mannie's wife, Sarah Osrin (Epstein), boarded with my Grandparents in Orange Grove many years ago, when she left the Arc, and my one grandson is friendly with Mannie's grandson in Melbourne.

I have four children, and six grandchildren. My eldest son Marc lives in Melbourne and has two sons

REMEMBERING OTHER ARCS

Sonia Scop (who is now Margolias) and I are very good friends. I met up with Sonia (after having lost contact with her when I left the Arc) when my husband and children came back to live in Johannesburg after having lived for 22 years in Zimbabwe. Our two daughters became very friendly (Sonia and I hadn't yet met again) and Sonia kept telling her daughter that she knew my daughter. In fact it was me as a young girl that she kept seeing and then we met up again through the girls, and have remained good friends since. Isn't that a wonderful story?

I know the 'Auntie Shirley', Selwyn Dembo's mother-in-law who lives in Melbourne so very well. She is related to my daughter-in-law who also lives in Melbourne. I also know Selwyn Dembo and his wife Sandy very well - Sandy is a very dear friend of mine.

Sonia was telling me about Wilhemina Joseph who lives in Bloemfontein - at first I didn't remember who she was but Sonia reminded me she was Dutch and wild and then it all came back to me. Yes you are right it seems as though we are connected by an invisible umbilical cord.

I became involved with all the *Old Arc News* while visiting my Mom at Sandringham Gardens. One Sunday we were sitting at the table in the garden and there were a few old dears sitting with us. Anyway one took a shine to me and we started talking and it turned out she was an Old Arc. She got so excited and went to her room to get me one of the newsletters to read - that is how it all started. Her name was Alma Goldstein (nee Lipman) and I say was, because sadly she passed away recently. But isn't it just so weird that she was sitting with me - I mean I didn't know her from Adam - makes your thoughts even more real! If not for her I would never have re-connected!

By Ronny Schreeuwer
I remember Barbara pretty well. I still have a picture of her in my mind with kind of lightish brown wavy hair. I think around the time of Molly Flink or just after around Tamara Salaman's time. I also remember David and Howard very well. They were good sportsman and I remember seeing David in Durban when we went down in December one year. It's very sad to hear that they both passed away so young.

1959 Ma giving the Senior girls cooking lessons
Rene Rothaus, Tamara Salaman, Barbara Ginsberg and Lorraine Rothaus

341

Chapter 92 – CAROL MERVIS (SOLOMON) (1945)

In January 1952 my brother Arthur Solomon aged five and I Carol Mervis (Solomon), aged 7½ were placed in the care of Arcadia. Our mother was ill with cancer and she passed away in May 1953. We were at the Arc for six years and we left in December 1957.

ARC MEMORIES

Upon arrival at the Arc we were put into the hospital section and had to have blood tests. Since then I have never been good at having my blood taken. The sister in charge was sister Conway and she had a daughter named Claire. They slept in the hospital section and Claire attended Parktown Convent, down Oxford Road. When we needed a haircut the Sister would cut our hair. We stayed in the hospital section for a few weeks and the children already there, used to come and ask "when are you coming over".

We were put into the Baby group, until a certain age (can't remember what age) and then transferred to the Junior Girls or Boys.

We used to go for outings on the bus. The bus driver's name was Charlie and he was very nice to all the children. He and his family lived at the top near where the cows were housed.

Ma and Doc Lichtigfeld were in charge at the time. Doc was a big man and always had warm hands. Ma was very strict, she called me to her room on the Saturday after my mother passed away (she died on Friday night 22nd May) to tell me and I told my brother. That Saturday Ma made me sit next to her in Shul. On our birthdays Ma would give the birthday person a big packet of sweets which we shared.

The dentists used to come and check our teeth and if you were really sick Dr Getz used to come to see you. Everyone was scared of Dr Getz.

On Saturday nights a film was shown in the dining room, and if a child was naughty during the week they were punished by Vic Klevansky and not allowed to see the film.

On Sunday afternoons we all used to go and sit on the wall in Oxford Road to wait for our parents' visit. We could see the cars or buses coming down the Oxford Road hill and there was great excitement. Some children did not have any visitors and we who had, felt so sad for them.

We used to have housemothers looking after us in the dormitories, and I remember one person in particular, Nurse Scotty, she used to drink whiskey and smoke Gold Flake cigarettes. She was very strict.

Carol and her brother Arthur

My brother and I went to Saxonwold Primary School. Some children went to Jewish Government, then on to Athlone or Parktown Boy's and Girls'.

I had an aunt who lived opposite the zoo and on Saturday after lunch I and a few friends used to bunk out, walk through the zoo and visit my aunt who usually brought us back before 4 o' clock when we had to attend an Oneg Shabbat. We were dropped off at Federation Road and walked up the steep hill behind the Babies and Junior Girls looking very innocent.

On a few occasions we would also bunk out and go to the Hamlet Home for retarded children. We did not know the name of the home, but it was and still is situated behind Arcadia. We saw the babies through the windows and the nurses allowed us to hold them.

There was a lady who used to come and make dresses for the girls. She had a little sewing room in the main house.

Sometimes a Committee member would have a party for the children at their house and it was really a wonderful outing. The Lubners had a big house in Houghton and it was so nice to go there.

During the movie on Saturday nights we were hungry and used to go to the bread cupboard and take bread. On Saturday afternoons we would go up the hill to see the workers make *tamaleke* which was a syrupy sweet or they made *skokiaan* (beer) with yeast.

There were lost of swings, a big slide and a merry go round, a sandpit and big swimming pool for the children, also a boxing ring and the late Donald Goldman would teach the boys to box.

Once a month you could go out for the day with your parent. That was really something special. Our father would take us to the war museum at the zoo – it was a fascinating place.

I took my husband to see the Arc when everything was being sold. It was so sad to see the buildings in such disrepair, the big kitchen and the main dining room, library and the upstairs where the senior girls stayed. I never went back before that as I was very sad. I had good memories as well as sad memories because I wanted to be at home with my mother and at the time couldn't understand.

I am sure there are still many old Arcs scattered around the world and sometimes one reads about them passing away, which brings back a flood of memories, good or bad.

My brother now lives in Jacksonville Florida, USA with his wife. I live in Johannesburg with my husband Ronnie, we have three children. Our eldest son Rael became a Rabbi and lives in Israel with his wife and family. Our other children are in Johannesburg and we have nine grandchildren. Thank G-d.

Our eldest son has lived in Israel for 20 years and we have visited Israel about 10 times over the years. He was married in 1971 during the Gulf War and at one of the Sheva Brocha dinners we met up with Yechiel Bortz. He was one of about eight Bortz children who lived in the Arc.

RULES OF THE HOME WHEN CAROL WAS ADMITTED

o On the admission of a child to the Orphanage the parent or guardian thereof agrees to abide by the Rules of the Home.

o Visiting is permitted on Sundays only, and then between the hours of 2.30 and 5.00 p.m.

o Visitors are not allowed to enter departments or dormitories.

o Children may be allowed out of the Orphanage on application to, and with the consent of, the Superintendent. In such event babies must be returned home by 5.00 pm and other children by 6.00 pm

o Pocket money must be left in the care of the Superintendent. Small quantities of fruit and confectionery may be brought on visiting days and must be handed to the Housemother for the child concerned.

o All clothes are provided for the children by the Committee. Any clothes brought by parents, relatives and friends shall be handed to the Matron for the child concerned.

o Children may not be permitted to leave "Arcadia" overnight except with the approval of the President, for which application must be made through the Superintendent.

Arthur and Carol with their Father

Carol and Ma

Chapter 93 - SHARRON LIPMAN (GETZ) (1946)

I was born 15 November 1946 and arrived at the Arc in 1952. (I don't remember the month). I was well cared for by Ma and Doc and Vicky.

I can still remember what Ma told me, "You will be very happy here just try." Ma was right. I can only thank the Arc staff for my good life. I left the Arc in January 1966 and left for Israel in February 1966 to the kibbutz and have stayed there ever since.

SHARRON REMEMBERS

I have read the *Arc Memory Booklets* and it has reminded me of the good days in the Arc. When I saw Marcel two years ago he remembered the Arc and our good years we spent together.

I have very good memories of the Arc. All the kids in the Arc were the same if they had family or not. We were all alike. I remember visiting day that came every Sunday when the families came to see the kids. There were a few of us that did not have someone to see. Ma and Doc always had sweets and cakes in their flat for us. When I was 12 years Ma told me she wants me to have my Batmitzvah with all the other children. I told her no because I would not have a family to be at my party. Ma told me that there would be people at my Batmitzvah. Ma was right. All the staff and the committee members came. At the end I saw Ma crying out of joy. Then I felt I do not need family and that Ma and Doc and the staff were my family.

We were woken up at six by a loud knock on the door. In came Miss Purward saying, "I will be back in 10 minutes". To get ready, wash and clean teeth and make up our beds. Miss Purward would take us to the dining room for breakfast.

Ma and Doc would give us a smile and a tap on the back. Breakfast would take about 30 minutes, we had a packet for lunch. Then we would go to our bus Ma and Doc would wave us goodbye.

My best school days were Sunday, Tuesday, and Thursday. I would have sport in all the other classes I would try my best because of Vicky. He would help me so I tried my best. At the end of the school day we would take the bus back to the Arc, where Doc and the staff waited to give us lunch, after which they would help us with our homework. Then I would spend time with my music

OUR TUCK SHOP

I cleaned my brother's shoes for two cents so that I could go and buy some sweets. I found all kinds of things to do so that I could get some sweets.

Sharron Getz – a school photo

On Sunday when it was a day that the people would come and see the kids, some of the committee members would come and bring some sweets and cakes for us.

OUR HOME

To many of us the Arc was the only home we knew. A love of a mother and father was given to us by Doc and Ma and Vicky and staff. Over and above all the committee is tireless in its efforts to provide us with all the extra luxuries that make Arcadia a home.

THE VISIT OF CLIFF RICHARD

We were all doing our homework when Ma came in to the lounge and told us to finish our work as there is a visitor coming to see us - he is a very good singer.

We finished our work and ran to our big lounge and waited. Then Doc came in and behind him came the one and only Cliff Richards.

I think that all of us could not speak. He spoke to us telling us about himself and then came the moment for him to start singing. He sang and we sang with him he then gave us all a big picture of himself after cakes and drinks. We had pictures with him it was a day to remember.

There was another day I cannot forget when another singer came it was an Israeli singer. I was not allowed to see her as I had to stay in my room, as I put a white mouse in the pocket of Sandra Markus. I was told by Vicky to say sorry but I would not. I found it very funny and to this day I don't think I apologised.

MY FAMILY

My husband Aubrey Michel Lipman was born in South Africa on 20 March1939. He died on 24 August 1977.

We were married in July 1967 and have three children, Yochanan, born 1968, Chedvah, born 1970 and Vered, born 1975.

My daughter was married in 1996 and has a daughter Shachar born 1998, and two sons Ron born 2000 and Ori born in 2002.

My brother Marcel Getz lives in Canada. His wife is Brenda and they have three children, two boys and a girl.

MY FIFTIETH BIRTHDAY

My children Yochanan, Chedvah and Vered wrote this poem for my 50th birthday. In January 1997 the kibbutz held a big party for moms who turned 50. I happened to be in South Africa, but when I returned home I was given the poem and the biggest bunch of flowers.

Sharron and Aubrey on their wedding day

You who know my mom she is the
best mom and the greatest

Also in her spare time she is in the police force
But our mom is so different
Soft warm and good and will always
Find time to help others night and day
And is always happy to help

A mom like this we will never never give up

A mom like this I will always keep
Mom this night is for you
If you were here tonight I would step
Down from the stage and give you
The biggest hug and kiss that can
Be given to a mom
Mom Mom we love you
Please stay with us for as long
As we need you and you need us.
We love mom

Sharron and her late husband Aubrey Michel Lipman with son Yochanan and daughter Vered

Chapter 94 – THE SCHREEUWERS (1943, 1946, 1949, 1951 and 1954)

Simon Schreeuwer, our father, was born in 1913, in Manchester, England, from Dutch parents. He moved to Holland as a young boy, where he met my mother, Clara Poppers, who was born in 1918 in Utrecht, Holland.

A little before the war broke out they got married and had a daughter Betty. Their whole family, including our parents and their parents and brothers and sisters were all rounded up by the Germans in Utrecht and transported to a waiting camp, Westerbork in the north of Holland.

Betty passed away during that time from dysentery and Raymond (Rafi) was born in 1943 in Westerbork. After a while they were transported to another camp, Bergen Belsen, in Germany. They spent some years there, and from there they were sent to Auschwitz. On the way they were rescued by the Russians and pulled off the train.

After the war ended it took them a few years to get back on their feet. Louis was born in 1946, Willy (Bracha) born in 1949, then Ronny born 1951 all in Holland.

Clare and Simon Schreeuwer immigrated to South Africa in June 1951 from Holland with the four children, to get away from the chaos and unpleasant memories of the war and to begin a new life. They'd both lost their parents and other members of their families in the holocaust

Our parents never fully recovered from their experience in the camps. They were not very healthy mentally and physically. It was very difficult for new immigrants to make a living and times were tough after the war. Dad worked as a travelling salesman and Mom as a housewife, but sad to say she was not able to cope emotionally.

In May 1952 the three oldest children were put into the Arc, but as Ronny was too small, he was put into Cotlands. We were there until June 1953, but Dad could not handle that we were not at home, so home we went. Mom could not cope again, so back we went for a second time and a third time. During one of our home stays we went to Allen Isaacs Camp and had a great time there. After a while we went home again, and stayed there for some time.

Shelley (Rachel) was born in 1954. In 1957 Willy, Ronny and Shelley were taken back to the Arc where they stayed until we finished school. Raymond and Louis went to hachshara and finally left South Africa for Israel.

Ronny, Shelley, Louis (in background) and Rafi with Mom (Claire) and Dad (Simon) in foreground – At the Arc

In the nine or ten years that we'd been in and out of the Arc we'd also changed schools just as often. It had made it very difficult for us to settle down in any way so when we finally moved to the Arc in 1961 it was the best thing that could have happened to us

During our period in the Arc we learned discipline, had lots of friends and support. We had many activities that we created for ourselves or were organised for us. We were truly fortunate to have a good supportive committee, Doc and Ma and Vicky at the time. Arcadia gave us a strong foundation of Judaism, values, education and culture.

Each year we enjoyed very much going to Durban in December. Shelley started to go to Bloemfontein in July when she was about 13. After all these years she still has good contact with her families from Durban and Bloemfontein.

Arc life for us was good. I don't think any of us would know where we would have been today if it was not for the Arc. We went through tough times there also, but we came out okay, all of us. It is very hard to have parents and not to be with them, even though a lot of the Arc kids had one or the other parent or none, we knew better.

Clare and Simon Schreeuwer returned to Holland in 1976, where they lived in Ijsselstein near Utrecht for a couple of years. Simon (Simian) Schreeuwer, passed away in Israel January 1986 at the age of 72. Clare Poppers Schreeuwer, in her later years lived in Holland, Den Haag in a Jewish home for the elderly and passed away in September 2005.

While Rafi, Ronny and Shelley now live in Israel, Louis lives in Sydney Australia and Willie in South Africa

RAYMOND (RAFI) SCHREEUWER

RAFI'S ARC MEMORIES

I don't remember the exact dates we came to the Arc. We came to SA in 1951, so I presume it was in 1952/53. I must have been 10 or 11 the first time and I was in and out the Arc. Ronnie must have been around three. I returned home for a while and then returned to the Arc at almost 14 years. I remember one of the ladies (Lubner I think) picking me up. Of course I did not want to go and kicked and screamed and of course it was of no help. Anyway I arrived at the Arc received by Doc and Ma.

The first question on arriving in the Arc the second time was "has he been Barmitzvahed?" "No" said my father, "we could not get him to go to the lessons". Well from that day on Doc never left my side till I learned my parasha. Doc encouraged me to have a Barmitvah. He used to sit with me for hours teaching me the short parasha that I had to say (I could never remember poetry etc). I still have the chumash I received. It was short because I could not remember poetry even then. In the end I was Barmitvahed.

I was also in Arcadia the year Jan Pierce came there and how I

A Young and Older Rafi

wanted to be the one to sing, but one of the other kids did. I would walk with him and teach him the song for days before the great day but I don't think he really needed my help. The last year I was there Doc took me to trade school in the centre of Johannesburg. I think it's still there. I must tell you it was the best thing that he could have done for me.

I shall never be ashamed of being in the Arc, especially after what Doc and Ma instilled in me. I know I was not very good at school due to personal problems but I think because of the Arc I managed to build myself up. I don't remember any hassles with kids at school or having fingers pointed at me.

I think we should all be proud of what we have become. For some it came easy and others more difficult. I for one look back many a time and am thankful for what I have today even though it may not be much by some standards. I have two wonderful boys and two grand children and a great wife who is much too protective of me (39 yrs of togetherness). What more can I want...

AFTER LEAVING THE ARC

I left the Arc in 1959, did some electrical training, immigrated to Israel in 1961 to a kibbutz (Yisreel) and married in 1964. I moved to the USA for 12 years and had a couple of photo studios. In 1976 things turned sour and we tried to continue till 1979 when we moved back to Israel. We have lived here ever since in Safad (Golan). I did medical photography (Pathology) for a while then I set up the computer department for the hospital in 1981. I retired at age of 56 due to ill health.

I have been living in Israel for the past twenty years and Ronny and Shelly are also here. I have two boys Ami and Ari. Ami is married and has a boy and a girl. Ari does not want to marry so he says, we shall see.

LOUIS SCHREEUWER

Louis as a young man

LOUIS' ARC MEMORIES

I must have been six or seven years old when I was in the Babies. There were some wooden benches that they used to put up at a slant on the wall by the steps and us kids used to slide down them. Well the one time that I tried it I got a bum full of splinters. Ruth at the hospital enjoyed herself pulling them out with tweezers.

I remember all the other *boeties* in our dorm; the Ginsbergs, Leslie Sacks, Manfred Stein, Hymie Aronouff, Hilton Rothaus Alan Levy (or that might have been in the juniors), Ralph who had Polio and many others.

Alan Levy and I used have boxing lessons with Donald, and Alan used to give me such a headache every time we boxed. He was smaller than me, but a tough *oke*. I wonder what happened to him.

Stelzner was my worst enemy because Thursdays was toasted cheese day when we came home from school for lunch. I hated cheese and she always tried to force me to eat it. So one time my brother Raymond came to the Arc and really told her off in not so many words.

My *mother* in the Arc was Sarah Farber, she was always there for me and I would imagine for the most of the kids as well.

I could go on and on, so many memories good and not so good. I wasn't very happy in the Arc always running away wanting to be with my parents and Raymond. It wasn't easy for any of us, waiting every Sunday by the soccer field hoping that our parents would come and see us, and very lucky and happy when they did, but I always felt so bad for those who didn't have anybody to visit them and bring them some goodies

The people that stand out most in my mind at that young age were: Ruth with her long fingernail, what a great person, Sister Conway and her daughter Claire and Sarah Farber, who was like a big sister and was always there for me.

I have lots of memories good and bad, but thank goodness for the Arc it really did a lot of good for lots of kids, especially with people like Ma and Doc around.

I went to Jewish Goverment School with Principal Aronstein and Vice Principal Paktor. Those were the good days. You used to get milk and a packet of peanuts in summer and hot chocolate in winter. It was really *lekker*.

Hymie Pearlman married the best looking girl in the Arc. There were lots of envious guys around when he was courting Tamara. I worked with Hymie for a short time at Prima meats in Jo'berg. I can still see him taking a swig of his Cod Liver Oil every day.

My wife Shelley nee Goldberg and I have been living in Sydney for the past 8$\frac{1}{2}$ years. Its been, hard but it's the greatest move I have ever made. I work for a company Harvey Norman as a Proprietor of the bathroom section and I'm always happy to help out old Arcs if I can.

I have two children a daughter Nikkie and a son Gregory. Nikki, married Ryan Basserabie and recently gave us our first grandson. My son Greg is studying Chiropractics at University.

Louis Schreeuwer's Daughter's wedding
Shelley and Louis with bride Nikki and husband Ryan Basserabia
and his parents, Dennis and Ros

RONNY SCHREEUWER

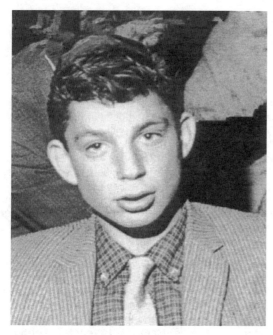

Ronny Schreeuwer

After leaving the Arc Ronny worked a few years as an articled clerk. He then went to the States and on to Israel where he went to an Ulpan and then carried on as a volunteer. There he met his wife, Dorothy, went to Holland for a while and got married there and then they went back to Israel to become members of the kibbutz.

Ronny and wife Dorothy, from Canada, have lived in Israel on Kibbutz Sdot Yam for over 20 years and they are blessed with four sons: Doron who looks like Ronny, Ilan, a surfer with a slightly olive complexion, Ayal very tall and blonde like a Viking and Nier the youngest who has just gone into the army.

Kibbutz Sdot Yam is right on the Mediterranean coast (half way between Haifa and Tel Aviv) and next to the Roman city Ceasarea that Herod built 2000 years ago. The Kibbutz, (besides all the regular things of a kibbutz) has a museum with many Roman artefacts found over the years, a ceramics factory and a yatch club. There is also a well known artist (a kibbutznic) who has her studios there overlooking the sea and there is a factory that copies in stone some of the Roman artefacts found. Ronny helped sell me at least 15 kg of these stone carvings and what a problem I had trying to carry them let alone getting them onto the plane.

SUNDAYS

Sundays was really special for us, it was visiting day. Our parents would come loaded with all kinds of tuck. We would wait at the bottom of the drive for our folks to come. Every car that passed that wasn't them was disappointing. It always seemed like ages until they would arrive and then they would be there. I used to enjoy playing soccer or tippy or just shooting at goal with my folks looking on, or we'd go up to the pool to show them how well we could swim. We'd walk around and greet other parents and talk a little bit until it was time to go. It was fun and we knew we weren't alone.

I used to look forward to Charlie's coming, (Mark and Shaun's father). He would bring them all those wonderful Marvel comics, which I couldn't get enough of. That's what I studied in form four, comics and classics, it's a shame I didn't get grades for that at school.

There were Sundays when my folks couldn't come. I would generally go up to the G's (Goldsmiths) and discuss cameras and developing techniques with Stanley. I would look at the latest photographic magazines. Mrs G would always have something good in the house to nibble on. I felt really at home there. It made the pain of not seeing my parents that particular Sunday a lot less.

SPORTS DAY

I remember when we had sports day at the Wanderers or sometimes somewhere else. We used to come off with all the trophies. It was great fun; we always used to run according to our size and not our age. I remember the sports committee complaining to Doc and how he would shrug it aside with a chuckle. The best part was travelling back to the Arc in the old Arc bus. We'd sing songs like "You can't go to heaven in the old Arc bus", "We'll be coming round the mountain" and we'd rant off the Arc war cry "1,2,3…. Arcadia boys are we….. 4,5,6… We got them in a fix ….. 7,8,9….. We lead them all the time….Arcadia. A R C A D I A Arcadia "

SCHOOL

I remember when we had to walk to school. We had these heavy cardboard suitcases with these uncomfortable metal handles, not like the backpacks that we have today. In the winter our fingers would freeze and we would change from hand to hand to prevent the blood flow from stopping in our fingers. We had about seven or eight periods a day, each one a different lesson or subject. We had to have all our books in the suitcase for all the subjects of that particular day. There was no such thing as leaving books at home or not doing homework.

We always had to be at school by 8.00 am sharp or before then, but no one liked to arrive at school early. To be a couple of minutes early in those days was just a waste of time. We wanted to be at school exactly on time and leave exactly on time. Our suitcases were heavy, I think it must have been at least a three kilometre walk. If we were fast walkers we could do it in 25 minutes, if not up to 35 minutes.

We had to be on time. At 8.000 am sharp the prefects would start writing down names of all late comers and we would become candidates for detention.

We would have to rush to the school hall for early morning prayers on Mondays. On Thursday we went to the play field for cadets or on other days we lined up in our "houses" where we would be inspected and given the latest sports news and the importance for us to participate as supporters at the rugby or cricket games was emphasised.

THE 1966 WORLD CUP

The 1966 the World Cup was hosted by England. Two kids from different homes were to be chosen to go to England, all expenses paid. One was chosen from Herber House (I think) and the other from the Arc. Who was it to be?

Les Durbach, Leon Goodman, some others and me were all fanatic soccer players. Every minute free we had we were playing tippy, soccer or kicking a rugby ball. At the time Les was the only kid representing the Arc at school playing rugby. For some unknown reason none of us were allowed to play sport at school in those years. Only finally when I got to matric was I allowed to play rugby at school. In matric I played for the first XV in my first year of rugby.

I was a soccer fanatic. My wall and ceiling were covered with soccer pictures. Anything I could find in any sport magazine of local or overseas teams and players..

Les was chosen and I think we were all as excited as he was. We followed every detail of Les's preparation for the trip. We listened to every broadcast of the games and were very excited when England beat Germany in the final. It was like World War II all over again.

Finally, when Les came back loaded with postcards, pictures and souvenirs, we couldn't wait to hear the stories. It was one of the most exciting periods of our stay in the Arc. To this day when I watch English football and I see a team manager who was a player in World Cup 1966, all those memories come rushing back.

Paul Cohen, Ronny, Jules Gordon and Les Durbach.

RONNY "OUR PROTECTOR WARRIOR HERO"
By David Sandler

Ronny told me of his exploits as a fighter and hero of the younger boys in the Arc which I faithfully recorded. So here is the story of Ronny, our protector warrior hero, where Ronny remembers some of the fights he got into at the Arc.

Ronny was in the same class at school as Robert Langman who was a notorious bully. Robert used to bully Ronny regularly and get him to do his homework until one day Ronny read the book "*Green Mantle*". In this book the hero was a small man who was very strong and used to fight larger baddies and win. Ronny related to this hero and decided to fight back against Robert Langman and Robert challenged him to a fight to be held on the verandah on the side of the Boys Department. Ronny says he did not beat Robert but he refused to give in and gave such a good account of himself that Robert never bullied him again.

On another occasion Neville Merwitz was apparently bullying some of the younger boys, Mark and Shaun Jacobs. Ronny our hero, (no doubt mindful of the large packets of grub and the Marvel comics the Jacobs boys received on Sundays,) decided to intercede on their behalf and to sort out Neville. Now Ronny is very short and Neville (Camel) was very tall, say 50% taller than Ronny, our hero, who attacked by diving at Neville's legs and toppling him to the ground. Then our hero jumped on top of Neville and pummelled him with punches and Neville was "knocked out".

Now Ronny was really worried. Neville would not come round and try as they may he responded to nothing. Time went by and eventually Mrs Stelzner appeared and wanted to know what was wrong with Neville. Ronny really started to panic and she was told that Neville had fallen. Eventually Neville came round. Neville was a great actor and I always wonder if he had decided to act his way out of the fight and get Ronny into trouble with this clever acting.

Ronny, Les Durbach, Michael Goldstein and Leon Goodman all repeated form four. Ronny tells me that the main reason was that they used to spend all their time playing soccer and tippy and he was hooked on those fantastic Marvel comics that Mark and Shaun Jacobs got from their Dad each week.

Ronny remembers fighting twice with Les Durbach and remembers the fights were stopped. He says that Les, (Taaibos,) was very tough. I think one fight was about whether the dormitory windows should be open or closed. Les wanted the fresh air and Vicky in his wisdom put the boys into different dormitories.

Ronny remembers Simon Woolf hitting him. Now Simon was very strong but would never bully anyone and was a very gentle person. Ronny says that Henry Shippel put Simon up to it as Henry fancied Willie, Ronny's sister, and Ronny discouraged the match. Ronny also says he teased Simon about his 'grunting' which to me seems a more logical reason.

Ronny says that Stanley Stein got into a fight with Simon because he saw Simon 'bullying' Ronny. I remember this fight where Simon had his nose bloodied but he gave Stanley a good account of himself. Also Ronny says that Stanley Stein gave Hymie Aronoff (Sonny Boy) a warning not to bully Ronny as Ronny had landed up with a bump on his face after being 'beaten up' by Sonny Boy.

By the way Ronny used to regularly bully Graham Stoler who was much younger than him because Ronny said, "Graham simply liked to be bullied".

I'm sure we all remember Graham regularly wailing out in his fog horn loud voice. I remember hitting Graham, who was more my equal in size, and getting bigger, and having to punch him hard to get him to stop annoying me. Now Ronny our hero picked me out for hitting Graham in his face.

I remember on another occasion Ronny and I were sparring with gloves on. Although Ronny had a much more powerful punch I think I had a longer reach and I was good at defending myself (thanks to Donald Goldman's boxing lessons) and quick to get out the way. While we were sparring someone called out to us and I was distracted momentarily and its then that Ronny landed me one on the jaw and my teeth chipped slightly as my jaw closed.

RONNY THE RUGBY HERO
By David Sandler

I remember Ronnie playing rugby. We were only allowed to play sports in the very last year of our school, in Form 5. I don't know why this happened and I suppose we were at a disadvantage in relation to everyone else who had been playing regularly throughout the years.

Anyway, Ronnie made the first team and on one occasion he saved what was a definite try. The opposing side was through and there was a guy with the ball and he was running to score a try and there was nothing between him and the line. Ronnie ran after him and took a full dive, like a dive that you would use to start off a swimming race and he just managed to tip the back of the guy's foot. That tripped him and he just sort of splat out on the field, short of the line and of course he did not score. Ronnie definitely saved that try with his magnificent dive.

CUTTING RONNY DOWN TO SIZE
By David Sandler

Another thing I remember about Ronnie was he loved himself. He thought he was the bees knees and he really fancied himself with the girls. I think to be perfectly honest the girls did fancy him too and I was, I suppose, a little bit jealous. Ronnie

was always standing in front of the mirror preening himself and at one time he used to cut his own hair. I think he even had his own mirror and we thought him to be very conceited.

One day he needed some help to cut the back of his hair because he could not see what he was doing. So on this occasion I remember volunteering "to help" and I thought this was a golden opportunity to cut him down to size. I took the scissors and calmly cut a big chunk of hair out of the back of his head. I then put the scissors down and I ran. By the time he realised what was going on, I was far away and he ran and eventually he caught me and he beat me up. He was much stronger than me and he really got stuck into me and I cried, but, I can tell you it was worth it. He was embarrassed for weeks and weeks until this big bald patch in his hair grew back again. It was worth every punch I got.

Ronny carrying the Torah

Shelley, Willy and Ronny

SHELLEY van den HOEVEN (SCHREEUWER)

Clara, Willy, Shelley and Ronny

I have been living in Israel since 1984 in the absolute north of Israel, on Kibbutz Misgav-Am. It is near Matula and the nearest town is Qiriat Shmone. We live on a mountain approximately 800 metres high up and it is cold in the winter.

I left South Africa in 1974, went to Holland for a three month holiday and stayed for almost 10 years. I married Gert, a Dutchman, in 1978 and had a daughter Elisa in 1981. I left for Israel 1984 had a son Benny in1987. My daughter, who is in the army at the moment, comes home every other week.

My sister Willy left the Arc around 1964 and got married a few years later. She has four children; Eve Ruth, David and Debbie. Her kids were at the Arc for a short time. Willy (Bracha) Jasven has changed her name, and is still living in Johannesburg, with her four kids. They are now all married and Eve has one girl and two boys, Ruth one boy and a girl, David, one girl two boys. Debbie does not have kids as yet and is still studying.

PLAYING SICK

There were the three of us in the junior department; Hannah Durbach, Helen Shaer and myself. Maybe Sadie Baitz was also there. We decided to be sick, as we did not want to go to school, so we decided to go up to the hospital and say that we were not feeling well. Sister Conway took our temperatures and put us into bed, as we did have slight temperatures.

What happened after that was amazing. By the next day we were all very sick and we all had chickenpox. By the end of the week the hospital was full. That was one joke on us. Our parents were not allowed to visit us in the hospital. We had to stay on one side and them outside so we were talking from the windows. But we had a great time, as there were so many of us in the hospital at one time. I think we must have been there for about two weeks. I remember Doc, coming into the hospital

Young Shelley Shreeuwer

every so often, bringing comics for us to read. That was also the last time we played sick.

ARC MEMORIES

The best time of my life was, when they started sending us off on holidays to Durban, and then later they started sending us to Bloemfontein. I had a great time, and the people really became my family. To this day I have contact with the families that I stayed with in both places. I am also very grateful that today that these families are still like family to me today.

Something that I do remember is that every year on our birthday Ma would come down to the Babies Department with her packet of sweets and a present for the birthday boy or girl. There was one particular year that I remember, but do not know how old I turned. It must have been my sixth or seventh birthday. I was waiting for Ma to come and wish me Mazal Tov, and eventually she arrived with her sweets and her present and till today I remember what I got as it made such an impression on me. It was a carousal music box with animals on it that turned and turned. I don't think I had it very long, but all I know is that it was the best present I had in years.

I used to keep to myself. I will never forget Pauline Kruger. We were very close. My dad had a soft spot for her when we were kids, we used to take her with us a lot when we were allowed home on Sundays, we used to go on picnics, I actually never forgot her.

After reading Bertha's letter I think that the children of that era really must have had a tough time. I believe that we went through the same, but in a different time and age. It was hard for everyone. I have never felt ashamed of where I came from and how I grew up, and I think I can speak for one or two of my siblings. It did make us stronger when we left the Arc and went to the big wide world, it took us a bit of learning to get where we are today. If it wasn't for the Arc where would we be today?

So I always say thank you for the help that I received as I know my parents would not have been able to do for us what the Arc did. We were five kids altogether, and it was hard for new immigrants to make a living and life was not easy for my parents coming from Holland after the war.

Raymond, Louis, Willy (Bracha), Ronny and Shelley Schreeuwer

Chapter 95 HYMIE ARONOFF (1947)

Hymie was born on the 15th November 1947 and was in the care of the Arc from 1952 to 1964, together with his older brother and sister, Julius born 1944 and Myrtle born 12946.

Hymie was a good sportsman and was always a friendly person with an even temperament. Although he was very strong I don't remember him ever bullying.

Hymie and Myrtle now live in Israel. Hymie has three daughters and four grandchildren. Two of his daughters live in Australia and one in Israel.

Julius married Vera Lozinsky also from Arcadia and they have a son Brian who is an attorney.

REMEMBERING HYMIE
Written by David Sandler

At Jewish Government School in the late 1950s my sister Jenny and I used to visit our uncle Ben's elderly parents who stayed near the corner of Bok and Nugget Streets every Wednesday afternoon after school and they used to give us a bag of sweets to share. They were always happy to see us and we would chat a bit and maybe they also had a little snack for us to eat.

I remember telling this to Hymie who immediately suggested 'we visit them everyday'. When we arrived there we made a noise knocking over some dustbins and the elderly couple told us to come back on Wednesday.

Once after school Hymie and I, with his encouragement, were throwing stones at some girls and they went to tell Mr. Pactor. Hymie was called in and got some cuts and Mr. Pactor warned me (who was much younger) not to throw stones at girls.

I do remember as a youngster being carried to hospital from the soccer field one Saturday morning by Hymie Aronoff when my face stopped a very hard soccer ball that had just been given a tremendous kick by a senior boy. By the time we reached the hospital the discomfort from being carried was more than the pain in my face but Hymie insisted he carry me which was a feat in itself.

At the Swimming Gala we had a few unusual events and one was a competition to see who went the furthest with a single dive and breath. Hymie Aronoff would win this as he had not only a good dive but could hold his breath a very long time as he drifted the furthest across the pool.

A CLEAN STORY
By Hymie Aronoff

I was on my way to supper one evening when Mrs Stelzner, who was walking just behind me said:
"Hymie, haf you bathed?"
"Yes, Mrs Stelzner, I have" I said.
"No you haf not! Go back and bath right now!" she said.

While muttering my protest that I had indeed bathed, I turned round and went back for another bath. While I was sitting in the bath (washing myself much more vigorously than before), in walked Mrs Stelzner. "Vosh yourself properly!! " she shouted, while proceeding to hit me on the head with her shoe!

I was absolutely shocked at this intrusion on top of being hit on the head and instinctively retaliated by punching Mrs Stelzner on the arm. This caused her to flee, calling for "Vickeeeeeeeee! Vickeeeeeeeeee!!" Vicky, on being told of this attack on Mrs Stelzner, called Doc, and a conference was held about how to deal with this "violent Sonnyboy".

I was sentenced to three months solitary confinement in the (haunted) hospital!

By M Perry Kotzen (2005)

Chapter 96 – JULES GORDON (1948)

Jules was born on the 16th of June 1948 and was in the care of Arcadia from 1959 to 1966, from age 11 to 18.

Jules married Vivienne Levy in December 1972 and they have a daughter Laurie who is a speech therapist and a son Darren, who produces movies and has made a movie 'Soldiers of the Rock' soon to be released.

GOOD AND BAD MEMORIES, OF MY ARC DAYS.

I think every person who was an Arc resented being there, resented the rules and rebelled either whilst there or after they left. Bear in mind that the Arc was responsible for so many individuals with different attitudes, personalities, temperaments and backgrounds, and everyone had their own aspirations for their futures when they would leave the rules and regulations behind and go out into the outside world. Only after you had left the Arc, did you realize why the rules HAD to be adhered to, via our house mother, Stelzner, Vicky, and obviously, Doc and Ma. Most of us left, took a while to get adjusted, and got on with what we had to do.

MY MEMORIES ARE DURING THE 1960s.

This was the swinging 60's....long hair and freedom....and there WE were, with short back and sides, compliments of Mr Kirshner, the Arc barber, who couldn't exactly cut a straight line, let alone be entrusted to give us a balanced haircut....his eyesight had started failing him 20 years previously!!

What bugged me was the fact that once you had had your Barmitzvah you were obliged to attend Shul twice a day, not of your own choice. You were told what time to go to sleep, what time to wake up, when you could do what, when to do homework, when and if you were allowed to go out. Rules, rules and more rules. For a youngster it's difficult to understand, especially having tasted the freedom of the outside.

ARRIVING AT THE ARC

On arriving at the Arc I was put into the hospital with Sister Conway and Ruth Dire (who by the way was quite a mean tennis player). All new residents were put through the same procedure. I was in Standard 3 and because it was mid year, could not be admitted to Saxonwold primary school until the beginning of the following year, so I went to Jewish Government school in Doornfontein for six months.

My grandmother lived in a flat in town; the Arc bus dropped us off in Doornfontein early in the morning, which now gave me the time to take a run to visit her for my second breakfast before school started. And so started my illustrious bunking out career.

Jules Gordon

We were officially allowed out on the first Sunday of the month only, and allowed visitors every Sunday afternoon. This made no difference to me, as I had made many out–Arc friends at school and we decided to start a band in Standard 5. The year was 1961, the year the Beatles turned the music world on its head. Our band, *'Image'* lasted until 2003, much longer than The Beatles, except we didn't make as much money as they did!

We practiced every Sunday morning at our drummer's house in Saxonwold, the neighbours being woken not only by our great music, but by the buzzing of the 49cc motor bikes some of our 'fans' drove to come and listen to our band.

Our fist big gig was to play at the Arc fete. We were supposed to play for one hour and ended up playing for five hours in an enormous tent which had been erected for the occasion in front of the main building, next to the Babies Section.

Of course I could not get permission to attend band practices, so I arranged with Adon Shalit to attend the earliest Hebrew class on Sundays. I had to bunk out down the hill, hitch a lift down Oxford Road, with my band equipment. I was lucky in hitching a ride and never waited longer than five minutes to get a lift. Guess I had a lucky thumb!

Dear Doc turned a blind eye, as long as I was back in time for lunch.

Talking about bunking out. In order to bunk out, Simon Wolf used to hop from the first floor bathroom window, over the rock pathway, onto the grass verge on the side of the driveway (only about 10 metres high and three metres across) from the windowsill. You could not take a run! Crazy? We weren't as brave!

We then arranged to have a spare key cut for one of the side doors of the Junior Boys building so a group of us could bunk out. The group included Henry Shippel, who had organised the key, Simon Wolf, Brian Langman, Brian Hough, Neville Murwitz, Keith Lang, Martin Katz, Stanley and Manfred Stein, to name a few, and whoever was lucky enough to crack an invite to join us. So we could bunk out to midnight shows in town, or just go *jolling* to Hillbrow late at night, especially during school holidays. When the moon was bright, I don't know how the watchman never saw our l-o-n-g shadows creeping across the soccer field on our way to where we would climb over the Oxford Road wall since the gates were locked at 6 0'clock.

We simply couldn't and wouldn't pay money into the public telephone box (tickey box) down the hill and across Oxford Road on the corner of Federation Road. I lost count of how many times I was caught as I jumped over the small gate into Oxford Road, either by Charlotte Sasto, or by Vicky Rabinowitz, who were Arc committee members, and taken back up to Doc's office to be reported for leaving the grounds without permission! He would give me a long lecture, and as soon as they were gone, give me a wink and tell me not to do it again.

The public phone box was our only way of communicating with the 'outside world' (this was many years before cell phones), and that is how 'the Georgie' was born. What was a Georgie? By using an insulated piece of wire, connecting it to the mouth-piece of the telephone and touching the other side on the metal of the tickey box, you heard a crackle, and presto, you could speak for three minutes, and re–crackle again to carry on speaking- FOR FREE.!!! (Legend has it that a guy named Georgie discovered this method of *shnying* a free call.)

One day the Post Office official came to clear the moneybox in the phone whilst I had a Georgie in my hand, and was busy on a phone call...damn cheek, he chased me all the way down the road! I ran around a corner, jumped over a wall, and almost landed in the mouths of three enormous dogs. I rather sat making friends with these dogs than to being liable for a R500 fine, or be shelled back to Doc to face the music! Many years later I told Doc what had happened, and he looked at me, thought a while, and just said, 'You scoundrel!' and burst out laughing. That was Dear old Doc.

The post office official drove up and down the road for almost two hours trying to find me and as a result, I was late for supper and had to create some long yarn as an excuse.

I recall when Polly Pearlman made some home-made mulberry and peach wine down the hill, and got Sidney Elkin to 'taste' and as a result of drinking just a little too much; Sid arrived in the dining room as drunk as a lord! At first they thought that he 'had gone crazy'. He was put into the hospital as punishment for refusing to split on Polly, and was banned from Arc Saturday night movies for a month.

Oh those 16 mm movies! We were given a handful of hard boiled sweets (to crack your teeth on). The serials to be seen (Zorro, Batman, etc etc) were normally out of sequence. As a result we couldn't exactly follow what was supposed to be happening from the week before. Sometimes inadvertently we'd be issued a "take–up reel" which was too small to take up the larger reel of the movie, so half the movie would end up in a pile on the floor and had to be untangled before we could carry on with the movie. Those of us who smoked used to slip out for a quick puff, and those guys who had a girlfriend used to also try to slip out past Ma Lich's "eagle eyes" just to meet for a quick smooch (and whatever!)

Midnight food raids were in! The pantry was the main target...why not also hit the fruit room while you were there as well?

The Arc tradition of not 'splitting or squealing' on fellow Arcs was adhered to strictly, and was punishable by being given a 'pile-in' in the boys long dormitory, which at one stage housed over 20 children. The guys would line up on each side of the dormitory armed with pillows (some of them used to put soccer boots and shoes in the pillow-slips for more impact!) and the perpetrator had to run down the line and get clobbered.

As you got older, you moved along the passage to smaller dorms until you got to the 'end senior room', which housed four senior boys. Unfortunately this room was right opposite Vicky's room (so he could try to keep an eye on us).

Vicky who was senior Latin master at Parktown Boys High School, (and also a sergeant-major in the army during the second world war, of which he always reminded us!) He was also a great yarn teller, and sent many guys to bed absolutely terrified after some of his 'spook yarns' on Friday nights! He was always available to lend an ear to your problems and to guide you with advice.

Upstairs in the boys building was the big and small homework rooms, more bathrooms (for senior boys only) as well as storage lockers .Oh yes there was also the "Ironing rooms" were our washing was ironed and sorted back into our cupboards by Stelzner and her staff of Monica and Betty.

The Arc swimming pool was a famous landmark, as this was the only pool heard of that was built on stilts! Below the pool was the large filter room were as we grew older, we used to meet the girls and smoke our lives away! That room, much like the cellar under the main building saw plenty of action!

The 'pond' which I never saw filled with water, was the venue for so many "tippy" (soccer with a tennis ball) matches and competitions. We also used to play 'soccer on the tar', outside the main building entrance, especially before Shul on Saturday mornings. Never mind the soccer, the main object was to try and not have your name taken by Ma Lich who sat at the upstairs bathroom windows with her notebook. If your name was noted then 'no movies' that night! Obviously, if you were caught, you would conveniently 'forget' who else was playing with you so they would also not get punished...the code of not squealing!

In September 1961, when I was in Standard 5, we were all called up to the front entrance of the main building on a Sunday afternoon. The pop idol of the day was Cliff Richard. Cliff arrived with two members of his band, The Shadows.

Cliff sang "*Living Doll*" to our great excitement, using Leonie Meyer's guitar, which was missing two strings! What struck me most about him was that he was very unassuming and modest, and down to earth and very humble. He answered all the questions we asked and was just like one of us; which is not expected of pop icons. And even more exciting, I sang "*A Voice in the Wilderness*", one of his hits. I remember being as nervous as I could ever be. This song stayed in our band's repertoire for many years to follow as it obviously had a very special meaning for me.

Jules singing, Neville on harmonica, Manfred on guitar, and Brian Socher on drums in front

Cliff Richard at the Arc. Jules is front left next to Adella Lozinski. Myrtle Aronoff is between them with Abe (Duck) Kupferberg on far right. Photo taken by Gingerer Stoler, Graham's father

Jenny Levin (Jennifer Fliess) and I were in Mrs Trott's class (Standards 4 and 5, 1959/60) at Saxonwold Primary School for a short while. That year, my hero and most of our idol of the day, Cliff Richard and two of The Shadows visited the Arc.

I sang "*Under the boardwalk*" at a prize giving ceremony together with Manfred Stein (guitar), Neville (Boom) Merwitz (harmonica), and Brian Socher (drums). All the instruments were borrowed from my band members who were not Arcs, but were always at the Arc, so that some of the guys from school thought they were together with us at the Arc.

I remember Melvin Katz could never be woken up in the mornings, so one Saturday morning we took him in his bed, together with his locker and left him in the middle of the soccer field. As usual after Shul we went down to the soccer field to play our game and there was Melvin, blankets pulled over his head, still fast asleep at 11 o'clock in the morning.

MEMORIES OF DOC AND MA LICHTIGFELD

I was admitted to the Arc in June 1959 at the age of 11, and was there until matric.

My first impression of the Arc was the famous Arc gates and long tree lined driveway up through the arch to the front entrance. There I was greeted by this man who was larger than life in his height, the size of his shoes, but mostly by the size of his heart.

This was Doc. He had a stern Germanic accent, yet a gentle voice and a very calming aura about him. He wore round glasses and had the biggest hands and fists I had ever seen and yet he was a very gentle quiet, and kind person.

Doc was well over six feet tall and at the stage that I first met him he already had a stoop in his shoulders especially when he walked.. I never knew his age, but he always seemed to be 'quite old' to me. Doc was known to us as 'the great guy', which to all of us at the Arc he really was.

He used to play soccer with us after Shul every Saturday morning. It was a standing arrangement amongst all the guys that he would always 'score' the final goal of each game and we all used to run around him and congratulate him on his 'winner'!! It was great to see him all chuffed in his size 12 soccer boots.

Doc used to come down to the Junior Boys building every weekday evening at 7.30, to teach each barmy boy his barmy portion separately, which took plenty of patience, (normally about six months) as a lot of the guys were actually tone-deaf. He used to sit next to us on the bench at the bottom of the stairs opposite Mrs. Stelzner's room and go patiently over and over (and over) our portions until we knew it backwards!

He made sure that none of the boys who had already had their barmy could even think of bunking going to Shul twice every single day! He loved blowing his whistle to get our attention (I always seemed to get it in the ear). Doc was always keen for everyone to further his or her studies, and was always there to guide us in any situation.

He knew that I always used to bunk out, but only made it an issue of it if I was caught by one of the members of the committee. He would give me a stern warning in front of them, made all sorts of punishment threats, and give me a sly wink when out of their sight. He truly was 'a great guy.'

Ma was quite short. She always wore her hair in a plait and a bun on her head. Rumour had it that it that it actually hung below her waist! She was always very thorough and had this tough exterior, but was actually a softie at heart.

She had the nickname of 'eagle eyes' and could spot you from across the opposite side of the Shul talking to your friend next to you, or 'checking out' the girls sitting opposite, or even worse would catch us with a penknife in our hands carving our names in the Shul benches.

On Saturday mornings, after breakfast we would have our weekly game of 'soccer on the tar' in front of the main building. The only problem was that Ma was taking our names from behind one of windows upstairs, and would get 90% of our names before she was spotted. Once this was done we were banned from movies that evening.

She was famous for making the barmy boys an 'egg-flip' at the barmy breakfast in her flat just before you sang your portion…this was supposed to settle and calm your voice, but actually made you feel more bilious than anything else!!!

I have nothing but very fond and dear memories of the couple we called Doc and Ma.

WHERE ARE THE ARCS OF OUR GENERATION?

What has happened to our generation of Old Arcs? Now that The Arc is no longer, you lose even more contact with the guys than ever, at least we used to see each other at Shul!

They do exist…Manfred Stein, the Kupferbergs, the Durbach clan; the Laskers and the rest of the guys who were with us. There are such great stories and characters from our era. Gershon and Max Rochlin, Sidney Elkon, the Sacks brothers. The Langman brothers, Howard and David Ginsberg (who have both passed away), and of course Sharon Getz. Simon Wolf, Marcel Getz. Also guys like Henry Shippel, Brian Hough and his brothers, Charles Resnick, Neville (Boom) Merwitz. These are names that spring to mind. These guys seem to have just disappeared!

TSUNAMI IN PHUKET - DECEMBER 2004

I'm sure you heard that I was caught in the tsunami in December in Phuket well anyway life goes on, but you just don't forget. I still find it hard to believe that I was on the spot when one of the worst natural disasters in history struck and have lived to tell the tale. The date, Sunday, 26th December, 2004.

My wife, Vivienne, cousin, Theressa and I were holidaying on the island of Phuket in Thailand at The Holiday Inn, which is situated across the road from the beach when the tsunami tragedy occurred.

As the death toll climbs all we can do is thank The Lord that we're back home safe, surrounded by our loved ones. Thousands of others weren't as fortunate. Physically we're all well after emerging from the ordeal without a single scratch, but mentally and emotionally we're still struggling to come to terms with the full extent of devastation that we witnessed first hand.

We're all undergoing trauma counselling to come to terms with it, but I find myself feeling very emotional at times when I speak of or think about the devastation of this beautiful island paradise and the hardship wreaked upon its hospitable, gentle and friendly inhabitants.

When I consider all that could have gone wrong I feel amazed and also very, very lucky and thankful. Another thing that this disaster made me realise, was just how many people cared for us. I thank all my friends and loved ones for their prayers and support. My thoughts and sympathy go out to all the people from all over the world who were affected by this tragedy.

There is a greater force even than nature which allowed us to survive and I thank G-d for sparring us. But perhaps the most important lesson that this experience has taught me is that I was thankfully spared, for some reason, and it is important to live each day to the fullest and never to take anything for granted. That's what I plan to do – starting right here and right now.

Jules still singing in a band (on right)
with Manfed Stein playing Guitar (on the left)

Darren, Jules, Vivienne and Laurie

Chapter 97 - MARTIN KATZ (1948-1998*)

Martin was born in 1948. He was placed in the care of Arcadia in 1954 and lived there until he matriculated at Parktown Boys' High in 1965.

Martin was a very placid person who was small for his age.. He never bullied the younger boys and always had a cheerful disposition.

He joined in when we played soccer or cricket and collected stamps and I remember him sharing some of the stamps that he 'found' in an album in a box of books that had been donated to the Arc.

I remember him volunteering to take me (about five years younger than him) to the movies in town during the school holidays as I was too young to be given permission to go by myself.

MARTIN KATZ
As remembered by Jules Gordon.

Martin was not a physically well person, and from the time that I knew him he was on medication and had to go for regular medical check-ups. He had contracted rheumatic fever as a baby and as a result of this he was a very small and thin guy.

Martin, Manfred Stein, and I shared our Barmitzvah together in June 1961 and in the photo of our Barmitzvah Martin looks a lot younger than Manfred and I.

Martin's nicknames were 'Kitty Kat' because of his gentle nature and also 'Bomber Katz' because of a medical condition that he suffered with no complaints.

He had a very bubbly personality and was very laid back. I actually can't recall him ever losing his cool with anyone, especially after he'd finished with one of his 'bombing raids' and taken a lot of flack from the guys as no one could go near the toilets for at least an hour after he had been there. This was as a result of a medical condition.

Martin was pretty bright at school. He always did my maths homework for me, for which I was eternally grateful!

He spent a lot of time down at the chicken *hoks* raising his brood of chickens of which he knew all the different types and breeds. He loved music and I remember him always asking me if I'd heard the latest song being played on the radio. He loved Cliff Richard especially. He was always saying he that he wanted to hear me singing on the radio one day

He was a generous guy and always shared his tuck, which his mother used to bring him every Sunday, with us, so we never had to raid his locker!

His mom was a rather big lady, and I always professed that he took after his father, who ran a barber shop in Hillbrow and was more of Martin's build.

I never saw Martin or heard of him after he left the Arc, which was a year before I did, and if I'm not mistaken he went to university to study accountancy.

I heard that he had passed away in the late 1990's.

Max Goldman remembers bumping into Martin in the 1970's at Saturday night discos and that Martin ran his own disco called Cream Cheese.. Max always found Martin to be a true mensch.

Martin Katz (2nd from left) with Bessie Bortz, Manfred Stein, Julius Gordon and Hymie Aronoff in 1961

Jennifer and Elizabeth lived in the Arc for almost a decade. They were admitted in February 1956, soon after their mother died of multiple sclerosis. The sisters left in 1965 when their father remarried. Jennifer was in the Arc from the age of six to almost 16 and Lizzie from two to 12.

THE HOSPITAL-THE ARC'S FIRST PORT OF CALL

I lived for almost a full decade at the Arc: from the age of six to almost 16; from 60 days after my mom died till a few days after my dad's second marriage. With no conscious recall of my life before the Arc, that decade pretty much was my childhood and youth. And with so much of that time still blurry, those years shrink to random moments, snapshots that have somehow survived. Reading my admittance papers a few years ago brought home in the starkest way that the Arc had rescued us from a life of abject poverty. Without their intervention my baby sister and I might have been shunted between foster homes, or struggling relatives. Worse still we might have been adopted and so permanently separated from the father we adored.

Instead we went into the Arc. Suddenly, one morning in February 1956, I found myself in this strange and vast place. A skimpy list of our clothes on admittance is the only testimony to our arrival. Our toys weren't listed, but I know that I had a Raggedy Ann doll and a doll's pram that was soon ripped apart by some boys whose need for go-kart parts was obviously greater than my need for remnants of my past life. Or, as is more likely, they were simply stronger than me.

And on that fateful day, was Daddy allowed to stay a while, to see where we would be living, to take his leave slowly and gently? When I think of the effort that parents, and I among them, put into preparing our children for our first separation, such as the start of nursery school, and how many of them scream and fuss anyway, I wonder at our being left there. After all the whole thing had only been arranged a couple of days beforehand at a time when we were still reeling from my mother's death only two months earlier. My best guess is that Daddy would have been sent away as quickly as possible and we would have told to be good girls and wave him off. Who knows? Will I ever know?

Next we would have been led to the hospital for a week or two in quarantine. So the Arc's very own little hospital would have been our real port of entry. Here, Sister Conway and Ruth ruled the roost.

Sister was later to play quite a friendly role in my life, but for the moment, an anecdote of her telling is the only episode I can recount of that time. Her curiosity was aroused, so she told me, when she saw me sitting on the floor reading aloud from the newspaper. Her initial thought was that I couldn't possibly be reading fluently at that age, and she quietly came up behind me to check her suspicions. She was amazed to find that I was indeed reading, and not making up stories.

Elizabeth and Jennifer with their Dad

Isn't it funny how a physical environment can remain so strongly etched in memory? Clearly the brick and mortar still cover the pain trapped beneath. Thus I can lead you beneath the vine-covered trellis past the conservatory used as dance studio and the archway opening into the courtyard where Charlie the bus driver lived. We continue down a few rough stone steps, with rosebushes either side and finally up a couple of polished stairs into the hospital. Immediately on the right was the dispensary where we called in at the appointed hour for the occasional aspirin or bandaging of wounds. At times, of course, we'd really be sick with flu, sore throats, mumps, measles and other childhood diseases. At other times, to avoid exams or the submission dates of projects, or generally to have a bit of a rest from school and its impositions, each of us would have had our own particular talents in pretending illness.

At around the age of 12, I was diagnosed with hay fever. Luckily for me, the ear, nose and throat specialist on the Arc's medical panel only provided his services in the morning at his rooms in town, so I had an excuse to miss school every Wednesday morning for an entire year. The beauty of hay fever was that I could claim a cold if I wanted a hospital break, or

Sister Conway

held a perfectly folded hand towel and a facecloth. In the lower part of the locker we stored the hospital dressing gown we'd been issued, and any personal bits and pieces we might have had with us. But there was no privacy here - for the lockers were opened and checked as part of the daily ward inspection. Our slippers had to be tidily placed below the locker. The top of the locker had to be kept clear. Here Ruth would place the large washbowls first thing in the morning, as we weren't allowed out of bed if we had a temperature. Once all the bowls were distributed, Ruth would do the rounds with a large jug and fill each bowl with piping hot water. As the facecloth would be hanging on the far side of the locker, and thus out of our reach, she'd helpfully drop it into the bowl, check we had a cake of brick-red carbolic soap, and leave us to our morning wash.

Once we were clean, she could turn her attention to our beds. Sister and Ruth were clearly determined that the occupied beds would be as spick and span as the empty ones. The skill with which they could change the sheets from under our feverish bodies with fresh, heavily starched ones, without baring our bodies to the cold morning air, was an amazing feat in itself. Our role was to firmly hold the blankets as they efficiently tugged the sheets out. Once they were done we were so tightly tucked in we could barely move and had to wriggle our way to freedom by partially loosening the taut bedclothes.

Despite the hospital's pristine formality, we were spoilt during our stays there. Steaming hot cocoa and breakfast in bed on a freezing winter morning causes a wonderful sense of well-being and, in my case, could almost make the hated porridge palatable. I seem to remember a radio, and the chance of listening to daytime serials and, in those pre-television days, endless hours in which to read or play board games such as Monopoly, Ludo, or Snakes and Ladders. There might have been visits from Ma or Doc to break up the monotony of the day. And after a couple of days in bed, depending on the seriousness of the malady, when the thermometer returned a normal reading, we'd be allowed out of bed for a couple of hours. Then we could visit friends in other wards or perhaps wander out into the sunshine on the patio that stretched the length of the hospital.

I'm sure that dispensary queues were longest on Monday mornings and gradually shortened as the week progressed. By Thursday evening we'd all want to be shipshape for discharge

insist that I only had hay fever if I was really sick but wanted to avoid having to stay in hospital. And so, as with any craft, after a while I honed this skill to its full potential. While this knack may have got me into the hospital when I chose to be there, or out when I chose not to be there, it did leave a residue of manipulative tactics that took years to struggle off.

There was one awful summer where things were totally out of my control – mumps kept me confined throughout December so there was no holiday that year, and no cause for celebration of my birthday late in that month. Given the contagious nature of mumps, it's unlikely that I was the only one there for the duration.

Beyond the dispensary there was a kitchen, Sister Conway's own apartment, a fully equipped dental clinic, a doctor's examining room, two private rooms and four wards. The largest was a mixed ward for the younger children. The second ward, with its cubicles, was meant for more contagious illnesses. Next came a ward for the senior boys and the last of the four was the domain for the Senior Girls.

But whichever ward you were in, was spotless! If only today's impoverished National Health Service looked as good: High hospital beds that must have been regularly repainted to maintain their perfect gloss; fat pillows in crisp pillowcases at the head of each bed; immaculate white counterpanes, with not a crease in sight were tightly tucked in at the base of beds, then their precisely folded corners smoothed into a 45 degree drop to a straight line hiding the bed's steel frames.

Ruth, Sister Conway's assistant would have done brilliantly in the army. That place sparkled. The under-shelf of the bedside lockers held an array of nursing paraphernalia, such as kidney-shaped stainless steel dishes for spitting out after brushing our teeth. A light blue plastic drinking cup matched the Arc's insignia and blue stripe woven into the counterpane. A side rail

The Wolf Hillman Hospital

on Friday, so if you still had a temperature you had to tamper with the thermometer during the evening's ward round. One way, of course, was to whip it out of your mouth if Sister or Ruth turned away. Or wriggle it about in your mouth to get it above rather than below your tongue. But they knew the tricks as well as we did so, on occasion, a weekend in hospital would have been inevitable. It was probably more the fear of missing the Saturday night film than aspirin and cough mixture that got us well by week's end

THE ARC

How clear the buildings and the landscape have remained in my mind. If only my memories of my parents, the chain of events that brought me to the Arc, and my companions and experiences while in the Arc had survived in equal measure. With absolutely no effort I can see the many different staircases in the main building, the enormous kitchen with its locked and bolted walk-in fridge, and the shiny steel cooking vats. On the senior girls' floor, upstairs in the main building, the dormitories and verandahs, one open, one enclosed for lunch and homework, are as clear to me today as if I had photographs in front of me.

I can visualise the sandstone colour of the dining room stone walls, see out through the tall windows to the black iron of the fire escape coming down form the girls' verandah, where you'd be sure to see our school bloomers and shirts hung out to dry every Wednesday and Friday afternoon. I can almost smell the wonderful aroma of the apple-green cake of Sunlight soap as we scrubbed at those granny bloomers and dirty collars trying to ignore our grumbling bellies, for the ritual was pre-ordained: laundry first, lunch last.

I can picture the long curving driveway along which Charlie, our friendly, smiling driver, drove us to school every day in the big blue and silver Mac bus, with its bulldog emblem. I went to Saxonwold Primary and later, Parktown Girls' High. Good schools, but then we lived in such a good neighbourhood. What a paradox – to live in an orphanage, in a stately aristocratic home, with the country's wealthiest family, the Oppenheimers, as neighbours! I have always been careful to explain that 'my' orphanage was a very far cry from the Dickensian one that we all know so well from Oliver Twist's sorry tale, but that doesn't make it any closer to having been a warm and loving home. It couldn't be. There's no replacement for dead parents and dismantled homes, but certainly our physical needs were well taken care of. Painful emotions and traumatic residue were never, to the best of my knowledge, treated or even acknowledged. We just got on with it, as children do, and survived.

Out beyond the main gates was the wide sweep of Oxford Road. When I was young, the driveway down to the entrance gates seemed never-ending. I think the gates usually stood open, but their being open was an illusion of freedom, for they kept us in more strongly than if they had been ten feet tall, chained and guarded by human and canine patrol. Bunking out, and there was plenty of that, wasn't via the main gates. We had quieter corners, walls and forgotten side gates far from Ma's all-seeing eyes. We needed our escape routes to freedom. How weak and unreliable today's smart security cameras are in

comparison to those eyes. Ma had a knack of crinkling them until they all but disappeared into the folds of her heavy eyelids. It seemed that the more her eyes narrowed to wafer-thin slits, the more she was able to see into our souls, and discover what we were desperately trying to hide. For example, on Saturday evenings, once supper and Shul were over, and Shabbat safely behind us for another week, we'd convert the cavernous dining room into a cinema hall. Two tidy columns of seats, boys on one side, girls on the other, firmly separated by a wide central aisle down which Ma would patrol. To the casual visitor it might have looked as if she was generously distributing hard-boiled sweets from the paper-lined brown carton she held. But we all knew that she was far more concerned with scrutinising our faces for any signs of guilt, of having crossed the dividing aisle under cover of darkness. Ma never let up.

There were several storerooms in the main building, all carefully bolted. We only gained access, one at a time, to try on donated clothes, some new, some used, under Ma's scrutiny. Then there was the dressmaker's eyrie. A steeped bright and airy attic with vistas to three sides: towards the main entrance, the narrower road curving up from the kitchen archway to the dairy and servants block at the top of the hill, and to the wildly overgrown area jutting over the open expanse in front of the impressive front doors to the mansion. But we girls weren't in that room to look at the view.

We were there, probably by appointment, to view the heavy McCall's books of summer and winter patterns from whose pages and Mrs Saphier's scissors, our Pesach and Rosh Hashanah dresses would emerge. For we girls were allowed to choose the dress of our dreams from the glossy pictures, select the material of our choice from bales piled high on the cutting table. Our tailored dresses were finished with hand-made accessories: covered buttons and belts and pretty lace trim. I remember that we were often disappointed, thinking that the finished garments never looked as good as the modelled versions. A recent discovery of an old colour slide led me to rethink that idea. I looked at that beautiful photograph of Daddy, Liz and me (I must have been about 14 at the time), arm-in-arm in front of a synagogue that I haven't been able to identify, and I am amazed at how beautiful that dress was and how perfectly it had been tailored to my petite frame. How sophisticated and graceful it made me look! Clearly that picture disproved any doubt as to the talents and professionalism of Mrs Saphier, our Belgian seamstress. She spent such long hours alone in that backwater and continued, despite our lack of appreciation, to turn out endless dresses as if she were still in Brussels, working priceless Belgian lace.

PORRIDGE

I wonder if anyone else remembers this in the same way. I do remember David Sandler saying that he loved the porridge so obviously my experience was pretty extreme. Any others feel the same?

Castor oil and other such childhood remedies have lodged firmly in my mind, and in my taste buds. Milk of Magnesia, that revoltingly thick white compound had the most amazing resemblance to whitewash. If the two were put to a taste test, I doubt they could be told apart. To avoid confusion, and the risk of poisoning, Milk of Magnesia came in a thick blue glass bottle from which it was carefully measured into a tablespoon, and then into our defenceless mouths.

But at least these remedies were not part of the daily menu. Jungle Oats most definitely was. Here in London, almost half a century later, I find it incredible that people actually choose to cook porridge every morning or even savour it as a weekend treat. Clearly, porridge has come a long way. I remember Jungle Oats (Quaker Oats) as a warm, grey, lumpy, gluey mass of heavy gruel. Oat husks were strategically hidden, ready to lodge themselves between our teeth or jab our palates. One way or another, the husks were difficult to dislodge and anathema to my sensitive taste buds. This heavy-duty material clearly belonged in a cement mixer, and should never have reached the table. I doubt that Oliver Twist would have asked for seconds!

On Saturdays, we had Corn Flakes or Rice Crispies. These were definitely a vast improvement on the mid-week alternative as long as one was quick enough to prevent the cereal being drowned under Hot milk that would turn it into a soft cardboard mash. A minor issue compared to the Oats. Occasionally, we'd have *Maltabella,* a chocolate-coloured porridge that had a distinctive sandy, gravel-like consistency that would have worked well with the Oats in the cement mixer! But at least *Maltabella* had a finer texture and gravel was easier to consume than nasty, sharp husks. *Mielie-meal* was probably the best of the hot breakfast bunch.

Ma took a very personal interest in everything we did. And our eating habits were no exception. Indeed I believe she nurtured my dislike of porridge into full-blown hatred. She followed my progress, or rather lack of it, with an eagle eye. In my experience, breakfast was a battleground and I was rarely victorious. What battles of will we had: Ma determined to get the entire bowl of porridge into my stomach; I was equally determined to sabotage her plans. So I spooned the stuff around, this way and that, trying to reduce its volume, hoping that I'd be able to outsmart Ma who, no matter where she was on her patrol of the vast dining room, could always be relied on to turn around at the very moment I had convinced one of the staff to take the brimming bowl away.

She of course had power on her side. For even if a kind member of staff managed to sneak my bowl off the table without being observed that was not the end of ordeal. To carry off the whole thing successfully, he would have to juggle the plates and get mine away from its top-of-the-pile visibility where it could still be spotted and returned.

On a school day, I had a better chance of making an escape, as Ma would not have prevented me from catching the school bus. I suspect it suited her purpose to turn a blind eye now and then. But during school holidays, time was on her side and there was no escape. I could be detained all morning, and all day too, until that bowl was empty. But knowing the score didn't make things any easier. Left alone, the breakfast things long cleared away, I could do no more than stare rebelliously into that hated grey glue. Occasionally Ma would take pity on me and compromise on two or three more spoonfuls, then set me free. More often than not she would insist that I finish the full portion under her gaze. A growing pile of sharp-pointed husks

in the bowl was testimony to the struggle, and proof of my princess-like fastidiousness. Had I enjoyed porridge more, and eaten it without fuss, I might have grown beyond the under-developed and thus painfully shy teenager that I was. I wonder now how much it was the porridge, and how much the rigidity and enforcement that set my teeth on edge. Both, I expect.

SHUL AT THE ARC

I wonder if the synagogue existed when Lord Phillips owned Villa Arcadia or if this building beyond the library, the fishpond and the open courtyard was a later addition. The smooth pillars on all four sides of the courtyard looked quite the same so I suspect the building was part of the original design but probably had a different purpose. For us, it was Shul.

Howard Ginsberg and Harry Kuperberg carrying the Torah

We spent so much time in the Shul's rich brown pews that we were absolutely familiar with every grain of wood. Here, as elsewhere, and perhaps a symptom of the times, separation of the sexes, and a most distinct hierarchy were the order of the day. Girls sat to one side of the central aisle with Ma occupying the first seat in the back row. The rest of the back row belonged to the most senior of the girls with ever younger and thus less important girls filling up each of the other rows towards the aisle, with the youngest filling the first row, immediately opposite the boys. In total, the girls only filled one section of seats. Two further sections stood empty most of the year but were used by visitors on the festivals and the old-Arcs who sometimes attended our Saturday morning services.

Opposite us girls, although I think they filled more than one section, were the boys. Again, ranging through the ages, youngest to the front rising in height and seniority to the back row. The boys of course had Fickey, who had a long, long time previously been an Arc boy himself. Fickey, unusually, had chosen to return to the Arc as a resident housemaster and part-time Latin tutor and so became a permanent fixture of the boys' existence. He took his supervisory role most seriously.

So Fickey, in a way was Ma's counterpart over on the boys' side. Fickey, however, did not stay put in a back seat as Ma did. He wandered about to check that all the boys were behaving themselves. But it was Doc who was star performer in our Shul. With a black flowing cassock over his suit, he restlessly strode about like a majestic lion, king of his domain. There was no doubt that he presided over the whole house. The Siddur seemed so small in his large hands, and though I seem to recall that he often had a finger holding the book open, he had no need to read its contents. I have no doubt that he knew every prayer and hymn by heart. Occasionally, to set us straight, he might open the Siddur to point out which page and verse we should have been attentive to, and the humorous look on his face and the twinkle in his eyes as he did so matched the performance of greater names than his from London's stage, or Hollywood's silver screen.

Doc was a character. A charismatic, intelligent and revered figurehead who could have presided in absolute fairness over any court in the land. A somewhat straggly moustache and a jauntily set beret, replaced by a black yarmulka in Shul and at meals, completed the picture.

Ma, in contrast, was of medium-height, with dark hair and eyes, well-tailored suits and a good collection of hats, invariably small, almost bonnet-sized. Most of all it was her hair that lent severity to her looks. For her hairstyle never changed. Parted in the middle and tightly pulled back into a thin plait that was twisted into a bun and the whole pinned low at the base of her head.

Ma's eyes were almost black. Doc's eyes seemed to twinkle and crinkle in endless humour, whereas hers seemed to almost disappear into their sockets.

Doc's great height and the sense of barely bridled power he imparted were softened by his humour and warmth. It would have been difficult to match his warmth, intellectual curiosity and affability. Ma's personality was probably over-shadowed by his larger than life one.

With hindsight, I suspect that Doc was so wrapped up in philosophy and theology that he blissfully lived on high with G-d and our biblical forefathers, leaving Ma with the practicalities and disciplinary aspects of all our lives.

As to our attendance at Shul, we girls got off relatively lightly - not out of any favouritism, merely in accordance with Jewish Orthodox practices. We certainly had to attend Shul every Friday evening and every Saturday morning and evening too.

And then there were the High Holy Days as well as every major and minor festival and fast day in the Jewish calendar. Once the boys had been Barmitzvah, they had to attend Shul on a daily basis. They enveloped themselves in the mystery of Tallit and Tefillin, learned how to open and read the Torah, and carefully roll it up again. They were allowed to open the Ark, remove the velvet and gold-bedecked scrolls and slowly carry them down the aisle towards the Bimah with Doc proudly bringing up the rear, beaming like a patriarch seeing a favourite son bearing his newborn son in his arms. In religious ceremony we girls, in the traditional orthodox way, played a smaller part.

The Arc Shul

Despite all its solemnity, the Shul offered opportunity for fun and even matchmaking. As the Torah scrolls were borne along the aisle to and from the Ark, we were allowed, indeed expected, to stretch out our fingertips to touch and kiss the sacred objects. If you happened to sit in the front row, you could just about reach the passing parade, although you often had to call out to attract the Torah bearers back from the boys' side. For the rest of us, seated out of reach of the aisle, we had the opportunity to spill out and mill about, ostensibly to touch the Torah scrolls, and I'm sure we did that too, for we held them in awe. But it was also the perfect opportunity to mingle with the boys and try to get closer to our current favourite. Sometimes it took quite an effort on Ma's part to restore order and get us all back to our seats and allow the service to continue.

Most fun of all, aside from Purim, was probably the Saturday night Havdalah service. It was undoubtedly one of the high romantic spots of the week when a boy and a girl would be called upon to come up to the Bimah and hold a lighted candle during the reading of the evening's prayers.

Havdalah Service with Gary Creighton, Minnie Baitz, David Sandler and Michael Goldstein with his back to us

Here there was plenty of opportunity for matchmaking and Doc played along gamely. At times, he would have been primed in advance so that when he called up a couple, they would be greeted with hoots of laughter from the young congregation. At other times, Doc would pretend that he had no idea who to call upon and there would be lots of whispered suggestions as he bent his head behind the wide sleeve of his cassock, avidly listening to suggestions. It wasn't all fun and games though. At times, it could be very embarrassing as for example when a 'friend' had divulged someone's secret longing and suddenly this passion became public knowledge. Worse was to come when everyone would laugh at the absurdity of such an unlikely match. But once up on that Bimah, enjoying the pleasurable warmth of fresh wax in the palm of one's hand, all embarrassment would be washed away. All our attention was taken up as we tilted the candle over as far as it would go to get as much wax in as little time as possible, without the flame dying. For here was real achievement: taking copious amounts of wax back to your seat! Sometimes we might share the wax with a friend, or repay a 'debt. Either way, it was a prize to show off. I wonder how many 'couples' came about by virtue of this Saturday evening ceremony.

ARC PETS

I was and remain a great animal lover. Ma was definitely aware of this – for I was the proud recipient of a pair of jodhpurs found among the used clothing donated to the Arc. More importantly, when two Kerry Blue puppies were donated to the Arc, I was more or less given charge of them, or so I thought. I wonder now if others didn't see Sooty and Lucky as being under their charge. Their warm, plump bodies and blue-back curls made them delightful and cuddly friends.

We had to collect their food from the main kitchen. Once I decided that the food the cook spooned into the dog dishes wouldn't appeal to them and, without further ado, began to tip the food back from the dog bowls into the cooking pot, into our dinner. Ma caught me in the act (she had that uncanny knack of appearing at all the wrong moments) and nearly blew her top. I couldn't understand what all the fuss was about as I'd washed the dogs' bowls. It just didn't occur to me that the spurned offering was no longer clean (or kosher!) enough to rejoin our food! I don't know how readily Ma had agreed to accept the pups, but I'm sure that on that day she must have regretted any momentary softness in having done so. My crime began with my entering the kitchen as I should have stayed on its outer edges, beyond the long stainless steel tables and never even approached the vast cookers.

At weekends and holidays we bunked out. We couldn't go very far because of the rigid structure to the day. There were no shops nearby, so either we had to jump over the gate at the furthermost corner of the Arc's grounds and head down to the shop at the zoo, which was tricky because you had to get in to the zoo first or, depending on the season, wander around the neighbourhood filching fruit off the neighbours' trees, a risky and not necessarily rewarding prank.

I remember mulberry bushes in the Arc grounds but with so many fruit-pickers about, there would have been little opportunity for the black berries to fully ripen. But at least they provided plenty of leaves to feed the silkworms that many of us kept, as I did for a season or two. These were fascinating and very busy little creatures. For all my fear and repugnance of insects, silkworms were in a class of their own. I could spend hours watching them chomping away at the mulberry leaves I picked for them, watching their warm round little bodies move, segment by segment, across the leaf, hunching up the middle section of their flexible bodies in camel-like humps to move across from leaf to leaf. I never lost the fascination of watching them spin themselves away into bright golden cocoons tenuously held across the corner of a shoebox by a few strands of bright golden thread.

Pet white mice weren't too bad either – although not quite tempting enough to keep any of my own. Some of the boys did and, to show they fancied you, they would allow you to hold a mouse in the palm of your hand and feel how ticklish its feet and whiskers were against your skin. All well and good for a few minutes, hopefully to be handed back before it urinated on your hand, because the strong smell of their urine was vile.

And then there were the rabbits. As I ruled the canine world, so Raymond Lang ruled the rabbit kingdom. These were actually wild rabbits in captivity, enormous grey and brown creatures held in a large hutch of concrete, bricks and mesh to which Raymond held the keys.

On a trip to town to the dentist, when I was old enough to be allowed out alone on the bus, I visited the pet shop at the bus terminus. Pet shops were probably top of my list of favourite shopping places anyway. On that particular day, I fell in love with a small black bunny, bearing an amazing resemblance to Pookie, the bunny hero of one of my favourite childhood books. I couldn't resist, and bought the animal naming her Pookie as I extracted her from her cage and took her snuggling in my arms to the cash desk and onto the bus. Bunnies make delightful pets, soft, cuddlesome, cute. I could spend ages watching her kick her way around the dormitory. I especially loved the feel of the carpet-like underbrush to her paws that allowed her to confidently leap around on the polished floors without mishap. Except of course for the mishaps of nature – for bunnies, cute as they are, will insist on leaving piles of shiny little black marbles of shit and puddles of urine that reek of ammonia. And so, giving in to the complaints of my dormitory mates, I eventually had to find a new home for my illegal resident. Obviously, Raymond was my first port of call, and so my sweet, delicate little pet joined the rough and tumble of the rabbit hutch where, as rabbits do, she was soon carrying young.

I spent a lot of time with Pookie down at the hutch, but gradually she became less tame and was soon part of the wilder bunch. A painful incident brought my rabbit period to an abrupt and unforeseen end. I had foolishly ignored all the hints from a large grey buck that he had no interest in being stroked. I tried to hold on to him, despite his growing animosity and suddenly he had sunk his great big rabbit teeth into the little finger of my left hand, making several deep and dirty gashes into the flesh. In pain, and quite frightened, I knew I had to get this properly treated but I had to do this without casting any slurs on the rabbits that would risk their expulsion from the Arc. That would have been too high a price for Raymond to have to pay for my silly stubbornness.

How on earth was I going to explain these horrible deep gashes that radiated all around my finger in such curious fashion? I headed off to the hospital, cupping my throbbing hand and developing my story as I went: I had chosen a place to sit down in some long grass and as I put my hands down to support myself, I had, or so I would explain, put my hand into a pile of broken glass and this was the outcome. Sister was no fool, and she and I had a special relationship thanks to our Wednesday escapades, so she accepted my story at its face value and doused the cuts well with antiseptic without any further interrogation. Later, I laughed at the thought of 'glass' jumping out of grass to 'bite' in such peculiar fashion. I still bear the scars and my finger is a little crooked, but the rabbits were safe.

Pets were warm and loving without any of the paradoxes of human relationship. Much as I loved the Kerry Blues, this didn't stop me rescuing a farm mutt when the occasion arose. We had all been out on a picnic on a farm at the Vaal River. I think it was organised and sponsored by the Vereniging Jewish Community and we'd all looked forward to the outing. There were games and races and boat rides and plenty to eat, probably a *braaivleis* too. The smell of cooking meat had attracted both children and dogs from the native kraal and a young scrawny dog, all skinny legs and slapping tail took my

fancy. With brown and orange patches on his otherwise white short coat and the saddest brown eyes imaginable Patches' charm outweighed any practical deterrents, such as his flea and tick inhabitants, or the difficulty of hiding a hyper-active animal of that size on a bus to 'sneak' back to the Arc. And yet I did it. I rescued Patches from that hot, arid kraal where the sparse food supply chain didn't stretch down to the lower rungs of the puppy kingdom. Thus Patches moved to suburbia, to start a new life in posh Parktown. Ma could not have been too impressed, but somehow the dog stayed on and grew up although he didn't remain at the Arc very long. I don't remember how his end came about.

And then there were horses. Not that the Arc ran to horses (why not I wonder, after all we had tennis courts, a swimming pool, and many other trappings of wealthy homes). Fortunately, our neighbours the Oppenheimers had several nearby. They could be visited in their field along a quiet tree-lined road just beyond the Arc wall, below the tennis courts. Adella Lozinski was definitely a partner to this particular crime, and there were others. Lucky and Sooty enjoyed coming along too but their interest lay elsewhere – in the horse droppings rather than stroking the soft fuzz of the horses' noble noses. It was here that I suffered my second injury at the Arc – although fortunately this wasn't related to the horses themselves. We'd been running along the road towards their field, building up speed, probably swept along by a sense of freedom and the exhilarating touch of a brisk wind. Suddenly, I found myself sprawled flat out on the road from where I picked myself up with a bloody knee. Mopping up the blood, I discovered a couple of deep holes that would clearly need the attention of Sister Conway. These wounds took weeks and weeks of regular doses of nasty yellow powder (was it an antibiotic or merely antiseptic?) and endless bandage changes, leaving scars that are visible to this day. I have no recall of the story that I must have told to explain this injury. Obviously it was far too flimsy to survive.

Ma had to have known of my love of animals. How else can I explain my luck in being sent off for holidays to a delightful family that owned a dairy and racehorse farm on the outskirts of Johannesburg? I think I spent more than one holiday with them. In fact, they lived so close to town that my dad occasionally took Liz and me to visit them on our Sundays out, forging his own friendship with them. Certainly, they gave me one or two holidays to remember. I had ample opportunity to study the racehorses in their boxes, and I loved watching the early morning training sessions in which they were put through their paces and coaxed into entering new-fangled starting gates. My dad of course was definitely aware of my love of animals and somehow, for a couple of years, came up with the money for riding lessons on our Sundays out.

All that remained of those years was my copy of Black Beauty with my dad's handwritten inscription, a present from him for my tenth birthday that I carried around the world on my many migrations. Finally, almost forty years later, sketchy memories of childhood emerge here and there.

THE RAND SHOW

Well into the 1960s, we were taken to the Rand Show every year - or rather we were each given a handful of free tickets for the rides in the Amusement Park (I think this was based on age - there was always a hierarchy involved) and then dropped off at the entrance and pretty much left to our own devices. Such freedom! I don't think we were much interested in the agricultural and industrial exhibitions (that's what the Rand Show was about wasn't it?) but spent all our time deliberating about how to make the tickets last as long as possible on the rides.

The Whip was an easy choice for a scaredy cat like me - but I did eventually manage to overcome my fear of heights and risk the Roller Coaster and my fear of ghosts and ride the Ghost Train... Not so the Dive-Bomber, I never set foot in that. Also there was that Fly Wall - where the whole thing was spun around like a human Mixmaster and as it slowed you were sort of glued to the walls by (I assume) centrifugal force. But I must confess that I left that ride to people of more scientific bent, or braver heart.

Candy floss, multi-coloured popcorn, and toffee apples were absolutely irresistible fairground delicacies if you had enough pocket money to buy any, and horrible torment if you didn't.

AFTERNOON SHIFT

Most of our Bat Mitzah preparations took place at the Arc. But we also had to sit the public exam at Johannesburg's central Synagogue. In addition to the new Pesach and Rosh Hashanah dresses made for us every year, a special dress was made for each of us in our Batmitzvah year. I had my Batmitzvah with Brenda Stein, Jenny Sandler and Hannah Goldstein. I've got no idea if we somehow collectively chose the bluish-green felt-like cloth from which our dresses were cut, or if this was standard Batmitzvah issue. When I look at those photographs now, I'm intrigued by the minor variations on the common style, some piping, slight differences in the collar shape, and the position of the covered buttons. More impressive still were the white gloves and white satin yarmulkes we wore on the big day. Actually, there were two big days - our day in Shul and our star performance at the Prize Giving ceremony that year.

In Shul, we each had an extract to recite from the scriptures. Here 'A woman of worth who can find, for her price is far above

rubies?' is still firmly entrenched in memory although for the life of me I don't know if it was the piece I recited or that of Brenda, Jenny or Hannah.

Aside from the religious aspects of the Batmitzvah, the year we turned twelve also gave us the opportunity, along with the 13 year old boys celebrating their Barmitzvahs, to get centre-stage at the Arc's annual prize-giving day to which all parents and committee members were invited. With a long table of dignitaries there to lend solemnity and perhaps funds to the occasion, we four took to the stage in our new dresses, white gloves, and white satin yarmulkes firmly clipped to our shoulder-length hair. All four of us wore our hair lightly teased and either glamorously flicked up or smoothed under in a sleek pageboy look.

And so, with just the right match of seriousness and glamour, we took to the stage for the prize-giving event. In turn, we stepped up to the microphone to say a few rehearsed words of thanks. No doubt it was all pretty formulaic: thanks for all we had learned, and been given in preparation for the Mitzvah. Were the yarmulkes a regular feature or did we four uniquely choose them? Certainly they would have been almost as chic as a Jackie Kennedy type pillbox hat and, firmly clipped to our hair, they did lend an extra touch of sophistication. But why on earth we wore white gloves, I have no idea. Perhaps it was to protect our hands as we moved along the line of dignitaries, nodding politely by way of response to their words, perhaps adding a few of our own to make the moment a reciprocal diplomatic exchange. And then at the end of the long platform we received our 'prize'- the real reason, as far as we were concerned, for all the fuss.

Whatever was packed into that schoolgirl suitcase remains shrouded in the mists of time. I would guess that it contained our Batmitzvah certificate, our exam results, maybe our own personal copy of the Siddur. Certainly they would have contained a book or two chosen for their enriching suitability. I seem to recall a wristwatch too. But a Batmitzvah was a one-off occurrence. Learning Hebrew was not.

Being blessed from left to right: Jennifer, Hannah Goldstein, Brenda Stein, Jenny Sandler, Paul Cohen, Hilton Rothaus and Boris Sedacca.

*Hebrew Classes with G'veret Sher on left and Gerber on right
Front row: Les Durbach, Keith Lang, Jennifer and Henry Shippel
Back Row: Unknown, Hymie Aronoff, Unknown,
Jenny Sandler and Brenda Stein.*

Hebrew was an integral and compulsory part of our lives throughout each school year. Three, perhaps even four afternoons a week we attended classes according to our different levels of progress. Doc could be likened to Chancellor of the Arcadia Hebrew campus. He had a team of three teachers who reigned in the three classrooms located below the Shul. Hebrew, as the modern incarnation of the ancient biblical language was seen as part of our Jewish education. It carried no hidden political agenda. Indeed, the Arc avoided any political stance and so we had nothing to do with Zionist Youth Movements. We cared little for Hebrew lessons, probably because we had so little free time and these classes took up such a big chunk of our afternoons. They took their toll with exams and report cards and years of study.

For me, at least, those Hebrew classes more than proved their worth when I went to Israel at 18 and could enjoy the fruits of all that grammar and vocabulary building. My conscience stung terribly when I first visited the beautiful Hullah Valley. As I toured the area, enjoying its rich bird life and the shade of the eucalyptus trees planted by pioneers to reclaim the precious valley, a picture of Mr Shalit, one of our Arc Hebrew teachers sprang to mind. For Mr Shalit had been one of those pioneers, contracting malaria for his efforts. He was lucky to have survived and I think it cost him his hearing.

I am sure that there were many afternoons, struggling with his hearing aid and a class full of cruelly inconsiderate pupils, me included, who cared not an iota for his story or his place in history. In those moments, I am sure he must have regretted coming anywhere near the Arc! I wonder if he ever heard that I went to live in Israel and finally came to appreciate his teaching and enjoy the fruits of his sacrifice! I do hope so.

As I said, we had very little free time. After school ended, at 2.00 pm perhaps even 3.00 pm once we were in high school, and later still if we had compulsory sports on the agenda, we were bussed back to the Arc. Before we could get a bite to eat, we had to deal with the daily chores. These were a rigid daily imposition, fluctuating with the seasons and growing ever more time-consuming as we scaled the hierarchical ladder. During the winter months of our high school years, we had to wash our long-sleeved cotton shirts, woollen stockings and thick school bloomers every Wednesday and Friday.

All this in addition to our underwear which we washed every evening and hung on the rail at the side of our lockers to dry. The summer blouses and winter shirts were heavy-duty work. We used Sunlight soap and a scrubbing brush to remove the thick line of dirt that formed on collars and cuffs. No easy task after having worn them for three days. We had to wash them in a small hand basin, rinse them and hang them out on the line to dry before we could get any lunch. In the evening, or more often, quite late at night after finishing our homework, we'd still have to iron our shirts, perhaps polish our shoes. From time to time we had to press the school gym and tie as well. No casual jeans and crumpled T-shirts for us in those days!

Lunch would be carried up from the kitchen and was often a bit of a free for all, followed by either a Hebrew lesson, or homework to prepare. Ma or Doc, or perhaps a member of the Committee, would drop in to see if anyone needed a helping hand. There were also courses on offer at different times -

ballet classes took place with Carole on Sunday mornings and we were all expected to be there at the appointed hour according to our age and ability.

Other classes seemed to have a shorter shelf life, or perhaps it was my notorious lack of commitment and life-long disinterest in physical exercise. On the musical side, I only remember piano lessons. I also remember giving them up with - or so it seemed at the time - good reason. In a battle of will with the piano teacher, I thought I'd won when she insisted I cut my fingernails short or give up the piano. I kept the long nails then, and the regret now at not being able to read music or play a musical instrument.

Deportment classes, with Renee Lacey and her son, founders of Johannesburg's best-known School of Deportment, were a passing fancy - probably theirs more than ours. Outdoors, we had tennis lessons but those I remember in my junior years, and I never really took to the sport. I could never hit a ball. And there was no shortage of opportunity to try to do so on the Arc's or Parktown Girls' many sports fields. For South Africans, sport was high on the curriculum. Swimming pools were standard issue at every school, as were umpteen tennis and netball courts, gymnasia and hockey fields.

And I'm only talking about the girls' schools here. The boys probably had even more facilities. For a pint-sized shrinking violet like myself, far more at home in my head than in my body, each and every one of these was a cleverly devised system of torture. I became quite adept at finding creative ways to avoid as many as possible. Swimming at least had some merit in a hot climate. But I preferred to keep my face out of the water, and my eyes open. The crawl stroke was therefore a slow struggle, with all my energy going into breathing. This meant that little energy actually reached my legs where it was most needed to propel me to the far side of the pool. No wonder I was invariably last to reach the far side in the Arc galas as, with eyes tightly shut, I had no chance of keeping a straight line or of reaching a pre-determined 'there'. When it came to diving for coins at the end of the gala, I had no hope. What with breathing in, pinching my nose, closing my eyes, and planning my dive immediately above a coin, by the time I actually got going all the coins had been collected. My dad would throw in a couple just for me when it was all over. Finally, in high school, I took a life-saving class, which I quite enjoyed. Fortunately, I've never been called on to test its value. It probably earned me some brownie points with the game's teacher and that was no small feat.

Netball, back at primary school, actually opened the door to my first catering experience.

When it was recognised that I brought no added value to the team, I was dispatched to the kitchen. There I could concentrate on carefully cutting oranges into eighths so that all pith was removed from their centres and they could easily be eaten out of their skins by the sweaty players at quarter and half-time. How nice it would have been if the warm welcome had been for me instead of for the tray of refreshing oranges I carried onto the court. With sport being high on every school's agenda, our teachers had obviously realised that we could sneak off after school and avoid the compulsory afternoon sports sessions. Thus we got gym classes, swimming, hockey

Netball Practice: Anne Flink, ?, Sandra Markus, Ma, ?, Brenda Stein, Jennifer Fliess, Rosalind Kupferberg and Janice Blumberg

and more interspersed between classes in English, French and Maths.

Escape was virtually impossible. How I hated the gym, with its ladders and ropes, mats and wooden horses, and its game's mistresses roaring at us to do better, try harder, move faster. Given a choice between sport and Hebrew, I would have gone for the latter every time. Maybe that's why my Hebrew is so good!

AFTER LEAVING THE ARC

Liz and I left the Arc in the middle of 1965 after $9^1/_2$ years there. I was six and she was two when our mother died and two months later we were residing at 22 Oxford Road. I don't remember visiting after leaving. Liz seems to have kept up contact more than me.

I finished high school at the end of 1966, learned to type, worked in Johannesburg for nine months and then went off to Israel for the whole of 1968. On the 31st March 1969, just three months after my return from my year in Israel, my father died --- he never went to Israel. In those three months, I met the guy I would marry and we got engaged within weeks of our first meeting. Then, a couple of weeks later, my dad died and I

turned to the Arc for a bit of financial help. I was only 19 so we went to court and my then fiancé got guardianship of Liz so we could all get passports. I got married two months later and we all left South Africa for Israel by the end of 1969. Liz finished high school and went to the army.

My three children - Ilan, Tali and Michal – were all born in Israel. I later divorced, and after living in Israel for the best part of 30 years, moved alone to England in 1997.

Liz also has three children – Sagit, Ronen and Na'ama. She's married to David Bar Mouha. They live in Menahemya, a village in the Jordan Valley.

Jenny with her Dog

369

Chapter 99 – NEVILLE MERWITZ (1950)

Neville was born in 1950. He was placed in the care of Arcadia in 1955 and lived there until he finished his schooling in approximately 1967.

Neville Merwitz was a character who stood out. He was a fantastic yarn spinner and could embellish any story. He also really knew how to tell a joke and would keep us all, including the senior boys, entertained for hours with his jokes, his mimicking and his endless repertoire of humour.

Our Saturday morning soccer games were sometimes interrupted by injuries, mainly kicks sustained. While many injuries were genuine, no doubt many an Oscar would have been won by 'injured' players. The best actor I think was Neville and his acting was also extended to saving and even more so to 'trying to save' goals when he was a goalie.

Not only was he skilful in entertaining us but he was very skilled in making things and experimenting. I remember him making a blowpipe, peashooter, catty, a pipe contraption that shot arrows, converting some sheepskin he found on a dead sheep into a beautiful clean sheepskin, pouring lead into shapes in a boiler and making perspex knick-knacks.

He was also part of the band with Julius Gordon and played the mouth organ. He explained to me in intricate detail how he was going to get a falcon and train it to catch birds and all the things he needed to look after it. He was able to turn his talents to many many things.

I remember Neville at Jewish Government School in the late 1950s and his Mom used to visit him before school and bring him something to eat and then would wash his hands.

LEARNING HOW TO SHOP
Written by David Sandler

After school we also had free time in grade one and two as we finished school before the other classes. Also we had free time as we waited for the Arc bus. This gave us the chance to look around and go shopping.

I remember Neville showing me a shining silver half crown (two and six) and persuading me to come to the shop with him and 'he'd buy me something'. Just before we got to the shop he revealed that it was 'only a penny (covered in silver paper) so he could not *opps* (give) me.

Neville "making things"
Looking on (L-R) Brian Sandler, David Lipschitz, David Sandler, Max Goldman and Offer Fein.

On one occasion when I was five I had two or three pennies and was going to go to the corner cafe to buy some penny lines

Now having two or three pennies was a big thing for a five year old in 1957 and I must have told all the other Arcs and was duly given instructions on how to buy sweets.

My instructor was Neville Merwitz who was a few years older than me. (Or was it Hilton Rothaus or Paul Cohen?)

The instructions were as follows: Go to the shop and sit down in front of the penny lines. Look at all the penny lines and choose very very slowly what you want. When the shopkeeper is not looking put some down your shirt. I went off to buy sweets and followed the instructions and was successful on two occasions.

On the third attempt a boy who was in my class at school spotted me stealing and told the shopkeeper. The shopkeeper was very angry and threatened to call the police and took the sweets out of my shirt front, missing the sweets that had gone to the back of my shirt.

He let me go. I was crying and never stole from that shop again. I was relieved that the boy in my class never told it as "*News*" in the class the next day.

NEVILLE MERWITZ
Written by Boris Sedacca

Neville Merwitz was like a big *boetie* to me at the Arc, especially from the time he carried me off to hospital when I broke my arm. Boy, did he tell some fantastic yarns!

The best one I remember is about his 'out of body' experience. He told me he was so good at playing dead that he once like, stepped out of his body, and while people were standing around him trying to revive him, he just stood there laughing behind their backs. He used to fashion things from very basic items, and because he was so good at manual work he decided to take up diamond cutting and finished his apprenticeship, but then moved on to other things. By some twist of fate he happened to meet a cousin of mine who still lives in South Africa, and they used to go parachuting! Nev always wanted to be a parabat, and used to tell the most amazing stories about them.

RUNNING AWAY FROM THE ARC
Written by Max Goldman for Neville

Me, Brian Socher and Arnold (Bear) Salmonson decided to run away from the Arc.

We chose to leave after lunch on a visiting Sunday as that would give us lots of time before the alarm was raised, not forgetting to take a siddur with us for the dark moments which would inevitably befall us!

We decided to head for Durban because we could always sleep on the beach and catch fish to eat! So we made our way to Park Station as that's where our train to Durban would be

specially scheduled for us - who needed tickets! Somehow our fairy godmother would lay on a train for us.

We got to the station and as luck would have it OUR train was leaving in ten minutes - what timing! We scouted around and decided to board at the quietest section (first class, no less). We never realised that the scarcity of passengers near the first class coaches was related to the cost of the fare! But hell - money was not an issue for us.

We locked ourselves in the toilet and waited for what seemed an eternity till the train started moving. We were going to Durban! Gingerly we left the toilet and found a compartment. Very foolishly we closed the door - just the sign the inspector needed to check on tickets. Within an hour we were accosted by the ticket inspector and the game was up!

Needless to say we received severe reprimands on returning to the Arc and were quarantined in the Arc hospital for some months!

So ended our beach adventure and our search for freedom!"

The game was up in the train

By M Perry Kotzen (2005)

MRS CHARLOTTE SASTO RECALLS
August 2002

I joined the committee of Arcadia in 1950 so a lot of the names brought back many memories. When I read the names I would see them as small boys and girls and now some are grandparents or have children of over 30, it suddenly struck me that I am older.

The one story by Neville Merwitz as related by Max Goldman of the three boys who ran away on Sunday afternoons and decided to go to Durban really made me laugh as I was concerned with it, being the chairlady at the time.

About eight o'clock on that Sunday evening I received a phone call from Ma to tell me that three boys were missing. The children had told her that they were most probably going to Durban on the 9 o'clock train. I rushed down to the station and got there at ten to nine, managed to find the ticket examiner and stopped the train from leaving. We went through the train but could not find the boys so the ticket examiner promised me that he would look out for them. Well a few hours later I received a phone call that they had been found in a first class compartment on the train.

I must say that I was also delighted to read how well many of our girls and boys have done. I really enjoyed reading about my old friends and I must say it has brought back many pleasant old memories especially the delicious chips on Thursday night. Although I am older I still do volunteer work everyday, some of which includes young children.

AFTER LEAVING THE ARC

I had been out of contact with everyone, and was also out of the country for four years and in Swaziland. This is where I first saw Les after so many years. I left Swaziland and I am back in Johannesburg.

After I left the Arc, I went into the diamond trade, and qualified as a Brilliandeer (Polisher), I spent nine years in the trade. The diamond trade started going down, so I left and went into the carpet trade with someone who was also an ex Arc, Mitch Cathro.

I worked for a few years fitting carpets, and then went into the InteriordDesign business with Anna Isaacs, one of South Africa's foremost Interior Designers, whose children were also in the Arc, Shana, Nadia and Maurice Lerman.

While I was with Anna, I was offered a position, by my brother-in-law, in the bicycle business. I started in 1978 not knowing anything about bicycles, but built up a reputation as one of South Africa's top bicycle mechanics and wheel builder.

I was married before, and have two beautiful children, Terry my daughter, who is now married and living in Toronto, Canada with her husband Lance and their son Shawn Michael. Brad, my son, is now in his 3rd year at Wits as a medical student.

I have since remarried, to the most wonderful woman, her name is Zonia. She has been a pillar of strength when I was down and didn't give up. She also has two children, but they live in Middleburg. I am back in the bicycle business. I work for a boss now, she is very good to both of us. I used to know her husband before from racing bicycles, and triathlons, which brings me to the topic of racing which you might want to hear about.

I started racing in 1979, just in club racing in Pretoria, and then provincial. I won my first race in 1981 which was an Inter-provincial race, and then opened a bicycle shop in Johannesburg with my brother-in-law, and asked Alan van Heerden, one of South Africa's top riders, to join us in our new venture.

I was invited to be a support mechanic for the teams in the Rapport Tour, which is the biggest cycle race in South Africa. Just to cut a long story short, I raced for approximately 11 years, and then three years Triathlons.

Neville and Zonia on their wedding day

Chapter 100 – THE DURBACHS (1950s)

The Durbach family consists of one brother and five sisters and they came from the Orange Free State where their parents Issie (Isaac) and Lily lived. Issie worked in a general dealer store, for a Mr Sacks in Wolvehoek, and their house was very close to a railway sliding.

Esther (Puddy) is the oldest born in 1949, then came Les (Taaibos) in 1951, Hilda in 1952, Myra in 1953, Hannah in 1954 and lastly Thelma the youngest in 1958.

The Durbachs were in and out the Arc a few times throughout the fifties and sixties and they all would have spent the major part of their school years including all their high school years in the Arc.

Issie was also a car trader who used to deal mainly in Peugeots and would always be discussing cars with Les, who initially qualified as a Diesel Mechanic.

I spent many a Sunday on the Vaal River with Les and his family especially after we had left the Arc and he and his sisters were all like family to me.

Les Leon and I were in the Birt Street Hostel together and later rented a flat together and we would all go jolling together.

LESLIE DURBACH (TAAIBOS)
By David Sandler

Les was always very interested in cars and he initially qualified as a Diesel Mechanic but then later went to work at his Uncle Sloam's clothing factory and became a Sewing Machine Technician. Les has been fixing sewing machines around the Johannesburg area for many years now.

Soon after we had left the Arc and finished with the army Les Leon and I were in the Birt Street Hostel (run by Arcadia) together and later we rented a flat in Bellevue (which we called upper Houghton) together and we would all go *jolling* together.

Les married Fleur, a school teacher, and they have two children Dani and Jarred.

The Durbachs with their Mother Lily -L-R Les, Esther, Lily with baby Thelma on her lap,, Myra at the back, Hilda on the end and Hannah in front.

LES THE RUGBY PLAYER AND SHLUPP

This is an Arc story that Les Durbach remembers well and which he related to me.

At one time he and Hilton used to have great fun sliding down the grass embankments with cardboard. These grassy embankments were up the hill and above the orchard.

On one occasion they went direct from school to do some sliding and Les took off his shoes and forgot them there and went home for lunch. The grass embankments up the hill of course are outside the Arc and are the properties of some richer folk of Johannesburg and they were strictly out of bounds for us.

After enjoying himself going up and down the embankment, Les, who was used to walking around barefoot, went downstairs to the Junior Boys and only after a while did he discover that his shoes were missing. When he went back to investigate he found his shoes but only one was okay. The other one had been chewed up into little shreds by a dog. As these were his school shoes he had a big problem and he had to go and explain it all to Mrs Stelzner.

She wanted to know what happened to his shoes and eventually he explained it to her and then she called Vicky. They wanted to know why he was there and they threatened to stop his rugby and that was a very big threat as Les was a mad keen rugby player. Eventually they relented and Mrs Stelzner told Les to look in the little cupboard under the stairs and find other shoes that fitted him.

Now you may be thinking how the title *shlupp* fits in. Les always volunteers that he was a *shlupp.* He was the only one who played sport, rugby, all his years in high school. The rest of his contemporaries, Ronny, Leon and I only played sport in the last year of school.

On another occasion we all agreed that Les, who was one of a group of us who had broken into William the handyman's workshop, need not own up. This was to protect his special rugby playing privilege.

I think while it is apparent, it is worth while mentioning here that Les is a very persuasive and convincing character. I think that this not only kept him out of trouble with Vicky and Stelzner but it allowed him to play rugby and also to keep on the right side of the other boys.

Les was quite fanatical about his rugby and being fit and healthy. At one time Les and Ronny had a big argument because Les always wanted the window wide open for fresh air while Ronny was cold. Fickey solved the problem by putting them in separate dormitories. We used to get a bottle or two of fresh milk and Les Durbach used to always want to drink first so he could have all the cream off the top.

AN ARC IS AN ARC IS AN ARC
By Les Durbach

Once when I tried to explain to an outsider what an Arc is, I got this army sergeant stare of Hollywood proportion. "It's got nothing to do with a part of a geometrical circle. It's basically an umbilical bonding of a circle of friends." "I'm totally confused", he said.

Well, let me try some of Docs' philosophy! "Who is this *oke* Doc?" he asked perplexed. Hell everybody knew him, cleverer than Windows 95 and before you had finished clicking the question to Doc the answer was already on hand.

Besides all that, a soccer ball feared most coming near Doc's boots on a Saturday morning after Shull. I could sometimes see that ball cringe in anticipation of contact with Doc's boot as he sent it on its path of destruction!

Where was I? Oh yes. All the Arcs were and still are by some biblical force part of a small arc of the big circle. Like a mystery we all gelled together in some form or another. Fruit salad at the Ritz had nothing on us.

"So what's the big deal" says my friend. I'll tell you what, "Could you give your buddies an *unjan* ten years down the line?" "What the hell is that?" he asks. "It is like a hello *klap.*"

No matter how poor or rich an Arc is he still remains part of the circle. We know all about one another, like old snotty (Hilton) who used a hammer drill to get into his nose, or this guy Les (the mother of all *shlups*), even this nerd David who had the kind of lips that we were to die for says Old Joe Baloyi, or little Helen who could easily have made the "mousetrap" still playing in London.

Hell I could go on forever, Chips I see Fish (Max) coming round the corner, or is it Klev?

A BIG HELLO! *'N GROOT HAAI!*
By Les Durbach - 1988

I so clearly remember the fun, the camping, the parties, the chicks, hell Dave, how could I ever forget. You were great and we were like brothers Mike, Leon, You those were the days, and so time chimes on.

I hear the odd news from those that are still brave to keep in touch [thank God] with you.

When Mike and Fel told me that they were going to Australia, I became so excited, I can just imagine the hugging, the handshakes, even the odd tear.

May I join in this experience with this letter.

Fleur and Les Durbach and their children Dani and Jarrad (Boetie)
Portrait by Shani Krebbs

375

ESTHER GOLDBERG (DURBACH) (PUDDY and KOEKSISTER NO 1)

Puddy married Bruce Goldberg and had twin sons, Bret and Darren. One of them sadly passed away in an accident. Puddy works as a diamond dealer.

Esther Durbach

THE AWAKENING OF THE WATER
By Esther Durbach

I was probably about ten years old at the time when I contracted chicken pox or measles and was put into isolation ward with the other girls.

We were, for some unknown reason, given potties to use by Sister Conway and unbeknown to me one of the girls put Enos fruit salt into the pot. Just imagine my shock when the water started to sizzle. I dived into my bed, said the Shma and hid under the covers until I heard the other girls laughing.

Esther Durbach, Willy Schreeuwer, Adella Lozinski

HILDA O'LEARY (DURBACH) - (ANGIE and KOEKSISTER NO 2)

Hilda married Vic O' Leary and has two children, Lance and Tamara. Hilda worked for many years for the South African Army.

MY FAMILY

My daughter Tamara has two boys Matthew and Dean. I live with Tam and her family in a beautiful home in Bedfordview. Gary her husband has a motor spares business and I think he is the only son-in-law that loves his mother-in-law.... aren't I just lucky?

My son Lance and his wife have a beautiful girl named Amber Erin. She is *dinkum* a Durbach. They presently have a lovely home in Highlands North. My mom (Lily) is still in Sandringham Gardens and we try to see her every weekend.

My daughter has a very unusual medical problem, Menieres, which is an imbalance of the middle ear. When she has this attack she is unable to walk, as she becomes unbalanced and must stay in bed, which can sometimes last for a few days. It is very sad...but nonetheless we all climb in and help with the children etc.

Esther and Hilda

ARC MEMORIES

I remember one evening while we were lining up for supper, Mrs van Rensburg (mevrou) kept on picking on me, I called her a "Stooge" and she then told Ma, who called me into the inter-leading dining room and *klapped* me across my face at least ten times. I had no idea what a Stooge was, so I refused to apologise. That's how stupid we were.

Puddy and I were waiting down at the bottom driveway one day during our July holidays when Puds met Bruce, and we were invited to his parents' home for a movie. We thought this was just great. Then Donny and Carine saw us sitting at the bottom and enquired what we were doing there, we politely told them and they shouted at us and called us "Trollops" another strange word and we had no clue what this meant. Anyway my father and mom were telephoned by Doc, and he must have given our parents a bull-bat story, because when they came to fetch us the next day, Michael Goldstein came with them and he told us that my father is the hell in and he has a doctor ready for us so that he can see if we are still "Virgins" that perplexed us even more.

I remember Robert Langman and I were kissing behind the big palm tree by the Tennis Courts and was caught by Ma...Oi Vey....more pooh to follow. But all in all I think I was a goody goody with just two big boobs.

I left the Army after 23 years and six months and thank heavens things have changed dramatically. So I am what you would call a "Full Time Boba" and I just love it.

MYRA DURBACH (KOEKSISTER NO 3)

Myra and Natie King, her partner of almost 30 years, have two beautiful children Warren and Tarren. Myra works in the printing industry.

Myra Durbach

ARC MEMORIES

Camel (Neville Murwitz) told us a story about a Saturday night at the movies, in the Arc, where they showed the first reel and before they put the next reel on, they did a random check to see that we were all there, only to discover that when Vicky called David Sandler's name he did not answer.

Only after they decided that they would not put on the next reel did he answer, but he had girl's clothes on and Boetie (Les) said that David stood up and said, "Here I am".

Elizabeth and I were best friend in the Babies – she taught me how to tell the time and I remember the two black dogs Lucky and Suki which we used to feed. I was very upset when David Sandler's dad came to fetch him and when he left the Arc.

On Sundays we all used to wait for our folks to pick us up at the main entrance – and my Dad used to come with all these fancy cars. Some of the other Arcs used to tell us - Durbachs your folks are here.

Late Leon and Max and also David used to come fishing with us on the Sunday we went out for the day, and we sure had a great time at the river.

Warren Myra and Tarren

Thelma has been gone 25 years 6th January 2006 and is still very much in our minds. Do you remember her boyfriend Brian? He is married with kids but never fails to remember her on that day.

HANNAH AND THELMA DURBACH

Hannah, since leaving the Arc, has spent her life travelling around the world with Manfred, her boyfriend since she was sixteen.

Thelma sadly passed away a few years after leaving the Arc.

The Durbachs as grown ups- Les and Hannah at back and Esther Hilda and Myra in the front.

Chapter 101 – THE LOZINSKI SISTERS – ADELLA NOLL (1949) AND VERA ANGEL (1950)

Adella and her younger sister Vera were born in Ireland in 1949 and 1950 respectively and came to South Africa in the late 1950s with their Mother and Aunt.

I remember it was in 1960 that Vera first came to Mrs Durbach's Standard 1 class in Jewish Government School. She came with her Mom on her first day of school and I also remember her waiting for Hebrew lessons that were held after school.

Very soon after that Vera and Adella were both placed in the care of Arcadia and I always remember their Mom and their Aunt coming together to visit them both on Sunday afternoons at the Arc.

I remember that Vera did very well in the diving competitions at the Arc Swimming Gala. She always won the event as she was the one with the smallest splash.

Adella and Vera stayed about ten years in the Arc and left in the late 1960s.

They both married and are now Adella Noll and Vera Angel. While Adella lives in the UK Vera lives in Cape Town.

MY FAMILY

Our mother Hannah who was known as Netta had three sisters and one brother and they were all born in Dublin.

After our parents divorced, my mother, who was basically alone, decided with her sisters that it would be better for us to be in South Africa with them. My two aunts Molly and June were already in South Africa; Molly was married to Jack Rachlevsky and June Carroll never married. The sisters never had any of their own children.

June and Netta shared an apartment in Hillbrow and as they had to go out and work it was decided by their sister Molly (who at the time knew one of the Hebrew teachers) to put us in the Arc as we would be in a safe environment.

1962 Girls Playing- Minnie Baitz and Vera with hands up
Linda Stoler the taller girl, Myra Durbach, Les Mark looking the other way and Marcia Salmonson at back
In Front Marilyn Stoler back to us, Shelley Grishkan and Elisabeth Fliess.

My aunt worked for Greatermans in town and Netta got a job in a factory sewing garments. She then worked in the Jewish Old age home for a while and later found a job in the staff canteen in Woolworths in Kerk Street, Johannesburg. When we (Adella and Vera) went to the dentist in town we used to run in and she would always give us some nice hot chips.

VERA REMEMBERS

I will treasure the *Arc Memory Booklets* and hopefully one day my son will read them and know what a wonderful childhood I had.

I just wanted to read and read and read. It brought back so many memories things that I had forgotten. In fact reading some of the articles I pictured myself being there all those years ago. Especially the Saturday night bioscope and of course not to mention the two hard sweets which were dished out – it was lucky we did not break our teeth. Not to mention the fruit raids and the guys when they used to go to the zoo and pinch a rabbit or two. The booklets are difficult to put down, every now and then when reading something I am laughing and my husband thinks I am a little crazy. He knows I was in the Arc but does not know the fun we had, it was truly one big family.

I must admit I forgot the names of the people who gave us Hebrew lessons, the boys' housemother, Sister Conway and reading these books make them all of a sudden come to life again. I even forgot little Georgie until I saw a picture of Bella Lubner holding him at one or other function. I am also saddened to read what happened to him. You really brought back a flood of memories, reading these books was so invigorating I just could not put them down.

If I remember rightly I think we were in the same class firstly at Jewish Government School and later in Roseneath Primary School. I think it was you, me and Paul. I remember Neville's mother coming to the Jewish Government School and brushing his teeth etc.

Something which stands out in my mind, how useless I was at maths at school but how good I was in the history class getting high marks for assignments on the American War etc, etc. I remember how brilliant you were with your high maths marks – that is one thing I remember about you. I am not surprised that you became an accountant. I can't remember if we were ever friends or spoke with each other in those days, but I remember you were always getting high marks for maths.

Ruth Dire was a big part of many children's lives. I personally never really got close to her and actually did not really have much to do with her in the old days. I think I was scared of her and Sister Conway, especially the way Sister Conway used to give us the needle when we needed it, she used our bottoms as though she was playing darts.

But there are one or two people who stand out and one was John the painter, who used to tell all us kids that he was Dr London and came from London Town. I don't know if you remember him, he was a short little round guy who used to do the painting and we had another name for him, Blackie. I remember, and I can still see him as if it were yesterday, when he was painting we would steal his brush and start painting and put paint on his face and tell him we were going to paint his face white. I am sure he cannot still be alive as he, if I remember, was not too young in those days. I often wonder if he had a family and what happened to him when he eventually retired.

Doctor London Painting by Michael Perry Kotzen

Also I remember some of the guys who used to work in the kitchen. I think one had the name of Phinias and he used to make the porridge, or should I say the horrible lumpy, glue type thing that we called porridge.

To this day I can't look at it and the greasy fried eggs swimming in the oil or butter but still hideous. Whenever I fry an egg, which is not very often, I still think of those greasy eggs.

Another thing that comes to mind was the special breakfast we always had on a Saturday morning, the corn flakes and the jam donut, not to mention the Saturday Oneg Shabat with the Oros. Doc walked up and down asking us religious questions, ie the names of the month, the five books of Moses etc etc, and he would basically give us the answers too.

I remember once that Doc had to go to Israel for some presentation and he asked me to stay in the flat with Ma. He also instructed me not to sleep until she got out of the bath as I think she had a habit of falling asleep in the bath. I actually stayed in the flat in a room that she made very comfortable for me. I can still remember all the newspapers piled high waiting for Doc to read and all the books too. When Doc returned he brought me a present of a broach and Mrs van Rensburg (who looked after the girls) a necklace. She did not like the necklace and I did not particularly like the broach, so we swapped and I still have the necklace to this day and treasure it.

I saw your brother Brian a few years ago, he was working at the Jewish Cemetery in Cape Town – he recognised me and believe it or not, if he did not come over to me, I would have walked right passed him.

Vera (centre) and Dorothy Sedacca winning the three-legged race

I keep in touch with Hymie Aronoff and write occasionally to Honey (Myrtle) in Israel. Other than that I have no further communication with any Arcs.

VERA'S FAMILY

My son Brian is over 30 years old and married Sharon Levitt in December 2000. They have a baby girl Amy, so I am now a gran. Brian is a lawyer and works in a firm in Cape Town.

I married for the second time. I am a secretary and my husband is a Science and Maths teacher. I work for a medical company, who import and distribute medical equipment. I was retrenched after 25 years and the company re-employed me after 18 months. My hubby to his day has not been able to get me to add and subtract. He teaches at the Herzlia High School, it is equivalent to King David.

My husband's name is Nissim – also known as Nick. He is a Sephardic Jew, whose parents originally came from Rhode Island, opposite Turkey.

Nick's parents have now passed away, his mother died on Yom Kippur 2005, she had just turned 89 years old. My late father-in-law used to go in a small boat with his father to the different little islands around Rhodes to sell Greek and Turkish delicatessen. They had such fascinating stories to tell about life on the Island. One of Nick's aunts, his late mother's sister is a survivor of the camps. A lot of Nick's family ended up in the camps and they did not survive. His parents settled in the Congo where they ran a shop (something along the lines of the mine shops where they sold anything and everything.)

Nick used to frequently come to Johannesburg, as he contracted polio when he was very small and had to have several operations in the Johannesburg Children's Hospital. He then recuperated in the Hope Home situated high up on the side of the zoo. He also has fond memories of the place even though he was left alone, not speaking a word of English as his father, may his soul rest in peace, had to go back to the shop.

When problems started in the Congo in 1960 the family jumped in their car and came to Cape Town but returned to the Congo as they had just left and needed to go back to see what had happened to their home and shop. Nick and his cousins, as well as friends landed up in our sister orphanage, Oranja, so we have a lot in common. A lot of the people from the Congo, when the problems started, went either to Rhodesia (know as Zimbabwe) and to Cape Town. Of course my parents-in-law and their brothers and sisters made for Cape Town as they loved Muizenberg, the sea and the fishing.

ADELLA IN LONDON

Adella has been living in London working as a debt collector for some time now. She has made contact with many Arcs living around London. She lives in Surrey (outside London) about five miles away from Boris and two hours away from Robert Langman, who lives in Essex.

Besides catching up with Boris and Robert she has been in touch with Jenny Levine and also is regularly in touch with Debbie Frogel.

Adella's daughter Tammy had a baby boy in October 2005, so that now makes it two grandchildren.

Minnie Baitz, Adella and Hilda Durbach

Chapter 102 – BORIS SEDACCA (1950)

Boris and his younger sister Dorothee were born in 1950 and 1952 respectively in Alexandria, Egypt, which was then French-speaking. Their family fled Egypt during the Suez Crisis in 1956 and lived in France for five years before coming to South Africa in 1962, where they only then learnt to speak English. Boris and Dorothee were both in Arcadia from 1962 to 1965.

LIFE BEFORE COMING TO THE ARC

As children we first lived in Alexandria's cosmopolitan community. This was made up of Arabs (both local and foreign), Greeks, Turks, Indians and French, whose language was adopted as the common tongue, much as English is used throughout India. There were also Jews in small numbers coming from all those groups.

You could say I had a somewhat traumatic childhood in Egypt during the 1956 Suez Crisis. You know the kind of thing that happens - a little runt comes up to you at school and pushes you, so you push him back. Next thing you're surrounded by bigger guys and one of them says: *"Quoi, tu a frappé un Musulman? Après école nous allons te tuer!"* ("What, you struck a Muslim? After school we're going to kill you!")

I told my teacher what happened and after school I was asked to stay behind. Then after a short wait of ten, maybe 15 minutes, I was told I could go home. As I stepped out of the school gate someone called my name, a car door opened, and I was whisked away to safety. I had never been in a car before, or even a taxi - my parents used to hire a coach and horse to get us home after a visit to friends or relatives.

On another occasion, my mother sent me out with a saucepan to get some milk from a stall a couple of blocks away. On the way back home, I was jostled by some Arab boys and spilt most of the milk. When I got back with just a tiny bit of milk at the bottom of the saucepan, my mother shouted at me, but when I told her what happened, she panicked.

Things were getting out of hand after Nasser nationalised the Suez Canal, provoking an invasion by Britain, France and Israel. We had a nightly blackout. Even the janitor came into our apartment and blew out a candle we were using to make a point of what he thought of us.

Alexandria did not see that much action - the main bounty was Cairo - but I remember sirens blaring in the streets one day and the sound of explosions with puffs of smoke in the sky from gun shells aimed at some aircraft flying overhead.

One night during the blackout, the sirens went off again, and as we were in one of the apartments higher up in the block, our English neighbours, who had a massive basement apartment invited us down to take refuge. As we were coming down the stairs in a bit of a panic, we could see tracer shells lighting up

On Train to Durban- Boris with arm in plaster, Willy Schreeuwer at back and Dorothee, Vera Lozinsky and Sadie Baitz in front.

the sky out of the staircase windows, trying to pick out allied aircraft. Because my father and all the other men in our group appeared scared out of their wits, I started panicking too, but just as I was about to get hysterical my mother, with incredible presence of mind, smiled and said: *"regarde les feux d'artifice."* (Look at the fireworks.) At that point, the men realised what big babies they were, calmed down a bit, which helped to calm me.

Anyway we left Egypt and went to live in France, but things were still traumatic. My father was in Paris one day and heading home, when an Algerian man was shot dead right next to him in the street by another Algerian.

I used to get into fights at school, both with Arabs and Christians. My mother started feeling the strain and was eventually hospitalised with mental illness.

My aunt, who had moved to South Africa persuaded my father (her brother) that life there was better, and this would help my mother get better. We moved to SA but that did not help my mother, and she was in and out of hospital all the time.

That is when my father turned to the Arc for help. A few months after Dorothee and I went in to the Arc, my mother was permanently committed to a mental home. About 35-40 years ago, she was moved to Fort England Hospital in Grahamstown, where she died in 1994.

STORIES ABOUT BORIS
By Ronny Schreeuwer

An episode I remember with Boris happened one evening after finishing homework upstairs in the homework room. Keith Lang and Manfred Stein paired us off together to have a fight with one another. I started wrestling with Boris and realised there was no point to it and stopped. For that I got beaten up. I used to really piss Boris off when I called him *Bolhairs*, I think that was one of the first words he understood in English. He would chase me and sometimes when he caught me he'd punch me in the back. It was all fun and games in those days.

I made contact with Boris and Dorothee, his sister, on MSN. We've had some really pleasant chats. Isn't it amazing how one or two years in the Arc with some kids seemed like we were together much longer and the difference in time 30-40 years has made no difference.

By David Sandler

I remember once going to hospital with a dog bite, which I think sister treated with much hidden amusement. I had been stealing fruit with Boris and been nipped by a dog on the back of my heel while climbing over a stone wall with the stolen fruit. Boris Sedacca had terrified me by telling me what happens when a dog with rabies bites you. Boris said that the dog had dripping saliva, which was a sure sign of rabies. I thought it was better to face sister than to go mad.

Boris, I can tell you that whenever I eat pumpkin, I remember you, especially when I see big white pumpkin pips. It's you who educated me and showed me one could eat these dried pips which are even better than sunflower seeds and were as tasty as peanuts. One sunny Saturday afternoon when we were exploring, we found the scooped out pips of a pumpkin drying in the sun on the window sill of the cow stable and that was my introduction to the taste.

I imagine that Dolly must have missed them and that she would have had to find a safer place to dry them away from us little Arc boys.

In the middle dormitory were the youngest Junior Boys which included Boris Sedacca, Leon Goodman (newly arrived) Paul Cohen, Hilton Rothaus, Max Goldman and me and very soon after our arrival in the Junior Boys we were introduced to shadow boxing. A little after 'lights out' the shadow boxing would start. We would pull out a torch and the boy on the end bed would shine the torch onto the opposite wall across the three other beds. Two of the boys on the other three beds would get up and stand on their beds and 'box'. Because the

light was on the one side, the guy nearest the torch would cast the biggest shadow on the wall and would be like a giant casting his shadow not only on the wall but on the ceiling too. The person closest to the wall and furthest would throw the smaller shadow and effectively you would have a giant fighting a little man when you looked at the shadows on the wall. The giant (shadow) would not have to do much at all. He would have a massive hand being closest to the torch while the person nearest to the wall would be jumping up and trying to hit him and his giant hand. The guy in the bed in the middle would be half way size between the other two and the trick was to play around so you could cast the best shadow of fighting on the wall. You did not really look at the people who were punching or moving their hands, you looked at the shadowed result on the wall which was very good. That was our shadow boxing.

By Les Durbach

A story Les Durbach remembers concerned Boris, Hilton and himself. There was a foofie slide right down the hill which Hilton and he used to use regularly. Boris who was French and spoke very little English was new in the Arc and the day came when he wanted to have a go. Unfortunately he did not wait until he was down to the ground level but jumped off about three quarters of the way down and tumbled and he broke his arm. He had to be taken up to Vicky and Stelzner and had to explain what had happened.

Boris had just come to the Arc and he was French speaking and he could not really talk English very well. Vicky and Stelzner questioned him as to what had happened and he was apparently taken all the way down the hill again (with his broken arm) to the scene of the accident and he had to explain to them what happened in his broken English.

BORIS REMEMBERS

Feels like a lifetime ago that we last met at the Arc. I had left and you were still "inmates" at the time, sometime around the mid-60s if I remember right. I used the term "inmates" in a purely jocular fashion, reminiscing about the condition which many of us felt we were in at the time, although I dare say that 40 years later we all realise the labour of love that was behind all the strict regimentation.

Ronny if I remember our little scraps, I would be the first to hit out, you hit back, I hit back (harder), you hit back (harder), then I'd go away and blub.

I was called "Ball-hairs" - because I couldn't understand, Keith Lang enlightened me by pointing in the region of his midriffs. That's how I know.

What I remember about your sister Willy is her expression when she sang *This Land is Mine* (Exodus). What power! I though she was cut out for opera.

I remember my fall from the tree. I was terrified because it started raining and thundering, and I was a bit slow getting off the tree, and everyone was shouting: "Hey Frenchie, the

382

lightning's gonna hit the tree. We're gonna have a *braai,* ha ha ha." Then there was a loud thunderclap and in my panic to get down quickly, I didn't hold on to a branch properly and fell back on my bottom holding out my arms to break the fall. I heard this crack and when I looked at my left wrist, it was well mangled. Someone said it was shaped like a bayonet and everyone burst out laughing.

Then, quite matter-of-fact, Neville Merwitz says: "Yep, that arm is definitely broken." I got vertigo and felt my knees caving in under me. When I said: "I feel faint," everybody burst out laughing again. Ha, ha: I was supposed to say: "I want to faint," or "I'm going to faint."

Anyway Neville grabs me under one arm and carries me off to the hospital. My English has improved somewhat since then. I never thought it would turn out to be such a damn useful tool for earning a living as a journalist.

Boy, were we bad! Do you guys remember when we had to go en masse to some guy to apologise for stealing fruits from his trees? He turned out to be quite friendly and engaged in some chat for a few minutes.

AFTER LEAVING THE ARC

For me, life has been like a mirage. I left South Africa in 1975 with R800 in my pocket and a B-stream Matric. I went to Israel for a couple of months and stayed on a Kibbutz, then went to England and worked as a volunteer for almost three years. Then got a job in computer journalism, met a girl, had babies, got separated in 1993, studied electronic engineering as a "very" mature student and graduated with honours.

I guess I'd never really pushed myself at the Arc because I was a bit of a dunce then. Do you remember David how I taught you to play chess, and then you beat me every time after that? That was incredible.

Anyway, I thought I would become an engineer because I was fed up with journalism, but at the ripe old age of 47, not many employers are going to take a second look. Took a job as a cab driver for a while, then went crawling back to journalism on my hands and knees, where I've been ever since.

Life's not too bad. Despite the stigma of coming from the Arc, which I am sure is very keenly felt by many old Arcs, I have managed to more or less come right in life. I've got two lovely girls, Natalie and Miriam.

Last year Natalie graduated with first class honours in social

anthropology from Cambridge University. Miriam started an English and philosophy degree at Warwick University a few months later, but decided to pack it in after three weeks. She's going to start again later this year, changing her studies to Sanskrit and Eastern philosophy:

I have been in contact with Adella Lozinski, who it turns out also lives in Surrey (outside London) about five miles away from me, and then Robert Langman, who lives a bit further away in Essex. Who would have thought, 40 years ago, that we'd end up here.

Natalie, Boris and his aunt

Sue and Miriam

Chapter 103 – THE SAIETS

Michael (born 22nd September 1951) and Adele Saiet (born 4th November 1952) were in the Arc from 1964 to 1969 and completed their high school years in the Arc.

Their parents were Mildred and Benny Saiet. The children were placed in the care of the Arc after their parents had divorced.

Michael and Adele lived in Bellevue for some years after leaving the Arc. Michael initially ran a retail shop selling Mama Lottie overalls for Sloum Durbach and then later worked in his clothing factory.

Michael married Felicia Durbach (Les Durbach's first cousin) and moved to Canada in 1986 with his young family. There he continued in the 'rag' trade.

MICHAEL SAIET

I married Felicia (nee Durbach) and I have been living in Toronto Canada for just over 18 years! We have two children Jason (28 years old) and Leigh (26 years old).

Jason is married to Linda (nee Rojas from Ecuador) and they have given Felicia and I the best gift in the world! They gave us a beautiful granddaughter Kayla Masha.

Leigh has been going out with Tom Flow for the last nine years and finally Tom proposed to Leigh last month! They plan to marry next year! Felicia and I have been 'empty nesters' for a few years but now that we have Kayla in our lives we feel that

we have been blessed! Imagine Zeida Mike and Boba Felicia!

FAMILY TREE AND THE ARC CONNECTIONS

Felicia is a first cousin to Leslie Durbach and sisters.

Leslie introduced me to Felicia 35 years ago we have been married for over 30 years! Felicia's parents Sonia and Sloum and their daughter Barbra followed us to Toronto 15 years ago. Barbra is married and she has two kids. I am very fortunate that I have a large family here numbering 27. Another family connection that I would like to mention is The Sandler connection! David Jenny and Brian are my cousins! My late Dad Benjamin and David's late Dad Michael were first cousins (Girty their Boba and Ann my Boba were sisters!)

My Dad, Benjamin Saiet passed away in August 2005 so Adele and I travelled back to South Africa for the funeral. Les Durbach met us at the airport and that same afternoon we had the funeral. The first night we slept at Graham Stoler's house I hadn't seen Graham in more then 30 years! The next day Adele and I moved in with Les and Fleur and they made us feel right at home, even through that difficult time! Even though I hadn't seen Leslie, Fleur Hilda Esther Myra Graham Stoler, Neville Merwitz in years the moment we met it was as though we had seen them yesterday!

As ex Arcs we have a special connection that binds us as brothers and sisters!

Boys playing Soccer – Michael with ball – 1967

384

ADELE WORKMAN-DAVIES (SAIET)

Adele first worked for Map Studio then at Wits Geology Department as a cartographer, where she met Clive Workman-Davies. They became friends and regularly used to take ice-skating classes at the Carlton Sky Rink. They married in 1982 and initially lived in South Africa and had a daughter Cheryl who was born in December 1987. Cheryl has just turned 18 and has just graduated from high school with a university entrance. Clive also has a daughter Tracy who is a Vice Principal at Allen Glen High School in Johannesburg, as well as a son Bradley who is a lawyer.

Adele, Clive and Cheryl emigrated to Australia in January 1998 and they settled in Kalgoorlie a mining town in Western Australia where Clive lectures in Mining Engineering at the Western Australian School of Mines, Curtin University.

They are now Australian Citizens and part of a large group of South Africans who have also joined the mining community in the Kalgoorlie Goldfields. They saw the Springboks beat the Wallabies at Subiaco in August 2005 and watched the Proteas draw against the Australian's at the WACA on the 20th December 2005.

Adele studied Art and Design at Curtin University, Kalgoorlie and is now an Artist and a Teacher of Art to school children. She is also working as a co-ordinator and provides occupational therapy to children who are ill at the hospital in Kalgoorlie.

Adele Saiet at school

ADELE'S ARC MEMORIES

It was Vicky Klevansky who introduced my family to the Arc as he used to play tennis at my aunt Lily and Julius Ostroff's house every Sunday. My aunt's house used to be next to Parktown Boys' High School. They had a huge double storey house with large grounds. I am sure that some of the Arc boys will remember it as she, and my cousin Sybil often used to talk about getting visits from the Arcs. Unfortunately the house was knocked down and there are now offices in its place. My aunt and uncle moved to Cape Town in the 80's and sadly they have now both passed away. My cousin Sybil Goldberger and her family now live in Lyndhurst, Johannesburg.

I have very fond memories of my time in the Arc. I especially enjoyed the open fields and trees. The jacaranda trees were just fantastic especially when they were in flower. The Big Tree next to the slide was my favourite and I often used to give it a hug. I always enjoyed the view of the main building and the Shul from the field below. There was a rabbit's hutch next to the slide with lots of baby rabbits, but they eventually disappeared because wild cats and rats killed them off.

One of my first memories at the Arc was playing baseball on the field next to the slide. Everyone joined in, the girls and the boys. We had some really good laughs, somehow that did not last very long as we were not encouraged to spend too much time with the boys. However when we were able to we did, but the girls were punished if we were caught spending too much time with the boys. One punishment was not being allowed to

go to movies on Saturday night. That was tough as it was the highlight of the week. I have many memories of watching the boys playing soccer with Doc on Saturdays. We would sit on the bench and spend time talking and watching while the boys played. And there were many times we would watch them play Tippy in the pond next to the swimming pool. We would also walk down to the wall next to Oxford Road and sit and listen to our radios and watch the traffic go by and count the cars as they went by.

Talking of the swimming pool, there are lots of memories that stick in my mind. One was a heat wave in Johannesburg one summer. Everyone was in the pool. Not a space to be seen. Even Doc was in the pool. Another memory was the swimming galas. One of my first memories was of everyone very eager to have a go (1965–1967) One thing we would get into serious trouble for was if we were caught wearing a bikini. That was punishable with every punishment Ma could think of. However that did not stop us, especially when we went away to Durban for our annual holiday. That was what made the best memories and would keep us going until the next year.

Sometimes we would to be taken out to movie premieres and one that I remember well was 'The Yellow Rolls Royce' in 1964 with Rex Harrison and Ingrid Bergman. I was still in the Junior Girls Department. It was a cold winter evening and Ma made us wear old fashioned scratchy coats. Mine had huge big buttons that made you feel like a stuffed cabbage. We were driven in the big, old, bumpy school bus and bundled out onto the red carpet.

I just could not believe it when I turned on the TV recently and there was '*The Yellow Rolls Royce*.' Forty two years later - I was able to watch it again after so many years.

'Mary Poppins' was another movie we went to see at the Colosseum Movie house. There was always something arranged for us to do in the holidays, for example, we all went in the bus to the Vaal River, we had fantastic motor boat rides all day, and plenty to eat! Speaking of which, Ma's tagalag and chopped herring was and still is the best!

Lesley Mark, Janet Miller and I sometimes used to take a bus ticket from Ma in the mornings and say we were staying after school for sports but instead of going to the activities we would go shopping, but with not very much money. So we would just walk around the supermarket, find a broken packet of food and have fun eating from the packet that just happened to be there conveniently. We would walk out quite satisfied, and just pay for one small thing like an apple. We would also sometimes visit some of our school friends on the way home. Sometimes we would steal carrots from the orchard veggie garden and be chased by the gardener who threatened to tell Ma. Not good!!!

I definitely remember Ruth Dire who in Jules Gordon's words was quite a mean tennis player. One Saturday afternoon after Shul she was practicing her swing. I very eagerly volunteered to hit back to her but it was a very bad move as instead of hitting them back I found myself jumping out the way dodging flying bullets.

We would often sit and listen to records on the record player that my Dad gave me for my birthday, when he visited us one Sunday. In those days we were only allowed out one Sunday a month. After visiting was over we would sit on the grass next to the swimming pool or on the steps next to the Boys Department, Paul Cohen, Leon Goodman, David Sandler, Janet Miller and Linda Stoler and would talk together and would listen to Leon's records of the Beach Boy's and get all nostalgic, and wish we were able to do all the things the Beach Boys were singing about.

I very sadly miss Leon, and I will always remember him singing happily to his Beach Boys' records.

All of the Arcs, David Sandler, Leon Goodman, Max Goldman, Leslie Mark, Janet Miller, Linda Stoler, the Durbach family, the Laskers are all very special people. David is in fact my third cousin. My Mom was the caretaker of Joldian Court, Yeoville. Some of the Arcs lived in that block for many years. Mom used to help everyone with accommodation and considered herself Mom to everyone. My mom passed away in July 1996 and is very much missed.

I have so many memories and they are all now very special, and so are all the Arcs that I came into contact with. It has been and is very special to be a part the Arc even though at times it was very difficult and like Michael, I say the very same, as ex Arcs we have a special connection that binds us together as brothers and sisters.

1969 Holiday to Bloemfontein
Adele Saiet, Marilyn Stoler Sharon Grishkan and Janet Miller

Chapter 104 – LEON GOODMAN (1951-1995)

Leon was born in 1951 and was placed in the care of Arcadia in 1963 following the break-up of his parents' marriage.

He lived in the Arc until he finished school at Parktown Boys' High in 1969 and then spent 1970 in the Air Force doing his National Service.

REMEMBERING LEON

David Sandler Remembers;

Leon was an excellent sportsman and whether we were playing soccer or cricket he was always one of the first selected. He was very quick off the mark and this gave him an edge in soccer. I remember once sparring with Leon. Basically I could keep out of his way (as trained by Donald as a youngster) as he did not have a far reach. However, one day he gave me an uppercut, which just lightly brushed my chin and nose. It was like a train rushing by and I believe he would have done serious damage to me if he connected me. I immediately gave up sparring with him and I believe out of all my contemporaries he threw the most painful punches. If he punched your arm it stayed lame, sore and bruised for weeks on end.

He came to the Arc when he started high school and although we were not so friendly in the Arc we were kind of thrown together when we left the Arc. We both worked for Leiman Teeger Gaddin Sifris and Co and studied accountancy together part time at university. We lived together, firstly in a residential hotel in Hillbrow, the Franklin, and then in the hostel in Birt Street. Later we shared a flat with Les in Sharp Street in Bellevue East. We all spent many holidays together and even went on our first dates together.

Leon used to look after his possessions very carefully and had a special knack for remembering names. He would know the names of all sportsmen (especially soccer players) film stars and remembered the names of everyone he came in contact with. He did very well in business and a few weeks before he died he called me up out of the blue to tell me how well he was doing.

He married Nadine and has three children; Jodie who is studying law, Wayne and Lisa.

Max Goldman Remembers

Leon's unveiling was held in February 1996. The stone was in the shape of a Magen David – very unique. This sad day left a mark on me. It is nine months since that terrible day in June 1995 when Leon was robbed and murdered at his business premises and I find myself often thinking of him.

Some of my thoughts:

o Leon's arrival at the Arc in 1963 and we immediately plundered his box of toys;

Ronny Schreeuwer, Les Durbach, Doc and Leon Goodman

o Leon was always a good player at Saturday morning soccer;
o Lesley Mark. Leon's girlfriend?
o Leon playing soccer at Parktown Boys' High (black/red checked shirt);
o Latin with Klev;
o Living in the house in Birt Street Raedene;
o Our time at Leiman Teeger with Henry van Wel, Saretzsky, Lockoff, Gaddins and trip to Marble Hall;
o Sharp Street Flat with Les David and the Saiets;
o Holidaying in Durban Cape Town, Lourenco Marques Cape town (Sandy Bay);
o Peugeots 404, 203, 504, Yellow Merc, Beetle;
o Trips to Unisa to hand in assignments or to receive exam results;
o Fishing trips to the Vaal and Free State;
o Leon's wedding where I was best man and made a great speech;
o Leon the bowls enthusiast;
o Leon's young family suddenly left alone;
o The mystery of life.

PHOTOS OF LEON ON NEXT PAGE

Leon with daughter Lisa
Next four photos all are of Leon
Nadine and Leon
Max Goldman, Brian and David Sandler, Les Durbach and Leon.
Leon and Brian Sandler

Chapter 105 - GARY BLACKMAN (1951)
Past Chairman and Honorary President

Gary was born in 1951 and his younger brother Tony was born in 1956. They lived in the care of Arcadia from January 1964 to March 1966.

Gary left the Arc a week after his Barmitzvah that he shared with Max Goldman and David Sandler.

Gary served 14 years on the Arc committee joining in 1988. He was Honorary Secretary from October 1990 to October 1992, Vice -Chairman from October 1992 to October 1994, Chairman from October 1994 to October 1996 and was made an Honorary President in Oct 1996.

GARY'S MEMORIES - INSIDE OUT AND OUTSIDE IN

My Mom and Dad separated when I was ten years old and I became quite independent and streetwise. Two years later my Mom dropped the bombshell that my brother and I were to go and live in Arcadia. I needed to be free and this admission to a "place of detention" was difficult to bear. Nevertheless we were admitted and I quietly endured this unfair termination of my freedom.

My memories from the inside looking out, although now somewhat hazy, were more of times of being bullied and punished than times of fun and enjoyment.

Saturday sport after Shul was compulsory and more often than not I was bowled over by the bigger boys and failed dismally to ever get to the soccer ball or cricket ball. I am not sure why we were ever forced to play, as I felt like part of a target practice with me as the target.

A Sunday visit 1963 – Brother Tony with Mom Shirley and Gary.

Les, Leon and Gary in 1965

The time indoors in the Junior Boys was no better. There seemed to be more mornings of lining up with the rest of the boys and bending over for a punishment with a mini cricket bat than satisfying breakfast meals. Punishment was the name of the game, and there was always some good reason for a punishment. I am sure there were also some good times but these faded into oblivion.

I looked forward to the Sunday visits from my Mom and Dad. I used to sit on the side of the entrance and watch each bus at it went past and dropped off the visitors hoping that the next parent to emerge would be mine.

My Mom must have been painfully aware of my sadness and use to promise that we would be reunited as soon as she could. True to her word after some two years in Arcadia, we packed up and moved back home.

I left Arcadia, never to set foot there again until one eventful day in 1988, some 22 years later, when Selwyn Dembo, with whom I had the privilege to be working on a new project with, discovered that I was an Old Arc. He coerced me to join the committee and there I discovered that Arcadia was graced with a dedicated committee and devoted and caring team of professionals and staff.

Now I was looking outside in. Slowly but surely my views of Arcadia changed and the unhappy bleak picture that I had painted was replaced with a bright picture of an organisation whose sole purpose was to improve the lives of the children in its care, prepare them for the future ahead and to achieve their maximum potential.

The committee was sorely hurt when the management of Arcadia was torn away from them and my membership of a group that I was proud to belong to came to a crashing halt after 14 years.

Today I have those good memories of Arcadia, memories of friends, memories of those that I admired and memories of children's laughter.

David, Max and Gary in 1996 – 30 years after their shared Barmitzvah

MY FAMILY

I married Miriam (nee Bass) in 1975 and have two children Seth and Dale. I practiced as a lawyer in Johannesburg and settled in Auckland, New Zealand in 2004.

My wife, Miriam also had some connection with Arcadia, in that her step mother is Zelda Gordon who was in Arcadia for many years, together with her siblings, Bobby, David and Cerisa.

Tony, my brother, also lives in Auckland, New Zealand and immigrated here some seven years ago. He is married to Sharon, nee Reeb, and they have two sons and a daughter, Brett, Caylie and Matthew who are 17, 15 and 13 respectively. Tony had his own business as an auto-electrician for many years in South Africa and continued in the same profession when he came to New Zealand. He quite recently decided that he needs to move on from the hands on work and has since become the area manager with an international car battery distributor.

Dale, Seth, Miriam, and Gary

Chapter 106 – DAVID SANDLER (1952)

Our mother, Myra Goldberg died on 27 March 1956 (aged 34) from cancer and Jenny and I were admitted to the Arc on 29 July 1956. Jenny was then six (born 1949) and I was about three and a half years old (born 1952). My brother Brian born 1954 was only one and a half when my Mom died and was not admitted to the Arc until he was two years old. He turned two on 6 November 1956 and was admitted to the Arc on 18 November 1956.

My Dad, Mayer Lipa Sandler, was 39 years old at the time and was the Manager of Cape Meat Supply and as he was in business he was unable to look after us.

My parents married in 1948 and at the time of my Mom's death we all lived in a house in Hunter Street in Yeoville.

After my Mom died my Dad tried keeping the family together and I remember one, then another elderly Jewish housekeeper coming to live with us but they did not work out. In terms of my Mother's will, the house had to be sold and we went to live with my Grandparents, Gertie and Solomon Sandler, in Johannesburg Street in La Rochelle, but they were too old to look after us. My Grandfather had been injured in a car accident and was described as a speculator.

My aunts and uncles had discussed looking after us and in fact decided which one of us should live with which family but in the end they thought it was better not to split us up, so we all went to the Arc. The Arc was to be our home for the rest of our childhood, until we finished school.

Jenny left the Arc at the end of 1968, I left and the end of 1969 and Brian left during 1970.

David with his sister Jenny

MY FAMILY HISTORY

Solomon Plein (1843-1904) (my great great grandfather) came from Poneves Lithuania, Russia around 1870 to South Africa where he established a few general dealer shops, leaving his wife, one son and three daughters behind. After about five years he sent for his 15 year old son, Yehuda, who came out by ship in order to evade conscription to the Russian army, as most conscripts never survived.

Yehuda (Julius Joshua Plein) (1865-1945) (my great grandfather) went back to Russia to find a wife and married Shauna Mathematics (my great grandmother). Later they returned to South Africa with Dora, their firstborn who was three. Two more children Barney and Janie (my grandmother) were born in South Africa.

Janie was born during the Boer War after Yehuda, her father had been made a prisoner of war. He was supposed to have sided with the Boers. It has been said that he was involved in corruption and profiteering and unscrupulous trading by supplying the government with food during the beginning of the war. The British deported him to Ceylon as a prisoner.

Shauna Mathematics, died about a month after giving birth to Janie when Dora was eight years old, Barney was two.

During the Boer War the three Plein children were then taken in and looked after by three different Jewish families.

At the end of the war Yehuda heard that his wife had died and went on to Australia. He then decided, (according to Barney Plein), that as there were not enough Jews in Australia, he would not be able to make a living and went back to Lithuania to find a wife. There he married Sonia (whose maiden name was Hotz). Her parents were big millers from Saville, Lithuania. She was a daughter of his first wife's sister. They returned to Johannesburg, set up a home for Dora, Barney, Janie and Sonia and to make a living, opened up a Kosher Boarding House with Dora's help.

They had four children - Sonia, Dulcie, Solomon Benny and Vera.

Janie (my grandmother) married Barney Goldberg (my grandfather) and they owned a shop and properties in Randfontein. They had two daughters Myra (my Mother) and Fay.

Barney Goldberg died in 1927 at age 48 from pneumonia and Janie remarried Sam Levitan who was a 52 year old shopkeeper living in the Central Hotel Buildings in Randfontein and who had arrived in South Africa in 1894.

Janie died in 1931 from septicaemia after giving birth to Roy Kenneth Levitan.

Myra Goldberg aged nine (my Mom) and her sister Fay aged eight, orphans, lived in the care of Arcadia from 8 February 1933 to 30 January 1934.

On the admission form Myra my Mom, is shown as nine years old, born 8 December 1923, in grade two and having had tonsilitis and whooping cough. Fay, her sister is shown as eight years old, born 12 April 1925 in grade 1 and also having had tonsilitis.

Roy, the son of Janie and Sam Levitan, on the death of Janie was brought up by Miss Fels, the midwife. Roy referred to her as his mother and he lived with her after his father died.

Dora (my gran's sister) and Willie Lewitton who lived in the Free State came up to the Rand and took the two girls out of the Arc after about a year. They made a home for them and looked after them till they married.

FAY'S MEMORIES OF ARCADIA

Fay remembers that both Myra and her hated Arcadia and initially had no desire to even try and remember her time there.

Fay remembers the Arc was more like a prison than a home and they were looked after by 'a cruel anti-Semitic Afrikaans nurse.' She says that they used to walk to the school which was down the road and she also remembers being hungry in Arcadia.

Fay started to sleep walk and was threatened that she would be locked in the laundry if she did so. As a result she would keep herself awake all night so that she did not sleepwalk. Myra, she says, in protest, refused to walk and used to crawl around.

Myra and Fay left Arcadia in January 1934 and they went to live with their auntie Dora and Uncle Willy Lewitton, who had been living in the Orange Free State (OFS) in Tweespruit (Tweefontein?) running a General dealer store. They had come up to Johannesburg to make a home for the girls. They were not so wealthy, but kept a kosher home. They moved from place to place and found it very hard to settle in the city after living in the OFS.

MY MEMORIES OF BEFORE THE ARC

Before we came to the Arc we lived in a house at 65 Webb Street in Yeoville, the house my parents inherited from my Great Aunt Dora. As the property sloped downwards away from the road it had steps going down at the back to an outside toilet. We had an African servant called Johannes and a maid whose name I don't remember. Lastly, we had a Collie called Rover.

Johannes was gentle and caring towards us children and always had a big smile. He walked Jenny to school down the road by the Yeoville Shul and I went along too holding on to his big finger. He used to call me *"kleinbaas"* and he stopped to chat with the friendly big nannies sitting on a little wall drinking their tea from shining silver tins and eating their bread for breakfast. They would always be talking and laughing loudly.

I have only one recollection of my Mom. I was sick in bed and she was sitting on the bed in her white flowing nightgown. She was feeding me tea from a saucer in which she cooled the hot tea which she poured from a teacup. She would carefully hold the saucer and I would then drink the cool tea from it. I think she herself was sick at the time and had got out of bed to look after me.

I remember sleeping with my Dad and him telling me to wake him if I wet the bed. This I duly did and then he hung the sheet over an electrical cord that came from the back of the bed and sloped up to the roof from where it hung with a light bulb on the end, which lit the bedroom.

I remember two old Jewish ladies coming (at different times) to stay with us as housekeepers, but they did not last long. One of them was bitten by Rover, the dog, who then had to be tied up and they did not like having to go to an outside toilet, especially at night. One of the old ladies landed up at the Arc some time later as a helper to the housemother.

I also remember playing in a large pile of yellow sand, which the bricklayers would mix with the cement to lay the bricks. We had great fun playing in the sand and my Aunt Fay tells me that the family doctor, a friend, used to come round to keep an eye on us. He saw us one cold day playing in the sand not properly dressed for the cold, and reported us to the Jewish Welfare.

MY FIRST DAY IN THE ARC

I remember the first day we were in the Arc and being driven up the long driveway in my uncle Ben's large car and seeing boys playing soccer right at the top of the drive. Jenny and I went to the Arc hospital with my Dad and were bathed, Sister Conway and a few senior girls looking on. My Dad was upset and I would not let him go or say goodbye. As he was unable to say goodbye directly, as this would upset me, he said he was 'going to the toilet' and then left. Some senior girls were ready to play with and distract me, so I did not really notice my Dad's departure and it was not traumatic.

Sister Conway ran the hospital and she was assisted by Ruth. They ran the hospital most efficiently and although strict they had a very gentle and kind side which we got to know over the years.

We had to stay in the hospital for a week or two, "in quarantine", during which we were checked by doctors and then we went down to the Babies. Sister used to call me a little gentleman and spent a few minutes now and then to talk to me and to befriend me. Also the senior girls came to see the 'new babies' and play with us as their natural motherly instincts kicked in. I remember I had a brown rubber monkey, which whistled when you squeezed it, and I used to chew and suck on its ear. I can still remember the rubbery taste of the ear.

SAYING GOODBYE ON SUNDAYS

Every Sunday was a traumatic goodbye, but especially the first Sunday each month when we went out and I would have spent the day with my Dad. I remember one particular Sunday goodbye.

I held onto my Dad's leg with all the might a three and a half year old could muster. I was only as high as his leg but I would not let go. I was crying and was very upset and did not want him to leave.

Suzie, the nanny, told me not to be a baby and to stop crying, and my Dad snapped at her in my defence saying "He is just a baby! What do you expect?" It was not normal for my Dad to be angry but he would have been upset too. He would have wanted to avoid these traumatic good-byes when he took us back to the Babies Department at the end of the Sunday outings.

My hanging on bought me some more time with my Dad and he stayed on a while, but then "had to go to the toilet." I awaited his return patiently at the front door and after a while when he did not come back, reality sunk in. He had gone home leaving through the back door.

I was struck with panic and a sense of deep loss and emptiness. I cried and screamed and stamped up and down..."did the *Zulu dance*" as my cousin Jonathan would have said.

After I had expended a lot of energy crying, screaming and stamping I was exhausted and calmed down to just the occasional sniffle. I was lead off to the dormitory where I changed into my pyjamas. Later we had a dinner of "Post Toasties" in milk and sprinkled with sugar, a treat, and then I went to bed with the other kids.

I can clearly remember one Sunday, while I was in hospital and before Brian even came to the Arc, another episode when my Dad tried to say goodbye. As soon as he said he was going home I would get upset. I would cling to him, I would cry and I would scream. It was always very difficult for him to get away because I would get so upset and he would have to invent ways to go home. I remember this Sunday he said he was just going to fetch Brian and bring him back. But he did not come back and I waited and waited, but waited in vain.

On another occasion when I was in hospital on the Sunday day-out he simply did not come in to see me in the morning when he picked up Jenny and Brian, as it would have been very difficult for him to leave again. So he came and saw me when he dropped them back in the afternoon. It was a rainy day and I had my head pressed against the glass door looking outside at the pathway that led down to Babies and along which my Dad would have to take Jenny and Brian home. My Dad surprised me by coming through the front entrance of the hospital and I remember Sister saying that I had been looking out for him for a long time.

THE BABIES

Boys and girls from the age of two went into the Babies Department till age ten and then they were separated into either Junior Boys or Junior Girls. I spent six and a half years in the Babies from July 1956 to December 1962.

When I came to the Arc, Auntie Botha was not yet there, but I only have a few memories of her predecessor. I remember Auntie Botha very well, and she was in charge for many years. She left at about the time I went to the Junior Boys.

For the much younger children after each meal was potty time when we had to sit on our pots in the bathroom area and do our 'business'. This was a time to be sociable and we would sit and talk and drag our pots around with our legs while still sitting on them and sometimes we would even race each other dragging our pots.

I remember we had a nanny, Rachel, and her job was to look after us at night and to do the ironing, mainly of all the school shirts. So she was there at night watching over us. She had to wake up a few of the children and take them to the toilet to try and stop them wetting their beds.

I remember having nightmares and screaming out in my sleep. On one occasion it was the roaring Metro Golden Meyer lion that made me scream out in fear and on another it was either the wolf from the three piglets' story or from Goldie Locks that was going to eat me. Rachel then let me sleep in the dining room where she was doing the ironing at night.

The person I remember most during this time was Max Goldman with freckles and ginger hair and one very clean thumb. There was also Elisabeth Fliess, who later I said was my "girlfriend", and Nadia Learman. The girls were slightly younger than us and we played with them. At that time Suzie, who was a very tiny African nanny, looked after us. Max and I never went to nursery school, but I remember Hilda Durbach who was also about our age did. I don't know why this was so.

Suzie encouraged Max and I to suck our thumbs (I suppose to comfort ourselves and to make us sleep) and Max always had a very clean white thumb. Max used to suck his thumb all the time. I used to suck my thumb too, but not to the same extent. She never smacked us, but she was at times a little impatient with us and spoke harshly to us, so we did as she asked.

We sat on the steps, at the front of the Babies, having lunch in the shade of an upright pencil pine tree. Lunch consisted of a little sausage roll, which was quite dry and a tomato. At about the time Hilda came home from nursery school we would have to go and rest until the other kids came home from primary school.

Here I remember Nadia's brother, Morris Learman and their older sister Shana, Hilton Rothaus, Neville Merwitz, Paul Cohen, Elizabeth's older sister Jennifer Fliess and a group of older kids including Bessie Bortz, Hymie Aronoff, Violet Solomon, David Ginsburg, Raymond Warshoski and Kenny Saus. Michael Goldstein and his sisters Valerie Hannah and Lauraine, Esther and Mark Lazralovich, Offer and Boaz Fein and the Schreeuwers, Ronny, Willy and Shelley came later.

I would call out, "Morris Learman ginger German." This is something I had learnt from some older boys. Morris would get angry and beat me up and I would go away crying. I remember crying quite a lot and was called a "cry baby". Some nights in bed I would think of my mother and feel this great emptiness and cry myself to sleep. Generally it would not take much to set me off crying. If I was upset and someone asked me what was wrong it would be hard for me to explain without reverting to crying again so I suppose I was a big cry baby. It even said so in one of the Arc magazines and when I met up with Ruth over 40 years later she reminded me.

There were two pedal cars, a jeep and a red one with a thick coat of paint. The jeep went very well but the red one was very difficult to pedal. Max and I always vied with each other to get the jeep, and I remember on one occasion, Max had been in the jeep a long time and did not want to give me a turn. I told him that the housemother (before Botha) was giving out sweets, so off Max ran to get his (in vain). Well, then it was my turn on the jeep and Max thought that was unfair.

The Senior Girls used "to save us" (sweets). We all had someone who would "save us" and I remember Eva Bortz used to save me. I remember her giving me the sugary fruity Pesach (Passover) sweets which she would have kept from Oneg. I would have to tell her rude stories about lemonade and chocolate cake and make her laugh to "earn" the sweets. She would pick me up and carry me on her hips like a baby and kiss and cuddle me. I think that at this time Bessie Bortz, Eva's sister "saved" Max.

Max and I used to vie with each other for Bessie's attention. Max was her favourite and I remember Bessie coming to me and telling me something to the effect that she was Max's friend, not mine, however she also added that Max had told her to say that. I tried to win her over by telling her that I was going to be rich when I was grown up and she laughed.

WHY I AM NOT A DOCTOR AND WHY I TAKE THREE SUGARS

From the very early age of three or four I used to tell everyone who asked what I would be when I was big, that I was going to be a doctor. I think the seed of this desire was planted by an aunt of mine who suggested I be a doctor. She probably also told me doctors made a lot of money and were very rich.

In those days we saw our parents once a week on Sundays. On the first Sunday of the month you could go out for the full day and for the rest of the Sundays parents could only visit us at the Arc in the afternoons. My Dad who was honest and righteous in his own way, was not very good with these rules and he would regularly each Sunday take us off to visit our grandparents.

Ma knew about this "bunking out" and told us kids we should not go out and that we should come and tell her if our father wanted to take us out. I also remember her explaining the rules to my Dad a few times. My Dad would initially say nothing when Ma spoke but he would nod his head with his mouth slightly open and his eyes open a little bit wider and his "voeseraai" buzzing and pressed on his ear. When Ma was finished the

telling off and the explaining of the rules, my Dad would sort of gently smile and laugh softly, like a naughty boy found out. He would then change the subject and would explain in an animated way, using his hands a lot, that his "voeseraai" (which was a wooden box (4x10x20cm) with batteries which made a buzzing noise) was to block out the noises that came from inside his head and that he could not hear too well. I'm not too sure what Ma made of my Dad who suffered from tinnitus.

We would still go visit my Gran regularly each Sunday. My Dad would park his Dodge, and later his van at the top of the drive by Dolly and the stables. We would hide under the dashboard and off we would go. My Dad would tell us not to worry and I think Ma had given up on us as she had explained the rules to my Dad a few times. We told her at the end of the day when she questioned us that we had visited our Gran. She was never angry with us about this bunking out, and I think she must have come to the conclusion it was good for us and my Dad to visit our grandparents. Ma would also have seen that it was a hopeless case to pursue the matter with my Dad as my Dad would nod in agreement in front of her and then simply take us to visit our Gran the next time when Ma was not around. I would like to have been a fly on the wall when Ma discussed the problematic Mr Sandler with Doc. Somehow I think Doc would have shrugged his shoulders and simply smiled.

We looked forward to these visits to my Gran, where we caught up to my Bobba (my Gran, Gertie)) and my great aunt, Auntie Feiga, who only spoke Yiddish and the rest of my aunts and uncles and cousins.

In the afternoon at tea time we would all be sitting around the dining room table. I would have watched my Gran going through the tea making ceremony. The water had to be boiled and the tea leaves added. There were no tea bags those days and the tea had to be poured through a strainer to remove the tea leaves. The milk was first poured into the cup and then the tea added and finally hot water added, if necessary. The big treat from my Gran was a lemon cream biscuit made by Bakers. We used to very carefully separate the two sides and then lick the entire lemon cream filling and finally eat the biscuit. If we were lucky we got a second biscuit. Funny how lemon creams nowadays do not taste as good.

My great aunt's daughter, my Aunt Silvia, would ask me in a loud and shrill voice, "Nu Dovidil, wot vil you be ven you are finished mit school?" I would tell them "I'm going to be a doctor." She would exclaim with a loud shrill, "Mmmmm !! Un doktor!!" Everyone would start laughing and there would be translations and discussions back and forth in English and in Yiddish.

This question and answer would come up many times when I visited my Gran or my grand Auntie Feiga who lived a block down from my Gran in La Rochelle. She was my grandfather's sister and in her backyard were two or three massive fig trees. Whenever I went there we would pick the figs and I always thought figs in Yiddish were Feiga and that's where she derived her name.

I remember falling on the back steps that went down to the outside toilet and grazing my knee and they got me to wee in a little container and then proceeded to clean the wound with the wee.

My grandfather (Solomon) would have also been there in the early days. He was quite a bit older than my grandmother and he passed away when I was quite young, after a car accident. I have two memories of him. One when he was sitting stooped in a chair with his arms in front of him holding onto a walking stick which would be just about chin level. He was sitting in an alcove with the morning sun streaming in through the lace curtains on the bay windows where the ferns grew very well in a large brass pot. The second memory was him sipping lemon tea with a sugar block held between his lips. I am digressing so let me get back to the story.

It was at one of these tea parties that I graduated from drinking a "bissen" milk to drinking tea. I must have been deemed old enough to drink tea because if we were short of milk my Gran would have sent my Aunt Rosie to buy the milk from the Indian shop half a block away and us kids would have all gone with her. My Gran poured the tea and asked my Dad how many sugars? Three was the answer he gave and since then it's always been three sugars for me. He would pour the tea into a saucer to cool it down and then I would shlurp it from the saucer.

It was about four years later and I must have been about seven or eight in the Babies and before the *kraal* was built. Sidney Lipschitz was giving me a ride on his shoulders on the netball field below the main building and the subject came up about what I was going to be when I grew up. When I told him a doctor he explained that I would have to study for seven long years before I become a doctor and could earn money. This was much too long he explained, and I could be something else and it would not take so long. After that day I decided not to become a doctor.

I landed up becoming a Chartered Accountant. I studied six years at Witwatersrand University and about four years in other institutions, a total of about 10 years. I can clearly say that the conversation with Sidney that day put me off from wanting to be a doctor.

IN THE BABIES

In the middle of the afternoons, very occasionally, 'tuck' would be handed out. On Sundays when parents visited some of them brought their children 'tuck', generally a brown bag of sweets. The tuck was all kept in the tuck cupboard in the passage and handing out the tuck was quite a difficult thing to do as some children received a very large bag of tuck while others received very little or none at all. In fact some children did not even get a visitor.

We would all stand in front of the open tuck cupboard and the Housemother would hand out the tuck. The children without any tuck would wait patiently towards the back. The Housemother would first give the children who actually had tuck something to eat and they would run off to eat their sweets. She would then slowly look through the packets and 'find' something for each child even those without any tuck. If you had been naughty you would probably be sent off with no tuck.

I also remember going up to the Senior Girls once or twice for elocution lessons and going swimming in the babies' pool (later the tippy pond) but it was only on one or two occasions as it was always getting blocked up.

After Hebrew lessons, which I found very boring, we would play till say 5:30 pm when it was bath time and the boys and girls were bathed separately. I remember the water being very dirty and there being a very thick layer of dirt on the top. We would be three in the bath and would climb out and stand on the bench to be dried. Then we got dressed in our pyjamas and had supper at about 6:00 pm and then brushed our teeth and went to bed.

Brushing teeth was not so strictly enforced or supervised and I think many of us did not have tooth brushes or tooth paste. Every now and then we were given new brushes and toothpaste. We did see the dentist regularly on a Sunday morning in the Dentist's room up in the hospital and if we needed fillings we would have to go to town. There the Dentist would often also give us toothpaste and brushes.

I remember being nicely tucked up in bed in the Babies and very late some nights listening to the animals from the zoo. On a quiet night one could clearly hear the roaring lion and the trumpeting elephant and also the shunting steam trains from the station in town. Also I remember one warm night kneeling on my bed and looking out of the window into the sky and seeing the entire sky filled with stars of all different colours and sizes. I believe I was dreaming as it was after hearing one day at school how beautiful the stars were at night.

ON THE WEEKENDS THE ROUTINE CHANGED

On Friday afternoons at bath time we used to have a change of clothes and this was the first time I dressed up as a girl. I must have been about four years old. The girls had had their baths and had been given clean clothes for the week and their dirty clothes were all in a big heap outside the bathroom. The boys were getting ready for their baths when Kenny Souse, a much older boy, suggested that we all dress up in the girls' clothes. There were about 15 boys ranging from three to ten years old all fighting for, and putting on assorted bits of girls' clothing. All of a sudden the housemother appeared and there was an even bigger scramble to take off the girls' clothing. I think she was very amused to see us little ones struggling to get out of the girls' clothes.

When we were a bit older I remember that on Friday afternoons we used to be invited to the homes of friends in our class. Mrs Edelman (Auntie Shirley) organised it and we would go to their home and have lunch and then spend the afternoon with them until about 5.00 pm. Sometimes during the holidays we would also be taken out by these friends for the day.

I remember many visits to my school friend Martin Woolf and one day playing with Melanie his cousin, who in later years married my first cousin Elliot, who is an Architect and for a few years was an Honorary Architect to Arcadia.

We all had our turn to go out for the day with Mrs Edelman (Auntie Shirley) and I remember her inviting us all to her house for a swim and an afternoon party.

On Friday night Ma used to come down to the Babies and light the Shabbat candles.

We used to go to Shul every Saturday morning and for all festivals. Shul was a little bit boring and here Doc would lead the service and read from the Torah. We would all go out and kiss the Torah when it was taken from the Ark to the Bimah and when it was taken back again. Janice Blumenfeld (a senior girl) and then later Sharon Getz used to look after the Babies and take us to Shul and bioscope. The older Babies also used to go to bioscope on Saturday nights, but often had to go to bed after the news and cartoons, as the main picture was deemed to be inappropriate.

I remember we used to get "opening medicine" regularly on Saturdays. Initially I think it was caster oil but then later we got "Milk of Magnesia". This did work and I remember spending ages on the toilet as the opening medicine did its work. Also I remember receiving a tonic. It looked like syrup, sticky and brown and thick and we each got a spoon full and slowly swallowed it. To this day I am still not sure why we used to get the opening medicine and tonic.

Marina, Marina, Marina

I remember Graham, Linda and Marilyn's (Stolers) mom. She used to come to the Arc on a Saturday as opposed to a Sunday and she used to sit by the steps outside the front of the Babies and wait for us to finish our rest to see her kids. The Senior Girls used to come and sit with her and then she used to sing to them and she had a very nice voice. I remember her singing a particular Italian song, "*Marina, Marina, Marina*" and even now I can sing it and I remember the words and I have remembered it ever since then, over 40 years ago.

The Oneg tree

Then there was the Oneg tree which was near the netball field and not far from the Babies. In summer in the afternoons, about four o' clock on Saturdays, the Juniors and Seniors would all have to gather for Oneg ('or fours') and *Lecol* (orange cordial with water) or milk and a piece of sponge-cake would be served. Then Doc would ask questions on the Bible and Torah and Jewish History etc and if we did not know the answer he would just hint at it and hint at it and give us more clues and more clues. He would never tell the answer, but he would give away so many hints and endless clues to lead the children to the answer.

On Sunday mornings the girls did ballet with Carol, while the boys went to boxing with Donald. The boxing room was under the Shul and I remember getting into trouble for hitting Maxie too hard. As a kind of punishment Donald got an older boy, Raymond Lang, to spar with me and he was a bit tough on me, but not too tough.

I remember life in the Arc as generally happy, except the Sunday afternoon trauma after my Dad's visits when I was first in the Babies.

I remember the Sunday afternoon feeling one grew up with. It was the excitement of looking forward to the visit and it was also the sadness, loneliness and emptiness afterwards. I remember hanging on to my Dad when it was time for him to go home, especially after a Sunday out (the first Sunday each month). I remember my Dad having to invent ways of going to avoid the trauma. Until only a few years ago I would still feel an emptiness on Sunday afternoons and I always felt I must go out and do something.

AROUND THE BABIES

Burning Rubber

I remember very clearly the Babies' area where we used to play. At the end of our play area, on the side close to the tennis court were two separate toilets and between them there were two washbasins. It was quite close to the tennis courts and I think originally it was a change room or just toilets to be handy to the tennis courts. This was at the end of the Babies Department and the end of the enclosed playground and our playing area, so Max and I used to go there quite often and we found quite a few interesting things there and did a few naughty things there too. Max loved to play with matches and so we got hold of some matches. I am not too sure where from. We went into one of these toilets with this rubber duck or rubber doll and I remember we had some newspapers and we lit the newspapers and we burnt the rubber. Although we did not really make a big fire the rubber had melted and we got it on our fingers and it burnt into our hands and it was really painful and sore. We couldn't really run and tell anyone because we had been naughty and we had done this to ourselves and I remember the dripping rubber burning on our little hands. I am looking at my hands now, I don't see any marks on them but I remember it being very sore.

Bougainvillea Bushes

On one occasion I climbed on top of the wall and stood and looked down the hill. Against the wall on the other side were large purple bougainvillea bushes. I remember walking along the wall and getting dizzy and losing my balance and actually falling over the wall. The drop was much higher on the other side of the wall because it was sloping downhill but when I fell, I fell into this bougainvillea bush. I didn't hurt myself at all and the bush cushioned my fall. Although the bougainvillea has got thorns, because it saved me, I have always thought of it as a nice protecting plant rather than a thorny horrible bush.

The Swing and the Pool

The swing at the Babies was eventually tied up so we could not use it. On one occasion I was having a bailing out competition with Graham Stoler to see who could jump off the swing the furthest. I was older than Graham and of course I would always beat him. This time he jumped further than me and not to be out-done, I really swung very high and I jumped. I jumped past him and told him so as I lay on the ground but in the process I broke my arm. Another occasion when someone was on the swing, Boaz Fein was walking by when the screws on the bottom of the swing caught him on the forehead. He had to go off to hospital with a vicious wound that left a bad scar. After that the swing was tied up.

We got a baby pool that was made out of zinc or corrugated metal and it was oval shaped and it had around it, a wall maybe a metre high. It was painted blue and it sat on a little stage, a raised platform. It was not very big and it did not last very long. It wasn't really practical because, although you could fill it with water, it was difficult to clean. It hung around a while, but then they got rid of it.

On one occasion Morris Learman and I collected a couple of zinc sheets. You could find zinc sheets all over the place. We put them up against the jungle gym so as to make a slide. Morris slid down and I slid down after him. When I slid down some jagged metal edges around some holes caught me just by the knee and I received quite a deep cut. There was a lot of blood and panic and screaming and off I ran. I had to be taken to the hospital and I blamed Morris Learman for pushing me and he received a smack. I still have the scar today.

In the earlier days our play area was open, but then later on we were enclosed in what we called, a *kraal*. William, the handyman came along and he built this *kraal* with upright poles, maybe about 80cm high and sharpened on the top. I don't know why they were sharpened on the top and it did not seem to make sense. We were confined within this *kraal* and in the *kraal* were the jungle gym and the swing and there we had to play.

Four Corners

Just outside the *kraal* on the side going up towards where the Succah was, and where the stage was for the prize giving, there were four metal posts. Here we used to play "four corners" which was a game played by five people. One was in the middle and the ones at the post would have to change sides (poles) and while they were changing sides, the one in the middle would have to try and grab the pole before the others could change sides. The one who lost out would be in the middle.

These four posts actually formed a boxing ring and on one occasion I remember them actually putting the ropes on the four poles, and having a boxing match. I only saw a boxing match there once.

Baseball

In this same area we used to play baseball. We used a tennis ball and a tennis racket. The base was the wall which backed onto the stage, where we had our prize giving. You would run from that point to first base, the door in the middle of the side of the Joe Louis Wing, then second base was the tree up against the *kraal* and third base was the stone L-shaped bench that was at the Oneg tree and back again would complete the diamond. We used to play baseball quite often and it was quite good fun there.

Setting up for the prize Giving

When it was prize giving time we would all help set up the chairs. The chairs would be carried down from the main building. I don't know exactly where they came from. They would be folded and we would unfold them and put them into lines and then the lines were straightened, re-straightened and straightened again. It was all good fun putting it all together and taking it down afterwards.

The stages would also be set up and a row of poles and cross-beams covered with branches and shrubs formed a wall behind the stage. There was an entrance out of which we would come onto the stage for the prize giving. This is also where we used to have our large Succah in the earlier times.

Wandering Around

On the one side near the corner of the Babies we used to sit by the steps and have our lunch with Susie and then further along was the Oneg tree. There was also a loquat tree at the bottom of the steps close to the Oneg tree and we would climb in it during summer and maybe early spring and try to get the loquats. I never climbed it but the older boys and maybe some of the braver younger boys did. The way I used to try and get loquats was to throw sticks and stones at the yellow ones.

There was also a "bread tree" which was near the swings which overlooked the hill. I am not too sure why we called it a bread tree or what tree it really was. It had a berry, same size as a loquat with a big pip inside. This was near Montgomery's cliff. It would be around this area that Max Goldman would have made his first fire which burned down half the hill.

A bit further down there was the slide and nearby another plaything which wasn't a jungle gym, but it was something where you could go across, hanging on by your hands. This contraption had ladders going up on each end and then had a ladder going across and you could go across by hanging and moving one arm at a time.

There were the *hok*s around there in earlier days and that's where Max and my brother Brian made another fire completing the job of burning down the rest of the hill.

There was stone work and terraces and little stone benches you could sit on by the netball field. If you went around towards the embankment leading up to the main building there was an electrical box and it had a certain smell about it.

Between the hospital and the Juniors or Senior Girls there was an area that was overgrown with grass and quite a few stones. Also there was a little area where there were these massive pots which were used for seedlings. Seedlings were planted here and there was like a little nursery and when the plants got bigger they would be transplanted into the gardens which were all around the Arc. There was this one African man, Bernard, I think his name was, and he used to look after this area and you would see him spending lots of time there and the story goes that he used to grow his *dagga* there. You could see he was always in a daze with glassy red eyes and drifting around and every now and then stop and have a little smoke. Now I don't know if that is real or this was made up, folk lore, but that's how I also remember it.

By the Tennis Courts

By the tennis courts just around by the toilets there was this palm tree with very sharp long thorns. We used to play a game called 'peggy' using these thorns. You broke off one of these thorns and two of you would stand opposite each other. Then you would have turns to peg the thorn into the ground. You would throw it and the idea was that you would throw it next to another person's foot. If it stuck in the ground that person would have to open their legs and the objective was to get the person to open their legs more and more until they could not open them anymore. You would have a turn and they would have a turn and the winner was the one who pegged it too far that the other one could not reach it. Sometimes you would peg that thorn into your opponent's leg by accident and it stung a bit because it was very sharp and hard.

Another thing that happened by the tennis court was collecting wire. Sometimes you would want wire because you could make a bow and arrow with the wire. Where did we get the wire? The tennis court of course. You would just worry the wire, move it back and forward until it broke. Then you would unwind the strand and by unwinding the strand you would leave a big hole in the side of the tennis court fence. As you unwound each piece it undid the diamond shaped fence and so I am sure the tennis court had a few holes in that side as we collected the wire to play with and also to make bows and arrows.

In the area just above the Senior Girls, below the hospital there was long grass. It was overgrown and that's where the seedlings were and that's where we also used to catch grasshoppers for Susie who would encourage us to do this.

I remember there once being a massive bean plant, with lots and lots of beans, planted by Sonia Scop that grew up on the tennis court fence. Initially I used to eat a lot of the beans that were growing there and I would simply take the pods and eat them. For some reason or other I got it into my head, that Sonia Scop was not nice, and I decided I would just break the plant and I did just that. It was quite stupid and silly of me and later on when she questioned me about it I admitted it quite proudly. She wasn't upset about it and she did not say anything to me about it but with a lot of hindsight, I was just a stupid little kid and I must have been 5 or 6 at the time.

Also around this area I remember seeing a bee flying and I caught it in my hand and of course it stung me. I had to go up to see Sister Conway at the hospital and she put some purple stuff on and she could not really understand why I actually caught it. There was a doorway leading from the Senior Girls towards the tennis courts. There were steps there with walls on the side and it was here that Beryl Lucking fell and broke her collarbone.

If you walked towards the hospital, at the corner of the tennis courts you came to a solid concrete wall. That wall we practiced on. You could actually hit the ball against the wall and have quite an energetic game with yourself by hitting the ball against the wall.

You then walked up towards the concrete stairs which were quite steep and on the one side were these vines which had these purple trumpet flowers and under the leaves you could

find silver ladybugs or golden ladybugs which we used to occasionally collect. In the vines you could go through a little hole and you could force yourself in there and be enclosed within the bush. This was very close to the area that was like the sun room on the side of the hospital which became the art room, where I remember we used to have our art lessons with Eileen Sasto, who was the daughter of Charlotte Sasto who was on the Arc Committee for many years.

The Hospital

Hospital was a nice place to be on the bitterly cold winter's days and I used to get in by rubbing my eyes and reporting in sick with pink eyes, which was some kind of allergy. I think sister got wise to me as I always had recovered by mid morning when the sun was shining and we were busy reading comics. She would then send me to school telling me that I had a little allergy, which was not contagious. Later I would have to invent " sore throat, sore tummy and headaches" to gain admittance.

All of us had chicken pox and mumps and German measles. Those kids who had not yet caught the latest sickness were encouraged to play with those who had, so that we all had it and that we would not get it when we were older. It was good fun being in hospital in groups when chicken pox and mumps and German measles were around. We did not have to go to school and would be able to play all day. We had masses of comics to swap as Doc kept us all well supplied.

While I enjoyed the days in hospital as a kid, I was terrified of the nights alone in the hospital. I had heard stories of the hospital being haunted from the older Arc boys. I remember Henry Shippel telling "true stories" about ghosts in the hospital and to this day I still remember very vividly two nightmares in the hospital.

I remember reporting to Sister one day as I was weeing red. I felt quite alright but I had heard somewhere that if you had bilharzia, which came from dirty and stagnant water, you would wee red. I was a bit worried as I had been playing in a fish pond at a park on the Sunday day out with my Dad.

Sister quickly diagnosed the problem with a single question, "Have you been eating red popcorn?" This indeed was the cause.

The hospital was the place where we had our vaccinations against the various diseases. It was terrifying for us children to line up for these injections. The long queue, the screaming of the ones in front when it was their turn and the smell of ether all added to the terror.

Also our teeth were examined at the hospital on a Sunday morning at least every six months. Dr Kussner would come in and Rosie or Bessie Bortz would act as the dental assistant. He would gently tell us to 'open wide' and poke around at our teeth. I often needed extra attention and would have to have an appointment at his rooms at Ingram's Corner in Hillbrow. This was a treat even though the drilling and filling of the teeth was sometimes painful and you had to sometimes wait a very long time for your turn. I remember first going to see the dentist when about four years old and over the years my minders included Sister, Sharon Getz and Anne Flink. Most times after seeing Dr Kussner I ended up with a few sweets that I could 'only suck'.

I remember other children were terrified of the dentist and specifically remember hearing Sharon Getz screaming while being treated. Dr Kussner was always very gentle and soft spoken. I remember he got a new drill that 'didn't hurt so much' and sprayed water on your tooth as he drilled.

Just to the side of the hospital I had a garden with Minnie Baitz. We planted potatoes given to us by Mrs. Westruid (who looked after the kitchen) in the same flowerbed that the dahlias were growing just above where they used to build the sukkah.

Before School

We were dropped off by the Arc bus at school at about 7.30 am while school only started at eight 'o clock which gave us some freedom and a chance to look around and also get up to mischief. It was a time to walk around the streets or look for treasures in the park or "explore" the school.

One morning before anyone was there Jenny and I went into the secretary's office early. We phoned my Aunt Mercia, who lived in Krugersdorp and we had a nice chat with her from school. We had looked up her number in the phone book and Jenny made me talk first and only spoke afterwards.

Early one morning I took Mrs Durbach's rubber which was in her top drawer and I played *charms* with it and later on in the class when she discovered it was missing she asked if anyone knew about it. One of the kids told her that I had it and I denied taking it and offered to allow her to search my bag for it. I had played *charms* with it and lost it. I think somehow she knew it was me, maybe the guilt was written on my face.

On another morning I stole some of the domino matchboxes from Mrs Levinson's room. She was my grade 2 teacher and had them in a little drawer in shelves in the side in her room and I knew where they were. I stole them from her because there was a competition to collect the most empty matchboxes and you could win a book as a prize. I actually gave them in as part of the ones I had collected.

Later on during the day Mr Pacter, our principal, called me in and asked me where the domino matchboxes came from. I denied stealing them. He did not believe me and he reminded me of the 10 commandments he used to quote at every assembly, especially "Thy shall not steal!" I was questioned about where I got these matchboxes. I said I had got them from my Dad. I think they knew I had stolen them but they never pushed the issue with me, but I did not win the book that was the prize for collecting the most matchboxes. Another boy in my class , Colin Zaiden won it.

On one occasion, I forgot my bag at home and when we arrived at school and I could not find my bag I cried. Christopher, the bus driver, who was nicknamed Dice, instead of coming back later with my bag must have gone straight back to the Arc and brought the bag to me, and as a result of that, the kids from Saxonwold were late at school. I thought that was a bit of a stupid way to do things. He should have taken the kids to school first and then brought my bag later. My bag was brought to me in my class after school had started and when I got home the kids from Saxonwold School who were late that morning were angry with me.

During School

Bessie Bortz used to ring the bell in the morning and I remember Maxie telling me once that Bessie let him ring the bell.

We used to assemble in the hall once or twice a week including on Fridays. During assembly Mr Pactor, the headmaster stood on the edge of the stage and read out a passage from the Bible. He would stand very close to the edge of the stage and rock forward and backwards as he read the Ten Commandments from quite a tiny little book. We thought he was going to fall off the edge of the stage.

During break my Dad occasionally came to visit us at school through the back gate. The back gate would be locked, but he would be there and somehow I would know he was there and we would have to ask the African groundsman, who used to look after the school, to unlock the gate. I used to have to find him and ask him to open the back gate, a thing he did quite willingly and my Dad would always give us some money and we would buy ice cream.

During break there was the ice cream man who sold ice cream suckers for a tickey. It was a long round ice lolly which you could suck and it was very cool and tasty. Because many of the kids did not have enough money he cut the ice lolly up so he could sell you a penny's worth or 1½ penny's worth instead of a tickey's worth. He could sell you what you wanted and all he would do was cut up the ice lolly.

There was quite a big fuss made because the principal got very angry about this and he announced at assembly that you shouldn't buy from him as the knife was very dirty. I don't know if the knife was clean or not, but anyway that's what happened so there was no more buying part ice creams or half ice creams.

I bought a tin of condensed milk from the corner Indian Store (the Coolie Shop) with my shilling that I received weekly for pocket money. I put it under my desk in the drawer ready for break time when I would have a special treat eating it by sucking it all out of the two little holes I would make in the tin. But when break time came I forgot about it and then I only remembered it later in the day.

On inquiring I discovered that Cecel Levine had taken it and he had drunk the whole lot. I was very upset and I told him he had to buy me another one, but he refused. He said he didn't have to buy me another one because I had been to his house lots of times, because I used to go there Friday afternoons, and I had eaten a lot of food there. There was nothing I could really do, so he had my tin of condensed milk and I was very upset.

In my class there was a guy called Mervin Sherman and once he went home early because he messed in his pants. I thought he had very good manners because he didn't say I pooed in my pants or anything bad. He just said in a very loud and clear voice, "I am not feeling well and I messed in my pants". I thought that was a very civilized way of asking to go home after messing your pants.

After School

After school we also had free time in grades one and two as we finished school before the other classes. Also, we had free time as we waited for the Arc bus. This gave us the chance to look around and go shopping.

Along Bok Street towards Joubert Park was a fish and chips shop. There we would sometimes go after school if we were fortunate enough to have a fortune (a sixpence) to buy fish and chips. We never used to buy the fish, we used to just buy the chips which were really nice and a very special treat. At the top of the park on Bok Street we waited for the Arc bus that used to stop and pick us up. Bessie swapped her Arc sandwiches with the ice cream man for ice cream. I thought that was very smart as we sometimes did not even eat our *sarmies* and we took them home and threw them away.

One special occasion my Dad gave me two and six (2 ½ shillings) and Max and I, who came out earlier than the other children, went off and we bought chips. We actually walked all the way up to Joubert Park and looked in at all the shops to see what we could buy. We looked at a kaleidoscope that we could not buy as it cost two and six and we had already bought these chips. Just as we were coming back to the corner we saw the Arc bus driving off. We ran and we shouted, but they did not hear us and just drove off and so we went back to Mr. Pactor's office. We told him we had missed the bus and he phoned the Arc saying he had two naughty boys with him and asking what he should do. It was decided that he should put us on the bus home and so Mr Pactor asked us to go with this prefect who took us to the bus stop at Joubert Park. There we were put on the bus to the Arc and then when we got off the bus at Oxford Road Susie was waiting for us at the bus stop. She walked us up the drive and we got a big smack for missing the bus.

THE JUNIOR BOYS

When we were about ten we were separated into either junior boys or junior girls. In the junior boys we were no longer confined to "*the kraal*" and were free to wander up and down the hill and had ample time to pursue our latest interests or to get up to mischief. As Junior Boys we not only had to obey the instructions of the housemother and Fickey, but also those of the senior boys.

ARC LAW AND LORE

When we were in the Babies and approaching 10 years old we were very keen to go to the Junior Boys. We had heard many many stories of the Junior Boys. Neville Merwitz, who was at school with us and a few years older than us was a fantastic yarn spinner, and could embellish any story and fed us many of these tails. Paul Cohen and Hilton Rothaus would confirm them. They explained to us about pilings which is what happened to

squealers and schlupps and the general goings on in the Junior and Senior Boys.

They explained to us the unwritten laws which were:
o   Thou shalt not squeal (tell on one another or dob in)
o   Thou shalt not schlupp (suck up to) the people in charge
o   Thou shalt own up (if you did something wrong and there was a witch hunt for the culprit and everyone was to be punished)
o   Thou shalt obey your elders (especially if they were bigger than you and short-tempered)

There were epic and fantastic tales about pilings and punishments, about fruit raids, bunking out, raiding the orchard the bread room and the cellar. Also there were various stories about the hospital being haunted, about the head boy, Hymie Pearlman who was tough and enforced the law and about Skellie (Julius Aronoff) who broke the law. There were stories about running away and catching trains to Durban. There were stories of adventure about the Rand Show and complimentary tickets to the rides, about up the hill and down the hill, about building huts and *hoks* and scotch carts and racing down the drive and having chickens and selling the eggs and also about cooking *tamalekie*. There were stories about fires and Stelzner and Vicky too.

As bine and 10 year olds we could not wait to go to the Junior Boys and take part in all these fantastic things and whenever a Junior Boy visited our *kraal,* we would ask them to tell us about the Junior Boys. While Neville, Hilton and Paul built the fantasy there were a few who painted a more sceptical picture. Arnold Salmonson told us it was not so nice and that Hymie Pearlman was a bully. This did not put us off and we were still very keen to move.

The girls my age, Linda Stoler and Minnie Baitz moved to the Junior Girls and I was dead keen to go to the Junior Boys. Then Auntie Botha called me a few days later and told me that I was staying in the Babies for another year. I started to cry and then she laughed and told me that Maxi and I were going. It was a very thrilling thing for us both. We had been in the Babies for seven and six years and had been fed these fantasies which would now be realized.

We met Stelzner and got our numbers (mine 16) and played with those just older than us and slowly got used to the Junior Boys and our new surroundings. There were never any pilings although we were shown the spot in the long dormitory where David Ginsburg was thrown up in a blanket and hit the roof and then came down to hit the floor. The floorboards had collapsed a little and there was quite a big depression on the floor. Hymie Pearlman had left and in charge was Mervyn Lampert, more a scholarly type than a tough athletic type like Hymie had been.

There were fruit raids, bunking out, raiding the orchard, the bread room and the cellar. There was the Rand Show and complimentary tickets for the rides. We did build huts and scotch carts. Cooking was tried unsuccessfully as the smoke from the fires attracted, in one case Vicky when we cooked under the pool and then Ma when we cooked down the hill.

One Sunday I met Hymie Pearlman who had then left the Arc. He was sitting in the shade of the enormous bougainvillea bush opposite the main entrance waiting for someone and beckoned me with his index finger. I was reluctant to go over, but did as he continued to beckon me.

He had a big warm friendly smile, which lit up his face and he asked me if I knew who he was and asked me many leading questions. I told him I knew who he was and that I was now in the Junior Boys. Because of his friendly warm smile and the gentle way he talked to me, I was not afraid of him and told him that I had been told he was a bully. He did not deny this, but laughed heartily and we had quite a long conversation and I left with the impression he was a very nice and friendly.

The Senior Boys at the time I arrived in the Junior Boys were Mervyns Lampert, Stanley Stein and his younger brother Manfred, Keith Lang, Simon Woolf, Les Sacks, Jackie Levine, Raymond Warshosski, Hymie Aronoff and Brian Langman (Flossy). I believe they would have been in the two end dormitories.

A bit younger were Henry Shippel, Martin Katz and then Julius Gordon and Brian Hough and if not in the end dormitories, were in the long dormitory together with, Raymond Lang, Robert Langman, Brian Socher, Les Durbach, Ronny Schreeuwer and Neville Merwitz.

There were unwritten laws that existed between the Junior Boys and the Senior Boys. Junior Boys had to show respect for the Senior Boys or would be quickly pulled back into line. Generally they were required to do what the seniors wanted and they had the right to order you about. Some of the older boys used to smoke and we would be sent to the zoo to buy them smokes. Maybe you were gang pressed to play cricket or soccer or to do something when you did not really want to. You would be obliged to share (opps) what you were eating (your grub) with the Senior Boys. Generally they exercised this right in moderation as long as you showed them respect.

Initially in the Junior Boys, and later when a new boy came along, there would be fights and challenges to sort out the pecking order. If someone was much stronger than you then you would know your order, but the problem arose when two boys were more or less equal in strength. This was the case with Max and I who were a few months apart in age and over the years we fought several times. When we were in the Babies we fought a few times and I think I always got the better of Max. I remember Manfred Stein hitting me "for hitting Max" as Suzie marched us up to catch the bus to school one morning. Also I remember Donald who taught us boxing reprimanding me for hitting Max too hard when we sparred.

I remember having a punching fight with Max in the bathroom in the Junior Boys where we fought on for quite a while with almost every punch going into the face. Hilton witnessed the fight and I think he encouraged both of us at different times. When I was getting the better of Max he would cover his face and head with his hands and arms and bend forward. Max did not give up, but would rest a while and then come back at me and I would back off when he rested. Although I think I got the better of him in that fight, he did not surrender and so the pecking order was not resolved.

Soon after we had another wrestling fight that took place in the changing room adjoining the bathroom. Max had me in a headlock and banged my head against the wall and I had a big cut on my head caused by a screw that stuck out of the wall. There was blood all over and so the fight was stopped and I had to go to hospital to have the wound attended to. The Senior Boys teased me about it and regarded it as a victory for Max.

The very same day Michael Saiet came to the Arc he challenged me to a wrestling match and soon had me in a headlock from which I could not escape. He was bigger than me and I noticed that he only challenged smaller boys than himself, except Ronny and Leon who he must have recognised as too strong for him.

It only took one punch from Leon on my arm to tell me how powerful Leon was. My arm remained "lame' for weeks and the bruise went from green and purple to black and then blue. I once stood up to Michael Goldstein who was picking on me. I was holding my own boxing him, but he soon got the better of me when he threw me to the ground and sat on me.

Bullying did go on and most of us were on the receiving end and on the giving end in some way at some time or other. There were some kids however, who would never bully younger kids; Merwyn Lampert, Hymie Aronoff, Simon Woolf, Martin Katz and Brian Langman (called Flossy because of his blond hair). There was only one boy that was a terrible bully.

In the middle dormitory were the youngest, which included Boris Sedacca, Leon Goodman (newly arrived) Paul Cohen, Hilton Rothaus, Max Goldman.

The character that stands out to me the most at this time was Simon Woolf. He was not like the other seniors. He was a bit of a loner, not as boisterous as the others were and he was gentle and never ever bullied the younger ones. He was also very industrious and disciplined. He had a *hok* and kept chickens and made sure they were properly fed. He told me how he had gone very early one morning to the market to buy them. When he kept silkworms they were the biggest, as he would feed them at least twice a day with fresh green leaves. I remember he used to go down the hill and do weight lifting with poles and with him would always be Henry Shippel who simply sat and watched. Simon was teased by the other Senior Boys and at one time used to go around making a kind of grunting noise from his throat.

ARC SOCCER AND SPORTS

Every Saturday morning we had our ritual game of soccer after Shul. While it was fun playing soccer on Saturday mornings when we were a bit older, it was not much fun when we were younger and smaller. The ages ranged from about 10 years to 18 years old. The smaller boys of 10 and 11 years old were naturally scared of getting in the way of, or tackling the larger boys of 16 and 17 years who were fast and determined. We had a choice of either getting hurt by the larger boys on the other side when we tried to stop them, or getting a punch from the older boys on our own side for being too chicken to tackle and letting through the opposition. Generally if the side lost we were at risk of being punched for being chicken or not playing well enough.

When we were new Junior Boys Max and I had our own way of scoring and we were a bit indifferent to the game going on around us. We competed by each counting the number of times we touched the ball and seeing who touched the ball the most. Although we wanted to beat each other in this count of touches, it was quite dangerous getting the ball as you could get hurt when the opposition took it from you and you could also get a clout from an older team mate if you miss-passed the ball.

Doc joined us every Saturday morning for our ritual soccer game and he would always play up forward more or less camping near the opposition's goal waiting for a pass. He wore very large rugby boots with metal studs, very large black or blue rugby shorts and his beret to protect his head from the sun. When he had the ball he would protect it by pushing any defender away with an outstretched arm, like a rugby player, and he would accentuate his strides by grunting and growling. The victim was usually a smaller boy as the older boys were wise enough to give Doc a wide berth to avoid getting kicked or being trodden on with the studs.

At halftime, which was when the older boys wanted a rest or were thirsty, we sat on the side of the field under a shady tree and next to the tap. The water from this tap and the one by the pool was always very cool and very sweet. Fickey did not believe Les when one night he caught Les outside and Les told him that he had gone to drink water from the tap by the pool 'because it was sweeter and cooler'. There we would banter with Doc discussing tactics and missed opportunities and joking and teasing and drinking the cool water and cooling off.

The game was sometimes interrupted when the ball was kicked over the fence and 'down the hill' or into the Gee's house with its barking dogs. When we first started playing soccer Max and I were the ball boys and our job was to retrieve just such balls. We would both rush to recover the ball and when it was over the fence and in the Gee's garden we would wait as the dogs barked until Mrs Gee came out and gave us the ball with a smile. The problem arose when the Gees were out because Max and I were scared of the dogs and would not jump the fence. Help came from Hilton, who was not scared and he would retrieve the ball in a flash.

The game did not finish until Doc had scored his goal. Sometime he had toe punted a few goals during the game but if he had not, the word would go out, "Give Doc a goal!" Then the opposition players would feign 'trying to stop Doc' with extra grunts and exclamations, the goalie would 'dive' the wrong way and Doc would score. Sometimes the show had to be repeated as the ball could go in any direction as Doc toe punted it as he aimed for goal. Doc would get annoyed if he was not passed the ball when he was 'unmarked and had a clear shot at goal' and he would tell off the one who had not passed to him.

Leon stands out as a very talented player and out of my contemporaries no one was faster off the mark or quicker between two points. He was a skilful dribbler and had a strong and accurate kick. Ronny was also very skilful, but would hold onto the ball a bit too long. Les, who played rugby, was very fit and had the most powerful kick, but he lacked the ball handling skills of Leon and Les.

Donald had instilled in us the rudiments of boxing when we were younger and we would sometimes put on gloves and do a bit of sparring. On one occasion Ronny and I were sparring. Although Ronny had a much more powerful punch than I, I had a longer reach and I was good at defending myself; with my fists protecting my face and quick to dance out the way of danger, as Donald had taught me. While we were sparring someone called out to us and I was distracted momentarily and it was then that Ronny landed me one on the jaw and my teeth chipped slightly as my jaw closed.

I also remember sparring with Leon. Basically I could keep out of his way, as he did not have a far reach. However, one day he gave me an uppercut, which just missed my chin and nose. It was like a train rushing by and I believe he would have done serious damage to me if he had connected with me. I immediately gave up sparring with him and I believe that out of all my contemporaries he threw the most painful punches. If he punched your arm it stayed lame, sore and bruised for weeks.

We played cricket both on the soccer field and in the tippy pond, but this was not as popular as soccer. We also had tennis courts where we played tennis, but our interest in tennis was spasmodic. We swam in summer and had galas and at school in our later years, we played rugby and hockey and did athletics.

LOOKING AFTER ANIMALS

Simon Woolf and some other older boys had *hoks* and kept chickens. The *hoks* were made of zinc (metal sheets) and poles that could be found lying around up or down the hill. I'm not too sure where the wire can from. Later I understand the *hoks* were removed because of the risk of disease.

The Arc got William, the handyman, to build a big chicken run. It was always fascinating to watch him go about his work and one got many ideas from observing him. Initially the *hok* was stocked with lots of chickens by the Arc. Over time the chicken numbers diminished and the *hok* then housed four ducks, rabbits, pigeons from Dolly, and guinea pigs. Leon had a cousin who owned a pet shop and we bought the animals from him. Occasionally we sold him pigeons and rabbits.

The *hok* was first "owned" by Raymond Lang and Hilton Rothaus but they did not look after it properly. Henry Shippel was then the prefect and he held a "court of enquiry" about the neglected animals. We all had our say and then Henry Shippel made his decision and took the *hok* from them and gave it to Leon and I.

We took the ducks to the swimming pool for a swim, but Vicky told us not to do this again as they were dirty. Raymond Lang slaughtered the ducks, which were our pets, just before we went to Durban for our holidays and I remember we were upset and I gave my Dad a duck as a present. In the new year we bought many small ducklings because the first four had done so well. Unfortunately, one night, rats attacked the ducklings and there were very few survivors. We were all quite shocked to see the carnage and had to kill one or two of the ducklings that were wounded, but still alive.

The rabbits used to sometimes fight and we would find one or two with flesh wounds. Initially we took them up to hospital for treatment but then were given a bottle of ointment to treat them with. Once we built a little den for the rabbits. It was a tomato box covered with rocks with a small entrance. Soon afterwards a large rabbit disappeared and there was a smell around the place. Only very much later did we discover that it had got stuck in the little den we had built and then we buried it. We fed the rabbits with carrots we stole from the orchard and also would get all the green vegetable waste cuttings from the kitchen. Sometimes we would let the rabbits out of the *hok* to nibble on the grass.

Dolly had lots of pigeons that were in the loft above the stables and in a *hok* just next to her house. She gave us pigeons which were nesting in her *hok* and these we quickly relocated to our *hok*. The pigeons were homing pigeons and after keeping them caged for say three weeks we would let them come and go as they pleased.

GARDENING

We also had vegetable gardens and Raymond Lang and I built a "water pipe" from the tap just below the verandah of the main building down a few terraces to "our" vegetable garden. The "pipe" consisted of gutters and pipes of various sizes scrounged from up and down the hill and strung together and sloping down to the garden. It was quite an engineering feat. We spent a lot of time tending our gardens and our interest would come and go in fits and starts. We collected cow manure from all over the grassed areas where the cows wandered and would dig it into the ground. Also we would mix the cow manure with water in a big drum and then pour it over the ground in an attempt to fertilize the ground. The gardener attending the orchard would sometimes help us with seeds and on one occasion we stole tomato seedlings and transplanted them into our garden. He was very cross as we had betrayed his trust. He had promised to give us some when they were big enough to plant out, but we were too impatient.

SCOTCH CARTS

We used to build scotch carts and race down the Arc drive and we were always scrounging materials for our carts. I remember us wanting to get into William's (the handyman) workshop. We wanted tools, nails and prams for their wheels and axles for building our scotch carts. Michael Saiet said he could tickle the lock and he opened it with a piece of wire. We helped ourselves and then faced the music when we came back from school on the Monday.

Mrs. Stelzner asked us when we came home from school if we had broken into William's workshop and when one or two of us owned up she asked who else was there. We would never squeal on each other and got a hiding, not only for doing the deed, but also for not dobbing each other in. We were sometimes questioned individually and holes would be picked

in our different versions of what happened. It came out that Michael Saiet had tickled the lock. We agreed not to insist that Les Durbach own up, as he was mad keen on rugby and he feared the punishment would stop him playing.

In the beginning a barber used to come to the Arc to give us haircuts, but later we went to have our hair cut in Rosebank about once a month. This was after being sent to one or two fancy places in town where they even did our nails. Haircuts were short back and sides and although we pleaded with the barber to not make it too short he gave us "the usual". This was a great opportunity to go shopping as the procedure took the whole afternoon, as any other customers were given preferential treatment and went ahead of us.

Besides our shopping we would visit the OK Bazaars and help ourselves (shoplift) to stamps. Michael Saiet who was a keen stamp collector and spent lots of money on stamps tried his luck after seeing the easy success of some younger boys. Unfortunately he was caught and the police were brought in. Because of these two events Michael Saiet was labelled a "criminal" by Mrs Stelzner, but in fact I think he was very unlucky and was caught twice, the only two times he stepped out of line.

MAGIC

One day Michael Goldstein, who was interested in magic, announced that he knew how to hypnotize people. A victim, Brian Sandler, my brother was chosen and he was duly slowly hypnotized, and now we had to prove that he was indeed under Michael's power. So Michael gave him very difficult things to do. We got him to go knock on Stelzner's door and ask for sweets. It was quite late and Mrs Stelzner told him to "Stop zis nonsense and go to bed immediately". The coup de grace was when Michael told Brian to sleep and he collapsed into a deep sleep on the floor outside Stelzner's door. Brian definitely was hypnotized and so too was Anthony Mark who was told to stand on a chair and then fall forward on his face. This he did and I remember catching him inches from the ground and saving him from smashing his face.

SMOKING PIPES

Simon Woolf used to put newspapers up into the downpipes from the gutters, at the Junior and Senior Boys, and then light them and run away and hide. What happened in these pipes was that the papers would burn and as the paper burnt it would cause a suction and vibration and a kind of roaring. So you would hear this roaring coming from who knows where. The roar would start off slowly and get stronger and stronger and reach a climax and then slowly abate as the newspaper burnt up.

Simon used to do this on a regular basis and this would cause Mrs Steltzner to come running out of her room looking and trying to find out what was causing all this roaring. She wouldn't know and she would look around and ask, "What is ziz noise? Who is doing it?"

If you looked higher at the top by the roof where the gutters join onto these downpipes you could see the smoke coming out. As a Junior Boy I remember doing this once or twice, because it was nice to hear this roar build up and then abate.

So Steltzner was always running out to find out what was going on and where the noise was coming from. She would ask the kids and we wouldn't know, or rather we'd say we didn't know. I think this worried and annoyed Steltzner and once or twice she would cross examine us, questioning us very carefully and aggressively to find out the cause of the noise.

Steltzner would ask, "What is zat, who is doing zat?" and of course we all played innocent and we said we didn't know. Simon got a lot of pleasure out of this because he had one up on her. I can imagine him laughing and really having a joke about it and I can imagine Steltzner being really angry about it and really upset and fuming. But she eventually did catch him.....

One day the inevitable happened, Simon got caught red-handed lighting the paper and he got into a lot of trouble and was duly punished.

MAKING MONEY

I remember bunking out and buying firecrackers in Hillbrow in packets of 40 for four cents and then selling them at the Arc for about four for a cent. I also remember lending out a shilling during the week to Hilton and getting back one and six on the next Sunday. I also sold hot coffee at night during winter. I would have to buy coffee, sugar and condensed milk, and the hot water would come from the tap or from Mrs Stelzner. Graham Stoler was my partner for a short time, but it did not last as he used to continually drink the condensed milk. Vicky knew that I was selling coffee and commented that that was how some businessmen started off.

THE LIBRARIAN

The Library

Initially Les Durbach was the librarian but later when he became the Prefect I became the Librarian of the Arc for about three or four years from about age 13/14 to about 17. I took my job as Librarian very seriously and I used to arrange all the

books by sizes. If you looked along the rows you'd see all the books were level with each other (the same height) and I thought that was the way to be a good Librarian and run the library. I also sorted books into sets, so all books that looked the same, I would put together. My idea was uniformity and straight lines and same size books together.

You could just take the books as you wanted them and there was no record kept of books taken out or a library card for each book. There were hundreds of books and very many old books and I don't think we really respected or appreciated the value of books or the knowledge to be gained from them. The library had a certain 'bookie' smell about it. It was a very big library and they had very old sets of books.

Periodically we would get new boxes of books coming in. I think it was from deceased estates or from couples or families moving overseas. These boxes of books would appear and it was always very interesting to see what we found. I was always on the look-out for stamp albums. Once or twice we got some really beautiful stamp albums and they disappeared very quickly because people wanted them. I remember once finding an old pornographic French book. It would have been from the 1920's, 1930's and there were all these very explicit pornographic pictures in them. I remember showing the book to my sister, Jenny, and she took it away.

HELPING YOURSELF

Helping yourself to the fruit was not so easy, as the shelves of apples in the fruit room were out of reach if we stretched our arms through the window. This required the invention of a simple tool that Max and I made. What was needed was a long thin stick with a needle on the end. One would put the stick through the gap in the window, peg an apple, turn the stick around so the apple sat on the needle on top of the stick and then gently retract the stick with the apple out through the gap. At times the needle would come out when we pegged the apple or the apple would fall off at the critical time we were carefully taking it out the gap. This would result in great laughter as we would run away and would have to fix our stick before the fun would start again.

Max reminded me about the one occasion we were so engrossed in what we were doing that we never saw the night watchman creep up on us. He stretched out his huge arms and with a loud roar he grabbed both of us. All three of us just burst out laughing at the comedy of it that he let us go scot free!!

On another occasion, after helping myself to apples and a cool drink, instead of going up the hill and around I decided to take a short cut through the kitchen as I thought no one was around. Unfortunately I walked almost straight into Ma coming the other way. She saw the apples and cool drink I was carrying and asked, "Ver did you get zat?" I replied immediately, "Ma I stole it." I don't know if she believed me but she responded "Ach get away." This I promptly did and that was the end of the matter.

PARKTOWN BOYS' HIGH

Parktown Boys' High was one of the better schools in Johannesburg with a very proud and long history. It was very much a traditional "English Grammar School" and being a boys' only school the emphasis was on sports. The pupils were placed into one of the houses; Romans, Thebans, Tuscans and Trojans and if your father or brother before you had been in a particular house, you could also select it. At my time all the Arcs were in Trojans. I spent my five years in high school there from 1965 to 1969.

THE SENIOR BOYS

Moving to the Senior Boys was a much less formal and exact event than moving to the Juniors. All we had to do was move to the end dormitories and the move would depend on your age, your year in school and also the number of other boys in the same group. We were not so strictly disciplined as the Junior Boys and we were given more latitude and could switch off our lights when we wanted to.

EXTRAS LESSONS

We used to have lots of extra lessons in English, Afrikaans and Mathematics. I think Doc worked on the theory that the key to our future success was through education and that we could never have enough extra lessons. If extra lessons helped even a bit, that was enough reason to have them. We regarded them as a bit painful as we saw them as the same as Hebrew lessons as eating into our free time.

SEDER NIGHTS

Seder nights at the Arc were a very special thing. We all got dressed in our smart clothes and wore ties for Shul. The Shul service was relatively short. There were quite a few Old Arcs around who were to join us for the Sedar and the atmosphere was very festive and exciting as we looked forward to the Seder food and singing.

Doc would lead the Seder and he would be walking around the tables and encouraging us all to sing. Ma worried more about the food and saw that there was enough food for everybody. In the large dinning room hall the boys used to sit on the one side and the girls on the other side. We always had a long main table that ran along the full length of the hall alongside the French windows, where all the guests and visitors were seated. These were mainly old Arcs that helped make the night good fun. We would have one little minute glass of wine each (empty fish paste containers), while the guests would have bottles of wine on the main table. The idea was to try and get some wine from the main table and sometimes we were friendly with the guests and they would sneak some of the wine to us.

Over the years the songs in the Hagadah were sung in a special Arc way. "*Echad mi yordea*?", the girls would sing in a nice sweet voice and the boys would respond in a very gruff voice . "*Echad ani yordea*!!" Also we would add our own words to Chad gad yad and at the end we used to substitute our own words to bizrei zuzzi and used to say instead "Who *vry* Susie."

Doc who always lead the singing, would be racing through the verses which became longer and longer and very few of us could keep up with him, but we would always be sure to slow him down as everyone joined in with the "Who *vry* Susie" part.

Besides the ceremonial food we had matzo balls or *kneidlach* and chicken soup and then we would have chicken and potatoes and maybe carrots. I remember the chicken always used to be so hard and dry. I think maybe it was kept in the oven too long or maybe on Friday nights or on Pesach the prayers went on too long and the timing wasn't really co-ordinated with the kitchen so the chicken was really hard and almost like chewing wood.

When it came to Kiddish in the morning after Shul at Pesach time we used to get a big fruity-like sugary sweet to eat, and we always looked forward to eating them. I am not too sure what the sweets were called, but I always associate these fruity sugary sweets with Pesach and it was the same sweet that the Senior Girls 'saved' for us when we were still in the Babies.

HOLIDAYS

Up to about the age of 10, while still in the Babies Department, I had been to various places on holiday. I had been to Pretoria and Knysna with the people from Pretoria, to Durban with my Auntie Ray and Uncle Ben and to Springs with my Auntie Sarah. I had also been several times to Somerset West near Cape Town to stay with my Auntie Fay, once when I was still very young with my Mom, once when I was very young and in the Arc, once when I was about seven and once when I must have been eight or nine. I never ever went away to camps.

My Mom, my old Auntie Ruth Jenny
and me, on the beach on holiday in Somerset West.
This photo was taken around 1955, a couple of years before I "lost Brian".

When I was around 14 I went to Krugersdorp for a few days with my Auntie Mercia and that was when her son Rodney had his Barmitzvah. The caterers were Gloria's and it was a very posh affair with a marquee in their garden.

HOLIDAYS IN DURBAN

From about the age of about 10 or 11 I went to Durban every December till I left the Arc. The Durban HOD (Hebrew Order of David) organised families to host the children from the Arc. We would go down to Durban by train and we would spend around three weeks there.

It was always exciting looking forward to the holidays and to a prize giving where we had a selection of gifts we could ask for. You could ask for a towel, a shirt, a pair of trousers or it was generally something you would want for your holiday. A Mrs Evans, who I think was connected to one of the big department stores would present us with our gifts. When you got on the train to go down to Durban you would have your gift and new clothes all packed in a suitcase.

Going down to Durban was a great adventure in itself. We had the run of the train and had a lot of fun running up and down, looking out the windows and visiting each other's compartments. We were on the train a long time because we always used to take the 'milk train' that used to stop at all the stations.
Going through the Valley of a Thousand Hills with all its tunnels and views, going up and down the mountain and all the greenery, the water and the waterfalls was indeed a magical experience.

Eventually we would get to Durban and from there we would be taken to the Durban HOD where we would all gather in the big reception centre and we meet our hosts. Some would have new hosts while others would meet their old hosts that had hosted us before.

The holidays were always very well organised and besides organising hosts, outings were also organised. In the three weeks we had about three or four group outings and also there was a social, a dance, at the Durban HOD which we would all go to.

I stayed for three or possibly even four years with the Swils; Eric and Rivka Swil and their children Robert and Rochie. They lived in Berea in a beautiful house and they treated me very well and as part of the family. Eric was a pharmacist and Robert was a couple of years older than me.

KEITH LANG AND JENNY SANDLER

When I first arrived in the Junior Boys I think all the Senior Boys at the time fancied Bessie Bortz, but as she did not reciprocate they looked elsewhere. I think this is why Keith took up with Jenny, my older sister. Jenny and Keith "went steady" together for quite a long time and they often met by the Arc swimming pool.

While this benefited me a bit, because Keith (a Senior Boy) was nice to me (a Junior Boy) as he was going out with my sister, it also had its costs me two and six. Keith was going to take

Jenny to bioscope one day in town during the holidays and I lent him the money to do so.

A little bit later when we all three were together talking, Keith said he had not forgotten that he owed me the money and Jenny responded something like, "No Keith, you don't need to pay it back. David won't mind." I said nothing but I was angry that my sister had given away my pocket money.

LEAVING THE ARC

After the end of the year when I had done my matric we all went down to Durban as per normal and were hosted by families organised by the Durban HOD. Those of us going to the army were sent back to Johannesburg by train a bit earlier so we could be there on our official army call up date. We went to the drill hall and then landed up in the army where we spent the next nine months.

During my time in the army I remember receiving two letters from Doc. The one was greetings and congratulations with my matric results and the second was to tell me that Brian (my brother) had run away. I had already been shown an article on Brian's running away in the newspaper by a fellow "roofie".

It was only after I had finished the army and came to see Doc at the Arc that "good-byes" were said. Doc was very happy to see me and we talked for a while. He was very happy with, and complimented me on my matric results. He explained to me that I must go see M. Goldsmith in town to get my Barmitzvah money and he also arranged for me to see Mr Teeger about a job and university. He then gave me a purple 3-cent school bus ticket and with his arm on my shoulder we walked through the main entrance to the two pillars at the top of the long Arc drive. There he wished me good luck and shook my hand and bade me farewell.

I was very upset and felt a great sense of loss as I walked down the drive and I cried. Here I was 17 years old, leaving my home of the past 14 years behind and walking out into the world where I had no means and I knew very few people. I felt very vulnerable and lonely. The Arc was all I ever knew and it had sheltered me and had provided for all my needs and now I had to start all over again and had to learn to fend for myself.

Although I did not know it at the time, what was to help me in the outside world was the education and upbringing that had been given to me through the tremendous caring and generosity of the Jewish community and also my many Arc brothers and sisters. There was no doubt about me going to university and this seed had long ago been planted by Doc.

M. Teeger the one time chairman of the Arc and also a partner at Leiman Teeger Gaddin Sifris and Company, a firm of chartered accountants, gave me a job. He suggested I work for three months during which I could decide whether I wanted to do a Bachelor of Commerce full time or do a Certificate in the Theory of Accountancy part time. Later I agreed to do the latter part time, partly influenced by Mr. Teeger who said it was better to be a 'mensch' and earn your money than to go to university full time and live on a pittance of an allowance.

I went to see Mr Goldsmith, the long time secretary of the Arc, in town. He gave me my Barmitzvah money and arranged for me to buy a suit from a shop in town. I bought a brown one.

I lived with my Dad and stepmother for around six months. Leon Goodman, who had been living with his uncle, and I then moved into a residential hotel in Hillbrow where Myra, Hilda and Esther Durbach also stayed. We both worked for Mr Teeger and went to university part time doing accountancy.

What sustained me when I first left the Arc was mainly the friendship and camaraderie of other Arcs. Les Durbach stands out here. He would pick me up on Sunday mornings and off we would go with a carload of other Arcs, mainly his sisters, to spend a day with his parents on the Vaal River. It was also my great pleasure each weekend to visit the Arc and spend time with the kids I grew up with and in the place I grew up.

Les, Leon and I shared a flat together in Bellevue East, (upper Houghton we called it) and we all used to go "*jolling*" together. We became fast friends who accepted each other warts and all. Leon was killed tragically in later years and when I visit SA and I am with Les, I feel at home.

LIVING IN PERTH

I have lived in Perth since 1981 and since 1988 have lived in a 'home amongst the gum trees'. I live on a hectare block (2.5 acres) about 30 minutes from the Perth City centre in Western Australia. My home is my sanatorium. Maybe I was looking for another Arc with lots of space as my house is surrounded by bush and several eucalyptus (gum) trees. There is a 40-metre drive way and a big open parking area..

It's a pity there are no Arc boys around as I have a few mulberry trees and also loquat trees in the garden. While I try to eat the fruit, the parrots that fly around in the wild, also help and lots of fruit simply drops off and goes to waste. There is also a fig tree, an avocado tree and a mango tree that have all borne at least one fruit. Also there is a lemon tree that never runs out of lemons throughout the year.

There are always strange animals in the pool and I have rescued quite a few snakes, bobtail lizards and a racing goanna.

I have found many scorpions and frogs in the pool, not to mention a mice and many spiders. Some ducks wintered in my pool and had a nest in a flowerbed next to the pool and even flew into the pool when I was swimming. In the morning I would see their foot prints in the frost.

MY FAMILY

My sister Jenny left South Africa to go on holiday when she was 21 and she settled in the UK.. She has a daughter Katie of around 26 and lost her first daughter Kirsty (three years older than Katie) when Kirsty was about 16. It was a tragedy that one can never forget. Jenny has never been a good correspondent and many many people have complained to me about her not writing.

Brian, my younger brother, is still in SA. He worked and lived in Cape Town for a few years and now lives in Johannesburg.

I separated from my wife Barbara for the last 12 years. I am a qualified chartered accountant.

I have two very special daughters thanks to Barbara who has always been a very good mother and over the years we have always put them first.

Sarah is 22 and is a few minor credits away from completing a four year Bachelors Degree in Interior Architecture.

Esther, (who was Dux in her last year of school and won five first prizes for five out of her six subjects) is 19 and now 2nd year in TAFE doing Fashion and Design. She plans to have her own label.

Whenever I go back to South Africa I have always been most welcome by fellow Arcs and I am in touch with lots of Arcs around the world. Life in Perth is relatively quiet and it is now my home and I consider myself to be very lucky to have landed up here 'down under'.

Lastly, if you have not noticed yet, I have an obsession (or a Meshugas) and that is to collect and record Arc Memories.

David with his daughters Sarah and Esther (Portrait painted by Shani Kreb

Chapter 107   BRIAN SANDLER (1954)

Brian was born in 1954 and lived in the care of Arcadia from 1956 to 1970.

Since leaving the Arc Brian has tried his hand at many things to earn a living including working at the Jewish Cemetery in Cape Town and entertaining children as a clown.

LOSING MY BROTHER, BRIAN
By David Sandler

Now we are going back in time to when Brian was two or three and I was about four or five in 1957/58. My brother, Brian, my sister, Jenny, and I were taken down to Somerset West (which is near Cape Town) for a holiday as my Late Mom's sister, my Auntie Fay, had invited us to come down to the Cape to spend the summer holidays with her and her family. My aunt was married to Monty Teperson and she had four sons but only three at that time.

We travelled down to Cape Town by train with my Auntie Ruth there to look after us. She was to us a big fat Yiddisha Mamma. She was a very old woman at the time and she would talk with a Yiddisha accent and she was very 'Jewish', speaking Yiddish from the old school. I don't know if she was actually born in South Africa, I imagine she came out to South Africa as a young kid from Lithuania and she still had her ways from Lithuania.

In 1957 she was well into her sixties and she brought us by train down from Johannesburg to Cape Town. I am not too sure exactly how she was related, but she looked after us and shared the compartment with Jenny, Brian and me.

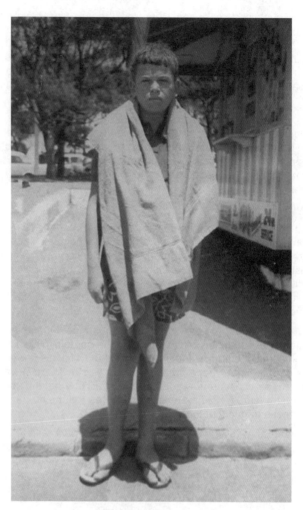

Brian on holiday at Durban Beach

David, Jenny and Brian

Going down to Cape Town she sat by the window and spoke about the "beautiful scenery" and pointed to this "beautiful scenery" thing and we looked for this "beautiful scenery" thing. We were not too sure what we had to look for but there was the *veldt* and the country rushing by us and it was thrilling for us kids to be on a train on holiday and going down to the cape for our holiday.

She used to sing songs to us and the one I remember "I give to you a golden egg, with 45 niggers behind your beg, if you will marry me, me me, if you will marry me" It was an old Jewish song which I still remember.... the man offering to give to the woman, all these things and only when he offers her a lot of money then she says yes she will marry him.... and he turns around and says "you want my money but you don't want me, I won't marry, you, you you, so I won't marry you."

408

David and Brian

After arriving at Cape Town we were met by my Auntie Fay and driven down to Somerset West where we were to spend the holidays. My uncle and aunt held a liquor licence and they had a hotel, the *Helderberg Hotel*, which was in the main street of Somerset West. Across the road from the hotel my uncle's mom, Granny Jean, lived in a flat and so too did my uncle and aunt but they put us in the hotel in room number 1 right on the top floor.

One day my auntie Fay drove us to the beach, and as she was very busy in the hotel she left us on the beach with my old Auntie Ruth to look after us. So it was just us three kids, Jenny, Brian and me on the beach. We were all excited as we had these new buckets and spades. So off Brian and I went to build a sandcastle.

We started to dig this moat around and pile the sand up into a big castle in the middle. The tide had receded and there was no real water for the moat, so I asked Brian to go off and get some water to fill the moat. I can still see the picture of him walking off towards the sea. It was shallow and you had to go in for quite a while before it got deep and the tide was out and the water had receded quite a lot and it was very calm. He brought back a bucket or two of water.

I was very busy digging the moat and building the castle and I did not notice the time passing by. Eventually my Auntie Ruth, who was sitting not far off, came along and asked me where Brian was. Then it dawned on me, he had not brought back a bucket of water for quite some time. So then there was a search on to find Brian.

We started looking and walking up and down, but mainly just looking around where we were. We waded into the shallow water and amongst the bathers. We looked and looked and

could not find him, so we just walked up and down the beach a little bit further. Still we could still not find him and the panic set in.

My Aunt Ruth kept asking, "Ver is your brother? Ver is he? Ver is he?" and we kept on looking and looking with no Brian to be found. My old Auntie Ruth, had come all the way from Jo'burg, especially to look after us because my Auntie Fay was very busy with the hotel as it was Christmas time and there were a lot of guests. Old Auntie Ruth was panicky and was embarrassed that she had lost my brother. She gave me a slap and again and again asked, "Ver is your brother?"

So we went up and down even further along the beach and I was looking in the water, looking for a head bobbing out there. I was shivering and cold and I'm sure half an hour to an hour had passed and there was a wind blowing up. We were going up and down the beach looking and she was stopping at every group who was sitting on the beach telling them the story.

"He (pointing at me) lost his brother!"
"He (pointing at me) sent his little brother into the water with a bucket!"
"Have you seen a little boy wandering around with a bucket?"

I was past shivering and was shaking and crying because it was cold and I was worried and upset as I had lost my brother. I remember a man pointing to me and saying to my aunt "Look he is cold and shivering, give him a towel." but she replied "No he has lost his brother. He can't have a towel."

We kept walking up and down and repeating our story and increased the area that we were looking in. After a long long time when we still could not find Brian, my Auntie Ruth decided that we had to inform my Auntie Fay. This would have been a great loss of face for her. She went across the road to the tickey box (the public telephone) and phoned and very soon afterwards Fay was there.

Now Fay was very loud and also panicking and she arrived and greeted me with "How can you lose your brother?" in a very shrill voice, "How can you lose your brother?" She would say, "*Got man*!!", because she came from the Cape and she would stand there looking at me with a screwed up face because obviously she was upset

The Teperson family had lived in the Cape for many years and they knew the police. Fay went and explained to the police that this boy had disappeared and she gave them a description. The police were very co-operative and they were very friendly, as it was a small community. The next thing you saw and heard was this police car driving up and down the main beach road, broadcasting on a loudspeaker "Has anyone seen a little boy with a bucket?" So it went on up and down and up and down the road announcing, "A little boy missing, and please can you report to the police station if you find this little boy."

This all took place at the Strand as opposed to Somerset West, which were about five kilometres apart. My Auntie Fay walked along the main road of the Strand and she went into the hotels and she spoke to the receptionists and told them about the lost boy.

All this took ages. It was only much later and well into the afternoon maybe 2.00 pm to 3.00 pm that they found Brian again.

When they found him I was already back at the hotel and I was extremely upset and sad about losing him. Everyone, including my sister and cousins accused me, a five year old, of losing Brian. I did feel responsible because he was with me when we were playing in the sand and I sent him off to get the water. The picture of him walking off towards the sea was still fresh in my mind. We have often over the years spoken about "How I lost Brian" and now it is part of our family folk lore.

A woman found Brian wandering on the beach and she had taken him up to her hotel room. She explained that she had found him and she was looking after him. I suppose the bottom line is Brian was found and we were all very relieved.

BUNKING SCHOOL
By Brian Sandler

I remember the time I decided to bunk school - one of the many times.

I took a set of clothing from my locker the night before and put them in my school bag. The next morning after breakfast I waited at the bottom of the driveway for all the guys to leave for school. I quickly ran up the hill by the gate to get changed and hid my bag and went to the houses above the Arc. I went to the movies and came back the same way I had left. When I reached the place where I hid my bag I found someone had taken it.

Now I was getting worried and scared – what was I going to do?

I decided to go back to my dorm and think what to do. All of a sudden I heard someone shouting my name. It was Les Durbach. He was coming to tell me. I had no chance to escape. He then took me to Doc who was very cross. He flapped six of the best. He sent me back to the Boys' Department. When I reached my bed I found my school uniform on my bed and my bag. Still to this day I do not know who put it there.

Babies at play 1961
Brian on bicycle on left, David Lipschitz on horse,
Max Goldman reading

SHOT FOR STEALING FRUIT
By Brian Sandler

One day I decided to go on a fruit raid. I was with Mark Jacobs. We came to one of the houses we often stole fruit from. I climbed the wall and jumped in the garden. Mark kept watch. I was picking fruit, not noticing a guy come out of the house. Mark shouted at me "chips". I saw him with a rifle. I ran towards the wall and chucked over the bag. I was halfway over with my backside showing facing the guy when I heard a loud bang. All of a sudden the top part of my leg started to sting. It was a salt and pepper gun. Without thinking I was over the wall and limping down the road, screaming, we ran all the way back home. I, still screaming ran straight for the swimming pool and dived in. The top part of my leg was burning and it was very painful. I swore I would never steal fruit again. But the next week I was at it again!

ARCADIAN PYROMANIAC CONFESSES
By Brian Sandler

One balmy summer Saturday evening I decided to have some fun and proceeded to the bottom of the driveway thinking about what I could do to relieve the boredom. "A fire will help clear my thoughts and perhaps provide some inspiration."

So I collected some kindling and lit just a small one and was enjoying the warm glow. My thoughts were a million miles away and I was feeding my fire with more combustibles without being aware that the fire had taken its own path, igniting some dry grass and spreading down the driveway towards Mr G's cottages.

After trying in vain to exercise some control over what was rapidly becoming an inferno and realising that I was losing the battle, I turned on my heels making towards the boys dorm. I was greeted by mass hysteria obviously my fire had been noticed and everybody who was anybody was making their way towards the now out of control blaze. I pretended that I knew nothing about it and joined the masses, after all there is safety and anonymity in numbers.

By the time we reached the "scene of the crime" the fire brigade was already there. The sight of the stalwart firemen encouraged the pyromaniac to light yet another fire. The adrenaline rush was great. I enjoyed the crowd watching the firemen going about their work.

As they were about to pack up and leave, my second fire was spotted by one of the crowd. We all mounted the fire truck making like firemen and approached the sight of the second fire in order to douse it.

I decided that enough was enough and I ended the evening with my secret close to my chest. I went to watch movies with my friends as if nothing had happened. Now you all know who was responsible for the mystery fires at the Arc.

Jenny, David and Brian with their Dad Mayer Lipa Sandler

BRIAN RUNS AWAY
By David Sandler

I remember Brian running away one day or, to be more exact, he did not return from school. I was about 14 or 15 at the time and Brian, would have been 12 or 13. We were both going to Parktown Boys' at the time and it was a Friday. Very simply we all came back to the Arc and Brian was not there. We thought he had bunked out to Hillbrow or town to buy something and that he would be back a bit later.

I was concerned and I waited next to the pool, on the grass on the little embankment. From there you could see the buses coming down Oxford Road and the passengers alighting at the bus stop. If Brian came home by bus I would see him getting off the bus. If he walked up the Arc drive or across the soccer field I could also see him from that position.

I sat and waited and waited endlessly for him to come home. With the passing of time I became worried. In the back of my mind I thought something was wrong and I also did not want him to get into trouble, but I knew he was in trouble already. I felt partly responsible for Brian as I always did. That Friday afternoon I waited in vain because he did not come home. I was very worried and I was getting sick. I had a headache as I had been sitting in the sun and was concerned that something had happened to Brian, as he had never done this before

Everyone would ask "Where is Brian? Where is Brian?" They all gave their suggestions of what could have happened and we never imagined that he would just so blatantly not come back home. We all thought that something must have happened.

The next day was Saturday and the worrying continued. We did our normal Saturday things, went to Shul, played soccer and had lunch. No doubt the Arc had contacted the police to look for him but still no Brian. On Saturday afternoon lots of Arcs were sitting next to the pool on the embankment. We had long discussions and many suggestions were put forward as to what had happened to Brian.

Then all of a sudden at around three 'o clock he appeared. He had come home 24 hours late.

I remember Puddy, (Esther Durbach), told me not to worry and told me it was not my fault, but, that did not make me feel any better

I think that was quite a pivotal time for me, because from that time I worried less about Brian. After that if he was missing or if he did something wrong, while I would care about it and I would be concerned, I would not let it get the better of me. I would partially dissociate myself from it and not take it too personally.

Previously he had done a few naughty things and it had embarrassed me and I felt guilty for him and it would have cut into me and it would have hurt me. I would have worried about things that he had done and almost worried in his place but after all that worrying and not feeling well, and in fact feeling sick from this worrying, I changed. From that time on I cut myself off from worrying too much about Brian.

Brian came home 24 hours late and he said he had been in the *koppies* looking for snakes. He had found this cave in the *koppies* but he did not find any snakes. He explained that the snakes were harmless so you did not have to worry about them biting you. I did not really know what to believe

Brian dressed as a Clown

Chapter 108 – MAX (MAXIM) (1953) AND CHARLES GOLDMAN (1960)

Max was born on 6th of January 1953 and was placed in the care of the Arc before his second birthday, in 1954. He left Arcadia when 17 years old after completing his Matric at the end of 1970.

Max attended Parktown Boys' and later qualified as a B Comm. He is married to Sabrina Stroman and the two of them have been in business together, running an Employment Agency since 1988.

While they don't have any children, they do have pomeranian dogs which they dote upon.

ARC MEMORIES

ROOM FOR CHANGE

At about age seven or eight, David Sandler and I found ourselves in the vicinity of the swimming pool (the one on stilts). We had often noticed that some of the junior girls, on their way to the swimming pool, would first disappear into the filter room beneath the pool for a short time, and then emerge in their swimming gear. We deduced that they must obviously be using the filter room as a change-room. Our curiosity was certainly aroused (I know that I for one had not yet seen any girl in her birthday suit!) and so I was very keen on David's suggestion that we try to observe the change-room procedure. We waited

Back row: Paul Cohen, Hilton Rothaus, Raymond Lang, Linda Soler, Jennifer Fliess. Hannah Goldstein
Middle row: David Sandler, Max Goldman, Lorraine Goldstein, Offer Fein
Front row: Marcia Salmonson, Elizabeth Fliess

for one of the girls to arrive and sure enough, along came Sylvia Gordon!

What transpired thereafter must have been quite a shock to my system as to this very day my mind is a total blank - I do not recall seeing anything!

EAGLE EYES

On Wednesdays we finished school early (12.30 pm). Another nice thing about Wednesdays was that immediately after lunch (under the peppercorn tree) Mrs Stelzner used to give us sweets - now that was one queue we made sure of being in! If you happened to have been a naughty boy during that week you were faced with the dilemma of joining the sweets queue or not. One had to carefully consider one's misdemeanour and reach a decision as to whether it was a "no sweets" misdemeanour or not. Mrs Stelzner did not favour naughty boys.

The difficulty was that one's own assessment of your misbehaviour seldom corresponded with how Mrs Stelzner viewed the offence. Accordingly most boys decided that they should always "try their luck" and join the sweets queue, whatever their offence, using the premise of "Nothing ventured, nothing gained".

Now Mrs Stelzner, when dishing out these sweets, never looked up, all she saw were two open hands.

There were always naughty boys in the queue and that was a certainty. They would shuffle forward and place their open palms in front of Mrs Stelzner. Mrs Stelzner's eagle eyes would instantly recognise who the hands belonged to and instead of disgorging sweets into the waiting palms Mrs Stelzner would let fly with a stinging slap, while shouting out: "Nussing for you!! You did "such and such!"

The pain of no sweets and stinging hands was only exceeded by the embarrassment of having failed to buck the system in front of your fellows!

By M Perry Kotzen (2005)

MAX, GRAHAM AND THE BICYCLE

I'm sure David has written about his and my cellar raid that produced two bicycles! This story deals with the raid Graham Stoler and I made, also on the self same cellar.

This is what happened:

Saturday evenings before movies was a time for killing time. Either Graham or I hit on the plan to raid the cellar below the main kitchen - was this the precursor to or a copycat of my cellar raid conducted with David Sandler - I don't know.

Anyhow we somehow got hold of a torch and did our exploratory investigation which revealed one main storeroom which was well padlocked. We decided to unscrew the hasp and staple but not having a screwdriver, had to defer this part of the operation.

Some weeks later, with a screwdriver in hand we crept down the long flight of wooden stairs into the coal cellar. We could not risk using the stairway light, hence the torch. Our attempt at unscrewing the hasp revealed that we had the wrong size screwdriver!!

Another few weeks passed by. Eventually we arrived back in the cellar with the right screwdriver and started to undo the hasp. Alas! To our horror, the screws were so impacted into the wood that progress was slow (we only had the short window of time on a Saturday evening within which to operate!).

After another few weeks had passed my patience ran out and I decided to just use brute force and to hell with the damaged door which could be used in evidence! So we procured a steel rod and with a deft flip of my wrist the hasp and staple were history and the door creaked open. We were delirious with anticipation (it felt like we had broken into Tutenkamen's tomb)!

We snuck inside and peered into the virtually impenetrable gloom. Our torch was almost ineffectual in the blackness. Near the door we made out an object resembling a bicycle. Wow! This was the jackpot! It was still wrapped in its entirety in brown paper, covered in years of dust.

We tore away a piece of the wrapping to confirm our jackpot find overcome with excitement and the shine of a new bicycle peeked through! Gingerly we manoeuvred the bicycle up the coal chute and out into the quiet night. We found a hiding place in some bushes not far from Oxford Road. How we looked forward to riding this bicycle after returning from school!

Sadly, at that time, the M1 was under construction and when we returned to our hiding spot the next afternoon, our new bicycle, our jackpot prize, had disappeared - stolen by the road workers who must have accidentally stumbled on it. We cried and cried - boy were we heartbroken!

The moral of the story: If you steal a bicycle, keep it in your bed!

A NOSTALGIC TRIP

- The Arc bus - Charlie Miller - Christopher "Dice" - acorn fights from the bus windows.
- Cheder with Gverets Sher and Gerber ("don't complain about having to learn Hebrew - one day you will need it!") and Adon Shalit.
- Hebrew Schools Spelling Competitions - how did we do so well? Any ideas?
- Hebrew Day Schools athletics competitions -.how did we do so well? 16 year-olds running in U13 races?
- Swimming gala - Herzl vs Bial - Hat and Dress race - diving for coins at day's end - "throw them here Doc! "Cokes at the hospital - thanks Ruth!
- Daily Shul at 6.15 am - .tefilli LM Radio blaring from the girls' window: Long John Berks!!! Yikkel stikkel - *lekker lekker* luck.
- Evening Shul - again!
- If it's Thursday it must be fish and chips supper - save those chips for later!!
- Oneg Shabbat - sponge cake and Lecol.
- Doc and Ma, Mrs Van Rensburg, Mrs Stelzner, Mrs Lucas, Miss Marques, Mr and Mrs Duzzy, Mr Chait, Mr McKay, Auntie Botha, Mrs De Winnaar, Sister Conway.
- Dental exams at the Arc hospital - "Town!" "Town!" "Town!"
- Saturday morning soccer with "Pass the ball!!!" Doc and Eddie and "Miggie" Miller. Girls shouting and clapping.
- Girls' dancing lessons on Sunday mornings with Carol.
- Sewing lessons with Mrs Saffee.
- Art lessons with Eileen Sasto.
- Harmonica lessons with Effie Segal.
- The Arc Fete.
- Movies in town on public holidays.
- Movies on Saturday night - Arc boilies!!!!
- Celebrities brought to the Arc by Mr Stodel
  - Cliff Richard (The Shadows)
  - Marion Friedman (pianist)
  - Solomon King (singer)
  - Larry Adler (Harmonica)
- Rosh Hashanah and Yom Kippur services with Starkey and others.
- The Arc Sukkah (winner of many a sukkah competition)

- Some Staff:
  - Suzie Matwetwe, Gladys, Rachel, Mimi, Elias - (Babies Department)
  - Joe Baloyi, Elias Kaola, Lillian, Sophie - (Junior Boys)
  - Blackie (Doctor London), Nicholas, George, Andries - (Kitchen, Garden)
- Fruit tree raiding in Forest Town.
- Bunking out to Hillbrow.
- C Hollander Lodge (Vereeniging) annual picnic at Dickinson Park - speedboat rides, watermelon, games, zoo - singing in the Arc bus ("We're here because we're here because we're here" "There was playing in the storm, in the storm"

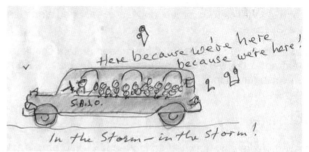

By M Perry Kotzen (2005)

CONFESSIONS OF AN ARSONIST
Written by David Sandler

This is a true report of what was told to me by my fellow Arc, Max Goldman, in December 1999

The First Time

I was sitting with Auntie Botha and Elisabeth Fliess by the Oneg Tree and she was listening to our reading. It was a school afternoon and it was my turn to read first. We were sitting facing the stairs that lead up to the ping pong room and the main building.

After I had finished reading, it was Elizabeth's turn and I wandered off towards the hill and decided to warm myself with a little fire which I knew I could easily put out. It must have been dry and windy as the fire quickly got out of control and raced away.

I went back to the Oneg Tree and sat down next to Elizabeth and Auntie Botha and as they finished reading pointed out that there was smoke coming from down the hill.

There was a large raging fire and half the hill was burnt. The guilty party had to be found. Luckily my alibi was watertight as I was "Reading to Auntie Botha."   Poor Paul Cohen. He was found to be guilty and was thrashed on his naked bottom.

I remember Hilton Rothaus and I looking through the window and watching the thrashing and saying "You know we could have all been burnt," and thinking, "Poor Paul".

The Second Time

I was much older now and in the Junior Boys. I was also much more experienced in making and putting out fires.

It was a cold wintry weekend so naturally I decided to make a fire to warm myself. I invited Brian Sandler to see how good I was in putting out fires and off we went to the downhill by the slide.

I made a little fire and put it out. Then I made a larger one and also put it out very easily. We continued to burn bigger and bigger patches as our confidence grew. Eventually we outdid ourselves.

The chicken *hok* was very close to the fire and was almost burned down!! The fire had raced away and the hill was alight. We both ran off in different directions.

I went and hid up the hill and could see people looking and hear them calling out for me. Did they know it was me? Had Brian squealed on me?

It started to get dark and I started to feel hungry so eventually I gave myself up to Les Durbach. He marched me off to Doc. The caning I got from Doc was a laugh!!! Doc produced this old cane which just disintegrated when he caned me.....there was no pain whatsoever!!!

Conclusion

While the confessor did not remember any more fires there were many many more. In fact on one occasion two together; one up the hill and one down the hill.

Now you may laugh at the saying "if you play with matches you will wet your bed" I know it is true.

Sabrina and Max

CHARLES GOLDMAN

Max has a brother Charles who is seven years his junior and who was born in 1960. Charles was also in the Arc from 1967 to 1977.

Charles works as a Computer Programmer and in 1988 married Aviva Abel of Port Elizabeth. They now have a son Eli who Barmitzvahed in 2005.

1971 Arcadia Bulletin Cover Page
Sammy and Charlie sitting in front and Carmen Lindy with glasses at back

Max, Eli and Charles

Chapter 109 – LESLEY BECKER (MARK) (1953)

I was born in 1953 and my brother Tony in 1957 and we were placed in the care of Arcadia in July 1963 as our parents were divorced.

My Mom wanted a better life for us and found it difficult to bring up two small kids on her own. I left the Arc in December 1970, just after Tony who went with my Mom to live in Israel.

My Grandmother (Mom's Mom) came to South Africa at the age of 16 from Latvia to search for her father, whom she never found. My grandfather was in South Africa already.

I do not have much information on my father's side and there never was much contact.

I met my husband, Guy, in Durban and in 1990 we moved to Israel with our two sons and we now are members on Kibbutz Revivim.

My Mom, Maisie Effune, is buried on the Kibbutz.

ARC MEMORIES

Its so super reading all the Old Stories from everyone, from my era, and from before and after. Whilst reading somehow, suddenly a name comes up and I remember the person; Neville Mervitz, Donald Goldman the boxer, and Vera Lozinsky,

I remember a story with Violet, one of the Salaman girls. While Fickey was talking to her, she was holding up a little umbrella (the ones put in cocktails). We all had a good giggle. I am not too sure what punishment she received, but she did. The Salaman sisters were beautiful girls.

I always followed Marion Shraga. around, like a shadow. I was very very young, and I am sure that she was unaware of it. One Succot, we were having dinner in the Succoth, and I offered her my roast potatoes, and her reply "What do I look like your dustbin?" what a bummer. Jenny Sandler always stood up for me, and gave her some reply.

One time Jenny's Aunt came to the Arc to visit the Sandlers and she thought that I was Jenny.

Reading the stories from Jennifer Fleiss' articles brought back many memories of the hospital, Shul and the Rand show.

I remember when Harry Kupferberg fell thru the trampoline

Julius Gordon sang with Cliff Richard, in 1963, the year that Tony and I came to the Arc.

Shelley Grishkan, used to spit her lumpy porridge into a serviette or down her uniform, at breakfast, and then hide it in her uniform to throw away later.

I remember going to town movies with Janet and Linda, with a skirt on and bobby socks, and then the minute we got to town,

Les in her favourite dress

we rolled down our slacks, which had been rolled up under the skirt. We never once thought how they must have looked!

I remember Mrs Lubner coming back from Overseas with pressies for us. She was very generous and used to buy us dresses for Yomtov. One unlucky girl received a half-full bottle of perfume. I remember being taken out by her, to her home in Houghton for lunch and being asked very sweetly questions regarding the Arc house-mothers etc etc. Boy did Linda, Janet and I *splab* it all out as usual. Next thing we know, we are being called into a Sunday Meeting, remember them, and being in lots of trouble!

Fish and chips on a Thursday night was the highlight of the week. We saved the chips in a serviette and left the dining room with the serviette between our knees, walking of course like models, can you imagine it, so that we could eat them later.

Hilda was once "klapped" by Ma while lining up for dinner. Janet, Linda and I (as usual) were counting each "klap" that she got....1, 2, 3, or something.

416

Front to Back: Myra Durbach, Sadie Baitz, Lesley Mark, Helen Sher, Janet Miller (trying to sort out her knitting, Valerie Goldstein, Beryl Sacks (looking down, Max Goldman

BUNKING OUT

One Friday night I bunked out with Linda Stoler and Janet Miller. We went to the bottom of the Arc drive, across the soccer field on our knees, lest someone should see us and were met by friends of Linda. We went to a Disco in Hillbrow, called the "Swinging Beach Club" which was covered in sand. We had a great time. When we got back to the Arc, our guard Adele Saiet, had fallen asleep, and we couldn't get in through the burglar guards but, after much yelling she woke. No-one was waiting for us and we climbed into bed, and fell asleep.

The next morning at breakfast, Ma came to our table and asked how we were, as we all looked a bit tired, as though we had been dancing all night. Talk about three red face girls. She told us that she suggests that we rest in the afternoon, and go to bed early, that evening. No Saturday movie, the worst punishment, and that was that.

Linda was not expelled from the Arc because of that. Not

another word was ever mentioned regarding the incident but the outside fire escape stairs leading from the Senior Girls upstairs down to the dining room below where the boys lined up were removed, rather quickly and quietly.

In the Arc I fancied Leon Goodman. He just used to tease me and make me cry. My best friend was Janet Miller, and we used to get into a lot of trouble together. When Janet was sent to the cottage, it was the worst, for me. I also wanted to go. The Arc Committee refused, parted us and said we weren't a good influence on each other. But we still got to see each other often; I was good at bunking out!

We got to bunk out plenty Janet Linda and I and I really miss those days. To this day Janet and I are best of friends.

The Arc gave us a good education, friends for life, and security. The food just was never part of the discussion.

Lesley and Helen Sher posing on Durban Beach

417

AFTER LEAVING THE ARC

After leaving the Arc I studied with Hilda Durbach Shorthand typing at Houghton College, in town and spent more time eating hot chelsea buns, then anything else! I stayed with my Auntie Shirley, my Mom's sister for a year, whilst studying, and then moved to a flat in Hillbrow with Janet.

I worked in Mr Teeger's accounting firm Leiman Teeger Gaddin Sifris and Company for many years as did Leon Goodman and David Sandler. Max Goldman also worked there for a short while.

I used to be a big flirt and broke many hearts until I met Guy!!!

Ryan Justin Les and Guy

KIBBUTZ REVIVIM

I met and married Guy who was born and bred in Durban and we had two boys. Guy had done two years army training and studied and worked in agriculture in South Africa.

In 1990 Guy and the boys and I moved to Israel. Initially we spent six months on Kibbutz Tzora studying Hebrew, and then moved to Kibbutz Revivim where we have became members.

On the Kibbutz Guy has studied Hotel and Restaurant Management and has become a qualified Electrician. I worked for 13 years in the Baby Department looking after the children.

We went to England (Isle of Man) in 2002 for two years, where Guy worked as a Farm Manager on a Diary Farm. I did this and that. We came back to the Kibbutz in September 2004 as my son, Ryan, had come back a year earlier to do his Army training. He has a year to go, which please G-d will pass peacefully, and quickly. He is at the moment stationed at Beit Lid, close to Netanya, and is a "Resup". I have no idea what that is in English but basically he is like a Unit Organiser. He enjoys giving out orders and telling soldiers what to do.

Justin is no longer working on the kibbutz. He is working on a fish farm, not far from here, where he also lives.

I would be back on the Isle of Man, tomorrow, but unfortunately Guy very much enjoys Kibbutz life. He is now in charge of the Electricity Department. I feel it is too Life Controlling, on the kibbutz just like the Arc but, I am happyish here, and have some very very good friends, and I suppose life is basically good to us here

Guy and Les

Chapter 110 - ANTHONY MARK (1957)

Lesley and Tony were placed in the care of Arcadia in July 1963 after their parents were divorced.

Tony who was born in 1957 spent eight years in the care of Arcadia from age six to age 14. He left the Arc in 1971 just after his Barmitzvah and joined his Mom Maisie (maiden name Effune) in Israel.

After he finished school in Israel in June 1976 he returned to South Africa and worked on the stage and made quite a name for himself.

In 1982 he went to Europe, settled in Paris, and continued to work in the entertainment business and was in cabaret, advertising, jazz singing and more recently has made his name in film.

Tony as Coppertone Man
Shooting of commercial for Coppertone Suntan Oil. 1989

ARC MEMORIES

I guess for many Arcs, we will always remember the good times. For instance the excitement of going away on holiday to Durban in the summer, Bloemfontein in the winter, or receiving our presents on Chanukah. We had quite a large selection, "goggles, flippers or beach towels."

Our Saturdays after Shul, playing soccer. Actually I remember

at those matches we were scared of playing opposite Doc. He always used to charge – whether the ball was there or not. We'd see him coming and we would kick the ball away as fast as possible no matter what side and then he'd give us hell for not playing properly.

Peter Hough, Martin Lasker, Beverly Collet, Sharon and Shelley Grishkan, Marilyn Stoler, Tony Mark and David Lasker - 1966 Prize giving.
"This is where my stage career began" Tony Mark

In the afternoon some of us used to sneak off to the zoo, to buy sweets and on the way back raid all the fruit trees from the houses along the way – no matter if the fruit was ripe or not.

One day we were playing cowboys and Indians. I ended up as a cowboy who received an arrow in the forehead and I still have the mark.

I remember the *mielies* we cooked under the pool in old pots.

And I especially remember our hair cut days in Rosebank when we used to raid the OK Bazaars. Boy did we know how to steal. We became so good at it that at Saxonwold School, one of us used to ask to be in the tuckshop, as a salesman, then another Arc used to come and buy. The buyer used to pretend he was giving money. He would buy chips, crunchies, flakies the works and he would get back some change (what chutzpah). Also we would try and sell the chicken noodle soup and when the Arcs came to buy we would go to the bottom of the tub and bring up tons of noodles, then the others would get only the soup.

On sports day the Arcs were the best, we would win quite often – egg and spoon races, three legged and the relays. I have to this day my swimming certificates – first for breaststroke and backstroke (the width) ha.

We also used to swap our sandwiches at school, ours bread soaked in syrup and peanut butter (ugh) for chicken or cheese sandwiches. I remember Vicky used to give us his sandwiches and sometimes some fruit, after homework time at night.

Friday after dinner we used to get together to listen to squad cars and then he used to scramble sweets, the best were the *boilies*.

The few incidents I find hard to forget were, and could have been very significant for my future. As I was a good swimmer, I used to swim for Saxonwold and Parktown Boys Std VI. I was often chosen with John John Park (son of Reg Park who was Mr Universe in body building) to present our schools. We used to go to Durban and Bloemfontein for different galas and races, but most of the times Ma refused to let me go. Heaven only knows why. The same for soccer, whenever we would play other schools, eight out of ten times I could never participate.

When I was in Primary School, Saxonwold, I used to be quite sad and sometimes felt very left out at school, because I was never quite sure whether I would be allowed to go with the others, on competitions to Cape Town or Durban. Gradually I got left out of the group, as they knew it would be touch and go with my situation. I can remember one time our coach did contact the Arc to request my participation, but Ma was Ma and I could not go.

The only memories I have left of the school days at Saxonwold Primary School are photos taken with the school teams. So yes, not all was rosy for us at the Arc.

MY STAGE CAREER

When I arrived in Israel in 1971 I guess I made up for lost time in the Arc.

I left the Arc in 1971 just after my Barmitzvah and followed my Mom to Israel where I finished school, on Kibbutz Beit-Hashitta, in the Emek Israel, between Afula and Beit Shean. When I graduated in June 1976 I decided that I wanted to return to South Africa, as I was getting more and more involved with the stage.

When I arrived back in South Africa I stayed with Les in Hillbrow for a while and started doing theatre and a few TV shows for the South African Broadcasting Commission (SABC). I auditioned for a Rock Musical called "*Let my people go*" at the Chelsea Theatre. I got the lead part with a singer "Jody Wayne". After that it was various cabaret shows in Cape Town, Jo'burg, Durban and also South African TV. In 1979 I auditioned for the first Sun City show, I got in, got quite a bit of publicity which made me *numero uno* in the papers.

After Sun City I went on tour doing cabaret in Durban and Cape Town for two years. I also did the a lead dance role in the musical "*South Pacific*" at the Nico Malan Opera House in Cape Town with "Graham Clarke."

In 1982 I decided to leave for Europe and ended up in Paris. I auditioned for a show at one of the big music halls, the "Paradise Latin". It's like the "Lido." I got in and got the principal role. During my first six years at this theatre I got involved in lots of films and TV commercials which I did until 1989. I then toured France and Europe for about ten years.

I also became a singer for Jazz clubs and still do so for various galas. I have now for some time decided to do something different – restaurant business and am running a very popular restaurant – Swiss and French Cuisine in Paris.

In 1985 I was invited to do a show in Berlin with Shirley Bassey, the Village People and Gloria Gaynor.

Queen Yahna , Tony and Gloria Gaynor - Germany 1989

In 1988 Sun City asked me to come back to SA, (The Wild Coast) to do another show which I did for six months. The

420

Choreographer was Roger Mesami who was also Liza Minelli's choreographer.

Cabaret "Millionaires Club " - Durban 1981

Rehearsal for a classical Jazz show in Switzerland 1992

MY MOVIE CAREER - SO FAR

After nearly 15 years of French Showbizz, I decided to take a small break, and helped some friends in their restaurant business, but I couldn't stay away from the stage too long and now its filming. What more can I say, I'm having fun, and who knows where my next path will lead.

Her name Is Arielle Domballe and she is a big name in France.
She Is also an Opera Singer. The Film Is Called Milady based on the Story of the Three Musketeers

So I'm now doing film full time, and have been on location quite regularly these last three years. Since May this 2005 I've done seven movies, not major roles, but small parts and worked with some big European directors.

I recently I finished a movie with the director of "*The Big Blue 3*" With Rosanna Arquette all about deep sea diving. It was a great hit. And not so long ago the director who's name is Luc Besson did "*The 7th Element*" with Bruce Willis. Any way, I was chosen out of quite a few guys for this role, and like I said not a biggy but enough to put down on my CV as having worked with him is quite *larney*.

A recent photo of Tony

MORE RECENTLY TONY WRITES

All is well here in Paris, and still filming as usual, actually had a small part in Spielberg's last picture, shot partly in Paris, called *Munich*. I guess you all know, the sad events surrounding this story? Should be a good picture. I was recently asked to play in a short movie, produced by the final year students, of the famous school of cinema here in France "*The Fimes*" I played an American GI style "MASH." It was lots of fun."

I'm up for a part, in a TV series, and play the role of an FBI agent here in Paris and so life goes on.

Tony dressed for his part in the film called The True Story of The Eiffel Tower.

Chapter 111 – SHARON KRAVETSKY (GRISHKAN) (1955)

In 1962 Sharon at age seven (born 6th September 1955) and her sister Shelley aged five (born 9th January 1957) were placed in the care of Arcadia following the death of their mother Rose.

Their father Hymie had come to South Africa from Lithuania as a seven year old child with his parents who had both passed away in the fifties. He always maintained a very strong attachment and remained an ever strong presence in Sharon and Shelley's lives until he passed away in 1974.

Likewise their mother Rose (Sparks) had come from Lithuania as a child and her father was Rav Sparks at the Doornfontein Shul in its earlier days.

Sharon and Shelley both left the Arc in 1973 and lived with their dad in Hillbrow and in 1974 were involved in an horrific accident. Sharon was in a coma for a long time and it took her years to recover.

The same year Hymie passed away suddenly never to witness Sharon's recovery or the success of their lives.

Sharon Grishkan

Sharon, Dad and Shelley Grishkan

ARC MEMORIES

I remember oh my G-d the dark room. When we were in the Babies we'd sit for hours and also we had to touch our toes in the hallway without bending our knees.

I wore bands and couldn't sleep one night, I was playing with them and got my lip caught so I had to stand and touch my toes for an hour. Helen de Winnaar really *balled me out*, what a bitch. One time I was talking at night past my bedtime, she nearly broke a bottle over my head she was so angry.

I remember Thursday nights were fish and chips and spinach and of course ice cream for dessert. I was not allowed ice cream cause I used to throw my fish and spinach on the floor until Helen de Winnaar found out, I thought she was going to kill me.

When we were in the Senior girls I remember Hannah Durbach and I decided to bunk out one night. We tied our sheets from our beds together and climbed out of the bathroom window. Martin Lasker was or I think Gary Crighton kept an eye so nobody would see us.

Anyway we ran like hell down the driveway to Oxford Road and we started to hitch hike and of course what a surprise, guess who picked us up? It was none other than Manfred Dankert. That was when he first met Hannah. He asked us where we wanted to go and neither of us really knew. So he said come to my apartment, we did. He had a condominium on some high rise building in Hillbrow on the top floor. We went in and wow the apartment was furnished with the finest of fine. The furniture was beautiful. We were afraid to do anything let alone sit.

Anyway I got really scared and told Hannah let's go, she said she wanted to stay so I left and met up with her later. I went back to the Arc. If she hadn't stayed she would probably be married with kids. Anyway it's quite a story. Unfortunately one escape lead to another escape, it got to a point where she

made arrangements. He would pick her up at the bottom of the drive. I used to help her escape, thank G-d, we were never caught.

For the record Hannah and Manfred have been together for the past 35 years.

MY FAMILY

I am married to Mark Kravetsky and live in Winnipeg, Canada with my seven children. They are a handful and I thank G-d they're all healthy.

Sharon's family (Photo taken in 2000)
Back row l-r: Shoshanna Toba 13, Sharon, Husband Mark, and Shmuel Mayer 16.
Girls in middle row: Shula Baila 12 and right Shifra Rosa 15
Boys in front; Mordechai Zvi 8, Ephriam Noah 6 and Avraham Leib 10

Chapter 112 – SHELLEY SEGAL (GRISHKAN) (1957)

Shelley married Stuart Segal in 1977 and they have three children; Darren born 1980, Ryan born 1982 and Lauren born 1986. They migrated to Australia in 1994.

ARC MEMORIES

I always remember our Arc spirit and our ever so insular lives. Some of our greatest "escapes" were our Bloemfontein holidays where most of us experienced our first French kiss, not too mention our Durban holidays where we all had at least one crush on the hot Durban guys. I recall some senior girls bunked out and the very next morning without warning the fire escape staircase was cut away and removed. Thereafter the main steps, that we never dared to tread on, became the next escape route. "They" could hardly remove those. The new senior girls were in total awe of the old senior girls.

A new recruit arrived and "they" told her she was not to come out of her room in her long pants since we do not wear that at the Arc. After three days and three nights they insisted she see the light of day and as she waltzed out in her long pants, the revolution began. We immediately all rolled down our long pants which had been concealed underneath our skirts and long pants were in to stay, forever after.

One thing that stands out most in my mind is toast. After I squealed to my Dad, Hymie Grishkan, that I hated cold, soggy, wet toast Mevrou van Rensberg, began her campaign of standing over me till I swallowed every last piece. I remember lining my school gym with serviettes so as to spit mouthfuls in as she turned her head and cutting the toast up into pieces so on distracting Mevrou, the girls at my table could snitch pieces off my plate to help me get through 'toast time'.

Remember our beautiful dog Lucky, and the silkworm who crawled out of his box to rest upon someone's tongue and the kid who climbed out of bed and peed into the slipper instead of the potty.

Sharon and Shelley

Young Shelley Grishkan

BERYL LUCKING

Beryl Lucking came to the Arc in the late 1950s at the very young age of about three years old. In the Babies she was a sickly child who was always given a lot of extra attention.

At one stage she fell and broke her collar bone and the house mother in charge of us at the time, "Auntie Botha", was very angry and no doubt embarrassed that this had happened.

Beryl spent a lot of time in the Arc hospital and one day when she was still quite young just disappeared, never to be mentioned again, even upon asking.

Many years later, as an adult I met a doctor socially and upon discussing my being an Ex Arc she told me about a patient she had many many years ago a little girl Beryl Lucking from the Arcadia who had died of cancer. I was stunned.

REVISITING THE ARC

On a recent trip to South Africa I caught up with several ex Arcs. I also visited the Arc, which has been sold. The main building and hospital, being heritage listed, are to be restored.

As kids, those high ceilings, huge carved wooden doors, perfectly formed arches, magnificent staircases, marble floors, vast expanses, aerial views and massive grounds were right out of a Harry Potter Movie. It still remains a magnificent architectural masterpiece. I remember the care, the kindness, the compassion, the joy and not so joyous and some 'not so nice' housemothers and a few naughty kids along the way.

I feel very privileged to have grown up at Arcadia. Whilst for most of us living at home was clearly first prize, the values, resilience, respect and compassion that we came to know has stood many of us in good stead!! The comradeship of our shared experience crosses all barriers from eye surgeons to housewives and there is a definite unspoken, but well understood bond between the many who for one reason or another might have had to share in the common experience of being an Arc. It is surely adversity that we all come to respect. There for the grace of G-d go any one of us, since as we know first hand, life at the flick of a finger, can change for any one of us!!

Do you remember the magnificent bathroom with the sunken bath upstairs outside Ma and Doc's flat? Only years after I left Arcadia did I discover what was behind that forbidden closed door.

Well with clothes on I proceeded to lay in it for a photographic session great fun we had! Walked through all the now empty dormitories, the kitchen, the huge, then locked up bread cupboard and locked fruit rooms. We used a nail on a stick to retrieve apples one by one through the wire bars. Mrs Saffer the ingenious dressmaker, used to alter our "hand downs" to look haute couture.

Since the Shul was being converted into an office theatrette, the seating had been removed, so we were unable to seek out our engravings which we tirelessly etched into the wood down through the years of every Shabbat and all the Chagim we spent in there. I finally got a bird's eye view from the balcony of the Lichtigfeld's flat. My G-d we never stood a chance of not being caught bunking out, Ma had an aerial view of the whole of Johannesburg from that vantage point!!

I couldn't access the Baby Department which the workmen told me, was next to be pulled down. The Boys' Department has been pulled down and replaced by huge Hollard office blocks as well as more office blocks on the soccer fields, including where the Goldsmiths once lived.

The very long tree lined driveway remains, and oh yes all those beautiful palm trees alongside the driveway we used for building the succah every Succot is all gone....

It was very very special and nostalgic visit down memory lane, a somewhat memorable journey.
....

1967 Girls Back Row: Lynette Sher, Lauraine Goldstein, Helen Sher, Shelley Schreeuwer, Hannah Durbach and Myra Durbach.
Standing: Valery Goldstein, Sharon Grishkan, Beryl Sacks, Estelle Besser and Ruth Jacobs.
Sitting: Sadie Baitz, Marilyn Stoler, Beverley Collett and Shelley Grishkan.

OBTAINING AUSTRALIAN CITIZENSHIP

In the second half of 2003 Shelley and her three children obtained their Australian Citizenship. This was after a tough three year legal battle that she had with the Australian Government who wanted to send her back to SA after her husband (the principal applicant) returned to SA. She was left with nothing and no support and had to struggle on her own to support and bring up her three children.

She started working again. Initially she worked as a full time Hebrew Teacher teaching Sidur, with baby sitting and teaching Hebrew in her spare time to get extra cash to support her family.

Shelley has guts and a real inner strength that perhaps she got from being in the Arc. She has not let her current circumstances get her down and always holds her head up high. She carries herself with a positive disposition and a smile. We all salute you Shelley and wish you well.

Following are two letters sent to Shelley for the occasion: The first is from Stuart Berkson, a long time friend of Shelley's and the second is from the Rabbi of the local congregation.

Letter from Stuart M Berkson, Chicago, USA
5 August 2003

Having to write this letter is a bit like the definition of mixed emotions (that is, watching your mother-in-law drive over a cliff in your new Mercedes). Mixed emotions because I am very sad that I cannot be there in person to share this momentous day with you and the kids but incredibly happy that this wonderful day has finally arrived.

We have known each other for more than 15 years. When we first met you were Shelley from Sandton, with three beautiful kids in tow destroying the children's department at Edgars. From that first encounter at the till you were incredibly warm and welcoming, inviting me into your home and making me a part of your extended family going forward. Without our chance encounter, I probably would have viewed South Africa as just another country on my list of business locations, which certainly would have had a significant impact on my practice and the enjoyment I have from it.

Through these years we have gone through all of the ups and downs that truly good friends experience. The joy of getting to know each other's families, the sharing of wonderful occasions and visits together, the hardships of illness and personal traumas, the dislocation of moves. However, through this all our friendship has only grown.

The fact that our friendship has grown is not a surprise – I could have predicted that 15 years ago. What is surprising is how much you have grown in this same period. When we first met you truly were Shelley from Sandton, a lovely South African girl who, although having experienced a difficult life (I have never forgotten the Arc), was certainly a *kugle*, complete with a beautiful home in Morningside Manor with a maid (oh, don't you miss Adelaide!), and a Merc in the driveway (although it was not yours – you were driving that ratty yellow car).

When you first talked of emigration your fears centred on having to clean your own home and losing the community that you knew. You were brought to Australia for all of the right reasons, but you were never told that you were going without the right papers. When you said goodbye to Judy Crescent, I doubt you ever imagined the battles you would have to fight simply to survive and remain in Australia that would stand in front of you.

It is this personal growth that makes me so incredibly proud of you. Being Shelley from Sandton may not have been a perfect world, but it was certainly a dream compared to the uphill fight you faced in becoming Shelley the Australian. I continue to marvel (and tell others, like my wife Linda, my girls and people like Linda Cooperman) at your ability to survive and cause your family to thrive in Australia. You have done all this with no help from anyone – giving your kids an education, making sure their needs are attended to, putting a roof (or as we say, ruff– remember how much your kids laughed at the way I talked; now I laugh at them because they sound like Australians) above everyone's head. Things you took for granted when you were Shelley from Sandton became your sole responsibility as Shelley from Melbourne, and you have managed to achieve these with a smile on your face and a determination in your heart. It is that type of determination and single-minded focus that leaves the rest of us in awe of your accomplishments.

It would have been easy to simply curl up in a corner and cry about the cards you were dealt. However, that was not something you were prepared to do. When it looked like you were not going to obtain resident status, you found a way to get this. At times when it looked like there was no money to even pay for the basics, you simply went off to baby sit. A girl who had never taken public transportation in South Africa learned to take it in Australia. You played all the roles in the house, even those you have never intended to fill. Throughout it all, your focus has always been on making a new life for your family, making their life in Australia better than what they could have expected in South Africa.

Besides the incredible pride I feel in all that you, and only you, have achieved personally, I also feel tremendous joy at the thought of you and the kids becoming Australians. Although I certainly love South Africa, there is no doubt in my mind that the payoff from all of your sacrifice, becoming citizens of Australia, is well worth the sacrifices you have made.

Our forefathers left Europe looking for more friendly shores where they could live safely as Jews, provide a good environment with good opportunities for their kids, and make a decent living. That was really all they wanted. My relatives thankfully took the boats to Canada and the US; yours picked the wrong ships and ended up in South Africa! You have now corrected that mistake and given your children (and future grandchildren) an opportunity to be part of a country in which they can live and prosper freely, where opportunities exist and the future is secure. Our ancestors left their homelands and made great sacrifices so that their children could have an easier life, even if it meant a harder life for themselves. You have done the same, and I am confident that this will pay great dividends for your kids, their kids and so on.

Although I will not be there to celebrate with you in person, I will certainly be there in spirit. Shel, I am so proud of you for what you have accomplished, and so excited for you and the kids for all the opportunities which lie ahead of you as Australians. Mazel tov on this wonderful occasion.

Letter from RABBI P HEILBRUNN, Chief Minister, St Kilda Hebrew Congregation - Melbourne Victoria Australia 12 August 2003

Although I will not be able to be with you tomorrow evening to witness your great achievement of becoming an Australian Citizen, I certainly offer you my warm and sincere congratulations.

Your path to residency and citizenship has been fraught with difficulties which seemed virtually insurmountable.

In congratulating you, I wish to commend the spirit and sheer guts you have displayed in meeting each one of the challenges successfully. Your spirit inspired a small group of concerned members of our community to try and help you the best way they knew how, and I am proud to have been amongst them.

Please G-d may the coming years be filled with the blessings of good health, achievement and contentment for you and your family.

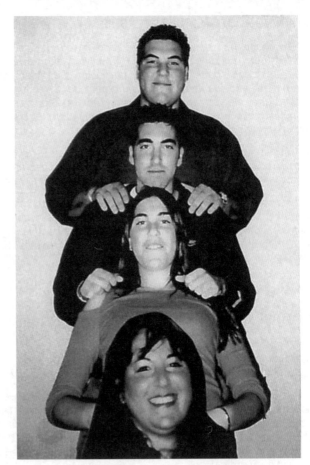

Shelley Segal with her three beautiful children, Darren Justin and Lauren

Darren Justin and Lauren and Shelley Segal

Written by Shelley Segal (nee Grishkan)

The Arc was an experience shared with some very wonderful children, some great staff and special committee members and *kol kavod* to each and every Ex-Arcadian and please G-d may we all continue to make successes of our lives, spread joy, happiness and love to all whom we encounter. We all deserve Hashems richest blessings!

Chapter 113   SHAUN (1956) AND MARK (1955) JACOBS

Our connection to the Arc began prior to living at the Arc, in two different ways, strange, but here goes. Mark and I were put in the Cape Town Orphanage when I was one and Mark was two - we lived there for about 18 months to two years.

Concerning the Johannesburg Arc, children were allowed to go home with a classmate, whose parent would then drop them off at the Arc by 5.00 pm once a week after school on a Friday.

Mark and I attended Saxonwold Primary School, the same school as many of the Arc boys and girls, so we all knew one another. One could not help knowing the Arcs, who would gather as a gang and beat upon the poor 'outsider' who would dare to start a fight with an Arc boy. Moreover, the old Arc bus was unmistakable to all and sundry, belching out black diesel fumes all over the northern suburbs of Jo'burg, not unlike the old Putco buses.

I think Gary Chrighton came initially, but then Alan Jacob, who shared a class with me, came on a regular basis. That was back in the beginning of 1964, and it lasted for months.

One Friday, our regular home visitor Alan, was dropped off, as usual, at the Arc. Then, a few days later, on the May 31st 1965 (Republic Day - RSA - happy holidays, an event to remember), Mark and I were dropped off at the Arc, to live.

Frankly speaking, we didn't quite know what was happening to us, but I suppose each Arc child has their own story. I was nine years old and Mark ten. We were taken out of the Arc for about four months in 1968, but were returned promptly.

We officially left the Arc in January 1969, ie when I was just about to turn 13, and when I entered high school and Mark 14.

Although we were taken out of the Arc, we were enrolled for high school at Parktown Boys', so our friendship, association with the Arcs, continued, since the boys went to the same school. The girls attended Parktown Girls' High, which, for some unexplainable reason was actually in the suburb of Greenside.

Shaun now lives in Israel on Kibbutz Tzora where Ruth (Jacob) and Sharon (Getz) live. Shaun is married with three kids, while his brother Mark lives in Sydney, and is married with two kids.

"UNFORGETTABLE THAT'S WHAT YOU ARE"
Shaun Jacobs remembers.

When my mind drifts back to years gone by, and the Pond, the *hok* and the Junior Boys come into clear sight, these images immediately link themselves to almost surreal or hallucinatory events such as aggressive chickens attacking small boys on the soccer field, daily early morning bed inspections, twice daily Shul attendance, compulsory nightly homework lasting literally hours - even if one was nine years old at the time.

Shaun by the Junior Boys

Then of course, a smile silently takes shape, and one thinks of those official and unofficial regular 'outings' – respectively; the visits to Rosebank to receive those uncharacteristically short razor haircuts in the days of long-haired Beatles, raiding parties to the OK Bazaars to steal fruit or to 'borrow' possibly unwanted low-hanging fruit from neighbourhood 'philanthropists'.

And yes, as per my title, I instinctively hum a tune. The Arc was certainly unforgettable, and it is possibly a twist of psychology that one's mind, in retrospect, tends to remember the positive, more than the negative. Clearly there were both aspects to those days back then.

I would be at fault not to dredge up some mildly humourous episodes that a fellow Arc may well have written about in the past.

SOME OF SHAUN'S ARC MEMORIES

Herewith a short passage concerning some memories, but where does one start? So many small anecdotes, stories, and incidents, that may or may not have changed over time, but they remain nonetheless so vivid in my memory.

The Junior Boys scrambling to be on top of the slide (located between the *hok* and the Babies), in order to get educated in the ways of the female form, ie the Senior Girls, changing before the Saturday night *fliek*, with the curtains wide open, displaying their wonderful all.

Only the boy at the top of the slide would be fully able to get an unimpeded sight of those wonderful sought-after bodies, but he would get pushed down the long slide, so the next in the queue could get his lustful look-in, so it would be a continual climb to the top of the slide, a few seconds glimpse, and a slide down, then back up again....

The four Barmitzvah Boys, standing on the Bimah on Saturday morning, singing their hearts away while one of the Senior Boys tied all their shoe laces together. When it was time to depart the Bimah, the four, walking ever so slowly in short steps so as not to fall over, resembled old men doing the soft-shoe-shuffle along a cobbled boardwalk, while the 'congregation' would fall about laughing.

'Arranging' that Doc always scored the last goal after Shul on Saturday mornings, was like a scene out of a Monty Python movie - skilled footballers tripped over themselves while others fell over sideways for no apparent reason; Doc would come charging through, and the inevitable goal was scored.

After the football game, the Senior Boys forcing the Junior Boys to sit in a circle, then determining who would fight with whom. A week after Mark's and my arrival, Peter Hough told Mark to fight Graham Stoler; from memory, before Mark realised what was going on, Graham, the hi-pitched wailer, was biting Mark's neck. Then, Leon Goodman selected me to fight Brian Sandler; all I remember was being pulled off Brian, who was lying under me with a bleeding nose and lip. Funny, but so sad and so unnecessary.

During the December holidays, Mark, Danny Lasker, Gary Crighton (if I remember correctly) and I went to see the Pink Panther (movie) in Rosebank, near the OK Bazaars. Returning home, I ran across Oxford Road to catch the bus, and was hit down by an oncoming car. I crawled to the side of the road, where someone from the nearby bottle store brought me in, and offered me sugar water (probably should have been a neat J&B). They asked if they should contact the Arc, and we all retorted 'no', fearing the worst. When we arrived back at the Arc, I limped in behind Danny and Mark. Ma was waiting, asked what happened, and without waiting for a reply, slapped Danny in the face. Why? Who knows, he surely didn't deserve it.

Julius ('The Silver Threads') Gordon, Neville Merwitz and a few other kind hearted folk, told Mark that the were-wolf comes out during the full moon. Mark, a believing kindly soul, landed up three days in the Arc hospital suffering from fear.

Our first year end holiday, and the arrival on Durban platform, armed with a metal ashtray (made at the school metal work classes) that would be given to the host family for keeping one for three weeks. I remember waiting on the platform, looking around in confusion, until a strange friendly face appeared with a photograph in their hand; looking at the photo, then back at me, and asking, "Are you Shaun?" The folk were nice and kind enough, but Mark and I had never been separated before, so it was a serious learning curve for me.

When the photographers came to take photographs for the Arc magazine, Ma and Mrs Stelzner put out jugs of juice and piles of sandwiches on each table, for obvious reasons. When the photographers disappeared, so did the extra food and drink.

Shaun on the train to Durban

Saturday nights at the movies in the dining room. Everyone waited anxiously, quietly, looking forward to the weekly entertainment. The Babies sat in the front row, then the Juniors, then the Seniors, who got up to all kinds of strange activities in the darkness. No-one ever knew what the movies were about, in advance. The first reel would click into life, eyes would focus on the screened wall - then, 20 seconds after the movie started, we would (for example), understand it was a war saga or a detective story, see a villain get shot or a soldier emerge and throw a hand grenade. Suddenly, stop! The lights would go on, the Babies would be ordered to stand up, and out they marched - no violence for them.

Those who remained got those two most sought after hard boiled sweets before the last reel was shown. What a joy, since those sought-after sweets could be given to a girl who would then pass them onto another girl, who was the object of one's desires. At nine or ten years old, desiring a girl was almost like a dog chasing a car. When he catches up with the car, the dog wouldn't know what to do with it...

So much more - Vicky's morning inspections with cane in hand, Neville carving the letter 'V' (for victory) with a red - hot mathematical compass, into selected Junior Boys, Shul twice daily even though no-one ever understood a word of what we were reading, Mrs. Stelzner doing the rounds at night and screaming at the top of her lungs to keep quiet, Jo Boloy pinching the hell out of us, mad chickens chasing us across the soccer field then we got our revenge back on those chickens by slaughtering them, and cooking them for the train ride down to Durban in December...... and so on and so forth.

It was one helluva ride.

SHAUN REVISITING THE ARC

Let me share my somewhat recent visit to The Arc in 2004, I happened to be in Johannesburg, and driving down Oxford Road, the car seemed to steer itself into the entrance of the Arc.

I hesitated, but drove up the tree-laned highway, hoping to enjoy the reminiscences of youth, when a security guard approached me as I was parking outside the Main Building.

He mentioned that Hollard Insurance had purchased the property, and intimated that they were refurbishing and upgrading the site. Building rubble was everywhere, and accordingly, he informed me, the property was out of bounds to 'the public'. After some discussion on the matter, I made a small contribution to his pension fund, and was thus allowed to meander around, albeit for a short period, although, quite frankly, much had already been demolished.

I drove away with mixed emotions, but with a feeling that despite its disappearance, The Arc lives on, in our collective memories.

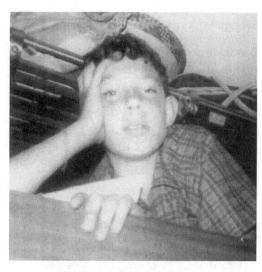

Mark Jacobs – on the train to Durban

MEMORIES OF MARK JACOBS

What stories can I tell you? There are many fond memories.
- Going on fruit raids
- Raiding the OK bazaars on haircut days
- Doc kicking us instead of the ball on our Saturday morning soccer games.
- My heroes were:
- Leslie Durbach – he slept with his window wide open to get fresh air (even when it was bloody cold) and played first team rugby.
- Ronnie Schreeuwer – a good friend to us younger guys. He had a strong sense of right and wrong.

MARK AND I NOW

Allow me to span over 35 years, and offer you a brief insight into what has transpired in the life of both Mark, my brother and I, since we left the Arc in 1969.

At the outset and in advance, let me apologise if what I have to say is boring, but facts are as they are - dry and irrefutable. I'll try and nonetheless offer some detail, since I have lost contact with almost all the Arcs, apart from Ronnie Schreeuwer and Ruth (Jacob).

Mark and I matriculated from high school at Northview High (Highlands North area), where Mark was selected as the Head Boy. Both Mark and I played 1st team rugby for the school, and as per extra mural activities, learned karate. Under our differing age divisions, we were both South African national karate champions.

Mark went on to direct studies at Wits University, while I went into the army, as was obligatory in South Africa at the time. I became an officer in a combat unit, spending most of the time in Angola, and took part in the war that was raging there in 1974 to 1975.

Mark completed his medical studies at Wits, then went to Cape Town University to study for Ophthalmic Surgery, as a specialisation. During his studies, Mark married, and thereafter with his wife and young son, emigrated to Sydney, Australia. Mark qualified as an Eye Surgeon in Australia, and thereafter proceeded to Great Ormond Street University Hospital in London for three years, where he started his PhD, which he completed after having returned to Australia (where he currently resides). Mark has two sons, one studying music at university, while the younger son is completing high school.

I married in RSA, and have three Children, approximately two years apart. When my eldest was about eight years old we migrated to Israel, where we have been living ever since, on kibbutz. I took the opportunity of completing my university studies while working, and subsequently went on to complete my MBA as well. With respect to my children, my eldest (daughter) is a lawyer, and the second eldest completed her four years at university recently in Nursing Science - she is currently a Staff Nurse, working at a large hospital near Tel Aviv.

My son recently finished six years in the army, and as an Officer in an elite unit, he benefited by the army sending him to university. Hence, he began his studies at a university near Tel Aviv, majoring in Government and Political Strategy, and he intends to go back to the army thereafter.

My Father, for those who remember him, died in 1999, and is buried at West Park Cemetery in Johannesburg.

Mark and Shaun Jacobs, Danny Lasker and Errol Hough showing off their trophy won in the relay on the Jewish day schools sports day

Chapter 114 – DANNY LASKER (1953)

Danny is the oldest of five brothers. He was born in Liverpool England, and his family were third or fourth generation English. His parents migrated to South Africa in 1957 when Danny was about three years old and Martin (the second oldest) was just a few months old. Their father found work as an electrician in Carltonville.

Danny says he grew up in a very unstable environment at home till the age of about seven when his Mother decided that it was best for her sons to be placed in the protection of Arcadia.

Initially in 1960 the three oldest brothers Danny, Martin and David were admitted to Arcadia and Sammy who was just a few months old came at a later date. Several years later a fifth son Reginald was also admitted into Arcadia.

Danny left the Arc in December 1972 after finishing school and went to Israel where he has lived ever since.

In 1981 Danny married an Israeli, Abigail and they have four children Maron, Evan, Shacked and Adiel. Danny is now a security guard and lives in Israel in a village, Kedumim.

Danny's brothers Martin David Sammy and Reginald left the Arc when they had finished school. Martin passed away in an accident. David Sammy and Reginald live in Johannesburg.

ARC MEMORIES

I remember playing tag – hide and seek- and the whole Arc was our boundary and sometimes even outside the Arc. It was an all day game. I remember chasing Graham through the "quadrangle" (stationery room and scullery) and coming out at the main road and no Graham. Vanished. Disappeared. A mystery. We were about the same running speed but I had more stamina than him and could eventually wear him down. He obviously knew that and planned accordingly. This episode in the quadrangle happened more than once and I was baffled as to how he simply vanished into thin air. Finally I was told, or caught him in the act. He simply ran at top speed because I was not far behind – grabbed the low lying eaves (gutter) with a jump and swung himself up onto the roof and over the peak in a few seconds!! Unbelievable guts!! That's how I remember it now.

Graham Stoler Clears up the Mystery Disappearance

I remember all this very well and make a true confession. Considering that Danny was fitter then me and considering that I was overweight, I surely couldn't run away from Danny. But after that quadrangle episode Danny asked me, "Where did you disappear to?" Well surely we were still going to carry on with

Danny Martin Sammy Reggie and David

the running and I was in no mood to tell him the truth so, I told him a little story. I was not letting out my secret. I told him I jumped on the roof, knowing that he would not have looked for me on the roof.

What I did Danny, instead of running straight to the street, I simply turned right into the kitchen area and hid up the side stairs where the girls would walk up to their rooms, just by the kitchen entrance - another mystery solved...

The older boys forced Graham and I to fight each other. We were more or less the same weight and height. He was slightly taller and heavier but younger than me. I hated it and the older boys who forced us into it.

I remember the two loquat trees at the bottom of the stone stairs leading from the area of Doc and Ma's apartment to the area of the Babies. Up until today I love loquats! I love all fruit! Fruit raids probably at fault. I remember mulberry stains on clothes and body. How did we ever get rid of them? I remember stomach pains and diarrhoea from stuffing myself with fruit - forbidden fruit always tastes better someone once said, but there is also the other side of the coin.

I also remember the "Bread Tree" near the swings on the verge of the downhill. Dry and tasty. I never quite tasted anything like that again – I loved that fruit.

At the ripe old age of seven, eight or nine I had my first girlfriend, Marcia. We were both thin, quick, fast and agile. I just remember us running around all the time. Later on in life I had a big crush on Beryl, but somehow I just did not know what to do with it.

I remember Beryl, Ruth and other Arc girls getting off early from school and "making their way home" via Parktown Boys' High. Our poor teachers did not stand a chance once they came by. Total lack of concentration in the classes. After a while this kind of performance was stopped by the authorities.

For me I confess it was quite embarrassing and I breathed easier when it stopped. Anyway their point was proved – they were all in their own ways pretty, and altogether the Arc girls could cause havoc with our emotions.

I loved the library, National Geographic, Hardy Boys and Enid Blyton's *Noddy*. I also remember massive jigsaw puzzles on the floor or table in the Boys'. Max and David were there with me. Great times.

I remember one of the older boys used to pick on us younger guys and Ronnie was my saviour and hero. Ronnie, even though he was a lot shorter, about half a metre I guess, would lay into him whenever he saw him bullying.

One day I decided to climb the big Oak Tree. It wasn't an easy decision for me. It was a big tree. I started slowly and finally reached the top. That's where my problems started. I looked down and around and enjoyed a fantastic sight. After a while I decided to descend but found out very quickly that descent, especially when you're looking down, is much more difficult mentally and physically than ascent.

Eventually my nerves gave out on me and I was paralysed – still on the top after a few unsuccessful attempts to descend. I started to shout for help and cry. Who knows how long I was stuck up there until someone – Ronnie? came and helped me down. I was a nervous wreck by then and I don't think I ever climbed the tree again.

Paradoxically I really liked parachuting in the Army, while 99% don't like it or hate it passionately. In a night jump with full equipment I had a mishap and I found myself hanging upside down looking at the beautiful dark sky and stars and only one shoulder harness in place. Yes I'm still alive.

I remember Boaz and Offer Fain. One of them had a very bad allergy to pollen and grass. We had to piggyback him everywhere.

Cowboys and Indians – I was usually the leader. One day we "raided" the Coops – emptied them. We got there stealthily and "conquered" it and carried on. I went into the walled sections and scouted down the hill. What did I see? A couple kissing. I quietly signalled everyone to take positions in the other sections. That picture still remains vividly in my mind.

Gary and myself playing darts outside the Senior Boys on the terrace of palm trees and garden. I threw up my dart practically vertical and it came down right on Gary's head – point first! Don't remember what happened after that.

Gary and I at school in arts and crafts class – we were nine years old I think – Gary got up to ask the teacher a question and before he sat down I held the big raffia needle – point up – on his seat. He sat. He didn't cry or scream. But we both dashed to the toilets and there he pulled down his pants and I saw my "handiwork". One nice small hole that was already going blue and purple. He was crying but not blatantly. He had real guts. Again I don't remember what happened afterwards! How did he manage to sit for the next few days? Who sterilised the puncture? Who gave him an anti-tetanus shot?

One Sunday Muffy and I started telling jokes to each other. It started early in the morning and finished hours later in the afternoon – late. It was just one of those days. No matter what he said we just laughed hysterically, we rolled over on the ground in fits of laughter. Every now and then we would have a slight pause and just by looking at each other we would burst out into more fits of never-ending laughter. By the end of the day our stomachs, throats and eyes were really and truly sore from laughter and tears.

Max always wanted me to sit next to him because I loved fish and he didn't! I remember him stuffing fish into his trouser pockets and pretending to cough and spitting the fish into serviettes. A dog coming into the dining room and eating his fish – How in hell did a dog get in? He had a fertile mind when it came to fish. I was constantly placed far enough away from him so that I couldn't help.

Broken bones – playing tag. Gary running away from someone with me. I ran ahead of him. I was already in the vast open area of the oak tree, slide and swings. Gary had jumped down from the dining room area into the terraced gardens. On his way down he tried to jump over a massive rock and came short.

He broke his arm. I was the first to get to him. You could see the bone sticking out at a strange angle. He didn't cry?

Lightning had struck down a big tree uphill opposite the main entrance. Gary and I climbed the fallen tree and sat on a thick branch some height from the ground, two to three metres. We had long sturdy poles that reached to the ground. Gary 'poled' first ie flung himself with the aid of the pole downwards and outwards. Pole vaulting comes to my mind. He landed safely and then it was my turn. I was scared chicken! I deliberated and deliberated and a few times nearly got up enough courage to pole. Eventually I got down. The branch snapped and I landed badly and sprained and fractured my arm. While I was in plaster Mouse (Helen) came by too often and pestered me. I gave her a plaster on her head non-too gently. She was surprised and hurt! I only hurt my arm again.

I remember playing soccer in the homework room, in the corridor, on the verandah and who knows where else? You could hear the thuds and bangs and shouts of play in Timbuktu.

I remember walking to Parktown Boys' every morning. Sometimes leaving it just too late – 12 minutes before eight! That steep incline outside the Arc gate. In winter we would freeze. In Saxonwold I remember being outside of class more than inside. The principal would sometimes stroll around and catch those that were outside the class for extra punishment. I got whipped with a cane more times than I can remember or count. Once Gary, Graham and myself and others were all caned for something or other. Even then I remember Gary as being strong willed and brave. The first to take the punishment and hardly a word out of him. I was "chicken" always being last and hoping he would be tired and maybe less angry after having spent his fury on others first. We used to compare bare arses afterwards. Red, blue, purple and welted with exact replicas of the cane. He broke more than one cane on us during those years.

I remember playing cricket at the Arc and dressing up in pads of all kinds; leg pads, ball guards, helmet? I didn't mind fielding too much as long as I was not too close to the batters. Batting I distinctly didn't like. Those hard cricket balls were often bowled at me too fast for my health.

At Parktown we used to sit on the concrete benches, which looked onto the main field, during 'breaks". One day I was messed on by pigeons three times in the less 30 minutes. I was promptly told that three times is meant to be lucky!

I remember the swimming pool and the vine that climbed the fence. I used to love to suck the flowers for juice - Honeysuckle. There was also a certain type of clover that grew wild at the Arc that I also loved to eat.

I could eat three or four bowls of porridge on winter mornings and remember fish and chips on Thursday nights. Yum Yum!

Where we used to wait for the Arc Bus at Saxonwold there were a few plum/apricot trees (not very tasty – sour!) The bees anyway always enjoyed themselves there at the cost of my brother David's lower lip which was nearly always chapped in winter. He always had chapped lips – open cuts in his lower lip

that the bees loved to sting – poor David. What agony and frustration for me!

I remember waiting in the *kraal* on Sundays expectantly for a visit from my parents. Standing and looking, searching and hoping and eventually disappointment. One Sunday I remember seeing my father come to visit us. He was still far away near the "massive" slide (how I feared that huge slide) but I ran like crazy to meet him and as I got nearer I even called out to him and nearly "jumped" him. What a shock and heartbreak to realise it was someone else – who I didn't know!

I remember Gary and his migraines – poor little Gary! I always liked him. He was small and I imagine bullied around a lot – not by me I hope. He took up karate and then no one messed with him and his migraines also vanished. He had fantastic self-control and guts. According to Mouse he's religious!

We had scary movies on Saturday night. Were they crazy at the Arc letting us younger guys see movies like *The Blob*, *Frankenstein* and *Dracula*. There was always some wise ass who at the most scary parts, with the music building up the tension, did or said something to scare us even more.

When the M1 was under construction a few guys – me included – decided to pour sand into the petrol tanks of the massive earthworks equipment. I remember after the weekend finished Doc was obviously informed by the M1 authorities and I don't exactly remember what happened to us – maybe I wasn't involved – but I have the faded memory of something more serious than just a talk by Doc. I remember frequent crashes into the Arc wall before the M1 was made. Still it was a "crime" to rob us of all that playing area and our direct route to the Zoo and the Zoo Lake and the orchards for raiding.

At one stage I used to go with Alan and Ruth Jacobs to their father's flat in Hillbrow mainly on Sundays. One day Alan showed me with his dad's binoculars a certain lady who lived across from them in another block of flats. It seems that Alan had quite a lot of "practice" with people who did not pull up their blinds or draw their curtains. In short this certain lady caught us spying on her and informed his father. I don't remember exactly the consequences but it was embarrassing.

Paul Cohen thought he was Cliff Richard but he could only play a few notes on his guitar - over and over again - and sing pop songs.

June 1966 it snowed in Johannesburg and we started pelting each other with snowballs on the soccer ground. Someone, maybe Ronnie, pelted snow on the back of Paul's head and there was a cry of "There's snow on Table Mountain" and there was much laughter and gaiety. How he hated that nick name and us little guys didn't dare say it to his face but the elders, naturally, had no problems with him.

I remember some older boys used to pick on us younger guys and Ronnie was our saviour and hero - Ronnie, even though he was a lot shorter would lay into them whenever he saw bullying.

I used to make catapults (like others as well). One day I lay in quite tall grass above the Babies and Girls on a terrace next to the steep stone stairs that lead to the girls' tennis courts from the Hospital. I took out my "Catty" and a few 'perfect' stones and aimed it at a group of guys and girls on the steps to the Girls. I obviously had a target - who I can't remember - in sight and I took my time and aimed carefully.

It was quite a distance to shoot and I deliberated somewhat. I pulled on my "Catty" and with perfect precision and coolness let go. What a shot! Bingo! Holy Moses! What a racket and fuss there was. He was screaming in pain - I hit him on the head - and everyone was trying to figure out what happened. I silently slipped away out of sight in the tall grass. I started to worry that I had caused serious damage to him.

I casually re-entered the scene a minute or so later and asked what happened. No one had the foggiest idea at all! There were all kinds of speculations! I was largely ignored. I was really worried about the damage to him. My only defence is - the devil got into me.

David Sandler gives his Version of Events

Let me tell the catapult story from my perspective…

I was walking down the tall staircase of concrete steps leading from the hospital (near the old art room) down to the tennis court. At the top, parallel with the stairs was a fence covered with a thick vine of purple trumpet flowers and if you looked under the leaves you could find gold or silver ladybugs. At the bottom of the staircase was a small tree stump sticking out of the embankment. I remember once catching a bumble bee, which nested in this stump. It was for Eva Bortz who was doing a project for school and she had a whole lot of different insects pinned to a board. She gave me a net to catch it with.

When I got near the bottom of the stairs I felt a sharp powerful and very painful sting on the left side of my temple. It was a stone hitting me. I cried out in pain and people came running. No one knew where it came from and someone suggested it was something that had fallen from a tree. Trouble was there were no trees around.

MOWING THE LAWN

Helen and I were visiting one Sunday in Germiston with this family - forget their name. They had a huge double storey house with a massive ground and all well enclosed by big trees. We must have been in our early teens then.

We were given the pleasure of mowing their lawn. I mowed with the electric mower and Helen with the petrol one. We were told and warned explicitly not to work close together and to be careful and not let the mechanical mower 'mow' the electric cable. I remember the two of us were really excited and enjoyed the mowing. I remember the couple, with their kids I think, looking on us now and then with happy faces at our pleasure.

Somehow in our excitement and joy Helen really 'mowed' my electric cable and it was a real 'shocking experience'. Probably just a few minutes of that couple's lapse in their watching us caused the two of us to get 'entangled'. Wow! What a sight it was! Helen - poor Helen, was blue from shock and was held

tight by the current to the mower. She had also wet herself from the shock which probably made matters worse.

That image of poor Helen 'dancing', blue and wet and shouts etc are even today engraved in my head. Don't ask me what happened, I have no more memory than that. But why do I feel guilty? What did I do wrong to cause such a mishap? Thank heavens for selective memories. Maybe it's better not to know the real story. How she survived I'm sure everyone would like to know. How come she's never mentioned this before? Maybe she's blanked it out? Or maybe I've got the wrong person involved. Anyway I hope I'm forgiven. I really meant no harm, it was truly an accident.

MORE ARC MEMORIES

In your *Arc Memory Booklets* is a picture of Vicky from 1938 at camp. I swear I remember that same robe on Vicky in the '60s and early '70s! I know in those days they made clothes to last [good quality], not like today. I tend to hang onto my clothes for a long time too.

In the Arc I remember how the cows used to graze in the big open area below the main building. There was a large ferocious looking bull with horns – big ones! We used to play 'matadors' with him. We would flash a red shirt at him and when he charged we would run for our lives. He had large wicked horns! We would try and see who would be the bravest and creep up the closest to him or stay the longest when he charged.

Hilton Rothaus and I were at friends or relatives of his in the suburbs on a Sunday. I remember a swimming pool. In short, while driving he used to sit next to the driver with a steering wheel in his hands and copy the exact movements of the driver. The car we were driving in was a bit higher than the normal car around and people from other cars, as we passed them, would look casually and boringly at another car passing them and then instantly recognise something abnormal.

What expressions on peoples' faces! I remember at least one face that kept up with us for a bit and couldn't quite make out who was the driver! Hilton's 'driving' was so real!

One older boy who was tall, lean and well built and I were alone in the swimming pool and somehow we got talking. He used to smoke like a chimneystack but he had very good stamina. He had incredible stomach muscles and would show off by 'rippling' them. He demanded from me to punch him in the stomach as hard as possible. I was about 14 years old I think. I was very reluctant but he insisted. I punched one half-heartedly, he encouraged me to punch harder and consistently – I did! He didn't budge! Just grinned! Solid as rock!

MY FRIENDSHIP WITH JONATAN SYDNEY LIPSCHITZ

My friendship of 30 odd years with a certain ex-Arc is unique I think for two reasons. One, because I have had, up till fairly recently practically no contact with Old Arcs and two, I figure he is about 12 years older than me and I believe he left the Arc before I entered! At the Arc he used to befriend me when he came to visit. Who was he visiting? He had no one in the Arc! I don't remember how our friendship started or even when or why. The fact is I saw him as an elder brother/father figure.

I remember at one stage visiting his brothers and others in Johannesburg with him at their home. I also remember him driving me places on Sundays – where to I don't remember. I remember our 'acquaintance' (I don't even know how to define our relationship then) was nothing permanent or pre-arranged. If he arrived – he arrived! I don't remember much of it .

We came on Aliyah more or less the same time I think. I visited him on kibbutz Merom Golan (Golan Heights) shortly before the Yom Kippur War. The Egged bus took me through the Israeli held part of Kuneitra – a big deserted town on the Golan – to the Israeli army post and then on to his kittubtz nearby.

Afterwards, when I lived on kibbutz Rosh Zurim in the Etzion Bloc (south of Jerusalem) he came to visit me in his car (on Shabbat?) On Shabbat he parked outside the kibbutz and visited me. If I remember correctly, I was really surprised to see him!

We kept in contact all those years. I visited him with my newly wedded wife and Mom on his kibbutz in 1981 and staying the night with him. Sometime after that he also got fed-up with kibbutz life – its pettiness, inequality etc and left. Next I remember him (the ultimate bachelor) inviting me to his wedding! He married an Israeli girl and they lived in Jerusalem. We then got to see each other a lot more frequently. I remember visiting them with my wife (and Maron later) and having supper together in their flat. He has a fantastic wife and she's also a great cook! Later on they moved out of Jerusalem to Meraseret Zion nearby, from a flat to a house.

When I worked in Jerusalem as a construction foreman, he worked in the Tax Department, which was next to my bus stop. I would pop up now and then to chat with him. I haven't seen him for a few years now as I don't get to Jerusalem often nowadays, but we're still in phone contact a few times a year.

I still today can't figure out a lot of things about our relationship! Socially, politically, religious-wise, age-gap we're worlds apart!! Anyway Yonatan (don't call him Sydney – he doesn't like that name at all) Lipshitz maybe you can enlighten me on our history.

Later I spoke to Yonatan (Sid Lipschitz) and he said that he doesn't know himself how our friendship came about. That's real puzzling for me because I thought I would get answers to a few questions. OK so that didn't happen! Big deal! Life will carry on without the answers, no?

AFTER LEAVING THE ARC

I left the Arc in December 1972/January 1973 after my matric exams earlier on had finished and I waited to go to BA (Bnei-Akiva) camp in the Cape. To back track a bit, a year or so earlier in 1971 I was in Form IV at Parktown Boys', battling through school with an average of about 55%. I swam for the school 'B' team and reserve for 'A' team – crawl and butterfly. I was in the rugby 2nd team as permanent hooker and certainty of next year's first team hooker. I ran the mile in athletics. At

that stage of my life only one thing was a certainly – no way was I going to the SA Army.

I was English born in Liverpool – third or fourth generation English – my parents emigrated when I was about three years old and Martin just a few months. My father found work as an electrician in Carltonville.

Why not the Army? I was drafted into the SBS/SAS, but my decision to dodge the draft was before that news! Why? I don't really know or remember! I just didn't see SA as my home or country. I couldn't see myself studying, living, or working there at all. I was dead against the apartheid policies and I couldn't live a life of lies as I saw it. My 'soul' was just not connected even though it was a beautiful country and I was on very familiar ground in a good Jewish society. I had no real reason not to stay and live my life like most other Arcs in SA. It was just a strong conviction then that as soon as I could I would leave SA.

I had no relatives in SA and as far as family was concerned I had very little attachment to my parents whom I saw maybe once or twice a year. I had more attachment to my mother than my father. I grew up in a very unstable environment at home till the age of about seven when my Ma decided that it was best for her sons, four by then, me the eldest and Sam just a few months old, to be in the protection of the Arc. Where would I go to without family, friends, relatives or money I had no idea whatsoever. I just knew I was leaving straight after matric.

Summer holidays 1970/1971 were coming up and the Arc had decided to send us to BA for the holidays. I objected to BA, but I was prepared to go to Habonim. My Germiston family's sons who were my age, all told me about the fun at Habonim Camp. No way could I persuade anyone to release me to Habonim, so I went heavy-hearted to BA summer camp. What a surprise it was for me - that summer camp, a way of life that I had never contemplated or tried before.

No one pressed me or bothered me at all about religion or anything else. I just floated along with the current and made good friends and had a real good time there. By the time I returned to school – matric year – I had a lot to think about. I battled with my conscience and myself in the first term and then finally decided I wanted to learn more about that mode of life.

I had decided that there was a G-d and Judaism offered the right answers. It wasn't an easy decision. It was so much easier just to carry on my 'normal' way of life like all the other Arcs. The moment I had made my decision and 'tied my boat' to BA and Judaism, I had a few other decisions to make. Tefillin, Prayers, Kashrut, Shabbat etc. Somehow everything fell very quickly into place even though I was still in a turmoil of emotions and thought. I gave up school sport because of games on Shabbat. I became a Madrich/leader in BA, although it was only of kids four to eight years old and I became very involved with BA friends and leader/management guys. School work as yet was not affected.

First term matric suddenly had no more meaning for me. I had decided to participate in a BA leadership program of one year study and work on a religious kibbutz in Israel. BA wanted me to return to SA and help them as a graduate of their leadership course, but I simply told them long beforehand that I had no intention of returning to SA. They, in spite of that, let me participate in that course.

The Arc put pressure on me to stay in SA and go to Uni or college or learn a trade or something. I was deaf to all pleas, pressures, good intentions etc from everyone, including family. What would I do after my year was up in Israel? Who knows? All I know was that I finally had a course and destination where I would feel at home – Israel! I had not the foggiest notion whatsoever of Israel, but it was in my soul.

I left SA to Israel with one suitcase and one small trommel and $400, which my father said was mine from my grandma's will, in traveller cheques in my pocket. Off to the wild blue yonder – bye! January 1973 El-al landed in Ben Gurion at night – dark, wet and cold. A car from the kibbutz – or taxi – I can't remember – with a representative of theirs met us (four girls and two boys) and took us to Kibbutz Shluchot in the Bet Shean Valley.

My first memory outside Ben-Gurion airport of Israel was seeing a road sign saying 'Baptist Village' (near Tikva). What a major letdown! Baptists in Israel! What's going on here? Later that night/morning I got to meet the Israeli Jews. On Shluchot I studied Judaism half-day and worked half-day, in the date trees – up before first light! Just like the Arc! I enjoyed the work, friends from all over the world. In this course were participants from the southern hemisphere – Brazil, Argentina, Australia, New Zealand. BA, studies, field trips and Ulpan. A whole new wonderful new world had opened up for me.

During the year I was approached cautiously as to what I was going to do in the future. I think there were people who wanted me to stay on kibbutz. I was a very diligent worker. I had realised by then that kibbutz life suited me but not that kibbutz. I wanted a young, new kibbutz where I could feel I was part of its growing. I shopped around quietly (four options only) which quickly reduced itself to one option. I decided on a quiet visit to Rosh Zurim in Gush Etzim, about 20 km south of Jerusalem, nearly 1000 m high in the mountains. It was established in mid 40s, devastated by Arabs in 1948 and re-established in '69 by religious Jews. There were 10 to 20 families maybe, and about 50 unmarried men and women of my age – mainly army personnel – Nachal.

Someone made the connections for me and I visited. Love at first sight! Mountain air, beautiful view of all the coastal area, an inland area and you could see to the horizon. There were young idealistic people and a kibbutz that was still at ground zero, growth wise. I remember the Israeli BA – Mizrahi representative was not at all impressed when he was informed by someone of my 'quiet' visit. How dare I usurp his function etc etc? Who do I think I am? Nothing did I know of Israeli bureaucracy and functionaries! Anyway, I'm just plain stubborn – ask my wife! There's my way and there's other peoples' way!

Unfortunately war broke out and Israel was in a major upheaval. About a month after war broke out I felt stranded and left out of everything. I wasn't happy at kibbutz anymore. Most of the young and capable were at war and some, if not all of my fellow BA participants had been rushed back home or were anyway

shortly on their way home. I had decided to leave for Rosh Zurim. Again without telling anyone, especially the representative or functionary. I remember some hassle about it all, but I got there somehow.

One of my Israeli friends in Shluchot encouraged me to enlist in the Israeli Army a few weeks after war broke out, but I realized I still was not ready for that. Rosh Zurim, by that time was nearly deserted – all in the army. Women and a few guys were all that was left. My first job that I remember was that I had to build a new set of guard fences around the kibbutz. About 2.5 m high mesh fence and then a double-sloped barbed wire fence of about one metre high. The length of the fences was a few kilometres.

I worked mainly alone. I had to bash these iron poles into hard ground and rock by myself! I had to *schlep* all these materials on my shoulders to wherever I was working. Sometimes when the tractor was available – rarely – me or someone else would hook up a trailer bed and drive over steep and terraced slopes to my work. Sometimes others worked with me, but they soon gave up. Real back breaking, teeth shattering, hand splitting tough work. These other volunteers were all strappy young guys, bigger and tougher looking than me but no one stayed the distance. This lasted a few months!

Today I look back on it and I'm astounded at my endurance, sheer bloody mindedness, toughness and capability. It's still standing today I think! Life there gradually got back to normal with the return of everyone after about six months. I worked here and there preparing terraces for new fruit trees, walnut and pistachio. Early 1974 I was convinced that here was my home and it was about time to enlist. August 1974 enlisted into Paras and was accepted after the usual army trials. I was then nearly 21 years old. My NCOS and officers were younger than me or about my age!

I remember the Gees meeting me in Jerusalem in the mid 1970s at the King David Hotel which is very central. They bought me a pair of very excellent long socks from Switzerland that till today serve me well. I go through socks and shoes very quickly.

Being religious, a new immigrant, without family, and living in Judea made me a complete stranger to the Israeli army. We were about five religious soldiers only out of about 100 in the beginning. It wasn't easy for me, language, culture, ideological, religious, family, socially etc etc, but I finished my 2½ year stint as best as I could. The current Chief-of-Staff was my vice Regimental Commander and gave me about ten days of camp prison for an alleged breach of discipline. Matin Vilnai – Minister of Staff was my Batallion Commander.

The army was my first real meeting with your average Israeli. What a surprise! It took me time to figure out who, what and why! After the army I was already not quite so sure about kibbutz life but after I turned down an option to work with El-Al security, because of religious reasons. I had definitely had enough of military like life and its restrictions and incursions, mostly justified, into religious life. As I didn't know what I wanted to do, a real big problem with newly released soldiers even today, I felt that kibbutz would do for the meantime.

I worked in our fields about 40 minutes drive into the coastal plains. I worked with irrigation, ploughing, sowing etc. long, long hours with little social contact and little reward – started to wear me down mentally, socially and psychologically.

I then decided to take a year's leave from kibbutz to find myself again. Add to my turmoil a fractured elbow from work, a broken heart, my Aussie girlfriend decided that her parents were more important in the long run than her for me. It was touch and go for a while! She returned to Aussieland. My Yank friends had always pestered me to visit them so I was on my way. Six months working holiday in US, six months same in Sydney, Australia with Aussie mate (We lived in kibbutz together and we are still friends today. He lives in nearby Kfar Saba) and one month in Johannesburg over Pesach 1980.

Half a year after returning to kibbutz I realised I had made a big mistake by returning to kibbutz. I was about to leave when I met this Israeli girl doing her National Service stint on kibbutz. Well, she was shy and I was smitten and somehow things got rolling which left me on kibbutz. This was my first and only real personal contact with an Israeli girl. Within a few scant months we decided to get married. I wanted to leave, but she wanted to stay – we stayed for three years. I worked in the cow shed and factory. In 1983 she finally gave in to my wishes and we left for K Arbu. There I was security officer for the Reth Sherash Energy Co (contractors for Air Force Lovi project of engines). Lovi Project was cancelled in 1986 – US pressure. How could they sell us inferior F-15 or F16s if we had the Lovi? I had to decide what to do with my life again. A building contractor from K Arba had decided that I was what he wanted for a foreman – he would teach me the trade so I took up his offer.

Finally I had found my field of interest. In 1989 I went to night school and learnt the trade in a serious level. With the good economy in those years I jumped ahead and earned a fortune. The problem with the building trade here is that (like everywhere else) it's a bit erratic. My wife was not too pleased with this erratic way of life. In 1991 I had decided I needed a new turn in life. I had been living in the Jerusalem-Hebron Hills for 18 years. I needed a different climate, different scene, air, social life and most importantly to get out of the building restrictions of stone and cement in the Jerusalem area.

There were plenty other methods of building and I wanted to learn more. We bought a house here in Kedumim, and finally moved here in 1994 and into our house in 1999. Government policies in Judea and Samaria prevented our house from being completed in 1991 – 90% finished then – till approximately 1997.

In December 1995 my wife and I were involved in major car crash. I was then an independent contractor for about eight months and managing. We were both extremely fortunate, especially my wife who was five months pregnant with Adiel, to be alive. That's another story by itself. Because of health problems my business went dead on me and because of those health problems I today am a simple security guard in my village. Life definitely has its ups and downs as all of us know. Some manage better than others while some are less fortunate.

I don't have time or patience for regrets and what I've done up till today is just that and nothing more.

I like to think that my decision to live here in Israel, and especially in Jehudah and Shomran, our ancient birthplace as a nation and the place where our foregathers trekked back and forth and later established the Jewish Kingdom, is and was the only decision a Jew like me can make with a clear conscience.

I live about 10 km from Shechem, not far physically or spiritually from Joseph's grave, which was abandoned last year by the IDF – an ongoing scandal in Israel- and Joshua's Alter on Mount Eval, where Joshua re-established the Covenant of God with the Jews as they entered Mt Irrad (Canaan) and circumcised everyone after their long journey throuth Sinai.

Yes here in Israel we live on the edge of a precipice all the time. No one, as of today and maybe never in my lifetime, has a workable plan as to how to forge us into a Jewish Nation with secure borders and all around peace. Kedumin has more than 600 families and growing all the time. Average family of five kids or maybe more. We've spread out over a large area with different neighbourhoods all over. It takes about 10 minutess to drive from one side to the other. Kfar Saba is approximately 20 – 30 minutes from here.

Danny Shacked, Evan, and Abigail with Adiel in front.

Danny's son Maron with his new bride

438

Chapter 115 - DAVID LASKER (1957)

David was born in 1957 and was in the care of Arcadia from age two till he finished school in 1975.

He was then in the South African army for 18 months and was a 2nd lieutenant, quite a rarity for a Jewish boy. David was at University for six years doing BA Teaching, preceded by a year in commerce and followed with a year in law.

During this time he also stayed in the Greenside cottage as a "housefather" to Ex Arcs who were in transition from school to work. This was run by the Arc for children who had left the Arc.

He then worked in commerce and after some time bought into a company and eventually bought the whole company called I Sandler & Co.

David is married to Karen (Osher) who was also in the Arc for two years.

David is one of five brothers while Karen has three sisters and one brother, Glen. All ten children were in the Arc. Karen's sister Colleen lives in Sydney while her two other sisters Adelle and Donna live in Johannesburg.

David and Karen have two children Josh and Gabi.

David Lasker, Desiree and Gary (at back) Creighton, Ashley Schubb and Michael Rothaus at play -. 1972

While I remember David well I did not really have much to do with him as he was five years my junior.

I do remember him as an Arc boy of say 15 borrowing my car, a Peugeot 404, ex Leon Goodman, and disappearing for a few hours with other Arc kids when he was 'just going down to Killarney for a short while'. I was really worried while waiting for him to come back and realised then that I had done the wrong thing.

Despite many requests, this is the only story I could coax out of David.

BED TIME STORY
By David Lasker

It's a bit late in the evening for stories - you should be in bed by now! Lights out at 7.30 pm.

Once upon a time in a fantasy land called "The Arc" a certain youngster called Max had shown some of the very junior boys, David Lasker amongst them, how to make a decent bow and arrow.

Having built a set that was his pride and joy, David proceeded to a shoot-out contest against said Max, to see who could shoot an arrow over the huge Oak tree, at the bottom of the garden, below the main building, next to the slide.

After a while this became a bit boring and some other attraction was sorely needed - this attraction soon showed up in the guise of another boy, called Anthony Mark.

David soon convinced Anthony to play Cowboys and Indians, and Anthony was given a broken toy gun to use, while David kept the bow-and-arrow.

Needless to say, David soon had the upper hand, as the arrows were fitted with cactus spike tips and Anthony was doing his best to flee the scene.

Anthony was struck in the back by an arrow and fell pole-axed to the ground. David thought he had killed the cowboy, and was very relieved to find him still breathing, though lying face down for some time.

So ends our story for tonight - sleep tight and dream sweet dreams.

Chapter 116 – LAURIE FINEBERG (1961)

Laurie was born in 1961 and his older sister Tania in 1958. They were in the care of Arcadia from 1964 to 1970.

ARC MEMORIES

I have not had contact with anybody from the Arcadia until I bumped into Alan Goldsmith who put me in contact with David who sent me *the Arc Memory Booklets*. They brought back so many memories both good and bad of the time spent there.

The memory that has never left me was my first day and watching that car carrying my mother away from me and that feeling of being deserted. I also remember the funeral of the Caretaker (I do remember I was friendly with his son). This was my first experience with death and all of us stood on either side of the driveway as the hearse drove past.

I was moved by the article of Martin, Thelma and Georgie, who have all passed away. Even though I can't picture Georgie's face I still can remember him. The one incident that sticks in my mind was his Barmitzvah when he had to say a speech and he stood up and just said "Thank You" that was it. That moment in time has stuck with me.

The one bad memory that will never leave me was the dark room in the Babies Section. Many a night I was sent there for punishment and to this day I don't understand why. I don't remember much about the Arc as I believe that I have blocked most of the memories out over the years, but I do have snippets that come back to me every now and again.

I remember the friendships I had with Sammy, Charles, Eric, and Leo to name but a few. The fun we had and what we got up to. Eric Niedermeyer and his brother Leo and sister Michelle were all in the Arc and so too was the girl Eric married, Moira Wassermann and her brother, also Eric. Other contemporaries were Deborah and Ruth Frogel, Pauline Kruger, Charlie Goldman, Sammy Lasker, Georgie Marshack and Carmen. I understand that Eric and Moira live at Umslanga and have twin daughters.

I remember the December holidays and going to stay at strangers, how they treated us with kindness and understanding. Also I remember Saturday night movies in the main dinning hall. I have vivid memories of Doc and Ma

I remember Shani Krebs who is in prison in Thailand. My thoughts and prayers are with him and I hope that some day soon he will be able to come home and be reunited with his family and friends."

I am married to Celeste Binder and we have two kids, David and Natasha, We live in Sandton.

I am in the computer business supporting the Microsoft Business Solutions products.

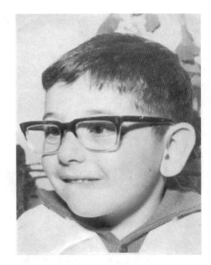

Laurie Fineberg

Laurie and his sister Tania

Prize Giving and Concert 1966

Chapter 117 – DEBORAH FROGEL (1963) AND RUTH FROGEL (1961-2002)

Debbie Frogel was born in 1963 and placed in the care of Arcadia inOctober 1965 as a very young child together with her older sister Ruth. They lived in the Arc for a very short period.

Debbie has no recollection of being in the Arc and lives in the UK with her many pets.

NO MEMORIES OF THE ARC

I have no recollection of anyone or anything at the Arc, except Aunt Helen (Mrs de Winnaar). She was for my entire adult life and until the day she died, my 'adopted' mother. Her sister, Aunt Sarie who is now 88 sent me this photo of myself with Auntie Helen and another girl. Adella Noll (Lozinski) prompted me to enquire about my past.

I think I was the youngest in the Arc, certainly still in a cot. I was there with my sister, Ruth Frogel who was nearly three years older than I.

Apparently as my Mum died before I was a year old, and according to my late Father, I first had to go to another orphanage (Cotlands) but then the Arc eventually accepted me even though I was not yet two years old. Adella remembers the day I arrived and Ruth hiding me under a table being very protective. Adella was in charge of the babies so she recalls it quite clearly that I was 'under age'.

Sadly Ruth passed away aged 40 of ovarian cancer - the history of my family.

I met Adella (Lozinsky) here in UK and we became very close friends. She introduced me to my first cousin Jenny Levin (Jennifer Fliess) who was also in the Arc with her sister Liz.

I lived and was educated in Cape Town. I studied interior design and worked in that line for about 15 years. I was married for 13 years to a decorator. I have no children except the four legged type. I am an animal fanatic! I immigrated to England in August 2002, am divorced and live happily with my partner, his dog and my South African cat. I keep busy by being a 'housewife' and am a mature hairdressing student. I live in a beautiful part of Essex in the country.

REMEMBERING DEBORAH AND HER SISTER RUTH
Written by Freda Cheilyk

I knew Debbie's mother and also her father. I know that Debbie was in Arcadia with her late sister Ruth who died a few years

Auntie Helen (Mrs de Winnaar) Sandra Newstead and Deborah Frogel 1968 Sandra Newstead, married Edgar (Adam Goldsmith's cousin) and they live in SA.

ago in Cape Town. Ruth could not have been much more than 40 when she passed away.

As it happens I was at her first birthday party and her mother was already ill then.

Written by Charles Goldman

I do remember Ruth and Debbie Frogel but since they left Arcadia while we were still in the Babies Department, I have not heard a single thing about them. I was very friendly with Ruthie. I do recall one particular Sunday night in the Babies Department when I was scared of the dark and I got into her bed to seek refuge. Well after that, I was teased for quite a while with people saying we were getting married and being 'fresh' and other things, all of which I did not understand. Oh for the innocence of childhood.

Standing: Leo Nedermeyer on his brother Eric's shoulders,
Pauline Kurger on Tanya Fineberg's shoulders
Kneeling: Laurie Fineberg, Charles Goldman (Carmen Lindy in front of him),
Sammy Lasker, Ruth Frogel, holding her sister Debbie and Georgie Marshak
(Others unknown)

Back Row left to right: Georgie Marshack, Charlie Goldman and Sammy Lasker
Front Row: Thelma Durback, Diane Joffee, Sandra Newstead, Michelle Williams,
Desiree Crighton, Ruth and Debbie Frogel.

MY SISTER RUTH

I don't recognise anyone from the photos (*above*) but it was wonderful to see Ruth (always a little tomboy) and myself as kids. I wish she were alive to share them with me.

I am so pleased to have some pictures of my beloved sister and me from those days.

I am still quite in awe of seeing the pictures of Ruth and I. I shall treasure them always. We had a very strong bond between us even though we lived different lives and often in another country. Ruth was the traveller, not I. In a nutshell throughout her life she was a fun loving, generous, non-conformist free spirit who loved to travel.

I was the cautious scared one, so I shocked even myself with immigrating to the UK all by myself. Ruth always told me I had blinkers on "See the world Debs" she would say and now I have seen a tiny piece which I like very, very much.

Ruth Frogel as a baby

Ruth Frogel age 39

Chapter 118 – THE COTTAGE SYSTEM

As a result of a change in philosophy towards supporting children within their family unit the cottage system was first introduced in 1969 with seven children from Arcadia initially moving into a house in Rosebank. Later there was a move to Greenside and the number of children fluctuated over the years. In later years the Cottage served as a half-way stage for ex-Arcadians, functioning in conjunction with the After-Care Committee.

THE HUGO STEINHART COTTAGE SYSTEM
Extract from the Annual Bulletin – 31 March 1970

In August 1969, five children - a brother and sister, two sisters, and another boy, all of varying ages - were moved from Arcadia to a rented house in 19 Cradock Avenue, Rosebank, under the supervision of the house-parents, Mr and Mrs J Berman. In December two more boys, brothers, were moved from Arcadia to make up the full complement of seven children. Before the children were transferred to the Cottage they and their parents or close relatives, were interviewed.

A small sub-committee, under the convenership of Dr C P Nelson, was appointed to supervise the Cottage and to ensure that everything needed was obtained and that the children were properly settled in. They made a special appeal to Committee members, members of the Branches and other well-wishers in order to obtain furniture, fittings, equipment and the linen required. The response was overwhelming for by the time the children moved in most of the items required had been donated.

The three girls, aged 17, 16 and 13 years respectively, attend the Parktown Girls' High School, in Forms 5, 4 and 2. Of the four boys, whose ages vary between 15 and 12 years, one is in Form 4 at Parktown Boys' High, another in Form 3 at the Oxford College and the other two are in Std 5 at the King David School, Victory Park. Where necessary, additional coaching has been obtained in various school subjects and the homework is regularly supervised.

The children's Hebrew and religious education is also fully catered for. Kashruth is strictly observed and orthodox religious practices strictly adhered to. One of the teachers from the Arcadia Hebrew School visits the Cottage regularly to give Cheder lessons. All the children attend service at the Oxford Synagogue.

The children are encouraged to play with the children in the neighbourhood, to visit them and to invite their friends to visit in turn. The girls are encouraged to help in the kitchen in order to learn the basic fundamentals of cooking, housekeeping and, most important, of Kashruth. They accompany the house-mother on occasional shopping expeditions and choose some of their own clothes. In this way we inculcate a useful knowledge of home economics.

It is our intention that the children will continue to stay in the Cottage even after they matriculate and go on to further studies or to work. If they wish they may remain until they get married

In brief, the Cottage sub-committee is attempting to establish a home environment that resembles any normal home.

Shortly after the close of the year under review (April 12 1970) the official opening of the Hugo Steinhart Cottage took place. A large gathering of distinguished visitors, including representatives of major organisations and Branches were present, Chief Rabbi B M Casper consecrated the Cottage and affixed a mezuzah to the main door. Councillor Sam Moss, Mayor of Johannesburg also addressed the gathering.

HUGO STEINHARDT COTTAGE:
Extracts from the Annual Bulletin – 31 March 1986

Some years ago we acquired a cottage in Rosebank through the munificence of Mrs Hugo Steinhardt to perpetuate the memory of her late husband. This, the Hugo Steinhardt Cottage subsequently moved to Troon Road in Greenside. Children were housed there in a quasi-family style for many years, and this proved to be a successful scheme. This gave way to a new need, that is, to provide a facility for young adults as a halfway house of self sufficiency. The Cottage is going strong in that guise to this day. - *1986 Annual Report*

After leaving Arcadia the senior children live at the cottage and are requested to contribute a nominal amount towards their board and lodging, only when they are financially able to do so.

We have between four and six residents most of the year and they are a fine group of young adults, some attending university, college or are already working. When they are financially ready and able, they leave the cottage. The atmosphere in the cottage is a happy one.

Kashrut is strictly observed and it is seen to that they receive a nutritious and balanced diet.

The day to day running of this home is in the hands of the young people themselves, thus equipping them better to cope when they go on their own in the outside world.

Our social worker is in daily contact with the cottage. I would like to thank Ruth Garb, our social worker, for her assistance and guidance, and to the members of the Hugo Steinhardt Cottage sub-committee for their regular attendance at the cottage. - *Meir Judeikin Chairman - 1986 Annual Report*

Janet and Marilyn Miller, Graham and Marilyn Stoler, Errol and Peter Hough, and Bernard Tanner went to live the Cottage in Rosebank. Joe Berman and his wife Ellen looked after the children from the Arc in the cottage.

Chapter 119 – THE MILLER SISTERS
JANET (1954) AND MARILYN (1953)

Janet was born in 1954 in Pretoria and together with her older sister Marilyn, who was born in 1953, were placed in the care of the Arcadia in 1965.

They both went to live in the Cottage in Rosebank in August 1969 together with Errol and Peter Hough, Marilyn and Graham Stoller and Bernard Tanner.

Joe Berman, and his then wife Ellen, looked after all these children from the Arc in the cottage.

Janet went to Saxonwold Primary School and Parktown Girls' High where she matriculated in 1971 and then left the Cottage.

Marilyn left after matriculating in 1970.

JANET (MEYER) MILLER 1954

ARC MEMORIES

Linda, Les and I bunked out one Friday night. We got Adele to open the bars and then close them behind us as we went down the fire escape. We crawled amongst the bushes to the entrance where Linda's boyfriend was going to meet us at 1.00 am. We waited until 2.30 am when he arrived. The three of us went to the Beach Club in Hillbrow. We danced the night away then were dropped off at 4.00 am or 5.00 am. We sneaked back in, up the fire escape, woke Adele up and went to sleep.

Next morning Ma asked us if we enjoyed our evening out. We were all grounded from Saturday night movies. The fire escape stairs were removed and to this day we don't know who bust us.

On Saturday nights when Mrs Van Rensburg was off duty, David Sandler used to come up to the Senior Girls before bioscope. One night he hid behind the cupboard and Lesley and I asked Myra to try on a bra so that David could see.

LES BECKER (MARK) AND JANET MEYER (MILLER)
Written by Lesley Becker (Mark)

Arc 'sisters' who were "a bit wayward and not easily manageable".

When I try and think back, I think that I was friendly with Jennifer's sister Elizabeth, they left in 1965 and we arrived in 1963, so it wasn't a long friendship. Not like the one that I have with Janet Miller.

Gee we went through a lot together, and to this day, thank G-d we are still as close as ever. Janet is the sister that I never had. We have the e-mail and phone connection. I remember our Durban December Holidays. We were placed together, with the

Janet Miller

Janet and Lesley at Durban

most wonderful family, the Lowenbergs. Now, how we got to them is a story. He (Bill) was a Lawyer, and his wife (Elaine) was a psychologist (I think).

Well. they were approached by the Arc Committee and this story we were told many many many years later, when Bill visited us, in Jo'burg and took us out to dinner. As I mentioned, they were approached, and were told that they had a problem finding accommodation for two girls, who were a bit wayward and not easily manageable, and if they agreed to try and have us, and it didn't work out after a couple of days, the Committee, would have us sent back to the Arc pronto.

After much discussion between Bill and Elaine, they agreed. Well to the Arc shock, disappointment, they survived us. After that year, we went and spent July and December holidays with them, for many happy years.

According to Bill, we were normal, healthy teenagers, whom the Arc did not know how to handle. And I can happily say that after 30 years or so, we are still in contact with Bill, that is.

I can't say that I have many memories of the Arc that rush out to the front, instantly, but when reading stories from others, they spring to mind immediately. Maybe blocked out somewhere.

Adel Saiet Raymond Lang and Janet

THE COTTAGE

Seven of us were chosen as the ones that supposedly needed a family environment most. Bernard Tanner, Peter and Errol Hough, Marilyn and Graham Stoler, my sister Marilyn and I.

Joe and Ellen Berman were our house parents. When they started the cottage they were young and enthusiastic. They had two daughters at the time Tal and Rama and they were like our little sisters. I still see them both and am in fact working as an Estate Agent for Joe who owns Executive Homes.

We bunked out, often to Hillbrow, where Joe seemed to know where we were and once even found us in Hillbrow at a place called *The Narnia* and bought us coffee and then took us home. They were very liberal in their way of raising us.

I for one needed my freedom, which I got. The only regret I had was that I had to leave my best friend behind, Lesley Becker (Mark) but we did move into a flat afterwards and are still the best of friends today even though we live miles away from each other. We went through a lot together and we are pretty much sisters.

Graham Stoler was the problem child. He and I used to fight like cat and dog. He drove me mad, but when anyone used to fight with him I used to take his side. We are still very close today and see each other every other week and he is pretty well adjusted.

AFTER LEAVING THE ARC

I am married to Carl Meyer. We have two children - Jacqui has her Honours in Psychology and is currently waiting to get into masters which in this country can take a few years. She has just come back from London where she worked in a Psychiatric hospital for 7 months. She loved it, but is now studying again doing Honours in English. She is the eternal academic.

Our son Brad has qualified as a personal fitness trainer. He has been working in a gym, Planet Fitness, but is also going off to London in April to find himself and make some money working in that field.

My husband Carl is also an Estate Agent. We work together at Executive Homes. We live in Sydenham, Johannesburg.

I am in contact with Helen Sher, Graham Stoler, Beryl Sacks, The Durbachs, Max Goldman, Stephan Weinstein. I regularly bump into Jules Gordon, Pauline Kruger, Beverly Collett, among others.

One thing I must say though, is that I was pretty happy in the Arc as well as the cottage. I had good friends, life-long friends, had fun bunking out, running away, getting up to mischief. I guess I was pretty normal.

Carl, Jacqui, Brad and Janet

MARILYN BERMAN (MILLER) 1953

Marilyn was born in 1953 and together with her younger sister Janet was placed in the care of the Arcadia in 1965. They both went to live in the Cottage in Rosebank in August 1969 and Marilyn left the Cottage in 1970 after completing her matric.

MARILYN REMEMBERS

Graham used to drive me crazy while I was studying for my matric. He used to bang on my door with a broomstick. He was no easy baby!

What I found interesting was reading about the idea of the Cottage system - that it would be like a home and that those living there would continue to live there while they go to university etc. Well I was asked to leave and had to go and board. That should never have happened. I should have been allowed to remain in the cottage and not told that I should leave. It messed up my University career, as I was not well and I was so lonely. Maybe that is what really angered me and pushed me away from ex Arcadians, except Shelley van der Hoven, whom I am communicating with in Israel.

Marily in school uniform

Marilyn on holiday in Durban. Shaun Jacobs on far right.

MY FAMILY

I lived in Israel for 10 years and I love Israel. I still hold the same position as Sales Manager for the company I worked for in Israel for many years, that means I get to travel all over the world at least four to six times a year. Not easy, but necessary.

I am also involved with the Union of Jewish Woman, as well as Tikkun, and I help a lot in Alexandra with the elderly as well as with HIV/Aids victims.

It is sad but rewarding work.

I have three wonderful kids, all grown up.

My middle child, Samantha lives in South Africa and is married to Brandon Starkowitz whose uncle is Starkey from Arcadia. They have given me a new grandson - he was born seven weeks early and his name is Daniel and my granddaughter is Alexa (Lexi). They are both gorgeous.

My son Warren, lives in Beersheva, Israel, and my youngest, Candice is married to a kibbutznik and lives on kibbutz Beeri (close to Ashkelon).

Arc girls at bioscope

446

Chapter 120 – GRAHAM STOLER (1955)

In 1957 Graham Stoler at age three (born 1955) was placed in the care of Arcadia together with his older sister Linda aged five (born 1953). Marilyn the younger sister (born 1956) being only one went to Cotlands initially and then to Arcadia when two.

They were placed in the care of the Arc following the divorce of their parents Abe Stoler (who was also in the Arc during Vicky's time) and his wife Marge.

Linda who was the oldest left the Arc (or was she pushed out) in 1969 and in August 1969 Graham and Marilyn were placed in the new 'Cottage' in Rosebank under the care of Joe and Ellen Berman together with Marilyn and Janet Miller, Errol and Peter Hough and Bernard Tanner.

ARC STORIES OF GRAHAM STOLER
Written by Kay Stoler

Graham and Linda Stoler

Linda was in charge of running a raffle to raise money. The prize was a jar full of chewing gum (probably *Chappies*). Anyway the object of the raffle was to buy a ticket and to guess how many *Chappies* were in the jar.

Graham desperately wanted to buy a ticket and take a guess how many there were inside the jar. He asked Linda for a ticket and she told him it was OK, she had already bought him a ticket. Graham went away very happy.

After the draw had taken place, Graham was approached by his friends who all congratulated him on winning the jar of chappies. Graham was so excited and he rushed off to claim his prize. Clutching the jar of *Chappies* Graham walked off, when Linda came tearing up behind him, snatched the jar off him and said "That's mine - give it to me, I won it".

I think somewhere along the line, little Linda Stoler knew how many there were in that jar! Linda in her youth was a shrewdie, I am glad to say though, she turned out to be an honest business lady.

How To Spend All Your Money At The Tuck Shop And Still Get Change

Linda Stoler was in charge of the Tuck Shop - Graham used to be a frequent customer - as it was the only place where you could spend all your money on tuck and still get change! I suppose this is one of the perks of having family run the Tuck Shop. - Linda also did this for other Arcs.

Anthony Marks and Graham Stoler

Anthony came to South Africa on a fleeting visit from Paris. Leslie invited some of the old Arcs round for lunch and to catch

1964 Arcadia Bulletin Cover - Elocution Lessons
Gary Creighton, Errol Hough, Graham Stoler, Sadie Baitz and Hannah Durbach.

up with Tony. Graham had not seen Tony since they left the Arc. They were sitting on the patio wall outside Lesley's lounge - Tony was looking down at his hands. He said to Graham. "There is one thing that happened in the Arc and I can't remember who did it to me. I was playing with a plastic plane when someone set it on fire. The plane hit me falling onto my hand. The plastic melted onto my skin and the more I rubbed my hand trying to get it off, the more the plastic burned through the layers of my skin. It was so sore, but for the life of me I can't remember who did it".

Graham at this stage was very quiet - which is unusual for Graham as he always chirps in. I had heard this story from Graham before, so I didn't say a word, wondering if Graham would own up that it was in fact him. Eventually, after mulling it over, Graham started laughing and nudged Tony and said "Tony it was me". Tony looked at him and said "Yes now I remember ..... I could not remember after all these years who was there - but now it comes back to me". Luckily all was forgiven and we ended up having a great day with him and Leslie's family.

THE BENEFITS OF BULLYING

Shelley Segal (nee Grishkan) managed to toughen up, probably because she was in the Arc. I would like to congratulate Shelly for getting her Australian citizenship. Well done Shelley! But I must add, "I knew there was some benefit to the Arc kids when I tormented them, as a kid." Whew, did we learn from each other. As it goes, there has been much written about Ronnie Schreeuwer etc, bullying me. In response, I also learnt from him; to keep away if they are bigger than you, and grow as fast as you can.

Michael Goldstein (Muffie) Paul Cohen, Zelva Bartlet, and Graham Stoler at back. Jenny Bartlett, Brian Sandler and Shelley Bartlett in middle. Marilyn Stoler sitting in front.

Graham and Muffie (Michael Goldstein)
Lynette Sheer, the wife of Muffie, relayed this story to Graham.

Muffie took a car in the Arc and took it for a joy ride. He eventually crashed it.
Graham said "I know".
Lynette said "How do you know".
Graham replied "because I was with him".
Muff told me to go for a ride, then we ended up crashing up the pavement.
I think this escapade stood them in good stead for driving on South African roads!

Maxi and Graham

I think these two were the naughtiest in the Arc - Maxi is well known for practicing arson at an early age - a trait he seems to have grown out of lately.

Graham relayed this story to me.

Maxi apparently was saving all his cents to try and get up to one rand - which in those days probably bought a lot of *Chappies*. Every day Maxi showed Graham his stash - and every time a cent was added to the pile he took great pride in showing it to Graham. This didn't really perturb Graham - he wasn't really interested. The day arrived when Maxi finally saved enough cents to make up a full Rand. He was really excited and as usual wanted to show Graham.

Now a Rand to Graham was really enticing - the cents mounting up hadn't bothered him - but now Maxi had a whole Rand. Graham decided this was too much to bear and he took Maxi's Rand.

I don't know if Maxi ever knew this - but now he does. I wonder how much that comes to with interest!!!! Graham didn't turn out

to be a bank robber - in fact he went the other way - he's too honest!!

David Sandler's Comment:

I think Graham is confusing Max for me. David Lipschitz and I were in the Babies and saving up together. Perhaps Max was also saving up with us, but I don't remember him being involved. When we had ten shillings together I swapped it for a ten-shilling note from my Dad and we kept the note under our metal cupboard.

One day it disappeared and I was very upset. Some time later found out that Graham had "found it" and given it to Doc. I explained to Doc that David Lipschitz and I had saved it together, but I think he did not believe it possible that two small children in the Arc and in the Babies could save ten shillings.

THE STIGMA OF BEING IN THE ARC

Just a story about the Arcadia stigma, which once upon a time was a concern, until I realised that the way the world is out there, there are and were so many people more unfortunate than ourselves. The Arc for me, is a past strength not a weakness.

A hard working client friend of mine, with whom I was working one night, was telling me that he works hard today, because as a child he had nothing. His parents gave very little to the kids. He never had shoes, he went to bed sometimes without supper, and he grew up, without much. As we were talking openly that night I decided to tell him, that I also had a bit of a tough childhood, when he said "nothing like he had", no food etc.

So I said to him, that I do not wish to challenge him about how tough a childhood we both had, but that I had grown up in an Orphanage and even that we did have food we.........well he interrupted me, and apologised to me and agreed that I (Graham) had had a much harder childhood than him. Well he couldn't stop apologising about the challenge about the hard childhood he had.

But I couldn't accept that apology easily, and believed that his childhood was much harder than mine. We had food, we had meals, we went to bed with many friends amongst us. (Some were bullies but we had to keep their interests in mind as well.)

People have an incorrect impression of how we grew up in the Arc. I never got no discount (except from an Arc) from society out there because I was an Arc. So stigma, is in the eyes of the beholder, not in the place where we grew up and I can live with that.

A BIG CHANGE FOR A BIG FISH
Written by David Sandler

Graham loved to be bullied (he was always looking for trouble) and also loved to bully. When Graham was in the Arc you always heard him before you saw him and he was always 'asking' older boys to beat him up by provoking them and nagging them. Here Ronny Schreeuwer stands out but many others were also guilty, including me. It was almost as if

Graham needed that physical contact and attention and then would cry and comfort himself and then he would be OK for a while.

Graham got the name Big Fish (from Joe Baloy the African Help) and was really a bit of a problem child. Later on he went to stay in the cottage run by Joe and Ellen Berman in Rosebank and there I understand he terrorised smaller Peter Hough and Bernard Tanner, who had to gang up on him to protect themselves. Also he drove Janet and Marilyn Miller crazy.

I later caught up with Graham in the 'Young Mens' Hostel' in Birt Street, Raedene, where he attended Damiline College and finished his schooling in 1972. Also there for a short time was Ronny Schreeuwer, Leslie Durbach, Leon Goodman, Simon Woolf, Brian Hough and I.

Here I remember Solly Farber who was the Arc Committee member in charge of the Boys' Hostel talking to us. Solly Farber made a special appeal to the older boys to be patient with Graham, who was still very difficult and disruptive. He explained that we could not simply kick him out, explaining that Graham had nowhere else to go. So Graham you also unwittingly taught us tolerance. That was in the early seventies.

Graham did two years of National Service and worked as a baker and a chef. Later he worked for 12 years in a hair care product company before going into business on his own. During this time he went to university completing a commerce accounting degree.

Graham is now over six feet tall, has a voice like a foghorn and he writes in large capitals. You can never beat him in an argument; not only is he quick witted, but he simply drowns you out. Today Graham is truly someone to look up to, not only because of his size but because he has provided, and continues to provide employment to several fellow Arcs including Lynette, Sammy and Marilyn in his Hair Care Products business, which has been running for the past 10 years.

Graham married Kaye in 1985 and they have a daughter Jenny born in 1991.

Doc and Solly Farber would undoubtedly be smiling down proudly from heaven to see the way the 'problem child' Graham has turned out.

GRAHAM'S SISTERS

Linda got married at quite an early age to Tim Hornby in 1972 and they live in Natal, Durban. They have three children and four grandchildren.

Marilyn stayed in the Cottage until 1973 and returned to the Arc for a year where she completed her matric. Marilyn recently married John Scott.

Girls at Dancing Lessons - Linda Stoler and Minnie Baitz at back Myra Durbach, Elizabeth Fliess, Hannah Durbach and Lesley Mark in the Middle and Marilyn Stoler sitting in front.

1959 Babies at play
Linda Stoler top right, Elisabeth Fliess in white, Morris Learman with black jersey, David Sandler behind, Melanie Learman, with Max Goldman at the back. In front is Nardia Learman, Lorraine Goldstein, Lesley Mark and Valerie Goldstein with Marilyn Stoler right in front.

Written by Ursula Rembach

Brian and his two little brothers Errol and Peter were placed in Arcadia in September 1961 after the tragic death of their mother. The family lived in Acropolis in Louis Botha Avenue, Orange Grove (just past the bend near the Orange Grove Hotel). Brian would be in his mid 50s now.

My maiden name is Ursula Rosenblatt. I lived in the same block of flats together with my mother, sister and brother. Brian and I were good friends."

My cousin Lionel Slier's mother Sarah, and my mother Leah (Altuska), as well as their other siblings were Ochberg orphans who lived at Arcadia. I live in Melbourne and travel to Sydney quite often as I have a son living there

Errol and Peter went to stay in the Cottage in Rosebank with Joe and Ellen Berman in 1969.

Brian left the Arc at the end of 1966 when he finished his Matric and in 1971/72 he lived in the Boys' Hostel in Raedene and still lives in South Africa.

Peter lives in Canada, but lived in Australia for a year.

Errol passed away some time ago.

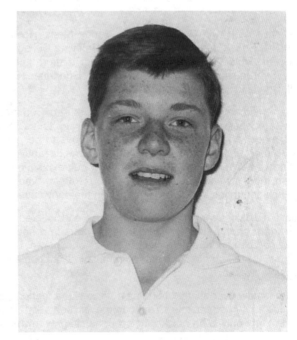

Errol Hough

ERROL HOUGH
As remembered by Max Goldman

Errol was an amiable, likeable, helpful, reserved and intelligent guy as well as being a Parktown Boys' hockey player of some note!

I don't recall when Errol arrived at the Arc - I guess it must have been around 1963/64 as I don't remember him as being in the Babies Department, which I left in 1963. Errol had an older brother Brian, and a younger brother Peter.

I believe Brian now lives in Durban and Peter lives in either Canada or Australia.

Anyhow I will say that Errol was, like me, a fairly reserved guy and so we soon became very firm friends. Errol was one year my junior and I suppose I was a type of mentor to him. We used to spend most of our free time together, whether it was bunking out or exploring the endless caves around the Arc - there was no shortage of caves and "unexplored" topography.

Whenever we found a suitable location we would immediately set about building our "Hut".... a piece of our very own real estate over which we were the masters - what a grand feeling!

Saturday mornings were soccer days, but both Errol and I were not too keen to join in as we felt that the soccer was taken far too seriously and not worth fretting about - so we would avoid it and would do our own thing - climbing trees and the like.

One of the traditions of Simchat Torah in the Arc was the ascribing of suitable nicknames when being called up to collect a miniature Torah for the procession - year-in and year-out Errol and I were known as "Mr and Mrs Goldman!" as we were virtually inseparable!!

Each December, starting in the early 1960's, the Arc kids got on the train to spend the holidays with the very special Jewish community in Durban!!

Errol and I would always arrange get togethers in Durban and I spent many a lazy pool day at his hosts, "Bubbles" and Havis Perling of "Orchid Meats" fame.

Errol was one the "guinea pigs" of the Arc's Cottage System and he left the Arc for the Cottage in Rosebank in 1969.

I was indeed heartsore at this turn of events and from this point on, we all but lost contact with each other except for our meetings at Parktown Boys' High.

* Approximate date

There followed a hiatus of some years during which we had little contact until one day in the late 70's when we suddenly bumped in to each other at an accountancy lecture at Wits University. We also met at Mark's Park when we were on opposing teams of the Accountants' Football League.

After leaving university Errol left SA for the UK and we were unfortunately no longer in touch with each other. A few years thereafter I was suddenly shocked to learn of Errol's passing in the UK.

I remember Errol with much fondness and miss him greatly!!!!! MHDSRIP

Errol and Max Goldman

PETER HOUGH

1963 Peter checking the Mayor's Medallion.
Sharon Grishkan under Mayor, Marcia Salmonson on left.

It was in 1969 that my brother Errol and I moved from the Arc to the Cottage System in Rosebank. I was 12 and Errol was 15. I remember that this was one of the happiest days of my life. A number of kids had already been moved to the cottage a few months earlier. If memory serves me correct Marilyn and Janet Miller, Graham and Marilyn Stoler, Bernard Tanner and Errol and I made up the full complement. Ellen and Joe Berman were the foster parents at that time. We lived across the street from the Rosebank Shopping Centre (OK Bazaar) on Cradock Avenue. We were free to roam about and I had a sense of a new kind of freedom which was different from being told when and where you had to do something or be somewhere.

Going to Durban by train (1963)
Jules Gordon, Mervin Lampert and Peter at back with
Ruth Jacobs Manfred Stein and Ronny Schreeuwer in front.

Bernard and I attended King David School in Victory Park and were picked up by Barney Meyers (the then Head Master) each morning. He had a small mini into which about five kids and he used to cram into. Errol attended Parktown Boys; High at that time. Errol, Graham, Bernard and I were all in one bedroom at the time.

Bernard and I had our Barmitzvah at Oxford Shul and the Arc put on a big catered luncheon in the gardens of the house after

451

Shul – what a fantastic experience. These initial experiences really gave me a sense of being which I believe hugely impacted on me in future years.

The Cottage System was later moved to Greenside where Mr and Mrs Kaye and Rabbi Levy and his wife were the foster parents at different times. Janet and Marilyn Miller and Graham had left by this time and I believe it was Beverly Collett who moved into the house in Greenside.

After completing High School at King David I stayed on at the cottage for about a year while attending Wits University and then moved out and rented a flat in Yeoville with Errol.

The one thing I can say about the Cottage System is that in my mind it moulded me into the person that I am today. What I mean is, that the people who lived there, the foster parents and the committee involved in the running of it all had a huge impact on me. There obviously were also some not so good memories, but overall all the people involved were good people all trying to do their best under the circumstances and the circumstances involved a lot of different personalities.

The one person that stands out to whom I owe a huge amount of gratitude to was Dr Nelson. He headed the committee who oversaw the cottage and always had all of us kids' interests at heart – what a kind, patient and gracious man.

1963 Arc children at play
Tony Mark directing traffic, Peter in middle, Georgie Marshak on right and Sammy Lasker in front

!962 Chedar Lessons.
Brian Hough, Martin Katz, Bessie Borts and Rosalind Kupferberg in back row,
David Ginsberg, Michael Goldstein, Raymond Lang and Boris Sedaca in middle row and Les Durbach and Jenny Sandler in front.

Chapter 122 – BERNARD TANNER (1958)

Bernard was born in 1958 and was placed in the care of the Arc in 1966 at age eight after the death of his father.

In August 1969 he moved to the Cottage and lived there until 1975 when he matriculated.

After Bernard completed his national service he studied law and did his articles and qualified as a lawyer in 1980.

REMINISCING

I remember spending a short time in the Arc and then the best thing for me was being sent to the cottage. Graham Stoler was also at the cottage and he used to bully Peter Hough and I. The only way to sort him out was for Peter and I to gang up against him." Over the years I have had many dealings with Graham (since

the Arc days) and he is a wonderful human being .We get on very well and have daughters the same age. I have even met him "on court" and enjoyed some tennis with him over the years.

I felt that the Old Arc forum should be used to pay tribute to all those that contributed to the cottage system. Too often, we tend not to acknowledge those who have made a real difference.

For me, the cottage represented a turning point. I would rather use the opportunity to praise those people who were involved rather than recount some meaningless story concerning Graham's antics.

It was Brecht who once stated: "*because things are the way they are, things will not stay the way they are.*" How right he was.

1967
*Standing; Errol Hough, Michael Saiet (at back) Brian Sandler, Graham Stoler, Alan Jacobs, Mark Jacob, Gary Creighton,
David Sandler, Danny Lasker and Shaun Jacobs.
Sitting; Tony Mark, Sammy Lasker, Peter Hough, Bernard Tanner and David Lasker*

TRIBUTE TO UNSUNG HEROES

There are certain defining moments in our lives and for me such a moment came at age 11.

I remember being called into the library in the main building at 22 Oxford Road and being asked if I would be interested in being placed in an experimental system which I was told was called the "Cottage System".

I immediately identified this as an opportunity of a lifetime realising that I would be placed in a more "normal" environment and that in all probability such a move would be beneficial to me. I had no hesitation in agreeing to be placed in this experimental system

.During the time that I lived at "the cottage", I had three sets of "house" parents namely Mr and Mrs Joe Berman, Mr and Mrs Kaye and Rabbi and Mrs Levy. They were vastly different in their outlook and approach, however notwithstanding their differences; their collective common goal was to provide a "normal" home life for all of us that were placed in the cottage.

I have over the years remained in constant touch with Joe and Ellen Berman and their family and I have from time to time been in contact with Rabbi and Mrs Levy, although that contact has been somewhat erratic. I have had no contact with Mr and Mrs Kaye.

The most liberating memory I have when I first arrived in the Cottage System was when Joe Berman showed me my room and I realised that I would have my own bedside light which I could control. In future I would determine when "lights out" took place. For me this was euphoric and probably the most memorable item, as I had control of the light. It empowered me in a strange type of way and also inculcated a love of reading. No one realises the difference a seemingly small item can make to a person and the impact it can have.

The cottage experience also enabled me to go on regular everyday outings and I learnt everyday things such as the fact that tea, coffee and sugar were not bought in tea, coffee and sugar shops but in stores such as Checkers and the OK Bazaars. I began to realise how sheltered and removed my few years in Arcadia had been.

It was the simple everyday activities which I believe "normalised" my day to day life and also assisted me in integrating in a new school (King David) and enabled me to obtain a completely new perspective on my day to day life and a new self image generally.

I am of the view that my years in the cottage were invaluable and I wish to salute and thank everyone who was involved in the Cottage System, both directly and indirectly. In particular, Mr and Mrs Joe Berman, Mr and Mrs Dave Kaye and Rabbi and Mrs Joshua Levy. There were also various other members of the committee such as Dr Nelson, Mrs Lubner, Mrs Sasto and various others of whom I am currently unaware. I am firmly of the view that the cottage concept was enormously beneficial to all of us and had a major and extremely positive effect on each of our lives.

Each of your contributions indelibly changed our lives in ways that you cannot imagine and I wish to express my personal appreciation and an enormous "*kol hakavod*" to each and every one of you.

The slogan that appeared on the Arcadia letterhead went something as follows: *"No one stands as erect as he who stoops to help a child."*

You are all giants and deserve to walk tall and be honoured for a contribution that made a real and significant difference to each of our lives.

In preparing this short article, no adverse inferences should be drawn in regard to life in Arcadia as opposed to life in the Cottage System and I am merely expressing my own personal opinion in regard to the manner in which the Cottage System benefited me and my own personal feelings in regard to my experiences. My comments are not to be misconstrued, as Arcadia itself is a wonderful institution, however, a large group of children could never have had the same type of day to day experiences as a small group living at the time in Rosebank and being privy to common everyday experiences "on the outside".

I believe that my years at "the cottage" certainly equipped me to deal with all aspects of my life and again I wish to pay tribute to each and every individual who was involved.

I realised that these were indeed unsung heroes who deserve to be heaped with praise for their unselfish acts and for assuming roles which certainly contributed in the most material way to each of our lives.

AFTER LEAVING THE ARC

I completed my National Service in 1976 and commenced studying law and serving articles simultaneously from January 1977. I qualified as a lawyer in 1980 and have practiced uninterrupted since then. Throughout the years I have continued studying law at various universities as I have always enjoyed the academic side of law. I am married with two children, a son of 19 and a daughter of 16. As a family we have travelled fairly extensively over the years, which we have loved. I am a regular "gymgoer" and "Shulgoer". I am extremely grateful to all those that helped me along the way and hence the tribute.

CHAOS AND 'VERKRAMPTE'
1973 - 1978

After Doc and Ma left the Arc, the period of enlightenment which they had ushered in disappeared for a short period.

Children at play

Chapter 123 - PHILIP AND SYLVIA DUZZY
At Arcadia 1972-1977

Philip and Sylvia Duzzy were appointed Superintendent and Matron of Arcadia in 1972. They resigned in 1977.

Here is how the children of the day remember them.

Joan Sacks (Krebs) writes:

Ma and Doc were not there too long after we arrived at the Arc, but what I do remember of them was that they were very warm people.

The Duzzys were not suitable for the job in any way, as they were cold people who were really not interested in the children. It was just a nice cushy job for them.

I remember that the Duzzys where not really well liked by anyone. They certainly did not like my brother or me. The year that my brother was Head Boy and I was Head Girl we decided to terrorise the Duzzys. They did not come out of their flat for nearly one week. My brother and I ran the Arc together.

Sammy Lasker writes:

The superintendent couple who took over from Ma and Doc were Philip and Sylvia Duzzy who arrived from Cape Town after Ma and Doc retired in the early seventies. From what I can remember about the era, as I was still in the Arc, they weren't very popular or tough enough to handle some rather, should we say boisterous young guys and girls.

After the rigorous, but fair, discipline set by the Lichtigfelds (Ma and Doc) there was no way that they (the Duzzys) were ever going to reign in these guys and girls.

Related by Sammy Lasker:

Phillip Duzzy had a glass eye and the kids used to mock him. In the dining room one morning, the boys started mocking him about his glass eye. He got upset and started threatening them. Shaun Krebs took a grapefruit and threw it at Duzzy - it missed Duzzy but hit the back of the wall and soaked his wig with grapefruit juice. He blamed me. He grabbed me by the collar and total chaos erupted in the dining room. The police were called in to quell the situation. I was then 13 years old.

Helen Sher writes:

I was there with the Duzzys and don't remember them as being very nice, even though they tried.

Two stories I do remember about them are:

1975- Presentation of TV.
Mr Duzzy on left and Mrs Duzzy and Mr Teeger on right.

The Arc got very progressive after Doc and Ma, and the dining room became very co-ed, the boys and girls were allowed to sit at the tables together. Shelley Grishkan and Gary Creighton were at the same table and one supper they were laughing hysterically during the meal. After supper Mrs Duzzy called Shelley over and the conversation went something like this:

Mrs Duzzy: What was so funny during dinner?
Shelley: I can't remember.
Mrs Duzzy: You might as well tell me, because Gary told me what he said and I want to know if he told me the truth.
Shelley: "Gary said that you look like a platypus" (or some words to that effect).
Mrs Duzzy: Thank you very much, because I didn't ask Gary." Needless to say Gary got told off.

When I was in matric I had the dormitory all to myself, being 'Prefect' and it went with the privilege. It was my matric dance and Gaby Edery was going to another matric dance at King Edward School. As I was allowed home later than her, we arranged that she would wait up for me in my room. Mrs Duzzy caught her sneaking into my room and sent her back to her room.

Gaby wrote me this note saying: "Come to my room because the fat sneak is prowling around" (or words to that effect). Of course Mrs Duzzy found the note and was furious. When I came home she stood outside her room like a guard waiting to see if Gaby would come to my room. We did eventually find a way.

Chapter 124 – SAM LASKER (1959)

In 1961 Sammy's three oldest brothers Danny, Martin and David were admitted to Arcadia and Sammy who was then just a few months old came to the Arc in 1962. Several years later a fifth son Reginald was also admitted into Arcadia.

SAMMY RECALLS

My four brothers and I, three older than me and one younger, were all in Arcadia. I was there for 17 years and not once have I been embarrassed about it. We all received a good education good upbringing and *nachas* from an excellent Jewish organisation.

What Jules Gordon has written about Doc and Ma is very moving as they were a very special couple. Nothing negative can ever be said about them.

I recall that there was a Portuguese housemother who replaced Mrs Stelzner, after she passed away in her sleep. This lady was Mrs Marques and I do remember her waking up her charges (us young boys) by tickling our toes at 6.00 am every morning. I was one of them along with Charles Goldman, the late George Marshak, Eric and Leo Niedermayer, Laurie Fineberg, Glen Osher and others. This was in 1972 in the Boys' Department and there were about 12 of us in the first dormitory.

I remember both Mandy Livingstone and David Graf. Mandy was very pretty and talented in her hairdressing career. I was aware that they are no longer with us.

Colin Hurwitz was never in Arcadia. His mother Minnie and her brother Sidney (Beans) Levine were and he knows many Old Arcs as he visited a lot during those years.

STORIES OF SAMMY LASKER
Written by Kay Stoler

The Fete

There was a fete at Oxford Shul grounds. The Arc boys including Sammy invited themselves to the fete. They arrived with no money and when they left, they were laden with half the stock at the fete. Sammy, Shaun, Leo, Eric and Charles had their dorm stocked for the month with chips, cold drinks, biscuits, sweets etc. *Nogal,* they also hitched a ride home in a taxi as their loot was too heavy to carry.

Borrowing the Arc van

The usual mob of that time loaned the Arc van to go gallivanting in Killarney. Eric drove the van and drove pretty well at that.

Tok Tokkie and horse play

They played *tok tokkie* on the flat doors. Their usual ploy was to

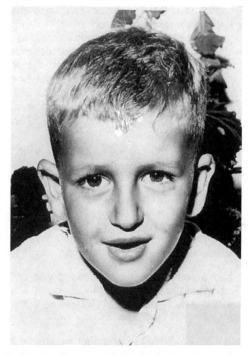

Sammy Lasker

leave a pile of dog poo on the front door steps. Knock on the doors, run away, the owner would open the door and stand on the poo.

To this day they have never been found out. I hope they have progressed to another game!!

Shaun, Leo, Eric and Charles took Georgie Marshak into Oxford Road, tied him up and pretended to beat him up when they saw a car coming. As soon as the driver got out, Georgie screamed and they all ran away. One day a guy pulled out a gun. They still continued having fun with Georgie. They never really hurt him - they just wanted to have fun!! If you tried doing this today - I doubt if anyone would stop, they wouldn't turn a blind eye!

Sammy David and Reggie

Chapter 125 – JOAN SACKS (KREBS) (1957)

Joan was born on 14th November 1957 and her brother Alexander Krebs (Shani) was born on the 15th October 1959. Their parents were Hungarian immigrants who fled the 1956 Hungarian uprisings and went to South Africa to make a new life. When Joan was three and Shani was one when their father died, leaving the children in the care of their mother who was unable to speak English and struggled to find work. In 1970 they were put in the care of Arcadia as their mother had to return to Hungary. Shani left the Arc in 1979 after he matriculated and Joan left in 1977.

MEMORIES OF THE ARC

I remember that the Duzzys where not really well liked by anyone. They certainly did not like my brother or me. The year that my brother was Head Boy and I was Head Girl we decided to terrorise the Duzzys. They did not come out of their flat for nearly one week. My brother and I ran the Arc single handedly.

They also had a pompous son who used to visit and flirt with the girls. They were not suitable for the job in any way, as they were cold people who were really not interested in the children. It was just a nice cushy job for them.

Ma and Doc were not there too long after we arrived at the Arc, but what I do remember of them was that they were very warm people.

I was not very liked by the girls, at one stage not one of them spoke to me for about six months and I coped very well with this. Wow it was peaceful.

We had sewing lessons in that little sewing room upstairs. I made my first long sleeve shirt in that room, the collar was so big, it looked like I was going to take off any minute. I was so proud of this shirt but of course could never wear it.

I remember the one housemother we had, a Mrs Bouwer. Wow what a wonderful lady this was. She loved me and she was very good to the girls and I would say the warmest of all house mothers. I did not get one with Van Rensburg at all. She had her favourites and whenever donations of clothing came in, she would first choose stuff for herself and then her favourites would get to choose so very little was left for me and those she did not like.

Overall, I really enjoyed my stay at the Arc. The food was always very good and we got a good education.

MY CHILDREN

Both my children are good loyal people. Not because they are mine but I put a lot into bringing them up. No-one, but I mean no-one was allowed to touch them, feed them, talk to them or look at them when they were babies, I did everything for them and I loved it. I never ever left them with anyone. I have truly enjoyed my children. I was there for every little thing that they learnt or did for the first time. Yes for one year I did not get out of my pyjamas I was so exhausted but I would not do it differently if I did it over again. Their names are Darren and Keri. They are unique children with qualities that very few have. I am so proud of them.

My daughter looks a little like me, because she too is blonde but my son, does not look like any of us.

Portrait of Joan and Daughter Keri - By Shani Krebs

Chapter 126 – ALEXANDER (SHANI) KREBS (1959)

Shani was born in 1959 and was placed in the care of Arcadia, together with his sister, Joan, in 1970. Shani left the Arc in 1979 after completing his matric.

In April 1994 Shani was incarcerated in prison in Thailand to serve a 40 year prison sentence on drug related charges.

When you read this book he will have been incarcerated for twelve years.

I ask you to please support him and not to judge him.

BOYS WILL ALWAYS BE BOYS

The following episode transpired roughly when I was 14 years old at the prime of puberty. Whenever I have reminisced of past events this particular event never failed to bring a smile to my face. At 14 my attraction for the opposite sex had become fervently apparent, Sammy Lasker, Charles Goldman and I had begun our unrelenting reign of mischief. There wasn't a single room in Arcadia or building in its vicinity that we couldn't get into, however most our attention was focused on the girls especially the seniors. We would stalk a specific girl, one of us would distract her while the other would come from behind and look up her dress.

This daring scheme we even practiced on our school teachers, another ideal location where all girls fell victim to prying eyes was at the public telephone. Most girls spent hours on end speaking to their boyfriend, a pen-size flashlight became an indispensable commodity. Charles Goldman kept a small mirror in his possession permanently. But the excitement soon faded and we began to feel an urgency to see the real thing, a totally naked woman. At that time I was secretly in love with one of the girls.

She oozed femininity and had all the qualities that appealed to me. So we began to devise a plan to see her naked. After several failed attempts we figured that the best time would be on a Saturday morning just before lunch and before the Senior Girls returned from a morning basking in the sun at the swimming pool, which had become a regular activity. On a Saturday morning, while we innocently swam and sunbathed we inconspicuously kept an eye on her. She was the type of girl you couldn't help staring at, she had become accustomed to probing eyes no doubt. Anyway she began gathering her things, Sammy and I sprinted to the Senior Girls' dormitory.

After some painstaking manoeuvring we managed to sneak into her room unnoticed. I hid under her bed while Sammy crawled under Joan's bed (my sister) and there we were anxiously awaiting her arrival. I was extremely nervous and could hear my heart beating. I was starting to become apprehensive and wasn't sure if I could go through with all this. I mean, what if we were caught. We were dead quiet, the silence was almost

Shani in prison in his Soccer kit

deafening, sweat was forming on my forehead, my ambivalence was shattered by the sudden creaking of the wooden floor boards, which intensified with the approaching footstep that seemed to reverberate with the pounding of my heart.

I was too young for so much excitement. I thought I wanted to get out of there, how on earth did I land up here in the first place. I couldn't blame Sammy. It was too late, the door opened, I recall covering my eyes with both my hands and pulling my knees to my chest, panic was setting in, any second I was expecting to be caught. I vowed not to open my eyes and remain in that position, nothing happened, only the methodical movements of her were distinct, curiosity got the better of me, I straightened my legs and removed my hands from my face, I took a peep in the direction of Sammy. His eyes were beaming with pleasure, he winked and gave me a thumbs up, my eyes darted towards her dainty feet, I edged forward a little more and there right before my very eyes was her full naked body in all its splendour.

It was a breathtaking moment, she was everything I imagined her to be and even more. She had obviously just taken a shower as the towel she was using to dry her hair covered her eyes. I could feel my own breath growing heavier, I wanted to touch her in what seemed like a moment of passion, but instead retreated into the shadows under the bed she took her time dressing, which enabled us a few good peeps, soon she was fully dressed and then silence. I couldn't understand what she was doing that she was taking so long, I edged forward again simultaneously moved the bed covering, there she was her face close to the mirror and was applying mascara. From the angle of the mirror she had a clear view directly under the bed, her eyes caught my movement, she shrieked. I almost had a heart attack, and she reacted by grabbing the cover off the bed and yelled "What the hell are you doing!!"

I innocently whispered and gestured with my index finger over my lips "ssshshoot, keep your voice down". A mixture of confusion and bewilderment came over her, I spoke even softer "we are playing catches and I'm hiding from Charles, her face went totally blank and she responded with a simple Oh!. I hurriedly added "Do me a favour and please go and check if Charles is anywhere outside or near the stairway", almost as if she was in a trance she suggested that I stay where I was while she goes to look if Charles is anywhere to be seen.

Luck was on my side. By the time she returned and assured me that he was nowhere to be seen, I had come out from under the bed, I thanked her and was out of there in a flash. Sammy had made his own escape undetected. At lunch when she saw me she was furious. She had realised what I had got up to and angrily pointed her finger in my direction and said "Watch out my boy!!"

That became the dramatic end to our secret romance as did our peeping Tom days abruptly end. I guess boys will always be boys.

"CROSSING THE LINE"

While reading the article about the sale of Arcadia and its relocation to RAEDENE, the mention of which triggered a horrific recollection, an occurrence that none of those involved would ever forget. For those of you who don't know and presuming it is the same RAEDENE in question, it is an area situated adjacent to the General Hospital, opposite Arcadia and is accessible via the Sunnyside Hotel. I've decided to call this story "Crossing the line."

I was roughly 16 years old at the time and we were at a phase in our adolescence when night excursions became the order of the day, which added an element of danger to our adventures. Such outings compromised of hi-jacking parked cars or anything with wheels, house-breaking which isn't altogether an appropriate description, more like trespassing. The challenge was getting in and out of buildings undetected, and never with the intention of stealing something, and if caught escaping was imperative and the ultimate adrenaline rush all part of the game.

There were countless occasions when we were chased by either security guards, landlords, gardeners, milkmen and even police and as such became great athletes, getting caught was also a loss of face to the other boys. At school we Arcs always

took first, second or third place in the cross country races, which was much to the surprise of our colleagues who never saw us at training and couldn't quite understand why the Arcs were such formidable opponents.

Friday nights had routinely become a bunking-out night. Watching the Brady Bunch on TV had lost its moments and on this particular night we were looking to do something out of the ordinary. Without opposition it was decided that we would explore the hospital, which was still under construction and the area within its immediate vicinity which happened to house a girls' boarding school called *Raedene*. The location itself was charming and the botanical gardens, known as *The Wilds* bordered its property, enhanced its splendour and tranquillity, which at night had taken on a menacing transformation and looked more like a setting for a horror movie. I recall at the time a man's mutilated body being found amongst the abundant foliage of *The Wilds* and a few rapes had taken place there. Crime was on the increase and even Killarney had become notorious as a playground for unsavoury characters and as such the police patrolled the area constantly. And so with the increased element of risk and as a preventative measure, night raids, as we called them, had taken on a whole new dimension and we were compelled to carry weapons which took the form of batons, nunchakas, knives and sometimes even baseball bats. We were extremely resourceful and were renowned for our courage and determination, our motto was "Do or Die". Little did I know of the impact and influence our comradeship would have on my character in later life.

On this particular Friday night we were more in number than usual, and it was unanimously decided to allow certain junior boys to join the expedition as part of their initiation into manhood. Barmitzvahs were a spiritual thing and were for *bagels,* survival in a precarious situation was the real test. Straight after dinner our usual crew, which consisted of myself, Sammy Lasker, Charles Goldman, Eric and Leo Niedermayr, Colin Coats who wasn't actually an Arc, but had proved his loyalty and become a staunch friend, and two junior boys who joined us for the first time were David Graff and Steven Landsman A.K.A. Fanny assembled in the driveway. Taking the junior boys with us was way irresponsible, but nothing new for the harum scarum boys we were becoming. Sooner or later they would be bunking out on their own anyway, none of us really considered the consequence of our actions.

Armed with our weapons, some of us even donned balaclavas, we stealthily made our way out of the grounds, via the hill passing on the side of the Goldsmith residence. From there we went through Mr White's house then we entered the General Hospital, which provided a maze of adventure, our relentless quest for excitement was insatiable and the fact that we were fearless made us unpredictable, our defiance for authority was an inherent trait in most Arcs.

Parked and chained to one of the street lamps inside the premises of the hospital was a three-wheeled bicycle type cart with a huge bin in front and used by the milkmen to do their deliveries, some of the boys tried to pull the chain apart but with little success.

Colin Coats approached and said "Let me have a go". He grabbed the chains with both hands and pulled with all his strength and to our amazement the lock popped open with what seemed like minimal effort. Triumphantly he mounted the saddle and gestured us to jump into the bin, we all piled in and raced down the hill screaming our heads off, because of the excessive weight and the speed we were travelling at, he lost control and crashed into the side-walk, we went flying in different directions, what a gas. We laughed our heads off and bolted from the scene.

We then made our way to *Raedene* girls' where on previous outings some of us had actually met a few of the girls who quite fancied us. Having been familiar with the terrain around the property, getting in and out of the home was only a matter of manoeuvring from one side to the other. The only obstacle that presented any difficulty was the 6 ft steel fences adorned with barbwire which we climbed with relative ease. We entered the grounds which were dimly lit and made our way to the front of the building. I was feeling uncomfortable, there was something eerie about the place. The silence was unnatural.

Unbeknown to us lurking behind and hidden in the shadows was someone watching our movements. We all congregated in front of the main building, on top of our voices and in concert we began reciting the song "The German officers crossed the line, *palles vous* and so on…." Lights were coming on in different sections of the building which was simultaneously followed by a dog barking. It wasn't very convincing and sounded like some poodle.

Rising above the bark echoed a coarse masculine voice and seemed awfully close, "What the hell are you doing here?" I could have sworn it was a German accent, we turned and like lightning ran in the opposite direction. The next thing we knew there was a gunshot. Colin was a little to my right, we were pretty close to each other and I heard him utter under his breath, "Ouch my leg, I've been hit," then there was another shot, I remember saying "Nonsense that was a cap gun or a fire-cracker".

Fanny, one of the juniors was further back and just off Colin's right side. I had taken the lead, Colin was keeping up with me and again pleaded that he had been hit, we all ran in different directions and had agreed before that, if anything happened and we were separated we would meet in *The Wilds* by the fish ponds.

I kept thinking to myself, what kind of lunatic would shoot on a bunch of kids. Minutes later we all frantically met at our rendezvous, everyone was accounted for, a small victory. I hurriedly explained that Colin had been shot and we proceeded to inspect his leg, true to his word. A mixture of shock and surprise came over us, there before our very eyes was a hole in the rear of his jeans covered in blood, just below his right buttock and had exited on the other side travelling straight through his thigh. Colin pulled his jeans to his knees, it wasn't a pleasant sight. Red and white flesh was hanging out of the wound.

He was in pain and we needed to get back to the Arc before a decision of our next course of action could be made, as we automatically presumed that whoever shot at us would have

called the police. We quickly made our way through the back of *The Wilds*, which was quite a climb, and ran along the outskirts of Killarney and around Harry Oppenheimer's property. Colin kept up with me all the way. I remember thanking G-d that it wasn't one of the junior boys that got hit, Colin was quite tall from an early age and had it been that Fanny got shot, the bullet would have entered his spine and might have been fatal.

We got back to the Arc in reasonably good time, it wasn't very late, if I am not mistaken it was around 10.00 pm, we sent the Junior boys back to their dormitories while we smuggled Colin into the toilets under the stairway that led to the senior girls. I then unmindfully rushed up the stairs to call my sister Joan, who just happened to be coming out of her room. I frantically ran up to her, a sight, I was covered in black jacks, panic stricken and sweating like a pig. I hurriedly blurted a thousand words a second at her. I could see a mixture of anger and confusion came over her and was infuriated by my sudden intrusion and reprimandingly queried what the hell had we done this time. Without saying anything further I grabbed her arm and gestured her to follow me.

Once in the toilet, Sammy explained in a controlled tone what had transpired. I've always known Joan to be squeamish, and to my surprise she took charge of the situation. She started assigning duties, Sammy and I were instructed to keep vigil watch for Vicky. Eric and Sandra Newstead were told to fetch towels, a bowl of hot water, bandages etc etc and then ordered Colin to remove his pants, while Joan was performing first aid on him.

Suddenly Vicky appeared and made his way into the adjoining area to the toilet. Immediately I thought we were busted as Vicky had a clear view of Colin's naked bum and Joan's profile was in full view through the slightly ajar toilet door. Vicky started stamping his feet and wanted to know what was going on and in one movement tried to push his way into the toilet. I grabbed the handle of the toilet door and pulled it closed simultaneously. Sammy and I asked Vicky not to enter and said that he shouldn't go in because Colin didn't have his pants on. Vicky was startled, as he had seen Joan in there and looked at us suspiciously.

He obviously suspected that something was wrong, but couldn't quite figure out what it was. He then went on to say, "Well then finish whatever it is that you are doing and get back to dormitory" and proceeded to leave, we all sighed with relief.

By this stage Colin was in great pain and Joan strongly suggested that we get him to a hospital. So we phoned a close friend of Colin's, Steven Penn whose father was a pharmacist and lived in Greenside. Within 15 minutes, they arrived and whisked Colin off to hospital. Fortunately he recovered without any complications and even though we may literally have crossed the line, the incident never deterred us from future escapades and Colin remained a staunch friend with a few of the Arcs especially Eric.

In September 2001 Colin Coats paid me a surprise visit in Thailand He lives in Chicago and is a single parent with four children and is a successful diamond-dealer.

A REBEL WITHOUT A CAUSE

It was during the autumn of 1977, my matric year. I was then the so called Head Boy of Arcadia. I was at an age where most of my contemporaries were either driving their parents' cars and or had their own. Unfortunately the only mode of transport we as Arcs had at our disposal was the Arc van and bus, and only as a passenger. It had become a custom handed down by our predecessors to take the Arc van on a joy ride in the late hours of the evening. David Lasker was an accomplished driver from an early age and a mentor to those that followed in the years to come.

It was forbidden to leave the premises on Shabbath. It was late that Friday evening, a slightly chilled autumn wind broke the silence of the night. As I lay restlessly on my bed I decided that a night out and around in the Arc van would add to the excitement of a mundane weekend. I encouraged Mark Wasserman to join me.

Around midnight after everyone had gone to sleep we hijacked the Arc van, off we went gallivanting aimlessly through the deserted suburbs. In retrospect one can only wonder what possessed me to be so irresponsible, there I was an unlicensed driver, putting both our lives in jeopardy while the thrill might elude us, the fact remains that my defiance of authority was a driving force in all my pleasure seeking endeavours. Around 1.00 am somewhere in Bramley, we got stuck in a dead-end, what made matters worse was that it was at the bottom end of an uphill. There was no way of push-starting the van, the arduous task of getting the van out of this dead end began. Eventually we managed to get it out. We were on a straight and level road exhausted and sweating like pigs.

Suddenly in the distance appeared one of those blue Valiants, with dimmed lights. We both spotted it at the same time, I could hear Mark utter under his breath "It's the Police". My heart stopped for what seemed like eternity. As the Valiant approached, I leapt into the drivers seat of the van, Mark remained at the rear and kept pushing on my instruction, the pursuing Valiant pulled alongside the Arc van. It was the police alright.

The policeman then proceeded in a half English/Afrikaans accent to ask what the problem was. My chest was pounding, I tried to speak but there were no words and then as if from a distance, I heard myself saying "She wont start do you think you could help push"? Talk about having chutzpah. I wasn't very convincing. His voice grew stern as he ordered me to pull to the side of the road and had pulled the Valiant in front of me forcing me to a standstill. Before I knew what was going on my door had been flung open and I was blinded by the beam of a flashlight. He then shone the torch in the direction of the ignition, simultaneously asking me for my licence, then in a much harsher tone, as he looked at the ignition he said "Where are the keys"?

My whole body began to shake and I began to stutter "Ke, ke, ke, keys, there are no keys, a scuffle pursued and all hell seemed to have broken loose. I heard shouting at the rear end of the van "put your hands in the air". At this stage. I must have gone into shock. I began fighting the cops off and telling them that I could explain everything, they kept coming at me but

couldn't get me out of the van, one of the cops produced what looked like 9mm automatic and stuck it between my eyes. I immediately froze and was literally wrenched out of the van. Mark was already seated and cuffed at the back of the Valiant. I've never forgotten that desperate look in his eyes.

We were taken to the Bramley Police Station. During the interrogation I was slapped and punched in the stomach. Mark was two or three years my junior and wasn't touched. After telling them that we were from Arcadia, it just so happened that the sergeant on duty was familiar with the Arc and knew Vicky, what a relief as neither of us entertained the prospect of spending the weekend in the cells, our prayers were answered and around 2.00 am we were escorted back to the Arc.

On our return Vicky never said a single word, his disappointment was obvious. I had let him down. Before retiring to his room Vicky came into my dormitory, he said without even looking at me "I cannot understand your mentality" which he repeated as he exited the room, seeing the expression on Vicky's face made me realise the severity of the situation.

The Monday following, an emergency session was held by the senior members of the Arc committee which if I'm not mistaken was chaired by Sidney Nochumson. We enjoyed a mutual dislike for each other. On several other occasions I had been brought in front of the chairman for various other misdemeanours. One such incident that was instigated by yours truly and was still very fresh in his mind was the mass uprising and forced retirement of the hypocritical rule of the tyrant couple know as the Duzzys.

Having become a familiar sight, leniency was far from our chairman's agenda. This was the final straw, I was formally expelled and it was decided that I be sent to Norman House, a reformatory or haven for juvenile delinquents.

During the period Arcadians enjoyed the privilege of attending any school of their choice and the majority of us chose King David, Victory Park. The arbitrary decision by the committee to have me expelled left me extremely distraught. I was devastated and strongly felt that a great injustice had befallen me, a view shared by the fellow matric students of Victory Park, headed by Roy Lotkin, then my best friend. The students of King David drafted a petition pleading with the Arc committee to retract my punishment and allow me to complete my matric, as my future was at stake. Another meeting was arranged and Mr Woolf who was head principal of Victory Park High School had by choice attended the meeting in my defence. Luckily I had a good reputation at school and was a keen sportsman. Not only was I in the swimming team, but also played in the 1st XV rugby team for two consecutive years and was awarded half colours for my performance. I was house captain and during the year we had won all the inter-house sports activities, except for the rugby where we took second place.

Thanks to Mr Woolf I was given permission to stay on in Arcadia for the remainder of my matric on the condition that I be *gated* for three months and my allowance be withheld for the same period. It was further agreed that I attend counselling with the current psychologist of Arcadia whose name was Vivien Budlinder. She turned out to be a lovely person and a strong friendship ensued. She was compassionate and never accepted anything at face value. We remained friends for years. Thanks to Mr Jeffrey Woolf, Vicky and the King David matric students I had the opportunity to make amends.

Vicky informed me soon after the meeting that he had never before heard a person speak so highly of another individual as Mr Woolf had spoken of me, which I was extremely humbled by. I never did too well in my prelims, however I did pass and attained a distinction in Art.

During that period skate boarding had just become the new craze. Most of my time and energy was channelled into skating, I had a snowy-smith board with alpha wheels, then the Mercedes of skate-boards. What a trip it was. Imagine skating down Oxford Road and overtaking the double-decker buses. Just for the record I did manage to pass matric.

Many years have elapsed since our days in Arcadia and yet memories that are deeply rooted in our hearts still prevail. Arcadia and its people will always hold a special place in my heart. My prayers and wishes are that you all continue to live a healthy and happy life and may you succeed in all your endeavours.

I would also like to take this opportunity to honour those special friends and relatives whose sudden departure never had any real sense, and whose deaths affected so many lives. We can never forget you, Thelma Durbach, Martin Lasker, Georgie Marshak, David Graf and Mandy Livingstone.

My fondest regards to Vicky Klevansky, Goldie and Stan Goldsmith, Ruth Dire (Conway) and Nicholas, Joe Balor and William also Rommy and Doreen. Then a big hello to the Laskers, Danny, David, Sammy and Reggie. Sharon and Shelley Grushkin, Beryl Sacks, Helen Sher, Sandra Newstead, Jenifer and Beverley Ling, The Ederys Terry, Gaby, Louise and Pierre, the Landsmans, Steven, Morris, Eleanor and Crystal, my sister Joan and her husband Malcolm Sacks, their children Darren and Kerry. I miss you all terribly and love you lots.

To the Niedermayers, Eric and Moira, Leo and Jance and all their children, the Joel sisters, Adrienne and Charmaine, the Woolf sisters, Babette and Myra, Lynnette Bark, Sandra Klevansky, the Ginsbergs, Charles Goldman, The Wainsteins, Stephen, Gavin, Darren and Paul, Mark Wasserman, Leonard Botes, Wendy Rubenstein, The Sulmans, Louise, Ingrid and Lawrance. The Oshers, Glen Karen, Colleen, Adelle and Dona, Bernard Tanner, Graham Stoller, The Durbachs, Les, Ester, Hannah and Myra, Michael Rothaus, David and Brian Sandler, Gary and Desiree Crighton. You are all never too far from my thoughts, if I've left any of your names out please forgive me.

WE REMEMBER THELMA MARTIN AND GEORGIE

It was great seeing so many Arcs again in the same place at the same time in the *Old Arc's Scrapbook*, I feel privileged to have appeared in it. It brings so many of us together in thought and spirit and imbues a greater sense of belonging to a more meaningful past.

My delight was over shadowed by a great sense of remorse when seeing the photographs of Thelma Durbach, Martin Lasker and the mention of Georgie Marshak. Martin and Thelma were at the very prime of their youth when they were tragically taken from their loved ones. Death is always a heart rending affair, especially when it's a family member or close relative and those who have never experienced such a misfortune cannot relate to the loss and identify with the pain that accompanies such tragedy.

Thelma was young, vivacious and beautiful and would always listen to what you had to say. She was kind caring and considerate and wouldn't harm a fly. Martin who was extremely close to Thelma was the gentlest of souls and was always willing to give a helping hand, his tranquil nature and good sense of humour stood him apart from others, he was an individual of immense integrity. Their absence has left a void in many of our lives. Here were two people who were innocent to the ways of the world and had outstanding character, traits, which makes their deaths that much more difficult to understand and accept. It's almost as if they never belonged to this world but rather to a higher plain of existence, closer to G-d, may their souls rest in peace and may we forever cherish their memory.

For those of you who remembered Georgie Marshak will recall him being mentally retarded. I left Arcadia in December 19 77 and in the years to follow, Georgie became a problem, his age exceeded that of the other children and he was also physically over-powering which frightened some of the younger children. The Arc committee decided that it was in the best interest of all concerned to send him to Selwyn Segal, a home for the mentally handicapped.

Having spent most of his life in Arcadia the sudden change of environment was most unsettling and Georgie went into a state of depression which was intensified by the daily sedatives he was forced to consume, with the result that he attempted to burn the section in which they kept him. He became a threat to those around him and was transferred to a place called Cresset house which was situated near Hartebeespoort Dam.

When I finally got to hear about everything that had happened I became deeply concerned and feared the worst on visiting him at Cresset House I was shocked beyond belief, the transformation was unbelievable. He was a walking zombie and could hardly recognise me, he was so heavily sedated. This wasn't the Georgie I knew so well. Soon afterwards I learnt of his sudden demise. When inquiring to the cause of his death I was told that it was a common occurrence for retarded people to pass away at a young age. I never really came to terms with his death.

Georgie as I remembered him was a fighter and had a strong will to live. I've always strongly suspected that he was a victim of involuntary euthanasia, nobody cared, which was evident by the attendance at his funeral. I would like to say this Georgie, I have never forgotten you and you will always hold a very special place in my heart, you were like a brother to me, I never got the chance to tell you but there were some of us who loved you, you crazy son of a bitch.

Being a misfit and all Georgie affected most our lives. I learnt a very important lesson from him, Georgie never gave up, he had guts and determination, he saw things differently to us and did things his own way, whatever he set his mind on doing, no matter how difficult or far reaching he nearly always achieved his objectives, some of the things he used to do really amazed me. I will never forget a specific incident.

Georgie had this tendency of just wandering off and I had taken him under my wing so to speak; which consisted of numerous obligations, a responsibility that nobody cared to undertake. One of my tasks was taking him on outings and on this particular day we caught a bus to the centre of town to see a movie at the newly built Kine Centre which was opposite the Carlton. The centre was one of the first complexes that housed eight different theatres under one roof. It was the middle of the holiday season and there were literally thousands of people around. The show commenced at about 10.00 am and ended around 11.40 am which gave us approximately 30 minutes to get back to the Arc for lunch.

After the movie ended we worked our way to the exit. I was holding Georgie around the wrist and guiding him along, finally we dismounted the escalators, I tightened my grip and gestured that we should hurry to the bus stop. I don't know why but he yanked his arm from my grip and simultaneously delivered a half blow, half shove to my chest which caught me by surprise and by the time I had composed myself he disappeared into the already scurrying crowd. It happened in a matter of seconds. I frantically searched the immediate vicinity. It was impossible to find him in the flow of people.

I then decided to walk along the route that the Oxford Road bus normally travelled and still no sign of him. I caught the next bus home, I was worried as hell, what if something drastic happens to Georgie and what will Vicky say. I was in trouble and I was scared as I always imagined the worst. I arrived a couple of minutes late for lunch and as I entered the dining room, I

searching glanced around and there to my relief Georgie was sitting at his table as if nothing had happened. As our eyes met a fat grin appeared on his face almost as if he knew what I had just been through. After lunch I confronted him and asked him why he had run off and how did he get home so quickly, he simply answered that he wanted to run home and beat the bus back to the Arc, thinking about it, I realised what an incredible feat that was.

There was another incident that was quite funny, Georgie normally got home earlier than the rest of us from school and as usual would have his lunch before us. It so happened that on that day we had chocolate pudding for dessert which was always served in a huge bowl and could dish up 11 healthy portions. I had just arrived through the side entrance of the Boys Department and proceeded to my bedroom. No sooner one of the younger boys came running into the room kicking up a fuss about Georgie polishing off the whole bowl of chocolate pudding. I found him in his room sitting on his bed with chocolate all over his face and clothing. At first he denied eating all the pudding. I then severely reprimanded him and before I knew it he grabbed a pair of nunchakas and threw them at me, fortunately for me he missed. I retrieved the sticks and managed to subdue him. There was never a dull moment having Georgie around. Shame he really had it rough. We were always taking the mickey out of him.

I remember him having this blue photo album inside which he meticulously arranged pictures between the cellophane. I think from *Hustler* porn magazine, of naked ones and an assortment of provocative sexual scenes. We couldn't have been more than 15 or 16 years old. One day Sammy, Charles, Eric and I decided to ask Georgie if we could look through his album which he proudly handed to us. While he wasn't looking we

Georgie Marshak, David Graaf, Eric Niedermeyer, Shani Krebs, Sammy Lasker and Charlie Goldman

carefully removed one of the pages and then innocently returned it to him. The outcome, after he discovered the missing pages was predictable. He went berserk. Georgie grabbed a brick and chased us for I don't know how long. It was the funniest thing because to Georgie this was an unacceptable invasion of his privacy. In the end we had no choice but to succumb to his uncontrollable pursuit to retrieve his picture. After that episode Georgie never parted with his blue photo album.

When I first came to the Arc there were about 43 children and the fact that there were quite a few of us of roughly the same age, made life that much more interesting and exciting. There would always be something to do which turned out more often than not to be of a mischievous nature. Our reputation for being wild preceded us. At school we enjoyed a special respect amongst our peers, also the average Arc excelled more at sports than in academics.

In retrospect one can admit that life was great. We were like a huge family but many of us were not content and couldn't wait to finish school and to make a life for ourselves in the real world. I recall Vicky saying on numerous occasions, that our years in Arcadia and school were the best years of our lives and that life in the real world wasn't as easy as we all assumed, and how right he was, if only we could have those years again.

REMEMBERING DAVID GRAF

When David Graaf first arrived at the Arc around 1973 he was a self conscious temperamental little boy who was sadly, almost completely deaf. This impairment he sustained in an explosion as a mere infant during the six day war in Israel of 1967 in which he tragically lost his father.

David and his sister Sharon and mother resettled in South Africa. According to David his stepfather was cruel and abusive and one of the reasons why David and his sister were sent to the Arc. Initially life was equally difficult for him at the Arc. As in most juvenile institutions there are those who readily prey on the weak and naturally, David fell victim to the unrelenting bullying of his peers, myself included.

There were times when you would call out or speak to David and he would ignore you, almost spontaneously you would react by saying, "Are you deaf or something" and inevitably it would be said with a raised voice to ensure that he heard you. This happened frequently with different people, which wasn't a nice thing to say and in the beginning he would sulkily shy away in tears. Only to be bombarded by more verbal abuse.

David attended St Vincent's School for the Deaf, and as the years passed he became stronger both physically and emotionally and started to stand up for himself. He participated in various sports activities, such as rugby, athletics and swimming. One day after ignoring me when I called out to him, as usual by mistake, I angrily asked him that same question that he had more than likely heard a thousand times over, "Are you deaf?" I have never forgotten, he replied assertively, "Yes I am deaf and why do you keeping asking me when you know I am".

I retaliated by saying "Then answer me", to this he responded equally annoyed, "Have you ever considered that I may not be interested in what you have to say". I was startled, I thought to myself, the son of a bitch all these years he deliberately pretended not to hear me when all along he knew exactly what you said. David had finally become one of the boys, the transformation was incredible.

David had loved his music and used to play the guitar pretty well. We had a lot of fun together. He joined us on most of our escapades while in the Arc. Besides knowing sign language, David had this incredible talent of being able to lip-read someone from anything up to about 15 metres. David's mother was a lovely woman and cared deeply for her children and visited regularly. On Sundays she would fetch David and Sharon and often took me along for the day.

After David left the Arc he went his own way, every now and again we bumped into each other. I recall him having a very beautiful girlfriend with whom he had been together for quite some time. David also had a regular job and everything seemed normal. On one occasion I and a fellow Arc went to visit David after we learnt that he was in a bad way. Apparently he and his girlfriend had broken up. On our arrival I was shocked, David looked terrible.

He was totally out of it, he admitted to having become a Welcanol addict, which he was injecting intravenously. We tried to reason and talk sense into him. It's difficult to establish a timeframe when all this transpired. David did stop using and got back together with his girlfriend. Then I'm not really sure whether weeks, months or years later I heard that David had died from an overdose.

I will always remember David as a kind, sensitive and caring human being who still found a degree of happiness in a sometimes ruthless world, if only I had been a better friend he may still be with us. Please forgive me for not caring in the way you cared for others, we miss and love you and cherish the memories we have of you. David Graaf I always think of you as the brother I lost. The truth is we Arcs are all family.

REMEMBERING MANDY LIVINGSTONE

It is a privilege to honour the memory of two of our beloved friends, Mandy Livingston and David Graff who tragically passed away some years ago. Understandably trying to figure out the order of events when all this took place is extremely difficult, so I stand to be corrected if the years I have mentioned are inaccurate.

If anyone would know or remember when Mandy Livingston came to the Arc that person would be Wendy Rubinstein. I left the Arc in 1977 and my call up for the army was in January 1978. During and after my two years in the military, there were many Arcs from my generation and others who frequently visited Arcadia on the weekends, whether to play football, tennis, enjoy a dip in the pool or visit a girlfriend and/or just to meet each other. The Arc was a popular venue to hang out.

My earliest memory of Mandy around this time, is that she was this gorgeous little redhead who always gave the impression of being content and happy. She had this incredible vivacious laugh, she loved to talk and when given the opportunity she spoke a thousand words a minute. She was also a good listener and many confided in her, she seemed to always have a solution to everyone's problems.

Around the early 1980's I broke my leg playing football, a result of which I went to stay at the Arc cottage in Greenside. David, Reggie and Sammy Lasker, Mark Wasserman, Wendy and Mandy all stayed there. I was confined to bed and needed assistance with everything. Although everyone was very accommodating, Mandy for some reason took it upon herself to be my very own nurse. I was very grateful. Later she admitted that she had a crush on me.

She brought me my meals, she bathed me, dressed me and even helped me to the toilet. I remember so clearly here I was with a full plaster on my leg, taking a bath was a mammoth task, the pain was excruciating and here was this petite, dainty girl trying to manoeuvre not only me but also my leg, while I am screaming from the pain. Actually whenever I think about it, I laugh, it was a real sight. She was an angel in disguise, we became good friends.

At the time Mandy was an apprentice hairdresser. She never made a lot of money, but somehow even with the little she made, she often bought me something to cheer me up. On my way to recovery she helped me take my first steps without crutches.

Mandy was a workaholic, she eventually qualified and worked at Carlton Hair in Hyde Park where she had established a huge clientele. She was a very talented hairdresser and well known in those circles, even though she was somewhat eccentric with her own hairstyles, I never ceased to be amazed at how exquisite she always looked.

In the mid 80's and here again I stand to be corrected, Mandy's best friend and mentor, Laura Berkowitz also from Greenside, tragically died in a car accident. Mandy was shattered, she cried for months on end. She became totally withdrawn and distanced herself from everyone. The day Laura was taken something inside Mandy died. She was never the same after that, she lost interest in everything and eventually we lost contact with each other.

I then saw Mandy again in the early 90's. She had changed considerably, although still very pretty, she was no longer the energetic cheerful little girl I knew and loved. I stayed and spent some time with her, she was cutting hair privately and seemed comfortable, but life for Mandy had become purposeless without her friend Laura. As we were both of free spirits, we as usual parted and went our different ways. I never saw her again. I was arrested in 1994 and a year or so into my confinement, I learnt that Mandy had taken her life.

Mandy will always be a part of me, I know in my heart wherever Mandy is she would have found the happiness she so aboundly gave to others.

MESSAGE TO JENNY LEVIN (FLIESS)

Ever since reading your descriptive versions of the events that transpired during the course of your time at Arcadia, for reasons I cannot fully grasp, and without wanting to impose, I have felt a strong urge to contact you and extend a hand of friendship to you, but refrained till now. Before I proceed I am compelled to applaud your spell-binding compositions, the rhythmic flow of your sui-generis style of writing is totally captivating and no doubt ranks amongst the finest writers of our times. I sincerely mean that! Your account of Shul at the Arc was of particular significance to me, as Solly Farber rightfully commented that Shul played a central role in all our lives.

The religious aspects of the different generations that filtered through Arcadia remained constant and unchangeable. It's our traditions that has over the eons in effect contributed to the strength and survival of our people, as has the bond that bounds each and everyone of us.

Your vivid recollection of the order and sequence in which the shabbat service was conducted evoked some of the more celebrated times I had in Arcadia. I enjoyed a measure of popularity amongst the girls, and being Head Boy and the chazan for the remainder of my senior years January 1976 to December 1977 were the most memorable. The unique atmosphere inspired by kiddush and the singing of the shabbat songs blended with the intimate moments so many of us secretly shared during the service with our female counterparts, added and enhanced the festivities and the spiritual elevation of shabbat.

Shabbat is likened to a bride, and we were routinely expected to wear our finest clothes. We boys would go to great lengths, preparing ourselves for the occasion. I recall how some of us would blow-dry our hair or borrow matching shirts or trousers to look our best. Yom Tov was equally significant and rendered itself the rare opportunity of acquainting ourselves with girls from outside of Arcadia.

I recall on several occasions making eye contact with one of the girls I fancied, and in my quest to win over their hearts I would hold their hands longer than usual and when wishing them Shabbath Shalom I would kiss them more passionately than what was normal. The innocence of adolescence, what an intriguing and beautiful phase that was in our lives. Pesach seders were equally memorable. In those days, as tradition had it, each person was required to read a portion from the Haggadah. Normally, the dining room, during every seder, was filled with an array of guests that would range from ex-Arcs to committee members and from friends to family and relatives, reading your allotted portion in the midst of all these people was as nerve-racking as having your Barmitzvah all over again. What made matters worse and more challenging was that it was customary for the kids sitting in your immediate vicinity and opposite you, to by whatever means, distract your attention whilst reading. This was executed by various means such as pushing and pulling on your clothing or punching and tickling on whatever part of your anatomy was available. Another tactic was mimicking your reading and even going as far as throwing things at you. One can only imagine what a task it was to contain yourself. For the more confident readers it was the ultimate test and for the less accomplished it was most embarrassing.

After consuming a fair amount of kiddush wine I can assure you that very few of us could restrain the mumbling and fits of laughter we inevitably succumbed to. One would literally have had to be there to appreciate the hysterics of what could be described as an unscripted drama, reality TV at its best, we had such a gas. Vicky on the other hand never failed to express his disapproval and as a rule would peek angrily over the rim of his glasses and give you this "I will deal with you later" look, but never actually imposed the punitive measures his gaze conveyed.

During my years at Arcadia we had a Russian cook by the name of Zena, who epitomised your average stereotype post second world war Russian bureaucrat, she was short and corpulent and an inveterate smoker. Her bright red lipstick, matched the colour of her hair, combined with her hardened anaemic facial appearance managed to instil a degree of fear in most of us.

I remember one day Sammy Lasker and I being on the receiving end of one of her backhands. She caught us breaking into the pantry. Actually quite a few of us fell victim to her clutches. Auntie Zena, as she was known by most, prepared the most amazing Friday night meals, her roast potatoes and chicken was the best. She also served concocted Russian fried-rice which consisted of grated carrots, chopped onions, fried together with rice and was incredibly palatable.

While in Arcadia I developed an unusual habit and I couldn't help wondering if there were any of you who cultivated a similar tendency. It doesn't matter where I am and with whom, and as far back as I can remember, whenever I'm eating and or being served a meal I polish it off nearly as fast as it was served. This habit started when I was a Junior. We would always rush to finish our food, either out of fear that one of the Seniors would help themselves, or, so that we would be first for seconds. Friends of mine are continually amazed at the speed I'm able to consume my meals.

I see further in your account of events Jenny that in essence our experiences were in fact very similar. The annual outing to the Rand Easter Show was also a major occasion on our calendar. I couldn't have been more than 13 or 14 years old when I first visited the show, and quite enjoyed dropping in on the various countries' exhibitions, after which we all descended upon the amusement park.

After enjoying a few of the fairly normal rides, Sammy, Charles, Glen Osher, Eric and some of the others talked me into going with Georgie Marshak on the dive bomber. Whatever possessed me to acquiesce to their devious suggestion still eludes me to this day. The illustrious dive bomber was one of the most horrific rides I've ever been on. Imagine this. There we were, Georgie Marshak and I, in this rocket shaped capsule spinning and twirling backwards and then forward in a 360 degree circle. With every dive I honestly thought, due to its incredible momentum and the almost deafening sound of the monstrous motor and chain that drove it, that any second the

capsule was about to break loose from its structure, leaving us plummeting to earth.

I had uttered a thousand curses under my heavy breath, next thing I know Georgie began shrieking like a suicidal maniac. This all happened in a fraction of a second, within the start of the ride. I remember seeing Georgie's horror stricken face as he kept grabbing me and holding on for dear life. If only he knew that I was feeling equally as desperate and frightened, we were totally helpless and at the mercy of the steel monster, in a state of stupor. I too began screaming and shouting, hoping that the attendant would sympathise with our pleas and end the ride. The stupid attendant misinterpreted our cries and assumed that we were having a great time so what does he do, he extends the time. We survived the experience and fortunately for everyone the following year the menacing dive bomber was banned nation wide.

MESSAGE TO SOLLY FARBER AND OTHERS (2003)

I liked what you wrote, "*our Arc-ness defines us*" we are like none other, Thanks for all your compliments and the display of compassion towards my incarceration. Much time has passed since we last saw or spoke to each other. Although we never saw eye to eye during those years that you presided as the incumbent chairman, any notions of resentment that I may have harboured have obviously faded with the years, and I hope to still see you again one day.

It's been a rare privilege having had the occasion of having a glimpse into your life as an Arcadian, I was profoundly moved by the exceptionally well narrated account of your brother Moozy's life. My heart goes out to you. One can only imagine the pain and trauma you endured by his passing away, and the effect his loss had on you at such a vulnerable age. Your story brought tears to my eyes and all I can say is that Moozy would have been proud of you, for not only your achievements but as importantly for all the years you have devoted to Arcadia, and its children. If you wish I would happily paint his portrait in honour of not only his memory but also in respect of a unique brotherly bond that exists between you to this very day. I wish you strength and health.

One of the Ex-Arcs whose memory sticks out most in my mind was Donald Goldman. What a guy he was. He never missed Yom Tov. I remember him so well, always a friendly smile on his face and he holstered a mighty handshake.

SHANI'S LETTERS

Below are extracts from some of his letters

Letter To Vicky - April 1999 - It was only recently that I received a copy of the character reference that you had written on my behalf, which has subsequently been submitted as part of my personal petition for a Royal Pardon. Before I proceed, it is with greatest reverence that I would like to take this propitious moment to thank you for your highly acclaimed recommendations. Was I really such a commendable child? I kind of perceived myself somewhat differently.

On reading your support letter, not only was I overcome with a multitude of emotions, but also many memories came flooding to mind. Isn't it uncanny, just how swiftly time eludes us all, what may seem like a mere moment in endless time and space inescapably becomes years and even though the world is ever changing, everything remains the same, it is only the way that we perceive it that it changes.

It hasn't been an easy undertaking to write this letter, admittedly I feel a great sense of shame, I feel this for many reasons, which wouldn't be proper for me to delve too deeply therein. Many, many years have passed, yet my memory of you and everything you stood for is still so apparent. As we grow up we all go our separate ways, no two people are alike, every man an island unto himself, like none other. Having mostly led an obstreperous life-style, I continually found myself subjected or being left to the vicissitude of chance, and thus I find myself in this present predicament.

We all have a purpose in this life and there are times when people are completely blameless and undeserving, yet they are afflicted with great suffering, for reasons which are beyond our comprehension, perhaps it's to attenuate the material barriers that obscure their light, to strengthen them spiritually, whatever it may be, my present existence serves as an environment of challenge, growth and accomplishment.

On the 26th April 1999 will be five years that I've been incarcerated, absurd as it may seem, but I have managed to create a life here, one which has become of the greatest significance on so many levels. I have furthered my artistic skills in that I have mastered the art of portraiture, I have excelled in this field to a standard of excellence that surpassed my wildest dreams, my art compilation stands at over sixty pieces, I have developed an unrelenting passion for poetry and I've written in the vicinity of nearly one hundred poems. More importantly I have also been studying Torah for what's going on for nearly two years, which has changed my whole outlook on life and way of thinking, I feel spiritually elevated and with the knowledge and understanding that I have attained, I feel that I have enhanced a greater sense of serenity, I've also grown in wisdom. In Judaism we strongly rely on the traditions of our forefathers, yet it is imperative that at the same time we also arrive at our faith through our own philosophical endeavours. Even though my hopes for the future are looked upon with certain trepidations, I've learned to live in perfect faith, because Hashem has the perfect time for each and everyone of us, I know in my heart that in time my eventual emancipation will be a reality. May Hashem always be with you.

2000 - I'm going for 42 next year and I'm still very active. I exercise and play football six days a week. I'm physically in incredible shape and I've somehow managed to maintain a positive attitude, which is rather difficult under these circumstances, obviously I long for my freedom. There is a book written by an Australian called "*Damage Done*". His name is Warren Fellows. He spent about 12 years in Bangkwang Prison, if you read the book it will give you some idea of what one has to contend with. Anyway, I am not the type of person who complains. I do miss my family and friends very much, some days are harder than others, but generally I am well and thankful for my good health. Art has become my life and most days I'm either painting or drawing. I do correspond with numerous people around the world. Unfortunately we don't even have access to telephone, let alone computers. Our mail service it terrible and gets delayed for no reasons besides incompetency so most of my letters are smuggled out by the guards - at a price of course.

March 2001 - I'll be damned if life isn't full of surprises. You better believe it, but I have often thought of you and the ex-Arcs and wondered how many of you know about my predicament. Thanks for initiating a communication between us and also the enclosed copy of your recently published booklet of "*Arc Memories*".

Even though we were from a different generation after glancing at the photographs and reading the personal experiences of some of the ex-Arcs, I was overcome with an overwhelming sense of nostalgia, memories of my own life in Arcadia and my childhood as a whole sprung to thought. Besides Morris Landsman who has visited me here in Thailand and with whom I'm in regular contact with, I've lost contact with most of the other Arcs, which is rather sad, but also understandable.

As with most Arcs my childhood was filled with excitement and adventure. No doubt each and every one of us has a story to tell each unique in their own right.

Besides the long-term psychological affects of leading a life of continual deprivation most of us will agree that we had it relatively good. While the non disciplinary aspect of our upbringing is open to criticism, which set us apart from other children, we were different. This distinction is particularly obvious in the environment I presently find myself in. I'm not advocating that this disparity is considered an impediment, but rather the contrary. I'm serving a life sentence in one of the world's most notorious maximum security prisons where conditions are beyond human comprehension, for a crime I was unaware of committing. Anyway, the point I'm trying to make is, as with any type of institution it is the finest and strongest that always survive. In addition to our capacity to endure extreme levels of suffering whether physical or mental, we Arcs grew up with high standards and strong morals, we always stood up for what we believed was right, such loyalty that exists between Arcadians is rarely found anywhere, and I'm proud of the fact that I'm an Arcadian.

On 26 April, 2001 it will be seven years that I've been incarcerated, it's a crazy world, yet somehow I managed to create a life for myself which very few of you could relate to, I have utilised my time constructively in that I have furthered my artistic skills and have become quite a prolific painter.

Art is an experience of the inner self, an infinite journey of the mind, where the parameters are defined by the imagination, Every picture has become a process of discovery and challenge, an exploration of the unknown. My own inspiration became a means of penetration deeper and deeper into an understanding of people and the world that has forsaken me, and with every creation not only did my spirit become more and more free but as importantly my anger dissipated. While none of us can fathom what the future holds in store, and while I may look upon my own future with certain trepidations, I've learnt to live in perfect faith, my life is in the hands of Hashem.

September 2001 - No doubt most of you are cognizant of the so to speak "inevitable sale of Arcadia". I don't know about the rest of you but personally I was quite distraught and even exasperated by this most unwelcomed revelation, no defence can justify the ruthless disposal of part of our heritage. I had envisaged a grander destiny for the home that became a monumental relic and a link to the past for so many. Surely other alternatives could have been pursued such as declaring it a national museum or converting it into an art gallery which would adequately finance its restoration and day to day maintenance. A sad moment in time. Where will we congregate to celebrate Yom-Tov. It is clear that we have become a dying breed widening an already deepened rift between so many of us.

Gone are the days when reminiscing of past events filled us with a sense of nostalgia and a belonging to a more meaningful past. Compelling memories that can never be erased will now be a lingering figment of the imagination, a mere illusion that can only be accentuated by our shared knowledge of those experiences.

Ever since the success of the *Arc Memory Booklets,* I have felt an uncontrollable urge to make contact with many of my contemporaries as these booklets provide the perfect forum for us Arcs to become re-acquainted and to communicate with each other by sharing thoughts, ideas and experiences. While many of us stand alone in this world no man is an island, and while some of us openly preserve past memories, there are many of you who are reticent of your own.

Like it or not we are all part of a greater family and there is so much we can learn from each other. So many of us are driven by material gains and success that we never stop to contemplate the meaning of life and our purpose in G-d's master plan, and how often do we consider those who are less fortunate than ourselves. In my readings I came across a thought provoking aphorism that had a profound impact on my own attitude towards people, and would like to share it with you, I believe it came from the Teachings of the Talmud, "If I am not for myself, who is for me? And if I am only for myself, what am I

That's powerful stuff and if I may take this propitious moment to thank those Ex-Arcadians who took the time and effort to write to me, mainly being, David Sandler, Shelley Grishkan, Lynette Bark, Glen Osher, Morris Landsman, Hymie Sacks, Barney Segal, Michael Perry Kotzen from Israel and Mary and David Kotzen from the United States. Making contact with you all was like finding a long lost family member and as such I cherish our correspondence and newfound friendships.

On request from David I once again find myself putting pen to paper and delving into the past in search of some memorable events. Whoever said that David *(Sandler)* was not a demanding person, and at this rate he will more than likely have us writing a book about our experiences. I think it is great and I really hope that more of you will step forward in the future and share your own encounters. Reveal yourself.

Shani as Prefect making a thank-you speech at the Vereeniging Picnic

February 2002 - With restrained forbearance I waited for more than three and a half interminably tedious years for an answer to my personal petition requesting a Royal Pardon, then like a lightning bolt from the heavens on August 17 calamity struck its hardest blow yet. I was callously informed, by the prison authorities, that my personal petition requesting a Royal Pardon had been rejected. My immediate concern was for my family, who I know would be shattered by the news, I on the other hand have grown accustomed to adversity and affliction and accepted the outcome with surprising equanimity.

Having served nearly eight years of my sentence and still not knowing my eventual day of release, and especially when so many other western foreigners are being transferred to prisons in their own country, and are being released after a few months, certainly makes my situation that much worse. Unmoved by the horrific reality of my fate, I have still managed to retain a sound state of mind and that ever-burning vestige of hope that the bonds of my captivity will one day be lifted and I will once again breathe the air of freedom.

Yet despite my misfortune and the constant hardships I've been subjected to during the course of my life, my ideals and principles remain unsullied, as have my aspirations and dreams survived. I am driven by the knowledge that my journey in life is only beginning, and while I may not fully understand the order of occurrences and their reasons, as the situation stands, I have little choice but to accept what transpires, and maybe years from now in the distant future it will all make sense.

January 2003 - A heartfelt thank you for yet another great booklet, in what appears to have evolved into the continued saga of a coterie of people, whose trials and tribulations are a testimony of their distinguished personalities and unshakable virtues. I am constantly imbued with an immense sense of pride by our association, and overwhelmed by the unconditional acceptance of the majority of ex-Arcs, who have tenaciously contributed their literary disquisitions to your much acclaimed prodigious works.

Few words can describe the immeasurable delight we have derived through your unrivalled devotion in spanning an interest, and laying the foundations for a playground where ex-Arcadians from around the globe, are given the opportunity to share their lives and perpetuating an unforgettable past, of a people whose memories and experiences have their rightful place in the archives of South Africa's Jewry. Additionally, you have not only encouraged, supported and promulgated my circumstances but also inspired many aspects of my existence. I thank you for that.

While I enthusiastically read through "*More of Arcs* and *Arc Memories*", as with previous editions, I found myself being effortlessly transported into another world, an alluring age of innocence and untainted beauty

December 2005 - I was ecstatic to learn that you finally decided to write a book. I'm real excited for you and honoured that you want to devote an entire chapter to me. You are more than welcome to use any extracts from my letters and feature whichever pictures of my art you want.

I'm definitely in a far better frame of mind than before. Seeing my family after so many years has unquestionably revived my

enthusiasm for life and awakened a legion of longings. As my nephew Darren would say 'It was totally awesome'. I hadn't seen my niece and nephew for almost 12 years. Initially I was extremely apprehensive and nervous as to how they would react to me, as fortune would have it we all got on really well, and I sensed that the kids who are basically all grown up, were impressed with their uncle. They are such wonderful and well mannered children. I felt so proud on one hand and ashamed on the other for bringing such dishonour to my family, not to mention the suffering and torment they have endured through my blunders.

All our futures are determined by Hashem. Hashem in all his goodness is bound to show his abundant mercy and until such time I believe with a strong conviction that a greater purpose awaits me. But if I may add the fact that there are people who care and are willing to offer assistance whether moral or financial is reassuring and of great comfort and eases my suffering.

On the 9th of June 2006, the King of Thailand will be celebrating his 60th anniversary on the throne making him the longest reigning monarch of modern times. We are praying and hoping that an amnesty will be decreed and that drug offenders will benefit equally.

Children alighting bus at Vereeniging Picnic

POEMS BY SHANI KREBS

SHADOWS

Man may sculpt a rose
our destiny nobody knows
only shadows follow us
where one goes
A divine fool!

DAYS AND DAYS

There is no such day as tomorrow
Every day has become the same
If there was a day that one could borrow
the day after today
would be the same as tomorrow

THE SEA-GULLS CRY

In my dreams I hear the mermaid's songs
she calls me all night long
The ever-changing tides
Awake the sea-gulls cries

Frail my emotions have come to be
For it is the sunset I cannot see
Oh! how beautifully the stars would shine
if only you were mine

STARLESS MOON

If you gazed into my tearful eyes
you would hear my fearful cries
if you felt my aching heart-beat
you would know my never-ending need

When thou art not near me
I feel as barren as a withered tree
I see not the stars nor the moon
the wind carries my lovers tune

The sun does not shine for me
Whilst we cannot be
I feel your breath
an enchantment of my death

WALLS

My life revolves around walls
walls that seem so high
that you cannot see the sky
yet the sky is not so high
as the walls seem to touch the sky
Oh! how I wish I could fly

A MESSAGE TO ACCOMPANY MY ART

September 2001 - Although my experiences in life have been extremely diversified, prison life by contrast is very different to anything I've ever encountered. It can either make you or break you, I chose to avoid the latter. From the very onset of my incarceration I firmly believed that this was my destiny and my primary objective was survival.

My journey hasn't been an easy one. I have devoted uninterrupted years to developing my artistic skills, any less of a commitment would simply never had yielded the escalating ascendancy that has arisen from my dedication and an appreciation for the depth of understanding of my purpose in this so called mysterious puzzle that most of you know as life. Without allowing my emotions to exceed my talents, it is my dream to make my mark on leaving behind a legacy of paintings before I depart, or choose to, from this planet.

My art is fundamentally an exploration of the self and nothing more than but a means of escaping my reality. At first the only medium available to me was a black ball point pen, as the colour black became a symbol of my despair and oppression. It has never been about fame or fortune, and here I must ask you, what is fame without freedom.

2004 - Art is my passion and I must confess, as would be any artist's dream, that over the years I wanted nothing more than to be recognised, at an appropriate time, as an artist. Just recently the South African Ambassador, after viewing some of my work, asked me if I would be interested in exhibiting some of my art at their forthcoming 10 year anniversary celebration, and also commissioned me to do portraits of the Thai Monarchy, which I enthusiastically agreed to do. While I may secretly harbour visions of success, I have never taken my talent for granted, my humility is undiminished by the adulation I've received, yet as time draws closer I am overcome by a sense of apprehension. My art, a form of self-expression and exploration has always been very private and it seemed only right that it remained concealed from the eyes of the world. It belonged in the shadows of the realm that inspired its very existence, or perhaps the degree of reluctance I feel, is the fear of exposure, the very recognition I once longed for now haunts me, who knows? Where do we go from here?

Shani Krebs is still in prison in Thailand and in April 06 it will be 12 years of his 40 year sentence served. I urge you all to write to him and not to judge him. I think any support we give him will help him and will strengthen his will to continue with his art, which is his escape.

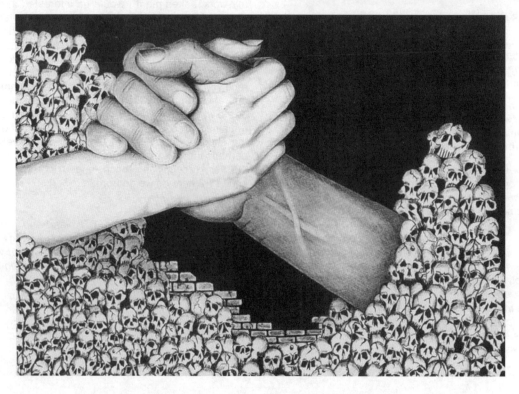

King Bhumibhul of Thailand -- "The Strength of the Nation

The Queen of Thailand –" The Mother of the Nation"

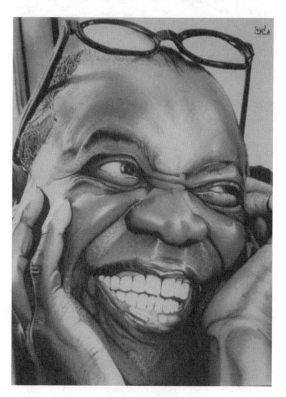

Louis Armstrong

Cary Grant et Ingrid BergmanDans les enchaines

26 January 2001 (Watercolour)

Battle scarred faces" in four-walled city towns
9 January 2001(Watercolour)

"Still life" 2 November 2000 (Pastel)

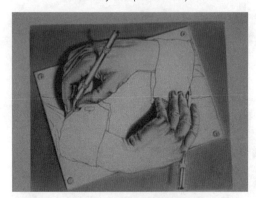

March 2002

"Child Slaver y"The children of Etireno
born into the clutches of greed

30 October 2001

Loana – Verse's from a gypsy's song

The Virgin Mary

19 October 2001

475

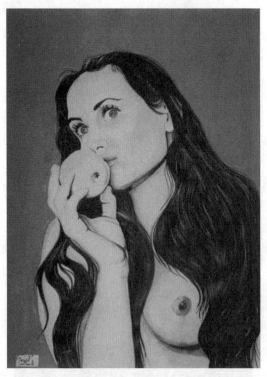

"En dessous d'un oranger" (From under an orange tree.)
February 2001 (Watercolour)

"Unmasked beauty" emerges from the snow storm
4 February 2001 (Watercolour)

"Soul searcher" 30 October 2000 (Pastel)

25 February 2001 (Watercolour)

CHANGES IN CHILDCARE PHILOSOPHY – AND *'VERLIGTE'*
1980s ONWARDS

"The days when a children's home was essentially only a place for the kids to live, have passed. We now have to provide a therapeutic environment in which to bring up the kids and to handle all facets of their care"

S A Farber, Chairman 1983

"In Arcadia we have our full time staff. The Director, Clinical Psychologist, Social worker, Child Care workers and Domestic Assistants. All play their part in the day to day care of the children."

Dr Shalom Faber, Chairman of Arcadia, 1997

1987 Seder Rehearsal

New Name
Bulletin for Year Ended March 31st, 1982

Arcadia South African Jewish Orphanage is now Arcadia Jewish Children's Home

New mission statement
Bulletin for Year Ended March 31st, 1984

Arcadia cares for Jewish children in need of a specialised residential or daycare environment.
We respond to the needs of children in this community who require specialised treatment in order to achieve a healthy family life.

Arcadia provides opportunities on physical, social, emotional, academic and spiritual levels so that our children can develop to their full potential.

Arcadia shares this parenting task with families, so that healing and family re-unification can be achieved".

I have as yet collected very few Arc Memories covering this period because of the low number of children in residence and because these children would all be caught up with the daily struggles of making a living and they would not have had time to look back and reflect over their childhood in Arcadia. I'm confident that with the passage of time these memories will emerge.

In the late 1970s and onwards there were various factors at play which completely changed the dynamics at Arcadia and as a result the need for the large estate disappeared.

With a change in childcare philosophy there was a dramatic reduction in the number of children in residence at Arcadia and at the same time new modern childcare philosophies and methods were introduced in Arcadia.

The extracts from the Annual Bulletin tell about the changes that occurred in the childcare philosophy of Arcadia and the plan to sell the estate and relocate to the north eastern suburbs.

REDUCTION THE NUMBERS OF CHILDREN

The philosophy of childcare in Arcadia changed and it was deemed to be more beneficial to support the children in their family environment. The introduction of the Cottage Scheme in August 1969 was an extension of this Philosophy.

The number of children actually in residence in Arcadia decreased gradually from an average of 107 in the 1950s, to 74 in the 1960s, 36 in the 1970s, 30 in the 1980s and steadied out around the 25 mark thereafter.

The number of "children in need and never in Arcadia" increased from 62 in 1950, to 127 in 1963 but generally ranged between the 80-120 children from 1960 to 1993 when the number shot up from 147 to 264 in 2001.

ARCADIA'S NEW NAME
Bulletin for Year Ended March 31st, 1982

The decision to change our name was taken at the last Annual General Meeting of the Institution. After 75 years Arcadia has ceased to be the Arcadia SA Jewish Orphanage and is now Arcadia Jewish Children's Home. This change reflects more than a mere change of name; it reflects a new image of ourselves, and certainly describes more accurately our place and function in the community.

Arcadia is not, and has not for many years been an orphanage. It is a children's home, with all that that warm appellation implies.

Annual Bulletin 1988-1989

Report and Balance Sheet for year ended 31st March 1989

ARCADIA

The change of name and status is perhaps the most important single development in Arcadia's recent history.

ARCADIA MISSION STATEMENT
Bulletin for Year Ended March 31st, 1984

Arcadia cares for Jewish children in need of a specialised residential or daycare environment.

We respond to the needs of children in this community who require specialised treatment in order to achieve a healthy family life.

Arcadia provides opportunities on physical, social, emotional, academic and spiritual levels so that our children can develop to their full potential.

Arcadia shares this parenting task with families, so that healing and family re-unification can be achieved.

THE CHILD DEVELOPMENT COMMITTEE
Bulletin for Year Ended March 31st, 1984
By SA Farber CHAIRMAN

As I stated in last year's bulletin, the days when a children's home was essentially only a place for the kids to live, have passed. We now have to provide a therapeutic environment in which to bring up the kids and to handle all facets of their care. I believe that this, the Child Development Committee plays a huge part in that direction.

The Child Development Committee meets every month at a supper meeting. The matters discussed revolve mainly around the children and problems they are encountering.

As the problems are often of an emotional or sociological nature the committee itself is comprised of professionals. We have medical men and our social worker, together with the Director and Matron and the Chairman of Arcadia. The Education sub-committee chairman is also an important member.

A unique feature of our meetings is the opportunity they afford for the many people involved with the kids to meet each other and plan an integrated approach to each individual child and to the child's problem.

This ensures that we are not pulling in different directions and hence not undermining each other's efforts. Social workers from the Transvaal Jewish Family Council also attend. This liaison is very fruitful and ensures an easy passage for children either entering or leaving Arcadia's care.

The sub-committee was instituted only three years ago and has repeatedly proved its value. We have, as it were, learnt on the job and have developed an efficient modus operandi. Acute problems are dealt with as they arise and matters of general principle are discussed regularly.

Each member of the team has brought their own particular expertise to our deliberations and this provides the best chance for making sensible and all embracing decisions when required.

As Chairman of the group I would like to thank all the members who have so readily given their time to help us and Arcadia do well by the children.

A new idea which has been instituted is for one of our psychiatrists to hold a clinic at Arcadia once a month. This is usually held a few days prior to this sub-committee's meetings. The doctor concerned can then give up to the minute reports and advice to the group at our meetings. For this I thank Dr Allan Miller who has really been a fountain of knowledge and expert advice to us.

Another innovation has been meetings of the Chairman of this group with the Housemothers in Arcadia. An exchange of views takes place and the ladies who have the 24-hour-a-day care of the kids need no longer feel that they are working in isolation.

We will continue to do our best for Arcadia and the Arcadians and work towards our ultimate goal which is to assist Arcadia to nurture happy and healthy children who can take their place in society or with their own families as well balanced Jewish South Africans.

CHILD DEVELOPMENT COMMITTEE
Bulletin for Year Ended March 31st, 1990
By Dr S A Farber - Chairman - Child Development Committee

The Child Development Committee has been in existence for the past ten years. It has become an integral part of the management of Arcadia and plays a most important role in the Care of our Children.

The people who serve on this committee include all those members of the Staff who are involved in the care of the children; the director, the Social Worker, the House-parents, the Clinical Psychologist, the Doctors on our Medical Board, and certain members of the Committee. As such we regard this as our Professional Committee.

This Group has the responsibility to ensure the best care for the children; to plan for and enhance the emotional wellbeing of the Arcadians; and to deal with their medical sociological and related problems.

In planning for a particular child we invite any other experts and interested parties to help us. This may be teacher or Headmaster, School Social worker, parent or even friend of the family.

In effect, therefore, we gather together all the people who may be concerned with the child. This approach has been the main committee strength of this and has made it so very effective. We have the full history available to us and all the differing attributes of the child. This enables us to make decisions which are valid and comprehensive.

We like to think that out of all this comes the best possible plan for our precious charges.

In the past year Arcadia has made another change designed to rationalise our Childcare Program. The sub-committees that have impact on the welfare of the children now report directly to this Committee. They include the Education Committee, the Day-Care-Centre Committee, the Aftercare Committee and most importantly, the Clinical Committee.

The Clinical Committee is convened by Michael Niss our Psychologist. He meets with the Senior Staff of Arcadia and they formulate a plan for the future of each child. The plan takes into account the abilities, the needs and the wants of that boy or girl. The very fact that we have a 'life-plan' makes it more certain that we will handle the child in a consistent manner and consistency is precisely what our children so desperately need.

Of course we realize that people and times can change and so we regularly update our plan for each child. We also do not want to force a child along a particular route. Our philosophy is that we must lay out the road ahead, but it is up to the child to step onto the path and to go along that path. The road is not set in concrete and we are delighted if a youngster indicates an interest in a different direction.

In Arcadia we have a warm caring approach to the children. This warmth is generated by the wonderful staff. Everybody plays their special part to give that special Arcadian feeling. This is perhaps the most important thing that The Arc does for the children.

For this we have to thank Gerry, Dianiella, Vicky and the Housemothers.

Michael Niss has been our Clinical Psychologist for the past two years and has been a marvel. His expertise is really important to us.

Of the doctors, those who have been particularly involved are Doctors Joe Teeger and Robyn Friedlander. Their help is invaluable and we thank them for their time and their interest.

We have had a busy and interesting year and look forward to the challenges of another year of service to Arcadia and the Arcadians.

EXTRACT OF THE CHAIRMAN REPORTS
Bulletin for Year Ended March 31st, 1997
By Dr Shalom Faber

Another year has passed and here we are at the start of another year, another year of caring for children.

We live and function in a world that is constantly changing. The style and manner of caring for children goes through paradigmal shifts as deep and wide as those in any other sphere of human activity. In former years it was deemed sufficient to provide food, a warm and dry place to sleep and a roof over the head for children and admission to Arcadia was easily resorted to. Now we regard the removal of a child from the family and admission to an institution [even one as excellent as Arcadia] as the very last resort.

This attitude has brought about profound changes for us. Now we have fewer children in our Home, but we have more children under our care. The need is to provide funds [and other resources] to assist these children in their own homes rather than admit them to Arcadia.

Back Row, L to R: Mr A Saul, Mr J Esekow, Mr S Goldsmith, Mr M Kaplan, Dr S Farber (Chairman)
Dr S Milner, Mr M Gaddin, Mr S Paikin, Mr B Meyers, Mr S Chalmers, Mr J Orelowitz
Front Row, L to R: Mr E Osrin, Mrs D Shulman, Ms D Shulman, Ms D Kanareck, Mr S Dembo, Mr S Klevansky, Mr L L Lipschitz, Mr H Harris
Away Overseas: Ms D Nightingale

Top row: Mrs L. Katz, Mrs A. Kaplan, Mrs M. Lazarus, Mrs D. Keplushnik, Mrs S. Edelman

Middle row: Dr S. Nelson, Mr G. Blackman, Mr H. Shaff, Mr H. Kabe, Mr M. Ladier

Bottom row: Mrs S. Stein, Mrs M. Perrer, Mr A.B. Treisman, Miss S. Chalmers, Mr G. Chalmers

General Committee and Senior Staff 1997

Arcadia in Action

Our activities are many and varied and can be summarized as follows:

We provide a safe, therapeutic environment for children who need that type of care. This involves many people and is fully described in the other reports in this bulletin.

Arcadia is an integral part of the community

An organisation such as Arcadia cannot function without the active involvement of many people. One can say that ultimately everyone in the community plays some part either big or small in the activities of Arcadia. In Arcadia we have our full time staff. The Director, Clinical Psychologist, Social worker, Child Care workers and Domestic Assistants. All play their part in the day to day care of the children.

From all that I have said it is clear that Arcadia has deep roots in the fabric of the Jewish and secular communities of this region of our land. We are indeed a well known and well loved part of the local scene.

We look forward to many more years of serving the Community and caring for those children in the Community who may need our help.

Thank you for all your support. Please continue to help us in our dear task.

EXTRACT OF THE CHAIRMAN REPORTS
Bulletin for Year Ended March 31st, 1998
By Dr Shalom Farber

New times - New ideas

We have reached a watershed in the Arcadia epic. Time has moved on. The needs of the community have changed. The Child Care paradigm has changed. The number of children requiring Institutional Care has diminished.

For these and other reasons we have come to the realisation that it is time for us to move our activities to a smaller facility where we can provide a more intimate environment for the children and a more affordable home for the Institution. To this end our Forward Planning Committee has been working for the past two years to map out a new future for Arcadia. The Estate is being offered for sale. Our staff structure is being revised and we will have to function with a much smaller 'team'. Hopefully this will enable us to survive the severe economic plight which encompasses us at present. As this scenario unfolds we will keep our members and our community ;'au fait' with developments.

It is clear that Arcadia depends on many, many people to carry on her exquisite and essential duties. My thanks to each and everyone who has contributed in whatever manner to our cause.

THE CHAIRMAN WRITES
Year Ended March 31st, 1999
By Dr Shalom Faber

In trying to conserve the funds of Arcadia, we have attempted to decrease our expenses, and we have reduced our staff complement. Our ex-Director, Gerry Orelowitz, is emigrating and our long-standing Secretary, Stanley Goldsmith, has retired. We have reduced the staff to maintain the estate and look after the children. The staff of Arcadia are very well aware of the financial problems and there has been close attention given to reducing the costs of running Arcadia as regards food, clothing and other expenses.

Arcadia is now run with two co-directors. Selwyn Chalmers has been appointed Director of Arcadia and runs the office, and is directly in control of all of the finances of the institution. Our Social Worker, Daniella Kanareck, has become the Program Director and she is directly responsible for the care of the children, and is fully informed as to the finances so that we can carefully choose what outsourcing is needed to look after our most precious possessions, our children. These two new posts replace four previous posts in keeping with our need to protect our funds. The new management style has resulted in a distinct improvement in communication. We are certain that there will be a great change in the way that Arcadia is run.

The nurturing of the needs of our children in respect of their health, psychological wellbeing, their education and development is superbly taken care of. I must compliment and thank all of the staff concerned: Daniella Kanareck, Adina Menhard, our beloved Vicky Klevansky and our newest Child Care worker Mmule Mashiyane.

We are proud of our good name in the Jewish and secular communities.

FORWARD PLANNING COMMITTEE
Bulletin for Year Ended March 31st, 2000

As its name implies, this committee has to anticipate Arcadia's future needs and plan and provide for those needs. The members of this sub-committee are the office bearers of Arcadia and a number of other members who have special expertise or enthusiasm to offer.

The community we serve has become smaller in recent years, but the number of families and individuals requiring assistance has actually increased. This reality is reflected in our finances which, have - to say the least - become most parlous. We are providing an increasing service load from a decreasing 'fiscus'. These are some of the matters that have concerned us recently:

The Arcadia Property

The Villa Arcadia has been our home for many decades. It is a most beautiful and valuable property, but has become unsuitable for our needs. The property is large and the maintenance of the numerous buildings and the extensive grounds is a heavy burden on our finances. In addition to this, it has been apparent to us for some years that the present campus is not ideal for the housing of our children.

For the past five years we have been attempting to sell the Arcadia property or to use the asset in a practical and favourable way. Thus far we have not been able to achieve our aims. The campaign to sell Arcadia has moved into a new phase and you may have noticed the very large sign on our grounds, facing the M1 motorway advertising Arcadia 'For Sale or Rent'. We are most serious in our intent to sell.

Relocating our children

We need to house our children differently and in a different environment, this is very clear to us. With our diminishing reserves and poor income we have only been able to dream about achieving this aim until and unless we could sell our property. Thankfully we now have another option to move forward with our plan. Due to a most generous donation that was made to us from the Liberty Life Trust - through the good offices of Hilton Applebaum and of the Chevrah Kadisha - we can achieve that dream. We have been seeking, and have already earmarked two lovely houses in the north eastern suburbs to purchase. This will place our children right in the middle of a Jewish 'medinah' where they can interact with the local community, make friends and have easy access to Shuls, sport clubs, libraries and the like.

The wheels are already in motion and we hope to make the move within the next six months. Once we have the houses we will undertake repairs and improvements to satisfy the needs of a rather 'large family'.

Planning the Big Move

As desirable as the move is, it does require careful planning. It is not simply a matter of loading the children and the staff onto buses and dropping them off in our new premises. We will have to plan and co-ordinate the various aspects. A new style of living will necessitate a new staffing structure. Our present staff have given us years and years [and in some cases, decades] of service. Their needs have also to be considered.

The security and integrity of the Arcadia property has to be ensured during the move. For a while we will have to manage our new home[s] and Arcadia. This will further stretch our resources. Our administrative offices are at present on the Arcadia campus. The office will most probably need a new home base. This will be researched, planned and provided. In addition to these cardinal issues engaging our attention there are many other problems and issues for us to sort out. We meet regularly to try to plan for all of these real and potential needs. My sincere thanks to all the members of this committee, to Mike Kirchmann for his valuable input, to Hymie Moross our honorary architect, Steve Jaspan our town planner and to the many other people who have helped us in our work.

We are looking forward to a very full and a most significant year for Arcadia and for this Forward Planning Committee.

ANNUAL BULLETIN 2000-2001 – GENERAL COMMITTEE

OFFICE BEARERS:

Honorary Presidents:

Dr C P Nelson, Mr L Teeger, Mr E Osrin, Dr S A Farber, Mr A P Hepker, Mr S Dembo, Mr G Blackman, Dr S Milner

Honorary Vice-Presidents: - Mesdames C Sasto, S Stein

Chairman: -	Mr M Gaddin
Vice-Chair: -	Mr S Paikin
Honorary Treasurer: -	Dr S Farber
Honorary Secretary: -	Mrs M Ferrer
Trustees: -	Mr M Ladier, Mr A B Treisman, Mr B Meyers

Other Members of Committee:

Mr S Arenson	Mr S Klevansky
Mr D C Datnow	Mr K Lang
Mr J Esekow	Mr D R Levy
Mr S Goldsmith	Dr M Niss
Mr D Kapeluschnik	Mr A Saul
Mr M Kaplan	Mr G Saul
Mr D Shulman	

Ex-Officio Members of the General Committee:

Dr H Utian, Chairman Medical Board, Dr Z Isenberg, Chairman Dental Board,
Chief Rabbi C K Harris, Rabbi M D Standfield

Auditors: -	Messrs Horwath Leveton Boner
Honorary Solicitors: -	Moss-Morris Inc
Honorary Architects: -	Moross and Partners Inc

Honorary Life Members of Arcadia:
Mrs D Gilchrist, Mrs L Bader, Mrs F Marks, Mrs S Stein, Mrs C Sasto, Mrs B Krasin, Mr A B Treisman, Dr M Davimes, Mr S Goldsmith, Mr S Klevansky, Mr M Ladier, Mr B Meyers, Mr Henry Harris.

Chapter 128 – JAVIN WEINSTEIN (1965)

My brothers Paul (born 1967), Darren (born 1966) and Stefan (born 1963) and I were all in the care of Arcadia from 1977 to 1984. I was there from 1977 to 1983 when I completed my matric at King David Victory Park.

We were all there with the Laskers, Oshers, Krebs, Landsmans (van Zyls) and Mandy Livingston.

My younger brother Darren became an athletics icon, winning the Arcadia marathon and six cross country's at school. He also won numerous awards on the soccer, rugby and cricket fields, unfortunately his knees weren't strong enough for the rigors of professional sport.

Paul won a place in the Transvaal schools rugby team at the provincial tournament and I and Stefan were pretty average at everything we did and contemplated playing in various sports teams. Paul and Darren both live is Israel somewhere close to Alec and Gooti Saul (G-D bless them both) on Kibbutz Hanita and Sa'ar respectively and are both married to Israeli girls.

Stefan is in the furniture business with my oldest brother Lewis and my sister Marlene. They are also married with two children each.

I'm in the life assurance industry with Liberty Life and am enjoying myself immensely. I'm married to Angie de Aguiar and have three beautiful children (two daughters and a son).

We are still very good friends with the Laskers and Oshers and have contact with them often. When you are blessed with friends like we have and a wonderful family then you realise Hashem has smiled on me.

Javin, Reg Lasker and Paul Weinstein - 1980

Javin, Reg Lasker, the Deputy Mayor of Jhb and Calvin Quinto at our Barmizvah - 1979

1981 Boys- Adrian and Grant Kruger are at the back and Michael Gordon and Steven Kapaluschnik in the front.

Bneimitzvah-Verna Smith, Wendy Rubenstein, Eleanor Landsman and Darren Weinstein with the late Chief Rabbi Casper - 1980

Chapter 129 – STEVEN IAN KENIGSBERG (1982-2002)

Steven was born in Johannesburg on the 17th of July 1982 and was in the care of Arcadia from 1995 to 2000.

Steven was killed in Israel on the 3rd of March 2002 at the age of 19 on active duty as a Magen David Adom (MDA) volunteer in the Israeli Army.

REMEMBERING STEVEN

Steven went to primary school at King David, Linksfield and stayed at the hostel. Later he came to Arcadia and went to KES (King Edward High School). He was Chairman of the Arcadia Youth Committee He had a very good nature with many positive attributes which was recognised by his peers. He had a wonderful sense of humour and Adina Menhard says that he made everyone laugh a lot.

One of his peers writes: "Steven was exceptionally intelligent and mature far beyond his years. He was sensitive - a great confidante - always thoughtful and kind. He was always helpful and was there for anyone who needed help. He was great company, great to be with, with a wonderful sense of humour. He was very patriotic to Israel and always planned to make Aliya."

Selwyn Chalmers wrote: "Writing about the death of Steven Kenigsberg brought back the feeling of sadness and shock we felt when this happened. I know that people always speak well of someone in circumstances like this, but he was truly a really likeable young guy, with a gentle nature. I was at Arcadia when Steven Kenigsberg first arrived and of course when he left for Israel. He was indeed a lovely young man - gentle and sensitive. We were all devastated when we heard the news of his death.

According to Vicky he was a truly lovely person, and very proud to be in the Israeli army.

Steven, as an Magen David Adom (MDA) volunteer, in the Israeli Army, ran to help those wounded by sniper fire and was killed as well by the sniper.

He is survived by his parents; Kevin and Linda-Ann Kenigsberg, his grandmothers Hannah Kenigsberg and Ray Segal and his brothers Mark and Joel Kenigsberg.

NEWSPAPER ARTICLES

Selwyn Chalmers sent two articles from Israeli newspapers.

The front page of the newspaper is covered with the photos of 21 Israelis killed that week by the Intafadah. According to the article (dated 8 March 2002) 21 soldiers and citizens were killed that same day, including 12 soldiers and citizens at a military checkpoint near Ofra in the Shomron which was targeted by a

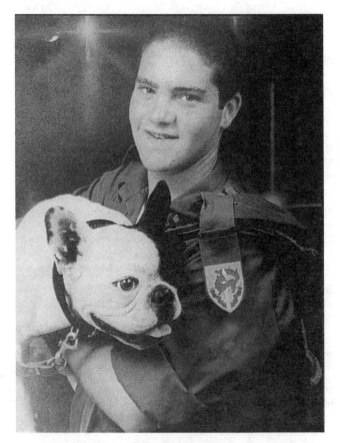

Steven Kenigsberg

sniper. Steven, as an MDA volunteer, ran to help the wounded and was killed as well by the sniper.

The articles are from the *Ma'ariv* newspaper and translate as follows.

STEVEN KENIGSBERG OF BLESSED MEMORY

Steven's father was interviewed yesterday. He said that Steven's death was not in vain and that because of soldiers like his son Steven, we are able to live securely in this country, Israel, which is the only country we Jews have.

Steven was nineteen and a half and from Hod Hasharon. Steven Kenigsberg was killed yesterday in a shoot-out on the army post of the Kissofim area.

Steven and his father immigrated to Israel two and a half years ago. The father said yesterday that Steven loved the life in Israel from the moment that he arrived in Israel - he wanted to go into the army and to prove himself on the battlefield, and to defend Israel. He was praised for being an excellent soldier.

At Succoth he was honoured by an invitation to meet the Prime Minister. He was extremely proud of that. He phoned us to say that he was involved in an incident with terrorists who had cut through fence at Kissofim. We were worried and frightened for him but we knew that he was doing his duty in spite of the danger.

The father said, that he and Steven immigrated to Israel because they were Zionist and that they believed that Israel was the only Jewish country.

Steven joined the Betar movement at an early age in South Africa. He was brought up on Zionist ideals. At sixteen and a half he immigrated to Israel with his father. They left their family in South Africa.

Tal Glazer, the shaleach of Betar at the time and Steven's madrich, said; 'Steven always wanted to be a soldier. It was not surprising that he chose to serve on the battlefront!'

The Caption under picture reads: Steven Kenigsberg was chosen as an excellent soldier.

A NATIONAL HERO OF ISRAEL

Steven Kenigsberg's father, Kevin, told reporters that Stephan's dog Shmaltz, walks about the house restlessly and obviously misses Steven. We all miss him. Everyone loved Steven. He was very sociable and friendly. In the absorption centre Steven was a 'success story'. When we came from South Africa, Steven was very South African in manner and personality.

An ex-South African acquaintance told me two months ago that Steven walks and talks in the same way and intonation as an Israeli. He had become a thorough Israeli. He had integrated completely in two and a half years. In the 24 hours after Steven's death a further 20 Israeli soldiers and civilians lost their lives. Each one with a tragic story and their life experiences and memories.

Aidene, Steven's step-mother, remembers Steven as facetious and funny and full of life. 'Steven was well able to please and amuse everybody' said Aidene. 'He always volunteered. He was particularly sensitive to the 'underdogs' and the less fortunate in society. He was a most responsible young man'

Friends said that Steven was always very kind and helpful. He never wanted to fail or to disappoint. 'We took our problems to Steven'. 'He was always a smiling, happy, well mannered and modest young man'.

Tearfully his father, Kevin, said 'Steven would help old people to cross a street!' Steven will forever be a young hero of Israel. We will love him always. We are very proud of Steven. He protected us in Israel and now he will protect us from heaven!

Steven Kenigsberg aged $19^1/_2$ took a direct hit of a bullet in his throat. The four other Israeli soldiers with Stephan were injured light to medium. The terrorist managed to escape.

Steven's father, Kevin, remembers the first time Steven went to Gaza. He telephoned me from the bus to tell me he was travelling to Gaza. He said 'I love you Dad'. I told him that I loved him, said Kevin. I could sense that he was afraid.

Steven was critically injured by the lone terrorist. He was rushed to Saroka hospital in Beer Sheva. But all efforts by the doctors to save him were sadly in vain. Israeli investigators revealed that the terrorist had entered the outpost at night and without setting off the alarm.

Chapter 130 – DOREEN KAPELUSCHNIK – At Arcadia 1971-1988.

Doreen was first employed in 1971 to look after the children, but after Mr and Mrs Duzzy resigned in 1977 she acted as Matron, and Sidney Klevansky as Principal

Doreen was Matron from 1977 until 1988 when she joined the Arcadia committee after resigning as Matron. She was active on the House and Aftercare Committees until the old committee was dissolved on 22 July 2002. She is still active with the Old Arcs and assists with their regular book sales.

DOREEN KAPELUSCHNIK

In February 1971 my husband and I and our son arrived at Arcadia to take up the position of House Parents at the Arcadia Jewish Orphanage, now known as Arcadia Children's Home. Our section was the Joe Lewis Wing and we were given 19 children in our care boys and girls and their ages ranged from three years to 11 years. This new system was introduced to enable children to be housed as a family. Rather a large family, but soon the older children were transferred to the Boys' Department, formerly the Hospital and the girls went to the main building.

My husband went out to work and I, together with two domestic workers, Rachelle and Mimi cared for the children and their needs.

In 1972 I gave birth to my second son and the children were always around to see the baby and watch him develop.

Nursery School was at Oxford Shul and the Saxonwold Primary School.

In 1979 we all moved to the main building, while renovations took place at the Joe Lewis Wing, which was converted from large dormitories to rooms which housed two children. The rooms were comfortable, new beds were bought and pretty curtains and bedspreads adorned the rooms. There was great excitement when the children were able to have a lounge and their own TV. Prior to that they were always welcome to come and sit in our lounge.

I was promoted to Matron and Vicky Klevansky was the Principal in 1977 and I attended all general meetings with the committee and sub-committee on a regular basis.

Communal Seders for Pesach were held in the Main Hall and Yom Tov was always celebrated. New clothes were bought for the children. Visitors were welcome to Shul and to a meal afterwards.

Every Friday night and Saturday morning Shul services were held and all the children participated. Refreshments were always looked forward to after the service. In summer all the children enjoyed the swimming pool. Once a year we all looked forward to the picnic at Vereeniging and a

Doreen Kapeluschnik

great time was had by all. Summer youth camps were attended in December.

Sadly I resigned in May 1988 to set up a home for my family.

A day to remember was being 'unter firer' for Wendy nee Rubenstein and Alan Norman. The Chupah took place at the Arc Shul. As Wendy was my first intake to Arcadia in 1972 it was very meaningful for me when she was able to leave from my home to get married.

In 1991 I was co-opted to join the General Committee and later I became the Chairlady of the After Care Committee until it was taken over by the Chevrah in 2002 and we were told our services were no longer required.

1981 Junior Boys

Chapter 131 – SELWYN CHALMERS - IN TIMES OF CHANGE
At Arcadia 1996 to present times

Selwyn Chalmers has been in the service of Arcadia for almost ten years in various capacities but in fact his connection with Arcadia goes back many years as his father and uncle were in the care of the Arc in the 1930s.

Selwyn has worked for Arcadia over a very difficult period of change. The once beautiful Villa Arcadia was looking very tired and, become too expensive to maintain and was not being fully utilised. More importantly the estate had outgrown its use because of the dwindling number of children in residence at Arcadia.

Selwyn was present when very dramatic changes took place:

○ *The Arcadian committee resigned and Arcadia fell under the umbrella of the Chevrah Kadisha;*
○ *The children were relocated to the two refurbished houses in Sandringham;*
○ *Villa Arcadia, the home of the Arcs for almost eighty years, was sold.*

JOHNNY (1920-1966) AND CYRIL CHALMERS (1921-1956).
Written by Selwyn Chalmers

When I started working at Arcadia in 1996 Vicky Klevansky informed me that he had known my father at Arcadia in the 1920's. On checking records I was surprised to find out that my father and his brother had both indeed been at Arcadia.

Johnny Chalmers, my dad, and his brother Cyril (known as Sid) were admitted to the Arc in 1926. Johnny was born in 1920 and Cyril in 1921. Unfortunately I know nothing about their stay at Arcadia but both Vicky and David Aginsky have told me they remember them. Judy Rosenberg (Rushowitz) living in Tel Aviv also remembers Cyril, which is quite amazing after about 50 years ago.

My father left the Arc in 1931 and went to live in the UK with his mother. He spent a few years there before coming back to South Africa. During the war years he enlisted in the "cavalry" and had the rank of sergeant. During the war he met my mother and they were married in 1941 in Pretoria.

In 1947 my father and his brother Sid went to Israel and fought in the Israeli War of Independence. My parents were divorced round about this time. My father later remarried an Israeli woman and they went to live in what was then Southern Rhodesia, in Bulawayo. He passed away at a very young age in 1966 at the age of 46.

Sid Chalmers served in the fledgling Israeli Air Force and later was a flight engineer for El Al. His plane was shot down over Bulgaria and he and all passengers and crew were killed. This was in 1956 when he was at the young age of about 35.

Selwyn Chalmers

Selwyn Chalmers et al at Shul

SELWYN CHALMERS

Selwyn Chalmers was appointed as Assistant Secretary in 1996 to Stanley Goldsmith, an ex-Arcadian who had served as Secretary for 44 years, and retired in 1998.

In 1999 Selwyn was appointed as Administrative Director of Arcadia with the departure of Mr Gerald Orelowitz. and worked for many years in the rooms under the Shul at the Arc, the location to which the offices which had been in the city for decades had been relocated.

THE ADMINISTRATIVE DIRECTOR'S REPORT
Extract from the 2000 Annual Bulletin
By Selwyn Chalmers

We have long had the desire to move the children to a more suitable location. Our hope has been over the past few years to sell our property in order to purchase two houses in the heart of the Jewish area. Unfortunately we have not had the funds to accomplish this goal. We are now in the position to make the initial purchase of the houses, but we would need to appeal to the community for funds in order to renovate, alter and furnish the buildings.

In common with many other Jewish organisations we have been struggling financially. With the ever dwindling and ageing community less able to support us adequately it is becoming ever more difficult.

We can only hope that this will be the year in which we finally sell our property and relocate our children in the near future.

THE ADMINISTRATIVE DIRECTOR'S REPORT
Extract from the 2001 Annual Bulletin
By Selwyn Chalmers

The last few years have seen major changes in the welfare organisations of the Jewish Community. We have seen most of the major organisations consolidating and relocating. This flux has had many positive consequences with major administrative savings and most groups being now located in the heart of the Jewish area.

Arcadia has also taken positive but painful steps in that direction. We had hoped at this time to already occupy our new houses in Elary Street, Raedene. Unfortunately the amount of red tape with the Council has necessitated a slow and cautious approach.

Our previous director once quoted the 1996 Draft Discussion Document for the Transformation of the Child and Youth Care system, concerning the geographical location, size and milieu of a children's home. It is advised that *'residential care centres should not be located in isolated areas and away from communities'*. The report went on to say *'Young people, families and the community should have easy access to the facility, and the facilities should have easy access to community resources.'*

This is soon to take place when we move our children to Raedene, near the community Shuls, Kosher shops and restaurants, etc.

All our energies are focused on our forthcoming move, and also the sale of our property in Parktown. At the same time, we need to strengthen our capabilities for our main function, which is looking after children in need. We have been looking after children - most successfully - for ninety five years, and we have built up a large store of knowledge and experience. However, we are continually striving for excellence and our professional staff are always attempting further improvements.

I would like to take this opportunity to wish Daniella Kanareck, our previous Program Director, best wishes for her future in Australia after more than ten years dedicated service to Arcadia.

To our new Program Director, Jacqui Chesler, we wish the best of luck in her challenging and demanding post. I am sure that her professionalism and experience will stand her in good stead hopefully for many years to come.

My thanks to the small band of administrative staff for their loyalty and dedication. Lynda Swartz, Naomi Rachelson, Gillian Edelstein and Elizabeth Munene - thanks for your care. A job well done also by Adina Menhard and her team of child care workers Mmule Mashiyane and Flora Mulaudzi. Also the domestic staff Thomas Baloyi, Mary Matsiu, Emily Xaba, Magdelina Ndlovu. I would be remiss if I left out our three drivers, Jonas Madue, Nicholas Mashaba and Robert Mashele. They cheerfully and competently *'schlep'* the children, deliver gifts from the Gift Shop and drive around for the office as well.

I would like to say a few words about Vicky Klevansky whom I'm proud to call my friend and colleague. After an association with Arcadia spanning many decades, Vicky is always available with advice, reminiscences and practical help. Many thanks to Vicky.

Last but not least, I extend my thanks to our Chairman Mike Gaddin, our Committee in general and the Executive in particular, for their support and interest, their guidance and advice.

THE CHANGES

THE CHANGE IN THE COMMITTEE

On the 6th March 2002 a special meeting of the Arcadia committee was held to hear a proposal that "Arcadia fall under the umbrella of the Chevrah Kadisha." This meeting was addressed by Denis Levy and Lawrie Brozin of the Chevrah Kadisha. After a debate the proposal was voted on and the motion adopted.

On the 9th March the last of the signatures by all Arcadia Committee members were obtained and the takeover became effective. The old committee effectively resigned on this date and had no more management rights or signing powers.

New mandates were given to the bank virtually immediately and the "new committee" became effective a little later.

Colin Datnow became the Chairman of Arcadia, Denis Levy the CEO and Marion Pohl's official title is Group Operations manager. All decisions are now made by the professional management, who report directly to Colin Datnow.

THE RELOCATION OF THE CHILDREN

When Arcadia relocated to Sandringham on 22 May 2002, there were 14 children in residence.

The children were moved on 22nd May 2002 to the two refurbished house on George Avenue in Sandringham in the heart of the Jewish Community. The remainder of the Arc office staff and gardening staff remained at Arcadia until 30th June 2002. Two of the office staff and all the garden staff were retrenched and the remaining office staff, except Selwyn were transferred to Sandringham Gardens.

Selwyn remained alone on the property for a full month before Arcadia was vacated on 31st July 2002 and he was appointed Administration Manager and his office relocated to Sandringham Gardens,

THE SALE OF PROPERTY

The property was sold in 2004 and the transfer was effected on 22nd February 2005. The purchasers, Hollard Insurance then commenced the excavations and demolitions necessary to build its new headquarters.

FOR SALE
PRIME HISTORICAL SITE

Don't miss an excellent opportunity to participate in the conservation of history by securing this site for a head office or office development.

Situated on Oxford Road, with superb visibility from, and access to, the M1. This low density, well established 52 250m² site, with turn of the century Herbert Baker designed structure, features stunning views of Johannesburg.

Chapter 132 – THE END OF "ARCADIA" at 22 Oxford Road, Parktown and the Start of the New Arc in Sandringham.

In the previous chapter we spoke about the changes that took place:

○ The Arcadian Committee resigned and Arcadia fell under the umbrella of the Chevrah Kadisha

○ The children were relocated to two refurbished houses on George Avenue in Sandringham.

○ Villa Arcadia the home of the Arcs for almost 80 years was sold.

In this chapter we see it all through the eyes of the Old Arcs.

Many Old Arcs and friends were traumatised by the events as;

○ The committee of Arcadia consisted of many Old Arcs who had served Arcadia faithfully for many years. In 2001 these included Sam Paikin, Solly Farber, Barney Meyers, Jeff Esekow, Stan Goldsmith, Sidney Klevansky, Keith Lang and Alec Saul. Past Committee who were Old Arcs included Elli Osrin, Selwyn Dembo, Gary Blackman and Sidney Nochumsohn.

This came to an abrupt end.

○ Old Arcs had for decades attended the High Holy Day Services which were run by our own 'three tenors'; Abe Starkowitz (Starkey), Solly Farber and Mannie Osrin (and previously Leonard (Joss) Lipschitz). Shul was always a chance to catch with our old friends to sing those old tunes and to listen to Starkey. Many Old Arcs would have notched up over 50 years of going to Arc Shul with some even over the 60 year mark. I'm sure Starkey was Chazan for over 50 years too.

This came to an abrupt end.

○ Old Arcs often used to visit Arcadia, looking around and reliving their past experiences. I'm sure we all remember as children seeing Old Arcs visiting and wandering around the Arc and looking around and visiting the memories of the past. Also many of us after we first left the Arc and then as adults and even with our children have visited the Arc to look around and renew old memories.

This came to an abrupt end.

To add to this trauma, in the middle of all this, our informal leader and the personification of Arcadia, Solly Farber, and his life long Arc friend David Kotzen passed away within a day of each other.

It was traumatic for many Old Arcs to see the home of their childhood being excavated and knocked down and them being denied access to the estate to wander around.

I let the correspondence I received tell the story.

Villa Arcadia

Jeff Esekow, RSA - 25 April 2002

Very briefly the news is:

1. Arcadia has been taken out of the hands of the Arc Committee as you knew it, ie some of the old Arcs such as Solly Farber, Gary Blackman, Keith Lang, Alec Saul and myself.
2. The Arc is now administered by Chevra Kadisha. The whole take-over was very quick and traumatic for the old Committee.
3. We have been trying without success to sell the property for about eight years.
4. Solly Farber is very ill. I am trying to persuade him to write his book on Arcadia. Time is of the essence.
5. My son used the Arc Shul for his wedding in December. I believe he is the first person who had both his Barmitzvah and wedding in the Arc Shul.

Solly Farber RSA - 9 June 2002

David Sandler and I are putting together a book about Arcadia. We will use material from the various *Old Arc Memory Books* that David has compiled over the past two years. We would like more material and appeal to you as Old Arcs to write about your time in Arcadia, or about some episode you remember and would like to share with others. We want funny stories, sad stories, family histories perhaps explaining why you were put into the Arc, romantic stories, heroic stories and stories about what happened in your life after you left the Arc. We think this will be a wonderful book. Make your story known and write to me (Solly Farber)

As you know, the Chevrah Kadishah here in Jo'burg have taken over the management of Arcadia. The children have been moved to two houses in Sandringham.
Ciao for now

Max Goldman, - RSA 10 June 2002

I'll say that there is a lot of concern over what has transpired with the Arc.

The silence in the media is rather "deafening" to say the least - getting louder with the passage of time. Is it not possible to issue a brief statement covering:

o   Future Shul services
o   Right of access to the property for old Arcs
o   Fickey's placement
o   Goldsmith's placement
o   Arc office location

Max Goldman, RSA - 8 July 2002

AUCTION OF ARC CONTENTS this SUNDAY, 14 JULY 2002

For those of you who do not yet know, the contents of the Arc is to be auctioned this Sunday at the Arc. So, if you want to acquire pieces of Arc memorabilia then be there on Sunday. That metal hand basin which you had to wash with while "sick" in the Arc hospital can now belong to you for a small sum!!!! Doc's ("in disrepair") and Klev's ("still packs a wallop") canes can also be yours, as well as that famous "wake-up" referee's whistle Fickey used every morning!

There are even some of Doc's philosophy books available (Jung, Nietsche etc!!) for all you thinkers. Items can be previewed on Friday, 12 July 2002 at the ARC. Unfortunately no pre-auction selling is allowed.

Max Goldman, RSA - 15 July 2002

I never attended the Arc auction but Janet tells me that there was a huge crowd. I previewed on Friday, but found no books for you.....the "Nietsche" note of mine was just a joke....I remember Doc carrying that book around for quite awhile. I did see the projector I operated 32 years ago!!!

Dave Kotzen, - 19 July 2002

Reading about the Arc being sold was not something new for me. Solly Farber had told me of these plans some years ago. For me it takes on the same perspective, as if one were to compare it to a life experience of a family member or very dear friend who is suffering of a fatal illness. From a humane stand point we only want peace for this person.

However, when the ultimate takes place, we are left with a severe pain that sometimes can never be replaced. Frankly, this is the way I feel about the Arc, having spent 19 years of my life in this environment, it is nevertheless so sad to learn about the fate of the Arc. It was a time in our past for all of us, and clearly something we will all carry with us to our death. History has a wonderful way of recording events and perhaps one day, our grandchildren will look back at our history with special significance.
Always,

Len (Dave Kotzen's son) - 24 July 2002

It is with much sadness that I wanted to let you know that my father, Dave Kotzen, passed away suddenly and without notice yesterday, Tuesday July 23, from a heart attack.

My mother, who is not familiar with the computer, asked me to please communicate this to you so that you would know what has happened and also to know that Dave from zenpugs@aol.com will not be writing to you again.

My mother wanted me to also express her thanks for the contact that you provided for my Dad with his friends from the Arc.

Best wishes and many thanks,

Tanya Farber - 26 July 2002

My beloved father Sholom Abe Farber passed away yesterday evening after a struggle with cancer. He died in the arms of his three loving daughters and his wife. We were at his side and held him with love. How fitting that he should die so soon after his ever-lasting best friend/brother Dave Kotzen.

I will let you know when this address is no longer in existence, but I will keep it going for some time so that his friends can still communicate with his family.
His youngest daughter,

Mannie Osrin - 25 July 2002

Dear all Old Arcs,

To all those who haven't heard the sad and tragic news, I have to tell you that within 24 hours of the sudden death of Dave Kotzen, his close friend, and our very wonderful brother Solly Farber passed away peacefully after a long and difficult illness, endured with great fortitude and dignity.

To Dave and Solly's family, on behalf of Old Arcs everywhere, I pass on our heartfelt condolences, and wish them long life.

On a personal note, I remember Dave Kotzen with fondness, but I never knew him very well. It was always great to read his contributions to this contact forum.

Solly on the other hand was a very dear friend of mine, someone I will miss terribly. He was truly the most remarkable person, in all aspects, that I was ever privileged to be associated with.

My wife, Sarah, joins me in my sympathies.
May they both rest in peace.

Bertha Kronenberg (Klevansky) Canada - 1 September 2002

You'll be pleased to know that Vicky is happily ensconced in an hotel in Berea, his movements somewhat more restricted than when he was in Arcadia: The area is not so savoury beyond the gates of the hotel. He says the food is good, there are plenty of old-timers for conversation, and his quarters are most comfortable.
Kind regards:

Max Goldman, RSA – 4 September 2002

The Arc Shul is now sadly consigned to history...and all we now have are the memories. I believe a sale of the Arc is fairly imminent. The Torahs were relocated to Sandringham Gardens.

Your hard work on all the Arc books was timely indeed!!

Hard to think Solly Farber is gone from this world. It seems so recent that I had my hand on his shoulder, trying to console him at his sister Sarah's grave. Dear Sarah, who Nadia used to call "Selah".

I can't believe that they auctioned off the *Arcadia* sign!!!!

Mannie Osrin, RSA - 10 September 2002

Most of you, I'm sure, know that we didn't hold any services at the Arc this year, and in fact it looks as though we never again will do so. With the passing of Solly Farber, the closing of the Arc and Starkey and I having "lost our jobs" so to speak, this was a Rosh Hashana that was certainly tinged with sadness. Still it's heartening that so many Old Arcs can and do keep in touch.

"Once an Arc, always an Arc" as someone once said!! I'll certainly write again after Yom Kippur. In the meantime, "well over the fast"

Willie Isaacs, USA - 12 September 2002

I did voice my regrets to my family about the possibility that the services at Arcadia could have stopped. Mannie, I am truly sorry that you lost your job over so many years. It is the end of a very long journey for all of you that were lucky enough to be able to attend for so long.

Fondest Regards to you all and best wishes for the New Year once again.

David Sandler, Australia - 23 December 2002

Brian, my brother, tells me he visits Vicky at the hotel in Berea every week and does his shopping for him.

Jeff Esekow, RSA – 24 December 2002

As you no doubt know the Arc is now a branch of the Chevra Kadisha in Johannesburg and is no longer autonomous. There is nobody on the Arc Committee who was in any way connected to the Arc, and this is very sad. Your emails and the Old Arcs newsletters are all that holds the family together. In fact the Arc Shul is no longer in use and the home has been moved to Sandringham Gardens on George Avenue.

The Arc as we knew it, is standing empty and all the contents has been sold. Please send me a list of the Arc contacts so that I can communicate with my contemporaries by email or post.

Best regards and peace to all.

Max Goldman, RSA - July 2003

I would be very interested to hear your comments on the following (maybe crazy) idea: "Rosh Hashana/Yom Kippur 2003 back at the Arc Shul.
Obviously there are four essential preconditions:

1. Mannie and Starkey's willingness to hold the services,
2. That the furniture is still there (I did hear that it had been earmarked for donation).
3. That the Shul can be reconsecrated as a Shul; and
4. That the Arc remains unsold."

Mannie Osrin RSA October 2003
Old Arc Association Newsletter

Well now another Rosh Hashana and Yom Kippur have come and gone.

For a lot of us who grew up in Arcadia with the Shul there as the only Shul they ever knew, and for those who continued to attend services there for most of our post Arcadia days, it was really a time of sadness, and in some ways confusion, not having the Arc Shul to go to for the Yom Tovim.

Last year with the "shock" of not having the Shul for the first time, it was too soon and too raw an experience to really sink in. This year however the reality truly set in. No Starkey, no Jonah, no Ficky, no seeing friends and brothers and sisters, whom you hadn't seen for a year or two. Lots of emotions. And in amongst all these feelings of course, you had to let Hashem know that you weren't "there" any more but you were now sitting in this or that particular Shul. I sincerely hope all the messages got through!

I myself went to the Oxford Shul ("down the road" from the Arc as it were) with my brother Elli. I was very impressed with the services. Apparently there were a few other Old Arcs there, but I saw only Jules Gordon and Max Ladier from a distance.

**Selwyn Chalmers, RSA - 10 September 2003
(Admin Manager [previously Director] of Arcadia)**

As you no doubt know the Chevrah Kadisha in Johannesburg has taken over control of Arcadia.

We have been trying (unsuccessfully) to sell the Arcadia property for a number of years. We have a company looking at purchasing the property and they have asked us to take all the seating, Bimah etc from the Shul. We have now done this and we desperately need to do something with all this furniture. We would ideally like this to be used in a Shul somewhere. We thought about Australia. We have heard of the contents of entire Shuls which have been shipped to Australia to be used in a Shul there.

Do you think there is any possibility of anyone needing this stuff in Australia?"

Mannie Osrin, RSA - February 2004

I spent a most enlightening and interesting hour with Selwyn Chalmers, who was the Superintendent at Arcadia for the last seven years before it closed. He is now the Admin Manager at the "new" Arcadia, so to speak, and he took me to see the two cottages where the children are now residing, all 20 of them. I am sure most of you remember where the Sandringham Old Age Home is and also where the Selwyn Segal Hostel is.

Well the Arc is now situated between the two and consists essentially of two houses, one of which is home to the juniors, numbering 11 and the other to the seniors, nine in all. There is nothing fancy about the set-up, but very comfortable and very good security. There are a few lounges with TV and the seniors all have computers in their rooms. There is a smashing swimming pool as well and a communal games building.

Unfortunately, there are no other grounds to speak of. Certainly no uphill and downhill! Those few kids that I did meet all seemed relaxed and perfectly normal in every way. They and their rooms were all neat and tidy at the same time, and greeted Selwyn and me in a well mannered, cool sort of way (the one youngster had to interrupt his cell phone conversation!) As we left Selwyn said to me "quite different from your days, isn't it?" to which I could only lamely reply "sure, but so is everything today."

Selwyn tells me, incidentally that when he came to work at Arcadia, Ficky, on hearing that his name was Chalmers went to the archives and pulled out Selwyn's father's file. This was the first time he learnt that his dad had been in Arcadia (1920's)".

Max Goldman, RSA - February 2004

Construction work has started at the Arc on field opposite the main dining room looking towards the zoo.

Brian Sandler, RSA - February 2004

The Arc has been sold to Hollard Insurance Company. Vicky and I were there today, having a look around. There are about 400 workers there clearing. They are going to put up office blocks."

Bertha Kronenberg, Canada - February 2004

I just read this from my son in Johannesburg and thought I must pass it on.

"Drove past Arcadia on the highway last night to dinner. It was quite sad to see that they've started dismantling and demolishing the place. All the roof tiles, window frames etc.etc. are stripped out of the buildings and resold. Remember those big palm trees down by the pool. They are excavated out of the ground and sold. I've heard of prices in the 10's of thousands for those old trees. I explained to Josh (our grandchild aged 11) about your life and upbringing at Arcadia."

Surely they're not dismantling the main building! Isn't there anyone in Jo'burg (an Old Arc) who can report further??

David Lasker - 17 March 2004

Arc sold to Hollard Insurance - Rosebank/Killarney Gazette 1 March 2004.

Max Goldman, RSA - 15 March 2004

For those of you who are unaware, construction at the Arc has now begun in earnest. The Boys' Department was demolished this past week - it is now but a memory!!!

Tons of soil have been dumped on the soccer field to raise its level to that of the now demolished Boys' Department.

David Lasker, RSA - March 2004

I drove past today and took this picture.

The soccer field is ploughed up and the Boys' Department is demolished. The swimming pool that stood on stilts below the Boys' Department was demolished many years ago.

Golde, Stan and Adam Goldsmith, RSA - 15 March 2004

Yes, about two weeks ago they started on earthworks and demolitions at the Arc.

I must be honest that when I drove past the first time and saw what was happening I got very emotional because even though I was not in the Arc I was part of the Arc and it struck me that 45 years of my life have been connected to the Arc. I have contacted the local Heritage agency who told me that the Boys' Department and the Babies' Department buildings are to be demolished. I was also told that the Shul is going to be turned into a museum depicting the history of "*Villa Arcadia*". The main building facade cannot be changed at all, however inside the building can be changed which is where the insurance company, which bought the property will be creating their headquarters.

Golde, Stan and I will be travelling to Cape Town to spend Pesach with Maxine and her three sons, the youngest of whom will celebrate his 21st while we are in Cape Town. Stan is not as healthy as we would like him to be, but he and Golde carry on Baruch Hashem.

May everyone have a good and peaceful Pesach and carry on communicating.

Selwyn Chalmers, RSA– March 2004

An update on the New Arc set-up

I was indeed the secretary in the offices under the Shul and I did meet you more than two years ago at the Arc. The Chevrah Kadisha have taken over Arcadia - from 9 May 2002. They had two houses next door to the property of Sandringham Gardens

which they renovated for the children. These two houses are completely separate from Sandringham Gardens and are surrounded by walls all around and leads onto George Avenue with its own (guarded) entrance.

The set-up is as follows:

The Chev have complete admin and financial control. We have a Program Director who is a Social Worker and looks after the needs of the children, with staff under her. The Admin is theoretically under my control and I report directly to the management of the Chevrah Kadisha. We now have 20 children at the Arc, which is the highest number for many years. They range in age from four to 17. We also have an aftercare program and we look after the children's needs when they finish school. We pay for tertiary education and provide rent and subsistence money until the age of 25 or until they can support themselves.

The latest on the Old Arc:

The Boys' Department and the house that was occupied by the Gees have now been demolished and the purchaser is now excavating the soccer field. I understand that the Hospital will be refurbished and not destroyed while the Babies - the Joe Lewis Wing, will be demolished at a later stage.

Selwyn Chalmers, RSA - May 2004

I went past Arcadia again today and there is a lot of activity going on there. The soccer field has been excavated and there are two large cranes busy at work. It looks like there will be a large building there. It seems like there may be a section in the main building set aside for the history of Arcadia-boards plaques etc perhaps photos. As soon as I know more I will let you know.

Chevrah News for September 2004

Arcadia Jewish Children's Home is expanding. At the moment thee additional bedrooms and a bathroom are being added to the Junior house.

Most of the children who live at Arcadia today are placed there for their own protection, either by order of the Children's Court or through private placements. These children are dependent upon Arcadia for their every need - physical, educational, emotional and medical. They have nowhere else to go and no one else to depend upon.

The current situation at Arcadia is as follows:

o   20 children live in residence.
o   18 of those in residence are statutory placements.
o   The Day-Care Centre has 22 additional children who live at home and spend their days at Arcadia in a supervised, constructive and stimulating environment.
o   The After-Care program caters to 11 adolescents who have completed their schooling and are now being assisted by Arcadia with tertiary education, accommodation and the kind of support and guidance normally provided by parents."

Selwyn Chalmers - Admin Manager of Arcadia
21 November 2004

I went to see The "Old Arcadia" yesterday morning. I went to remove all the old mezuzahs all over the buildings. In fact I found 66 old mezuzahs. I was astounded at the scope of the building which is going up there. One can see from the Highway the new building which covers what was JSUP (the Senior Boys) and virtually the whole of the soccer field. This will be a three storey building and is massive. There is also a smaller building being erected over the whole area of what was Stan Goldsmith's house and the old orchards.

The Friedman Cottage (The Old Hospital) is being changed into a gym. It is really large and an impressive development. One of the senior guys there told me that the company is very concerned and sensitive to the heritage of Arcadia. They are busy restoring the main building and I believe that they intend to replace all the boards and placards.

I nearly forgot something else. Our driver Nicholas Mashaba who everyone will remember as the Chef/Cook at Arcadia is retiring at the end of the year. Nicholas has been working at Arcadia for 46 years and I'm sure that many old Arcs will remember him.

Selwyn Chalmers - April 2005

I have what I consider very exciting news: I have just had a conversation with a gentleman by the name of Andrew Munro from Hollard Insurance. As you no doubt know, Hollard is the company that bought our old property in Parktown.

He told me that they expect the work on the main house to be completed in the next couple of months. He wants to know if there are any Old Arcs who would like to attend the official opening of the building. This will be held towards the end of the year, in the spring. I also mentioned to him that next year is Arcadia's centenary year, and he seemed as if he would be amenable, in fact happy to have some sort of function for us to celebrate this wonderful event.

Freda Cheilyk (Koppel) Australia - April 2005

May I tell you that I know Adina and every year that I visit Johannesburg I have also visited the children and Adina at Sandringham.

The place looks good. The children look happy and generally there is a good atmosphere. They also have an after school care on the grounds.

Max Goldman, Johannesburg – 1 August 2005
An Arc boy (1954 - 1970)

A Walk Down Memory Lane (The Arc Revisited)

I was privileged to visit Arcadia in the role of service-provider to the new owners, Hollard Insurance, through my company, Kgotso Recruitment Solutions.

A mammoth office complex, several storeys high, has now replaced the Boys' Block and the Soccer Field.

What a strange experience it was, nostalgia simultaneously intermingling with awe, horror and happiness...to mention a few of the emotions my presence evoked!

I was unable to gain access from the old Oxford Road entrance as this was temporarily closed, so back down Oxford Road I drove to enter via Federation Road. Happily it seems that Hollard intend to retain the name "*Arcadia*". Access was via a steep inclined tar road with reinforced concrete covering the entire side of the old "down the hill". Through the security gates at the top and then along a winding road laid along the edge of the old soccer field, now buried under many metres of thousands of tons of earth.

Signs showed the way to "*Visitors Parking*" (along the old driveway), and "*Villa Arcadia*", among others. My visit was for business purposes, but I made an instinctive beeline for "*Villa Arcadia* ", eager to see what had transpired over these last few years. The tar road joins the old driveway at the same place the soccer field did. The original concrete slabs which constituted the driveway still remain, for now. A paved walkway now runs parallel to the old driveway - flanked on either side by the age-old lines of jacarandas and palms (most of which are untouched). In the old orchard/Goldsmiths house (now demolished) stands a huge monolith, several storeys high, presumably a parking garage.

The peppercorn tree under which countless Arc boys enjoyed their school-day lunches (Mrs Stelzner et al) has also survived, one of the few remaining witnesses to the old boys' block, now just a memory. Many trees have not survived the onslaught of "progress".

On entering the main parking area at Villa Arcadia one is struck by the sparkling "old lady in new garb"! The renovation of the building has been done very professionally and it sports a new gleaming coat of white paint. The front upstairs section overlooking the parking area has been remodelled and now boasts an open air balcony.

The fish pond also remains - all the fish long since sold off by Sam Bartlett to a pet shop in town!

The former Shul seems now to be an employee training room. Devastating!! - Thoughts of Doc, Starkey, Jonah, Mannie, Solly et al go through my mind.

The downstairs of the main building (to which I did not gain access) appears to be in use as a recreational area. The kitchen is still a kitchen, albeit now boasting the finest in decor and equipment!

The stone pathways and walls have been extensively retained, though the plants that "graced" these areas have been decimated and these areas are mostly denuded of vegetation. Surely new flora is on its way soon!

Alas! The Oneg tree is no more - though what I remember of it was that it was not in good condition some years ago when David Sandler and I went on a nostalgic "traipse" of the Arc on his visit from Oz. Luckily we took many photos, that day.

The area outside the old Joe Lewis wing stretching down below the northern side of the main building has been totally cleared and raised - presumably the initial stages of another building soon to rise there. The Joe Lewis wing still stands, but rumour has it that its days too, are numbered! I never got a look at the tennis courts or the Woolf Hillman Hospital. The hospital it is said, will be utilised as a gymnasium.

A glance up at the old laundry and compound areas reveals no apparent changes except that they are now devoid of all people. Thoughts of Dolly and Charlie Miller, sons Willy and Miggie, daughter Funu. The smell of manure, the cows, the old Arc bus!

I arrived at Arcadia on 2 December 1954, as a toddler. I could never have imagined that 51 years later I would be visiting the Arc and witnessing such vast changes, some good, some bad.

In my opinion, bearing in mind the sorry state of the Arc's finances at the time, more good than bad has resulted, as the "grand old lady is now in good hands" after many years of situational neglect.

This "Old Lady" is destined to adorn the skyline of Parktown for many, many more years into the future.

Au Revoir Arcadia!!

Photos of the Restored Arc Buildings
From Jules Gordon, Max Goldman and David Lasker.

Chapter 133 - VILLA ARCADIA RENEWED

Written by Susan Ford from Hollard Insurance

HOLLARD NURTURES VILLA ARCADIA BACK TO HEALTH AND RENEWED PURPOSE

Villa Arcadia has found a new life and purpose under the stewardship of Hollard Insurance.

For eight decades, 1922 to 2002, it nurtured over 3000 Jewish children in need. Previously, 1908 to 1922, it was an elegant venue for social occasions in the then rough-and-ready mining camp-like town of Johannesburg. But by 2003 Villa Arcadia had lost its lustre and its once lofty purpose was hidden from view.

That's when Hollard Insurance saw it neglected on its 15 acres and fell in love. Without hesitation they bought Villa Arcadia from Arcadia Jewish Children's Home equally passionate about its past history and its future potential.

"It was love at first sight," says Hollard CEO Paolo Cavalieri. "There was a marvellous *feeling* about the place and we knew immediately that here was the future home for our Hollard family. At the time our people and seven divisions were housed in four different buildings around Johannesburg. We were turning 21 and the time had come for all of us to merge together in one place."

"We loved the fact that there was a meaningful and important history imbedded in every rock and brick at the Villa. We could feel it! We were also excited about the prospect of restoring the historic building to its former glory while capturing and preserving the history of nearly a century – 80% of which involved the Jewish children in need who had been nurtured there and gone on to become successful citizens – not only in South Africa but in other parts of the world.

"So, with enthusiasm and passion we set about nurturing the magnificent Villa back to health, vitality and former glory. We assigned architects to design new buildings that would harmonize with the elegant Sir Herbert Baker mansion while providing every modern convenience and technical advancement of the 21st century. We formed no less than 32 sub-committees to see that every detail of our passion and vision would be translated into reality and in June 2005 we moved in."

VILLA ARCADIA NOW ... and then

What Old Arcs may not have noticed – or been too young to care about – as they moved (probably ran!) through the grand double doors in Villa Arcadia to watch movies, attend synagogue or go about their daily business, is that the overhead carved fanlights of those magnificent double doors were crafted by the now famous and greatly admired artist, Anton van Wouw. These carved masterpieces have been carefully restored with the guidance of leading heritage

architects ... as has all the handmade brasswork by the famous George Ness.

Another of the Villa's claims to fame is that Sir Herbert Baker designed the Parliament Buildings in Pretoria immediately after designing Villa Arcadia. Many features of the mansion reflect that later design and are said to be the fore-runner of this landmark building in South Africa's capital city.

WHAT IS WHERE?

Downstairs: Old Arcs will probably enjoy knowing that the rooms on the ground floor have been turned into elegant meeting rooms where business conferences and social gatherings are frequently held not only by Hollard, but by prominent organisations where celebrities are frequent guests. The Villa has now become a sought after venue for certain types of gatherings because of its incredible view, beautiful environment and significant history. On a clear day the view stretches to the Magaliesberg Mountains 70 kilometres away.

Upstairs: The well-travelled, wide corridor, now leads to smaller meeting rooms and has been turned into an art gallery that changes every eight weeks to showcase and nurture South African artists, giving them much-needed exposure.

Art on the Walls: Throughout the restored mansion a unique collection of extraordinary artwork adorns the walls. With the aim of merging the historic with the contemporary, and fostering long-term partnerships, Hollard commissioned fine artists to collaborate with skilled Xhosa beaders to create unique artworks using beads as the fine art medium.

What's happened to the hospital? - The orphanage's hospital has been transformed into the Hollard Hollsome Centre, including a fully equipped gym designed by an Athens Olympic rowing medallist. This is where Hollard staff have easy access to personal trainers, the gym, family planning, nutritional counselling, HIV/AIDS counselling and management as well as physiotherapy and various free health support services.

MORE NURTURING IN MODERN HOLLARD HOUSE

In the lobby in the new Hollard House, yet another form of nurturing is going on. A massive collection of 294 *Creative Blocks* – 180 mm x 180 mm each – are displayed in the busy and impressive, double-volume, foyer. They are created by struggling artists and sold off the wall to staff and visitors. *Hollardites* enthusiastically act as salespeople for the artworks which provide the sole income for many of the artists.

And so the nurturing that started 80 years ago by the South African Jewish Orphanage continues – in another form – and the memories live on. In addition, with Hollard's enthusiastic support, the local Heritage Society guides tours through Villa Arcadia from time to time – admiring the beauty and remembering the people who have lived there.

*Villa Arcadia's elegant veranda and elevated position provides a
breathtaking view of Johannesburg – including, on a clear day,
the Magaliesburg Mountains 70 kilometres away.*

The main entrance to Villa Arcadia glitters like a jewel at night and greets frequent visitors to social functions and conferences.

This Chapter has been submitted by the Johannesburg Jewish Helping Hand – The Chevrah Kadisha.

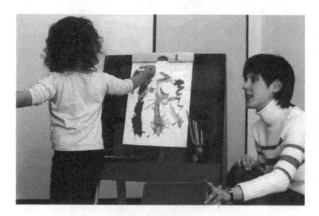

In the interests of the Jewish community, and at its request, the Johannesburg Jewish Helping Hand – Chevrah Kadisha, assumed financial, legal and management responsibility for Arcadia Jewish Children's Home in March 2002.

Arcadia had reached maximum capacity in 1939 when, due primarily to the influx of refugee children from Europe fleeing the nazi persecution, there were 400 children in its care.

As time went by the practice of placing children in the orphanage for financial reasons became increasingly undesirable. Progress in Social Services dictated the advantages of, as far as possible, keeping children at home with their parents by providing them with the financial means to do so.

With the war behind them and a new, enlightened approach to the importance of family, the 1950's -- with its general improvement in the socio-economic situation and increased life expectancy -- brought fewer orphans into Arcadia and numbers in the Jewish orphanage dwindled. By Arcadia's 75th Jubilee year in 1981 only 40 children resided there.

Long before the Johannesburg Jewish Helping Hand officially assumed responsibility for Arcadia, the organisation played a pivotal role in providing the funds that enabled parents to house, feed and educate their children themselves. Now, in 2006, the only children housed there are those whose parents are not able to take care of them.

Today almost every child at Arcadia is placed there for their own protection either by order of the Children's Court or through private placements.

By 2002 only a small section of Arcadia's sprawling 17-acre property in Parktown was occupied by the children who lived there.

IT WAS TIME FOR CHANGE.

One of the first efforts undertaken by the Johannesburg Jewish Helping Hand on behalf of the children was to relocate them to two renovated residential houses in Sandringham. Here the children enjoy a domestic, suburban environment that bears no semblance of institutionalisation. An intimate and homely atmosphere has been carefully created and nurtured.

The large, rustic log cabin on the Arcadia grounds houses a fully- equipped Day Care Centre which provides supervised care not only for children resident at Arcadia, but also for children of working parents in the community.

In residence and at the Day Care Centre, full time and well-trained child-care workers supervise and tend the children by day and night. Healthcare, education, therapy, play and homework supervision are all part of the deal. Enormous energy is invested in offering Arcadia's children every opportunity for their futures.

Being located in a Jewish neighbourhood, in close proximity to youth movements and synagogues, the children are encouraged to take full advantage of their exposure to communal life.

The After Care Program is designed to care for the financial, educational and emotional needs of post-matric youths who no longer live on campus. Arcadia provides them with tertiary education, accommodation and the kind of support and guidance normally provided by parents.

TODAY'S NUMBERS:

○ 20 children live in residence – of which 18 are statutory placements
○ The Day-Care Centre has 22 additional children who live at home and spend their days at Arcadia in a supervised, constructive and stimulating environment.
○ The After-Care programme caters to 11 adolescents who have completed their schooling

Arcadia's children receive excellent care. They also receive love, support and a warm, comfortable home. Schooling is selected to meet the needs of each individual child and counseling, religious studies, medical and dental care, and even exciting holiday programs, are all made available.

While no effort is spared to provide these children with every advantage of growing up in a normal family home, in truth we know that nothing can ever really replace that.

These children have nowhere else to go and no-one else to depend upon.

YOU CAN HELP

The Arcadia Jewish Children's Home is not able to generate income in the form of fees and therefore the children are totally dependent on the facility for all the requirements - physical, emotional, intellectual and spiritual.

The support of the community is essential to their ongoing care. Your donation would be deeply appreciated.

For direct deposits, our banking details:

Arcadia Jewish Children's Home:

Bank:	First National Bank
Branch:	Parktown
Branch Code:	250-455
Account No:	54860054731

NB: Please Help Us To Identify Your Contribution By advising us by email or fax of any direct deposits made.

Fax: 011 640 2919
Email: Selwync@jhbchev.co.za

Or mail your contribution to:
Private Bag X7, Sandringham 2131

THANK YOU FOR CARING AND SHARING

SALE OF ARCADIA PROPERTY

The Arcadia property in Parktown was sold in 2004 and has become the new headquarters of Hollard Insurance Company.

Designed by Sir Herbert Baker in 1905, the jewel on the site, Villa Arcadia, was the historic home of Sir Lionel Phillips, mining magnate and politician, before it was converted into the **Arcadia Jewish Children's Home**. Hollard has restored the house to its former splendour and features it as the main attraction of the site. *Hollard House* is a low-rise development which covers 6.5ha. The offices accommodate up to 12,000 workers. Conservation experts were employed to ensure that the heritage of the property was retained.

Chapter 135 ~ GROUP PHOTOS

1930 Juniors

1931 Babies

503

1931 Babies

504

1933 - Girls

505

1941 Girls

506

1941 Boys

507

1941 Group Photo

508

1942 Senior Boys

509

1943 Concert Participants

510

1949 Group Photo

511

1952 Boys by Pond

512

1949 – Visit of Reg Park

513

1957 Group photo

514

1950 - Visit of Okkie Geffen

515

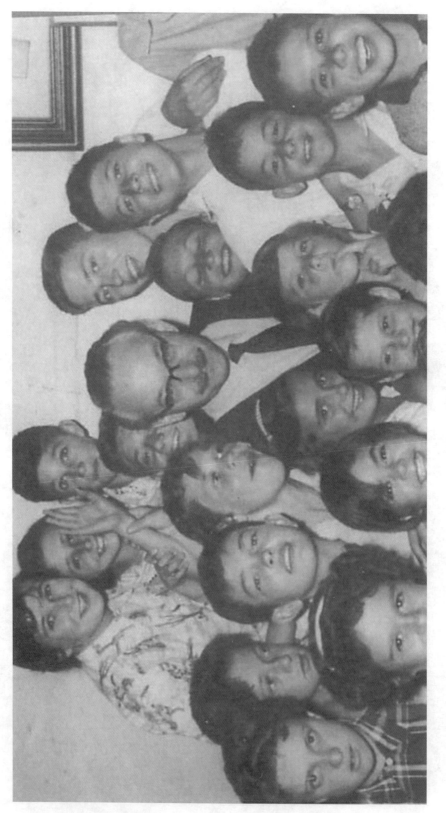

1957 – Visit of David Koseff

516

1957 – Visit of Claudio Arrau

517

1959 - Tickey and Sixpence (the Clowns) visit the Arc

518

1959 - Visit of Menachem Begin

1961 - Visit of Carmela Corren

1961 - Visit of Gina Bachauer

521

1962 – Visit of Jan Peerce

522

1965 Group of Children

523

ACKNOWLEDGEMENTS

This book completes a journey started in November 1999, when I first started collecting Arc photos and stories, and my first and greatest thanks go to all my Arc Brothers and Sisters who entrusted me, initially with the photos of their childhood and then later with their Arc Memories, especially those who bravely opened their inner hearts and shared their more sensitive and private stories.

Thanks go to two very close Arc 'brothers', David Kotzen and Dr Solly Farber who have passed away in July 2002 a day apart. They both inspired and encouraged and helped me and contributed to the booklets that I put together and as mentioned previously I sometimes feel that it is not by chance that I share with them my names David and Solly.

Shorly before his death, Solly and I had agreed to write a book on the Arc together and Solly has indeed written the book with me as many of his articles from past Arcadian publications are included in this book. I hope that David and Solly, as well as Doc and Ma enjoy the book from above.

Back to earth and thanks go to Michael Perry Kotzen, the octogenarian, initially from Israel and more recently from Sydney, who has been the most prolific contributor of Arc Memories. I could always depend on his weekly letters, together with a sketch on the back of the envelope. He has always given me endless help and has been the proof reader marking with a red cross all the errors in both initial and later drafts. He also supplemented some other Arcs' stories with his sketches. He is an actor who is always busy and recently got a leading role in a play in Sydney.

Thanks must also go to Freda Cheilyk (Koppel) from the Goldcoast who is a mine of information and could always be relied upon to help with details and information of Arcs over many generations. Freda also encouraged others to write.

A big thank you also to Alec Saul hailing from Israel and the previous editor of the Old Arc Association Newsletter. Like Freda, he has been a mine of information and has encouraged others to sent in their Arc Memories. Alec has also been helpful and very generous in raising funds to pay for the book.

Thanks go to Dr Mannie Osrin who recently settled in Melbourne with his wife Sarah, and he too was the editor of the Old Arc Association Newsletter. He has always helped with information and advice.

Thank you also to Marcelle Plaut from Perth for all the endless hours and days she spent typing, to Jenny Levin (Jennifer Fliess) from the UK who edited the foreword and to Max Goldman from Johannesburg, who 'from his unique position' helped with the spelling of the names and by sending me photos from fellow Arcs.

Next I must thank my daughter Sarah, who helped design the cover and a very great thanks must go to Antoinette Weber who gave very generously many months of her time, including giving up her annual leave, to help knock my initial draft into shape. Antoinette assisted with the typing and editing and was responsible for formatting, scanning and placement of photos and proofreading of the book.

We had many heated arguments about what should stay in the book and what should be deleted and many times I was told that I was "not writing the newsletter!!!" We would at times disagree about which words to use or not use and these chapters remained unfinished for weeks and even months. Many a photo had to be rescanned because it was not straight and many times I had to search through my piles of papers and boxes of letters to find the original photos. I dreaded the question that arose many many times, "What is the correct spelling for so and so's name?" or the statement, "You can't put this in. I've seen this somewhere else before!!"

On the positive side I had a very good excuse for not cleaning my house and many routine things were placed on hold, as the book slowly but surely took over our lives. Without Antoinette the book would be twice as long and Vicky would be spelt five different ways.

At this juncture I need to also thank my employers, Advantage Air, and fellow employees for being very patient with me and covering for me and for allowing me to devote more of my time to the book than to my work over the past six months. They have also kindly offered to assist in sea-freighting the books to South Africa.

Lastly I must thank all those who have helped so far in sponsoring the printing of the book. At the time of going to print they are Freda Cheilyk (Koppel), Alec Saul, Eli and Estelle Zagoria from Perth, Graham Stoler from Johannesburg and finally Peter Hough from Canada who immediately and most generously stepped forward to help. No doubt there are others who will help, and my thanks go to them also.

Thank also to the Old Arcs who have come forward, albeit too late, with their Arc Memories. When I have collected enough of these we can do another book of "*More Arc Memories*"